Betjeman's
Best British Churches

BETJEMAN'S
BEST BRITISH CHURCHES

UPDATED BY RICHARD SURMAN

With photographs by Michael Ellis and Richard Surman

Collins

Collins

Published in 2011 by Collins
An imprint of HarperCollins*Publishers*
77–85 Fulham Palace Road
London W6 8JB

First published in Great Britain by William Collins Sons & Co. Ltd, 1958

A catalogue record for this book is available from the British Library.

ISBN 978-0-00-741567-0

Printed and bound by South China Printing Co Ltd

CONTENTS

HOW TO FIND A CHURCH

This book includes Ordnance Survey (OS) and Global Positioning System (GPS) coordinates to help readers locate the churches with precision.

USING THE OS COORDINATES

The OS grid references work on all the paper Ordnance Survey maps and the Ordnance Survey's OpenData service on its website (www.ordnancesurvey.co.uk). If using the website, simply type the full grid reference into the OpenData search bar – e.g. ***SE966710*** – which will take you directly to a map page showing the church, usually identifiable as 'PW' for 'place of worship'.

If you are using an Ordnance Survey paper map, the same six-digit grid reference will work as follows:

- **THE FIRST TWO LETTERS** – e.g. the ***SE*** of ***SE966710*** – refer to the Ordnance Survey's division of Great Britain into 100 x 100 km major grid squares, each identified by two letters. On the paper maps, the letters can be seen in large lettering in the corner 1km grid squares and also where the major squares butt up to each other.
- **THE FIRST TWO DIGITS** – e.g. ***96*** – refer to the horizontal grid lines, called the 'eastings', which are numbered left to right on the paper maps.
- **THE THIRD DIGIT** – e.g. ***6*** – refers to the eastings grid in tenths. Thus the 6 in this example is six-tenths east of grid line 96.
- **THE FOURTH AND FIFTH DIGITS** – e.g. ***71*** – refer to the vertical grid lines, called the 'northings', which are numbered bottom to top on the paper maps.
- **THE SIXTH DIGIT** – e.g. ***0*** – refers to the northings grid in tenths. Thus the 0 in this example is within one-tenth north of grid line 71.

The division of tenths on the six-digit OS references in this book should be accurate to within 100 metres of the church.

USING THE GPS COORDINATES

These references give the latitude and longitude of locations in a digital format used by many car SatNav systems, mobile devices with GPS, and major online mapping applications such as Google and Bing.

Car SatNavs

First check if your SatNav allows the input of latitude and longitude / GPS coordinates. There are several reference systems in operation, so select 'digital' if given the option. In some SatNavs you will need to key in the full GPS coordinates with letters – e.g. ***54.12669N, 0.52226W*** – while in others the letters may have to be selected separately.

Note that the GPS coordinates given in this book are centred on the church building itself, rather than an access point into the grounds or the nearest car park. Churches sited in remote fields, woods or parks may be some distance from the nearest public highway, and in such cases SatNavs won't necessarily guide you to the best access point or parking place, although they should indicate where the church stands.

If your car SatNav does not offer the option to input the coordinates, we would suggest that you search for the village name and then the church name as a point of interest within the village, or, failing that, searching for 'Church Street' in a village often yields results!

Google Maps and Bing

Google Maps, Bing and some other online maps directly read the digital coordinates given in this book. Simply type the coordinates – e.g. ***54.12669N, 0.52226W*** – into the map's search bar.

Mobile phones and Other GPS Devices

Handheld devices that support GPS can read the GPS coordinates. On an iPhone, BlackBerry or Android device, for example, open the Google Maps application and type the coordinates into the search bar. Devices that use Full GPS (linking directly to satellites) are more accurate than those using Assisted GPS (via mobile phone masts).

If your device does not recognize the letters in the references, try leaving out the letters and substituting a minus sign before the longitude reference – e.g. ***54.12669, -0.52226***. (The minus sign is not necessary for longitude references ending in E.)

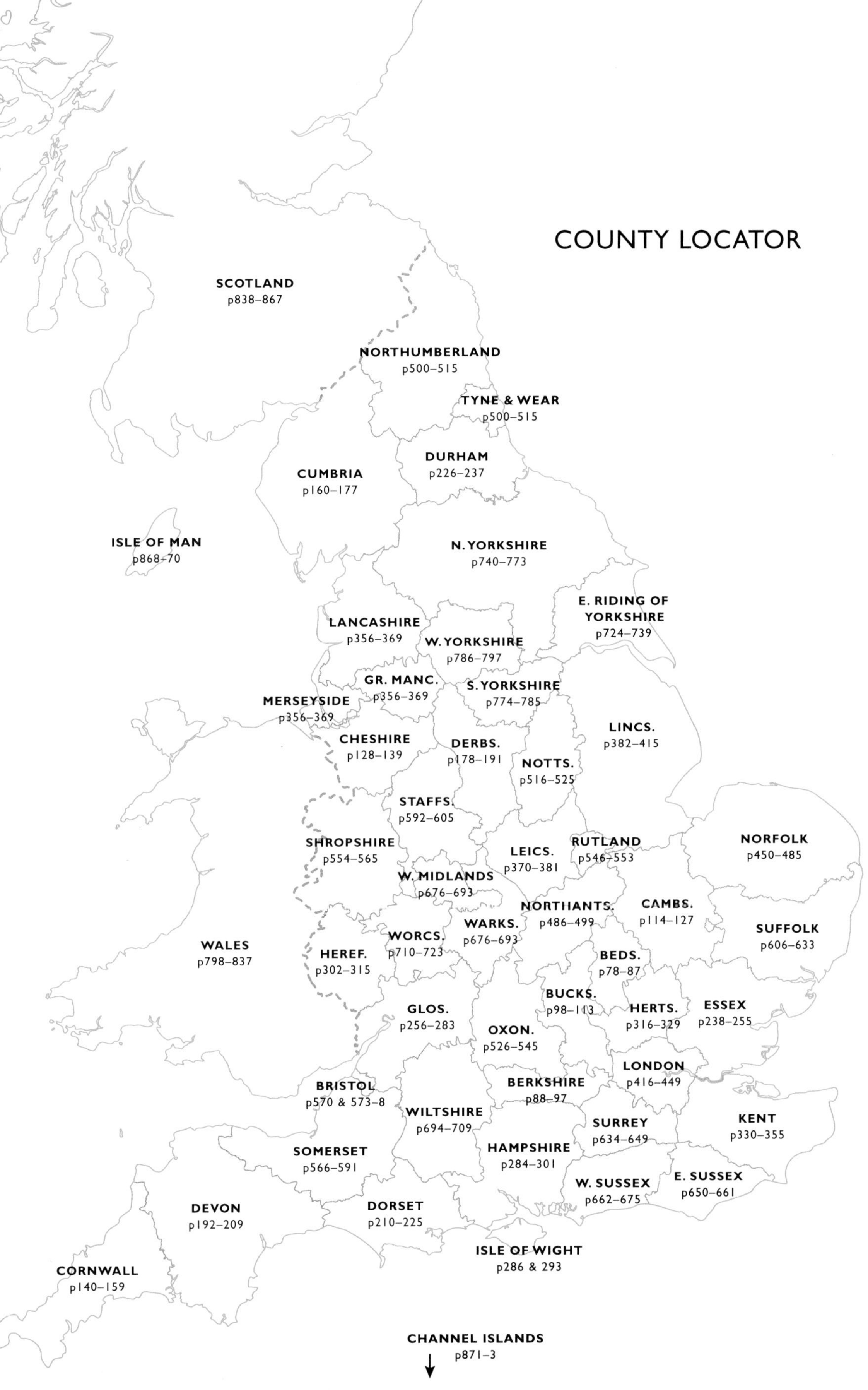
COUNTY LOCATOR
SCOTLAND p838–867
NORTHUMBERLAND p500–515
TYNE & WEAR p500–515
DURHAM p226–237
CUMBRIA p160–177
ISLE OF MAN p868–70
N. YORKSHIRE p740–773
E. RIDING OF YORKSHIRE p724–739
LANCASHIRE p356–369
W. YORKSHIRE p786–797
GR. MANC. p356–369
S. YORKSHIRE p774–785
MERSEYSIDE p356–369
CHESHIRE p128–139
DERBS. p178–191
NOTTS. p516–525
LINCS. p382–415
STAFFS. p592–605
SHROPSHIRE p554–565
LEICS. p370–381
RUTLAND p546–553
NORFOLK p450–485
W. MIDLANDS p676–693
NORTHANTS. p486–499
CAMBS. p114–127
SUFFOLK p606–633
WARKS. p676–693
WORCS. p710–723
HEREF. p302–315
WALES p798–837
BEDS. p78–87
BUCKS. p98–113
HERTS. p316–329
ESSEX p238–255
GLOS. p256–283
OXON. p526–545
LONDON p416–449
BERKSHIRE p88–97
BRISTOL p570 & 573–8
WILTSHIRE p694–709
SURREY p634–649
KENT p330–355
SOMERSET p566–591
HAMPSHIRE p284–301
W. SUSSEX p662–675
E. SUSSEX p650–661
DEVON p192–209
DORSET p210–225
ISLE OF WIGHT p286 & 293
CORNWALL p140–159
CHANNEL ISLANDS p871–3

PREFACE

BY RICHARD SURMAN

Since John Betjeman compiled the first 1958 edition of the *Collins Guide to English Parish Churches*, it has become a classic of its kind, and has been reprinted several times, most notably in the two-volume *Collins Pocket Guide to English Parish Churches*, published in 1968, and the 1980 edition, in which the scope of the book was extended to take in churches in Wales. The background to the book is a story all of its own. To many, Sir John Betjeman was latterly the Poet Laureate, whose work was reviled and adored in equal measure. But Betjeman was many things apart from being a poet: as a young boy holidaying in Trebetherick he went church-hunting, and in adolescence, churches became a passion for him. He would always talk about his childhood impressions of buildings as being crucial in determining his later responses to architecture.

Friendships with James Lees-Milne, the noted architectural advisor to the National Trust, Betjeman's work on the *Architectural Review*, where he met and formed a life-long friendship with the artist John Piper, a spell as the film critic for the *Evening Standard* – all these fed Betjeman's limitless and sometimes mischievous imagination, which was equally exercised by his colourful private life.

His working life would take a different emphasis however, when he proposed the idea of a series of county guides to Jack Beddington, publicity manager of Shell-Mex BP. Beddington was known for his patronage of artists and writers, and Betjeman found himself working alongside Paul Nash and a coterie of friends to whom he handed out work on the *Shell Guide* series. What always characterised Betjeman's reactions to architecture and countryside was a sense of place – the setting – as well as architectural and topographical detail. However mannered Betjeman might sometimes appear, one of his great gifts was to let landscape, architecture and art speak for themselves. After the war, Betjeman worked on many magazines, as well as writing poetry, and appearances on television became more and more regular. His presenting of the *ABC of Churches* programmes was a great success, not least to the crew, with whom he got on famously (although he did disconcert at least one member of the crew by taking his teddy bear Archibald Ormsby Gore wherever he went).

This new version – *Betjeman's Best British Churches* – takes Betjeman's original idea and moves it in a slightly different direction, but with great respect for his fundamental love of parish churches. The volume has much of a 21st-century feel about it – the age of satellite navigation and precision mapping have allowed us to create very precise locations for each of the churches featured herein. Betjeman

◁ **COLN ST DENYS: ST JAMES THE GREAT** – *sunk into the picturesque Gloucestershire landscape, the church retains its Norman ground plan and tower*

would have found this odd, I'm sure, but it is our hope that in 'modernising' the format of the book, we might appeal to a new audience more familiar with the digital age, as well as re-invigorating those familiar with earlier versions.

There are three radical departures from previous editions. The first is that we have introduced a much stronger pictorial element: full colour photographs are used throughout the book, as are accurate and clear maps of each county. The second radical difference arises from the first: with a large number of colour illustrations, the extent of the book has had to be considerably reduced. Betjeman's original book contained some 4,500 entries, and in some respects was a gazetteer. We decided to considerably modify this present edition, cutting down to some 2,500 entries. The criterion for retaining entries has been, wherever possible, to refer to the very simple star system that Betjeman employed in the 1968 edition, as the basis for first selection. Although the most recent 1993 edition discarded this form of rating, we have re-introduced it here, refining it so that throughout the book there is now a one- and two-star rating. Naturally there are many other churches included that were not starred in Betjeman's 1968 edition – some of those have been revised too. There are also new churches included, and to these we have applied rating criteria that reflect those of which Betjeman would have approved.

The third radical departure from previous versions is the creation of an entirely new section for Scotland. Though Scottish religious history differs quite significantly from that of England and Wales, we believe that there is a sufficient number of fine churches in Scotland to merit a place alongside their English and Welsh counterparts.

Another distinct feature of this present book is the inclusion of several notable Roman Catholic churches: these have been selected as being of outstanding historical, architectural or artistic merit. The medieval abbey of Pluscarden in Scotland qualifies on both counts, first as the only medieval monastery in the British Isles in continuous use – barring a hiatus after the Reformation – by a Roman Catholic monastic community, and second as a centre of design and production of outstanding contemporary glass. The Church of the Immaculate Conception, Farm Street, London has an entry, based on the excellent work of A. W. N. Pugin to the altar and reredos and the chancel chapels by H. Clutton and J. F. Bentley. London's Brompton Oratory gets an entry too; it would be remiss to ignore this extraordinary piece of Rome in London. In common with earlier editions we have also included churches in the care of the excellent Churches Conservation Trust, the Friends of Friendless Churches – especially in Wales – and English Heritage.

As regards the structure of counties, we have followed all the modern ceremonial boundaries: this has necessitated a considerable re-ordering of Yorkshire, the merging of Westmorland and Cumberland into Cumbria, changes to Berkshire and Oxfordshire and several other counties. Rutland, the country's smallest and fiercely independent county, has been retained, whilst Huntingdonshire and the Soke of Peterborough have been brought together within Cambridgeshire.

Bristol is with Somerset, and London is in two parts, Central and Greater London (the latter containing Middlesex and the inner parts of Essex, Kent and Surrey). Greater Manchester and Merseyside are together with Lancashire.

Considerable effort has gone into checking the facts about each entry, and wherever possible we have corrected errors. For errors that we have inadvertently introduced or have failed to correct, we both apologise and welcome comments.

To those people who may be disconcerted by the disappearance from this edition of their familiar churches, we ask for their forbearance, and hope that we have explained with sufficient persuasion the reasons why. Above all what we have striven to achieve is a book that captures the spirit of the earlier editions, in a 21st-century context.

A book such as this is not possible without the work of many people, not least those who have contributed to the various counties over the years. In particular I would like to thank Sam Richardson and Helena Nicholls at Collins Reference for their enthusiastic support for a long and complex project. I would also like to express my gratitude to Mike and Ros Ellis at Thameside Media: their hard and painstaking work on the planning, design, mapping, checking and photography have been essential. Their enthusiasm and expertise has taken them, I suspect, way beyond their brief. I am also very grateful to Michael Lynch, former Sir William Fraser Professor of Scottish History and Palaeography, for his eagle-eyed and helpful observations on my attempts to disentangle Scottish religious history.

Many others have contributed more indirectly – those hard-working souls that keep (some) of our fine churches open, that write the individual church guides, many of which are of a very high standard, and the various organisations, particularly the Churches Conservation Trust, the Friends of Friendless Churches, the National Churches Trust and the many county historic church trusts, all of whom work tirelessly to preserve a priceless heritage – the parish church.

Richard Surman 2011

INTRODUCTION

BY SIR JOHN BETJEMAN

PART ONE: THE OLD CHURCHES

To atheists inadequately developed building sites; and often, alas, to Anglicans but visible symbols of disagreement with the incumbent: 'the man there is "too high", "too low", "too lazy", "too interfering"' – still they stand, the churches of England, their towers grey above billowy globes of elm trees, the red cross of St George flying over their battlements, the Duplex Envelope System employed for collections, schoolmistress at the organ, incumbent in the chancel, scattered worshippers in the nave, Tortoise stove slowly consuming its ration as the familiar 17th-century phrases come echoing down arcades of ancient stone.

Odi et amo. This sums up the general opinion of the Church of England among the few who are not apathetic. One bright autumn morning I visited the church of the little silver limestone town of Somerton in Somerset. Hanging midway from a rich-timbered roof, on chains from which were suspended branched and brassy-gleaming chandeliers, were oval boards painted black. In gold letters on each these words were inscribed:

TO GOD'S
GLORY
&
THE HONOR OF
THE
CHURCH OF
ENGLAND
1782

They served me as an inspiration towards compiling this book.

The Parish Churches of England are even more varied than the landscape. The tall town church, smelling of furniture polish and hot-water pipes, a shadow of the medieval marvel it once was, so assiduously have Victorian and even later restorers renewed everything old; the little weather-beaten hamlet church standing in a farmyard down a narrow lane, bat-droppings over the pews and one service a month; the church of a once prosperous village, a relic of the 15th-century wool trade, whose soaring splendour of stone and glass subsequent generations have had neither the energy nor the money to destroy; the suburban church with Northamptonshire-style steeple rising unexpectedly

◁ **WALPOLE ST PETER: ST PETER** – *the porch to the church is vaulted in a beautiful sandstone, the bosses sculpted into the sleeping forms of foals, sheep and suchlike*

above slate roofs of London and calling with mid-Victorian bells to the ghosts on the edge of the industrial estate; the High, the Low, the Central churches, the alive and the dead ones, the churches that are easy to pray in and those that are not, the churches whose architecture brings you to your knees, the churches whose decorations affront the sight – all these come within the wide embrace of our Anglican Church, whose arms extend beyond the seas to many fabrics more.

From the first wooden church put up in a forest clearing or stone cell on windy moor to the newest social hall, with sanctuary and altar partitioned off, built on the latest industrial estate, our churches have existed chiefly for the celebration of what some call the Mass, or the Eucharist and others call Holy Communion or the Lord's Supper.

Between the early paganism of Britain and the present paganism there are nearly twenty thousand churches and well over a thousand years of Christianity. More than half the buildings are medieval. Many of those have been so severely restored in the last century that they could almost be called Victorian – new stone, new walls, new roofs, new pews. If there is anything old about them it is what one can discern through the detective work of the visual imagination.

It may be possible to generalize enough about the parish church of ancient origin to give an impression of how it is the history of its district in stone and wood and glass. Such generalization can give only a superficial impression. Churches vary with their building materials and with the religious, social and economic history of their districts.

The Outside of the Church – Gravestones

See on some village mount, in the mind's eye, the parish church of today. It is in the old part of the place. Near the church will be the few old houses of the parish, and almost for certain there will be an inn very near the church. A lych-gate built as a memorial at the beginning of this century indicates the entrance to the churchyard. Away on the outskirts of the town or village, if it is a place of any size, will be the arid new cemetery consecrated in 1910 when there was no more room in the churchyard.

Nearer to the church and almost always on the south side are to be found the older tombs, the examples of fine craftsmanship in local stone of the Queen Anne and Georgian periods. Wool merchants and big farmers, all those not entitled to an armorial monument on the walls inside the church, generally occupy the grandest graves. Their obelisks, urns and table tombs are surrounded with Georgian ironwork. Parish clerks, smaller farmers and tradesmen lie below plainer stones. All their families are recorded in deep-cut lettering. Here is a flourish of 18th-century calligraphy; there is reproduced the typeface of Baskerville. It is extraordinary how long the tradition of fine lettering continued, especially when it is in a stone easily carved or engraved, whether limestone, ironstone or slate. The tradition lasted until the middle of the 19th century in those country places where stone was used as easily as wood. Some old craftsman was carving away

△ **ST JUST-IN-ROSELAND: ST JUST** – *coastal lichen and moss on one of the headstones*

while the young go-aheads in the nearest town were busy inserting machine-made letters into white Italian marble.

The elegance of the local stone carver's craft is not to be seen only in the lettering. In the 18th century it was the convention to carve symbols round the top of the headstone and down the sides. The earlier examples are in bold relief, cherubs with plough-boy faces and thick wings, and scythes, hour glasses and skulls and cross-bones diversify their tops. You will find in one or another country churchyard that there has been a local sculptor of unusual vigour and perhaps genius who has even carved a rural scene above some well-graven name. Towards the end of the 18th century the lettering becomes finer and more prominent, the decoration flatter and more conventional, usually in the Adam manner, as though a son had taken on his father's business and depended on architectural pattern-books. But the tops of all headstones varied in shape. At this time too it became the custom in some districts to paint the stones and to add a little gold leaf to the lettering. Paint and stone by now have acquired a varied pattern produced by weather and fungus, so that the stones are probably more beautiful than they were when they were new, splodged as they are with gold and silver and slightly overgrown with moss. On a sharp frosty day when the sun is in the south and throwing up the carving, or in the west and bringing out all the colour of the lichens, a country churchyard may bring back the lost ages of craftsmanship more effectively than the church which stands behind it. Those unknown carvers are the same race as produced the vigorous inn signs which were such a feature of England before the brewers ruined them with artiness and standardization. They belong to the world of wheelwrights and wagon-makers, and they had their local styles. In Kent the chief effect of variety was created by different-sized stones with elaborately-scalloped heads to them, and by shroud-like mummies of stone on top of the grave itself; in the Cotswolds by carving in strong relief; in slate districts by engraved lettering. In counties like Surrey and Sussex, where stone was rare, there were many wooden graveyard monuments, two posts with a board between them running down the length of the grave and painted in the way an old wagon is painted. But most of these wooden monuments have perished or decayed out of recognition.

'At rest', 'Fell asleep', 'Not dead but gone before' and other equally non-committal legends are on the newer tombs. In Georgian days it was the custom either to put only the name or to apply to the schoolmaster or parson for a rhyme. Many a graveyard contains beautiful stanzas which have not found their way to print and are disappearing under wind and weather. Two of these inscriptions have particularly struck my fancy. One is in Bideford and commemorates a retired sea-captain Henry Clark, 1836. It summarizes for me a type of friendly and pathetic Englishman to be found hanging about, particularly at little seaports.

For twenty years he scarce slept in a bed;
Linhays and limekilns lull'd his weary head
Because he would not to the poor house go,
For his proud spirit would not let him to.
The black bird's whistling notes at break of day
Used to wake him from his bed of hay.
Unto the bridge and quay he then repaired
To see what shipping up the river stirr'd.
Oft in the week he used to view the bay,
To see what ships were coming in from sea,
To captains' wives he brought the welcome news,
And to the relatives of all the crews.
At last poor Harry Clark was taken ill,
And carried to the work house 'gainst his will:
And being of this mortal life quite tired,
He lived about a month and then expired.

The other is on an outside monument on the north wall of the church at Harefield, near Uxbridge, one of the last three country villages left in Middlesex. It is to Robert Mossendew, servant of the Ashby family, who died in 1744. Had he been a gentleman his monument would at this time have been inside the church. He was a gamekeeper and is carved in relief with his gun above this inscription.

In frost and snow, thro' hail and rain
He scour'd the woods, and trudg'd the plain;
The steady pointer leads the way,
Stands at the scent, then springs the prey;
The timorous birds from stubble rise,
With pinions stretch'd divide the skies;

The scatter'd lead pursues the sight
And death in thunder stops their flight;
His spaniel, of true English kind,
With gratitude inflames his mind;
This servant in an honest way,
In all his actions copies Tray.

The churchyard indeed often contains cruder but more lively and loving verses than the polished tributes inscribed in marble tablets within the church to squires and peers and divines of the county hierarchy. The Dartmoor parish of Buckland Monachorum displays this popular epitaph to a blacksmith which may be found in other parishes:

My sledge and hammer both declin'd,
My bellows too have lost their wind.
My fire's extinct, my forge decay'd,
And in the dust my vice is laid,
My coal is spent, my iron's gone,
My nails are drove, my work is done.

Though such an epitaph can scarcely be called Christian, it is at least not an attempt to cover up in mawkish sentiment or in crematorial good taste the inevitability of death.

The Outside

The church whose southern side we are approaching is probably little like the building which stood there even two centuries before, although it has not been rebuilt. The outside walls were probably plastered, unless the church is in a district where workable stone has long been used and it is faced with cut stone known as ashlar. Churches which are ashlar-faced all over are rare, but many have an ashlar-faced western tower, or aisle to the north-east or south-east, or a porch or transept built of cut stone in the 15th century by a rich family. Some have a guild chapel or private chantry where Mass was said for the souls of deceased members of the guild or family. This is usually ashlar-faced and has a carved parapet as well, and is in marked contrast with the humble masonry of the rest of the church.

Rubble or uneven flints were not considered beautiful to look at until the 19th century. People were ashamed of them and wished to see their churches smooth on the outside and inside walls, and weather-proof. At Barnack and Earl's Barton the Saxons have even gone so far as to imitate in stone the decorative effects of wooden construction. Plaster made of a mixture of hair or straw and sand and lime was from Saxon times applied as a covering to the walls. Only the cut stone round the windows and doors was left, and even this was lime-washed. The plaster was thin and uneven. It was beautifully coloured a pale yellow or pink or white

△ **EAST SHEFFORD: ST THOMAS** – *plaster on exterior walls would once have been common but is now a rarity; here too is a use of many materials: brick, stone, tile and timber*

according to the tradition of the district. And if it has now been stripped off the church, it may still be seen on old cottages of the village if any survive. The earlier the walls of a church are, the less likely they are to be ashlar-faced, for there was no widespread use of cut stone in villages until the late 14th century when transport was better, and attention which had formerly been expended on abbeys was paid to building and enlarging parish churches.

And this is the place to say that most of the old parish churches in England are building rather than architecture. They are gradual growths, as their outside walls will shew; in their construction they partake of the character of cottages and barns and the early manor house, and not of the great abbey churches built for monks or secular canons. Their humble builders were inspired to copy what was to be seen in the nearest great church. The styles of Gothic came from these large buildings, but the village execution of them was later and could rarely rise to more than window tracery and roof timbering. Even these effects have a local flavour, they are a village voluntary compared with the music played on a great instrument by the cathedral organist. Of course here and there, when the abbeys declined, a famous mason from an abbey or cathedral might rebuild the church of his native place, and masons were employed in rich wool districts of East Anglia, the Midlands and parts of Yorkshire and Devon to build large churches which really are architecture and the product of a single brain, not the humble expression of a village community's worship. Much has been discovered about the names and work of medieval architects by Mr John Harvey in his book *Gothic England* and in the researches of Messrs. Salzman, and Knoop and Jones.

These outside walls on which the sun shews up the mottled plaster, the sudden warm red of an 18th-century patching of brick, the gentle contrast with the ashlar, the lime-washed tracery of the windows, the heating chimney-stack in local brick climbing up the chancel wall or the stove pipe projecting from a window, these are more often seen today in old watercolours in the local museum, or in some affectionate and ill-executed painting hanging in the vestry shewing the church 'before restoration in 1883'. Most of our old churches have been stripped of their plaster, some in living memory. The rubble has been exposed and then too often been repointed with grey cement, which is unyielding and instead of protecting the old stones causes them to crack and flake in frosty weather, for cement and stone have different rates of expansion. To make matters worse the cement itself has been snail pointed, that is to say pointed in hard, flat lines, so that the church wall looks like a crazy pavement.

Old paintings sometimes shew the external roofs as they used to be. The church roof and chancel are scarcely distinguishable from the cottage roofs. If the original steep pitch survives, it is seen to be covered with the local tiles, stones or thatch of the old houses of the district. 15th-century and Georgian raisings or lowerings of the roof and alterations to a flatter pitch generally meant a re-covering with lead, and the original pitch may be traced on the eastern face of the tower. Victorian restorers much enjoyed raising roofs to what they considered the original pitch, or putting on an altogether new roof in the cathedral manner. The effect of those re-roofings is generally the most obviously new feature on the outside of an old church. Red tiles and patterned slates from Wales or stone tiles which continually come down because they are set at a pitch too steep for their weight, are the usual materials. Instead of being graded in size, large at the eaves and getting smaller as they reach the ridge, the stone tiles are all of the same size so that the roof is not proportioned to the walls. The ridges are usually crowned with ridge tiles of an ornamental pattern which contrast in colour and texture with the rest. The gable ends are adorned with crosses. The drainage system is prominent and there will be pipes running down the wall to a gutter. On the rain-water heads at the top of these pipes there will probably be the date of the restoration. The old way of draining a roof was generally by leaden or wooden spouts rushing out of the fearsome mouths of gargoyles and carrying the water well beyond the walls of the church into the churchyard. If the water did drip on to the walls the plaster served as a protection from damp. Butterfield, a comparatively conservative and severely practical Victorian restorer, in his report on the restoration of Shottesbrooke church (1845) remarks of the flint walls of that elegant building, 'There are no parapets to any part of the Church, and the water has continued to drip from the eaves for five centuries without any injury to the walls.' On the other hand the water has continued to drip from the eaves of Sir Edwin Lutyens' fine church of St Jude-on-the-Hill, Hampstead Garden Suburb, London, and over its Portland stone cornice with considerable injury to the brick walls in less than half a century. The nature of the wall surface, the pointing, and the means devised for draining the water clear from the wall foundation once it has reached the ground, have much to do with keeping out the damp.

Sometimes we may find on the outside walls a variety of scratches, marks and carvings. The only ones of any beauty will probably be the consecration crosses, where the Bishop anointed the walls with oil when the church was newly built. They are high up so that people would not brush them in going past. Similar crosses may be seen on stone altars inside the church. The small crosses which are cut roughly in the jambs of doorways were, according to the late E. A. Greening Lamborn, an angry antiquarian with a good prose style, probably put there not for consecration but 'to scare away evil spirits and prevent them crossing the threshold'. There is a whole literature devoted to masons' marks on the walls of churches, outside and in, and to the 'scratch dials' or 'mass clocks' which look like sundials lacking a gnomon, to be found on the outside south walls of many churches. The masons' marks are triangles, diamonds, bent arrows, circles, squares and other shapes looking rather like boy scout signs, cut into ashlar in some churches, notably the large ones, and surviving where stone has not been re-tooled by the Victorians. Often they may be only scribbles. But they seem to help some antiquaries to give an exact date to buildings or portions of a building. Scratch dials or mass clocks were used generally to show the time when Mass was to be said (usually 9 a.m. in medieval England). Others are primitive clocks. But they, like the parish registers, belong to the non-visual side of church history and it is with the look of a church that this book is primarily concerned.

Finally there are on the outside of churches the gargoyles spouting water off the roof and the carved heads to be found either side of some windows and the figures in niches on tower or porch. Gargoyles can be fearsome, particularly on the north side of the church, and heads and statues, where they have survived Puritan outrage and Victorian zeal, are sometimes extremely beautiful or fantastic.

The church porch flapping with electoral rolls, notices of local acts, missionary appeals and church services (which will occupy us later) gives us a welcome. Though the powers of the parish vestry have been taken over by parish councils and local government, church doors or the porches which shelter them are often plastered with public announcements. Regularly will the village policeman nail to the church door some notice about Foot-and-Mouth Disease when the British Legion Notice Board has been denied him or the Post Office is shut. Most church porches in England are built on the south side, first as a protection for the door from prevailing south-west gales. Then they were used as places for baptism, bargains were made there, oaths sworn, and burial and marriage services conducted. Above some of them, from the 14th century onward, a room was built, usually for keeping parish chests and records. In these places many a village school was started. At first they may have been inhabited by a watchman, who could look down into the church from an internal window. In counties where stone is rare there are often elaborate wooden porches, notably in Sussex, Surrey and Essex.

Professor E. A. Freeman, the great Victorian ecclesiologist, thought little of a man who went up the churchyard path to the main door, which is more or less

△ **ASHTON: ST JOHN THE BAPTIST** – *the 15th-century screens at the church have some of Devon's best figurative panel painting*

what we have done, and did not go round the whole building first. But he was an antiquary who took his churches slowly, speculated on them and did detective work about dates of extensions. On a day when the wind is not too cold and the grass not too long and wet, a walk round the outside of the church is always worth while. On the farther side, which is generally the north, there may well be extensions, a family mausoleum for instance, of which there is no sign inside the church beyond a blocked archway. Mr John Piper and I had a peculiar experience through not going round the outside of the derelict church of Wolfhamcote near Daventry in Warwickshire. The lovely building was locked, the windows smashed, and the sun was setting on its lichened stone. There was only one cottage near and we could make no one hear. So we climbed through a window in the south aisle. Bat-droppings were over rotting floors and damp stains on the ochre-plastered walls, and in the fading light we saw that the altar cloth had been raised and revealed a black tunnel with light at the end, a most peculiar thing to see beyond an altar. We approached and saw there were stairs going down under the table leading to a passage in which brass-studded coffins lay on shelves. When we went round the outside of the church we saw that beyond the east end was a Strawberry Hill Gothick extension, the mausoleum of the Tibbits family. Vestries are more usual on the north side of churches than mausolea, and very ugly most of them are, hard little stone sheds leant against the old walls. There will be almost for certain a north door blocked or bricked-up long ago, with the trace of its arch mouldings still there. There may even be a north porch. But unless the village and manor house are to the north of the

△ **ROCK: ST PETER AND ST PAUL** – *like many churches, it has retained its Norman doorway while the church around it has been fully Gothicised*

church this side of the churchyard will be gloomy and its tombs will be, at the earliest, 19th century, except for a very few near the east end. And so round by the sexton's tool-shed and the anthracite dump and the west door of the tower, we return to the south porch.

Notice the stonework round the outside doors. Often it is round-headed and of Norman date, an elaborate affair of several concentric semi-circles of carved stone. It may even be the only Norman work left in the church and may originally have been the chancel arch before the chancel was enlarged and a screen put across its western end. The later medieval rebuilders respected the Norman craftsmanship and often kept a Norman door inside their elaborate porches.

There is often difficulty in opening the door. This gives the less impatient of us a chance of looking at the door itself. Either because the business of transferring the huge church lock was too difficult, or because here was a good piece of wood older than any of the trees in the parish, church doors have survived from the middle ages while the interiors on to which they open have been repaired out of recognition. The wood of the door may be carved or be decorated with old local ironwork. If it is an old door it will invariably open inwards. So first turn the iron handle and push hard. Then if the door seems to be locked, turn the handle the other way and push hard. Then feel on the wall-plate of the porch for the key. Church keys are usually six or eight inches long and easy to find. If there is no sign of the key and all vestry doors are locked, call at a house. If the path leading through the churchyard to a door in the vicarage wall is overgrown and looks unused, you may be sure the vicarage has been sold to wealthy unbelievers and there is no chance of getting the key from there. The houses to choose are those with pots of flowers in the window. Here will be living traditional villagers who even if they are chapel will probably know who it is who keeps the church key. Men are less likely to know than women, since men in villages are more rarely church-goers. Villagers are all out on Saturday afternoons shopping in the local town. Only an idiot and the dog remain behind.

The Porch and Bells

Down one step – for the churchyard will have risen round an old building – and we are in the church itself.

The practised eye can tell at a glance how severe the restoration has been, and often indeed who has done the damage. For instance almost every other church in Cornwall, beside many farther east, was restored by Mr J. P. St Aubyn late in the 19th century, and he has left his mark at the church porch in the form of a scraper of his own design, as practical and unattractive as his work. We must remember, however much we deplore it, that the most cumbersome bit of panelling bought from a Birmingham firm without regard for the old church into which it is to go, the sentimental picture for the Art Shop, the banner with the dislocated saint, the Benares ware altar vases, the brass commemorative tablet, the greenish stained-glass window with its sentimental Good Shepherd – often have been saved up for by some devout and penurious communicant.

It must be admitted that spirituality and aesthetics rarely go together. 'Carnal delight even in the holiest things,' says Father R. M. Benson, founder of the Cowley Father '(habits of thought and philosophy, acquisition of knowledge, schemes of philanthropy, aesthetic propriety, influence in society) hinders the development of the Christ-life by strengthening the natural will.' So when one is inclined to lament lack of taste and seemingly wilful destruction of beauty in a church, it is wise to remember that the incumbent, even if he be that rarity a man of aesthetic appreciation, is probably not to blame for modern blemishes to the fabric. He is primarily a missioner and he cannot offend his parishioners on so unspiritual a matter. The reader who casts his mind back to his early worship as a child will remember that a hymn board, or a brass cross or a garish window were, from his customary gazing on them Sunday after Sunday, part of his religious life. If as an older and more informed person his taste and knowledge tell him these things are cheap and hideous, he will still regret their passing with a part of him which is neither his intellect nor his learning. How much more will an uninformed villager, whose feeling always runs higher where the church is concerned than a townsman's, cling to these objects he has known as a boy, however cheap they are. When the vicar or rector felt himself entitled to be a dictator, he could with more impunity and less offence than now, 'restore' the old church out of recognition. He could hack down the box-pews, re-erect a screen across the chancel, put the choir into surplices and move it from the west gallery to the chancel, and substitute a pipe organ for the old instruments. Even in those days many a disgruntled villager left the church to try his voice in chapel or to play his instrument in the old village band. It is a tribute to the hold of our church that congregations continued to use their churches after restorations in Victorian times. Perhaps the reason for the continued hold is that the more ritualistic performance of the Church Services made church more interesting. There is no doubt that Evangelicals were worried at the success of Tractarian methods. But picture your own childhood's church whitewashed on the advice of the Diocesan Advisory Committee, your pew gone and a row of chairs in its place, the altar different, and the chancel cleared of choir-stalls and the choir non-existent as a consequence. Were it not your childhood's church, you would consider this an improvement. One part of you may consider it an improvement despite associations, but not the other. Conservatism is innate in ecclesiastical arrangement. It is what saves for us the history of the village or town in wood and glass and metal and stone.

Let us enter the church by the tower door and climb to the ringing chamber where the ropes hang through holes in the roof. Nowhere outside England except for a very few towers in the rest of the British Isles, America and the Dominions, are bells rung so well. The carillons of the Netherlands and of Bourneville and Atkinson's scent shop in London are not bell ringing as understood in England. Carillon ringing is done either by means of a cylinder worked on the barrel-organ and musical box principle, or by keyed notes played by a musician. Carillon bells are sounded by pulling the clapper to the rim of the bell. This is called chiming, and it is not ringing.

Bell ringing in England is known among ringers as 'the exercise', rather as the rearing and training of pigeons is known among the pigeon fraternity as 'the fancy'. It is a class-less folk art which has survived in the church despite all arguments about doctrine and the diminution of congregations. In many a church when the parson opens with the words 'Dearly beloved brethren, the Scripture moveth us in sundry places...' one may hear the tramp of the ringers descending the newel stair into the refreshing silence of the graveyard. Though in some churches they may come in later by the main door and sit in the pew marked 'Ringers Only', in others they will not be seen again, the sweet melancholy notes of 'the exercise' floating out over the Sunday chimney-pots having been their contribution to the glory of God. So full of interest and technicality is the exercise that there is a weekly paper devoted to it called *The Ringing World.*

A belfry where ringers are keen has the used and admired look of a social club. There, above the little bit of looking-glass in which the ringers slick their hair and straighten their ties before stepping down into the outside world, you will find blackboards with gilded lettering proclaiming past peals rung for hours at a stretch. In another place will be the rules of the tower written in a clerkly hand. A charming Georgian ringers' rhyme survives at St Endellion, Cornwall, on a board headed with a picture of ringers in knee-breeches:

We ring the Quick to Church and dead to Grave,
Good is our use, such usage let us have
Who here therefore doth Damn, or Curse or Swear,
Or strike in Quarrel thogh no Blood appear,
Who wears a Hatt or Spurr or turns a Bell
Or by unskilful handling spoils a Peal,
Shall Sixpense pay for every single Crime
'Twill make him careful 'gainst another time.
Let all in Love and Friendship hither come,
Whilst the shrill Treble calls to Thundering Tom,
And since bells are our modest Recreation
Let's Rise and Ring and Fall to Admiration.

Many country towers have six bells. Not all these bells are medieval. Most were cast in the 17th, 18th or 19th centuries when change-ringing was becoming a country exercise. And the older bells will have been re-cast during that time, to bring them into tune with the new ones. They are likely to have been again re-cast in modern times, and the most ancient inscription preserved and welded on to the re-cast bell. Most counties have elaborately produced monographs about their church bells. The older bells have beautiful lettering sometimes, as at Somerby, and South Somercotes in Lincolnshire, where they are inscribed with initial letters decorated with figures so that they look like illuminated initials from old manuscripts interpreted in relief on metal. The English love for Our Lady survived in inscriptions on church bells long after the Reformation, as did the use of Latin. Many 18th- and even early 19th-century bells have Latin inscriptions. A rich collection of varied dates may be seen by struggling about on the wooden cage in which the bells hang among the bat-droppings in the tower.

Many local customs survive in the use of bells. In some places a curfew is rung every evening; in others a bell is rung at five in the morning during Lent. Fanciful legends have grown up about why they are rung, but their origins can generally be traced to the divine offices. The passing bell is rung differently from district to district. Sometimes the years of the deceased are tolled, sometimes the ringing is three strokes in succession followed by a pause. There are instances of the survival of prayers for the departed where the bell is tolled as soon as the news of the death of a parishioner reaches the incumbent.

Who has heard a muffled peal and remained unmoved? Leather bags are tied to one side of the clapper and the bells ring alternately loud and soft, the soft being an echo, as though in the next world, of the music we hear on earth.

I make no apology for writing so much about church bells. They ring through our literature, as they do over our meadows and roofs and few remaining elms. Some may hate them for their melancholy, but they dislike them chiefly, I think, because they are reminders of Eternity. In an age of faith they were messengers of consolation.

The bells are rung down, the ting-tang will ring for five minutes, and now is the time to go into Church.

The Interior Today

As we sit in a back pew of the nave with the rest of the congregation – the front pews are reserved for those who never come to church – most objects which catch the eye are Victorian. What we see of the present age is cheap and sparse. The thick wires clamped on to the old outside wall, which make the church look as though the vicar had put it on the telephone, are an indication without that electric light has lately been introduced. The position of the lights destroys the effect of the old mouldings on arches and columns. It is a light too harsh and bright for an old building, and the few remaining delicate textures on stone and walls are destroyed by the dazzling floodlights fixed in reflectors from the roof, and a couple of spotlights behind the chancel arch which throw their full radiance on the brass altar vases and on the vicar when he marches up to give the blessing. At sermon time, in a winter evensong, the lights are switched off, and the strip reading-lamp on the pulpit throws up the vicar's chin and eyebrows so that he looks like Grock. A further disfigurement introduced by electrical engineers is a collection of meters, pipes and fuses on one of the walls.[1] If a church must be lit with electricity – which is in any case preferable to gas, which streaks the walls – the advice of Sir Ninian Comper might well be taken. This is to have as many bulbs as possible of as low power as possible, so that they do not dazzle the eye when they hang from the roof and walls. Candles are the perfect lighting for an old church, and oil light is also effective. The mystery of an old

[1] I have even seen electric heaters hung at intervals along the gallery of an 18th-century church and half-way up the columns of a medieval nave.

church, however small the building, is preserved by irregularly placed clusters of low-powered bulbs which light service books but leave the roof in comparative darkness. The chancel should not be strongly lit, for this makes the church look small, and all too rarely are chancel and altar worthy of a brilliant light. I have hardly ever seen an electrically lit church where this method has been employed, and we may assume that the one in which we are sitting is either floodlit or strung with blinding pendants whose bulbs are covered by 'temporary' shades reminiscent of a Government office.

Other modern adornments are best seen in daylight, and it is in daylight that we will imagine the rest of the church. The 'children's corner' in front of the side altar, with its pale reproductions of water-colours by Margaret W. Tarrant, the powder-blue hangings and unstained oak kneelers, the side altar itself, too small in relation to the aisle window above it, the pale stained-glass figure of St George with plenty of clear glass round it (Diocesan Advisory Committees do not like exclusion of daylight) or the anaemic stained-glass soldier in khaki – these are likely to be the only recent additions to the church, excepting a few mural tablets in oak or Hopton Wood stone, much too small in comparison with the 18th-century ones, dotted about on the walls and giving them the appearance of a stamp album; these, thank goodness, are the only damage our age will have felt empowered to do.

The Interior in 1860

In those richer days when a British passport was respected throughout the world, when 'carriage folk' existed and there was a smell of straw and stable in town streets and bobbing tenants at lodge gates in the country, when it was unusual to boast of disbelief in God and when 'Chapel' was connected with 'trade' and 'Church' with 'gentry', when there were many people in villages who had never seen a train nor left their parish, when old farm-workers still wore smocks, when town slums were newer and even more horrible, when people had orchids in their conservatories and geraniums and lobelias in the trim beds beside their gravel walks, when stained glass was brownish-green and when things that shone were considered beautiful, whether they were pink granite, brass, pitchpine, mahogany or encaustic tiles, when the rector was second only to the squire, when doctors were 'apothecaries' and lawyers 'attorneys', when Parliament was a club, when shops competed for custom, when the servants went to church in the evening, when there were family prayers and basement kitchens – in those days God seemed to have created the universe and to have sent His Son to redeem the world, and there was a church parade to worship Him on those shining Sunday mornings we read of in Charlotte M. Yonge's novels and feel in Trollope and see in the drawings in Punch. Then it was that the money pouring in from our empire was spent in restoring old churches and in building bold and handsome new ones in crowded areas and exclusive suburbs, in seaside towns and dockland settlements. They were built by the rich and given to the poor: 'All Seats in this Church are Free.' Let us now see this church we have been describing as it was in the late 1860s, shining after its restoration.

Changed indeed it is, for even the aisles are crowded and the prevailing colours of clothes are black, dark blue and purple. The gentlemen are in frock coats and lean forward into their top hats for a moment's prayer, while the lesser men are in black broad-cloth and sit with folded arms awaiting the rector. He comes in after his curate and they sit at desks facing each other on either side of the chancel steps. Both wear surplices: the Rector's is long and flowing and he has a black scarf round his shoulders: so has the curate, but his surplice is shorter and he wears a cassock underneath, for, if the truth be told, the curate is 'higher' than the rector and would have no objection to wearing a coloured stole and seeing a couple of candles lit on the altar for Holy Communion. But this would cause grave scandal to the parishioners, who fear idolatry. Those who sit in the pews in the aisles where the seats face inward, never think of turning eastwards for the Creed. *Hymns Ancient and Modern* has been introduced. The book is ritualistic, but several excellent men have composed and written for it, like Sir Frederick Ouseley and Sir Henry Baker, and Bishops and Deans. The surpliced choir precede the clergy and march out of the new vestry built on the north-east corner of the church. Some of the older men, feeling a little ridiculous in surplices, look wistfully towards the west end where the gallery used to be and where they sang as youths to serpent, fiddle and bass recorder in the old-fashioned choir, before the pipe organ was introduced up there in the chancel. The altar has been raised on a series of steps, the shining new tiles becoming more elaborate and brilliant the nearer they approach the altar. The altar frontal has been embroidered by ladies in the parish, a pattern of lilies on a red background. There is still an alms dish on the altar, and behind it a cross has been set in stone on the east wall. In ten years' time brass vases of flowers, a cross and candlesticks will be on a 'gradine' or shelf above the altar. The east window is new, tracery and all. The glass is green and red, shewing the Ascension – the Crucifixion is a little ritualistic – and has been done by a London firm. And a smart London architect designed all these choir stalls in oak and these pews of pitch-pine in the nave and aisles. At his orders the new chancel roof was constructed, the plaster was taken off the walls of the church, and the stone floors were taken up and transformed into a shining stretch of red and black tiles. He also had that pale pink and yellow glass put in all the unstained windows so that a religious light was cast. The brass gas brackets arc by Skidmore of Coventry. Some antiquarian remains are carefully preserved. A Norman capital from the old aisle which was pulled down, a pillar piscina, a half of a cusped arch which might have been – no one knows quite what it might have been, but it is obviously ancient. Unfortunately it was not possible to remove the pagan classical memorials of the last century owing to trouble about faculties and fear of offending the descendants of the families commemorated. The church is as good as new, and all the medieval style of the middle-pointed period – the best period because it is in the middle and not 'crude' like Norman and Early English, or 'debased' like Perpendicular and Tudor. Nearly everyone can see the altar. The Jacobean pulpit has survived, lowered and re-erected on a stone base. Marble pulpits are rather expensive, and Jacobean is not wholly unfashionable so far as woodwork is concerned. The prevailing colours of the church are brown and green, with faint tinges of pink and yellow.

Not everyone approved of these 'alterations' in which the old churches of England were almost entirely rebuilt. I quote from Alfred Rimmer's *Pleasant Spots Around Oxford* (c. 1865), on the taking down of the body of Woodstock's classical church.

> 'Well, during the month of July I saw this church at Woodstock, but unhappily, left making sketches of it till a future visit. An ominous begging-box, with a lock, stood out in the street asking for funds for the "restoration". One would have thought it almost a burlesque, for it wanted no restoration at all, and would have lasted for ever so many centuries; but the box was put up by those "who said in their hearts, Let us make havoc of it altogether". Within a few weeks of the time this interesting monument was perfect, no one beam was left; and now, as I write, it is a "heap of stones". Through the debris I could just distinguish a fine old Norman doorway that had survived ever so many scenes notable in history, but it was nearly covered up with ruins; and supposing it does escape the general melee, and has the luck to be inserted in a new church, with open benches and modern adornments, it will have lost every claim to interest and be scraped down by unloving hands to appear like a new doorway. Happily, though rather late in the day, an end is approaching to these vandalisms.'

The Church in Georgian Times

See now the outside of our church about eighty years before, in, let us say, 1805, when the two-folio volumes on the county were produced by a learned antiquarian, with aquatint engravings of the churches, careful copper-plates of fonts and supposedly Roman pieces of stone, and laborious copyings of entries in parish rolls. How different from the polished, furbished fane we have just left is this humble, almost cottage-like place of worship. Oak posts and rails enclose the churchyard in which a horse, maybe the Reverend Dr Syntax's mare Grizzel, is grazing. The stones are humble and few, and lean this way and that on the south side. They are painted black and grey and the lettering on some is picked out in gold. Two altar tombs, one with a sculptured urn above it, are enclosed in sturdy iron rails such as one sees above the basements of Georgian terrace houses. Beyond the church below a thunderous sky we see the elm and oak landscape of an England comparatively unenclosed. Thatched cottages and stone-tiled farms are collected round the church, and beyond them on the boundaries of the parish the land is still open and park-like, while an unfenced road winds on with its freight of huge bonnetted wagons. Later in the 19th century this land was parcelled into distant farms with significant names like 'Egypt', 'California',

'Starveall', which stud the ordnance maps. Windmills mark the hill-tops and water-mills the stream. Our church to which this agricultural world would come, save those who in spite of Test Acts and suspicion of treachery meet in their Dissenting conventicles, is a patched, uneven-looking place.

Sympathetic descriptive accounts of unrestored churches are rarely found in late Georgian or early Victorian prose or verse. Most of the writers on churches are antiquarians who see nothing but ancient stones, or whose zeal for 'restoration' colours their writing. Thus for instance Mr John Noake describes White Ladies' Aston in Worcestershire in 1851 (*The Rambler in Worcestershire*, London, Longman and Co., 1851). 'The church is Norman, with a wooden broach spire; the windows, with two or three square-headed exceptions, are Norman, including that at the east end, which is somewhat rare. The west end is disgraced by the insertion of small square windows and wooden frames, which, containing a great quantity of broken glass, and a stove-pipe issuing therefrom impart to the sacred building the idea of a low-class lodging house.' And writing at about the same time, though not publishing until 1888, the entertaining *Church-Goer* of Bristol thus describes the Somerset church of Brean:

> 'On the other side of the way stood the church – little and old, and unpicturesquely freshened up with whitewash and yellow ochre; the former on the walls and the latter on the worn stone mullions of the small Gothic windows. The stunted slate-topped tower was white-limed, too – all but a little slate slab on the western side, which bore the inscription:
>
> JOHN GHENKIN
> Churchwarden
> 1729
>
> Anything owing less to taste and trouble than the little structure you would not imagine. Though rude, however, and old, and kept together as it was by repeated whitewashings, which mercifully filled up flaws and cracks, it was not disproportioned or unmemorable in aspect, and might with a trifling outlay be made to look as though someone cared for it.'

Such a church with tracery ochred on the outside may be seen in the background of Millais' painting *The Blind Girl.* It is, I believe, Winchelsea before restoration. Many writers, beside Rimmer, regret the restoration of old churches by London architects in the last century. The despised Reverend J. L. Petit, writing in 1841 in those two volumes called *Remarks on Church Architecture*, illustrated with curious anastatic sketches, was upbraided by critics for writing too much by aesthetic and not enough by antiquarian standards.

He naturally devoted a whole chapter to regretting restoration. But neither he nor many poets who preceded him bothered to describe the outside appearance of unrestored village churches, and seldom did they relate the buildings to their settings. 'Venerable', 'ivy-mantled', 'picturesque' are considered precise enough words for the old village church of Georgian times, with 'neat', 'elegant' or 'decent' for any recent additions. It is left for the Reverend George Crabbe, that accurate and beautiful observer, to recall the texture of weathered stone in *The Borough, Letter II* (1810):

But 'ere you enter, yon bold tower survey
Tall and entire, and venerably grey,
For time has soften'd what was harsh when new,
And now the stains are all of sober hue;
and to admonish the painters:
And would'st thou, artist! with thy tints and brush
Form shades like these? Pretender, where thy brush?
In three short hours shall thy presuming hand
Th' effect of three slow centuries command?
Thou may'st thy various greens and greys contrive
They are not lichens nor light aught alive.
But yet proceed and when thy tints are lost,
Fled in the shower, or crumbled in the frost
When all thy work is done away as clean
As if thou never spread'st thy grey and green,
Then may'st thou see how Nature's work is done,
How slowly true she lays her colours on . . .

With the precision of the botanist, Crabbe describes the process of decay which is part of the beauty of the outside of an unrestored church:

Seeds, to our eye invisible, will find
On the rude rock the bed that fits their kind:
There, in the rugged soil, they safely dwell,
Till showers and snows the subtle atoms swell,
And spread th' enduring foliage; then, we trace
The freckled flower upon the flinty base;
These all increase, till in unnoticed years
The stony tower as grey with age appears;
With coats of vegetation thinly spread,
Coat above coat, the living on the dead:
These then dissolve to dust, and make a way
For bolder foliage, nurs'd by their decay:
The long-enduring ferns in time will all
Die and despose their dust upon the wall
Where the wing'd seed may rest, till many a flower
Show Flora's triumph o'er the falling tower.

Yet the artists whom Crabbe admonishes have left us better records than there are in literature of our churches before the Victorians restored them. The engravings of Hogarth, the water-colours and etchings of John Sell Cotman and

△ **WILLEN: ST MARY** – *a Classical church of the 1670s by Robert Hooke, it points the way to the Georgian interiors of the following century*

of Thomas Rowlandson, the careful and less inspired records of John Buckler, re-create these places for us. They were drawn with affection for the building as it was and not 'as it ought to be'; they bring out the beauty of what Mr Piper has called 'pleasing decay'; they also shew the many churches which were considered 'neat and elegant'.

It is still possible to find an unrestored church. Almost every county has one or two.

The Georgian Church Inside

There is a whole amusing literature of satire on church interiors. As early as 1825, an unknown wit and champion of Gothic published a book of coloured aquatints with accompanying satirical text to each plate, entitled *Hints to Some Churchwardens*. And as we are about to enter the church, let me quote this writer's description of a Georgian pulpit: 'How to substitute a new, grand, and commodious pulpit in place of an ancient, mean, and inconvenient one. Raze the old Pulpit and build one on small wooden Corinthian pillars, with a handsome balustrade or flight of steps like a staircase, supported also by wooden pillars of the Corinthian order; let the dimensions of the Pulpit be at least double that of the old one, and covered with crimson velvet, and a deep gold fringe, with a good-sized cushion, with large gold tassels, gilt branches on each side, over which imposing structure let a large sounding-board be suspended by a sky-blue chain with a gilt rose at the top, and small gilt lamps on the side, with a flame painted, issuing from them, such Pulpits as these must please all parties; and as the energy and eloquence of the preacher must be the chief attraction from the ancient Pulpit, in the modern one, such labour is not required, as a moderate congregation will be satisfied with a few short sentences pronounced on each side of the gilt branches, and sometimes from the front of the cushion, when the sense of vision is so amply cared for in the construction of so splendid and appropriate a place from which to teach the duties of Christianity.'

And certainly the pulpit and the high pews crowd the church. The nave is a forest of woodwork. The pews have doors to them. The panelling inside the pews is lined with baize, blue in one pew, red in another, green in another, and the baize is attached to the wood by brass studs such as one may see on the velvet-covered coffins in family vaults. Some very big pews will have fire-places. When one sits down, only the pulpit is visible from the pew, and the tops of the arches of the nave whose stonework will be washed with ochre, while the walls will be white or pale pink, green or blue. A satire on this sort of seating was published by John Noake in 1851 in his book already quoted:

O my own darling pue, which might serve for a bed,
With its cushions so soft and its curtains of red;
Of my half waking visions that pue is the theme,
And when sleep seals my eyes, of my pue still I dream.
Foul fall the despoiler, whose ruthless award

Has condemned me to squat, like the poor, on a board,
To be crowded and shov'd, as I sit at my prayers,
As though my devotions could mingle with theirs.
I have no vulgar pride, oh dear me, not I,
But still I must say I could never see why
We give them room to sit, to stand or to kneel,
As if they, like ourselves, were expected to feel;
'Tis a part, I'm afraid, of a deeply laid plan
To bring back the abuses of Rome if they can.
And when SHE is triumphant, you'll bitterly rue
That you gave up that Protestant bulwark – your pew.

The clear glass windows, of uneven crown glass with bottle-glass here and there in the upper lights, will shew the churchyard yews and elms and the flying clouds outside. Shafts of sunlight will fall on hatchments, those triangular-framed canvases hung on the aisle walls and bearing the Arms of noble families of the place. Over the chancel arch hang the Royal Arms, painted by some talented inn-sign artist, with a lively lion and unicorn supporting the shield in which we may see quartered the white horse of Hanover. The roofs of the church will be ceiled within for warmth, and our boxed-in pew will save us from draught. Look behind you; blocking the tower arch you will see a wooden gallery in which the choir is tuning its instruments, fiddle, base viol, serpent. And on your left in the north aisle there is a gallery crowded under the roof. On the tiers of wooden benches here sit the charity children in their blue uniforms, within reach of the parish beadle who, in the corner of the west gallery, can admonish them with his painted stave.

The altar is out of sight. This is because the old screen survives across the chancel arch and its doors are locked. If you can look through its carved woodwork, you will see that the chancel is bare except for the memorial floor slabs and brasses of previous incumbents, and the elaborate marble monument upon the wall, by a noted London sculptor, in memory of some lay-rector of the 18th century. Probably this is the only real 'work of art' judged by European standards in the church. The work of 18th-century sculptors has turned many of our old churches into sculpture galleries of great interest, though too often the Victorians huddled the sculptures away in the tower or blocked them up with organs. No choir stalls are in the chancel, no extra rich flooring. The Lord's Table or altar is against the east wall and enclosed on three sides by finely-turned rails such as one sees as stair balusters in a country house. The Table itself is completely covered with a carpet of plum-covered velvet, embroidered on its western face with IHS in golden rays. Only on those rare occasions, once a quarter and at Easter and Christmas and Whit Sunday when there is to be a Communion service, is the Table decked. Then indeed there will be a fair linen cloth over the velvet, and upon the cloth a chalice, paten and two flagons all of silver, and perhaps two lights in silver candlesticks. On Sacrament Sundays those who are to partake of Communion will leave their box-pews either at the

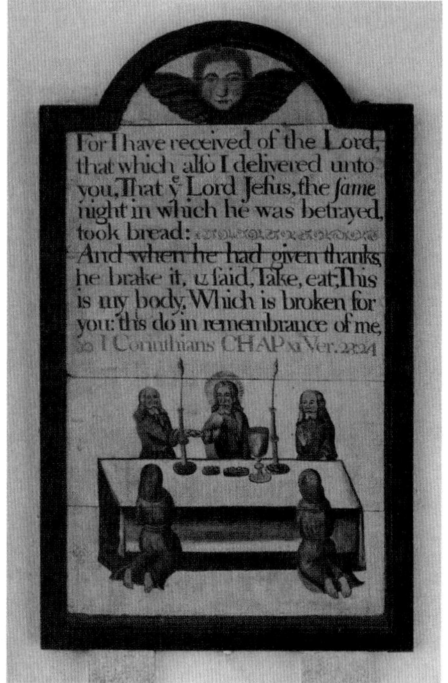

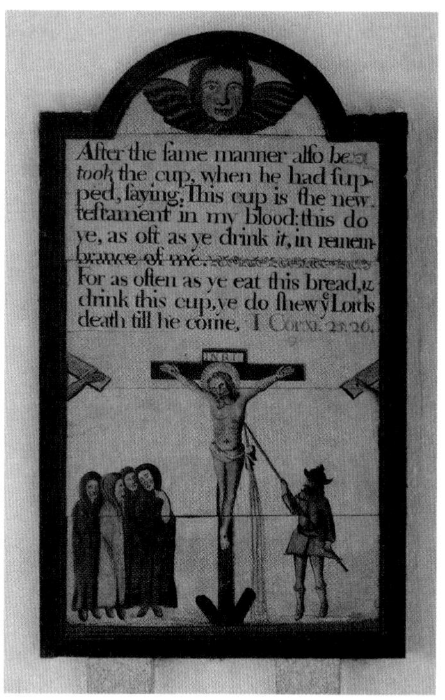

△ **ALTARNUN: ST NONNA** – *painted panels with biblical texts and images became popular from the 17th century; these from Cornwall hang either side of the high altar*

Offertory Sentence (when in modern Holy Communion services the collection is taken), or at the words 'Ye that do truly and earnestly repent you of your sins, and are in love and charity with your neighbours', and they will be admitted through the screen doors to the chancel. They will have been preceded by the incumbent. Thereafter the communicants will remain kneeling until the end of the service, as many as can around the Communion rails, the rest in the western side of the chancel.

The only object which will be familiar from the Victorian church is the font, still near the entrance to the church and symbolical of the entrance of the Christian to Christ's army. Beside the font is a large pew whose door opens facing it. This is the christening pew and here the baby, its parents and the god-parents wait until after the second lesson, when the incumbent will come forward to baptize the child in the presence of the congregation. Some churches had Churching pews where mothers sat.

Our churches were, as Canon Addleshaw and Frederick Etchells have pointed out in *The Architectural Setting of Anglican Worship*, compartmented buildings. So they remained from 1559 (Act of Uniformity) until 1841 onwards when Tractarian ideas about the prominence of the altar, the frequent celebration of Holy Communion and adequate seating for the poor – for the population had suddenly increased – caused a vital replanning of churches. What we see in 1805 is a medieval church adapted to Prayer Book worship. The object of having the Prayer Book in our own language was not so doctrinal and Protestant, in the

Continental sense, as is often supposed, but was to ensure audible and intelligible services. The compartments of the building were roughly three. There is the font and christening pew which form a Baptistry. There is the nave of the church with the pews facing the pulpit which is generally half-way down the church against one of the pillars, and the nave is used for Matins, Litany and Ante-Communion. Some of the larger churches have one end of an aisle or a transept divided off with the old screens which used to surround a Chantry chapel in this part. This the parson might use for weekday offices of Matins and Evensong when the congregation was small and there was no sermon.

The lime-washed walls form a happy contrast with the coloured baize inside the box-pews, the brown well-turned Stuart and Georgian wood-work and the old screens, the hatchments which hang lozenge-shaped on the wall above family pews, and the great Royal Arms in the filled-in tympanum of the chancel arch. Behind the Royal Arms we may see faintly the remains of a medieval painting of the Doom, the Archangel Michael holding the balance, and some souls going to Heaven on one side of him, others to Hell on the other side. In other parts of the church, too, the pale brick-red lines of the painting which once covered the church may be faintly discernible in sunlight. Mostly the walls will be whitewashed, and in bold black and red, with cherubs as decorative devices, will be painted admonitory texts against idolatry. The Elizabethan texts will be in black letters; the later and less admonitory Georgian ones will be in the spacious Roman style which we see on the gravestones in the churchyard. In the Sanctuary on either side of the altar are the Lord's Prayer and the Commandments painted in gold letters on black boards, and perhaps Moses and Aaron flank these, also painted on boards by a local inn-sign painter. An oil painting of the Crucifixion or The Deposition of our Lord or some other scriptural subject may adorn the space above the altar table. Far more people could read than is generally supposed; literacy was nearly as rife as it is today. There was not the need to teach by pictures in the parish church that there had been in the middle ages.

The lighting of the church is wholly by candles. In the centre of the nave a branched brass candelabrum is suspended by two interlocking rods painted blue, the two serpent heads which curl round and interlock them being gilded. In other parts of the church, in distant box-pews or up the choir gallery, light is from single candles in brass sconces fixed to the woodwork. If the chancel is dark, there may be two fine silver candlesticks on the altar for the purpose of illumination. But candles are not often needed, for services are generally in the hours of daylight, and the usual time for a country evensong is three o'clock in the afternoon, not six or half-past six as is now the custom.

Outside the church on a sunny Sunday morning the congregation gathers. The poorer sort are lolling against the tombstones, while the richer families, also in their best clothes, move towards the porch where the churchwardens stand with staves ready to conduct them to their private pews. The farmworkers do not wear smocks for church, but knee breeches and a long coat and shoes. Women wear wooden shoes, called pattens, when it is wet, and take them off in the porch. All the men wear hats, and they hang them on pegs on the walls when they enter the church.

How still the morning of the hallowed day!
Mute is the voice of rural labour, hushed
The ploughboy's whistle, and the milkmaid's song.
The scythe lies glittering in the dewy wreath
Of tedded grass, mingled with fading flowers,
That yester morn bloomed waving in the breeze.
Sounds the most faint attract the ear, – the hum
Of early bee, the trickling of the dew,
The distant bleating, midway up the hill.
With dove-like wings, Peace o'er yon village broods:
The dizzying mill-wheel rests; the anvil's din
Hath ceased; all, all around is quietness.
Less fearful on this day, the limping hare
Stops, and looks back, and stops, and looks on man
Her deadliest foe. The toilworn horse, set free,
Unheedful of the pasture, roams at large;
And as his stiff unwieldly bulk rolls on,
His iron-armed hoofs gleam in the morning ray.

So the Scottish poet James Graham begins his poem *The Sabbath* (1804). All this island over, there was a hush of feudal quiet in the country on a Sunday. We must sink into this quiet to understand and tolerate, with our democratic minds, the graded village hierarchy, graded by birth and occupation, by clothes and by seating in the church. It is an agricultural world as yet little touched by the machines which were starting in the mills of the midlands and the north. The Sabbath as a day of rest and worship touched all classes. Our feeblest poets rose from bathos to sing its praises. I doubt if Felicia Hemens ever wrote better than this, in her last poem (1835), composed less than a week before she died.

How many blessed groups this hour are bending,
Through England's primrose meadow paths, their way
Towards spire and tower, midst shadowy elms ascending,
Whence the sweet chimes proclaim the hallowed day:
The halls from old heroic ages grey
Pour their fair children forth; and hamlets low,
With whose thick orchard blooms the soft winds play,
Send out their inmates in a happy flow,
Like a freed rural stream.
I may not tread
With them those pathways, – to the feverish bed
Of sickness bound, – yet, O my God, I bless
Thy mercy, that with Sabbath peace hath filled
My chastened heart, and all its throbbings stilled
To one deep calm of lowliest thankfulness.

One is inclined, seeing the pale whites and ochres and greys, relieved here and there with the warm brown red of local bricks, which we associate today with Georgian England, to forget how highly coloured were the clothes of the people. Thomas Hood's early poem *The Two Peacocks at Bedfont* (1827) describes with the colours of an aquatint the worshippers entering that then countrified Middlesex church:

So speaking, they pursue the pebbly walk
That leads to the white porch the Sunday throng,
Hand-coupled urchins in restrained talk,
And anxious pedagogue that chasten wrong,
And posied churchwarden with solemn stalk,
And gold-bedizened beadle flames along,
And gentle peasant clad in buff and green,
Like a meek cowslip in the spring serene;
And blushing maiden – modestly array'd
In spotless white – still conscious of the glass;
And she, the lonely widow that hath made
A sable covenant with grief, – alas!
She veils her tears under the deep, deep shade,
While the poor kindly-hearted, as they pass,
Bend to unclouded childhood, and caress
Her boy, – so rosy! – and so fatherless!
Thus as good Christians ought, they all draw near
The fair white temple, to the timely call
Of pleasant bells that tremble in the ear, –
Now the last frock, and scarlet hood and shawl
Fade into dusk, in the dim atmosphere
Of the low porch, and heav'n has won them all . . .

The Lord of the manor and his family have entered their private pew, hidden in a transept and with a separate entrance. Their liveried servants sit on a bench behind them. All round the church is an array of hats hanging on pegs on the walls above the pews. The parson, who has entered the church in his long white surplice and red silk hood of an Oxford Master of Arts, takes his place in the second desk of the three-decker. The parish clerk is below him to say 'Amen'. He begins Morning Prayer, facing the congregation. He then mounts to the pulpit and preaches a sermon, which is usually read. Extempore preaching was a sign of 'enthusiasm'. The Devon poet N. T. Carrington well describes a morning service in *My Native Village* (1830):

Ah, let me enter, once again, the pew
Where the child nodded as the sermon grew;
Scene of soft slumbers! I remember now
The chiding finger, and the frowning brow
Of stern reprovers, when the ardent June

Flung through the glowing aisles the drowsy noon;
Ah admonitions vain! a power was there
Which conquer'd e'en the sage, the brave, the fair, –
A sweet oppressive power – a languor deep,
Resistless shedding round delicious sleep!
Till closed the learned harangue, with solemn look
Arose the chaunter of the sacred book, –
The parish clerk (death-silenced) far-famed then
And justly, for his long and loud – Amen!
Rich was his tone, and his exulting eye
Glanced to the reedy choir, enthroned on high,
Nor glanced in vain; the simple-hearted throng
Lifted their voices, and dissolved in song;
Till in one tide, deep welling, full and free
Rung through the echoing pile, old England's psalmody.

The singing is from metrical psalms which are bound with every prayer book. The versions used were generally those awkward quatrains by Tate and Brady. They are easily committed to memory. The minister or clerk reads out the stanzas and then the congregation sings, stanza by stanza, those few who cannot read committing the lines to memory. The custom, still prevailing in some Evangelical churches and many chapels, of the minister's proclaiming the first verse of the hymn, is doubtless a survival of these days. Two of Tate and Brady's metrical psalms, 'Thro' all the changing scenes of life' and 'As pants the hart for cooling streams', survive, cut down, in modern hymn books. An appendix to the Psalms was also printed, consisting of rhyming doxologies and a few hymns for special occasions such as 'While Shepherds watched'. From this appendix grew the separate hymn book, of which the most famous and successful was *Hymns Ancient and Modern* (1861), which consisted first of 273 hymns.

The parson's sermon is the end of the service unless it is 'Sacrament Sunday'. For the sermon has come after the Nicene Creed and not at the end of the office of Morning Prayer. It was the custom to have Morning Prayer, Litany and Ante-Communion. The whole service lasted about two hours. As the time of eating was at three o'clock, this was no great inconvenience. But one can understand where the deep-rooted English idea that church worship is boring had its origin. The layman was asked to take part in the monkish offices of Morning and Evening Prayer (an anglicized and potted version of the daily offices of monks and nuns) as well as in the celebration of Communion, always the central act of worship of the Church. The English habit of attending but not receiving Communion was the origin of the Ante-Communion service alone being read, and 'Sacrament Sundays' being special and rare occasions; for it was ordered in the Prayer Book that two or three people must be willing to partake of the Sacrament before it could be celebrated. This order was made with the intention of encouraging people to communicate. But the habit of abstaining was too strong, hence the diminution of the service to Ante-Communion.

The Church in the Fifteenth Century

There will be no end to books on the Reformation. It is not my intention to add to them. Rather I would go back to the middle of the 15th century, when the church we have been describing was bright with its new additions of tower, porch, aisles and clerestory windows, and to a medieval England not quite so roseate as that of Cardinal Gasquet, nor yet so crime-ridden as that of Dr Coulton.

The village looks different. The church is by far the most prominent building unless there is a manor-house, and even this is probably a smaller building than the church and more like what we now think of as an old farm. The church is so prominent because the equivalents of cottages in the village are at the grandest 'cruck houses' (that is to say tent-like buildings with roofs coming down to the ground), and most are mere hovels. They are grouped round the church and manor-house and look rather like a camp. There is far more forest everywhere, and in all but the Celtic fringes of the island agriculture is strip cultivation, that is to say the tilled land is laid out in long strips with no hedges between and is common to the whole community, as are the grazing rights in various hedged and well-watered fields. There are more sheep than any other animals in these enclosures. The approaches to the village are grassy tracks very muddy in winter. Each village is almost a country to itself. Near the entrance to the churchyard is the church house where the churchwardens store beer or 'church ales' for feasts. This is the origin of so many old inns being beside the churchyard in England. The graveyard has no tombstones in it. The dead are buried there but they are remembered not in stone but in the prayers of the priest at the altar at mass. Everyone goes to mass, people from outlying farms stabling their horses outside the churchyard. The church itself looks much the same. The stone tower gleams with new cut ashlar; the walls of the church when they are not ashlar are plastered.

Not only does everyone go to church on Sunday and in his best clothes; the church is used on weekdays too, for it is impossible to say daily prayers in the little hovels in which most of the villagers live. School is taught in the porch, business is carried out by the cross in the market where the booths are (for there are no shops in the village, only open stalls as in market squares today). In the nave of the church on a weekday there are probably people gossiping in some places, while in others there are people praying. There was no privacy in the middle ages, when even princes dined in public and their subjects watched them eat. The nave of the church belonged to the people, and they used it as today we use a village hall or social club. Our new suburban churches which are used as dance halls during the week with sanctuary partitioned off until Sunday, have something in common with the medieval church. But there is this difference: in the middle ages all sport and pleasure, all plays and dancing were 'under God'. God was near, hanging on his Cross above the chancel arch, and mystically present in the sacrament in the pyx hanging over the altar beyond. His crucifixion was carved on the preaching cross in the churchyard. People were aware of God. They were not priest-ridden in the sense that they bowed meekly to whatever the priest

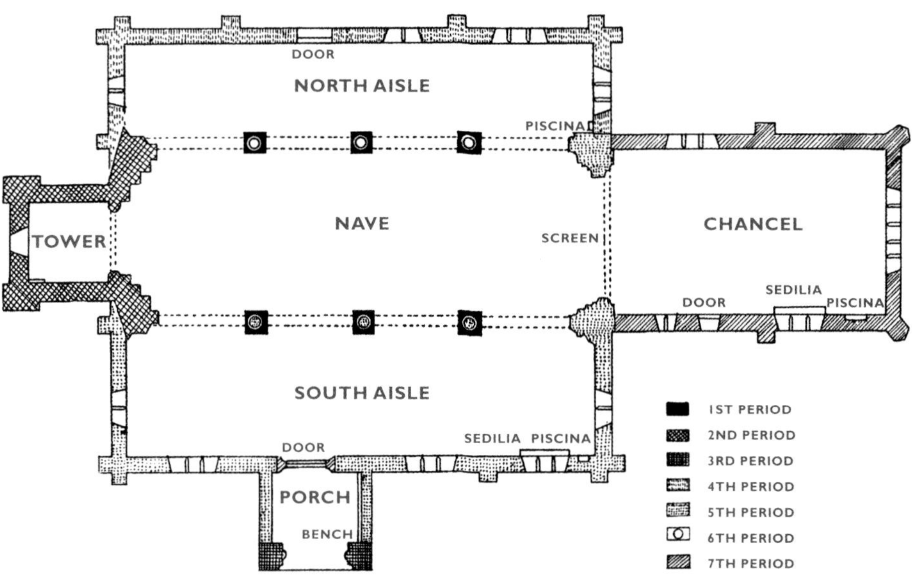

△ **THE GROWTH OF A MEDIEVAL CHURCH** – *'At Harringworth in Northamptonshire there had been an aisleless church, to which a tower had been added at the end of the 12th and aisles early in the 13th century. In about 1300 a new north aisle had been built with a new altar at the east end. Soon after the whole of the south aisle and arcade were built. The work was done in a very conservative spirit. During the next few years, the north arcade was entirely rebuilt so as nearly to match that on the south. Thus the work, beginning with the north aisle, and extending over some 30 or 40 years, finished on the side on which it began.' (From* The Ground Plan of the English Parish Church, *by A. Hamilton Thompson, 1911)*

said. They had decided opinions and argued about religion and the clergy, and no doubt some went to church reluctantly. But no one thought of not going to church. They believed men had souls and that their souls must be exercised in worship and customed by sacraments.

Let us go in by its new south porch to our parish church of five-hundred years ago. Many of the features which were there when we last saw it are still present, the screen and the font for instance, but the walls are now painted all over. Medieval builders were not concerned with 'taste'. But they were moved by fashion. If the next village had a new tower, they must have one like it. If the latest style at the nearest big abbey or bishop's seat made their own building seem out of date, then it must be rebuilt. At the time of which we are writing, the style would be Perpendicular. Only the most shewy features of earlier building – a Norman chancel arch removed in a few instances to the south door, a 'decorated' window with rich tracery, and perhaps a column with sculptured foliage capital of Early English times – might be spared if they could be made to look well. The builders were chiefly concerned with making the interior of the church as rich and splendid as possible, something to bring you to your knees. Most parish churches, even the smallest, had three altars, one in the chancel and one on either side of the chancel arch.

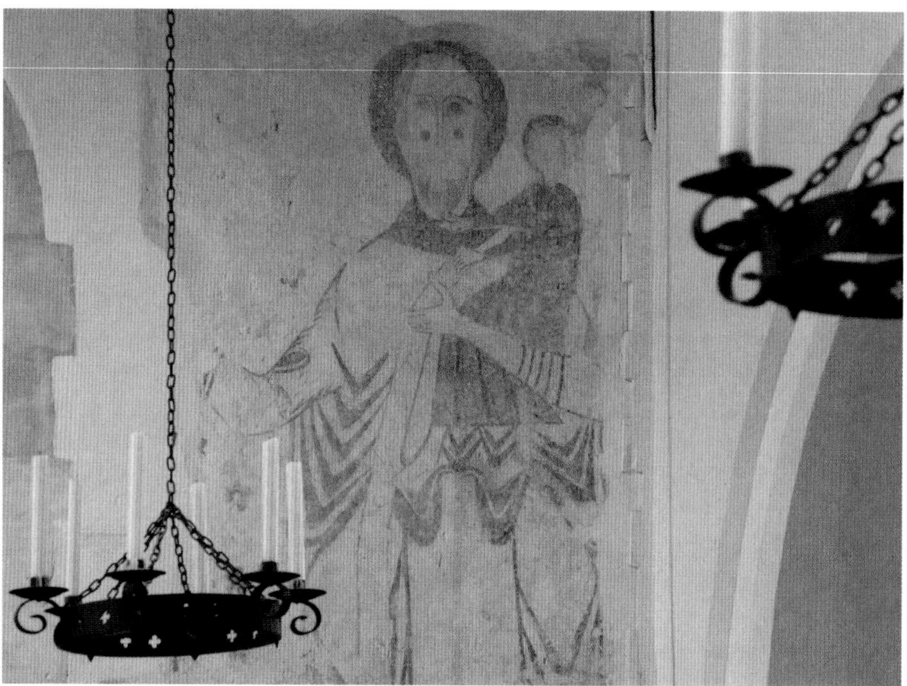

△ **WEST HORSLEY: ST MARY** – *St Christopher carrying an infant Christ on his shoulder was a common theme for medieval wall-paintings; this one could be as early as 13th-century*

Where we go in, there is a stoup made of stone or metal, containing Holy Water. And somewhere near, very prominent, is the font. Over it is a painted wooden cover, rising like a church steeple and securely clasped down to the basin of the font and locked. This is because the font contains Baptismal Water, which is changed only twice a year at Easter and Whitsun when it is solemnly blessed. The cover is raised by means of a weight and pulley. The plaster walls are covered with paintings, mostly of a dull brick-red with occasional blues and greens and blacks. The older painting round any surviving Norman windows is picked out in squares to resemble masonry. Chiefly the paintings are pictures. There will be scenes in the life of Our Lady on the north wall, and opposite us probably a huge painting of St Christopher carrying Our Lord as a child on his shoulders and walking through a stream in which fishes are swimming about and fishermen hooking a few out around St Christopher's feet. It was a pious belief that whoever looked at St Christopher would be safe that day from sudden death. The belief is kept alive today on the dashboards of motor-cars. All the windows will be filled with stained glass, depicting local saints and their legends. Our Lord as a baby and receiving homage as the Saviour will be painted somewhere on the walls. But chiefly there will be pictures and images of Our Lady, who will probably be portrayed more often in the church than her Son. Our Lady was the favourite saint of England, and more old churches are dedicated to her than to anyone else. The Christianity of late medieval England was much concerned with Our Lord as Saviour and Man, and with Our Lady as His mother.

The wooden chancel roofs will all have painted beams, red, green, white and gold and blue. The nave rood may not be painted but over the rood-beam just above the chancel arch it will be more richly carved and painted than elsewhere. The stone floor of the church is often covered with yew boughs or sweet-smelling herbs whose aroma is stronger when crushed underfoot. Strong smells were a feature of medieval life. People did not wash much or change their clothes often, and the stink of middens must have made villages unpleasant places in hot weather. Crushed yew and rosemary must have been a welcome contrast in the cool brightness of the church. Five-hundred years ago, most churches had a few wooden benches in the nave. In some districts, notably Devon, Cornwall and parts of East Anglia, these were elaborately carved. In most places they were plain seats of thick pieces of oak. People often sat along the stone ledges on the wall or on the bases of the pillars. And the pillars of the nave had stone or wooden brackets with statues of saints standing on them. Everywhere in the church there would be images of saints. Though some worshipped these and thought of them as miraculous, such was not the teaching of educated priests of the Church. John Mirk, prior of Lilleshall, who flourished c .1403, wrote thus:

'Men should learn by images whom they should worship and follow. To do God's worship to images is forbidden. Therefore, when thou comest to church, first, behold God's Body under the form of bread upon the altar; and thank Him that He vouchsafe every day to come from the holy heaven above for the health of thy soul. Look upon the Cross, and thereby have mind of the passion he suffered for thee. Then on the images of the holy saints; not believing on them, but that by the sight of them thou mayest have mind on them that be in heaven: and so to follow their life as much as thou mayest.'

And here in the nave, the people's part of the church, we have not yet looked eastward to Our Lord upon the Cross. His figure hanging on a wooden cross over the chancel arch, with St Mary and St John weeping on either side of Him at the foot of the cross, looks down from above the screen. This dominates the nave, and behind it or above it, painted on the east wall, is the depiction of the Doom. There, above His Body on the Rood, is a painting of the Resurrected Christ, the severe judge. His wounds are shewn, His hands are raised with the nail prints in them, and His eyes fix you as you stare up. Angels blow trumpets around Him, and there rising from their graves are naked souls, painted as naked bodies but wearing head-dresses, tiaras, crowns and mitres to shew their rank in life. On one side they enter rather joylessly the gates of heaven. On the other, with terrible imagery, are shewn devils with sharks' teeth and rolling eyes, hauling off the helpless souls to the gaping mouth of hell, a yawning cauldron in the bottom corner of the picture. The artists had a far more enjoyable time drawing devils and hell than angels and heaven. For one sweet-faced saint or tender portrait of Our Lady surviving in the wall-painting in our islands, there must be two or three alarming devils.

It is appropriate that here in the nave, with Our Lord looking down sadly from the Cross and sternly from His glory, people should be reminded of how to live while on earth if they wish to escape Hell. And while we look at the judgement on the wall, let us listen to John Bromyard, a Dominican Friar of c. 1390, preaching against the rich:

'Their souls shall have, instead of palace and hall and chamber, the deep lake of hell, with those that go down into the depth thereof. In the place of scented baths, their body shall have a narrow pit of earth; and there they shall have bath more black and foul than any bath of pitch and sulphur. In place of a soft couch, they shall have a bed more grievous and hard than all the nails and spikes in the world; in place of inordinate embraces, they will be able to have there the embraces of the fiery brands of hell . . . Instead of wives, they shall have toads; instead of a great retinue and throng of followers, their body shall have a throng of worms and their soul a throng of demons. Instead of large domain, it shall be an eternal prison house cramped for both.'

Heaven is represented in the chancel beyond the richly-painted screen, where the priest murmurs scarcely audible Latin and where the Body of Our Lord under the form of bread, hangs above the altar in a shrouded pyx. Much chatting goes on in the church during sermon and Mass, and we may now approach the screen to examine it and the jewel-like blazing richness beyond, in the holiest part of the church.

Through the screen which runs across the whole width of the church, you may glimpse the richest part of all this teaching imagery. The altars at the end of the aisles are either guild chapels, or family chapels, each with their paid priests. The Shoemakers may have an altar dedicated to Crispin, and will subscribe for its upkeep and to keep its lights burning. Another chapel may be kept up by a guild which pays a priest to say Mass for the Souls of its departed members. The secular descendants of these guilds are the trade unions and burial societies of today. The big town churches such as those at Coventry, Stamford and Bristol had many guild chapels with priests maintained to serve them. And many altars contained a relic of a saint. The walls round the altars were painted, the roofs above them were richer and more elaborately painted than those in the people's part of the church, the altar hangings were of the richest silks and threaded with jewels, the fair linen-cloth laid upon the altar itself a white, plain contrast with the elaborate hangings. The floors of the chancel are of marble or tiles. Brasses of dead priests shone bright among them. You may see what they looked like in illuminated missals. The ornaments on the altar were few, candles perhaps, and if a cross, then a small one to help the priest in his devotions – for here in the chancel we meet the risen Lord. Only in the nave is He dead on the cross, as large as life.

Few people will make their communion at Mass. Indeed it is rare for anyone to make his communion except at Easter. People think of the Mass as something offered for them rather than something of which they partake the sacred elements.

On a hot summer Sunday morning in the country, when I have been reading Chaucer to the sound of bells pouring through the trees, I have been able dimly to imagine this late medieval religion. Life is short for everybody. It is matter of fact. The pictures on the church walls are not thought of as 'art', but are there to tell a story. Small parish churches were not consciously made beautiful. They

△ **COVENTRY: HOLY TRINITY** – *only rediscovered in 1999 and now restored, this extraordinarily intact Doom painting is dated to the early 15th century*

were built and decorated for effect, to be better than the church in the next village, to be the best building in the village itself, for it is the House of God, and God become Man – that was the great discovery – offered here upon the altar. All sorts of miraculous stories were invented about Him, and even more about His mother. Because He was Man born of woman, he becomes within the grasp of everyone. Few of the extravagances of German and Spanish late medieval art are found in English representations of the scourging, the crucifixion and the deposition. Jesus is thought of as the baby of poor people who received the tributes of a king. His mother is the most beautiful woman in the world – and how many lovely, loving faces of Our Lady we may see in the old glass, wall-paintings and statues which survive in England. And she bore a Spotless Son who was God and Judge of all. No wonder she was loved by the pious English.

The miracles of Our Lord were not so interesting to these people as the miracles they ascribed to His saints. Here extravagancy knew no bounds. St Petroc sailed in a silver bowl from Cornwall to an isle in the Indian Ocean. St Winifred was beheaded by an angry lover, but her head was reunited to her body and she became an abbess. There were saints like St Quintin who cured dropsy, saints for toothache, and for colds and fever, and for finding things. There were patron saints for every craft and trade. There were miraculous images which winked, or flew to bedsides; there were statues of saints that had never been, like the Maid Uncumber in old St Paul's Cathedral.

Though for the everyday things of life there were friendly saints who helped, life itself must have been terrifying, a continual rush to escape hell. Our Lord and His Mother were the loving and human part of it; hell was the terrifying

△ **WINCHCOMBE: ST PETER** – *the church has a fascinating array of grotesques and gargoyles that seem to mix anguish, fear and broad comedy*

part. The Devil was seen. His fellow devils yawned as gargoyles with bats' wings on the north walls of the church, black against the evening sky. The white teeth of devils and their red eyes gleamed out of the darkness. Evil spirits lurked behind stones on lonely moors and ranged the deep woods. Good and evil fought together in the roar of the storm. All thought, all sight, every breath of the body, was under God. The leaping sciapod, the man-eating mantichora, the unicorn, might easily be met in the forest by men with imaginations, which as easily would expect to see Our Lady flying through the air, or the local saint, for centuries enshrined in his altar, walking down the street. The witch cast her evil spells, blood and death lay around everywhere, the entrails of a man hung, drawn and quartered, shone black with flies in the sun, silvery lepers tinkled their bells, creating loneliness around them. The fear that men felt is expressed in the grotesque carvings over the north walls of churches, and in the corbels and bosses of roofs, and in bench-ends, screens and miserere stalls. Their humour is shewn there too. Chiefly in the figure of Our Lady do we see the tenderness and sweetness of this late religion.

So when we walk down a green lane like an ancient cart track towards the ringing church-bells, we can see the power of God in the blossom and trees, remember legends of the saints about birds and stones, and recall miracles that happened in the parish at this or that spot. And on a feast day we can see the churchyard set out with tables for the church ale when Mass is over, and as we enter the nave we can see it thronged below the painted roof and walls with people in the village, young and old, and the rest of the parish crowding in with us. Human nature may not have been better. Life was as full, no doubt, of wrong and terror as it is today. How different it was is expressed in the words of Froude:

'For, indeed, a change was coming upon the world, the meaning and direction of which even still is hidden from us, a change from era to era. The paths trodden by the footsteps of ages were broken up; old things were passing away and the faith and the life of ten centuries were dissolving like a dream. Chivalry was dying; the abbey and the castle were soon together to crumble into ruins; and all the forms, desires, beliefs, convictions of the old world were passing away never to return. A new continent had risen up beyond the western sea. The floor of heaven, inlaid with stars, had sunk back into an infinite abyss of immeasurable space; and the firm earth itself, unfixed from its foundations, was seen to be but a small atom in the awful vastness of the universe. In the fabric of habit which they had so laboriously built for themselves, mankind were to remain no longer.

And now it is all gone – like an unsubstantial pageant faded; and between us and the old English there lies a gulf of mystery which the prose of the historian will never adequately bridge. They cannot come to us, and our imagination can but feebly penetrate to them. Only among the sleeping on their tombs, some faint conceptions float before us of what these men were when they were alive; and perhaps in the sound of church bells, that peculiar creation of medieval age, which falls upon the ear like the echo of a vanished world.'

The Churches Before The Fifteenth Century

To imagine our church in earliest times of Christian England is, alas, to enter the controversial world of archaeology. There was a Christian Church in the Roman settlement at Silchester, Berkshire, and its remains have been excavated. It had an apse at the west end instead of the east where one would expect it to be, and the altar which is supposed to have been wooden and square, was also in the west. The east end was square. The church is said to be 4th century. Only the foundations remain. The form of worship was probably more like that of the Orthodox church today than the western rite.

But there are enough later pre-Conquest churches remaining to give us an idea of the architecture of those times. They are called Saxon. There are two types. The southern, of which the earliest churches are found in Kent – three in Canterbury, St Mary Lyminge, Reculver, and, most complete, Bradwell, Essex, all of which are 7th century – were the result of the Italian mission of St Augustine, and were reinforced after the coming of St Theodore in 669. In plan and style they resembled certain early Italian churches. The northern group found in Northumberland and Durham are survivals of the Celtic church, and their architecture is said to have come from Gaul, and is more barbaric looking than that of their southern contemporaries. Their three distinctive features were, according to Sir Arthur Clapham, an unusual length of nave, a small chancel, less wide than the nave, and very high side walls. In the northern group, the most complete is Escombe, Durham (7th and early 8th century?), a stern building, nave and chancel only, with squared rubble walls, small windows high up and square or round headed, and a narrow and tall rounded chancel

△ **EARLS BARTON: ALL SAINTS** – *a rare surviving Saxon tower, with characteristic stripwork and crude arched bell openings in the top stage; the parapet above is later*

arch. We have a picture of the interiors of these northern churches from near contemporary accounts. The walls and capitals and arch of the sanctuary were adorned 'with designs and images and many sculptured figures in relief on the stone and pictures with a pleasing variety of colours and a wonderful charm'. We learn, too, of purple hangings and gold and silver ornaments with precious stones. Elsewhere in England the most considerable remains of pre-Conquest work are those at Monkwearmouth (Durham), Jarrow (Durham), Brixworth (Northants), Deerhurst (Glos), Bradford-on-Avon (Wilts), the tower of Earls Barton (Northants), Barton-on-Humber (Lincs), Sompting (Sussex), the Crypts at Repton (Derby), Wing (Bucks), and Hexham (Northumberland). From the pre-Conquest sculpture, like the crosses at Bewcastle and Ruthwell, and the carvings at Langford (Oxon), Romsey (Hants), Bexhill (Sussex), St Dunstan's Stepney (London), and the moving relief of the Harrowing of Hell in Bristol Cathedral, and from such enrichment as survives in such objects as St Cuthbert's stole (Durham), the Alfred Jewel in the Ashmolean Museum, Oxford, the beautiful drawing in the Winchester Psalter and Lindisfarne Gospels in the British Museum, we know that these Romanesque masons, sculptors and illuminators were very fine artists, as fine as there have ever been in England.

However, it is safer to try to imagine our parish church as it was in Norman times, as far more of our old churches are known to be Norman in origin than pre-Conquest, even though as in the church of Kilpeck (Herefordshire) the pre-Conquest style of decoration may have continued into Norman times. It is narrow and stone built. Let us suppose it divided into three parts. The small,

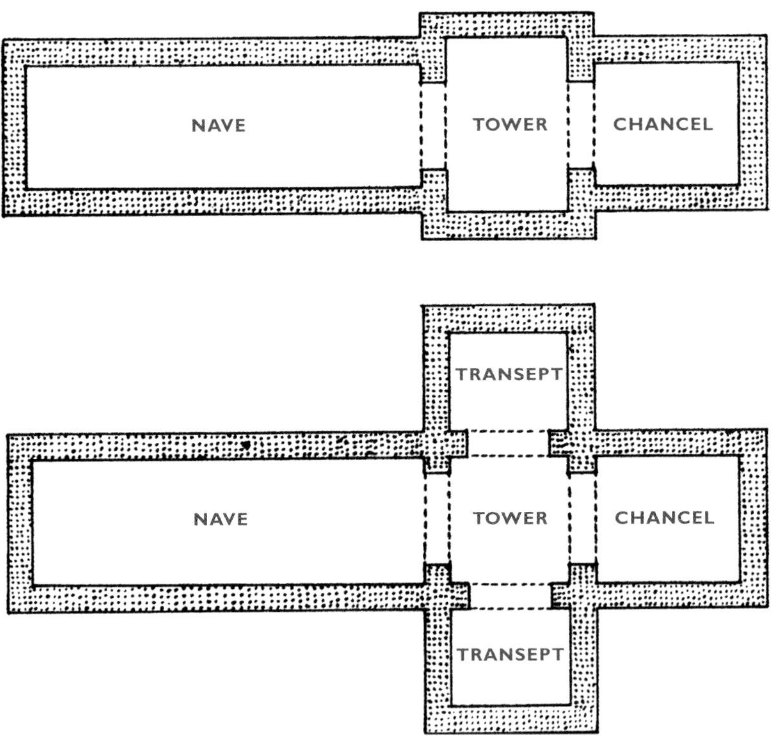

△ **ANGLO-SAXON AND NORMAN** – *Two aisleless plans with central tower. (Top) tower between nave and chancel; (Bottom) tower over crossing of transepts with nave and chancel*

eastward chancel is either square-ended or apsidal. Then comes the tower supported internally on round arches. The nave, west of the low tower, is longer than the chancel. The windows are small and high up. The church is almost like a fortress outside. And it is indeed a fortress of Christianity in a community where pagan memories and practices survive, where barons are like warring kings and monasteries are the centres of faith. These small village churches are like mission churches in a jungle clearing.

There are no porches, and we enter the building by any of the three doors to the nave on the north, south or west. Inside, the walls of the nave are painted with red lines to look like blocks of stone. The raftered roof is hidden by a flat wooden ceiling which is painted with lozenges. The floor of the nave is paved with small blocks of stone or with red tiles. There are no pews. We can only see the chancel through a richly moulded round arch, that very arch which is now the South Door of your parish church. Above this chancel arch is a painted Doom, not quite so terrifying as that of the 15th-century church, for all the painting here is in the manner of the mosaics still seen in basilicas of Italy and eastern Europe.

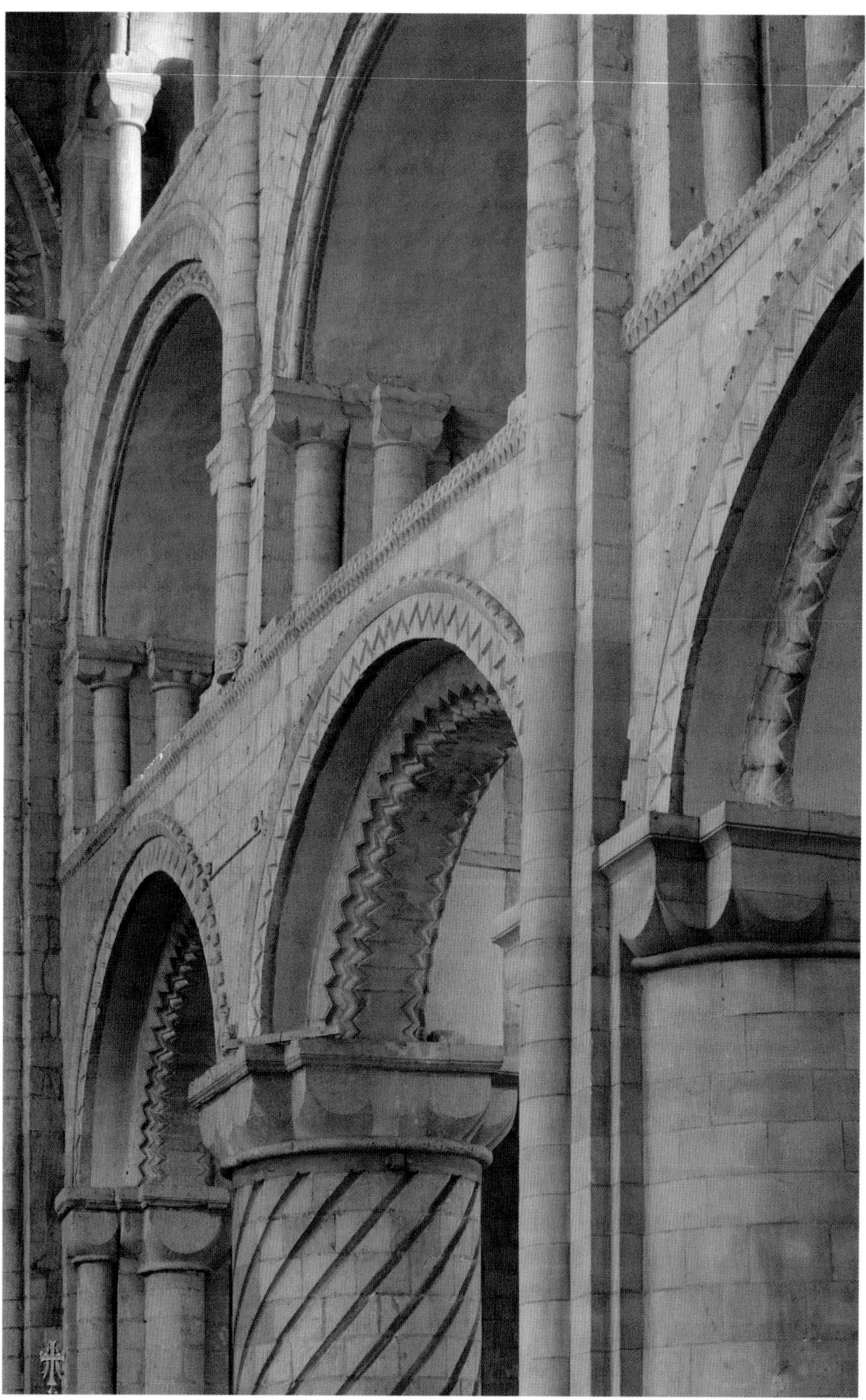

△ **WALTHAM ABBEY: HOLY CROSS** – *sturdy Norman arcades sometimes survive in churches that have been much altered in later centuries, though not all are carved with as much grace as these very decorative columns for the abbey church*

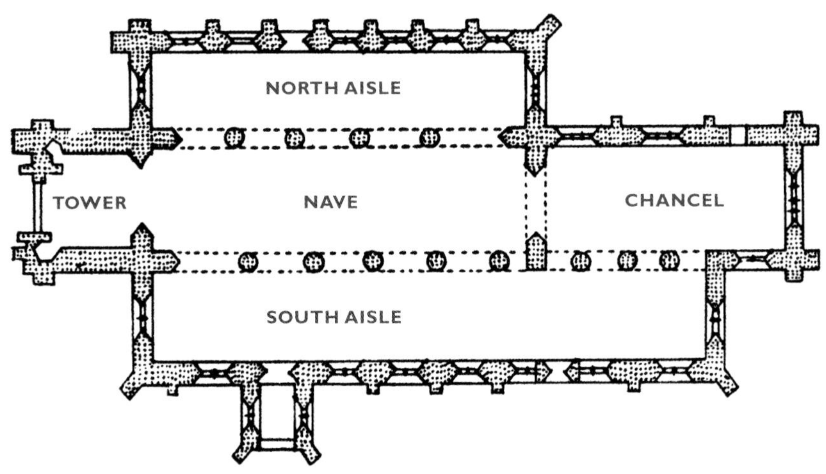

△ **GOTHIC ADDITIONS TO A NORMAN PLAN** – *Based on Raunds, Northamptonshire: probably this was a Norman aisleless church consisting of nave and chancel of equal width. A tower and north aisle ot the nave were added in the 13th century. In the 14th century a south aisle was added. The original Norman walls were pierced and turned into arcades.*

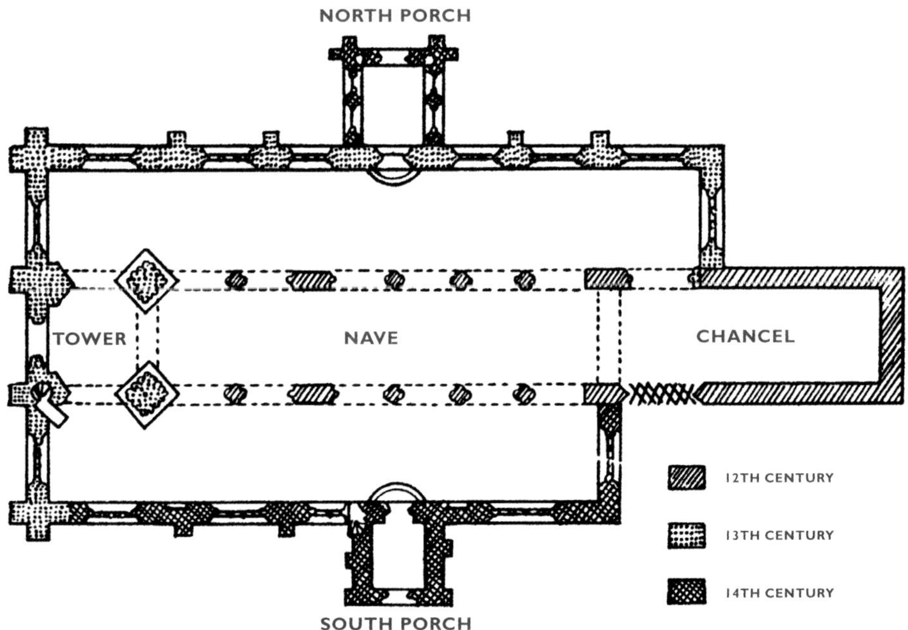

△ **A TOWN CHURCH ENLARGED IN THE 13TH AND 14TH CENTURIES SO AS TO PROVIDE GUILD CHAPELS** – *Based on Grantham, Lincolnshire*

The splays of the windows in the nave have figures of saints painted on them. But it is through the chancel that we see the greatest riches. Stained glass is rare. If there is any it is in the sanctuary and black with much leading and giving the impression of transparent mosaics. The walls are painted everywhere with figures, also recalling mosaic pictures. There are bands of classic style, patterns dividing them. The altar is of stone, small and box-like, recalling the tombs of Christians in the catacombs of Rome in the very earliest days of Christianity. The altar stands well away from the eastern, semi-circular end of the apse. It is covered with a cloth hanging over its four sides, decorated with vertical bands.

Our Lord is depicted on the cross as a King and Judge, not as a man in anguish as in later crucifixions. The religion of the time was less concerned with Him and Our Lady as human beings, more concerned with the facts of Judgement, Death and Hell. It was more ascetic and severe.

PART TWO: THE NEWER CHURCHES

Of the 16,000 parish churches in England more than half have been built since the 17th century, and the majority of these were erected in the 19th and 20th centuries. Guide books, almost wholly antiquarian in outlook, still dismiss even 18th-century churches as 'modern', while Victorian buildings are usually beneath their consideration. Yet some of the noblest churches are post-Reformation, from cathedrals like St Paul's and Truro and Liverpool, to the great town churches designed by such architects as Hawksmoor, Gibbs, Street, Butterfield, Pearson, Brooks, Nicholson and Comper.

The first post-Reformation churches differed little in plan from those of medieval times. Wren in some of his churches for the City of London seems to have tried to build uncompartmented churches, where Baptism, Morning and Evening Prayer and Holy Communion could all be conducted in an undivided space, without the priest and his assistants moving out of sight and earshot.

Usually the plan was the nave with three-decker pulpit dominating for Matins, Litany and Evensong, a screen through which the congregation passed for Communion, and a Bapistry at the west end. The earliest post-Reformation churches usually had west galleries for organ and choir and also side galleries, because by the 17th century the population had begun to increase, especially in the towns where many new churches were built. The churches of the 17th and 18th centuries were mostly built on the English medieval plan. The only noticeable new feature in the more traditional churches was that the chancels were shallower and broader than those surviving from earlier times.

The style of tracery and decoration and wood-carving certainly changed. Windows were square-headed in the 16th century, and thereafter became round-headed. Grapes and cherubs and a cornucopia of fruit cascaded down the sides of altar-pieces, wreathed round the panelling of pulpits, and flattened themselves into patterns on the ceiling. The Renaissance style of Italy became the fashion. But it was an English version. Wren's Portland stone steeples and lead spires, so happily clustering round St Paul's Cathedral, are a recollection of Gothic architecture, though most of them are Renaissance in detail.

The interior of even the most room-like classic church of the 17th and early 18th centuries generally differs from its contemporary Dissenting interior. In the former there is provision for the expounding of the Word, and for the two chief sacraments; in the latter there is provision for the Word, but there is no suggestion of an altar about the table that is set for Communion. There may be some significance in the hour-glasses so often found beside the Anglican pulpits. They were intended as a check on the length of the sermon, and perhaps as a reminder to parson and people that there were other offices of the Church to be performed than preaching. Only for the short period when the Commonwealth ejected ordained priests of the Church, who returned with the Restoration, can these interiors have resembled Dissenting meeting houses.

Some of our finest scuplture is to be found in the monuments erected in all parish churches new or old during the 17th, 18th and early 19th centuries. A whole illustrated literature of this has been developed by the late Mrs Esdaile and Mr Rupert Gunnis. The work of great sculptors ignored or despised by the Victorians, such as Roubiliac, Rysbrack, Stone, Wilton, the Bacons, Hickey and Paty, has received recognition owing to their writings.

From the middle of the 18th century until its end, new churches were Classic, usually in the manner of the Brothers Adam, with chaste decorations in low relief in interior plaster and woodwork, and comparatively plain exteriors. The individuality of architects was beginning to assert itself over traditional plan and local styles. Cross-shaped churches were built with altar at the eastern axis and there were square and octagonal churches as well as proprietary chapels with the pews all arranged for a view of the occupier of the pulpit. These last buildings came as near to a Dissenting chapel as Anglicanism permitted.

Gothic never died. The style was driven by the Renaissance out of churches and houses into barns, farms and cottages. It was revived in a romantic form, suggesting Strawberry Hill (1733), even in the 17th century. And a slender case might be made for its never having died even in ecclesiastical building. There are Stuart churches which are Tudor Gothic, such as Low Ham in Somerset (1624), and Staunton Harold in Leicestershire (1653), which are like late Perpendicular medieval churches, and not a conscious revival but a continuance of the old style. St Martin-in-the-Fields, London, until its rebuilding by Gibbs in 1721, had been continuously rebuilt in the Gothic style since the time of Henry VIII. There are churches like St John's, Leeds (1632), and Compton Wynyates (1663), which are a mixture of Classic and Tudor Gothic. Then there are the first conscious imitations of old forms by architects, such as Sir William Wilson's tower of St Mary's, Warwick (1694), and Wren's tower and steeple to St Dunstan-in-the-East (1698), and his towers of St Mary Aldermary (1711) and St Michael's Cornhill (1721). There is an interesting and well-illustrated chapter on this subject of the earlier revival of Gothic in M. Whiffen's *Stuart and Georgian Churches*. The plan of these buildings was almost always traditional with an emphasized chancel. Now and then a Lutheran element crept in. In the Gothic church of Teigh in Rutland

(1783), the small font is fixed by a brass bracket to the Communion rails. But the seats face north and south and the pulpit is at the west end.

In the reign of Queen Anne Parliament passed an act to remedy the insufficiency of accommodation for worship in London and the vicinity. Leading architects of the time like James Gibbs, Archer and Hawksmoor were employed, and several fine churches which challenge those of Wren were the result. Other large towns, for this was a time when the population of the midlands was rapidly expanding, followed London's example.

Throughout the 18th century there was great interest in theology. Anyone looking through the library of a country house can verify this, for he will find rows of superbly bound volumes of sermons and controversial pamphlets and histories of religion. In the spas and the richer parts of London, private chapels were built for favourite clergy. They are well described by T. Francis Bumpus in *London Churches, Ancient and Modern*:

'Well pewed, well warmed, undedicated, unendowed, unconsecrated, here captivating preachers of the Morphine Velvet, lavender-kid-glove school of theology dispensed the most comfortable doctrines. The pews were filled, and the good promoters were amply repaid by the pious tenantry, but accommodation for the poor was never thought of.'

Not all proprietary chapels were like this. Some were undoubtedly missions for teaching the Faith to the rich and indifferent or for bringing the Gospel to the poor. When town parishes grew very large in the 18th century, it was sometimes the custom for a chapel to be rented or built, and, if it did not succeed, to be sold again, or in some instances taken over by dissenters. St Martin-in-the-Fields had two such chapels which have now disappeared, and there were three in the parish of St Margaret Westminster and seven in the parish of St Pancras.

Few of these proprietary chapels survive as such today. Sometimes there is, in a large provincial town, one very Evangelical church, in classic style, whose patronage is in the hands of private trustees. This may well once have been an 18th-century proprietary foundation. In 1746 there were nineteen in London, excluding chapels belonging to Royal and Episcopal Palaces, Almshouses, Prisons, Livery Companies and Inns of Court. Those which have not been pulled down or become Dissenting places of worship, have been consecrated and turned into parish churches. I remember one in Bath called Kensington Chapel, which was Calvinistic yet Anglican, but which is now a furniture store. At another in Homerton, London, known as Ram's Episcopal Chapel, I attended worship, and the clergyman wore a black gown and bands for preaching. This charming 18th-century chapel is now, alas, demolished. At Christ Church, North Brixton, London, is an extremely original and impressive episcopal chapel re-erected in 1904 in the Byzantine style from designs by Professor Beresford Pite. It was built privately and in it the black gown was still used in 1952.

Another reason for the erection of new churches in the 18th century was the inadequacy of medieval buildings. They could sometimes hold galleries erected in the aisles and at the west end, but no more. Old prints shew us town churches which have almost the appearance of an opera house, galleries projecting

△ **WING: ALL SAINTS** – *this monument was sculpted by Roubiliac, a French artist of the 18th century who worked mostly in England; his work fell out of fashion by the 19th century*

beyond galleries, with the charity children away up in the top lighted by dormers in the roof, pews all over the aisles and in the chancel, and only here and there a pointed arch or a bit of window tracery to shew that this was once a gothic medieval church. Walls began to bulge, stone decayed, structures were unsound and ill-behaved children could not be seen by the beadle and clerk. The only thing to do was to pull down the building. A surviving interior of this sort is the parish church of Whitby. To go into it is like entering the hold of a ship. There are box-pews shoulder high in all directions, galleries, private pews, and even a pew over the chancel screen. Picturesque and beautiful as it is, with the different colours of baize lining the pews, and the splendid joinery of varying dates, such an uneven effect cannot have pleased the 18th-century man of taste. Therefore when they became overloaded with pews, these old churches were taken down and new ones in Classic or Strawberry Hill Gothick style were erected on the sites.

In the country there can have been little need to rebuild the old church on the grounds of lack of accommodation. Here rebuilding was done at the dictates of taste. A landlord might find the church too near his house, or sited wrongly for a landscape improvement he was contemplating in the park, or he might simply dislike the old church on aesthetic grounds as a higgledy-piggledy, barbarous building. Most counties in England have more than one 18th-century church, now a sad relic in a park devastated by timber merchants, still crowning some rise or looking like a bit of Italy or ancient Greece in the pastoral English landscape.

Eighteenth-century churches are beautiful primarily because of their proportions. But they were not without colour. Painted hatchments adorned the walls, gilded tables of the Commandments were over the altar, with Moses and Aaron on either side, the Royal Arms on painted wood or coloured plaster was above the chancel opening, coloured baize lines in the pews, rich velvets of all colours were hanging from the high pulpit and the desks below it, an embroidered velvet covering decked the altar in wide folds, gilded candles and alms dish stood on the altar. The art of stained glass was not dead in the 18th century as is often supposed. East windows were frequently coloured, with pieces of golden-yellow 16th-century foreign glass brought back from a Grand Tour, and gold, blue and dark green glass, partly pot-metal and partly coloured transparency, such as went on being made in York until late in the century. Another popular kind of window was the coloured transparency – a transparent drawing enamelled on to glass, like the Reynolds' window in New College, Oxford, by such artists as Eginton of Birmingham, Peckitt of York, James Pearson and Jervais.

After 1760 country churches were often rebuilt in the Gothick taste. Pointed windows, pinnacled towers and battlemented walls were considered ecclesiastical and picturesque. They went with sham ruins and amateur antiquarianism, then coming into fashion. The details of these Gothick churches were not correct according to ancient examples. Nor do I think they were intended to be. Their designers strove after a picturesque effect, not antiquarian copying. The interiors were embellished with Chippendale Gothick woodwork and plaster-work. Again nothing was 'correct'. Who had ever heard of a medieval box-pew or an ancient ceiling that was plaster moulded? The Gothick taste was but plaster deep, concerned with a decorative effect and not with structure. The supreme example of this sort of church is Shobdon, Herefordshire (1753).

Amid all this concern with taste, industrialism comes upon us. It was all very well for the squire to fritter away his time with matters of taste in his country park, all very well for Boulton and Watt to try to harness taste to their iron-works at Soho, as Darby before them had tried at Ironbridge; the mills of the midlands and the north were rising. Pale mechanics, slave-driven children and pregnant women were working in the new factories. The more intelligent villagers were leaving for the towns where there was more money to be made. From that time until the present day, the country has been steadily drained of its best people. Living in hovels, working in a rattling twilight of machines, the people multiplied. Ebenezer Elliott the Corn Law Rhymer (1781–1849) was their poet:

The day was fair, the cannon roar'd,
Cold blew the bracing north,
And Preston's mills, by thousands, pour'd
Their little captives forth . . .
But from their lips the rose had fled,
Like 'death-in-life' they smiled;
And still, as each pass'd by, I said,
Alas! is that a child? . . .
Thousands and thousands – all so white! –
With eyes so glazed and dull!
O God! it was indeed a sight
Too sadly beautiful!
A Christian himself, Ebenezer called out above
the roar of the young industrial age:
When wilt thou save the People?
O God of mercy, when?
The people, Lord, the people,
Not thrones and crowns, but men!
Flowers of thy heart, O God, are they;
Let them not pass, like weeks, away, –
Their heritage a sunless day.
God save the people!

The composition of this poem was a little later than the Million Act of 1818, by which Parliament voted one million pounds towards the building of churches in new districts. The sentiments of the promoters of the Bill cannot have been so unlike those of Elliott. Less charitable hearts, no doubt, terrified by the atheism consequent on the French Revolution and apprehensive of losses to landed proprietors, regarded the Million Act as a thank-offering to God for defending them from French free-thinking and continental economics. Others saw in these churches bulwarks against the rising tide of Dissent. Nearly three hundred new churches were built in industrial areas between 1819 and 1830. The Lords Commissioner of the Treasury who administered the fund required them to be built in the most economical mode, 'with a view to accommodating the greatest number of persons at the smallest expense within the compass of an ordinary voice, one half of the number to be free seats for the poor'. A limit of £20,000 was fixed for 2,000 persons. Many of these 'Commissioners' or 'Waterloo' churches, as they are now called, were built for £10,000. The most famous church of this date is St Pancras in London, which cost over £70,000. But the money was found by private subscription and a levy on the rates. For other and cheaper churches in what were then poorer districts the Commissioners contributed towards the cost.

The Commissioners themselves approved all designs. When one reads some of the conditions they laid down, it is surprising to think that almost every famous architect in the country designed churches for them – Soane, Nash, Barry, Smirke, the Inwoods, the Hardwicks, Rickman (a Quaker and the inventor of those useful terms for Gothic architecture, 'Early English', 'Decorated' and 'Perpendicular'), Cockerell & Basevi and Dobson, to name a few. 'The site must be central, dry and sufficiently distant from factories and noisy thoroughfares; a paved area is to be made round the church. If vaulted underneath, the crypt is to be made available for the reception of coals or the parish fire engine. Every care must be taken to render chimneys safe from fire; they might be concealed in pinnacles. The windows ought not to resemble modern sashes; but whether Grecian or Gothic, should be in small panes and not costly. The most favourable position for the minister is near an end wall or in a semicircular recess under a half dome. The pulpit should not intercept a view of the altar, but all seats should be placed so as to face the preacher. We should recommend pillars of cast iron for supporting the gallery of a chapel, but in large churches they might want grandeur. Ornament should be neat and simple, yet variable in character.'

In short, what was wanted was a cheap auditorium, and, whether Grecian or Gothic, the solution seems always to have been the same. The architects provided a large rectangle with an altar at the end in a very shallow chancel, a high pulpit on one side of the altar and a reading desk on the other, galleries round the north, west and south walls, an organ in the west gallery, and lighting from two rows of windows on the north and south walls, the lower row to light the aisles and nave, the upper to light the galleries. The font was usually under the west gallery. The only scope for invention which the architect had was in the design of portico and steeple, tower or spire.

Most large towns have at least one example of Commissioners' Churches, particularly in the north of England, where they were usually Gothic. None to my knowledge except Christ Church, Acton Square, Salford (1831) survived exactly as it was when its architect designed it. This is not because they were badly built. But they were extremely unpopular with the Victorians, who regarded them as cheap and full of shams and unworthy of the new-found dignity of the Anglican liturgy. The usual thing to do was to turn Grecian buildings into 'Byzantine' or 'Lombardic' fanes, by filling the windows with stained glass, piercing the gallery fronts with fretwork, introducing iron screens at the east end, adding a deeper chancel and putting mosaics in it, and of course cutting down the box-pews, thus ruining the planned proportions of the building and the relation of woodwork to columns supporting the galleries. The architect, Sir Arthur Blomfield, was a specialist in spoiling Commissioners' Churches in this way. Gothic or Classic churches were 'corrected'. In later days side chapels were tucked away in aisles originally designed for pews. Organs were invariably moved from the west galleries made for them, and were fitted awkwardly alongside the east end.

One can visualize a Commissioners' Church as it was first built, by piecing together the various undisturbed parts of these churches in different towns. The Gothic was a matter of decoration, except in St Luke's new church, Chelsea, London, and not of construction. A Commissioners' Church will be found in that part of a town where streets have names like Nelson Crescent, Adelaide Place, Regent Square, Brunswick Terrace and Hanover Villas. The streets round it will have the spaciousness of Georgian speculative building, low-terraced houses in brick or stucco with fanlights over the doors, and, until the pernicious campaign against Georgian railings during the Nazi war, there were pleasant cast-iron verandahs on the first floor and simple railings round the planted square. Out of a wide paved space, railed in with Greek or Gothic cast iron according to the style of the building, will rise the Commissioners' Church, a brick structure with Bath stone dressings, two rows of windows and a noble entrance portico at the west end. Such churches are generally locked today, for the neighbourhood has often 'gone down'; the genteel late Georgian families who lived there moved into arboured suburbs at the beginning of this century, and their houses have been sub-let in furnished rooms.

But Commissioners' Churches, which provided worship for nearly five million people, had a dignity and coherence which we can appreciate today now that the merits of Georgian Architecture are recognized. They were the last auditory buildings of the Establishment to be erected for about a century. Through the rest of the 19th century, most new churches might be considered inauditory buildings, places where the ritual of the service could best be appreciated, where sight came first and sound second.

By 1850 began a great period of English church building, which is comparable with the 15th century. Much as we regret the Victorian architect's usual 'restoration' of an old building, when he came to design a new one, he could produce work which was often original and awe-inspiring. To name only a few London churches, All Saints, Margaret Street; St Augustine's, Kilburn; St James the Less, Victoria; St Columba's, Haggerston; Holy Trinity, Sloane Street; Holy Redeemer, Clerkenwell; St Michael's, Camden Town; and St Cyprian's, Clarence Gate, are some large examples of the period which have survived Prussian bombing. To understand the inspiration behind these churches, we must leave architecture for a while and turn to the architects and the men who influenced them; architects such as Pugin, Street, Butterfield, Pearson, Gilbert Scott, Bodley and the Seddings, and priests such as Newman, Keble, Pusey, Neale, Wilberforce, and later Lowder, Mackonochie and Wainwright.

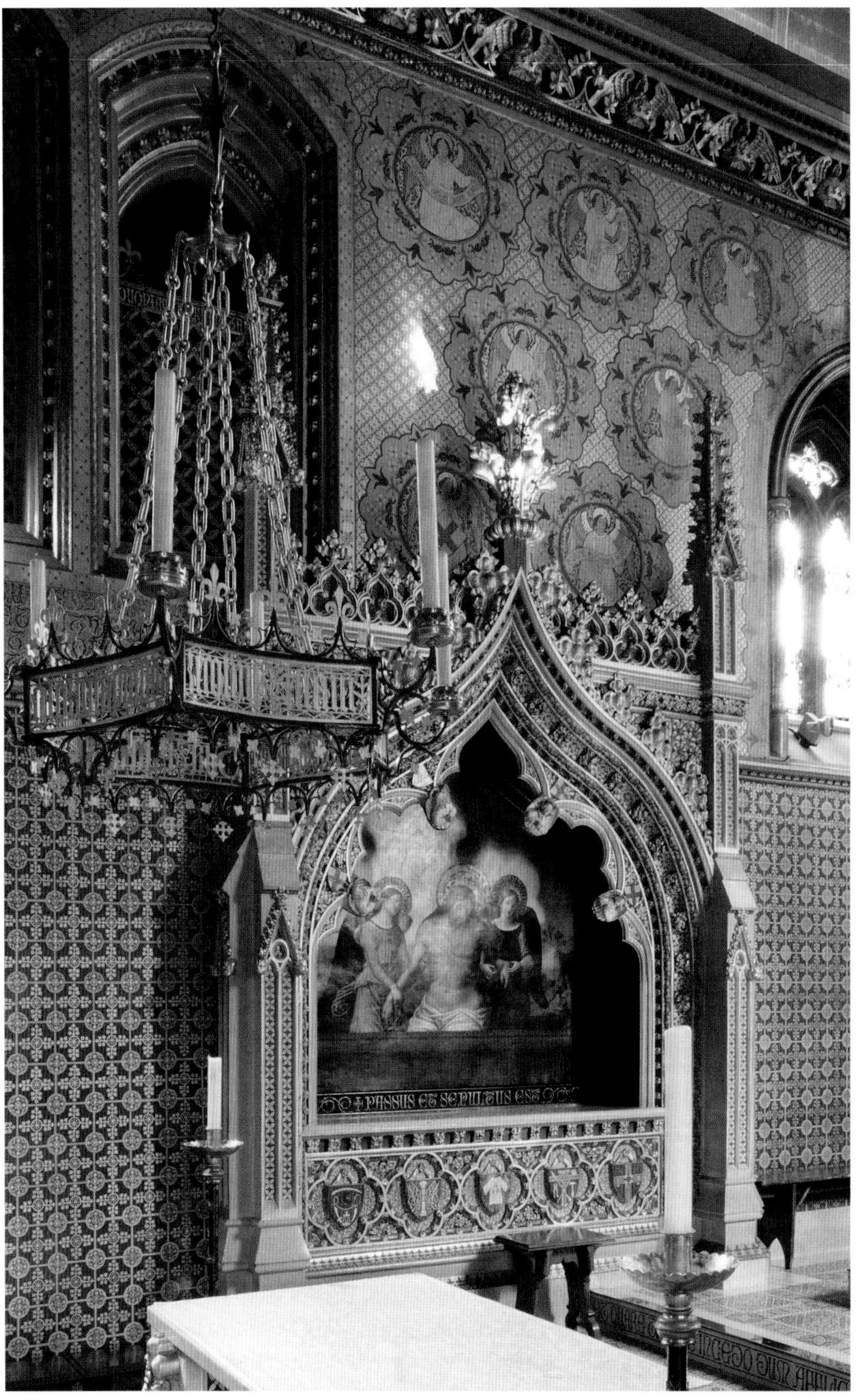

△ **CHEADLE: ST GILES** – *one of A. W. N. Pugin's most complete schemes, a meticulous recreation of medieval Gothic*

The Commissioners' Churches were built to provide more space for the worship of God. But in what way was God to be worshipped? And even, who was God? Those 19th-century liberals who survived the shock of the French Revolution took up a line which we can still find today in the absurd Act inaugurated by R. A. Butler (1944) about the teaching of religion in State Schools. The liberal view was, as Newman described it, 'the doctrine that there is no positive truth in religion, but that one creed is as good as another.' This view commended itself to Dissenters in the beginning of the last century, since they saw in it the liberty to expound their doctrines, and perhaps to win the world to believe them. It commended itself to those whom scientific discovery was driving to unwilling agnosticism. And, of course, it commended itself to materialists who had not yet made a dogma of materialism.

In the late Georgian Church there was little of such liberalism. People were divided into Low Church Evangelicals and old-fashioned 'High and Dry'. By the 1830s the great Evangelical movement was, as W. S. Lilly says, 'perishing of intellectual inanition'. Beginning, in Apostolic wise, with 'the foolishness of preaching, it had ended unapostolically in the preaching of foolishness.' The evangelical tea-parties, revelations, prophecies, jumping, shaking and speaking in strange tongues which went on in England in those days within and without the Church make fascinating reading. But they have left no enduring architectural monument, except for some of the buildings belonging to the Catholic Apostolic Church. The other party in the Church of England, the 'high and dry', was orthodox and uninspiring. Once a quarter, after preparing themselves by means of those Queen Anne and Georgian manuals of devotion which we sometimes find bound up in old prayer books, its members moved through the chancel screen on Sacrament Sunday to partake of the outward and visible signs of inward and spiritual grace. Their parsons wore the surplice and the wig, and abhorred change. They were not quite so negative as they are made out to be. There are several instances in the late 18th and early 19th centuries of screens being erected across chancels to shut off from the nave the place where the Sacrament was partaken.

The Church of England at this time drew its ministers from men who were scholars or gentlemen, usually both. Harriet Martineau's acid biography of Bishop Blomfield (1786–1857) in her *Biographical Sketches*, rather cattily says: 'In those days, a divine rose in the Church in one or two ways, – by his classical reputation, or by aristocratic connection. Mr Blomfield was a fine scholar;...'

Let us try to put ourselves into the frame of mind of somebody living in the reign of King William IV. Let us suppose him just come down from Oxford and still in touch with his University. The grand tour was no longer so fashionable. A squire's son usually went abroad for sport. Few came back with works of art for the adornment of their parks or saloons. Most country house libraries stop at the end of George IV's reign, except for the addition of sporting books and works of reference on husbandry, law and pedigrees of family and livestock. A studious man, such as we have in mind, would have turned his attention to antiquity and history. The novels of Scott would have given him a taste for England's past. The antiquarian publications of Britton would have reinforced it. In Gothic England he would have found much to admire. And the people of his village were still the product of agricultural feudalism. Tenantry bobbed, and even artisans touched their hats. Blasphemy shocked people, for many believed that Christ was the Incarnate Son of God.

Our young man would undoubtedly read *The Christian Year* by the Reverend John Keble (1827). It is hard to see today how this simple and unexciting, oft-reprinted book could have fired so many minds. Perhaps the saintly life of the author, who had thrown up academic honours and comfort to live among simple villagers as their minister, had something to do with it. At any rate, Newman regarded that book as the foundation of the Tractarian movement. The verses of *The Christian Year* were a series composed to fit in with the feasts, fasts and offices of the *Book of Common Prayer*. They drew people back to the nature of the Established Church. And the *Tracts for the Times* which followed, from Keble's Assize Sermon of 1833 up to Tract XC by Newman on the Thirty-nine Articles in 1841, would certainly influence him greatly. In these he would learn how the Church was finding herself part of the Catholic Church. Although many great men, greatest of all Newman, have left her for the Church of Rome, others remained faithful. Their witness in England in the last century is apparent in the hundreds of churches which were built on Tractarian principles in new suburbs and towns, in the church schools, public and elementary, in the Sisterhood buildings, in the houses of rest erected by good people of the kind one reads about in the novels of Charlotte M. Yonge, who was herself a parishioner and friend of Keble.

English architecture was also beginning a new phase of professionalism in the reign of William IV. Architects had in the past been regarded either as builders or as semi-amateurs who left the details of their designs to masons and plasterers. There had been great architects since the time of Wren. There was also a host of lesser men who in domestic work were pursuing their local styles and imitating the splendid designs of the metropolis, rather as village builders in monastic times had tried to reproduce in village churches the latest styles at the abbeys. But for years now architecture had been becoming a profession. Architects designed buildings and produced their own beautiful, detailed drawings. Less was left to the builder and the gifted amateur. In 1837 the Institute of British Architects was incorporated by Royal Charter. Architects were by now rather more like doctors and lawyers than artists.

The most influential was Augustus Welby Northmore Pugin (1812–52), who was said by his doctor to have crammed into his forty years of existence the work of a hundred years. Pugin's life has been entertainingly described by his contemporary Benjamin Ferrey in *Recollections of Augustus Welby Pugin*, 1861, and lately his life has been written by Michael Trappes-Lomax, who stresses his Roman Catholicism. Sir Kenneth Clark in *The Gothic Revival*, the Revd. B. F. L. Clarke in *Nineteenth Century Churchbuilders*, and John Summerson in an essay in *The Architectural Review* (April 1948), have all written most illuminatingly about him.

In 1841 Pugin published his *Contrasts* and his *True Principles of Christian Architecture.* Herein he caricatured in skilful drawings the false Gothick of the Strawberry Hill type, and lampooned everything that was classical. To contrast with these he had made beautiful shaded drawings of medieval buildings, particularly those of the late 14th century. He did not confine his caricatures to architecture, and peopled the foregrounds with figures. In front of pagan or classical buildings he drew indolent policemen, vulgar tradesmen and miserable beggars; before the medieval buildings he drew vested priests and pious pilgrims. He idealized the middle ages. His drawings were sincere but unfair. The prose accompaniment to them is glowing and witty.

Pugin's own churches, which were almost all Roman Catholic, are attempts to realize his dreams. But for all the sincerity of their architect, the brass coronals, the jewelled glass by Hardman of Birmingham, the correctly moulded arches and the carefully caned woodwork have a spindly effect. St Chad's Roman Catholic Cathedral at Birmingham, St Augustine's Church, Ramsgate, and St Giles's, Cheadle, are exceptions. It is not in his buildings but in his writing that Pugin had so great an influence on the men of his time.

Pugin is sometimes supposed to have joined the Church of Rome for aesthetic reasons only. It is true that he saw in it the survival of the Middle Ages to which he desired the world to return. But the Roman Catholics of his time were not whole-heartedly in favour of the Gothic style he advocated, and to his annoyance continued to build in the classic style of the continent or else in the plaster-thin Gothick he despised. The Church of England, newly awakened to its Catholicism, took more kindly to his doctrines, so that although he came in for some mild criticism from *The Ecclesiologist* (the organ first of the Cambridge Camden Society, and from 1845 of Catholic-minded Anglicans in general), Pugin contemplated writing an essay called: 'An Apology for the separated Church of England since the reign of the Eight Henry. Written with every feeling of Christian charity for her Children, and honour of the glorious men she continued to produce in evil times. By A. Welby Pugin, many years a Catholic-minded son of the Anglican Church, and still an affectionate and loving brother of the true sons of England's church.'

I do not think it was solely for aesthetic reasons, or even for doctrinal reasons, that Pugin joined the Church of Rome. He possessed what we now call, 'social conscience'. He deplored the slums he saw building round him. He abhorred the soullessness of machinery, and revered hand craftsmanship. His drawings of industrial towns contrasted with a dream-like Middle Ages, his satire on the wealthy ostentation of a merchant's house – 'On one side of the house machicolated parapets, embrasures, bastions, and all the show of strong defence, and round the corner of the building a conservatory leading to the principal rooms, through which a whole company of horsemen might penetrate at one smash into the heart of the mansion! – for who would hammer against nailed portals when he could kick his way through the greenhouse?' – are summed up in the two principles of Gothic or Christian architecture which he delivered to the world. These are they. 'First, that there should be no features about a building which are not necessary for convenience, construction, or propriety; second, that all ornament should consist of enrichment of the essential construction of the building.' Pugin's principles, and his conviction that the only style that was Christian was Gothic, are fathered by popular opinion on Ruskin. But Ruskin was not fond of Pugin. He disliked his Popery, and he thought little of his buildings. If one must find a successor to Pugin, it is the atheist William Morris. Both men liked simplicity and good craftsmanship. Both had a 'social conscience'. Pugin dreamed of a Christian world, Morris of a Socialist world, but both their worlds were dreams.

Let us imagine our young man again, now become a Tractarian clergyman. His convictions about how best to honour the God he loves, and how to spread that love among the artisans in the poorer part of his parish, are likely to take form in a new church. And, since he is a Tractarian, it must be a beautiful church. His reading of Pugin, the publications of the Cambridge Camden Society and *The Ecclesiologist*, will have inspired him. He will have no truck with the cheap Gothic or Norman Revival of the Evangelical school. A pamphlet such as that of Revd. W. Carus Wilson's *Helps to the Building of Churches, Parsonage Houses and Schools* (2nd Edition, Kirby Lonsdale, 1842) will have digusted him. Here we find just the sort of thing Pugin satirized: 'A very neat portable font has been given to the new church at Stonyhurst, which answers every purpose; not requiring even the expense of a stand; as it might be placed, when wanted, on the Communion Table from which the ceremony might be performed. The price is fourteen shillings; and it is to be had at Sharper's, Pall Mall East, London.' Such cheese-paring our clergyman would leave to the extreme Protestants who thought ostentation, stained glass, frontals, lecterns and banners smacked of Popery, and who thought with Dean Close of Cheltenham that 'the Restoration of Churches is the Restoration of Popery'. This explains why, to this day, unrestored churches with box-pews are generally Evangelical and locked. But the Evangelical did not wholly reject Gothic. Ullenhall (Warwicks) and Itchen Stoke (Hants) are Victorian Gothic churches designed to have the Table well away from the East wall and the lectern and pulpit dominant. Ullenhall retains its Protestant arrangement, and this arrangement was originally, we must remember, the 'High Church' of the 17th and 18th centuries. The Early English style was regarded as plain and primitive. Very few churches were built in a classic style between 1840 and 1900. The choice before young vicar is no longer Gothic or Classic, but what sort of Gothic?

Architects were turning their attention to churches. And the younger men were all for Gothic. Most architects were God-fearing folk of the new middle class. They felt privileged to build churches to the glory of God. Many of them were instructed in theology; they subscribed to *The Ecclesiologist* and to various learned antiquarian publications. They delighted to discuss the merits of Norman, and Decorated, Early English and Perpendicular, or Early, Middle and Late Pointed, according to which terminology they favoured. In the early 'forties they were still following Pugin. Pugin's chief Anglican equivalents were Benjamin Ferrey, Carpenter and Gilbert Scott. These men, and many others,

△ **LONDON: ALL SAINTS MARGARET STREET** – *Butterfield's masterpiece is an industrialised version of Gothic Revival, a medieval sensibility allied to modern materials and methods*

were capable of making very good imitations of a medieval fabric. With the aid of the numerous books of measured drawings that were appearing, it was possible to erect almost exact copies of such famous monuments of the Middle Ages as the spire at Louth, the tracery of the Angel Choir at Lincoln, and the roof of Westminster Hall. The scale was different it is true, and architects had no compunction about mixing copies of what they considered the 'best' features of old churches in their new ones. They thought that a blend of the best everywhere would make something better still.

The earlier Gothic revival churches, that is to say those of late Georgian times, were in the late 14th-century style. One may see in some prim and spacious Georgian square, brick imitations of King's College Chapel and Bathstone dressings. But in the late 1840s architects were attaching moral properties to Gothic styles. Pugin had started the idea and his successors surpassed him. Since Gothic was the perfect style, what was the perfect style of Gothic? I do not know who it was who started the theory that early Gothic is crude, middle is perfection, and late is debased . But – certainly from the middle of the 1840s – this theory was held by most of the rising young church architects. Promoters of new churches who could afford it were advised to have something in the Middle Pointed or Decorated style. This is the reason why in mid-Victorian suburbs, while speculative builders were still erecting Italianate stucco mansions, in the last stuccoed gasp of the Georgian classic tradition – South Kensington and

Pimlico in London are examples – the spire of Ketton or Louth soars above the chimney-pots, and a sudden break in the Palladian plaster terraces shews the irregular stone front, gabled porch and curvilinear tracery of a church in the Decorated style. Church architecture was setting the fashion which the builders followed, and decades later, even employing church architects (such as Ferrey at Bournemouth), they erected Gothic residences in the new winding avenues of housing estates for the upper middle classes. Most of the work of the late 'forties and early 'fifties was in this copying style. When an architect had a sense of proportion, there were often impressive results. Carpenter and his son and their partner Slater were always good. Their Lancing School Chapel must be regarded as one of the finest Gothic buildings of any period in England, and their London church of St Mary Magdalen, Munster Square, so modest outside, is spacious and awe-inspiring within.

The most famous copyist was Gilbert Scott. He and his family have had a great influence on English architecture over the past century. Gilbert Scott was the son of a Buckinghamshire parson, the grandson of the Calvinist clergyman Thomas Scott, whose Commentary on the Bible greatly influenced Newman as a youth. There is no doubt of Scott's passionate affection for Gothic architecture. He pays a handsome tribute to Pugin's influence on his mind: 'Pugin's articles excited me almost to fury, and I suddenly found myself like a person awakened from a long, feverish dream, which had rendered him unconscious of what was going on about him.'

Our young clergyman would almost certainly have applied to Gilbert Scott for his new church. He would have received designs from Scott's office. They would have been a safe, correct essay in the middle pointed style, with tower and spire or with bellcot only, according to the price. Scott himself, except when he first started in private practice, may not have had much to do with the design. He collected an enormous staff, and from his office emerged, it is said, over seven hundred and forty buildings between 1847 and 1878 when he died. When one considers that an architect in private practice today thinks himself busy if he has seven new buildings to do in a decade, it seems probable that Scott eventually became little more than an overseer of all but his most important work. His 'restorations' were numerous and usually disastrous.

Yet Scott, who was eventually knighted for his vast output, had a style of his own – a square abacus to his columns, Plate tracery in the windows, much stone foliage mixed up with heads, and for east or west windows, three equal lancets with a round window above them. In five churches of his, St Giles, Camberwell; St George's, Doncaster; Leafield, Oxon; Bradfield, Berks, and St Anne, Alderney, I can trace it clearly. He liked to build something big. He dispensed with a chancel screen. Instead of this, he often interposed between the congregation in the nave and the rich chancel, a tower or transept crossing which was either darker or lighter than the parts it separated. Add to this a sure sense of proportion and a workmanlike use of stone, and the dull mechanical details of his work are forgotten in the mystery and splendour of the interior effect. Scott realized some of Pugin's dreams for him. But he never did more. He was at heart a copyist and not a thinker in Gothic.

Church architecture by the 'fifties was very much an affair of personalities. The big London men and a few in the provinces had their individual styles. As Sir Charles Nicholson remarked in his comments on Henry Woodyer's beautiful building St Michael's College, Tenbury (1856), which was designed as a church choir school: 'It was never, of course, intended that the College should be mistaken for anything other than a 19th-century building: for Gothic revival architects did not attempt such follies, though their enemies accused them of doing so.' What is true of St Michael's College, Tenbury, is true also of most of the churches built in England after 1850. The chief of those architects who 'thought in Gothic' are listed below.

William Butterfield (1814–1900) was the most severe and interesting of them. He first startled the world in 1849 with his design for All Saints, Margaret Street, London, built on the cramped site of an 18th-century proprietary chapel where lights had been used on the altar since 1839, and a sung celebration of the Holy Communion introduced. All Saints embodies architectural theories which Butterfield employed in most of his other churches throughout his long life. It is constructed of the material which builders in the district were accustomed to use, which in London at that time was brick. Since bricks do not lend themselves to the carving which is expected of a Gothic building, Butterfield varied his flat brick surfaces with bands of colour, both within and without. In those days the erroneous impression prevailed that Gothic decoration grew more elaborate the higher it was on a building. The patterns of bricks in Butterfield's buildings grew, therefore, more diversified and frequent towards the tops of walls, towers and steeples. But their arrangement is not usually capricious as it is in the work of some of the rather comic church architects who copied him, like Bassett Keeling. Where walls supported a great weight, they were striped horizontally, where they were mere screen walls, diaper patterns of bricks were introduced. Inside his churches Butterfield delighted to use every coloured stone, marble and other material he could find for the money at his disposal. He was a severely practical man, and a planner and constructor first. His decoration was meant to emphasize his construction.

The plan of All Saints is in the latest Tractarian manner of its time. The high altar is visible from every part of the church. Indeed to this day not even the delicate and marked style of Sir Ninian Comper's side altar in the north aisle takes one's eye from the chancel. Butterfield disapproved of side altars and never made provision for them in his churches. The chancel is the richest part of the building, and the chancel arch, higher than the arcades of the nave, gives it an effect of greater loftiness than it possesses. There is, of course, no screen. The other prominent feature of any Butterfield church is the font. That sentence in the Catechism on the number of Sacraments, 'Two only, as generally necessary to salvation, that is to say Baptism, and the Supper of the Lord', is almost spoken aloud by a Butterfield church; altar and font are the chief things we see. But when we look up at arches and roofs, we see Butterfield the builder with his delight in construction. His roofs are described by that fine writer Sir John Summerson as 'like huge, ingenious toys'. The phrase is as memorable as all

Butterfield's roofs, of which the ingenuity and variety seem to have been the only sportiveness he permitted himself.

In person Butterfield was a silent, forbidding man who looked like Mr Gladstone. He was an earnest Tractarian with a horror of everything outside the liturgy of the *Book of Common Prayer*. Except for one Noncomformist chapel in Bristol, designed when he was a youth, and unlike the rest of his work, he built only for Tractarians. He supplied no attractive drawings to tempt clients. He was a strong disciplinarian in his office, and on the building site, scaffolding and ladders had to be dusted before he ascended to see the work in progress. He was averse to all publicity and show, and had little to do with any other architects. People had to take Butterfield or leave him. And so must we. Yet no one who has an eye for plan, construction and that sense of proportion which is the essential of all good architecture, can see a Butterfield church without being compelled to admire it, even if he cannot like it.

George Edmund Street, R.A. (1824–81), is chiefly remembered now for the Law Courts in London. He was in Gilbert Scott's office before setting up on his own. Early in his career he received the patronage of such distinguished High Churchmen as Prynne, Butler of Wantage, and Bishop Wilberforce of Oxford. Street himself was a Tractarian, singing in the choir at Wantage and disapproving of ritual without doctrine. The churches he built in the late 'fifties and throughout the 'sixties, often with schools and parsonages alongside them, are like his character straightforward and convinced. They are shorn of those 'picturesque' details beloved of the usual run of architects of the time. The plan of Street's buildings is immediately apparent from the exterior. Some of his village schools of local stone built early in his career in the Oxford Diocese are so simple and well-proportioned, and fit so naturally into the landscape, that they might be the sophisticated Cotswold work of such 1900 architects as Ernest Gimson and F. L. Griggs. Street's churches are built on the same principles as those of Butterfield, one altar only, and that visible from all parts of the church, a rich east end, and much westward light into the nave. Street had a sure sense of proportion, very much his own; his work, whether it is a lectern or a pulpit or a spire, is massive, and there is nothing mean about it nor over-decorated. This massive quality of his work made Street a bad restorer of old buildings, for he would boldly pull down a chancel and rebuild it in his own style. He was a great enthusiast for the arts and crafts. With his own hands he is said to have made the wooden staircase for West Challow Vicarage in Berkshire. His ironwork was drawn out in section as well as outline, and there were some caustic comments written by him in the margin of his copy of Gilbert Scott's *Personal and Professional Recollections* (in the RIBA Library) where Scott confesses to leaving the detail of his ironwork to Skidmore of Coventry, the manufacturer. Street was an able sketcher of architecture, and clearly a man who could fire his pupils with his own enthusiasm, even though he never allowed those pupils a free hand in design, doing everything down to the smallest details himself. Street's influence on English architecture is properly appreciated in H. S. Goodhart Rendel's *English Architecture Since the Regency*. It comes down to us through his pupils, among whom were Philip Webb and Norman Shaw, whose domestic

△ **WATERFORD: ST MICHAEL AND ALL ANGELS** – *Morris & Co. produced much of the glass in this church, some designed by William Morris and some, such as this example, by Burne-Jones*

architecture brought about the small house of today, William Morris, to whom the Arts and Crafts Movement owes so much, and J. D. Sedding, the church architect and craftsman.

The third of the great mid-Victorian church builders was John Loughborough Pearson (1817–97). His later buildings are of all Victorian churches those we like best today. He was, like Street and Butterfield, a Tractarian. Before designing a building he gave himself to prayer and receiving the Sacrament. He seems to have been a more 'advanced' clergyman than his two comparable contemporaries, for in his later churches he made ample provision for side altars, and even for a tabernacle for the reservation of the Blessed Sacrament. Pearson was articled in Durham to Ignatius Bonomi, the son of an elegant 18th-century architect. His early work in Yorkshire is competent copying of the medieval, and just distinguishable from the work of Gilbert Scott. But somewhere about 1860 he paid a visit to France, and early French Gothic vaulting seems to have transformed him. He built St Peter's, Vauxhall, London, in 1862. Like most of his later work it is a cruciform building with brick vaulting throughout and with a clerestory. St Peter's seems to have been the pattern of which all his subsequent churches were slight variants. Sometimes he threw out side chapels, sometimes he made aisles under buttresses. The Pearson style was an Early English Gothic with deep mouldings and sharply-pointed arches; brick was usually employed for walls and vaulting, stone for ribs, columns, arches and window tracery. Pearson also took great trouble with skyline, and his spires, fleches and roofs form beautiful groups from any angle.

One more individualistic Gothic revivalist was William Burges (1827–81), who was as much a domestic architect and a furniture designer as an ecclesiastical man. He delighted in colour and quaintness, but being the son of an engineer, his work had a solidity of structure which saved it from ostentation. His east end of Waltham Abbey and his cathedral of St Finbar, Cork, are his most beautiful church work, though Skelton and Studley Royal, both in Yorkshire, are overpowering in their rich colour and decoration, and very original in an early French Gothic manner.

Neither Butterfield, Street, Pearson nor Burges would have thought of copying old precedents. They had styles of their own which they had devised for themselves, continuing from the medieval Gothic but not copying it.

These big men had their imitators: Bassett Keeling who reproduced the wildest excesses of the polychromatic brick style and mixed it with cast-iron construction; S. S. Teulon who, in his youth, did the same thing; E. Buckton Lamb who invented a style of his own; Henry Woodyer who had a fanciful, spindly Gothic style which is original and marked; William White and Henry Clutton, both of whom produced churches, strong and modern for their times; Ewan Christian, the Evangelical architect, who could imitate the style of Pearson; or that best of the lesser men, James Brooks who built several 'big-boned' churches in East London in a plainer Pearson-esque manner. There was also the scholarly work in Italian Gothic of E. W. Godwin, and Sir Arthur Blomfield could turn out an impressive church in almost any style.

There is no doubt that until about 1870 the impetus of vigorous Victorian architecture went into church building. Churches took the lead in construction and in use of materials. They employed the artists, and many of the best pictures of the time had sacred subjects. The difficulties in which artists found themselves, torn between Anglo-Catholicism, Romanism and Ruskin's Protestantism, is described well in John Steegman's *Consort of Taste.*

After the 'seventies, Norman Shaw, himself a High Churchman, became the leading domestic architect. The younger architects turned their invention to house design and building small houses for people of moderate income. Bedford Park was laid out by Norman Shaw in 1878. It was a revolution – a cluster of picturesque houses for artistic suburbanites. And from this time onwards we have a series of artistic churches, less vulgar and vigorous than the work of the now ageing great men, but in their way distinguished: slender, tapering work, palely enriched within in Burne-Jonesian greens and browns. The Middle Pointed or Decorated style and variants of it were no longer thought the only correct styles. People began to admire what was 'late' and what was 'English', and the neglected glory of Perpendicular, long called 'debased', was revived, and even the Renaissance style was used. For as the Reverend B. F. L. Clarke says in his *Church Builders of the Nineteenth Century*, 'the question of Style was coming to be regarded as being of small importance'.

The last quarter of the 19th century was a time when the Tractarian movement firmly established itself. Of the eight Religious Communities for men of the Anglican Church, six were of the 1890s, and one, the 'Cowley Fathers' (Society of St John the Evangelist), was founded in 1865. Of the forty-five Communities for women, the first two, the Society of the Holy and Undivided Trinity and the Society of the Most Holy Trinity, Ascot, were founded in 1845, and well over half the rest are of Victorian origin. There are now in the Church of England more religious Communities than there were in medieval England, and this does not include Communities in Scotland, Wales, Ireland, America, Asia, Africa and Australia.

This was a time when the church was concerning herself with social problems, and building many new churches in England as well as establishing dioceses abroad. Many, and often ugly, little churches were built of brick in brand new suburbs. Cathedral-like buildings, subscribed for by the pious from wealthy parishes, were built in the slums. At the back of *Crockford's Clerical Directory* there is an index of English parishes with the dates of their formation. If you look up an average industrial town with, say, ten churches, you will find that the majority will have been built during the last half of the 19th century. Oldest will be the parish church, probably medieval. Next there will be a late Georgian church built by the Commissioners. Then there will be three built between 1850 and 1870, three built between 1870 and 1900, and two since then, probably after the 1914 war and in new suburbs.

It is entertaining, and not completely safe, to generalize on the inner story of the Church and its building in Victorian and later times. In, let us say, 1850, the vicar of the parish church had become a little old for active work, and left much to his curates. His churchmanship took the form mainly of support for the Establishment and hostility to Dissent. The word 'Dissenters' applied to Nonconformists always had a faint note of contempt. Methodists and Baptists were building chapels all over the rapidly growing town. Their religion of personal experience of salvation, of hymn-singing, ejaculations of praise; the promise of a golden heaven after death as a reward for a sad life down here in

△ **CARSHALTON: ALL SAINTS** – *Ninian Comper produced some of his finest work in this surburban London church, including this gilded and painted triptych for the high altar*

the crowded misery of back streets, disease and gnawing poverty; their weekday socials and clubs which welded the membership of the chapels in a Puritan bond of teetotalism, and non-gambling, non-smoking and welldoing: these had an appeal which today is largely dispersed into the manufactured day-dreams of the cinema and the less useful social life of the dance hall and sports club. Chapels were crowded, gas-lights flamed on popular preachers, and steamy windows resounded to the cries of 'Alleluia, Jesus saves!' A simple ceremony like total immersion or Breaking of Bread was something all the tired and poor could easily understand, after their long hours of misery in gloomy mills. Above all, the Nonconformists turned people's minds and hearts to Jesus as a personal Friend of all, especially the poor. Many a pale mechanic and many a drunkard's wife could remember the very hour of the very day on which, in that street or at that meeting, or by that building, conviction came of the truth of the Gospel, that Jesus was Christ. Then with what flaming heart he or she came to the chapel, and how fervently testified to the message of salvation and cast off the old life of sin.

Beside these simple and genuine experiences of the love of Christ, the old-established Church with its system of pew rents, and set prayers and carefully-guarded sacraments, must have seemed wicked mumbo-jumbo. No wonder the old Vicar was worried about the Dissenters. His parish was increasing by thousands as the factories boomed and the ships took our merchandise across the seas, but his parishioners were not coming to church in proportion. He had no objection therefore when the new Bishop, filled with the zeal for building which seems to have filled all Victorian bishops, decided to form two new parishes out of his own, the original parish of the little village which had become a town in less than a century. The usual method was adopted. Two clergymen were licensed to start the church life of the two new districts. These men were young; one was no doubt a Tractarian; the other was perhaps fired with the Christian Socialism of Charles Kingsley and F. D. Maurice. Neither was much concerned with the establishment of churches as bulwarks against Dissenters, but rather as houses of God among ignorant Pagans, where the Gospel might be heard, the Sacraments administered, want relieved, injustice righted and ignorance dispelled. First came the mission-room, a room licensed for services in the clergyman's lodging, then there was the school, at first a room for Sunday school only, and then came the mission church made of corrugated iron. Then there was an appeal for a church school and for a permanent church. For this church the once young clergyman, now worn after ten years' work, would apply to the Incorporated Church Building Society, and to the Church Building Fund of his own diocese; he would raise money among his poor parishioners, he would give his own money (this was a time when priests were frequently men of means), and pay his own stipend as well. The site for the church would be given by a local landowner, and who knows but that some rich manufacturer whose works were in the parish would subscribe. Whatever their Churchmanship, the new parishes formed in the 'fifties generally had their own church within twenty years.

All this while the Commissioners' Church in the town, that Greek Revival building among the genteel squares where still lived the doctors, attorneys and merchants, had an Evangelical congregation and disapproved of the old 'high and dry' vicar of the parish church. The congregation and incumbent disapproved still more of the goings on of the Tractarian priest in charge of one of the two new districts. He lit two candles on the Table which he called an 'altar', at the service of the Lord's Supper he stood with his back to the congregation instead of at the north end of the Table, he wore a coloured stole over his gown. He was worse than the Pope of Rome or almost as bad. The ignorant artisans were being turned into Roman Catholics. The pure Gospel of the Reformation must be brought to them. So a rival church was built in the Tractarian parish, financed by the Evangelical church people of the town, and from outside by many loyal Britons who throughout England, like Queen Victoria herself, were deploring the Romish tendency in the Established Church.

Many years have passed since this controversy, and the rival Evangelical fane probably has now a clergyman who always wears a surplice and sometimes a coloured stole, who has lights on the altar and faces east to celebrate Holy Communion, while the priest and congregation of the neighbouring Tractarian church, who now have incense, reservation of the Blessed Sacrament, daily mass, confessions and a High Mass on Sundays, still regard him as 'low church'.

If one may generalize about the ecclesiastical works of the last half of the century, when so many new churches were built, so many new dioceses established at home and abroad, one can say this. From the 'forties to the middle 'sixties, the majority of the new churches were built as missions to the poor in towns; from the middle 'sixties until the end of the century, and increasingly since then, most new churches have been built in the suburbs. This is not to say that the poor became neglected. Rich manufacturers, settled down as squires in country near Birmingham, Manchester, Liverpool, London, the Potteries and the East Riding, also often rebuilt their country parish church as did those established landowners who were pious and still wealthy. Hence the many rebuilt churches in the Home Counties, Cheshire, Shropshire, Warwickshire and Worcestershire. The 'Lux Mundi' group of the 'nineties, the Christian Socialism of such men as Father Adderley, Canon Scott Holland and Bishop Gore whose theology emphasized the Incarnation, laid great stress on the idea that the Catholic faith must play a part in the everyday life of factory and shop and not be a matter of Sunday worship only. Thus we find many slum Tractarian parishes building new mission churches on their smoky, overcrowded outskirts, churches with the names of black letter saints in the Calendar who always seem to be 'high': St Anselm, St Cyprian, St Erkenwald, St Mary Magdalen.

We like to think that the reason for the missions to the suburbs from the middle 'sixties onwards was that there were fewer poor. There may be some truth in this, but the reason lies more in the great growth of the middle classes – clerks, rich wholesalers and retailers, the Pooters, those dear, solid bits of English backbone. Few of them were more than one generation from a country village, and the churchgoing habit was ingrained in them from youth. They are the reason for the tall Perpendicular walls of St Philip's Church, in red brick with stone dressings, rising above the oak paling and evergreens where Victoria Drive intersects Tollemache Avenue. The Tollemaches, deriving an unexpected income in house rents from what had been a sandy warren, gave the site; the merchants in the detached houses at the richer end of Victoria Drive gave the woodwork; the rich brewer whose family have by now been absorbed into the country squirearchy gave the stained glass; and either George Gilbert Scott Junior, John Olrid Scott, G. F. Bodley, J. D. Sedding, Norman Shaw, or, if it is in the North Country, Paley & Austin, designed the church. These architects were the young men who emerged from the enormous office of Sir Gilbert Scott, or the gay craftsman's studio of Street. They carried the faith of their masters with them. They were generally Tractarians, of a more advanced sort than their masters. They were musical and artistic. They knew such men as Burne-Jones and Rossetti, and, much as they abhorred his atheism, they admired the decorative work of Street's pupil William Morris.

I think that the well-spring of this later church architecture is the work of George Gilbert Scott Junior, who was a close friend of G. F. Bodley. This talented man was a scholar who wrote that learned and interesting History of English Church Architecture until the Reformation. He was not only a medievalist. He was one of the first Victorians to appreciate again the work of the

Renaissance. The few churches he built are a foretaste of the work of Bodley and his followers. In 1877 he dared to build St Agnes, Kennington, London, in the despised Perpendicular style. What is more, he used brick walls, put a screen and rood across the chancel arch, and had a chancel under the same roof as the nave. He designed side chapels for daily services, he had no capitals to the piers in the nave arcades, and he filled the windows with glass by an unknown young artist called Kempe.[2]

But we can see other churches influenced by the Neo-Perpendicular movement, and many of these are very fine buildings, no more imitations of medieval than were the works of the older Victorians. They are, however, less Victorian than the daring experiments of the 'fifties and 'sixties, and they seem, like the small houses designed by Norman Shaw, to come into our time or at any rate into the 1920s. Because they are near us, we do not appreciate their originality. In our desire to see a new style emerge from new materials, we notice only that the mouldings and fittings are copies of medieval Gothic. We do not realize that the proportions, plan and liturgical arrangement are nothing like our old churches.

See in your mind's eye a church built in the neo-Perpendicular style by G. G. Scott Junior, Bodley, W. H. Bidlake of Birmingham, Edgar Wood, Sir Ninian Comper, W. D. Caroe, Sir Charles Nicholson, Temple Moore, J. D. Sedding, Edmund Sedding, Charles Spooner, E. P. Warren, Walter Tapper, Niven and Wigglesworth, Paley & Austin, to name a few of these later Victorian architects. If you cannot see it, I will try to re-create such a church, and you will remember it in some newish suburb of a provincial town where you stayed with an aunt, or on a holiday in the outskirts of a south-coast watering place, and you can read of it in Compton Mackenzie's *Sinister Street*. 'Ting-ting' the single bell calls to Sung Eucharist, because the tower, designed for a full peal of bells, was never completed. Rather gaunt without it, the church rises above the privet and forsythia and prunus of its little garden, for there is no churchyard to these churches; we have reached the era of municipal cemeteries, and it is in their marble acres that the dead of this new parish are to be found. Inside the church, the tall nave is filled with chairs, and the narrow aisles are not used on a Sunday, as they give a view only of side altars where the weekday Celebrations and the very early Sunday masses are said. The floor is of oak blocks, the walls are cream and clean, the woodwork of the thick Devonshire style chancel screen, carved by Harry Hems of Exeter, is unstained. In more recent times a coloured statue of Our Lady under a gilded canopy is seen against one of the eastern-most pillars of the nave. Through the screen we glimpse a huge reredos painted green and red and gold, with folding doors. The high altar has a purple frontal, because just now it is Lent. The floor of the sanctuary is paved with black-and-white marble. Riddel posts with gilt angels on them – the famous 'English altar' introduced by Sir Ninian Comper in the 'eighties – hold curtains round the north, south and east of the side altars. The windows are filled with greenish glass in which are patches of dark blue, red and gold. These are the work of Kempe,

[2] This church was destroyed by the Southwark Diocese after war damage.

and they allow more light into the church than earlier Victorian windows. The chief beauty of the church is its proportion. These architects favoured two kinds of proportion when they were building in the Gothic style – almost all of them designed Byzantine and classic churches as well – and they were either height and narrowness, or breadth and length. Their churches either soar or spread.

The Sung Eucharist is probably from the Prayer Book and with a crowd of acolytes at the altar. Blue incense rises to the golden reredos and the green Kempe window. The English Hymnal is used, and plain-song or more probably, Eyre in E [flat] or Tours in C. Candlelights twinkle in the mist. The purple Lenten chasuble of the priest is worn over amice, alb, stole and maniple, and there is discussion of these things after the service and before among servers and the initiated. We are in a world which feels itself in touch with the middle ages and with today. This is English Catholicism. There is much talk of Percy Dearmer, correct furnishings and vestments, the Prayer Book and how far one is justified in departing from it. After church the acolytes in their Sunday suits hang round the porch, and the young curates too, and there is a good deal of backslapping and chaff. For months the Mothers' Union and women's guilds of the church have been working on banners and a frontal to be ready for Easter. From these suburban parishes much of the Church life of modern England has sprung. They have trained their people in faith and the liturgy, they have produced many of the overseas missionaries and parish priests of today.

We are in modern times, out of the older and rich suburbs with their garden city atmosphere of guild craftsman and Sarum Use, and into the big building estates. The large areas of semi-detached houses, built by private speculators or councils, have been eating up our agricultural land since 1920. They have been brought about by the change in transport from steam to motor-bus and electric train. People are moving out of the crowded early Victorian industrial lanes and terraces, into little houses of their own, each with its little patch of garden at the back and front, each isolated from its neighbour by social convention, in districts where miles of pavement enlivened by the squeak of perambulators lead to a far-off bus route and parade of chain stores, and a distant vita-glass school, used as a Community Centre in the evenings. To these places, often lonely for all the people in them, is the new mission Church.

Just as there is today no definite modern style in England, except in what is impermanent – exhibition buildings, prefabs, holiday camps and the like, so there is no definite modern church style. In the period between the two wars church architects were too often concerned with style, and they built places of worship which vied with the local Odeon or with by-pass modern factories in trying to be 'contemporary'. They now look dated, and will, I fear, never look beautiful. But the purpose of the church remains the same as it was at the beginning of this book, to be a place where the Faith is taught and the Sacraments are administered.

△ **TUDELY: ALL SAINTS** – *one of the windows created by Marc Chagall to commemorate Sarah Venetia d'Avidgor Goldsmid, who drowned in the 1960s*

BEDFORDSHIRE

The north-bound train traveller from St Pancras retains a poor impression of Bedfordshire, the verdict generally being one of flat Midland scenery, at its more unrelieved; this is as unfair as it is uninformed. Sadly, many of the villages and small towns within easy reach of the M1 or major stations have been engulfed by large modern housing estates. However, it must be admitted at once that the central clay vale is a wilderness, raped for brick-making, and with a similar fate awaiting still-virgin land. Otherwise the county, for its limited area, is varied to a degree that is unique.

In the north the Ouse winds through a landscape of gracious tranquillity, a summer country of stone villages and broad water meadows which rises in the north-east to a continuation of Walpole's 'dumpling hills' of Northamptonshire. This is often surprisingly lonely country and, though the woods are now few and far between, the ghost of the old 'Bruneswald' forest still haunts the land.

In the centre of the county lies the Greensand ridge, a corridor of fifteen miles which historian W. G. Hoskins (1908–92) in his book *Midland England* considered 'unsurpassed in sanctity and peculiar purity'; it broadens in the west to the ducal country of Woburn, scenically magnificent with pine-woods and open heaths. In the east, being in part overlaid by clay and dissected by the River Ivel, the scenery is even more varied. Old Warden in particular retains a delightful Victorian picture-book quality almost unimpaired.

Beyond the Greensand the Gault clay valley is a prelude to the chalk hills, and, save around Toddington where a considerable elevation is reached, is subdued to them; it is largely unspoiled country, much of it formerly marsh of which Flitwick Moor remains as a fragment. There are one or two chalk outliers in the valley, of which Shillington church hill is the most renowned, and Billington the most beautiful.

The chalk reaches its greatest development at Dunstable, but its greatest beauty in the folded coombes and open windswept downs around Barton. At Totternhoe Knolls, a promontory of the lower chalk overlooking the vast Aylesbury Vale and the line of the Chilterns to the west, lies the site of the old quarries that gave to this area a building stone of poor external weathering quality, but one which served as inspiration for a local school of 13th-century carving, little known, but of high artistic merit.

Luton forms an industrial and suburban area 'as unexpected as it is unprepossessing', and with the dreadful tentacle that links it to Dunstable has straddled a large area of the foothills to the Downs. Much of the surrounding countryside is losing the battle against suburbia, and unforgivable crimes have been committed in the hills, the worst perhaps the cutting of the skyline at

◁ **DUNSTABLE: ST PETER** – *a red brick wall now stands where the church's eastern end was abruptly truncated*

NORTHAMPTONSHIRE
CAMBRIDGESHIRE
A14
A45
Shelton
Dean
Wellingborough
Rushden
Swineshead
Wymington
Podington
Knotting
A45
A6
Sharnbrook
Thurleigh
Odell
Felmersham
A428
A428
A509
Pavenham
Stevington
Clapham
A428
A421
Turvey
Blunham
Willington
BEDFORD
A603
BUCKINGHAM-
SHIRE
Kempston
Northill
M1
Biggleswade
Elstow
Old Warden
MILTON
KEYNES
A600
Marston Moreteyne
A1
A421
BEDFORDSHIRE
A507
A5
Shillington
Woburn
A6
A600
A5
A4012
A5120
A4146
Hitchin
M1
A1(M)
A6
A505
Leighton
Buzzard
Chalgrave
LUTON
STEVENAGE
Totternhoe
Dunstable
Eaton Bray
LUTON
HERTFORDSHI
A5
A418
A4146
0
5 miles
0
5 km
Tring
Hemel
Hempstead
A41

Totternhoe. In spite of all this, however, much charming country remains, particularly around Studham and Kensworth, where at 700 feet the chalk attains its highest elevation in the county.

The varied geology of Bedfordshire is echoed in the variety of its churches; in the north of the county the influence of Northamptonshire masons appears in the number of stone spires, fine ashlar masonry, and the use of the ferruginous brown stone which has been the scenic ruin of the iron-mining districts of the neighbouring county. Wymington is the finest example, but Swineshead and Podington have churches of very great merit. Two of the grandest buildings in the county, Felmersham church of the 13th century, and Odell of the 15th, lie in this area. The sandstone country has contributed a building stone which gives great character to the churches of the district; Northill is one of the most perfect examples. The churches of the south of the county are sometimes not very convincing from the outside, since the Totternhoe stone has often weathered so badly that they have been encased in 19th-century cement plaster with frightful aesthetic result. Flint used in chequer-board pattern with clunch, a soft chalky limestone, is a feature here and there, and a very attractive one. The showplaces of the area are Dunstable Priory, and the churches of Leighton Buzzard, Eaton Bray and St Mary's, Luton.

Until the 20th century Bedfordshire escaped the overbuilding of, for example, Hertfordshire, and in consequence Victorian church building is limited to Bedford, Luton and one or two examples connected with the big estates, of which Clutton's magnificent St Mary's, Woburn is outstanding. Scott gave Turvey church a chancel which it would be a euphemism to call a vigorous example of his mature style; more suitable to some rich inner London suburb than a village church, it is saved by impeccable craftsmanship, and a Collyweston (limestone slate) roof. Scott also worked at Eversholt in 1864 but on a more limited scale. There is one building that must be seen by those who like their Victorian architecture 'neat', and that is the Bury Park Congregational church of 1895, an early example of art nouveau Gothic which is one of Luton's many architectural surprises; it is difficult to imagine it ever having been on paper! There is one interesting 20th-century church, St Andrew's, Blenheim Crescent, Luton, a fine work by Sir Giles Gilbert Scott in his Cambridge University library manner, with red brick and pantile roofs.

There has been a certain amount of ill-considered restoration in the county, but in the main, save for the barbarous rebuilding of Cardington, the county has been well served by its church restorers.

△ **FELMERSHAM: ST MARY** – *clustered piers of the crossing and delicate rood screen*

△ **DUNSTABLE: ST PETER** – *the western front freely mixes Norman and Early English forms*

BEDFORD † St Mary ★

On corner of Cardington Road and St Mary's Street
OS *TL051493* **GPS** *52.1328N, 0.4656W*

St Mary's is from the Saxon/Norman period, with 16th- and 19th-century additions. There is a Norman crossing tower with Perpendicular top.

BEDFORD † St Paul

St Paul's Square
OS *TL049496* **GPS** *52.1354N, 0.4675W*

This, the largest church in Bedford, is in its final form mainly a work of the 19th and early 20th centuries, but its magnificent silhouette and striking scale justify the process. The S. aisle with its porch is medieval, the former a fine two-storeyed structure of the 15th century. It is from this side that one first appreciates that the building is a 'hall church', its clerestory windows being directly over those of the aisles. The tower and spire are 19th century, a somewhat enriched reconstruction of an original 14th-century feature. F. C. Eden did much to improve the interior in the early 20th century, and the chancel is now a model of rubrical correctness. The late 20th-century W. door, a slightly anachronistic combination of 14th- and 15th-century details, is very fine in effect.

BLUNHAM † St Edmund and St James

7ml/1km E. of Bedford
OS *TL153511* **GPS** *52.1462N, 0.3163W*

The church has a massive yet delicate sandstone and limestone tower, and is charmingly set in this thatch and whitewash village. The W. door is Norman, otherwise the predominant style is Perpendicular, including the fine stone screen between the chancel and the S. chapel.

CHALGRAVE † All Saints

6ml/10km N.W. of Luton
OS *TL008274* **GPS** *51.9362N, 0.5343W*

Set on an isolated site on a plateau overlooking the Chiltern hills, All Saints has a wonderful unspoiled interior, no doubt due to its poverty. The 13th-century carving of the nave arcade capitals is very fine and belongs to the Totternhoe stone group mentioned later. There are 15th-century traceried bench-ends in the old pewing. The tower was reduced to its present height in 1889, consequent upon the failure of the Totternhoe stone as at Eaton Bray. Wall-paintings, impressive as an overall scheme, unusually feature St Martin, and heraldic shields fill the spandrels in the nave.

CLAPHAM † St Thomas of Canterbury

2m/3km N.W. of Bedford
OS *TL034524* **GPS** *52.1609N, 0.4898W*

Important for the enormous Saxon tower with Norman top stage, St Thomas of Canterbury has a 13th-century font and a 17th-century communion table. The chancel is by Sir George Gilbert Scott, 1861–2.

DEAN † All Saints

11m/18km N. of Bedford
OS *TL046676* **GPS** *52.2969N, 0.4664W*

Dean is a scattered and unspoiled village embowered in trees, and its church has a perfect country interior; the roofs are wonderful specimens belonging to the 15th-century remodelling, from which only the 13th-century chancel arch and the 14th-century tower and spire were retained. Fine screens are at the W. end of both chapels and across the chancel arch.

DUNSTABLE † St Peter

5m/8km W. of Luton
OS *TL021218* **GPS** *51.8860N, 0.5175W*

This truncated fragment of Dunstable Priory still has a grandeur, particularly in its fine Norman nave of c. 1150, which makes the disappearance of the eastern parts a tragedy. The W. front is a magnificent makeshift, Norman and Early English in combination, of which the most lovely feature is the N.W. door, a sumptuous 13th-century creation loaded with ornament. Restored by Bodley in 1900 and later by Richardson. Scholarly re-creation of the Norman vaulting of the S. aisle, based upon the survival of three bays at the E. end. How much of the original material has been re-used is hard to tell, but the general effect greatly enhances the monastic character of the building.

△ **EATON BRAY: ST MARY THE VIRGIN** – *decorative corbel in the south arcade*

EATON BRAY † St Mary the Virgin

3m/4km W. of Dunstable
OS *SP969207* **GPS** *51.8767N, 0.5925W*

A complete 15th-century reconstruction and W. tower effectively conceal the interior core of the original 13th-century building, which has nave arcades of absolute and quite unexpected magnificence. That on the N. is the richer, with deep mouldings and conventional leaf-carving on the capitals, a tour de force of craftsmanship. On the S. arcade the decoration is simpler and the mouldings plainer, but the corbels at each end are wonderfully detailed. The 13th-century font is richly carved to match the N. arcade. The village may well have been the centre of the Totternhoe stone school of carving. Thomas of Leighton may have been responsible for the 13th-century foliated ironwork on the S. door; similar scrollwork can be found at All Saints, Leighton Buzzard.

ELSTOW † St Mary and St Helen

2m/3km S. of Bedford

OS *TL049473* **GPS** *52.1149N, 0.4693W*

A church of monastic foundation, this truncated but magnificent remnant of a Norman cruciform church is the central feature of an attractive village. The W. front was begun in the 13th century, but was never finished; it decayed until sensitive restoration by Professor Richardson in the mid-20th century. Two coeval 13th-century bays remain at the W. end inside, the rest being massive Norman work. The detached 15th-century bell-tower, witness to the religious doubts of the young John Bunyan, who was born nearby, completes a noble composition.

FELMERSHAM † St Mary ★

6m/10km N.W. of Bedford

OS *SP991578* **GPS** *52.2099N, 0.5505W*

On a superb site looking out over the Great Ouse, St Mary's was begun in 1220 and finished in 20 years – the finest Early English church in the county. The W. front is a noble arcaded composition. The raising of the nave walls in the 15th century to give a low pitched roof and clerestory, with a tower in place of an intended spire, created a fine four-square composition. There is competent restoration in the chancel, carried out by J. Brandon in 1853–4, when he reinstated lancet windows to match the existing. The interior is wonderful, particularly the great clustered piers of the crossing contrasting with the delicacy of an excellent 15th-century screen.

KEMPSTON † All Saints

2m/3km S.W. of Bedford across R. Ouse

OS *TL015479* **GPS** *52.1209N, 0.5185W*

Set by the river, All Saints is Perpendicular outside, including the tower. Inside are a 12th-century chancel arch and Early English arcades.

KNOTTING † St Margaret

4m/6km S.E. of Rushden

OS *TL002634* **GPS** *52.2603N, 0.5324W*

Churches Conservation Trust

A delightful church with Norman nave, 13th-century chancel and transept and W. tower dated 1615. There are simple 16th- and 17th-century furnishings, and chancel gates dated 1637.

LEIGHTON BUZZARD † All Saints ★

11m/18km N.W. of Luton

OS *SP919248* **GPS** *51.9148N, 0.6653W*

The finest parish church in the county, in an attractive market-town setting; 13th-century, of cruciform plan and with a gigantic spire. It had an excellent restoration after a major fire in 1985.The walls were raised in the 15th century and the magnificent timber roofs of typical flattish pitch were then constructed. The complete collegiate late 15th-century chancel, with seating and screens intact, is the great treasure of All Saints. Medieval graffiti on the piers, including a drawing of a Decorated window in the S. chapel. The elaborate ironwork on the W. door may be by Thomas of Leighton, creator in 1294 of the delicate grille at the tomb of Queen Eleanor in Westminster Abbey. There are good Kempe windows, 1887–1905.

LUTON † St Andrew ★

Blenheim Crescent

OS *TL082227* **GPS** *51.8928N, 0.4279W*

A fine church by Sir Giles Gilbert Scott, 1931–2, it is built of red brick with pantile roofs and a massive W. tower, and effectively lit by grouped clerestory windows.

LUTON † St Mary ★

Between Church Street and St Mary's Road

OS *TL095212* **GPS** *51.8787N, 0.4102W*

This magnificent church resists, by sheer architectural merit, the desolation of its setting. Begun in the 13th century, enlarged in the 14th, it reached its present form in the 15th when Lord Wenlock built his sumptuous chapel. Octagonal 14th-century baptistry, a work of great richness and competence. The W. tower has flint and clunch chequerwork panels, the latter, in part, replaced by harder limestone in modern times. Street's work in the chancel is of a dark richness, but the external refacing of the E. end was heartless. 14th-century font and canopy; Wenlock tombs.

△ **ELSTOW: ST MARY AND ST HELEN** – *sturdy Norman arcades run down the nave*

MARSTON MORETEYNE
† St Mary the Virgin

6m/10km S.W. of Bedford
Village also spelt Marston Moretaine
OS *SP996411* **GPS** *52.0598N, 0.5484W*

A magnificent building practically rebuilt in 1445, in a decade that yielded much rich architecture. The nave is very grand, with slender pillars, and a roof resplendent with bosses and angels. Detailing is bold and confident, though lacking the full richness of stained glass and screening. The detached bell-tower is a fine massive building; the whole is reminiscent of neighbouring Elstow.

NORTHILL † St Mary the Virgin

6m/10km E. of Bedford
OS *TL149465* **GPS** *52.1054N, 0.3238W*

The church is a blend of Totternhoe clunch and ironstone. Inside are 14th-century collegiate stalls. The golden glass of 1664 was commissioned by the Grocers' Company. Originally this formed the E. window, but the three panels were moved to the S. aisle in 1880.

ODELL † All Saints ★

8m/12km N.W. of Bedford
OS *SP966580* **GPS** *52.2118N, 0.5865W*

Set on an eminence in a good stone village, this is an excellent example of a unified 15th-century church. Grand W. tower of Northamptonshire type; the gentle incline up to a pinnacled parapet relieves what might otherwise be an overpowering bulk. The interior is marked by tall arcades, an original rood screen and very satisfying diamond-pattern flooring in nave and aisles. A group of seraphs in the 15th-century stained glass E. window of the S. aisle of a rare and naive beauty.

OLD WARDEN † St Leonard

7m/11km S.E. of Bedford
OS *TL136443* **GPS** *52.0856N, 0.3424W*

Perpendicular mostly, St Leonard's was substantially renovated in the 19th century. A Norman tower arch remains, and the interior has Jacobean panelling and an abundance of other carved woodwork, much of it culled from abroad, especially Belgium.

△ **LEIGHTON BUZZARD: ALL SAINTS** – *refined medieval graffiti and rich carving in the choir*

Monuments include a lifesize Classical statue of Sir Samuel Ongley, d. 1726.

PAVENHAM † St Peter ★
5m/8km N.W. of Bedford
OS *SP991559* **GPS** *52.1929N, 0.5510W*

On the hillside above one of the loveliest of the riverside villages, Pavenham church, like Old Warden, is full of carved panelling and rich woodwork, most of it installed in 1848; Jacobean in the main, consisting of everything from marquetry to high relief. There is a two-storey 13th-century S. porch, otherwise everything is mostly Perpendicular.

PODINGTON † St Mary the Virgin
5m/8km S.E. of Wellingborough
OS *SP941626* **GPS** *52.2543N, 0.6218W*

Mostly 13th-century, with 14th-century leaning spire, the church contains a Norman font, monuments and Orlebar wall-plaques.

SHARNBROOK † St Peter
7m/11km N.W. of Bedford
OS *SP993595* **GPS** *52.2256N, 0.5468W*

Perpendicular outside, including the noble spire which surmounts a Decorated tower, St Peter's is a sensitive modern restoration. Massive 19th-century Magniac Mausoleum stands in the churchyard.

SHELTON † St Mary the Virgin ★
11m/18km N. of Bedford
OS *TL033687* **GPS** *52.3076N, 0.4852W*

Remote and rustic, and delightfully chaste inside, the building is a mixture of Norman and later fabric. Pews, screen and clear glass form a comely assemblage, and there are a few wall-paintings.

SHILLINGTON † All Saints ★
8m/13km N.E. of Luton
OS *TL123339* **GPS** *51.9926N, 0.3647W*

This is a wonderful hill-top site, typical of many similar church-crowned hills along the line of the Chilterns. Alas, it was rather too long to fit the top comfortably, a factor which doubtless caused the failure of the tower footings in 1701. The present red-brick erection of 1750 is not really worthy of the church. A clerestoried hall, hardly interrupted in its continuity from W. to E., is mainly a work of the 14th century, only slightly altered subsequently, though with much 19th-century window tracery. The rood screen (15th-century with some later repairs) inside forms the only actual division and, save for the loss of its loft, is perfect. A vaulted crypt lies under the chancel; there are brasses, pews and screens to delight the eye.

STEVINGTON † St Mary the Virgin
4m/6km N.W. of Bedford
OS *SP990536* **GPS** *52.1722N, 0.5532W*

On a terrace above the Ouse, the church has a pre-Conquest tower complete with long-and-short quoins, augmented in the 15th century with an upper stage. There is a 14th-century nave roof with shield-bearing supporters, and a brass to Sir Thomas Salle, d. 1422.

SWINESHEAD † St Nicholas
10m/16km N. of Bedford
OS *TL057658* **GPS** *52.2806N, 0.4508W*

St Nicholas is a handsome Decorated church, including the tower, slender recessed spire and arcades. Inside are a richly carved Easter Sepulchre, good misericords and a fine W. door.

THURLEIGH † St Peter
6m/10km N. of Bedford
OS *TL051584* **GPS** *52.2144N, 0.4626W*

By a castle motte, St Peter's has an early Norman central tower with S. doorway, and a crude Adam and Eve carved in the tympanum. Otherwise the church is mostly Perpendicular with some early glass, a nave floor brass of c. 1420 and a 1590 wall brass to Edmond Daye in the S. aisle.

TOTTERNHOE † St Giles ★
2m/3km W. of Dunstable
OS *SP988208* **GPS** *51.8778N, 0.5656W*

This church, built from the quarries in the village, has an unusually fine exterior. In the gable of the nave is flint flushwork in the Chiltern style. Begun in the 14th century and adorned in the 16th by a pinnacled skyline, it provides a most satisfactory silhouette. Inside, all is space and light with carved roofs and woodwork, brasses and a good E. window by John Piper.

TURVEY † All Saints
7m/11km W. of Bedford
OS *SP940525* **GPS** *52.1632N, 0.6267W*

The Ouse Valley village is Victorian-Jacobean in character; its pre-Conquest church with 14th- to 15th-century additions was sumptuously 'improved' by Sir George Gilbert Scott in the mid-19th century. Exuberant scrolled ironwork by the local man, Thomas of Leighton, decorates the S. door, and there is a fine collection of 15th- and 16th-century brasses and monuments, largely to the Mordaunt family.

WILLINGTON † St Lawrence
4m/6km E. of Bedford
OS *TL106498* **GPS** *52.1360N, 0.3847W*

A grand early 16th-century church, St Lawrence was paid for by Sir John Gostwick, d. 1545, who was in the service of Henry VIII; his tomb is beside the altar. A memorable N. chapel contains helmets and monuments. The 1876–7 restoration was by Henry Clutton.

WOBURN † St Mary ★
5m/8km N. of Leighton Buzzard
OS *SP948332* **GPS** *51.9896N, 0.6199W*

St Mary's was erected in 1865–8 by William, eighth Duke of Bedford, to the designs of Henry Clutton, Bath stone being used throughout. It is an absolutely magnificent building; the interior is vaulted in stone and the echoes of the Ile de France are strong. The tall reredos by Caroe, choir-stalls and pulpit are later additions.

WYMINGTON † St Lawrence ★
2m/3km S. of Rushden
OS *SP955643* **GPS** *52.2695N, 0.6016W*

St Lawrence was begun in the mid-14th century by wool merchant John Curteys, who, with his wife, is buried in the chancel. This church must be an example of work carried out by masons based on jobs in the neighbouring county of Northamptonshire, but working here on a slightly tighter budget. All the Nene Valley features are to be seen, though delightfully out of scale, particularly in the tower and spire which are lavishly ornamented. The interior is rich and complex: a fine nave roof; the remains of a suitably horrific Doom painting; old pewing and some colour still on capitals and arches. The building provides the county's best instance of the luxuriant spirit of the 14th century.

BERKSHIRE

Berkshire has several types of scenery. In the east of the county, on the London side, is much wild heath and pine-wood, the sort of country which, almost uninhabited until the 19th century, now grows public institutions like schools, prisons and barracks, and small modern villas along the main roads and by railways. The Thames forms the northern border, and here is orchard-land extending several miles south until the downs are reached. The south-west and west of the county are mostly chalk downs, and the scenery is similar to the Wiltshire downland into which it merges.

The older houses and farm buildings of these districts are timber, brick and cob, and generally thatched or red-tiled. The towns are all built of brick and are all, except for Reading, comparatively small.

Until the end of the 19th century, when transport from London turned half of the county into a semi-suburb, Berkshire was thinly populated. There the churches were cottage-like with wooden belfries, thatched barns, farms and houses of downland hamlets. A few small flint towers arose from pleasant red-brick towns beside the Thames and Kennet, and there still are a great many commons and heaths, such as were so beautifully described in the 1820s by Mary Russell Mitford in *Our Village*. The brickwork in Berkshire was never so impressive as that of Kent and Sussex. The eastern and London half of the county was transformed first by railways and again by buses, bringing more monied people from London, who settled down in detached residences wherever the train service was convenient. These people built themselves new churches, and rebuilt old ones.

Berkshire is not a great county for ancient churches. The only grand example is St George's Chapel at Windsor (Perpendicular). Avington and Padworth have complete and small Norman churches. The best old churches will be found not in the Kennet valley, where these two are, but along the north slopes of the downs, to which stone for building could be brought fairly easily by river and then by trackway. The few big medieval churches of Berkshire, with the exception of Lambourn and Newbury, are in the northern half of the county. The churches on the downs and commons were nearly all small cottage-like buildings. One may see aquatints of some of them in *Views of Reading Abbey and the Principal Churches Connected Therewith* (1805), and in Buckler's drawings in the British Museum. They had flint and rubble walls, rendered (or plastered) outside (the flint Norman tower of Great Shefford) were built circular, like many church towers in East Anglia, because of the lack of stone for the corners); the roofs were of tile with dormer windows, and there was usually a wooden belfry at

◁ **GREAT SHEFFORD: ST MARY** – *beautifully set on the slope of a shallow valley, the round tower as charming as it is rare in the county*

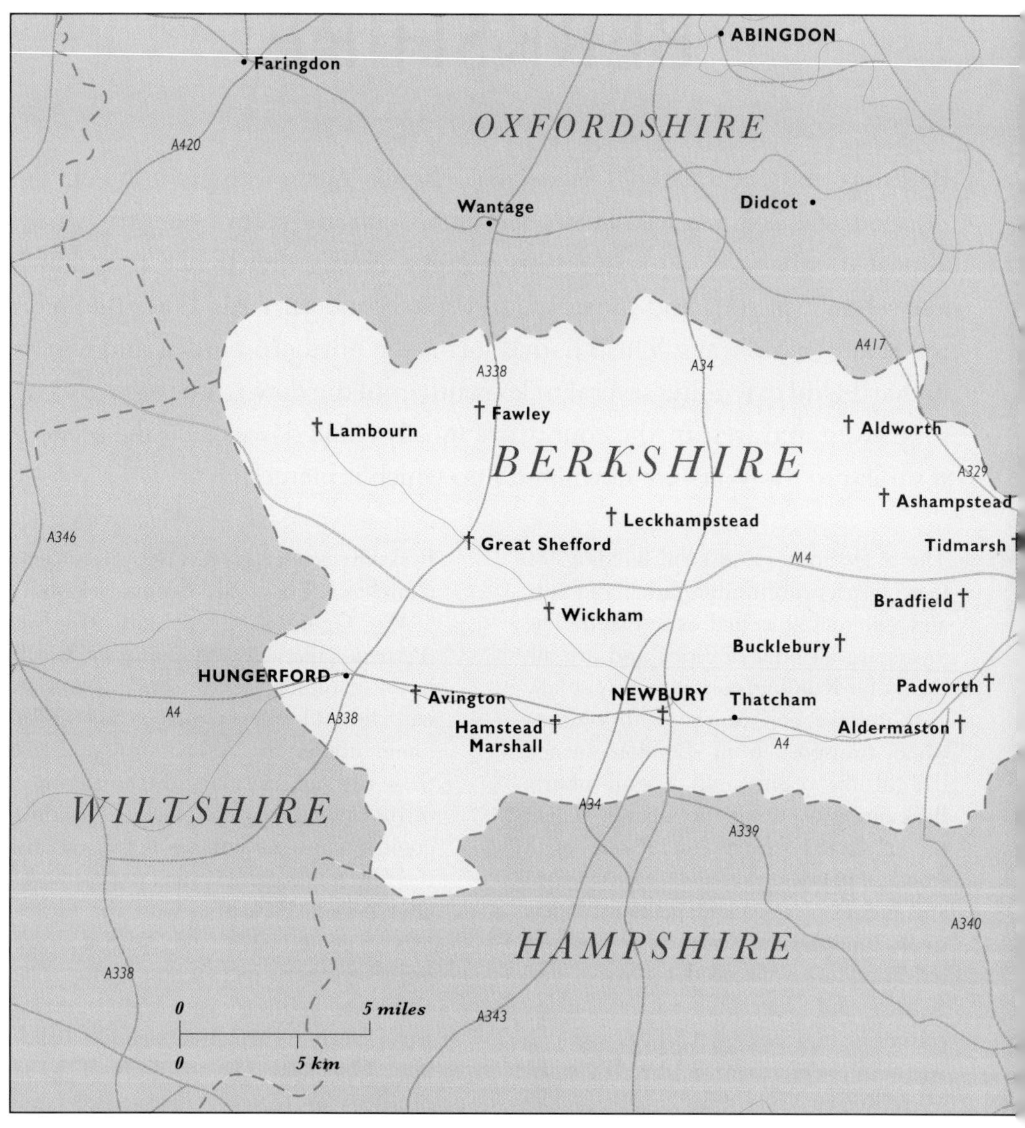

the west end, and a 17th- or 18th-century porch in brick. Such buildings must have seemed very unecclesiastical to rich and pious landowners long or newly settled in Berkshire, which by the 19th century had become a 'home county' influenced by the prosperity of the metropolis. So they were pulled down or else vigorously restored, stripped of their external and internal plaster, retaining perhaps only an arcade or a window of the original building. Some churches of this small cottage type survive, as at Avington, East Shefford and Padworth.

The great Victorian architects left their mark on Berkshire. But because the county was not much industrialized until the 20th century, there is less Victorian building than in old Middlesex, Surrey or Kent. The architect G. E. Street, who lived at Wantage at the beginning of his successful career, designed many charming church schools and vicar-ages in the area and a bold new church

and adjoining buildings at Boyne Hill, Maidenhead. Butterfield beautifully and conservatively restored Shottesbrooke and published a monograph about it. The best work of Victorian architects, together with that of the 18th and 19th centuries, is noted in the entries that follow. On the whole Berkshire has not been well served by those who rebuilt its churches. They had more money at their disposal than sensibility. But at least they built churches.

△ **EAST SHEFFORD: ST THOMAS** – *a barn-like church, alone in a field between a farmhouse and a manor house, it holds within it the remnants of some fine wall-paintings*

ALDERMASTON † St Mary the Virgin

8m/12km E. of Newbury
OS *SU596649* **GPS** *51.3807N, 1.1442W*

The church has Norman details, and there are 13th-century painted glass roundels of the Annunciation and the Coronation of the Virgin in the N. windows, as well as 14th- and 15th-century wall-paintings.

ALDWORTH † St Mary the Virgin

10m/16km N.W. of Reading
OS *SU554793* **GPS** *51.5107N, 1.2030W*

Huge 14th-century stone effigies of the De La Beche family occupy the interior, set beneath wonderfully carved cusped canopies along the N. and S. walls and under the arcade in the nave.

ASHAMPSTEAD † St Clement ★

8m/13km N.E. of Newbury
OS *SU564767* **GPS** *51.4873N, 1.1888W*

Originally a chapel of ease to St Bartholomew's in Basildon, St Clement's main interest is in its extensive 13th-century wall-paintings, including the Annunciation and Christ in Majesty. In a county not noted for medieval wall-paintings, these are very good – possibly of the 'Windsor School'.

AVINGTON † St Mark & St Luke ★

2m/3km E. of Hungerford
OS *SU372679* **GPS** *51.4095N, 1.4654W*

A delightful small church of the 12th century, with nave and aisle, all unspoiled. The S. doorway and chancel arch are decorated with zigzags and beak heads, and there is a fine Norman font with blind arcading and carved figures.

BISHAM † All Saints

3m/5km N.W. of Maidenhead
OS *SU848854* **GPS** *51.5612N, 0.7779W*

The church setting is superb, best seen from the other side of the River Thames. It was heavily restored by Benjamin Ferrey, 1849. The tower is 12th-century, embellished in the 15th century with a parapet and brick quoins. The Hoby Chapel contains family monuments of the 16th and early 17th century, and and a 1609 heraldic window of enamelled glass. In the churchyard are several burial stones of interest.

BRADFIELD † St Andrew ★

3m/4km S.W. of Pangbourne
OS *SU603725* **GPS** *51.4490N, 1.1332W*

In a brick and timber village and public school in a high, gravelly district, the church was almost wholly rebuilt by Sir George Gilbert Scott in 1847–8, and turned into something which, inside, is long-drawn, mysterious and vast in his transitional style, known as 'square abacus'.

BUCKLEBURY † St Mary

6m/10km N.E. of Newbury
OS *SU553708* **GPS** *51.4341N, 1.2058W*

The church is mostly 15th-century flint and chalkwork, with an early 18th-century interior, high box pews and hatchments, and good Stuart Royal Arms over the chancel arch. The S. doorway is Norman – well and interestingly carved – and on the tower are more carvings, of the 15th century. The glass in the chancel windows (1912) and N. aisle (1917) is by Frank Brangwyn.

EASTHAMPSTEAD
† St Michael and St Mary Magdalene

S. district of Bracknell
OS *SU863676* **GPS** *51.4013N, 0.7601W*

J. W. Hugall rebuilt the church in 1867, at the behest of the incumbent, Osbourne Gordon, who was a keen follower of the Anglo-Catholic revival. It has exceptional Burne-Jones windows, some produced jointly with William Morris. The largest and finest of them, the E. window, depicts the Last Judgement and was installed in 1876. There are 15th- and 16th-century brasses and ledger stones, and a very verbose monument to Sir William Trumbull, d. 1716.

EAST SHEFFORD † St Thomas

By East Shefford Farm, 1m/2km S.E. of Great Shefford
OS *SU390746* **GPS** *51.4697N, 1.4391W*
Churches Conservation Trust

A small, simple rustic church with wooden bell-turret, the church is set well in meadows by the River Lambourn. A fine wall-painting over the chancel arch was discovered by Eve Baker, and there are good 14th- and 15th-century monuments to members of the Fettiplace family. Now almost clear of pews, it has a lovely and peaceful atmosphere.

FAWLEY † St Mary

4m/6km S. of Wantage
OS *SU391813* **GPS** *51.5300N, 1.4374W*

Well set on the Berkshire Downs, this is a fine church by G. E. Street, 1865–6. Sombre in rock-faced ashlar, the high apse and offset S. tower are reminiscent of France. It has excellent contemporary furnishings, and the stained glass in the W. window is by Morris & Co.

GREAT SHEFFORD † St Mary

5m/8km N.E. of Hungerford
OS *SU380753* **GPS** *51.4761N, 1.4540W*

This is a Norman church with a round tower, rare in Berkshire, with a tub-shaped font of the 12th century on a 19th-century base. Lovely setting in the North Wessex Downs.

HAMSTEAD MARSHALL † St Mary ★

4m/6km W. of Newbury
OS *SU420667* **GPS** *51.3982N, 1.3977W*

An adjunct of a vanished country house, whose large brick-walled garden and sculptured piers remain, this is a little rustic and medieval church, mostly Jacobean and Georgian inside with some old high pews, three-decker pulpit and brick floors.

HURST † St Nicholas ★

5m/8km E. of Reading
OS *SU794729* **GPS** *51.4502N, 0.8575W*

Set among trees and old brick and timber cottages, the church is Norman and later; the brick tower was added in 1612. The interior is full of 17th-century woodwork – of note being the painted and gilded chancel screen – and there are many grand 17th- and 18th-century monuments.

LAMBOURN
† St Michael and All Angels

12m/19km N.W. of Newbury
OS *51.5086N, 1.5316W*

Set in a small downland town of racing stables, this is a grand cruciform medieval

LANGLEY MARISH: ST MARY THE VIRGIN – *a very private pew, leading through to the Kederminster Library; the door to the right leads into the main body of the church* ▷

"I HEARD A VOICE FROM HEAVEN, SAYING UNTO ME, WRITE,
BLESSED ARE THE DEAD WHICH DIE IN THE LORD:
SAITH THE SPIRIT: FOR THEY REST FROM THEIR LABOURS."
MEMORIÆ SACRUM
ROBERTI BATESON HARVEY
BARONETTI
OBIIT QUINTO DIE JUNII
ANNO
SALUTIS 1825, ÆTATIS 78.
Ostende nobis

church of various dates, starting with late Norman, to which were added the 15th- and 16th-century chapels. Running around the chamfer of an arch in the S. transept is a small but lively carving of hounds coursing a hare. There is a fine memorial to Thomas and Anne Garrard on the N. Chancel wall. Street's chancel restoration of 1861 destroyed the 15th-century oak beam ceiling and raised the floor (now restored to its original level).

LANGLEY MARISH
† St Mary the Virgin ★★

E. district of Slough
OS *TQ004795* **GPS** *51.5058N, 0.5536W*

The church is sandwiched between two lovely groups of brick and plaster almshouses – the old on the S. built by Sir John Kederminster in 1617; the new on the N. by Sir Henry Seymour about 1670. It is not far beyond the tentacles of Slough but packed with interest. The 17th-century tower is brick; there are remains of a nave arcade, c. 1200, replaced by a timber one dated 1630 and a spacious and rich 14th-century chancel. Above all, though, is the Kederminster and Seymour transept, pew and library, all of the first half of the 17th century and largely unaltered, with books on their shelves, painted panelling and grille, and heraldic overmantel over the fireplace. There are hatchments, glass, carved Royal Arms, monuments and everything a church should have.

LECKHAMPSTEAD † St James

6m/10km N. of Newbury
OS *SU439759* **GPS** *51.4809N, 1.3687W*

A church by S. S. Teulon, 1859, it is cruciform, of flint with red-brick dressings and bands. The interior is rich in polychromatic brick, and the well-crafted timber roof has huge cusped trusses.

MAIDENHEAD † All Saints

Boyn Hill, 5m/8km W. of Slough
OS *SU877808* **GPS** *51.5199N, 0.7366W*

A Tractarian grouping, all by G. E. Street, 1854–7, of vicarage, school, church buildings and church. The separate tower and spire (1865) is in local red brick. The buildings look well from all directions. The interior of the church is vast, violently coloured, richly dark with, as in all Street buildings, careful detail in ironwork, wood and coloured decoration.

NEWBURY † St Nicholas

West Mills, 16m/25km W. of Reading
OS *SU470670* **GPS** *51.4010N, 1.3249W*

The church is an imposing example of town Perpendicular, much restored, with Gothic archways in the churchyard. The fine carved pulpit is of 1607 and there are some good 16th-century brasses. The Caen stone reredos is by Comper, and shows Christ and the four Evangelists.

PADWORTH † St John the Baptist ★

8m/12km S.W. of Reading
OS *SU613661* **GPS** *51.3912N, 1.1199W*

A simple and charming Norman church, with windows and roof replaced in Tudor times and a porch added in 1890. The exterior is still plastered and with charming limewash on the tracery of the five Perpendicular windows. The interior is impressive, with a Norman chancel arch and a semi-domed apse, now thankfully free of the overbearing Brightwell and Derby-Griffiths monuments that once cluttered it. The remains of a 13th-century wall-painting of St Nicholas are discernable by the chancel arch.

READING † Christ Church

Christchurch Road
OS *SU722721* **GPS** *51.4440N, 0.9623W*

H. Woodyer designed this spirited High Victorian essay, 1861–2, with rich reredos by Birnie Philip and Hardman glass. The upper part of the chancel arch is filled with Reticulated tracery in carved chalk, possibly symbolizing the Lifting of the Veil of the Temple. The church was originally a chapel of ease to cater for an expanding parish.

SHOTTESBROOKE
† St John the Baptist ★★

3m/5km S.W. of Maidenhead
OS *SU841771* **GPS** *51.4867N, 0.7895W*

One of the grand medieval churches of the county, St John's is surrounded by parkland in flat country near Maidenhead. From a distance it is like a miniature Salisbury.

△ **SHOTTESBROOKE: ST JOHN THE BAPTIST** – *north transept, with the elegantly carved canopy in Decorated Gothic over the tomb of the founder, Sir William Trussell, and his wife*

Externally and internally it is a singularly complete cruciform Decorated design with central tower and lofty, elegant spire, all after 1337, with deeply moulded Curvilinear window tracery. The church is clearly the work of one man, and he an architect with an outstanding sense of proportion. The white interior is tall and light and full of delicately carved 14th-century details, particularly the founder's tomb (hard white chalk) in the N. transept, and the sedilia in the chancel. This complete church is just the sort of thing the more medievalist Victorians tried to copy and could not quite manage. The Victorian restoration by G. E. Street, 1854, did little harm.

TIDMARSH † St Laurence

1m/2km S. of Pangbourne
OS *SU634745* **GPS** *51.4664N, 1.0875W*

The main features of note are the Norman S. doorway of two carved orders (chain and chevron patterns) and the rare 13th-century polygonal apse. The intriguing timber bell-turret arch bears wood carving by a former incumbent's wife. A series of medieval wall-paintings has been restored.

WARFIELD † St Michael the Archangel ★

2m/3km N. of Bracknell
OS *SU880722* **GPS** *51.4420N, 0.7351W*

This is large and fine for Berkshire, mostly 14th-century Decorated, with a light, spacious and stately chancel, E. window with beautiful tracery and much carved chalk. There are remains of 14th-century glass, a 15th-century wooden screen and a loft in the N. aisle. The graceful 19th-century stone screen is by G. E. Street, who restored the whole church most carefully.

WICKHAM † St Swithun

6m/10km N.W. of Newbury
OS *SU394715* **GPS** *51.4413N, 1.4335W*

On a hill above the village stands an 11th-century tower to which has been added a church rebuilt in expensive knapped flint with stone dressings, by Benjamin Ferrey, 1854–9. The sumptuous interior is a mid-Victorian extravaganza. Lifesize elephants' heads in papier mache decorate the N. aisle roof, and there are lime-wood angels in the nave roof; the windows are of mid-Victorian purple and red stained glass. The only inharmonious note is the later E. window.

BUCKINGHAMSHIRE

Buckinghamshire is a somewhat curious county as regards its church architecture. It has never had a cathedral or any major monastic church. There are few large town churches to compare with those in many other counties – Aylesbury, High Wycombe, Chesham and Amersham being about the largest. There are few outstanding churches of major architectural note. But what the county lacks in this respect is more than made up for in variety.

There is no 'Buckinghamshire type' of church, spire, tower or window, and in this county the architecture follows, in most instructive and interesting fashion, the geological formations of the land. The churches in the extreme south, in or bordering the Thames Valley, have an enormous variety of materials where stone is absent – brick, in such places as Dorney, Hitcham, Penn and elsewhere. The earliest brickwork in the county, though it does not appear in the Chapel, is at Eton College, 1442. Then in the Chiltern belt there is, as one would of course expect, extensive use of clunch, chalk rubble and flint, with stone employed only for the dressings.

The Vale of Aylesbury provides a further variety of materials, while the north of the county, penetrating into the limestone belt, produces good stone building in many of its churches, comparable with that in the neighbouring counties of Northamptonshire and Oxfordshire.

The only 'groups' that can be identified in Buckinghamshire are those of stone-carvers. At Ivinghoe there is a very fine set of mid or late 13th-century carved capitals in the nave, which obviously came from the same mason's workshop as Pitstone, Eaton Bray, Flamstead, Chalgrave and several other churches in the neighbourhood.

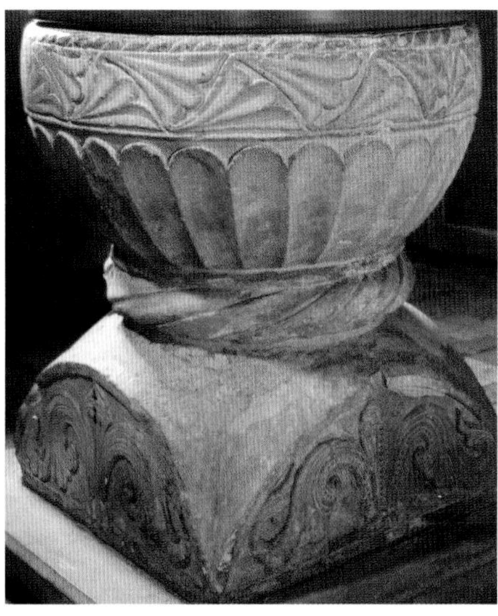

△ **LITTLE MISSENDEN: ST JOHN BAPTIST** *– an Aylesbury font*

Masons' marks also relate work at Eton College, North Marston and Hillesden with a group of travelling masons.

Then there is the series of Aylesbury fonts – a fine late 12th-century group taking its type-name from the font in Aylesbury church. Others may be seen at Bledlow, Buckland, Chenies, Great Kimble, Great Missenden, Little Missenden, Wing, Pitstone and Weston Turville, with some in Bedfordshire and Northamptonshire, besides several more obviously deriving from the same source.

◁ **NORTH CRAWLEY: ST FIRMIN** *– a noble church dating from the 13th century*

0
5 miles
0
5 km
NORTHAMPTONSHIRE
BUCKINGHAMSHIRE
BEDFORDSHIRE
HERTFORDSHIRE
OXFORDSHIRE
BERKSHIRE
Towcester
Olney
Clifton Reynes
BEDFORD
Hanslope
Gayhurst
Chicheley
Lathbury
North Crawley
Newport Pagnell
Great Linford
Willen
Broughton
MILTON KEYNES
Biddlesden
Lillingstone Dayrell
BUCKINGHAM
Tattenhoe
Chetwode
Hillesden
Twyford
Winslow
Stewkley
Dunton
North Marston
LEIGHTON BUZZARD
Bicester
Wing
Quainton
Edlesborough
Ivinghoe
Pitstone
AYLESBURY
Bierton
Nether Winchendon
Chearsley
Dinton
Haddenham
Weston Turville
Tring
Wendover
Berkhamsted
HEMEL HEMPSTEAD
Thame
Little Kimble
Monks Risborough
Princes Risborough
Bledlow
Little Hampden
Little Missenden
Chenies
AMERSHAM
Radnage
Bradenham
Ibstone
West Wycombe
HIGH WYCOMBE
Terriers
Penn
Chalfont St Giles
Fingest
BEACONSFIELD
Little Marlow
Fawley
MARLOW
Hedgerley
Stoke Poges
HENLEY-ON-THAMES
MAIDENHEAD
Hitcham
SLOUGH
Dorney
Windsor
A5
A428
A509
A43
M1
A508
A422
A413
A421
A507
A4012
A4146
A5120
A4421
A418
A41
A40
M40
A4129
A4010
A416
A404
A4130
A4
A329
M25
M4

AYLESBURY † St Mary ★
St Mary's Square
OS *SP817139* **GPS** *51.8179N, 0.8160W*

The church stands on the highest point of the town in a large churchyard surrounded by 17th- and 18th-century houses. It is large, handsome and cruciform, with an interesting outline to its lead spirelet, and has an intriguing plan full of surprises, with side chapels in unusual places. Substantially 13th-century, its character is a good deal spoilt by over-heavy Victorian restoration. A major re-ordering has closed off the W. bays of the nave and added a gallery. The fine font, c. 1180, is the prototype for a group in this and surrounding counties.

BIDDLESDEN † St Margaret ★
6m/10km N.W. of Buckingham
OS *SP632398* **GPS** *52.0535N, 1.0783W*

The little box-like church is remote, on the Northamptonshire border. It was once the private chapel of Biddlesden Park, part of the stable block, and is of the same date as the house, 1730, which occupies the site of a Cistercian abbey. There are undistinguished 18th-century fittings and clear glass; its charm subsisting in its situation and pleasant texture.

BIERTON † St James the Great ★
2m/3km N.E. of Aylesbury
OS *SP836152* **GPS** *51.8297N, 0.7880W*

Here is a really good architectural composition, with lofty 14th-century arcades and central tower on clustered piers. The walls retain much old plaster and whitewash, with glimpses of paintings peeping through here and there; the floor is a pleasant mixture of square red tiles or bricks and stone. There are several good details and fittings, including the Bosse monuments by W. Stanton.

BLEDLOW † Holy Trinity ★
2m/3km S.W. of Princes Risborough
OS *SP778021* **GPS** *51.7129N, 0.8747W*

Splendidly placed on the lower Chiltern slopes, on the brink of the Lyde – a chalk coombe – Holy Trinity overlooks the Vale of Aylesbury. The church contains many worthwhile things – nave arcades with carved capitals of about 1200; an Aylesbury font; fragments of wall-painting, including an amusing Adam and Eve; and a splendid S. doorway and porch, 13th–14th-century, with traces of original colouring. The whole plan is very irregular, and the inclusion of the tower within the aisles lends interest and importance to the interior at the W. end.

BRADENHAM † St Botolph
4m/6km N.W. of High Wycombe
OS *SU828971* **GPS** *51.6668N, 0.8037W*

St Botolph occupies a perfect village green setting. There is a Norman S. door, and the N.E. chapel has monuments and Tudor heraldic glass. Restored by Street, 1863–5.

BROUGHTON † St Lawrence
3m/5km E. of Milton Keynes
OS *SP893401* **GPS** *52.0522N, 0.6979W*
Churches Conservation Trust

This 14th-century church with 15th-century tower is notable for its extensive 14th- and 15th-century wall-paintings, which include St George and the Dragon, a Doom and an unusual work combining a Pietà with the Wounds of Christ.

CHALFONT ST GILES † St Giles
3m/4km S.E. of Amersham
OS *SU991935* **GPS** *51.6316N, 0.5695W*

In a village green setting, the church is approached through an old lych gate that passes under a 16th-century house. It affords an interesting development of plan throughout the Middle Ages; there are some wall-paintings.

CHEARSLEY † St Nicholas ★
7m/12km W. of Aylesbury
OS *SP720103* **GPS** *51.7869N, 0.9572W*

A charming place, the church lies at the foot of a steep lane below the village, which overlooks the Valley of the Thame and its rich water meadows not far from Nodey Abbey. The nave is 13th-century, the tower and chancel are from the 15th. Like Nether Winchendon nearby, it has mercifully escaped serious restoration and has a gallery which features the wooden support for the serpent, the largest of the instruments played by the band before the days of organs. There are

△ **CHETWODE: ST MARY AND ST NICHOLAS** – *this remnant of an Augustinian priory contains some exceptionally fine Early English work, such as the five-lancet east window (above right)*

two sets of Royal Arms, excellent modern pews and glass, a Norman font and a brass of 1462. The step down into the chancel is unusual, and the whole place has a pleasant, mellow, uneven quality.

CHENIES † St Michael ★

4m/6km E. of Amersham
OS *TQ015983* **GPS** *51.6748N, 0.5325W*

The church must be included here; for while it is, in the main, architecturally unimportant and somewhat spoiled by 'improvement', it stands most delightfully among the trees above the Chess Valley, hard by the mellow brick manor house of the Cheneys and Russells and the 'model' cottages of the village. Its principal feature is the fabulous series of monuments to the Russells, Dukes of Bedford, and their connections, in the N. chapel. Regrettably difficult to see, they are kept separate in the locked Bedford Chapel. Nikolaus Pevsner described them as 'a rich a store of funeral monuments as any parish church of England'.

CHETWODE
† St Mary and St Nicholas ★

5m/8km S.W. of Buckingham
OS *SP640298* **GPS** *51.9630N, 1.0693W*

The choir or chancel of a small Augustinian priory, it became a parochial church as long ago as 1480, when the then parish church was ruinous and the monks were hopelessly impoverished. It has the best 13th-century work in Bucks., and, though some of it is reset and restored, the range of dog-toothed and deeply cut sedilia, the great five-lancet E. window, and the triple-lancet on the S. with 13th- and 14th-century glass, would be notable anywhere. The 14th-century N. chapel has become the manor pew with fireplace. There are hatchments and other good things, including the earliest heraldic glass in any English church, depicting Henry III's coat of arms.

CHICHELEY † St Laurence ★

2m/3km N.E. of Newport Pagnell
OS *SP904458* **GPS** *52.1037N, 0.6807W*

Here is one of those splendid mixtures of dates and styles, from medieval to Comper,

that make so many English village churches the delightful places they are. The church stands near the Hall and has a Decorated nave and N. aisle, a 15th-century central tower not unlike Sherrington, and a Classical chancel with delicate detail dated 1708, probably by Francis Smith of Warwick, who built the Hall. The central space is early Comper, and is effective. There are good Renaissance monuments to Caves and Chesters.

CLIFTON REYNES
† St Mary the Virgin ★

9m/14km N. of Milton Keynes
OS *SP899513* **GPS** *52.1534N, 0.6873W*

Awkwardly placed (from the tourist's point of view) on the S. side of the Ouse, away from Olney and thus happily secluded, the church is of great interest. A Saxon origin is suggested by the odd proportions of its tall nave, though most of what we see is 13th-, 14th- and 15th-century. The principal features are the font, with figures of saints (14th-century), and the series of medieval monuments to the Reynes family, including the great rarity of two pairs of early 14th-century wooden effigies.

DINTON † St Peter and St Paul ★

4m/6km S.W. of Aylesbury
OS *SP766110* **GPS** *51.7930N, 0.8895W*

Late Perpendicular predominates here, with the exception of a celebrated Norman door with inscribed tympanum bearing a Tree of Life and beasts.

DORNEY † St James the Less ★

3m/4km W. of Slough
OS *SU924790* **GPS** *51.5024N, 0.6688W*

The church dreams away in a backwater beside the splendid timbered house of Dorney Court. With its Tudor brick tower and bits of every period of architecture before and since, from Norman times to a 19th-century window of King Charles the Martyr, everything is on an intimate and miniature scale. Note especially: the 12th-century font; W. gallery, 1634; S. porch, 1663; 15th-century stalls and base of screen brought from elsewhere; 17th-century communion rails and other woodwork; and the fine Garrard monument, 1607, by Nicholas Johnson, in the little N. chapel.

DUNTON † St Martin ★

4m/6km S.E. of Winslow

OS *SP823243* **GPS** *51.9118N, 0.8038W*

A church with hardly any village, St Martin's is small and pleasantly unrestored. There are box pews and a W. gallery with texts and rectors' and churchwardens' names of the 18th century painted on the front. The ceiling shows a hint of medieval timbers above. Many Bucks. churches must have been like this 150 years ago.

EDLESBOROUGH

† St Mary the Virgin ★

10m/16km E. of Aylesbury

OS *SP970190* **GPS** *51.8617N, 0.5927W*

Churches Conservation Trust

Below the Chiltern scarp and sited on a great mound, isolated and exposed to all the winds that blow across the vale, the church was horribly maltreated in the 19th century (plaster stripping inside, cement rendering out) but contains the most wonderful things – complete screen, stalls, pulpit and tester, and roofs of the 15th century; transverse arches in the aisles, and a series of exceptionally interesting brasses, as well as a complicated succession of medieval building periods.

FAWLEY † St Mary

3m/4km N. of Henley-on-Thames

OS *SU753867* **GPS** *51.5743N, 0.9140W*

In a scattered Chiltern hill-top village, the chancel of St Mary's, rebuilt in 1748, contains fine woodwork thought to be by Grinling Gibbons: font, pulpit, stalls, rails and panelling – all were formerly in the chapel of Canons House, old Middlesex. There are two formidable mausolea in the churchyard and Piper stained glass.

FINGEST † St Bartholomew

6m/10km W. of High Wycombe

OS *SU776911* **GPS** *51.6138N, 0.8796W*

The mighty Norman tower, with unusual twin saddleback roof, dwarfs the rest of this well-known church, which is set in a delightful village nestling in the Chilterns.

GAYHURST † St Peter ★

6m/10km N. of Milton Keynes

OS *SP846462* **GPS** *52.1082N, 0.7653W*

A complete rebuilding in 1728 of a medieval church in the grounds of the great Elizabethan house nearby – designer unknown. The tower has urns at the corners, and a charming, airy little cupola in the centre. The sides of the nave are unusual, with a central pediment, pilaster and doorway. The interior is practically unaltered, with good plasterwork, pews, pulpit and panelling. There is a splendid monument to Speaker Wright and his son, variously attributed to Roubiliac and William Palmer.

GREAT LINFORD † St Andrew ★

2m/3km N. of Milton Keynes

OS *SP850423* **GPS** *52.0728N, 0.7602W*

Pleasantly situated, it is reached past a handsome manor house and a 17th-century range built as village school and almshouses, and is a happy blend of the early 18th century and Decorated Gothic. The alterations inside to accommodate an increasing congregation are understandable but regrettable. At least the changes resulted in the discovery of a 15th-century tiled floor, part of which can still be viewed beneath the modern one.

HADDENHAM † St Mary the Virgin

3m/4km N.E. of Thame

OS *SP741080* **GPS** *51.7658N, 0.9267W*

A good 13th-century and later church, it lies at the extreme end of one of the most remarkable and complicated villages in Bucks., where many of the houses and walls are largely composed of wichert – a hard, compressed chalk marl. The W. tower overlooking the green is a good Early English composition, and inside the spacious church, work of this date as well as of many other periods is found. Note the 15th-century glass in the N. transept window. A flat plaster ceiling of early 19th-century date tantalizingly hides a 14th-century timber roof. A rewarding mixture.

△ **LITTLE MISSENDEN: ST JOHN BAPTIST** – *a wall-painting of the 13th century depicts St Christopher on the left and episodes from the life of St Catherine on the right*

HANSLOPE † St James the Great

6m/10km N.W. of Milton Keynes

OS *SP803467* **GPS** *52.1129N, 0.8274W*

Set in a windy village on high ground, the steeple is seen for miles around and is the tallest in Bucks. With a Norman chancel, the 13th, 14th and 15th centuries are all represented here; the 15th-century N. aisle added great width to the body of the church. The spire was rebuilt to only two-thirds of its original height after being storm-damaged in 1804. Despite scraping, the interior has good fittings – pulpit, Royal Arms, hatchments, an unusual family pew and brasses.

HEDGERLEY † St Mary the Virgin ★

3m/4km S.E. of Beaconsfield

OS *SU970873* **GPS** *51.5766N, 0.6006W*

The best Victorian Gothic church in the county – by Benjamin Ferrey, 1852 – it is built of the local flint, with a little stone and conglomerate, and stands high on a grassy slope surrounded by trees. It is the third church on the site, and has some oddments from the older buildings: a medieval font with Jacobean cover; an old painting of the Commandments; some brasses; and a reputed piece of Charles I's cloak.

HILLESDEN † All Saints ★

3m/4km S. of Buckingham

OS *SP685287* **GPS** *51.9531N, 1.0036W*

This is another of Buckinghamshire's lovely and lonely places. The church is almost entirely of the 15th century, and of a quality encountered hardly anywhere else in the county. There are contemporary roofs, seats, a screen and glass (legend of St Nicholas) and a Te Deum frieze of alternate instrument-playing and scroll-bearing angels in the

LITTLE MISSENDEN: ST JOHN BAPTIST – *the south chapel* ▷

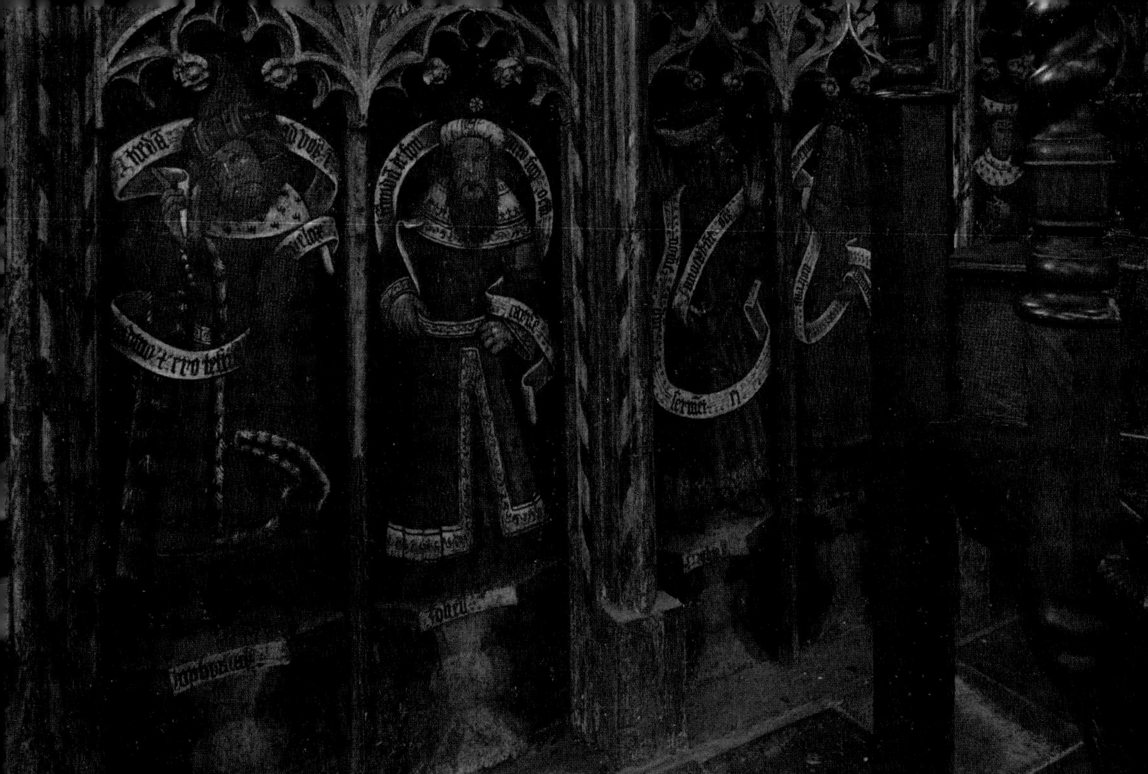

△ **NORTH CRAWLEY: ST FIRMIN** – *the 15th-century screen, with images of prophets, saints and kings, is Buckinghamshire's only such screen to remain complete*

chancel. Note also good monuments, and the lovely canopy over the stair turret attached to the two-storey vestry and sacristy. This is the church that inspired Sir George Gilbert Scott with his Gothic passion – his father was a clergyman at Gawcott nearby – and it was he who gently restored it in 1874–5.

HITCHAM † St Mary ★

4m/6km W. of Slough
OS *SU920825* **GPS** *51.5347N, 0.6750W*

This small church has an admirable mixture of materials and styles, lending both texture and interest: much of it is flint, with a 16th-century brick tower and chalk and plaster nave. The chancel arch is Norman, and the chancel itself a 1330–40 rebuilding. The chancel windows retain much of their original glass, depicting the Nine Orders of Angels and the Four Evangelists. Good monuments and brasses; the whole set among trees in a well-kept churchyard surrounded by ancient tawny brick walls.

IBSTONE † St Nicholas

6m/10km W. of High Wycombe
OS *SU756923* **GPS** *51.6248N, 0.9092W*

This small, intriguing church is sited away from the main village, overlooking the beautiful Turville Valley. It is primitive, mainly 12th- and 13th-century, and has a Norman S. doorway, weather-boarded bell-turret and Perpendicular pulpit.

IVINGHOE † St Mary the Virgin

8m/13km E. of Aylesbury
OS *SP945161* **GPS** *51.8362N, 0.6291W*

A noble cruciform church, 13th–15th century, St Mary's is set in a large churchyard. Particularly fine are the stiff-leaf capitals of the nave arcades, the carved Apostles on the roof wall-posts, and the poppyheads on the benches, which include a mermaid and some haunting Green Men.

LATHBURY † All Saints ★

3m/5km N. of Milton Keynes
OS *SP874449* **GPS** *52.0964N, 0.7248W*

Another dead-end place down by the Ouse just outside Newport Pagnell, All Saints church is dark and mysterious, with fragments of painting and robust carvings from its Norman past. Outside it is pleasantly embattled with a good stone texture.

LILLINGSTONE DAYRELL

† St Nicholas

4m/6km N. of Buckingham

OS *SP705398* **GPS** *52.0523N, 0.9729W*

Reached by a long cart track, this interesting church has an 11th-century chancel and tower arches. The tower is 13th-century, as is the chancel which contains a curious Easter Sepulchre, Dayrell brasses, a Renaissance tomb chest, old tiles and a funeral pall of 1699.

LITTLE HAMPDEN

† dedication unknown

7m/12km S. of Aylesbury

OS *SP860035* **GPS** *51.7241N, 0.7556W*

Humble and withdrawn among a few cottages and scattered farms, its simple interior is decorated with 13th- to 15th-century wall-paintings, including the earliest St Christopher in England. It leaves a great impression of the medieval hamlet church. The timbered, two-storey N. porch is unique in Bucks. There is a tombstone by Eric Gill to his neighbour Mary Bernadette Nuttgens.

LITTLE KIMBLE † All Saints ★

4m/7km S. of Aylesbury

OS *SP826064* **GPS** *51.7504N, 0.8041W*

Small and undistinguished externally, with a little W. bell-turret, All Saints stands amidst beeches and greenery on the edge of Chequers park. Inside are to be found, artistically, the best wall-paintings in Bucks., including St Christopher, St James major, St George (a notable standing figure), St Lawrence, St Francis preaching to the birds (only two in England), St Clare, St Bernard, and assorted ecclesiastics, plus part of a Doom, and a life of St Margaret and St Catherine, all early 14th-century. There is also a square of Chertsey tiles under a mat in the chancel, with enchanting scenes from the life of King Mark of Cornwall and other Arthurian romances.

LITTLE MARLOW † St John Baptist

2m/3km N.E. of Marlow

OS *SU874878* **GPS** *51.5825N, 0.7399W*

St John Baptist is in a good Thames-side village at a dead end and consequently almost unspoiled. The church has the unusual feature of a triple-gabled E. elevation, reminiscent of Devonian or Cornish churches; and has a light, limewashed interior. The chancel shows good 13th-century detail; the S. aisle and chapel were 'beautified' by Sir Nicholas Ledewich, so the inscription on his tomb tells us, about 1430.

LITTLE MISSENDEN † St John Baptist

3m/4km W. of Amersham

OS *SU920989* **GPS** *51.6821N, 0.6694W*

The church stands by the manor house and a number of pleasant houses in the village. Externally it is very picturesque; of flint and brick with a dormer window in the nave roof. An exquisite E. window has three double-shafted lancets. The church is principally renowned for its series of 13th- and 15th-century wall-paintings, which include St Christopher, a vivid Martyrdom of St Catherine and a Crucifixion.

MONKS RISBOROUGH

† St Dunstan ★

Adjoins Princes Risborough to N.

OS *SP812044* **GPS** *51.7326N, 0.8246W*

The general effect of this church is especially pleasing from the exterior, as it stands in a good churchyard with high hedges and trees and the old Rectory hard by. The main part of the structure is 15th-century; inside there are good things to see, such as the 12th-century font, 14th-century tower arch and brass, a somewhat reduced painted screen and remains of old glass.

NETHER WINCHENDON

† St Nicholas

4m/6km N.E. of Thame

OS *SP732122* **GPS** *51.8042N, 0.9388W*

One of the most attractive church interiors in the county and entirely unspoiled, in a rural village setting, at the foot of a steep hill. The structure is medieval, but the atmosphere is of the 18th century, all lit by brass Jacobean candelabra, with gallery and high pews, hatchments, sentences and a Jacobean three-tier pulpit. Recent restorations to the nave floor, gallery stairs, pews and pulpit are sensitive and of fine quality. Notice an unusual modern memorial to Lieut-Colonel Francis Tyringham Higgins-Bernard, a 20th-century version of a medieval knight's tomb.

NORTH CRAWLEY † St Firmin ★

6m/10km N.E. of Milton Keynes

OS *SP926446* **GPS** *52.0924N, 0.6485W*

An important medieval church, it was restored in the 18th century. The rebuilding of the chancel in the 13th century is recorded by a rare carved inscription outside the E. window. The nave has a S. arcade of c. 1200 with good carved capitals and a 14th-century N. arcade. The 15th-century screen is the only painted one to remain complete in the county; the figures on the panels are those of prophets, kings and saints.

NORTH MARSTON

† Assumption of the Blessed Virgin Mary

6m/10km N. of Aylesbury

OS *SP777227* **GPS** *51.8974N, 0.8721W*

The church is associated with John Schorne, rector in the late 13th and early 14th century, who performed miraculous cures of the gout and became venerated as a saint. The S. aisle contains the original (14th-century) remains of his elaborate shrine, and the nave has good medieval work of various dates. The canons of Windsor filched Schorne's relics and, probably as a sop to the disgruntled parishioners, paid for the building of the superb chancel and two-storey vestry and sacristy in the late 15th century. The church was restored in 1855 at Queen Victoria's expense in memory of John Camden Neild, a local landowner who left his fortune to the Queen after his death in the 1850s.

OLNEY † St Peter and St Paul

8m/13km N. of Milton Keynes

OS *SP889509* **GPS** *52.1499N, 0.7008W*

The view from the S. across the water meadows of the Ouse is memorable. The tall broach spire and the splendid chancel windows, all of the 14th century, remind one that Northamptonshire is only a mile or two away. Inside is large and airy, but heavily scraped. The pulpit in the S.W. corner was used by John Newton, vicar in the 1760s, who, with his friend William Cowper, wrote the *Olney Hymns.*

PENN † Holy Trinity ★

3m/4km N.W. of Beaconsfield

OS *SU916932* **GPS** *51.6309N, 0.6775W*

There are splendid views from the churchyard. The church, of wonderfully varied textures and materials, with two great porches, has a medieval structure, the roof of

△ **TATTENHOE: ST GILES** – *some of the stonework and architectural details of this humble little church are thought to have come from nearby Snelshall Priory, a ruin by the mid-16th century*

c. 1400 being one of the finest in the county. But it was much altered by the Penns and Curzons in the 18th century, which is the date of the chancel and its fittings, and many of its monuments. The great treasure is the 15th-century Doom painting on oak boards set over the chancel arch; it was found in the roof in 1938. The series of brasses is good for costume; and in the centre aisle is the tombstone of a descendant of William Penn, Quaker and founder of Pennsylvania.

PITSTONE † St Mary ★

8m/13km E. of Aylesbury
OS *SP942149* **GPS** *51.8251N, 0.6341W*
Churches Conservation Trust

This small church lying in chalk fields below the Chilterns has a most satisfactory interior, with work of many dates and textures; 13th-century capitals like Ivinghoe, 15th-century nave arcades, a 12th-century font – the whole dominated by a fine Jacobean pulpit and tester.

QUAINTON
† Holy Cross and St Mary ★

6m/10km N.W. of Aylesbury
OS *SP749201* **GPS** *51.8749N, 0.9120W*

The church stands a little apart from the village in a group with almshouses and a Carolean rectory, and commands a lovely view over the vale. It was badly mauled by 19th-century restorers, who endowed it with a monstrous roof and hideous tiles, but it is notable for the finest 17th- and 18th-century sculpture in the county. In the nave are monuments by Stayner, William Stanton, Leoni and M. C. Wyatt, but inside the tower (too often locked) are the moving figures of Justice Dormer and his wife sorrowing over their dead son – a work of genius long attributed to Roubiliac, but more latterly believed to have been sculpted by Michael Rysbrack, c. 1728.

RADNAGE † St Mary ★

6m/10km N.W. of High Wycombe
OS *SU786979* **GPS** *51.6748N, 0.8646W*

Perched on the wooded slopes of the tumbled ground behind the Chiltern scarp below

△ **WING: ALL SAINTS** – *the compelling classical monument to Sir Robert Dormer, d. 1552*

Bledlow Ridge is a scattered village of several 'endships', one of which is clustered around the church and rectory. The exterior, of partly plastered chalk and flint with brick repairs, fits perfectly into the landscape. Much of the structure is of about 1200, with aisleless nave and chancel and a plain tower between. The simple village interior retains its original plaster, covered with a medley of medieval paintings and post-Reformation texts.

STEWKLEY
† St Michael and All Angels ★★

5m/8km W. of Leighton Buzzard
OS *SP852261* **GPS** *51.9269N, 0.7622W*

This very fine Norman church, with central tower, is comparable with Iffley, Oxon. The W. front is particularly rich Norman work, with blind arcades and an odd hanging keystone. Inside, a restoration by Street took away something of the texture, but enhanced the lofty scale, culminating in a distant, dark chancel, whose chevron-carved stone vaulting is very fine.

STOKE POGES † St Giles

3m/4km N. of Slough
OS *SU975827* **GPS** *51.5351N, 0.5949W*

The poet Thomas Grey wrote his *'Elegy Written in a Country Churchyard'* here, and the association rather obscures the main points of interest: a 14th-century timbered and traceried porch; the limewashed walls of the oddly placed 13th-century tower; and the renovated Hastings chapel in which one rather regrets the disappearance of a good gallery. Fine panels of 17th- and 18th-century glass have been placed here.

TATTENHOE † St Giles

4m/7km S. of Milton Keynes
OS *SP829339* **GPS** *51.9979N, 0.7938W*

Tiny St Giles used to stand wistful and remote in the midst of moats, banks, ditches and other evidences of a deserted village. That remoteness has been compromised in recent years, and the church now stands on the edge of a much-reduced patch of scrubland, primarily for the use of dog walkers, on the edge of a late 20th-century housing development. There is a simple interior with box pews for each of the three farming families that formed the nucleus of Tattenhoe from the 14th century to the 20th. Betjeman's 'authentic aroma of the past – stale paraffin and mouldy hassocks' has now succumbed to the 2007 installation of electricity and heating.

TERRIERS † St Francis

N.E. district of High Wycombe
OS *SU877944* **GPS** *51.6423N, 0.7337W*

By Sir Giles Gilbert Scott, the church was consecrated in 1930, and is one of his best designs. Light and shade are artfully employed within, and the impressive exterior is suitably enhanced by a lofty central tower.

TWYFORD † St Mary

5m/8km S. of Buckingham
OS *SP665266* **GPS** *51.9346N, 1.0340W*

A church of exceptional interest for its details and fittings, whose various architectural styles have created something of a jumble. The Norman doorway is notable, and inside there are fine 13th-century arcades, with a good deal of 15th-century woodwork – roof, pews and screen with some painting. There are worthwhile monuments, both medieval and later.

WEST WYCOMBE † St Lawrence ★

2m/3km W. of High Wycombe
OS *SU827949* **GPS** *51.6474N, 0.8056W*

Medieval in origin, the church is dramatically placed within an Iron Age earthwork; the curiously wrought flinty Dashwood Mausoleum lies to the E. Much of the church, including nave, upper part of the tower and mausoleum, were rebuilt and rededicated in the mid-18th century on the direction of local landowner Sir Francis Dashwood, one of the founders of the secretive Knights of St Francis – later and more commonly known as The Hellfire Club. There were several such clubs at the time, based upon a philosophy of licentiousness. Dashwood's Hellfire Club met on several occasions in the caves beneath the church and, if perhaps only to play cards, in the golden globe that tops the tower. The nave walls are lined by engaged Corinthian columns and there is good plasterwork and ceiling painting. The furnishings, though, are more curious than beautiful.

WESTON TURVILLE

† St Mary the Virgin ★

3m/4km S.E. of Aylesbury
OS *SP859102* **GPS** *51.7847N, 0.7557W*

The church is at the end of a lane near the 18th-century manor house in whose grounds is the motte of a Norman castle. The building is of many styles and of an attractive irregularity with things in it to please everyone – a 12th-century Aylesbury font, 13th-century arcades, 14th-century chancel with good window tracery, 15th-century tower, fragments of old glass (a tantalizing medley, this), 17th-century pulpit, and so forth.

WILLEN † St Mary Magdalene ★

2m/3km N.E. of centre of Milton Keynes
OS *SP878412* **GPS** *52.0624N, 0.7200W*

Like a city church transported to the remote countryside, with dramatic effect, this delightful church is a confection of brick, stone, Classical pilasters, urns, high pews, pedestal font and all the rest; the apsidal chancel is Victorian. The church is to the design of Robert Hooke – Curator of Experiments to the Royal Society and architect of The Monument in London – and was built around 1680 through the munificence of Dr Busby, the famous headmaster of Westminster School. Now the church stands as a bulwark against the sprawling housing of Milton Keynes.

WING † All Saints

3m/4km S.W. of Leighton Buzzard
OS *SP880225* **GPS** *51.8949N, 0.7221W*

With a polygonal apse like the prow of a ship, this is the most important Saxon church in the county, and contains much of interest from many dates. The Saxon crypt was opened in 1878, and there is a fine 15th-century carved oak roof, ornamented with back-to-back angels. Conspicuous and flamboyant monuments to the Dormer family abound; in contrast a touching simple brass memorial to 'Honest Old John Coats that sometime was porter at Ascott Hall, hat now (alas!) left his key, lodge, fure, friends and all to have a room in Heaven.'

CAMBRIDGESHIRE

Modern Cambridgeshire includes the historic county of Huntingdonshire and the Soke of Peterborough, although all three areas retain distinctive characteristics, and Huntingdonshire continues to insist on its separate identity. Perhaps because Cambridge University and Ely Cathedral are so outstandingly beautiful, people underrate the county that contains them. Cambridgeshire scenery is nowhere obvious or dramatic – the famed Gog Magog Hills, south of Cambridge, are modest, nowhere reaching 300 feet. The southern part of the county is rolling and chalky, giving surprisingly fine and wide views. In the north, the fens dominate, where the eye sees mostly sky.

As Olive Cook, author and champion of rural preservation, wrote in *Cambridgeshire: Aspects of a County* in 1953, 'It would not be possible to find elsewhere so unexpected a contrast between the chalk uplands with their carpets of delicate grasses and rare flowers, wild yet amiable, and the expanse of the Fens, dyked, drained and filled, yet still boundless, awe-inspiring and alien.' The towers and spires of the 14th century, the great time of church building here, show the sense of skyline peculiar to the Middle Ages and still dominate much of the landscape, despite the inevitable impact of 21st-century light industrial development, and the unstoppable tide of suburban housing developments.

Cambridgeshire is not a unity. In the south it is like its neighbours, Essex, Suffolk and Hertfordshire. Steep-roofed cottages are reed-thatched, and their walls colour-washed. Parish boundaries are long strips, parallel to the Anglo-Saxon Devil's Dyke and so designed as to make best use of a variety of resources on every strip. In this rolling scenery are country houses in well-wooded parks, and the thatched villages, which are seen best in sunlight when their colour washes are shown up, cluster round flint churches whose mouldings and carvings are of hard chalk. In the west of the county a coarse rubble is used for the churches.

Until 1836 the northern part of the county, the Isle of Ely, was separate from Cambridgeshire. Until the 17th century, when the Fens were drained on a grand scale, the Isle was mostly shallow water with monastic settlements and churches on raised banks and islands. The greatest of these is the Benedictine Abbey of Ely itself. Whittlesey, Sutton, Thorney, Swaffham Prior, Wisbech and St Wendreda's March are other examples of island or peninsular medieval churches which rose over the shallow water like ships, made of limestone from Lincolnshire and Northamptonshire. Beside them, the houses and churches of modern Fen settlements seem mean and unimportant.

In 1839 two Cambridge undergraduates, J. M. Neale and Benjamin Webb, formed the Camden Society for

◁ **MARCH: ST WENDREDA** – *double hamer-beam roof with its host of flying angels*

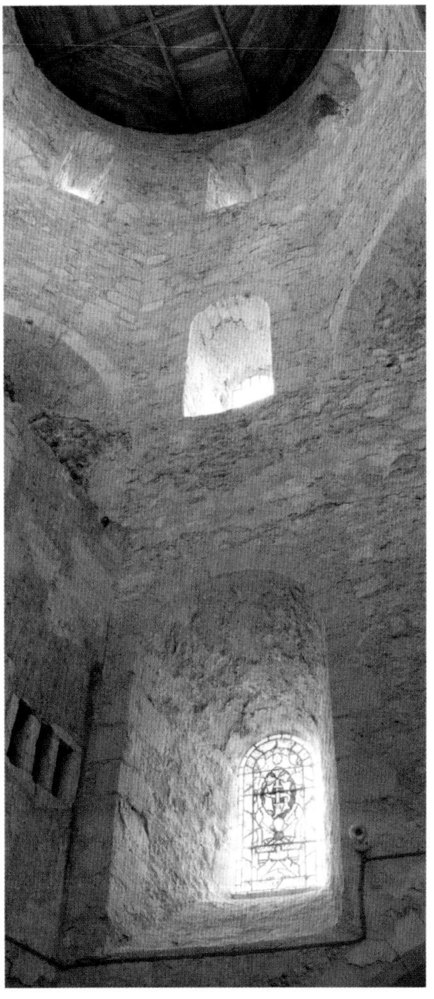

△ **SWAFFHAM PRIOR: ST MARY** – *inside the late 12th- / early 13th-century tower*

the restoration of old churches on what were thought 'correct' principles – the abolition of box pews, the removal of plaster and whitewash, the adornment of the sanctuary with stained glass and colour, and the promotion of 13th–14th century Gothic (Early English and Decorated) above every other style. Yet Cambridgeshire remained Low Church with a good deal of Perpendicular Tudor cement affixed to crumbling fabrics. The Camden movement was not without its effect on local churches, though its influence spread later all over England. The Cambridgeshire churches, for this and other reasons, were subject to more than usually vigorous Victorian retooling and refurbishing.

Historically, Huntingdonshire was small – the third-smallest old county in England – and is now a local authority district of Cambridgeshire. Its scenery is uneventful, either flat or very gently rolling; it has few recognized 'beauty spots'. Perhaps because of this, Huntingdonshire has been less able to defend itself than others against the more hideous and cheap manifestations of modern 'progress'. Bisected by the A1 from north to south, the soulless anonymity and the garish adjuncts of motor traffic have slashed the gentle landscape across and across; though many of the aerodromes and abandoned wartime installations that irritated Betjeman have long since gone. And, of course, in a county where there is so much sky in the landscape, pylons and poles are particularly intrusive.

Yet the Huntingdonshire district still has much beauty. In the west and south its remote, hilly landscape has many oaks and ash trees. The Huntingdonshire elms (*ulmus glabra*) originated here in the mid-8th century. The churches and cottages in the west and south are of yellowish-grey limestone and approach the excellence of those in neighbouring Northants. From St Neots to St Ives, near the slow windings of the sinuous Ouse, are willowy meadows and villages of reed-thatched cottages where the churches are the only old stone buildings, the stone having been brought here by water in medieval times. The north-east is fen: 'When first drained (and much Hunts. fen was drained in the last century) the spongy peat stood some feet above the rivers and channels, but it has so shrunk that a water-course may now be higher than your head. It is a new land, and though the soil is rich, much of it coloured with flowers and vegetables,

LINCOLNSHIRE
Spalding
A151
Bourne
The Fens
A1101
A6121
A16
A15
Leverington
Wisbech
A1073
amford
Barnack
A15
PETERBOROUGH
A47
A1101
Thorney
A47
Wittering
PETERBOROUGH
A605
NORFOLK
Castor
A1
Fletton
Whittesley
March
Orton Longueville
A10
A1101
A141
Yaxley
CAMBRIDGESHIRE
Oundle
Glatton
Littleport
Chatteris
Ramsey
Sawtry
Little Gidding
A141
A10
A142
SUFFOLK
A1(M)
ELY
A1101
HUNTINGDONSHIRE
Sutton
A1421
A142
Isleham
Leighton Bromswold
Alconbury
A1123
HUNTINGDON
A14
St Ives
Soham
Fordham
Brampton
A10
Chippenham
A11
Kimbolton
Snailwell
Buckden
A14
Burwell
Waterbeach
Great Paxton
Swaffham Prior
A1
Elsworth
NEWMARKET
A14
St Neots
Madingley
Bottisham
A428
A428
CAMBRIDGE
Dullingham
Kirtling
BEDFORDSHIRE
Westley Waterless
M11
A1198
A1307
Harlton
Hauxton
A421
A603
A11
Balsham
Babraham
BEDFORD
Wimpole
Little Abington
Hildersham
A10
Biggleswade
Bartlow
Haverhill
A600
Bassingbourn
Ickleton
A6
A1
Royston
Saffron Walden
ESSEX
A505
0
5 miles
Baldock
120
0
5 km
Letchworth
A600
A10
A507
Hitchin
A1(M)
M11

△ **BARNACK: ST JOHN THE BAPTIST** – *11th-century carving of Christ in Majesty*

it has a bleak empty look. The villages are modern and poor…' (Andrew Young, *A Prospect of Britain*, 1956).

Huntingdonshire has five attractive old towns. St Neots, St Ives, Huntingdon, linked with the old red brick of Godmanchester by a bridge and meadows, and Kimbolton – two parallel streets, one Georgian and the other medieval, with the great Vanbrugh house of the Dukes of Manchester at one end of them. The brick industry is long established in the district, and old red-brick houses make a happy contrast with silvery medieval stone and humbler plaster-walled cottages and inns.

When it is remote, Huntingdonshire is more remote and countrified than anywhere in England, and for Betjeman there was always a strong atmosphere in the county of the Civil War. The towns, one feels, stand for Parliament, the villages for the King. Oliver Cromwell was born at Huntingdon, where a chapel spire is higher than the church towers. He has a statue at St Ives and several of his chief supporters came from the county. The 17th-century High Church movement is represented by George Herbert, who rebuilt and refurnished his village church at Leighton Bromswold in 1620, and Nicholas Ferrar, who founded an Anglican religious community, of which Little Gidding church survives as a tender memorial. In the Civil War, Barnabas Oley, Vicar of Great Gransden, smuggled the Cambridge College plate through Huntingdonshire to Charles I at Nottingham.

The Soke of Peterborough – traditionally associated with the Diocese and city of Peterborough – is now a unitary authority within the ceremonial county of Cambridgeshire. In the east it is fen country, becoming hilly and wooded as it stretches westward to Stamford. Here lies the park and immense Elizabethan house of Burghley. The Manor of Burghley and other lands in the Soke (together with wide jurisdictional rights over the whole area) formerly belonged to the abbots of Peterborough, and were granted by Elizabeth I to her treasurer Lord Burghley.

The industrialized city of Peterborough is not half so dull as those who pass through it in the train may think. It is a grey town – grey limestone, lightish-grey and grey-yellow brick. The west front of the Cathedral was described as 'the grandest and finest in Europe'. Its Norman nave and roof and the splendid 'New Building' in Perpendicular at the east end, the tree-shaded ramifications of the close, are all hidden from the main road; so is the excellent local museum.

The churches of the Soke and their villages are almost all built in local limestone, the churches with stone spires. Vestiges of Norman work in many of the churches recall the influence of the Benedictine Abbey.

△ **BARNACK: ST JOHN THE BAPTIST** – *as an 'inspired architectural hotch-potch', it typifies what's so appealing about the English parish church*

ALCONBURY † St Peter and St Paul ★

4m/6km N.W. of Huntingdon

OS *TL184761* **GPS** *52.3703N, 0.2615W*

The village is watered by Alconbury Brook running down the long village green, with the church on the northern fringe of a cluster of colourwash-and-tile cottages. The inside of the 13th-century chancel is noble and serene, enhanced by an attached and embattled arcade along each side, the 15th-century roof marrying well with the older work. There is good contrast between the plaster of the chancel and the pebbly walls of the nave, where the plaster was stripped. The tower has one of the county's many good broach spires.

BABRAHAM † St Peter

7m/11km S.E. of Cambridge

OS *TL509505* **GPS** *52.1324N, 0.2041E*

St Peter's occupies a secluded riverside site beside a Jacobean-style mansion of 1832. Its plain unbuttressed W. tower is claimed as pre-Conquest but is more probably 13th-century; there is a lofty Perpendicular nave and assorted woodwork. The Bennet monument in the S. aisle (second half of 17th century) is highly individual and attractive, and John Piper designed the E. window glass.

BALSHAM † Holy Trinity

6m/10km N.W. of Haverhill

OS *TL587508* **GPS** *52.1332N, 0.3185E*

Here is a fine, large, early medieval tower, and a dignified, somewhat austere, nave dating from the rectorship of John of Sleford, d. 1401; richly carved choir stalls were also commissioned by him. His brass is in the chancel, which is separated from the nave by a late medieval rood screen with loft.

BARNACK † St John the Baptist

3m/4km S.E. of Stamford

OS *TF079050* **GPS** *52.6326N, 0.4066W*

Originally a grand Saxon church, as evidenced by the spectacular stone stripwork decoration of the tower and the magnificent tower arch, the church has since acquired the characteristics of the succeeding centuries, and so is

△ **BOTTISHAM: HOLY TRINITY** – *18th-century monument to Sir Roger and Lady Elizabeth Jenyns*

typical of that inspired architectural hotchpotch which is the English parish church. The Barnack stone quarries fed the greatest of the medieval building projects in the Nene Valley and farther afield. In the N. aisle is a beautiful late Saxon or early Norman carving of Christ in Majesty.

BARTLOW † St Mary

5m/8km W. of Haverhill

OS *TL585451* **GPS** *52.0823N, 0.3132E*

Much restored by Rowe in 1879, there is a Norman round tower, and inside extensive 15th-century wall-paintings, the finest of which is of a dragon – 'ferocious and antediluvially large' was Pevsner's impression.

BASSINGBOURN † St Peter & St Paul

3m/4km N.W. of Royston

OS *TL330440* **GPS** *52.0790N, 0.0596W*

A fine mid-14th-century Decorated chancel of individual design contains much flowing tracery and widespread use of ogees, notably on the sedilia and piscina. There is a good rood screen and a poignant monument to Henry Butler, d. 1647.

BOTTISHAM † Holy Trinity ★

6m/10km E. of Cambridge

OS *TL545604* **GPS** *52.2209N, 0.2612E*

Perhaps the best of the county's churches. An unmistakeable sight from the nearby A14, it is mainly 13th- and early 14th-century with W. tower and tall galilee porch, finely moulded arcades, stone chancel screen and wooden parcloses. Here also is the indent for what must have been the very sumptuous brass of Elias de Bekyngham, said to be the only honest judge in the reign of Edward I. There are many 16th- to 18th-century monuments.

BUCKDEN † St Mary ★

4m/6km S.W. of Huntingdon

OS *TL192676* **GPS** *52.2941N, 0.2526W*

The church has a graceful steeple, overshadowed by the 15th-century brick tower of Buckden Palace nearby. The bulk of the nave is in a good, sober Perpendicular, and the double-storey S. porch has a workmanlike vault. Inside, the plaster has been scraped away showing the coarse rubble beneath and throwing into prominence the ashlar of a lofty arcade. Some interesting 16th-century panels with Passion scenes have been imported, and there are 15th-century roofs and painted glass.

BURWELL † St Mary ★

4m/6km N.W. of Newmarket

OS *TL589660* **GPS** *52.2697N, 0.3282E*

This is excellent Perpendicular. The stately nave, roofed in 1464, stands as a monument to the 15th-century imagination, all line and glass with splendid carved roofs, blank traceried panels, and slim shafts. The exterior is best seen when approached from Cambridge by the Swaffhams; all is unified 15th-century apart from the bottom of the Norman tower.

CAMBRIDGE † Holy Sepulchre

Bridge Street

OS *TL448588* **GPS** *52.2084N, 0.1190E*

One of four remaining round churches in England, it is impressive without and within. Of 12th-century origin, the church was mainly rebuilt in the 15th century, then extensively restored by Salvin in 1842, when some 'ecclesiological' fittings were introduced.

CAMBRIDGE † St Bene't

Bene't Street

OS *TL448582* **GPS** *52.2037N, 0.1183E*

The 10th-century tower with typical Saxon long and short quoins is perhaps the county's oldest extant fabric. The tower arch has cavorting Saxon beasts; the nave and aisles, c. 1300, have suffered from heavy Victorian restoration.

CASTOR † St Kyneburgha

2m/3km W. of Peterborough

OS *TL124985* **GPS** *52.5730N, 0.3419W*

This small village stands near a Roman settlement and in Norman times was evidently still important, to judge by the fine tower of the period, crowned by a stumpy Germanic spire. Few Norman cathedrals have a more richly ornamented steeple than this, with all four walls of the tower panelled in two stages of characteristic Romanesque detail. There are fragments of Saxon carving and a rare inscription recording the dedication of the church in 1124.

CHIPPENHAM † St Margaret

4m/6km N. of Newmarket

OS *TL663698* **GPS** *52.3012N, 0.4383E*

Set in a model village, St Margaret's church is mostly a 14th–15th-century post-fire rebuilding; there is a delightful interior with a memorable 15th-century wall-painting of St Christopher, and good Perpendicular window tracery.

DULLINGHAM † St Mary the Virgin

4m/6km S. of Newmarket

OS *TL631576* **GPS** *52.1934N, 0.3856E*

This is an Estate-village setting; flint and field stone, mainly Perpendicular, with a fine N. porch. Inside is an unexpected and rather incongruous late Victorian pulpit of green Italian marble, and numerous 18th- and 19th-century Jeaffreson monuments.

ELSWORTH † Holy Trinity

7m/11km S.E. of Huntingdon

OS *TL318635* **GPS** *52.2546N, 0.0697W*

The church is set high, overlooking this pretty village with a stream coursing through the green, and has good Decorated work with much Reticulated tracery. There are fine Tudor choir stalls with linenfold carving, and a curious mid-18th-century Ionic reredos, moved by the Victorians to the W. end.

ELY † St Mary

14m/23km N.E. of Cambridge

OS *TL538802* **GPS** *52.3986N, 0.2599E*

Of the church built by Bishop Eustace (1198–1215), the seven-bay Early English nave arcade remains, as does the finely carved N. doorway: all of excellent quality.

FLETTON † St Margaret

S. district of Peterborough

OS *TL197970* **GPS** *52.5584N, 0.2350W*

This has a good share of Norman work, not over-plentiful in the county, but is chiefly remarkable for the series of 9th-century Saxon carvings now reset in the chancel. These are wonderful products of the Mercian

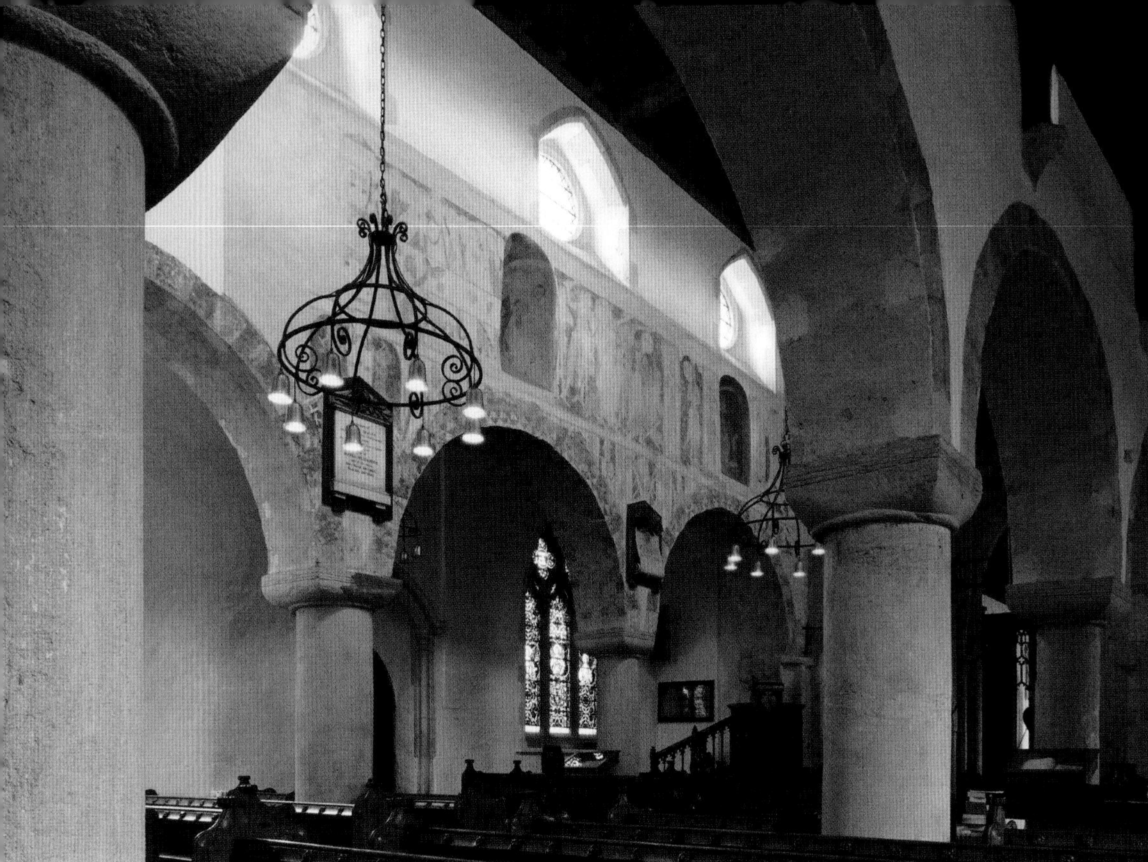

△ **ICKLETON: ST MARY MAGDALENE** – *frescoes above the Norman arcade depict the Passion of Christ in the upper tier and the martyrdom of saints below, in the space between the arches*

school, and their birds, beasts and patterns bear comparison with the glories of Breedon-on-the-Hill, Leicestershire.

FORDHAM
† St Peter and St Mary Magdalene
5m/8km N. of Newmarket
OS *TL633707* **GPS** *52.3103N, 0.3947E*

The Lady Chapel is the pièce de résistance – strangely set over a vaulted porch, altered in the 15th century, but redolent of the apogee of the Decorated style. Colourful Edwardian decorations enliven the chancel.

GLATTON † St Nicholas
7m/12km S. of Peterborough
OS *TL153861* **GPS** *52.4607N, 0.3035W*

St Nicholas has a noble ashlar-faced Perpendicular W. tower with frieze, battlements and pinnacles with animal supporters. Inside are arcades of c. 1300, with scalloped capitals, benches with carved poppyheads, wall-paintings and a vaulted vestry.

GREAT PAXTON † Holy Trinity ★
3m/4km N.E. of St Neots across R. Ouse
OS *TL209641* **GPS** *52.2624N, 0.2285W*

A dark and cavernous church of the Conqueror's time conceived on a thrilling scale – the arches of the crossing stupendous when compared with the man-sized nave arcade. There's no hint of all this outside, since the central tower has disappeared and there is now a stubby 14th-century tower at the W. end. The nave rising towards the E. is an original Saxon feature and provides a link with contemporary German churches.

HARLTON
† Assumption of the Blessed Virgin Mary ★
6m/10km S.W. of Cambridge
OS *TL387525* **GPS** *52.1536N, 0.0262E*

The church – a complete 14th-century rebuild of clunch and field flint – and adjoining Manor Farm make a pleasant group. Inside is a stately instance of Decorated-Perpendicular transition, with a fine stone screen, late 14th-century reredos, statue niches, crocketed canopies and

△ **ICKLETON: ST MARY MAGDALENE** – *some of the kneelers on the pews record the momentous events in the life of the church and parish, including the 1979 fire and subsequent restoration*

a good alabaster wall-monument to Sir Henry Fryer, who died in duel in 1631.

HAUXTON † St Edmund

4m/6km S. of Cambridge
OS *TL435521* **GPS** *52.1492N, 0.0973E*

This is a lovely and simple church, whose Norman nave and chancel are separated by a grand arch. A well-preserved wall-painting of St Thomas à Becket, c. 1250, fills a niche on the S. wall.

HILDERSHAM † Holy Trinity ★

10m/16km S.E. of Cambridge
OS *TL545488* **GPS** *52.1162N, 0.2556E*

Standing in a woodland setting overlooking the River Grant, the church is worth a visit to savour the effect of its attractive and characteristic 13th-century plan. The Victorians left their mark here, not least in the richly frescoed chancel. There are brasses to the Paris family in the chancel but, alas, the pair of lifesize wooden effigies, c. 1300 and once such a feature of the church, were stolen in 1977.

HUNTINGDON † All Saints

Corner of High Street and George Street
OS *TL237718* **GPS** *52.3307N, 0.1850W*

One of two surviving medieval churches in the town, and set close by pleasing Georgian town houses, All Saints is a 15th-century rebuilding of an earlier 13th-century church, with the 14th-century tower retained. There is pleasing Perpendicular tracery; the nave, aisles, chancel and porch are all embattled. Oliver Cromwell was baptised here.

ICKLETON † St Mary Magdalene ★★

10m/10km S. of Cambridge
OS *TL494438* **GPS** *52.0729N, 0.1795E*

In a village-green setting and victim of a horrid fire in 1979, this church was yet the beneficiary, since it uncovered a remarkable series of 12th-century frescoes. Already celebrated for its Saxon-Norman arcades, the paintings of the Life of Christ mark Ickleton as an apogee of the rural Romanesque.

△ **LITTLE GIDDING: ST JOHN** – *the narrow nave and chancel are fitted out as a miniature college chapel, with wooden panelling, Classical arcading and a ribbed barrel-vault roof*

ISLEHAM † St Andrew ★

8m/13km S.E. of Ely

OS *TL643744* **GPS** *52.3431N, 0.4115E*

Spacious and cruciform, St Andrew's is Decorated without, save for the W. tower by Street. The nave is resplendently panelled, clerestoried and roofed to unusual design by the mercantile family of Peyton, 1495, to whom there are some monuments. There is also a very fine Jacobean communion rail.

KIMBOLTON † St Andrew

7m/11km N.W. of St Neots

OS *TL099678* **GPS** *52.2979N, 0.3894W*

A large town church with a 14th-century tower and broach spire. A delightful Decorated oak screen with paintings, c. 1500, stands between the chancel and S. chapel, which is dominated by Montagu monuments. There is also stained glass by Louis Tiffany, 1901.

KIRTLING † All Saints

5m/8km S.E. of Newmarket

OS *TL686576* **GPS** *52.1910N, 0.4664E*

Here was once a Tudor mansion built by the Norths; the surviving gatehouse and moated site are impressive. The Norman S. doorway to the church bears a carving of Christ in Majesty on the tympanum; the door ironwork is also Norman. There are good North hatchments and monuments in the 16th-century brick-built family chapel.

LEIGHTON BROMSWOLD

† St Mary ★

8m/13km W. of Huntingdon

OS *TL115752* **GPS** *52.3642N, 0.3629W*

The nave and tower of this 13th-century and later church were rebuilt in 1626 by the poet George Herbert, when St Mary's 'was so decayed, so little and so useless that the parishioners could not meet to perform their duty to God in public prayer and praises'. The old aisles were sacrificed and the new nave was married to the medieval transepts, which perform their proper function in giving breadth and freedom to the whole design. The church had in fact become a true Protestant 'preaching space'. The roof design is bold with sturdy tie beams.

LEVERINGTON † St Leonard
1m/2km N.W. of Wisbech
OS *TF444114* **GPS** *52.6811N, 0.1359E*

A four-staged tower of many styles crowned with a Victorian spire marks out this Silt Fen church, whose Perpendicular nave supports a later clerestory. A good 14th-century porch is two-storeyed and decorated with a fine carved frieze underneath an elaborate battlement.

LITTLE ABINGTON † St Mary
9m/15km S.E. of Cambridge
OS *TL529491* **GPS** *52.1199N, 0.2326E*

Restored by St Aubyn, 1885, the church is Early Norman, especially the N. and S. nave doorways with simple chip carving. There is Kempe glass, 1901, in the chancel depicting the Adoration of the Magi.

LITTLE GIDDING † St John ★
10m/16km N.W. of Huntingdon
OS *TL127816* **GPS** *52.4211N, 0.3441W*

In undulating country relieved from the extreme flatness of the Fens and sheltered by a grove of trees, the tiny church survives the depopulated village and the hall, now levelled. Little Gidding is linked with Nicholas Ferrar and his unique experiment in the contemplative life. From outside the red brick is disappointing, but within there is richness in a collegiate style, the fabric mostly of the early 18th-century. Embroidered texts on the walls quote from Ferrar and from T. S. Eliot, who visited here and made a poem of his recollection of that event, which formed the last of the *Four Quartets*. The lines read more like an admonition on the wall than in their original context: 'You are not here to verify, / Instruct yourself, or inform curiosity / Or carry report. You are here to kneel / Where prayer has been valid.'

MADINGLEY † St Mary Magdalene
4m/6km N.W. of Cambridge
OS *TL395603* **GPS** *52.2236N, 0.0409E*

An idyllic park setting above a little lake; the tower parapet incorporates Saxon tomb fragments. A fair mixed bag of fittings includes a 14th-century bell, and there are monuments to the Hyndes and Cottons. Interesting for its location as much as the building.

MARCH † St Wendreda
14m/22km E. of Peterborough
OS *TL415952* **GPS** *52.5364N, 0.0850E*

The crowning glory of St Wendreda's is the double hammer-beam roof with a host of angels; the finest in the county. The church is all Decorated and Perpendicular, apart from the chancel by W. Smith, 1872.

ORTON LONGUEVILLE † Holy Trinity
S.W. district of Peterborough
OS *TL168965* **GPS** *52.5540N, 0.2783W*

This is a 13th- and 14th-century church with W. tower built in 1672. In the N. chapel is an early 17th-century funeral helm with vizor and spike; in the N. aisle a fine early 16th-century wall-painting of the upper half of St Christopher.

RAMSEY † St Thomas of Canterbury
10m/16km S.E. of Peterborough
OS *TL290851* **GPS** *52.4491N, 0.1022W*

The church is a monastic relic from the old abbey and was actually built as a hospitum, standing on the fringe of the compact little town. The body of the structure is early 12th-century, and the vaulted chancel late-Norman; the W. tower dates from 1672. The presence of a 13th-century font and re-used materials of that date in the tower suggest parochial use from that time. There is late glass by Morris & Co.

ST NEOTS † St Mary ★
8m/12km S.W. of Huntingdon
OS *TL184601* **GPS** *52.2269N, 0.2670W*

Tucked away on the fringe of this small market community, the church is a luxurious 15th-century building with perhaps the finest tower in the county. The church is faced in ironstone and pebbles with ashlar dressings, an agreeable contrast in colour and texture. The roof is almost flat, not over-elaborate but very English and most satisfying. Almost everything a good town church should be.

SNAILWELL † St Peter
3m/4km N. of Newmarket
OS *TL642675* **GPS** *52.2818N, 0.4059E*

Set against a backdrop of trees, the church has a 12th-century round tower with tall belfry

WHEN THE BLAST OF THE TERRIBLE ONES
IS AS A STORM AGAINST THE WALL
THOUGH THEY CLIMB UP TO HEAVEN
THENCE WILL I BRING THEM DOWN
WHATSOEVER THY HAND FINDETH TO DO
DO IT WITH THY MIGHT
THERE IS NEITHER SPEECH NOR LANGUAGE
BUT THEIR VOICES ARE HEARD AMONG THEM

△ **SWAFFHAM PRIOR: ST MARY** – *two windows in the north aisle commemorate the First and Second World Wars with images and textual messages of resolute strength*

lights. There is a good deal of 14th-century work, a Perpendicular clerestory and a hammer-beam roof.

SOHAM † St Andrew

5ml8km S.E. of Ely
OS *TL593731* **GPS** *52.3335N, 0.3370E*

Celebrated 15th-century tower rising high above the fenland, the top resplendent with flushwork, battlements and pinnacles.

SUTTON † St Andrew

6ml10km W. of Ely
OS *TL448789* **GPS** *52.3897N, 0.1269E*

The tower, with its odd two-stage octagonal lantern, stands majestically on a ridge above the fen. Bishop Barnet of Ely began the rebuilding c. 1370, and there is good Decorated tracery.

SWAFFHAM PRIOR † St Cyriac ★

5ml8km W. of Newmarket
OS *TL568638* **GPS** *52.2509N, 0.2959E*
Churches Conservation Trust

Two churches in one churchyard stand on a little hillock above the village street. Both are large with good towers. St Cyriac has a distinctive late 15th-century octagonal upper stage with flushwork parapet.

SWAFFHAM PRIOR † St Mary ★

5ml8km W. of Newmarket
OS *TL568639* **GPS** *52.2512N, 0.2956E*

St Mary, next to St Cyriac (see previous entry) is 12th-century, partly octagonal and formerly crowned by a stone spire. Entrance is through the W. tower, with views up through the stages.

THORNEY ABBEY
† St Mary and St Botolph

7ml11km N.E. of Peterborough
OS *TF282042* **GPS** *52.6205N, 0.1071W*

Its atmosphere is ascribable in part to fine trees growing in and around the little town. The church is a fragment (five bays of the nave) of the Romanesque abbey, taken over as a parish church in 1638. The E. end was added by Blore in Norman style in 1840–1, and includes an effective window copied from glass in Canterbury Cathedral.

WESTLEY WATERLESS
† St Mary the Less ★
5m/8km S. of Newmarket
OS *TL617562* **GPS** *52.1805N, 0.3650E*

It stands high on the chalk, and has some of the deepest wells in the county. The neat little church has lost its small round tower, and the west gable wall that replaced it was rebuilt in the mid-19th century. It is in an original if somewhat finicky Decorated idiom. There is a good early 14th-century brass to Sir John and Lady de Creke.

WHITTLESEY † St Mary
5m/8km E. of Peterborough
OS *TL269969* **GPS** *52.5557N, 0.1282W*

The church has the best tower and spire in the county; it can be seen for miles around, though it is rather dwarfed by the forest of chimneys to the left as you approach by road from the S. There is a selection of stained glass and a monument to General Sir Harry Smith, d. 1860, by G. C. Adams of London, in the Westminster Abbey tradition. Another monument in the chancel, to Elizabeth Kentish, d. 1792, was designed in Rome by her sorrowing husband, Richard Kentish.

WIMPOLE † St Andrew ★
6m/10km N. of Royston
OS *TL336509* **GPS** *52.1411N, 0.0484W*

A church in the squire's back yard, 14th-century in origin but almost entirely rebuilt by Henry Flitcroft in 1749. It was restored in the Decorated style in 1887. Fine 14th-century heraldic glass is in the N. chapel, and there is a remarkable series of monuments by Scheemakers, Banks, Bacon, Flaxman, Westmacott and others.

WISBECH † St Peter and St Paul ★
12m/19km S.W. of King's Lynn
OS *TF462095* **GPS** *52.6640N, 0.1618E*

With handsome 18th-century and later houses on the 'brinks' fronting the River Nene, Wisbech cuts a dash under favourable conditions. The large town church has three nave arcades and is rather dark within. There is a bit of everything from the 12th century onwards, but the early 16th century provided the free-standing N. bell-tower and the ornate S.E. vestry, perhaps originally a guild chapel. Numerous wall-plaques include one by Joseph Nollekens. The reredos depicting the Last Supper is by Salviati, 1885, to a design by Basset-Smith.

△ **WITTERING: ALL SAINTS** – *sculpted head in the north aisle arcade*

WITTERING † All Saints ★
3m/4km S.E. of Stamford
OS *TF056020* **GPS** *52.6057N, 0.4416W*

This lovely two-celled late Saxon church has a tremendous chancel arch and original nave and chancel quoins. The good Norman nave arcade has roll mouldings and zigzags. There is a late 13th-/early 14th-century W. tower.

YAXLEY † St Peter
4m/6km S. of Peterborough
OS *TL177918* **GPS** *52.5118N, 0.2671W*

There is some agreeable colour in the village, with black-and-white timber cottages thrown against brick and tile. The church, noble and large for the size of the community, has an elegant steeple with flying buttresses crowning an impressive composition. The many components – aisles, transepts and porch – mass together most fittingly. The plan is complex, with an aisled chancel and transepts, all of differing roof levels. Inside, there is a series of fragmented medieval narrative wall-paintings and a good 15th-century East Anglian chancel screen. The E. window, altar and reredos are by Sir Ninian Comper. Outside is a good scattering of carved figures, grotesques and gargoyles.

CHESHIRE

Cheshire is crossed by many whose eyes are on a target beyond. It is on the way to Wales, on the route north and south, and for such travellers Cheshire does little to arrest the unseeing eye. It is flat except at the edges, and the roads are so good and the corners so hideously made safe that the visitor is almost hustled through it. To those, however, who treat Cheshire as an end rather than as a means, the county is surprisingly rewarding.

Elsewhere the county has an almost regular pattern. The background is always richly pastoral, and, from north to south down the centre, chemical works have followed the line of the three salt towns, Northwich, Middlewich and Nantwich. The smaller elements in the pattern are more ancient, and stem from Welsh as well as English settlement: there are few villages, and many scattered farms and hamlets.

The typical medieval parish church, especially in the south and west of the county, served a vast area, often as much as 30 square miles in extent. Malpas, Great Budworth, Bunbury, Acton and Astbury are churches of this kind. It is not surprising, therefore, that there should be so many interesting private chapels and former chapels of ease, nor that some of the ancient parochial churches of the county should be of such splendour.

It is not only, however, for size or interest that some Cheshire churches are remarkable. A great many of them are cleverly sited, using slight eminences to dominate their surroundings, and most of them are built of red sandstone, a stone never much used for houses. The typical 15th-century Cheshire church must have looked fine when its mouldings were sharp and the houses beneath it half-timbered. Now the detail is frayed or replaced, the surrounding black and white is yearly giving way to a modern uniformity, and it is to the untypical church that one is attracted, to Astbury, built of millstone grit, to the brick churches of Tushingham, to the Peovers, to curious Baddiley and freakish Birtles. Here, perhaps, in these untypical Cheshire churches, the county is now typified, a county that only reveals itself to those who leave the fast through roads, and rewards them handsomely.

◁ **ASTBURY: ST MARY** – *the corbel heads lining the nave arcades are thought to represent some of the church's medieval benefactors*

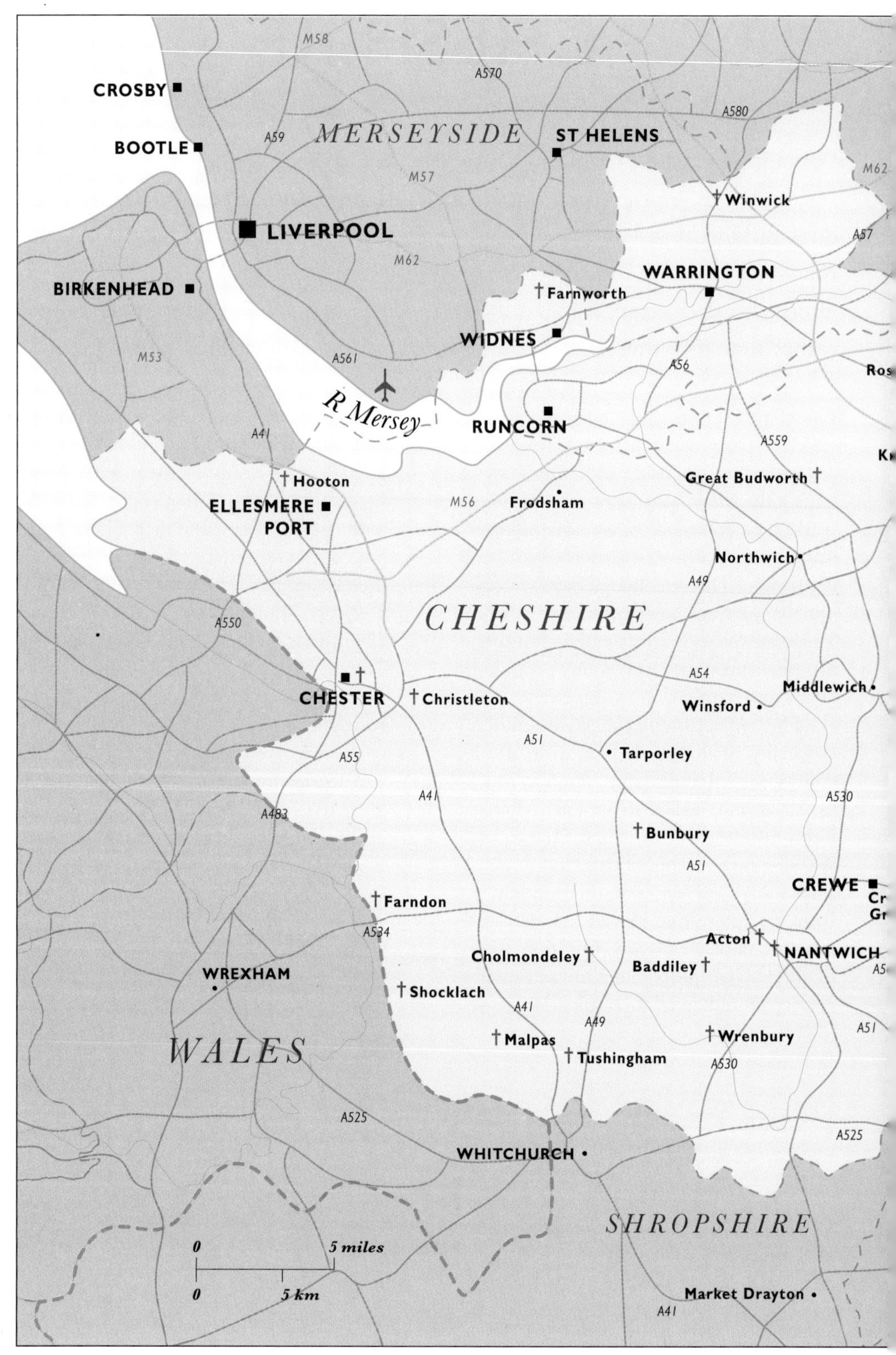
CROSBY
BOOTLE
MERSEYSIDE
ST HELENS
LIVERPOOL
BIRKENHEAD
WARRINGTON
Winwick
Farnworth
WIDNES
R Mersey
RUNCORN
Hooton
ELLESMERE PORT
Frodsham
Great Budworth
Northwich
CHESHIRE
CHESTER
Christleton
Middlewich
Winsford
Tarporley
Bunbury
CREWE
Farndon
Acton
NANTWICH
Cholmondeley
Baddiley
WREXHAM
Shocklach
Malpas
Tushingham
Wrenbury
WALES
WHITCHURCH
SHROPSHIRE
Market Drayton
0 5 miles
0 5 km
M58
A570
A580
A59
M57
M62
A57
M53
A561
A56
A41
A559
M56
A49
A550
A54
A51
A55
A530
A483
A534
A525

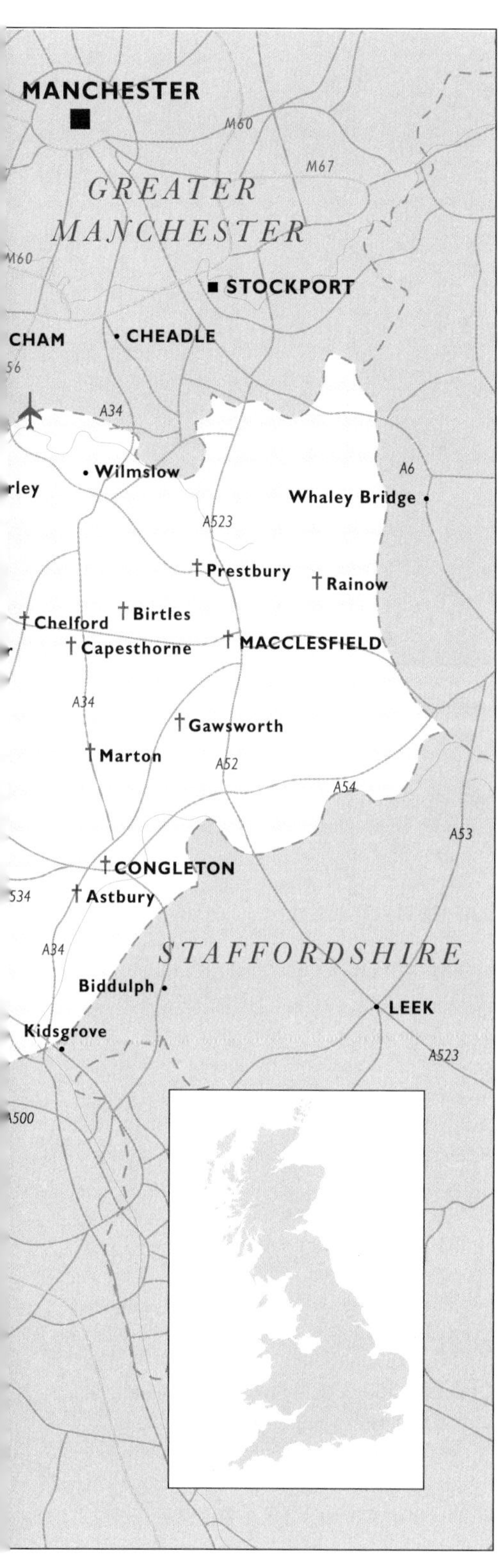

ACTON † St Mary ★

1m/2km W. of Nantwich

OS *SJ631530* **GPS** *53.0737N, 2.5511W*

The great church, mostly of the 13th and 15th centuries, dwarfs its tiny village. The tower, rebuilt in 1757, is an early instance of Gothic Revival. The low screen and other chancel furnishings are partly late 17th-century, although they look older. There is a Norman font, a 15th-century canopied wall-tomb and some fine 17th-century effigies.

ASTBURY † St Mary ★

1m/2km S.W. of Congleton

OS *SJ846615* **GPS** *53.1507N, 2.2314W*

The great battlemented church makes the sloping village green look like a glacis and the lych gate like a barbican. Outside details are sharp and well-preserved because the building stone is millstone grit – rare in Cheshire. The N.W. tower became detached during a c. 13th-century rebuilding of the church, at which time the main body was moved further south. Inside are superb oak roofs, Perpendicular in style, but with inscriptions of 1616 and 1702 to indicate installation or possibly alteration. The N. aisle roof, though – with its overabundance of angels for the space it occupies – was brought from elsewhere and is likely to be 15th- or early 16th-century. There are 15th-century stalls, a screen, wooden eagle lectern, 17th-century altar rails, Royal Arms and a font with mechanical cover. Sir G. G. Scott used a light touch in the 1862 restoration.

BADDILEY † St Michael ★

4m/6km W. of Nantwich

OS *SJ605503* **GPS** *53.0489N, 2.5905W*

By farm lanes in flat country, St Michael's is neither easy to find nor to interpret. The timber-framed chancel dates from 1308 and the brick nave of 1811 has a ceiled roof of 15th-century type. The tympanum is one of the most interesting in England – pre-Reformation in structure, with painted Creed, Commandments and a Coat of Arms dated 1663. It is some 20 feet square and is supported on an eight-foot screen; it divides the lower chancel from the nave with claustrophobic thoroughness. Elsewhere there is a W. gallery, box pews and a pretty pulpit.

△ **ASTBURY: ST MARY** – *the woodwork throughout is exceptional, topped off by magnificent ceilings that are divided into patterns of rectangles by moulded beams with richly carved and gilded bosses*

BIRTLES † St Catherine ★
4m/6km W. of Macclesfield
OS *SJ862747* **GPS** *53.27N, 2.2074W*

A freak brick church of 1840 with octagonal tower in a wooded parkland setting, it was built originally for the squire, Thomas Hibbert, but has been parochial since 1890. The inside is all self-confident vitality and Victorian treasure hunting. There is good 16th- and 17th-century Netherlandish glass and an ornate pulpit of 1686; the family pew and reader's desk are made up of carved pieces and the baptistry is decorated with painted panels.

BUNBURY † St Boniface ★
3m/4km S. of Tarporley
OS *SJ569580* **GPS** *53.1182N, 2.6452W*

A large, well-sited 14th-century collegiate church, with nave arcades and wide aisle windows of about a hundred years later, St Boniface's was well restored after severe war damage. Four of the original doors have survived, and there are also 16th-century oak doors with lattice panels in the stone screen of the chantry chapel. An important early alabaster effigy of Sir Hugh Calveley is in the chancel, and there are many interesting fittings.

CAPESTHORNE † Holy Trinity ★
6m/10km W. of Macclesfield
OS *SJ840727* **GPS** *53.2513N, 2.2411W*

The chapel of a great house, Holy Trinity was designed by William Smith and built in 1722. The drive to the house and chapel sweeps through a park with views over woods and a lake. The chapel itself, of brick with stone dressings, is rectangular, with a balustrade and cupola. The interior is somewhat darkened by injudicious Victorian glass, and there is a mosaic reredos of 1886–8. The pews were arranged college-fashion in 1877, and there is a raised family pew at the W. end, original rails and a good font.

CHELFORD † St John the Evangelist
6m/10km W. of Macclesfield
OS *SJ819739* **GPS** *53.2624N, 2.2727W*

A stone-dressed brick church of 1774–6; the tower was added in 1840. Inside are box pews, a splendid Art Nouveau pulpit, altar rails, choir stalls and mural decorations with sprays of flowers and saints, all by Percy Worthington, 1903, and some stained glass by Morris & Co. The W. Gallery is now a meeting room.

CHESTER † St John the Baptist

St John Street

OS *SJ409661* **GPS** *53.1891N, 2.8856W*

A Victorian exterior hides this dignified Norman cruciform church, with its early 12th-century arcades. There is a painted reredos by Heaton, Butler & Bayne to a John Douglas design, 1876. The church stands adjacent to a Roman amphitheatre and Grosvenor Park.

CHOLMONDELEY † St Nicholas

6m/10km N. of Whitchurch

OS *SJ544516* **GPS** *53.0600N, 2.6809W*

The private chapel of the castle, St Nicholas's is set on a plateau in park – cruciform and built of brick and stone. The nave and walls encasing an older structure have been attributed to Vanbrugh, but in fact they were built by Fetherston in 1716, with transepts added in 1829. The hammerbeam roof is medieval, and the rails, screen and other furniture 17th-century. The Family Pew or State Gallery has cushions fashioned from robes worn at the coronation of William IV.

CHRISTLETON † St James

Suburb, 3m/4km E. of Chester

OS *SJ440657* **GPS** *53.1856N, 2.8383W*

In a rich, pretty village is W. Butterfield's only complete Cheshire church, 1875–7. The late 15th-century tower was retained at Butterfield's own request: 'This country is an old country, but if we don't take care it will soon be as new a one as America… You had better keep the old tower and so look a little different to the modern new churches which are generally so noisy and pretentious.' What giants those Victorians were! His new church honours its site with warm red and white polychromy and excellent fittings.

CONGLETON † St Peter ★

Chapel Street, 11m/18km N. of Stoke-on-Trent

OS *SJ859627* **GPS** *53.1618N, 2.2115W*

This is an unspoilt town church of 1740–2, whose Gothic tower was added in 1786. The lower part of the 14th-century tower was retained during the 1786 Gothic tower restoration. It is plain outside and most pleasing within: galleries on three sides, supported on piers with columns above. There are fine box pews throughout, those in the galleries steeply tiered, a William III Arms, a particularly good brass candelabrum of 1748 and interesting 18th-century glass. The font is original, as are the altar rails.

CREWE GREEN
† St Michael and All Angels

2m/3km E. of Crewe

OS *SJ726553* **GPS** *53.0947N, 2.4092W*

By Sir George Gilbert Scott, 1857–9, the church stands in one of Crewe Hall's modest hamlets, a colourful church of red and blue brick, stone shafts and a steeply tiled roof. The interior with apsed chancel is polychromatic, with lots of good carving and excellent glass.

ELLESMERE PORT – HOOTON
† St Paul ★

Near Hooton, 3m/4km N.W. of Ellesmere Port

OS *SJ367774* **GPS** *53.2906N, 2.9509W*

By James K. Colling, 1858–62, and formerly part of the Hooton Hall estate, now on the fringes of Ellesmere Port, this is a prodigious Romanesque church of red and white ashlar with octagonal crossing tower. Many of the details are French and Italian, including the Lombardic frieze across the W. front. Inside are granite arcades and, over the crossing, an astounding ashlar dome. Rich fittings include good stained glass and the serpentine font, which won a medal at the Great Exhibition.

FARNDON † St Chad

6m/10km N.E. of Wrexham

OS *SJ413544* **GPS** *53.0841N, 2.8775W*

The church, set in a big riverside village, was badly damaged in the Civil War and was rebuilt, apart from the 14th-century W. tower. The remarkable 17th-century E. window depicts prominent local Royalists, pikemen and trophies of war.

△ **LOWER PEOVER: ST OSWALD** – *the c. 14th-century bog oak chest in the south aisle was hewn from a single, solid piece of timber, pulled up from a peat bog in a partly fossilized state*

FARNWORTH † St Luke

1m/2km N. of Widnes
OS *SJ517877* **GPS** *53.3844N, 2.7275W*

This is a village setting for a red sandstone church with work of all periods. There are good Tudor wooden ceilings in the chancel and S. transept, and the Bold Chapel, rebuilt in 1855, has good monuments, including one to Peter Patten Bold by Chantrey, 1822.

GAWSWORTH † St James ★

3m/4km S.W. of Macclesfield
OS *SJ890696* **GPS** *53.2241N, 2.1661W*

The Perpendicular church adjoins the garden earthworks of the Elizabethan Hall. The 17th-century monuments to members of the Fitton family, with life-like grouped effigies, are outstanding. The nave roof is panelled oak.

GREAT BUDWORTH † St Mary and All Saints ★

2m/3km N. of Northwich
OS *SJ664775* **GPS** *53.2936N, 2.5043W*

An imposing village church standing on a hill, St Mary and All Saints is a 14th- and 15th-century structure, of good proportions and very light inside. The 16th-century oak crown-post and wagon roofs are impressive; there are some 13th-century benches, and a medieval stone altar in the S. chapel.

LOWER PEOVER † St Oswald ★

6m/10km E. of Northwich
OS *SJ743741* **GPS** *53.2639N, 2.3864W*

The churchyard forms the green of a very pretty hamlet, with inn and school, at the end of a cobbled lane. Although tidied up by Anthony Salvin in 1852, it is still one of the finest examples in the county of a half-timbered church of c. 1370. The tower attached to it is 16th-century Perpendicular. The effect inside is of dark oak and whitewash. Very good 17th-century furnishings include box pews, some with the lower halves of the doors fixed to retain the rushes. Marquetry panels decorate a fine 17th-century pulpit.

△ **LOWER PEOVER: ST OSWALD** – *the interior woodwork is a mix of ages, with a c. mid-14th-century nave arcade at its core and very well carved 17th-century pulpit, box pews and screen*

MACCLESFIELD
† St Michael and All Angels
Church Street
OS *SJ917737* **GPS** *53.2603N, 2.1244W*

Late 13th-century, but largely rebuilt by Sir A. Blomfield in 1898–1901; the church has a sumptuous early 16th-century three-storeyed S. porch, but is chiefly noted for an array of 15th–17th-century monuments, including one by William Stanton, 1696.

MALPAS † St Oswald ★
8m/12km E. of Wrexham
OS *SJ486471* **GPS** *53.0195N, 2.7670W*

The large handsome church, mainly late 15th-century, stands by a motte at the highest point in the village. It is spacious, light and well-proportioned, with a magnificent angel roof. The splendid interior contains a superb 13th-century iron-bound chest, misericords and box pews. The Cholmondeley and Brereton family chapels are separated from the nave by fine Perpendicular screens, and contain contrasting pre- and post-Reformation monuments from 1552 and 1605.

MARTON † St James and St Paul
3m/4km N. of Congleton
OS *SJ850679* **GPS** *53.2088N, 2.2257W*

Black and white, built c. 1370, this is the most complete timber-framed church in Cheshire. The tower lobby has massive posts, and the nave and aisles are under one roof. There are traces of a 14th-century Doom.

MOBBERLEY † St Wilfrid ★
2m/3km E. of Knutsford
OS *SJ790801* **GPS** *53.3182N, 2.3162W*

A green village setting with inn and cottages; the design is a typical late medieval one for E. Cheshire; the aisle walls have small three-light square-headed windows. There is a magnificent rood screen of 1550 bearing carved Coats of Arms, and on the screen pillars can be seen a carved Green Man. The roof is fine, with 15th-century carving on the king-posts, and there is 14th-century glass, now on the S. side of the chancel.

LOWER PEOVER: ST OSWALD – *the church was re-roofed in 1852 and the exterior timberwork made more decorative* ▷

IN
MEMORY OF

△ **MOBBERLEY: ST WILFRID** – *the 13th-century church was aggrandized in the 15th and 16th centuries, when first the clerestory was added and then the sturdy, Perpendicular tower*

NANTWICH † St Mary ★

Between Hospital Street and Monks Lane
4m/6km S.W. of Crewe
OS *SJ652523* **GPS** *53.0670N, 2.5206W*

A beautifully set large cruciform church built, like so many Cheshire churches, of soft red sandstone which weathers badly. The exterior is impressive, however, despite extensive restoration by George Gilbert Scott, with a striking pinnacled octagonal tower at the crossing. The vaulted interior is rare in Cheshire, with a superb chancel containing carved and gorgeously canopied late 14th-century choir-stalls with misericords.

OVER PEOVER † St Lawrence ★

In grounds of Peover Hall,
6m/10km E. of Northwich
OS *SJ772735* **GPS** *53.2582N, 2.3431W*

In a park, near splendid 17th-century stables and backed by the Tudor hall. The oldest elements of the church are the two chapels: the S. chapel is mid-15th-century, the ashlar N. chapel mid-17th. The N. chapel in particular is outstanding and the earliest true Classical work in the county. The nave was rebuilt in brick, with a pleasantly pitched roof, in 1811. The W. tower – red brick with stone quoins and dated to 1741 – was retained. Rich furnishings and excellent tombs with effigies create a delightful, haunting atmosphere.

PRESTBURY † St Peter

2m/3km N.W. of Macclesfield
OS *SJ900769* **GPS** *53.2893N, 2.1505W*

The church, by the pretty village street, looks 15th-century, but has 13th-century nave arcades. There are oak roofs, a Jacobean pulpit and, in the spandrels of the arcades, dainty paintings of the Apostles, dated 1719. In the churchyard is a small Norman chapel rebuilt in 1747 and restored in 1953.

RAINOW † Jenkin Chapel (St John) ★

Near Saltersford Hall, 2m/3km E. of Rainow;
3m/4km N.E. of Macclesfield
OS *SJ983765* **GPS** *53.2863N, 2.0257W*

This remote mountain chapel built in 1733 looks like a converted farmhouse; a low tower was added to the gable end in 1755. The roof is of heavy Kerridge slabs, the windows are square, sash and domestic, and there is a chimney stack halfway along the S. wall. The gallery, box pews and fittings are intact.

ROSTHERNE † St Mary

2m/3km S.W. of Altrincham

OS *SJ742836* **GPS** *53.3495N, 2.3880W*

In a large churchyard beautifully set between village and mere, the church is mainly Perpendicular outside, with a handsome Georgian tower of 1742–4. The chief delights here are the monuments: a 13th-century knight, a spirited wall monument to Samuel Egerton, dated 1792, by Bacon, and an affecting sculpture by Richard Westmacott Jnr of local woman Charlotte Lucy Beatrix Egerton, who drowned in Rostherne Mere on the eve of her wedding in 1845; an angel kneels over her recumbent figure.

SHOCKLACH † St Edith

6m/10km E. of Wrexham

OS *SJ431501* **GPS** *53.0459N, 2.8490W*

This is a small rustic church in the fields, with a double bellcote on the W. wall. The Norman S. doorway is crudely decorated with zigzags and lozenges. The church dates from at least the mid-12th century, but is perhaps Saxon in origin. The chancel was added in the 14th century. Inside are good, plain fittings and a pleasing 18th-century nave ceiling with rosettes; scratched on a pane of glass originally in the E. window, 'I, Robert Aldersey was here on 1st day of October 1756 along with John Massie and Mr Derbyshire. The roads were so bad we were in danger of our lives.'

TUSHINGHAM

† Old St Chad Chapel of Ease

4m/6km N. of Whitchurch

OS *SJ527462* **GPS** *53.0117N, 2.7057W*

Along a field path, half a mile E. of the Victorian church and parsonage which replaced it, the brick chapel of 1689–91 stands in a numinous oval enclosure. The superb interior has many things fashioned from Cheshire oak, including the W. Vaudrey gallery, decorated roof trusses, chancel screen, panelled pulpit, altar table with high-backed family pew to either side, and even an oak font!

WINWICK † St Oswald

3m/4km N. of Warrington

OS *SJ603928* **GPS** *53.4308N, 2.5978W*

St Oswald's is mostly 14th-century, with a buttressed tower and large spire, and has richly panelled 16th-century roofs in the nave and S. chapel. The celebrated chancel is in the Decorated style, added by A. W. N. Pugin in 1847–8, with richly decorated barrel-vaulted ceiling and sedilia. Ornate iron screens separate the E. end chapels from the nave. In the Legh Chapel are good 16th–19th-century monuments, and part of a Saxon cross is in the Gerard Chapel. The enigmatic Winwick Pig, carved on the exterior of the tower next to a niche, is perhaps an emblem of St Anthony.

WRENBURY † St Margaret ★

5m/8km S.W. of Nantwich

OS *SJ593477* **GPS** *53.0257N, 2.6073W*

St Margaret's is an early 16th-century Perpendicular church that overlooks a village green, its tower, nave and aisles all conspicuously battlemented. The interior is pleasing, and must have been very fine indeed before the renovations of the 1920s and 30s. The pink masonry looks, however, less scraped than is usual when the plaster is removed, and the box pews, though lowered, are of a good colour. There are crests on pew doors, hatchments, some signed monuments and a W. gallery.

THEY THAT GO DOWN TO THE SEA IN SHIPS
THESE MEN SEE THE WORKS OF THE LORD

CORNWALL

Cornwall is a Duchy, separated from England by the picturesque Tamar Valley, and has more sea coast than anywhere else in Britain. The prevailing building materials are slate and granite. The granite bursts up through the slate and forms Bodmin Moor, which is mostly desolate except for prehistoric remains and the beehive cells of Celtic Christians. A district of half-granite and half-great white pyramids of decomposed granite, known as China clay, is near St Austell. Moorland covers the far western granite promontory between St Ives and Land's End. The Scilly Isles, where the churches are small, simple and comparatively new, are the nearly submerged tops of granite hills, between which and Land's End was the lost territory of the Lyonesse.

The rest of the county is slate, varying from bluish silver to deep green. The peninsula of the Lizard is made of coloured rocks called Serpentine. Tin mines have brought 19th-century industrial scenery, with its chapels and streets, to the districts around Camborne and Redruth. Visitors of our own generation have pocked the tremendous coast with bungalows, but they have also preserved the humble slate-grey fishing ports because of their picturesque qualities. The two most attractive inland towns in Cornwall are Launceston, a border fortress to which have been added Georgian houses, and Truro, where Pearson's noble Victorian cathedral rises in the French manner out of the old houses and shops. Truro has its Georgian streets and so have Helston, Penzance and Falmouth. Calstock, on the border with Devon, is the least-known and most uninterruptedly Cornish town. The Duchy becomes its native self in winter, and that is the time to see it.

Inland, Cornwall is mercifully considered dull. The wooded valleys like those of the Allen, Camel, Inny, Fowey and Lynher, with their steep slopes of thin Cornish elms, carpeted underneath with spring anemones, their slate-hung houses, whose gardens in summer are bright with hydrangea, veronica and fuchsia, are remotest and loveliest Cornwall. The coast is awe-inspiring. Rocks fall sheer into the peacock-blue Atlantic and English Channel, and rock pools are full of many-coloured seaweeds and marine life.

Before Southern England was Christian, Cornwall had been visited by Celtic missionaries from Wales and Ireland. Their names survive as those of saints, though little is known about many of them. The Cornish are the same sort of Celts as the Welsh and Bretons, but the Celtic field system makes the Duchy look different from England. The Celtic saints were hermits who lived in beehive cells and are said to have recited the Psalms

◁ **ST IVES: ST IA** – *one of four similarly styled angels in the roof of the church's north aisle*

waist-deep in cold streams. The crosses of their age survive, and so does the siting of their churches, for the parochial system came late to Cornwall, and the church on the site of a Celtic hermit's cell is often remote from the chief village in the parish. It is in the larger villages that one finds the chapels of Methodism, which has made as deep an impression on Cornwall as it has on Wales.

The old Cornish churches are rugged and windswept, and their charm is in their storm-resisting construction and their lichen-crusted texture. The Cornish historian T. S. Attlee (who contributed to an earlier edition of this book) thought that the rather unenterprising nature of Cornish churches, which were nearly all rebuilt or added to on the same pattern in the 15th century, was for two main reasons. The first reason was that the local stone was hard to work. Cornwall is deficient in lime and so the mason used mud, and walls had therefore to be kept low. Roofs had to be barrel-vaulted so as to distribute their weight evenly along the walls. This sort of roof suited a boat-building people and their tools – the adze and spokeshave. Hence Cornishmen never reached realization of wall and window, voids and solids, as a composition. They stuck at the stage of regarding them as an aggregate of lumps with holes left in it, as did their Celtic forebears. The second reason was that most Cornishmen made their living from the sea, so they saw no pattern in town and village, as for instance did sheep and wool masters who lived off the surface of the land. So the true village church can only be found far inland, as at Altarnun, Blisland, St Neot and Bodmin.

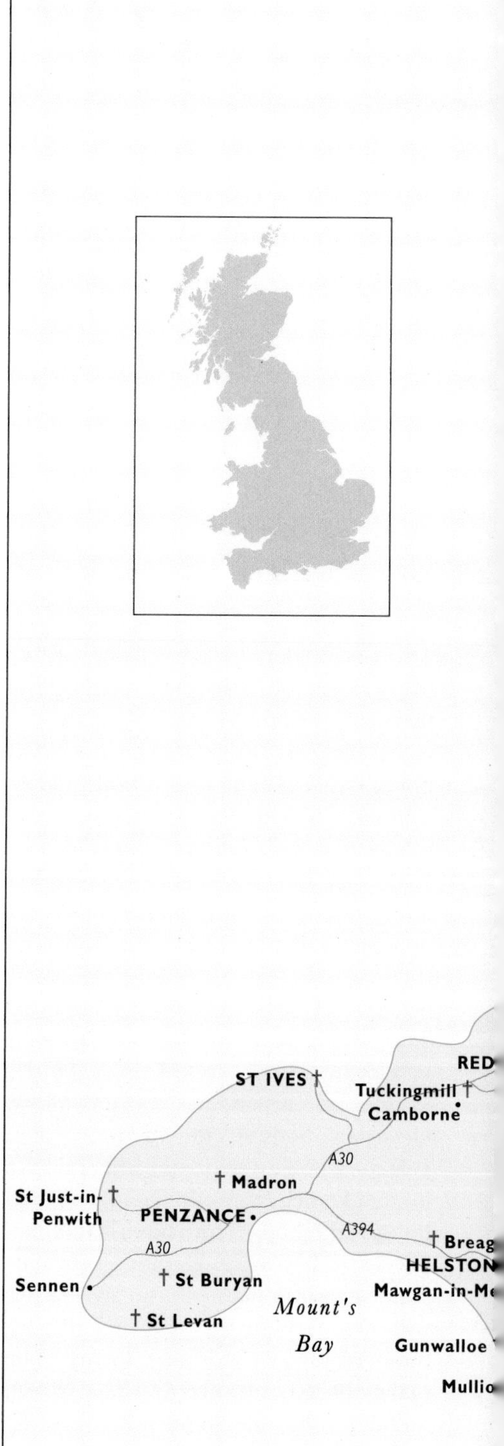

A39
Morwenstow
Kilkhampton
DEVON
BUDE
Launcells
Bude Bay
Holsworthy
A3072
A388
A3079
CORNWALL
A39
A30
Tintagel
A395
LAUNCESTON
Laneast
Camelford
Port Isaac
Altarnun
A388
A386
St Endellion
Trebetherick
St Minver
A30
PADSTOW
Bodmin
Linkinhorne
Wadebridge
Blisland
Moor
TAVISTOCK
A389
A390
A39
A389
Calstock
St Neot
BODMIN
A388
A386
Mawgan-in-Pydar
A38
LISKEARD
St Columb Major
Landulph
EWQUAY
A390
A30
A38
Lostwithiel
Lanlivery
Saltash
St Winnow
St Germans
A391
PLYMOUTH
Golant
Torpoint
Looe
Par
ST AUSTELL
Fowey
Lanteglos-by-Fowey
A39
A390
Probus
TRURO
St Clement
A3078
Dodman Point
St Just-in-Roseland
St Mawes
St Anthony-in-Roseland
TH
0
10 miles
0
10 km
everne

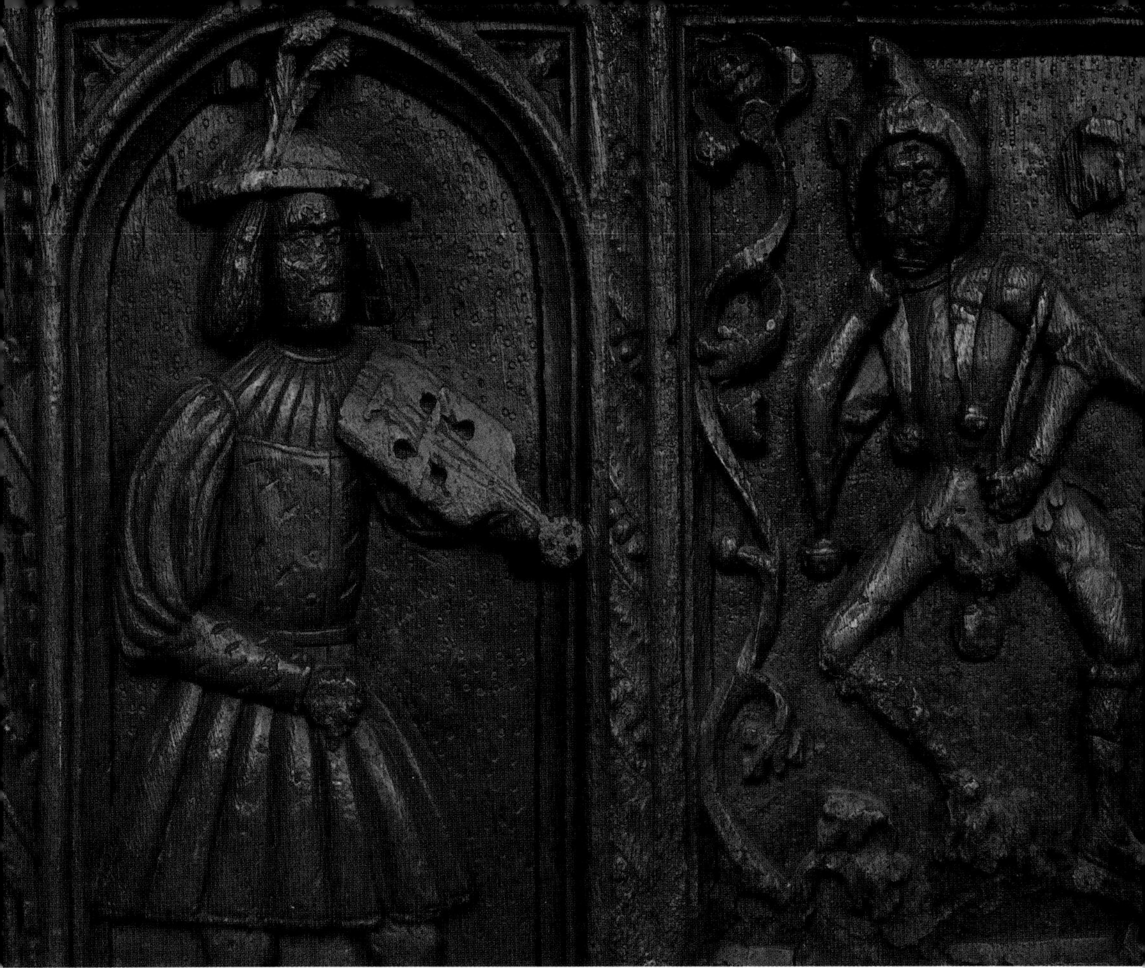

△ **ALTARNUN: ST NONNA** – *two of the richly carved and highly characterful bench-ends; the one on the left shows a musician with a viola-like instrument, the one on the right portrays a jester*

ALTARNUN † St Nonna ★

7m/11km W. of Launceston
OS *SX222813* **GPS** *50.6046N, 4.5129W*

Large, cathedral-like 15th-century church with lofty tower, it contains a fine display of 16th-century bench-ends by a known carver, Robert Daye. There is a huge Norman font of local type, 17th-century Communion rails extending across chancel and aisles, and a noble rood screen. Early 17th-century panels on the E. wall depict the Holy Communion and the Crucifixion.

BLISLAND † St Protus and St Hyacinth

4m/6km N.E. of Bodmin
OS *SX100731* **GPS** *50.5270N, 4.6815W*

The village of old granite and slate houses has a green with ash trees on it. The church, with a 15th-century tower made of enormous blocks of local moorland granite, looks out over a steep wooded valley. It has two transepts, a S. aisle and two chancel chapels. The old carved wagon roofs remain throughout, and the nave floor is of slate; the walls are white; a few old carved bench-ends survive; otherwise there are chairs. The Georgian wine-glass pulpit was restored by F. C. Eden, and virtually all the amazingly rich screen with loft which extends the whole width of the church, a blaze of red and gold and green and white, with a rood over its centre, is his. The screen gives to this weather-beaten village building, with its 15th-century S. arcade of granite sloping this way and that, an unforgettable sense of joy and mystery. Through the delicate tracery of the screen may be glimpsed splendid altars by Sir Ninian Comper and harmonious windows by F. C. Eden. As a restoration and even improvement on a medieval church, this holy and peaceful place on the edge of Bodmin Moor can hardly be bettered in the kingdom.

△ **BLISLAND: ST PROTUS AND ST HYACINTH** – *the interior is a mix of the highly decorative and the rustic, the panels of the wagon roofs reminiscent of fishing nets stretching over the nave*

BODMIN † St Petroc

26m/42km W. of Plymouth

OS *SX073670* **GPS** *50.4714N, 4.7167W*

The largest parish church in Cornwall, the lower part of the tower is Norman; otherwise the structure is mainly late medieval. Though the interior was much refurbished in Victorian times, it retains its old wagon roofs and a grand Norman font of local type, with severe-looking angels at the corners. Note the splendid table-tomb in black Catacleuse stone of Thomas Vyvyan, 1533, Prior of Bodmin and titular Bishop of Megara, a delightful blend of Gothic and Renaissance decoration.

BREAG † St Breaca

3m/4km W. of Helston

OS *SW618284* **GPS** *50.1084N, 5.3320W*

A fine 15th-century granite church, with buttressed W. tower carved with gargoyles. Medieval wall-paintings portray saints Ambrose, Christopher, Corentine and Hilary, and there is a Warning to Sabbath Breakers. A 3rd-century Roman milestone is preserved within the church, and in the churchyard is a badly weathered Saxon cross head.

CHACEWATER † St Paul

4m/6km N.E. of Redruth

OS *SW750440* **GPS** *50.2538N, 5.1565W*

A church was built here in 1828, repaired in 1886, greatly damaged by lightning in that same year, and entirely rebuilt (except the tower) by Edmund Sedding in 1892. The church is a few yards S. of the main Truro–Redruth road on a steep knoll. The tower, a gaunt shaft, bare of windows except in the uppermost of four lightly indicated stages, is impressive. Inside, the church is remarkable for the colour of the unplastered walls of local stone, buff, grey, yellow and brown setting off effectively the shallow seawater-green of

the octagonal shafts of Polyphant stone and granite arches. The nave has a wagon roof, 43 feet high, the aisles lean-to roofs. An arched recess in the E. wall provides a bent eyebrow to the five-light E. window, whose bright stained glass comes from St Mary's, Truro. There are lancets in the clerestory and square-headed windows in the aisle walls which have shallow recesses inside and corresponding projections without. A satisfying sense that Sedding here knew what effect he wanted to get; and got it.

FOWEY † St Fimbarrus
8m/12km E. of St Austell
OS *SX125517* **GPS** *50.3354N, 4.6357W*

Built in the mid-14th century, it was greatly altered and enlarged in the 15th, when the clerestory was added – a rarity in Cornwall. The tower is the second tallest in the county. Inside is a wonderfully carved 15th-century wagon roof, an unfinished Norman font, a pulpit fashioned of wood salvaged from a Spanish galleon, and 17th-century Rashleigh monuments.

GOLANT † St Sampson ★
2m/3km N. of Fowey
OS *SX120551* **GPS** *50.3663N, 4.6440W*

This snug little church, consecrated in 1509, occupies an airy situation on height above the Fowey River; trim, stiff box pews, extremely uncomfortable, recall the fidgets of Gus and Flora in Henry Kingsley's 1861 novel, *Ravenshoe*. There are three-sided altar rails and fragments of 16th-century glass.

GUNWALLOE † St Winwaloe ★
3m/4km S. of Helston
OS *SW660205* **GPS** *50.0390N, 5.2690W*

Romantically sited alone near the sea, with a detached tower built into the rock; St Winwaloe is 14th- and 15th-century and typical of the area. By the N. and S. doors are the remains of a screen with attractive tracery and figure-painting of eight Apostles depicted in a Moorish style (restored in 1977). The screen is said to have been made from wreckage wood of 'The St Anthony of Lisbon (or Padua)', which sunk off the coast in 1526 while en route from Flanders to Portugal. St Winwaloe is a gently restored, unforgettable place.

KILKHAMPTON † St James the Great
4m/6km N.E. of Bude
OS *SS252113* **GPS** *50.8751N, 4.4851W*

A large church in the village centre, it was mostly rebuilt in the 16th century, but retaining an elaborate Norman doorway. Lofty arcades of seven bays with tall granite monolithic columns; rich wagon roofs and the largest collection of carved bench-ends in Cornwall. The organ is by Father Smith, the nucleus of which is thought to have come from Westminster Abbey. The Grenvilles were responsible for the 16th-century restoration, and in the Grenville Chapel is a particularly grandiose monument to Sir Bevil Grenville.

LANDULPH † St Leonard & St Dilpe
3m/4km N. of Saltash
OS *SX431615* **GPS** *50.4324N, 4.2104W*

In a sylvan setting on the River Tamar between two inlets, the church has a well-carved rood screen, bench-ends, manorial pew of the Lower family, and monument to Theodore Palaeologus, descendant of the last Christian emperor of Greece. Plaster walls and slate floors remain.

LANEAST † St Sidwell & St Gulvat
7m/11km W. of Launceston
OS *SX227839* **GPS** *50.6286N, 4.5069W*

Laneast should be visited first among Cornish churches, as it gets one's eye in for the general run of them. Originally 12th-century cruciform, the fabric was enlarged and refashioned in the 15th century. Set in a secluded nook not far from the Polyphant quarry, the church exhibits the standard Cornish arrangement at its best: four centered arches of arcade with a wagon roof. The pulpit has earlier 15th-century carved panels, and the bench-ends are mutilated. There are extensive if fragmented remains of 15th-century painted glass. In spring the surrounding churchyard is a mass of wild daffodils.

LANLIVERY † St Brevita
2m/3km W. of Lostwithiel
OS *SX079590* **GPS** *50.3999, 4.7031W*

Standing high with a lofty granite tower overlooking the Fowey Valley as it widens towards the estuary, and in spite of considerable

◁ **GUNWALLOE: ST WINWALOE** – *tucked in among the dunes, the church appears to have been washed in with the tide; it houses an intriguing screen (above left), Byzantine in style*

renewal, this is one of the great churches of Cornwall. As usual, a cruciform fabric was refashioned in the 15th century, when an aisle replaced the S. transept. The masonry is granite ashlar masonry, there is an unspoilt wagon roof in the S. aisle, and a ringers' rhyme board in the tower.

LANTEGLOS-BY-FOWEY † St Wyllow ★

1m/2km E. of Fowey
OS *SX144515* **GPS** *50.3344N, 4.6083W*

St Wyllow is difficult of access, both by the ferry across the Fowey River and the narrow, winding and precipitous lanes from Lostwithiel. It is a 14th-century church, refashioned in the 15th century. The font is 13th century, and there are early 16th-century bench-ends, and a 15th-century altar tomb with brass. The church is remarkable for the very effective arrangement at the W. end where the N. and S. aisles are prolonged to embrace the tower, to which they give arched access. Edmund Sedding gave a graphic description of the condition of the church before he undertook its restoration in 1909, and it remains an outstanding example of careful and conservative repair – the dilapidated roof with decay arrested, the leaning walls stabilized in the act. The panelling from family pews, removed from the E. end of the church and erected at the W., is interesting and unusual.

LAUNCELLS † St Swithin ★★

2m/3km E. of Bude
OS *SS243057* **GPS** *50.8243N, 4.4947W*

In a wooded valley, this is the only Cornish church wholly undisturbed by Victorian 'restoration'. Outside it is like other churches in the district, but the interior comes as a welcome surprise; old plaster on the walls, ancient roofs intact; the finest bench-ends in Cornwall; box pews, pulpit in Strawberry Hill Gothic, three-sided altar rails, reredos and organ case; granite and Polyphant arcades; Norman font with 17th-century cover.

LAUNCESTON † St Mary Magdalene

20m/32km N.W. of Plymouth
OS *SX332846* **GPS** *50.6378N, 4.3601W*

The church was erected by Sir Henry Trecarrel in the early 16th century; the tower is older. It is chiefly remarkable for a profusion of carved ornament on its exterior – painstaking work in inappropriate material, because granite, with its coarse and conglomerate structure, does not allow precision in delineation. A recumbent figure of St Mary Magdalene in a niche under the E. window may be seen to be covered with pebbles thrown up by the local people. The vicar says that the old custom is to stand with your back to the figure and try to throw a stone so that it will land on the back of the recumbent figure. This is supposed to bring you good luck for the rest of the week. The scraped interior has an early 16th-century pulpit, easily the best in Cornwall; elsewhere are 17th- and 18th-century monuments, carved with Royal Arms, and the organ case is early 18th-century.

LINKINHORNE † St Melor

8m/13km S. of Launceston
OS *SX319735* **GPS** *50.5376N, 4.3728W*

The noble 16th-century granite tower of this spacious church, set in a remote village, is one of the highest in Cornwall. Inside the church are wagon roofs (that of the nave with some original colour), a large wall-painting of the Works of Mercy, mural monuments of 1688 and 1735, and memorial slate slabs of local type. A holy well in late medieval granite structure can be found in a nearby field to the southwest of the church.

LOSTWITHIEL † St Bartholomew ★

5m/8km S.E. of Bodmin
OS *SX104597* **GPS** *50.4074N, 4.6691W*

Both the tower and the body of the church are different in character from the usual Cornish type. The tower and lantern spire – of Breton influence – make a most satisfying composition when viewed from the S.W. There are short, stout buttresses to the lowest stage; narrow lancets in the next; little louvred openings just below the transition by bold set-offs from the square to the octagon; and, at

LAUNCESTON: ST MARY MAGDALENE – *rugged Cornish granite, carved in a rustic, no-nonsense style* ▷

△ **LAUNCELLS: ST SWITHUN** – *thankfully overlooked by the restoring eye of Victorians*

the junction of tower and spire, eight traceried, gabled, unglazed window-like features, which successfully carry the vertical lines of the tower into the pyramid of the spire. Inside the church, the arcade on piers without capitals lacks emphasis, and the little irregularly spaced clerestory windows are insignificant. But the great five-light E. window is fine. (Some historians consider the church French, both in style and in stone employed.) The c. 13th-century Pentewan font is outstanding.

MADRON † St Maddern

2m/3km N.W. of Penzance
OS *SW453318* **GPS** *50.1316N, 5.5647W*

The mother church of Penzance looks at its best in hydrangea time, when it stands amid a blaze of colour looking towards St Michael's Mount. Though now mainly late medieval, its core is far older; on the whole it has fared better than many of its neighbours, and the interior is quite atmospheric. Wagon roofs; a rood screen richly carved with 16th-century base and modern upper part; carved bench-ends; a coloured alabaster panel from a reredos; early 17th-century brass and 18th-century altar rails.

MAWGAN-IN-MENEAGE

† St Mawgan ★
3m/4km S.E. of Helston
OS *SW709250* **GPS** *50.0817N, 5.2029W*

A glorious situation above colour-washed cottages on the slope of a beech-covered vale; the church is of granite, 13th–15th-century with a three-stage tower topped with fine finials; a good wagon roof covers the nave. The recumbent crusader effigy in the S. transept is a member of the Carminow family. Also in the S. transept is a hagioscope. Other monuments include those to the Vyvyan family.

MAWGAN-IN-PYDAR

† St Mawgan and St Nicholas
4m/7km N.E. of Newquay
OS *SW872659* **GPS** *50.4547N, 4.9987W*

This mainly Perpendicular church stands in a picture book setting on a slope running down to the River Menalhyl. The embattled tower with stair turret stands to the S., adjoining a broad S. aisle that runs the full length of the church. The carved screen separating the S. aisle and nave from the chancel bears the Arms of Arundel quartering those of Carminow. Set in the chancel floor is a brass effigy of a vested priest, and at the E. end of the S. aisle are brasses depicting George Arundel and his wife Elizabeth. In the churchyard, mounted on a stout base, stands a lantern cross, whose square head contains bold carvings of the Annunciation and the Crucifixion. Behind is a memorial in the shape of a boat's stern to 11 seamen "who were drifted ashore in a boat frozen to death, at Beacon Cove". Butterfield restored the church well in 1861–2.

MORWENSTOW

† St Morwenna and St John the Baptist

6m/10km N. of Bude

OS *SS205153* **GPS** *50.9093N, 4.5545W*

Near cliffs high above the sea: the poet R. S. Hawker was vicar here from 1834 to 1875. The N. arcade is Norman, with crude but strong carvings of heads, both men's and animals'; the S. porch and doorway are also Norman, and interestingly carved. The walls are scraped. The arcade arches bear carved spandrels including an antelope, a monk and a hippopotamus. The carved and painted rood screen was re-assembled by Hawker from fragments of 16th- and 17th-century carving and given cast-iron tracery. A short walk takes one to Hawker's driftwood hut, where he spent time with Charles Kingsley and Alfred Lord Tennyson.

MULLION † St Mellanus ★

5m/8km S. of Helston

OS *SW678192* **GPS** *50.0276N, 5.2421W*

Set on a windy hill above the cove, long and low in the Cornish manner, this is a mainly late medieval church. The inside was restored and adorned by F. C. Eden, who designed the screen and loft, S. aisle, glass and altars. There are wagon roofs and many old bench-ends.

MYLOR † St Mylor ★

2m/3km N. of Falmouth

OS *SW820352* **GPS** *50.1770N, 5.0542W*

Delightfully set just above a creek, St Mylor is Norman in origin and refashioned later; it was 'restored' by Victorians. There is a 16th-century carved screen and pulpit. The best that happened during the Victorian restoration was the discovery of a 17-foot Celtic cross, in use at the time as a make-shift flying buttress. The churchyard is full of seafarers, and in a separate area, a graveyard for men and boys from the training ship HMS Ganges, moored nearby for 30 years, and a byword for harshness.

PAR † St Mary the Virgin

By St Blazey Gate, Biscovey

4m/6km E. of St Austell

OS *SX058535* **GPS** *50.3502N, 4.7309W*

This is G. E. Street's first church, 1848–9, when he was just 24, and among his most successful. Early English predominates in a dramatic square tower with broached octagonal belfry and stone spire, perhaps inspired by Lostwithiel, which early called forth Street's admiration. Simple materials and the starkest lancet style give this church a freshness all its own. Inside there are vistas, depth and mystery, and delightful Wailes glass.

PROBUS † St Probus & St Grace ★

5m/8km N.E. of Truro

OS *SW899477* **GPS** *50.2920N, 4.9510W*

The magnificent early 16th-century tower is the tallest in the Duchy; Somerset rather than Cornish in character. Emphatically moulded at the base, its soaring lines have a firm foundation. Lavishly ornamented on granite, there is enough plain surface to escape any impression of over-elaboration. The interior, though without clerestory, is more lofty than most. The arcades between nave and aisles are composed of slender and graceful piers, delicately moulded between shafts and crowned with chaplet capitals. The three great E. windows are impressive, and, on turning to the W., one is delighted by the lofty arch into the tower and the vision of the tall window through it: there is an early 16th-century brass and mural monument to Thomas Hawkins, 1766.

ST ANTHONY-IN-ROSELAND

† St Anthony

On the opposite side of the R. Percuil estuary from St Mawes

OS *SW854320* **GPS** *50.1495N, 5.0040W*

Churches Conservation Trust

St Anthony's stands behind Place House, home to generations of the Spry family, tucked down below the headland in a wooded cave, looking across the creek to St Mawes.

△ **ST BURYAN: ST BURIANA** – *the rood beam is a riot of wild animals and imaginary beasts*

Despite an extensive 19th-century restoration, the church has retained its original medieval cruciform form. Pevsner thought it "the best example in the county of what a parish church was like in the 12th and 13th centuries": the Norman doorway is from Plympton Priory. The amateur architect the Rev. Clement Carlyon oversaw the 19th-century restoration, rebuilding the chancel, installing wooden roofs, floor tiling and stained glass. The carved 'woodwork' at the top of the walls is tin stained to resemble wood. The N. transept contains monuments to the Spry family.

ST BURYAN † St Buriana

4m/6km E. of Land's End

OS *SW409257* **GPS** *50.0750N, 5.6224W*

Its lofty tower rising above the village square is a landmark; the church is mainly 15th-century reconstruction. The rood screen, of Devon type, stretches the width of the church, with a richly carved rood beam above that graphically depicts animals and mythical beasts hunting, fighting and devouring one another. The screen, which has traces of original colour, had been taken down during an early 19th-century restoration, but was gradually pieced back together – the central section between 1880 and 1909, the Lady Chapel section a few years later by Belgian refugees; the northern end was restored in 1922 in memoriam to the dead of the First World War. A 13th-century font rests on a 15th-century base.

ST CLEMENT † St Clement ★

2m/3km E. of Truro

OS *SW850438* **GPS** *50.2557N, 5.0167W*

Whitewashed cottages with bushes of mauve and pink hydrangeas form two sides of a little forecourt and hold in the angle a slate-hung lych gate. On the walls of the lych gate, inside, are fixed slate headstones, and in the churchyard are many others, all worth scrutiny. Their lettering is free and sinewy, diversified with endearing errors in spelling and spacing. Most have ornament, fanciful and cut with precision. Inscriptions show originality in sentiment and rhyme. The church was reconstructed (except the tower) in 1865; and it was very well done. The roofs of nave and aisle are carried on 32 arch-braced principals four feet apart. The E. part of the nave roof is top-lighted by a course of glass instead of slate each side of the ridge; an unusual expedient. The glazing of the windows is all of the same character – clear glass leaded in elaborate geometrical patterns with borders and lozenges of emerald-green, hot red, midsummer-sky-blue, gold and violet. While a single window may strike one as garish, the sparkle and shimmer of the whole is extremely pleasing. The device of the Foul Anchor, which the Admiralty shares as an emblem with St Clement, appears more than once in windows and walls, appropriate to two admirals and a naval lieutenant commemorated in the church.

ST COLUMB MAJOR † St Columba

6m/10km W. of Newquay
OS *SW912636* **GPS** *50.4358N, 4.9403W*

In the 19th century Butterfield drew up plans to turn St Columba into the cathedral church of Cornwall, but the church was pipped at the post in 1876 by Truro. Nevertheless this remains a fine church, if much, and not altogether well, altered. The tall Perpendicular tower is imposing, with the first stage pierced by two archways, possibly to allow access to the nearby medieval college. Interesting carved 15th-century bench-ends depict a variety of figures, including a dancing bear and a musical monkey. The screen is Victorian, replacing an earlier Tudor screen removed at the whim of an incumbent. Inexplicably, a fine 16th-century pulpit was replaced in the early 20th century. The overall external impression is elegant, with fine Perpendicular and Geometric tracery in all the E. windows.

ST ENDELLION † St Endelienta ★

4m/6km N. of Wadebridge
OS *SW997786* **GPS** *50.5733N, 4.8301W*

The church stands almost alone on a hill-top, a long way from its nearest village, Trelights, and its nearest town, Port Isaac. One steps down from the lichened granite exterior into a light and airy building with two aisles, slate floors, grey walls and light oak benches of a modern and impressively simple design. There are three single altars, that in the S. aisle being a 15th-century table-tomb of blackish-blue Catacleuse stone, possibly the shrine of St Endelienta. The font is Norman. The glass is unstained; the old roofs survive. Indeed, the church gives the impression that it goes on praying day and night, whether there are people in it or not. St Endelienta's touching hymn by Nicholas Rosscarrock, c. 1550, is pasted into the hymn books. In the tower is a Georgian ringers' rhyme on a painted board. It is a prebendal church which somehow escaped all reformations. The low slate houses for the prebendaries survive around the church.

ST GERMANS † St Germanus of Auxerre

8m/12km S.E. of Liskeard
OS *SX359577* **GPS** *50.3967N, 4.3096W*

Different from other churches in Cornwall, it is of monastic origin and was attached to an Augustinian priory founded in the 12th century; earlier St Germans was the seat of the bishops of the S.W. before Crediton and Exeter. It consists of the nave and S. aisle of what must have been an imposing structure. The W. front has a magnificent Norman doorway with Art Nouveau ironwork by Henry Wilson, and is flanked by two towers. The N. tower is 13th-century and octagonal, and the S. tower 15th-century and four-sided. Interior scraped and refurbished by St Aubyn, 1887–94, and interesting rather for its architecture than its contents. Inside is a monument to Edward Eliot, 1722, by Rysbrack, dramatically lit, and a fine Burne-Jones ten-light window at the E. end.

△ **ST IVES: ST IA** – *on the harbour's edge, the church stands proud in the pleasant seaside town, its tower one of the tallest in the county*

ST IVES † St Ia

St Andrews Street
OS *SW518405* **GPS** *50.2125N, 5.4799W*

Built in 1410–34, St Ia is a prominent landmark among the narrow roads that make up the heart of St Ives. Like the town itself, it bustles with visitors in the summer. It has a rather lovely interior, with good carving throughout: on the capitals of the sandstone piers, as well as in the woodwork – deeply carved on the bench-ends, more delicate in the choir stalls and the 1930s parclose screen. Best of all is the wagon roof, decorated with vines and other patterns and populated by sculpted figures of saints, apostles and angels. Much of the woodwork was painted and gilded in the 1960s, with some further restoration to paintwork in the 1990s. In the Lady Chapel is Barbara Hepworth's Madonna and Child, a tender sculpture created in memory of her son Paul, who was killed in active service with the RAF in 1953.

ST JUST-IN-PENWITH † St Just

4m/6km N. of Land's End
OS *SW371314* **GPS** *50.1247N, 5.6788W*

St Just-in-Penwith is a mostly 15th-century Perpendicular church, with stout square tower, battlements and pinnacles – a no-nonsense church for a town rooted in tin mining. The heavily restored interior, back to uneven stone walls, contains an early wall-painting of St George and the Dragon. Good atmosphere, though: the light a salty haze across the cool, gloomy interior.

ST JUST-IN-ROSELAND † St Just

2m/3km N. of St Mawes
OS *SW848356* **GPS** *50.1821N, 5.0150W*

A 13th-century church overlooking the tidal creek of the R. Percuil, more to be appreciated

△ **ST JUST-IN-PENWITH: ST JUST** – *a sea-salty air pervades the interior, which, though scraped, has a compelling atmosphere that seems part of the windblown landscape on the western headland*

for its setting than anything else. The churchyard slopes steeply down: it is adorned with luxurious sub-tropical plants, and the path is lined with granite slabs bearing biblical quotations.

ST KEVERNE † St Keverne

9ml/15km S.E. of Helston
OS *SW791212* **GPS** *50.0507N, 5.0867W*

Dominates the village square, with its good tower and spire. The spacious 15th-century interior has a wall-painting of St Christopher on the N. wall. There are many memorials to local families who served in the Honorable East India Company, early 16th-century bench-ends, and in the churchyard the Mohegan Stone, an engraved Cornish cross.

ST LEVAN † St Levan

6ml/10km S.W. of Penzance
OS *SW380222* **GPS** *50.0423N, 5.6602W*

Possibly 13th century, the church is cut into the slopes above Porthchapel. The two-stage tower is 15th-century, embattled and pinnacled. The six-bay arcade is supported on monolithic rough cut granite pillars, and the roof has gilded and painted bosses. The Victorian pews made use of older bench-ends with shepherds, eagles and a hatted jester. J. D. Sedding did the Victorian restoration.

ST MINVER † St Menefreda

3ml/4km N.W. of Wadebridge
OS *SW964770* **GPS** *50.5580N, 4.8747W*

In an attractive wooded church-town, the church is mainly 13th–15th-century, with a tall octagonal spire; the octagonal slate pillars and arches of the N. aisle are Norman. The granite pillars and arches of the S. aisle date from the 15th century, when the church was enlarged. The tower and spire were there before this, but became dilapidated and were

rebuilt in 1875. The porch was built in the 14th century and probably rebuilt in the 15th. The carved bench-ends are 15th-century too – mostly secular figures, and one of Henry VIII. The rich Victorian E. window is by Michael O'Connor.

ST NEOT † St Neot ★

5m/8km N.W. of Liskeard

OS *SX186678* **GPS** *50.4824N, 4.5582W*

A slate and granite village in a wooded valley below Bodmin Moor and dominated by the church with handsome Decorated tower and buttressed 16th-century double-aisled exterior. This is the Fairford of the West and has 15 windows of medieval glass sensitively renewed by W. Hedgeland, 1829; the most interesting show the lives of St Neot and St George. There are old roofs and a rood screen. The walls are scraped.

ST WINNOW † St Winnow ★

2m/3km S. of Lostwithiel

OS *SX115569* **GPS** *50.3824N, 4.6522W*

A lovely situation on the Fowey River, which laps the churchyard wall. There are woods in tiers across the wide river, an old stone boathouse and, by the church, a farm that was once the rectory. There is a fine early 16th-century rood screen restored by E. H. Sedding and a splendid E. window to the S. aisle filled with 15th- and 16th-century glass, whose wealth of imagery may well occupy the wandering attention of the congregation. The old stained glass depicting the Crucifixion, in the E. window of the chancel, is to be noted; also the shape of the arches of the arcade – slightly stilted.

TINTAGEL † St Materiana

4m/6km N.W. of Camelford

OS *SX050884* **GPS** *50.6630N, 4.7597W*

All alone on the open cliffs above the Atlantic, it still retains an atmosphere of early Christianity. A large Norman cruciform church refashioned in the 13th century and later, it retains its original plan. The scraped interior contains a late 15th-century rood screen and Norman font decorated with grotesques. The iron hinges to the N. door are 12th-century, and there is an ancient stone altar in the vestry.

TREBETHERICK † St Enedoc ★★

By the mouth of the R. Camel, near Trebetherick, 6m/10km N.W. of Wadebridge

OS *SW931772* **GPS** *50.5582N, 4.9216W*

A small, crooked 13th-century spire peers myopically through the grassy hillocks on the golf course, and over Daymer Bay. St Enedoc is the place where John Betjeman himself is buried, his grave marked by a delightful slate headstone beside the gate. The church is 12th-century, but most is now from the 15th century. The restored interior, dark and ancient, was rescued from drifting sands in the 19th century.

TUCKINGMILL † All Saints

1m/2km N.E. of Camborne

OS *SW657407* **GPS** *50.2201N, 5.2855W*

A strong church suitable for this former tin-mining area, it was built for the Bassett family, in Romanesque style, by J. Hayward of Exeter, 1843–5. A whitewashed stone interior, with large granite chancel arch and arcade form a rather plain interior. The glass is by Robert Beer of Exeter.

◁ **ST NEOT** – *filled with richly coloured medieval glass, this north aisle window depicts 12 scenes from the life of St Neot*

CUMBRIA

The present county of Cumbria comprises the two traditional counties of Cumberland and Westmorland, as well as incorporating the Furness part of Lancashire, sometimes known as 'Lancashire North of the Sands', which has happily restored Cartmel Priory to its ex oficio position of being the 'true' cathedral of Cumbria. Not for nothing is the county's motto *Ad Montes Oculos Levavi* – 'I shall lift up mine eyes to the hills'.

A largely glacial landscape of mountains, valleys, lakes, tarns and fells, fringed in the west by a coastal plain, this part of England has been a source of awe for some. In the 18th century Daniel Defoe found the Westmorland landscape to be 'the wildest, most barren and frightful of any that I have passed over in England', bounded by unpassable mountains, with straggling paths on which the unwary traveller was likely to be waylaid.

By the mid-18th century the beauties of the area were being acknowledged by John Brown and Thomas Gray, although some, notably Thomas de Quincy, were still dismayed by the remoteness and savagery of the Lakeland landscapes. It was principally Wordsworth who gave romantic voice to the Lakeland landscape, and Turner and Constable who captured its mysterious beauty on canvas.

Slate sandstone and limestone are the rocks that define many of the area's churches. The soft sandstone of the west doorway of St Bees Priory has weathered into its own abstract grotesques. In lonely Martindale, St Martin's is rough-hewn slate, a tiny church that offers a peaceful pause to the fell walker. Sandstone features in the east of the county, notably in the beautifully situated church of St Lawrence in Appleby. In the north-east, hard by Hadrian's Wall, is the glowing stone of Lanercost Priory, whilst at Cartmel the limestone tower of the Priory can be seen from Morecambe Bay, outlined against the distant hills.

North of St Bees, the Georgian town of Whitehaven testifies to Cumbria's industrial past. Enriched by coal mining and ore extraction, the town was developed to a grid plan by Sir John Lowther in the 17th century. It was a successor's principal colliery steward, Carlisle Spedding, who designed the fine Georgian church of St James – which Pevsner considers to be one of the finest Georgian interiors of the county.

But it is the little upland and valley churches of the Lakeland fells that draw many: the idyllic setting of St Michael at Isel and the quiet charm of St John's at Ulpha, more or less as Wordsworth knew it. Old Westmorland's open and remoter places contain churches of infinite charm too. St Ninian Ninekirks, redundant but still open, requires a good walk along an indistinct track to a meadow overlooking the River Eamont, about one and half miles round trip but hugely rewarding. For the less energetic, the 'Cathedral of the Dales' – Kirkby Stephen's parish church of St Stephen, with its glorious Early English arcades – is easy to access.

◁ **APPLEBY-IN-WESTMORLAND: ST LAWRENCE** – *the light-hued sandstone and modest tower give a real charm to the church, which stands on the banks of the River Eden*

SCOTLAND

NORTHUMBERLA

Bewcastle

A74(M)

Kirkandrews-on-Esk

Longtown

Gretna

A7

A6071

Lanercost

A69

Brampton

Burgh-by-Sands

A689

A689

Solway Firth

CARLISLE

A69

A686

A595

Wigton

Wreay

Armathwaite

Alston

A596

A595

M6

A6

A689

Boltongate

Crosscanonby

Torpenhow

Kirkoswald

CUMBRIA

Maryport

Dearham

A686

Bridekirk

Isel

DUR

A591

Greystoke

Brougham (Whinfell Park)

Cockermouth

PENRITH

Bassenthwaite

Brougham

WORKINGTON

A66

A66

Kirkby Thore

Long Marton

Lowther

Crossthwaite

KESWICK

A5091

Morland

Bolton

A5086

A592

APPLEBY-IN-WESTMORLAND

Ormside

WHITEHAVEN

Martindale

Bampton

A66

A591

Brough

A6

St Bees

Egremont

Lake District

A592

Kirkby S

Grasmere

Orton

Nether Wasdale

Gosforth

Ambleside

A685

Ravenstonedal

A595

A6

A593

Seascale

Windermere

A683

Coniston

M6

A591

Waberthwaite

A685

Ulpha

KENDAL

Sedbergh

A593

A684

Hav

A592

A65

Broughton-in-Furness

A5084

Cartmel Fell

Witherslack

A590

A683

Millom

A595

Cartmel

Ulverston

Kirkby Lonsdale

Urswick

GRANGE-OVER-SANDS

NORTH YORKSHI

Dalton-in-Furness

A687

A590

A5087

BARROW-IN-FURNESS

A65

M6

A683

Morecambe

A6

Settle

LANCASTER

0 10 miles

0 10 km

LANCASHIRE

△ **BASSENTHWAITE: ST BEGA** – *an ancient church with pre-Conquest origins*

APPLEBY-IN-WESTMORLAND
† St Lawrence ★
12m/19km S.E. of Penrith
OS *NY683204* **GPS** *54.5782N, 2.4915W*

This large Decorated and Perpendicular church is set in a beautiful and unspoiled town between the River Eden and the Norman castle on the bluff dominating the ford. The chancel and other works are by Lady Anne Clifford, 1654–5, who lies here with her mother Lady Margaret. There are 15th-century Parclose screens, 17th-century monuments and a celebrated 16th-century organ case, removed from Carlisle Cathedral.

ARMATHWAITE
† Chapel of Christ & St Mary ★
9m/15km S.E. of Carlisle
OS *NY505462* **GPS** *54.8082N, 2.7701W*

The chapel stands on a hillock in fine scenery by the River Eden. The original chapel fell into a ruinous state and was used as a cattle-shed until rebuilt c. 1688 by Richard Skelton of nearby Armathwaite Castle. Today it is a plain stone building, consisting of undivided nave and chancel, and small W. turret containing one bell. There is still something about it of the manger and the cattle in the straw that makes one think of it as a true church of the Nativity. The glass in the E. window is by William Morris and Co, to designs by Dearle and Burne-Jones.

BAMPTON † St Patrick ★
7m/11km S. of Penrith
OS *NY521180* **GPS** *54.5553N, 2.7412W*

Built in 1726–8, with the church interior much altered in 1885. The W. tower has a doorway with an interrupted segmental pediment. Inside are elegant oak Georgian arcade columns and a cut-down Jacobean pulpit.

BASSENTHWAITE † St Bega ★
6m/10km N.W. of Keswick
OS NY226287 GPS 54.6479N, 3.2000W

A short walk down a sloping track leads to a church with one of the loveliest of Lakeland settings, beside a vigorous stream, visited by the Wordsworths and Tennyson. Pre-Conquest in origin, c. 950, it has a slight lopsided feel, with two S. arches opening into the mid-14th-century chantry chapel endowed by Sir Adam de Bastenthwayt. Squeezed into the S. aisle is a 14th-century monument to Sir Robert Highmore. A beautiful replica of the original 14th-century lead crucifix hangs over the octagonal pulpit on the N. side of the chancel arch. On the other side is an iron hourglass bracket: a charming simple church in an inspiring setting.

BECKERMET † St John the Baptist ★
3m/4km S. of Egremont
OS *NY018067* **GPS** *54.4463N, 3.5145W*

By J. Birtley, 1878–9, St John the Baptist

occupies a striking situation high above the confluence of two becks. It is a most successful example of a small Victorian church, with a pleasing and well-designed interior. There is a collection of Anglo-Danish sculpture and later coffin lids. The nearby 13th-century St Bridget's, now a mortuary chapel, has two shafts of Norman crosses in the churchyard.

BEWCASTLE † St Cuthbert

9m/15km N. of Brampton
OS *NY565745* **GPS** *55.0636N, 2.6819W*

Although dramatically set among Border fells, the church itself is not particularly interesting, dating originally from the 13th century and rebuilt in the 18th century, at which time it was dedicated to St Cuthbert. But beside it is the celebrated late 7th-century Bewcastle Cross, an outstanding monument to the Golden Age of Northumbria.

BOLTON † All Saints ★

4m/6km N.W. of Appleby-in-Westmorland
OS *NY639234* **GPS** *54.6046N, 2.5598W*

An ancient little stone edifice, All Saints somehow achieves nobility. It has a late Norman chancel, nave and S. porch with doorway; over the N. door is a charming and celebrated Norman carving of knights jousting – a little treasure. The bell-turret, 1693, has a saddleback roof. The font and cover are from 1687, and an unusual chancel screen of open tracery is probably local work of the late 18th century.

BOLTONGATE † All Saints ★

5m/8km S.W. of Wigton
OS *NY229407* **GPS** *54.7560N, 3.1986W*

Originally Norman, and outwardly unremarkable, the church was rebuilt in the late 14th or early 15th century with a thrilling, steeply pointed tunnel vaulted nave which is supported on thick stone walls, themselves steadied by stout external buttressing. There is good glass by Kempe and Willement, and from the outside a fine view of Skiddaw.

BRAMPTON † St Martin ★

9m/15km N.E. of Carlisle
OS *NY528610* **GPS** *54.9417N, 2.7378W*

Built of red sandstone in indefinable style, with mixed Gothic and vernacular elements, this is Philip Webb's only commissioned church, 1874–8. The wide and spacious interior has woodwork by local craftsmen and spectacular Pre-Raphaelite coloured glass by Burne-Jones and the Morris firm.

BRIDEKIRK † St Bridget ★

2m/3km N. of Cockermouth
OS *NY116336* **GPS** *54.6905N, 3.3722W*

Rebuilt by Cory & Ferguson, 1868–70, in a neo-Norman style, St Bridget's is a large cruciform church with crossing tower and apse. The original tympanum and chancel arch were incorporated into the new church. The chief glory is the mid-12th-century font with an inscription recording its maker, 'Richard he me wrought, and to this beauty me brought', and some lively carvings of scenes and dragons.

BROUGHAM † St Ninian ★★

1m/2km walk along river from Whinfell Park Farm, 2m/3km E. of Penrith
OS *NY559299* **GPS** *54.6628N, 2.6846W*
Churches Conservation Trust

Unforgettable: known locally as 'Ninekirks', St Ninian's stands surrounded by trees in the middle of a field in a lonely meadow by the River Eamont. This was the site of a Saxon church, then a Norman, but today it is just as Lady Anne Clifford rebuilt it in 1660. It is a restrained instance of Gothic Survival, with whitewashed interior, oak box and canopied pews, pulpit with sounding board, oak seats with carved arm-rests and screens. Lady Anne's initials, in a laurel surround, appear in the plasterwork over the altar.

BROUGHAM † St Wilfrid ★

By Brougham Hall, ½m/1km S. of Penrith
OS *NY527284* **GPS** *54.6485N, 2.7335W*

An ancient, plain little building of chancel, nave and bellcote, this one too was restored by Lady Anne Clifford (see previous entry) in the mid-17th century. It is filled with a collection of European antiques by the first Baron Brougham and Vaux in the 1840s, who also redid the windows in Norman style. The contrast between the interiors of these neighbouring churches is almost unbelievable.

CARTMEL: ST MARY THE VIRGIN AND ST MICHAEL – *the richly carved choir stalls* ▷

△ **CROSTHWAITE: ST KENTIGERN** – *primarily a church of the mid-16th century, it houses a memorial to the poet Robert Southey*

Here is rich cathedral opulence, the church as full as it can be of beautifully carved oak – an elaborate parclose organ casing, pillars, tall pews and a screen with rich round posts and beautiful cornice. The gilt oak reredos has a magnificent 15th-century altarpiece with superb carvings bordered by medieval woodwork of the finest craftsmanship. The pulpit is enriched with medieval carving; the oak roof is divided into panels, each with richly emblazoned shield or crest. Nothing in Cumbria, or indeed anywhere, compares with this juxtaposition of plain and simple building without and opulence within.

BURGH-BY-SANDS † St Michael

5m/8km N.W. of Carlisle
OS *NY328591* **GPS** *54.9221N, 3.0489W*

Built largely of stone from the Roman wall and strongly defensive against the Scots – particularly the broad 14th-century tower with its iron gate to the nave – St Michael's is largely Norman and Early English. 1½ miles to the N.W. is a monument to Edward I, who died whilst encamped on Burgh Marsh in 1307.

CARTMEL
† St Mary the Virgin and St Michael ★★

2m/3km W. of Grange-over-Sands
OS *SD379787* **GPS** *54.2012N, 2.9523W*

Among the fields of a pleasant little town in a wide valley of the Cartmel Peninsula stands what was once Lancashire's finest parish church, part of a long-vanished priory. It is a massive Transitional cruciform building with 15th-century Perpendicular windows installed when the upper stage of the central tower was added. The crossing arches are pointed, but the chancel arcades are still round. The S. choir aisle, rebuilt c. 1350, has good Decorated windows. There are magnificent Renaissance screens and stall canopies of 1618 restoration, after it had stood roofless for 80 years, and fine choir stalls with misericords. Many monuments include 14th-century Harrington effigies, and that to Dame Katherine Lowther – a fine Baroque work of 1700.

CARTMEL FELL † St Anthony ★

6m/10km S.W. of Kendal
OS *SD416880* **GPS** *54.2849N, 2.8977W*

This small, low, rustic limestone church of

△ **GRASMERE: ST OSWALD** – *the two-tier arcade in the nave; the church is the burial place of another of the 'Lake Poets', William Wordsworth*

1503 is cut into the fell side. The windows are mullioned and there is a saddleback tower. Inside are two very handsome screened pews and a three-decker pulpit of 1698; the 15th-century glass is from Cartmel Priory. All very charming in its simplicity.

CROSSCANONBY † St John the Evangelist

3m/4km N.E. of Maryport
OS *NY069390* **GPS** *54.7374N, 3.4472W*

This is a Norman church that incorporates Roman stones. Other stones include a hogback gravestone, carved like a little house of the dead, and a 10th-century cross fragment with dragons biting themselves. The South aisle was added in the 13th century. The tomb of John Smith, local salt tax collector, is a reminder of the importance of the nearby coastal salt pans, which produced salt over some 700 years.

CROSTHWAITE † St Kentigern ★

½m/1km N.W. of Keswick
OS *NY257242* **GPS** *54.6083N, 3.1512W*

The present church, built on an ancient site, achieved its present form c. 1553, though it includes 14th-century arches. Twelve consecration crosses outside and nine inside were found in 1915. A recumbent white marble carving of the 19th-century Poet Laureate Robert Southey, by J. G. Lough, bears an epitaph written by William Wordsworth. The church was restored as part of the memorial to Southey by Sir George Gilbert Scott, and the Baptistry is a memorial to Canon Hardwicke Rawnsley, Vicar here for 34 years, founder of the National Trust, lifelong friend of John Ruskin and mentor to a young Beatrix Potter.

DALTON-IN-FURNESS † St Mary

4m/6km N.E. of Barrow-in-Furness
OS *SD225738* **GPS** *54.1549N, 3.1870W*

By Paley & Austin, 1882–5, this is a spectacular Decorated sandstone church with large W. tower and jolly limestone diapering. The assymetrical interior has octagonal piers and a broad moulded chancel arch.

DEARHAM † St Mungo ★

Suburb, 2m/3km E. of Maryport
OS *NY072363* **GPS** *54.7140N, 3.4413W*

This is a 12th- and 13th-century church with

△ **KENDAL: HOLY TRINITY** – *a fine array of Perpendicular windows stretch across the east end*

a Pele tower used as a refuge during cross-border skirmishes with the Scots. Inside is a carved Norman font and copious Anglo-Danish sculpture, including the Kenneth Cross and the Adam Stone, both found during a late 19th-century restoration.

GOSFORTH † St Mary

2m/3km N.E. of Seascale
OS *NY072035* **GPS** *54.4193N, 3.4313W*

A red sandstone church, St Mary's was mostly rebuilt in the Decorated style in 1896–9. Inside are two 10th-century Norse hogback tombs, carved with battle scenes, and in the churchyard stands the wondrous Gosforth Cross, a soaring Anglo-Norse creation of the later 10th century. The cross is 14 ft in height; the lower part of its shaft is round and represents the ash tree Yggdrasil, which in Norse lore is the tree that supports the universe.

GRASMERE † St Oswald

3m/4km N.W. of Ambleside
OS *NY337073* **GPS** *54.4575N, 3.0236W*

Wordsworth and members of his family are buried in the churchyard, and Woolner's monument to the poet is in the church. The rough, massive old church has a notable two-tier arcade, the upper dating from the 17th century. The resulting jungle of black beams is an object lesson in elementary building, ingenious and almost indescribable except by Wordsworth, who had a shot at most things, and declared that the roof was upheld: 'By naked rafters intricately crossed / Like leafless underboughs, mid some thick grove / All withered by the depth of shade above.' A curiously partisan feature of being the parish church for Grasmere, Rydal and Langdale is that each has its own separate entrance into the churchyard.

GREYSTOKE † St Andrew ★

5m/8km W. of Penrith
OS *NY443307* **GPS** *54.6691N, 2.8646W*

Made collegiate in 1382, the church is vast and gracious. The chancel arch is Early English, otherwise all mostly 15th-century. The tower and chancel were rebuilt in 1848. There are 20 canons' stalls with interesting misericords and 15th-century glass in the the E. window. Of the Victorian glass, that by Kempe is the most interesting; on the W wall is a 20th-century figure of the crucified Christ by the Brazilian-born sculptress Josefina de Vasconcellos, whose work also adorns St Paul's Cathedral in London, as well as Liverpool and Gloucester cathedrals.

△ **ISEL: ST MICHAEL**– *the fabric of the church is largely Norman*

ISEL † St Michael

4m/6km N.E. of Cockermouth
OS *NY162333* **GPS** *54.6879N, 3.3008W*

St Michael's is a largely Norman church, with a 15th-century window bearing three sundials to mark the monastic hours. The chancel arch stonework is reminiscent (at a very small scale) of St Bees Priory. The Anglo-Danish cross shaft bearing the rare three-armed symbol known as the triskele, one of the earliest symbols found on Christian monuments, was stolen in 1986. The old church stands on the banks of the Derwent, and nearby is an ancient bridge of three arches, rebuilt in 1812. The church thankfully survived the catastrophic flooding of 2009.

KENDAL † Holy Trinity ★

Between Kirkland and river
OS *SD516921* **GPS** *54.3225N, 2.7443W*

This prosperous Perpendicular town church stands, nearly as broad as York Minster, above the River Kent, and is Cumbria's largest parish church. Nothing is older than the 13th century here and most dates from the 15th century. Five aisles and 32 pillars create the impression of a walk through a stone forest. The 20th century is well served by Josefina de Vasconcellos' moving sculpture *The Family of Man*, situated near the E. window of the northernmost aisle.

KIRKANDREWS-ON-ESK
† St Andrew ★

1m/2km N. of Longtown, 8m/12km N. of Carlisle
OS *NY391719* **GPS** *55.0386N, 2.9543W*

In an attractive setting, St Andrew's is an estate church of local red sandstone. It was built in fine style in 1776 by the Rev. Robert Graham of Netherby Hall, which the church overlooks across the River Esk. The interior was sensitively restored by Temple Moore in 1893, when the Italianate chancel screen, reredos and new organ were provided.

KIRKBY LONSDALE
† St Mary the Virgin ★

14m/22km N.E. of Lancaster
OS *SD611788* **GPS** *54.2037N, 2.5975W*

Hidden behind Market Street in this enjoyable small town, the church is approached through 19th-century iron gates below an iron arch. In a lovely setting in the Lune Valley, the view from the churchyard is perhaps the finest in the county, praised by Ruskin, painted by Turner and endlessly satisfying. The church has been much modified since

△ **LANERCOST PRIORY** – *it became a parish church in the 18th century, when the main surviving parts of the former priory were restored*

its days of Norman greatness from which, however, it retains S. and W. doorways. The latter is a fine example of late Norman work, recessed in four orders and much enriched with zigzags and other ornaments. In the N. arcade are three powerful early Norman piers and arches bearing Durham-style diapering. There is a charming six-sided pulpit of 1619, and, in the S. aisle, glass of Faith, Hope and Charity by Henry Holiday, who took over from Edward Burne-Jones as stained glass designer at Powell's Glass Works when Burne-Jones left to work for Morris & Co.

KIRKBY STEPHEN † St Stephen ★

9m/15km S.E. of Appleby-in-Westmorland
OS *NY775088* **GPS** *54.4742N, 2.3484W*

Known as 'The Cathedral of the Dales', St Stephen's was probably founded in the 8th century. Rebuilt in the 13th and 15th centuries, it was heavily restored in 1847. Stately and impressive Early English arcades separate the nave from the aisles. The embattled W. tower of c. 1506 replaced a central Early English tower which fell in the 15th century. Inside, an 18th-century bread cupboard is curved around a pier and there are 15th- and 16th-century monuments to the Musgraves and Whartons. Most interesting of all is the Loki stone, a relief carving of the Norse God of Mischief.

KIRKBY THORE † St Michael

8m/13km S.W. of Penrith
OS NY638259 GPS 54.6273N, 2.5621W

In the lovely Eden Valley, this is a simple church of red sandstone. The base of the tower is early Norman, while the chancel, nave and upper parts of the tower are 13th-century. There is reused stone from the nearby Roman fort of Bravoniacum incorporated into the fabric. Inside is a pulpit made of reused finely carved 17th-century panels, and an octagonal font of 1688. The rather odd pointed and moulded chancel arch is from a Victorian restoration, and the bell, said to be the county's largest, is thought to have come from Shap Abbey.

KIRKOSWALD † St Oswald ★

7m/11km N. of Penrith
OS *NY555409* **GPS** *54.7611N, 2.6928W*

The little sandstone town with its moated castle and house, now a museum, is one of the best in the county. Like many churches dedicated to St Oswald, this one is associated with a spring, but it is almost certainly the only one in which a pure spring of water rises from the conical hill at the foot of which the church stands, flows under the length of the nave and issues as a drinking-well outside the W. wall. The tower of 1897 stands oddly at the top of the hill 200 yards away from the church, which has interesting medieval fabric and a collegiate chancel of c. 1523.

LANERCOST

† Priory of St Mary Magdalene

3m/4km N.E. of Brampton

OS *NY555637* **GPS** *54.9662N, 2.6952W*

Beautifully situated in the quiet wooded valley of the River Irthing and entered through an ancient gatehouse, the nave and N. aisle of the priory were restored and refitted in the 18th century to serve as the parish church. The priory was founded about 1169 by Robert de Vallibus (de Vaux). Edward I, Queen Eleanor, Robert the Bruce and David King of Scotland cross and re-cross its history in the 14th century. The earliest portions, such as the base course on the S. of nave and transept, are Transitional; the remainder elegant Early English. It has a beautiful clerestory and W. front with bold recessed doorway and arcading. Inside are Burne-Jones lancets in rich colours, and monuments by Boehm; in the S. chapel is the tomb of Lord Dacre of Battle of Flodden fame. The E. end of the present church, built after the priory was dismantled, has a little 16th-century glass, but is mostly clear. In low evening sunlight, the priory glows: a place of magic.

LONG MARTON

† St Margaret & St James

3m/4km N. of Appleby-in-Westmorland

OS *NY666239* **GPS** *54.6100N, 2.5177W*

The building is early Romanesque in origin, especially the nave with huge quoins. Parts of the S. doorway, with its crude tympanum adorned with winged beast and dragon, might be as early, but this part of the church was reset during a 19th-century restoration.

LOWTHER † St Michael

4m/6km S. of Penrith

OS *NY519244* **GPS** *54.6129N, 2.7462W*

Beautifully placed above the River Lowther, the church has portions dating from the 12th, 13th and 17th centuries. The shell was almost completely rebuilt by Sir John Lowther in the 17th century with a dome and lantern on the tower, unfortunately since removed. The church has some splendid Lowther monuments, including William Stanton's John, Viscount Lonsdale, d. 1700, a fine semi-reclining figure now behind the organ. Outside, in rather dismal isolation, a figure of the 2nd Earl – William – is seated in a frankly sinister late 19th-century mausoleum.

MARTINDALE

† St Martin Old Church ★

In hills above Ullswater, 10m/16km S.W. of Penrith

OS *NY434184* **GPS** *54.5577N, 2.8761W*

One of the loneliest churches in Cumbria, St Martin's stands at 1,000 feet above the sea; it was for a time disused. The Old Church, originally 11th-century, was renewed in 1633. With its simple bellcote, porch and rustic slatework, it has an almost domestic appearance; inside is 17th-century woodwork, a good carved pulpit and massive beams. It is used for services about three times a year and has neither heating nor electricity; it is often visited by walkers seeking peace and solitude.

MARTINDALE † St Peter New Church

In hills above Ullswater, 10m/16km S.W. of Penrith

OS *NY436191* **GPS** *54.5644N, 2.8736W*

With only a few farms for company at the top of the Hause Pass, the present church of St Peter was erected in a sort of Early English style in 1880–82 by B. Cory. There is good 20th-century glass by Jane Grey. Another 20th-century window, dedicated to St Nicholas, commemorates the loss of HMS Glorious off the Norwegian coast during the Second World War.

MILLOM † Holy Trinity

N. of Millom town centre,
5m/8km S.W. of Broughton-in-Furness

OS *SD171813* **GPS** *54.2207N, 3.2728W*

This late Norman sandstone church shelters against the ruins of the 13th-century castle. There is some later medieval work, including Curvilinear and Reticulated window tracery. The Victorian restoration did the church no favours, but a 12th- to 13th-century chancel arch remains, and in the Huddleston Chapel there is a fine alabaster monument, 1494, commemorating Richard Huddleston and his wife Lady Mabel Dacre.

△ **ORTON: ALL SAINTS** – *the church is dominated by the limewashed Perpendicular tower*

MILLOM † St George

St George's Road, town centre; 5ml8km S.W. of Broughton-in-Furness
OS *SD171799* **GPS** *54.2089N, 3.2717W*

Inspired perhaps by the rapid expansion of Millom through mining and ironworks in the late 19th century, the new church of St George was built by Paley & Austin in an elaborate Decorated style, with blind arcades and geometric tracery. There is a fine central tower with recessed spire – a landmark visible for miles around – and a good wagon roof to the nave. Stained glass commemorates the life of the poet Norman Nicholson, who is buried in the nearby town cemetery.

MORLAND † St Lawrence

6ml10km W. of Appleby-in-Westmorland
OS *NY598225* **GPS** *54.5965N, 2.6235W*

This delightful church has a fine Saxon W. tower. Its plan is unusual: nave, N. and S. transepts are mostly Norman, the chancel was rebuilt in the 16th century. From outside the church has the look of a miniature minster, and is beautifully set adjacent to Morland House and gardens.

NETHER WASDALE † St Michael

15ml8km N.E. of Seascale
OS *NY124040* **GPS** *54.4245N, 3.3504W*

St Michael's plain external appearance conceals a surprisingly elegant, simple, gas-lit Georgian interior, with plaster reliefs of cherubs on the coved ceiling. It was originally a chapel of ease for St Bees Priory, and dates from the 16th century – a single-cell building with bellcote. The pulpit and lectern came from York Minster, and there are traces of wall-paintings on the S. wall.

ORMSIDE † St James ★

2ml3km S.E. of Appleby-in-Westmorland across R. Eden
OS *NY701176* **GPS** *54.5532N, 2.4632W*

Strikingly situated on a conical knoll W. of the River Eden with fine views of Roman Fell, St James's is predominantly Norman and no-nonsense, with a robust Scot-repelling tower only 11 feet square. The arcade to the N. aisle is formed of stout columns topped with crudely carved capitals, and the oak king-post chancel roof is 400 years old. Set in the N. chancel wall is a 14th-century hagioscope.

The famous 9th-century Ormside Bowl, a Saxon treasure of gold and enamel, was dug up in the churchyard in 1823, and is now in York Museum.

ORTON † All Saints ★

12m/18km N.E. of Kendal
OS NY622083 GPS 54.4695N, 2.5845W

On a site that has grand views towards Orton Scar and the Howgills, the white-washed rustic Perpendicular tower of the church is unmissable, supported by bulky stepped buttresses. The bulk of the church is 13th-century, its nave and aisles long, broad and low, with roof lights set over the chancel arch (the old crossing). The 1662 font is carved out of sandstone, and of particular note is a charming window in the baptistry by Beatrice Whistler, wife of the painter J. MacNeill Whistler. The principal restoration was by Paley and Austin, 1877, and there is good 19th-century glass.

PENRITH † St Andrew ★

Between Friargate and Market Square
OS *NY516301* **GPS** *54.6642N, 2.7511W*

Hawksmoor modelled his designs for this stately red sandstone Classical church of 1720–2 on St Andrew's Church in Holborn. The 13th-century W. tower was retained from the earlier church on the site. The nave has two tiers of round-arched windows and a Tuscan doorway through the base of the tower. Inside are three galleries on Tuscan columns, an elegant tower staircase and a large Venetian E. window. Wall-paintings in the chancel are by Jacob Thompson. Outside in the churchyard is the Giant's Thumb, a Norse cross from 920, erected as a memorial to his father by Owen Caesarius, King of Cumbria 920–37. There is also a cluster of hogback stones.

RAVENSTONEDALE † St Oswald ★

4m/6km S.W. of Kirkby Stephen
OS *NY722042* **GPS** *54.4330N, 2.4296W*

Approached by a long straight path, the church is delightfully set among imposing trees among the moorland heights, overlooking the Scandel Beck. Fragments of the old church were incorporated in the present Georgian structure of 1738–44. The almost intact Georgian interior has a three-decker pulpit, benches arranged in collegiate fashion, facing into the central aisle, Royal Arms, text boards and a W. gallery. Beyond the N. wall outside are remains of the Gilbertine Abbey, built here c. 1200.

△ **ST BEES** – *the weathered but magnificent carving around the west doorway*

ST BEES † Priory/St Mary and St Bega ★

4m/6km S. of Whitehaven
OS *NX968121* **GPS** *54.4939N, 3.5935W*

This is a cruciform monastic church of soft red sandstone with a choir of six bays, transepts, central tower and clerestoried nave of c. 1250. Although much restored, the church is unassailably imposing. The original E. end was not demolished during the Reformation and now forms part of the school library. The Norman W. front is magnificent, and the three principal orders of the doorway are carved with rich chevron mouldings and beak-heads. Inside are many pre-Conquest carved stones. W. Butterfield restored the tower space and transepts in 1855–8 and built the Romanesque spire; he later added the fine Art Nouveau wrought-iron chancel screen.

ULPHA: ST JOHN – *a church of rustic appeal and solitude* ▷

△ **WREAY: ST MARY** – *carvings of flora and fauna abound in the architectural details*

TORPENHOW † St Michael ★

6m/10km S.W. of Wigton

OS *NY205398* **GPS** *54.7469N, 3.2353W*

A church with superb views of Solway, Scotland, Lake District and Pennines, St Michael's is a broad-shouldered, bulky building with a finialled bellcote. Norman in origin, it retains many fine Norman features, of which the chancel arch is undoubtedly the best, with red sandstone carvings of demonic figures on the N. side, whilst on the S. side of the arch are human figures and animals in a lighter sandstone. The wooden nave ceiling is Baroque, brought here by Thomas Addison in the late 17th century. It is adorned with painted flowers, cherubs and scrolls, and is believed to have come from a livery hall in London. Odd and completely out of place, but with a certain eccentric charm.

ULPHA † St John ★

4m/6km N. of Broughton-in-Furness

OS *SD198932* **GPS** *54.3285N, 3.2347W*

A lovely old simple church, more or less as Wordsworth knew it, with fragments of 18th-century decoration and old timbers in a black and white roof. It is built of local stone in a beautiful spot, overlooking the River Duddon. See Wordsworth's sonnets on the subject, especially the one beginning 'The Kirk of Ulpha to the pilgrim's eye'.

URSWICK † St Mary and St Michael ★

3m/4km E. of Dalton-in-Furness

OS *SD268741* **GPS** *54.1583N, 3.1218W*

This ancient church overlooks Urswick Tarn, and has a massive 13th-century (possibly Pele) tower with Perpendicular top stage. The aisleless nave with fine rustic king-post timber roof is dated 1598. There is an enigmatic and interesting carved 9th-century runic stone, but the exciting thing here is the woodwork: lots of it, very fine, carved in 1909–12 by Alec Miller to the designs of C. R Ashby at the Guild of Handicrafts.

WABERTHWAITE
† St John the Baptist ★

1m/2km S.E. of Ravenglass across R. Esk, 6m/10km S.E. of Seascale

OS *SD100951* **GPS** *54.3436N, 3.3855W*

A lonely, simple and typical dale church, snug under Muncaster Fell and a surrounding screen of trees, the church is tucked into a bend of the upper reaches of the Esk estuary. It has a homely unadorned interior, lit by oil lamps and furnished with box pews, Royal Arms, a 17th-century pulpit and Norman font. Outside is an Anglo-Norse cross shaft from the 9th or 10th century. This is a perfect setting for a tiny church.

WHITEHAVEN † St James ★★

High Street

OS *NX976184* **GPS** *54.5508N, 3.5834W*

St James's Church overlooks the town – a Georgian statement to Whitehaven's coal-fuelled prosperity in the 18th century. It was designed by Carlisle Spedding, principal colliery steward to Sir James Lowther. Outwardly rather dour, the interior is superb. Stucco roundels decorate the pastel (1970) ceiling, and the rows of Classical pillars supporting the three galleries lead to a domed apse and a beautiful painted altarpiece of the Transfiguration by Correggio's pupil Procaccini.

WIGTON † St Mary

11m/18km S.W. of Carlisle

OS *NY255482* **GPS** *54.8238N, 3.1595W*

Built in 1788, the church is a triumph of painting inside. The work of the Rev. John

△ **WREAY: ST MARY** – *a unique work of the mid-19th century by Sara Losh, who designed and crafted the church as a memorial to her sister*

Ford in the 1950s, it is a study in grey, gold and strawberry-pink. There is a handsome pulpit with swags. Nothing of the church it replaced remains, except traces of original stonework used in nearby buildings.

WITHERSLACK † St Paul ★

6m/10km S.W. of Kendal
OS *SD431841* **GPS** *54.2502N, 2.8736W*

The church was built and endowed in 1669 by John Berwick, a Royalist who became Dean of St Paul's, and his brother, who was physician to Charles II. The roof was raised in 1768. Pews, rails and other fittings were added in the 19th century. The marble figure of a baby, Geoffrey Stanley, who died as an infant in 1871, sleeps on one window sill. There are good hatchments with angles at the corners, and a fine Royal Arms of Queen Anne with a jolly lion. The canopied pulpit was once a three-decker, and the altar table is 17th-century. The plain white Classical interior is a perfect foil to the romantic setting of hanging woods and limestone outcrop.

WREAY † St Mary ★★

5m/8km S.E. of Carlisle
OS *NY435489* **GPS** *54.8319N, 2.8807W*

Pevsner called Wreay the best in church architecture during the years of Queen Victoria. It was designed by talented amateur Sara Losh as a memorial to her sister Katherine, d. 1835. The church was consecrated in 1842 and is of unique design, drawing on Losh's European travels and unusually extensive education. The result is what Jenkins calls a 'Lombardic' church, rich in Italian Romanesque and early Christian ideas. Local masons were employed, and there is abundant exotic sculpture. Excellent details include the W. doorway, enriched with flowers, birds and beetles, the green marble altar table, supported by brass eagles, and the alabaster font, mostly carved by Sara herself. All here prefigures the Arts and Crafts movement by almost 50 years. In the churchyard is the cyclopean mausoleum for Katherine.

DERBYSHIRE

Derbyshire is a microcosm of England except that it has no sea. In the south it has pastoral country which merges into Leicestershire across the Trent, and here the older cottages and farms are of a dark red brick and the churches are of pale limestone. In the northern half of the county, stone never seems far from the surface, and stone of such variety of colour and quality as is found nowhere else in England.

There is the silvery white stone of the White Peak, where the drystone walls seem to take up more room than the grass in the little fields, and where the windswept farms are of a blue-grey limestone with mullions and transoms of a darker stone. There are limestones and ironstones of pale yellow, orange and brown, and great rock formations suddenly intruding into landscaped gardens such as at Chatsworth. The Saxons delighted to carve the stone into crosses, and build it into their churches, the crypt at Repton being the most perfect survival. The Normans used it for churches as at Steetley and Melbourne. And north of a line between Buxton and Chesterfield is the darker millstone grit of the High Peak.

With all this stone goes the remarkable scenery of the Peaks and Dales and of the moors of Derbyshire, a wild and windswept landscape generous enough to absorb the numerous holidaymakers and day trippers to the region. Derbyshire has been mined for lead and alabaster and Blue John and coal, and quarried for monumental stone as at Hopton Wood. It is still mined and quarried for its pure limestone, though thankfully the landscape is ample enough to accommodate the massive scars of quarries such as that at Wirksworth.

Derbyshire also has its industrial districts – the earliest are Georgian and associated with the spinning-mills of Crompton and Belper and the names of Arkwright and Strutt. On the eastern borders are the former coal districts, sooty, wire-strung and upheaved with excavations, and pitted with those sudden semi-towns one finds in neighbouring Nottinghamshire. It still has railway works at Derby and, although the iron industry is no longer, there is a major foreign presence in the car industry.

After its wonderful natural scenery and its less wonderful industrial districts, Derbyshire is chiefly a place of great houses. Chatsworth, a palace set in magnificent landscaped park and gardens, Hardwick Hall ('more glass than wall') and the dramatically sited castle at Bolsover are all associated with the Cavendishes. Haddon Hall, ancient and intimate, and Sudbury Hall, mellow and friendly, both belonged to the Vernons. Kedleston is the 18th-century ancestral home of the Curzons. There is also Calke, curious and remote, and the more modest hall at Melbourne in the south.

Here and there on hill-slopes are the Gothic Revival castles and abbeys of the Georgian and later industrialists, mostly now converted into institutions. In the

◁ **MELBOURNE: ST MICHAEL AND ST MARY** – *outstanding Norman arcades, enlivened by zigzags, with rough carved cushion capitals*

△ **DETHICK: ST JOHN THE BAPTIST** – *a 13th-century church with later tower in a splendid setting*

north, too, it is a county of wells, dressed with pictures made of flowers at Whitsun and summer festivals. There are mineral springs and the hydros that go with them, the boarding-houses, conferences, conventions, kiosks, souvenirs and car parks of holidaymakers.

Churches are lower on the list of the county's attractions than scenery and houses. Those least spoiled by Victorian restoration are private chapels – that at Haddon, with its wall-paintings, monuments and old woodwork and glass, like an untouched country church; and that at Chatsworth, sumptuous Renaissance of 1694 with marble and wood carving and a painted ceiling by Verrio. The parish churches, besides the Saxon and Norman work mentioned, are mostly small and severely restored, because there was plenty of money here in Victorian times, and the churches were generally stripped of their plaster and had their windows filled with greenish-tinted glass.

Large, cruciform 13th-century churches are at Ashbourne, Bakewell and Wirksworth. Grand 14th-century work is at Chesterfield, Tideswell, Norbury, Sandiacre and Whitwell. Spires are not typical of Derbyshire; the best is at Breadsall. Perpendicular 15th-century architecture, so common in the rest of England, is rare here, and the tower of Derby All Saints is its noblest expression. Several churches were built in the troubled century following the Reformation, still Gothic in style, at Risley and Foremark.

The 18th century produced much good wrought-iron work, particularly that of Robert Bakewell. Gibbs' design for All Saints, Derby, 1723–6, now the Cathedral, is the most distinguished Classical church in the county, and there are a few unrestored chapels of great charm. The 19th-century churches of Derbyshire are not of first rank; the best are Sir George Gilbert Scott's work at Edensor, the more individual and un-Derbyshire church at Bamford by Butterfield and, by the local Derby firm of Stevens and Robinson, the grand estate church at Osmaston and the more individual St Luke's, Derby.

In the last century, another Derby firm, Currey and Thompson, are worth looking out for, especially at St Mary the Virgin, Buxton.

A6024
A629
Stocksbridge
M1
SOUTH
YORKSHIRE
GLOSSOP
A57
A624
A57
SHEFFIELD
A625
Castleton
A6
Whaley Bridge
Peak District
Dronfield
Eckington
Steetley
A5004
A6
Eyam
Tideswell
A623
A621
A61
Whitwell
Staveley
A60
BUXTON
A6
Hassop
CHESTERFIELD
A619
Taddington
Edensor
A619
BAKEWELL
A632
A54
DERBYSHIRE
M1
Monyash
A632
A61
Ault Hucknall
A53
A515
Youlgreave
Ashover
Clay Cross
Hartington
MATLOCK
A615
MANSFIELD
A5012
Bonsall
Dethick
LEEK
A523
Alfreton
Brassington
Crich
Tissington
WIRKSWORTH
NOTTINGHAM-
SHIRE
A515
Ripley
STAFFORDSHIRE
Belper
A38
Ashbourne
A517
A52
A6
Norbury
Morley
Ilkeston
NOTTINGHAM
Kedleston
Breadsall
Dale Abbey
A515
Stapleford
A50
Trusley
Radbourne
A52
A50
Risley
Sandiacre
DERBY
UTTOXETER
Doveridge
Dalbury
Long Eaton
Church Wilne
Sawley
A453
Marston-on-Dove
A50
A515
Weston-on-Trent
A511
Repton
Foremark
A38
Melbourne
BURTON UPON
TRENT
A6006
M1
LOUGHBOROUGH
0
5 miles
0
5 km
Ashby-de-
la-Zouch
LEICESTERSHIRE
A444
A42

△ **ASHBOURNE: ST OSWALD** – *partially mutilated figures on the sides of the Bradbournes' tomb in the north transept's Boothby Chapel*

ASHBOURNE † St Oswald ★

13m/21km N.W. of Derby
OS *SK176464* **GPS** *53.0150N, 1.7387W*

Approached through 18th-century wrought-iron gates from Church Street, with its 16th-century grammar school and 18th-century houses, the graceful church has an attractive setting on the edge of town, and a breathtaking tower and spire. The chancel is Early English, dedicated in 1241, with noble lancet windows. Other parts are Decorated, and there are great Perpendicular windows. The whole building has a curious irregularity, but ever-changing vistas. The S. aisle is so wide that it appears as a second nave. There is plenty of Victorian stained glass and Arts and Crafts glass in a S. aisle window, 1905. Monuments, mostly in the N. transept, include the little girl Penelope Boothby, 1781, whose portraits became famous as a symbol of innocence.

ASHOVER † All Saints ★

6m/10km S.W. of Chesterfield
OS *SK348631* **GPS** *53.1641N, 1.4799W*

The church is beautifully placed among trees, the E. end framing the view at the end of the broad village street, with the characteristic Derbyshire outline – low and embattled, its tower with a spire set behind battlements. The church is mainly of the 14th and 15th centuries, the spire and rood screen given by the Babingtons. There are good alabaster tombs and brasses, and a lovely Norman lead font with figures in an arcade.

AULT HUCKNALL † St John the Baptist

5m/8km N.W. of Mansfield
OS *SK467652* **GPS** *53.1822N, 1.3020W*

In the winter the boastful towers of Hardwick Hall can be seen a mile to the S. The churchyard is nicely cluttered and random, and the church picturesque in its varied outline. Although Norman in origin, externally all is Perpendicular, while the inside is dark and holy, with a Norman arcade and crossing arches, and a very narrow, possibly Saxon, arch opening into the small chancel. In the W. wall outside is set a Norman carved tympanum depicting St George and the Dragon, and St Margaret emerging from the body of the Devil. There is a fine monument to the first Countess of Devonshire, 1627, and a memorial to Thomas Hobbes, the philosopher. William Butterfield restored the church in 1885–8, and furnished it excellently.

BAKEWELL † All Saints
7m/11km N.W. of Matlock
OS *SK215684* **GPS** *53.2130N, 1.6787W*

Well set above this ancient town and crowned by a distinctive octagonal crossing tower and spire, the church was originally Norman and on a grand scale – see the fragmentary blank arcade at the W. end. The rest is 13th- and 14th-century, but was rebuilt (not well) in the 19th century. There is much to see inside: a rare medieval wall-monument to Godfrey Foljambe and wife, c. 1385, and interesting Vernon monuments. There is important Saxon sculpture, including the handsome early 9th-century churchyard cross, and an interesting jumble of fragments in the S. porch.

BONSALL † St James ★
2m/3km S.W. of Matlock
OS *SK279581* **GPS** *53.1196N, 1.5833W*

Perched on a hill above the stone village, which has a fine cross in its marketplace, the church is embattled and pinky-grey, the spire a flight of fancy. The exterior is largely rebuilt, but inside are tall 13th-century arcades, the N. slightly later than the S. The stone is silvery, the walls cream-plastered, the texture and colour soft everywhere.

BRASSINGTON † St James
4m/6km W. of Wirksworth
OS *SK230543* **GPS** *53.0857N, 1.6577W*

In a commanding position at the top of the stone-built village, the church is basically Norman, with additional work in the 14th century and much restoration in the 19th. The S. arcade is especially fine, with circular piers, waterleaf and scalloped capitals. The W. tower is refaced. Otherwise it is mostly 19th-century and somewhat harsh, but with some good detailing.

BREADSALL † All Saints
2m/3km N.E. of Derby
OS *SK371397* **GPS** *52.9543N, 1.4491W*

The fine steeple is a landmark across the broad Derwent Valley north of Derby. The early 13th-century tower is four-square and plain, with an elegant 14th-century spire. There are handsome S. windows to the 14th-century nave. W. D. Caroe restored the church well in 1915 after fire damage by suffragettes the previous year.

BUXTON † St Mary the Virgin
7m/13km E. of Macclesfield
OS *SK059729* **GPS** *53.2536N, 1.9130W*

Built in 1914–15 by the Derby Arts and Crafts architects Currey and Thompson, the church is original and attractive, with pretty eyebrow dormers rather than a clerestory in the sweeping roof. Within are good contemporary furnishings.

CASTLETON † St Edmund
10m/16km W. of Sheffield
OS *SK150829* **GPS** *53.3428N, 1.7757W*

Standing in the middle of a close-knit village, in the lee of Peveril Castle, is this church with 14th-century tower. The nave is something of a surprise, shorn of its aisles in 1831, giving the appearance of a Commissioners' church of the period. The 19th-century Gothic porch is charming, leading to a plain plastered interior with Norman chancel arch and 17th-century box pews.

CHESTERFIELD
† St Mary and All Saints ★★
St Mary's Gate, 10m/16km S. of Sheffield
OS *SK385711* **GPS** *53.2362N, 1.4244W*

St Mary and All Saints is a town church on a prodigious scale; cruciform, with long nave and chancel, flanked by various chapels, it reflects the wealth of the town's guilds. Its crooked spire of timber and lead, which long since warped into its present ungainly shape, is a landmark from all around. The crossing was dedicated in 1234, but most of the church dates from 100 years later. The interior – lofty, spacious and elegant – has a 14th-century nave of six bays with tall, graceful columns, and appears almost sophisticated after the Norman homespun of many Derbyshire churches. In the Lady Chapel are alabaster tombs of the Foljambes – strange, fascinating and of delicate workmanship. Everywhere there are rich furnishings: medieval screens, a Jacobean pulpit and exquisite 18th-century candelabra of wrought iron. The stained glass is by Sir Ninian Comper and Christopher Webb.

CHURCH WILNE † St Chad

6m/10km S.W. of Derby
OS *SK448318* **GPS** *52.8822N, 1.3343W*

The church is set in meadows by the Derwent, with the well of St Chad nearby. A substantial three-stage tower with a stair turret seems to grow out of the upper part. The church is mostly 14th-century, the S. aisle extended eastward in 1622, and all is tied together by 15th-century battlements. The nave and aisles are spacious and light, having wide three-light lancet windows and clear glass, in contrast to the 17th-century Willoughby Chapel, which takes its sombre colour from the original Flemish glass. The church was restored by Currey and Thompson after a fire in 1917, and has some of their Arts and Crafts furnishings. There are bad but amusing alabaster monuments and, in the churchyard, good 17th- and 18th-century slate headstones.

CRICH † St Mary

4m/7km E. of Wirksworth
OS *SK348546* **GPS** *53.0880N, 1.4818W*

Externally a handsome if standard composition, with pleasant unrestored Decorated tracery, a Perpendicular W. tower and Norman nave. There is a rare stone lectern in the N. wall of the chancel, a massive Norman font and monuments in the chancel. The organ pipes, now no longer used, are housed in a fine casing.

DALBURY † All Saints ★

6m/9km W. of Derby
OS *SK263342* **GPS** *52.9053N, 1.609W*

A narrow lane leads to a farming hamlet with a small church at the end, 13th-century in origin, though heavily restored in the 19th century. At the W. end is a sweet little castellated tower like a toy castle, and a loveable interior with box pews and late 17th-century font and pulpit of 1862.

DALE ABBEY † All Saints ★

5m/8km N.E. of Derby
OS *SK437385* **GPS** *52.9429N, 1.3506W*

Romantically set in a secluded valley beyond the village, near the ruined arch of the 12th-century abbey with a hermitage close by, this tiny church and farmhouse coexist under one roof and are pleasant to behold. The interior is a delight – minute and higgledy-piggledy, with box pews, a gallery in the roof, a 'cupboard' altar, and a pulpit dated 1634. There is a late 13th-century mural of the Annunciation, Visitation and Nativity.

DERBY † St Mary's Bridge Chapel

Duke Street
OS *SK353367* **GPS** *52.9271N, 1.4758W*

A picturesque view from across the river has been unforgiveably compromised by Derby's inner ring road, which has been routed to within a hair's breadth of the chapel. Nonetheless, it is one of only five surviving bridge chapels, dating from the 14th century and later.

DERBY † St Mary RC

Between St Alkmunds Way and Darley Lane
OS *SK351367* **GPS** *52.9274N, 1.4790W*

Following the Catholic Emancipation Act of 1829, St Mary's Roman Catholic Church was designed and built in 1838–9 by A. W. N. Pugin, who was newly converted to Roman Catholicism. Unusually it is set on a north–south line. Pugin lamented the uncanonical necessity of this, imposed by constraints of the site. The whole building is imposing and very correct Perpendicular. The Gothic W. tower, with ornamented finials, has a fine window. The sanctuary is apsidal, and its lofty archway is echoed by a curved rood. The Lady Chapel, as large as a modest country church nave, was added in 1853 by Joseph Hansom – he of the Hansom Cab. There is stained glass by Hardman; the general effect is elegant and dignified.

DETHICK † St John the Baptist ★

2m/3km S.E. of Matlock
OS *SK327579* **GPS** *53.1179N, 1.5127W*

In a fine position on a hill over Cromford, the remarkable W. tower, modest in scale

△ **DALE ABBEY: ALL SAINTS** – *the church adjoins a farmhouse that, in the past, served as an infirmary and later as the Blue Bell Inn; the church interior is a ramshackle delight*

but lavish in detail, was built by Sir Anthony Babington in the 1530s; it has a curious stair turret which rises above the rest. There is a clerestory, but no aisles. The manor house has gone, but a 16th-century tithe barn remains.

DOVERIDGE † St Cuthbert

2m/3km E. of Uttoxeter
OS *SK113341* **GPS** *52.9042N, 1.8322W*

St Cuthbert is approached beneath the cover of a venerable yew and set in the former grounds of the demolished manor hall. The 13th-century work is memorable – a tall chancel and massive W. tower, the spire a 14th-century addition. The rest is mostly 14th-century too. The absence of a chancel arch or screen adds to the spaciousness of the interior.

ECKINGTON † St Peter and St Paul

6m/10km N.E. of Chesterfield
OS *SK432797* **GPS** *53.3132N, 1.3530W*

The church is distinguished by a massive tower, c. 1300, with a round-arched W. doorway, lancet windows, and low, thick-set 14th-century spire. The Classical S. aisle and porch, 1763, are by John Platt. Inside, too, there is history in stone. The E. bays of the nave arcades date from the late 12th century, the rest 13th; the N. aisle 14th and 15th; the chancel Classical also – but turned Gothic again in 1907.

EDENSOR † St Peter

2m/3km E. of Bakewell
OS *SK250699* **GPS** *53.2256N, 1.6260W*

Sir George Gilbert Scott rebuilt this in 1867 for the 7th Duke of Devonshire; it is set in a pretty model village in Chatsworth Park and provides an impressive essay in the Early English style with its tall spire and interior with Hardman glass. The alabaster pulpit is supported on black and red local marble, also used for the sedilia and font. On the W. wall is a massive florid monument to William, 1st Earl of Devonshire, d. 1625, and Henry Cavendish, d. 1616. The W. window is by Hardman and a fine example of his glass.

EYAM † St Lawrence ★
5m/8km N. of Bakewell
OS *SK217764* **GPS** *53.2843N, 1.6749W*

Eyam is famous as the village that halted the plague in 1666, when the village closed itself to the outside world. The Mompesson chair in St Lawrence's chancel commemorates the event – it is named after the rector at the time of the plague, who convinced the villagers to quarantine themselves to prevent the disease spreading. The 13th-century chancel was restored by Street in 1868-9. There is a huge sundial of 1775, 16th- and 17th-century wall-paintings, and texts on the nave walls. An 8th-century cross is in the churchyard. Look for the wonderful tombstone to the cricketer Harry Bagshawe, showing stumps flying and the umpire's finger pointing to heaven.

FOREMARK † St Saviour ★
6m/10km S. of Derby
OS *SK329264* **GPS** *52.8348N, 1.5120W*

Built by Sir Francis Burdett, 1662, in his park at Foremark Hall, this is a Gothic church without, except for window-spacing and some strapwork, but completely Renaissance within. The furnishings are original, neither Gothic nor Carolean, but rather the Jacobean style of 50 years earlier. They include a screen, triple-decker pulpit, box pews and a wrought-iron communion rail by Robert Bakewell, c. 1710.

HARTINGTON † St Giles
9m/15km N. of Ashbourne
OS *SK129604* **GPS** *53.1413N, 1.8077W*

Raised above the spreading village, the large cruciform church straddles the mound on which it sits, with proud, ashlar-faced tower looking out over the roof-tops. Inside there are vistas through arcades and into transepts, and a sense of interconnecting parts making up the whole.

HASSOP † All Saints RC
3m/5km N. of Bakewell
OS *SK223723* **GPS** *53.2474N, 1.6666W*

By Joseph Ireland, 1816–18, for Francis Eyre of Hassop Hall, the church is unusual and unexpected in this little hamlet – an Etruscan temple in the Peak District. With echoes of Inigo Jones's Covent Garden church St Paul's, it has a monumental and rather severe W. portico over which sits a disproportionately overhung roof. The interior is gentler and more ornate, with an early 19th-century chamber organ in the W. gallery and an elaborate altar of French origin.

KEDLESTON † All Saints
4m/6km N.W. of Derby
OS *SK312403* **GPS** *52.9592N, 1.5367W*
Churches Conservation Trust

The old village was moved, but the medieval church still stands cheek by jowl with the grand 18th-century hall by Robert Adam. It is essentially a late 13th-century cruciform church, with crossing tower and transepts, Norman S. doorway and a Classical E. end. The memorial chapel to Lady Mary Curzon, Vicereine of India, was added by Bodley in 1907–13. The Curzon family monuments include effigies designed by Robert Adam and Michael Rysbrack and span some 700 years.

MARSTON-ON-DOVE † St Mary
4m/6km N. of Burton upon Trent
OS *SK233296* **GPS** *52.8637N, 1.6551W*

St Mary sits in a flat plain near the confluence of the Dove and the Trent. It has a fine recessed 14th-century steeple, 13th-century chancel and 14th-century nave. The interior is spacious, as the N. aisle was given an upper storey in the 15th century. The 19th-century organ came from Sudbury Hall. The church has the oldest bell in the county, cast in 1366.

MELBOURNE
† St Michael and St Mary ★★
7m/11km S. of Derby
OS *SK389249* **GPS** *52.8211N, 1.4242W*

A singularly ambitious cruciform Norman church of c. 1130 with twin W. towers and taller crossing tower and lofty stone-vaulted narthex. Traces of the original apses can be seen at the E. end. The Norman bishops of Carlisle made this their seat when their own city was threatened by the Scots, and it reflects their status. An austere and noble interior is rich with Norman carving, with monumental circular piers, stilted arches, and much zigzag. The crossing is even better: carved capitals

REPTON: ST WYSTAN – *the alabaster figure of a 14th-century knight at the north-east end of the nave, by the stairway to the crypt* ▷

depicting the 'Melbourne Cat' and a Sheela-na-Gig. Fragments of paintings can be seen on the W. piers.

MONYASH † St Leonard ★

4m/6km W. of Bakewell
OS *SK151664* **GPS** *53.1951N, 1.7748W*

Beneath the high moors, the church is built of attractive contrasting stone. It is cruciform, though on a small scale, the N. transept being originally a chantry. Of the 13th and 14th century, the earliest features are the chancel arch, sedilia and piscina. Butterfield restored the church in 1887, rebuilding the N. transept on its old foundations. The 10ft-long parish chest is believed to be from the 13th century.

MORLEY † St Matthew

4m/6km N.E. of Derby
OS *SK396409* **GPS** *52.9643N, 1.4109W*

A spired country church among lawns and trees outside the village, with an attractive 18th-century rectory. W. of the church is the beautiful Bateman Mausoleum, 1897, by G. F. Bodley. Inside, there is golden light and much texture. The S. nave arcade is Norman; the rest 14th- and 15th-century. The glass, from Dale Abbey, was made in 1482. Fascinating brasses, monuments and incised slabs tell 500 years of family history, mainly of the Stathums, Sacheverells and Babingtons; Katherine Babington, d. 1543, is the best.

NORBURY † St Mary and St Barlok

4m/6km S.W. of Ashbourne
OS *SK125423* **GPS** *52.9788N, 1.8145W*

This small church occupies a quiet, leafy setting above the River Dove, close by the manor with its late 13th-century hall. The church has a splendid 14th-century chancel – spacious and wide, with the windows fine and tall. Much of the original glass survives, with patterns and heraldry in grisaille and soft colours. In the chancel are altar tombs of the Fitzherberts, with good effigies and enchanting figures of weepers; a bedesman sits under Sir Ralph's foot.

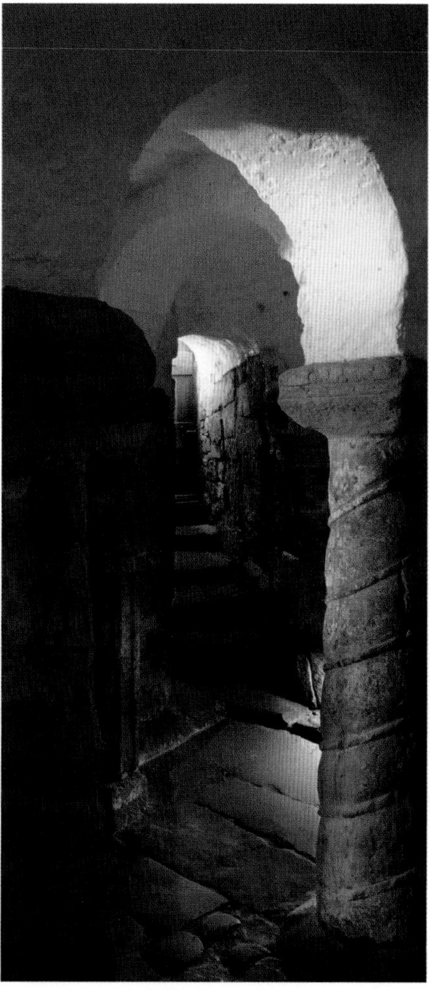

△ **REPTON: ST WYSTAN** – *the Saxon crypt, with vaulted ceiling and barley-twist pillars*

RADBOURNE † St Andrew

4m/6km W. of Derby
OS *SK286359* **GPS** *52.9206N, 1.5760W*

St Andrew's is in Radbourne Park and has a fine old yew tree in the churchyard. Small and mainly of the 13th and 14th centuries, there is a mixture on the S. side of Tudor windows and an 18th-century porch. The zigzagged sedilia has a bishop's crozier marked on the shaft. The medieval benches came from Dale Abbey. Pole monuments and hatchments are proudly displayed.

REPTON † St Wystan ★★

5m/8km N.E. of Burton upon Trent

OS *SK303271* **GPS** *52.8412N, 1.5516W*

A graceful spire marks this fine church, which sits by an old priory arch leading to the school – a satisfying group in a pleasant country town with market cross. The church has all types of architecture from the 8th century to the 15th, but the most exciting part is the Saxon chancel and, beneath it, the crypt, discovered accidentally in the 18th century. Winding stairways lead down to the crypt; it has a rough stone vault and pillars wreathed with barley twists.

RISLEY † All Saints

2m/3km N.W. of Long Eaton

OS *SK461357* **GPS** *52.9168N, 1.3158W*

Of curious and delightful appearance, there is some confusion over the actual dates of All Saints. Suffice it to say that the church owes its existence to the Willoughby family who lived in Risley Hall from the 16th century. The tower, topped with outside crocketed pinnacles, has a tipsy lean. The N. aisle and vestry were added in the 1841 restoration. Inside are hatchments and painted commandment boards.

SANDIACRE † St Giles ★

2m/3km N. of Long Eaton

OS *SK480372* **GPS** *52.9307N, 1.2873W*

Set on a hill, with the industry of the Erewash valley below, the church has a memorable silhouette – a high Norman nave and still higher Decorated chancel of almost cathedral proportions, with tall pinnacled buttresses. Inside, the same contrast; the simple whitewashed nave, robust Norman chancel arch, and breathtaking chancel, bathed in light, with star and leaf shapes in the tracery, and richly ornamented sedilia and piscina.

SAWLEY † All Saints

Adjoins Long Eaton, 7m/13km S.E. of Derby

OS *SK472313* **GPS** *52.8777N, 1.2994W*

An avenue of limes leads from the main road to this church, which stands on a small rise by the river. It is mostly 13th- and 14th-century with Perpendicular flourishes. The dignified Perpendicular chantry chapel, like a domestic bay window, is panelled and vaulted inside, with the tomb of John Bothe, d. 1496.

△ **TIDESWELL: ST JOHN THE BAPTIST** – *19th-century carving of Zacharias, John's father*

STEETLEY † All Saints Chapel ★★

2m/3km W. of Worksop

OS *SK543787* **GPS** *53.3027N, 1.1858W*

J. L. Pearson brought this astonishingly complete showpiece of a small Norman church of nave, chancel and apse back to life. Built about 1160, it was left roofless after the Commonwealth, standing alone in the fields. Inside, the vaulted apse, lavishly decorated nave and chancel arches, the capitals scalloped, or carved with leaves, animals and people, all create a delight that J. Charles Cox described as 'the most perfect and elaborate specimen of Norman architecture to be found anywhere in Europe'.

TADDINGTON † St Michael

5m/8km W. of Bakewell

OS *SK141711* **GPS** *53.2373N, 1.7898W*

The moor drops down sharply to the church and village and the Dale below. This handsome church with spire is largely 14th-century

△ **TIDESWELL: ST JOHN THE BAPTIST** – *the magnificent carving of the chancel stalls in the late 19th century was the work of Suffolk craftsmen from Bury St Edmunds*

with an impressive chancel and E. window; the interior is scraped. A stone lectern is built into the chancel wall.

TIDESWELL † St John the Baptist ★★

6m/10km E. of Buxton
OS *SK152757* **GPS** *53.2787N, 1.7726W*

'The Cathedral of the Peak', sheltered in a hollow on the bleak moors, is a grand and inspiring church of the 14th century. The Perpendicular tower has character, with immense turrets and pinnacles, and the fine chancel compares with Ashbourne, Norbury and Sandiacre. The Perpendicular style allowed for large windows and light to flood in – at its very best with an autumnal or late winter sun. A fine stone screen stands behind the altar, with canopied niches, and, at the W. end of the chancel, is a mighty arch into the nave and a great panelled window; interesting tombs and brasses vie with 19th-century Suffolk joinery and delightful 20th-century bench-ends by local carvers Advent and Hunstone.

TISSINGTON † St Mary ★

4m/6km N. of Ashbourne
OS *SK176522* **GPS** *53.0674N, 1.7381W*

A Jacobean manor house, grey stone cottages, triangular green and five wells (dressed with flower mosaics on Ascension Day), form a perfect feudal village setting for the church, which, with a sturdy Norman tower, stands on a bank in the midst. The interior had too much restoration in 1854. There is an extravagant 1643 Fitzherbert monument with ladies in Jacobean dress that cuts off part of the chancel arch – no doubt here about what was considered the more important. There is also a two-decker pulpit and a Norman font with incised creatures.

TRUSLEY † All Saints ★

6m/10km W. of Derby
OS *SK253355* **GPS** *52.9166N, 1.6243W*

Approached along a grassy path, the small Georgian brick church of 1713, together with the old hall and manor house, forms one side of this small village. The interior is delightfully all of a piece with communion rails, three-decker pulpit, box pews and font.

WESTON-ON-TRENT † St Mary ★
6m/10km S.E. of Derby
OS *SK397275* **GPS** *52.8444N, 1.4110W*

Alone among trees by the river, St Mary's is small and mostly 13th-century. The nave and aisles are wide rather than long with very tall, slim pillars, unexpectedly dignified and impressive. An embattled and buttressed tower supports a recessed spire. Inside is a Jacobean pulpit and fragments of a monument to Richard Sale in the gruesome taste of the early 17th century – a skeleton with hour-glass, pick and shovel. The 18th-century timber-framed porch adds a domestic touch.

WHITWELL † St Lawrence ★
4m/6km S.W. of Worksop
OS *SK526768* **GPS** *53.2858N, 1.2121W*

Pleasantly placed by open farmland on the edge of a once pretty village, now surrounded by a landscape shaped by coal mining. The core of the church – W. tower, S. doorway, nave and clerestory – is Norman. The interior is a delight, light and cheerful with whitewashed walls and an absence of stained glass. The chancel arch is round, but with keeled shafts, preparing one for the Decorated chancel with rich sedilia; the transepts are Decorated too. Altogether it is a rewarding building, full of texture and interest, set in an attractive graveyard and fortunately not spoiled by too much tidying up.

WIRKSWORTH † St Mary ★
4m/6km S. of Matlock
OS *SK287539* **GPS** *53.0819N, 1.5723W*

A grey market town with a maze of steep, winding streets and 'ginnels' (passageways), and set below some cruel quarries, Wirksworth clawed its way back from dusty semi-dereliction to being a fine town with a thriving cultural life. The town's large cruciform church, dating from the 13th century, was much added to and restored by George Gilbert Scott in 1876. It is at the hub of the town, set in a graveyard enclosed by railings and surrounded by a ring of houses, rather like a miniature cathedral close. The interior is impressive, with lovely vistas. An exceptionally interesting 9th-century or even earlier coffin lid sculpted with scenes from the gospels is displayed on the N. wall of the nave. On the W. wall is a carved figure of a leadminer with pick and kibble. There are two fonts – one Norman, one 17th-century – brasses and good monuments.

YOULGREAVE † All Saints ★
3m/4km S. of Bakewell
OS *SK212643* **GPS** *53.1760N, 1.6842W*

The massive, stately Perpendicular tower stands four-square to the winds of the Peak. Inside is a wide Norman nave, a particularly impressive S. arcade and fine Norman carving. The font of c. 1200 has a separate holy-water stoup supported by a salamander. There are two delightful alabaster monuments; a miniature tomb chest to Sir Thomas Cokayne, d. 1488, with effigy only 3½ feet long, and a panel of great charm to Robert Gylbert, d. 1492, who stands with his wife and 17 children and the Virgin and Child in their midst. The fine E. window is by Burne-Jones. Opposite the S. door is an early carved pilgrim figure, set into the wall.

DEVON

The popular idea of this large south-western county is not far from the right one. The steeply banked lane, stuffed with fern and foxglove and honeysuckle, winds down through oaks which interlace their lichened branches to an old stone bridge over a stream which babbles against boulders. Soon we come to the barton or farm, pink-washed and snug, cob-walled and thickly thatched among its steep little fields of red earth. On the hill-slope higher up is the village. Here are thatched walls too, and cob cottages with rounded corners and bulging hearths and hollyhocks and fuchsias in the garden. Out of the sycamores near the hill-top peep the tall pinnacles of a thin church tower.

Inside the church, low 15th-century arcades of clustered columns support a barrel-shaped wooden roof whose timbers are carved. And right across the east end, for we do not expect to see a chancel arch in Devon, will be a wooden screen with carved base and painted saints on its panels, and through the wooden tracery above the panels we can see the altar. Above the tracery is a beam carved with grapes and vine leaves from which wooden vaults over-arch to support a loft which has painted panels. Above this once stood the rood, looking down the chancel into the nave. And out into the scented warmth of the churchyard we will go, back to the village for Devonshire tea, with strawberries and cream, where people will call us 'my dear'.

Such places may indeed be found inland in south Devon. This part of the county has luscious vegetation; flowers seem bigger and brighter than in the rest of England, and the sheltered estuaries on the south coast are almost tropical. But the uplands of west Devon are bare and flattened, to quote the historian Sir John Fortescue, 'between the hammer of west wind and the anvil of the yellow clay'. Even so the stony valley villages have the sheltered look of the south. But there are other sorts of Devon scenery: Exmoor with its smooth moorlands; Dartmoor with its sharp outcrops of granite; Lynton and Lynmouth with their Alpine steeps; south-coast seaside towns like Sidmouth, Teignmouth, Dawlish and Torquay, where stucco Georgian terraces and Gothic cottages look through boughs of ilex to the Channel. In Plymouth one can find maritime Georgian at its best. The city was formed from the amalgamation of three towns: Devonport, of marble pavements and Greek Revival public buildings; slate-hung Stonehouse, with its Royal William victualling yard; and Plymouth itself, old as the sea, pseudo-simple in its arid new centre. At Tiverton there is fine architectural evidence of a long-prosperous agricultural market town.

Nearly all the old churches of Devon were rebuilt or enlarged in the 15th century. The inspiration behind Exeter Cathedral, with its square Norman towers and beautiful nave and choir, rebuilt in the late 13th and early 14th centuries, and behind that miniature cathedral, the collegiate church of Ottery St Mary, did not survive into

◁ **BRENTOR: ST MICHAEL** – *a spectacular setting on the fringes of Dartmoor, with views over Devon and west to Cornwall*

the 15th-century prosperity of country parishes, for it was monastic in origin. The 15th-century Devon churches have the low West Country proportions of Exeter Cathedral and Ottery, but they are much of a pattern. The towers, though often graceful, have less variety than those of Somerset.

Devonians seem to have been primarily carvers of wood and stone, and only secondarily architects. Almost every old church has remains of wooden screens or pulpits or benches. Painting seems to have interested them less than carving, and screen-painting is not as impressive as that of East Anglia. The county was conservative and Catholic, and in 1549 the Prayer Book Rebellion, a gallant attempt to reinstate the old missal after the Reformation, started at St Andrew's Church in Sampford Courtenay. Love of the old ways probably accounts for the survival of screens in so many churches, and even the building of them as late as the 18th century, as at Cruwys Morchard. But it does not account for the disappearance of almost all old stained glass in the county.

In the 19th century, Devon was High Church under the autocratic reign of the great Bishop Philpotts, 'Henry of Exeter'. It is not surprising, therefore, to find work of the London Tractarian architects, Street and Butterfield, and the talented local church architect, F. Hayward, building new churches and making good use of the various marbles available in the county. Plymouth remained what it had long been, Puritan and iconoclastic.

Devon is different from the rest of Britain. It is brighter-coloured, more West Country than Somerset, where one still feels the pull of Bristol, and less Celtic than sea-swept Cornwall. Exeter is not only its county and cathedral town – vilely developed of recent years on its outskirts, and in the centre – but it is the capital of a country, the country of Devon, and the mother city of the ancient Celtic kingdom of Dumnonia.

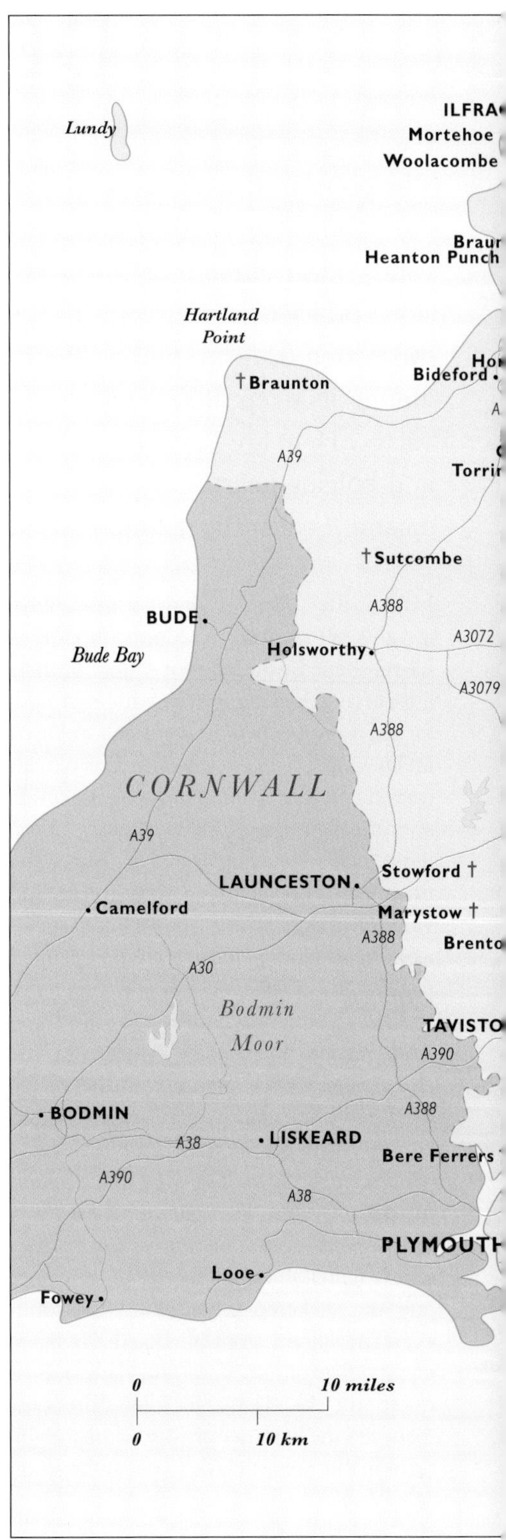

Lynton
Lynmouth
Parracombe
Burnham-on-Sea
MINEHEAD
Watchet
Exmoor
SOMERSET
BRIDGWATER
TAPLE
Swimbridge
Molland
South Molton
Langport
TAUNTON
Bickington
Wellington
Burrington
DEVON
Chulmleigh
Cruwys Morchard
TIVERTON
Cadeleigh
Cullompton
Kentisbeare
Chard
Coldridge
Upton Hellions
Honeychurch
Sampford Courtenay
Sandford
Plymtree
Crediton
HONITON
Colebrooke
Newton St Cyres
Upton Pyne
Gittisham
Axminster
HAMPTON
Hittisleigh
Cheriton Bishop
EXETER
Ottery St Mary
Sidbury
LYME REGIS
Seaton
Salcombe Regis
Branscombe
Sidmouth
Bridford
Doddiscombsleigh
Ashton
Kenton
North Bovey
EXMOUTH
Manaton
Ashcombe
Dawlish
Widecombe-in-the-Moor
Buckland-in-the-Moor
TEIGNMOUTH
Shaldon
Newton Abbot
Haccombe
Ashburton
West Ogwell
Torbryan
Buckfastleigh
TORQUAY
Babbacombe
TOTNES
PAIGNTON
Harford
Harberton
Cornworthy
BRIXHAM
DARTMOUTH
Kingsbridge
SALCOMBE
Start Point
A39
A399
A396
A38
A358
A361
A378
M5
A303
A377
A373
A30
A375
A3122
A379
A381

ASHCOMBE † St Nectan ★
8m/13km S. of Exeter
OS *SX912795* **GPS** *50.6056N, 3.5386W*

At the head of the long combe of Dawlish Water stands this originally small 13th-century cruciform church – traces seen in the tower, S. transept and chancel. In the 15th century the Kirkhams enlarged the N. transept into an aisle. Salvin's renovation of 1824–5 removed much of its medieval character, including the rood screen, though the carved 15th-century bench-ends remain. It is now light, charming, and Gothic, with delicate plaster panelling and colouring everywhere. The adjacent vicarage is of the same happy period.

ASHTON † St John the Baptist ★
5m/8km S.W. of Exeter
OS *SX856846* **GPS** *50.6506N, 3.6194W*

A singularly attractive church in every way and worth going 50 miles to see. It lies on the luxuriant W. slopes of Haldon, where they cascade down to the Teign Valley. Entirely rebuilt and refurnished between about 1400 and 1485, Ashton is the 'typical' Devonshire church at its best and unrestored, although late 19th-century work replaced parts of the building. The plastered walls and white Beer-stone arcade set off the rich colouring of the medieval screens, glass and wall-paintings. The lavish carved woodwork so characteristic of Devon churches is here in abundance. The 15th-century rood screen and parclose screens have some of the best figure-paintings in Devon, especially those on the N. parclose screen and on back of the aisle screen. Carved bench-ends, heraldic glass and wall-painting are all of same period. There is an Elizabethan pulpit with canopy, 17th-century communion rails and a wooden monument to Sir George Chudleigh, 1657, who lived nearby. Note also the original 15th-century S. door and wagon roofs. The groined canopy of the rood screen, added in 1908, alone mars the scene.

ATHERINGTON † St Mary ★
7m/11km S. of Barnstaple
OS *SS591231* **GPS** *50.9902N, 4.0087W*

Located on a hilltop in the village, the fabric is not exciting structurally, mostly plain Devon Perpendicular over-restored by Pearson, 1884. It is notable, however, for its screens, original wagon roofs and fine series of 15th-century carved and crocketed bench-ends. The N. aisle screen, all that remains of a screen that once spanned the N. aisle and chancel, supports a fine rich original rood loft, the only one left in Devon, the work of John Parres, c. 1530. The chancel section of the screen was replaced c. 1800 by an inferior and earlier type from Umberleigh Chapel nearby. There is an altar tomb to Sir John Bassett and his two wives, as well as 13th- and 14th-century effigies.

BABBACOMBE † All Saints
Adjoins Torquay to N.
OS *SX924652* **GPS** *50.4774N, 3.5167W*

This is a fine example of a Butterfield Gothic Revival church, 1868–74, incorporating polychromatic Devon marbles, notably in the pulpit, font and chancel floor. The mosaics behind the high altar are by A. Salviati.

BERE FERRERS † St Andrew ★★
7m/11km S. of Tavistock
OS *SX459634* **GPS** *50.4503N, 4.1714W*

Mostly rebuilt about 1300–30, St Andrew's is unusual for Devon in retaining so much 14th-century work. Note the early 14th-century glass in the E. window, with interesting and varied tracery – Reticulated, Perpendicular and Intersecting. There are also early 16th-century benches, with Ferrers heraldry carved on one, and the tombs of the Ferrers, who built the church and lived in the medieval house nearby. The handsome table-tomb in the N. transept is that of Lord Willoughby de Broke, 1522. The lovely estuary of the River Tavy should be seen here.

BRANSCOMBE † St Winifred ★
5m/8km E. of Sidmouth
OS *SY195884* **GPS** *50.6902N, 3.1403W*

A delightful place sited in a combe about a mile back from the sea in a long, narrow village, this church is important for the antiquary, as it shows a process of continuous development from the 11th century to the 16th, though the dominant features are the crossing tower, mostly Norman, the 13th-century work in transepts and nave, and the 14th-century

ASHTON: ST JOHN THE BAPTIST – *Devon through and through, with rustic plastered walls, sublime wood carving on the screens and good quality panel-painting too* ▷

△ **ASHTON: ST JOHN THE BAPTIST** – *the figure painting on the screens shows a deftness of touch and an expressive quality*

chancel. The woodwork is worth studying, especially the Elizabethan W. gallery, the communion rails enclosing the table on four sides, the excellent three-decker pulpit – rare in Devon – and the box pews in the N. transept. There are monuments to the Wadhams and other local gentry.

BRAUNTON † St Brannock ★

5m/8km N.W. of Barnstaple
OS *SS489370* **GPS** *51.1130N, 4.1598W*

Set in the largest village in Devon, now virtually a suburb of Barnstaple, St Brannock's is a large barn-like church, not very prepossessing but well worth visiting. The Celtic missionary-saint Brannoc (who came across from South Wales) founded a minster here in the 6th century and is almost certainly buried under the high altar. The present church is mostly 13th-century, but with much later detail. Note the Norman S. tower with lead-covered broach spire. The remarkably wide nave is covered by a fine roof enriched with 15th-century bosses, including one of a sow feeding her litter. The N. transept gallery was the private pew of the Snow family.

BRENTOR † St Michael

5m/8km N. of Tavistock
OS *SX470804* **GPS** *50.6033N, 4.1623W*

A wonderful site, perched on the very summit of an extinct volcanic cone, 1,100 feet above the sea, St Michael's has a lonely and remote setting, with views over half of Devon and Cornwall. The first church was founded here c. 1140 by the Gifford family, but most is 14th century and heavily restored by the Victorians.

BRIDFORD † St Thomas à Becket

4m/6km E. of Moretonhampstead
OS *SX816863* **GPS** *50.6650N, 3.6766W*

St Thomas à Becket is a granite Perpendicular church set in a granite village with Dartmoor in its views to the west. There is some late-medieval glass, carved stalls and bench-ends, wagon roofs and other medieval woodwork. Best of all is the splendid rood screen, made about 1530, which retains much of its soft, ancient colouring.

BUCKLAND-IN-THE-MOOR † St Peter
3m/4km N.W. of Ashburton
OS *SX720731* **GPS** *50.5440N, 3.8072W*

In a romantic moorland setting in the National Park, St Peter's is mostly 15th-century granite, with a carved Norman font and crude early 16th-century paintings. The 14th-century traceried screen is particularly fine, despite Fellowes Fynne's intrusive restoration: an interesting if unnecessary jigsaw of the old and new.

BURRINGTON † Holy Trinity
4m/6km N.W. of Chulmleigh
OS *SS637166* **GPS** *50.9332N, 3.9400W*

Largely 15th-century Perpendicular with good woodwork, Holy Trinity was restored in 1884. The tower is earlier: 13th- to 14th-century with a 15th-century top stage. Inside is a well-preserved screen with carved pomegranates and inverted Green Men, and a traceried S. door. The N. and S. ceilings have Tudor angels and bosses.

CADELEIGH † St Bartholomew
4m/6km S.W. of Tiverton
OS *SS914079* **GPS** *50.8605N, 3.5444W*

Well-set with good views. The church is mainly 15th-century, but the inside walls are decorated with plaster panels from the mid-18th century, when the box pews were fitted. In the N. aisle is a fine canopied altar tomb to Sir Simon and Lady Catherine Leach.

CHERITON BISHOP † St Mary
6m/10km S.W. of Crediton
OS *SX773935* **GPS** *50.7287N, 3.7395W*

Set in a tight fold between hills, the church has a good collection of fittings: a Norman font, 16th-century pulpit, coloured rood screen, bench-ends and a rare Elizabethan painted Royal Arms over the S. door.

CHULMLEIGH † St Mary Magdalene
8m/12km S. of South Molton
OS *SS686141* **GPS** *50.9119N, 3.8693W*

Standing high above the River Dart, this church was collegiate from the 13th century, but its fabric dates mainly from the 15th century now. It has a tall W. tower and a long and notably complete rood screen. The chancel tiles and fittings are by Gould, 1879–81, all set off with Hardman glass.

COLDRIDGE † St Matthew ★
20m/32km N.W. of Exeter
OS *SS698076* **GPS** *50.8537N, 3.8504W*

Both church and village are set on the summit of a high ridge, with views across to Dartmoor. Some Norman work, but mostly late 15th- to early 16th-century. Highly interesting contents include medieval screens (flamboyant work in the parclose screen as at Colebrooke), a fine medieval carved pulpit, late medieval bench-ends, tiles, glass, wagon-roofs with carved bosses, and the table-tomb of Sir John Evans, who gave many of the fittings in 1511–12.

COLEBROOKE † St Andrew ★
5m/8km W. of Crediton
OS *SS769000* **GPS** *50.7867N, 3.7463W*

The 14th-century church, enlarged in the 15th, stands boldly by itself. It has a good W. tower. The unusual, crudely carved bench-ends date from the late 15th century, as do the fine screens – a rood with linenfold panelling, and screens to the Copelstone Chapel with an unusual Curvilinear design.

COMBE MARTIN † St Peter
4m/7km E. of Ilfracombe
OS *SS586463* **GPS** *51.1984N, 4.0248W*

St Peter's is set in a rather dull village but is an unusual and pleasing example of the old and new. The rood screen, decorated with painted saints, has contemporary carved saints in the niches. The loft is by Herbert Read, 1911, the reredos by Doris Downing, 1972, and the rood figures above the screen by Colin Shewring are inspired by an illustration from the *Book of Hours*.

CORNWORTHY † St Peter ★
4m/6km S.E. of Totnes
OS *SX829555* **GPS** *50.3881N, 3.6479W*

This is a 15th-century building in a Dartside village, with a Norman font and much-restored medieval screen. Most of the rest of the interior dates from 1788, with later modifications, including the box pews, a canopied pulpit, altarpiece, clear glass and altered window tracery. Delightful repose everywhere, and quite unharmed by Victorian meddlers.

CREDITON † Holy Cross ★★
8m/12km N.W. of Exeter
OS *SS836002* **GPS** *50.7897N, 3.6522W*

A splendid collegiate church in a sleepy little town, Holy Cross is the successor to a Saxon minster and cathedral. Built of red sandstone, it has a Norman central tower incongruously set within a mainly 15th-century Perpendicular fabric. The clerestory is very beautiful; unusual even in good Devon churches. The unfortunate memorial by Caroe above the chancel arch to Sir Redvers Buller, who was vastly admired by Devonians if not by the outside world, is described by the writer Simon Jenkins as a 'mix of Perpendicular and Pre-Raphaelite in what could be the backdrop for an Arthurian romance'. Other examples of Gothic revivalism are here too. Original Gothic is represented in the sedilia, carved figures in the vaulting and traces of early paintwork. There are tombs for Sir John Sully, 1387, Sir William Peryam, 1604, and John Tuckfield, 1630.

CRUWYS MORCHARD † Holy Cross
5m/8km W. of Tiverton
OS *SS874121* **GPS** *50.8980N, 3.6021W*

Highly 'atmospherick', for it stands beside the ancient house of the Cruwys family who have lived there since the 12th century. Mostly 14th-century and early 16th, the interior is nevertheless quite Georgian in feeling, all done after the great fire of 1689, with plastered walls, a remarkable Georgian chancel and parclose screens. The chancel fittings show continuity of traditional forms. The cut-down box pews are all named, some marked as being for boys, others for girls.

CULLOMPTON † St Andrew ★
5m/8km S.E. of Tiverton
OS *ST021071* **GPS** *50.8558N, 3.3910W*

Another splendid town church, but unlike Crediton, St Andrew's is 15th- and 16th-century Perpendicular. The fine red tower – one of the things one looks for from the train dashing down to Exeter – was finished in 1549. The second S. aisle was built in 1526 by John Lane, a wealthy cloth merchant. A rich fan-traceried roof has carvings of ships, sheep-shears, and so forth. The gorgeous coloured roof runs unbroken throughout the entire length of the church, and the splendid coloured rood screen runs across its entire width. Cullompton brings home to one the lavish colour of a medieval church against the white background of the Beer-stone arcades.

DARTMOUTH † St Petrox ★
7m/11km S.E. of Totnes
OS *SX886503* **GPS** *50.3422N, 3.5661W*

A splendid site at the very mouth of the Dart, the church makes a highly effective grouping with the castle and the wooded cliffs. This is an ancient Christian site, but the present church was entirely rebuilt in Gothic style, 1641–2, with much woodwork of that period and fine brasses to Dartmouth merchants.

DODDISCOMBSLEIGH † St Michael
6m/10km S.W. of Exeter
OS *SX857865* **GPS** *50.6674N, 3.6179W*

The N. aisle of this church has the best medieval glass in Devon outside Exeter Cathedral. A set of five large Perpendicular windows are painted in pale yellow and white with touches of red, green and blue. Here are delicately drawn saints, the Seven Sacraments and heraldry.

EXETER † St David ★★
St David's Hill
OS *SX915931* **GPS** *50.7274N, 3.5382W*

W. D. Caroe's best church, 1897–1900, St David is a Romantic essay much influenced by the Celtic twilight as well as Art Nouveau. The interior is gargantuan in its expression, with powerful limestone ribs accentuating the bays of the narrow aisles and timber tunnel vault. The tall reredos is also by Caroe; the glass by the Kempe Studio.

EXETER † St Mary Arches ★
Mary Arches Street
OS *SX918925* **GPS** *50.7223N, 3.5338W*

Restored in 1950 by S. Dykes-Bower after war-time bomb damage, it is the only Devon parish church to retain two full Norman arcades, with plain piers and square scalloped capitals. The reredos, altar and rails date from 1696. There are many fine monuments

◁ **CREDITON: HOLY CROSS** – *at ease in the afternoon sunlight, the recumbent figure of Sir John Sully on his late 14th-century tomb*

to most of the mayors of Exeter. The rebuilt barrel-vaulted roof uses timbers recovered from a U.S. landing craft. Externally the church was poorly served by its restoration, which used imitation stone.

GITTISHAM † St Michael ★

2m/3km S.W. of Honiton
OS *SY133983* **GPS** *50.7784N, 3.2300W*

Luxuriant colouring is everywhere in this cob and thatch village in deepest east Devon. St Michael's is the usual Perpendicular village church, but the atmosphere is 18th-century with the box pews, ceiled roofs, hatchments and a gallery. There are several pleasant 16th- to 19th-century mural monuments.

HACCOMBE † St Blaise ★

3m/4km E. of Newton Abbot
OS *SX898701* **GPS** *50.5212N, 3.5558W*

In an estate setting in parkland of the Carews, St Michael's is a small 14th-century church with bellcote, modest porch and brightly coloured lancet windows. The church is notable for its fine collection of medieval effigies and brasses, 13th- to 17th-century, of various lords of Haccombe and members of the Carew family. There is some 14th-century glass, a stone screen, pulpit and reredos by Kendall of Exeter, 1821–2.

HARBERTON † St Andrew ★

2m/3km S.W. of Totnes
OS *SX778586* **GPS** *50.4150N, 3.7209W*

A large, unspoilt village in a fertile landscape, and a splendid 14th–15th-century church, with a handsome tower and a fine late-medieval rood screen; the vaulting and cornices are especially rich. The saints and angels depicted in the lower screen panels are said to be modelled on young ladies of the congregation in 1870, and are on metal plates. Some of the original painted wooden panels of saints thankfully survive, and can be seen on the N. aisle. The pulpit is 15th-century, octagonal and carved – one of Devon's best. The richly painted 17th-century panels are of the Apostles, possibly replacing figures lost after the Reformation.

HARFORD † St Petroc

10m/16km E. of Plymouth
OS *SX638594* **GPS** *50.4193N, 3.9181W*

A 15th-century moorland church, it stands on the edge of Dartmoor and has a modest W. tower and ceiled wagon roofs. There is a tomb chest of 1566 with a brass of Thomas Williams, Speaker of the House of Commons.

HARTLAND † St Nectan

12m/19km N. of Bude
OS *SS235247* **GPS** *50.9949N, 4.5165W*

Not in the old borough but two miles W. at Stoke, overlooking the open, restless Atlantic; the tower was built as a landmark for mariners. It is a large 14th-century church with late 15th-century embellishments. The Norman font is splendid, as are the carved bench-ends of 1530; the wagon roofs are partly ceiled and coloured. The priest's chamber above the N. porch is where the poet Parson Hawker wrote *The Cell by the Sea* in the 19th century. There are numerous modest little monuments and ledger slabs to local gentry, in which the parish abounded for centuries. The magnificent late 15th-century rood screen spans the entire width of the church.

HEANTON PUNCHARDON
† St Augustine

4m/6km N.W. of Barnstaple
OS *SS502355* **GPS** *51.1000N, 4.1406W*

Set above an estuary, St Augustine's is mostly late medieval with a plastered interior and richly carved Perpendicular tomb to Richard Coffin, d. 1523, in the N. wall of the chancel.

HIGH BICKINGTON † St Mary ★

7m/11km S. of Barnstaple
OS *SS599205* **GPS** *50.9670N, 3.9963W*

St Mary's, like so many in north Devon, is a hill-top church. The 12th-century building was altered and enlarged in the early 14th and early 16th centuries; the original wagon roofs were restored in the 19th century. There is a magnificent series of about 70 carved bench-ends of two distinct types: late Gothic, c. 1500, and Renaissance, c. 1530.

CULLOMPTON: ST ANDREW – *the carved Beer-stone arcades, with a view through to the Lane Aisle, the skull and cross bones of a Gothic Golgotha at its west end* ▷

HITTISLEIGH † St Andrew ★

7m/11km S.W. of Crediton
OS *SX733954* **GPS** *50.7448N, 3.7962W*

An ordinary little Devonshire farmers' church in lonely country bordering Dartmoor, St Andrew's has been restored late and lovingly. The nave and chancel are late 13th- or early 14th-century, the granite aisle 16th-century and the tower late 15th-century. Inside are plastered, cream-washed walls, ceiled roofs with some carved bosses, and the usual floor-slabs to Tudor and Stuart yeomen and small gentry of the parish. An endearing little church.

HOLBETON † All Saints

10m/16km E. of Plymouth
OS *SX613501* **GPS** *50.3352N, 3.9503W*

This simple church stands on a slope above the village. Sedding did the very good restoration for the Mildmay family and, as well as restoring the old, introduced a fine Arts and Craft feel. The carved bench ends, chancel roof and sedilia all bear Sedding's touch. The screens are post-Reformation, with fine tight-carved tracery. It's a pity he didn't attend to the glass, which is poor. In the N. chapel is a memorial to Sir Thomas Hele; all 22 of his children are shown praying.

HONEYCHURCH † St Mary

7m/11km N.E. of Okehampton
OS *SS629028* **GPS** *50.8086N, 3.9470W*

Far from any village and as delightful as its place name, St Mary is a simple Norman building, done up in the 15th century and given three new bells, new benches and a little tower – all still there. The pulpit is Elizabethan; the Norman font has a Jacobean cover. The blackest-hearted pagan would smile at Honeychurch as he pushed open the door and saw this touching little interior.

HORWOOD † St Michael ★

3m/4km E. of Bideford
OS *SS502276* **GPS** *51.0290N, 4.1373W*

A delightful little church up in the hills; again no village. All dates from about 1500, decently kept. The mid-15th-century alabaster effigy of a lady is probably Elizabeth Pollard, hence the Pollard Aisle. There are 16th-century bench-ends, 17th-century altar rails, some medieval glass and tiles, and numerous floor-slabs and memorials to centuries of squires. Nothing at Horwood is outstanding, but all is in rustic harmony.

KENTISBEARE † St Mary ★★

6m/10km N.W. of Honiton
OS *ST068081* **GPS** *50.8650N, 3.3257W*

This is a good Perpendicular church throughout in luxuriant countryside. Its beautiful checkered tower is of red sandstone and white Beer-stone. A pier capital in the S. aisle has a carved ship and woolpack, and the early 16th-century rood screen is one of the county's best. There is also refined tracery and some original colour, and a fine W. gallery of 1632.

KENTON † All Saints ★

4m/6km N. of Dawlish
OS *SX957833* **GPS** *50.6401N, 3.4750W*

A fine late 14th-century church in a large, rich village. This is red sandstone country, and the church is built of it to a fully aisled Devonshire plan at its best. There is a handsome tower and S. porch, and a Beer-stone arcade with carved capitals. The massive and stately rood screen and loft were restored by Read of Exeter; he also restored the fine medieval pulpit. Henry Wilson made the central cross.

MANATON † St Winifred

3m/4km S. of Moretonhampstead
OS *SX749812* **GPS** *50.6178N, 3.7690W*

St Winifrid's is an engaging granite church in a picturesque village. The tower and nave were much repaired after storm damage in 1779. The celebrated 11-bay rood screen is enriched by painted panels of saints and, unexpectedly, small statuettes above the central doorway.

MARYSTOW † St Mary the Virgin

6m/10km N.W. of Tavistock
OS *SX434828* **GPS** *50.6244N, 4.2144W*

In a lonely setting among the trees, the church has remains of a Norman S. doorway and an early 14th-century chancel. There is a good free-standing monument to Sir Thomas Wyse, d. 1629.

MOLLAND † St Mary ★★
6m/10km E. of South Molton
OS *SS807283* **GPS** *51.0425N, 3.7018W*

St Mary's stands on the Exmoor foothills in quiet farmland. An unremarkable 15th-century exterior, but inside is Georgian and complete – plastered and whitewashed, with a three-decker pulpit, box pews and ceiled roofs. The chancel is shut off by a rustic 18th-century 'screen' with plastered tympanum above. There are 17th- and 18th-century monuments to the recusant Courtenay family, lords of the manor.

MORTEHOE † St Mary the Virgin
4m/6km W. of Ilfracombe
OS *SS456451* **GPS** *51.1851N, 4.2093W*

A wild windswept outcrop close by the Atlantic coast is the setting for this dark, cruciform church, of an older period than usual in Devon. It has largely escaped the restorer and is mostly Early English. The two-bay N. aisle is rustic; the S. aisle more refined, with Perpendicular windows illuminating a strange passage connecting transept and nave. In the S. transept is the traceried tomb chest of Rector William de Tracey, d. 1322. The chancel arch is filled with a memorial mosaic by Selwyn Image.

NEWTON ST CYRES
† St Cyres and St Julitta
3m/4km S.E. of Crediton
OS SX879979 GPS 50.7707N, 3.5907W

On a bold site above an unusually attractive village of cob and thatch, the church, of local volcanic stone, dates from the early 15th century. The arcade is of Beer-stone. There is an 18th-century canopied pulpit and striking monuments to Northcotes, especially that of John Northcote, d. 1632, a lifesize male figure, seemingly in Wellington boots.

NORTH BOVEY † St John the Baptist
2m/3km S.W. of Moretonhampstead
OS *SX739838* **GPS** *50.6405N, 3.7842W*

An attractive green village with old oaks. The chancel is 13th-century, otherwise this is a 15th-century granite church with broad low interior, ceiled wagon roofs and a good screen with statuettes under crocketed canopies similar to those at Manaton.

OTTERY ST MARY
† St Mary the Virgin ★★
11m/18km E. of Exeter
OS *SY098955* **GPS** *50.7528N, 3.2792W*

This is a grand town church of even higher rank than Crediton and Cullompton. With a somewhat French exterior and collegiate in appearance, it was closely modelled on Exeter Cathedral by the munificent Bishop Grandisson, who rebuilt the original church in 1342. The Dorset Aisle with its beautiful fan-vaulted roof was added in about 1520. The interior is all impressive with much detail for study: the roof-bosses in the crossing vault are particularly fine. Dating from the 14th century are the clock in the S. transept, the excellent canopied tombs of Sir Otho de Grandisson, d.1359, and his wife, Lady Beatrix de Grandisson, choir-stalls, altar screen, sedilia, minstrels' gallery and wooden eagle given by Bishop Grandisson. There was a thorough restoration by Blore and Butterfield in 1850; they did less harm than might be expected. The same could not be said for the 1977 repainting, which is disturbing and disruptive.

PAIGNTON † St John the Baptist ★★
3m/4km S.W. of Torquay
OS *SX886608* **GPS** *50.4368N, 3.5695W*

Mainly 15th-century, St John the Baptist retains some 12th-century remains of the previous church. The long interior is a cheerful mix of red sandstone and white plasterwork. A medieval stone pulpit has ogee panelling, and the sedilia is very good Victorian Decorated. The Kirkham chantry screen, c. 1526, is one of the finest in the country – a mass of carved figures, fan vaults and gables. In the two side arches are tombs of the Kirkham family.

PARRACOMBE † St Petrock ★
4m/6km S.W. of Lynton
OS *SS674449* **GPS** *51.1884N, 3.8978W*
Churches Conservation Trust

John Ruskin saved this outwardly plain church from destruction when a new church was built close by in 1870. It has a completely unspoiled whitewashed Georgian interior; everything is irregular and just as it was 200 years ago,

△ **MOLLAND: ST MARY** – *a lovely Georgian interior, the box pews like flood water surrounding the outward-leaning pillars of the 15th-century arcade*

including the box pews, a screen with tympanum above, set with Royal Arms, commandments, creed and Lord's Prayer. Elsewhere are hat pegs, text boards and mural tablets to local yeomen. The walls and ceilings are whitewashed and there are some 16th-century benches. At the W. end are five raked box pews for the church band and children.

PLYMOUTH † St Andrew

Catherine Street
OS *SX479543* **GPS** *50.3698N, 4.1398W*

A fine 15th-century town church, St Andrew's was gutted in 1941 during the war, but beautifully restored by Frederick Etchells. The W. window is by John Piper.

PLYMTREE † St John the Baptist

8m/13km N.W. of Honiton
OS *ST051029* **GPS** *50.8179N, 3.3474W*

One of the most attractive medieval interiors in Devon, with excellent woodwork, coloured capitals in the arcade and original colouring. The screen is very fine with its faded gilding and intricate carving. There are paintings of 34 saints, rustic but charming.

REVELSTOKE
† St Peter the Poor Fisherman

Noss Mayo, 10m/16km S.W. of Plymouth
OS *SX563464* **GPS** *50.3004N, 4.0177W*
Churches Conservation Trust

Dramatically sited on the cliff-edge overlooking the estuary is this medieval church with Saxon origins. Rather romantic in its part-ruined state, the nave and chancel are roofless, whilst the aisle and porch have fine carved medieval roofs. Open air services are held twice a year.

SALCOMBE REGIS † St Peter

2m/3km N.E. of Sidmouth
OS *SY148888* **GPS** *50.6929N, 3.2071W*

Set in a combe, St Peter's has Norman work including the circular piers of the N. arcade with scalloped capitals, and the ghost of a doorway in the chancel S. wall. There is a 15th-century oak lectern.

SAMPFORD COURTENAY

† St Andrew ★

5m/8km N.E. of Okehampton

OS *SS632012* **GPS** *50.7948N, 3.9418W*

In a cheerful whitewashed cob and thatch village, St Andrew's is silvery granite and mostly early 15th-century, with an elegant lichened tower. The interior is spacious and light with much clear glass, which suits a granite interior. Part of the S. arcade is very beautiful dove-grey Polyphant stone from east Cornwall. There is a screen in the S. aisle – a fragment of the original that spanned the width of the church – a Norman font, and carved bosses and wall-plates to the roofs. The Prayer Book Rebellion of 1549 began and ended here.

SANDFORD † St Swithun

2m/3km N.W. of Crediton

OS *SS828025* **GPS** *50.8104N, 3.6639W*

The church has an elaborate W. gallery of 1657 with carved arcaded front and fluted columns, conservative for the date, and fine 16th-century bench-end.

SHALDON † St Peter

On S. side of R. Teign, connected by bridge to Teignmouth

OS *SX931724* **GPS** *50.5421N, 3.5093W*

By E. H. Sedding, 1893–1902, this is a superb Arts and Crafts church in banded red sandstone and grey limestone, overlooking the Teign estuary. The majestic interior is alive with colour and craftsmanship. Note the outstanding pulpit and the altar in the apsidal E end.

SIDBURY † St Peter & St Giles

3m/4km N. of Sidmouth

OS *SY139917* **GPS** *50.7190N, 3.2201W*

In an attractive village setting, this is an intriguing structure with plain Saxon crypt and Norman tower adorned with two repositioned statues. The main part of the church has Norman origins, but there has been a 15th-century reworking. Inside are good wagon roofs and late Kempe glass.

STOWFORD † St John

7m/11km E. of Launceston

OS *SX432870* **GPS** *50.6617N, 4.2189W*

In a fold of hills, St John's is Perpendicular, thoroughly restored by Sir George Gilbert Scott in 1874. There are good wagon roofs and profuse Victorian woodwork. Monuments include a Baroque marble sculpture of a diminutive Mr Harris posed as a Roman soldier in full-bottomed wig.

△ **OTTERY ST MARY** – *the tomb of a knight: Sir Otto de Grandisson, d. 1359*

SUTCOMBE † St Andrew ★

5m/8km N. of Holsworthy

OS *SS346116* **GPS** *50.8808N, 4.3512W*

Sutcombe is a dullish village in a remote, unvisited part of Devon, but it has an excellent granite church. Part of the church is Norman, otherwise it is mostly late 15th- to early 16th-century. There is a large collection of early 16th-century carved bench-ends commemorating local families of Norman origin. The 16-sided pulpit bears fine carving by a local man, and there are many late medieval floor tiles of Barnstaple manufacture. Granite, sandstone and oak are the predominant materials.

△ **SWIMBRIDGE: ST JAMES THE APOSTLE** – *the magnificent full-width rood screen, in which the most recent repairs are both easy to identify and appreciate*

SWIMBRIDGE

† St James the Apostle ★★

5m/8km S.E. of Barnstaple

OS *SS620299* **GPS** *51.0527N, 3.9689W*

Known as the 'hunting' vicar's church, St James the Apostle's was restored in the 19th century by Jack Russell, its lively and keen hunter vicar. It has one of the three medieval spires of north Devon. The tower and leaded broach spire are 14th-century; the rest is 15th. Furnishings are unusually rich and interesting, including a stone pulpit, c. 1490, with some original colour, a splendid 15th-century rood screen, restored by Pearson, and a remarkable Renaissance font cover. There are some bench-ends and wagon roofs.

TAWSTOCK † St Peter ★★

2m/3km S. of Barnstaple

OS *SS559299* **GPS** *51.0506N, 4.0561W*

St Peter's is a fine cruciform church, nearly all 14th-century (and therefore unusual in Devon) in the former park of the earls of Bath, with a good Georgian rectory some way off. Those who like church monuments will be rewarded at Tawstock – it has a splendid collection, mainly of the earls and countesses of Bath, their connections and household officers. In the N. transept is a ceiling of Italian plasterwork, medieval glass, a beautiful 16th-century gallery, a Renaissance manorial pew of the earls of Bath, carved bench-ends and monuments. In the S. transept are a similar ceiling and monuments. In the S. chancel aisle is a fine open roof, c. 1540, Burman's figure of Rachel, Countess of Bath, 1680, and the tomb of Lady Fitzwarren, 1589, which carries a most beautiful effigy.

TEIGNMOUTH † St James

15m/24km S. of Exeter

OS *SX939730* **GPS** *50.5480N, 3.4983W*

Except for its 13th-century sandstone W. tower, the church was rebuilt c. 1821 by W. E. Rolfe, a pupil of Soane. Octagonal in shape, it has a delightful light and airy interior with slender clustered cast-iron piers supporting a lantern.

TIVERTON † St George ★
12m/19km N. of Exeter
OS *SS954124* **GPS** *50.9021N, 3.4885W*

The best Georgian church in Devon, by John James, 1714–30, its symmetrical yellow sandstone exterior has rusticated quoins. Inside are Ionic columns, galleries and panelling.

TORBRYAN † Holy Trinity ★
4m/6km S.W. of Newton Abbot
OS *SX819668* **GPS** *50.4894N, 3.6650W*
Churches Conservation Trust

An imposing Perpendicular exterior gives no hint of what bursts upon the eye on pushing open the door – the most completely characteristic Devon interior in plan, fittings, colour and atmosphere. The first impression is of uninterrupted light from the large windows of clear glass, whitened walls and ceilings, and the white Beer-stone arcades. Then against this background is the vivid colouring of the rood screen, pulpit and altar, nearly all 15th-century, though the altar is actually made up from the original pulpit. 18th-century box pews encase earlier benches and have brass candle-holders, all very charming.

TORQUAY † St John the Evangelist
Montpellier Road
OS *SX918636* **GPS** *50.4627N, 3.5246W*

Torquay's magnificent high church, by G. E. Street, 1861–71, dominates the harbour. There is extensive use of Devon marble, a rare total immersion font, mosaic panels by Burne-Jones and Salviati, and Morris glass.

UPTON HELLIONS
† St Mary the Virgin ★
2m/3km N. of Crediton
OS *SS842033* **GPS** *50.8176N, 3.6449W*

This unsophisticated country church is set in deep country, though not far from Exeter. Plastered and whitewashed walls, always a good start for a country church, support 15th-century wagon roofs; there are some carved benches of the same date. The pulpit is Georgian and a country-made monument commemorates a country squire and his wife.

UPTON PYNE † Church of Our Lady
3m/4km N. of Exeter
OS *SX910977* **GPS** *50.7687N, 3.5468W*

In a setting near cottages, the church is built of 'trap', a local volcanic stone. The 14th-century W. tower is unusually decorated with figures of the four evangelists, set in niches above the buttresses. Inside, set into the S. wall, are two canopied 16th-century tombs of the Larder family. The attractive interior was restored in 1867–8.

WEST OGWELL † Dedication unknown
4m/6km W. of Newton Abbot
OS *SX818700* **GPS** *50.5183N, 3.6677W*
Churches Conservation Trust

This delightful little church stands in a park, an unaltered early 14th-century cruciform building with a late-Georgian interior. The plastered and whitened walls, clear glass, box pews, altar rails and Jacobean pulpit are all very appealing.

WIDECOMBE-IN-THE-MOOR
† St Pancras ★★
5m/8km N.W. of Ashburton
OS *SX718767* **GPS** *50.5768N, 3.8108W*

A fine granite church in the heart of Dartmoor, it is best seen in winter against the austere lines of the moorland above. It is essentially early 14th-century cruciform; the original transepts enlarged into aisles in the late 15th century or early 16th. This was a common development in the larger Devon churches, which are not as purely Perpendicular as they seem. Widecombe has a noble tower – granite at its most graceful, and odd for such a remote village – probably built by prosperous tinners. The surviving dado of the rood screen has 32 figure-paintings. In the W. end is a small village museum.

DORSET

This is a county of small churches and enormous scenery. Its long extent of shadowy coast, so varied and dramatic, is in most places too steep or too strange – one thinks of the sixteen miles of pebbles called the Chesil Beach from Portland to Bridport – to admit many colonies of hideous holiday bungalows. Only at three places, the Poole-Bournemouth conurbation, Weymouth, still with remains of Georgian dignity, and Swanage is there very much 'development'. This beautiful little county divides itself into three kinds of scenery, for long described as Felix, Petraea and Deserta, and the ghost of that immortal fatalist, Thomas Hardy, haunts all three. More recently the National Grid and the Army and other Government departments have done their best to lay his ghost and kill the remoteness.

Felix is the clay vales of the west and north-west, with Beaminster, Bridport and Sherborne as their chief towns, all in rich farming country abounding in oaks, a land of rivers and stone manor houses and butter pastures and, in the Blackmore Vale, of hunting people.

Petraea is the chalk downs and rocky formations of Purbeck and Portland. The chalk comes in from Wiltshire and crosses the county diagonally from north-west to Lyme Regis in the south west. The hills are higher and steeper than those of Wiltshire, and topped by a marvellous series of earthworks, including Maiden Castle, with its two miles of ramparts, one of the biggest pre-historic earthworks in the world. From the chalk heights you may often see the English Channel on one side and the azure blue of the rich vales inland. The red-brick 18th-century town of Blandford Forum and the white limestone county town of Dorchester are in the chalk. The Isle of Purbeck, with Wareham at its gate and Swanage on its coast and Corfe Castle in the middle, is a hilly diversity of geological formations which makes the crumbling cliffs, with their boulder-strewn shores, strange indeed. Purbeck marble, such as supplied columns for Westminster Abbey, the Temple Church, London, Salisbury Cathedral, and many a medieval font and effigy, may be seen at Durlston Head near Swanage. The loveliest part of the island of Purbeck is cut off by the military. The Isle of Portland, with its own tall, fair-haired people a separate race from the mainland, is a block of limestone nearly four miles long and with hardly any trees. Here was quarried the white stone Wren used for St Paul's Cathedral and many of his churches. It is quarried today.

Deserta is south-east Dorset behind the Isle of Purbeck, 'a thousand furlongs once of sea, now of barren ground, ling, heath, furze, anything'. Hardy's Egdon Heath is part of it; so is that inland sea with the town of Poole on its shore, looking over to wooded Brownsea Island.

◁ **SHERBORNE: ST MARY** – *exquisitely detailed fan vaulting above the choir*

In all this variety of material, it is not surprising to find much beauty of many coloured building stones, varying from the deep gold of Sherborne to the silver-white of Portland and the lavender of Milton Abbey, in churches, manor houses and cottages. And even in the centre of the county, where flint was most easily available, the church builders varied their outer walls with bands of limestone. Brick was not used till the 18th century.

Most of the Dorset churches are mainly Perpendicular; few have clerestories, and many have squat and sturdy towers with a prominent stair turret carried up to or above the battlements and pinnacles. The only grand monastic buildings still used as churches are those of Wimborne, Sherborne and Milton.

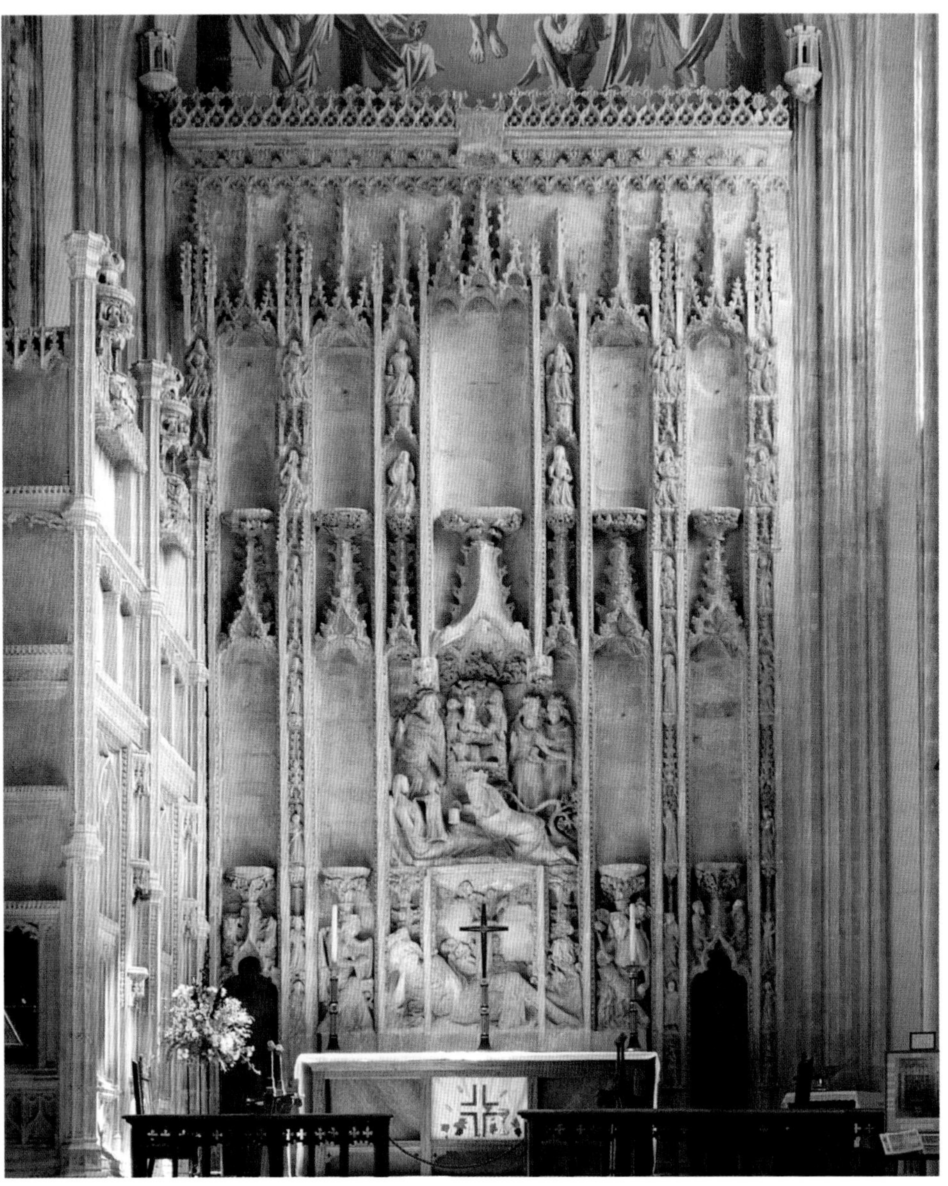

△ **CHRISTCHURCH: PRIORY CHURCH** – *carved Jesse screen of 1360 behind the high altar*

ABBOTSBURY † St Nicholas ★

8m/12km S.W. of Dorchester
OS *SY577852* **GPS** *50.6650N, 2.5989W*

The church adjoins the scattered remains of the former Benedictine Abbey in a large and picturesque village. The fabric is mainly late Perpendicular. In the N. porch is a stone effigy of an abbot. The chancel has a fine 17th-century ornamental plaster ceiling and handsome Georgian altarpiece; there is 15th-century painted glass with an upper portion of the Blessed Virgin from a Crucifixion.

AFFPUDDLE † St Laurence

8m/12km E. of Dorchester
OS *SY805937* **GPS** *50.7427N, 2.2772W*

A picturesque thatched village in the Piddle Valley below the great heath. The church and the former parsonage with its spreading lawns form a charming picture on the river bank. The church is mainly a 13th-century fabric enlarged with aisle and comely tower in the 15th century. The S. doorway is notable – a trefoil arch with two carved faces. Linenfold bench-ends date from 1548, and the pulpit of the same time, polygonal and carved with the Evangelists and other figures.

BATCOMBE † St Mary

8m/12km S.E. of Yeovil
OS *ST618038* **GPS** *50.8331N, 2.5430W*

A romantic setting under Downs. Altogether Perpendicular with stately W. tower, little altered and little spoiled, though restored in 1864 when pews and glass were renewed; there is a 15th-century stone screen.

BEAMINSTER
† St Mary of the Annunciation ★

5m/8km N. of Bridport
OS *ST478012* **GPS** *50.8084N, 2.7408W*

The spectacular W. tower of St Mary's is its glory, covered with pinnacles arising from everywhere. The W. front still has its carved reliefs of the Crucifixion and Ascension. The Perpendicular interior was restored in 1860 and contains two fine monuments, one to Thomas Strode and the other – an obelisk and sarcophagus – to George and Catherine Strode by Scheemakers, 1753.

BERE REGIS † St John Baptist ★

7m/11km N.W. of Wareham
OS *SY847947* **GPS** *50.7522N, 2.2176W*

St John the Baptist's is all the more impressive for its dreary setting, surrounded by characterless council housing. The church is a fine fabric of Saxon origin, largely rebuilt in the 12th century, refashioned and enlarged in the three succeeding centuries. The S. side has capitals adorned with peculiar figures, whilst the N. side is more restrained early Gothic. Grim Victorian glass contributes nothing here. The tower exhibits the stone and flint chequerwork characteristic of the district. The elaborate timber roof of the nave is said to have been given by Cardinal Morton. In the chancel are 16th-century Purbeck marble monuments to the Turbeville family, and a window containing Turbeville heraldic glass.

BLANDFORD FORUM
† St Peter & St Paul ★★

16m/25km N.W. of Bournemouth
OS *ST885063* **GPS** *50.8562N, 2.1638W*

A devastating fire destroyed the church and town in 1731, and the whole place was rebuilt in a pleasing manner by the Bastards, a local family of builder-architects. John and William were responsible for the church, 1731–9, a fine specimen of Georgian design in ashlar. The interior has largely escaped Victorian interference and retains its W. gallery, font, pulpit, numbered box pews and mayoral seat. In 1893 the apsidal sanctuary was cleverly moved out on rollers to newly prepared foundations and a chancel inserted; the newer work is in complete harmony with the rest.

BOTHENHAMPTON
† Holy Trinity (new church)

1m/2km S.E. of Bridport
OS *SY470919* **GPS** *50.7247N, 2.7517W*
Churches Conservation Trust

An interesting Arts and Crafts design by E. S. Prior, 1887–9, with large transverse arches across the nave and deep reveals to the windows. Contemporary font and pulpit; altar front by W. R. Lethaby; E. window by Christopher Whall, though possibly with the input of Lethaby.

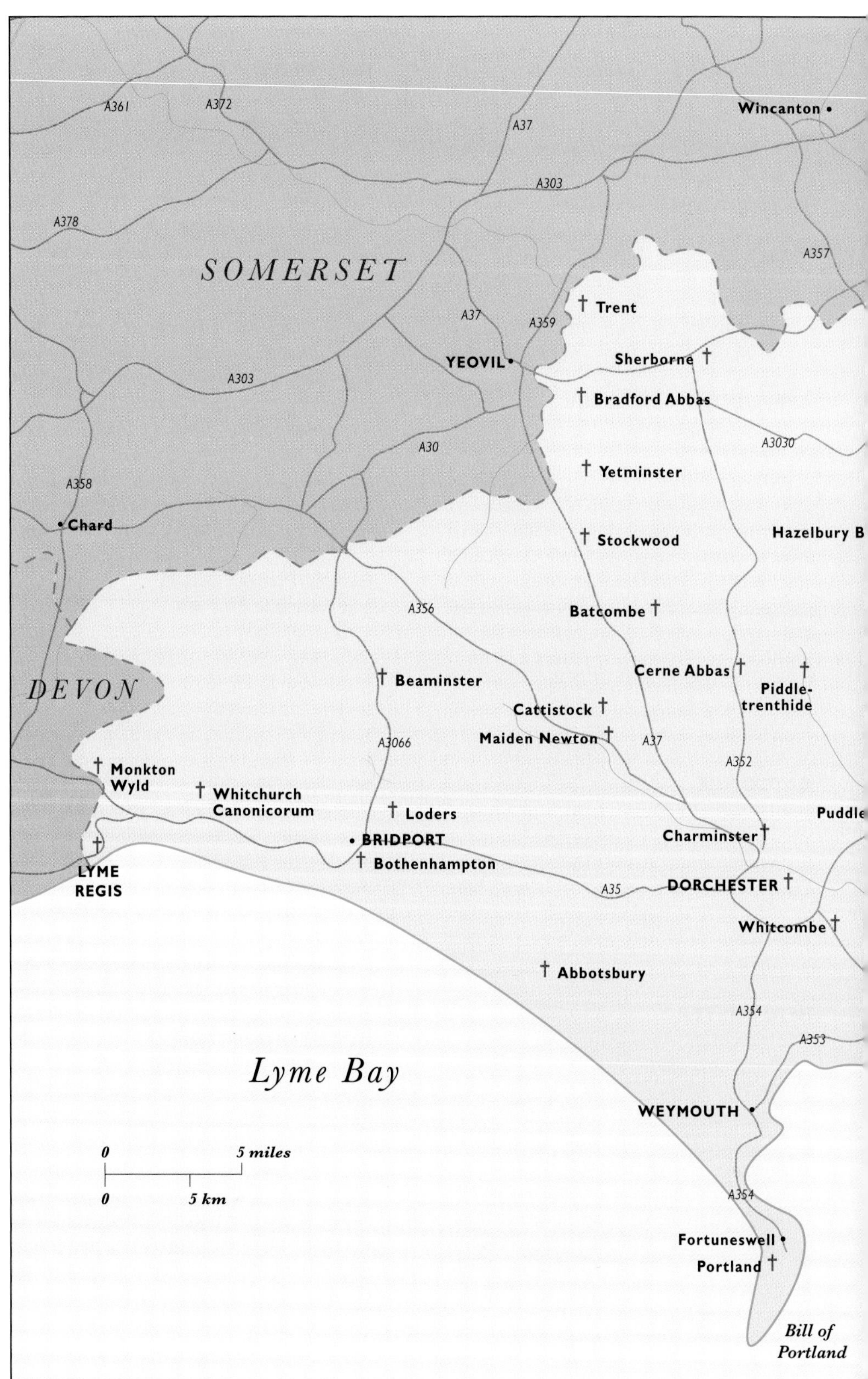
A361
A372
Wincanton
A37
A303
A378
SOMERSET
A357
Trent
A37
A359
YEOVIL
Sherborne
A303
Bradford Abbas
A3030
A30
Yetminster
A358
Chard
Stockwood
Hazelbury B
A356
Batcombe
Cerne Abbas
Piddle-
trenthide
DEVON
Beaminster
Cattistock
Maiden Newton
A37
A3066
A352
Monkton
Wyld
Whitchurch
Canonicorum
Loders
Puddle
BRIDPORT
Charminster
Bothenhampton
LYME
REGIS
A35
DORCHESTER
Whitcombe
Abbotsbury
A354
A353
Lyme Bay
WEYMOUTH
0
5 miles
0
5 km
A354
Fortuneswell
Portland
Bill of
Portland

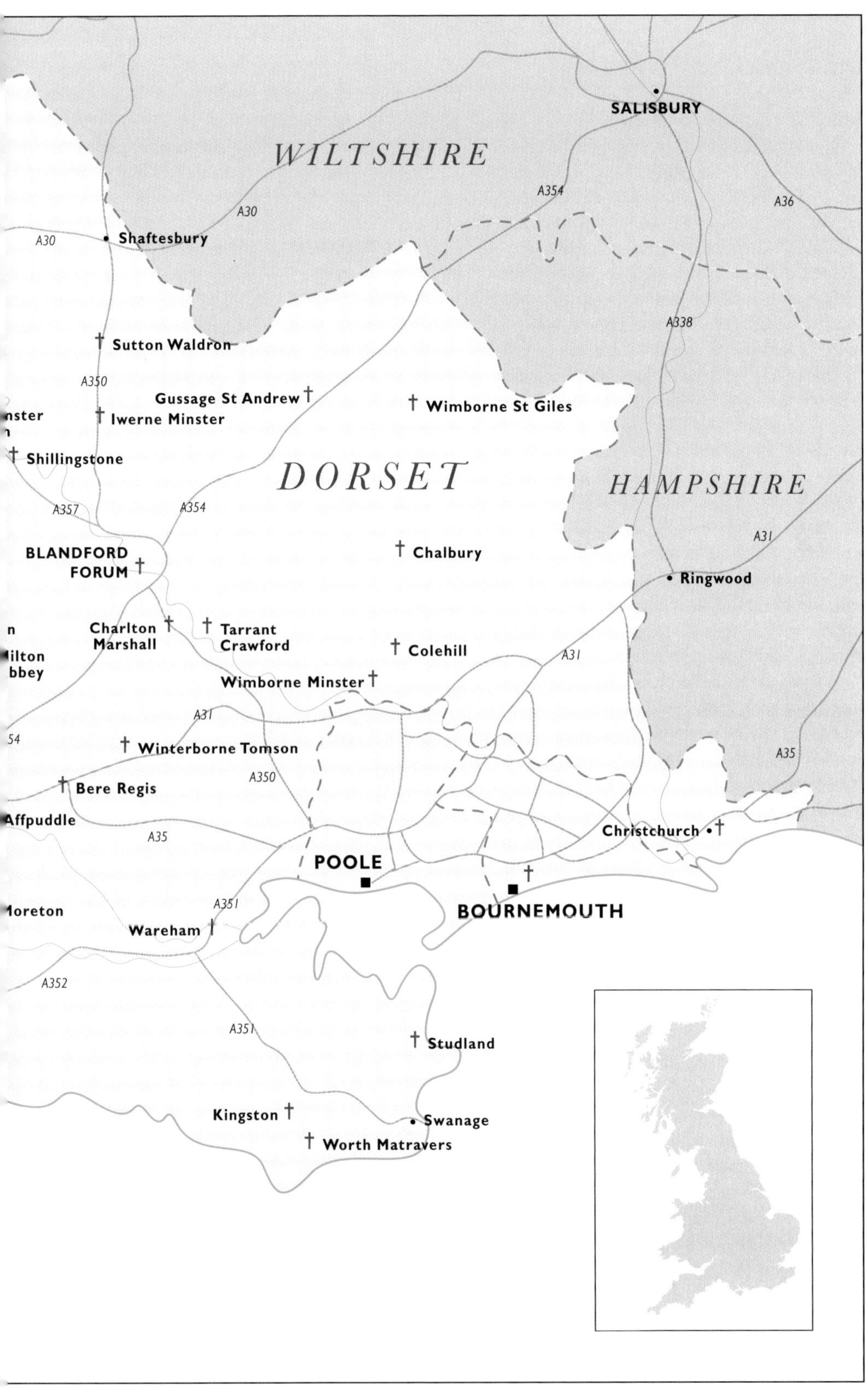
SALISBURY
WILTSHIRE
A354
A36
A30
A30
Shaftesbury
A338
Sutton Waldron
A350
Gussage St Andrew
Wimborne St Giles
Iwerne Minster
Shillingstone
DORSET
HAMPSHIRE
A357
A354
A31
BLANDFORD FORUM
Chalbury
Ringwood
Charlton Marshall
Tarrant Crawford
Colehill
A31
Wimborne Minster
A31
Winterborne Tomson
A35
A350
Bere Regis
Affpuddle
A35
Christchurch
POOLE
BOURNEMOUTH
A351
Wareham
A352
A351
Studland
Kingston
Swanage
Worth Matravers

BOURNEMOUTH † St Peter ★★
St Peter's Road
OS *SZ088912* **GPS** *50.7206N, 1.8755W*
A handsome polychromatic Gothic Revival creation by Street, 1854–74. The recently restored chancel and S. transept are a flourish of alabaster, marble and stone: carved angels and foliage decorate everything. Richly ornamented choir stalls by Bodley are set beneath screens and crocketed arches, all under a fine vaulted roof. In the S. chapel, the sanctuary by T. G. Jackson is rich in colour too. Street did the pulpit, and Burne-Jones the S. chapel window.

BOURNEMOUTH † St Stephen ★★
Corner of St Stephen's Road and St Stephen's Way
OS *SZ085915* **GPS** *50.7232N, 1.8806W*
In contrast to St Peter's, Pearson's Gothic Revival church has more in common with the style of G. G. Scott – more concerned with architectural authenticity than decorative art. The result is as restrained as St Peter's is flamboyant: the interior is a unified Gothic design – finely proportioned piers, a rose window in the N. transept, the S. transept being enclosed with an organ loft over a vaulted chapel. A clerestory of elegant clear glass lancet windows forms an unbroken line from the N. side, through the W. end and along the S. side. Nothing jars in this refined space.

BOURNEMOUTH † St Clement ★
St Clement's Road
OS *SZ107921* **GPS** *50.7286N, 1.8494W*
By John Dando Sedding, 1871–3; tower added 1890–3. Sedding was a founder-member of the Arts and Crafts Movement, and this was his first major church; a fine design in free Gothic style. Tower with traceried battlements, cloister link to original vicarage, sadly demolished. Good furnishings of wood, stone and alabaster, glass in W. tower window by Henry Holiday.

BRADFORD ABBAS
† St Mary the Virgin ★
3m/4km S.E. of Yeovil
OS *ST587142* **GPS** *50.9265N, 2.5884W*
With its embattled parapets, pinnacled tower and large Perpendicular windows, the church is characteristically north Dorset. The interior has been scraped, to the loss of much atmosphere. Note the handsome panelled roofs, stone rood screen, late 15th-century bench-ends and 17th-century pulpit.

CATTISTOCK † St Peter & St Paul ★
9m/15km N.W. of Dorchester
OS *SY591995* **GPS** *50.7939N, 2.5810W*
A pleasant village in the upper valley of the Frome with an attractive group of cottages near the church. The church was mostly rebuilt by Sir George Gilbert Scott in a rather gloomy Decorated Gothic style, but its claim to fame is the work done in 1874 by his far more able elder son and namesake. This consists of the tower, porch, N. aisle and vestry. The tower is superb in the best local manner, fine Perpendicular, 'Even if second-hand Perp,' says Pevsner. At the base of the tower is a bapistry, containing a lofty Gothic font cover by Temple Moore, 1904. Excellent, too, are the N. arcade, the open porch with its wooden vault, and a stone screen. In the S. aisle is quite outstanding Pre-Raphaelite stained glass by Morris and Burne-Jones, 1882.

CERNE ABBAS † St Mary ★
7m/11km N. of Dorchester
OS *ST665012* **GPS** *50.8095N, 2.4755W*
The handsome 15th-century tower dominates this delightful little mid-Dorset town, once the seat of an important Benedictine Abbey of which there are still some scattered remains. The fabric is of late 13th-century origin, but was largely rebuilt in the 15th century and early 16th century, and partially reconstructed in the 17th century. Note the stone screen, the 14th-century wall-paintings in the chancel, the 17th-century pulpit with tester, and the great E. window, which probably came from the Abbey and has been cut down to fit its present position.

CHALBURY † All Saints ★
4m/6km N. of Wimborne
OS *SU018068* **GPS** *50.8611N, 1.9750W*
A charming little hamlet church set in typical east Dorset scenery, with plastered walls and

△ **CHRISTCHURCH: PRIORY CHURCH** – *a misericord depicting what seems to be a singing elf*

timber bellcote. The fabric is of 13th-century origin with a 14th-century E. window. The interior was refitted in the 18th century and has escaped Victorian 'restoration'. Note the box pews, three-decker pulpit, W. gallery and clear glass. In place of the chancel arch is a triple opening supported on slender wooden columns.

CHARLTON MARSHALL
† St Mary the Virgin ★★

2m/3km S.E. of Blandford Forum
OS *ST900040* **GPS** *50.8361N, 2.1428W*

With the exception of the late-medieval tower, the church was rebuilt in 1715, probably by one of the Bastards of Blandford. The plan and elevations are medieval in manner, with chequered flint and ashlar walling, but the details are entirely Classical, owing much to Wren. The grand reredos at the E. end is worthy of a London church, and the interior retains a good balance between the medieval and the Classical.

CHARMINSTER † St Mary the Virgin ★

1m/2km N. of Dorchester
OS *SY679926* **GPS** *50.7330N, 2.4559W*

An aisled 12th-century church, St Mary's was partly rebuilt early in the 16th century, with a fine W. tower of Ham stone which obviously influenced G. G. Scott, Jnr, when he designed that of Cattistock; the long paired belfry windows are particularly effective. The diminutive chancel is early 19th century and quite attractive; there is a 12th-century arcade and chancel arch, remains of wall-paintings, 16th-century Purbeck marble monuments and a good Kempe window.

CHRISTCHURCH † The Priory ★★

7m/11km E. of Bournemouth
OS *SZ160925* **GPS** *50.7322N, 1.7742W*

This cathedral-like Priory Church – parochial since the Reformation – mercifully transcends the swamp of dreary housing that has engulfed the coastline between Lymington and Poole. The nave and transepts are Norman, the W. tower a 15th-century replacement for the original central tower, and the rebuilt chancel is Perpendicular. The arcading on the stair turret is exceptional, each level having a different design. The N. porch is impressive Early English, with double doors and Purbeck shafts, and the nave is monumental Norman, leading under a grand Decorated stone carved reredos at the old crossing to the Perpendicular chancel, whose choir has outstanding stalls and misericords. The S. aisle contains two chantry chapels, to Robert Harys and John Draper, and the N. aisle contains the great Salisbury Chantry, to Margaret Pole, Countess of Salisbury.

COLEHILL † St Michael and all Angels

1m/2km N. of Wimborne
OS *SU024012* **GPS** *50.8105N, 1.9662W*

A pleasing little essay in Arts and Crafts style by W. D. Caroe, 1893, of brick, half-timber and plaster. The interior is like a timbered barn.

DORCHESTER † St Peter ★

7m/12km N. of Weymouth
OS *SY692907* **GPS** *50.7156N, 2.4369W*

A Perpendicular church, stately, but not large, St Peter's is well placed in the centre of town. Built of Portland stone with Ham Hill stone dressings, it has a magnificent tower with tall belfry lights; the interior is lofty with a wagon roof; there is a Jacobean pulpit and good 14th- and 17th-century monuments.

GUSSAGE ST ANDREW † St Andrew

12m/19km N.E. of Blandford Forum
OS *ST976142* **GPS** *50.9277N, 2.0354W*

St Andrew's is a small 12th-century church in a farmyard setting. A single-cell building, the E. end was altered in the 13th century. There are important 13th–14th-century wall-paintings, recently restored; the nave roof is 15th century, and there is a 17th-century pulpit and 18th-century chandelier.

HAZELBURY BRYAN † St Mary & St James ★

5m/8km S. of Sturminster Newton
OS *ST753082* **GPS** *50.8736N, 2.3520W*

This is a good example of a Dorset village church in a typical Blackmoor Vale setting. It is mainly Perpendicular with embattled parapets and a sturdy W. tower. Nave and aisles have Perpendicular roofs. Note the late 12th/13th-century octagonal font with an 18th-century cover, the canopied pulpit and the remains of 15th-century painted glass. The interior was well restored by Sir Charles Nicholson.

HILTON † All Saints ★

7m/11km S.W. of Blandford Forum
OS *ST781029* **GPS** *50.8259N, 2.3114W*

Another typical Dorset country church, it is picturesquely situated above the thatched roofs of the village in the heart of the Downs. As typically in these parts, it is mainly late Gothic – although now over-restored – and incorporates in the N. aisle a fine range of 15th-century windows from the destroyed cloister of Milton Abbey. The fan vault of the porch probably comes from the same source. In the tower are 12 tall panels with figure-paintings of the Apostles which also came from Milton Abbey.

IWERNE MINSTER † St Mary

5m/8km N. of Blandford Forum
OS *ST868144* **GPS** *50.9295N, 2.1887W*

So restored by T. H. Wyatt and J. L. Pearson that it is difficult to tell what was where, and who did what. The tower has a 14th/15th-century spire, one of three in the county, while the interior is a good illustration of Norman and early Gothic. The S. chapel is a Pearson reconstruction, very good Victorian Decorated Gothic, but difficult to tell how authentic.

KINGSTON † St James ★★

5m/8km W. of Swanage
OS *SY955795* **GPS** *50.6156N, 2.0642W*

This is one of Street's final – and certainly one of his best – churches, 1873–80. Though more suggestive of the Ile de France than Purbeck, with its apsidal chancel and W. rose window set above a narthex, it is built of local materials, and the lofty central tower is among the most successful of the Victorian era. Street's fittings include much beautiful ironwork in the screen.

LODERS † St Mary Magdalene ★★

2m/3km N.E. of Bridport
OS *SY491942* **GPS** *50.7458N, 2.7225W*

Delighfully set at the end of a handsome village street, the church is reached by way of a profusely planted pathway. It was gifted to monks from Montebourg Abbey by the Duke of Devon in the 12th century; the monks are believed to have introduced the art of cider-making to England. Evidence of an earlier Saxon door was uncovered during the 1899 restoration. Three Norman openings in the chancel gave access to the rood loft and pulpit, and a fine Easter Sepulchre adorns the N. chancel wall. The S. chapel is 14th-century Perpendicular. Remnants of the ambulatory that connected to the chancel are visible. The outside is decorated with gargoyles – a bagpiper, imps and demons, and a man suffering from toothache.

LYME REGIS † St Michael the Archangel

8m/12km W. of Bridport
OS *SY343922* **GPS** *50.7257N, 2.9317W*

An attractive little seaside resort on the borders of Devon with many late 18th- and early 19th-century houses and a few earlier survivals. The church has an interesting architectural history. Originally a 12th-century

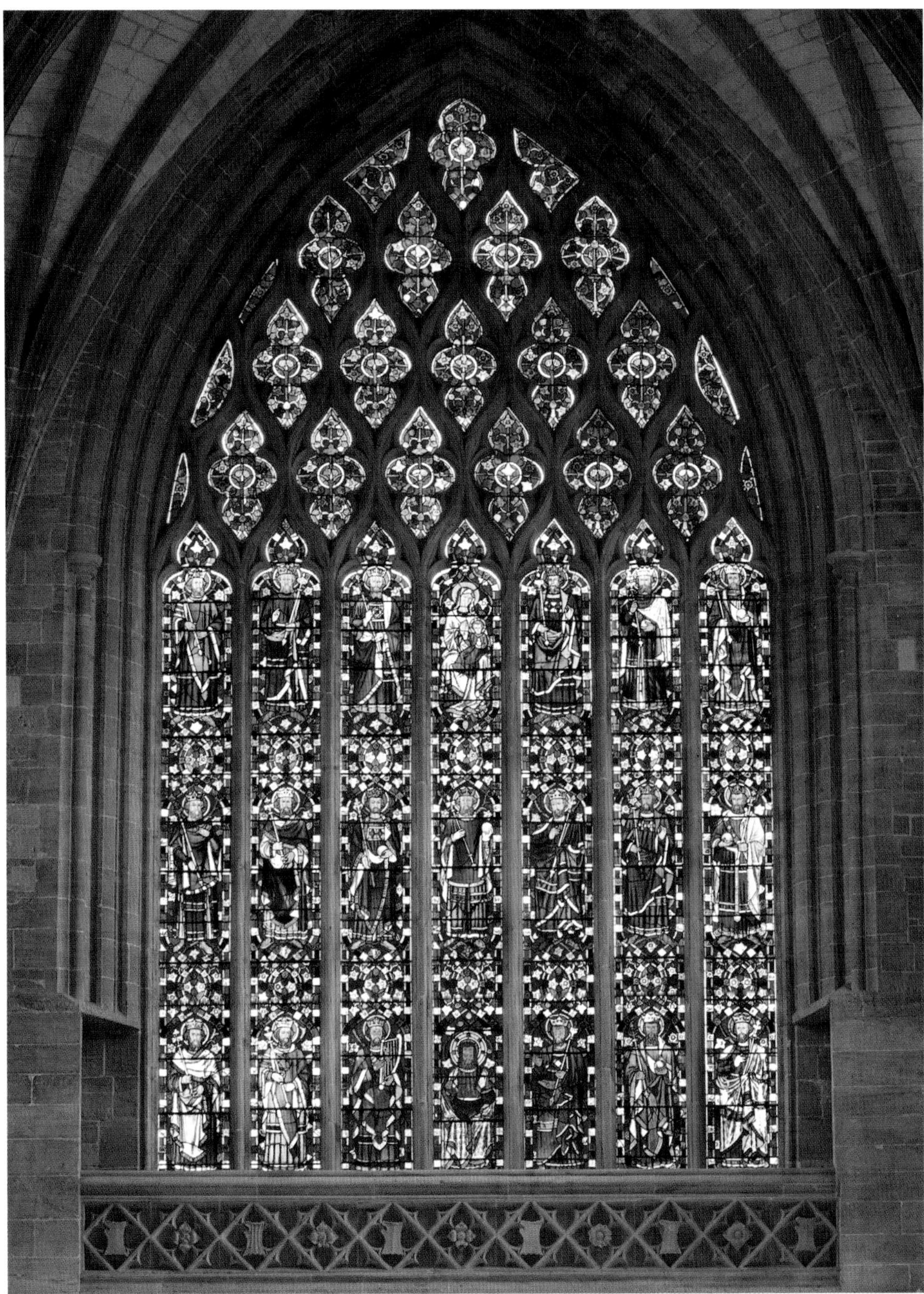

△ **MILTON ABBEY** – *Pugin's dazzling Tree of Jesse window in the south transept*

tripartite structure with axial tower, transepts were added c. 1200 and, later in the 13th century, aisles to the nave. Early in the 16th century a new church was erected to the E. of the tower, and the transepts, aisles and old chancel removed. Early in the 19th century the Norman nave was shortened. The later church is typically Devonian with continuous

nave, chancel and aisles. Tudor arcades, canopied pulpit, W. gallery and lectern, all of the 17th century, and an early 16th-century tapestry panel add to its interest.

MAIDEN NEWTON † St Mary
8m/13km N.W. of Dorchester
OS *SY596978* **GPS** *50.7792N, 2.5740W*

The church is 12th century in origin, with 15th-century enlargement and refashioning, with an axial Norman/Perpendicular tower. The N. doorway has zigzags, and the wooden door is believed to date from the 12th century. The chancel arch has scalloped capitals.

MILTON ABBEY † Milton Abbey ★★
7m/11km S.W. of Blandford Forum
OS *ST798023* **GPS** *50.8204N, 2.2873W*

The present abbey church is only a small part – aisled chancel, tower and crossing with transepts – of a much larger original building destroyed by fire in 1309. The chancel is separated from the crossing by a pulpitum on which, on the choir side, are two 15th-century painted panels depicting the founder of the monastery, King Aethelstan, and his mother, Egwynna. The windows are mostly Decorated, and the S. window is a Tree of Jesse by A. W. Pugin, a fine combination of tracery and glass.

MONKTON WYLD † St Andrew ★
3m/4km N. of Lyme Regis
OS *SY336963* **GPS** *50.7628N, 2.9421W*

By R. C. Carpenter, 1848–9, this is a handsome Decorated church in a romantic wooded setting, with a well-proportioned nave and chancel, and a central tower with a broach spire. The interior is all Ecclesiological correctness, with octagonal piers, chancel screen, brass altar rail and rich glass.

MORETON † St Nicholas ★★
7m/11km E. of Dorchester
OS *SY805892* **GPS** *50.7028N, 2.2769W*

A delightful 1776 'Gothick' church by James Frampton,'restored' by a descendant, William Frampton, who added the N. aisle and porch in the 1840s. The N. wall was destroyed by a stray bomb in WWII, and, in the 1950s, Laurence Whistler was commissioned to design replacement glass for the windows. The results are exquisite: clear engraved and etched glass, whose subjects range from Christmas candles and corn stooks to a crashed fighter plane under a blazing sun. The W. Glaxay window is arguably the finest, a whorl of swirling light. Outside is the burial place of T. E. Lawrence (Lawrence of Arabia).

PIDDLETRENTHIDE † All Saints
6m/10km N. of Dorchester
OS *ST702007* **GPS** *50.8054N, 2.4241W*

A fine village church of 14th-century fabric on a Norman core. The 15th-century tower is replete with pinnacles and gargoyles. Thomas Hardy worked here as an architect's assistant.

PORTLAND † St George ★
4m/6km S. of Weymouth
OS *SY686720* **GPS** *50.5470N, 2.4438W*
Churches Conservation Trust

Situated in a bleak position on the W. side of the 'island', this Georgian church was built in the heyday of Portland stone quarrying. Built by Thomas Gilbert, a local architect, in 1754–66, the church is cruciform, with a central dome and W. tower with cupola. The interior is quite unaltered, with box pews, galleries and twin pulpits. A most satisfying church.

PUDDLETOWN
† St Mary the Virgin ★★
5m/8km N.E. of Dorchester
OS *SY758943* **GPS** *50.7483N, 2.3433W*

A large village with some good groups of rural architecture and a fine early 18th-century parsonage in the Blandford manner. The church has one of the most 'atmospherick' interiors in Dorset, and is mainly late medieval with an earlier core. The nave has a fine panelled roof. Note the beaker-shaped font, probably of the 11th century, and the box pews, canopied pulpit and gallery, all 17th century, as well as a fine array of 15th- and 16th-century brasses and monuments in the Athelhampton Chantry.

◁ **MILTON ABBEY** – *the light-filled north transept, with the Damer Monument, a tomb in honour of Joseph Damer's wife Caroline, by Agostino Carlini*

△ **PUDDLETOWN: ST MARY THE VIRGIN** – *alabaster tombs in the Athelhampton Chantry*

SHERBORNE † St Mary ★★

5m/8km E. of Yeovil

OS *ST637164* **GPS** *50.9467N, 2.5168W*

Formerly the church of a Benedictine abbey, it became parochial after the Dissolution. The large cruciform fabric is externally mostly 15th-century, but it is actually a Norman church transformed, with slight remains of Saxon work at the W. end: the old portion of the Lady Chapel and Bishop Roger's Chapel are 13th century, and the fan vaults of the nave and choir are among the finest in existence. The interior was vigorously restored and decorated by Carpenter and Slater in the middle of the 19th century, and the nave and transepts are crowded with seating. In the S. transept is the imposing monument of the Earl of Bristol, d. 1698, and his two wives. The mainly modern stalls possess an interesting series of 15th-century misericords. Note the 15th-century painted glass in the Leweston Chapel, the 12th–14th-century abbatial effigies and the 18th-century mural tablets. Considerable remains of the monastic buildings are incorporated in the school to the N. of the church. The W. window bears new stained glass by John Hayward, 1998, and Laurence Whistler did the charming engraved glass reredos in the Lady Chapel. The town, pleasantly sited on a slope above the Yeo, has many attractive houses of various dates and styles.

SHILLINGSTONE † Holy Rood ★

6m/10km N.W. of Blandford Forum

OS *ST824114* **GPS** *50.9024N, 2.2506W*

A large village in the Stour Valley with many picturesque cottages and a restored cross. The church stands somewhat away from the main part of the village and is of 12th-century origin. Note the banded flint and ashlar masonry. There was the usual refashioning in the 15th century, and restoration and enlargement throughout the 19th century. Bodley made further alterations in 1902 – note the painted ceiling and pleasant Bodley fittings. There are several 12th-century windows, 12th-century font, and 17th-century pulpit. A worshipful church.

△ **PUDDLETOWN: ST MARY THE VIRGIN** – *effigy of a knight, thought to be Sir William Martyn*

STOCKWOOD † St Edwold

7ml11km S. of Yeovil
OS *ST590069* **GPS** *50.8604N, 2.5837W*
Churches Conservation Trust

This attractive little church, the smallest in Dorset, stands in a beautiful setting with stream and footbridge, all set under a hanging wood. It is mostly 15th-century, with a porch and bell-turret added in 1636. Inside, a late medieval font and Jacobean communion table.

STUDLAND † St Nicholas ★

3ml4km N. of Swanage
OS *SZ036825* **GPS** *50.6423N, 1.9498W*

Of Saxon origin, rebuilt in the 12th century, it is the most complete Norman church in Dorset, with low axial tower, vaulted chancel and sanctuary. There is much good 12th-century detail, but the interior has been scraped; the chalice-shaped font is 12th-century, the E. window is 13th-century, the mutilated pulpit is 18th-century and there is text over the chancel arch.

SUTTON WALDRON † St Bartholomew ★

5ml8km S. of Shaftesbury
OS *ST862157* **GPS** *50.9406N, 2.1977W*

By G. Alexander, 1847, with an interior decorated by Owen Jones, the church is a 'beau ideal' of mid-Victorian Romanticism. Rich colours scintillate in the modified light. This is one of the prettiest churches in the county.

TARRANT CRAWFORD † St Mary

3ml4km S.E. of Blandford Forum
OS *ST922034* **GPS** *50.8307N, 2.1107W*
Churches Conservation Trust

A simple chapel now, with nave and chancel hard to tell apart – all that remains of a once great Cistercian convent. The setting is pleasing, with the adjacent house and medieval barn. The crude 14th-century wall-paintings deserve attention, part of a sizeable scheme: the upper part shows scenes from the life of St Margaret of Antioch; below are three skeletons of kings – warnings of mortality, even for the privileged.

TRENT † St Andrew ★
3m/4km N.E. of Yeovil
OS *ST589185* **GPS** *50.9648N, 2.5859W*

The village, formerly in Somerset, abounds in good architecture – medieval, Tudor and later – with plenty of well-established trees as a background. This aisleless church is interesting architecturally and is full of excellent fittings. A lateral tower is crowned by one of the three ancient stone spires of Dorset. The 13th-century fabric was enlarged and refashioned in the 14th and 15th centuries. The chancel is good Somerset Perpendicular; the fine rood screen has its vaulting intact; and the pulpit is of Continental origin, possibly Dutch. A Regency-style ceiling and chancel decorations, c. 1840, are the work of the Rev. William Turner. The E. window contains interesting old painted glass, mostly 16th- and 17th-century foreign work, and there is a fine array of early 16th-century carved bench-ends and Gerard tombs in the N. transept.

WAREHAM † St Martin ★
6m/10km W. of Poole
OS *SY922876* **GPS** *50.6889N, 2.1115W*

Well-situated at the N. end of the town, near the Saxon ramparts, St Martin's is a rare survivor of the Great Fire of Wareham in 1762. It is a small pre-Conquest church with typically high Saxon nave, refashioned in the 13th century and later. After a long period of neglect, it was well restored by W. H. Randoll Blacking in the 1930s. Note the remains of 12th-century wall-paintings in chancel and a fine monument to Lawrence of Arabia by Eric Kennington, rejected by St Paul's Cathedral, Westminster Abbey and Salisbury Cathedral because of controversy over Lawrence's involvement with the Arabs during the First World War.

WHITCHURCH CANONICORUM
† St Candida & Holy Cross ★★
4m/6km N.E. of Lyme Regis
OS *SY396954* **GPS** *50.7554N, 2.8565W*

A large church in the heart of Marshwood Vale, it is mainly Early English with some good detail, especially in the arcades; waterleaf and scalloped capitals crown the Norman S. arcade, whilst the later N. arcade capitals are carved with stiffleaf, trumpet-scalloped and, in one bay, zigzag carving round the entire arch. The church is probably unique in this country in that it retains the relics of its patroness, St Wite, in a 13th-century shrine. Note the late 12th-century font, early 17th-century pulpit, fragments of 15th-century painted glass and a tomb to Sir John Jeffrey in the chancel.

WHITCOMBE † dedication unknown
3m/4km S.E. of Dorchester
OS *SY716883* **GPS** *50.6937N, 2.4027W*
Churches Conservation Trust

By the roadside with an old farm and thatched cottages to keep it company: the nave is 12th-century, the chancel 15th-century and the tower and windows late medieval. Its interior is less spoilt than many in Dorset. Note the Saxon cross shaft, 13th-century font and a 15th-century wall-painting of St Christopher. William Barnes, the Dorset poet and scholar, 1801–86, preached his first and last sermons in this church.

WIMBORNE MINSTER
† St Cuthberga ★★
7m/11km N.W. of Bournemouth
OS *SZ009999* **GPS** *50.7990N, 1.9881W*

St Cuthberga's stands in the heart of a small market town with many pleasant Georgian houses. Formerly a collegiate church, it is the only instance of a two-towered fabric in Dorset. It has a Saxon cruciform plan, although the nave and crossing are Norman; the aisles are Decorated. The Early English E. windows have good Flemish painted glass. A Jacobean monument to Sir Edmund Uvedale stands in the N. chancel aisle, and, close by, is a Saxon chest. On a wall near the Norman font hangs an early 14th-century astronomical clock.

WIMBORNE ST GILES † St Giles ★
11m/18km N.E. of Blandford Forum
OS *SU031119* **GPS** *50.9071N, 1.9560W*

In a small village in undulating country between Cranborne and Wimborne, the church is well-placed on the E. side of a green, flanked by a row of almshouses on the N. It was completely rebuilt in excellent Georgian style in 1732. Bodley 'gothicized'

△ **STUDLAND: ST NICHOLAS** – *a church of Saxon origins, reworked in the 11th and 12th centuries*

the interior in 1887, but a fortunate fire in 1908 necessitated reconstruction – superbly carried out by Sir Ninian Comper. The interior is a treasure-house of Comper work: screens, pulpit, seating, altars and glass. There are some fine 17th-century monuments, well restored after the fire.

WINTERBORNE TOMSON
† St Andrew ★★

6ml/10km W. of Wimborne Minster
OS *SY884974* **GPS** *50.7762N, 2.1648W*
Churches Conservation Trust

A small 12th-century hamlet church in the Winterborne Valley, sandwiched between the old manor house and a farmyard. This little single-cell Norman church still has the apsidal E. end and plastered wagon roof. It was refashioned early in the 18th century and, after long disuse, was found and restored well by the Dorset architect A. R. Powys in 1931. The restoration was mostly paid for through the sale of a manuscript by Thomas Hardy. Inside is a complete set of early Georgian fittings. The W. gallery incorporates a fragment of the old rood loft.

WORTH MATRAVERS † St Nicholas ★

4ml/6km W. of Swanage
OS *SY972774* **GPS** *50.5967N, 2.0397W*

The stone village of Worth Matravers is austere, and its church is, next to Studland, the most complete Norman fabric in Dorset. Here the tower is at the W. end and not axial like Studland. The chancel was altered in the 13th century and has a fine 14th-century E. window. The external corbel tables, the inner S. doorway and chancel arch are all good Norman work.

YETMINSTER † St Andrew ★

5ml/8km S.W. of Sherborne
OS *ST594106* **GPS** *50.8939N, 2.5780W*

A large village on high ground which, in spite of some modern development, is attractive, with thatch and stone, slate roofing and mullioned windows. St Andrew's is a good type of Dorset village church. Its chancel is late 13th-century and the rest was rebuilt in the 15th century, with embattled parapets and good roofs retaining much original colour. There is some early 16th-century seating and a good brass of 1531. The churchyard is rich in table-tombs and headstones of the late 17th and 18th centuries.

DURHAM

Durham is a grey, gaunt, curiously withdrawn county. To strangers it means little except a succession of pit-heaps along the Great North Road or a heart-stirring view of Durham Cathedral glimpsed from the train. You must live in County Durham or grow to love the gauntness and the greyness before you can properly appreciate its highly individual beauty, a beauty of contrast and paradox, to be found where rows of workmen's cottages sprawl across the heather of the open fells, or where a Saxon church stands neighbour to a council estate.

Durham people do not wear their hearts on their sleeve, and Durham county conceals its treasures from the casual passer-by. How many of the tourists who visit the Yorkshire Dales and Roman Wall know anything of the barren and beautiful land that lies between, the high fells of Weardale and upper Teesdale, where the Romans mined for lead and the prince-bishops hunted the red deer, and where today, if you know the country well enough, you may come upon blue pools of gentians spilled in the hollows of the hills?

Eastwards, too, where the grim shipbuilding towns edge the cliffs between the mouths of Tyne and Tees, unexpected rewards await the discerning explorer: the foundations of a Roman fort lying exposed to view between rows of little red-brick houses; a railway station in the high Grecian style standing elegant and aloof in a dismal urban setting; a wooded valley, one of those steep, secretive denes so characteristic of the Durham countryside, winding its way down to the coal-blackened sea. Coal and the sea – these two were the kings of County Durham. But it would be a mistake to picture the county as a solid industrial area like south Lancashire; the villages have open country around them and the shipyard towns have fine stretches of sandy beach for a playground. Country and town live side-by-side in odd but not unhappy contrast.

This element of contrast, so characteristic of Durham, gives a peculiar charm to her medieval churches. One of these ancient and seemingly indestructible buildings is often to be found standing a little lost in an industrial landscape, and the bizarre contrast between church and setting can be strangely moving. Especially is this so in the case of those Saxon churches which are the particular glory of County Durham.

In Durham the pre-Conquest period is of the first importance. In any medieval church it is the rule rather than the exception to find Saxon work still in existence, and it is always worthwhile to enquire for Saxon crosses and carved stones. By contrast Norman work is rare and seldom of the first class. (Kirk Merrington, the most complete Norman church in the

◁ **BILLINGHAM: ST CUTHBERT** – *the battlements are a 14th-century adornment to the Saxon tower and 12th-century nave*

Gosforth
A69
Corbridge
NEWCASTLE UPON TYNE
A68
TYNE & WEA
NORTHUMBERLAND
A692
Chester
Stanley
Consett
Edmondbyers
Hunstanworth
Lanchester
A689
A68
DURH
Brandon
Brancepeth
DURHAM
Spennymoo
Kirk
Merringto
Escomb
Bishop Auckland
Newton
Heighington
Staindrop
A688
Gainford
Barnard Castle
A67
High
Coniscliffe
Brough
Wycliffe
DARL
A66
CUMBRIA
A66
NORTH YORKSHIRE
0
5 miles
0
5 km
A1
A6108

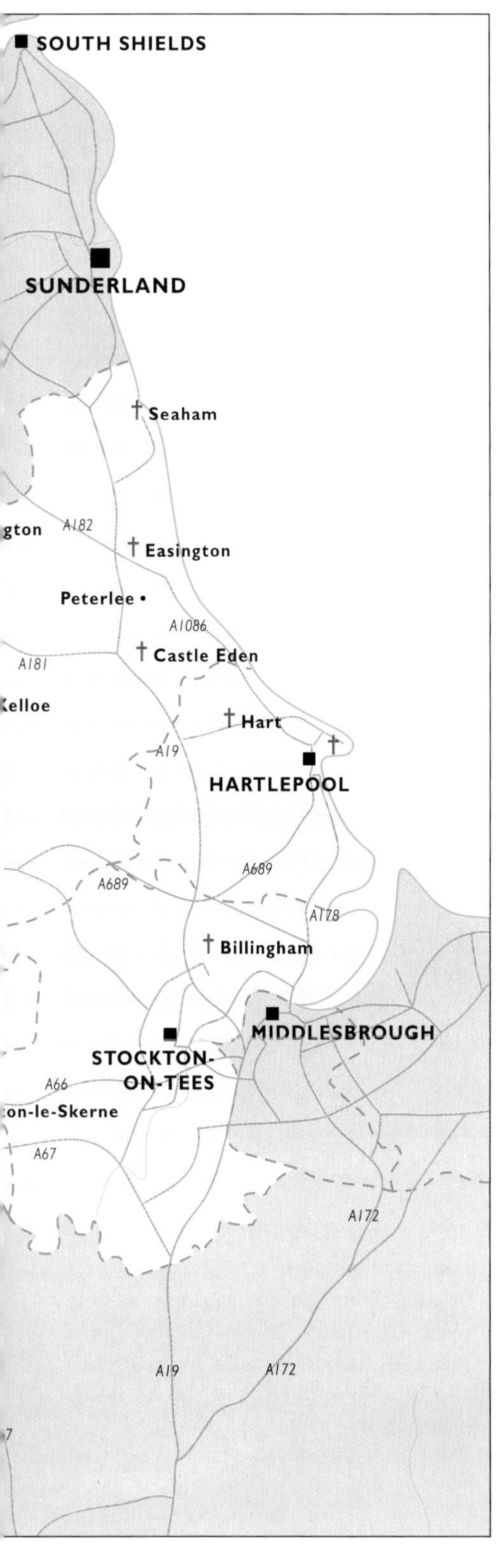

county, was deliberately destroyed during the 19th century.) With the exception of Pittington, there is no church worth a visit for the sake of the Norman work alone, and the great Norman cathedral in Durham seems to have provoked few imitators.

From the Conquest until the Reformation Durham remained a poor and isolated area, so that it is not surprising to find that St Hilda's, Hartlepool, St Cuthbert's, Darlington, and the parish churches of Staindrop and Chester-le-Street are the only large medieval churches that can stand comparison with those of the wealthier South.

The most notable post-Reformation development was the appearance of a school of wood-carving peculiar to County Durham. The carvers worked in a Gothic rather than a Classical tradition, a fact partly accounted for by the northern 'time-lag', which allowed artistic styles to continue to flourish here long after they had fallen out of fashion in the more sophisticated South. The chief patron of these wood-carvers was Bishop Cosin, and when he gave orders for the construction of new stalls for the Cathedral he decided to reproduce as nearly as possible the design of the medieval ones destroyed during the Commonwealth. 'Cosin' woodwork is to be found in many churches throughout the county, much of it clearly influenced by the design of these stalls.

Of classical churches the most notable is Stockton. Following the Industrial Revolution came an outburst of church-building, but the results are disappointing in the extreme. Architects of the Victorian Gothic school did their best work under the influence of the Oxford Movement, and often at the behest of a pious squire whose hobby was ecclesiology. Neither of these factors was powerful in County Durham, where the typical pit-village church is a bare,

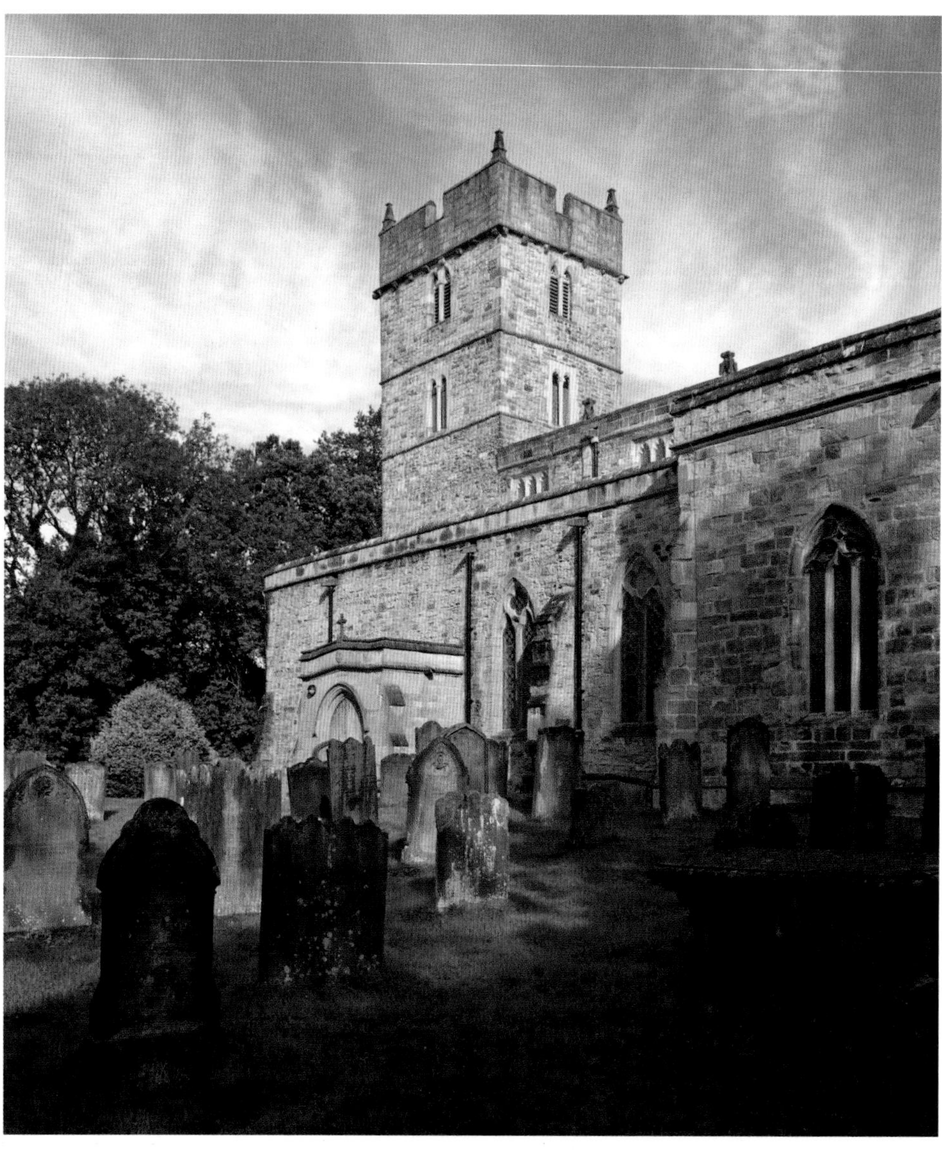

△ **BRANCEPETH: ST BRANDON** – *founded in the 12th century, it was rededicated in 2005 following the 1998 fire and the church's subsequent restoration*

barn-like structure usually designed by one of the local architects, the best of these being Hodgson Fowler.

The poverty of the Victorian churches has at least the negative virtue of plainness, and where the proportions of the buildings are good an imaginative scheme of redecoration can work an astonishing transformation. Unhappily such transformations are rare. Durham remains a comparatively poor county, remote from contemporary artistic influence, and, with a few notable exceptions, the 20th-century work is as undistinguished as the 19th.

BARNARD CASTLE † St Mary

15m/24km W. of Darlington

OS *NZ050162* **GPS** *54.5417N, 1.9230W*

The ancient market town rises dramatically above the Tees, with its main street presided over by the delightful octagonal market cross and town hall. The church stands a little way back. The Norman S. doorway has zigzags; there is a good Transitional N. arcade, and impressive Perpendicular chancel arch and W. tower, its base crowded with 18th- and 19th-century monuments. The whole church was extensively restored in the 19th century.

BILLINGHAM † St Cuthbert

2m/3km N.E. of Stockton-on-Tees

OS *NZ457223* **GPS** *54.5942N, 1.2933W*

A typical County Durham town church setting – a large industrial town with dense council housing, and a secretive old corner, with cottages, old rectory and tree-shielded churchyard. St Cuthbert's Saxon tower and high narrow nave are topped with 14th-century battlements. The nave was altered in the 12th century, leading up to a wide, light chancel, vaguely Perpendicular in style, rebuilt by G. E. Charlewood, 1939. The sudden emergence from the darkness and constriction of the nave into the light and space of the chancel is very dramatic and satisfying.

BISHOP AUCKLAND

† St Andrew Auckland

9m/15km S.W. of Durham, 1m/2km S. of the town centre

OS *NZ217284* **GPS** *54.6509N, 1.6644W*

This dominating building, long and impressive with W. tower, transepts and two-storeyed porch, stands in a large churchyard with trees. It is almost entirely 13th-century with a long interior. There is a fine Saxon cross fragment, a 14th-century carved wooden effigy and a set of 28 stalls with misericords in the chancel, the gift of Cardinal Langley.

BRANCEPETH † St Brandon ★★

4m/6km S.W. of Durham

OS *NZ224376* **GPS** *54.7338N, 1.6524W*

Prettily situated in a park, a few hundred yards from the prodigious Victorianized block of Brancepeth Castle. This church of many dates was distinguished for its unusual and beautiful woodwork given by John Cosin, rector here from 1626 and later Bishop of Durham. However, most of the church's furnishings and contents were destroyed in a 1998 fire. Since then it has been the subject of an extraordinarily bold and imaginative restoration, using local craftsmen and sculptors. The result, now complete, is the recreation of a space evocative of a time before churches were crammed with the furnishings of the Tudor time onwards.

CASTLE EDEN † St James

2m/3km S. of Peterlee

OS *NZ428384* **GPS** *54.7393N, 1.3367W*

'This sacred edifice which consuming time has now reduced to ruinous decay was rebuilt by Rowland Burdon in 1764' – so reads the inscription over the vestry door of this early Gothic Revival church of 1764, probably by William Newton, which stands in a pretty setting near a park gate. The aisles, with Corinthian columns painted blue, the capitals gilded, were added in 1800.

CHESTER-LE-STREET

† St Mary and St Cuthbert ★★

6m/10km N. of Durham

OS *NZ276513* **GPS** *54.8559N, 1.5716W*

The church presides over a dreary suburban vista. Thought to have once housed the remains of St Cuthbert and the *Lindisfarne Gospels*, it is mostly 13th- to 16th-century and has the finest spire in County Durham, rising from an octagon that in turn crowns a heavily buttressed Early English tower. The Early English nave is long and dark. At the N.W. end of the church is an anchorite's cell with squint window, now the Anker House Museum. In the N. aisle is a long line of effigies of the Lumley family, placed here by John, Lord Lumley during the reign of Elizabeth I. Two are medieval, brought from the graveyard of Durham Cathedral; the others are Elizabethan and deliberately archaic in style, representing ancestors going back to the time of Edward the Confessor. To squeeze them in, some of the older effigies had to have their feet cut off in Procrustean fashion. The N. chapel, by Ignatius Bonomi in 1829, has a colourful and charming altar and reredos by Sir Charles Nicholson, 1928. Here lie the Lambtons, once the earls of Durham. There is a facsimile of the *Lindisfarne Gospels* that can be viewed in the church.

DARLINGTON † St Cuthbert

Market place

OS *NZ291144* **GPS** *54.5244N, 1.5518W*

Standing austerely beautiful at the lower end of Darlington's market-place, this is an important and beautiful Early English church with very large and fine transepts. It was probably begun in 1192 by Bishop Pudsey, who intended to make it a great collegiate church; the construction including aisles was completed by the mid-13th century. The 15th-century stalls have good misericords, and there is a spectacular 'Cosin' Gothic font cover. The 14th-century stone rood screen somewhat obscures the view of the chancel. The church was extensively and carefully restored by George Gilbert Scott in the 1860s.

DURHAM † St Oswald King and Martyr

Church Street

OS *NZ275419* **GPS** *54.7714N, 1.5727W*

Outwardly all Perpendicular except for the elaborate Victorian E. end, but the three E. bays of the nave are late Norman. The church was largely rebuilt in 1834 by Ignatius Bonomi and restored after a fire. The W. window is by Morris & Co., with panels by Ford Madox Brown. A Kempe window in the N. aisle commemorates Hodgson Fowler, architect, d. 1910, who worshipped here. J. B. Dykes, hymnologist and a pioneer of the Catholic revival, was vicar here from 1826–75.

EASINGTON † St Mary

2m/3km N.W. of Peterlee

OS *NZ414434* **GPS** *54.7842N, 1.3573W*

Perched on a hill with wide views of cottages and collieries to the sea, St Mary's is a nobly proportioned Early English church with Norman W. tower, richly furnished with Cosin-style woodwork. There is a 14th-century Frosterley marble effigy of a lady and a 13th-century effigy of a knight. The E. end, with its five lancets, is a scholarly restoration of c. 1850, with stained glass by O'Connor.

EDMONDBYERS † St Edmond

Also spelt Edmundbyers; 5m/8km W. of Consett

OS *NZ014499* **GPS** *54.8441N, 1.9791W*

An altogether delightful church in peaceful wooded surroundings. It is Norman, built of freestone from the nearby quarry, and the present appearance owes much to a very thorough rebuilding and restoration c. 1859, an excellent example of how a restoration can preserve the original character and atmosphere of a church fabric. One of the most pleasing features is the Victorian chancel arch – more like an arcade with a central round-headed arch and two flanking half-length arches that serve as a reading desk and pulpit respectively. The chancel roof has Victorian king-posts, and all in all the interior is a delight.

ESCOMB † The Saxon Church ★★

1m/2km N.W. of Bishop Auckland

OS *NZ189301* **GPS** *54.6660N, 1.7080W*

Another Durham surprise: at the bottom of a steep hill in a rebuilt former pit village is a circular site suggesting Celtic influence, at the centre of which stands this tiny 7th-century Saxon church. Very bare, very simple, with a typical tall, narrow nave and chancel, it is almost untouched since Saxon times, except for the insertion of windows and the addition of a S. porch. The chancel arch is thought to have been built of blocks of stone removed from the Roman fort at Binchester. A Saxon sundial can be seen on the S. wall, marked with mass times. After Durham Cathedral, it is the most impressive ecclesiastical building in the county and a moving memorial to the age of Bede.

GAINFORD † St Mary

8m/12km W. of Darlington

OS *NZ169166* **GPS** *54.5451N, 1.7392W*

The church stands at the S.W. corner of the green in a pretty village by the Tees. It is a rugged composition with its low tower and wide roof, mainly 13th-century with good lancets in the chancel. It has a collection of carved stones, mostly Saxon, and a good monument of 1709 to John Middleton, resplendent with garlands and cherubs.

EDMONDBYERS: ST EDMOND – *a 12th-century church, though much restored in the mid-19th* ▷

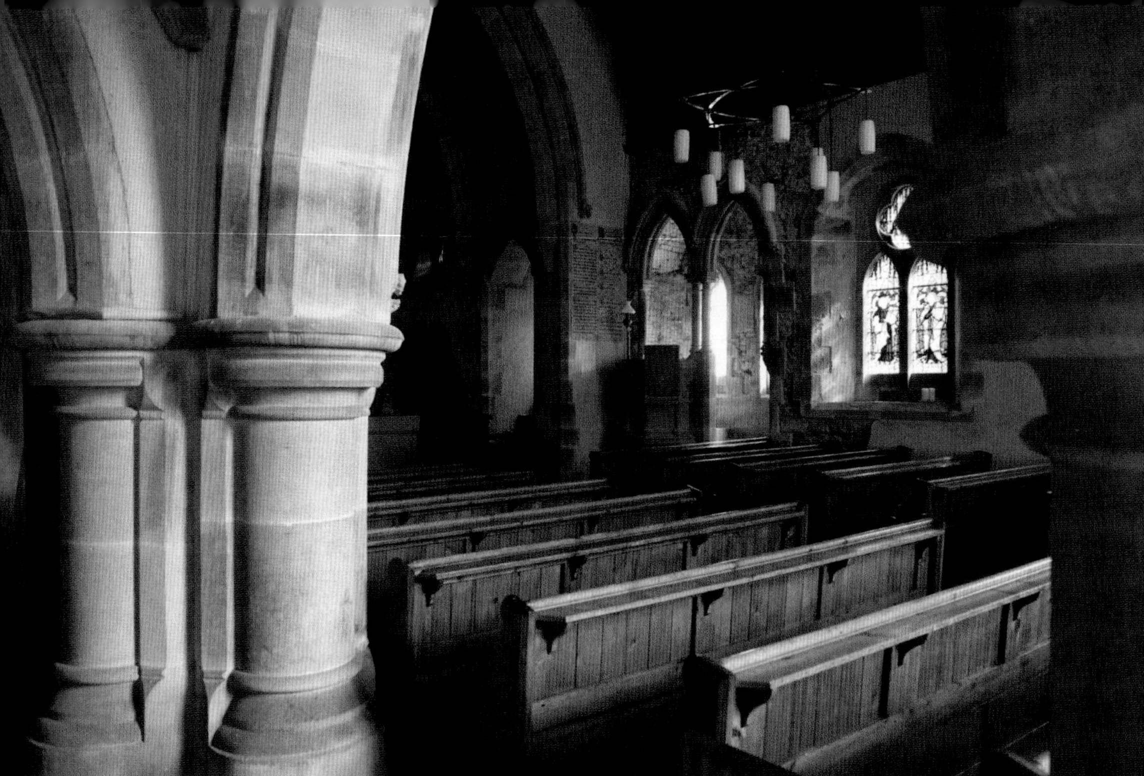

△ **HUNSTANWORTH: ST JAMES** – *a well-realized work of Gothic Revival by S. S. Teulon, the interior is unified by painted plaster walls with ashlar dressings*

HART † St Mary Magdalene ★

3m/4km N.W. of Hartlepool
OS *NZ470351* **GPS** *54.7088N, 1.2713W*

The mother church of Hartlepool, it stands on the edge of a village on sloping ground with wide views across fields to the sea. This is a church of many dates, with Saxon baluster shafts and carved stones, and an early 16th-century sculpture of St George set into the S. wall. The interior is scraped but full of atmosphere, with two fonts, one plain Norman, the other 15th-century and ornate.

HARTLEPOOL † St Hilda ★★

On headland overlooking Hartlepool
OS *NZ528336* **GPS** *54.6954N, 1.1817W*

This is a magnificent Early English church by the sea with views of the docks. There is a fine tower with enormous buttresses, a splendid long nave with seven bays and clustered Early English columns, and a single-lancet clerestory. The chancel was rebuilt in 1870, and the furnishings are good, with sympathetic modern fittings. There is a famous 7th-century Saxon namestone associated with the early monastery here, and the tomb of Robert Bruce, the founder, is behind the altar.

HAUGHTON-LE-SKERNE † St Andrew ★

District of Darlington, 2m/3km N.E. of town centre
OS *NZ308158* **GPS** *54.5373N, 1.5251W*

Set in a pretty village, at the end of a street of handsome 18th-century houses, this is a medieval church with some Norman work, including the chancel arch, which has a curious Victorian arch cut through the wall above it. The interior is beautifully furnished with 'Cosin' woodwork, a pleasant example of an ancient church adorned in post-Reformation manner. There are interesting Saxon and medieval carved stones, and a rare Royal Arms of George II, erroneously displacing the Stuart quarterings – a heraldic howler.

HEIGHINGTON † St Michael

2m/3km S.W. of Newton Aycliffe
OS *NZ249223* **GPS** *54.5959N, 1.6161W*

At the centre of a spacious village green, with attractive cottages around, St Michael's is mainly pre-Conquest and Norman, with a chancel arch of c. 1100, and a 16th-century pulpit and stalls. There is a crude painted and carved heraldic wall monument to George Crossyer, d. 1669, south of the chancel arch.

△ **KIRK MERRINGTON: ST JOHN THE EVANGELIST** – *a speculative 19th-century rebuilding of a Norman church by George Pickering*

HIGH CONISCLIFFE † St Edwin ★

4m/6km W. of Darlington
OS *NZ225152* **GPS** *54.5319N, 1.6526W*

St Edwin's makes a dramatic sight from across the Tees – the church, spire and gabled Victorian rectory standing perched together on a rocky cliff above the river. It is essentially Early English but with a Norman N. doorway and S. windows. There are also 15th-century chancel stalls and fragments of 10th-century cross shafts.

HUNSTANWORTH † St James

8m/13km S. of Hexham
OS *NY949490* **GPS** *54.8360N, 2.0808W*

This appealing Victorian church stands next to the overgrown remains of a Pele tower, a delightful 19th-century rebuilding by S. S. Teulon of an 18th-century church. The roof is diaper-patterned with purple and green slate. The pyramidal tower roof is topped with a peacock weather vane and, taken with the apsidal E. end, has a rather French look. The interior is all painted plaster and ashlar: dusty pink in the nave complements the deeper blue of the apse roof. A lovely Gothic N. arcade and chancel arch lie below a fine wooden arch-braced roof.

KELLOE † St Helens ★

5m/8km N. of Sedgefield
OS *NZ345365* **GPS** *54.7227N, 1.4657W*

Away from the terraces of miners' cottages, the church stands in an unspoilt green combe, the sole survivor of the medieval village of Church Kelloe. It is mainly 12th-century with an Early English chancel and 14th-century chantry. The treasure is the richly carved Caen stone 12th-century cross depicting the Life of St Helena. A tablet commemorates the birth of Elizabeth Barrett Browning in 1806 at Coxhoe Hall, now demolished. The church now holds an annual festival in E. B. B's honour, which attracts an international audience to this unlikely spot.

KIRK MERRINGTON
† St John the Evangelist

4m/7km N.E. of Bishop Auckland
OS *NZ262314* **GPS** *54.6776N, 1.5948W*

St John's occupies a commanding position on a high ridge with good views over the surrounding countryside. Its interest is in the almost complete and controversial Victorian rebuilding by George Pickering, 1850–1, of what had been a very fine Norman church.

NEC TEMERE NEC TIMIDE

The result is a speculative Victorian Norman pastiche, giving some idea of the original building, with odd bits of Norman and Saxon stonework inserted seemingly at random. Inside is a good example of 'Cosin' work, a finely carved screen, combining Classical and Gothic elements.

LANCHESTER † All Saints ★★

7m/11km N.W. of Durham
OS *NZ167473* **GPS** *54.8211N, 1.7406W*

A large village church, with tall tower facing the green, elegant and embattled with a pretty weather-vane. The church is essentially Norman and Early English. In the porch is a Roman altar dedicated to Garmangabis. The monolithic columns of the N. nave arcade are presumably from Lanchester Roman station. A spectacular zigzag-carved Norman chancel arch leads to the raised choir and sanctuary. Curious arches pierce the side walls of the chancel. There is a carved tympanum above the vestry door, and 13th-century glass. The general effect is high, light and spacious, complemented by well-designed and well-spaced modern pews.

PITTINGTON † St Laurence ★

4m/6km E. of Durham
OS *NZ328435* **GPS** *54.7860N, 1.4902W*

St Laurence's is set in a rural oasis between two pit villages. It is chiefly remarkable for a strange and exuberant late Norman N. nave arcade. The arcade was inserted below Saxon windows; a 12th-century wall-painting survives in the splay of one of them. The font cover is Jacobean and there are many carved stones including a tiny 13th-century tombstone carved with two swords.

SEAHAM † St Mary the Virgin

5m/8km S. of Sunderland
OS *NZ422505* **GPS** *54.8475N, 1.3436W*

This tiny gaunt church is surrounded by trees bent and stunted by easterly gales. Saxon, and similar in plan to Escomb, it has Roman stones built into its walls. The late 12th- or early 13th-century chancel has a double piscina with a priest's hand raised in blessing incised within its arch. The pleasant windows are by Kempe, and the parish register contains an entry of Byron's marriage to Arabella Milbanke, which took place in the drawing-room of neighbouring Seaham Hall.

STAINDROP † St Mary ★★

5m/8km N.E. of Barnard Castle
OS *NZ131206* **GPS** *54.5808N, 1.7988W*

Prettily situated in a large village beside Raby Park, this spacious and airy collegiate church was rebuilt by the Nevilles, incumbents of nearby Raby Castle, whose presence in the church overwhelms all else. There are traces of the original Saxon church of St Gregory, now enclosed by the later Norman building. The nave arcades are Early English, the E. bays having scalloped capitals. A 15th-century clerestory brings light into the nave, the N. aisle windows have Reticulated tracery, and elsewhere are lancet and Perpendicular windows. The choir stalls are pre-Reformation, and the medieval chancel screen is said to be the only one in the county. The two-storey priest's dwelling is now a vestry. Dominating everything, particularly at the W. end, are the Neville tombs: the large alabaster tomb of Ralph Neville, 1st Earl of Westmorland, d.1425, and his two wives; the oak tomb of Henry Neville, d. 1564, with carvings of his children on the sides; and near the N. door, a monolithic 18th-century monument to William Harry Vane, 1st Duke of Cleveland, carved by Richard Westmacott, President of the Royal Academy.

WYCLIFFE † St Mary

4m/6km E. of Barnard Castle
OS *NZ116143* **GPS** *54.5241N, 1.8210W*

A small and humble 13th- to 14th-century building close to the Tees, St Mary's stands in a beautiful situation near the dignified Georgian former rectory. The long, low church has a bellcote and porch and much medieval glass in the S. windows. The well-furnished interior has an interesting 1963 coffered ceiling by William Whitfield and a gaily painted chancel. There are several small monuments and inscriptions to the Wycliffe family; according to tradition, John Wycliffe, 'morning star of the Reformation', was born here.

◁ **STAINDROP: ST MARY** – *the tomb of William Harry Vane, 1st Duke of Cleveland*

ESSEX

Essex is a large square with two sides water. It is a stronger contrast of beauty and ugliness than any other southern English county. Most of what was built east of London in the 19th and 20th centuries has been a little bit cheaper and a little bit shoddier than that built in other directions. Southend is a cheaper Brighton, Clacton a cheaper Worthing, and Dovercourt a cheaper Bournemouth. With the gradual spread of Greater London, towns such as Leyton, Canning Town, Silvertown, Barking, Ilford and West and East Ham have all been lost to the county (see the London chapter). Only the Norman parish church of East Ham and the scant abbey remains of Barking and Leyton parish church tell us that these were once country places.

Our age has added the planned and congested dormitories of Becontree and Harold Hill. Along the Thames bank, factories and power stations can be seen for miles over the mudflats, and the hills of Kent on the opposite bank look countrified by comparison.

But Essex is a large county and the industrialisation is only a part of it. The county also has the deepest and least disturbed country within reach of London. Between the Stour, Blackwater, Crouch and Thames estuaries is flat agricultural scenery with its own old red-brick towns with weatherboarded side streets like Maldon, Georgian Harwich and Rochford – the headquarters of an Essex puritan sect known as The Peculiar People. Colchester was, as Pevsner said in his *Buildings of England: Essex* volume, more impressive than any town in England for 'the continuity of its architectural interest' – extensive redevelopment has changed that.

The flat part of Essex has not the man-made look of the fens. It is wild and salty, and its quality is well described in S. Baring-Gould's novel of Mersea, *Mehalah: A Story of the Salt Marshes*, 1880. It is part of that great plain which stretched across to Holland and Central Europe. Most of inland Essex, east and north of Epping Forest, is undulating and extremely pretty in the pale, gentle way suited to English watercolours. Narrow lanes wind like streams through willowy meadows past weatherboarded mills and unfenced bean and corn fields. From oaks on hill-tops peep the flinty church towers, and some of the churches up here are as magnificent as those in neighbouring Suffolk – Coggeshall, Thaxted, Saffron Walden and Dedham are grand examples of the Perpendicular style. Thaxted, for the magnificence of its church and the varied textures of the old houses of its little town, is one of the most charming places in Britain.

Chiefly, Essex is a place of varied building materials. 'It would be an interesting study for an antiquary of leisure

◁ **GREAT WARLEY: ST MARY THE VIRGIN** – *built in a style that elegantly straddles Arts and Crafts and Art Nouveau*

CAMBRIDGESHIRE
A1307
Haverhill
Hadstock
Pentlow
A1092
Belchamp St Paul
Strethall
Saffron Walden
A1017
Wendens Ambo
Great Sampford
Castle Hedingham
Debden
M11
Finchingfield
Little Maplestead
A10
Thaxted
Great Bardfield
Halstead
Gosfield
ESSEX
Elsenham
Chickney
Tilty
Little Easton
Stebbing
Stansted
BRAINTREE
A120
Bishop's Stortford
A120
A120
Little Dunmow
A10
Great Canfield
White Notley
Rivenha
Hatfield Broad Oak
A131
Fairstead
A130
HERTFORDSHIRE
Sheering
Great Br
Abbess Roding
Broomfield
Boreham
HARLOW
A1060
CHELMSFORD
A12
Epping
A414
A414
Greensted
A10
Blackmore
Margaretting
Purle
Waltham Abbey
Stondon Massey
Fryerning
Ingatestone
South Woodham Ferrers
Buttsbury
Navestock
M11
A130
A12
Chigwell
Billericay
BRENTWOOD
A128
Ingrave
A129
Great Warley
Rayleigh
A127
Laindon
GREATER LONDON
East Horndon
BASILDON
Hadleigh
A13
M25
A13
Corringham
Canvey Island
A13
South Ockendon
R Tham
Woolwich
A102
KENT
A282
Tilbury
A2
GRAVESEND

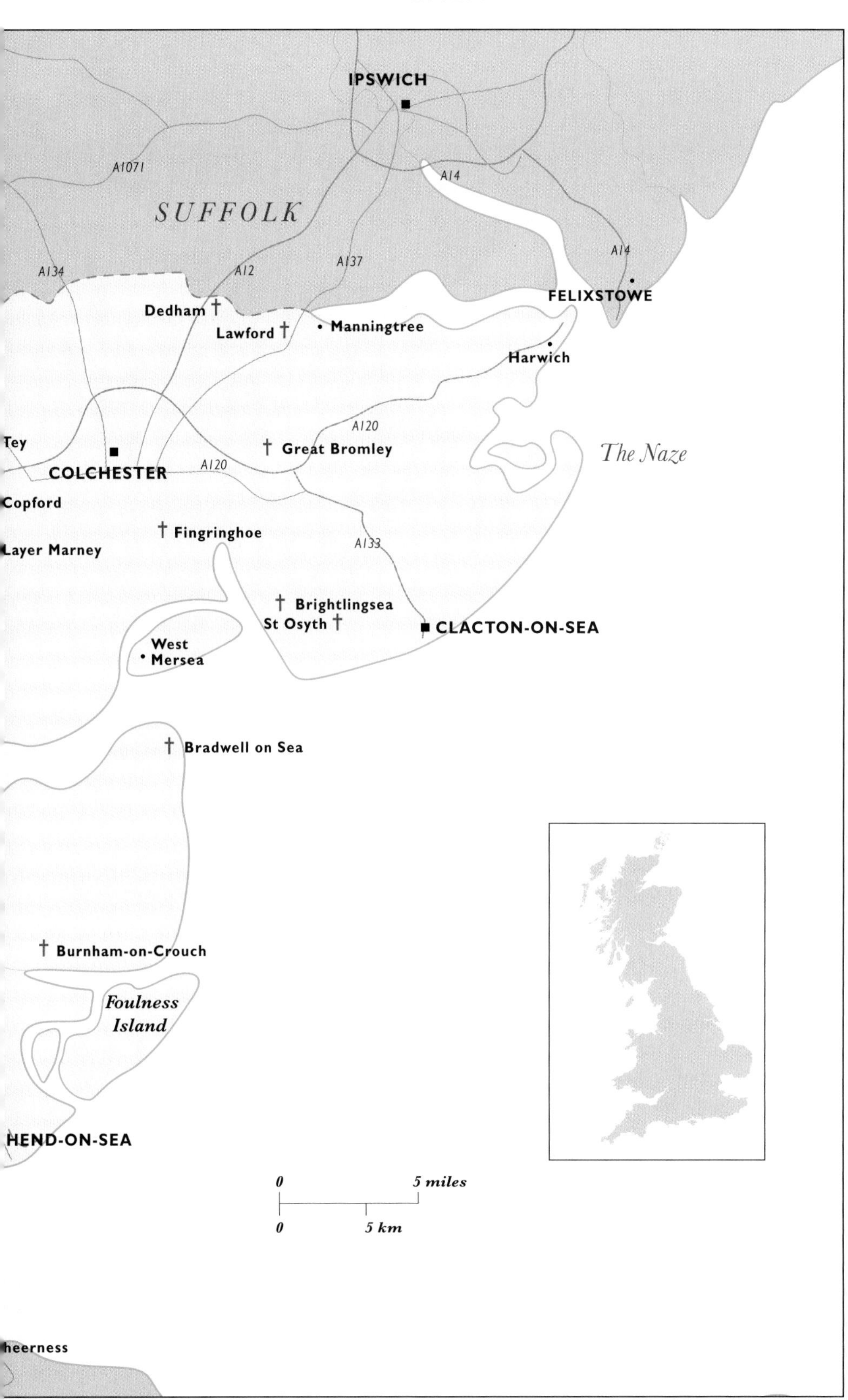
IPSWICH
A1071
A14
SUFFOLK
A134
A12
A137
A14
FELIXSTOWE
Dedham
Lawford
Manningtree
Harwich
A120
Tey
Great Bromley
The Naze
COLCHESTER
A120
Copford
Fingringhoe
Layer Marney
A133
Brightlingsea
St Osyth
CLACTON-ON-SEA
West
Mersea
Bradwell on Sea
Burnham-on-Crouch
Foulness
Island
HEND-ON-SEA
0
5 miles
0
5 km
heerness

△ **FINCHINGFIELD: ST JOHN THE BAPTIST** – *the church's Norman tower topped with 18th-century cupola stands above the picturesque village, which remains much as depicted on the sign*

to trace the various sources of materials employed in Essex church building, and the means by which they were brought to their destination.' (G. Worley, *Essex, a Dictionary of the County*, 1915) To build their churches, the east Saxons and the Normans used any material that came to hand – Roman tiles, split oak logs (as at Greensted), pudding stone taken from the beach deposits, and flint. The 15th-century tower of South Weald was made of ragstone brought across from Kent on the opposite shore. But chiefly Essex is a county of brick, which was made here as early as the 13th century. There are many brick church towers of unrivalled beauty, red as a bonfire; there are brick arcades and brick porches and brick window tracery. And when they left off building churches in this beautiful red brick, moulded into shapes and patterned with blue sanded headers, the Essex people continued it in houses until the 19th century.

Essex looks its best in sunlight, when the many materials of its rustic villages, the brick manor houses, the timbered 'halls' and the cob and thatched churches, the weatherboarded late-Georgian cottages, the oaks and flints, recall Constable. The delightful little town of Dedham and one half of the Stour Valley, be it remembered, are in Essex, and were as much an inspiration to Constable as neighbouring Suffolk, where he was born, and to which Essex is often so wrongly regarded as a poorer sister. It may be poorer in church architecture, but what it lacks in architecture it makes up for in the delicacy and variety of its textures.

△ **BRADWELL ON SEA: ST PETER-ON-THE-WALL** – *a remote place of worship built in the 7th century using ancient Roman bricks and stones*

ABBESS RODING † St Edmund

9m/15km N.E. of Epping
OS *TL571114* **GPS** *51.7795N, 0.2770E*

A fine late 15th-century church with earlier elements, it has 15th-century glass, including a bishop in Mass vestments, a late 12th-century font and good 17th-century monuments.

BELCHAMP ST PAUL † St Andrew

5m/8km W. of Sudbury
OS *TL798434* **GPS** *52.0603N, 0.6218E*

A Perpendicular church with a handsome W. tower, good chancel roof and octagonal font; also fine 15th- and 16th-century chancel stalls with misericords.

BLACKMORE † St Laurence ★★

3m/4km N.W. of Ingatestone
OS *TL603016* **GPS** *51.6904N, 0.3178E*

In an attractive little village and close to a fine house known as 'Jericho' stands the Norman church, which was once a small priory of Augustinian canons. There is a very impressive 15th-century timber bell-tower of intricate and elaborate construction, with three diminishing stages terminated by a broach spire.

BOREHAM † St Andrew

4m/6km N.E. of Chelmsford
OS *TL756096* **GPS** *51.7577N, 0.5430E*

The Norman central tower of St Andrew's incorporates a pre-Conquest E. arch. There is an unusual monument of 1589 with three Radcliffes, Earls of Sussex, on one alabaster tomb chest.

BRADWELL ON SEA
† St-Peter-on-the-Wall ★

7m/11km N.E. of Burnham-on-Crouch
OS *TM031081* **GPS** *51.7353N, 0.9400E*

Approached by a cart track through fields, and situated on the sea wall at the mouth of the Blackwater, this is one of the oldest churches in the county, having been built by St Cedd in about 654. Its materials were mostly taken from the ancient Roman fort of Othona, on the gateway of which the church is said to stand. The 7th-century nave remains.

BRENTWOOD † St Paul ★
In Bentley district, 1m/2km N.W. of Brentwood
OS *TQ566966* **GPS** *51.6469N, 0.2630E*

By E. C. Lee, 1878, a severe Early English essay in flint and stone, set in parkland. It has a shingled broach spire and good carved details; the sumptuous fittings include a reredos of the Way of the Cross.

BRIGHTLINGSEA † All Saints ★
8m/12km S.E. of Colchester
OS *TM077187* **GPS** *51.8286N, 1.0130E*

An attractive little town of old buildings on the Colne estuary has as its parish church, situated on a modest hill about a mile inland, a building whose exterior has fine flint flushwork. The late 15th-century tower is, unusually for the region, embattled, and is buttressed diagonally – one of the finest in the county. Inside, a Victorian frieze records local sailors lost at sea: in the N. chapel are brasses to the Beriffe family – medieval merchants and benefactors of the church.

BROOMFIELD † St Mary the Virgin
2m/3km N. of Chelmsford
OS *TL705104* **GPS** *51.7670N, 0.4699E*

The 11th–12th-century church of St Mary's contains a fair quantity of Roman brick and has a round tower which is an unusual feature in Essex.

BURNHAM-ON-CROUCH
† St Mary the Virgin
9m/15km S.E. of Maldon
OS *TQ948970* **GPS** *51.6383N, 0.8147E*

Best for its setting, the church is principally 14th- and 15th-century; the embattled S. aisle has good Perpendicular tracery with a pretty early 16th-century brick N. porch. The S. porch door has linenfold panelling, and the 19th-century nave has a plastered vaulted ceiling.

BUTTSBURY † St Mary
1m/2km E. of Ingatestone
OS *TQ663986* **GPS** *51.6617N, 0.4043E*

St Mary's is a small church, set in lonely farmland in the Wid Valley. It is mostly 14th-century, with Perpendicular arcades, medieval ironwork on the N. door, and an 18th-century chancel. Fragments of 15th-century painted boards – the upper portions of a Doom – were discovered in 1977 in the roof and can now be seen on the S. wall.

CASTLE HEDINGHAM
† St Nicholas ★★
4m/6km N.W. of Halstead
OS *TL784356* **GPS** *51.9902N, 0.5978E*

A large Norman church standing in the middle of the village, close to the remains of the De Vere castle. Three of the 12th-century doorways still have their original wooden doors. There is a fine hammer-beam roof to the nave of early 16th-century date; a wheel window is at the E. end of the chancel. An elaborate 14th–16th-century rood screen separates the nave from the chancel, on the S. side of which are some 15th-century stalls with misericords. The altar tomb in the chancel is of the 15th Earl of Oxford, d. 1539, and has low relief figures. The Tudor brick tower incorporates a stone inscribed 'Robert Archer the master builder of this stepell 1616'.

CHICKNEY † St Mary the Virgin ★
3m/4km S.W. of Thaxted
OS *TL574280* **GPS** *51.9287N, 0.2882E*
Churches Conservation Trust

A pre-Conquest church set in an isolated position far from any village and screened by trees, St Mary's has an unsymmetrical charm of its own. The Saxon nave retains two double-splayed windows, and the skewed chancel has small Early English lancets. Above the pre-Reformation stone altar are set two captivating carvings of a man and woman.

COPFORD
† St Michael and All Angels ★★
5m/8km W. of Colchester
OS *TL934227* **GPS** *51.8693N, 0.8092E*

Remotely situated and somewhat difficult to find, since it lies some way from the main road, this church must not be missed. An important 12th-century church, its nave and chancel originally had tunnel vaults – very rare in Norman parish churches. These have been removed, though some springers remain. The S. aisle of c. 1300 contains what must have been some of the earliest medieval bricks in

◁ **FINCHINGFIELD: ST JOHN THE BAPTIST** – *the fine early 15th-century rood screen*

England. The fame of this church lies in the remains of wall-paintings over the whole of the original building. They date from the middle of the 12th century, though have been considerably over-restored since their discovery in 1865. Of great interest, above the pulpit, is a scene depicting the healing of Jairus's daughter. In the half-domed vault over the apse is a Byzantine painting of Christ in Majesty, with unnecessary embellishments by Daniel Bell, who restored the paintings in the 1870s.

CORRINGHAM † St Mary ★

4m/6km S. of Basildon
OS *TQ709832* **GPS** *51.5226N, 0.4633E*

Petrochemical storage has industrialized this parish, but its village atmosphere is still preserved in the group of buildings consisting of the Saxon church, some old cottages and the 15th-century inn. Though dating from pre-Conquest days, the greater part of the church is 14th-century. There is a good screen of that date and some furnishings by Martin Travers.

DEBDEN
† St Mary the Virgin and All Saints

4m/6km S. of Saffron Walden
OS *TL551332* **GPS** *51.9759N, 0.2568E*

Alone in landscaped grounds, the church is mostly 13th–14th-century, enhanced by an elegant Gothic W. front and delectable octagonal E. chapel of 1793. There are good 18th-century monuments.

DEDHAM † St Mary the Virgin ★

6m/10km N.E. of Colchester
OS *TM057331* **GPS** *51.9585N, 0.9928E*

This large Perpendicular church stands in an attractive village, witness to the prosperity of the 15th-century cloth trade. The magnificent tower has octagonal buttresses ending in tall pinnacles, much painted by Constable. The fine monument of c. 1500 is to Thomas Webbe, merchant and benefactor of the church.

EAST HORNDON † All Saints ★

4m/6km S.E. of Brentwood
OS *TQ635895* **GPS** *51.5808N, 0.3592E*
Churches Conservation Trust

Standing in an isolated position on the top of a hill, this all-brick church is particularly worth seeing. Rescued from dereliction in the 1970s, it has a cruciform plan with the unique feature of a gallery room above each transept that was used as a family pew. There is an early 16th-century Tyrell Chapel, and the fittings include a beautifully incised stone slab dated 1422, bearing a portrait of Alice Tyrell.

ELSENHAM † St Mary the Virgin

4m/6km N.E. of Bishop's Stortford
OS *TL542259* **GPS** *51.9105N, 0.2408E*

St Mary's is mainly Norman, with a finely decorated 12th-century chancel arch and S. doorway with zigzags and chip-carved tympanum.

EPPING † St John the Baptist ★

5m/8km S. of Harlow
OS *TL459021* **GPS** *51.6987N, 0.1105E*

By Bodley & Garner, 1889, a very dignified Bath-stone church in the Decorated style, standing alongside an attractive, wide high street. The prominent tower was added by Bodley in 1908. Inside are round barrel vaults with painted texts and good furnishings by Bodley's partner, Cecil Hare. The glass is by Kempe and Burlison & Grylls.

FAIRSTEAD † St Mary

4m/6km S. of Braintree
OS *TL767166* **GPS** *51.8209N, 0.5637E*

St Mary's is one of the earliest Essex churches, and the tower, nave and chancel have Roman brick quoins and dressings. Important wall-paintings of c. 1275 were discovered during the restoration of 1890; the painting above the chancel arch depicts the Passion, whilst on the S. wall is St Christopher.

FINCHINGFIELD
† St John the Baptist ★★

8m/12km N.W. of Braintree
OS *TL686328* **GPS** *51.9682N, 0.4532E*

The church is in a lovely setting on a hill. The massive Norman tower, with its quaint 18th-century cupola, dominates one of the most attractive villages in the whole county. The church does not entirely come up to the standard of its setting, though contains many good things. The stonework is a random mix

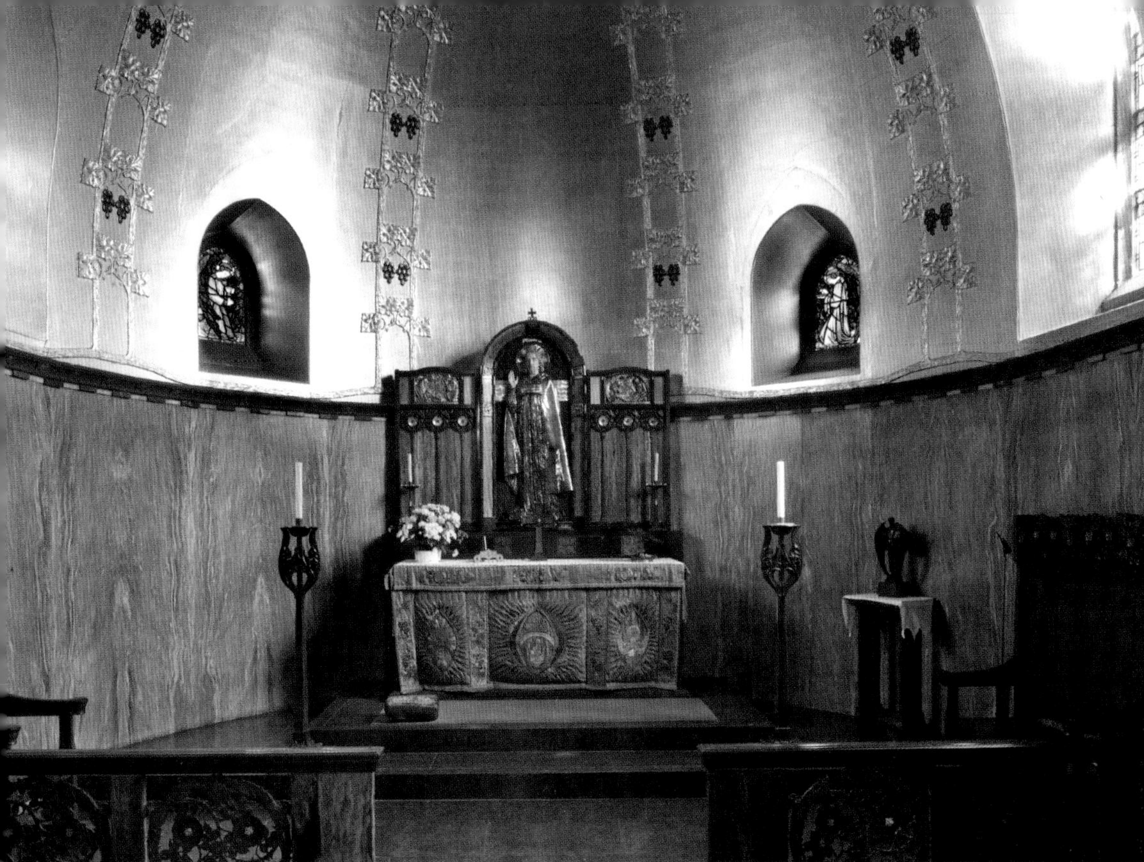

△ **GREAT WARLEY: ST MARY THE VIRGIN** – *bronze, silver gilt, ormolu, enamel, mother-of-pearl and marble are used in the apsidal chancel, and the vault is finished with aluminium leaf*

of brick, flint and stone. The W. door into the tower, with its three orders of columns and chevron ornament in semi-circular arched head, is a good example of Norman work. The rest of the church is mostly 14th-century. There are two fine screens – early 15th-century and perhaps the best in Essex. The S. aisle screen has carved grotesques, and peering from the walls all round the church are corbel heads, whose expressions cover the gamut of human emotions.

FINGRINGHOE † St Andrew ★

4m/6km S.E. of Colchester
OS *TM029203* **GPS** *51.8452N, 0.9452E*

Dominating the ancient settlement, this is one of the county's most impressive marshland churches. It is largely 14th-century, with a tower of banded flint and stone, nave roof with carved heads, extensive wall-paintings and 17th-century monuments.

FRYERNING † St Mary ★

½m/1km W. of Ingatestone
OS *TL638001* **GPS** *51.6759N, 0.3683E*

A large red brick tower with diapering in blue bricks marks out this 16th-century church. Traces of its Norman origins are to be found in some of the windows and doorways, and, inside, a Norman font with cross and crown, and a Jesse Tree. A former parishioner is commemorated in the N. wall window – Airey Neave MP, killed by the I.R.A. in London, 1979.

GOSFIELD † St Catherine

4m/6km N.E. of Braintree
OS *TL777294* **GPS** *51.9347N, 0.5846E*

St Catherine's is entirely 15th–16th-century, with a remarkable brick squire's pew-cum-family chapel added in 1735–6. Lit by a Venetian window, it has something of the appearance of a theatre box. Good monuments include one by Rysbrack to John and Anne Knight, and an altar tomb against the S. wall to Thomas Rolf, 1440.

△ **GREENSTED: ST ANDREW** – *the timber walls of this dark woodland church are 11th-century*

GREAT BARDFIELD
† St Mary the Virgin ★
2m/3km S. of Finchingfield
OS *TL678303* **GPS** *51.9465N, 0.4401E*

The church looks down on one of the most attractive villages in Essex, full of beautiful old houses. Mostly 14th-century, and rather dark inside, it is remarkable for the stone rood screen of excellent craftsmanship filling the whole of the chancel arch, surmounted by Victorian figures by Bodley.

GREAT BRAXTED † All Saints
12m/18km N.E. of Chelmsford
OS *TL850154* **GPS** *51.8069N, 0.6834E*

All Saints has a wonderful picturesque setting in the grounds of Braxted Park. Principally Norman with a 13th-century tower, the timber belfry stage was added in 1883. The 19th-century Du Cane Chapel contains many monuments, some with traceried canopies.

GREAT BROMLEY † St George ★★
6m/10km E. of Colchester
OS *TM083262* **GPS** *51.8962N, 1.0269E*

A church of considerable architectural interest, St George's dates principally from the 15th century. There is a magnificent tower supported with angled and diagonal buttresses, and a S. porch with fine flint and stone flushwork. The S. arcade has Decorated capitals of intricate detail – grotesques and swirling foliage. The glorious double hammer-beam nave roof is filled with carving in every space, and there is original paintwork and a very fine brass of a priest in Mass vestments.

GREAT CANFIELD † St Mary ★
7m/11km E. of Bishops Stortford
OS *TL593180* **GPS** *51.8379N, 0.3121E*

Remotely set along tree-bordered lanes, near a motte-and-bailey castle, the church is essentially Norman. The S. door carving with a patterned tympanum is of interest: the outer order is billeted, as is the fine chancel arch, with scalloped capitals and cable mouldings. The treasure here is the beautiful 13th-century wall-painting of the Virgin and Child, described by Pevsner as 'full of tenderness'.

GREAT SAMPFORD † St Michael ★
4m/6km N.E. of Thaxted
OS *TL642353* **GPS** *51.9924N, 0.3906E*

Pleasantly situated by some old cottages, the church was almost entirely rebuilt in the 14th century. Six consecration crosses still remain, and there is a fine tomb recess in the S. chapel. The plain 15th-century font bowl stands on a Decorated stem.

GREAT TEY † St Barnabas ★
7m/11km W. of Colchester
OS *TL891257* **GPS** *51.8985N, 0.7485E*

The church's main feature is the magnificent Norman tower of four stages, with Roman brick dressings at the crossing of nave and chancel. The chancel is a good example of Decorated work.

GREAT WARLEY † St Mary the Virgin ★
2m/3km S.W. of Brentwood
OS *TQ588899* **GPS** *51.5864N, 0.2921E*

By Charles Harrison Townsend, 1904. A modest exterior belies a lush display of craftsmanship inside, mostly by Sir William Reynolds-Stevens, with glass by Heywood Sumner: an excellent example of Art Nouveau in the English Arts and Crafts manner.

GREENSTED † St Andrew ★★
1m/2km W. of Chipping Ongar
OS *TL538029* **GPS** *51.7044N, 0.2255E*

A famous church in a wooded setting, this is the only surviving example of a timber Saxon church. The walls of the nave consist of split oak logs, and this part of the church is said to be possibly the oldest wooden structure in Europe. Its dating has been revised somewhat, with tree-ring dating in 1995 suggesting construction in the 11th century. The chancel is early 16th-century, of Tudor brick. The roof and much woodwork was drastically restored in the 19th century. Within these walls the body of St Edmund is said to have rested on its way from London to Bury St Edmunds.

HADLEIGH † St James the Less
4m/6km W. of Southend-on-Sea
OS *TQ810870* **GPS** *51.5531N, 0.6095E*

Almost stranded on an island site between two carriageways of the A13, this is a complete Norman church with apse, whose plan has remained structurally unaltered. There is a 13th-century wall-painting of St Thomas of Canterbury, and the 13th-century remains of a figure on the arch of an E. window.

HADSTOCK † St Botolph ★
4m/6km N. of Saffron Walden
OS *TL558447* **GPS** *52.0791N, 0.2733E*

This is most likely the minster erected by Canute in 1020 to commemorate his victory at the Battle of the Assendun over Edmund Ironside. The neighbouring parish of Ashdon is said to be the scene of the battle. It is a remarkable Saxon cruciform church, built on the remains of an earlier Anglo-Saxon church, perhaps of the monastery founded by Abbot Botolph in 654.

HATFIELD BROAD OAK
† St Mary the Virgin ★
5m/8km S.E. of Bishop's Stortford
OS *TL546166* **GPS** *51.8268N, 0.2431E*

South of Hatfield Forest and dominating a village of attractive old houses, this church formed the nave of the priory founded by Aubrey de Vere c. 1135. Here is good 14th- and 15th-century work, with a fine tower and a notable sculptured monument to Robert de Vere, 1221. The reredos, panelling and communion rails are excellent examples of early 18th-century work, probably by John Woodward, a pupil of Grinling Gibbons. A library has been built onto the church to house some 200 books given in 1680; among them is an *Aldine Aristode*, 1498.

INGATESTONE
† St Edmund and St Mary ★
5m/8km N.E. of Brentwood
OS *TQ651995* **GPS** *51.6708N, 0.3865E*

Here is the finest of the many brick towers of Essex – black diapering on red Perpendicular brickwork. Inside, generations of the Petre family dominate, including Sir William Petre, Secretary of State to Henry VIII, in alabaster by the chancel: he rebuilt the S. chapel as a family vault.

INGRAVE † St Nicholas
2m/3km S.E. of Brentwood
OS *TQ623920* **GPS** *51.6037N, 0.3426E*

One of the best 18th-century churches in Essex, St Nicholas's was built in 1735, in red brick with an incongruously militaristic tower. Though by an unknown hand, the church is reminiscent of the work of Hawksmoor.

△ **GREENSTED: ST ANDREW** – *the split oak logs on the nave wall have been dated to Saxon times, making this possibly the world's oldest surviving wooden church*

LAINDON † St Nicholas

W. district of Basildon
OS *TQ687895* **GPS** *51.5792N, 0.4347E*

St Nicholas's is mainly 13th-century, with one of the best timber steeples in Essex and a sturdy timber-framed belfry. An unusual 17th-century priest's house is attached to the church.

LAWFORD † St Mary ★

1m/2km W. of Manningtree
OS *TM089315* **GPS** *51.9434N, 1.0380E*

The chancel, sedilia and the N. side E. window command attention in this otherwise unremarkable 14th-century church. The Decorated windows in the chancel are idiosyncratic, with carved birds, animals and foliage ornamenting the arches and shafts, each window with its own form of tracery. The sedilia are similarly fine in detail, and around the E. window on the N. side of the church is an interconnected sequence of acrobats, each one holding the leg of the one above.

LAYER MARNEY
† St Mary the Virgin ★★

6m/10km S.W. of Colchester
TL928174 **GPS** *51.8221N, 0.7965E*

The church was rebuilt by Lord Marney early in the 16th century, close to his house, Layer Marney Towers, and is an excellent example of Tudor brickwork with blue diapering. An unusual feature is the priest's lodging at the W. end of the N. aisle. An appealing painting of St Christopher is on the N. wall, and there are two medieval screens of moderate quality. The Marney Chapel is of great interest, with a recently discovered Tudor fireplace, and the tomb of Sir William Varney, d. 1414. Lord Henry Marney's tomb, d. 1523, sits between chapel and chancel, an odd mixture of Gothic and Classical.

LITTLE DUNMOW † St Mary ★

2m/3km E. of Great Dunmow
OS *TL656212* **GPS** *51.8651N, 0.4039E*

A place well-known for its flitch of bacon awarded to the man and woman who had not repented of their marriage for a year and a day, the church is all that remains of an Augustinian priory of which it formed a chapel on the S. side of the choir, and from which it was separated by a beautifully proportioned arcade, which remains. Some excellent 14th-century stone carving, mostly of animals and flowers, can be seen in panels along the S. wall. The Dunmow Flitch Chair in the sanctuary is made up from a 13th-century stall. Two fine 15th-century altar tombs to the Fitzwalters with alabaster effigies are at the back of the church.

LITTLE EASTON † St Mary ★

2m/3km N.W. of Great Dunmow
OS *TL604235* **GPS** *51.8870N, 0.3301E*

First impressions of St Mary's are of an unexciting Victorian church with 'Norman' windows to the S. Internally the fabric is similarly uninspiring, but the contents are of great interest: wall-paintings of the 12th century; Gothic panels; the tombs of Viscount Bourchier, d. 1483, whose brass still holds remnants of its original colour; effigies of Henry Maynard and William Maynard in the Bourchier/Maynard Chapel; and a painted panel above the pulpit recounting visits to the nearby manor house of the Shakespearean actress Ellen Terry. A jingoistic memorial to wartime American bombers is in the N. transept.

LITTLE MAPLESTEAD † St John the Baptist ★

2m/3km N. of Halstead
OS *TL822339* **GPS** *51.9746N, 0.6520E*

Built by the Knights Hospitaller c. 1340, it is one of the five 'round churches' in England. The hexagonal nave is separated from the circular aisle by a well-proportioned 14th-century arcade, much restored in 1850. There is an apsidal chancel and Norman font.

MALDON † All Saints ★★

9m/15km E. of Chelmsford
OS *TL849070* **GPS** *51.7318N, 0.6767E*

In the midst of an attractive little hill town above the Blackwater, this 13th-century church has a unique triangular tower surmounted by a hexagonal spire. The 14th-century S. aisle survived a hard 18th-century 'restoration', in which the N. aisle and nave were recombined. The Purbeck marble arcade is very fine, and the S. wall bears a profusion of Decorated arcading encompassing the sedilia and windows. The window in the S. chapel was presented to the church by the town of Maldon, Massachusetts in the USA.

MARGARETTING † St Margaret ★

4m/6km S.W. of Chelmsford
OS *TL665004* **GPS** *51.6779N, 0.4070E*

The 15th-century timber W. tower and shingled broach spire of St Margaret's are supported on freestanding posts connected by arch braces, and the timber N. porch is Tudor. The inside E. wall is covered with ornamental plasterwork illustrating the the Miracle of the Loaves and Fishes, which makes a frame for a near-complete 15th-century Jesse window, made up of Flemish glass.

NAVESTOCK † St Thomas

4m/6km N.W. of Brentwood
OS *TQ540983* **GPS** *51.6630N, 0.2259E*

A Norman and later church with an impressive 13th-century timber-framed tower and spire. Inside the church is plastered wooden arcading to the nave.

PENTLOW † St Gregory & St George ★

3m/4km W. of Long Melford
OS *TL812461* **GPS** *52.0841N, 0.6442E*

The church has an early Norman nave and chancel, whose apse retains three original windows, and a 12th-century round tower – one of six in the county. To the N. is a curiously disproportionate 16th-century Perpendicular chapel, tunnel vaulted, containing a very fine altar tomb with recumbent effigies of Judge

George Kempe, d. 1606, John Kempe his son, d. 1609, and Elinore his wife.

PURLEIGH † All Saints
3m/4km S. of Maldon
OS *TL841020* **GPS** *51.6869N, 0.6625E*

Delighfully situated on top of a hill, the church is principally 14th-century, including the fine W. tower and rare white brickwork. It is of great interest to Americans because its rector from 1632–43 was Lawrence Washington, who was great-great-grandfather to George Washington.

RIVENHALL
† St Mary and All Saints ★★
5M/8KM S.E. of Braintree
OS *TL828177* **GPS** *51.8288N, 0.6514E*

This church was extensively remodelled in 1838, and the stuccoed exterior gives nothing away, but it is actually an almost complete 11th-century two-cell building. It also possesses the finest medieval stained glass in the county. In 1840 the then incumbent brought over from France some 12th-century glass from a church near Tours and fitted it into the E. window, thus giving St Mary's some of the earliest surviving glass in Europe. It was fashionable at the time for wealthy English clergymen to purchase items abroad to be incorporated into their restorations. A visit to the church should not be missed.

SAFFRON WALDEN † St Mary ★★
12m/19km N. of Bishop's Stortford
OS *TL537386* **GPS** *52.0247N, 0.2393E*

The crocketed spire of Essex's largest church can be seen for miles around. Designed in the grand East Anglian manner, St Mary's is the height of Perpendicular, consisting of a lofty nave – 54 feet high – flanked by soaring arcades to the N. and S. aisles, and a raised chancel separated from the nave by a rood screen designed by Nicholson, 1923. Vast Perpendicular windows flood the interior with light – it is a church of structure rather than content. There is a great architectural link between this church and King's College, Cambridge, not many miles away.

ST OSYTH † St Peter and St Paul ★
3m/4km W. of Clacton-on-Sea
OS *TM122155* **GPS** *51.7985N, 1.0771E*

Situated delightfully close to the old abbey, the gateway of which is a noted monument. Though the church dates from the early 12th century, its most remarkable architectural feature is the fine 16th-century brick arcades separating the nave from the aisles. The furnishings include some very fine alabaster monuments to the D'Arcy family. There are also some early 19th-century 'sheep fold' communion rails on a horse-shoe plan.

SHEERING † St Mary the Virgin
2m/3km E. of Sawbridgeworth
OS *TL508136* **GPS** *51.8008N, 0.1864E*

The church is Norman and later Perpendicular. In the E. window is a fine late 14th-century stained-glass depiction of the Coronation of the Virgin.

SOUTH OCKENDON † St Nicholas
suburb 3m/4km N.W. of Grays
OS *TQ595829* **GPS** *51.5226N, 0.2977E*

St Nicholas has a 13th-century circular flint tower, rare in Essex. Inside there is a good alabaster wall-monument of 1601 to Sir Richard Saltonstall, Lord Mayor of London. The majority of church dates from a Victorian restoration of 1866.

STEBBING † St Mary the Virgin ★
3m/4km N.E. of Great Dunmow
OS *TL663240* **GPS** *51.8898N, 0.4166E*

At the S. end of a typical Essex village of attractive old buildings stands the church of mainly 14th-century date in brick and stone. The interior is light and spacious, with graceful arcades and a rare three-arched Decorated early 14th-century stone screen filling the whole chancel opening. The timber roofs bear carved angels.

STONDON MASSEY
† St Peter and St Paul
3m/4km S.E. of Chipping Ongar
OS *TL572015* **GPS** *51.6910N, 0.2739E*

An early Norman nave and chancel church with a late medieval timber-framed belfry. Inside are two 16th-century brasses, one of

THAXTED: ST JOHN THE BAPTIST – *the Lady Chapel, c. 1510, in the south aisle of the chancel* ▷

THOMAS

△ **WALTHAM ABBEY: HOLY CROSS** – *spiral and zigzag decoration embellish the pillars of the splendid Norman arcades lining the nave of this former abbey*

which, to John Carre, d. 1570, bears the Arms of the Ironmongers' Company.

STRETHALL † St Mary the Virgin ★

4m/6km W. of Saffron Walden
OS *TL485398* **GPS** *52.0370N, 0.1643E*

This is a small, late Saxon church in a very beautiful setting, in one of the most rural parishes in the county, with probably the smallest population. The nave is separated from the chancel by a finely proportioned and decorated archway of the time of Edward the Confessor.

THAXTED † St John the Baptist ★★

6m/10km S.E. of Saffron Walden
OS *TL610310* **GPS GPS** *51.9543, 0.3422*

Standing high up above a town of attractive old houses is one of the grandest churches in the county. Approaching the town from the S.E. is an unforgettable sight as the houses converge towards the old Moot Hall, above the roof of which is seen this magnificent parish church. Principally of 14th-, 15th- and early 16th-century dates, it consists of a narrow nave with much wider aisles, a crossing with N. and S. transepts and a spacious chancel with N. and S. chapels, whose arcades have delightful open spandrels. The N. and S. porches each have a parvise room above. The interior has a fine play of light and shade. There are good fragments of old stained glass remaining, and two windows by Kempe. The absence of customary pews gives a great feeling of spaciousness. Good craftsmanship can be seen in the roofs. The font is completely hidden by the font case and cover of late 15th-century date. For much of the 20th century, its two vicars Jack Putterill and Conrad Noel created here a centre for Anglo-Catholicism.

TILTY † St Mary the Virgin ★★

3m/4km N.W. of Great Dunmow
OS *TL599265* **GPS** *51.9142N, 0.3248E*

Formerly the chapel by the gate of the neighbouring Cistercian Abbey, St Mary's has

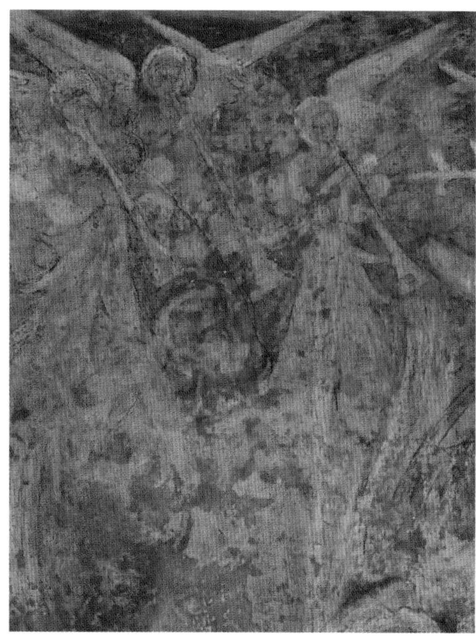

△ **WALTHAM ABBEY: HOLY CROSS** – *figures of saved souls ascending heavenward and of angels blasting trumpets on the Day of Judgement, from the 15th-century Doom painting*

a 13th-century nave with regularly spaced lancet windows leading into a very large 14th-century chancel – a work of great architectural beauty. The E. window has some of the loveliest Reticulated tracery in the county, and the sedilia have a fine canopy. Outside, the belfry is surmounted by a charming 18th-century cupola.

WALTHAM ABBEY † Holy Cross ★★

7m/11km S.W. of Harlow
OS *TL381006* **GPS** *51.6876N, -0.0034W*

Only the nave, aisles and S. chapel remain of what must have once been a most imposing monastic establishment. The tower was added after the Dissolution. The splendid Norman nave is comparable with the nave of Durham Cathedral and has spiral and zigzag ornament on the pillars. There are too many Victorian pews, but some have now been removed. Much 19th-century restoration was undertaken by William Burges, who commissioned Sir Edward Poynter to recreate Peterborough's medieval roof here. There is an excellent E. window by Burne-Jones – early work depicting the Creation, a Tree of Jesse and the Creator. The Lady Chapel, 14th-century, has an important 15th-century Doom painting, discovered during restoration works. There are many fine monuments throughout the church, including that to a ship owner, thought to be by Grinling Gibbons. Queen Eleanor's body rested here on the way to Westminster Abbey.

WENDENS AMBO
† St Mary the Virgin ★

2m/3km S.W. of Saffron Walden
OS *TL512363* **GPS** *52.0053N, 0.2027E*

Dating from the end of the 11th century, this delightful little country church has a most attractive setting and is approached by a lane bordered with typical Essex thatched cottages. Furnishings include 14th-century wall-paintings, a Perpendicular pulpit and carved benches.

WHITE NOTLEY † St Etheldreda

3m/4km S.E. of Braintree
OS *TL785182* **GPS** *51.8342N, 0.5900E*

An attractive small 11th- and 13th-century church with a 14th-century S. porch, and some early 13th-century stained glass and 16th-century paintings.

GLOUCESTERSHIRE

Gloucestershire is richer than any other county in variety of colour and outline. Indeed, rich is the adjective that best suits it. The Severn and Avon brought vessels to Gloucestershire from Spain and later from America. The wool trade in the late Middle Ages brought prosperity to the limestone Cotswold Hills, and many fine Perpendicular churches rose in the little wool towns of which that at Northleach is an impressive example.

Before that, the Normans had built the great naves of Gloucester Cathedral and Tewkesbury Abbey with their cylindrical columns, and many a country church has a Norman arch or window or tympanum. The Black Death came to the county and some work was stopped; even so, a great building tradition was maintained, and nowhere else are there such fine farm buildings, enormous barns and stone-built manor houses as in Gloucestershire. The medieval tradition continued in the construction of tithe barns, dovecotes and outbuildings until early in the 18th century.

In the 16th and 17th centuries there was what the historian Anthony West has called a water-power industrial revolution, when the rapid streams of the south Cotswold valley were used to turn mills employed to make cloth. These old mills, stone-built equivalents of the card mills of the north of England, survive in the deep Stroud valley and are still, some of them, used as factories. At this time, in the western half of the county and near Bristol, there was an iron industry. Later came the coalfields to the oak woods of the Forest of Dean.

The greatest richness of the county is in its stone and scenery. As you enter Gloucestershire from the east, you continue with the limestone scenery of Oxfordshire and north Wiltshire. This is a warm yellowish-grey that breeds a delicate patina of lichens. In the little piece of Gloucestershire north of Moreton-in-Marsh, the limestone takes on a golden tinge as though bathed in perpetual late sunlight. Further west and north of Bristol, the stone is a cold grey, and houses have red tiles in the Somerset manner. The most spectacular scenery of all is in the middle of the county, by the Stroud valley and Minchinhampton Common and Amberley. Here the stone is silver-white, and at Painswick it is almost as white as Portland stone, but with a warmth in it that Portland lacks. The central tower of Gloucester Cathedral is built of Painswick stone.

As may be expected in this part of the country, where stone is so plentiful and where it has been worked for centuries, the workmanship is of high quality. Stone-tiled roofs have graded tiles, large at the eaves and small at the ridges; stone is used for mullions and transoms of windows as easily as if it were timber; moulded stone arches are used for doorways. Nobly carved tombstones in a local Baroque style diversify country churchyards.

◁ **EASTLEACH: ST MICHAEL AND ST MARTIN** – *the hipped west tower rises above water meadows*

Everywhere you descend from barren heights, which once tinkled with sheep bells, to enclosed valleys shaded by beech where the stone villages cluster. At the western heights of this stone kingdom you may look over miles of the Severn Valley below you to the blue mountains of Wales and the gigantic outline of the Malvern Hills.

The Severn Vale and Vale of Berkeley (in the second the famous double-Gloucester cheeses are made) are a complete contrast with the eastern stone area. The Severn winds through muddy flatness; willows abound, as do orchards and pastoral scenery. Stone used here for churches, barns and causeways raised above flood-level could easily be carried up the Severn. But humbler buildings were timber-framed, and many old cottages survive among drabber brick cottages of the last century.

The least visited part of the county is the north-west, which has the Georgian red-brick town of Newent as its capital. Here on the Herefordshire border are oak-woods and wild daffodils and steep hills and forgotten farms down steep-banked lanes and red earth and pink sandstone. The land between the muddy flatness of the Severn and the steep-wooded splendour of the Wye Valley is occupied by the Forest of Dean. Mitcheldean to the north might be a small Welsh town with its high, narrow streets and weather-worn appearance. The Forest itself is among high hills and has a rather unpleasantly large quota of conifers, but once you leave these you find oak-woods and brown streams and grass-grown mineral lines leading to ruined industries, and then suddenly and unaccountably a coal-tip and a mine and a township of miners' red-brick cottages. One might be in Durham. Architecturally, the churches are mostly poor late-Georgian and Victorian buildings, which have the used and highly

reat Malvern
Pershore
Evesham
WORCESTERSHIRE
Shipston-on-Stour
Chipping Campden
Todenham
Wormington
Buckland
Great Washbourne
Stanton
Ashchurch
TEWKESBURY
Teddington
Oxenton
Toddington
Forthampton
Chacely
Deerhurst
Hailes
Winchcombe
Moreton-in-Marsh
Bourton-on-the-Hill
Longborough
Stoke Orchard
Bishop's Cleeve
Ashleworth
Chipping Norton
Stow-on-the-Wold
Oddington
Bledington
Naunton
CHELTENHAM
GLOUCESTERSHIRE
Highnam
GLOUCESTER
Shipton Solers
Withington
Northleach
Windrush
Little Barrington
Brimpsfield
Elkstone
Stowell
Chedworth
Painswick
Rendcomb
Coln Rogers
Coln St Denys
North Cerney
Bibury
Carterton
Duntisbourne Rouse
Daglingworth
STROUD
Baunton
Hatherop
Eastleach
Southrop
Selsley
Bussage
CIRENCESTER
Ampney Crucis
Ampney St Mary
Fairford
Minchinhampton
Meysey Hampton
Lechlade
Avening
South Cerney
Down Ampney
Kempsford
Faringdon
Ozleworth
Ashley
Beverston
Tetbury
Cricklade
Didmarton
Malmesbury
Great Badminton
Chippenham
Calne
Corsham

△ **AMPNEY CRUCIS: HOLY ROOD** – *tomb of the resplendently moustachioed George Lloyd*

polished interiors of industrial churches. Forest of Dean stone is a pink sandstone which does not weather well.

With such richness of natural and man-made beauty, it is not surprising that Gloucestershire has attracted artists and art-workers. Chipping Campden and Painswick, Sapperton and Cirencester, have, for a century and more, been the homes of artists and handicraftsmen, stained-glass artists, potters, weavers and cabinet makers – such famous men as Ernest Gimson, Peter Waals, the Barnsleys and Christopher Whall, F. L. Griggs and C. R. Ashbee. Their love of the native crafts of the county, though it may have unwittingly inspired much arty craftiness of the aubretia and staddle-stone variety, has saved Gloucestershire from much vandalism.

One exotic in the county of Gloucestershire is the late Georgian spa of Cheltenham, set in flat land at the foot of the Cotswolds. It is a stucco and limestone town of ample tree-shaded squares and crescents and streets, a town of gardens and sunlight, where the stately houses are adorned with most delicate and inventive ironwork verandahs and porches, designed to give lightness to the Classic severity of their architecture. Cheltenham is, as it were, St John's Wood and Regent's Park set down over square miles of Gloucester meadowland. But inevitably the raw red brick of housing developments spreads ever wider: Cheltenham's new suburbs are not perhaps as densely packed as the meadows surrounding Tewkesbury, which have almost disappeared under a tide of cramped villas: Gloucester has long overwhelmed its surrounding villages. The restraint that encouraged a local council to build council houses in local stone has been abandoned by the private developers.

AVENING: HOLY CROSS – *a cruciform Norman church of great charm* ▷

AMPNEY CRUCIS † Holy Rood

3m/4km E. of Cirencester
OS *SP065018* **GPS** *51.7158N, 1.9073W*

A cruciform church with work of all periods from Saxon to 19th-century, it has a good Norman chancel arch and a celebrated gabled churchyard cross of c. 1415, which escaped the Puritans by being carefully walled up. There are remains of wall-paintings in the N. transept, which also contains the tomb of George Lloyd, shown in full armour with fine moustache.

AMPNEY ST MARY † St Mary ★

4m/6km E. of Cirencester
OS *SP075015* **GPS** *51.7125N, 1.8919W*

An isolated little church on the main road with no village visible, St Mary dates from the 12th century, its boldly carved N. doorway with a strange primitive tympanum. There are splendid 12th- to 15th-century wall-paintings, including Christ of the Trades, St Christopher and St George. The church was restored in 1913 when F. C. Eden added stained glass to the flowing Decorated windows.

ARLINGHAM † St Mary the Virgin ★

9m/15km N.W. of Stroud
OS *SO706106* **GPS** *51.7939N, 2.4269W*

This is a very remote spot, situated in a loop of the Severn. The Decorated chancel with piscina and credence shelf has fine 14th-century glass with paintings of saints. Good monuments include one by Nollekens.

ASHCHURCH † St Nicholas

2m/3km E. of Tewkesbury
OS *SO927334* **GPS** *51.9991N, 2.1069W*

The church has a long nave, short chancel and a 14th-century battlemented W. tower. The decorous 15th-century rood screen has traceried panels and cornice decoration of grape vines; somewhat restored, but a rare survival in this county. The roofs are old; a painted Tudor frieze and stained glass by Hardman and Kempe add to the interest.

ASHLEWORTH
† St Andrew and St Bartholomew ★

5m/8km N. of Gloucester
OS *SO818251* **GPS** *51.9249N, 2.2653W*

A superb setting next to a court-house of c. 1460 and tithe barn; the spire is 14th-century, the roofs 15th-century. Inside is a 15th-century font, painted Royal Arms of Elizabeth I, a 17th-century holy table, communion rails and reading desk. Extensive restoration took place here after the floods of 2007.

ASHLEY † St James the Greater

3m/4km N.E. of Tetbury
OS *ST931947* **GPS** *51.6512N, 2.1001W*

This is a small Norman church with a carved S. doorway, Early English arcade and chancel arch of c. 1100. Rustic monuments abound.

AVENING † Holy Cross ★★

2m/3km S.E. of Nailsworth
OS *ST879979* **GPS** *51.6806N, 2.1755W*

Holy Cross is a beautiful cruciform Norman church with central tower, carefully restored in 1902 by John Micklethwaite. The chancel was delightfully rewrought in the 14th century, with a fine vault. There is a Commonwealth holy table, small sculpted panels set into the walls, glass by Clayton and Bell and Christopher Whall, and a kneeling effigy of a notorious pirate, Henry Brydges.

BAUNTON † St Mary Magdalene

2m/3km N. of Cirencester
OS *SP021046* **GPS** *51.7408N, 1.9700W*

This is a small Norman and later church, restored in 1876. A well-preserved 14th-century wall-painting depicts St Christopher crossing a stream with fishes frolicking at his feet, a hermit with lantern on one bank and a female figure on the other.

BERKELEY † St Mary the Virgin ★★

10m/18km S.W. of Stroud
OS *ST684990* **GPS** *51.6891N, 2.4575W*

St Mary's is a robust edifice standing above the castle, overlooking the Severn estuary. The bell tower stands some distance from the main church, which has a splendid Early English W. front with ramped lancets and buttresses. The Early English arcades inside have finely carved stiff leaf. Comper did the stone reredos in the chancel, 1918. The elaborately carved 15th-century Berkeley Chapel contains the canopied tomb of James, 11th

△ **CHACELEY: ST JOHN THE BAPTIST** – *Norman at its core, the tower and sandstone spire are additions of the 13th and 14th centuries*

Lord Berkeley, d. 1463, and a feast of other monuments; angels hold the Berkeley Arms over the small priest's doorway.

BEVERSTON † St Mary ★

2m/3km W. of Tetbury
OS *ST861940* **GPS** *51.6448N, 2.2013W*

High on the Cotswolds, near the picturesque ruins of the castle, St Mary's shelters behind a surrounding screen of trees: ruined itself, it was rescued by the Victorians. A very weathered 10th-century sculpture of the Resurrection is set into the S. side of the tower, and inside is a beautiful restored 15th-century rood screen (recovered from the rector's garden). The large Decorated windows have clear glass, and the walls are lime-washed. The 19th-century roof by Lewis Vulliamy is an odd affair, with beams going this way and that.

BIBURY † St Mary

6m/10km N.E. of Cirencester
OS *SP118065* **GPS** *51.7571N, 1.8301W*

William Morris thought the village to be England's most beautiful, with its honey-coloured stone weavers' cottages. The church dates from the 8th century and overlooks the square. Sadly many of its Saxon artefacts have been replaced by replicas, but there is still much of interest: traces of a carved Saxon pilaster in the chancel, sections of pilasters above the N. arcade, and Saxon jambs to the 13th-century chancel arch, which breaks through a Saxon string course. There is much of interest here of the 12th and 13th centuries too: a reset Norman doorway with chevron carving, 13th-century lancet windows, and Transitional and Early English arcades. Of a much later date, and of real note is the Arts and Crafts window, 1927, by Karl Parsons, who was apprenticed to Christopher Whall. The window was featured in a set of Royal Mail Christmas stamps in 1992.

BISHOP'S CLEEVE
† St Michael and All Angels ★★

4m/6km N. of Cheltenham
OS *SO960277* **GPS** *51.9481N, 2.0585W*

This magnificent late 12th-century church has been sympathetically restored; its striking Norman W. front has turrets and a handsome doorway with zigzag carving. The rib-vaulted S. porch has an ornate carved door surround and a Green Man, and in the parvise are battle scenes painted by a schoolmaster in 1818. The Decorated chancel has fine ball-flower mouldings, and there is good window tracery of various styles. The W. gallery is a fine piece of Jacobean carving; where once the church band played, now the choir sings.

BITTON † St Mary ★

6ml/10km E. of Bristol
OS *ST681693* **GPS** *51.4221N, 2.4588W*

A Saxon, Norman and Early English church with a markedly long nave, it has a splendid Perpendicular tower with arcaded parapet, battlements and pinnacles, and was restored in 1846 by the enterprising Rev. H. N. Ellacombe, who designed the angelic nave roof. He and his father, both vicars, spanned 99 years between them. Above the chancel arch, Saxon but reworked by the Normans, are two sculpted feet, possibly traces of a vast and early – c. 1000 – rood screen. Other evidence of the church's Anglo-Saxon origins can be seen in the former porticus arch, which gives an idea of the width of the early church.

BLEDINGTON † St Leonard

4ml/6km S.E. of Stow-on-the-Wold
OS *SP245225* **GPS** *51.9010N, 1.6453W*

Set in an attractive village, the church is mainly Perpendicular with a beautiful clerestory containing brilliant 15th-century glass. There is a tiny chantry chapel, a Transitional S. arcade, Norman bellcote and an Early English E. window. The interior is limewashed, very light and unspoiled, restored by F. E. Howard of Oxford, 1923.

BOURTON-ON-THE-HILL
† St Lawrence

2ml/3km W. of Moreton in Marsh
OS *SP175325* **GPS** *51.9908N, 1.7461W*

A delightful village setting, with the long main street running up a steep hill. St Lawrence's has a Norman S. arcade with drum pillars and scalloped capitals; the pointed arches are later. The chancel is 14th-century, and there is much 15th-century alteration, including new roofs to the nave and chancel. The gallery is late 18th-century.

BRIMPSFIELD † St Michael

6ml/10km S. of Cheltenham
OS *SO942128* **GPS** *51.8141N, 2.0854W*

High up in the Cotswolds close to the tree-covered foundations of the Giffords' castle stands St Michael's church. It is Norman and later with an unusual Commonwealth pulpit, 1658. The interior is pleasantly plastered, and there is an ancient barrel-shaped nave roof, and good 17th- and 18th-century table-tombs in the churchyard.

BUCKLAND † St Michael ★★

1km/2km S.W. of Broadway
OS *SP081360* **GPS** *52.0224N, 1.8823W*

St Michael's is a little gold and grey church set in a shallow fold of the north Cotswolds. Although scraped, it almost completely escaped the hands of restorers and is full of treasures: the Buckland Pall, a medieval cope; Cotswold carpentry throughout; 17th-century oak panelling complete with tester heads in the S. aisle; the shepherds' pews; and hat pegs in the gallery. There is also 15th-century glass in the E. window depicting three of the Seven Sacraments, restored by William Morris, and, in the S. aisle, 15th-century tiles.

BUSSAGE † St Michael and All Angels

2ml/3km S.E. of Stroud
OS *SO882035* **GPS** *51.7301N, 2.1715W*

Attractively set on a steep hill, this church was built in 1846 by J. P. Harrison, largely from the subscriptions of Oxford undergraduates. A sound ecclesiological job, the S. aisle and porch were added in 1854 by G. F. Bodley, an accomplished first work. The reredos is also his.

CHACELEY † St John the Baptist

3ml/5km S.W. of Tewkesbury
OS *SO855306* **GPS** *51.9743N, 2.2123W*

This is a charming, mainly Norman, church in the flood plains west of the River Severn. The Norman chancel arch is outstanding. The S. aisle is 14th-century, and the church contains old village stocks and a large drum, possibly a relic of the church band.

△ **CIRENCESTER: ST JOHN THE BAPTIST** – *a glorious manifestation of Perpendicular Gothic*

CHEDWORTH † St Andrew ★★

4m/6km S.W. of Northleach
OS *SP051121* **GPS** *51.8077N, 1.9264W*

The church is situated above the straggling village and at some distance from the famous Roman villa. First impressions suggest another 'wool' church, as indicated by the fine Perpendicular windows of the nave, but inside there is a Norman arcade and aisle. In spite of this curious lack of balance, the church has considerable dignity. The 15th-century carved stone pulpit is really fine and shaped like a wine glass. The Norman tub font has interlacing arcades.

CHIPPING CAMPDEN † St James ★★

8m/12km S.E. of Evesham
OS *SP154394* **GPS** *52.0533N, 1.7757W*

Set at the end of this unspoiled little town, this is a great golden Perpendicular 'wool' church with a magnificent tower. Inside, the tall nave arcades have concave chamfers on the columns and very pretty capitals in consequence. There are brasses to the wool staplers and a great monument of 1664, the finest work of Joshua Marshall; macabre swathed figures in grave clothes are revealed by the open doors of the tomb. A late 15th-century embroidered altar frontal and dorsal is kept under the tower.

CHIPPING SODBURY
† St John the Baptist

10m/16km N.E. of Bristol
OS *ST727823* **GPS** *51.5390N, 2.3943W*

Mostly Perpendicular, with an Early English chancel, the church has a S. porch with re-inserted medieval carved figures of the Virgin and Child flanked by John the Baptist and John the Evangelist. Under the

△ **DUNTISBOURNE ROUSE: ST MICHAEL** – *distinguished by a diminutive saddleback tower, the church stands on a slope overlooking the River Dunt*

Perpendicular tower is interesting tierceron vaulting. The church was extensively restored by Street in 1869.

CIRENCESTER † St John the Baptist ★★

14m/22km W. of Swindon
OS *SP023021* **GPS** *51.7177N, 1.9669W*

The largest and most splendid of the Cotswold 'wool' churches, and perhaps one of the most beautiful Perpendicular churches in all England. The nave and aisles have pierced traceried battlements interspersed with tall crocketed pinnacles – as exciting a skyline as at Gloucester Cathedral. The remarkable three-storeyed S. porch of c. 1490 is bedecked with oriel windows, niches and tracery, once used as the town hall. Inside, one is immediately struck by the enormous height of the clerestoried nave of six bays and the characteristic 'Cotswold' window over the chancel arch. Other features are the rare painted and gilded 'wine glass' pulpit of c. 1450, the early 18th-century Bristol brass candelabra, the Lady Chapel monuments, the fan vaulting of St Catherine's Chapel, the 15th-century glass in the E. window and everywhere the Arms and devices of the church's many patrons.

COALPIT HEATH † St Saviour ★

8m/13km N.E. of Bristol
OS *ST673807* **GPS** *51.5248N, 2.4717W*

In a once notorious colliery town, in which 'frequent scenes of continual dread of outrages on property and public peace then prevailed', St Saviour's was built as a mission church. Completed in 1845, it was designed by William Butterfield, his first Anglican commission. The fabric is uncompromising early Decorated revival, with pointed arches and octagonal piers, and much of the furnishing is Butterfield's. The screen now under the tower was Butterfield's original chancel screen, replaced by a 1932 wooden screen by Harold Brakspear, whose work was normally on a much grander scale.

COLN ROGERS † St Andrew ★
6m/8km N.E. of Cirencester
OS *SP087096* **GPS** *51.7858N, 1.8746W*

A charming country church, with Saxon nave and chancel almost intact apart from the altered windows, and with a simple chancel arch and panelled Perpendicular pulpit – a rare delight. The small W. tower is late Perpendicular.

COLN ST DENYS
† St James the Great ★
6m/8km N.E. of Cirencester
OS *SP085109* **GPS** *51.7970N, 1.8768W*

Prettily situated in the Coln Valley near the Fosse Way, the church is both picturesque and interesting, for it retains its original Norman ground plan and central tower. The tower itself is massive, as wide as the church and heavily buttressed, with a 15th-century belfry stage.

DAGLINGWORTH † Holy Rood ★
3m/4km N.W. of Cirencester
OS *SO993049* **GPS** *51.7436N, 2.0110W*

A Saxon Cotswold church with long-and-short quoins, it has a crucifix on the E. gable and a sundial over the S. door. But most important of all are three very beautiful pre-Conquest stone panels in the walls of the nave and N. aisle, which are spirited depictions of the Crucifixion, Christ in Majesty and St Peter.

DEERHURST † St Mary ★★
7m/11km N.W. of Cheltenham
OS *SO870299* **GPS** *51.9680N, 2.1899W*

In pleasant, sleepy, riverside country is one of the most celebrated Anglo-Saxon churches in England. Originally a monastery, founded in the 8th century, it was rebuilt in the 10th after the Viking invasion and later given Early English and Perpendicular windows. The tall, slender tower, Saxon in the lower part and medieval above, is very striking as one approaches across the large churchyard. Inside, the unusual height of the nave is further emphasized by the blocking of the E. end, originally an apse, and by the double triangular-headed window high up in the W. wall. The chancel has seating on three sides of the altar in the 17th-century manner, and the late 9th-century font is a wonderful piece, a cylindrical bowl covered with patterning. Nearby is the chapel of the Holy Trinity, dedicated by Earl Odda on 12 April 1056 in memory of his brother. Recently discovered is a Saxon painted figure on a stone panel, set high in the E. nave wall, comparable in age to that at Nether Wallop.

DIDMARTON † St Lawrence ★
6m/10km S.W. of Tetbury
OS *ST822874* **GPS** *51.5856N, 2.2578W*

Standing next to the manor in an attractive churchyard, this is one of the churches the Victorians happily forgot. Instead they built a new one, and this precious place was allowed to sleep on in Georgian bliss; an almost complete 18th-century interior.

DOWN AMPNEY † All Saints ★
2m/3km N. of Cricklade
OS *SU098965* **GPS** *51.6675N, 1.8593W*

The church stands close to the manor, forming a pretty group in flat Upper Thames country. The Early English tower has a 14th-century spire with a gilded weather-cock. Inside are fine 13th-century arcades and lavish 19th-century oak fittings in the chancel. The transepts are noteworthy; on the N. side, behind a beautifully carved and painted Jacobean screen, is the elaborate tomb of Sir Anthony Hungerford, 1637, and on the S. are two 14th-century recumbent effigies beneath a rich canopy. This is the birthplace of composer Ralph Vaughan Williams.

DUNTISBOURNE ROUSE
† St Michael ★★
3m/4km N.W. of Cirencester
OS *SO985060* **GPS** *51.7532N, 2.0226W*

On the steep side of a valley overlooking the River Dunt, this is an enchanting place and the site of a small Saxon church. The saddleback tower, nave roof and chancel step down the hill, but even so, the chancel added by the Normans is so high at the E. end that there is room for a crypt below, which is now approached down fern-covered steps in the churchyard. The crypt has a narrow unglazed Norman slit window, while those in the chancel are little bigger. The interior is unspoiled by antiquarianism, with

△ **DUNTISBOURNE ROUSE: ST MICHAEL** – *a fragment of Norman wall-painting*

17th-century box pews in the nave, misericords in the choir and fragments of Norman wall-painting, uncovered in 1872.

DYMOCK † St Mary the Virgin

4m/6km N.W. of Newent
OS *SO700312* **GPS** *51.9787N, 2.4375W*

Here is important Norman work; a fine S. doorway with Tree of Life tympanum and chevroned head, and matching chancel arch. It was wickedly scraped during Middleton's 1870s restoration. There is glass by Kempe.

DYRHAM † St Peter

4m/6km S. of Chipping Sodbury
OS *ST741758* **GPS** *51.4806N, 2.3737W*

In a splendid setting on a terrace by Dyrham House, the church is mainly 13th- and 15th-century. Clear glass gives a beautifully light interior. There is a Jacobean pulpit with tester, a Norman font, some medieval tiles and fine tombs, a brass to an armour-plated Sir Maurice Russell, d. 1416, and a robust canopied tomb to George Wynter, d. 1581.

EASTLEACH † St Andrew ★

4m/6km N. of Lechlade
OS *SP202053* **GPS** *51.7465N, 1.7088W*

Eastleach is a village with two Norman churches either side of a clear brook in one of the most charming spots in the county. The flat stone bridge spanning the stream is known as Keble's Bridge after the saintly poet who was curate at St Michael and St Martin's (following entry). St Andrew's has a richly carved Norman S. doorway with a Christ in Majesty tympanum over it and a simple saddleback tower of later date.

EASTLEACH
† St Michael and St Martin ★★

4m/6km N. of Lechlade
OS *SP202052* **GPS** *51.7453N, 1.7084W*
Churches Conservation Trust

St Michael and St Martin's is situated on the N. bank of the stream. The church is of Norman origin, though much of the building was reworked in the 13th century – that is the date of the three lancets at the E. end of the broad chancel. Now redundant, but all plain, simple and delightful.

ELKSTONE † St John the Evangelist ★★

6m/10km S. of Cheltenham
OS *SO967122* **GPS** *51.8093N, 2.0490W*

In the high Cotswolds, this is one of the most famous Norman churches in the county. There is a tall Perpendicular W. tower, the original Norman tower having collapsed. This is built of huge freestone blocks, which contrast with the rubble walls of the Norman nave. The S. doorway has a richly carved Christ in Majesty in the tympanum and a prominent beakhead above. Inside there are two beautifully carved zigzag arches that formerly supported the central tower and which effectively divide the exquisite little sanctuary, with original rib-vaulting, from the tall body of the church. The chancel arch terminates with two dragons' heads. The E. window has highly coloured glass by Henry Payne of Stroud, 1929, giving a beautiful light to the tiny sanctuary. Elsewhere, carved faces gaze down from the corbel-table.

FAIRFORD: ST MARY THE VIRGIN – *the church has the finest 15th-century glass in England* ▷

△ **GREAT WASHBOURNE: ST MARY** – *Maltese cross in the tympanum over the south door*

ENGLISH BICKNOR † St Mary
6m/8km N.E. of Monmouth
OS *SO581158* **GPS** *51.8393N, 2.6091W*

Set high above a river on the site of a Norman castle, the church's rebuilt Victorian exterior conceals good Norman work inside. There are splendid 12th-century arcades with elaborate capitals, beak heads and chevrons, a Norman font and three stone figures from the 1300s.

FAIRFORD † St Mary the Virgin ★★
8m/12km E. of Cirencester
OS *SP151011* **GPS** *51.7090N, 1.7821W*

A complete and perfect Perpendicular church. The chancel, aisles, porch and clerestoried nave have continuous embattled parapets with pinnacles; the smooth freestone is warm and mellow. The parapet of the central tower is pierced with quatrefoils and has pairs of pinnacles at the corners, and there is much good stone carving outside. Although smaller than the other great Perpendicular 'wool' churches in the county, Fairford has the best late 15th-century glass in England, and in sufficient quantity to be judged apart from its antiquarian interest; it is exceedingly beautiful, and its restoration was completed in 2010.

FORTHAMPTON † St Mary
2m/3km W. of Tewkesbury
OS *SO858325* **GPS** *51.9914N, 2.2070W*

Of Norman origin, now mostly 14th-century and later. Great interest attaches to the free-standing stone altar of c. 1300. There is a beautiful pre-Raphaelite E. window by Henry Holiday; the W. window is by Clayton and Bell; another window, by Burgess, depicts the Virtues.

GLOUCESTER † St Mary-de-Crypt
Southgate Street
OS *SO830184* **GPS** *51.8641N, 2.2471W*

The church is 14th-century and Perpendicular, to a cruciform plan. The enriched chancel has an Easter sepulchre; there are stone screens and monuments, including one by Scheemakers.

GLOUCESTER † St Nicholas
Westgate Street
OS *SO829187* **GPS** *51.8673N, 2.2497W*
Churches Conservation Trust

Most prominent is the Perpendicular three-stage W. tower. The Norman S. doorway has an Agnus Dei tympanum and on the door itself a 14th-century bronze knocker with grotesque head. Among many civic monuments is a splendidly self-confident tomb to Alderman John Walton and his wife.

GREAT BADMINTON
† St Michael and All Angels
5m/8km E. of Chipping Sodbury
OS *ST806828* **GPS** *51.5444N, 2.2799W*

This is a Classical church of 1785 attached to

GREAT WASHBOURNE: ST MARY – *the church dates to the early 12th century* ▷

△ **LECHLADE: ST LAWRENCE** – *another of Gloucestershire's magnificent Perpendicular churches, St Lawrence's spire is particularly fine, rising proudly from the meadows*

the great house of the dukes of Beaufort and approached through the garden. The chancel and apse were added in 1875 and furnished by Temple Moore in 1908. A shrine to the Beauforts, the church is plastered with marble monuments, including a very grand one of the 1st Duke of Beaufort in full Garter robes and beauty queens pretending to be Fates.

GREAT BARRINGTON
† St Mary the Virgin

2m/3km W. of Burford
OS *SP205134* **GPS** *51.8196N, 1.7037W*

A Norman church with many Early English and Perpendicular embellishments, it is noted for its 17th-century Fettisplace wall tombs and a fine marble monument by Nollekens.

GREAT WASHBOURNE † St Mary ★

7m/10km N.E. of Tewkesbury
OS *SO986344* **GPS** *52.0085N, 2.0207W*

This small hamlet near Alderton Hill on the Worcestershire border has a tiny Norman church with 18th-century box pews, reading desk and two-decker pulpit. The dividing wall between chancel and nave is pierced by a small Norman arch similar to those of the N. and S. doorways. At either end of the chancel arch are two Gothic squints; the Perpendicular font is set directly between this arch and the altar. Over the S. door is a tympanum carved with a Maltese cross, symbol of the order of the Knights Hospitaller.

HAILES † Hailes Chapel of Ease ★

7m/10km N.E. of Tewkesbury
OS *SP 050301* **GPS** *51.9698N, 1.9280W*

The little church near the Abbey ruins is one of the most unspoilt in the county. Inside everything is old – Elizabethan benches; 17th-century pulpit and tester; 15th-century tiles, glass and screen; 14th-century wall-painting. It has its own special atmosphere.

HATHEROP † St Nicholas ★

3m/4km N. of Fairford
OS *SP153050* **GPS** *51.7444N, 1.7786W*

Hatherop's church dates from 1854, by Henry Clutton in a Perpendicular style with French Gothic overtones. The central tower has a saddleback roof and the pretty vaulted mortuary chapel, enriched by Burges, has a stone frieze of castles and the letter 'B' for Barbara, Lady de Mauley, whose impressive effigy it contains.

HAWKESBURY † St Mary ★

4m/6km N.E. of Chipping Sodbury
OS *ST768869* **GPS** *51.5807N, 2.3359W*

This great church is set in a remote valley like a wrecked ship at the foot of the Cotswold cliff. It has a fine 14th-century tower, Norman N. door and 15th-century stone pulpit. The interior is scraped, but there are several monuments, one to the 2nd Earl of Liverpool, who was prime minister at the time of Waterloo and died in 1828.

HIGHNAM † Holy Innocents ★★

3m/4km W. of Gloucester
OS *SO796195* **GPS** *51.8741N, 2.2971W*

Set in a park, the church was built by Thomas Gambier Parry and Henry Woodyer in 1850 of a grey-green limestone in Decorated style. The magnificent spire is covered in ballflower motifs and has crocketed pinnacles. Inside, it is pleasantly dark with walls painted by Parry to simulate drapery. There is a continuous frieze of Biblical characters, all with golden haloes. The chancel arch is tall and elegant, with painted mouldings, and the chancel is brilliant with shining tiles, painted organ, and walls with texts, vines and symbols of the Passion. The jewel-like stained glass is by Clayton and Bell, Hardman and Wailes. This is the Anglican fulfilment of the Pugin ideal.

IRON ACTON † James the Less ★

3m/4km W. of Chipping Sodbury
OS *ST680834 51.5491N, 2.4619W*

A church of dark sandstone, it was substantially restored by Sir T. G. Jackson, 1879. The W. tower was built by Robert Poyntz, Sheriff of Gloucestershire, d. 1439; in the churchyard is a uniquely beautiful 15th-century memorial cross, mutilated and lichen-covered. Good interior fittings include Laudian altar rails, an 18th-century brass candelabrum, a Jacobean pulpit, medieval effigies of the Poyntz family and 19th-century mosaic floors in Roman style. The reredos and side chapel screen are full of colour and joy, part of F. C. Eden's restoration of c. 1930.

KEMPLEY † St Edward the Confessor ★

6m/8km N.E. of Ross-on-Wye
OS *SO671296* **GPS** *51.9640N, 2.4798W*

By Randall Wells, 1903, St Edward is a stone-built church with steeply pitched tiled roof. It is a fine design, with a large Reticulated W. window, heavy rood and beautiful contemporary fittings and sculpture by Ernest Gimson, Ernest Barnsley and local craftsmen in accordance with the precepts of the Arts and Crafts Movement, to which the church is a shrine.

KEMPLEY † St Mary ★

6m/8km N.E. of Ross-on-Wye
OS *SO669312* **GPS** *51.9788N, 2.4820W*
English Heritage

The old church of St Mary is an unforgettable place, with an 11th-century nave and chancel, and its walls aglow with some of the finest Romanesque frescoes in England. In the barrel-vaulted chancel in particular, an almost complete cycle survives with Christ in Majesty at the centre surrounded by the Symbols of the Evangelists and other themes from the Revelation of St John the Divine; a heavenly vault indeed. In the nave are further wall-paintings of the 15th century. An interesting tympanum is set over the S. door, almost obscured by the Tudor porch.

KEMPSFORD † St Mary ★

8m/12km E. of Cirencester
OS *SU161964* **GPS** *51.6670N, 1.7681W*

On the upper Thames with a fine three-stage tower reputedly built by John of Gaunt, St Mary's has large Perpendicular windows and a parapet with trefoil-headed openings and crocketed pinnacles, all with weather-vanes. Entering the Norman S. doorway, the church seems dark though lofty, chiefly because of the large amount of Victorian stained glass (some of it very good, by Kempe), and the tessellated tiles. The vaulting under the central tower has painted heraldic shields. The chancel aisle was added by Street during his restoration of 1858. On the walls of the nave are framed Puritan texts. This is the only English church where an Irish peer is buried under the organ.

KEMPLEY: ST MARY – *the Norman church is entered through a charmingly ramshackle Tudor porch* ▷

LECHLADE † St Lawrence ★★
10m/16km N.E. of Swindon
OS *SU214995* **GPS** *51.6939N, 1.6904W*

Modestly placed at the corner of the market place of this pleasant town, St Lawrence's is one of the great Perpendicular 'wool' churches, all 15th- and 16th-century, with a splendid chancel roof, fine bosses and corbels, angels, a blacksmith, wrestlers and evangelists' symbols. The 19th-century screen detracts from the spacious interior.

LEONARD STANLEY † St Swithin ★
3m/4km W. of Stroud
OS *SO802032* **GPS** *51.7277N, 2.2876W*

Leonard Stanley is set under the escarpment of the Cotswolds. The large church was part of a Norman priory, cruciform in plan with a massive central tower, and Perpendicular windows inserted in the N. nave wall, all with clear glass. The walls are lime-washed. The crossing has splendid Norman arches with carved capitals; that featuring the woman washing Christ's feet in the chancel is especially good. The former cloisters are now in the farmyard of a very fine farmhouse.

LONGBOROUGH † St James
3m/4km N. of Stow-on-the-Wold
OS *SP179297* **GPS** *51.9659N, 1.7408W*

The church is Norman and later, with a beautiful embattled early 14th-century S. transept and reredos with canopied niches. There are medieval and later monuments, one by Sir R. Westmacott, to the architect C. R. Cockerell, who designed the completely sealed-off Sezincote private pew, 1822–3.

MEYSEY HAMPTON † St Mary
6m/8km E. of Cirencester
OS *SP117000* **GPS** *51.6992N, 1.8320W*

Consecrated in 1269, it has a cruciform plan and was perhaps built by the Knights Templar. The fine early 14th-century Decorated chancel has ballflowers, piscina, sedilia and a tomb recess.

MINCHINHAMPTON † Holy Trinity
2m/3km S.E. of Stroud
OS SO872008 GPS 51.7059N, 2.1863W

Set in a thriving hilltop town between the

△ **PAINSWICK: ST MARY THE VIRGIN** – *clipped yews surround the church*

Golden Valley and the Nailsworth Valley, the truncated spire of Holy Trinity is unmistakeable. The tower and transepts are 14th-century, the rest rebuilt 1842 by Thomas Foster. The broach spire was reduced in 1563, the upper part being replaced by a battlemented corona. Foster's Gothic sits uneasily against the fine medieval crossing with tierceron vaulting. The best features are in the S. transept, whose stone slab roof is supported by stone cross-arches with scissor bracing. There is a fine rose window in the transept, and below are two ogee-arched Decorated tomb recesses with effigies of a knight and his lady, each on a chest with quatrefoil front panelling.

MITCHELDEAN
† St Michael and All Angels ★
10m/18km W. of Gloucester
OS *SO663185* **GPS** *51.8650N, 2.4898W*

One of the largest churches in the Forest of Dean, it dates from the 14th to 15th century and was restored by H. Woodyer in 1853. The notably slender spire was rebuilt by N. Wilkinson of Worcester, c. 1760. The reredos,

◁ **PAINSWICK: ST MARY THE VIRGIN** – *one of the church's monuments*

△ **RENDCOMB: ST PETER** – *a late Perpendicular church, built in fine, honey-coloured ashlar with heavy battlements to the roofline*

by W. Storr-Barber in 1913, is monumental, with lifesize white marble figures. An excellent Doom painting is above the chancel arch, showing eight scenes of the Passion below Heaven, the Last Judgement and Hell. The splendid E. window is by John Hayward, 1970, and there is glass by Kempe.

NAUNTON † St Andrew

5m/8km W. of Stow-on-the-Wold
OS *SP112234* **GPS** *51.9092N, 1.8383W*

Set in the lovely wooded valley of the Windrush, St Andrew's is chiefly 16th-century with a Perpendicular tower and richly decorated stone pulpit of c. 1400.

NEWLAND † All Saints ★★

4m/6km S.E. of Monmouth
OS *SO552095* **GPS** *51.7826N, 2.6498W*

This great church in hilly country on the edge of the Forest of Dean is sometimes called the Cathedral of the Forest: imposing without, and with the most noble proportions within. It was built during the 13th and 14th centuries, given later chapels and restored in 1862. The width of the aisles gives it a tremendous feeling of spaciousness. The graceful, handsome W. tower is finely pinnacled. There is a diverse group of effigies, tombs and memorials in the church, including an archer, a forester and the unique 'Miner's Brass' – hod and pick in hand, he has a candlestick in his mouth.

NORTH CERNEY † All Saints ★★

4m/7km N. of Cirencester
OS *SP018077* **GPS** *51.7688N, 1.9745W*

Set in the Churn Valley, the church and its rectory can be seen from the Cheltenham–Cirencester road. It is chiefly Norman, with an Early English upper stage to the saddle-back W. tower and three windows with 15th-century glass. The church was refurbished through a collaboration between the churchwarden William Iveson Croome and

F. C. Eden in the early 20th century, and is the most beautifully furnished and colourful little church in the county. The painted rood is by Eden, though the Christ is Italian work of c. 1600, and in the Lady Chapel are three 15th-century statues of St Martin, St Urban and the Virgin. Outside is an inscribed manticore (mythical beast) near the S. transept.

NORTHLEACH † St Peter and St Paul ★

10m/16km N.E. of Cirencester

OS *SP111145* **GPS** *51.8296N, 1.8390W*

Once an important centre of the wool trade, Northleach has one of the most beautiful of the Perpendicular 'wool' churches in the Cotswolds; its S. porch has been called the most lovely in all England, with its tall pinnacles and statue-filled niches. The nave of five bays has columns with concave chamfers and a tall clerestory with a very broad window over the chancel arch. All was built by John Fortey, d. 1458; his brass is under the N. arcade.

ODDINGTON † St Nicholas ★

3m/4km E. of Stow-on-the-Wold

OS *SP234255* **GPS** *51.9280N, 1.6598W*

The church is away from the village, surrounded by lovely trees. For many years after 1852 it was in disuse. However, it was given a new reredos as a 1918 memorial and is now a most beautiful church, with nave, chancel and S. aisle. All the windows have clear glass and, in the S. aisle, Reticulated tracery. There is a large 14th-century Doom painting on the N. wall, William IV Arms over the chancel arch, and the Jacobean pulpit, set high on a single pillar, is a beauty.

OXENTON † St John the Baptist

6m/10km N. of Cheltenham

OS *SO958314* **GPS** *51.9817N, 2.0619W*

In a lovely setting under the Cotswold scarp is this almost unspoilt medieval church, mostly 13th-century with Elizabethan linenfold carving, floor tiles and wall-paintings which once covered the whole interior.

OZLEWORTH † St Nicholas of Myra ★

2m/3km E. of Wotton-under-Edge

OS *ST794932* **GPS** *51.6380N, 2.2987W*

Churches Conservation Trust

Standing next to a Georgian house in a circular churchyard, the church has a rare Norman hexagonal central tower, 14th-century chancel and later monuments.

PAINSWICK † St Mary the Virgin ★

3m/4km N.E. of Stroud

OS *SO866096* **GPS** *51.7853N, 2.1948W*

A large church with spire at the centre of the Cotswold town, it is surrounded by fine houses. The churchyard has ancient clipped yews and a unique collection of carved table-tombs, many marked with the trade symbols of their occupants. The interior has a Classical reredos in the S. chapel and a 19th-century iron screen in the S. aisle. The S. entrance is now covered by a rather odd modern porch.

RENDCOMB † St Peter ★

5m/8km N. of Cirencester

OS *SP018097* **GPS** *51.7868N, 1.9745W*

A lovely late Perpendicular church built of fine ashlar, it consists of a nave and S. aisle of almost equal breadth with contemporary roofs, divided by an arcade, the columns of which have delightful concave chamfers. There is a restored 16th-century screen across both nave and aisle. Depressing glass on the E. side is somewhat relieved by some colourful old glass on the N. side, with Renaissance motifs. The noteworthy Norman font carved with the 12 Apostles is of the Herefordshire School of stone carvers.

RUARDEAN † St John the Baptist

4m/6km S.E. of Ross-on-Wye

OS *SO621176* **GPS** *51.8565N, 2.5515W*

This is a hill-top site in the Forest of Dean with spectacular views north over Herefordshire. The early 12th-century church was restored in 1890; its treasure is the celebrated tympanum of St George and the Dragon.

ST BRIAVELS † St Mary

20m/30km S.W. of Gloucester

OS *SO558046* **GPS** *51.7388N, 2.6406W*

This late 11th-century church built of forest sandstone stands next to the castle high above the River Wye, with wonderful views of the Wye Valley. Of the original fabric only the S. aisle, a heavy Norman crossing and an

△ **RUARDEAN: ST JOHN THE BAPTIST** – *over the south door, the 12th-century tympanum shows St George slaying the dragon*

unusual font remain. The tower dates from 1830, the N. arcade is Norman, the S. arcade is Early English with a triforium above, and the chancel was rebuilt in 1861. In the S. transept is a tomb recess, and in the S. aisle is an impressive monument with recumbent figures of William Warren and his wife, and three kneeling children.

SELSLEY † All Saints ★

1m/2km S.W. of Stroud

OS *SO829038* **GPS** *51.7328N, 2.2487W*

Set in a spectacular position on the edge of the Cotswold escarpment, the church was intended as a copy of the church at Marling in Tirol, commissioned by Samuel Marling, but Bodley produced a fine French Gothic building instead. The windows by Morris, Philip Webb, Burne-Jones and their fellow Pre-Raphaelites are the glory of the church. The lych gate is based on Butterfield's at Coalpit Heath.

SHIPTON SOLLARS † St Mary ★

Also spelt Shipton Solers; adjoins Shipton, 5m/8km S.E. of Cheltenham

OS *SP031184* **GPS** *51.8649N, 1.9560W*

Churches Conservation Trust

A pretty little 13th-century church with Perpendicular features, most sympathetically restored in 1929 and with glass by Geoffrey Webb.

SOUTH CERNEY † All Hallows

4m/6km S.E. of Cirencester

OS *SU049973* **GPS** *51.6748N, 1.9292W*

Near the upper Thames gravel pits, a large Norman and later church, with a reset 12th-century doorway depicting Christ in Majesty and the Harrowing of Hell. The 14th-century chancel is rich with ballflower decoration, and the wooden head of Christ on the 12th-century rood is a work of poignant intensity. The S. aisle was added by J. P. St Aubyn in 1862.

SOUTHROP † St Peter

3m/4km N. of Lechlade

OS *SP202034* **GPS** *51.7291N, 1.7088W*

The famous font bears spirited figures of virtues and vices from the medieval *Psychomachia*. The Early English chancel and Keble monuments remind us that John Keble ministered faithfully in this place.

△ **STANTON: ST MICHAEL AND ALL ANGELS** – *Sir Ninian Comper designed this reredos along with the church's rood screen and gallery*

STANTON † St Michael and All Angels ★
10m/16km N.E. of Cheltenham
OS *SP068343* **GPS** *52.0073N, 1.9010W*

Set in a specially pretty village below the banks of the north Cotswolds, the church has a Perpendicular S. aisle and porch, embattled, and of a beautiful brown and golden texture. The W. tower has a spire. Inside, Sir Ninian Comper designed the rood screen, reredos, gallery and some stained glass.

STOKE ORCHARD
† St James the Great ★
4m/6km N.W. of Cheltenham
OS *SO917282* **GPS** *51.9522N, 2.1211W*

This is a small and lovely Norman chapel of ease, with 12th-century ironwork on the N. door and a decent square font. But the wall-paintings are superb; the assured Life of St James of Compostela links this humble place with the best of the Continental Romanesque.

STOWELL † St Leonard
8m/12km N.E. of Cirencester
OS *SP087130* **GPS** *51.8162N, 1.8746W*

St Leonard's is a late Norman cruciform church containing a spirited Romanesque Doom painting and, on the N. nave wall, Our Lady, the Apostles and the Heavenly Court observing the Saved and the Lost.

TEDDINGTON † St Nicholas
5m/8km E. of Tewkesbury
OS *SO964329* **GPS** *51.9951N, 2.0533W*

This is a church full of surprises. There is a Norman chancel arch and a tower dated 1567, incorporating a fine Early English tower arch and W. window from Hailes Abbey. Inside are 17th-century wall-paintings and unexpected Commonwealth fittings, and a Royal Arms of William and Mary, 1689, painted very large on the S. wall.

TETBURY † St Mary ★★
5m/8km N.W. of Malmesbury
OS *ST890929* **GPS** *51.6353N, 2.1597W*
Churches Conservation Trust

Francis Hiorn's church, finished in 1781 except for the steeple, is one of the triumphs of the early Gothic Revival. The thin, tall columns, like giant bamboos, give one a keen feeling of the period. They are made from Forest of Dean oak, sunk 20 feet below ground and encased in plaster moulding.

△ **WORMINGTON: ST KATHARINE** – *the Savage Brass of 1605, which depicts one Anne Savage in bed with her swaddled baby*

The interior is unspoiled, retaining most of its original furnishings, especially the reredos and brass chandeliers. There are galleries on every side except the E., and box pews throughout.

TEWKESBURY † St Mary the Virgin ★★

8ml/12km N.W. of Cheltenham
OS *SO890324* **GPS** *51.9904N, 2.1606W*

Tewkesbury's abbey church is in the flat meadows where the Avon joins the Severn, which once ran red with Lancastrian blood. With the proportions of a cathedral, the abbey is a monumental expression of Norman power, with a grand Norman nave, W. front and tower, an early 14th-century apsidal choir with chapels forming a chevet, and superb vaulting to the nave and transept of 1349–59. Through all run echoes of England's longest and most futile Civil War. There is a memorable set of 14th-century monuments, second only to Westminster – most notable of which is that of Hugh le Despenser, d. 1348, and his wife Elizabeth Montacute, d.1359 – and a great deal of delicate stonework in the chantry chapels. Wonderful 14th-century glass can be seen in the presbytery clerestory, with knights in armour, brilliant in heraldic surcoats.

TODDINGTON † St Andrew

6ml/8km N.E. of Cheltenham
OS *SP035330* **GPS** *51.9962N, 1.9504W*

Set in the park of Lord Sudeley's fantastic Gothic Revival house, this is a good example of G. E. Street's work. In a lovely deep golden-coloured ashlar, with a tall broach spire and rich Decorated style, it contains a forest of Purbeck marble columns with a background of white ashlar and 19th-century marble effigies by Lough.

TODENHAM
† St Thomas of Canterbury ★

3ml/4km N.E. of Moreton-in-Marsh
OS *SP243363* **GPS** *52.0248N, 1.6470W*

Almost completely rebuilt in the early 14th century, the church is a triumph of the Decorated style. The N. arcade, chancel and string courses are perhaps the most cherishable items among so much that is outstanding.

UPLEADON † St Mary the Virgin ★
8m/12km N.W. of Gloucester
OS *SO768269* **GPS** *51.9407N, 2.3377W*

The church has a delightful Tudor timbered and brick nogged tower with mullioned windows and overhanging pyramidal roof. The church's origins are 12th-century, and inside the tower is fully open to the nave, affording a good view of the wooden cross bracing. The interior is whitewashed, light and airy, with a nave roof supported by rough cut king posts. The N. Norman door is very good, with the string course curving gracefully to accommodate the outer arch. The tympanum depicts an Agnus Dei flanked by two jolly lions. All this survives because of a spirited rescue by the parish in 1966.

WESTBURY-ON-SEVERN
† St Peter and St Paul ★
6m/8km S.W. of Gloucester
OS *SO717139* **GPS** *51.8232N, 2.4118W*

The remarkable detached tower of c. 1270 was probably intended for a watch or garrison in view of the heavy buttresses; the whole is surmounted by a 14th-century shingled oak spire, which is a landmark from the river. The tower stands to the W. of the main body of this mostly 14th-century church.

WINCHCOMBE † St Peter
6m/10km N.E. of Cheltenham
OS *SP023282* **GPS** *51.9525N, 1.9679W*

In the middle of an attractive small town, this is a typical Cotswold 'wool' church, begun c. 1460. The embattled, pinnacled tower has the finest weather-cock in the county, richly gilded, and there is a particularly grotesque collection of gargoyles, the odd one with toothache. The E. end has been rebuilt, and has a fine seven-light window; there is no structural division between nave and chancel. There is a fine brass candelabrum of 1753, a late 17th-century organ case and a richly painted Royal Arms of George III.

WINDRUSH † St Peter
16m/24km S.E. of Cheltenham
OS *SP193130* **GPS** *51.8157N, 1.7210W*

St Peter's is Norman and Decorated; the celebrated 12th-century S. doorway is replete with double beak-heads, and there is an elaborate chancel arch and magnificent table-tombs. Thomas Keble was curate here in 1817.

WITHINGTON
† St Michael and All Angels
5m/8km S.E. of Cheltenham
OS *SP031156* **GPS** *51.8392N, 1.9562W*

This is a good Cotswold church in an interesting village. Norman in origin, the nave is almost entirely lit by a Perpendicular clerestory. There is a fine carving of Sir John Howe and his wife, signed by Edward Marshall, 1651. A splendid exterior, though the interior is a disappointment, spoiled through too much Victorian restoration.

WORMINGTON † St Katharine
3m/5km S. of Evesham
OS *SP039364* **GPS** *52.0265N, 1.9439W*

A small church, Perpendicular and later, it was reputedly built by the abbot of Hailes in 1475. In the S. aisle is a late Saxon sculpture of the Crucifixion with the Hand of God above – intense of expression though crudely made. Of great interest on the chancel's S. wall is the Savage Brass, 1605, depicting Anne Savage with an infant at her side in her bedchamber. Gimson did the oak pews and pulpit in 1926, though some Jacobean carved oak benches remain.

WOTTON-UNDER-EDGE
† St Mary the Virgin
9m/15km S.W. of Stroud
OS *ST760934* **GPS** *51.6392N, 2.3479W*

Of many styles – Decorated, Perpendicular and 19th-century – with a great W. tower, good plaster ceilings of c. 1800 and a noble 18th-century organ brought here from St Martin-in-the-Fields in London. There is a beautiful early brass to Thomas Berkeley, d. 1417, and his wife, d. 1392. He wears a collar of mermaids.

HAMPSHIRE
& THE ISLE OF WIGHT

Hampshire falls naturally into four divisions. The main portion of the county consists of chalk downs, through which the swift-flowing Itchen, Test and Meon cut their way. All along these valleys the villages cluster thickly, sometimes not a mile apart, many of them boasting an ancient church, while on either side of the valleys the vast rolling uplands stretch away for miles. The churches in this region are chiefly built of the local flint, with wooden belfries supported internally upon great baulks of timber. Notable among them are the Saxon churches of Corhampton in the Meon valley and Headbourne Worthy in the Itchen valley.

The western part of the county, beyond Southampton Water, consists largely of the New Forest. Here the magnificent Romsey Abbey bears witness to one good result of the Norman invasion, though the area also includes such varying churches as the perfect Saxon example at Breamore, the Early English parish church of Beaulieu (once the refectory of the monastery), the delightful 'unrestored' Minstead, with its box pews and galleries, and the 'copy book' example of the Gothic Revival at Lyndhurst.

The third division of Hampshire, lying along the Sussex border, is characterized by the great steeply wooded hills known as the 'hangers'. Only here in the county is there any local stone, and Selborne is the most perfect ensemble of village and church lying under its Hanger, the whole district enshrining the memory of the 18th-century naturalist Gilbert White. Here too, Goodhart-Rendel left a learned Victorian restoration at the isolated chapel of St Hubert at Idsworth, with its fine 14th-century wall-paintings of the saint.

Finally, there is the border region of the north-east, an extension of the Surrey pine and heather country, now much bitten into by the vast military conurbation of Aldershot and its jet-propelled over-spill of Farnborough, all marred by the M3 and associated ribbon development. All Saint's at Crondall and St Mary and St Michael's at Stoke Charity are worthy of attention here.

As regards its coast, Hampshire is not remarkable, although the salt marshes are of international importance to wildfowl. For the most part it consists of broad tidal creeks and a seemingly endless straggle of dreary houses.

In the county there is almost nothing remarkable of the Perpendicular – in fact very little Gothic architecture at all. Of the 18th century, the interior of St Mary's, Avington, is fine Georgian; the

◁ **IDSWORTH: ST HUBERT** – *isolated on a ridge of farmland, St Hubert's was probably built in the early or mid-11th century and is home to an important cycle of 14th-century wall-paintings*

19th century is gloriously celebrated in the Pre-Raphaelite interior of St Michael and All Angels at Lyndhurst, and the Stanley Spencer murals in the almshouse chapel at Burghclere are a testament to 20th-century religious art.

ISLE OF WIGHT

Whereas Hayling Island is a bit of Hampshire that has slipped into the sea, the Isle of Wight has a personality of its own, and this persists despite caravans, flash shop-fronts and shoddy bungalows, which have spread over so much of its 150 square miles. From east to west there stretches a high chalk ridge, from Culver Cliff to the Needles, as noble as the Sussex Downs and known as the 'back' of the island. South of this, and facing the open sea, are a very few old buildings and the modernised Victorian towns of Ventnor, Shanklin and Sandown. Inland, the chalk slopes gently to a lower range of hills, and then slopes still more gradually until it reaches the low coast along the Solent. Newport is the ancient capital of the island, and here the Medina River divides it into two, Cowes at its mouth. Yarmouth and Brading are the other old ports, and Newtown, once large for its date, has almost disappeared.

What strikes one about the island is the luxuriance of its vegetation after the comparative aridity of Hampshire. Myrtles, fuchsias and geraniums grow unprotected in the open air. In the undercliff, beyond the back of the island, there is a steamy tropic richness. And next one notices the variety of local building stone, differing in colour from village to village, almost as much as those amazing streaks to be seen on the cliffs when the afternoon sun strikes Alum Bay. This stone and the style of building shown in old churches and cottages have affinities more with Dorset than Hampshire, and is best of all seen in West Wight, the most countrified part of the island.

The island became popular in the 18th century, though families like the Worsleys of Appledurcombe (now a Baroque ruin), the Barringtons of Swainston, the Holmeses and Oglanders, had lived here for many generations. But in the 18th century a handful of artists settled here. In the next century came Keats and later Tennyson. First the more gentle and less 'horrid' scenery was preferred, so that most Georgian buildings are on the Solent side of the island. The Victorians favoured the open sea, and not even the example of Queen Victoria at Osborne could tempt holidaymakers back to the tamer Solent coast. That was left to the yachtsmen, who have created a nautical civilization of their own at Cowes, Ryde, Yarmouth and Bembridge.

The old churches of the island are humble stone buildings with a West Country look, and their beauty is largely in their texture. The characteristic of their plan is aisles extending the full length of the chancel. Their prevailing style is 15th-century. The Georgian churches are mostly in unsophisticated Gothic, and have the look of proprietary chapels for Evangelical valetudinarians.

The Isle of Wight entries are grouped under 'I' in this chapter.

A346
BERKSHIRE
M4
READING
A329(M)
Marlborough
Hungerford
NEWBURY
BRACKNELL
A4
A338
A327
A34
Silchester
A345
Burghclere
Tadley
WILTSHIRE
Kingsclere
Pamber End
Bramley
CAMBERLEY
Ashmansworth
Wolverton
A30
A338
M3
A339
A340
A33
A343
BASINGSTOKE
Basing
Winchfield
A34
Odiham
lisbury
Plain
A342
ALDERSHOT
Whitchurch
HAMPSHIRE
Crondall
ANDOVER
SURREY
A303
Dummer
A31
Amesbury
A303
A339
Froyle
A287
A343
A3057
Stoke Charity
Northington
ALTON
A360
A345
Nether Wallop
A33
M3
A30
A325
A30
A34
Avington
A31
A32
Selbourne
Easton
Itchen Stoke
Empshott
Liphook
Headbourne Worthy
Priors Dean
Hawkley
WINCHESTER
Tichborne
SALISBURY
A3057
Mottisfont
Farley
Chamberlayne
Chilcomb
A272
A354
A36
PETERSFIELD
A27
A3090
East Meon
A272
Romsey
Breamore
Hale
Buriton
A27
EASTLEIGH
A32
A338
WEST
SUSSEX
Corhampton
A3
Chalton
Fordingbridge
SOUTHAMPTON
Idsworth
Ellingham
A31
Minstead
A35
A3(M)
A286
A326
M27
Boarhunt
Lyndhurst
Southwick
HAVANT
New
Forest
Hythe
Titchfield
Cosham
Warblington
Ringwood
FAREHAM
Portchester
Brockenhurst
Beaulieu
Fawley
A31
PORTSMOUTH
A35
Boldre
GOSPORT
South Hayling
New Milton
Lymington
Cowes
A3021
Ryde
Milford-on-Sea
BOURNEMOUTH
Selsey
Bill
Yarmouth
Newport
Carisbrooke
Brading
Freshwater
Poole Bay
ISLE OF WIGHT
Sandown
Shorwell
Godshill
Shanklin
A3055
Ventnor
St Catherine's
Point
0
10 miles
0
10 km

ASHMANSWORTH † St James ★
8m/13km N.E. of Andover
OS *SU410566* **GPS** *51.3073N, 1.4122W*

An endearing small rustic Norman church whose un-restored interior has early 13th- and 15th-century wall-paintings; the brick porch is of 1694. The memorial porch window is to the composer Gerald Finzi, d. 1956, engraved by Laurence Whistler, whose most remarkable work can be seen in neighbouring Dorset, at St Nicholas, Moreton.

AVINGTON † St Mary ★
4m/6km N.E. of Winchester
OS *SU532322* **GPS** *51.0871N, 1.2405W*

This is the most perfect 18th-century church in the county – a neat, simple and decent design of sturdy tower and rectangular nave, built of brick on the edge of the Park by Margaret Brydges, Marchioness of Caernarvon, in 1768–71. The interior retains all its original fittings in Spanish mahogany, said to have been salvaged from an Armada galleon, and a barrel-organ in the gallery which still works.

BASING † St Mary ★
2m/3km E. of Basingstoke
OS *SU665529* **GPS** *51.2716N, 1.0467W*

This large and handsome 15th- and early 16th-century rectangular church of mellow brick with stone dressings was built around the vestiges of a Norman central tower by the wealthy Paulet family. Their heraldic key is ubiquitous throughout, and their four tombs are set between chancel and chapels. The N. chapel, unusually, has chestnut windows – a rare use of wood and evidence of the local scarcity of good building stone. The church was damaged in the Civil War siege of Basing House. Miraculously, the beautiful statue of the Virgin and Child on the W. front survived; it was hidden by ivy at the time.

BASINGSTOKE † All Saints
Victoria Street
OS *SU637516* **GPS** *51.2608N, 1.0883W*

By Temple Moore, 1915, this is a dignified ashlar church in the Decorated style with a restrained interior, rich furnishings and golden E. window.

BEAULIEU
† Blessed Virgin and Holy Child ★★
6m/10km N.E. of Lymington
OS *SU388025* **GPS** *50.8212N, 1.4501W*

The refectory of the great Cistercian Abbey makes a splendid parish church; in it Early English architecture is seen at its best. The foliated reader's pulpit and graceful arcaded stairway in the W. wall are the finest features of the spacious interior.

BOARHUNT † St Nicholas ★
2m/3km N.E. of Fareham
OS *SU603082* **GPS** *50.8709N, 1.1438W*

This small, simple, late Saxon church is set in isolated farm and woodland under Portsdown Hill. The Saxon doorways, though blocked, can still be seen on the N. and S. sides. Inside, a plain Saxon archway leads to a simple chancel, with a 13th-century lancet E. window, and Norman splay on the S. wall. The complete Prayer Book furnishings of 1853 include a three-decker pulpit, squire's pew and W. gallery.

BOLDRE † St John ★
2m/3km N. of Lymington
OS *SZ326994* **GPS** *50.7937N, 1.5379W*

Isolated from habitation, St John's is set on a hill overlooking the wooded valley of the Lymington River, on the edge of the New Forest. A church of gradual growth, it is very attractive externally. The tiled roof of the nave sweeps down to cover the S. aisle, and the tower, in S. transeptal position, has an upper stage of 1697 in brick. The writer and artist William Gilpin was rector 1771–1804.

BRAMLEY † St James
5m/8km N. of Basingstoke
OS *SU644589* **GPS** *51.3263N, 1.0758W*

An engaging church with a pretty brick W. tower, 1636, and dormer-windowed Norman nave, with a large Gothic brick S. aisle (the Brocas Chapel), 1802, by Soane. The interior fulfils the external promise, having a handsome W. gallery of 1738, with organ case by Temple Moore, medieval wall-painting, 16th-century pews, rood screen and old roof. In the Brocas Chapel, lit by some old Flemish glass, is a big monument of 1777, the tomb of Bernard Brocas, attributed to Thomas Carter.

△ **AVINGTON: ST MARY** – *a very satisfying red-brick church of the 18th century*

BREAMORE † St Mary ★★

3m/4km N. of Fordingbridge

OS *SU153188* **GPS** *50.9693N, 1.7831W*

This important Saxon church of c. 1000 is set in parkland with noble cedars, close to a mellow red-brick Elizabethan manor house. The church was originally cruciform, but the N. transept has gone. Over the archway to the S. transept is an Anglo-Saxon inscription which translated means 'Here the Covenant becomes manifest to thee'. Among other Saxon features are double splayed windows, long-and-short quoins, and the great stone rood over the S. door. The rood, sheltered by a later porch, was defaced after the Reformation, but traces of the 15th-century painted background survive.

BURGHCLERE
† Sandham Memorial Chapel ★★

3m/5km S. of Newbury

OS *SU463608* **GPS** *51.3446N, 1.3362W*

The chapel is home to one of the 20th century's great works of religious art. Stanley Spencer's

△ **AVINGTON: ST MARY** – *a delightful Georgian interior, with a three-decker pulpit of Spanish mahogany, box pews and many wall pegs for the hanging of hats and wigs*

deeply moving depiction of war, inspired in structure by Giotto and Michaelangelo, was commissioned by the Behrend family. Painted on canvases affixed to the walls, it is rightly hailed as a masterpiece.

BURITON † St Mary the Virgin

2m/3km S. of Petersfield

OS *SU740200* **GPS** *50.9748N, 0.9471W*

In a beautiful setting by a duck-pond and manor house under steep wooded hillsides, the church has 12th-century arcades, a chancel of c. 1280 and a triple sedilia, unusually fine for Hampshire.

CHALTON † St Michael and All Angels

6m/10km N. of Havant

OS *SU732159* **GPS** *50.9383N, 0.9596W*

This is an attractive 13th-century downland church near a half-timbered and thatched inn; it has a fine E. window with Geometrical tracery c. 1270.

CHILCOMB † St Andrew

2m/3km S.E. of Winchester

OS *SU507279* **GPS** *51.0484N, 1.2779W*

A small late Saxon church in lonely downland setting, it has flint and stone walls, an appealing roofline of red-brown tiles and a weatherboarded bellcote. There is also a Norman pillared piscina, octagonal Gothic font and an early 17th-century screen.

CORHAMPTON † Dedication unknown

adjoins Meonstoke to N., 9m/14km N. of Fareham

OS *SU610203* **GPS** *50.9791N, 1.1324W*

The small Saxon church of c. 1035, spoilt only by the 1855 brick E. end, is best seen from the N.W., where the characteristic Saxon proportions, pilaster-strips and 'long-and-short' work are most evident. The S. side, hidden by a huge old yew, has a Saxon sundial. Inside, the original chancel arch and 12th-century murals are of greatest interest.

COSHAM † St Philip ★

N. district of Portsmouth

OS *SU665047* **GPS** *50.8389N, 1.0556W*

By Sir Ninian Comper, 1936–8, and one of his last designs, achieving 'unity by inclusion'. The exterior is of brick and artificial stone. Inside, the focus is on the altar, which is covered by a gilded baldacchino, or ciborium, decorated with painted angels and apostles. The decorated windows and Corinthian columns combine in a masterly display of eclecticism.

CRONDALL † All Saints ★

3m/4km N.W. of Farnham

OS *SU794484* **GPS** *51.2300N, 0.8631W*

Approached by a lime avenue, the heavily buttressed exterior, dominated by a proud brick N. tower of 1658, is promising. Though scraped and refurnished in three Victorian restorations, the noble Transitional interior does not disappoint, for the clerestoried nave leads to a splendid rib-vaulted chancel with an Agnus Dei boss, lit in part by clear glass, and full of Norman detail.

DUMMER † All Saints

5m/8km S.W. of Basingstoke

OS *SU588460* **GPS** *51.2103N, 1.1588W*

The homely interior has a fine Early English chancel and chancel arch, above which is the 15th-century rood canopy. On the S. side of the chancel arch is a squint, re-opened in 2000. The deep W. gallery dates from the time of Charles II.

EAST MEON † All Saints ★★

5m/8km W. of Petersfield

OS *SU680222* **GPS** *50.9959N, 1.0315W*

All Saints is a striking, boldly massed Norman church set above the village on the slopes of a green down. The burly, enriched Norman tower is crowned by a patterned lead broach spire surmounting a cruciform plan, the nave and transepts of which are largely Norman. The splendid Tournai marble font was presented by Henry de Blois. The chancel and S. chapel were rebuilt in the late 15th century; the glass and fittings are mostly by Comper.

EASTON † St Mary

2m/3km N.E. of Winchester

OS *SU509322* **GPS** *51.0874N, 1.2744W*

Almost entirely c. 1200, with a remarkable vaulted apsidal chancel and richly moulded S. doorway, the church was rather flamboyantly restored by Woodyer in the 1860s, who 'improved' the Norman.

ELLINGHAM † St Mary and All Saints ★

2m/3km N. of Ringwood

OS *SU143082* **GPS** *50.8738N, 1.7972W*

A simple rustic ironstone and honey-coloured rubble church in water meadows by the Avon. The brick W. end is 1746, and the Georgian S. porch has a blue- and gold-painted sundial. The screen completely closes off the chancel, and carries a 16th-century tympanum painted with the Decalogue, Elizabethan texts and Royal Arms of 1671. A reredos ascribed to Grinling Gibbons is now at the W. end.

EMPSHOTT † Holy Rood

5m/8km N. of Petersfield

OS *SU753312* **GPS** *51.0756N, 0.9261W*

Set among deep woodlands, the church has a distinguished Early English chalk chancel arch and arcades, a fine timber roof, an unusual openwork bell-turret and a spire of 1884. The Norman Purbeck marble table font with cover is dated 1626. A 15th-century bench and a screen of 1624 are now under the tower.

FARLEY CHAMBERLAYNE † St John

6m/10km S.W. of Winchester

OS *SU397274* **GPS** *51.0450N, 1.4346W*

This is a remote, deserted village set high on the chalk Downs. The interior is Georgianized Norman, lightly restored by A. Marshall Mackenzie in 1910.

FAWLEY † All Saints ★

5m/8km E. of Beaulieu

OS *SU458032* **GPS** *50.8271N, 1.3505W*

A Norman W. doorway and early Decorated E. window of the chancel are the finest features of this basically late 12th-century church. The E. end was bombed in 1940 and well restored by W. H. R. Blacking in 1954. There is a fine Jacobean pulpit.

△ **IDSWORTH: ST HUBERT** – *the millennium fresco in the tympanum makes reference to the 14th-century paintings in the chancel beyond, particularly in the depiction of Christ within a mandorla*

FORDINGBRIDGE † St Mary

6m/10km N. of Ringwood
OS *SU145138* **GPS** *50.9236N, 1.7949W*

St Mary's is Norman to Perpendicular. Its Early English chancel has a huge E. window of three lancets; the N. chapel, nave and aisles, spacious throughout, are Decorated. The 15th-century tie-beam truss roof of the N. chapel is similar to the hammer-beam roof of the nave at Bere Regis, Dorset. A handsome carved Georgian Royal Arms is set over the N. door, and a 12th-century carved ox head can be seen over the vestry door.

FROYLE † Assumption of the Blessed Virgin Mary

4m/6km N.E. of Alton
OS *SU755428* **GPS** *51.1801N, 0.9203W*

The church forms a group with the grey-stone-gabled manor house at the upper end of a park. The nave and tower are red-brick Georgian and contrast with the grey-stone early Decorated chancel. The good Reticulated tracery of the E. window is filled with heraldic glass of the same period. All is sumptuously furnished in the Baroque taste by Sir Hubert Miller.

GOSPORT † Holy Trinity

1m/2km W. of Portsmouth across entrance to Portsmouth Harbour
OS *SZ621995* **GPS** *50.7931N, 1.1199W*

The building dates to 1696; it was enlarged in 1734 and again c. 1835. It was then restored in 1887 by A. W. Blomfield, who at the same time added the fine campanile, a local landmark for mariners. Externally of stern red brick; but internally bright, white walls, a good barrel roof, and oak columns encased in Ionic plasterwork, and a marble high altar with 18th-century reredos. The real treasure here is Handel's organ from Canons Park, Stanmore.

HALE † St Mary ★

4m/6km N.E. of Fordingbridge
OS *SU178186* **GPS** *50.9670N, 1.7473W*

Beautifully situated in woodland near a manor house above the River Avon, the church was rebuilt in 1633 in a pretty, rustic Classical style, and altered and enlarged, with transepts added by Thomas Archer in 1717. It is Victorianized inside, and the monuments include that of Archer, in Roman toga, flanked by his two wives.

HAWKLEY † St Peter and St Paul ★

4m/7km N. of Petersfield
OS *SU745291* **GPS** *51.0570N, 0.9371W*

Built by S. S. Teulon and completed in 1865, St Peter and St Paul's is one of his best churches – solid, vigorous Romanesque with a Rhenish helm tower. Inside are richly carved capitals and corbels.

HEADBOURNE WORTHY † St Swithin

2m/3km N. of Winchester
OS *SU487319* **GPS** *51.0852N, 1.3055W*

St Swithin's is a charming small Saxon church, beautifully set in meadowland; it originally served as a wayside chapel for pilgrims. The large, mutilated and important rood of c. 1000 is now placed above the vestry doorway.

IDSWORTH † St Hubert ★★

5m/8km N.E. of Havant
OS *SU742140* **GPS** *50.9213N, 0.9446W*

A highly picturesque small Norman and 16th-century chapel alone in a field in downland country. A pretty 18th-century white-painted bell-turret is at the E. end of the nave. Its 18th-century atmosphere was heightened in 1913 by Goodhart-Rendel. The nave has fine Georgian and 1913 fittings, including box pews, Jacobean pulpit, Royal Arms and a W. gallery. The chancel has a stucco ceiling with pictorial panels of 1913 and a highly important series of 14th-century wall-paintings depicting the legend of St Hubert and the life of John the Baptist. The contemporary millennium fresco in the tympanum is by Fleur Kelly.

ISLE OF WIGHT – BRADING
† St Mary the Virgin ★

2m/3km N. of Sandown
OS *SZ606873* **GPS** *50.6824N, 1.1427W*

Well-sited on a ridge at the N. end of the little town, this is the largest medieval church on the island. The 13th-century W. porch-tower stands on arches made to include a processional way around the church. The spacious interior, restored by Hellyer and Blomfield, is most interesting towards the E. In the 15th-century Oglander Chapel are the monuments and hatchments of the Oglander family, established at nearby Nunwell. There is an engraved Purbeck marble slab to John Cherowin, d. 1441, Constable of Portchester Castle.

ISLE OF WIGHT – CARISBROOKE
† St Mary the Virgin ★

Adjoins Newport to S.W.
OS *SZ485882* **GPS** *50.6919N, 1.3139W*

The stately 15th-century W. tower, the most beautiful on the island, is the finest feature of a church once both monastic and parochial. The priory was suppressed in 1414; the conventual buildings N. of the church have vanished. The church, with its broad, airy Norman nave and Early English S. aisle divided by a fine Transitional arcade of five bays, has a truncated look, for the chancel was pulled down c. 1565. The tomb of Lady Margaret Wadham, c. 1520, has a small kneeling effigy beneath a rich canopy.

ISLE OF WIGHT – GODSHILL
† All Saints ★

4m/6km W. of Shanklin
OS *SZ527818* **GPS** *50.6337N, 1.2559W*

Narrow lanes sweep uphill beneath trees to this well-known group of church tower and cottages. The mostly Perpendicular church might qualify as the least restored on the island. The interior, with old plaster and much clear glass, is unexpectedly spacious, a double nave divided end-to-end by a dignified arcade of six bays. Among its finest features is a rare 15th-century wall-painting in the S. transept of Christ crucified on a triple-branched lily. A fine 16th-century tomb of Sir John Leigh has effigies beneath a rich

MINSTEAD: ALL SAINTS – *a 13th-century church, overrun by the Georgians, who crowded the interior with benches, box pews and galleries painted with texts* ▷

Mr Thos Brown Bequeathed to the
Poor of this Parish a Donation of
arising from the Rent of a
Messuages & Lands at Hinton in the
Parish of Christchurch to be
Given annually in Bread or
Otherwise on New Years Day
The Revd S Berdmore DD
Bequeathed to the Poor of this
Parish £200-0-0 per Cent
Consols the Interest thereof
To be distributed annually by the
Rector according to his discretion
On or about the 6 of April
AD 2000
ON THE FIRST OF JANUARY
THIS CONGREGATION
ON BEHALF OF ITSELF & THOSE WHO
TO CARRY OUT ONE
FOR THE BENEFIT OF
THIS PROMISE MADE
LASTS UNTIL IT IS

arched canopy; elsewhere are self-important 18th-century monuments to the Worsleys of Appledurcombe.

ISLE OF WIGHT – NEWPORT

† St Thomas

4m/6km S. of Cowes

OS *SZ499891* **GPS** *50.6998N, 1.2937W*

By S. W. Dawkes, 1854–5, this is a large town church in the Decorated style. The richly carved pulpit was made by Thomas Caper of Salisbury in 1636; it is one of the finest in England and came from the old church.

ISLE OF WIGHT – SHORWELL

† St Peter ★

5m/8km S.W. of Newport

OS *SZ457829* **GPS** *50.6449N, 1.3546W*

This is a largely 15th-century Perpendiculasr church of mellow texture in a lovely village of thatched cottages in multi-coloured local stone. The exterior is weathered and unrestored; the interior quite dark and crowded with Victorian poppy-headed pews. Over the N. door is a fine and carefully restored 15th-century wall-painting of St Christopher. In the N chapel are monuments to the Leigh family.

ISLE OF WIGHT – YARMOUTH

† St James

OS *SZ354896* **GPS** *50.7055N, 1.4991W*

The church stands in the old part of this largely unspoilt harbour town. Mostly Jacobean, it is full of dark wood. The oddly elongated tower was raised some 30 feet in 1837 so as to act as a landmark for mariners. The main interest is in the S. chancel chapel, which contains a vault and memorial to Sir Robert Holmes, governor of the island in the latter part of the 17th century, who had a captured sculpture of Louis XIV 'decapitated' and a sculpture of his own head put in its place.

ITCHEN STOKE † St Mary ★★

4m/7km N.E. of Winchester

OS *SU559324* **GPS** *51.0884N, 1.2031W*

Churches Conservation Trust

By H. Conybeare, 1866, St Mary's is Gothic Revival, modelled on Sainte Chapelle in Paris, and exuberantly Victorian. The W. window is very striking – a wheel design set with vividly coloured glass. The roofs are painted, and glazed tiles form a complex pattern on the sanctuary floor.

LYNDHURST

† St Michael and All Angels ★★

6m/10km W. of Southampton

OS *SU298081* **GPS** *50.8725N, 1.5766W*

By William White, 1858–68, this is a splendidly mid-Victorian church in polychromatic brick, its tall brick-banded spire dominating the little New Forest town. Inside is a gallery of Pre-Raphaelite art; a fresco reredos by Lord Leighton; glass by Burne-Jones, Kempe and Morris; and monuments by Flaxman and S. P. Cockerell Jnr.

MILFORD-ON-SEA † All Saints ★

3m/4km S.W. of Lymington

OS *SZ290919* **GPS** *50.7263N, 1.5894W*

St Michael's is largely Early English. Of the cruciform Norman church, two bays of the S. arcade and the ends of the transepts remain. The 13th-century W. tower has a short lead spire and odd flanking penthouses with arched openings into it. Many windows show early forms of tracery. The interior with its low arcades, transverse crossing arches, barrel- and rib-vaulted roofs, is spacious and quite impressive. The chancel roof has very late bosses, 1640.

MINSTEAD † All Saints ★★

2m/3km N.W. of Lyndhurst

OS *SU259094* **GPS** *50.8843N, 1.6327W*

Well set on a knoll slightly away from the tiny New Forest village, this is perhaps the most obviously quaint of the several 'unrestored' churches in the county. To a 13th-century nave and chancel have been added a Georgian brick W. tower, S. transept and two squires' pews, complete with fireplaces. The highly atmospheric interior is crowded with open benches, box pews and two galleries, one two-tiered under the tower. A primitive Norman font, carved with an Agnus Dei, stands on a brick floor in front of the two-decker pulpit.

ROMSEY: ST MARY AND ST ETHELFLEDA – *the soaring nave and crossing, with light flooding in from the Early English west window* ▷

MOTTISFONT † St Andrew
10m/16km N.W. of Southampton
OS *SU325267* **GPS** *51.0392N, 1.5365W*

The church is Norman and Perpendicular, with a splendid Norman chancel arch. There is 15th-century glass in the chancel, and a monument of 1584.

NETHER WALLOP † St Andrew ★
6m/10km S.W. of Andover
OS *SU303363* **GPS** *51.1261N, 1.5670W*

This late Saxon to Perpendicular church with a fine flint W. tower was rebuilt in the 18th and 19th centuries. Over the chancel arch is an important Anglo-Saxon wall-painting from the Winchester School of artists, depicting flying angels supporting a mandorla containing Christ – perhaps the earliest surviving in England.

NORTHINGTON † St John the Evangelist
6m/10km N.E. of Winchester
OS *SU564373* **GPS** *51.1327N, 1.1948W*

Finely set on a hillside in rolling country, this is one of the finest Gothic Revival churches in the county. It is by Sir T. G. Jackson and was built by Lord Ashburton in 1889. The tall, commanding pinnacled tower and angular apse are impressive and look well together from across the valley, their flint and stone chequer being particularly good.

ODIHAM † All Saints ★
7m/11km E. of Basingstoke
OS *SU740509* **GPS** *51.2527N, 0.9405W*

This large, mainly Perpendicular church stands at the highest point of the small country town. To its south are 17th-century almshouses whose mellow old brickwork blends with the fine 1647 church tower. The spacious, but slightly chilly, interior has good 17th-century galleries and pulpit and many small brasses. Two E. windows are by Patrick Reyntiens.

PAMBER END † St Mary and St John the Baptist
4m/6km N. of Basingstoke
OS *SU608581* **GPS** *51.3192N, 1.1276W*

In a lovely sylvan setting away from the village, the church was built in c. 1130 for the alien priory of West Sherbourne. Of the former cruciform monastic church, the superbly proportioned Early English choir and the massive tile-capped Norman central tower remain. The spacious interior is lit by clear glass in long lancet windows and furnished with a 15th-century screen and pews. There are several Purbeck marble coffin-slabs and a wooden cross-legged effigy of a knight, c. 1270.

PORTCHESTER † St Mary ★
On N. shore of Portsmouth harbour
OS *SU625044* **GPS** *50.8366N, 1.1134W*

St Mary's stands in the S.E. corner of the old Roman fort of Portchester Castle, a romantic setting. This austere Norman church was built for a priory of Augustinian canons founded in 1133 by Henry I. Despite the loss of the S. transept and N. chapel, and the reduced chancel, the immense nave remains impressive; of particular note are the carved capitals surmounting the crossing piers. The W. front has a fine doorway, and the Norman font is the most uninhibited feature of the church.

PRIORS DEAN † Dedication unknown
4m/6km N. of Petersfield
OS *SU727296* **GPS** *51.0611N, 0.9628W*

A rustic Norman and Early English structure on Saxon foundations, this little church is set in a remote corner of well-wooded country. The whitewashed interior is lit by windows of plain glass; restoration took place in 1857. Of note are numerous 17th-century monuments to the Comptons and Tichbournes, including a relief wall monument to Sir John Compton, 1653, and his wife Dame Bridget Compton, d. 1634.

ROMSEY † St Mary and St Ethelfleda ★★
7m/11km N.W. of Southampton
OS *SU350212* **GPS** *50.9897N, 1.5014W*

The abbey church became the parish church at the Dissolution, when it was bought by the townspeople for £100. It had previously been the church of a nunnery founded by Edward the Elder, c. 907. A visit to this magnificent church is not easily forgotten, for here is great Norman architecture, grand in scale and rich in detail. The formidably blunt, massive exterior, with its squat central tower crowned by a wooden bell-cage, hardly prepares one for the grandeur of the interior. The church, which is largely 12th-century except for an Early English W. end, has many treasures: a wonderful Saxon rood and a smaller Saxon carving of the Crucifixion, Norman capitals, an early 16th-century painted reredos, a fine 13th-century Purbeck marble effigy of a lady, and the St Barbe monument by Thomas Stanton, 1660. The N. aisle E. window is Kempe at his very best. The image of Our Lady above the high altar is by Martin Travers.

SELBORNE † St Mary ★

4ml/6km S.E. of Alton
OS *SU741337* **GPS** *51.0985N, 0.9429W*

St Mary's is beautifully set behind a gigantic old yew between the village and a wooded ravine. The largely 12th- and 13th-century church is worth visiting for its own sake as well as for the 18th-century naturalist Gilbert White, who is buried here. Entered through a fine Early English S. doorway, the well cared for interior, restored by Gilbert's great-nephew, William White, is full of interest. A window of St Francis and the birds commemorates the author of *The Natural History and Antiquities of Selborne*, whose humble grave in the churchyard is inscribed simply 'G. W.', 1793.

SILCHESTER † St Mary ★

7ml/11km N. of Basingstoke
OS *SU643623* **GPS** *51.3567N, 1.0774W*

A charming little Norman to Perpendicular church, it stands near a portion of the wall of the lost Roman city of Silchester. The 15th-century screen survived a Victorian restoration that removed box pews and dormer windows. The 19th-century bench-ends are Art Nouveau, and the pulpit, with very odd domed canopy, Jacobean. The pre-Reformation screen is finely carved with delicate tracery, roses and pomegranates symbolising Henry VIII and Catherine of Aragon, and angels. The Early English chancel has painted patterning on the splays of S. windows. There is a beautiful 14th-century effigy of a lady.

SOUTH HAYLING † St Mary ★

on Hayling Island between Langstone and Chichester Harbours
OS *SU693056* **GPS** *50.7955N, 0.9769W*

Second only to Pamber as the finest Early English church in the county, this former priory church is large and well-proportioned, of Sussex type, with a central tower and shingled spire. The chancel E. window of five lancets has a good Tree of Life glass by Bryans, 1925.

SOUTHWICK † St James ★

4ml/7km N. of Portsmouth
OS *SU625086* **GPS** *50.8739N, 1.1117W*

Much of the old atmosphere remains, but nothing can compensate for the 1950s removal of the fine box pews which had been affected by death-watch beetle. The white-painted W. gallery on twisted 'barley-sugar' columns, pulpit, altar rails and handsome painted reredos are the remaining Georgian features of interest. Pride of place goes to the 18th-century reredos, painted to simulate marble and full of cheerful cherubim.

STOKE CHARITY
† St Mary and St Michael ★

6ml/10km N. of Winchester
OS *SU488392* **GPS** *51.1506N, 1.3025W*

Alone in a field by watercress beds, but once in company with the manor house of the de la Charite family, the church is of Norman and later date, restored in 1848, and is most remarkable for its lovely array of contents. In the Hampton Chapel, the least restored part with old plaster and clear glass, is a 15th-century sculpture of the Mass of St Gregory and a brightly coloured Perpendicular tomb. Medieval fragments decorate the floors and walls.

TADLEY † St Peter ★

6ml/10km N.W. of Basingstoke
OS *SU597599* **GPS** *51.3358N, 1.1432W*

Small, rustic and completely isolated, the church has a humble brick tower of 1685 and dormer windows. The gallery, pulpit, seats and altar table are all 17th-century. The church was restored in the 19th century.

△ **WINCHESTER: ST CROSS** – *the church amply displays the transition from Norman to Gothic; the windows in the transept (above right) are late Norman below and Early English above*

TICHBORNE † St Andrew ★
5m/8km E. of Winchester
OS *SU568302* **GPS** *51.0688N, 1.1897W*

St Andrew's is a delightful 11th-century and later 'atmospherick' church with prominent 17th-century brick tower, on the hillside above a village of neat thatched cottages. The interior has an unrestored look, with box pews of various dates, old plaster, clear glass and Royal Arms of 1735. The railed-off N. aisle belongs to the RC family of the Tichbornes, whose monuments it contains.

TITCHFIELD † St Peter ★
3m/4km W. of Fareham
OS *SU540057* **GPS** *50.8491N, 1.2330W*

The church stands off the former market-place of a village now threatened by suburbs, and is rich in interest. The Saxon base of a W. tower with shingled 1688 spire may be the oldest church fabric in the county. It shelters a Norman doorway. The tall, narrow nave is suggestive of Saxon origins, and Roman tiles are set into the W. front. Above the chancel arch is a painting of the Crucifixion by Kempe. The N. arcade and aisle are Perpendicular – gracious and unusual for such a modest church. The Wriothesley Chapel is on the S. of the chancel; it contains a carved triple tomb to the Countess of Southampton, her husband and son, and a memorial to Lady Mary Wriothesley, who died aged four.

WARBLINGTON
† St Thomas à Becket ★
1m/2km S.E. of Havant
OS *SU729054* **GPS** *50.8437N, 0.9659W*

St Thomas's stands in a secluded setting near Langstone Harbour, with only a farm and the ruined castle for company. The church is set in a large graveyard with two watchers' huts from body-snatching days, and many well-carved headstones. It has a partly Saxon tower riding between the Early English nave and chancel. The 15th-century timber N. porch is dark, grainy and weathered. Inside are good Early English arcades and tower arches, and there are two beautiful effigies.

WINCHESTER † St Cross ★★

St Cross Road

OS *SU476277* **GPS** *51.0475N, 1.3222W*

The chapel of the hospital founded by Henri de Blois, Bishop of Winchester, in 1133, is now a parish church. Dominating the hospital quadrangle, it is one of the county's noblest churches, ample in form and rich in content. Large-boned cruciform with central tower and vaulted throughout, it was built from E. to W. from 1160–1345. The transition in style is gradual, from enriched Norman, rippling with zigzag at the E. end, to Decorated at the W. end. Notable among its treasures are old wall-paintings, glass and tiles, beautiful Renaissance woodwork, a Flemish triptych and some brasses. Butterfield did the sensitive restoration in the 19th century.

WINCHFIELD † St Mary the Virgin ★

7m/12km E. of Basingstoke

OS *SU767536* **GPS** *51.2764N, 0.9004W*

This remote church is essentially Norman, though restored in 1849, when the N. aisle was added, neo-Norman windows replaced some medieval ones, and the brick top stage of the broad tower gave way to the present belfry stage and pyramid cap. The Norman S. doorway has good mouldings extending beneath the soffit and leaf capitals of exotic Saracenic character. There are some original windows, a Jacobean pulpit and old oak seats.

WOLVERTON † St Catherine ★

2m/3km E. of Kingsclere

OS *SU551585* **GPS** *51.3236N, 1.2094W*

In its assured Wren manner, the noble, handsomely proportioned W. brick tower, with its nicely detailed belfry windows and cornices, contrasts with the low-built cruciform church beneath it. Both tower and church were built in 1717. Two altars and two pulpits occupy the W. and E. ends. The gallery and chancel gates were removed in the late 19th century, but the box pews remain, each with an individual candleholder, giving the interior a strong period flavour.

HEREFORDSHIRE

This secret, partly Welsh county is so deeply silent in its many remote places that those who know it cannot be blamed for wishing to protect its rustic beauty from the crowds. Medieval farms, timber-framed and tiled, are isolated down narrow hilly lanes; hopyards and cider orchards abound; some churches are spared electricity. The Victorian Hereford of Francis Kilvert's diaries of rural life in the 1870s has suffered: suburbs all round, and an unsightly sprawl of housing developments has straggled west of the Wye, almost engulfing the Benedictines at Belmont.

But even if the county's towns have suffered from suburbanization and over-dense peripheral housing developments, the countryside remains special – rural landscapes to be cherished, from the sparse hills of the Welsh borders to the Malvern hills, its eastern ramparts, with the Rivers Wye, Lugg, Frome and Arrow creating rich valleys in its pastoral heart.

From the south of this county the Welsh were never driven out by the Saxons and they assimilated the Normans in their own way, for here is that curious group of Norman churches of which Kilpeck is the best known, where the carving of fonts, tympana and capitals seems to be a distillation of Continental Romanesque, Celtic and Norse, and unlike any other Norman work in England. Besides Norman churches, red fields, red-and-white Herefordshire cattle, cider, hops and barley, a chief feature of this woody landscaped county is the prevalence of old timber-framed buildings. These are rarely thatched but have roofs of stone slates or old tiles. Weobley, Eardisley and Pembridge are complete villages of them. Building stones are many and were used chiefly for churches, and they vary from the pale pitted tufa to red sandstone. There are few big country houses. Moccas, partly by Robert Adam, and Berrington, by Henry Holland, are fine examples. Downton Castle (1780–5), built by Richard Payne Knight, the exponent of the 'picturesque' theory, and Hampton Court, Hereford, are 'Gothick'. Eastnor Castle, by Sir Robert Smirke, 1808, is a very early example of Norman Revival. And Tudor is seen in Hellen's, Much Marcle.

The Cathedral of Hereford, still largely Norman, is square and West Country-looking; for many years it has been sadly bereft of its glorious screen by Scott and Skidmore (now restored and at the V&A). It is not so much admired as Gloucester and Worcester, with which it is usually compared. The county itself contains grand churches of every age, from Norman to early 20th-century, and of every style, although only a few 15th-century Perpendicular. This is odd since most of the medieval churches of the rest of England were added to in this century, and in many counties the most impressive parish church is wholly 15th-century. Hereford was not

◁ **GARWAY: ST MICHAEL** – *in a beautiful setting, the 13th-century tower was linked to the main body of the church in the 17th century*

△ **PEMBRIDGE: ST MARY** – *the church itself is good Decorated Gothic, but the compelling feature is the free-standing wooden bell tower, resembling a Scandinavian structure*

a rich county in the 19th century, so that Victorian 'restorations' are often cheap and ugly or else the churches were spared restoration altogether. For its size, Herefordshire has more 17th-century woodwork than elsewhere and a fair amount of Georgian box pewing. The county seems to have gone straight from 'High Church' to Evangelical, and 19th-century Tractarianism is rare.

As may be expected in so unspoiled a county, the settings of almost all the churches are attractive, and in the Welsh districts the old parish church is Celtic-fashion, some way off from the village. There is no 'typical' Herefordshire church. The churches are either curiously beautiful or dull inside. No county has a church so wonderful as Abbey Dore, that solemn Cistercian Early English abbey with its 17th-century woodwork making a rich contrast; nor is there parochial Decorated to compare with the S. aisle of Leominster. No county has so delicately moulded and joyfully coloured examples of Georgian as the Rococo-Gothic church of Shobdon, and for unrestored remoteness there is little to compare with Clodock and Richards Castle. Brinsop, so excitingly restored by Sir Ninian Comper, Brockhampton, Lethaby's bold design in the William Morris Arts and Crafts manner, and Seddon's strange Victorian effort at Hoarwithy, are all possessions which help to make the county so full of the unexpected.

John Betjeman's memory of the perfect Herefordshire is a spring day in the foothills of the Black Mountains, finding among winding hill-top lanes the remote little church of St Margaret's, where there was no sound but a farm dog's distant barking. 'Opening the church door I saw across the little chancel a screen and loft delicately carved and textured pale grey with time.'

0
5 miles
0
5 km
SHROPSHIRE
WORCESTERSHIRE
HEREFORDSHIRE
WALES
GLOUCESTERSHIRE
Bishop's Castle
Ludlow
nighton
Presteigne
Kington
Bromyard
HEREFORD
Ledbury
Ross-on-Wye
Abergavenny
Monmouth
-on-Wye
Richards Castle
Croft
Yarpole
Aymestrey
Shobdon
Leominster
Edvin Loach
Pembridge
Dilwyn
Birley
Sarnesfield
Eardisley
Kinnersley
Much Cowarne
Castle Frome
Mathon
Bosbury
Bredwardine
Monnington-on-Wye
Moccas
Brinsop
Bishopstone
Bridge Sollers
Peterchurch
Tyberton
Madley
Eaton Bishop
Vowchurch
Craswall
Eastnor
Fownhope
Much Marcle
Brockhampton
How Caple
Bacton
Llanveynoe
Abbey Dore
Kilpeck
Hoarwithy
Clodock
Sellack
Rowlestone
Garway
A489
A49
A4113
A488
A4110
A4112
A44
A4111
A438
A480
A465
A417
A4103
A466
A449
M50
A40

△ **BROCKHAMPTON: ALL SAINTS** – *a church of the Arts and Crafts movement, it makes use of vernacular materials and methods, including cedar tiles on the tower and thatching to the roof*

ABBEY DORE † St Mary ★★
10m/16km S.W. of Hereford
OS *SO387304* **GPS** *51.9688N, 2.8936W*

Surrounded by the small orchards of the Golden Valley are the presbytery, with its wonderful square red sandstone ambulatory and chapels, and the crossing and transepts of a great conventual church of the Cistercian order. The interior is alight with colour from the 17th-century glass in the lancet windows – a perfect example of Early English architecture with 17th-century fittings. The great oak screen was designed by John Abel for Viscount Scudamore in 1634, when he restored the abbey as a parish church, thus saving for posterity one of the most beautiful buildings in Herefordshire.

AYMESTREY
† St John the Baptist and St Alkmund ★
6m/10km N.W. of Leominster
OS *SO426651* **GPS** *52.2813N, 2.8428W*

A 12th-century red sandstone church with spacious plastered interior and a lovely, tall 16th-century rood screen.

BACTON † St Faith
7m/11km S.W. of Hereford
OS *SO370323* **GPS** *51.9863N, 2.9176W*

A pretty place buried in the Golden Valley where once lived Blanche Parry, maid-of-honour to Queen Elizabeth I. Her alabaster effigy can be seen in the church; the charming inscription ends: 'Allwaye wythe maeden quene a maede dyd ende my liffe.'

BIRLEY † St Peter
4m/6km S.W. of Leominster
OS *SO453533* **GPS** *52.1757N, 2.8005W*

This is an attractive red sandstone church, mottled with yellow lichen – but, alas, the interior has been scraped. The chancel arch is enriched with ballflower motifs; the airy S. chapel with three windows is Perpendicular, and there is a lovely Norman font.

BISHOPSTONE † St Lawrence ★
7m/11km N.W. of Hereford
OS *SO415438* **GPS** *52.0903N, 2.8539W*

In a country churchyard with no signs of any village: the church has an unusually broad nave

△ **CRASWELL: ST MARY** – *a barn-like rustic church of the 14th and 15th centuries, in the peaceful Olchon Valley*

with a fine Jacobean roof. Great Transitional stone arches lead to the transepts. The reredos is Jacobean, as is the nicely carved pulpit. The interior of the church is plastered.

BOSBURY † Holy Trinity ★
4m/6km N. of Ledbury
OS *SO695434* **GPS** *52.0886N, 2.4458W*

Set in the middle of a black and white village – one of the chief hop-growing centres – this is a large red sandstone church with late Norman arcades, a Perpendicular chantry chapel and two very grand Elizabethan tombs in the chancel. The detached 13th-century tower has a fortified look about it.

BREDWARDINE † St Andrew
11m/18km N.W. of Hereford
OS *SO334445* **GPS** *52.0948N, 2.9725W*

The church is close to the castle ruins and River Wye. A large Norman church, it is partly built in tufa, and has a Georgian tower of 1790 in small-coursed stones. Diarist Francis Kilvert was rector here from 1877 until he died in 1879.

BRIDGE SOLLARS † St Andrew
Also spelt Bridge Sollers;
6m/10km N.W. of Hereford
OS *SO414426* **GPS** *52.0788N, 2.8553W*

Norman church with boldly carved S. doorway and a chancel of c. 1300. An 18th-century sundial reads, 'Esteem thy precious time, Which pass so swiftly away, Prepare thou for eternity, And do not make delay.'

BRINSOP † St George ★
5m/8km N.W. of Hereford
OS *SO442447* **GPS** *52.0986N, 2.8155W*

In a delightful setting above an orchard, and some distance from the road, the church is of c. 1300–50. A somewhat unpromising exterior, but inside all is redeemed: a celebrated Norman tympanum is carved with St George and the Dragon by the Herefordshire School; there is a 14th-century screen and glass of the same period; windows in memory of the Wordsworths (the poet frequently visited); and there is a glowing alabaster reredos and glass by Sir Ninian Comper. Everything, new and old, is beautiful.

△ **CROFT: ST MICHAEL AND ALL ANGELS** – *hard at the heels of Croft Castle*

BROCKHAMPTON † All Saints ★

6m/10km S.E. of Hereford
OS *SO594321* **GPS** *51.9863N, 2.5924W*

By W. R. Lethaby, 1902; this is his last and greatest building, a richly symbolic church imbued with primeval sacredness. The central tower, with cedar tiles, and impressive, well-composed thatched roof are respectful of the local vernacular as advocated by the Arts and Crafts movement. The astounding interior is vaulted and supported by cruck-like concrete arches. The tapestry is by Burne-Jones, the glass by Whall and the carved wildflower panels on the choir stall are by George Jack, who taught carving at the RCA.

CASTLE FROME † St Michael ★★

6m/10km S. of Bromyard
OS *SO667458* **GPS** *52.1101N, 2.4868W*

Overlooking ranges of hop fields to the W., the church contains a superb 12th-century font of the Herefordshire School, richly carved with the Baptism of Christ and the signs of the four Evangelists, supported by three crouching figures which were reassembled with difficulty by Victorian restorers. The figure of the Christ child has a thin moustache, reflecting the practice of the time of portraying Christ as a miniature man. The carving is fluid and sophisticated, and shows many elements of influence. This work compares closely with the font at Eardisley, which might be by the same hand. In the chancel is the 17th-century alabaster tomb of the Unett family.

CLODOCK † St Clydog ★

8m/12km N. of Abergavenny
OS *SO326275* **GPS** *51.9420N, 2.9812W*

On the eastern edge of the Black Mountains and on the banks of the Monnow, this Norman and later church is broad, aisleless and altogether delightful, with great transverse tie beams giving stability to a rather unsteady appearance. The tower is a 'frontier' tower – embattled, with arrow slits. The wonderful interior is an essay in oak, with extensive late 17th-century furnishings: a three-decker pulpit, stalls and box pews, some of which contained small charcoal stoves.

CRASWELL † St Mary

6m/10km S.E. of Hay-on-Wye

OS *SO281362* **GPS** *52.0203N, 3.0485W*

Altogether modest, charming and prettily situated, St Mary's is a long, low structure of rough sandstone under a tight-fitting slate roof that dates from the 14th and 15th centuries. Its churchyard has no graves, as the ground is too stony; burials took place nearby at Clodock. Consequently, parishioners used the church grounds for playing 'fives', and more irreverently for cock fighting. Inside is plain and charming: four bays and a simple wooden W. gallery.

CROFT † St Michael and All Angels ★

5m/8km N.W. of Leominster

OS *SO449654* **GPS** *52.2842N, 2.8079W*

The pretty little church is set close by the front door of Croft Castle and is quite dwarfed by its huge bulk. It contains the magnificent tomb of Sir Richard Croft, d. 1509, veteran of the Wars of the Roses. There are early 18th-century box pews and a W. gallery.

DILWYN † St Mary the Virgin ★

6m/10km S.W. of Leominster

OS *SO415546* **GPS** *52.1872N, 2.8568W*

An attractive village with a spacious church, full of light as only the chancel has stained glass, along with lofty 13th-century arcades and a clerestory. The tower of c. 1200 has a small later spire which may be 18th-century.

EARDISLEY † St Mary Magdalene ★★

5m/8km S. of Kington

OS *SO312491* **GPS** *52.1361N, 3.0060W*

The centre of a large parish in which medieval houses abound. The church has a wonderful font carved in c. 1150 with the Harrowing of Hell, two men fighting with sword and spear, and a large lion, second only to that at Castle Frome, and possibly the work of the same stone carver who worked at Kilpeck.

EASTNOR † St John the Baptist ★

1m/2km E. of Ledbury

OS *SO731372* **GPS** *52.0328N, 2.3930W*

The church has a 14th-century tower but, apart from that, was rebuilt by Sir George Gilbert Scott in 1852. It is Scott's 'Middle Pointed' style with an E. window by Kempe. The church contains a Crucifixion attributed to Van Dyck, a Venetian altar frontal and sculpture by Scheemakers under the tower.

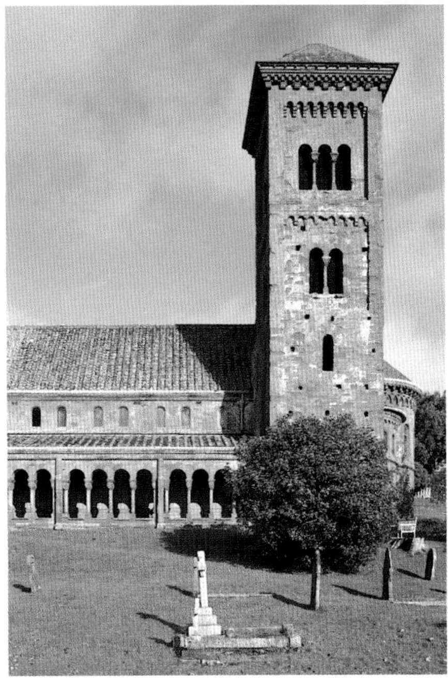

△ **HOARWITHY: ST CATHERINE** – *Seddon's Lombardian vision for the Wye Valley*

EATON BISHOP
† St Michael and All Angels ★

4m/6km W. of Hereford

OS *SO443391* **GPS** *52.0475N, 2.8135W*

A spacious church with tall 13th-century arcades, it has, like some Cotswold churches, a window over the chancel arch. Its chief glory is the early 14th-century glass in the E. window – the finest in the county.

EDVIN LOACH † St Mary the Virgin

2m/3km N. of Bromyard

OS *SO662584* **GPS** *52.2230N, 2.4957W*

The work of Sir George Gilbert Scott, 1859, on a wonderful hill-top site with fine views. The church was built to replace a small early Norman building of pink herringbone masonry and white tufa quoins, the ruins of which can be seen nearby. Scott's church is modest but well-contrived, with a polygonal

apse, W. tower and broach spire. The tower is embraced by the nave and is supported inside on two fat columns with foliate capitals. Good roofs, a timber arch to chancel, fine fittings and Hardman glass.

FOWNHOPE † St Mary ★★

6m/10km S.E. of Hereford
OS *SO581342* **GPS** *52.0053N, 2.6117W*

Set in the village street in a pleasant churchyard, this is perhaps the longest of the county's churches – a large Transitional work, with Norman central tower, later spire and a delightful Herefordshire School tympanum of c. 1150 depicting the Virgin and Child with decorative trails inhabited by a bird and a fierce lion. This is placed inside on the N. end of the W. wall. There is a considerable amount of Romanesque detail outside, and inside a very pleasing sense of space, with a broad, brightly lit S. aisle, a Norman arch to the choir and Early English chancel arch.

GARWAY † St Michael ★

8m/12km W. of Ross-on-Wye
OS *SO455224* **GPS** *51.8982N, 2.7934W*

A wonderful Norman church, associated with the Knights Templar, St Michael's stands on the hill-slopes above the Monnow. The chancel arch has three orders of richly carved chevrons carried on shafts with water-leaf capitals. The 13th-century detached tower was joined to the church by a corridor in the 17th century. To the S. is the Templars' fine circular stone columbarium of 1326; there are also nesting spaces for 666 birds.

HEREFORD † All Saints ★★

High Street, Hereford
OS *SO508400* **GPS** *52.0566N, 2.7176W*

All Saints is late 13th- or early 14th-century, with a spacious lime-washed interior entered directly from the street – a real city church. It has a noble 13th-century tower and spire, whose famous twist was rectified in 1992. The S. chapel has an interesting Wren-style reredos. The fine canopied 14th-century choir-stalls have excellent misericords, and there is a welcoming cafe at the W. end – perhaps everything a modern city church should be.

HOARWITHY † St Catherine ★★

5m/8km N. of Ross-on-Wye
OS *SO545294* **GPS** *51.9613N, 2.6625W*

An important and impressive work by J. P. Seddon in the 1870s, and a bit of Italy in the Wye Valley. Originally a brick church of 1843, Seddon was commissioned by the eccentric and autocratic Parson, and transformed it with Italian Romanesque windows, a campanile, cloisters with mosaic floors and half-apses at the E. end. Inside are Byzantine capitals, a superb gold mosaic of Christ Pantocrator, and rich fittings of marble, lapis lazuli and tesserae; both Italian and local craftsmen were employed.

HOW CAPLE † St Mary

4m/6km N. of Ross-on-Wye
OS *SO611305* **GPS** *51.9720N, 2.5668W*

The church and nearby court are set in a beautifully wooded slope in a loop of the Wye. The church contains a wooden screen supporting the Arms of William III and a pulpit with red-lined canopy; also much fine 20th-century woodwork.

KILPECK † St Mary and St David ★★

7m/11km S.W. of Hereford
OS *SO445305* **GPS** *51.9703N, 2.8091W*

Apart from a corner of the nave which is Saxon, some medieval windows and a bell-cote restored in the 19th century, it all dates from the third quarter of the 12th century. This is one of the most celebrated examples of the rich, late Romanesque style in England, showing influences from all over Europe and Scandinavia, and it marks the highest point of the Herefordshire stone carvers. The S. doorway has a Tree of Life tympanum and carvings of Welsh warriors in Phrygian caps. There is an exceptionally varied carved corbel table with a Sheela-na-Gig, entertainers, a dog, doves, hares, embracing lovers – as Jenkins says, 'all the life of a bawdy and busy Herefordshire village'. The chancel arch has draped and nimbused Apostles. During the restoration by Lewis Cottingham in 1848 some of the grotesques and carved figures around the S. doorway were 're-worked'.

◁ **KILPECK: ST MARY AND ST DAVID** – *the ornamentation around the south door is a tour de force of 12th-century Herefordshire stone carving*

KINNERSLEY † St James ★

10m/16km N.W. of Hereford

OS *SO345496* **GPS** *52.1410N, 2.9577W*

This lovely 14th-century church with a fortified saddleback N.W. tower stands near the imposing Elizabethan castle. The well-executed chancel and nave decoration was by Reverend Andrews, the rector in the late 19th and early 20th centuries, to designs by G. F. Bodley. On the chancel wall is a monument to Francis Smallman and his wife, both flanked by trumpeting angels.

LEDBURY

† St Michael and All Angels ★★

12m/19km E. of Hereford

OS *SO712377* **GPS** *52.0370N, 2.4201W*

This fine church in rich golden sandstone keeps well back from the town centre, which can be reached by a cobbled walk past medieval buildings. Some Norman work, but mostly early 14th-century, with lavish use of ballflowers. The early 13th-century detached tower stands to the N. of the church, imposing and lofty with a high 18th-century spire. The W. front of the church is Norman, with zigzags, and inside is a very rudimentary Norman chancel, much at odds with the spacious Decorated nave and aisles, with their fine Reticulated windows. The N. chapel was once a chapter house, and it too has magnificent windows. There is a good collection of monuments with works by Flaxman and Westmacott; the stained glass is by Kempe and others.

LEOMINSTER † St Peter and St Paul ★★

12m/19km N. of Hereford

OS *SO498592* **GPS** *52.2294N, 2.7356W*

Built of local sandstone, St Peter and St Paul's is only a part of the original priory, but a very fine one. There is a large tower at the W. end, with a marvellous 12th-century carved doorway. The N. side is the old monastic church, with fine Norman arches; in the centre is the 13th-century parish church, and to the S. is a 14th-century aisle with magnificent Decorated windows ornamented with a profusion of ballflowers both inside and out: an instructional mix of every building style.

LLANVEYNOE

† St Beuno and St Peter ★

12m/19km S.W. of Hereford

OS *SO303313* **GPS** *51.9764N, 3.0161W*

This small, delightful church is worth visiting for its beautiful hillside setting, and a wonderfully crude 10th-century carved panel of the Crucifixion.

MADLEY

† Nativity of the Blessed Virgin Mary ★★

6m/10km W. of Hereford

OS *SO419387* **GPS** *52.0438N, 2.8471W*

Set in a large, partly black and white village that has a cross retaining its original shaft, this is a superb large sandstone church, built in the 13th and 14th centuries and structurally unaltered. The polygonal apsidal chancel has a wealth of reinstated 14th-century glass windows, and the Decorated and Reticulated tracery of the nave and S. chapel windows is outstanding.

MATHON † St John the Baptist

3m/4km W. of Great Malvern

OS *SO733458* **GPS** *52.1103N, 2.3903W*

Of Norman origins; there is a good medieval W. tower, and a 14th-century tie-beam roof with cusping; the S. porch is timber, and there is a Jacobean pulpit.

MOCCAS † St Michael and All Angels ★

10m/16km N.W. of Hereford

OS *SO357432* **GPS** *52.0841N, 2.9391W*

Set in the park of Moccas Court – a house built to the designs of Robert Adam – stands an excellent example of a Norman church with rounded apse. Most lovingly restored by G. G. Scott Jnr, it was built of calcareous tufa in the second quarter of the 12th century. There are two carved Norman doorways and some 14th-century glass.

MONNINGTON-ON-WYE † St Mary

10m/16km N.W. of Hereford

OS *SO373433* **GPS** *52.0847N, 2.9156W*

Set in lush water meadows by the Wye, this is a Gothic Survival church of 1679, with a 15th-century tower. The church is a period piece, with twisted balusters everywhere, delightful oak benches, pulpit and a Royal

LEOMINSTER: ST PETER AND ST PAUL – *this valuable remnant of a former priory contains traces of every style of Gothic architecture* ▷

△ **YARPOLE: ST LEONARD** – *the detached bell-tower, which could be 12th-century*

Arms of Charles II. The timber-framed lych gate is of the same date.

MUCH COWARNE

† St Mary the Virgin ★

5m/8km S.W. of Bromyard

OS *SO618471* **GPS** *52.1212N, 2.5584W*

Set on top of a hill in undulating hop country, the church has a tall, graceful Early English arcade between nave and S. aisle, in which are the early 17th-century effigies of Edmund Fox and his wife lying on an altar tomb of fine design. The interior is light and beautiful.

MUCH MARCLE † St Bartholomew ★

7m/11km N.E. of Ross-on-Wye

OS *SO657327* **GPS** *51.9921N, 2.5008W*

The church, with its 13th-century nave, clerestory, central tower and very long chancel, has some fine monuments, including a lovely mid-14th-century woman, Blanche Mortimer, d. 1347, and, in the Kyrle Chapel, John Kyrle, d. 1660, and his wife Sybille Scudamore. In the nave is an unusual effigy of a yeoman named Walter de Helyon, d. c. 1357, carved from a solid oak block.

PEMBRIDGE † St Mary the Virgin ★

6m/10km E. of Kington

OS *SO390580* **GPS** *52.2174N, 2.8929W*

Set in a compact village of old timber-framed houses, this church is a fine example of the early Decorated style. But the most celebrated thing here is the remarkable detached 13th-century bell-house of Swedish type, the inside of which resembles a dark forest of ancient timbers. The stone walls and outlying trusses of the bell-house were added in the 15th and 16th centuries. The N. porch of the church is 14th-century, and has a ribbed, stone-vaulted ceiling. On the door is the original sanctuary knocker.

PETERCHURCH † St Peter ★

9m/13km W. of Hereford

OS *SO344385* **GPS** *52.0412N, 2.9564W*

On the banks of the River Dore in the Golden Valley stands this large, well-preserved Norman church, with traces of earlier Saxon work in the apse. Nave, double chancel and apse are all linked by tall, plain, rounded arches that progressively diminish in size, enhancing the feeling of distance between the nave and apse. The austere interior is enhanced by the blacksmith-made light-fittings, though the walls are scraped and badly pointed. The spire, visible from miles around, is a fibreglass replacement for the original, which was reduced and eventually dismantled in the mid-20th century.

RICHARDS CASTLE

† St Bartholomew ★

3m/4km S. of Ludlow

OS *SO484702* **GPS** *52.3282N, 2.7581W*

Churches Conservation Trust

Set on the hill near the earthworks of a Norman castle and the woods haunted by John Milton's treacherous Comus character, the detached early 14th-century tower is a splendid foil to the great bulk of the church. Inside, there are 17th-century box pews and, in the N. chapel, a family pew and some 14th-century glass. The E. window has the most lovely flowing tracery.

ROWLESTONE † St Peter ★

9m/14km N.W of Abergavenny
OS *SO373271* **GPS** *51.9391N, 2.9123W*

On the hills between the Monnow River and Dulas Brook stands a 12th-century church with finely carved S. doorway, tympanum and chancel arch. The capitals of the openings are carved with birds and intertwining foliage of great character. Late 15th-century candle-brackets illuminate the chancel.

SARNESFIELD † St Mary ★

11m/18km N.W. of Hereford
OS *SO374509* **GPS** *52.1531N, 2.9153W*

This is a very pretty grey-stone 12th-century church, with a lime-washed interior, elegant candelabra and wall monuments. The churchyard tomb is of John Abel, King's Carpenter, 1577–1674.

SELLACK † St Tysilio

3m/4km N.W. of Ross-on-Wye
OS *SO565276* **GPS** *51.9457N, 2.6337W*

A Norman and later church with a Decorated W. tower and fine broach spire. There is a good Jacobean gallery, pulpit and communion rails, and set in the E. window is a stained-glass composition of 1630, possibly re-assembled by Richard Scudamore, whose monogram can be seen in the glass.

SHOBDON † St John the Evangelist ★★

6m/10km N.W. of Leominster
OS *SO401628* **GPS** *52.2605N, 2.8788W*

The celebrated Georgian Gothic Revival church of 1752–6 is the work of The Hon. Richard Bateman of Shobdon Court, friend of Horace Walpole. Whimsical Rococo-Gothic interior with enormous pews painted white, two tiny transepts containing the family and servants' pews and a chancel framed by a 'proscenium' arch. The pulpit is in similar vein, and appears to float in mid air. The whole effect is extremely pretty and is now much admired, though in the past antiquarians have suffered anguish because its Romanesque predecessor was despoiled; the weather-beaten remains of its carved arches are in a field close by, but the Norman font has been restored to the church.

TYBERTON † St Mary

8m/12km W. of Hereford
OS *SO380398* **GPS** *52.0539N, 2.9053W*

Rebuilt in 1720, it retains a late Norman doorway. Built of brick, with a pretty tower surmounted by a stone cornice, pediments and urns, the exterior has been spoiled by ugly windows of 1879. Inside, however, the magnificent carved panels in the apse were designed by John Wood in 1728 and bear the Symbols of the Passion in a spirit of mysticism and communion most uncommon for the period. The other furnishings are contemporary, and there are monuments to the Brydges family.

VOWCHURCH † St Bartholomew ★

8m/12km W. of Hereford
OS *SO361364* **GPS** *52.0229N, 2.9313W*

Largely 14th-century fabric with a black and white bellcote of c. 1522, surmounted by a diminutive broach spire. The roof, supported on an internal oak frame, was reconstructed as part of a major re-ordering of the church, c. 1613. The timbers create a pleasing if eccentric impression of a copse. The rustic screen, stalls and communion rail are all 17th-century; there is a crude rendition of Adam and Eve on one of the screen posts.

YARPOLE † St Leonard

4m/6km N.W. of Leominster
OS *SO469648* **GPS** *52.2794N, 2.7785W*

The bell-tower with pyramidal roof is possibly the earliest known example of a detached bell-tower in England, with weatherboarded bell-stage, quatrefoils and a spire. Inside are free-standing posts with scissor bracing, and the door has long iron hinges; it could all be as early as the 12th century. Ancient though it may be, St Leonard's may represent the future of many rural churches: not only does it serve as a church, but also as a village shop, post office, café and art gallery.

HERTFORDSHIRE

At first sight Hertfordshire has little to offer in the way of churches: for a number of reasons there are, with the exception of Hemel Hempstead, no churches of outstanding merit in the county. Indeed, like the landscape in which they are set, these churches are distinguished rather for their seemliness and moderation than for more dramatic qualities.

Physically, Hertfordshire is a county of undulating chalkland with some deposits of glacial clay in the river valleys of the south and east. The only strongly marked features are the Chiltern Hills; entering the county in the south-east above Tring, they form a diagonal ridge across to the north-east, dying away beyond Royston into the Essex uplands. Because of the geological formation there is, except for flint rubble, no building stone, and the cost of transporting stone precluded its use, except for piers, tombs, window tracery and dressings. Where stone was used it was generally Totternhoe or other clunches from the lower and middle chalk, and, because of their poor weathering qualities, there is very little original stonework to be seen externally. A hardness in the appearance of many of the old churches is due to the replacement of weathered stone.

Formerly the county was heavily wooded, large areas being covered by the Chiltern, Middlesex and Essex forests. This had more effect on secular than ecclesiastical work, but there are some good roofs and screens, and timberwork found in porches.

Historically and socially, Hertfordshire suffered from three things: firstly, St Albans Abbey; secondly, good roads that divided the county; and thirdly, the lack of any strong central influence.

It might have been expected that St Albans Abbey – one of the wealthiest in the country – would have been the dominant source of architecural influence in the area. This, however, was not the case: due to the constant mismanagement of its finances and estates, the Abbey was kept in a state of chronic insolvency, and the county in a state of incessant agrarian disturbances. No abbot was ever able to embark on any vigorous building programme which might have influenced local masons.

The second and third factors are, to a large extent, interrelated. Except for the ancient Icknield Way, the main roads of the Middle Ages, which followed the lines of the older Roman roads – Watling St, Ermine St, Stone St, Akeman St and the later Great North Road – all ran roughly north to south. Even today cross-country journeys are awkward and inconvenient; in the Middle Ages they must have been almost out of the question. The result is that the county has developed architecturally in strips. The best buildings are to be found in the long one-street towns and villages. Family traits are found in groups of churches along one road which are not found in churches along the others. This has led to comparatively unspoilt areas between the main traffic lanes; once away from

◁ **KNEBWORTH: ST MARY AND ST THOMAS** – *presiding over the Lytton Chapel, the monument to the doubly named Lytton Lytton, d. 1710*

these roads the county retains much of its rural character unchanged.

Admittedly there are bad patches, which are getting worse: motorways have blighted large areas, and the road from London out through Waltham Cross is an eyesore. New Towns are spreading; and Watford was vulgarized by the 20th century. On the whole, however, Hertfordshire has been luckier than might have been expected from its proximity to London.

Today few country churches are so convincingly the 'village church' as those of Hertfordshire. Fabrics are generally in good repair; and churchyards, by present-day standards, not ill-kept. The most striking feature is generally the tower, sturdy and battlemented, usually with a taller stair-turret and crowned with the ubiquitous spirelet, known locally as a 'snuffer' or 'spike'.

Most churches in the county can show something of interest – often in the shape of magnificent monuments of the 16th, 17th and 18th centuries. The many country houses – especially those of retired London merchants – meant a number of wealthy, if not always distinguished, dead, whose taste for tombs of a modest piety has led to many fine and not a few extraordinary examples of funereal sculpture.

Woodwork, too, is widespread and interesting, and often – as at Hitchin – of a very high standard. Of pre-Reformation figure-carving there is little, and of old glass even less. Brasses, though, are to be found in most churches.

The Victorians were, on the whole, kind to Hertfordshire. Restorations, if lacking in character, are seldom out of period or locality: most of the great names of the period are represented, but seldom in a manner to cause comment.

Of the four or five Gothic Revival churches of merit, the finest in the county is the Roman Catholic Church

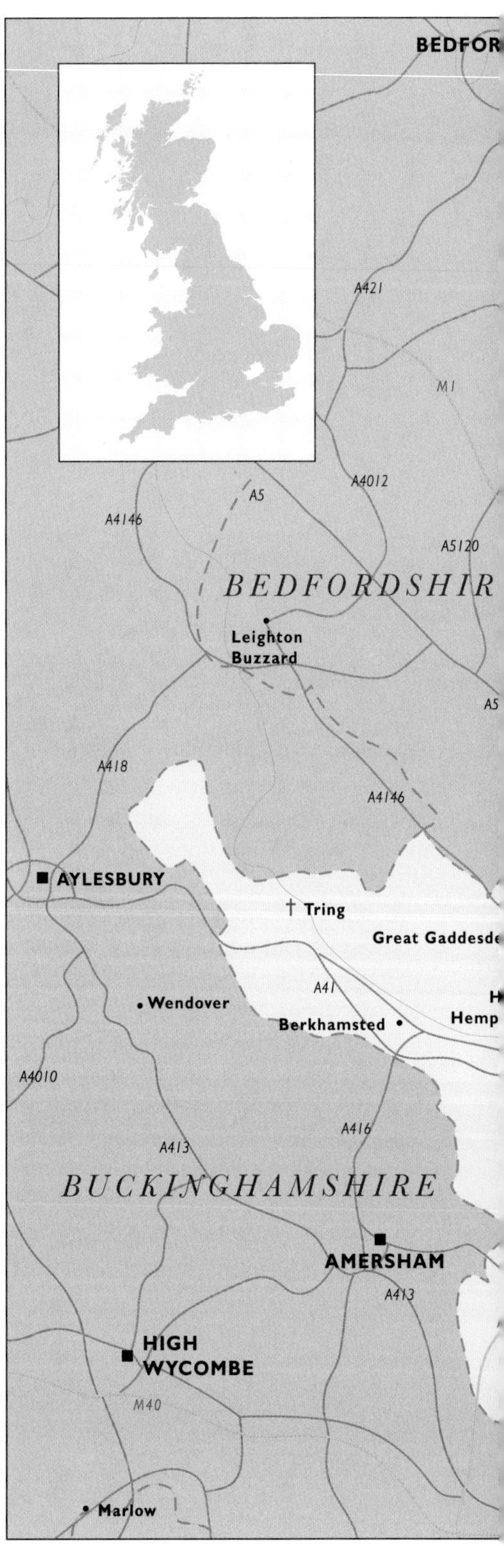

CAMBRIDGESHIRE
HERTFORDSHIRE
ESSEX
GREATER LONDON
Biggleswade
Ashwell
Royston
Baldock
Letchworth
Anstey
Hitchin
Little Hormead
Offley
STEVENAGE
St Paul's Walden
Benington
Bishop's Stortford
Stansted
Knebworth
Woolmer Green
Much Hadham
Ayot St Lawrence
Ayot St Peter
Waterford
Ware
Sawbridgeworth
Wheathampstead
Bengeo
Welwyn Garden City
Hertford
Great Amwell
Stanstead Abbots
Redbourn
HARLOW
Hatfield
Hoddesdon
St Albans
Broxbourne
South Mimms
Potters Bar
Barnet
Enfield
Chigwell
Harrow
A603
M11
A1
A505
A600
A507
A10
A1(M)
A602
A120
M10
M25
A111
M1
A41
A406
A12
0
5 miles
5 km

of the Holy Rood at Watford; it is by Bentley, and should not be missed. And, of course, the seeker after curiosities should visit St Albans for the work of Edmund Beckett, 1st Baron Grimthorpe, whose unsympathetic and controversial 'restorations' to parts of St Alban's Cathedral gave rise to the creation of the perjorative verb 'to grimpthorpe'.

△ **WATERFORD: ST MICHAEL AND ALL ANGELS** – *two of the windows made by Morris & Co. to designs by Burne-Jones; on the left is Prophetess Miriam and on the right King David*

ANSTEY † St George ★
5m/8km S.E. of Royston
OS *TL404328* **GPS** *51.9767N, 0.0431E*

This is a strangely impressive building which appears larger at first sight than it actually is, and is pleasingly free from restoration. The lower stages of the central tower, c. 1200, show the transition from Romanesque to Gothic. The chancel is a roomy 13th-century design, with 16th-century stalls and misericords, and unusual sedilia and piscina. The transepts, with squints to the chancel, are 13th-century. The nave is of 14th-century design with a clerestory and 15th-century roof. In the churchyard is the 15th-century lych gate.

ASHWELL † St Mary the Virgin ★★
4m/6km N.E. of Baldock
OS *TL267397* **GPS** *52.0419N, 0.1539W*

This magnificent 14th-century church belongs more to East Anglia than Hertfordshire. Both its design and the clarity of light, due to a lack of stained glass, remove Ashwell in feeling from the Home Counties. The W. tower is remarkable for its height, its buttresses, the use of clunch as a facing material, and its extremely elegant timber and lead spirelet. The interior shows a steady development from E. to W., the large aisleless chancel having been begun c. 1340, and the nave being finished c. 1380. The narrow W. bay of the nave was formed between the W. buttresses of the tower, which were decorated with blind full-height arches. There are 15th-century sedilia, 15th-century screens in the aisles, and a 17th-century pulpit and communion table. In the tower are two interesting graffiti – an inscription from the time of the plague of 1665 and a drawing of old St Paul's Cathedral.

AYOT ST LAWRENCE
† St Lawrence ★★
2m/3km N.W. of Welwyn Garden City
OS *TL191168* **GPS** *51.8380N, 0.2717W*

St Lawrence's church, which looks like a Greek temple with flanking pavilions and linking screens, was designed in 1778–9 by Nicholas Revett to terminate a view in the park in which the old church was left to be a Gothic ruin. It is an exercise in the application of Greek detail to a Palladian composition. Internally the Classicism is of Rome and not of Greece: a Rome, however, which has been tempered to unexceptionable Anglicanism of the 18th century. The rectangular nave is entered from the vestibule through a columned screen. The nave has a coffered ceiling and is flanked by two deep arched recesses; the E. end is a coffered apse.

AYOT ST PETER † St Peter ★★
1m/2km N.W. of Welwyn Garden City
OS *TL218149* **GPS** *51.8201N, 0.2335W*

This isolated polychromatic patterned brick church was designed by J. P. Seddon to replace an earlier church destroyed by fire. The external brickwork is bold – lozenge patterning on the apse, banding on the main body of the church and panels on the tower. Inside is Arts and Crafts combined with Victorian Gothic: a ceramic chancel arch by Walter Martin leads to a richly decorated apse, with painted roof panels showing sun, stars and angels, highly coloured organ pipes and ceramic floor tiles; and at the W. end, a font decorated with mosaic stands on coloured shafts. The detail is excellent, and the whole is a fine example of Seddon's originality.

BENGEO † St Leonard
N. district of Hertford
OS *TL330136* **GPS** *51.8056N, 0.0721W*

Built of flint and stone dressing, St Leonard's is one of Hertford's oldest buildings, a largely unchanged survival from the 12th century. After 1855 the church stood empty, until the Gosselins of Bengeo Hall undertook a restoration in the late 19th century, replacing the chancel roof and adding a small timbered belfry at the W. end. The brick porch is 18th-century. Remnants of medieval wall-paintings were discovered by William Weir during his 1938 restoration.

BENINGTON † St Peter
4m/6km E. of Stevenage
OS *TL296235* **GPS** *51.8957N, 0.1166W*

In a beautiful tree-shaded setting off the village green, this is a simple 13th–15th-century church, restored in 1889, with a fine Decorated N. chantry chapel containing good altar tombs to the de Benstede family. There are also pre-Reformation pews and interesting corbel heads supporting the roof timbers.

BISHOP'S STORTFORD

† St Michael ★

8m/12km N. of Harlow

OS *TL486213* **GPS** *51.8708N, 0.1574E*

Externally this large 15th-century church shows an amusing contrast between the solidity of the original work and the flimsiness of the upper stages of the tower and spire, which were added in 1812. It dominates the town in distant views. The roofs are original – that of the nave having finely traceried spandrels and resting on stone corbels carved as Apostles and shield-bearing angels. In the aisles a more secular note is struck, and the corbels include a cook, a woodman and a gardener. The label-stops of the nave arcade still bear their original head carvings. The greater part of the richly carved rood screen and the original choir stalls survive, with carved misericords and traceried backs.

BROXBOURNE † St Augustine ★

S. suburb of Hoddesdon

OS *TL371069* **GPS** *51.7444N, 0.0147W*

Attractively set on a bank of the River Lea, St Augustine's is flint-walled except for the ashlar-faced N. chapel and vestry of 1522: the tiled and leaded roofs are largely 15th-century. Inside, the nave and chancel are of six bays without a break and with original roofs. The altar tomb in the chancel of Sir John Say, d. 1474, and his wife has brasses and much original colour, and there are other later Say tombs in the chancel, among them the 16th-century tomb of Sir William Say. There are a number of brasses and monuments, and the S. door is an exuberant piece of work of c. 1640 with pilasters and segmental pediment.

FLAMSTEAD † St Leonard

5m/8km N. of Hemel Hempstead

OS *TL078145* **GPS** *51.8192N, 0.4362W*

The 13th-century nave has stiff-leaf capitals and a good 15th-century screen supporting carved wooden Rood figures from Oberamagau in Bavaria, donated in 1909 by Sir Edgar Saunders Sebright. There are fragmentary medieval wall-paintings in the N. aisle and nave, 13th–15th-century, with Apostles, St Christopher, the Passion and bits of a Doom. Elizabethan graffiti can be seen on some of the pillars, and there are fine monuments by William Stanton and John Flaxman.

GREAT AMWELL † St John the Baptist

1m/2km S.E. of Ware

OS *TL371125* **GPS** *51.7944N, 0.0122W*

Picturesquely set above a water garden created in 1800 to celebrate Sir Hugh Myddelton, 17th-century originator of the New River, this country church is as attractive as its setting, with Norman apsidal chancel and 15th-century tower. In the churchyard are good Georgian monuments, including that to Robert Mylne, architect and creator of the water garden.

GREAT GADDESDEN

† St John Baptist ★

3m/4km N.E. of Berkhamsted

OS *TL028112* **GPS** *51.7906N, 0.5099W*

A comparatively unspoilt building, but its development is obscure – probably a 12th-century fabric enlarged in succeeding centuries. S. nave arcade shows stiff-leaf capitals similar to Flamstead and Offley, and a 15th-century clerestory and roof. The N. chapel, a particularly mean little building of 1730, was built to house the remains of the Halseys of Gaddesden Place, to whose memory there are at least 22 monuments in the church. As most of them are white marble it is not surprising that it seems a chilly little place.

HATFIELD † St Etheldreda ★★

Next to Hatfield House

OS *TL235084* **GPS** *51.7615N, 0.2118W*

To the Glory of God and the House of Cecil: The enormous unaisled nave of St Etheldreda's is a 19th-century rebuilding on the original lines. The interest is in the S. transept with its stiff-leaf capitals and very good Burne-Jones glass, and the Brockett Chapel – essentially still Tudor, with much colour and heraldry, where Sir John Brockett, d. 1598, is commemorated by a wall memorial (his

△ **BENGEO: ST LEONARD** – *a Baroque monument for Humphrey Hall in the chancel; the wall behind has a medieval diaper pattern, itself superimposed upon an earlier white block pattern*

helmet hung high above). The 17th-century N. chapel is a complete contrast. Here lies Robert Cecil, 1st Earl of Salisbury, his effigy on a slab carried by four kneeling Virtues with a cadaver below, by Maximilian Colt, c. 1612. A fine 18th-century iron screen from Amiens guards the chapel.

HEMEL HEMPSTEAD † St Mary ★

7m/11km N.W. of Watford

OS *TL055078* **GPS** *51.7591N, 0.4728W*

This large 12th-century town church, with central tower and 14th-century timber spire, is the finest in the county. It stands at the end of the old town, farthest removed from New Town development. Begun c. 1140 and about 40 years in the building, it is, apart from the porches, vestries and spire, all of the one period. The nave of six bays with aisles is unusual for possessing a clerestory (not common in a building of that period), and the chancel has a rare 12th-century rib vault. The chancel was vivaciously decorated by Bodley in 1888, but has since been whitewashed; the glass is by Clayton & Bell.

HITCHIN † St Mary ★

8m/12km N.E. of Luton

OS *TL184291* **GPS** *51.9480N, 0.2773W*

The size of the church and the richness of its surviving fittings show that late medieval Hitchin was a town of some wealth; the early street plan and a number of good old buildings survive. The church is a most pleasantly textured building, showing great variation in material, including a 12th–13th-century W. tower and spectacular 15th-century vaulted S. porch of two storeys. It bears the Arms of the Staple of Calais and was probably paid for by Nicholas Mattock, a merchant. Good 14th–15th-century roofs, a fine set of traceried Perpendicular screens, 12-sided apostles' font and a panelled pulpit all signify a church of importance. The woodwork is without equal in the county.

KNEBWORTH † St Martin ★

1m/2km S. of Stevenage

OS *TL252200* **GPS** *51.8654N, 0.1817W*

A capricious and engaging mixture of Gothic and Classicism, Lutyens' 1915 church has a character all of its own. Inside are elements of the Byzantine, Doric columns, a broad and

△ **KNEBWORTH: ST MARY AND ST THOMAS** – *a mix of rusticism and refinery*

shallow apsidal chancel, and the organ pipes are a helical swirl arising from what appears to be an umbrella stand. Arches predominate, and, although Lutyens did not finish the church (it was completed in the 1960s by his friend Sir Albert Richardson), the furnishings are mostly his.

KNEBWORTH

† St Mary and St Thomas ★★

By Old Knebworth village, 1m/2km S. of Stevenage
OS *TL230210* **GPS** *51.8741N, 0.2135W*

The church stands in the grounds of Knebworth House and dates in part from the 12th century. Outwardly plain, it contains some outstanding contents: a Georgian pulpit with 16th-century Flemish panels, fine 15th-century oak pews, a 17th-century Italian painting of The Last Supper behind the altar, and the imposing Lytton Chapel, with its Lutyens screen and monuments. Here is a spectacular muster of the Lyttons; Lytton Strode Lytton, d.1710, Sir William Lytton, d. 1705, Sir George Strode, d. 1707, and William Lyton Strode, d. 1732, with his wife.

LITTLE HORMEAD † St Mary

3m/4km E. of Buntingford
OS *TL398291* **GPS** *51.9429N, 0.0332E*
Churches Conservation Trust

This is a small, largely Norman church set on high ground, with a remarkable display of lavish 12th-century ironwork on the N. door – now preserved inside the church. There is a Charles II Arms of 1660 over the fine Norman chancel arch, and a well-carved 14th-century font.

MUCH HADHAM † St Andrew

4m/6km W. of Bishop's Stortford
OS *TL430196* **GPS** *51.8573N, 0.0756E*

Next to the palace that had been the country retreat of Bishops of London for some 800 years, St Andrew's is a much rebuilt 12th-century church, with the chancel, c. 1220, the S. aisle, c. 1250, and the N. aisle, c. 1300, culminating with the tower of c. 1380. In the 15th century the clerestory, roofs, S. porch and many windows were renewed. The roofs are very good and have hardly been touched since they were first built. The screen and chancel stalls are also 15th-century, and

△ **KNEBWORTH: ST MARY AND ST THOMAS** – *Sir William Lytton's monument by Edward Stanton*

there is a sprinkling of brasses, and charming embroidered padded kneelers.

OFFLEY † St Mary Magdalene
3m/4km S.W. of Hitchin
OS *TL145268* **GPS** *51.9281N, 0.3357W*

This strange church looks as though it is the result of a random assembly of Gothic, medieval and Georgian. Sir Thomas Salisbury was responsible for both the Gothic brick tower and the extraordinary Portland stone Georgian chancel of c. 1777. The latter is rectangular and almost windowless, being lit by a roof light. Though hideous from outside, inside a sumptuous stucco baldacchino is set over the E. window. On the S. wall is a delightful monument by Nollekens to Sir Thomas Salisbury. The Gothic brick W. tower is of 1800.

REDBOURN † St Mary
4m/6km N.W. of St Albans
OS *TL099115* **GPS** *51.7920N, 0.4065W*

In an attractive village setting, this is a charming church in a pleasing green setting. The stocky tower is Norman and the church was enlarged in the 14th and 15th centuries. The E. window has good Reticulated tracery, and is set in chequered stonework. Much Norman work can be seen in the N. arcade, and there is a well-preserved rood screen of 1478, an early 18th-century font and monuments in the chancel.

SAWBRIDGEWORTH † Great St Mary
4m/6km N.E. of Harlow
OS *TL485148* **GPS** *51.8123N, 0.1528E*

This is a spacious, principally Decorated church, with a Tudor tower and 15th-century screen. There is a remarkable collection of medieval and later brasses and monuments, including brasses of the family and friends of Ralph Jocelyn, twice Lord Mayor of London in the 15th century.

SOUTH MIMMS † St Giles ★
2m/3km W. of Potters Bar
OS *TL222011* **GPS** *51.6962N, 0.2328W*

This flint-knapped church, built in stages from the 12th to the 15th century, was restored by Street in the 1870s; the pulpit reflects his time. The font cover and chapel window are

WATERFORD: ST MICHAEL AND ALL ANGELS – *the mosaic-tiled and gilded chancel with reredos behind the altar table by Powell & Sons* ▷

HOPE
AWAKE

REJOICE

△ **ST ALBANS: ST MICHAEL** – *a figure rising from her grave in the Doom painting*

by Comper (early 20th century), and there is medieval glass in the N. aisle windows. In the Frowke Chapel, formerly the chantry, is a fine Tudor monument to Henry Frowke the Younger, whilst in the chancel is a similarly fine early Classical monument to his father, Henry Frowke the Elder.

ST ALBANS † St Michael

St Michael's Street
OS *TL135073* **GPS** *51.7529N, 0.3561W*

The 10th–11th-century nave has the remains of a Saxon doorway and window arches of Roman brick; there are Norman arcades, an Early English clerestory and a fine 15th-century roof. Like St Albans Cathedral, St Michael's received the attention of Lord Grimthorpe, who extended the nave and built the tower. There is a very fine Elizabethan oak pulpit, and a marble effigy – possibly by Nicholas Stone – of Sir Francis Bacon, d. 1626, in the chancel. The remaining portion of a Doom, rather beautifully painted on wooden panels, now hangs on the nave wall over the doorway.

ST PAUL'S WALDEN † All Saints

3m/4km W. of Stevenage
OS *TL192222* **GPS** *51.8864N, 0.2687W*

This is the parish church of the Bowes-Lyon family, where Elizabeth the Queen Mother was baptised in 1900. The modest Decorated and Perpendicular collide abruptly with the exuberantly Classical chancel, frothy Baroque screen and lofty reredos, all of 1727 and by Gilbert White, related by marriage to the Bowes of Durham.

STANSTEAD ABBOTS
† (Old) St James ★

3m/4km S.E. of Ware (the old church is not in the village, but 1m/2km out on the road to Roydon)
OS *TL399110* **GPS** *51.7807N, 0.0277E*
Churches Conservation Trust

Steeped in atmosphere, the church has a completely unspoilt interior, with 18th-century box pews, altar rail and three-decker pulpit. The tower is 15th-century, as is the handsome timbered S. porch. There are good early 19th-century memorials

TRING † St Peter and St Paul

5m/8km N.W. of Berkhamsted
OS *SP924114* **GPS** *51.7945N, 0.6611W*

The distinctive nave piers with attached shafts are actually replicas of the 16th-century originals, which had been painted to simulate blue marble c. 1715; in 1815 the rector, Charles Lacey, had them repainted white. The painted chancel ceiling, rood screen and choir stalls are by G. F. Bodley in 1899–1900. Inside is a spectacular monument to Sir William and Lady Gore, 1707.

WARE † St Mary ★

2m/3km E. of Hertford
OS *TL356144* **GPS** *51.8120N, 0.0332W*

St Mary's is very large, very handsome and externally very much restored. Inside, what one can see today dates from the late 14th century and early 15th century. It is unusual that the transepts should be carried to full nave height and endowed with clerestories. The nave arcades are particularly fine, with the main mouldings running unbroken to the floor. Between the chancel and S. chapel is a handsome fan arch, similar to one at

Luton. The S. chapel also possesses some fine 17th-century panelling, with openwork scrolling and 17th-century communion rails and table. The octagonal font of c. 1380 is the most elaborate in the county, with panelled sides in high relief. The carving has considerable vigour, well above the usual 'shop work' standard.

WATERFORD
† St Michael and All Angels ★

2m/3km N.W. of Hertford

OS *TL312146* **GPS** *51.8152N, 0.0971W*

By Henry Woodyer, 1871–2, the church has a modest medieval exterior with timber bell-turret and shingled broach spire. But inside is a display of Victorian ecclesiological fireworks, with brilliant gilded mosaics in the chancel and a rich reredos by Powell & Sons. Best of all, though, is the set of excellent stained-glass windows by Morris & Co. in conjunction with Burne-Jones and Ford Madox Brown.

WATFORD † St Mary

Church St, Watford

OS *TQ110963* **GPS** *51.6547N, 0.3957W*

An oasis of quiet in Hertfordshire's largest, ugliest and noisiest town. The churchyard has 16th-century almshouses and an 18th-century Free School around it. The church is over-restored outside, but this treatment is not so apparent inside – basically a large 13th-century church, to which clerestory, new arcades and S. chancel chapel were added in the 15th century. Of the 13th century, there remains the chancel arch, the arches and responds of the S. arcade, and the beautiful double piscina in the chancel. The woodwork, except for the 15th-century nave roof and the pulpit of 1714, is generally 19th-century, very good of its period, and quite unusual restraint is shown in the design. The pride of St Mary's is the Morison Chapel of 1597, separated from the chancel by a Tuscan arcade. The Morison tombs, largely of alabaster, are the work of Nicholas Stone. Both show semi-reclining lifesize figures under rich canopies, with kneeling mourners.

WATFORD † Holy Rood RC ★★

Market St, Watford

OS *TQ108963* **GPS** *51.6548N, 0.3986W*

When J. F. Bentley built this lively and fine late 19th-century church, he was at the height of his career, and it is arguably one of the finest 19th-century churches, showing creative ingenuity in its use of a restricted floor area and a sensitivity to furnishing and decoration. The restraint of the nave, lit by Art Nouveau light fittings, serves to accentuate Bentley's monolithic and dramatic rood, and the vaulted and painted chancel beyond. The chancel is alive with wallflowers, carved vines and foliage on the capitals; there is green and gold diaper work in the piscina alcove, and paintings of saints and angels; all this is set under a ceiling of powdery blue. The Holy Ghost Chapel, at the N.W. end, is a masterpiece: intricately painted fan vaulting, and a dignified mural of the Pentecost set above the altar.

WHEATHAMPSTEAD † St Helen

3m/4km E. of Harpenden

OS *TL176140* **GPS** *51.8125N, 0.2947W*

Originally a Norman cruciform church, it is now mostly 13th-century onward. The richly Decorated N. transept is the best work of its date in the county. A 14th-century reredos of seven canopied niches was uncovered in the Lamer Chapel during the 1865 restoration.

WOOLMER GREEN † St Michael

2m/3km N.E. of Welwyn

OS *TL254184* **GPS** *51.8506N, 0.1801W*

A red brick essay in the Arts and Crafts tradition, this is the work of R. Weir Schultz, 1899–1900. It has an effective interior, with a panelled wagon roof, tiled chancel and traceried screen. There are good bronze and wooden fittings in the apsidal sanctuary, which is approached up green marble steps.

KENT

This is the county that seems the longest inhabited in historic times. The Romans lived here, St Augustine landed here, Saxons and Normans have left their mark. The two ancient sees of the county, Canterbury and Rochester, were both founded in the reign of the Saxon King Ethelbert (d. 616). The shrine of St Thomas à Becket in Canterbury Cathedral was the greatest place of medieval pilgrimage in England, and even today, when London has engulfed much of the north of the county, there is a feel of Kent about its suburban corner, and of pilgrims setting out down the Old Kent Road.

The long civilization of the county is summarized in the soaring stateliness of Canterbury Cathedral, whose architecture from Norman to Perpendicular is magnificent, and whose 13th-century glass in quality, if not quantity, equals that of Chartres and Bourges.

Kent has always been the doorstep of England from the Continent; it is the county one thinks of when invasion is threatened, from Roman times till the Battle of Britain. And seen first, after arrival home from abroad, with white chalk cliffs, the hops and orchards and oast-houses, the warm red-tile-hung houses and timbered yeoman's farms, the oaks and filbert copses of the Weald, the flint and ragstone churches are a graceful sight. Right across the county from west to east runs a high range of chalk hills, from Surrey to Dover, cleft in two places by Kent's chief rivers, the Medway and the Stour, with Maidstone on the Medway and Canterbury on the Stour. On the hilly Sussex borders was ironstone and once an iron industry. On the northern border along the Thames estuary are marshes with old-fashioned towns like Gravesend, Sheerness and Whitstable, and the Medway ports of Strood and Chatham, all of which are still weatherboarded and Dickensian in their older side streets. Far away in the south-east corner is the Romney Marsh, a flat sheep-nibbled kingdom with oak posts and rails, few trees and wind-swept salty churches. The rest of the county inland is what is always called 'The Garden of England'.

Kent's oldest towns are associated with pilgrims, beer and the sea. In late Georgian and early Victorian days, the coast became popular as a seaside resort. Heme Bay, Margate, Ramsgate and Dover have their stucco, Brighton-style terraces. Later, Folkestone was developed as a mid-Victorian resort. In this century the electrification of the railways has turned all the parts of the county on the London border into a near-suburb, and many an old cottage and farmhouse has been saved from destruction by the businessman in search of country life.

After the splendour of Canterbury Cathedral, the rest of the Kent churches, Rochester Cathedral itself included,

◁ **LYMPNE: ST STEPHEN** – *a fine mix of Early English and Norman, the latter most noticeably in the strong axial tower*

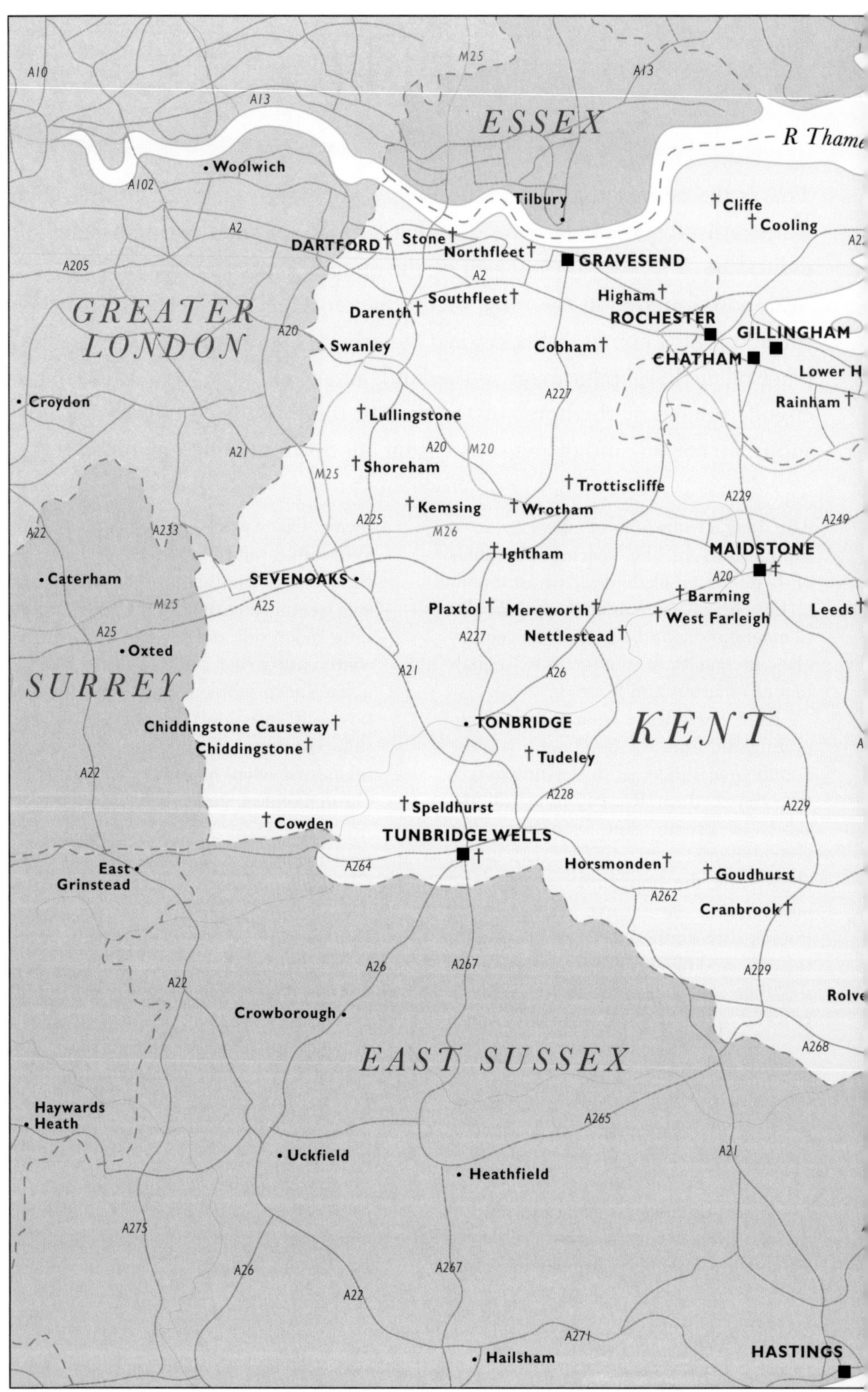
ESSEX
GREATER LONDON
SURREY
KENT
EAST SUSSEX
R Thames
Woolwich
Tilbury
Cliffe
Cooling
DARTFORD
Stone
Northfleet
GRAVESEND
Southfleet
Higham
Darenth
ROCHESTER
GILLINGHAM
Swanley
Cobham
CHATHAM
Lower H
Croydon
Rainham
Lullingstone
Shoreham
Trottiscliffe
Kemsing
Wrotham
Ightham
MAIDSTONE
Caterham
SEVENOAKS
Barming
Plaxtol
Mereworth
West Farleigh
Leeds
Oxted
Nettlestead
Chiddingstone Causeway
TONBRIDGE
Chiddingstone
Tudeley
Speldhurst
Cowden
TUNBRIDGE WELLS
East Grinstead
Horsmonden
Goudhurst
Cranbrook
Crowborough
Haywards Heath
Uckfield
Heathfield
Hailsham
HASTINGS
A10
M25
A13
A102
A2
A205
A20
A227
A21
M20
A229
A22
A233
A225
M26
A249
A25
A26
A228
A264
A262
A267
A268
A265
A275
A271

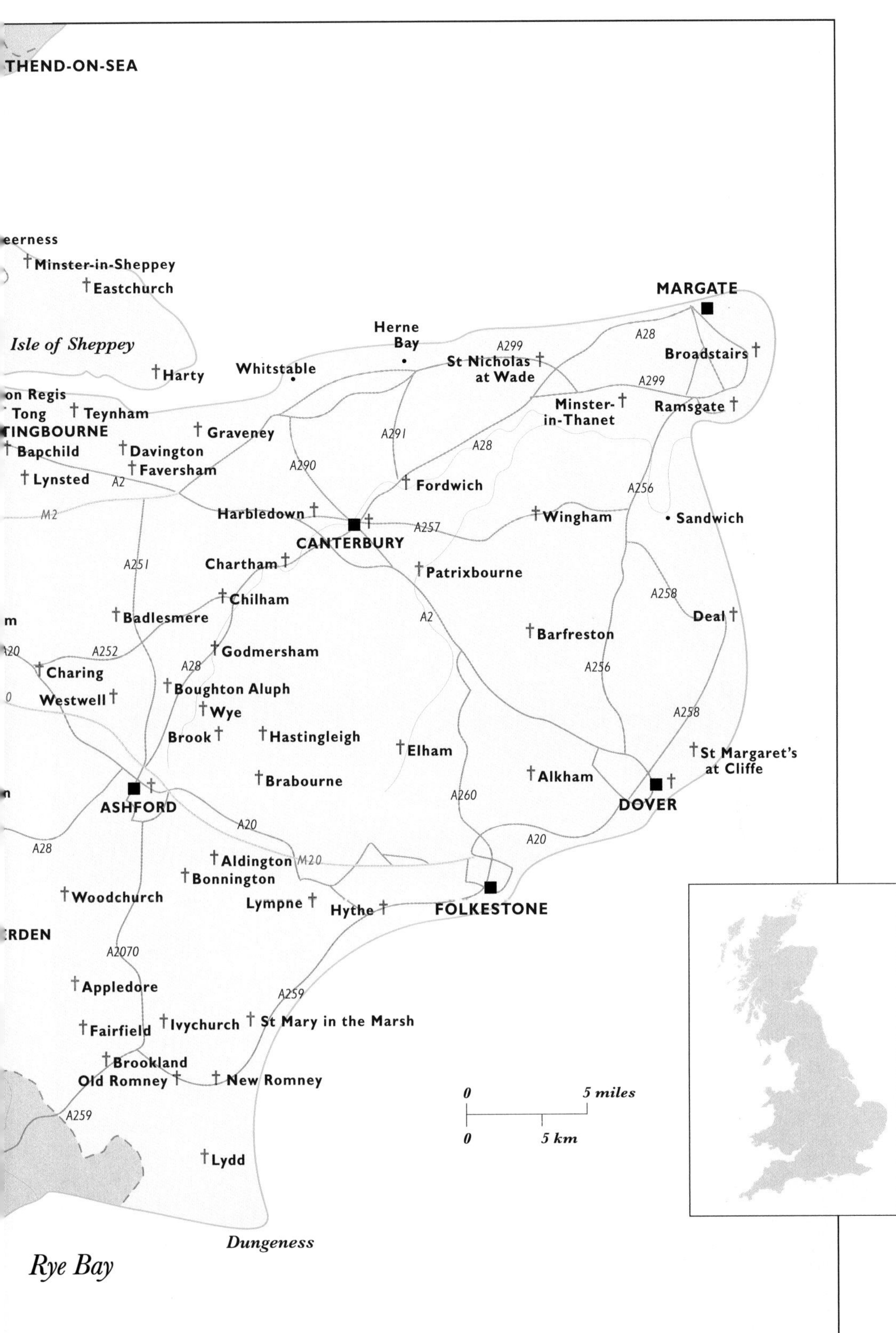

THEND-ON-SEA
eerness
Minster-in-Sheppey
Eastchurch
Isle of Sheppey
Harty
Whitstable
Herne Bay
St Nicholas at Wade
MARGATE
Broadstairs
Ramsgate
Minster-in-Thanet
on Regis
Tong
Teynham
TINGBOURNE
Bapchild
Davington
Faversham
Graveney
Lynsted
Fordwich
Harbledown
CANTERBURY
Wingham
Sandwich
Chartham
Patrixbourne
Chilham
Badlesmere
Deal
Barfreston
Godmersham
Charing
Westwell
Boughton Aluph
Wye
Brook
Hastingleigh
Elham
St Margaret's at Cliffe
Alkham
Brabourne
ASHFORD
DOVER
Aldington
Bonnington
Woodchurch
Lympne
Hythe
FOLKESTONE
RDEN
Appledore
Fairfield
Ivychurch
St Mary in the Marsh
Brookland
Old Romney
New Romney
Lydd
Dungeness
Rye Bay
A2
A20
A28
A251
A252
A256
A257
A258
A259
A260
A290
A291
A299
A2070
M2
M20
0 5 miles
0 5 km

are an anti-climax. In the Weald and the west, the churches are built of Kentish rag; on the Sussex borders near the chalybeate 17th-century spa of tile-hung Tunbridge Wells, sandstone is used; and on the chalk hills flint and clunch. Few of the churches have clerestories. Roofs are steep and large enough to cover nave and aisles in one. The Early English style predominates, and tracery is a county speciality in the old churches. The largest group of comparatively 'unrestored' churches is that on Romney Marsh.

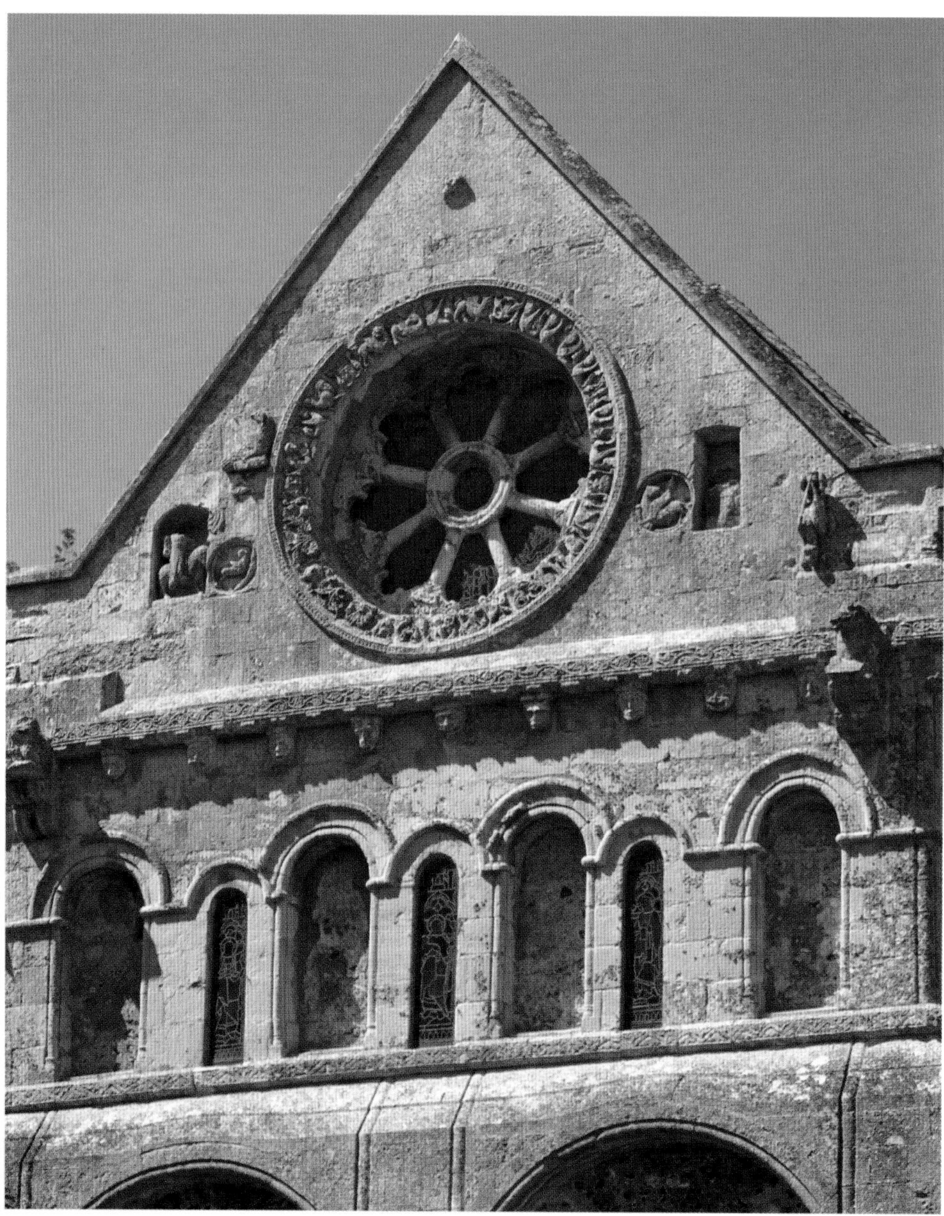

△ **BARFRESTON: ST NICHOLAS** – *the stone carving here is magnificent – the south of England's answer to the Herefordshire School*

ALDINGTON † St Martin
6m/10km W. of Hythe
OS *TR074361* **GPS** *51.0874N, 0.9615E*

The church has a large, fine W. tower built c. 1525–50, and a good set of 15th-century chancel-stalls with misericords and poppy-heads. The base of the medieval rood screen also survives.

ALKHAM † St Anthony
4m/6km W. of Dover
OS *TR255423* **GPS** *51.1361N, 1.2226E*

On a hill overlooking the village, this is a handsome 13th-century flint church with a grand N. chapel in the 'High Early English' manner of S.E. Kent, containing the finest blank arcading in the county, with lancets, tre-foiled arches and rich mouldings.

APPLEDORE † St Peter & St Paul
5m/8km S.E. of Tenterden
OS *TQ957292* **GPS** *51.0296N, 0.7904E*

A delightfully situated church, and originally Early English, but largely reconstructed after a French raid of 1380. Remnants of medieval floor tiles from that time have been placed in the Horne Chapel. The screens are good 14th-century; the font in the S. aisle is 15th-century.

ASHFORD † St Mary
13m/21km S.W. of Canterbury
OS *TR010427* **GPS** *51.1486N, 0.8729E*

This is a large cruciform town church, dating from the late 12th century, but mostly 1350–1475 with a magnificent central tower. The chancel screen is by Caroe, 1919, and there are 14th–17th-century monuments.

BADLESMERE † St Leonard ★
5m/8km S. of Faversham
OS *TR013550* **GPS** *51.2594N, 0.8849E*

Despite the harsh external render, this is a small church of great charm. The walls and choir stalls are older than the 18th-century interior, and the twin E. lancets are a local feature. The complete interior is of a rare beauty, with box pews rising in levels at the W. end, hat pegs round the walls and a three-decker pulpit.

BAPCHILD † St Lawrence
1m/2km E. of Sittingbourne
OS *TQ927629* **GPS** *51.3331N, 0.7653E*

A Norman, Early English and Perpendicular flint church with unusual 12th-century octagonal piers and an early 14th-century wall-painting of the Crucifixion behind the Lady Chapel altar. There is some E. W. Pugin work here, including a fine altar.

BARFRESTON † St Nicholas ★★
10m/16km N.W. of Dover
OS *TR264501* **GPS** *51.2056N, 1.2401E*

This is the best late Norman church in Kent, and is virtually unaltered. The S. doorway has a striking tympanum, showing Christ in Majesty, and fine carving in the orders – zodiacal symbols, musicians and Labours of the Months. The wheel window at the E. end is outstanding, with carved spokes and, round the outside, a parade of mythical creatures. Inside, the rich quality of stone carving continues in the chancel arch and flanking niches, and in the string courses round the nave – yet again with animals and mythical creatures. A joy to visit.

BARMING † St Margaret
3m/4km W. of Maidstone
OS *TQ720542* **GPS** *51.2612N, 0.4639E*

This isolated church has a fine Perpendicular W. tower and needle spire. There are Norman windows in the E. wall and, inside, 14th-century Flemish choir stalls with richly exaggerated carving in deep relief. The N. aisle is 19th-century, and Comper restored the chancel, though much of his work has been spoilt by later interventions.

BONNINGTON † St Rumwold ★
6m/10km S.E. of Ashford
OS *TR057344* **GPS** *51.0723N, 0.9351E*

St Rumwold's is claimed to be the oldest of the marsh churches. It is set in a beautiful and lonely spot, by the Royal Military Canal, and is of mostly Norman origin. Its timber belfry is topped by a 17th-century cupola. Inside, high in the gable of the steeply-pitched roof at the W. end is a Jacobean gallery, set on a curious framework of upright timbers: there is a good Georgian pulpit and tester. Most of

△ **BROOKLAND: ST AUGUSTINE** – *the curious detached belfry*

the glass is clear, apart from some medieval fragments in the nave and Victorian glass in the three E. windows.

BOUGHTON ALUPH † All Saints ★

4m/6km N.E. of Ashford
OS *TR033481* **GPS** *51.1963N, 0.9087E*

This large and distinguished cruciform church is set on a lovely slope of downland. Mainly 13th- and late 14th-century, it retains some original glass in the E. window and N. transept. Condemned as structurally dangerous in the 1950s, it has been the subject of major restoration. It is now open for services in the summer, and plays host to the Stour Music Concerts.

BRABOURNE
† St Mary the Blessed Virgin ★

6m/10km E. of Ashford
OS *TR103416* **GPS** *51.1357N, 1.0055E*

Situated in downland, St Mary's has a bulky, stunted Norman tower, the upper stages of which have been removed. Inside is fine Norman work with rich details, notably the tall and finely carved chancel arch and 12th-century glass in the N. wall of the chancel. The Scot family is commemorated throughout the building: the 16th-century altar tomb, an Easter Sepulchre and once the tomb of Sir John Scot, and very fine brasses in the S. chapel to other family members, now under protective coverings.

BROADSTAIRS † St Peter in Thanet

2m/3km N. of Ramsgate
OS *TR380684* **GPS** *51.3652N, 1.4189E*

The Norman church, with its long Norman nave and fine Perpendicular tower, was used as a naval signal station in Napoleonic times, and still reserves the right to fly the White Ensign. Extensive restoration took place in the mid to late 19th-century, variously attributed to Joseph Clarke and J. P. Seddon.

BROOK † St Mary ★

4m/6km E. of Ashford
OS *TR066442* **GPS** *51.1604N, 0.9538E*

Simple and grand, as if it had strayed across the Channel, this early Norman church has a remarkable stepped W. tower, the staircase of which leads up to a chapel, complete with altar and wall-paintings. Later windows let in sufficient light to view the remarkable monochrome wall-paintings of the life of Christ in the chancel. The 1986 reordering did much to restore the building's original Norman appearance.

BROOKLAND † St Augustine ★★

5m/8km W. of New Romney
OS *TQ989258* **GPS** *50.9973N, 0.8339E*

Picturesque and quite unspoilt, with its long, low roofs and two E. gables, St Augustine's has a remarkable detached belfry, octagonal in plan and built entirely of timber in three stages, like candle-snuffers stacked one on another. It is shingled from top to bottom, and the interior is spacious and airy. At the back of the church is the 12th-century lead font, one of the showpieces of Romney Marsh.

CANTERBURY † St Martin ★

St Martin's Hill
OS *TR158577* **GPS** *51.2781, 1.0937*

On a hillock alongside a handsome Georgian rectory, this is the church of Queen Bertha, where St Augustine worshipped. It is also the oldest continually used church in the

△ **CLIFFE-AT-HOO: ST HELEN** – *at the village edge, the church backs on to the estuary marshes*

English-speaking world. The nave is large for a Saxon building, and leads through a Perpendicular arch to a long, tunnel-like chancel with blocked Saxon windows. The Norman font, of Caen stone, is carved with intersecting and interlocking patterns, and is thought to have come from the nearby cathedral.

CHARING † St Peter and St Paul ★

6m/10km N.W. of Ashford
OS *TQ954493* **GPS** *51.2102N, 0.7967E*

The church stands among the ruins of the archbishop's manor-place and is approached down a lane off the pretty main street. The magnificent W. tower, c. 1465–1505, with its turret staircase, leads one to expect an impressive interior, and we are not disappointed. Both ensemble and detail are good, 13th–15th-century, restored after a fire in 1590. Notable are the vaulted porch, 17th-century bench-ends – now placed under the tower, highly decorative stencilled roofs, Early English, Decorated, Reticulated and Perpendicular window tracery, and chandeliers. The vamping horn, an early megaphone, is one of very few in the country.

CHARTHAM † St Mary ★

3m/4km S.W. of Canterbury
OS *TR106550* **GPS** *51.2559N, 1.0181E*

Cruciform and mainly 13th–14th-century, the church has a splendid chancel, with late 13th-century glass, arranged by Street in 1873–5. There is a huge and handsome brass to Sir Robert de Septvans, d. 1306, and a large monument to Sarah Young by Rysbrack, 1751.

CHIDDINGSTONE † St Mary

4m/6km E. of Edenbridge
OS *TQ500451* **GPS** *51.1863N, 0.1462E*

In an unspoilt village, St Mary's is mainly 14th-century, rebuilt after a fire in 1624. The large Perpendicular tower is adorned with carved gargoyles, and there is an interesting combination of Gothic and Renaissance detail in the porch. In the S. aisle are iron gravestone slabs, including one to Richard Streatfield (ironmaster, d. 1601), and in the churchyard is the Streatfield family vault, sheltered by a gazebo.

CHIDDINGSTONE CAUSEWAY
† St Luke
1m/2km N.E. of Chiddingstone
OS *TQ521465* **GPS** *51.1975N, 0.1758E*

The work of J. F. Bentley in 1897–8, this is his only 'Protestant' church. Outwardly Gothic, the church is of Bath stone in the Perpendicular style; the nave, chancel and N. tower are simple, solid and distinguished. In the E. window is powerful and vividly coloured German Expressionist glass by Wilfrid de Glehn, 1906.

CHILHAM † St Mary ★
6m/10km S.W. of Canterbury
OS *TR068536* **GPS** *51.2445N, 0.9628E*

The village, castle and church stand on high ground, set round a large square with black and white houses. The church, chiefly Perpendicular with a dominant W. tower, contains a remarkable series of monuments, including: a pair from the early 17th century in nielloed, black and white, Bethersden marble; a handsome group by Francis Chantrey; two children by Alexander Munro; and, most unusual of all, a pillar to Lady Digges with the four, rather lumpy, Cardinal Virtues seated around it – the work of Nicholas Stone, 1631. There is 15th-century glass in the N. aisle, an old school table and churchyard monuments.

CLIFFE-AT-HOO † St Helen ★
5m/8km N. of Rochester
OS *TQ735766* **GPS** *51.4620N, 0.4975E*

On the Hoo peninsula, St Helen's stands remote and large among trees above the marshes of the Thames estuary. Cruciform with aisles, long transepts and W. tower, the church is Early English with a Decorated chancel of collegiate configuration, and a Perpendicular porch. The 14th-century sedilia has finely formed ogee arches, and the choir stalls with misercords are magnificent. On the sturdy pillars are the remains of painted bands of colour.

COBHAM † St Mary ★
4m/6km S.E. of Gravesend
OS *TQ669683* **GPS** *51.3899N, 0.3984E*

The church is set overlooking the village. The 13th-century chancel of spacious proportions was enlarged in the 14th century by John de Cobham. Some 20 adults and 40 children of the Cobham family are commemorated here. There is a carved and painted altar-tomb set immediately before the altar, and throughout the church the finest collection of brasses in the county. The turreted and embattled tower, de Cobham's final work, is regarded as the best west Kentish tower.

COOLING † St James the Greater ★
5m/8km N. of Rochester
OS *TQ756759* **GPS** *51.4553N, 0.5264E*
Churches Conservation Trust

On the skyline to the N. are sprawling oil refineries, but around the church all is much is as it was when Dickens came here. The Early English chancel is very fine, with blind arcading enclosing sedilia and piscina on the S. wall. The churchyard has changed little since Dickens's time, and still has the unmarked headstones referred to in Dickens's *Great Expectations*.

COWDEN † St Mary
5m/8km E. of East Grinstead
OS *TQ466404* **GPS** *51.1447N, 0.0947E*

Once a centre of the Wealden iron industry, Cowden is now a remote and pretty village. The restored medieval timber-shingled tower and spire of St Mary's is carried on six massive posts. The E. window has pleasing Reticulated tracery, the pulpit dates from 1628 and there are cast-iron grave-slabs.

CRANBROOK † St Dunstan
7m/11km W. of Tenterden
OS *TQ776361* **GPS** *51.0973N, 0.5363E*

This is one of the best of the Weald churches, the church of the Wealden capital. Mainly late medieval, it has a baptistry of 1725 for the immersion of adults. The arcades are lofty Perpendicular, and the general impression is not unlike an East Anglian wool church. Three 13th-century wooden carved Green Men stare down from the tower wall. There are many monuments: in the S. chapel tombs of the Roberts of Glassenbury.

ELHAM: ST MARY THE VIRGIN – *Eden's furnishings, such as this well-wrought chancel rail with beautifully carved cherubs, are of a tremendous quality* ▷

△ **HYTHE: ST LEONARD** – *looking through to the Early English, aisled chancel*

DARENTH † St Margaret

2m/3km S.E. of Dartford

OS *TQ560712* **GPS** *51.4190N, 0.2433E*

The nave of St Margaret's is late Saxon with tiled quoins and in the N. wall double-splayed windows and a blocked doorway. The square, two-storey chancel is early Norman, and there is a large decorated drum font of the late 12th century.

DARTFORD † Holy Trinity ★

Overy Liberty

OS *TQ544739* **GPS** *51.4439N, 0.2204E*

The 12th-century tower has a 15th-century top; the rest of Holy Trinity is mainly 13th- and 14th-century. Here Henry V led soldiers in thanksgiving for his victory at Agincourt. On the E. wall of the S. chapel is a large 15th-century mural of St George, and there is a striking sculptured tomb to Sir John Spilman, d. 1626, jeweller to Elizabeth I. Richard Trevethick, the early pioneer of steam locomotion, is commemorated here in a wall memorial.

DAVINGTON

† St Mary Magdalene and St Laurence

On N.W. side of Faversham

OS *TR010617* **GPS** *51.3193N, 0.8845E*

A former church of a Benedictine nunnery of which considerable remains survive. Of the church, only the 12th-century nave and aisles remain, restored in 1845 by Thomas Willement, who also designed the stained glass. The E. end has a simple spoked wheel window, and the interior has a monastic simplicity in keeping with its origin.

DEAL † St George

8m/12km N.E. of Dover

OS *TR376528* **GPS** *51.2253N, 1.4020E*

This is a Classical church, built by Samuel Simmons in 1706: the roof is supported by massive ship's timbers, and there is much interesting furniture, including the corporation pew in the N. gallery pew. The fine organ case is by Sir T. G. Jackson. Outside is the tomb of Captain Edward T. Parker, paid for by Nelson. The inscription reads, 'My gallant good friend and able assistant'.

DOVER † St Mary in Castro ★

Dover Castle

OS *TR326418* **GPS** *51.1284N, 1.3234E*

Perched on the cliff tops above Dover, within the confines of the castle, St Mary's is an important Saxon church of cruciform plan, 800-1000, adjacent to the famous Roman lighthouse (used as the church bell-tower from the 13th to the late 17th century). It was restored by Sir George Gilbert Scott in 1860–62, and William Butterfield added his distinctive mosaic work in 1889 – neither work of the best quality.

EASTCHURCH † All Saints

2m/3km S.E. of Minster

OS *TQ988714* **GPS** *51.4071N, 0.8575E*

All Saints was built by Minster Abbey, 1432, of Kentish rag and flint. It is a fine example of Perpendicular in the county. The Perpendicular rood screen extends across the entire width of the church, and the nave roof is decorated with angels; there is a 17th-century Belgian tower screen and a good Corinthian monument with effigies, 1622.

ELHAM † St Mary the Virgin ★★

6m/10km N.W. of Folkestone

OS *TR177438* **GPS** *51.1522N, 1.1119E*

To many this is the most beautiful parish church in Kent, and this is a tribute to the careful restoration by F. C. Eden in the early 20th century. The 13th-century arcades were pierced through the Norman walls when the aisles were added; the clerestory is Perpendicular and the Early English chancel has a triplet in the E. wall. Eden oak-panelled the chancel and nave. Over the S. aisle altar is a 15th-century alabaster triptych of St Catherine. There are good corbels, old tiles, text boards and fine modern fittings.

FAIRFIELD

† St Thomas à Becket ★

2m/3km S. of Appledore

OS *TQ966264* **GPS** *51.0042N, 0.8018E*

A tiny barn-like structure of timber and plaster with red and blue brick walls stands in a field on Romney Marsh surrounded by ditches and sheep. It is of the 14th century, was refashioned in the 18th and carefully

△ **HYTHE: ST LEONARD** – *a nautical bench-end for a church overlooking the sea*

restored by Caroe in 1913. The delightful interior has original roof timbers, text boards, white painted box pews, three-decker pulpit and three-sided communion rail.

FAVERSHAM † St Mary of Charity ★

10m/16km W. of Canterbury

OS *TR018615* **GPS** *51.3171N, 0.8948E*

This is a large Norman and later cruciform church, whose nave was rebuilt by George Dance Snr in 1755; the elegant corona W. spire is by Charles Beazley, 1799. The Doric columns of the nave contrast starkly with the Gothic of the crossing and transepts, the scale of which is massive, and are in Decorated style. On one of the piers in the N. transept is a surviving medieval painting. The choir stalls have some of the county's best misericords, and the church purports to be the resting place of King Stephen, d. 1154.

FORDWICH † St Mary

2m/3km N.E. of Canterbury

OS *TR181598* **GPS** *51.2958N, 1.1271E*

Churches Conservation Trust

A small structure of Norman origin, St Mary's is unusually attractive with good texture outside and inside: a tall, narrow 13th-century tower arch, old tiles, box pews, corporation pew, a well-furnished sanctuary and 1688 Royal Arms. There is some 14th-century painted glass and a rare Norman sarcophagus.

FAIRFIELD: ST THOMAS À BECKET – *standing isolated, with only sheep for company, the church is of 14th-century origin* ▷

△ **LOWER HALSTOW: ST MARGARET** – *a Saxon church that looks out over the Medway*

GODMERSHAM

† St Lawrence the Martyr

6m/10km N.E. of Ashford

OS *TR062504* **GPS** *51.2160N, 0.9512E*

Old and cold in pretty surroundings, the church is perhaps best known for its Jane Austin family connections. In the 1720s rebuilding, raised pews were installed in the S. transept for Eggerton Manor and Godmersham Park. An early Norman N. tower with E. apse adjoins the nave, whose E. end is Early English and has three tall lancet windows. Inside is a 12th-century bas-relief of St Thomas à Becket.

GOUDHURST † St Mary ★

4m/6km N.W. of Cranbrook

OS *TQ723378* **GPS** *51.1137, 0.4616*

A good example of a Wealden church, with a long, low nave and yellowing stone; the church occupies the summit of a hill above the village and has distinguished monuments. The tower lost its top stage and spire in the 17th century, and the W. face of the tower is a curious conglomeration of Classical tinkering and Gothic. Inside is severely scraped, but the interest is in the memorials to the Culpepers and Campions.

GRAVENEY † All Saints ★

3m/4km N. E. of Faversham

OS *TR052626* **GPS** *51.3262N, 0.9449E*

A well-weathered church in a pretty churchyard, All Saints has sweeping views over the marshes. It is Norman in origin, of flint and stone, but now chiefly 14th-century and later. The clear glass and pale woodwork of the box pews make the interior light and spacious.

HARBLEDOWN † St Nicholas ★

W. suburb of Canterbury

OS *TR130581* **GPS** *51.2827N, 1.0536E*

Originally the church of a leper hospital founded by Lanfranc in 1084, it is still known locally as the 'leper church'. Its stark external appearance is actually very appealing, with long steep-pitched roofs to the nave and chancel, and a plain square Norman tower. Although restored in the 19th century, it is remarkably free from Victoriana.

HARTY † St Thomas the Apostle ★

Isle of Sheppey

OS *TR023662* **GPS** *51.3595N, 0.9045E*

On one of Kent's most romantic and remote church sites, St Thomas's overlooks the Swale estuary, and is Norman and later; there is a fine Decorated niche in the E. wall of the chancel and a good 14th-century rood screen, and the finely carved 14th-century Harty Chest in the Lady Chapel.

HASTINGLEIGH † St Mary the Virgin

6m/10km E. of Ashford
OS *TR101444* **GPS** *51.1611N, 1.0048E*

An isolated gem in a fold of the downs, St Mary's has an Early Norman nave and 13th-century chancel with lancets; one retaining its original grisaille glass.

HIGHAM † St Mary ★

5m/8km E. of Gravesend
OS *TQ716742* **GPS** *51.4408N, 0.4683E*
Churches Conservation Trust

Distinctive for its stone and flint banding, St Mary's is most notable for its woodwork. The pulpit is a robust and rustic work, carved in a similar style to the intriguing medieval S. door, decorated with heads, flowers, birds and other animals. Inside, the old nave has become the N. aisle, and both aisle and nave have fine rustic medieval screens.

HORSMONDEN † St Margaret ★

4m/6km S.E. of Paddock Wood
OS *TQ703381* **GPS** *51.1170N, 0.4330E*

A pleasing rural 14th-century sandstone church, whose unspoilt Perpendicular tower with staircase turret rises 70 feet above the surrounding fields. Inside, the tower and chancel arches form a fine balanced pair. The W. doorway is Perpendicular, bearing heraldic devices of Poynings and Fitzpayn. The mid-14th-century brass is of Henry de Grofhurst, rector for fifty years from 1311 to 1361, and in the nave hangs a beautiful Flemish-style candelabra.

HYTHE † St Leonard ★

4m/6km W. of Folkestone
OS *TR161349* **GPS** *51.0728N, 1.0841E*

St Leonard's is a Norman fabric, largely rebuilt in the 13th century, with further refashioning in the 14th. The W. tower was rebuilt in 1751. The superb elevated chancel has the best Early English work of any parish church in Kent; the celebrated crypt beneath contains vast quantities of bones.

△ **LOWER HALSTOW: ST MARGARET** – *decorative scheme on the 12th-century font*

IGHTHAM † St Peter

4m/6km E. of Sevenoaks
OS *TQ594569* **GPS** *51.2892N, 0.2858E*

The present church is an early 15th-century rebuilding, but with some Norman remains. There is a splendid monument to Sir Thomas Cawne, d. 1373; he lies in full-plate armour beneath a beautiful window in the N. side of the chancel, paid for in his will. Also under the E. window, a fine hanging monument of 1741 to Dame Dorothy Selby, celebrated needlewoman, by Edward Marshall. Elsewhere is a large collection of hatchments, Jacobean family pews from the James family of Ightham Court and a fine double-tiered candelabra.

IVYCHURCH † St George ★

3m/4km N.W. of New Romney
OS *TR028276* **GPS** *51.0126N, 0.8899E*

St George's is a large, low late Decorated church of rag-stone, the tower and turret covered with lichens of different colours. Restoration after the flying-bombs had damaged it did not impair its strange beauty. The wonderful empty interior has original plaster, with odd screens, text boards and a crude graveside shelter in the nave.

KEMSING † St Mary ★

3m/4km N.E. of Sevenoaks

OS *TQ556587* **GPS** *51.3069N, 0.2310E*

The church, of Norman origin with later additions, sits in a village at the foot of the N. Downs, and is marked by a distinctive shingled bell-tower and broach spire. It is full of beautiful craftsmanship; most of the modern work is by Sir Ninian Comper, 1902, including the colourful chancel decorations. The screen uses some 15th-century woodwork but mostly dates from the 1890s; Comper provided the rood figures above it. There is a 13th-century stained-glass medallion, some early 14th-century brass, a Jacobean font cover, and a 13th-century chest. The church's most recent acquisition is a tapestry of Kemsing life by Al Hart, 1991.

LEEDS † St Nicholas ★

4m/6km E. of Maidstone

OS *TQ825533* **GPS** *51.2500N, 0.6143E*

A grand Perpendicular church with tall, slender arches, St Nicholas's has a massive Norman tower with ten bells, and the oddest spire in the county, rivalling even that of St Augustine in Brookland for eccentricity. There are Saxon windows above the N. nave arcade, and the 15th-century roof is supported by crown posts. The 15th-century rood comprises eleven bays and spans the entire width of the church.

LENHAM † St Mary ★

10m/16km S.E. of Maidstone

OS *TQ899521* **GPS** *51.2367N, 0.7192E*

A village rich in old and picturesque houses, with a church notable more for its fittings than its fabric: it is chiefly 13th- and 14th-century, with 15th-century carved stalls and font; a 14th-century wall-painting of the Weighing of Souls; a medieval lectern and handsome pulpit of 1622 with tester. The stone altar was found buried in the chancel floor and reinstated in the 20th century.

LOWER HALSTOW † St Margaret ★

4m/6km N.W. of Sittingbourne

OS *TQ860674* **GPS** *51.3754N, 0.6713E*

This little and charming Saxon church is almost afloat in the Medway. The late Saxon nave and chancel with tile dressings are complete, and there is a 12th-century lead font, decorated with figures in arcades; the S. porch of 1913 is by W. D. Caroe, who restored the church.

LULLINGSTONE † St Botolph ★★

Adjoins Eynsford, 3m/4km S.E. of Swanley; entrance via the gatehouse of Lullingstone Castle

OS *TQ529644* **GPS** *51.3584N, 0.1960E*

The little white 14th-century church rises from the castle lawns – almost a family chapel and mausoleum, with monuments to the ancestors of the Hart-Dykes. The N. chapel is 16th-century, and the porch early 18th-century Classical; the 16th-century rood screen is complete, with coping and an early 18th-century open parapet. Flemish glass can be seen above the tomb of Sir George Hart, and, in the S. wall of the nave, 16th-century glass showing St George and the Dragon.

LYDD † All Saints

4m/6km N.W. of Dungeness

OS *TR042209* **GPS** *50.9518N, 0.9069E*

The largest parish church in Kent, and chiefly of the 13th century. The fine, lofty Perpendicular tower with a delicate Heme vault is the work of Thomas Stanley, a senior mason at Canterbury Cathedral. At the back of the church are traces of early Saxon work. There are numerous brasses, a 14th-century effigy of a knight and a bust of Anne Russell by Flaxman, 1781.

LYMPNE † St Stephen ★

3m/4km W. of Hythe

OS *TR119346* **GPS** *51.0721N, 1.0244E*

With superb views over Romney Marsh, the church, which groups well with the medieval manor on the W. side, is chiefly Norman and Early English, with a massive axial Norman tower and crown-post roof.

LYNSTED † St Peter and St Paul

3m/4km S.E. of Sittingbourne

OS *TQ942608* **GPS** *51.3138N, 0.7861E*

The village abounds in Tudor cottages and Elizabethan manor houses. The church, mainly Decorated and Perpendicular, has two chapels, the N. chapel being dedicated to the

△ **LULLINGSTONE: ST BOTOLPH** – *the Flemish screen of c. 1500–1520*

Hugessens, the S. chapel to the Teynhams. The exquisite Teynham monument of 1622 is by Epiphanius Evesham.

MAIDSTONE † All Saints ★

Between River and Mill Street
OS *TQ759554* **GPS** *51.2707N, 0.5216E*

A large broad town church, All Saints was formerly collegiate. It is situated above the Medway and flanked by the archbishop's manor-place and the former college – a wonderful medieval group, 15th-century and of admirable proportions. The choir stalls have misericords and the sedilia incorporate the founder's tomb with a contemporary painting behind. Many monuments include the massive indent of a brass to Archbishop Courtenay, d. 1396, and four fabulous shrouded figures by Edward Marshall, 1639.

MAIDSTONE † St Luke

St Luke's Road
OS *TQ765564* **GPS** *51.2800N, 0.5299E*

A confident, muscular Art Nouveau design by W. H. Seth-Smith, 1896–7, with Decorated window tracery. Broad, low arcades are supported on coupled columns. There is good detailing and craftsmanship throughout; the wall-paintings are by Ivon Hitchens, c. 1918.

MEREWORTH † St Lawrence ★

6m/10km W. of Maidstone
OS *TQ660537* **GPS** *51.2588N, 0.3779E*

Built for John Fane, Earl of Westmorland, in about 1740 by an unknown architect, St Lawrence's is a Classical church of distinction, with a Tuscan nave and W. portico of real elegance; the spire is a copy of St Giles-in-the-Fields, London. The Doric interior has a painted barrel vault in the nave and plaster ceilings to the aisles, and there are interesting monuments and splendid golden 18th-century and earlier armorial glass.

MILTON REGIS
† Holy Trinity with St Paul ★

W. suburb of Sittingbourne
OS *TQ908654* **GPS** *51.3557N, 0.7402E*

The surroundings are unattractive, yet this is a handsome building with Saxon core and massive W. tower, the best flint tower in the county, chiefly 14th-century with some good window tracery and brasses.

△ **LULLINGSTONE: ST BOTOLPH** – *the tomb of Sir George Hart, d. 1587, is dominated by the accompanying deathly, angelic and cherubic figures*

MINSTER-IN-SHEPPEY

† St Mary and St Sexburga ★

N. coast of Isle of Sheppey

OS *TQ956729* **GPS** *51.4221N, 0.8120E*

Occupying a commanding site on the highest point of Sheppey, this is two churches in one; the S. is parochial and Early English, the N. is the nunnery church founded in 670. There is Saxon work in the chancel and the N. nave wall. It was restored in 1880 by Ewan Christian. Of particular note is the effigy of Sir Robert de Shurland, c. 1300, and two large Northwode brasses, c. 1330.

MINSTER-IN-THANET

† St Mary the Virgin ★

5m/8km W. of Ramsgate

OS *TR310642* **GPS** *51.3304N, 1.3158E*

The W. entrance leads through a massive Saxon wall into a Norman nave. This was a rebuilding on a monumental scale of the abbey founded in 669. The church is cruciform in plan, with impressive Norman nave arcades and an Early English vaulted chancel with a full set of fine misericords with carved arm-rests. The excellent E. window is by Willement, 1861.

NETTLESTEAD † St Mary ★

5m/8km N. of Paddock Wood

OS *TQ685521* **GPS** *51.2434N, 0.4128E*

Standing a little apart, near Nettlestead Place, and with its 14th-century gateway, the church itself is 15th-century, with an older tower and wide aisleless nave. Some windows contain reassembled 15th-century painted glass of a high quality.

NEW ROMNEY † St Nicholas ★

9m/15km S.W. of Hythe

OS *TR065247* **GPS** *50.9851N, 0.9412E*

The only town church in Romney Marsh now has steps down to the entrance – a legacy of a massive storm inundation in 1287. It is mostly Norman and 14th-century, with a tall stately tower, W. door, nave arcades and a glorious Geometrical E. window. William Morris championed the retention of the most westerly bays, much to the annoyance of the incumbent of the time and his architect John Oldrid Scott.

NORTHFLEET † St Botolph ★

1m/2km W. of Gravesend
OS *TQ623741* **GPS** *51.4430N, 0.3347E*

St Botolph's stands in a dramatic setting on the edge of a disused quarry, and is mostly Decorated and Perpendicular, with a fine clerestory, although some Saxon long-and-short work can be seen by the tower. The early 14th-century carved oak screen is magnificent – one of the oldest in the county. In the chancel is a brass to Peter de Lacey, 1375, chaplain to the Black Prince, and is thought to be one of the county's best.

OLD ROMNEY † St Clement ★★

2m/3km W. of New Romney
OS *TR034251* **GPS** *50.9901N, 0.8982E*

There is no village, but a number of pretty houses; the 13th- to early 16th-century church stands apart in fields, partly sheltered by trees. Inside are 18th-century box pews, pulpit, reading desk, W. gallery, text boards and other delights, including a pastel colour scheme left in place after the filming of *Dr Syn* in the 1960s. Few churches are more picturesque than St Clement.

PATRIXBOURNE † St Mary ★

3m/4km S.E. of Canterbury
OS *TR189551* **GPS** *51.2534N, 1.1365E*

A small but very fine late Norman church of flint and Caen stone, St Mary's has a wheel window, rich sculpture to the tower and an outstanding S. doorway set into the tower. The doorway is decorated with a tympanum showing a seated Christ with figures from the Apocalypse: the orders of the arch bear a variety of Norman motifs and figures. Inside is interesting 16th–17th-century Swiss enamelled glass.

PLAXTOL † No dedication

5m/8km N. of Tonbridge
OS *TQ601536* **GPS** *51.2594N, 0.2945E*

In a village that is rich in old houses, this is one of the few churches built during the time of the Commonwealth. It is Gothic Survival, with a hammer-beam roof, and much enlarged in 1894. The ancient reredos is of foreign provenance.

RAINHAM † St Margaret ★

S.E. district of Gillingham
OS *TQ817658* **GPS** *51.3629N, 0.6091E*

With a tower visible for miles around, the church has a 13th-century chancel with traces of Norman work; the rest is mainly 14th- and 15th-century., with medieval N. and S. doors. The E. bay of the nave roof is panelled and painted with the Sun in Spendour, symbol of Edward IV, to form a ceilure over the altar. Some painted consecration crosses remain on the walls, and there are other 14th-century wall-paintings. An admirable carved 15th-century parclose screen separates the chancel and N. chapel, which contains monuments to the Tufton family.

RAMSGATE † St George

Church Hill
OS *TR381652* **GPS** *51.3361N, 1.4179E*

By H. T. Kendall from designs by H. Helmsley, 1825–7, this is a very distinguished Georgian version of Perpendicular in white brick and stone. The rib-vaulted interior has panelling and galleries supported on cast-iron columns.

ROLVENDEN † St Mary the Virgin ★

3m/4km S.W. of Tenterden
OS *TQ845312* **GPS** *51.0507N, 0.6311E*

Best approached from the east, this is a fine church, mainly Decorated and Perpendicular, the stone almost chocolate-coloured in places. The three E. gables are the best example of a common effect in Kentish churches. Above the S. chapel is a gallery with the Gibbon family pew, complete with carpets, chairs and table. Below, in the chapel, is a memorial to Robert Gybbon, d. 1719, whose descendant Edmund Gibbons wrote the *Decline and Fall of the Roman Empire*.

ST MARGARET-AT-CLIFFE
† St Margaret of Antioch ★

4m/6km N.E. of Dover
OS *TR358447* **GPS** *51.1535N, 1.3716E*

A complete and impressive Norman church, rich in ornament, with a fine W. door, arcades along the length of the nave at clerestory level, and, inside, sumptuously decorated arches. On the piers are carved maritime graffiti, including an early (and accurate) depiction of a galleon.

LYMPNE: ST STEPHEN – *set high above Romney Marsh, the church is almost adjoined by medieval Lympne Castle on its western side* ▷

△ **OLD ROMNEY: ST CLEMENT** – *box pewed, pastel-hued and a bit of a warren*

ST MARY-IN-THE-MARSH
† St Mary ★

2m/3km N. of New Romney
OS *TR064279* **GPS** *51.0142N, 0.9425E*

Exhibiting all the texture typical of a marsh church, St Mary's is mainly 14th- and 15th-century, with an earlier core. The interior is simple, with clear glass, white walls, old tiles and early 18th-century furnishings. A tonsured monk stares out from the sedilia. The childrens' author E. Nesbitt is buried here; her husband, 'the skipper', carved the memorial board now in the porch.

ST NICHOLAS-AT-WADE † St Nicholas

6m/10km W. of Margate
OS *TR265666* **GPS** *51.3542N, 1.2518E*

A large and impressive church, with a clerestoried nave and a striking contrast between N. and S. arcades. The S. arcade is Norman, with finely carved detailing that includes Green Men and stiff-leaf; the N. arcade is Early English and plain, unlike the Decorated arches supporting the tower. The Jacobean pulpit is attached to the wall, and the N. chapel contains many monuments to the Bridges family.

SHOREHAM † St Peter and St Paul ★

4m/6km N. of Sevenoaks
OS *TQ522615* **GPS** *51.3330N, 0.1845E*

Pleasantly sited in the Darenth Valley, St Peter and St Paul's is mainly 15th-century. The arch of the porch is formed of a great split oak, and a famous screen – one of the best in England – runs the full width of the church; panelled doors give access to the rood loft. The wooden drum pulpit of 1827 is by Blore from Westminster Abbey. There is a Burne-Jones window in the S. wall and monuments with portrait busts of the Borrett family by Cheere.

SMARDEN † St Michael

7m/11km S.W. of Charing 8m/12km W. of Ashford
OS *TQ879422* **GPS** *51.1490N, 0.686E*

A lovely village with a large, handsome 14th-century church, probably built after Edward III licensed a market here in 1332. The nave roof span is incredible – 'the barn of Kent'. To the N. and S. of the chancel arch are strange Victorian two-tier rows of blank arcading – presumably as reredos for side altars. An ancient medieval alms box is

△ **WESTWELL: ST MARY** – *the 13th-century interior with its alternative to the single chancel arch*

set on a carved tree trunk, the weight being a deterrent to thieves.

SPELDHURST † St Mary ★

2m/3km N.W. of Tunbridge Wells
OS *TQ553413* **GPS** *51.1507N, 0.2196E*

J. O. Scott's 1871 rebuilding of St Mary's is competent but not exciting. All the interest is concentrated in the glass, installed as an integral part of the church rather than as an afterthought; it is Morris & Co. at its best. The E. window is a Burne-Jones design of the Crucifixion, and in the chancel are two more, the Baptism of Christ and the Cleansing of Naaman. The Morris glass in the W. window is best of all – the Window of Praise.

SOUTHFLEET † St Nicholas

3m/4km S.W. of Gravesend
OS *TQ613711* **GPS** *51.4165N, 0.3193E*

This is a complete Decorated church, with brasses, sculptured sedilia and, in the chancel, two paintings, probably 17th-century, of Latimer and Ridley, and a lovely Reticulated E. window. A large alabaster wall-monument to John Sedley, d. 1605, stands in the S. aisle.

STONE † St Mary ★★

2m/3km E. of Dartford
OS *TQ576748* **GPS** *51.4503N, 0.2673E*

Overlooking the M25 Dartford Crossing from the edge of a modern housing estate, high up above a former chalk quarry that has since been transformed into the Bluewater shopping centre, the location is as unpromising as the church is impressive. Believed to have been built by the masons of Westminster Abbey, it has a perfect harmony of proportions and is richly decorated – all 13th-century, with a fine Geometrical E. window. The chancel vault by Street completed the work of the original masons. There is a brass to John Lombard, 1408, and traces of mural paintings, but the architecture is the main glory of the building.

TEYNHAM † St Mary ★

3m/4km E. of Sittingbourne
OS *TQ966636* **GPS** *51.3378N, 0.8213E*

Originally a pre-Conquest minster church, St Mary's stands between cherry orchards and the sea; the present-day 13th-century cruciform church is very large, with immense transepts. The naves, arcades and aisles are 15th-century work. The W. tower is 13th-century with a 15th-century upper stage. The S. transept has some very good brasses.

TONGE † St Giles

Adjoins Sittingbourne to E.
OS *TQ934640* **GPS** *51.3425N, 0.7758E*

St Giles's church is Norman with 13th-century and 19th-century refashioning. A steep sweep of cat-slide roof covers the nave and aisles; combined with the bulky tower it makes the outside look like a great barn. There is 13th-century ironwork on the tower door and a wall-painting of St Christopher; Kempe did the glass in the S. chancel window.

TROTTISCLIFFE † St Peter and St Paul

6m/10km W. of Maidstone
OS *TQ646605* **GPS** *51.3202N, 0.3612E*

A simple charming church in W. Kent, the building is largely Norman. The W. wall was rebuilt in 1885 and is an amazing example of elaborate knapped flint work. A fine high-canopied and carved pulpit of 1775 was brought from Westminster Abbey in 1824. There is much good glass for such a small church. In the churchyard is the burial place of the painter Graham Sutherland.

TUDELEY † All Saints ★★

2m/3km E. of Tonbridge
OS *TQ621454* **GPS** *51.1849N, 0.3188E*

All Saints at Tudeley keeps its treasure reserved for those who venture inside. Every window is filled with glass by Marc Chagall – a memorial to Sarah Venetia d'Avidgor Goldsmid, drowned in a sailing accident in 1963. Inside is a world of marine hues. The glass, made by Charles Marc of Rheims, replaces Victorian glass that is preserved in the vestry. This ranks as one of the greatest works of art in a British church.

TUNBRIDGE WELLS
† King Charles the Martyr ★★

Corner of Nevill Street and London Road
OS *TQ581388* **GPS** *51.1267N, 0.2594E*

The oldest church in the town, erected in 1678, enlarged in 1696 and again in 1882 by Ewan Christian, who added the chancel. The woodwork in the new chancel came from one of Wren's London churches, and there is a beautiful moulded plaster ceiling by Doogood, 1690, for which alone it would be well worth visiting; he was chief plasterer to Sir Christopher Wren, and it shows.

WEST FARLEIGH † All Saints

3m/4km S.W. of Maidstone
OS *TQ715535* **GPS** *51.2549N, 0.4571E*

All Saints is in a pleasant setting on the S. bank of the Medway. It is all early Norman, except for the Perpendicular W. tower of c. 1525 and an 18th-century vestry. The chancel arch is of note, being constructed of tufa, as are some windows and the original W. door surround. On the W. wall is a Royal Arms to George III.

WESTWELL † St Mary ★★

3m/4km N. of Ashford
OS *TQ990474* **GPS** *51.1919N, 0.8474E*

Rightly called a village cathedral, it is one of the most exciting architectural churches in Kent, despite the harsh external render and over-restored porch. The fabric is 13th-century with a few later alterations, including a 16th-century timber-framed porch. The lofty chancel is vaulted, and in place of a single chancel arch there are three tall and narrow openings with cusped heads and round columns. The chancel has a lovely Decorated sedilia, and in the E. window is finely conserved glass depicting the Jesse Tree.

WINGHAM † St Mary the Virgin ★★

6m/10km E. of Canterbury
OS *TR242574* **GPS** *51.2723N, 1.2130E*

The village is large, with many timber-framed houses; the church too is large. Conspicuous by its handsome spire, St Mary's is formerly collegiate, 13th-century, with surviving choir stalls and misericords. The arcade to the S. aisle is wood, a consequence of financial shenanigans from the 16th-century rebuilding. In the N. chapel is a monument to Sir Thomas Palmer, d. 1624, by Nicholas Stone: the virtuoso Oxenden family monument of 1682 is in the S. transept, its obelisk standing above horned oxen and mourning cherubs, possibly by Arnold Quellin.

△ **WOODCHURCH: ALL SAINTS** – *two corbel heads supporting an arch over the west door*

WOODCHURCH † All Saints ★

4m/6km E. of Tenterden
OS *TQ941349* **GPS** *51.0807N, 0.7711E*

All Saints is another of the county's large churches. It is also one of the most beautiful in Kent, in the main a masterly work of the 13th century. The arcades have alternate round and octagonal columns, and the triple lancets at the E. end, with banded marble shafts, are most effective. The interesting priest's brass of 1320 is to Nicholas Gore, d.1333. In the S. aisle is a roundel of 13th-century glass.

WROTHAM † St George ★

8m/12km N. of Tonbridge
OS *TQ611591* **GPS** *51.3090N, 0.3111E*

The tower rises straight off the old London road and has a vaulted passage beneath it from N. to S. The church is 13th-century, refashioned in the 15th. There is a vaulted porch with room above, and the massive door has a lock block of oak and a key nearly a foot long. The E. window, late Gothic of 1633, was brought from St Alban in Wood Street, London in 1958. There is a Perpendicular screen, an interesting series of brasses and Lady Chapel reredos by Sir Ninian Comper.

WYE † St Martin and St Gregory ★

4m/6km N.E. of Ashford
OS *TR054469* **GPS** *51.1844N, 0.9378E*

The church is an interesting disparity between John Kempe's 15th-century Perpendicular and the Queen Anne style of the early 18th century. The fall of the central tower in 1685 destroyed the chancel, and was replaced about 20 years later by a massive brick and flint S. tower entirely covering the original S. transept. The lofty Perpendicular nave has a grand timber roof. The delightful apsidal chancel has good clear glass.

LANCASHIRE

MERSEYSIDE & GREATER MANCHESTER

The county of Lancashire emerged from the mid-12th century, a conglomeration of Saxon and Norse burghs given by William the Conqueror as reward to the Norman barons who had supported his invasion of Britain in 1066. Principal among these was Roger de Poitou, whose lands stretched between the River Ribble and the River Mersey. William's son William Rufus added Cartmel, Lonsdale and Furness. These territories formed more or less the extent of the original county of Lancashire, and the 13th-century land enclosures and establishment of rights of way were the basis for the subsequent development of the county.

Early commerce emerged in the market places that grew up around churches in many of the county's towns, such as at St Peter's in Burnley and St Michael's at Kirkham. However, by the mid-16th century many of the numerous markets had disappeared, victims to fierce competition. A clear urban infrastructure was beginning to emerge by the end of the medieval period.

Although trade and prosperity had increased, Lancashire remained sparsely populated and remote from the rest of the country, and when the Tudors broke from Rome, it was the Lancashire Catholic gentry who remained obstinately true to the 'old' faith, defying the penalties imposed against 'Popish recusants'. Among their number were the Blundells of Crosby, the Townleys, Southworths and Sherburns. It was only in Manchester that Protestantism really thrived at this time, but the 16th-century philanthropic founding of grammar schools – Bishop Oldham's Manchester grammar school, Haigh's grammar school in Wigan, and later, Sir Humphrey Chetham's Manchester school and library – succeeded where repression had failed, establishing a firm Anglican-based system of education. Before the Civil War there were some 77 grammar schools throughout the county. Other influences established themselves: Calvinism in Bolton, the Quakers in Pendle, and these movements gave rise to a different class of church building, the chapel and meeting house.

Industrialisation came to the county in the 18th century. Its pace was fast and furious, and with it came profound social and economic changes. Water and steam power, canals and railways fuelled the development of Lancashire as the manufacturing and industrial heart of Britain: King Cotton ruled supreme.

It was only in the county re-organisation of the 1970s that Lancashire assumed its present form, losing Manchester and Mersyside, and – to the indignation of many – the Furness and Cartmel peninsulas, whose occupants still regard themselves as Lancastrians.

◁ **WHALLEY: ST MARY** – *the beautifully carved choir stalls with their fine canopies of c. 1430 were brought to the church from Whalley Abbey in 1536*

0
10 miles
0
10 km
CUMBRIA
LANCASHIRE
NORTH YORKSHIR
MERSEYSIDE
CHESHIRE
Kendal
Sedbergh
Ulverston
Grange-over-Sands
Kirkby Lonsdale
Melling-with-Wrayton
Carnforth
Morecambe
Heysham
LANCASTER
Overton
Isle of Walney
Slaidburn
Skipton
Fleetwood
Garstang
Clitheroe
Colne
Poulton-le-Fylde
Singleton
Great Mitton
Stydd
Ribchester
Whalley
Nelson
BLACKPOOL
Woodplumpton
BURNLEY
Kirkham
PRESTON
Samlesbury
Accrington
Lytham St Anne's
Warton
BLACKBURN
Much Hoole
Leyland
Tarleton
Euxton
Edenfield
SOUTHPORT
Chorley
Rufford
ROCHDALE
Rivington
Halsall
Standish
BURY
Ormskirk
BOLTON
Formby
Skelmersdale
MIDDLETON
Aughton
Up Holland
Hindley
WIGAN
OLDHAM
Pendlebury
Sefton
Worsley
SALFORD
Billinge
CROSBY
Kirkby
Barton upon Irwell
MANCHESTER
BOOTLE
ST HELENS
Moss Side
Haughton
WALLASEY
Everton
Tuebrook
Sale
LIVERPOOL
Warburton
WARRINGTON
BIRKENHEAD
Sefton Park
Allerton
Altrincham
Cheadle
STOCKPORT
Aigburth
WIDNES
Wilmslow
R Mersey
RUNCORN
Whaley Bridge
River Dee
ELLESMERE PORT
Flint
Northwich
Macclesfield
CHESTER
A684
A683
A6
A65
M6
A588
A682
A629
A59
A56
A586
A585
M55
A584
A6068
M65
A674
A666
A671
A675
A570
M66
M62
A565
M61
M60
M58
A580
M57
M67
A57
A540
M53
A41
M56
A34
A523
A537
A49
A550
A535
A58

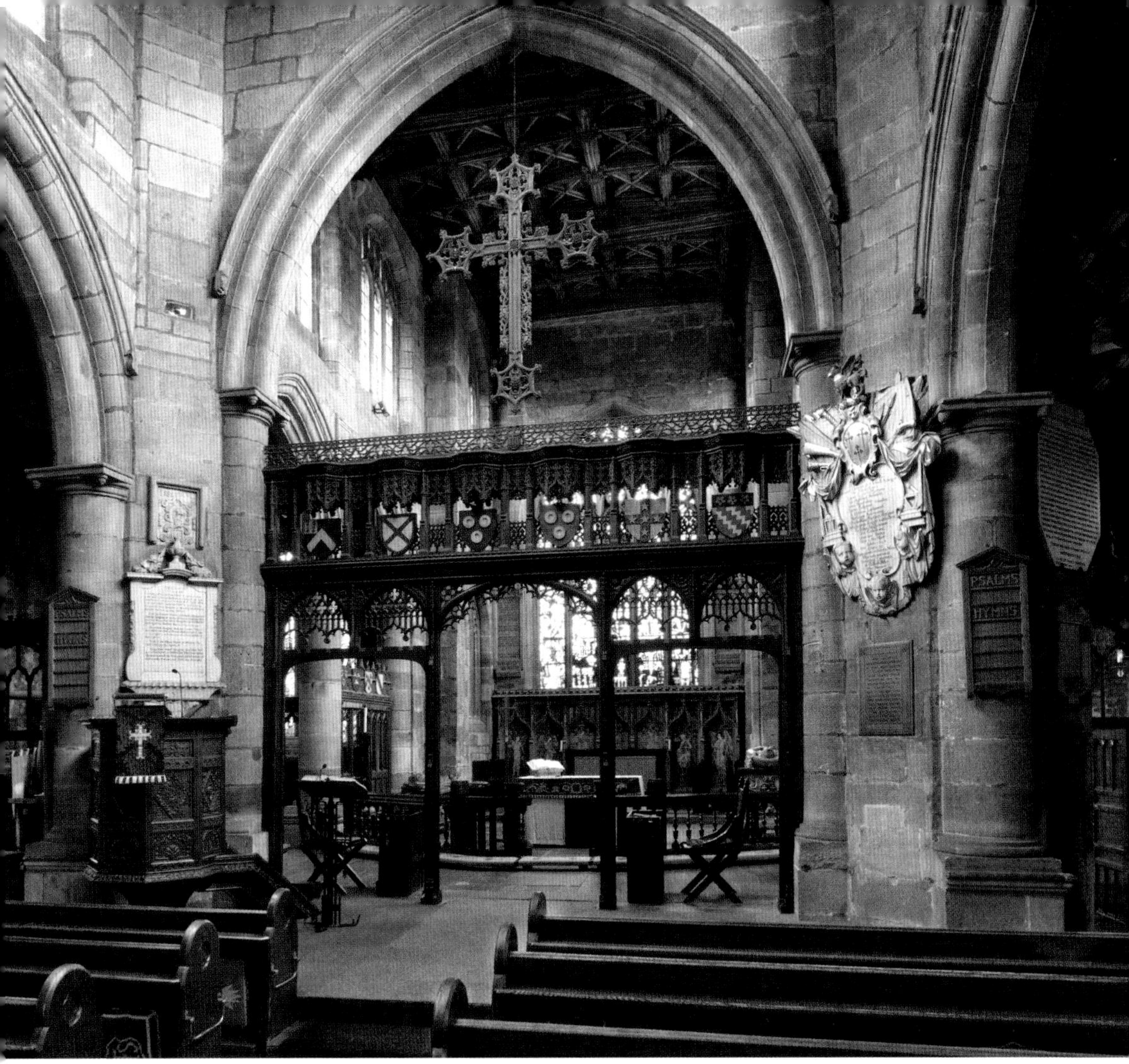

△ **STANDISH: ST WILFRID** – *much of the interior, especially at the chancel end, is 19th-century, including the screen and reredos; the fine oak roof, though, is of about 1580*

It is not surprising that many of the county's churches reflect such rapid social and economic change. Many medieval churches have been rebuilt, although small churches of the 17th and 18th centuries have fared better. For example: Much Hoole, 1628, which is complete save for the Victorian chancel; Billinge, 1717, with its small transepts added in the early 20th century; and Tarleton, 1719, which is a complete and delightful early Georgian work.

However, it was the impact of the 1820 Church Building Act, inspired by a survey showing little or no church building since the time of Queen Anne, and the great Victorian Ecclesiological movement that have left a legacy of Church Commissioners' and Gothic Revival churches throughout the county: E. W Pugin, Sir George Gilbert Scott, Paley & Austin, J. L. Pearson and G. F. Bodley are all names that resound through the county's many fine Victorian churches, and later, Sir Giles Gilbert Scott, whose cathedral for Liverpool, finally completed in 1978, is the glory of modern Gothic.

AUGHTON † St Michael ★

2m/3km S.W. of Ormskirk

OS *SD391054* **GPS** *53.5419N, 2.9197W*

Of grey-brown stone, the church stands low, among shady lanes. It has a mid-14th-century Decorated spire on the N. tower, an Early English nave and a 16th-century N. aisle with round-headed windows and N. chapel. The roof beams in the nave are Tudor, and adjacent to the S. porch is the original Norman doorway.

BARTON UPON IRWELL

† All Saints RC ★★

Redclyffe Road, Trafford; 5m/8km W. of Manchester city centre

OS *SJ766974* **GPS** *53.4734N, 2.3530W*

E. W. Pugin was commissioned by the recusant Catholic de Trafford family to build All Saints as a parish church with attached chantry. The resulting masterpiece, 1867–8, is one of Pugin's finest, in French Early Gothic style. Its W. front is adorned with a rose window and arch of banded stone over niches; the apsidal end has Plate tracery (exemplified at Soisson Cathedral). The resplendent interior includes a reredos with a flock of angels, intricate carved capitals to the nave, whose piers have painted stonework, and the N. chapel, with fine reredos and recumbent Christ below the altar.

BILLINGE † St Aidan

3m/4km N.E. of St Helens

OS *SD533006* **GPS** *53.5009N, 2.7051W*

In a long, hill-top village, St Aidan's is a greenish-cream limestone church of 1717, with urns on its embattled parapet, a clock turret over the W. door and a huge bell in the cupola above. There is unusual Gothic tracery in the rounded windows, and a Gothic flavour to the small transepts added in 1908 by Sir T. G. Jackson. Otherwise all is Classical with Doric columns, pilasters and entablature. The light, arcaded interior has round arches on Doric columns.

BOLTON † St Stephen and All Martyrs ★

Lever Bridge, Radcliffe Road

OS *SD732084* **GPS** *53.5722N, 2.4050W*

By Edmund Sharpe, 1842–5, this is a charming if bizarre Decorated terracotta church, created at the whim of a local colliery owner to demonstrate the versatility of terracotta. The strange appearance of the W. end was caused by the removal of the openwork spire in 1939, and the lower part of the tower in 1966. The interior also has many terracotta touches, including the corbels and bench-ends with poppyheads. The glass is by Wailes and Willement.

COLNE † St Bartholomew

6m/10km N.E. of Burnley

OS *SD888401* **GPS** *53.8572N, 2.1703W*

Founded in the 13th century, the church has an Early English and Decorated interior, and a mainly Perpendicular exterior. The N. aisle was replaced with a double aisle by Paley & Austin in 1883. In the chancel is an obelisk memorial to Christopher and John Emmott, by Sir Robert Taylor.

EDENFIELD † No known dedication

5m/8km N. of Bury

OS *SD798198* **GPS** *53.6744N, 2.3064W*

In a stone moorland village, this parish church has the dimensions and appearance of a domestic Georgian building, with the addition of a small crenellated tower. It was built in 1778 using dark masonry, with galleries, square pews, and mostly clear glass, and it exemplifies unspoiled, unspruced Georgian.

EUXTON † No known dedication

2m/3km N.W. of Chorley

OS *SD555189* **GPS** *53.6651N, 2.6743W*

An ancient-looking little 14th-century church of rough pink stone standing high above the main road, with an aisleless nave, it was largely rebuilt in the 16th century, with small Decorated windows (restored). There is a square 18th-century corbelled belfry, a chancel of 1837, an excellent Tudor roof, double piscina and scraped, outward-leaning walls.

GREAT MITTON † All Hallows ★★

8m/12km N.W. of Burnley

OS *SD715389* **GPS** *53.8462N, 2.4339W*

An Early English church in the Ribble Valley, whose nave slopes from west to east. There is a fine 15th-century screen from Sawley Abbey, and a good E. window with Intersecting tracery. A chapel to the recusant Shireburns was added in the 15th century, which contains striking tomb chests of the Shireburn family carved by the London sculptor William Stanton, from 1594 onwards.

HALSALL † St Cuthbert ★

3m/4km N.W. of Ormskirk

OS *SD370102* **GPS** *53.5854N, 2.9523W*

An important W. Lancashire village church of buff-coloured dressed stone. The Perpendicular spire rises from the tower with an octagonal top stage. Steep 14th-century roofs cover the nave and chancel; they are buttressed, pinnacled and of exceptional beauty. Spired turrets, one with a rood loft stair, stand to either side of the chancel arch. There is a finely ornamented 14th-century tomb recess in the N. wall containing a later, mutilated effigy, and a beautiful Decorated doorway of three continuous moulded orders, with an original panelled and traceried oak door.

HAUGHTON † St Anne

1m/2km S.E. of Denton, Greater Manchester

OS *SJ933955* **GPS** *53.4570N, 2.1012W*

By Medland and Henry Taylor, 1881–2, an unusual timber-framed church with bold, sweeping, patterned tile roofs converging on a curious tile-clad spire, and polygonally-topped stair turret. The windows in the broad nave have strange tracery, elaborate roofs and a general air of the unexpected: a pleasing essay in brick and tile.

HEYSHAM † St Peter

3m/4km S.W. of Morecambe

OS *SD410616* **GPS** *54.0474N, 2.9019W*

Overlooking Morecambe Bay, St Peter's is a low, rugged church on a site of high antiquity. The W. doorway is Saxon, there are early Norman capitals on the chancel arch, and the hoard of early sculpture includes a Viking hogback tomb and a strange 'house cross' in the churchyard, perhaps depicting the Raising of Lazarus. At the ruined St Patrick's Chapel nearby are curious recessed grave slots, carved into solid rock.

HINDLEY † All Saints

2m/3km S.E. of Wigan

OS *SD622043* **GPS** *53.5341N, 2.5706W*

Hindley is a large colliery village with an endearing Georgian church of 1766 with round-headed windows, Gothic tracery and a good doorway. The N., S., and W. sides are taken with galleries, the whole interior being painted in cream and white.

MUCH HOOLE † St Michael ★

6m/10km S.W. of Preston

OS *SD463223* **GPS** *53.6946N, 2.8147W*

St Michael's church is by a quiet lane in low, pastoral country, and dates from 1628. The embattled stone tower and W. front with corner urns is from 1720 and supported inside the church on two substantial Doric columns. The rest is of pink patterned brickwork with low stone-mullioned round-headed windows; the chancel is of 1859. There are box pews, a two-decker pulpit of 1695, galleries, a hatchment and Victorian glass. Jeremiah Horrocks, astronomer, was curate here when he discovered the transit of Venus in 1639.

KIRKBY † St Chad

6m/10km N.E. of Liverpool

OS *SJ408989* **GPS** *53.4843N, 2.8930W*

By Paley & Austin, 1869–71, this is a powerful Norman-Gothic church of local red sandstone. The prominent square central tower has a saddleback roof and square-ended chancel. There is a handsome neo-Norman S. doorway and bold interior with soaring, vaulted tower space. The effective chancel has blank arcading, lancets and Henry Holiday's Last Supper, 1898, in stone mosaic; he also did the glass. The very fine early Norman sandstone font with saints and Adam and Eve is at the back of the church.

LANCASTER † St Mary ★

St Mary's Parade
OS *SD473619* **GPS** *54.0507N, 2.8055W*

The large and impressive 15th-century Perpendicular exterior of St Mary's is accentuated by the grimness of the church's surroundings. Originally a Benedictine foundation, it has a Gothic Revival W. tower by Henry Sephton, 1754, and ornate two-storeyed S. porch by Paley & Austin, 1903. The fine interior is of later, 14th-century character: excellent details and good furnishings include the W. gallery, fine chandeliers and the remarkable and exuberantly carved Decorated choir stalls. There is a good deal of Saxon sculpture in the N. chapel. A most rewarding church.

LIVERPOOL – SEFTON PARK
† St Agnes and St Pancras ★★

On corner of Ullet Road and Buckingham Ave, Sefton Park (Toxteth Park), L17
OS *SJ375884* **GPS** *53.3896N, 2.9398W*

By J. L. Pearson, 1883, this is a noble church in the Early English style: all accentuated verticals and tall lancets. It is built of red brick with sandstone dressings and has a steep red roof from which rise a lead fleche and two stone spirelets flanking the polygonal apse. At the back of the apse is a tall reredos carved by Nathaniel Hitch, whose work also adorns Westminster Abbey and Truro Cathedral. Pearson's interior is outstanding.

LIVERPOOL – ALLERTON
† All Hallows ★

Between Allerton and Greenhill Roads, Garston, L25
OS *SJ399874* **GPS** *53.3807N, 2.9037W*

A late Decorated essay in rock-faced sandstone, by G. Enoch Grayson, 1872–6. The tower has large pinnacles and tall, perforated windows, and diminishes upward in five stages. The interior is mostly of Storeton stone, enriched with an important unified scheme of Burne-Jones glass. The chancel is of red and green jasper with stone and alabaster stripes above, and an arched and gilded wooden ceiling supported by golden angels. The sculptured group by F. Fabiani in the S. transept is a memorial to Mrs Bibby, as is the church itself. The marble memorial of 1840 by William Spence is to John Bibby, builder of the church.

LIVERPOOL – AIGBURTH
† St Anne ★

Church Lane, off Aigburth Road, Garston, L19
OS *SJ381862* **GPS** *53.3693N, 2.9305W*

St Anne's is like a country church, with fields behind it sloping down to the river. By Cunningham & Holme, 1836–7, it is a neo-Norman building of red sandstone, whose matching chancel and transepts were added in 1853. On the outside are a multitude of little round arches and wall arcades, even on the gateposts, and the tower has a scalloped overhanging parapet. The interior is spacious and galleried, with wide transepts and good grotesque corbels.

LIVERPOOL – EVERTON
† St George ★

Grecian Terrace, L5
OS *SJ355924* **GPS** *53.4252N, 2.9714W*

This is Thomas Rickman's light iron Gothic of 1812–14, one of the first of its kind. The Commissioners' sandstone exterior conceals a wonderful interior, with lavish and delicate use of cast iron in the galleries, arcades and traceried roofs; Rickman worked here with John Cragg, ironmaster.

LIVERPOOL – TUEBROOK
† St John Baptist ★★

West Derby Road, L13
OS *SJ382924* **GPS** *53.4248N, 2.9300W*

St John Baptist's is an early – and largely unknown – dignified essay in the Decorated style, by G. F. Bodley, 1868–71, built of red and white sandstone to a simple plan. Bodley concerned himself closely with the sumptuous interior: colour is everywhere, with exquisite furnishings and murals by C. E. Kempe, and early pale glass by Morris and Burne-Jones.

MANCHESTER – CITY CENTRE
† St Ann ★

St Ann's Square, M2
OS *SJ837983* **GPS** *53.4817N, 2.2458W*

A fine city church of 1709–12 founded by Lady Ann Bland, St Ann's was built in the style of Wren, by John Barker. It stands

△ **RIBCHESTER: ST WILFRID** – *the dominant feature of the 14th-century chancel is the group of three Early English lancet windows at the east end*

across one end of St Ann's Square, which was laid out at the same time. The distinctive pink sandstone exterior has a square W. tower, whose cupola was declared unsafe and demolished in 1777. There is an arcaded and galleried interior with flat, coved ceiling and tall Corinthian pilasters. The handsome apsidal E. end has good carving in the frieze. Much original woodwork includes pew backs and the magnificent pulpit. The marble font is of 1711.

MANCHESTER – MOSS SIDE

† Holy Name of Jesus RC ★

On corner of Ackers Street and Oxford Road, M13
OS *SJ847964* **GPS** *53.4645N, 2.2311W*

This is a Jesuit foundation, 1869, by J. A. Hansom – monumentally French Gothic outside and, inside, white terracotta, with a five-bay nave and N. and S. aisles, the slender piers of which rise to a finely vaulted roof. Numerous side chapels lead off both aisles. In the apse, the altar is alabaster inlaid with green Russian malachite, and behind is the lofty Caen stone reredos, bearing statues of the Jesuit saints: Hansom's son completed this. The baptistry is delicately moulded terracotta. The font is alabaster, with a counter-weighted oak cover.

MELLING-WITH-WRAYTON

† St Wilfrid

5m/8km S. of Kirkby Lonsdale
OS *SD598711* **GPS** *54.1347N, 2.6165W*

A largely Perpendicular church on a sloping site in the Lune Valley, necessitating three groups of steps to the altar. The 1762 clerestory was altered in 1866. There is Saxon sculpture, good 17th-century benches and good glass by Powell. Clementine Rumph, the German 'Florence Nightingale' of the Franco-Prussian War of 1870–71, is commemorated at the W. end of the S. aisle. The 15th-century Morley Chantry Chapel was heavily dealt with by the Victorians.

△ **RIBCHESTER: ST WILFRID** – *this mostly Early English church with a Perpendicular west tower stands on the site of a Roman fort*

MIDDLETON † St Leonard

6ml10km N. of Manchester
OS *SD872063* **GPS** *53.5533N, 2.1945W*

On a hill above the town, St Leonard's was reconstructed in 1523–4 by Sir Richard Assheton, whose Arms and initials appear on the elaborately panelled porch. The extraordinary wooden bell-chamber of c. 1667 is 'like a dovecote'. Note the 15th-century glass commemorating Flodden Field, and the fine Perpendicular rood screen with the Assheton Arms.

OVERTON † St Helen

2ml3km S.E. of Heysham
OS *SD440575* **GPS** *54.0112N, 2.8553W*

This is a simple church of charm, in a remote village on the banks of the River Lune. It has a gabled belfry, Norman doorway, a wider chancel of 1771, when square-headed windows were made, and a W. gallery. The N. transept was added in 1830.

PENDLEBURY † St Augustine

N.W. suburb of Salford
OS *SD787016* **GPS** *53.5107N, 2.3223W*

By Bodley & Garner, 1870–4, an outstanding Victorian church, modelled on Albi Cathedral in France, but faithfully translated into the English Decorated and Perpendicular styles. The austere red-brick and stone exterior has a canted E. bay; the projected tower was never built. The awesome interior has tall arcades, internal buttresses and a wooden barrel vault, the details simple so as not to spoil the lines. The impressively raised sanctuary has superb Bodley furnishings of reredos, sedilia and rood screen, and the glass is by Burlison & Grylls.

POULTON-LE-FYLDE † St Chad ★

3ml4km N.E. of Blackpool
OS *SD348394* **GPS** *53.8472N, 2.9921W*

St Chad stands in the middle of an old market town. It is a rebuilding of 1752–3,

△ **RIBCHESTER: ST WILFRID** – *in the north side chapel are traces of a 14th-century wall-painting of St Christopher carrying Christ on his shoulder; it is partly overlaid with later wall texts*

retaining an early 17th-century Perpendicular tower; the Romanesque chancel is of 1868. The doorways have Tuscan pediments, and the Georgian interior retains galleries with square pews and a good contemporary staircase. The pedimented entrance to the vault is dated 1699.

PRESTON † St Peter

St Peter's Square
OS *SD534299* **GPS** *53.7636N, 2.7081W*

By Rickman & Hutchinson, 1822–5, a stone and iron Decorated Commissioners' church, upstanding and well-composed; the crocketed S.E. spire was added by Mitchell in 1851. Inside, everything is cusped: the iron gallery arcade, the door panels and even the door handles. The church is now an arts centre, but a visit to view the outside is rewarding in itself.

RIBCHESTER † St Wilfrid ★

5m/8km N. of Blackburn
OS *SD649350* **GPS** *53.8103N, 2.5332W*

A lovely Early English church on the site of a Roman fort. The fine chancel has stepped lancets, and in the 14th-century N. chapel are remnants of a medieval wall-painting of St Christopher. The 1736 W. gallery is supported on stone columns, and there is a well-carved Jacobean pulpit – scene of a confrontation between the Royalist rector Christopher Hindle and the Parliamentary nominee Mr Ingham. Hindle was ejected.

RIVINGTON † Rivington Church ★

2m/3km N. of Horwich
OS *SD624144* **GPS** *53.6252N, 2.5685W*

The church, which no longer has a dedication and thus is known simply as Rivington Church, is a charming little aisleless structure in a moorland village, built c. 1540 and remodelled c. 1666. It has mullioned windows, a detached 16th-century bell-house, octagonal belfry, a late Perpendicular screen, linenfold pulpit and splendid 18th-century chandelier. On the N. wall is an 18th-century reproduction of a 16th-century painting depicting the Pilkington family, fire-damaged in 1834.

RUFFORD † St Mary

6m/10km N.E. of Ormskirk
OS *SD464156* **GPS** *53.6350N, 2.8118W*

This is a perfect small brick and stone Victorian church of 1869 by Dawson & Davies, with a spire suggesting a child's box of coloured bricks. The low aisles are lit by small pointed windows, mostly filled with good contemporary pictorial glass, and the nave piers have bold, attractive capitals. Memorials include a Flaxman figure of Lady Sophie Hesketh, d. 1817. The Royal Arms and brass chandelier are both from 1763.

SALFORD † St Philip with St Stephen

St Philip's Place
OS *SJ826986* **GPS** *53.4840N, 2.2631W*

By Sir Robert Smirke, 1825, in Greek style, and similar to his church of St Mary, Wyndham Place, London. The domed cylindrical steeple rises from a semi-circular Ionic peristyle on the S. side of the church, closing the vista from Bank Place, and defying the dreary surroundings. The interior is pleasant Greek Doric, with galleries, a wreathed frieze and flat ceiling.

SAMLESBURY † St Leonard the Less

3m/4km E. of Preston
OS *SD589303* **GPS** *53.7680N, 2.6237W*

Low down near the Ribble, this is a compact stone church comprising clerestoried nave of 1558 and aisles, N. tower and porches of 1899–1900. The 17th- and 18th-century box pews have been lowered, and the three-decker pulpit is now a two-decker. There is a fine monument of 1801 by J. Kendrick, with urn and draped figure, and Sir Thomas Southworth's funerary armour of helmet, sword and shield.

SEFTON † St Helen ★★

3m/4km N.E. of Crosby
OS *SD356012* **GPS** *53.5044N, 2.9712W*

The church stands among flat meadows that for the moment hold the housing estates and shops at bay. The large 14th-century spire rises from a buttressed tower, the outlines unified by spirelets. Of brown-grey stone, the church is otherwise late Perpendicular, c. 1535–40, with long, horizontal lines and an almost flat roof behind an embattled parapet. A fine Tudor interior contains glorious early 16th-century woodwork, including the canopied rood and chancel screens, the screens to the N. and S. chapels and, to the S., the Sefton pew. The chancel stalls of 1500 are complete, and there is a canopied pulpit of 1635. The Molyneux monuments commemorate the family's courage in battle, and range from a mailed effigy of c. 1296 to a table-tomb with brasses of 1568.

SINGLETON † St Anne

2m/3km E. of Poulton-le-Fylde
OS *SD385383* **GPS** *53.8379N, 2.9360W*

By E. G. Paley, 1860–1: a handsome Early English cruciform estate church with lofty N.E. steeple and Plate tracery. The glass in the E. window is by Frederick Preedy.

SLAIDBURN † St Andrew ★

6m/10km N. of Clitheroe
OS *SD710521* **GPS** *53.9642N, 2.4435W*

Buried deep in the Bowland Forest district, St Andrew's church is externally plain, but contains fine Jacobean woodwork. The screen, possibly by Francis Grundy, has finely detailed open tracery and is set into equally pleasing box pews. There is an elegant Georgian pulpit and an old oak chest. At the W. end of the church is an organ, with finely decorated pipes, which was played at the Great Exhibition of 1851.

SOUTHPORT † Holy Trinity

16m/25km N. of Liverpool
Manchester Road
OS *SD342175* **GPS** *53.6502N, 2.9966W*

A very grand town church By Huon Matear, 1903–13, of pink brick and sandstone, with a lofty tower topped by an octagon and

△ **WHALLEY: ST MARY** – *the church is Early English with later additions, including the tower and clerestory, and a Perpendicular refashioning of the aisle windows and east window*

pinnacles. The dramatic French-style interior is like a cathedral, with soaring octagonal piers, pointed, ribbed barrel vaulting and flamboyant stone tracery in the chancel roof.

STANDISH † St Wilfrid ★

3m/4km N.W. of Wigan

OS *SD563102* **GPS** *53.5871N, 2.6613W*

An imposing dark stone Gothic survival church of 1582–4, St Wilfrid's has an excellent Tudor roof, panelled and braced, with a fine range of individual bosses. There is some Renaissance influence apparent in the arcades, which use elegant Tuscan columns.

STOCKPORT † St George

Buxton Road

OS *SJ899889* **GPS** *53.3971N, 2.1520W*

By Hubert Austin of Paley & Austin, 1892–7, it is a magnificent church of cathedral-like proportions in uncompromising late Gothic style; cruciform, with a tall crossing tower, spire and flying buttresses. The seven-light E. window is the climax of the exterior, with massed Reticulated tracery and panelled decoration above and below. Inside, six bays of clustered shafts support a galleried clerestory, all culminating in the huge panelled piers of the crossing. A beautiful alabaster reredos stops the view up the nave, and beyond is the great E. window with glass by Shrigley and Hunt.

STYDD † St Saviour ★

5m/8km N. of Blackburn; adjoins Ribchester

OS *SD653359* **GPS** *53.8189N, 2.5273W*

A small, plain and remote 12th-century church, it was originally associated with a preceptory of the Knights Hospitaller. There are Norman windows in the N. side, and a doorway with zigzag decoration. On the S. side is a splendid Early English S. doorway; the screen and nine-sided pulpit are 17th-century.

△ **WHALLEY: ST MARY** – *the chancel is of about 1220, but for the Perpendicular east window, which replaced the original three lancet window in the 15th century; the glass is 19th-century*

TARLETON † St Mary ★

8m/12km E. of Southport
OS *SD456201* **GPS** *53.6748N, 2.8239W*
Churches Conservation Trust

This is a tidy, early Georgian brick church of 1719, with a stone bell-turret and elegant cupola added in 1824, together with porch and vestry. The roof has corner finials, and round-headed windows with clear glass light the interior well. The S. and W. panelled galleries are supported on fluted columns, and there is a handsome cast-iron stove.

UP HOLLAND † St Thomas the Martyr

4m/6km W. of Wigan
OS *SD523051* **GPS** *53.5404N, 2.7210W*

Originally a Benedictine priory, St Thomas's was founded in 1307; building continued through the 14th century, the tower being added in the 15th century. The interior is excellent, with slender Decorated piers and a refined plaster ceiling of 1752. The present chancel is an addition of 1882–6. There are pew ends dated 1635 with family initials.

WARBURTON † Old St Werburgh

5m/8km W. of Altrincham
OS *SJ696895* **GPS** *53.4021N, 2.4573W*
Churches Conservation Trust

The Old Church is small, secluded and of great interest. The building is of timber, with some walls replaced with stone in 1645, and some with brick in 1711, the date also of the brick tower. The roof is of Kerridge slabs. Inside, the constructional timbers divide off the aisles. The screen, pulpit, altar and rails are Jacobean; the box-pews are 1813 but look earlier.

WHALLEY † St Mary ★★

6m/10km N.E. of Blackburn
OS *SD732361* **GPS** *53.8212N, 2.4077W*

St Mary's is a large Early English church in the middle of the village, and close to the site of an old abbey. The tower, clerestory and aisle windows are all Perpendicular. Inside is splendid carved woodwork, including the canopied stalls with misericords of 1418–34 from the adjacent abbey, screened pews of

△ **WOODPLUMPTON: ST ANNE** – *popping up above this bungalow of a church is a Baroque octagonal lantern atop the most modest of towers against the west wall*

the 17th and 18th centuries, and the organ case of 1729, originally in Lancaster parish church. There are good later monuments and three Saxon crosses in the churchyard.

WOODPLUMPTON † St Anne ★

4m/6km N.W. of Preston

OS *SD499344* **GPS** *53.8039N, 2.7617W*

In low Fylde landscape, green and wooded, is this mainly Perpendicular church, with its S. aisle and W. tower a handsome Baroque rebuilding of 1748. It is a long, low building of warm cream-coloured stone with octagonal domed belfry and Gibbsian surrounds to the doors and windows in the 18th-century parts. The broad interior is lit by dormers in the roof of 1900, and has three aisles divided by Perpendicular arcades. The tasteful oak pews and screen also date from the 1900 restoration.

WORSLEY † St Mark

6m/10km W. of Manchester

OS *SD745006* **GPS** *53.5023N, 2.3849W*

By Sir George Gilbert Scott, 1846, St Mark's is a delightful estate church in his favourite Middle Pointed style: archaeological but relieved by jolly details like the gargoyled and crocketed spire. The splendidly eclectic interior has much carved woodwork, tiles and bright glass by Hardman.

LEICESTERSHIRE

To most outsiders Leicestershire used to conjure up images of a flat, featureless country strangely beloved by hunting men, for boots and shoes, and a kingdom of red brick. The truth is different. Far from being flat, the county stretches up on its eastern side to the high wolds that it shares with Lincolnshire – part of the limestone spine of England; and on the west it has its own, unique Charnwood Forest, whose granite hills rise to 900 feet above the sea, and which is now a part of the National Forest. The county is a great mix of livestock farming and engineering.

Leicestershire is where John Taylor cast the 'Great Paul' bell – the largest in the country – for St Paul's Cathedral: the Loughborough bellfounders have been casting bells in the county since the 1300s. This is where Stilton cheese comes from; but Leicester let the glory go to Stilton, where it was merely sold, never made. That is a characteristic wry Leicestershire joke, and it goes for other things in the county too. Belvoir – an incredible castle, standing up on its hill like something in a fairy-tale – is popularly supposed to be in Lincolnshire, or in Rutland.

Twenty-first-century Leicester is one of England's most diverse cities, whose South Asian population has added Hindu, Sikh and Muslim places of worship to the county's religious landscape. There is no great Roman Catholic family here, though a Cistercian monastery hides in Charnwood Forest.

△ **STAUNTON HAROLD: HOLY TRINITY** – *the church picturesquely set in the manorial grounds*

◁ **BOTTESFORD: ST MARY THE VIRGIN** – *weepers at the tomb of the 4th Earl of Rutland*

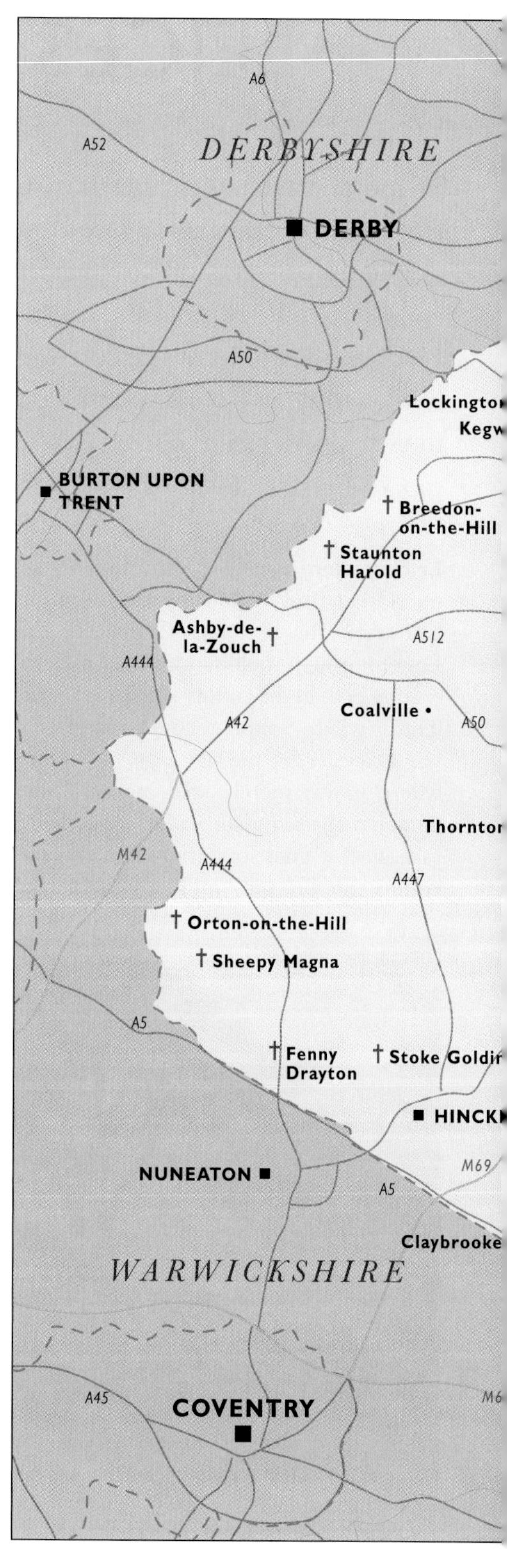

ASFORDBY † All Saints

3m/4km W. of Melton Mowbray

OS *SK708189* **GPS** *52.7634N, 0.9520W*

This is a 13th- to 14th-century amber-coloured ironstone church restored in 1866–7. The tower has Perpendicular tracery, pinnacled battlements, gargoyles and a fine limestone tower. The 15th-century oak roof is supported by angel corbels, and there is a Green Man boss. There is a rare coloured 15th-century bench-end, and fragments of a Saxon cross.

ASHBY-DE-LA-ZOUCH † St Helen ★

16m/25km N.W. of Leicester

OS *SK360167* **GPS** *52.7473N, 1.4668W*

Adjacent to the castle ruins, St Helen's is a prosperous Perpendicular church with outer aisles by J. P. St Aubyn, 1878–80. The interior has a splendid pedimented reredos of 1679, and the Hastings Chapel contains fine family monuments, beginning with an alabaster tomb of 1561 and including works by Kent and Rysbrack. At the back of the church is a finger-pillory.

AYLESTONE † St Andrew

District of Leicester, 2m/3km S. of centre

OS *SK571010* **GPS** *52.6039N, 1.1570W*

St Andrew's has a huge chancel of c. 1300, longer and higher than the nave, and one of the largest chancels in any village church. It has a fine Reticulated E. window and good 1930s glass by Harry Payne in Pre-Raphaelite style. The nave is an interesting blend of Early English and Decorated, with entertaining, crudely carved corbels. The carvings on the Tudor roof were gilded and repainted at the millennium.

BOTTESFORD † St Mary the Virgin ★★

7m/11km W. of Grantham

OS *SK807391* **GPS** *52.9434N, 0.8000W*

The approach to the church is delightful, across a brook and through a screen of trees. The nave and spire are handsome 15th-century ironstone work, reminiscent of several over the Lincolnshire border, a few miles away. The chancel was rebuilt in the 17th century to accommodate the magnificent monuments of the earls (later dukes) of

NOTTINGHAM
A46
A1
Bottesford
A52
NOTTINGHAMSHIRE
A607
Croxton Kerrial
A60
Buckminster
Wymeswold
A606
LINCOLNSHIRE
A6006
HBOROUGH
Asfordby
Stapleford
Kirby Bellars
MELTON
MOWBRAY
A1
A6
A607
A606
Gaddesby
RUTLAND
LEICESTERSHIRE
OAKHAM
A606
STAMFORD
Withcote
LEICESTER
A6121
Aylestone
Oadby
Kings Norton
A47
Uppingham
A43
Hallaton
Blaby
Wistow
A5199
Church Langton
A6003
A426
Peatling Magna
A6
A427
CORBY
OUNDLE
Lubenham
MARKET
HARBOROUGH
A427
A4304
A508
0
5 miles
0
5 km
NORTHAMPTONSHIRE

△ **BOTTESFORD: ST MARY THE VIRGIN** – *the chancel is packed with monuments of exceptional quality and power, dwarfing the modest altar*

Rutland, whose home, Belvoir Castle, looms up on the hills to the S. The monuments completely fill the chancel, blocking the sight of the altar from the nave. They afford a fascinating view of changing aristocratic taste in the 16th and 17th centuries.

BREEDON-ON-THE-HILL
† St Mary and St Hardulph ★★

5m/8km N.E. of Ashby-de-la-Zouch
OS *SK405233* **GPS** *52.8062N, 1.3995W*

The church stands within a great Iron Age camp on top of the hill, keeping watch on the Trent Valley. The hill itself is being steadily quarried away, the workings now approaching close to the edge of the churchyard. There was a Saxon monastic foundation here. The present church is Norman and 13th-century; its nave has been destroyed. From the Saxon church came the wonderful 8th-century carved stones, now set high up under the clerestory, in the S. aisle, and inside the tower (arrange to see especially the Breedon Angel set into the wall on the first floor). The N. aisle contains monuments and a Jacobean canopied pew of the Shirley family of Staunton Harold.

BUCKMINSTER † St John the Baptist

6m/10km N.E. of Melton Mowbray
OS *SK879230* **GPS** *52.7981N, 0.6976W*

The church is a stately early 13th-century building in a village setting, with a later 13th-century tower, broach spire and Perpendicular chancel. In the churchyard is the Gothic Dysart mausoleum of c. 1875.

CHURCH LANGTON † St Peter ★

4m/6km N. of Market Harborough
OS *SP724934* **GPS** *52.5338N, 0.9340W*

The tower is a landmark for miles around, a fine and imposing structure, tapering by stages from the ground and panelled at the sides. The proportions of the building throughout are excellent: the characteristic Leics. nave, short and high, is seen here to perfection. The fabric is Decorated with 15th-century remodelling, and the windows are a text-book illustration of the development of stone

△ **BREEDON-ON-THE-HILL: ST MARY AND ST HARDULPH** – *inserted into the stonework of the church are various Saxon carvings such as this one with its depiction of cat-like creatures*

tracery – from Plate and Geometrical to simplified Victorian Perpendicular.

CLAYBROOKE PARVA † St Peter ★
5m/8km S.E. of Hinckley
OS *SP496879* **GPS** *52.4869N, 1.2708W*

The nave has good Perpendicular work, rose-coloured piers supporting limestone arches and a 15th-century roof ornamented with carved animals and grotesques. The chancel is perfect early 14th-century, as beautiful inside as out. The best exterior view is from the S. side of the churchyard, where the treatment of the walls and the flowing Decorated tracery of the windows can be studied.

CROXTON KERRIAL
† St Botolph and St John the Baptist ★
7m/11km S.W. of Grantham
OS *SK835294* **GPS** *52.8565N, 0.7609W*

A gentle village setting, 15th-century central tower and much else besides. Inside is an astounding collection of Perpendicular bench-ends, some 45 in total, believed to have come from Croxton Abbey – hunters, grimacing heads, animals – by far the best in the county.

FENNY DRAYTON
† St Michael and All Angels ★★
3m/4km N. of Nuneaton
OS *SP350971* **GPS** *52.5707N, 1.4844W*

The church has early Norman origins, with a late 12th-century S. door, but otherwise it is mostly Decorated, all heavily restored in 1860. There is an excellent series of Purefoy monuments, 1545–1628; a memorial of 1736 records a grim struggle with the gout, 'attended with Exquisite Pain and Torture'. George Fox, founder of the Quakers, is said to have been baptised here.

GADDESBY † St Luke ★★
6m/10km S.W. of Melton Mowbray
OS *SK689130* **GPS** *52.7107N, 0.9805W*

Perhaps the most exciting medieval church in the county, dating mainly from about 1290 to 1340. The ornamentation of the exterior of the S. aisle is unique – a brilliant and riotous exhibition of the 14th-century stone carver's art. The exterior also has the largest collection of masons' marks in the county. The interior has been sympathetically and lightly restored, leaving the old, partly medieval seating and brick floors. The light pours in through clear glass, illuminating the wide empty spaces of the nave. In the chancel is a lifesize statue of Colonel Cheney on his horse at Waterloo, removed from the hall nearby.

HALLATON † St Michael and All Angels
7m/11km N.E. of Market Harborough
OS *SP786965* **GPS** *52.5606N, 0.8396W*

The main body of the church in this charming village is 13th-century ironstone, including the delightful tower and spire; the aisles are a 14th-century addition. At

BOTTESFORD: ST MARY THE VIRGIN – *the early 17th-century tomb of Roger, 5th Earl of Rutland, and his wife Countess Elizabeth* ▷

E ITALIE, SVISELAND, & Y LOW CVNTRIES WHERE HE
INVED 3 YEARES, AFTER HE WENT VOLVNTARIE
GE, HE WAS COELONEL OF Y FOOT IN Y IRISH WARRES
NNO 1598 HE WAS MADE LORD LIEVTENANT OF
OLNSHIRE IN ANO 1603 BEING Y FIRST YEARE OF
IGNE OF KING IAMES, IN W SAID YEARE HE WENT
SSADO FROM HIS MA INTO DENMARK, TO Y CHRISTNING
KINGS FIRST SONNE, & W Y ORDER OF Y GARTER
Y KING THERE. HE MARIED ELIZABETH SOLE
HTER TO S PHILLIP SYDNEY, HE DEPARTED Y LIFE
MBRIDGE Y 26 DAYE OF IVNE 1612 FROM WHENCE
PS WAS CONVEYED TO BELVOIR CASTLE & HERE
D Y 22 OF IVLIE FOLLOWING HE DIED WTHOVT
LEFT TO SVCCEED HIM IN HIS EARLDOM AND
IIS HO BROTHER FRANCIS NOW EARLE OF RVTLAND
OF HAMLACK TRVSBVTT & BELVOIR.

△ **BREEDON-ON-THE-HILL: ST MARY AND ST HARDULPH** – *the Early English aisled chancel is now used as the main body of the church, with private chapels railed off in the north aisle*

the E. end of the N. aisle there is an elaborately Decorated Gothic turret, surmounted by a little spire, and in the N. porch is a Norman tympanum of St Michael and the Dragon. The interior is spacious, with good 13th-century ornamentation in the chancel. At the E. end of the N. aisle is a small 15th-century rib-vaulted crypt, now used as a boiler room. At the W. end is a Saxon grave marker.

KEGWORTH † St Andrew ★

5m/8km N.W. of Loughborough
OS *SK487267* **GPS** *52.8357N, 1.2777W*

The church stands well, in the centre of a little town on a hill above the water meadows of the Soar. The lower part of the tower is 13th-century, the whole of the rest of the building early 14th-century, giving it a striking architectural coherence. Chapels at the E. end of the aisles look like transepts and help to build up the impressive external view from the E. The interior is somewhat bare, although there are good Royal Arms of 1685.

KINGS NORTON
† St John the Baptist ★★

7m/12km S.E. of Leicester
OS *SK689004* **GPS** *52.5979N, 0.9841W*

A startlingly lovely Gothic Revival church of 1720 in a beautiful setting on a hill, built for William Fortrey by John Wing the Younger. The original spire was struck by lightning in 1843, and its replacement suffered the same fate in 1850. The interior, of Norwegian oak, is almost untouched Georgian, lit by clear glass.

KIRBY BELLARS † St Peter

3m/4km W. of Melton Mowbray
OS *SK717182* **GPS** *52.7570N, 0.9377W*

Beautifully placed on rising ground above the little River Wreak, the iron and limestone church is best seen from the road leading from Melton Mowbray or from the N. across the river. The tower tapers in four stages to a tall broach spire. The building is mostly 13th-century, enlarged and embellished in the 14th, when it became the church of a small collegiate foundation.

LEICESTER † St Margaret

St Margaret's Way

OS *SK585050* **GPS** *52.6404N, 1.1363W*

The most handsome of the city churches, with a S. doorway and S. nave arcade of the 13th century. The tower and the chancel are particularly good examples of Perpendicular work. By the altar is the alabaster tomb of Bishop Penny, d. 1520. As a composition the church appears best from the N.E. corner of the churchyard.

LEICESTER † St Mary de Castro ★★

Castle Green

OS *SK582041* **GPS** *52.6323N, 1.1402W*

The church stands on the edge of the green. Its good Perpendicular spire, much repaired and rebuilt, dominates the river front of the old town. Except on days of brilliant sunlight, the interior is gloomy and mysterious. The history of the fabric is complicated, and at some points perplexing. There is Norman work in the nave, decorated with Norman and Victorian carved animals. The sumptuous chancel, separated by a Jacobean screen, is late Norman in its present form, its splendid sedilia with zigzags and foliate patterns. The wide S. aisle is mainly 13th-century with a Perpendicular roof. The tower is 'engaged' into this aisle, its ground floor forming a baptistry.

LEICESTER † St Nicholas ★

St Nicholas Circle

OS *SK582045* **GPS** *52.6351N, 1.1409W*

Viewed from the W., this church is unforgettable; it towers over Leicester's Roman foundations and core of the Jewry Wall, which is thought to have been part of the public baths of Roman Leicester. The Roman wall survived because it formed part of the narthex of this early church. The nave is Anglo-Saxon, and there are doubled-splayed windows in the N. wall, whose arches are formed of Roman tiles. The church was heavily restored between 1875 and 1898 and again in 1905, when the Saxon-Norman tower was restored very poorly.

LOCKINGTON † St Nicholas

6m/10km N.W. of Loughborough, 1m/2km E. of Castle Donington

OS *SK468279* **GPS** *52.8469N, 1.3065W*

The church dates from the early 13th century, but the aisles were widened in the early 14th to give the present spacious interior. There is an impressive five-light Reticulated E. window in the N. aisle. Excellent fittings include a good Perpendicular screen beneath a huge Royal Arms of 1704, a two-decker 18th-century pulpit, box pews, benches and an 18th-century W. gallery.

LUBENHAM † All Saints ★

2m/3km W. of Market Harborough

OS *SP705870* **GPS** *52.4770N, 0.9631W*

All Saints escaped the attention of Victorian restorers, leaving a charming muddle of the 12th, 13th, 16th and 17th centuries. Long, and almost flat-roofed, with a stout two-stage tower, the church has a simple attractiveness, with unrestored Georgian rustic furnishings. Plaster and whitewash still cover the walls, and even the 13th-century piers and capitals of the nave. The three-decker pulpit and box pews of 1812 survive as a set, together with a little medieval seating in the chancel. Uncovered fragments of medieval wall-paintings can be seen by the chancel arch and behind the pulpit.

MARKET HARBOROUGH
† St Dionysius

13m/21km S.E. of Leicester

OS *SP733872* **GPS** *52.4786N, 0.9213W*

The 160-foot spire of St Dionysius rises straight from the street in the centre of the town. The church shares the market square with red-brick Georgian town houses and an Elizabethan grammar school. The tower and crocketed spire are very good 14th-century Gothic, constructed with slight convexity to counteract the visual illusion of concavity created by a straight shaft. The main body of the church is later, c. 1470, of iron and limestone, and heavily embattled. It contains little of principal interest.

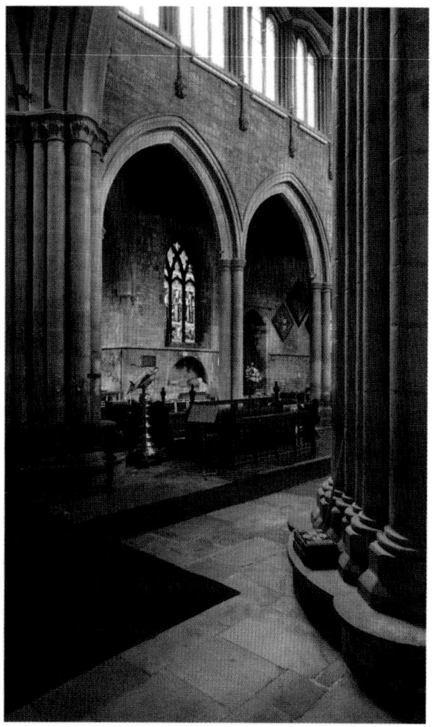

△ **MELTON MOWBRAY: ST MARY** – *clustered piers at the crossing*

MELTON MOWBRAY † St Mary ★

14m/22km N.E. of Leicester
OS *SK752190* **GPS** *52.7636N, 0.8858W*

This is a stately cruciform town church with a tall central tower, marred only by a very clumsy external stair turret on the N. side. The transepts have E. and W. aisles, a rare extravagance denied to many cathedrals, and the aisle windows have good Intersecting and Geometrical tracery. The most striking features are Perpendicular, including the lavish clerestory of 48 windows and the top stage of the tower. The interior has suffered much from bad Victorian restoration; the chancel is dingy and almost wholly without interest.

ORTON-ON-THE-HILL
† St Edith of Polesworth

9m/15km N.W. of Hinckley
OS *SK304039* **GPS** *52.6323N, 1.5519W*

An impressive 14th-century fabric of ashlar, whose embattled tower supports a rather odd obelisk tower. Inside are Georgian furnishings, 18th-century box pews, a three-decker pulpit, font and a small Bevington organ in the chancel. Set in the N. wall is a 14th-century effigy of an abbot of Merevale.

PEATLING MAGNA † All Saints ★

7m/12km S. of Leciester
OS *SP594924* **GPS** *52.5268N, 1.1247W*

This largely late 13th-century church is not of great note from the outside, though well seen from the road to the E. Inside, the walls, lined with texts and hatchments, have been scraped, but the pearly colour and texture of the stone are as delightful, in their different way, as plaster. The woodwork includes some 15th-century and Jacobean seating, a fine 17th-century pulpit, altar rails and reredos.

SHEEPY MAGNA † All Saints ★

6m/10km N.W. of Hinckley
OS *SK326013* **GPS** *52.6087N, 1.5198W*

A Perpendicular church with W. tower, whose main interest is in the four stained-glass windows in the S. wall, two by Morris and Co. to designs by Burne-Jones, 1879, and two by Kempe, 1897.

STAPLEFORD † St Mary Magdalene ★

4m/6km E. of Melton Mowbray
OS *SK811182* **GPS** *52.7554N, 0.7987W*
Churches Conservation Trust

St Mary's stands in a glade of the woods of Stapleford Park. It should be seen in the spring when the daffodils are out. The church was wholly rebuilt in the Gothic taste to the designs of George Richardson and at the expense of the Earl of Harborough in 1783. The interior is distinguished. The seats face inward, as in a college chapel. All the original fittings remain and the woodwork is good, especially the W. gallery. A 15th-century brass and a Caroline monument survive from the earlier church, both of high quality. On the N. side of the chancel is a superb monument by Rysbrack. The glass is clear throughout, but there is constant colour and movement in this church from the play of trees outside.

STAUNTON HAROLD † Holy Trinity ★

3m/4km N.E. of Ashby-de-la-Zouch
OS *SK379208* **GPS** *52.7841N, 1.4381W*
National Trust – Entrance to the park is ½m/1km S.E. of location

This is the private chapel of Staunton Harold Hall, set at an oblique angle to it, on a grass bank rising from the lake. The chapel was built at the expense of Sir Robert Shirley in 1653–65, as an Anglican gesture of defiance to the Commonwealth government. 'When', as the inscription over the W. door proclaims, 'all things sacred were throughout the nation Either demollisht or profaned.' Sir Richard died in the Tower of London in 1656 and the church was only completed after the Restoration. Though not the only church in England originating during the Cromwellian period, it is unique in preserving all its fittings, including pews, painted ceilings and altar hangings. The 17th-century pale-green glass survives in some of the windows. There is also an early 18th-century organ, and an iron chancel screen, probably by Robert Bakewell.

STOKE GOLDING † St Margaret ★★

3m/4km N.W. of Hinckley
OS *SP397972* **GPS** *52.5718N, 1.4145W*

A building of exceptional perfection, showing Decorated design and carving at its best, both outside, in the openwork parapet and buttresses, and inside, especially in the S. nave arcade with clustered columns and capitals carved with foliage and Green Men. The windows are notable throughout, particularly the Geometrical E. windows of the nave and aisle, and the N. windows, with their flowing tracery, which are a little later.

THORNTON † St Peter ★

6m/10km N.W. of Leicester
OS *SK468076* **GPS** *52.6647N, 1.3090W*

St Peter's occupies a charming situation, on the side of a hill overlooking a reservoir. The 14th- and 15th-century church has been very little restored, retaining its plastered walls, old floors and seating. The tympanum was last painted in 1820, and there is an enormous S. door from Ulverscroft Priory, complete with sanctuary ring. In the S. aisle the traceried heads of the E. window contain 14th-century glass. The linenfold bench-ends of 1560 are very fine. The only Victorian intervention is the shallow chancel added in 1864.

WISTOW † St Wistan ★

6m/10km S.E. of Leicester
OS *SP643959* **GPS** *52.5579N, 1.0519W*

A small church on the edge of the park at Wistow Hall, formerly the home of the Halfords; the tower is 15th-century, but the appearance of the fabric is now mainly of the 1746 remodelling, with some early 19th-century fiddling. The interior is near-perfect Georgian with plaster ceiling, painted ironwork altar rails, reredos, pulpit and box pews, all rounded off by a Royal Arms and Halford memorials.

WITHCOTE † Dedication uncertain ★

5m/8km S.W. of Oakham
OS *SK795057* **GPS** *52.6441N, 0.8253W*
Churches Conservation Trust

A small rectangular building, embattled and with crocketed corner finials, it served as the chapel for Withcote Hall, which it adjoins, and dates probably from about 1520–30. The windows are filled with excellent 16th-century glass. Restored in 1744, there is a noble reredos incorporating monuments on either side.

WYMESWOLD † St Mary

5m/8km N.E. of Loughborough
OS *SK603234* **GPS** *52.8054N, 1.1067W*

An early 14th-century and Perpendicular church, it was much decayed before A. W. N. Pugin's celebrated restoration of 1844–6. His are the deep-green roofs with the golden stars, the furnishings of font, sedilia and pulpit, the glass, the chandeliers and even the binding of the Bible.

LINCOLNSHIRE

This is the second-largest county in England and the least appreciated. The broad estuary of the Humber cuts it off from Yorkshire, so that it is on the way to nowhere except to the city of its glorious cathedral and its own fishing-port of Grimsby. It has pleasure resorts like Skegness on a very few of those 90 miles of low sandy coast, extremely rich agricultural towns like Spalding and Boston among their flat fields of bulbs and roots, and the industrial borough of Scunthorpe. The county town and cathedral city of Lincoln is ancient on the hill and industrial in the valley.

The A1 now bypasses the limestone town of Stamford with its fine churches, stone-tiled roofs, and substantial 17th-century and Georgian houses built in hilly streets, and goes on by Grantham, whose elegant 14th-century spire rises above the old red-brick and red-tiled roofs of the town.

Those who think of Lincs. as dull and flat are wrong. The scenery runs from north to south down the whole length of the county in varied bands. Along the inland western border is a limestone cliff extending from Stretton in Rutland to Winteringham on the Humber. Along its ridge, known locally as The Ramper, runs the Ermine Street in a straight line, and on the slopes below are the country houses, parks and feudal villages. From this ridge was quarried the beautiful white Ancaster and Lincoln limestone, of which so many of the churches were built. From Barton-on-Humber almost as far as the forgotten port of Wainfleet extend the chalky hills known as the wolds, which are an unexplored variant of the Sussex Downs. Here at Somersby, near the old red-brick town of Louth with its silver spire, Tennyson was born. The limestone ridge looks west, and the chalky heights look east to:

'Calm and still light on yon great plain
That sweeps with all its autumn bowers,
And crowded farms and lessening towers,
To mingle with the bounding main.'
(Tennyson, from *In Memoriam.*)

The 'great plain' is the Fen and the marsh north of it between the wolds and the sea. The coast is mostly dunes and samphire moss against the cold North Sea. In fen and marsh the landscape is three-quarters sky, as it is in so many of Tennyson's poems. A further type of Lincolnshire scenery is the heath between the chalk and the limestone. In places it creates something as unexpected as Woodhall Spa, that half-timbered Bournemouth-like settlement, among silver birches, heather and rhododendron.

The county has 700 churches and was historically divided into three parts, the Kingdom of Lindsey, Kesteven and Holland. Lindsey was the northern half of the county, and Kesteven and Holland the south-western and south-eastern quarters. Then these parts were sub-divided into sokes and wapentakes, and the whole county was Anglo-Saxon, though largely Scandinavian in dialect and place-names.

◁ **SKIDBROOKE: ST BOTOLPH** – *an isolated setting in marshland near the coast*

Hessle
Goole
Barton-upon-Humber
Thornton Curtis
A161
A1077
M18
LINCOLNSHIRE
A15
Thorne
SCUNTHORPE
A18
A18
Barnetby-le-Wold
M181
Bigby
BRIGG
A1084
M180
A15
Scotter
Scotton
Redbourne
A614
A161
Laughton
Northorpe
Blyborough
Bawtry
A159
Kinger
A631
Corringham
Glentham
A631
Gainsborough
Harpswell
Market Ra
Middle Rasen
A156
A620
Snarfo
Marton
Coates-by-Stow
Retford
Stow
A15
A46
A1500
A638
A158
Nettleham
Barlings
A57
A614
A57
Cherry Willingham
NOTTINGHAMSHIRE
LINCOLN
WASHINGBOROU
A46
A1133
A1
A46
A607

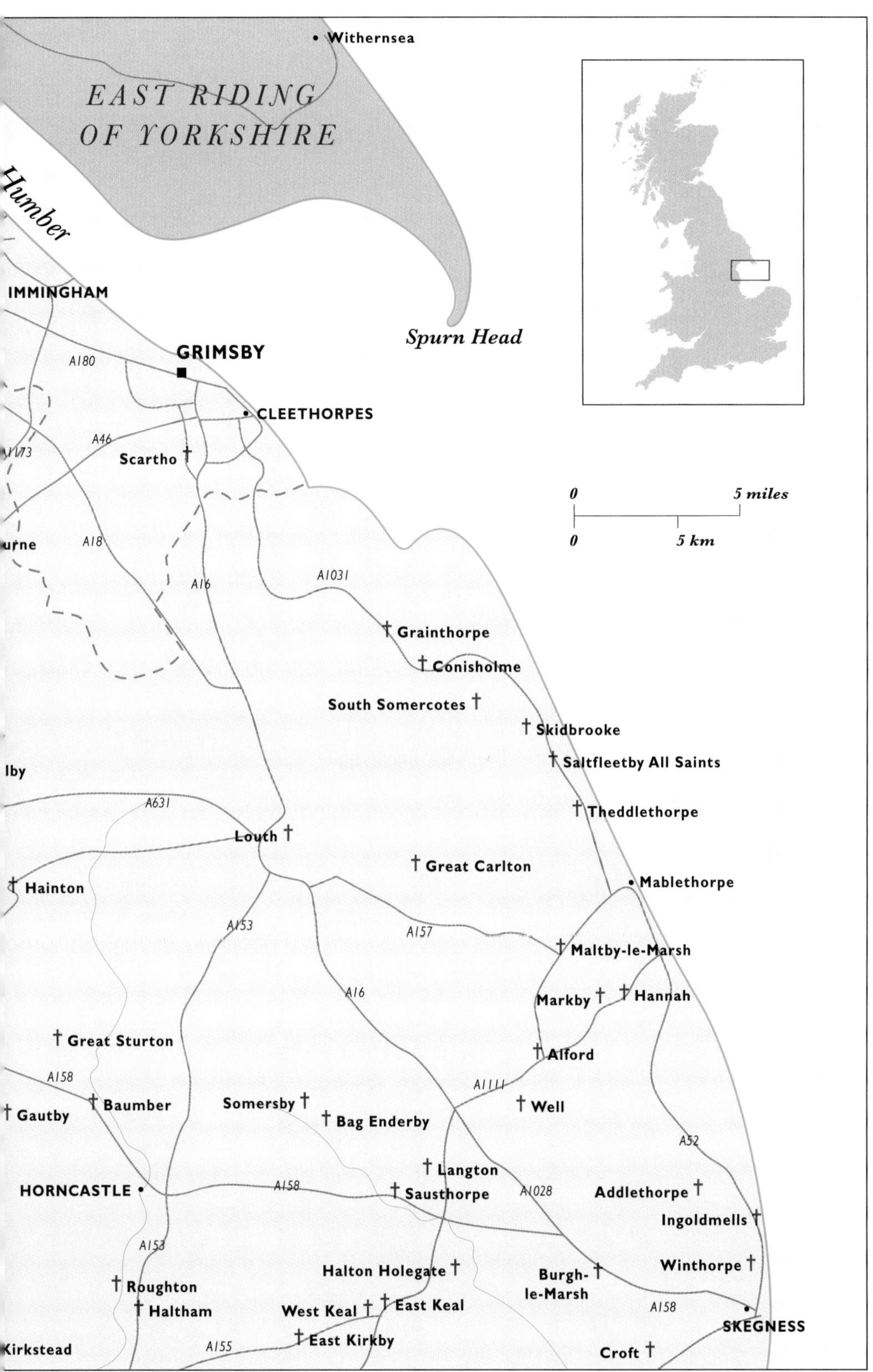

See following spread for southern Lincolnshire

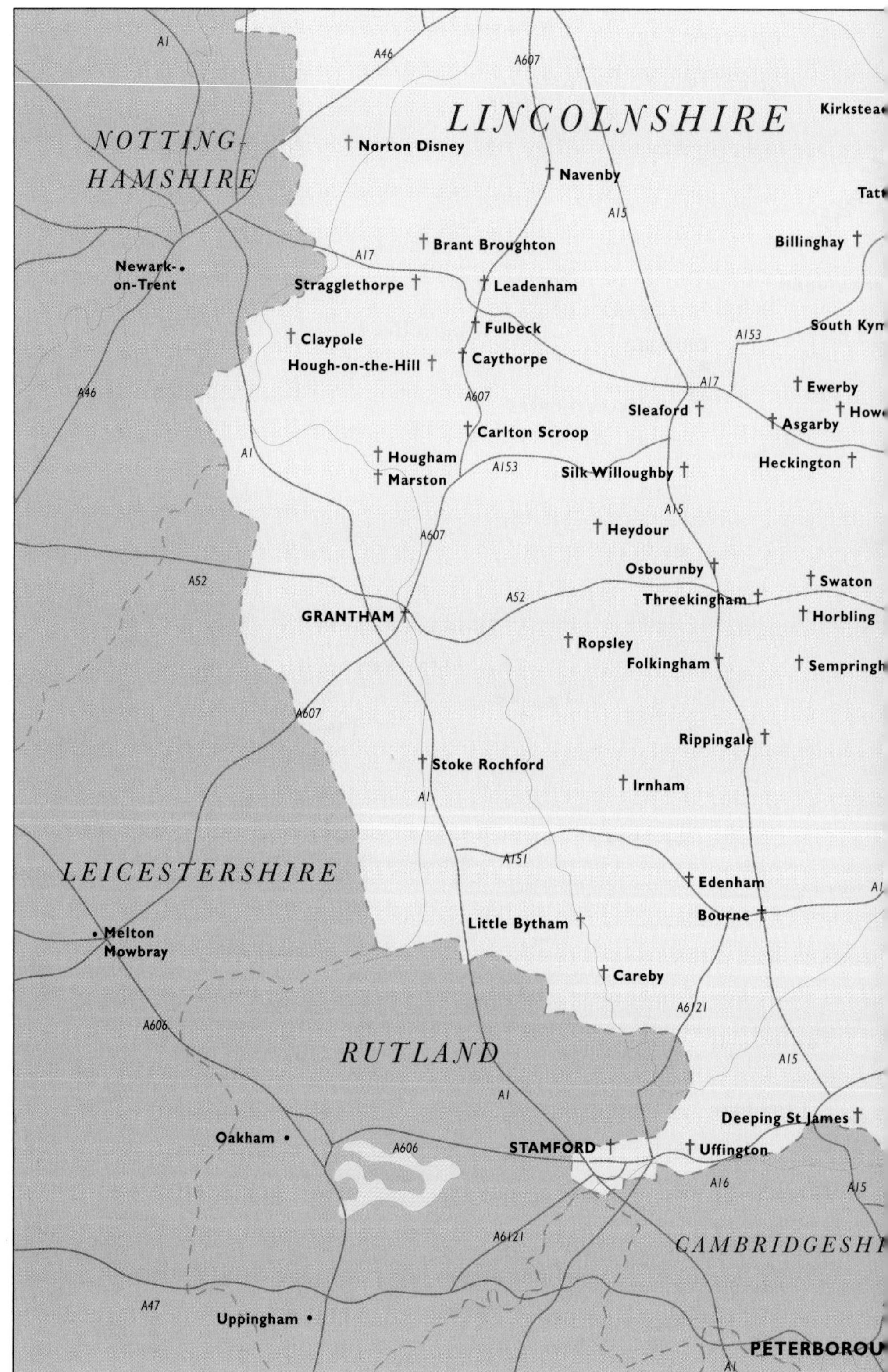
LINCOLNSHIRE
NOTTINGHAMSHIRE
LEICESTERSHIRE
RUTLAND
CAMBRIDGESHI
Kirkstea
Tat
Norton Disney
Navenby
Brant Broughton
Billinghay
Newark-on-Trent
Stragglethorpe
Leadenham
Fulbeck
South Kym
Claypole
Hough-on-the-Hill
Caythorpe
Ewerby
Sleaford
How
Asgarby
Carlton Scroop
Heckington
Hougham
Marston
Silk Willoughby
Heydour
Osbournby
Swaton
Threekingham
GRANTHAM
Horbling
Ropsley
Folkingham
Sempringh
Rippingale
Stoke Rochford
Irnham
Edenham
Bourne
Little Bytham
Melton Mowbray
Careby
Deeping St James
Oakham
STAMFORD
Uffington
Uppingham
PETERBOROU
A1
A46
A607
A15
A17
A153
A52
A151
A6121
A606
A16
A47

See previous spread for northern Lincolnshire

Except for the Cathedral and Louth, the old churches of Lindsey are smaller than those in the south of the county; and on the wolds and heath, where there was only local sandstone, they consist simply of nave and chancel, the weathered sandstone churches of the wolds having a crumbled and patched look. Kesteven, being full of limestone and a prosperous wool district, abounds in splendid 14th-century churches, most of which have enormous towers and spires. The part known as Holland was navigable fen, and stone was brought here by water to build some of the finest late medieval churches in England, such as Boston, Spalding and Gedney, which look all the more magnificent for the flatness of the landscape.

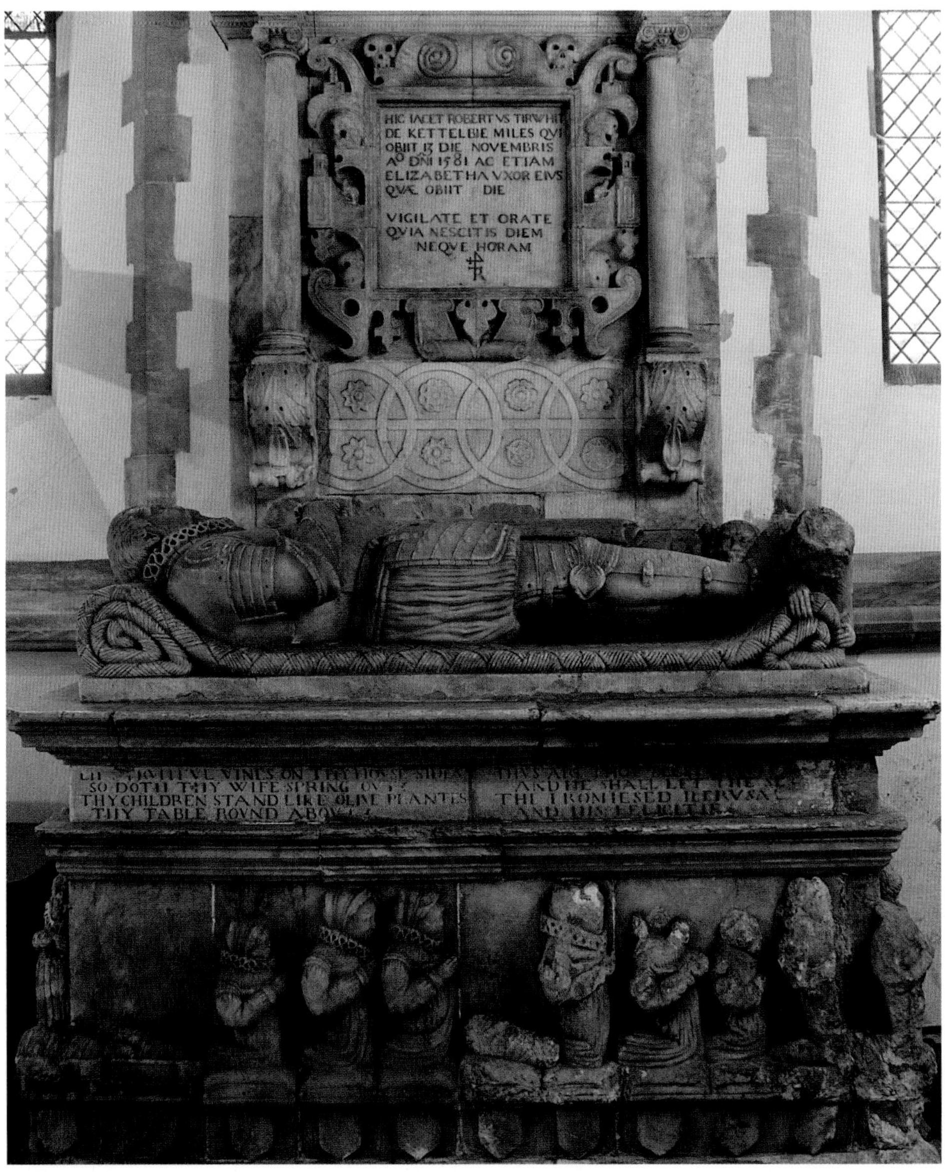

△ **BIGBY: ALL SAINTS** – *the alabaster memorial to the Tyrwhits, their 22 children represented as weepers around the base of the tomb*

△ **ADDLETHORPE: ST NICHOLAS** – *the bricked-up wall shows where the original chancel was located, before it fell into disrepair and was removed in 1706*

ADDLETHORPE † St Nicholas ★

4m/6km N. of Skegness

OS *TF550690* **GPS** *53.1963N, 0.3202E*

This is a grand 15th-century marsh church, with a bold W. tower and spacious sparkling-white interior, but no chancel – a lazy 18th-century incumbent pulled it down, to save the trouble of repairing it. There is, however, a great array of medieval screens and pews; the rood screen, with its rood and figures, has been reused as a reredos for the high altar at the E. end of the nave.

ALFORD † St Wilfrid ★

11m/18km S.E. of Louth

OS *TF455760* **GPS** *53.2616N, 0.1807E*

This good 14th-century church is notable for three things: the chamber over the S. porch; the fine alabaster monument of Sir Robert Christopher, d. 1668; and a drastic restoration by Sir George Gilbert Scott in 1867, when a second N. aisle was added and the tower heightened.

ALGARKIRK † St Peter and St Paul ★★

6m/10km S.W. of Boston

OS *TF291352* **GPS** *52.8995N, 0.0818W*

One of the stateliest cruciform churches in the northern fenland, it is Early English, Decorated and Perpendicular, with a central tower and low leaded spire, double-aisled transepts, and great traceried windows. The church was grandly restored by R. C. Carpenter in 1850–4, and is a complete realisation of the conservative Victorian restorer's aims – with highly coloured interiors, vistas everywhere, a well-furnished chancel and a skilfully placed and gaily painted organ case. The chancel and S. transept windows are by Hardman; the rest by Clayton & Bell.

ASGARBY † St Andrew

3m/4km E. of Sleaford

OS *TF116453* **GPS** *52.9942N, 0.3383W*

In a little park bordering the A17 stands a farmhouse with Gothic windows and a Decorated church with a huge Perpendicular crocketed spire dwarfing the rest. The untouched interior has clear glass, old floors and oil lamps.

BAG ENDERBY † St Margaret ★

5m/8km E. of Horncastle

OS *TF349720* **GPS** *53.2284N, 0.0197E*

A little and slightly battered-looking greenstone church in a remote village in the heart of the wolds, it has a 14th-century nave, chancel and windows, and 15th-century tower, porch and E. window. The inside is simple, with clear glass: its treasure is an outstanding Perpendicular octagonal font, with carvings of a Pietà and a hart and emblems of the Passion. In the early 1800s Alfred Lord Tennyson's father, George Clayton Tennyson, was vicar here.

BARLINGS

† St Edward King and Martyr ★

7m/11km E. of Lincoln

OS *TF075748* **GPS** *53.2600N, 0.3890W*

This church is pleasantly placed in a green field near the ruins of a Premonstratensian monastery, whose abbot was hanged for his part in the Lincolnshire Rising of 1536. There is a Norman doorway and some 13th-century work. It was restored by Charles Kirk of Sleaford in 1876, when the E. bay of the nave was heightened.

BARNETBY-LE-WOLD † St Mary

4m/6km E. of Brigg

OS *TA061090* **GPS** *53.5675N, 0.3986W*

Churches Conservation Trust

St Mary's is a lovely forlorn church on a hill-top, with Saxon work in the S. wall and a unique sculpture depicting an unidentified animal rather like a cat. The furnishings are mostly early 19th-century.

BARTON-UPON-HUMBER

† St Mary ★

Burgate 6m/10km S.W. of Hull across the Humber

OS *TA033220* **GPS** *53.6844N, 0.4367W*

Originally a chantry chapel, this is one of the most magnificent churches in the county. There is a nice illustration of the transition from Norman to Early English here: an elaborate Norman N. arcade with round columns and zigzag carving, and an Early English S. arcade with pointed arches, clustered shafts to the piers and water-leaf capitals. The chancel has good carving too in the arcade capitals, including Green Men. Two memorials of note in the chancel are a brass to a local vintner, Simon Seman, and an odd column and plaque to Jane Shipsea, d. 1626.

BARTON-UPON-HUMBER † St Peter ★

Beck Hill

OS *TA034219* **GPS** *53.6838N, 0.4347W*

English Heritage

The tower with its W. extension is one of the earliest pieces of ecclesiastical architecture in the county and is similar to that of Earls Barton, Northants. St Chad founded the original church here in the 8th century. Apart from the Saxon work, most of the present building is 14th-century, surmounted by a fine Perpendicular clerestory. Perhaps the most notable feature is the un-glazed E. window of the N. aisle, which bears the Crucifix and attendant figures on its three mullions. The church now has a new ossuary, housing bones dating back to the 11th century.

BAUMBER † St Swithin

4m/6km N.W. of Horncastle

OS *TF221744* **GPS** *53.2531N, 0.1699W*

An intriguing church, it is outwardly odd, with an enormous square red-brick tower and bare brick walls pierced with traceried Gothic windows. But under the tower is a Norman W. door, and Early English nave arcades reveal that it is in fact a spacious medieval church, enclosed in Georgian brick. Three ogee Gothic arches, playfully adorned with foliage, divide the nave from the Georgian Gothick chancel, and resemble similar work at Shobdon in Herefordshire – perhaps by the same hand.

BICKER † St Swithin ★

5m/8km S.W. of Boston

OS *TF224378* **GPS** *52.9242N, 0.1799W*

This cruciform church was described by Pevsner as 'truly amazing'; it boasts a truncated but impressive Norman nave, central tower, long chancel and much else. At the W. end there is a fragment of a carved 10th-century cross shaft. Trees and rows of cottages line the drainage channels through the village, which was a medieval port.

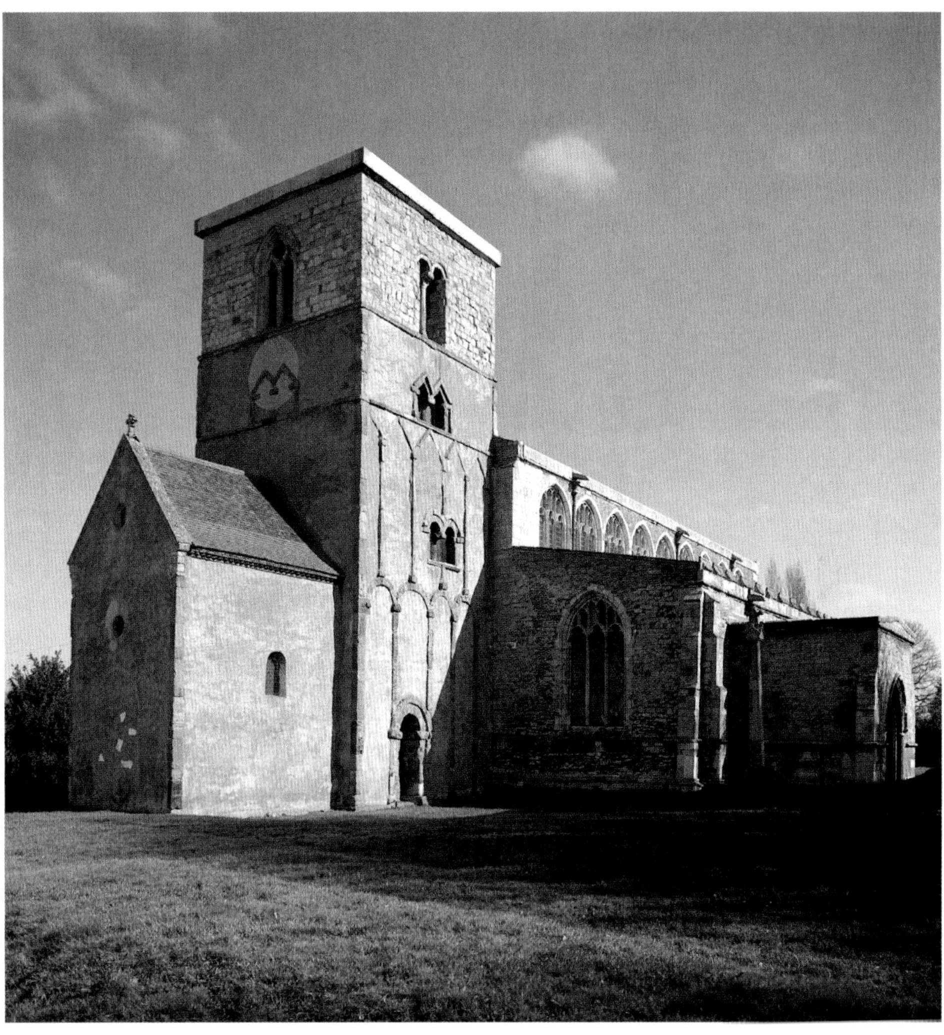

△ **BARTON-UPON-HUMBER: ST PETER** – *one of the county's earliest examples of Saxon architecture*

BIGBY † All Saints ★

4m/6km E. of Brigg

OS *TA059074* **GPS** *53.5532N, 0.4018W*

A long, low church in Early English style, it stands in a beautiful setting at the foot of the wolds near Brigg. Apart from the nine-sided font, the most interesting features are the monuments, including a massive alabaster tomb dated 1581 to Sir Robert and Elizabeth Tyrwhit, which bears the figures of their 22 children as weepers, and a brass of 1632 to Edward Naylor, 'a faithful and painefull minister of God's word'. At the E. end is a fine but sadly headless limestone carving of the Virgin and Child.

BILLINGHAY † St Michael ★

8m/12km N.E. of Sleaford

OS *TF156549* **GPS** *53.0791N, 0.2745W*

The heavily banked dyke, called the Billinghay Skirth, flows past the village; the church has a dumpy spire with slender flying buttresses from the pinnacles which, with the upper part of the tower, was rebuilt in 1787: an interesting example of 18th-century medievalism. The nave has a fine 16th-century roof, with carved roof bosses, and there is a nice modern stained-glass window showing rural life in the area and celebrating two millennia of Christianity.

△ **BRANT BROUGHTON: ST HELEN** – *medieval carved figures on the exterior*

BLYBOROUGH † St Alkmund

12m/18km N. of Lincoln
OS *SK933945* **GPS** *53.4395N, 0.5954W*

Pleasantly set on a lakeside in a well-wooded park, the church is best seen in spring, in a sea of daffodils. It was restored in 1877–8 by James Fowler of Louth, who retained the odd Georgian tower with its reused medieval gargoyles. Of great interest is the early 15th-century tomb of a former rector, Robert Conyng, d. 1434, shown in mass vestments; also the interesting rood, set on a beam brought from Thornton Abbey. Part of the figure of Christ was lying amongst lumber in the church some years ago, and the rest was dug up in the rectory garden.

BOSTON † St Botolph ★★

Church Close
OS *TF326441* **GPS** *52.9786N, 0.0251W*

'The largest and most important parish church in England', wrote the great antiquarian Dr Cox in the early 20th century. It dominates the town; it dominates the countryside. Its chancel projects, elegant, enormous, into the market-place; its tower stands sentinel on the very bank of the River Witham, 288 feet high: the largest parish church in England, and the loftiest medieval tower in England, albeit it is nicknamed 'The Stump'. The church is Decorated, the tower Perpendicular, and the scale of everything is tremendous. Inside, the eye is carried on up to the E. end with 14th-century stalls in the chancel, all with fine misericords, crowned with 19th-century canopies and a splendid Victorian reredos. The tower is dizzyingly open from inside, up to the lantern vault. There is a whole range of monuments, of every period, and rich furnishings, from John Cotton's fine pulpit to E. W. Pugin's extravagant confectionery of a font.

BOURNE † St Peter and St Paul

10m/16km W. of Spalding
OS *TF096199* **GPS** *52.7663N, 0.3757W*

This is one of the few surviving monastic churches in Lincs., although the present building contains only the nave of the abbey church. The nave arcades are good examples of 12th-century work; there are twin towers of which one is incomplete, and a 15th-century clerestory.

BRANT BROUGHTON † St Helen ★★

7m/11km E. of Newark
OS *SK915538* **GPS** *53.0745N, 0.6350W*

This is a major church with two distinct aspects. The exterior, mostly 14th-century in date, is late Decorated and early Perpendicular in style; the tower is grand, with lavish pinnacles and a soaring crocketed spire. The porches have very fine carvings, from ballflowers to bawdy figures, offering a wonderful and rather

◁ **BOSTON: ST BOTOLPH** – *some of the grandest proportions to be found in any parish church*

△ **BURGH-LE-MARSH: ST PETER AND ST PAUL** – *the tower clock face*

irreverent portrait of medieval life. The interior is extraordinary too: in 1873 Canon F. H. Sutton invited his friend G. F. Bodley to rebuild the chancel, and the wonderful partnership of rector and architect resulted in the church we possess today. It has a perfectly conceived chancel, medieval colour restored everywhere, the grandest furnishings and the most splendid glass, designed and made by Canon Sutton himself. The eye is led up to the sanctuary where Bodley's reredos frames the celebrated picture by the Master of Leisburn. Lit by candles, the interior is like a medieval dream.

BURGH-LE-MARSH
† St Peter and St Paul ★

5m/8km W. of Skegness
OS *TF500650* **GPS** *53.1611N, 0.2434E*

The lofty tower of this late 15th-century handsome greenstone church serves as a seamark near Skegness. It has an unusual ornamented parapet and exceptionally fine windows in the bell-storey. The chancel screen and other screens, pulpit and font cover are mostly early 17th-century. The N. doorway is earlier than the rest of the church and belongs to the period of the Black Death; the S. porch, now used as a vestry, was built of brick in 1702 and is picturesque, with a Dutch gable. The clock on the N. face of the tower has an inscription that reads: 'Watch and pray for ye know not when the time is'.

CABOURNE † St Nicholas

6m/10km W. of Grimsby
OS *TA139019* **GPS** *53.5016N, 0.2831W*

The Saxon tower has an original W. doorway with massive imposts and plain tympanum, and a bell stage of 1872. The church was extensively restored by A. W. Blomfield in 1872.

CAISTOR † St Peter and St Paul ★

8m/12km N. of Market Rasen
OS *TA116012* **GPS** *53.4963N, 0.3180W*

The lower stage of the tower is late Saxon or early Norman, the nave arcades are 13th-century, and the N. arcade bears corbels identical with those in the choir aisles of Lincoln Cathedral. There is a noble Early English S. door. One of the oddities here is the Gad whip – possibly used in a penitential ceremony relating to an old land dispute. In the Hundon Chapel at the E. end of the N. aisle are some 14th-century stone effigies and, in the chancel floor, a brass to John Ousterby, d. 1461, and his wife. The vestry contains a coloured alabaster monument to Sir Edward Maddison, who died at the age of 100 in 1553.

CAREBY † St Stephen

6m/10km N. of Stamford
OS *TF025164* **GPS** *52.7363N, 0.4823W*

The church is prettily set on the edge of its tiny village in meadows watered by the infant River Glen. Its early 13th-century tower with low tiled roof gives the whole composition a French look; on the S. door is a 14th-century sanctuary knocker. Inside there are 14th-century arcades, two 14th-century effigies, a rare medieval crimson cope embroidered with the Assumption of the Virgin Mary, made into an altar frontal, and a most unusual 19th-century pitch-pine vaulted roof.

CARLTON SCROOP † St Nicholas

6m/10km N.E. of Grantham
OS *SK947450* **GPS** *52.9940N, 0.5896W*

The lower part of the tower is Norman; the upper was rebuilt in 1632. The nave arcades

BRANT BROUGHTON: ST HELEN – *the restored ceiling with its beautifully painted angel roof* ▷

and porch are 13th-century. The E. window contains figures of the donor and his wife, surprisingly dressed as a nun, in medieval glass.

CAYTHORPE † St Vincent ★

8m/12km N. of Grantham
OS *SK938485* **GPS** *53.0261N, 0.6015W*

A church of much interest, its nave is divided into two by an early 14th-century arcade, running straight down the centre of the church. The stonework is most unusual – horizontal bands of ironstone and limestone. The central tower is surmounted by an exceptionally tall crocketed spire, rebuilt by Sir George Gilbert Scott in 1860 after having been struck by lightning. There are remains of a Doom painting over the tower arch, and late 17th- and early 18th-century memorials to the Hussey family.

CHERRY WILLINGHAM † St Peter and St Paul

4m/6km E. of Lincoln
OS *TF031724* **GPS** *53.2387N, 0.4554W*

Built in 1753 by Thomas Beck, it is the best example of a Georgian country church in the county, now gradually being encroached upon by ubiquitous suburban housing. Its founder is commemorated in a memorial that states his fortune was made 'without the sordid means of avaricious parsimony'. Inside it is much as it was, with original 18th- and 19th-century furnishings, and an ornate 20th-century altar.

CLAYPOLE † St Peter ★

5m/8km S.E. of Newark
OS *SK845489* **GPS** *53.0316N, 0.7405W*

Another richly crocketed spire, though not of the same quality as Caythorpe. The S. porch is striking, decorated with rich foliate motifs, and foliage is the dominant feature inside. Much stiff-leaf and Decorated carved foliage adorns the capitals, all of which have individual features – Green Men, a nun and other more enigmatic carved heads.

CLIXBY † All Hallows

2m/3km N. of Caistor
OS *TA102043* **GPS** *53.5242N, 0.3386W*
Churches Conservation Trust

A sensitive restoration of 1889 rescued the chancel of the ruined 13th-century church. The W. porch is now the filled-in chancel arch. On the floor is a 14th-century ledger slab with an incised cross and chalice, and traces of a Lombardic inscription to the memory of Robert Blanchard, priest. On the ceiling are Latin texts in praise of the Virgin.

COATES-BY-STOW † St Edith ★

6m/10km N.W. of Lincoln
OS *SK908830* **GPS** *53.3370N, 0.6377W*

This is a tiny church, Norman and later, far away among farm buildings E. of Stow, tactfully restored by J. L. Pearson in 1884 and containing a Perpendicular rood screen complete with loft and tympanum – the only one in the county. Some of the boards of the latter have been renewed, but traces of the painted figures can still be seen on the older wood. The pulpit and box pews are also 15th-century, and there are some fragments of medieval glass, and old brick floors.

CONISHOLME † St Peter

7m/11km N.E. of Louth
OS *TF402953* **GPS** *53.4365N, 0.1100E*

The small, mainly 14th-century church has been rescued from decay and admirably restored. Pantiles have been substituted for the cracked lead on the roof, and the walls plastered and whitened inside and out. There is a brass, 1515, to John and Anne Langholme and their 14 children. Part of an 11th-century wheel cross is propped in the S. window of the chancel.

CORRINGHAM † St Lawrence ★

4m/6km E. of Gainsborough
OS *SK871916* **GPS** *53.4145N, 0.6903W*

An important Saxon-Norman tower marks the location of this modest church on the edge of its ribbon-like village. Inside are Norman and Early English arcades with a Perpendicular clerestory – all splendidly restored by Bodley, together with a lively painted ceiling, rood screen, organ case and chancel stalls, and good Victorian glass, particularly the Jesse Tree by Kempe.

CROFT † All Saints ★

3m/5km W. of Skegness
OS *TF509618* **GPS** *53.1325N, 0.2545E*

A lovely church near Skegness, it is full of good 15th-century woodwork, including screens and

△ **CROWLAND ABBEY** – *the ruined west façade of the original nave is still of great interest*

box pews. The brass eagle lectern, found in the mud at the bottom of a moat some years ago, is late pre-Reformation. Among the excellent monuments is a small brass in the S. chapel, showing the upper part of a knight in chain mail, which is one of the oldest in England. In an unusual position, against the S. jamb of the chancel arch, is a monument to William Bonde, 1559, erected by his son Nicholas, President of Magdalen College, Oxford.

CROWLAND † St Mary with St Guthlac and St Bartholomew / Crowland Abbey ★★

8m/12km N.E. of Peterborough

OS *TF241103* **GPS** *52.6764N, 0.1651W*

Of the great Benedictine Abbey church there remains the Early English W. front, a frontispiece of great beauty even in its fragmentary state, together with the enormous Perpendicular N.W. tower with its grand two-storeyed porch and afterthought of a spire. The N. aisle became the parish church after the Reformation: it is early 15th-century, and the ceiling has very good tierceron vaulting. The W. front was conserved by Prof. R. Baker in the 1980s. Inside is a fine late 13th-century mason's tomb-slab with square and dividers.

DEEPING ST JAMES † St James ★
Adjacent to Market Deeping
OS *TF157095* **GPS** *52.6717N, 0.2896W*

Originally a priory church, this displays well every architectural style from Norman to 18th-century. It was originally cruciform but the transepts have gone. The tower and spire were built in 1717 and altered in 1819. The late Norman font is adorned with a design of intersecting arches.

EAST KEAL † St Helen
10m/16km W. of Skegness
OS *TF382639* **GPS** *53.1546N, 0.0661E*

Standing on the edge of the wolds, the church was almost entirely rebuilt in 1853–4 by Stephen Lewin, who also added the Early English-style tower. Only the 13th-century S. arcade and 14th-century N. arcade were retained, together with a richly carved 16th-century octagonal font.

EAST KIRKBY † St Nicholas
6m/10km S.E. of Horncastle
OS *TF332630* **GPS** *53.1479N, 0.0086W*

A very good restoration of 1903–5 by Caroe of this 14th-century greenstone church: inside there is a restored 14th-century screen with cusped panel tracery, and some 15th-century poppyhead bench-ends. The pulpit, decorated with biblical texts, is early 19th-century.

EDENHAM † St Michael and All Angels
3m/4km N.W. of Bourne
OS *TF062218* **GPS** *52.7836N, 0.4267W*

The church has a Perpendicular tower of Somerset type, good Perpendicular window tracery and interesting traces of the early 8th-century church – Saxon roundels in the S. aisle, string courses and, at the W. end of the nave, an 8th-century base of an Anglo-Saxon cross shaft. The church also contains very important and magnificent monuments to the dukes of Ancaster by Scheemakers, H. Cheere, Roubiliac, Charles Harris and Nollekens.

EWERBY † St Andrew ★★
4m/6km E. of Sleaford
OS *TF121472* **GPS** *53.0111N, 0.3296W*

The church represents Decorated architecture at its finest, and its spire is one of the best of its date in England – 172 feet high, with delicate buttressing and gargoyles. The 14th-century font is contemporary with the church, but appears to be mounted on the inverted bowl of a Norman font. There is a late 14th-century effigy in the N. aisle, and in the N. chapel an interesting recessed 14th-century tomb niche. There is also a good 19th-century lime-wood reredos, with carved figures set into gilded niches, and a memorable early 1300s rood screen with faint traces of early paintwork.

FOLKINGHAM † St Andrew ★
8m/12km S. of Sleaford
OS *TF071337* **GPS** *52.8904N, 0.4092W*

The picturesque village, once a town of importance, stands on a hillside; it has an enormous market-place and old coaching inn, and its church stands in a lane leading off the market-place. It has a splendid rood screen and S. porch with parvise. The arcades are 14th-century; the windows early 15th-century. The chancel is Early English with traces of Norman work. The late Perpendicular tower, one of the best in the county, is a conspicuous landmark.

FREISTON † St James ★
3m/4km E. of Boston
OS *TF377437* **GPS** *52.9736N, 0.0497E*

The stately Fen church is the remains of a Benedictine priory, founded from Croyland in 1114. The Norman nave is very striking, with fine arcades, a huge row of Perpendicular clerestory windows and an elaborate reset corbel table. The wooden Perpendicular font cover is a delight, with pinnacles, crockets and pierced tracery.

FRISKNEY † All Saints ★
8m/12km S.W. of Skegness
OS *TF460553* **GPS** *53.0759N, 0.1789E*

This church on the edge of the Fens contains architectural features of all periods from Norman onward, good Perpendicular screen-work and a Commonwealth pulpit. In the chancel is a splendid monument to the Booth family, and in the Perpendicular E. window, good glass by Wailes & Co., 1850. Some particularly interesting wall-paintings were discovered here in 1879, when Butterfield was restoring the church; but they have almost disappeared.

FULBECK † St Nicholas ★

9m/15km N. of Grantham

OS *SK947504* **GPS** *53.0428N, 0.5881W*

The particularly attractive village is claimed to be the prettiest in Lincs. The church has a grand Perpendicular tower and excellent Decorated tracery. Inside there is a late Norman font and an array of monuments to the Fane family, as well as one to Thomas Bell, 1674, a servant of the family who toured Europe with his master.

GAINSBOROUGH † All Saints ★

15m/25km N.W. of Lincoln

OS *SK814901* **GPS** *53.4015N, 0.7764W*

The 15th-century tower of the medieval church survives; the rest was rebuilt in Classical style in 1736, modelled on St Martin-in-the-Fields in London, and the architect was almost certainly Francis Smith of Warwick. It is a splendid building inside, even if a touch remote, and unfortunately lost some of its 18th-century fittings in a Victorian 'restoration', which replaced some 'atrocious' glass – according to Bodley in 1903, who installed some equally poor glass. Nearby is the Old Hall, an amazing, enormous 15th–16th-century house of brick and timber, former seat of the Burgh and Hickman families, which after many vicissitudes is now restored and open to the public.

GAUTBY † All Saints ★

4m/6km N.W. of Horncastle

OS *TF174724* **GPS** *53.2360N, 0.2414W*

An 18th-century church, it stands in a romantic setting within the old garden walls of the vanished Gautby Hall. It was rebuilt by Sir Robert Vyner, 1754, re-using some of the medieval features, notably the 15th-century font. There are some beautiful furnishings: the panelled pulpit and vicar's pew came from Skelton in W. Yorkshire, and the Vyner monuments were brought by Sir Robert Vyner from St Mary Woolnoth, London.

GEDNEY † St Mary Magdalene ★

3m/4km E. of Holbeach

OS *TF402243* **GPS** *52.7985N, 0.0792E*

There is 'more glass than wall' in this confection of early Gothic overlaid with airy Perpendicular. The Early English tower is surmounted by an unfinished Perpendicular spire. The E. window is an example of 14th-century work of a Continental type. The S. porch has an upper storey, approached by a turret stairway, and there is important 14th- and 15th-century glass in the N. aisle: the tracery is an eclectic mix of Curvilinear and Intersecting. The monuments include a late 14th-century brass, some coloured alabaster effigies to members of the Welby family, and a 13th-century figure of a knight in armour.

GLENTHAM † St Peter ★

7m/11km W. of Market Rasen

OS *TF003904* **GPS** *53.4015N, 0.4927W*

The church is a 14th-century building of considerable charm, its tower rebuilt in 1756. Two notable features are the Pietà over the door of the S. porch and the brass effigy of Elizabeth Tournay, 1452, in the chapel at the E. end of the N. aisle.

GOSBERTON † St Peter and St Paul

6m/10km N. of Spalding

OS *TF237317* **GPS** *52.8691N, 0.1630W*

This is a Fen church of great magnificence, Decorated and Perpendicular, cruciform with a central tower and crocketed spire, grand transepts, great traceried windows and a spacious and many-vistaed interior.

GRAINTHORPE † St Clement

7m/11km N.E. of Louth

OS *TF387965* **GPS** *53.4477N, 0.0881E*

The church has 12th-century origins, evident in the responds in the N. arcade, but most here is of the 14th and 15th centuries. There is good stout medieval timberwork in the nave and aisle roofs, and in the aisles are traces of 15th-century wall-paintings and texts. There are high pews and a brass on the chancel floor consisting of a cross with an elaborate head. The stem is lost, but part of the foot remains and stands on a rock in some water, wherein fish are swimming.

△ **HALTHAM: ST BENEDICT** – *emerging snowdrops and crocuses herald the end of winter at this atmospheric church set in a water meadow in the heart of Lincolnshire*

GRANTHAM † St Wulfram ★★

Between Castle Gate & Swinegate
OS *SK914361* **GPS** *52.9149N, 0.6407W*

Sir George Gilbert Scott regarded the spire of St Wulfram's as 'second only to Salisbury in beauty'. Not only is the spire of great beauty, the whole W. front is as distinguished as that of any parish church in England. Here Ruskin stood spellbound. Above soars the spire, slender, crocketed and 282 feet high, built between 1230 and 1300 – before Salisbury, 404 feet, and before Norwich, 345 feet. In its day it was the loftiest spire in England, the first of our great English spires. On either side are the enormous Geometrical windows of the two engaged aisles, and these wonderful traceried windows continue all around the exterior. The church is enormously wide, with aisles almost as broad as the nave, divided by early 13th-century arcades; the power of the grand interior is horizontal rather than vertical. There is a 14th-century crypt, an interesting collection of monuments and splendid Victorian furnishings by Sir G. G. Scott, Arthur Blomfield and Walter Tapper – the whole sits in a spacious churchyard, surrounded by Georgian and earlier buildings.

GREAT CARLTON

† St John the Baptist ★

6m/10km E. of Louth
OS *TF408855* **GPS** *53.3485N, 0.1139E*

In a particularly pleasant setting, the church is surrounded by fine trees and was rebuilt, except for the tower, in 1860–2 by James Fowler; an example of good Gothic Revival work. Those who look at the 15th-century tower are bidden, by a carved inscription, to pray for the soul of Robert Schadworth.

GREAT STURTON † All Saints

8m/12km S.W. of Louth
OS *TF215766* **GPS** *53.2730N, 0.1790W*

The hamlet is tiny, in a corner of the sparsely populated wolds, and the church is much reduced. The N. exterior wall shows the outlines of the former N. arcade (similar in appearance to St Cwfan, off the Anglesey coast). Inside, within the filled-in N. arcade, is an unusual, very faded 17th-century painting of Time and Death. On the mouldings of one of the former arcade arches is medieval decoration. J. T. Micklethwaite restored the church gently in 1904, adding the W. bellcote.

HAINTON † St Mary
6m/10km S.E. of Market Rasen
OS *TF180844* **GPS** *53.3441N, 0.2287W*

The hall and church make a delightful group across Capability Brown's Park; he may have been involved in the c. 1763 restoration. The Heneages have lived here since the 14th century, and the church contains a notable collection of their tombs and monuments from the 16th century to the present time. E. J. Willson's 1848 input was more of a rebuilding than a restoration.

HALTHAM † St Benedict ★
4m/6km S. of Horncastle
OS *TF246638* **GPS** *53.1571N, 0.1378W*
Churches Conservation Trust

This is a small church in a water meadow by a pretty village containing a former inn thatched with Norfolk reeds. The S. door is Norman and has a carved tympanum with geometric patterns. There is an Early English N. arcade, a remarkable Decorated E. window, a six-sided font and an ogee-headed priest's door. The wonderful interior has old pews and screens arranged facing this way and that, and a fine Decorated E. chancel window. With its humble bellcote, it is a church of great charm, not to be missed.

HALTON HOLEGATE † St Andrew ★
10m/18km W. of Skegness
OS *TF417651* **GPS** *53.1641N, 0.1195E*

The church stands on one side of the Hollow Gate and commands some of the best views in the county. It is almost entirely 15th-century, but there are some traces of 14th-century work, principally the Curvilinear E. window. It has been much, and carefully, restored at various times, most recently a rebuilding by J. Fowler to G. E. Street's plans. In the S. aisle there is an effigy of a cross-legged knight in armour.

HANNAH † St Andrew ★
4m/6km N.E. of Alford
OS *TF499794* **GPS** *53.2907N, 0.2486E*

An unsophisticated little mid-18th-century church of greenstone, it is set on a little knoll in marshland, not far from the coast, and is notable for its charming rustic Georgian interior. The E. end is surprisingly imposing, with a Venetian window and an altar rail with a 'jetty' in the middle to accommodate lots of communicants at once.

HARPSWELL † St Chad ★
6m/10km W. of Gainsborough
OS *SK935899* **GPS** *53.3982N, 0.5939W*

A small church at the foot of a hill, it has one of the few complete pre-Conquest Saxon towers. There is a 14th-century S. aisle, and the N. arcade has been built up. In 1891 an incised effigy of a priest was found in the floor. There is also a 14th-century effigy of a rector and a memorial to another, William Harrington, d. 1697; this last is inscribed on the ancient altar-slab. The 15th-century brass on the chancel wall depicts John Whichcot and his wife Elizabeth Tyrwhit, the latter with a windblown wimple-like head dress.

HECKINGTON † St Andrew ★★
5m/8km E. of Sleaford
OS *TF142441* **GPS** *52.9822N, 0.2991W*

A most famous Decorated church, it is perfect from the outside, with gargoyles, corbels and a multitude of carved statues on the tower. The inside is a little disappointing – severely scraped – but there are fine features too: the wonderful upright Easter Sepulchre, the superb carved sedilia and fine Curvilinear E. window. By an unusual arrangement, the transepts come W. of the easternmost bay of the nave.

HEYDOUR † St Michael
Also spelt Heydor; 6m/10km S.W. of Sleaford
OS *TF009396* **GPS** *52.9445N, 0.4989W*

The large church with its lofty spire is Early English, Decorated and Perpendicular, and contains an important quantity of 14th-century glass, and a wealth of 18th-century monuments to the Newtons of Culverthorpe. There are two by Rysbrack and two by Scheemakers that are easily missed, concealed by the organ and a red-baize door.

HOLBEACH † All Saints ★
7m/11km E. of Spalding
OS *TF359247* **GPS** *52.8035N, 0.0147E*

A little later than Heckington, this church is nearly all Decorated, with much Curvilinear tracery except for the Decorated window that is largely obscured by bell-ringing paraphernalia. It has a magnificent tower and spire and a good sandstone 14th-century tomb to Sir Humphrey Littlebury.

HORBLING † St Andrew ★

10m/16km N.W. of Spalding
OS *TF118351* **GPS** *52.9024N, 0.3380W*

This is a cruciform church whose tower has Norman work at the bottom and Perpendicular work at the top. The W. front is 1170, flanked by 15th-century aisle ends. There is a lot of 14th-century work and a good 15th-century octagonal font with emblems of the Passion. Among the many interesting tombs and monuments is an unusual medieval effigy of a kneeling knight, Sir Thomas la Laund, d. 1470, and a decorated brass wall plate to Thomas Brown, d. 1849, by A. W. N. Pugin.

HOUGH-ON-THE-HILL † All Saints ★

7m/11km N. of Grantham
OS *SK923464* **GPS** *53.0070N, 0.6255W*

A mighty Saxon tower, it has one of only four semi-circular extruded staircase turrets in all England; the others are at Broughton in Lincs, and Brixworth and Brigstock in Northants. The whitewashed, atmospheric interior is of distinguished Saxon proportions, with a tall nave. King John spent the last night of his life in a small priory at Hough after over-indulging himself on an unwise diet of peaches and new cider at Swineshead.

HOUGHAM † All Saints

6m/10km N. of Grantham
OS *SK886442* **GPS** *52.9880N, 0.6807W*

The church stands alone and stately close to the River Witham; here a Saxon cross shaft forms a lintel for the S. door. There is a lofty, spacious nave with a perfect Norman arcade, a Georgian chancel and a crusader tomb – all sympathetically restored by Temple Moore in 1895–6.

HOWELL † St Oswald ★

4m/6km E. of Sleaford
OS *TF135462* **GPS** *53.0016N, 0.3100W*

A very prettily situated church in a tiny parish near Heckington, it is still lit by candles. The architectural details are Norman, Transitional and Decorated. Notice the 14th-century bell-gable and the font, 1373, with shields and an incised memorial to John Croxby, a 15th-century rector. In the porch is a well-preserved mass dial.

INGOLDMELLS
† St Peter with St Paul ★

4m/6km N. of Skegness
OS *TF559688* **GPS** *53.1937N, 0.3329E*

One of a group of impressive churches near Skegness, whose 14th-century porch has rich carving and a wealth of notable woodwork. The arcades are c. 1200, with stiff-leaf capitals, and the pews are 15th-century, with poppyheads and traceried rear panels. Like Addlethorpe, Ingoldmells lost its chancel at the beginning of the 18th century through the negligence of the same incumbent. A unique feature is a brass to the memory of William Palmer 'wyth the stylt', 1520, on which he is represented as a civilian in a long-sleeved gown with his 'stylt' or crutch beside him.

IRNHAM † St Andrew ★

6m/10km N.W. of Bourne
OS *TF023266* **GPS** *52.8279N, 0.4824W*

This is a particularly interesting church, standing on the edge of a park and displaying architectural styles from the 13th–14th centuries. There is a fine brass to Sir Andrew Luttrell, 1390; parts are missing, but the figure of the knight and the cusped canopy over his head are especially good examples. The manor belonged for many generations to the Roman Catholic family of Thimbleby and their descendants, to whom there are some monuments.

KINGERBY † St Peter ★

4m/6km N.W. of Market Rasen
OS *TF057928* **GPS** *53.4219N, 0.4104W*
Churches Conservation Trust

This extremely picturesque church stands by the roadside opposite a wood which is carpeted with aconites in early spring. There is a very solid tower and a S. door, both of the 12th century. Reared against the S. wall is a specimen of what Boutell, a Norfolk antiquarian and vicar, described as 'semi-effigial' monuments. It shows the head and shoulders

HOUGH-ON-THE-HILL: ALL SAINTS – *the distinctive Saxon semi-circular extruded staircase turret, one of only four in the country* ▷

of a civilian, beneath which is a floreated cross in relief, with the feet of the figure protruding from its base and resting on a dog. There are four shields, one bearing the Arms of the Disney family, to which the subject of the monument belonged.

KIRKSTEAD † St Leonard ★★

6m/10km S.W. of Horncastle
OS *TF190613* **GPS** *53.1362N, 0.2224W*

The church is hard to find in its setting of bumpy fields: it adjoins the jagged fragments of the S. transept of Kirkstead Abbey, the chapel by the gate to the Cistercian Abbey. This exquisite, tiny, vaulted Early English church, with narrow lancets, delicately carved capitals and dwarf shafts, is one of Lincolnshire's most precious jewels. Inside is a very good roof – stone-vaulted with tierceron ribs and many well-carved bosses – and a very early half-effigy of a knight wearing a cask helm, an enclosed helmet with slits for breathing.

KIRTON † St Peter and St Paul

4m/6km S.W. of Boston
OS *TF304385* **GPS** *52.9283N, 0.0601W*

A grand Fen church, it was once much larger, but is still majestic with a nave of six Early English bays, Perpendicular clerestory and great Decorated traceried windows in the aisles. The splendid W. tower is a piece of brilliant early 19th-century pastiche, having previously been the central tower of the cruciform building.

LANGTON † St Peter and St Paul ★

Also known as Langton-by-Spilsby and Langton-by-Partney, 11m/7km N.W. of Skegness
OS *TF389703* **GPS** *53.2125N, 0.0799E*

The 18th-century lexicographer Dr Johnson used to worship here when he visited his friend Bennet Langton at the manor, and on one celebrated occasion he took off his coat and rolled down a grassy hill. If he revisited the church now he would still feel at home in it. The early 18th-century building, with tiered box pews in collegiate style, has a three-decker pulpit and a gallery, all unspoiled by restoration. In 2006 the church was repainted in the original Georgian colours.

LAUGHTON † All Saints ★

5m/8km N.E. of Gainsborough
OS *SK849972* **GPS** *53.4656N, 0.7224W*

Against the backcloth of woods, this is a medieval church gloriously restored and refurbished by Bodley in 1894 for Mrs Meynell-Ingram in memory of her husband. Bodley rebuilt the lofty chancel, installed the organ, designed the sumptuous reredos and rood screen, and provided the new roof. The altar ornaments are all due to him. It is a wonderful interior.

LEADENHAM † St Swithin ★

8m/12km N.W. of Sleaford
OS *SK950517* **GPS** *53.0546N, 0.5835W*

This is a handsome church, mainly 14th-century, with an impressive tower and magnificent crocketed spire. It forms one of the string of distinguished churches between Lincoln and Grantham. The attractive Flemish glass was inserted in the E. window in 1829, and Pugin painted the chancel ceiling in 1841. Outside in the churchyard are good slate headstones.

LINCOLN † St Peter-at-Gowts

High Street
OS *SK973704* **GPS** *53.2218N, 0.5438W*

An ancient landmark of the city, this is an important 11th-century church with a Saxon nave with long-and-short quoins, and a tall Saxon W. tower. The N. aisle and porch were added in 1852 by W. A. Nicholson, and C. H. Fowler enlarged the chancel in 1887.

LITTLE BYTHAM † St Medard ★

7m/11km N. of Stamford
OS *TF012180* **GPS** *52.7505N, 0.5007W*

A picturesque church in a pretty village near Stamford, it has some Saxon work at the S.E. corner of the nave. In the N. nave wall is a good Norman doorway, and over the S. door of the chancel is a unique tympanum, described as follows: 'In the centre is a sunk circular medallion said to have once contained the skull and arm bone of St Medard, the Patron Saint. On either side is an eagle within a circle, and below an animal adoring and some interlaced circles. On the lintel is a pattern of rectangular figures enclosing leaves.'

LONG SUTTON † St Mary ★★

9m/15km N. of Wisbech

OS *TF432228* **GPS** *52.7844N, 0.1223E*

The lead spire, according to the antiquarian Dr J. Charles Cox, is the highest, oldest, and most perfect lead spire in England, and crowns an early 13th-century tower of great beauty almost detached from the church. There is a handsome 15th-century S. porch of two bays with external turreted staircase, and a magnificent Norman nave with triforium and clerestory. The later work in the church is attributed to John of Gaunt. In the S. chancel aisle is fine medieval glass depicting St George and the Dragon.

LOUTH † St James ★★

14m/22km S. of Grimsby

OS *TF326873* **GPS** *53.3667N, 0.0081W*

Louth spire is one of the last great medieval Gothic masterpieces of England. It rises up stage after stage of almost impossible beauty to its great height of 295 feet. It was built of Ancaster stone between 1501 and 1515. 'For fifteen years, with scanty labour and scantier means, the work was carried on. They borrowed from the guilds and the richer inhabitants, they pledged their silver crosses and chalices. From the richest to the poorest all seem to have been affected with a like zeal.' (*The First Church Warden's Book of Louth*, Dudding, 1941.) The great pride of the townspeople in their achievement and their fear for its fate were largely responsible for the outbreak of the Lincolnshire Rising in 1536. Louth is a captivating town of Georgian streets and houses; the spire seems to float above it and the glorious countryside around.

MARKBY † St Peter ★

4m/5km S.W. of Mablethorpe

OS *TF487788* **GPS** *53.2855N, 0.2295E*

Markby's church is included as the only instance of a thatched church in Lincolnshire. A charming little building, it was probably a rebuilding of 1611 incorporating masonry from the Augustinian priory. The thatching is from 1672, when a churchwarden had the roof thatched in exchange for the tiles. Inside are box pews, a two-decker pulpit and three-sided communion rails.

MARSTON † St Mary ★

5m/8km N. of Grantham

OS *SK892437* **GPS** *52.9834N, 0.6715W*

St Mary's stands in a pretty setting by the Witham, a lovely glowing ironstone building with a lofty late 13th-century broach spire. The arcades are Early English, with off-the-shelf 19th-century heads in the spandrels; the 19th-century corbels of the nave and aisle roofs are much better. There are good 16th-century tombs and other monuments to the Thorold family, notably that in the S. chapel to Sir Anthony Thorold, d. 1594 – white and pink marble with Corinthian columns and an alabaster recumbent figure.

MARTON † St Margaret of Antioch ★

5m/8km S. of Gainsborough

OS *SK839817* **GPS** *53.3261N, 0.7407W*

The church is famous for its Saxon tower of herringbone limestone rubble masonry, and long-and-short quoins. Inside, a small section of the 11th-century nave can be seen between the tower and N. aisle. An 11th-century cross head is embedded in the chancel wall, and at the W. end of the S. aisle are fragments of an Anglo-Saxon cross. A simple, solemn early church, rich in texture and atmosphere.

MIDDLE RASEN † St Peter ★

1m/2km W. of Market Rasen

OS *TF087895* **GPS** *53.3913N, 0.3664W*

The finest part of this church is the Norman S. door, which came from the destroyed church of Middle Rasen Drax, in the same parish. There is a 15th-century screen and a 14th-century figure of a priest holding a chalice. The tower and windows of the S. aisle are good Perpendicular work.

MOULTON † All Saints ★

4m/6km E. of Spalding

OS *TF307241* **GPS** *52.7988N, 0.0627W*

This Fenland church has a magnificent late Perpendicular tower and spire, and many other features of great beauty, such as stiff-leaf foliage capitals and canopied niches containing figures of saints above the W. window. Apart from a very good and richly made screen, its great treasure is the remarkable early 18th-century Adam and Eve font, attributed variously to William Tydd, 1719, or as a Victorian copy of Grinling Gibbons' font at St James, Piccadilly, London.

NAVENBY † St Peter ★

9m/15km S. of Lincoln
OS *SK986578* **GPS** *53.1087N, 0.5278W*

The tower and spire fell in the mid-18th century, and the former was replaced by a poor substitute, but the remainder of the church is beautiful. The six-light Decorated E. window, somewhat resembling that at Heckington, is amongst the best of its kind. There is also an Easter Sepulchre on the N. side of the chancel, beneath which the sleeping soldiers are depicted with the Marys appearing above. At the E. end of the S. aisle is a disused font with a handsome carved cover designed by Charles Kirk of Sleaford and shown at the 1862 London Exhibition.

NETTLEHAM † All Saints ★

3m/4km N.E. of Lincoln
OS *TF007753* **GPS** *53.2653N, 0.4906W*

Nettleham is one of a few Lincolnshire villages with a stream running through it; beside the stream is the church, mainly 13th-century, with a chancel admirably rebuilt by Bodley and Garner in 1889. In the splays of the nave arcades are extensive traces of medieval wall-painting.

NORTHORPE † St John the Baptist ★

3m/4km W. of Kirton-in-Lindsey
OS *SK894971* **GPS** *53.4636N, 0.6538W*

A small church full of detail, with two Norman arcades, some scraps of medieval glass and two late brasses. The best feature is the early 14th-century S. doorway, enriched with a design of naturalistic foliage. The little picturesque village contains the ruins of a 16th-century manor house.

NORTON DISNEY † St Peter

7m/11km N.E. of Newark
OS *SK889589* **GPS** *53.1203N, 0.6717W*

Lost in the willows of the Witham and surrounded by woods, this romantic village was once dominated by the castle of the Disney family, whose name lives on in the creator of the famous film studio, a descendant of a junior branch. This is a perfect village church with old floors, benches, screen, altar rails, pulpit and a fine set of tombs and brasses of Disneys.

OLD LEAKE † St Mary the Virgin ★

6m/10km N.E. of Boston
OS *TF407502* **GPS** *53.0313N, 0.0974E*

A notable Fenland church, it suffered from settlement of walls by reason of continuous land drainage. It is mainly 14th-century with a spacious nave of six bays and N. and S. porches. Over the newel staircase to the rood loft there is an unusual and handsome octagonal turret which has been damaged by the use of iron cramps. Outside is open stone-work over the E. gable and a fine traceried frieze at the clerestory level; the niches sadly have lost their statues.

OSBOURNBY † St Peter and St Paul ★

5m/8km S. of Sleaford
OS *TF069381* **GPS** *52.9300N, 0.4102W*

The church here is principally 14th-century and possesses a Decorated sedilia and much 14th-century woodwork, including bench-ends depicting Adam and Eve, St George and the Dragon, and a fox preaching to geese.

PINCHBECK † St Mary

2m/3km N. of Spalding
OS *TF241255* **GPS** *52.8136N, 0.1587W*

This is a great Fenland church with noble W. tower and a grand nave; the roof is good – arched tie beams supporting queen posts, with gilded angels. Butterfield rebuilt the chancel in 1861, and there are handsome Victorian furnishings and earlier monuments. The E. and W. window glass is by O'Connor, 1851–5, while in the N. aisle and N. chapel is some 15th-century grisaille glass.

REDBOURNE † St Andrew ★

5m/8km S.W. of Brigg
OS *SK973999* **GPS** *53.4872N, 0.5344W*
Churches Conservation Trust

A fascinating church of medieval origin, it was gloriously redecorated in Strawberry Hill Gothic, 1775; with a charming plaster vault to the nave and chancel, a gaudy E. window of the Day of Judgement by William

△ **REDBOURNE: ST ANDREW** – *these rustically painted door panels are among the redecorations*

Collins, 1840, and other contemporary glass. There are good ducal hatchments of the St Alban family.

RIPPINGALE † St Andrew

5m/8km N. of Bourne
OS *TF097278* **GPS** *52.8367N, 0.3717W*

A pretty Kesteven village, in which the Perpendicular tower of the church is a prominent landmark. The architectural details of the church are worth studying, such as the nave formed of six bays, c. 1300. Inside is a series of medieval monuments: two knights in chain mail, a 15th-century deacon, an effigy of a lady and an altar tomb with figures of Roger de Quincey and his two wives.

ROPSLEY † St Peter ★

5m/8km E. of Grantham
OS *SK992342* **GPS** *52.8963N, 0.5258W*

The church still contains original Saxon parts, such as long-and-short work in the nave, and a carved crucifix at the N.W. angle. One chancel window and the N. arcade are late Norman; the clerestorey and S. chapel are Decorated; in the S. arcade is a pillar, 1380, commemorating the church's rebuilding. The Early English tower has an overset Decorated broach spire.

△ **SKIDBROOKE: ST BOTOLPH** – *now empty of furnishings and its stonework covered in moss, the church attracts bats and owls and the occasional visitor in search of atmosphere and solitude*

ROUGHTON † St Margaret ★

3m/4km S. of Horncastle
OS *TF241646* **GPS** *53.1649N, 0.1444W*

A patchwork of stone, brick and render, this is a small church of considerable charm in a small wooded village on the banks of the Bain. Doorways and capitals have been shifted and reset with abandon. Inside there are good fittings: a 12th-century font with 16th-century cover, an 18th-century panelled pulpit with barley-twist balusters, 18th-century candelabrum and Commandment boards.

SALTFLEETBY ALL SAINTS † All Saints ★

5m/8km N.W. of Mablethorpe
OS *TF455904* **GPS** *53.3906N, 0.1868E*
Churches Conservation Trust

Originally a late Norman church, it was rebuilt early in the 13th century. The lower stages of the tower, the nave arcade, the N. wall of the chancel and its two-light window are all 13th-century. In the 15th century the upper stages of the tower were added and the unusual windows in the N. side of the nave were put in. The nave roof was repaired in 1611 and the chancel rebuilt in 1873. In the S. porch is the Coat of Arms of John Grantham, patron of the church, flanked by shields bearing a crucifix and emblems of the Passion. Most of the 15th-century rood screen remains. On the E. wall of the side chapel is a rare stone reredos; there is a good 13th-century font, and two pulpits, one Jacobean and the other medieval.

SAUSTHORPE † St Andrew ★

10m/16km N.W. of Skegness
OS *TF382690* **GPS** *53.2010N, 0.0680E*

A handsome and well-proportioned church built of white brick by Charles Kirk of Sleaford in 1842–4. It has a tower with spire, more or less modelled on Louth, which is completely delightful and forms a conspicuous and charming feature of the landscape on the road from Horncastle to Skegness. The chancel has a colourful painted and gilded ceiling, and the reredos is similarly treated. The church is a very remarkable example of good work in an unpromising medium, by an architect who was also a practical builder.

SCARTHO † St Giles

District of Grimsby 2m/3km S. of centre
OS *TA267063* **GPS** *53.5387N, 0.0890W*

The church has a handsome Saxon W. tower; the belfry with mid-wall shafts and elaborate capitals somewhat later than the rest. There is a blocked W. door; its Early English replacement is on the S. side. The 20th-century N. aisle does not really do justice to the rest.

SCOTTER † St Peter ★

6m/10km S. of Scunthorpe
OS *SE887008* **GPS** *53.4966N, 0.6635W*

This is a church that contains work from Saxon to Perpendicular. The S. door and tympanum are pre-Conquest, and the arcade between the nave and the N. aisle is a perfect example of Early English work. There is a 15th-century rood screen and some interesting memorials, including a fine inscribed and decorated brass plate to Sir Marmaduke Tyrwhitt, d. 1599. Under the tower is the earliest known set of ringers' rules in verse.

SCOTTON † St Genewys / Genwys

7m/11km S. of Scunthorpe
OS *SK890990* **GPS** *53.4811N, 0.6598W*

A church of all dates from the 12th to 16th centuries, it was restored by G. E. Street in 1866. There is good Intersecting tracery in the S. aisle and throughout the spacious interior; of interest are four medieval Neville tombs with effigies.

SEMPRINGHAM † St Andrew ★

8m/13km N. of Bourne
OS *TF106328* **GPS** *52.8821N, 0.3571W*

In a splendid situation, the church stands isolated in fields beside the site of a Gilbertine monastery. It is a fine Norman building, the E. apse built by Edward Browning, 1868–9, after a lightning strike. The lavish S. doorway retains its 12th-century fir-wood door and ironwork, and there is an intact Norman corbel table of 'Lombard' type. The tower, originally 12th-century, was remodelled in the 14th-century in Somerset style. Lincolnshire's native saint Gilbert was born in this place, and his order began when seven village maidens asked to lead a sequestered life on the N. side of the church. In the churchyard is a holy well.

SIBSEY † St Margaret

5m/8km N.E. of Boston
OS *TF354507* **GPS** *53.0368N, 0.0186E*

This is a large church on the edge of the Fens, with two Norman arcades and a grand tower whose lower stages are 13th-century. Over the chancel arch is the original gable for the sanctus bell. The nave cancel and aisles were partly rebuilt in 1855. Annie Besant, wife of the rector Frank Besant, fled the area in 1873 to take up the cause of social reform, then became a Theosophist and ultimately a member of the Indian National Congress.

SILK WILLOUGHBY † St Denis ★

2m/3km S. of Sleaford
OS *TF057430* **GPS** *52.9740N, 0.4270W*

Everything about this church is beautiful; the 14th-century tower is surmounted by a slender and graceful spire with flying buttresses. Most of the building is late 14th-century; the S. door, with ballflower moulding, is particularly charming. The chancel was well rebuilt in 1878, and the woodwork includes 14th-century pew-ends, a 15th-century rood screen and a 17th-century pulpit.

SKIDBROOKE † St Botolph

1m/2km S.W. of Saltfleet
OS *TF439932* **GPS** *53.4162N, 0.1652E*
Churches Conservation Trust

The church stands across dyked fields in majestic isolation, a typical marshland setting more than a mile away from the village of Saltfleet Haven, which in the reign of Edward II was a thriving port. Green with moss, it has a spacious nave, aisles and chancel, all Early English or Decorated, with a Perpendicular clerestory and W. tower. Inside, all is textured like a deserted church in Tuscany. The quintessence of Lincs, at its remotest, solitary best.

SKIRBECK † St Nicholas ★

Suburb of Boston 1m/2km S.E. of centre
OS *TF337431* **GPS** *52.9686N, 0.0093W*

Standing on the bank of the Witham, this church is notable for its Early English nave, a tower, c. 1450, and an enormous, very fine Perpendicular W. window above the W. door of the tower. The Norman chancel was pulled down in 1598 and a beautiful substitute erected in 1933–5 to the designs of Temple Moore. There is a handsome Elizabethan pulpit of elaborate design. There are lovely views of the church from across the river.

SLEAFORD † St Denys ★★
11m/18km N.E. of Grantham
OS *TF068458* **GPS** *52.9997N, 0.4088W*

In the market-place is the splendid W. front of this church, pinnacled and niched, traceried and moulded; to its left and half-hidden is the Elizabethan vicarage. The spire is one of the earliest of all English stone spires: late 12th- or very early 13th-century. The nave is Decorated, the lofty arches supported on slender pillars, and all around, especially in the N. transept and S. aisle, is some of the finest Decorated tracery in England. Pugin described the rood screen as one of the most perfect anywhere – the rood itself and the figures are by Comper, 1922. To either side of the chancel are grand 16th- and 17th-century monuments to the Carre family – one of them by Maximilian Colt.

SNARFORD † St Lawrence ★
6m/10km S.W. of Market Rasen
OS *TF050824* **GPS** *53.3284N, 0.4239W*

Lost in the middle of nowhere: there is no village. The little church, with a farmhouse next door, is of little consequence in itself, but contains the breathtaking monuments to a family, the St Pauls. The interior of the church is dominated by their great Elizabethan tombs. Their wealth, their house, the family themselves, have long departed; only the church survives to recall their memory.

SOMERSBY † St Margaret ★
6m/10km E. of Horncastle
OS *TF343726* **GPS** *53.2340N, 0.0116E*

A small 15th-century church in the heart of the wolds, it stands opposite the former rectory in which Alfred Tennyson was born in 1809. The little church is altogether delightful and contains a bronze head of the poet by Thomas Woolner, 1873, and many souvenirs of interest.

SOUTH KYME † St Mary and All Saints
7m/11km N.E. of Sleaford
OS *TF168497* **GPS** *53.0326N, 0.2589W*

A wonderful spot – a grand tower stands by itself, relic of the castle of the Kymes and Umfravilles with church nearby, once the S. aisle of a priory church. A Norman door remains inside the porch, but the main part is 14th-century. Behind a little doorway in the panelling on the N. side of the chancel are astounding fragments of a 7th-century spiral-and-scroll decoration found during the restoration and rebuilding in 1890 by Hodgson Fowler.

SOUTH SOMERCOTES † St Peter ★
2m/3km S. of North Somercotes, and 8m/12km N.E. of Louth
OS *TF415938* **GPS** *53.4221N, 0.1293E*
Churches Conservation Trust

Known locally as 'The Queen of the Marsh', the church has a tall, graceful spire rising from a wide, flat landscape. It is mostly Early English and has a fine 15th-century font with emblems of the Passion.

SPALDING † St Mary and St Nicholas ★
Between Church Street and Love Lane
OS *TF250224* **GPS** *52.7850N, 0.1476W*

The church is mainly 14th- and 15th-century and has double aisles on each side of the nave, with a tower and spire at the S.W. corner. The whole interior is a maze of pillars. The N. porch has a vaulted roof and there is a chantry chapel at the S.E. corner. The church was restored by Sir George Gilbert Scott, who added a N. aisle to the chancel in 1864–6. Spalding is a prosperous Fenland town with many Georgian and earlier buildings, and unfortunate modern building wherever one looks.

STAINFIELD † St Andrew ★
7m/11km E. of Lincoln
OS *TF111732* **GPS** *53.2443N, 0.3352W*

A delightful Queen Anne church, it was built in 1711 by the Tyrwhitts. It was somewhat mutilated inside by the Victorians, but some panels of 17th-century needlework and funerary armour survive. The great house was burnt down in the early 19th century; a

△ **STAMFORD: ALL SAINTS** – *Early English blank arcading from the 1200s*

grass field near the church contains mounds which mark the site of a Benedictine nunnery.

STAMFORD † All Saints ★
All Saints Place
OS *TF028071* **GPS** *52.6524N, 0.4810W*

Without question, Stamford is one of the two or three most beautiful towns in England, built entirely of local limestone. It has five remaining churches, all of them outstanding. All Saints dominates Red Lion Square with its Perpendicular tower and lofty crocketed spire. At first sight the church appears all Perpendicular, but the unusual blank Early English arcades betray its earlier origins. There is a handsome Victorian reredos and a number of 18th-century monuments and earlier brasses – especially that to William Browne, 1489, founder of Browne's Hospital.

STAMFORD † St George ★
St George's Square
OS *TF032070* **GPS** *52.6517N, 0.4759W*

The church is surrounded by the delightful 18th-century houses of its own little square; in origin it is 13th-century, but the very fine chancel was rebuilt in 1449 by Sir William de Bruge, first Garter King of Arms, and in the E. window is an outstanding assembly of heraldic glass of members of the Order of the Garter, put here in 1732. There are distinguished 18th-century monuments, especially that to Sir Richard Cust by John Bacon, 1797.

STAMFORD † St Martin
High Street St Martin's
OS *TF031067* **GPS** *52.6490N, 0.4773W*

The only surviving medieval church outside the town walls, its tower can be seen in Turner's painting of the arrival of a stage coach in a storm. The 15th-century church is notable for the tombs of the Cecil family, housed in the Burghley Chapel. The earliest and best of these is that to William Cecil, d. 1598, canopied and vaulted. The only Victorian addition to this Perpendicular church was the extension of the N. chapel.

STAMFORD † St Mary ★★
St Mary's Street
OS *TF030070* **GPS** *52.6514N, 0.4782W*

The broach spire here is without doubt one of the most magnificent in England, early 14th-century on a 13th-century tower. The interior is glorious too – largely 15th-century, with its rare cradle roof in the Lady Chapel,

△ **TATTERSHALL: HOLY TRINITY** – *in 1439 King Henry VI licensed it as a collegiate church for seven priests, six secular clerks, six choristers and thirteen old people in the almshouses*

medieval tombs and delightful 19th-century furnishings. The rood screen, stalls and high altar are by Sedding, as is the gaily painted chancel ceiling. The glass is by Wailes and Christopher Whall. A devout, atmospheric interior.

STOKE ROCHFORD
† St Andrew and St Mary ★

5m/8km S. of Grantham
OS *SK920273* **GPS** *52.8358N, 0.6350W*

This is a large church with a Norman nave, at the heart of its later, mostly Perpendicular, fabric. It is noted for its monuments, particularly that of Sir Jon Neville, d. 1316, and his wife in the N. chapel, and in the S. chapel the monolithic monument to Henry Cholmely, d. 1641. The reredos is charming, painted by Mary Watts, champion of the Home Arts and Industries Association, who also designed the extraordinary cemetery chapel at Compton in Surrey.

STOW † St Mary ★

4m/6km N. of Saxilby
OS *SK881820* **GPS** *53.3276N, 0.6773W*

An impressive pre-Conquest church, it is cruciform in plan with a central tower and crossing arches of equal proportions. These arches, which are of the early 11th century, dominate the church, but there is notable Norman work in the nave, said to be by Remigius, first Bishop of Lincoln, 1072–94, and also in the spacious chancel, dating apparently from the early 12th century. The present crossing tower is Perpendicular.

STRAGGLETHORPE † St Michael

7m/11km E. of Newark
OS *SK913524* **GPS** *53.0612N, 0.6385W*

A little Saxon-Norman chapel with a later N. aisle, it is approached through a farmyard. Inside there are bleached box pews, a two-decker pulpit and a graceful 17th-century monument with an elegant verse; altogether a rare, undisturbed interior.

SWATON † St Michael ★
12m/19km E. of Grantham
OS *TF133375* **GPS** *52.9232N, 0.3161W*

One of the lesser-known marvels of Lincs., it is magnificent and cruciform with a central tower and enormous traceried windows. The nave arcades soar upward, with nave and aisles under a single roof. On the S. aisle wall is a faded Wheel of Life painting. A most distinguished church.

SWINESHEAD † St Mary ★
6m/10km S.W. of Boston
OS *TF237401* **GPS** *52.9449N, 0.1597W*

A vast Fen church, where the inset spire rises from a low octagon which surmounts a mighty square tower. The mostly 14th-century interior is very fine, spacious, wide and lofty, with a magnificent tower arch leading to the W. doorway. The nave arcades are gracious, under a clerestory with Reticulated tracery. The chancel was rebuilt in 1848 by Stephen Lavin.

TATTERSHALL † Holy Trinity ★★
8m/12km S.W. of Horncastle
OS *TF212575* **GPS** *53.1017N, 0.1910W*

Standing near the famous castle, this expansive church was entirely rebuilt in the middle of the 15th century. It was collegiate, and the chancel is divided from the nave by a heavy stone screen built in 1528. In the N. transept there are some good 15th- and 16th-century brasses of Continental manufacture. Originally every window was filled with contemporary glass, but most of it was removed in 1737, and 20 years later was taken to Stamford, where it may be seen in St Martin's Church and in the dining-hall of Burghley House. The little that remains in the church was transferred from the transepts to the E. window. Here 28 panels occupy seven lights in the lower half of the window, mostly consisting of isolated parts of various series representing the Sacraments, saints, angels and the corporal Acts of Mercy.

TEALBY † All Saints ★
3m/4km E. of Market Rasen
OS *TF157908* **GPS** *53.4022N, 0.2610W*

This medieval church is notable for the beauty of its setting on a slope above an attractive stone-built village and looking across to the park of Bayons Manor, built by Charles Tennyson d'Eyncourt, the uncle of Alfred Lord Tennyson, in 1836, and wantonly blown up in 1965 following decades of neglect.

THEDDLETHORPE † All Saints
3m/4km N.W. of Mablethorpe
OS *TF463882* **GPS** *53.3705N, 0.1985E*
Churches Conservation Trust

The main body of this attractive building is 14th- and 15th-century, although other periods are represented. In the E. chapels off the aisles there are Perpendicular windows, while those in the clerestory are unspoilt Decorated. The rood screen and the stone reredos in the S. aisle are both of the 15th century. There are two parclose screens belonging to the 16th century and some 18th-century monuments. There is also a brass of 1424 and fragments of medieval glass. On the aisle walls, which retain some of their original plaster, there are traces of early coloured decoration. The tower is surmounted by a curious pinnacle.

THORNTON CURTIS † St Lawrence ★
2m/3km S.E. of Barrow
OS *TA087178* **GPS** *53.6461N, 0.3556W*

This impressive church dates mainly from 1200–1300, with round-headed lancets in the chancel, simple flowing tracery in the S. aisle, and the most remarkable black Tournai marble font, with its amazing animal carvings – one of only 10 in England.

THREEKINGHAM † St Peter
6m/10km S. of Sleaford
OS *TF089361* **GPS** *52.9116N, 0.3812W*

A church which is notable for its tower and 14th-century broach spire, characteristic of the district. The chancel is late Norman, and the remainder of the building is Decorated, containing some fine mouldings. There are mutilated effigies of the Trikingham family.

TYDD ST MARY † St Mary ★
3m/4km S. of Long Sutton
OS *TF446185* **GPS** *52.7456N, 0.1409E*

A 14th-century Fenland church with a 15th-century brick tower and stone spire; the arcades are 12th-century relics of a former church. The large 14th-century chancel window has striking late Geometric tracery in the windows, and the 15th-century font is decorated with shields held by angels.

UFFINGTON
† St Michael and All Angels ★
2m/3km E. of Stamford
OS *TF061077* **GPS** *52.6570N, 0.4320W*

A lovely crocketed spire with flying buttresses stands above the Perpendicular tower of this elegant church. The 14th-century W. door has ballflower ornament, and inside are early 13th-century arcades, largely rebuilt in 1865, and a chantry chapel on the N. side. There are some monuments to members of the Manners family: of note on the S. chancel wall is that of Robert Manners, d. 1587, and his son Olyver – a marble and alabaster sideboard tomb – and opposite, a similar monument to Dr Stanton, Dean of Lincoln.

WALESBY † All Saints ★★
3m/4km N.E. of Market Rasen
OS *TF138923* **GPS** *53.4161N, 0.2888W*
Churches Conservation Trust

There is a good modern church in the village by Temple Moore, but the old one stands in solitary dignity on the top of a hill. For a long time it was practically a ruin, but was sympathetically restored in 1931. The arcades mark the transition from Norman to Early English. The substantial tower with stepped angle buttresses has double-lancet windows. There is a restored 15th-century chancel screen; a 17th-century pulpit was formerly used by the Presbyterians at Kirkstead. When the church was restored, the ravages of dry rot necessitated the removal of most of the box pews, but a few remain in the N. aisle. The view from this church across the valley of the Ancholme is superb.

WELL † St Margaret ★
11m/18km N.W. of Skegness
OS *TF444733* **GPS** *53.2378N, 0.1623E*

A delightful piece of 18th-century landscape gardening. A brief for £1,201 for its erection was issued in 1732. The surrounding country, which is undulating and well-wooded, is exceptionally beautiful, and the church, which has a portico with Tuscan columns and a fine Venetian window at the W. end, is an attractive example of early Georgian architecture. It is noteworthy that the orientation of this church was reversed in order to fit the landscape better!

WEST KEAL † St Helen ★
11m/18km W. of Skegness
OS *TF367637* **GPS** *53.1534N, 0.0435E*

This is perhaps the most advantageous site in Lincs., with grand views across Fens to Boston Stump. The fabric is mainly green sandstone, with a limestone chancel rebuilt in 1867 by Street, and brick patchwork on the S. aisle. The 15th-century porch has some outsized gargoyles. An ancient door is set in ascending carved stone figures. The capitals of the 14th-century arcades are its greatest glory, upon which can be seen dragons fighting, foxes stealing, pigs being chained and women almost bursting from their bodices. The tower collapsed in 1881 but was carefully rebuilt with appropriate gargoyles.

WESTON † St Mary ★★
3m/4km E. of Spalding
OS *TF292251* **GPS** *52.8085N, 0.0840W*

The church is almost entirely Early English, with a Norman-looking clerestory, 14th-century transepts and a 15th-century tower. The splendid S. porch has blind arcades on either side, and the nave arcades are extremely fine. The dark Victorian glass does not complement the completeness of this very good church. Of great interest is the font – circular and divided into eight sections, on each of which is a device of foliage in deep relief. One of the best of all Early English churches.

WHAPLODE † St Mary ★
2m/3km W. of Holbeach
OS *TF323240* **GPS** *52.7974N, 0.0384W*

This is a large and interesting church with a Norman chancel arch and a tower begun in the 12th century and finished in the 14th. The tower stands in an unusual position at the E. end of the S. aisle. The nave arcades are very interesting, showing a transition from round to quatrefoil piers, and from scalloped

△ **WHAPLODE: ST MARY** – *a small and rather perky griffin guards one end of the flamboyant tomb of Sir Anthony Irby and his wife*

to stiff-leaf capitals. In the N. transept is a very good Arts and Crafts oak traceried window, and in the S. aisle a magnificent highly coloured tomb to Sir Anthony Irby, 1623, and his wife Alice, 1625, with their five children as weepers below.

WINTHORPE † St Mary ★

2m/3km N. of Skegness
OS *TF559658* **GPS** *53.1669N, 0.3309E*

A late 15th-century church, it has a great expanse of glass and a magnificent collection of original woodwork, including a rood screen, carved pew-ends with poppyheads, very beautiful choir stalls and parclose screens at the ends of the aisles. There are also some early 16th-century brasses. The churchyard cross has been carefully restored.

WRANGLE
† St Mary the Virgin and St Nicholas ★

7m/11km N.E. of Boston
OS *TF424508* **GPS** *53.0360N, 0.1235E*

The fabric is Early English, Decorated and Perpendicular, with a grand 14th-century E. window and an Elizabethan pulpit. The glass was inserted between 1345 and 1371, and contains figures of kings and prophets, St George, St Cecilia, St Lucy, St Laurence, St Barbara and other saints. There is also an altar tomb to Sir John Read, 1626, whose family was for many generations resident here. Near the font is a ledger stone, dated 1705, commemorating William Erskine, an incumbent who built the beautiful former vicarage.

WYBERTON † St Leodegar

2m/3km S. of Boston
OS *TF328408* **GPS** *52.9484N, 0.0239W*

The church stands on the edge of a small park belonging to a handsome 17th- and 18th-century mansion which was formerly the rectory. Inside there are delicate clustered 13th-century arcades in the nave, and a small Georgian apsidal chancel.

LONDON

This chapter is divided into *Central London*, which includes churches in the City of London plus the central part of the area called 'Inner London' in previous editions of this guide, and *Greater London*, which includes churches in towns and suburbs that were once part of the historic county of Middlesex and the innermost parts of Essex, Kent and Surrey.

The only big medieval churches – old St Paul's, Westminster Abbey, St Bartholomew's, Smithfield, St Katherine by Tower (demolished 1825), The Temple Church and the various religious foundations along the banks of the Thames – were built mainly of imported stone brought by water from as far as Caen and Purbeck, since there was no available good local stone. The few medieval parish churches surviving in the boroughs of central London are not exceptional architecturally.

The old county of Middlesex had a humble Perpendicular style rather like that of Hertfordshire and south Essex. Surrey and the parts of Kent now within London had no fine parish churches except St Mary Overy, Southwark, which is now Southwark Cathedral.

London's first great church-building period after medieval times (and there were about 100 churches in the square mile of the City before the Great Fire of 1666) was in the 17th and 18th centuries. With few exceptions, the chief churches of these times were Classical. Sir Christopher Wren supervised the rebuilding of 50 in the City, of which 19 were destroyed by the Germans. Of 16 other churches built since the time of Wren, half were destroyed to pay for suburban churches. This is a great loss, as they were almost all more impressive and original, at any rate internally, than the lesser Wren churches.

In Westminster and Southwark and just outside the City, several handsome churches were built in the 18th century. These were in the Classical style. The usual building material in these parts for 17th- and 18th-century churches was Portland stone. This is well suited to the London climate and weathers black and brilliant white, so that it gives an effect of shadow on the greyest day. Brick was also used, and the London brick in the 17th and early 18th centuries was always of a variety of red and brown shades, which stood up to the soot of the mid-20th century remarkably well. Wren built lead steeples to some of his churches.

The next big phase of building was after the Napoleonic campaigns, when the usual materials were white stock brick for walls and Bath stone for portico, steeple and dressings.

Finally, there was the biggest church-building period in London since medieval times, from the mid-19th century onward. The churches of this period vary greatly in merit, and only exceptionally fine ones are listed.

◁ **ST PANCRAS NEW CHURCH** – *caryatids on the south porch styled similarly to those at the ancient Erechtheion in Athens*

CENTRAL LONDON

† All Hallows by the Tower ★

Byward Street, EC3 (City)
OS *TQ333807* **GPS** *51.5095N, 0.0793W*

Medieval, and largely destroyed by war, it was reconstructed in 1956–7 by Lord Mottistone of Seeley & Paget, who added an elegant spire to the brick tower of 1659. Formerly the church of the Port of London, it has a mariner's chapel in the S. aisle, and in the N. aisle a very fine triptych (whose central panel is missing) – Flemish, early 16th century. There is an exotic, florid Grinling Gibbons font cover in the baptistry.

† All Hallows on the Wall ★

London Wall, Broad Street, EC2 (City)
OS *TQ330814* **GPS** *51.5166N, 0.0844W*
Guild church

Designed by George Dance Jnr, 1765–7. The exterior is modest and apparently windowless. Inside, the church is elegance itself: a barrel-vaulted ceiling decorated with a flower pattern in Adam style, the plasterwork being lit by semi-circular windows above a broad frieze that binds the whole interior together, and below which are Ionic pilasters. Surprisingly and effectively, there is no cornice above the frieze. Above the panelled apse is a coffered semi-dome. Dance's method of lighting a church surrounded by high buildings was probably copied from Hawksmoor's at St Mary Woolnoth, and his apse from Gibbs's at St Mary-le-Strand, but he interpreted their themes in the restrained manner of the later Georgian age. The fittings are unobtrusive and unexceptional. It is now a guild church and home to several charities. There is a monthly service.

† All Saints Margaret Street ★

Margaret Street, W1 (Marylebone)
OS *TQ292814* **GPS** *51.5173N, 0.1390W*

By W. Butterfield, 1849–59, and often hailed as his masterpiece. The tall, unbuttressed tower, with its slate and lead spire and polychromatic brick had never been seen in London before; this is the pioneer church of the phase of Gothic Revival that ceased to copy medieval, but went on with new materials like cast iron and stock brick from where the medieval had left off. For the smallness and confined nature of the site, the effect of space, richness, mystery and size is amazing. The original plan was strictly Tractarian – one altar visible from all parts of the church, no screen, light from the W. end, and the chancel more sumptuous than anywhere else. Comper's side altar is wisely not in Butterfield's style and, excellent in itself, it does not compete with the huge mouldings and violent contrasts of texture and colour that make this building so memorable. The decoration on the E. wall is based on Dyce's original scheme; the large tiled pictures on the N., W. and S. walls are by Alexander Gibbs, just right for their setting. The roof, to quote the 20th-century art historian John Summerson, 'is like a huge ingenious toy'. The effect of this building is all achieved by scale – the huge but low arcades, the lofty chancel arch and reredos beyond. The thought and care over detail are best appreciated after long familiarity. An embarrassing screen has been put in the S. aisle.

† Brompton Oratory RC

Corner of Brompton Road and Cottage Place, SW3 (Knightsbridge)
OS *TQ271791* **GPS** *51.4971N, 0.1696W*

Unmistakable in Knightsbridge: Rome comes to London. The Baroque building, by H. Gribble in 1880–96, was modelled on the Church of the Most Holy Name of Jesus in Rome, and is second in size only to Westminster Cathedral. It was restored in the 1980s. Unlike the cathedral, it has a finished scheme of decoration, entirely late Victorian Italian, with marble panelling, side chapels, stucco and mosaic. Many of the statues were brought from the Gesù church in Rome.

† Christ Church Spitalfields

Corner of Commercial Street and Fournier Street, E1 (City)
OS *TQ337817* **GPS** *51.5191N, 0.0737W*

This is a huge, heavy galleon of white Portland stone by Nicholas Hawksmoor, 1723–9, anchored among the red-brick Queen Anne houses of the silk-workers. Two flights of steps lead to the immense

△ **HOLY TRINITY SLOANE STREET** – *reliefs in the chancel depicting saints, interspersed with the armoured figures of St George and St Alban*

barrel-vaulted portico, on top of which stand an oblong tower and spire. The body of the church is a separate composition, but towers, spire, portico and church hang together as one walks by. Everything is simple and gigantic. The aisled and columned interior is rich and grandly gloomy. A clerestory lights the flat and coffered nave ceiling; from the arcades below, the arches open onto transverse coffered tunnel vaults which overhang the aisles. To both E. and W. the great rectangle of the church is interrupted by transverse motifs; a beam on Corinthian columns, with a Royal Arms above, turns the E. end into a chancel, beyond which the walls curve to make a sanctuary. The church was in a dangerous condition in the 1960s and nearly demolished, but saved by the Friends of Christ Church and since expertly repaired.

† Holy Redeemer Clerkenwell

Exmouth Market, EC1 (Clerkenwell)
OS *TQ312824* **GPS** *51.5255N, 0.1092W*

By J. D. Sedding, 1887–8, in Italianate style, and as impressive as a big Wren church within – cruciform within a square shell. H. Wilson extended the church later, adding the distinctive campanile.

† Holy Trinity Sloane Street

Corner of Sloane Square and Sloane Street, SW1 (Chelsea)
OS *TQ280787* **GPS** *51.4932N, 0.1573W*

John Dando Sedding's last work, 1888–90, is a free and flowing Perpendicular interpretation, the cathedral of the Art Nouveau movement, furnished by Sedding's pupil Henry Wilson and associates from the Guild of Art Workers. The vast nave is alive with carving, the chancel gates are masterpieces of wrought iron and, beyond, the choir stalls have bronze relief panels – all a testament to Sedding's brilliant vision. And there is glass from Morris, Burne-Jones, Whall and W. Richmond – a unified scheme of outstanding composition. This church also was where Betjeman worshipped in London.

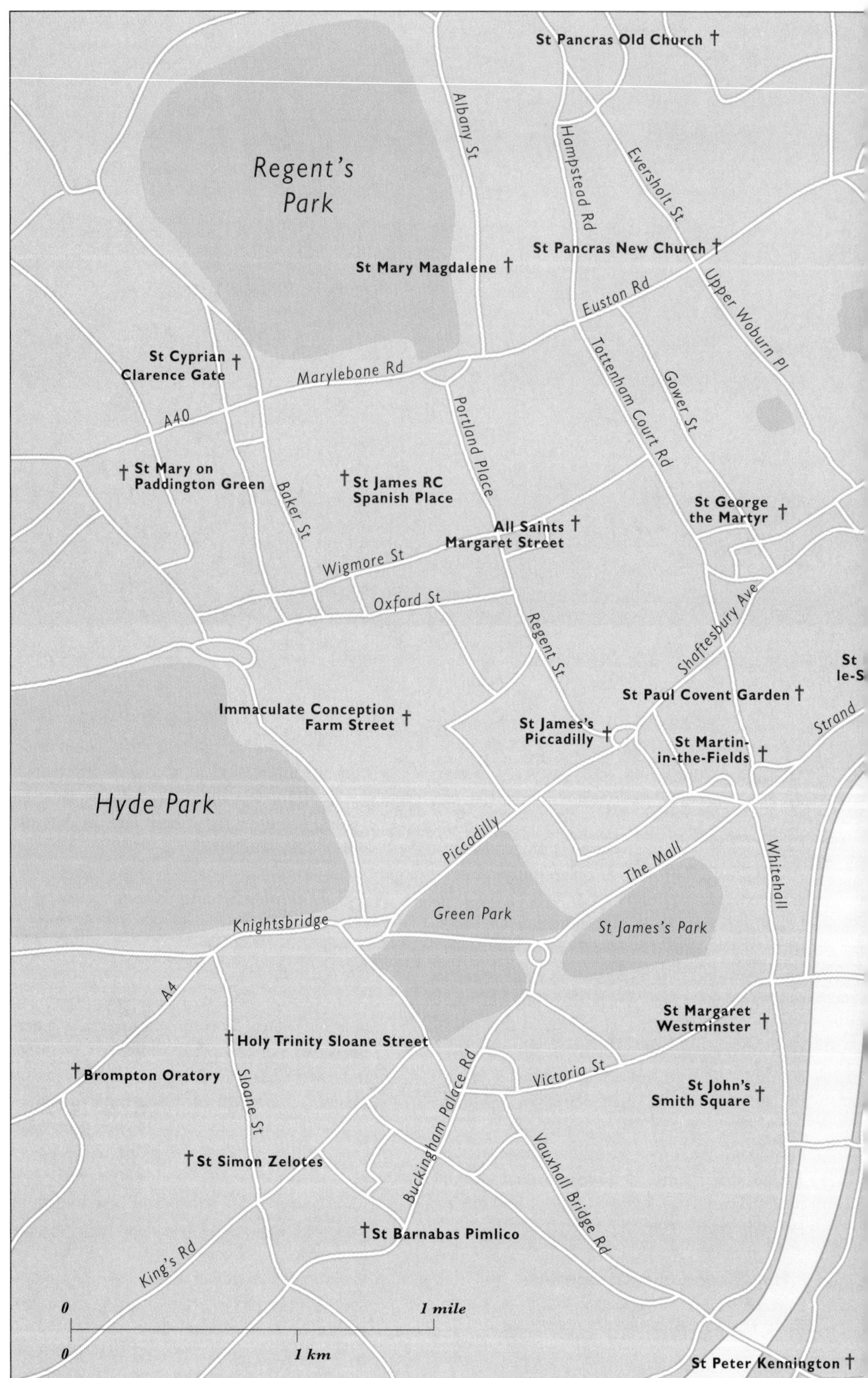
St Pancras Old Church
Regent's Park
Albany St
Hampstead Rd
Eversholt St
St Pancras New Church
St Mary Magdalene
Upper Woburn Pl
Euston Rd
Tottenham Court Rd
Gower St
St Cyprian Clarence Gate
Marylebone Rd
A40
Portland Place
St Mary on Paddington Green
St James RC Spanish Place
Baker St
St George the Martyr
All Saints Margaret Street
Wigmore St
Oxford St
Regent St
Shaftesbury Ave
St le-S
St Paul Covent Garden
Immaculate Conception Farm Street
St James's Piccadilly
St Martin-in-the-Fields
Strand
Hyde Park
Piccadilly
The Mall
Whitehall
Green Park
St James's Park
Knightsbridge
A4
St Margaret Westminster
Holy Trinity Sloane Street
Brompton Oratory
Victoria St
Buckingham Palace Rd
St John's Smith Square
Sloane St
Vauxhall Bridge Rd
St Simon Zelotes
St Barnabas Pimlico
King's Rd
0
1 mile
0
1 km
St Peter Kennington

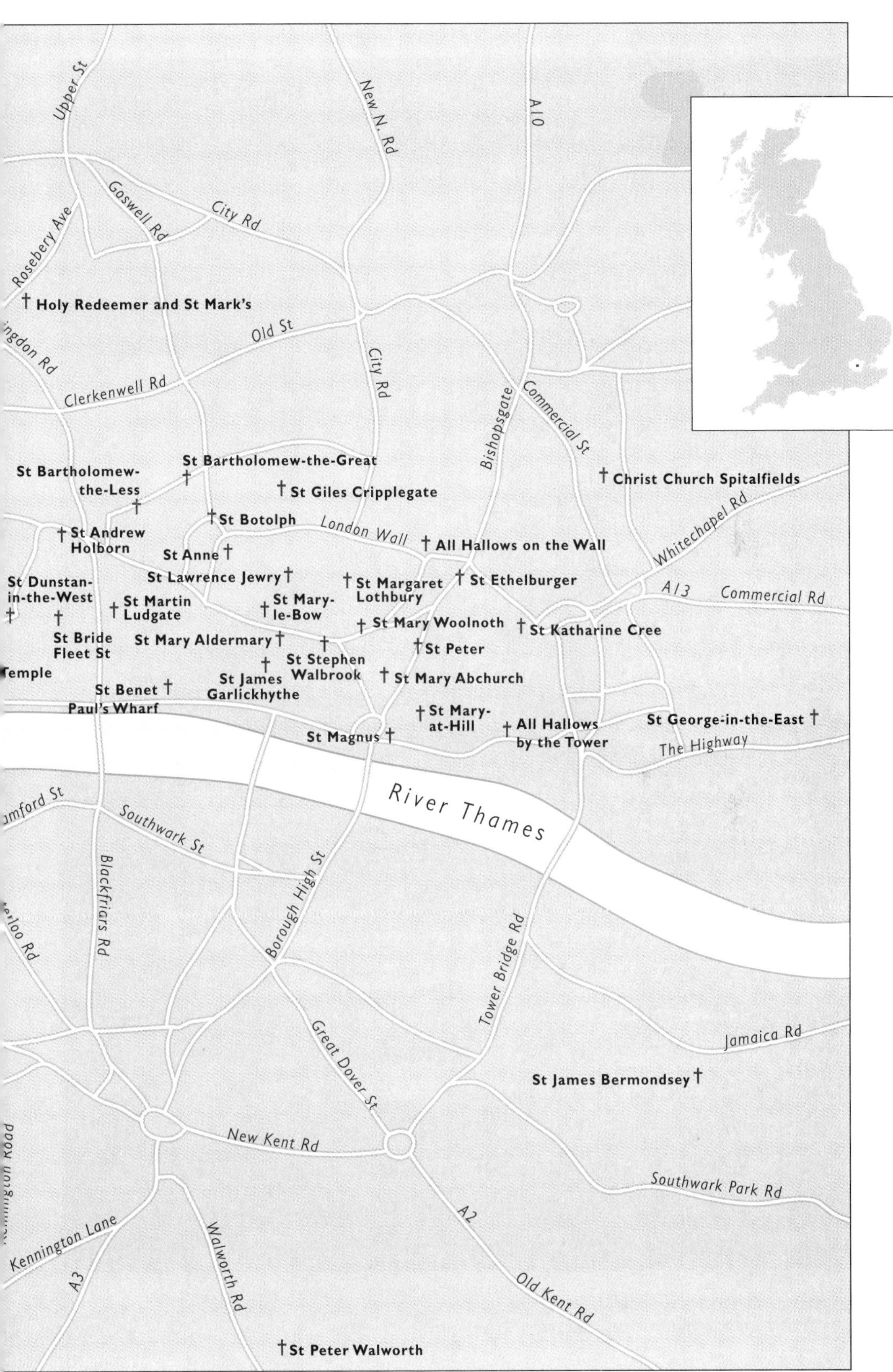
Upper St
New N. Rd
A10
Goswell Rd
City Rd
Rosebery Ave
Holy Redeemer and St Mark's
Old St
City Rd
Clerkenwell Rd
Bishopsgate
Commercial St
St Bartholomew-the-Less
St Bartholomew-the-Great
St Giles Cripplegate
Christ Church Spitalfields
Whitechapel Rd
St Andrew Holborn
St Botolph
London Wall
All Hallows on the Wall
St Anne
St Dunstan-in-the-West
St Lawrence Jewry
St Margaret Lothbury
St Ethelburger
A13
Commercial Rd
St Martin Ludgate
St Mary-le-Bow
St Mary Woolnoth
St Katharine Cree
St Bride Fleet St
St Mary Aldermary
St Peter
St Stephen Walbrook
St James Garlickhythe
St Mary Abchurch
St Benet Paul's Wharf
St Mary-at-Hill
All Hallows by the Tower
St George-in-the-East
St Magnus
The Highway
River Thames
Southwark St
Blackfriars Rd
Borough High St
Tower Bridge Rd
Jamaica Rd
Great Dover St
St James Bermondsey
New Kent Rd
Southwark Park Rd
A2
Kennington Lane
A3
Walworth Rd
Old Kent Rd
St Peter Walworth

△ **ST BENET PAUL'S WHARF** – *Wren's neat, red-brick church with contrasting pale stone quoins, now rather isolated by the traffic that swirls round it*

† Immaculate Conception Farm Street

Between Farm Street & Mount Street, W1 (Mayfair)
OS *TQ285805* **GPS** *51.5095N, 0.1491W*

By J. J. Scoles, 1844–9, this is the London headquarters of the Jesuits, an outstanding work of Gothic Revival by a relatively unknown architect. Marble piers support a nave of eight bays. The raised sanctuary is clad with Nottinghamshire alabaster and dominated by Pugin's altar and reredos; the entire church is rich in decoration and colour. The two chancel chapels are by H. Clutton and J. F. Bentley.

† St Andrew Holborn

Between Holborn Viaduct, Shoe Lane and St Andrew Street, EC1 (City)
OS *TQ314815* **GPS** *51.5173N, 0.1066W*
Guild church

The church, which stands between Holborn and Holborn Viaduct, is by Wren, 1684–90. The 15th-century tower was refaced in Portland stone, 1703. St Andrew's was gutted in 1941, restored by Seeley & Paget and re-opened in 1961. The classic organ and font are from the Foundling Hospital, and the reredos in the tower chapel from St Luke's, Old Street. Now a guild church, it also hosts several charities.

† St Anne and St Agnes

Cnr of Gresham Street and Noble Street, EC2 (City)
OS *TQ321814* **GPS** *51.5165N, 0.0963W*

This inconspicuous church, rebuilt by Wren in 1677–80, is justified by its interior. The plaster-vaulted ceilings are on the same plan as St Mary-at-Hill and St Martin Ludgate, except that the centre of the Greek cross has a wide cross vault instead of a dome. Some of the old woodwork remains, of which the best is the elegant altarpiece. Since 1966 this church has served the Lutheran community, and services are held here in Estonian and Latvian as well as in English.

† St Barnabas Pimlico ★

St Barnabas Street, SW1 (Pimlico)
OS *TQ284784* **GPS** *51.4904N, 0.1518W*

A mission church for the slums of Pimlico by T. Cundy Jnr, 1847–50, St Barnabas is Gothic Revival on Tractarian lines, with a S.E. chapel and sacrament house by Comper. The gilded reredos, splendidly monolithic, is by Bodley; the glass is by Kempe and Tower, and in the baptistry by Martin Travers. The nave walls are lined with mosaics of scenes from the Life of Christ. The spire was rebuilt in 2006–7.

† St Bartholomew-the-Great ★

Cloth Fair, off West Smithfield, EC1 (City)
OS *TQ319817* **GPS** *51.5189N, 0.0995W*

This great Norman church would be impressive anywhere. The 17th-century brick tower contains the oldest ring of bells in England. The flint and Portland stone refacing, added by Sir Aston Webb at the end of the 19th century, gives the outside an East Anglian look which the interior belies. This is vast, dark and Romanesque, with a triforium and apsidal end. Charmingly, the Perpendicular tomb of Rahere, founder of the great hospital, and a Perpendicular watching window in the triforium opposite, are inserted between rugged Norman columns. A cross-vaulted ambulatory leads round the church past an E. Lady Chapel. The church is the choir and transepts of a monastery whose nave was on the site of the present churchyard. The ancient W. gatehouse survived together with one side of the cloister.

† St Bartholomew-the-Less

Within grounds of Bart's Hospital, off West Smithfield, EC1 (City)
OS *TQ318816* **GPS** *51.5179N, 0.1006W*

The interior of the church was rebuilt in octagonal form by George Dance the Younger, 1789, and the plan was retained in Thomas Hardwick's 1825 rebuilding. Repaired after World War II by Seeley & Paget, the church reopened in 1951. The interior is chaste grey and white with Victorian fittings. It also serves as Bart's Hospital chapel.

† St Benet Paul's Wharf

Coner of White Lion Hill and Queen Victoria Street, EC4 (City)
OS *TQ320809* **GPS** *51.5117N, 0.0992W*

Remarkable as one of four Wren churches to survive the war unscathed, the red-brick exterior with stone dressings and swags above

ST BARTHOLOMEW-THE-GREAT – *the massive chancel with its Romanesque arcade was retained for parochial use after the Dissolution of the Monasteries* ▷

the windows, old tiled roofs, tower, lead dome and lantern look very well on the steep slope S. of Queen Victoria Street. It was finished by Wren in 1683. The interior, with galleries, W. organ and the usual carved Renaissance altarpiece, pulpit and wainscoted walls, is one of the least altered City interiors. It is the church of the College of Heralds and the London church of the Welsh Episcopalians.

† St Botolph Aldersgate

Corner of Aldersgate and Little Britain, EC1 (City)
OS *TQ321815* **GPS** *51.5170N, 0.0972W*

St Botolph's was rebuilt by Nathaniel Wright, 1790. Square pillars on each side support a gallery from which rise Corinthian columns – themselves supporting an arched ceiling delicately ornamented with bands and flowers. The ceiling is lit by semi-circular windows, as in Dance's church of All Hallows, London Wall. There is an apsidal E. end and the W. end with its organ case is an elegant composition. The pulpit and sounding board are also of the same date, and the beautiful transparency of the Agony in the Garden in the E. window was painted by James Pearson in 1788. The rest of the glass in the church is deplorable.

† St Bride Fleet Street ★

Bride Lane, off Fleet Street, EC4 (City)
OS *TQ315811* **GPS** *51.5138N, 0.1055W*

By Wren, 1671–1703. The church was gutted in 1940, restored by Godfrey Allen and rededicated in 1957. The elegant wedding-cake steeple of five octagonal stages is much admired. The interior is arcaded, and Doric columns support a clerestory and barrel-vaulted roof. The once galleried interior is now replanned on collegiate lines.

† St Cyprian Clarence Gate

105 Glentworth Street, NW1 (Marylebone)
OS *TQ277822* **GPS** *51.5244N, 0.1599W*

Designed and built by Comper and Bucknall, the church was consecrated in 1903, Comper's first complete one, considered by Betjeman to be the epitome of E. Anglian Perpendicular in London. A fine gilded screen and rood spans the entire church, and the chancel is rich in colour and fittings. The Perpendicular nave is refined, with tall arcades and a fine painted roof.

† St Dunstan-in-the-West

Fleet Street, EC4 (City)
OS *TQ312811* **GPS** *51.5142N, 0.1102W*

By John Shaw & Son, 1831, and rebuilt again in 1950. Its stump tower is a reduced version of Boston, Lincolnshire, and the famous 17th-century clock is a noted feature of Fleet Street. Inside, the body of the church is a spacious Gothic octagon, with much fine 17th-century Flemish woodwork. The Romanian Orthodox Church has its base here, its chapel distinguished by a very fine iconostasis from Bucharest.

† St Ethelburga

Bishopsgate, EC2 (City)
OS *TQ331813* **GPS** *51.5155N, 0.0820W*

This modest old church – dwarfed by its brash city neighbours – is interesting because it is what many of the 100 and more small churches in the City must have been like before the Great Fire. Following extensive damage caused by an IRA bomb in 1993, the church was rebuilt to its original plan – a nave and aisle divided by an arcade – and is now the St Ethelburga Centre for Peace and Reconciliation.

† St George-in-the-East

Corner of Cannon Street Road and The Highway, E1 (Stepney)
OS *TQ347807* **GPS** *51.5100N, 0.0597W*

One of Hawksmoor's six London churches, 1715–23, and perhaps the most original, built for well-to-do ship owners and ship masters. The church was gutted in 1941, although the distinctive pepper-pot towers survived, and Ansell & Bailey's restoration, 1960–64, is a combination of modern forms with surviving Georgian and Victorian decoration.

† St George the Martyr Bloomsbury

Bloomsbury Way, WC1 (Bloomsbury)
OS *TQ302815* **GPS** *51.5177N, 0.1248W*

A Commissioners' church, this was the last of Hawksmoor's London churches, 1720–30. It has a surprising stepped steeple, with porticoes on angled plinths, a statue of George I in Roman dress on top, and carved lions and unicorns symbolising the ending of the first Jacobite uprising. An impressive Corinthian portico leads to a dignified and solemn but bright interior of Greek cross plan.

† St Giles Cripplegate

Barbican, off London Wall, EC2 (City)
OS *TQ323816* **GPS** *51.5187N, 0.0938W*

Bombed and restored, St Giles is an oasis in the Barbican, a Jack Russell of a building holding its own against its over-powering neighbours. It is one of the few surviving medieval churches in the City, a large 16th-century double-aisled building with a 17th-century brick top stage to the tower. Note the new E. window from the Nicholson studios – lovely neo-Arts and Crafts. Cromwell was married here, and John Milton is buried near the pulpit.

† St James Bermondsey

Thurland Road, SE16 (Bermondsey)
OS *TQ342793* **GPS** *51.4970N, 0.0668W*

This is one of London's finest Commissioners' churches, by James Savage, 1827–9. The Greek exterior has an Ionic portico and slim W. tower modelled on the Wren tower at St Stephen Walbrook. There is a galleried interior, with pulpit and lectern raised high enough for the preacher to maintain contact with the galleries. The E. end is dominated by a painting of the Ascension by the little-known artist John Wood.

† St James Garlickhythe ★

Cnr of Garlick Hill & Upper Thames Street, EC4 (City)
OS *TQ323808* **GPS** *51.5111N, 0.0937W*

Finished by Wren in the same year as St Benet's, the church was Blitzed, then restored in 1967 by David Lockhart-Smith. The best exterior feature is the Portland stone steeple on the tower, which was added in 1714–17. The interior, which is columned, wainscoted and plaster-vaulted with much Renaissance woodwork, is grand and stately. Its plan is more medieval than most of Wren's City churches. This is the best post-war restoration in the City; new from old is undetectable.

† St James's Piccadilly

Cnr of Jermyn Street & Church Place, SW1 (Piccadilly)
OS *TQ294805* **GPS** *51.5087N, 0.1367W*

Sir Albert Richardson restored this Wren church, left roofless from the Blitz, in 1953. The modest old-brick exterior has a rebuilt tower: the spire, replaced in 1968, is a fibre-glass reproduction of the original, and there is an outdoor pulpit by Temple Moore. The pale, elegant galleried interior is Wren at his best, with slender Corinthian piers supporting barrel vaults. The font is by Grinling Gibbons, who also carved the reredos swags and lavish organ case, set above the choristers' gallery, and dominating the W. end.

† St James RC Spanish Place

Blandford Street, W1 (Marylebone)
OS *TQ282815* **GPS** *51.5182N, 0.1525W*

This is a fine example of Anglo-French Gothic Revival by Edward Goldie, 1885–90 – an enthusiastic essay in Early Gothic, with a lofty nave and triforium leading to a high vaulted heptagonal apsidal sanctuary. The rose window bears Royal heraldry of Spain, symbolising the historical connection with the chapel sponsored by the Spanish embassy since Elizabethan times. This connection is continued in spirit, with two Royal seats in the choir stalls, used by King Alfonso and Queen Ena of Spain on their visits to England. Of particular note is the Lady Chapel by J. F. Bentley, with a richly carved and gilded wood reredos of vines, angels and musical instruments, and a copy of Murillo's *Immaculate Conception*, a gift from the Count de Torre Diaz.

† St John's Smith Square

Concert Hall on Smith Square, SW1 (Westminster)
OS *TQ301791* **GPS** *51.4960N, 0.1271W*

Like so many London churches, St John's was bady damaged during the Blitz. It had been built by Thomas Archer, 1714–28, and post-war restoration was by Marshall Sisson, 1965–8. Four Baroque corner towers rise from graceful pedimented compositions on the N. and S. façades and flank more dominant projections on the other two. Thus this bold and strange church, islanded in the middle of a red-brick Queen Anne square, presents a different Portland stone and temple-like termination to each of the four streets that enter the square. It is now a concert hall.

† St Katherine Cree ★

Leadenhall Street, EC3 (City)
OS *TQ333811* **GPS** *51.5134N, 0.0790W*
Guild church

A fine Jacobean church of 1628, and the only Laudian church in London. The E. window, depicting a catherine wheel, dates from 1630. The interior is aisled with delicate Gothic vaulted ceilings sprung from Classical columns, all enriched with painted bosses of City livery companies.

† St Lawrence Jewry ★

Gresham Street, by the Guildhall, EC2 (City)
OS *TQ324813* **GPS** *51.5153N, 0.0924W*
Guild church

St Lawrence Jewry was built by Wren, 1671–7, and gutted in 1940; it was well restored and refitted by Cecil Brown, 1957, to Wren's original plans. The steeple is fibreglass, and the E. wall outside is based on Wren's modern design for St Paul's. Inside is light and airy – very fine.

† St Magnus the Martyr ★

Lower Thames Street, by London Bridge, EC3 (City)
OS *TQ329806* **GPS** *51.5093N, 0.0862W*

Wren, 1671–1705. The beautiful Portland stone tower and steeple mark the approach to Old London Bridge. Inside is a wealth of magnificent woodwork and ironwork – W. screen, gallery and organ case, doorcases, pulpit, altarpiece, sword-rests and communion rails. Wren's original was restored in the Baroque manner by Martin Travers, 1924, and again by Laurence King after war damage.

† St Margaret Lothbury

Lothbury, EC2 (City)
OS *TQ327812* **GPS** *51.5149N, 0.0888W*

One of Wren's later works in Portland stone with a tower and lead spire. The interior has a S. aisle and ingenious clerestory to the broad nave. It is filled with old woodwork from City churches destroyed by the Victorians. A Flemish-looking screen from All Hallows the Great (a Wren church) stretches across the E. end. The rich pulpit has a sounding board, also from All Hallows.

† St Margaret Westminster

Parliament Square, by Westminster Abbey, SW1
OS *TQ301795* **GPS** *51.4999N, 0.1267W*

Built in the late 15th to early 16th centuries, St Margaret's has been much restored. John James rebuilt the N.W. tower from 1734 to 1738, at which time the whole building was faced with Portland stone. J. L. Pearson added an E. and W. porch. The E. window, c. 1526, contains very good pre-Reformation Flemish glass of the Crucifixion; the reredos is by Kempe. There are two windows in the S. aisle by John Piper, 1967.

† St Martin-in-the-Fields

Trafalgar Square, WC2 (Westminster)
OS *TQ301805* **GPS** *51.5088N, 0.1267W*

One of London's best-known churches, by James Gibbs, 1722–6, 'the church with the ever-open door' of Dick Shepherd's ministry was built in 1722–6, a century before Trafalgar Square. Originally the awkward way the Portland-stone steeple bestrides the Corinthian portico was not apparent, as the church was glimpsed through narrow streets. Both the steeple and porticoed body of the church are compact and elegant as separate units. The much-visited interior has galleries and tall columns supporting a vaulted nave ceiling with graceful plasterwork, especially over the chancel arch, and shallow domes over the aisles. The church has triumphantly emerged from extensive restoration by Eric Parry Architects, and at the E. end is a controversial window by Iranian artist Shirazeh Houshiary, in collaboration with Pip Horne – a warped monochromatic grid, forming a cross.

† St Martin Ludgate ★

Ludgate Hill, EC4 (City)
OS *TQ318811* **GPS** *51.5141N, 0.1020W*

By Wren, 1677–84. The lead spire of this stone church is an elegant foil to the dome of St Paul's as one sees it from Fleet Street. The interior, though much rearranged in the last century, still contains its woodwork, including carved doorcases, reredos, panelling and choir stalls. The vaulted ceiling is a Greek cross in plan like St Anne and St Agnes and St Mary-at-Hill.

△ **ST MARY ALDERMARY** – *the particular joy of the church, built by Wren in Gothic style, is the plasterwork in the fan vaulting of the ceiling and in the spandrels of the arcade*

† St Mary Abchurch ★

Abchurch Lane, by Cannon Street, EC4 (City)
OS *TQ327809* **GPS** *51.5117N, 0.0883W*
Guild church

The brick tower, lead spire and plain brick exterior of the church are pleasant, but the inside is magnificent. It is one of the most richly decorated of Wren's churches, a great square room roofed by a dome painted by William Snow, springing from eight pendentives. The woodwork of pulpit, font cover and Grinling Gibbons altarpiece is richest English Renaissance.

† St Mary Aldermary

Queen Victoria Street, at Watling Street, EC4 (City)
OS *TQ324810* **GPS** *51.5127N, 0.0933W*
Guild church

St Mary's is Wren Gothic of 1682, with a fine tower. Inside are Gothic plaster ceilings consisting of a series of shallow domes supported on pendentives made to look like fan vaulting. The glass is by John Crawford and Lawrence Lee. Ornaments on the high altar are by Frank Knight.

† St Mary-at-Hill

Between Lovat Lane and St Mary-at-Hill Street, EC3 (City)
OS *TQ330807* **GPS** *51.5101N, 0.0837W*

The plain exterior of this Wren church of 1670–6 gives no idea of the riches within. Four fluted columns support broad arches over the transepts and E. and W. ends. Above the middle of the Greek cross thus formed rises a central dome from four pendentives, adorned with plasterwork. The plasterwork throughout is rich and bold, but the woodwork and ironwork are better still, particularly over the W. gallery and on the pulpit and altarpiece. The iron sword-rests of various Georgian dates are the best in the

City. The woodwork is mostly 17th-century, with skilful 1847 additions in the Renaissance style. The high pews survive.

† St Mary-le-Bow

Cheapside, EC2 (City)
OS *TQ323811* **GPS** *51.5137N, 0.0936W*

Wren, 1670–80, gutted in 1940. It has the most elaborate and famous Wren steeple rising from a tall tower with Roman Doric doorways set in a rusticated plinth and adorned with cherubs. The brick church, set back from the tower, was square with narrow aisles and wide nave; the crypt is Norman. The church was restored by Laurence King and re-opened in 1965. It includes good glass and a rood by John Hayward.

† St Mary-le-Strand

Strand, by Aldwych, WC2 (Westminster)
OS *TQ307809* **GPS** *51.5122N, 0.1168W*

James Gibbs's 1714–17 church was intended as the westerly termination of two narrow streets, now swept away. The stately Baroque owes much to Gibbs's time studying in Rome under Carlo Fontana. St Mary's is a Commissioners' church with a finely proportioned Classical tower. Outside, the effect is two-storeyed, Doric and Ionic. Inside is a vast open space, without galleries, under a rich, vaulted ceiling. The deep chancel is even richer than the nave and with even uglier glass, but it is a beautiful little church, islanded in traffic.

† St Mary Magdalene

Munster Square, NW1 (Regent's Park)
OS *TQ289824* **GPS** *51.5260N, 0.1425W*

Tucked away in Munster Square, the unpromising exterior of this rebuilt mission church conceals a fine Anglo-Catholic interior, with spacious nave and separately gabled aisles, all Early English. Slender arcades of clustered columns give views of the Hardman glass designed by Pugin, frescoes by Daniel Bell, paintings, an elegant screen and rood by Micklethwaite, and a perfect Tractarian chancel. By Richard Carpenter, 1849–52.

† St Mary on Paddington Green ★

Paddington Green, W2 (Paddington)
OS *TQ266817* **GPS** *51.5204N, 0.1753W*

A most satisfying exterior on its green mound on Paddington Green. By John Plaw, 1788–91, the church is shaped like a Greek cross with a shallow dome on top, and has yellow-brick walls, Portland stone semi-circular porches on three sides, and a Venetian window at the E. end. Inside is an octagonal gallery around three sides and the chancel on the fourth. As the art historian John Summerson said: 'The thing is thoughtfully worked out and quite undeserving of the scorn which later church builders heaped upon it.'

† St Mary Woolnoth

Corner of Lombard Street and
King William Street, EC3 (City)
OS *TQ327810* **GPS** *51.5128N, 0.0881W*
Guild church

This church, designed by Wren's talented clerk, Nicholas Hawksmoor, 1716–27, is original and impressive within and without. The W. tower is divided at its summit into two turrets surmounted by balustrades. The N. front is a splendid example of how to make a windowless wall interesting. The N. wall is quite plain because it originally had buildings against it. Inside, the church is square and for so small a site gives an amazing impression of sumptuousness and height. The effect is created by the fluted Corinthian columns rising in groups of three in the four corners of the church. They support a bold entablature and cornice above which rise semi-circular clerestory windows. There is a flat moulded plaster ceiling. The altarpiece has twisted columns and a canopy of wood with imitation tassels. The only projecting gallery to survive is at the W. end. The organ case, pulpit, gallery fronts and wrought-iron communion rails are all fine and part of Hawksmoor's compact design.

◁ **ST PANCRAS OLD CHURCH** – *this group of headstones surrounding a tree in the churchyard are believed to have been arranged thus by Thomas Hardy, when, as a junior architect under Blomfield, he supervised the removal of tombs in the churchyard for the navigation of the railway*

† St Pancras New Church

Corner of Upper Woburn Place and Euston Road, WC1 (St Pancras)
OS *TQ298825* **GPS** *51.5272N, 0.1300W*

St Pancras is the most expensive and the best of all English Greek Revival churches. Outside it is of Portland stone, with portico, steeple, apse, and two square projections at the E. end, that on the N. containing an elegant oval vestry, surrounded on the outside with caryatids. The portico is Ionic, and the steeple an adaptation 'free and astonishingly successful' (Summerson) of the Tower of the Winds in Athens. Rich Greek terracotta details from the Erechtheion adorn the outside. At the W. end are three impressive entrance lobbies, two for gallery staircases, and that in the middle an attractive Doric octagon under the tower. The interior is a vast flat-ceilinged hall, terminated by an Ionic apse and surrounded on three sides by galleries supported on columns decorated with lotus leaves. The church is needlessly dark because of Victorian stained glass introduced to dispel the 'Pagan' effect, as it was thought in those days, of the Greek detail. By H. W. and W. Inwood, 1819–22.

† St Pancras Old Church

Pancras Road, NW1 (St Pancras)
OS *TQ297834* **GPS** *51.5349N, 0.1302W*

An ancient church, with traces of Norman and earlier stonework, Old St Pancras was left to sink into decay, forsaken for the Greek glory of the New Church, and now literally overshadowed by the international rail terminal. A ferocious 1848 Norman Revival was undertaken by R. Roumieu and A. Gough, who removed the medieval tower and clad the ceiling timbers with plasterwork. The timbers were re-exposed and galleries were removed in the 20th century, restoring to the Old Church an element of its ancient dignity, and Martin Travers did some very pleasing Baroque decorative work in the 1930s. There is a 6th-century altar stone, and in the churchyard is Soane's excellent mausoleum for his wife, 1815.

† St Paul Covent Garden

Covent Garden Piazza, WC2
OS *TQ303808* **GPS** *51.5116N, 0.1237W*

Inigo Jones's barn church was rebuilt by T. Hardwick Jnr in 1795 after a fire. It is a huge brick box with wide eaves and Tuscan E. portico, and was described by Inigo Jones himself as 'the handsomest barn in England' (so reported Horace Walpole). The church is best known now as the actors' church.

† St Peter Kennington

Kennington Lane, Vauxhall, SE11 (Kennington)
OS *TQ307781* **GPS** *51.4868N, 0.1186W*

By J. L. Pearson, 1863–5 – the first French Gothic church by this great architect. Of yellow stock brick within and without, it is of Cruciform plan, the broad nave and apsidal chancel brick-vaulted with stone ribs. Massive low pillars crowd the nave and narrow aisles. The decoration and glass throughout is by Clayton & Bell. This is a most restrained and beautiful building to which later generations have done no harm.

† St Peter upon Cornhill

Cnr of Cornhill and Gracechurch Street, EC3 (City)
OS *TQ330811* **GPS** *51.5132N, 0.0846W*

By Wren, 1677–81. The brick tower, with its leaded cupola and spire with an enormous key as a vane, is hard to see among high buildings. Inside, the irregular oblong shape of the church, to which a regular Classical design of arcades and arched roofs has been applied, gives it a distorted appearance. But the woodwork, screen, organ gallery and pulpit are beautiful, and make it one of the most complete City church interiors.

† St Peter Walworth

Liverpool Grove, SE17 (Walworth)
OS *TQ325781* **GPS** *51.4866N, 0.0926W*

By Sir John Soane, 1823–5. Soane was not a church man and this was his first and best, and his plans are preserved in the Soane Museum. The style is Ionic outside with a stone steeple, the church is of yellow stock bricks with stone dressings. The interior is austere, in Soane's manner, but light and wide, with his original

△ **TEMPLE CHURCH** – *an effigy of one of the Knights Templars in the nave of the church, eyes wide and hand perpetually ready upon the hilt of his sword*

altar at the E. end. The brick-vaulted crypt, a scene of carnage during the Blitz, has been restored and is now a community arts centre.

† St Simon Zelotes

Moore Street, SW3 (Chelsea)
OS *TQ276788* **GPS** *51.4946N, 0.1622W*

By Joseph Peacock, 1859, and built to serve a relatively poor community, the church is of 'roguish' Gothic design, in which 'details of the Decorated period are piled up in a riotous conglomeration… never can there have been more architecture in less space.' (Goodhart-Rendel, Slade Professor of Fine Art, Oxford).

† St Stephen Walbrook ★

Walbrook, EC4 (City)
OS *TQ326810* **GPS** *51.5126N, 0.0899W*

By Wren, 1672–87. There is a stone tower with an elegant steeple, but the glory of this church is its interior. As G. H. Birch said in *London Churches* (1896), 'Nowhere else could one find a simple parallelogram… so admirably arranged'. Corinthian columns on stone bases divide the church into bays, aisles and sanctuary, leaving an open space in the middle to support a large coffered dome which is lit by a lantern. The plasterwork of the dome is arranged in horizontal bands, the broad and rich bands in the middle breaking up any effect of monotony. The organ case, font cover, altarpiece and pulpit are Renaissance woodwork, richly carved. The church was much damaged in the war but has been restored by Robert Potter; here is the infamous ten-ton marble altar by Henry Moore.

† Temple Church ★

By Inner Temple Lane and Kings Bench Walk, EC4
OS *TQ312810* **GPS** *51.5133N, 0.1102W*

Badly damaged in the Blitz, the circular nave, with its fine W. Norman doorway, triforium and arcades was re-dedicated in 1958. On the floor is a celebrated collection of knightly effigies. The rectangular chancel, a fine and atmospheric space with narrow piers rising to a vaulted roof, was re-dedicated four years before. The triple lancet E. windows have modern glass by Carl Edwards – a pleasing pastiche of the medieval.

GREATER LONDON

BATTERSEA † Church of the Ascension
Corner of Lavender Hill and Acanthus Road, SW11
OS *TQ280756* **GPS** *51.4655N, 0.1573W*

Begun by James Brooks in 1876, it was finally completed by J. T. Micklethwaite and Somers Clarke in 1888, a monumental brick Early English church with lancets and uninterrupted roof-line. The restrained Tractarian interior has round piers, plain nave capitals, and an ambulatory round the apse. The rood screen is by George Wallace, 1914, and the glass by Kempe & Tower.

BICKLEY † St George
1m/3km E. of Bromley, on Bickley Park Road
OS *TQ426690* **GPS** *51.4021N, 0.0497E*

Built of Kentish ragstone by F. Barnes, 1863–4, this Victorian Gothic Decorated church is large and handsome, clerestoried and with a hammer-beam roof. A 1989 fire destroyed much of the interior, so the fittings are now mostly modern. There is good modern glass by Lawrence Lee.

BOW † St Mary Stratford le Bow
On island in Bow Road, near A12 interchange, E3
OS *TQ376829* **GPS** *51.5288N, 0.0167W*

A weather-beaten stone and brick church dating from the 14th–15th centuries, altered later and well restored by Goodhart-Rendel. Though islanded by traffic, it has a countrified interior.

BRIXTON † Christ Church ★
Brixton Road, SW9
OS *TQ311770* **GPS** *51.4776N, 0.1129W*

By Beresford Pite, 1899–1902, an unmissable and highly original Byzantine-style cruciform church in brown brick with Portland stone stripes. The interior is domed, and there are careful details throughout.

BRIXTON † St Matthew
Between St Matthew's Road, Brixton Hill and Effra Road, SW2
OS *TQ309750* **GPS** *51.4597N, 0.1159W*

By C. F. Porden, 1822, St Matthew's is a Greek Revival Commissioners' church. The problem of combining the portico and tower was solved here by removing the tower to the E. end. The interior is galleried, and until the unfortunate introduction of a side chapel in the 1930s, it was pure Doric throughout without a curved line anywhere. Now extensively used by the local community.

CAMBERWELL † St Giles ★
Camberwell Church Street, SE5
OS *TQ329766* **GPS** *51.4730N, 0.0869W*

Designed by Sir George Gilbert Scott, 1844, St Giles is a stately and correct essay in Early English, cruciform with central tower and spire, and well proportioned within. The glass, furnishings and decoration are by Comper. The E. window was designed by Ruskin and Oldfield, a sequence of small biblical pictures from the Creation to the End of Time, and based on colours Ruskin saw at Chartres. It was made by Ward and Nixon.

CARSHALTON † All Saints ★★
1m/2km E. of Sutton, on Carshalton High Street
OS *TQ279644* **GPS** *51.3649N, 0.1630W*

The big church, redolent of Sir Aston Webb, is largely the late 19th-/early 20th-century work of A. and R. Blomfield (uncle and nephew) in Perpendicular style. It is, though, a surprisingly successful blend of many periods, with several medieval elements: the Lady Chapel, formerly the chancel; S. aisle, formerly the nave; outer S. aisle, formerly the S. aisle; and tower, topped by a Georgian spire. W. R. Corbould became rector in 1919, and his friendship with Ninian Comper resulted in a magnificent series of decorative works, some original, some embellishments to existing work by Bodley. Comper's work can be seen in the particularly rich reredos in the Lady Chapel, the painting and gilding of the high altar triptych, the rood and screen, organ case and colourful vaulted W. gallery; together, they make a fine composition. Comper produced some glass as well, but most in the church is by Kempe.

◁ **EAST HAM: ST MARY MAGDALENE** – *the Jacobean Nevill monument, with Edmund and his wife Jane kneeling in prayer and the figures of Hope and Prudence standing above*

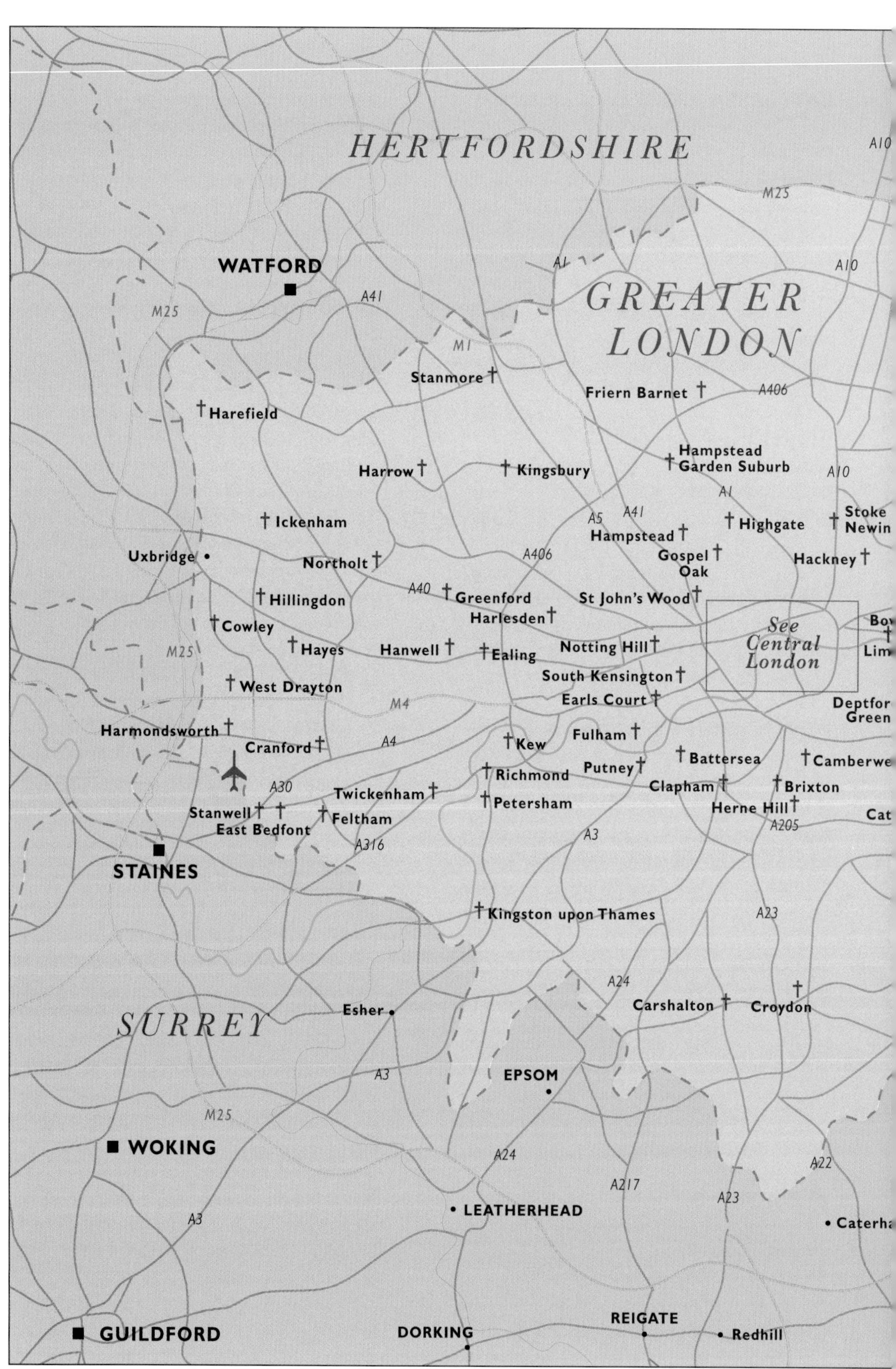

HERTFORDSHIRE
GREATER LONDON
SURREY
WATFORD
STAINES
WOKING
GUILDFORD
EPSOM
LEATHERHEAD
DORKING
REIGATE
Redhill
Caterha
Stanmore
Harefield
Friern Barnet
Hampstead Garden Suburb
Harrow
Kingsbury
Ickenham
Uxbridge
Northolt
Hampstead
Highgate
Stoke Newin
Gospel Oak
Hackney
Hillingdon
Greenford
St John's Wood
Harlesden
Cowley
Hayes
Hanwell
Ealing
Notting Hill
See Central London
South Kensington
West Drayton
Earls Court
Deptfor Green
Harmondsworth
Cranford
Kew
Fulham
Battersea
Camberwe
Putney
Richmond
Clapham
Brixton
Twickenham
Petersham
Herne Hill
Stanwell
East Bedfont
Feltham
Cat
Kingston upon Thames
Carshalton
Croydon
Esher
M25
A1
A10
A41
M1
A406
A5
A40
M4
A4
A30
A316
A3
A205
A23
A24
A217
A22

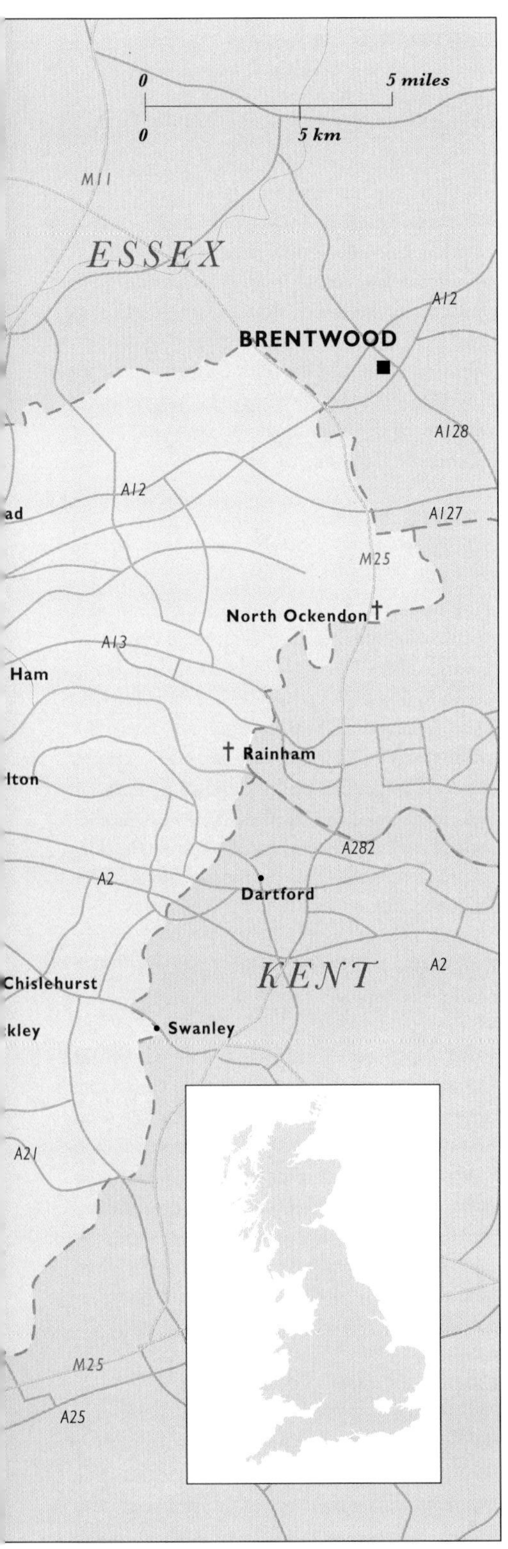

CATFORD † St Andrew
Sandhurst Road, SE6
OS *TQ389733* **GPS** *51.4419N, 0.0015W*

By P. A. Robson, 1904, 'an adaptation of 14th-century Gothic'. This was the latest and lumpiest phase of the Arts and Crafts Movement at its best. Outside, it is towerless and massive, dark red brick on a hill-top. Inside, all is spacious with brick piers, a wide nave, and the buttresses showing in the narrow aisle. The stained glass by Martin Travers matches the building well.

CHARLTON † St Luke
2m/3km E. of Greenwich, The Village, SE7
OS *TQ414778* **GPS** *51.4818N, 0.0358E*

Set in an old village centre within the S.E. London suburbs, St Luke's is a brick country church of c. 1630, standing in a charming old churchyard at the entrance to Charlton House. The 17th-century interior is comparatively unspoilt, with many monuments and memorials, among them Sir Henry Newton, and Sir William Congreve, d. 1814.

CHISLEHURST † The Annunciation
3m/5km N.E. of Bromley, on Chislehurst High Street
OS *TQ438709* **GPS** *51.4192N, 0.0672E*

By James Brooks, 1868, the church manages to maintain an illusion of distance from the hideous high street stores in the vicinity and is distinctive for its detached tower, set at an angle to the main body of the church. It is Gothic Romanesque in atmosphere, with a Continental-style spoked W. window, complete with Plate tracery. Inside, the chancel is particularly rich – a collaboration between Brooks and Nathaniel Westlake – with reredos, chancel screen and wall-paintings. The tympanum mosaic is by Salviati, 1890, to designs by Westlake.

CLAPHAM † Holy Trinity
Clapham Common North Side, SW4
OS *TQ291753* **GPS** *51.4625N, 0.1421W*

On Clapham Common, by Kenton Couse, 1774–6, the church is built of stock brick with stone dressings. An octagonal belfry stands at the W. end, and there are two tiers of windows; the galleried interior has a fine pulpit, now on the N. side. The chancel is by

Beresford Pite, 1903. The church has associations with the Clapham Sect, a local group concerned with the abolition of slavery, whose cause was taken up by William Wilberforce in Parliament.

COWLEY † St Laurence

1m/2km S. of Uxbridge, on Church Road, by Brunel University
OS *TQ059820* **GPS** *51.5274N, 0.4735W*

This tiny and primitive medieval church is a rare survival, with a 13th-century chancel and timber bellcote of 1780; the roofs are supported by 15th-century crown-posts. There is a Georgian double-decker W. gallery and early chancel pews.

CRANFORD † St Dunstan

By Junction 3 of M4, 3m/5km N.W. of Hounslow
OS *TQ101781* **GPS** *51.4919N, 0.4146W*

A fascinating church. The chancel and tower are 15th-century, while the nave was rebuilt in red brick with ashlar dressings after a fire in 1710. There are good fittings by Martin Travers, 1935–6, including the altar and terracotta-coloured reredos, the chancel arch with cherubs above and a new W. gallery. The extraordinary collection of monuments includes a grand work of c. 1613, the Aston Tomb by William Cure, Master Mason to the King, a Bernini-esque white marble effigy of Lady Elizabeth Berkeley by Nicholas Stone, 1635, and myriad later 17th- to early 18th-century cartouches, busts and tablets.

CROYDON † St Michael and All Angels

Poplar Walk, near West Croydon Station
OS *TQ322660* **GPS** *51.3783N, 0.101W*

Designed 1875–6, and built 1880–83 by J. L. Pearson, this is one of his loveliest churches. Outside it is of red brick, but made of stock brick for the vaulting. In one of the E. chapels there is Pearson's usual trick of using tall slim columns, two of which are functionless from the vaulting point of view, but make a screen to suggest complexity. The transepts are most magnificent on a small scale. The Baroque and Gothic fittings are by Bodley, Comper and Hare.

DEPTFORD † St Paul

Between Deptford High Street and Deptford Church Street, SE8
OS *TQ372774* **GPS** *51.4796N, 0.0244W*

To find such a rich Baroque church in such unpromising surroundings is an amazement. Built by Thomas Archer, 1712–30, it is a London Commissioners' church of imaginative and noble stature, with three pedimented porticos in Portland stone. The interior is cruciform and rich, with great Corinthian columns, fine plaster entablature, galleries and stately private pews. The E. end Venetian window with trompe l'oeil curtains above follows the curve of the apse.

EALING † St Mary

St Mary's Road, W5
OS *TQ176797* **GPS** *51.5044N, 0.3056W*

This medieval and 18th-century church was drastically enlarged and remodelled by S. S. Teulon, 1866–74. The huge W. tower has a pyramidal roof, and the 18th-century pediment is just visible above Teulon's Byzantine apse. The dramatic interior has iron columns supporting timber galleries and a mass of tracery in the roof. At the E. end are horseshoe arches and exotic fittings to match. The exquisite stained glass is mostly by Heaton, Butler & Bayne.

EALING † St Peter

Mount Park Road, W5
OS *TQ177817* **GPS** *51.5222N, 0.3044W*

By J. D. Sedding, 1889, completed by his partner, Henry Wilson, in 1892–3, this is an upper-class suburban church of highly original design, with a great W. window trisected by buttresses, with spirelets and little turrets along the roof. Inside is a triforium gallery and a painted framed ceiling. There are good early 20th-century fittings, including a carved oak reredos by Bodley & Hare, and glass by Kempe.

EARLS COURT † St Cuthbert

Philbeach Gardens, SW5
OS *TQ250784* **GPS** *51.4912N, 0.2005W*

This is a large red and black brick Gothic building with bright-green copper roof and fleche, a conspicuous landmark in Earls

△ **CARSHALTON: ALL SAINTS** – *the simplicity of the architecture combines effectively with Ninian Comper's brilliant decorative elaborations of the early 20th century*

Court by H. Roumieu Gough, 1884–7. It is chiefly remarkable for its interior Arts and Crafts decoration, where Tractarian devotion has given jewels, pictures, carving and inlay work to all available space. Many of Gough's fittings have survived: the rood screen, pulpit and Stations of the Cross. Particularly prominent are Geldart's overwhelming reredos and the Art Nouveau altar rails and 'neo-Viking' lectern by W. Bainbridge Reynolds.

EAST BEDFONT † St Mary the Virgin

3m/5km N.E. of Staines, on Hatton Road, S. side of Heathrow Airport
OS *TQ084736* **GPS** *51.4518N, 0.4402W*

Screened by trees on a green, the 12th-century and later church retains a Norman chancel arch with chevrons. The W. tower with timber top stage was added in 1865. There are fine mid-13th-century wall-paintings of the Last Judgement and Crucifixion.

EAST HAM † St Mary Magdalene ★

Corner of Norman Road and East Ham High Street South, E6
OS *TQ429823* **GPS** *51.5222N, 0.0588E*

This complete 12th-century church stands close to the former docks of E. London. It has interlacing arcades along the wall of the choir, and in the apse is a fine monument to Edward Neville, Earl of Northumbeland, and his wife. The apse is of particular note for its Norman timbered roof, the beams held together by wooden pegs. The elegant marble font is dated 1639, and there are remains of Cistercian wall-paintings. Above the chancel steps is a small opening to an anchorite's cell, which would have been used in the 13th or 14th century. The 10-acre churchyard is a designated nature reserve.

CARSHALTON: ALL SAINTS – *the west end of the church is as impressive as the east, with Comper's exquisite gallery and organ casing at the centre* ▷

FELTHAM † St Dunstan

4m/7km E. of Staines, on St Dunstan's Road, Lower Feltham
OS *TQ098722* **GPS** *51.4387N, 0.4207W*

By William Walker, 1802, St Dunstan's is a rustic building with round-headed windows, short tower and shingled spire. The aisles were given a 'Norman' cast in 1855–6. The simple interior has an original W. gallery supported on Roman Doric columns, the panels filled with charity inscriptions in elegant script.

FRIERN BARNET
† St John the Evangelist

2m/3km S.E. of Barnet, on Friern Barnet Road
OS *TQ278920* **GPS** *51.6131N, 0.1545W*

J. L. Pearson modelled part of this church on the derelict apse and choir of Heisterbach, a romantic Cistercian 13th-century ruin; it was completed by his son after his death. It is an ambitious early Decorated building with bold flying buttresses to the nave and aspidal chancel with ambulatory. The absence of the planned tower renders the exterior less interesting than inside.

FULHAM † St Alban

Margravine Road, W6
OS *TQ240779* **GPS** *51.4866N, 0.2146W*

A red-brick Arts and Crafts Gothic work by Sir Aston Webb and Ingress Bell, 1894–6, it is full of altars, confessionals and statues, including an unusually big Holy Child of Prague wearing a golden crown. This is a well-used church with an Italian ethos.

GOSPEL OAK † All Hallows

Savernake Road, NW3
OS *TQ278856* **GPS** *51.5556N, 0.1570W*

By James Brooks, 1881–9. The formidable, towerless and buttressed exterior of All Hallows rises from red Victorian villas and is overlooked by nearby tower blocks. Inside it is aisled, with very tall circular piers branching into ribs which support no vaulting, for the roof was completed after Brooks's death. The church is lit by bold lancets high in the side aisles, and a rose W. window. The chancel was completed in 1913 by Sir Giles Gilbert Scott, who also designed the massive stone font. It is a spacious interior, admirably suited to ceremony and sparing in its detail. Its cathedral-like effect is created by massiveness, simplicity and proportion. It is a frequent venue for music recitals.

GREENFORD † Holy Cross Old Church

Corner of Ferrymead Gardens and Oldfield Lane South
OS *TQ145831* **GPS** *51.5357N, 0.3503W*

One of the oldest buildings in the Borough of Southall, now faced in 19th-century flint, the core fabric dates from the 13th–14th centuries, with a 15th-century chancel roof and 17th-century wooden tower. There is a 17th-century W. gallery and tower staircase, and important heraldic glass showing the Arms of Mary I and Phillip II of Spain. In 1943 worship transferred to a new church, but occasional services are still held in the old.

GREENWICH † St Alphege ★

Greenwich Church Street, SE10
OS *TQ383776* **GPS** *51.4805N, 0.0097W*

The church, by Hawksmoor, 1711–14, is a massive four-square Portland stone building, with a fine Doric portico to the E. front. The tower and spire, added by John James in 1730, is feeble by contrast.

HACKNEY † St John of Jerusalem

Between Lauriston Road and Church Crescent, E9
OS *TQ355841* **GPS** *51.5404N, 0.0461W*

This is a large stone cruciform church in Early English style by E. C. Hakewill, 1845–8, with W. tower and polygonal apse. The interesting interior has wall-paintings, richly carved capitals and corbels, and strange tracery in the clerestory. Note the crossing, a rich space of clustered columns, moulded arches and angled, painted timber groins, by which are painted texts.

HACKNEY † St Mark ★

Between Sandringham Road and Colvestone Crescent, Dalston, E8
OS *TQ338851* **GPS** *51.5494N, 0.0704W*

By Chester Cheston Jnr, 1862–70, this is a huge brick and cast-iron hall full of pews, scalding glass, red baize emblazoned with fleur-de-lys, and original brass fittings. There are stained-glass angels in the vault, and the

△ **EAST HAM: ST MARY MAGDALENE** – *the chancel and apsidal sanctuary are a riot of architectural features, partially revealed Cistercian wall-paintings and Jacobean monuments*

lectern is adorned with a coloured stole. The vast and forbidding tower is by E. L. Blackburn, 1877, and has a barometer set on the outside.

HACKNEY † St Mary of Eton ★

Eastway, by A12 interchange, Hackney Wick, E11
OS *TQ366847* **GPS** *51.5454N, 0.0306W*

An Eton College mission church by G. F. Bodley, 1880, St Mary of Eton makes a picturesque group on East Way with a gate tower leading to court of Eton Mission buildings. The church inside has a broad nave with painted roof, tall, narrow aisles, and a S.E. chapel. It is full of vistas of arcades with strong, simple mouldings. It is colloquially known the the Cathedral of the East End.

HAMPSTEAD † St John

Church Row, NW3
OS *TQ261856* **GPS** *51.5553N, 0.1812W*

By H. Flitcroft, 1744–7, of stock brick with a castellated W. tower. Proposals to demolish the tower in the 1870s were dropped after a bitter row involving Sir George Gilbert Scott, Frederick Cockerell, Norman Shaw and the Rossettis. The result is a rich Victorian Classical effect looking E., but still Georgian at the W. end. There are many interesting tombs in both churchyards – the painter Constable and John Harrison, inventor of the marine chronometer, are among those buried here.

HAMPSTEAD GARDEN SUBURB † St Jude on the Hill

Corner of South Square and Central Square, NW11
OS *TQ255883* **GPS** *51.5801N, 0.1899W*

By Sir Edwin Lutyens, 1908–10, and one of his most successful, the church was designed as part of the Garden Suburb. It is a large silver- and red-brick basilican church with tall tower and pinnacled spire. The Byzantine interior has round arches, tunnel vaults, and brick piers, all covered with dignified murals of traditional Bible scenes by Walter Starmer. The Free Church and Institute in the same square are also by Lutyens.

△ **EAST HAM: ST MARY MAGDALENE** – *a cherub at the base of the Jacobean Breame monument on the north wall of the chancel*

HANWELL † St Mary
1m/2km W. of Ealing, at end of Church Road, W7
OS *TQ147807* **GPS** *51.5138N, 0.3474W*

An early church by Sir G. G. Scott, 1841, in a village setting, of flint with white-brick dressings and broach spire. The whitewashed interior has quatrefoil piers, galleries and monuments, and retains the wall-paintings attributed to W. F. Yeames.

HAREFIELD † St Mary the Virgin
4m/7km N. of Uxbridge, on Church Hill
OS *TQ053895* **GPS** *51.5953N, 0.4807W*

Pleasantly set away from the village, this is a modest medieval church, with 13th-century chancel and early 14th-century S. aisle. The N. aisle and tower were added soon after 1500, and the chancel, altered by Henry Keene, 1768, has a remarkable plaster ceiling. The glory of Harefield is its gallery of monuments – sepulchral art from the 15th century to 1800 – which yet does not overwhelm the church. The Newdigate and Ashby families are commemorated by William White, 1614, Grinling Gibbons, 1692, Sir Robert Taylor, 1760, John Bacon Jnr, 1800, and others unknown. The grandest monument is a canopied tomb to Lady Derby, 1636, with columns, stone curtains and much heraldry. The pulpit, communion rails, reredos and font cover are fine 17th- and 18th-century carving, some from Flanders.

HARLESDEN † All Souls
2m/3km N.E. of Ealing, on Station Road
OS *TQ216832* **GPS** *51.5353N, 0.2481W*

By E. J. Tarver, 1875–6, an octagonal brick church with small iron lantern and canted apse. The remarkable interior has a tie-beam and arch-braced timber roof with no internal supports, and the glass is by Selwyn Image, co-founder of the Century Guild of Artists.

HARMONDSWORTH † St Mary
4m/7km S. of Uxbridge, on N. side of Heathrow Airport
OS *TQ056778* **GPS** *51.4894N, 0.4790W*

Under seige from Heathrow Airport, the M25 and M4, St Mary's stands near the celebrated 15th-century Manor Farm Barn, one of the finest of its kind in England. It is a flint and rubble Norman and later church whose fine mid-12th-century S. doorway has shafts, beakheads and zigzags. The 16th-century S.W. tower is of brick in the upper stages, and has an 18th-century cupola. The pews are c. 1500, and there are good 18th–19th-century churchyard memorials.

HARROW † St Mary

Church Hill, Harrow-on-the-Hill

OS *TQ153874* **GPS** *51.5742N, 0.3374W*

Splendidly situated on Harrow Hill, this is the finest setting in old Middlesex. The pale-grey exterior and slim lead-and-timber spire can be seen for miles above the suburban villas. The lower part of tower is c. 1130, the chancel Early English and the nave roof fine Perpendicular, with corbels, carved posts and panels. The pulpit is well-carved Jacobean, with tester, and the original Norman font has been re-instated. The whole church was fiercely restored by Sir George Gilbert Scott, 1846–9, when the Decorated style was introduced. The interior is consequently hard, and the outside walls flinty. There are brasses from 1370, and monuments, principally to headmasters of Harrow School. The E. window is by Comper. Byron's daughter Allegra is buried in the churchyard, where he used to 'sit for hours and hours when a boy – this was my favourite spot'.

HAYES † St Mary

3m/4km S.E. of Uxbridge, between Church Road and Church Walk

OS *TQ097810* **GPS** *51.5180N, 0.4202W*

The church is 13th-century and later, of flint rubble. There is a good 16th-century open timber S. porch, Tudor roofs with carved Arms of Henry VIII and Catherine of Aragon, and a large wall-painting, c. 1500, of St Christopher. A 14th-century priest's brass commemorates Robert Lellee, and there are two table tombs of Walter Grene, d. 1456, and Sir Thomas Higate, d. 1576.

HERNE HILL † St Paul ★★

1m/2km S. of Camberwell, on Herne Hill, SE24

OS *TQ321745* **GPS** *51.4548N, 0.0993W*

By G. E. Street, 1858, who rebuilt the original Commissioners' church of 1843. 'One of the loveliest churches of the kind in the country,' declared Ruskin, who lived in the parish. Capricious capitals on the piers and marble reredos carved by Earp gave the Victorians equal delight. The glass is by Hardman, and the tower and spire from the earlier church by Stevens and Alexander, 1845.

HIGHGATE † St Augustine

Archway Road, at corner of Langdon Park Road

OS *TQ290875* **GPS** *51.5722N, 0.1394W*

By J. D. Sedding, 1880; completed by Henry Wilson, 1916; W. front by Harold Gibbons, 1925. Historically in Middlesex, it was one of the most beautifully furnished churches in that county.

HILLINGDON † St John the Baptist

1m/2km S.E. of Uxbridge, on Uxbridge Road

OS *TQ069829* **GPS** *51.5350N, 0.4599W*

St John the Baptist has origins in the 13th century – the chancel arch with stiff-leaf capitals dates from 1270. The nave and aisles date from the 14th century; the W. tower, 1629, replaced an earlier one and is topped with an open oak-carved cupola. Transepts and the E. extensions were added by Sir George Gilbert Scott during his restoration of 1847–8. The Le Strange Brass, 1509, is one of London's most impressive, and there are elegant 17th–18th-century monuments, including those to Sir Edward Carr, 1637, and the Earl of Uxbridge, 1743.

ICKENHAM † St Giles

2m/3km N.E. of Uxbridge, on High Road

OS *TQ079862* **GPS** *51.5649N, 0.4440W*

St Giles is an attractive 14th-century village church with a brick N. aisle of 1575–80, and mid-17th-century mortuary chapel on the N. side. The timber-framed S. porch and bell-turret are c. 1500. Inside is a carved 17th-century oak font, 16th-century brasses, and monuments including one to a sad shrouded infant, 1665.

KEW † St Anne

2m/3km N. of Richmond, on Kew Green

OS *TQ189774* **GPS** *51.4838N, 0.2879W*

George II, George III and William IV all

extended this initially simple 1714 Queen Anne fabric – a reflection of the Hanoverian court at Kew. The originally plain building acquired arcades and galleries, apse and mortuary chapel to the Duke of Cambridge. The domed chancel is Victorian, with Kempe glass, and there is later work by Comper. Gainsborough is buried here, and there are memorials to the Hooker family, who founded Kew Gardens.

KILBURN † St Augustine

Kilburn Park Road, NW6
OS *TQ255831* **GPS** *51.5331N, 0.1916W*

This is Pearson's largest London church, 1870–77, whose red-brick tower and white ashlar spire rises more than 250 feet over a drab neighbourhood. The church is red-brick and cruciform with a lead fleche at the crossing; all is Early English. Inside, one's first impression is of a multiplicity of brick-vaulted vistas of varying heights and with stone ribs. There are double aisles pierced through the buttresses, a triforium right round the church, carried across transepts by bridges. The low baptistry at the W. end and low ambulatory behind the three-bayed chancel increase the sense of height in the nave and choir. The paintings by Clayton & Bell and the ironwork are all in keeping. The way to see this church is to walk right round the inside, watching arch cutting into arch, giving a different vista with every step.

KINGSBURY † St Andrew

4m/7km E. of Harrow, on Church Lane, NW9
OS *TQ205868* **GPS** *51.5680N, 0.2618W*

By S. W. Dawkes & Hamilton, 1847; this was formerly St Andrew's, Wells Street, St Marylebone, and was brought here in 1933 to take the place of the old parish church, now redundant. Originally a leading church of the Catholic Revival, it is now a veritable museum of superlative Victorian furnishings. The reredos, pulpit, chancel screen and font are by Street; the litany desk, chalice and monument on the S. wall by Burges; a font cover by Pearson; lectern by Butterfield; W. window by Pugin; and panels on the W. gallery by Alfred Bell.

KINGSTON UPON THAMES
† All Saints

Between Clarence Street and Market Place
OS *TQ179693* **GPS** *51.4105N, 0.3061W*

Mostly 15th-century, its Perpendicular tower with pretty brick top added in 1708. It was restored by Brandon in 1862, and by Pearson in 1886–8. There is bright Victorian glass, a Comper altar and monuments including a Flaxman to Philip Meadows, with an almost detached cherub on a cloud, and a fine seated figure by Chantrey.

LIMEHOUSE † St Anne ★

Between Commercial Road and Three Colt Street, E14
OS *TQ367810* **GPS** *51.5117N, 0.0303W*

By Nicholas Hawksmoor, 1712–24. Another majestic masterpiece in Portland stone, lighter than Christ Church, Spitalfields, and with a tower composed of diminishing oblongs, emphasized horizontally by heavy cornices, and vertically by deep recesses for holding shadow. At the W. end is a beautiful pilastered apse, with semi-dome. From all sides this building looks magnificent. The interior, burnt in 1850, was beautifully restored by P. Hardwick. It is galleried, with a great oval ceiling hanging over the nave and a chancel whose E. window by Clutterbuck, dark and rich, is most surprisingly sympathetic to Hawksmoor's style and grand scale. This church won the first John Betjeman Award in 1990, given by the Society for the Protection of Ancient Buildings to honour Betjeman's memory – he was a committee member of long standing – and to promote the highest standards of repair to churches and chapels in England and Wales.

NORTH OCKENDON
† St Mary Magdalene

2m/3km E. of Upminster, on Church Lane
OS *TQ587848* **GPS** *51.5404N, 0.2876E*

A Norman church of ragstone and flint, it has been considerably added to and much restored in the 19th century, and is rich in brasses and monuments to the Poyntz family. The only surviving Norman feature is the S. doorway.

△ **PETERSHAM: ST PETER** – *the short and wide Georgian interior, with its plethora of box pews and galleries, tall pulpit and reading desk, and tiny chancel*

NORTHOLT † St Mary

4m/7km N.W. of Ealing, on Northolt Green
OS *TQ132840* **GPS** *51.5439N, 0.3689W*

St Mary's stands on a knoll by the old village green, tiny and charming in a sloping churchyard. The exterior of the church is whitewashed with brilliant red roof tiles, and the 16th-century bell-turret has a little spire; the nave, c. 1300, is aisle-less, and the chancel dates from 1521. The light and charming interior has a W. gallery, 1703, 14th-century font, Stuart Royal Arms and 15th–16th-century brasses.

NOTTING HILL † All Saints

Clydesdale Road, W11
OS *TQ247812* **GPS** *51.5165N, 0.2029W*

By William White in 1850–61, after he had built St Saviour's in Aberdeen Park, his best London church; now redundant. Although the spire is truncated, the tower is still dramatic with its polychromatic effects in stone and marble. The rich interior has been diminished by war damage and the removal of fittings, but it retains its reredoses by Cecil Hare and Martin Travers and chancel painting by Sir Ninian Comper.

PETERSHAM † St Peter

1m/2km S. of Richmond, on Church Lane, off Petersham Road
OS *TQ181733* **GPS** *51.4467N, 0.3013W*

A small church of great charm, it is set on the edge of a riverside village, overlooking meadows to the Thames and Richmond Hill. The chancel is late 13th-century, with a Cole monument, 1624, and 18th-century N. transept and tower with wooden octagonal lantern. The unrestored interior has box pews, a double-decker pulpit and a font of 1797.

PUTNEY † St Paul

Augustus Road, SW19
OS *TQ238730* **GPS** *51.4431N, 0.2186W*

St Paul's, red-brick and towerless in a rich, leafy suburb, is surprisingly simple and 'arty crafty' for its date, with Perpendicular tracery and a broad, spacious, light interior with octagonal piers. By J. T. Micklethwaite and Somers Clarke, 1877–8.

RAINHAM † St Helen and St Giles

Corner of Broadway and Upminster Road South
OS *TQ520822* **GPS** *51.5183N, 0.1906E*

The church is entirely Norman, with the whitewashed nave, aisles, chancel and tower all dating from around 1170. The nave piers have massive scalloped capitals. On the wall of the rood loft staircase is a large 16th-century graffito of a two-masted ship, or 'cog'.

RICHMOND UPON THAMES
† St Mary Magdalene

Between Red Lion Street and George Street
OS *TQ179748* **GPS** *51.4602N, 0.3038W*

Set quietly between two busy roads, this much-altered church was rebuilt in the late 15th- to early 16th-century. The N. aisle was added in 1699; the Tudor nave and S. aisle rebuilt in 1750. Blomfield replaced the nave ceiling, galleries and box pews, 1864–6, and Bodley replaced the Tudor chancel.

ST JOHN'S WOOD † St John

On corner of Wellington Road and Prince Albert Road, NW8
OS *TQ271828* **GPS** *51.5306N, 0.1684W*

Unmistakable in its setting by Lord's Cricket Ground, this elegant and simple Regency church by Thomas Hardwick Jnr, 1813–14, has an Ionic Portland stone portico of four columns with turret above. The lovely Tuscan interior, all white and gilded, was re-ordered in 1991, and has box pews and glazed galleries. Wall monuments record associations with the East India Company. The gardens behind the church, formerly the burial ground, are listed as a local nature reserve, a welcome oasis in a busy corner of N.W. London.

SOUTH KENSINGTON † Holy Trinity

Prince Consort Road, SW7
OS *TQ265794* **GPS** *51.5N, 0.1789W*

A beautiful Bodley church, 1900–3, the 14th-century-style Perpendicular W. front conceals Bodley's last and best interior – Edwardian Gothic Revival, reassuring and self-confident, full of rich detail. Bodley's triptych reredos, above the high altar, was carved by Laurence Turner, and is one of the church's outstanding features – gilded and canopied with carved figures depicting the Crucifixion. The wine glass-stem pulpit and choir stalls are Bodley's too, and his personal memorial, in puzzling Jacobean style, is to the left of the Lady Chapel.

SOUTH KENSINGTON † St Augustine

Queen's Gate, SW7
OS *TQ265787* **GPS** *51.4934N, 0.1780W*

This is a lofty stock-brick church, by W. Butterfield, 1865–71, the whitewashed interior now cleaned off to reveal the tiled murals on the aisle walls. The lovely gilded Baroque reredos is by Martin Travers, 1928. A polychromatic period piece of rare delight, celebrated by Betjeman in poem.

STANMORE † St John the Evangelist

4ml7km S.E. of Watford, on Church Road
OS *TQ167921* **GPS** *51.6162N, 0.3156W*

Two churches in one churchyard. The old brick church, consecrated by Archbishop Laud in 1632, is now a picturesque ruin. The new church, begun in 1849, by Henry Clutton, is in a Decorated style and contains some old furnishings and a number of good 17th- and 18th-century monuments removed from the old church.

STANMORE † St Lawrence

6ml10km S.W. of Watford, on Whitchurch Lane, Little Stanmore
OS *TQ185913* **GPS** *51.6083N, 0.2893W*

The church was built for the Duke of Chandos of Canons by John James in 1715; the 16th-century tower survives from the previous church. It is frescoed with panels and grisaille, probably by Laguerre and Belucci, c. 1720. There are many original fittings and a ducal pew at the W. end. On the N. side, the Chandos chapel is by Gibbs, 1735, the enormous tomb with statues is by Gibbons, and the organ by Jordan, c. 1720.

STANWELL † St Mary the Virgin

Between Staines Reservoir and Heathrow Airport, at end of Stanwell High Street
OS *TQ057741* **GPS** *51.4563N, 0.4799W*

A village church with slender spire standing

up from the flat plain of old Middlesex. The nave arcades date from c. 1260; most of the rest is 14th-century, with a N. aisle by S. S. Teulon, 1862. There is an imposing Knyvett monument by Nicholas Stone, 1622.

STEPNEY † St Dunstan and All Saints

Stepney High Street, E1

OS *TQ359815* **GPS** *51.5168N, 0.0417W*

This is a large, mostly 15th-century Perpendicular church, with Saxon carved stone slab over the high altar. Traces of 13th-century work can be seen on the S. side of the chancel. The large canopied altar tomb on the N. side of the chancel is of Sir Henry Collet. The curiously rural feel of the church is echoed in its village-like churchyard, full of monuments to Georgian sailors. The building was refaced with Kentish rag and knapped flint with stone dressings in Perpendicular style by Newman & Billing, 1872.

STOKE NEWINGTON † St Matthias

Wordsworth Road, N16

OS *TQ332854* **GPS** *51.5526N, 0.0794W*

Though bombed and sparingly repaired, this great brick church, 1853, is Butterfield at his boldest and simplest. From all angles the outside looks well, with its saddleback tower over the chancel, its high nave, lean-to aisles and low sanctuary E. of the tower. Inside the effect is of solemn grandeur, caused by two great transverse arches of low pitch over the choir; the W. narthex, the severe nave arcades and roof, modelled on Ely, are lit by a clerestory. William H. Monk (1852–89), musical editor of *Hymns Ancient and Modern*, and composer of *Abide with Me*, was organist here.

TWICKENHAM † All Hallows

Chertsey Road

OS *TQ158741* **GPS** *51.4542N, 0.3338W*

The original Wren church of All Hallows in Lombard Street was demolished in 1939, and the tower and cloisters re-erected here. The interior fittings and furnishings are from the original All Hallows: an interesting carved doorcase with figures of Time and Death leads to a gallery lined with wall-monuments, connecting the new church with the old tower.

TWICKENHAM † St Mary the Virgin

Between Church Street and Riverside

OS *TQ164733* **GPS** *51.4470N, 0.3251W*

In a lovely riverside setting, all that remains of the original fabric is the Kentish rag tower of the 15th-century medieval church. The rest is Classical, by John James, 1715. Alexander Pope was buried in the nave; there is a medallion portrait of him on the N. gallery wall.

WANSTEAD † St Mary

Overton Drive, E11

OS *TQ409877* **GPS** *51.5713N, 0.0325E*

The church was entirely rebuilt in 1790 by T. Hardwick. Virtually unaltered, it has a Tuscan porch and a well-designed bell-turret with Ionic columns, 1790. The nave arcades have tall Corinthian columns, and there are N., S. and W. galleries, original pews of 1790 and a fine pulpit with sounding board. The elaborate monument to Sir Joshua Child, d. 1699, and his son, d. 1698, came from the old church.

WEST DRAYTON † St Martin

3m/5km S. of Uxbridge, on Church Road

OS *TQ061795* **GPS** *51.5049N, 0.4718W*

Mainly of the 15th-century, there are some 12th- and 13th-century fragments in the flint rubble fabric. The tower has an external staircase turret, terminating in an open newel with wooden cupola above. Inside are octagonal piers and original roofs whose timbers are supported on corbels. The splendid octagonal Perpendicular font has relief-carved panels and grotesques at the base. There are monuments to the Pagets and Burghs, 16th-century brasses and a spirited carving of a ship to Rupert Billingsley, d. 1720, captain of the second Royal George. The church was extensively restored and refitted in 1850.

NORFOLK

The county of Norfolk has several characters: flat marshland to the west, flat Broadland to the east, flat Breckland to the south and, though there are no very high hills anywhere, the north is undulating. It was once a very empty county; this is so no longer, and there is much new building, not always of the highest quality. The development and conservation of Norwich has been well controlled, but King's Lynn, except for a small picturesque centre, has been tragically ruined.

In-filling in the villages is welcome, though the new houses are often second homes, for commuters or at best retreats for retired people, and the old community centres – the school, the post office, the shop, the pub and of course the railway station – no longer exist. The next on the list for closure are the Nonconformist chapel and the parish church.

The finest collection of churches are those to the west, in marshland – the Walpoles, Wiggenhalls, West Walton, Terrington and Tilney, and the Norman Walsoken. The architecture, from the 12th to the 15th century, is superb, and so are the fittings, especially the very elaborate carved bench-ends. In central and north Norfolk there are wonderful wooden roofs with angels, as at South Creake, Trunch, Necton and many others, and in the east exquisite painted screens, as at Ranworth and Barton Turf; and everywhere remarkable fonts, from a very fine carved Norman one at Burnham Deepdale to 25 superb 15th-century seven-sacrament fonts, some defiled, others almost perfect, as at Dereham. It can be truly said that there is not one Norfolk church without something worth seeing, which has made this selection appallingly difficult. Probably the most beautiful of all is Salle, near Reepham, a huge church in an almost deserted hamlet, built in the 15th century, with splendid roofs, font, font cover, brasses, remains of exquisite Norwich School glass and perfect proportions. To enter it at any time, but especially when it is empty, is an unforgettable experience.

Like Salle, many of the churches stand 'away in the fields', and are most important characteristics of the Norfolk landscape. There are over 100 round towers, not look-outs as people used to think, but built like that because flint, the only stone available locally, could not be used for corners; these are almost all Norman or Saxon. Then, when it was possible to import stone, came the great soaring towers, like Salle and, surprisingly, the highest of all in the prim seaside town of Cromer. There are few spires, apart from Norwich Cathedral, but there is a very splendid one at Snettisham and less important ones at Beeston and Tilney All Saints. There is flint flushwork on some of the towers, as at Westwick, and in many of the City of Norwich churches,

◁ **RANWORTH: ST HELEN** – *a 15th-century image of Archangel Michael on one of several brilliantly painted panels on the parclose screens that extend from the rood screen to create side altars*

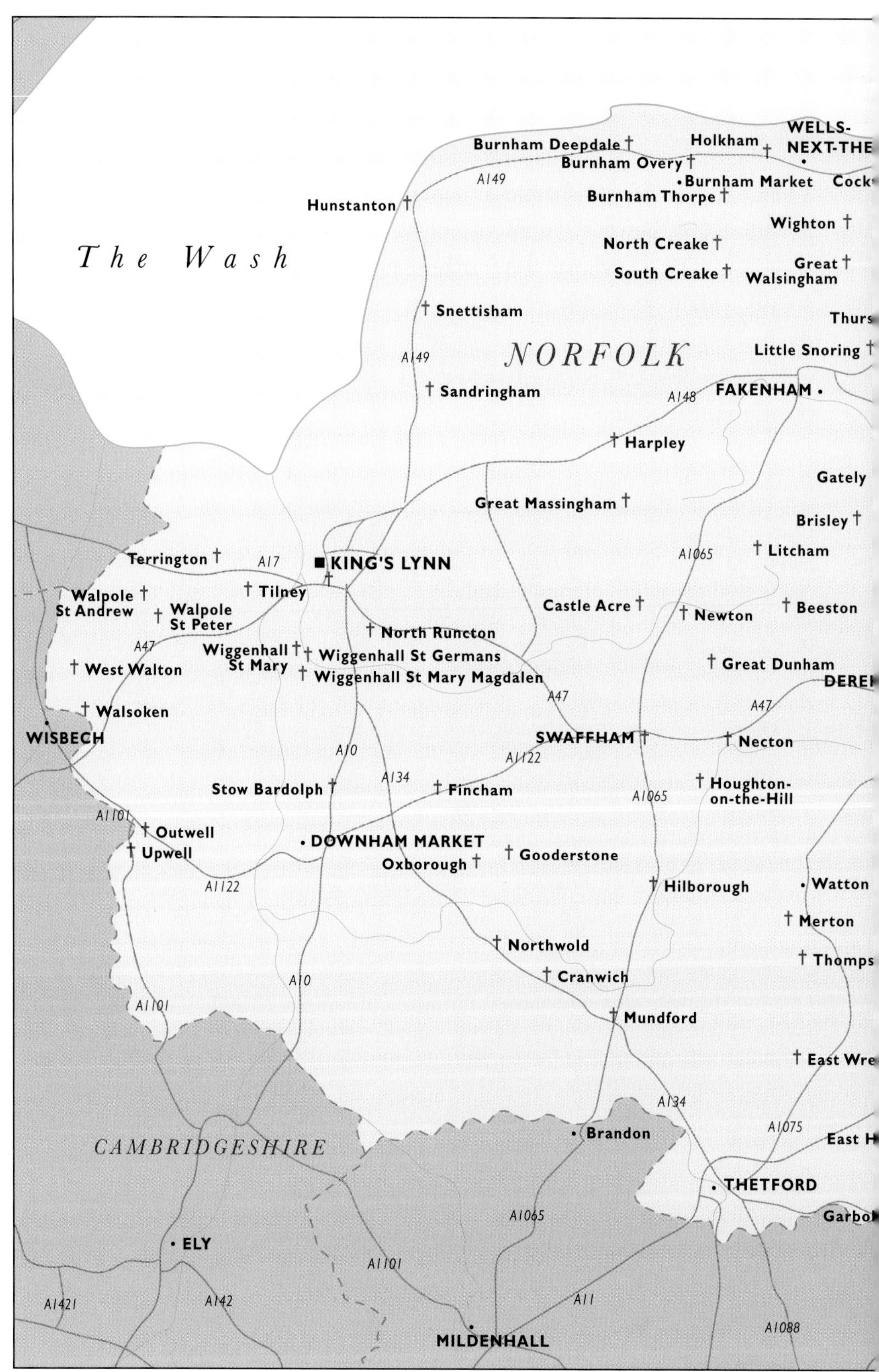

The Wash
NORFOLK
CAMBRIDGESHIRE
Hunstanton
Burnham Deepdale
Burnham Overy
Holkham
WELLS-NEXT-THE
Burnham Market
Burnham Thorpe
Wighton
North Creake
South Creake
Great Walsingham
Snettisham
Sandringham
Little Snoring
FAKENHAM
Harpley
Great Massingham
Gately
Brisley
Litcham
Terrington
KING'S LYNN
Tilney
Walpole St Andrew
Walpole St Peter
Castle Acre
Newton
Beeston
North Runcton
Wiggenhall St Mary
Wiggenhall St Germans
Wiggenhall St Mary Magdalen
West Walton
Great Dunham
Walsoken
WISBECH
SWAFFHAM
Necton
Stow Bardolph
Fincham
Houghton-on-the-Hill
Outwell
Upwell
DOWNHAM MARKET
Oxborough
Gooderstone
Hilborough
Watton
Merton
Northwold
Cranwich
Mundford
Brandon
THETFORD
ELY
MILDENHALL
A149
A148
A17
A47
A10
A134
A1122
A1065
A1101
A1075
A1065
A11
A142
A1421
A1088

on
keney
Cley-next-the-Sea
Salthouse
Weybourne
SHERINGHAM
landford
Upper Sheringham
Cromer
Letheringsett
HOLT
Felbrigg
Bessingham
Thorpe Market
Thwaite
Gunton
Trunch
Erpingham
Knapton
A149
Ingworth
North Walsham
Happisburgh
Thurning
Heydon
Aylsham
Worstead
Ingham
Cawston
Salle
Tunstead
Barton Turf
ey
Stratton Strawless
Catfield
Irstead
Sparham
Alderford
Ludham
A140
A1067
A1062
A149
Ringland
A1151
Ranworth
th Tuddenham
Mattishall Burgh
Caister-on-Sea
East Tuddenham
Acle
Mattishall
NORWICH
A47
GREAT YARMOUTH
Bawburgh
Wickhampton
A47
The Broads
A146
Gorleston
Framingham Earl
A143
am
Wymondham
Howe
A11
Saxlingham Nethergate
Loddon
Heckingham
A12
Hales
Haddiscoe
ttleborough
LOWESTOFT
Forncett St Peter
Fritton
Bedingham
Tibenham
Shelton
Ditchingham
Beccles
A146
A140
BUNGAY
A144
Pulham St Mary
A143
SUFFOLK
outh Lopham
DISS
Halesworth
A143
Southwold
EYE
0 5 miles
0 5 km

△ **NORWICH: ST PETER MANCROFT** – *some of the reset medieval glass*

notably the splendid St Michael Coslany, which is now redundant.

These churches, in the city and the county, are Norfolk's greatest treasure; there are fine stately homes and pretty villages, but nothing of the quality of this huge collection of church buildings, which is equal, if not superior, to anything in Europe. But owing to the shortage of clergy and the decline in church-going, there is an official move to 'rationalise' and to close any church which is inconveniently situated or not well supported. Some parishes resist, and officialdom does not always win, but the old happy situation of the church being a solid and absolutely permanent part of the parish, and a comforting witness to the Christian faith, has quite gone, and now anxiety has replaced that security. Norfolk is particularly conscious of this because it has so many churches to guard. It has a cause worth fighting for, and this has been recognised by the giving of generous grants from English Heritage as well as the local authorities, and many specially founded trusts, both local and national. Even so, it is always a struggle. Where a church is of great architectural importance, it may be vested in the Churches Conservation Trust – like the little Norman church at Hales in the south of the county or Thurgarton in the north – or else in the Norfolk Churches Trust, such as with West Rudham near Fakenham, or Cockthorpe near Stiffkey on the north coast.

It is in the city of Norwich that the modern is making its heaviest mark. Of the 31 pre-Reformation churches described in 1970 by Noel Spencer, author of *The Old Churches of Norwich*, most are now legally redundant. Seventeen of these are preserved by the Norwich Churches Trust and the City Council, to whom the freeholds were transferred by the Diocese. Viable commercial uses have to be found for the maintenance of these buildings.

Norwich is a fine city, and indeed has been carefully cherished, and the conservation is mainly sensitive and good; only in the matter of churches has there been no vision. There is no appreciation of their spiritual value, and no recognition of their historic importance as documents in the life of the community since Norman times. No city in England had as many churches within its walls, and few even in Europe; so, to put it at its lowest, the potential for tourism was enormous. The story of the Norwich churches is a very tragic one, of missed opportunities and lack of enterprise.

ACLE † St Edmund King and Martyr ★
6m/10km W. of Great Yarmouth
OS *TG401102* **GPS** *52.6372N, 1.5474E*

One of Norfolk's many round-towered churches, the tower has a 13th-century octagonal top stage. The Perpendicular rood screen is set into the chancel arch, its lower parts painted and decorated with motifs symbolising Edmund's martyrdom. The rood above is modern, but in keeping with the screen. The octagonal 15th-century font is remarkable despite its mutilation by the iconoclasts: eight relief panels with the Evangelists, angels and the Virgin with the dead Christ.

ALDERFORD † St John the Baptist
9m/15km N.W. of Norwich
OS *TG123187* **GPS** *52.7250N, 1.1435E*

Mainly of the 14th-century, St John's N. aisle was demolished, and traces of the arcade can still be seen. There is an exceptionally good seven-sacrament font with signs of the Evangelists and Crucifixion; it still retains some colour.

ATTLEBOROUGH † St Mary ★★
14m/22km S.W. of Norwich
OS *TM048953* **GPS** *52.5179N, 1.0183E*

This is a magnificent church, Norman at the E. end – where the tower is – with a late 14th-century nave. The early part contained the College of the Holy Cross, founded in the Norman church in 1368, after which the nave was built for the parish. But the great glories of this church, unmatched anywhere else in E. Anglia, are the rood screen, c. 1475, its loft still intact, stretching right across the church from N. to S., and the frescoes above. The screen, often restored, is the most beautiful silvery colour; one would have liked to have seen it before the 17th century, when the Arms of English bishoprics were painted on it. The much-mutilated frescoes above, of c. 1500, are still very remarkable for their colour and liveliness.

AYLSHAM † St Michael
12m/19km N. of Norwich
OS *TG192270* **GPS** *52.7961N, 1.2508E*

The church is in the centre of an exceptionally attractive small market town with many good Georgian buildings. The 18th-century landscape designer Humphry Repton is buried outside church on the S. side, with a delightful monument and poetic inscription. The church is Decorated and Perpendicular, has remains of a painted screen and good brasses, including Richard and Cecilie Howard, 1499, in shrouds.

BARTON TURF † St Michael ★
12m/19km N.E. of Norwich
OS *TG343218* **GPS** *52.7436N, 1.4704E*

This is a pretty church with a fine tower, but it must be visited for its screen, with an incomparably beautiful painting of the Nine Orders of Angels, second only to Ranworth. Some of the faces are mutilated but this hardly matters, so beautiful and so spiritual are these figures. Notice the seraphim with red feathers, archangels with sceptre and sword, and angels guarding the naked children who represent souls. As well as the Nine Orders there are depicted saints Apollonia, Osyth and Barbara. On the S. part of the screen are very interesting but less good paintings – they include a most charming portrait of King Henry VI.

BAWBURGH † St Mary and St Walstan
5m/8km W. of Norwich
OS *TG152086* **GPS** *52.6327N, 1.1797E*

The church has lost its chapel and shrine to St Walstan, but retains interest, including an 11th-century tower with conical tiled cap and some fine 15th-century glass.

BEDINGHAM † St Andrew
4m/6km N.W. of Bungay
OS *TM285933* **GPS** *52.4906N, 1.3645E*

This is a most rewarding and unspoilt church. There is a round tower with octagonal Perpendicular top, but most of the church is 13th-century. Of note is the priest's door into the chancel. There are old benches in the nave, one with an inscription on the back, box pews in the aisles, and very nice brick floors. There are many monuments and floor-slabs to the Stone family, and interesting glass in the E. window of the S. aisle – some medieval English and two later foreign panels. Over the chancel arch is an adventurous modern sculpture, a mirror set into a large spray of barley.

△ **BLAKENEY: ST NICHOLAS** – *the screens are 20th-century, though medieval in style, with just a hint of Continental Art Nouveau in the more sinuous carving*

BEESTON † St Mary ★

5m/8km N.W. of Dereham

OS *TF893152* **GPS** *52.7021N, 0.8016E*

Away in the fields, from which the village has withdrawn, stands one of the most beautiful 14th-century churches. Tracery in the nave and chancel windows recalls that at Great Walsingham; the clerestory, tower and spire are Perpendicular. The hammer-beam roofs have finely carved figures on the wall-posts. The 15th-century chancel screen has no top, but there are two fine parclose screens, both with remains of colour on their E. sides. There are lovely benches with pierced backs and good ends, and a nice crocketed font cover. A painted board sets out the deeds of John Forby, rector from 1595–1614, who renewed the chancel and sanctuary. But at either the Reformation or the Commonwealth a maniac – perhaps the infamous William Dowsing – must have been let loose in the church, for every single figure, even the angels in the roof, has been ruthlessly defaced or even decapitated.

BESSINGHAM † St Mary ★★

4m/6km S. of Sheringham

OS *TG166370* **GPS** *52.8873N, 1.2193E*

The church has a Saxon round tower, though the main fabric is an entire Victorian rebuild. It is all very simple and peaceful, with glass by Kempe dated 1897 and 1906, and excellent Powell & Sons glass in the E. window of Christ, the Saviour of the World. The setting is wonderful, on the edge of ploughed fields, the church lapped by bracken with contorted ivy clad oak trees all around.

BLAKENEY † St Nicholas ★★

5m/8km N.W. of Holt

OS *TG033435* **GPS** *52.9512N, 1.0249E*

This wonderful church dominates the very attractive village, and is visible from boats sailing in the harbour. The magnificent W. tower is 1435, and the Perpendicular nave and low Early English chancel culminate in a small beacon tower at the E. end. The church has been well restored with a modern German rood screen; there are old stalls with misericords in the chancel and a few poppyheads in the nave. The church's glory is a stepped seven-light lancet window in the chancel, and in the N. aisle is some good reset medieval glass.

BRISLEY † St Bartholomew ★★

6m/10km N.W. of Dereham

OS *TF950214* **GPS** *52.7558N, 0.8893E*

The village clusters around its church, which is distinguished by its fine tower. The church was rebuilt in sequence from the E. end, c. 1360, finishing with the tower in the 1430s. Inside it is refreshingly unrestored, with bits and bobs of everything: carved bench-ends, bosses, traces of wall-colouring, and a faded but discernible image of St Christopher on one wall. There is a 15th-century screen as well as box pews, a three-decker pulpit and a W. gallery of 1848. The font, unremarkable in itself, has a lovely coloured wooden pinnacle cover. In the chancel is a three-seat sedilia under ornamented ogees, and a celebrated brass of John Athorne in mass vestments, 1531. Under the chancel is the original crypt, once used for lodging prisoners en route to Norwich gaol.

BURNHAM DEEPDALE † St Mary

2m/3km N.W. of Burnham Market

OS *TF804443* **GPS** *52.9658N, 0.6854E*

Another church much like Bessingham, St Mary's has a Saxon tower and Victorian nave and chancel. Its treasure is the Norman Labours of the Month font, which is square with three out of the four sides panelled and carved in a charming rustic manner. There is good stained glass too, all reset but of great interest.

BURNHAM OVERY † St Clement

1m/2km N.E. of Burnham Market

OS *TF843429* **GPS** *52.9521N, 0.7420E*

Unusually for Norfolk, the church is set slightly higher than its surrounding countryside. The Norman central tower has a pretty 17th-century cupola. The S. arcade is c. 1200, and the chancel was remodelled in the 13th century with stepped lancets.

△ **CLEY-NEXT-THE-SEA: ST MARGARET** *– the church's newest addition, a white-crowned sparrow on the west window*

BURNHAM THORPE † All Saints

2m/3km S.E. of Burnham Market

OS *TF852417* **GPS** *52.9412N, 0.7549E*

This is a mostly Decorated and Perpendicular church where Admiral Lord Nelson's father was rector. He and Nelson's mother are buried in the nave, and all over the church are memorials to, or relics of, Nelson himself.

CASTLE ACRE † St James ★

4m/6km N. of Swaffham

OS *TF815150* **GPS** *52.7024N, 0.6863E*

Between the castle and the priory stands a church with a very fine Perpendicular tower. Inside are misericords, the base of a screen with early 15th-century painted panels, and an exceptional pulpit. This is hexagonal on a curved stem, with five panels, four of which show the four doctors of the church, Augustine, Ambrose, Jerome and Gregory, all vividly coloured and restored. Equally colourful is the soaring Perpendicular font cover.

CATFIELD † All Saints

15m/25km N.E. of Norwich

OS *TG381212* **GPS** *52.7363N, 1.5267E*

This is an attractive grouping of church and former rectory. The church is a fine

△ **CLEY-NEXT-THE-SEA: ST MARGARET** – *medieval glass in the south aisle depicting eight female martyrs, all saints, with their attendant symbols*

aisleless 15th-century building containing a Perpendicular screen with painted kings and faded wall-paintings.

CAWSTON † St Agnes ★★

4m/6km S.W. of Aylsham
OS *TG134238* **GPS** *52.7700N, 1.1620E*

A huge church looming over the village and surrounding countryside, it has an unusual and forbidding tower. The hammer-beam roof of the 15th century is outstanding, replete with angels and saints, and the screen is one of Norfolk's best: tall, with lovely tracery and painted dado panels, believed to be the work of Flemish artists. A wild man and dragon, symbols of the de la Pole family, are represented twice in this church, once in the spandrels of the W. door and again on the piscina in the S. transept.

CLEY-NEXT-THE-SEA † St Margaret ★

4m/6km N.E. of Holt
OS *TG044438* **GPS** *52.9464N, 1.0473E*

A squat tower, unusual clerestory of the 14th century, ruined transepts – this is a church of the sea now high and dry inland, and possibly never completed owing to the Black Death of 1348. The battlemented Perpendicular S. porch is very fine, with an upper floor that has seen use as a schoolroom, priests' chamber and library. The lower floor is vaulted, with an elaborately carved central boss. Inside is a very wide 14th-century nave and aisles, and above the arcades are canopied niches with richly carved and grotesque figures; there is carving of similar richness on the Tudor bench-ends. The W. window was recently restored, funds coming from the hundreds of birdwatchers who descended upon the village in 2008 to witness the rare appearance of a white-crowned sparrow on these shores. To honour the bird's assistance in the repairs, its image has been included as a small motif in the new window.

COCKTHORPE † All Saints

4m/6km E. of Wells
OS *TF981422* **GPS** *52.9408N, 0.9473E*

This is a very attractive 14th–15th-century church with a splendid monument to Dame Barbara Calthorpe, 1639, who 'was much comforted by the sight of 193 of her children and their offspring'. There is also a tomb chest to her husband, Sir James Calthorpe, 1615. This church was rescued from dereliction by the Norfolk Churches Trust.

CRANWICH † St Mary ★

7ml11km N.W. of Thetford
OS *TL782948* **GPS** *52.5225N, 0.6263E*

Surrounded by the trees of this possibly ancient circular site are the 18th-century rectory and thatched church. The Saxon tower is very special and pierced by round acoustic vents with simple knot tracery. The interior is dark and plain – a rather neglected Victorian left-over.

CROMER † St Peter and St Paul

4ml7km E. of Sheringham
OS *TG219422* **GPS** *52.9313N, 1.3013E*

The church gives character to the town grouped around it, with its tall tower, decorative flintwork and expanse of Perpendicular windows. Inside, it is a typical seaside church, restored with the Victorian tourists in mind, and now full of 19th- and 20th-century monuments and mediocre glass, excepting one Burne-Jones and Morris window in the S. aisle

DEREHAM † St Nicholas ★

Town historically known as East Dereham; 16ml25km W. of Norwich
OS *TF986133* **GPS** *52.6810N, 0.9379E*

This is an architecturally and historically interesting church, with a detached early 16th-century bell-tower. The S. doorway is Norman, and the nave is Decorated. Transepts lead from the crossing, over which is another tower, 15th-century. The chancel has sedilia, a piscina and aumbry niche. The S. porch and S. aisle windows are Perpendicular, as is the delightful Perpendicular sacramental font – one of the county's best. The execution of the carving, with miniature vaults to the panels, is of the best quality.

DITCHINGHAM † St Mary

1ml2km N. of Bungay
OS *TM329922* **GPS** *52.4782N, 1.4294E*

The church has a very tall Perpendicular tower, originally with figures in niches on either side of the door, and a 16th-century screen, very much restored. Inside is a black marble First World War memorial, with a life-size bronze figure of a dead soldier by Derwent Wood. There are also a few bits of old glass, and some from the early 19th century, and a window to Sir H. Rider Haggard (1856–1925), author of *She* and *King Solomon's Mines*, who lived in the village and was a church warden.

EAST HARLING
† St Peter and St Paul ★★

6ml10km S.W. of Attleborough
OS *TL989866* **GPS** *52.4419N, 0.9264E*

A magnificent church, it is basically 14th-century, although many of the windows are Perpendicular. The 15th-century alterations to the church are due largely to the beneficence of Anne Harling, d. 1498. She had three husbands; the first, Sir William Chamberlain, KG, d. 1462, is buried on the N. side of the chancel. He figures in the marvellous stained glass of the great E. window where he kneels, in armour, as does Anne's second husband, Sir Robert Wingfield in the lower lights. Above them there is a remarkable collection of Norwich School glass, placed in the church by Anne Harling. There are 15 scenes from the life of the Blessed Virgin Mary, a Te Deum panel, some angels in the tracery, the two donors and, for those who can find it, a scrap of a mantle, which is all that is left of the figure of Anne herself.

EAST TUDDENHAM † All Saints

10ml16km W. of Norwich
OS *TG085115* **GPS** *52.6613N, 1.0819E*

Approached from the road by a long lime avenue, the church has a beautiful S. porch with three niches and 'Gloria Tibi TR' in flint flushwork: the carved annunciation is like a firework display in the spandrels. Inside, all is plain and white, but one's eye is caught by a brilliantly coloured triptych – a very Tractarian piece that came from All Saints in Norwich. In the S. nave is some interesting Flemish glass, and in the chancel is a stone effigy of a knight in chain mail, 13th-century, holding his heart in his joined hands.

△ **EAST HARLING: ST PETER AND ST PAUL** – *Norwich School glass; part of 15 scenes from the life of the Blessed Virgin Mary*

EAST WRETHAM † St Ethelbert

5m/8km N.E. of Thetford
OS *TL915906* **GPS** *52.4800N, 0.8186E*

This is an elaborate and pretty church rebuilt by G. E. Street in 1865. The little saddleback neo-Norman tower is more French than East Anglian. Inside is very Tractarian, with polychromatic angel frescoes flanking the carved and gilded reredos. There are touching memorials to soldiers killed in the Great War, including a very grand one by Lutyens.

ERPINGHAM † St Mary ★

3m/4km N. of Aylsham
OS *TG198312* **GPS** *52.8339N, 1.2627E*

One is attracted to this church by its soaring tower, on a rise outside the village. It is full of splendid things, including a military brass to Sir John de Erpingham, dating from the early 1400s, and an E. window full of copies of 16th-century Lower Rhenish glass originally brought from Blickling Hall. The atmosphere in the church owes all to the Oxford Movement – a tabernacle on the high altar, statues of the Virgin and Child and a sanctuary lamp by the screen.

FELBRIGG † St Margaret ★

2m/3km S. of Cromer
OS *TG197390* **GPS** *52.9036N, 1.2662E*

In the park of Felbrigg Hall, this is a charming, beautifully cared for church surrounded by old trees. It has a famous collection of brasses dating from c. 1380 to 1612, and many monuments to the Windham family, including the fine bust of the statesman William Windham by Nollekens.

FINCHAM † St Martin ★

5m/8km E. of Downham Market
OS *TF688064* **GPS** *52.6296N, 0.4927E*

The church is built of flint and carstone, with flushwork battlements. The interior is almost entirely Victorian, with a good and delicately painted screen, and brass of a shrouded naked woman in the middle of the nave. The church's treasure is its Norman font – square, with three arcaded panels to each side in which are depicted biblical scenes of rustic but charming detail.

FORNCETT ST PETER † St Peter

8m/13km S.W. of Norwich
OS *TM164928* **GPS** *52.4904N, 1.1874E*

The 18th-century rectory and very interesting church stand well among trees. The church has a fine 11th-century round tower, and inside are 15th-century carved benches; the porch has carved emblems of the joint patrons, saints Peter and Paul.

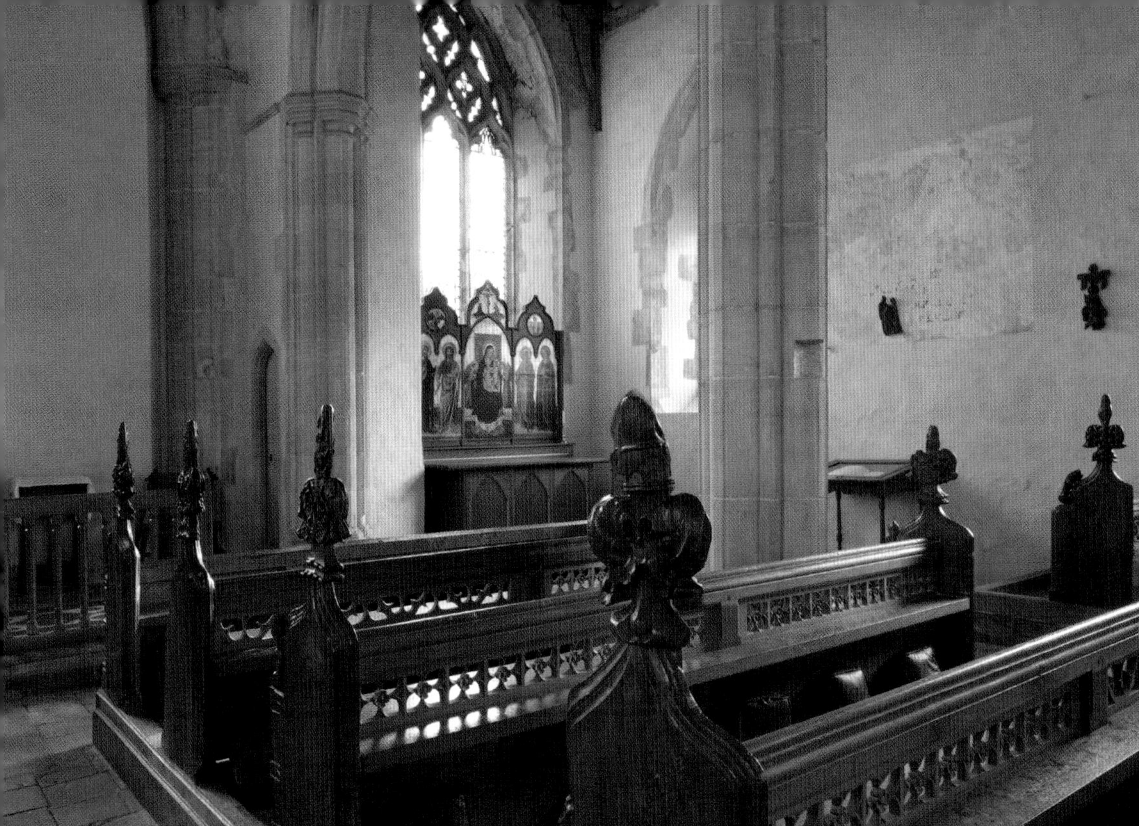

△ **GREAT WALSINGHAM: ST PETER** – *a subtle interior, with elegant Decorated window tracery, good stone and plasterwork and attractive poppyheads on the bench-ends*

FOXLEY † St Thomas ★

6m/10km N.E. of Dereham
OS *TG039217* **GPS** *52.7545N, 1.0208E*

An attractive village church, it stands in a lane of old houses. Inside is very unsophisticated, with a 13th-century chancel, and 14th-century nave and tower. The clear E. window gives the church a light and airy feel. The 17th-century benches are simple and rustic, the font is set under a fine W. gallery. The late 15th-century rood screen is simple and pleasing, but only when the gates are closed does it reveal its remarkable features, a set of painted panels with the four doctors of the Church – as at Castle Acre – with St Jerome holding a Gregorian chant manuscript.

FRAMINGHAM EARL † St Andrew

5m/8km S.E. of Norwich
OS *TG277027* **GPS** *52.5749N, 1.3597E*

Excavations here in 1984 revealed the original Saxon apse of this small, pretty church. There is a fine Norman inner S. door with beakheads and billets, and a Norman round tower and chancel arch; there is evidence of Anglo-Saxon work in the chancel windows and pilaster buttresses on the S. side.

FRITTON † St Catherine

7m/11km S. of Norwich
OS *TM227932* **GPS** *52.4920N, 1.2797E*

A round-towered church down a grassy track, whose outside is vaguely dull, with a raw piece of restored Decorated tracery in the chancel window. But inside there are wall-paintings of St George and St Christopher, and delightful 15th-century paintings on the screen bear pictures of the donor John Bacon and his wife, with a multitude of their children standing attentively behind. The font, though not out of the ordinary, has carvings of jovial lions' heads.

GARBOLDISHAM † St John the Baptist

7m/11km W. of Diss
OS *TM004816* **GPS** *52.3960N, 0.9444E*

The church has a beautiful tower, with fine flint and flushwork on the parapet, and shields and emblems set into the flushwork diagonal buttresses. The N. porch may well have been the original W. (Galilee) porch. Inside there are old benches and 15th-century screenwork, whose lower painted panels are very good, and in the windows is grand Victorian Gothic tracery.

GATELEY † St Helen
4m/6km S.E. of Fakenham
OS *TF960245* **GPS** *52.7828N, 0.9049E*

A church in a farmyard, with good benches that have carved backs and nice ends. The screen has eight good 15th-century painted panels, whose figures include King Henry VI and Master John Schorne, who holds a boot from which the Devil is emerging. There are Stuart altar rails and a Royal Arms of Charles I, and, in the chancel, a gilded and painted 20th-century reredos.

GLANDFORD † St Martin ★
3m/4km N.W. of Holt
OS *TG043414* **GPS** *52.9312N, 1.0396E*

This was a ruin until 1899 when Sir Alfred Jodrell started to rebuild it in memory of his mother. The angel roof, seven-sacrament font recreated in marble, elaborate choir stalls and screen are all of the traditional Norfolk Perpendicular type, and the church is very atmospheric. The stained glass is by Kempe and Bryans.

GOODERSTONE † St George ★
9m/14km E. of Downham Market
OS *TF762021* **GPS** *52.5885N, 0.6004E*

Near Oxburgh Hall, this is a church with a Norman W. tower, Early English chancel, Perpendicular nave and Decorated aisle. The porch has unusual round trefoiled windows. Inside it is lofty and light from much clear glass, and the view W. is taken up by a very tall Perpendicular screen with painted dado panels, prickets for candles and flowing tracery above. The 15th-century benches have pierced backs and poppyheads, and the E. window of the N. aisle has 14th-century glass showing the Resurrection of the Dead.

GORLESTON † St Andrew ★
2m/3km S. of Gt Yarmouth
OS *TG524044* **GPS** *52.5788N, 1.7247E*

This church, in what is virtually a suburb of Great Yarmouth, has been much restored, but is well worth a visit for the seven-sacrament font, the Stuart Royal Arms, a huge painting of Moses and Aaron, 14th-century Easter Sepulchre and the Bacon brass of c. 1320.

GREAT DUNHAM † St Andrew
5m/8km N.E. of Swaffham
OS *TF873147* **GPS** *52.6977N, 0.7718E*

St Andrew's has an impressive late 11th-century axial tower with many Roman bricks used in the arches. There is blind arcading of the same period on the nave's S. wall and Norman moulding around the triangular-headed W. entrance.

GREAT MASSINGHAM † St Mary
9m/15km N. of Swaffham
OS *TF798229* **GPS** *52.7742N, 0.6651W*

The church is largely 15th-century and overlooks an attractive village green. The Decorated W. tower is very stately, and the windows have a distinctive angular west Norfolk variety of early Perpendicular tracery with some Norwich School glass. The chancel and porch survived a thorough Victorian dismantling and restoration, retaining a lively Early English feel.

GREAT WALSINGHAM † St Peter ★★
4m/6km S. of Wells
OS *TF938375* **GPS** *52.9004N, 0.8807E*

Situated on a hillock outside the village is a most beautiful Decorated church with lovely and remarkable Decorated tracery of a kind rarely seen elsewhere. The old bench-ends with poppyheads and carved backs form a gallery of interest all their own. The tower has some 14th-century Norwich glass and elongated gargoyles.

GREAT YARMOUTH † St Nicholas ★★
Church Plain
OS *TG524080* **GPS** *52.6114N, 1.7273E*

This is the largest parish church in England, begun in the 12th century, added to, extended and widened in the 13th, 14th and 15th centuries. It was bombed and burnt out in 1942, and rebuilt by Stephen Dykes Bower, 1961, with a spacious, colourful and impressive interior, with stained glass by Brian Thomas. The pulpit, pews and tester over the font came from the church of St George, 1714–16; now closed.

GUNTON † St Andrew ★

In Gunton Park, 4m/6km S. of Cromer
OS *TG229341* **GPS** *52.8585N, 1.3097E*
Churches Conservation Trust

Surrounded by giant bamboos in the park of Gunton Hall is this small church with a Palladian portico by Robert Adam, 1769. It has a very elegant interior in dark wood with much gilding. Notice the binding of the prayer books of the Harbord family.

HADDISCOE † St Mary ★

4m/6km N. of Beccles
OS *TM439968* **GPS** *52.5153N, 1.5937E*

In a lonely corner of the county stands this church with a very fine round tower, Saxon at the base, then Norman and finally an upper 15th-century section with chequerwork. The 12th-century doorway has a carved relief seated figure above in mass vestments – a very fine piece of rustic Norman carving. In the S. wall is stained glass by Martin Travers depicting a young Baptist greeting the infant Christ – very fine 20th-century work by a great church furnisher and stained-glass artist.

HALES † St Margaret ★

10m/16km W. of Lowestoft
OS *TM383961* **GPS** *52.5107N, 1.5111E*
Churches Conservation Trust

This intact Norman thatched church sits surrounded by meadows in an idyllic rural setting. The round tower and apsidal chancel are virtually untouched. There are early 15th-century paintings of St Christopher and St James, and traces of what might have been an early Doom over the chancel, the arch of which is richly carved.

HAPPISBURGH † St Mary

6m/10km E. of North Walsham
OS *TG379311* **GPS** *52.8253N, 1.5309E*

The very handsome 15th-century tower stands as a bulwark against the horrible coastal caravan sites and the Bacton North Sea Gas Terminal. Its fabric is interesting, tapering in four buttressed stages to a simple battlemented parapet. The 19th-century restoration swept away much of interest inside, but nevertheless there is a very good screen and a fine font with angels, wild men and symbols of the Four Evangelists.

HARPLEY † St Lawrence ★

9m/15km W. of Fakenham
OS *TF788260* **GPS** *52.8025N, 0.6520E*

The church is notable for its bench-end carvings and the excellent S. door: the general fabric is a good example of Decorated, and the interior, though gloomy, is very atmospheric. The bench-ends include St Andrew with Saltire and St James the pilgrim. The rood screen was crudely and poorly repainted in the 1860s. The S. door is very fine, intricately carved with figures of the Evangelists and the major Latin doctors of the Church. Set into the door is the original wicket gateway.

HECKINGHAM † St Gregory

10m/16km W. of Lowestoft
OS *TM384988* **GPS** *52.5352N, 1.5143E*
Churches Conservation Trust

The tower is unusual, strange even: it has a round base, but the medieval upper half is mostly octagonal and looks very much like an afterthought. Most of the church, though, is essentially Norman, most notably the S. doorway, with excellently carved arched orders, very like its neighbour at Hales.

HEYDON † St Peter and St Paul ★

11m/18km S.W. of Cromer
OS *TG114274* **GPS** *52.8028N, 1.1347E*

The church is set in a delightful Norfolk estate village, and is entered through a S. porch that's vaulted, with carved bosses of Evangelists and angels – one or two like stone bats hanging from the roof – and a parvise above. The interior is mostly 17th-century,

HOUGHTON-ON-THE-HILL: ST MARY – *with the village which it served long since gone, the church now occupies a secretive spot, in a copse amongst farmland* ▷

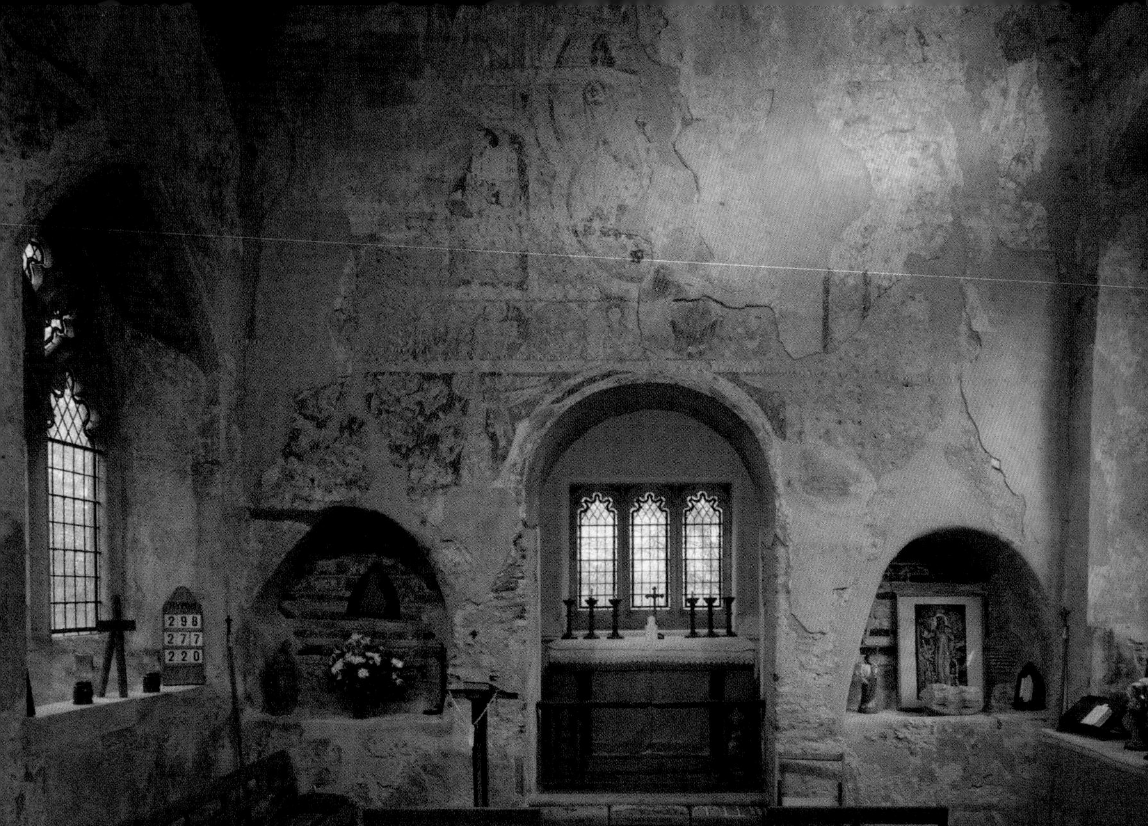

△ **HOUGHTON-ON-THE-HILL: ST MARY** – *the wall-paintings include a partly obscured Holy Trinity above the chancel arch, and roundels of Jesus, the Apostles and demons*

with a large squire's pew partially obscuring the chancel. The tomb chest in the N. aisle of Erasmus Earl is staggering: black, massive, some 12 by 6 foot in dimension. There are a number of wall-paintings here, most notably in the N. aisle, on themes of mortality: in the S. aisle is another good wall-painting showing the Annunciation, Nativity, the Magi bearing gifts and the Presentation at the Temple.

HILBOROUGH † All Saints

6m/10km S. of Swaffham
OS *TF825000* **GPS** *52.5673N, 0.6922E*

The church has a lovely Perpendicular W. tower with flushwork, angled parapets and an open-traceried parapet. The chancel of c. 1300 has a carved sedilia, and above the S. doorway is a tympanum that previously resided over the chancel arch; it has a sumptuous Royal Arms of James I. Inside there is a 17th-century brazier, which once solved the perennial problem of church heating. Lord Admiral Nelson's grandfather was rector here.

HINGHAM † St Andrew ★

6m/10km W. of Wymondham
OS *TG021021* **GPS** *52.5793N, 0.9826E*

Set in a charming country town from where Abraham Lincoln's family originated, this is a Decorated church built by Remigius of Hethersett, rector from 1319 to 1359. The tall nave has an excellent hammer-beam roof and stately 14th-century arcades. In the chancel is a monument to Thomas, Lord Morley, d. 1435, on the N. wall: it also serves as an Easter Sepulchre.

HOLKHAM † St Withburga ★★

2m/3km W. of Wells; access only when the park is open, except for special services
OS *TF878436* **GPS** *52.9572N, 0.7945E*

This church stands splendidly on a high mound inside the park N. of Holkham Hall, and is a most impressive and atmospheric Victorian rebuilding by James K. Colling, 1869, inspired by Juliana, wife of the 2nd Earl of Norfolk. Inside there are richly carved stalls and pews, a marble font and pulpit, rich floors, elegant hanging lamps and

△ **LITTLE SNORING: ST ANDREW** – *standing remote on the brow of a hill, the church has a detached Norman tower; the main body of the church is a mix of Early English and Norman*

many monuments, including some coffin lids. Behind a parclose screen in the N. aisle is a marble effigy of Countess Juliana (1870) by Boehm; across the chancel is a most interesting collection of Coke monuments from the earlier church. In the S.E. window is 18th-century heraldic glass commemorating an earlier restoration.

HOUGHTON-ON-THE-HILL
† St Mary ★

4ml/7km S.E. of Swaffham
OS *TF869053* **GPS** *52.6139N, 0.7595E*

Approached by a farm track, St Mary's can be visited most afternoons and by appointment with the warden. It is a lovely church of 11th-century origin, partly built with re-used Roman bricks. The nave remains, but the chancel, originally apsidal, was rebuilt in the 1760s in rectangular form. The present tower is 15th-century. For much of the latter half of the 20th century, the church was not used and sank into ruin. Nevertheless, when renovation began in the 1990s, significant wall-paintings were revealed; those that date from the 11th century are extremely rare instances of Romanesque painting. The painting schemes are full of interest, some of the figures depicted with curiously elongated fingers.

HOWE † St Mary

6ml/10km S.E. of Norwich
OS *TM275999* **GPS** *52.5499N, 1.3542E*

The round-towered Saxon church is set delightfully among old houses. Its conical cap is 17th- or 18th-century. The inside is Victorian and unexciting, but there is a triptych war memorial, a touch mawkish, and a brass plaque in the chancel on which the patron of the living sets out rules for the 18th-century incumbents.

HUNSTANTON † St Edmund ★

15ml/24km N. of King's Lynn
OS *TF674410* **GPS** *52.9409N, 0.4906E*

By F. Preedy, 1865, this is a very atmospheric seaside Victorian church in the Tractarian tradition. Externally the church is unremarkable, with banded flint and brickwork, but inside is colourful, devotional in the Highest

△ **NORWICH: ST HELEN** – *the south transept, with its vaulted ceiling of 1480 and large Perpendicular window flooding the church with light*

Anglican tradition, with traces of incense, and wonderful glass, including work by Comper and Kempe, and later glass by J. and W. Lawson and V. Flint. The furnishing is a bit spartan, with the exception of the font, which has a lovely banding of lead and brass round the rim.

INGHAM † Holy Trinity ★

7ml11km S.E. of North Walsham
OS *TG391260* **GPS** *52.7787N, 1.5438E*

The chancel of Holy Trinity is a rebuilding of c. 1350 as a conventual church of Trinitarian canons. The nave and tower, 1456 onward, followed. Inside there are splendid monuments, notably to Sir Oliver de Ingham, 1343, in the N. sanctuary, lying on a bed of stones, and early 14th-century effigies of Sir Roger du Bois and his wife on an altar tomb.

INGWORTH † St Lawrence

2ml3km N. of Aylsham
OS *TG192296* **GPS** *52.8196N, 1.2528E*

A pretty little Norman church whose tower collapsed in 1822. It was replaced by a rather charming Arts and Crafts vestry with a conical thatched roof to match the existing thatching on the nave and chancel. The S. porch is rudimentary but delightful, patched with brick, and with a stepped brick gable. Inside is simple but very appealing: pastel coloured walls, a simple screen, box pews and brick flooring and, best of all, an hour-glass for timing sermons set into a blue barley-twist columnar holder.

IRSTEAD † St Michael

7ml11km S.E. of North Walsham
OS *TG365204* **GPS** *52.7300N, 1.5019E*

This is a modest unspoilt thatched church in a remote rural corner, near Barton Broad. It has a narrow nave and S. aisle. Inside is a huge and rather intimidating wall-painting of St Christopher and some nice carved bench-ends, including a rather melancholy rabbit, but the great feature is the font: octagonal and richly carved, with traces of colour. Rather more curious is a set of screens painted by the Victorians, with the faces scrubbed out.

KING'S LYNN † St Margaret ★★
Saturday Market Place
OS *TF617198* **GPS** *52.7517N, 0.3955E*

In spite of much poor modern building, this is still the most beautiful town in Norfolk. It contains three fine medieval Gothic churches and one Victorian one. In the natural centre of the town, this is actually a Norman foundation, with some Norman work at the W. end. It has two W. towers and once had a spire, which fell in 1741. Round the churchyard are nice iron railings and gateways. The interior, though much restored at many periods, still has some marvellous things. Most famous are the two great Flemish brasses, tribute to Lynn's Continental trade. There are very fine 14th-century screens, a good Georgian pulpit with sounding board and a Snetzler organ of 1754. The reredos in the sanctuary is by G. F. Bodley.

KING'S LYNN † St Nicholas ★
St Ann's Street
OS *TF618204* **GPS** *52.7575N, 0.3970E*
Churches Conservation Trust

St Nicholas is not strictly a parish church, but it would be pedantic to omit it. It was built as a chapel of ease to St Margaret's, which shows what a place Lynn once was. The fine tower is Early English, with a spire by George Gilbert Scott, 1871, but the main church is of 1419, with a huge W. window of 11 lights, nine lights in the E. window and a fine angel roof. The two-storey S. porch is marvellous: lierne-vaulted and with bosses. The ledger stones include one to Robinson Crusoe: this is the church of the Lynn merchants, and is full of their monuments.

KNAPTON † St Peter and St Paul
3m/4km N.E. of North Walsham
OS *TG307341* **GPS** *52.8556N, 1.4260E*

Here is the most wonderful double hammer-beam angel roof, amongst the best in Norfolk, featuring 160 angels with outspread wings, though counting them correctly has challenged several church commentators. The font cover has a Greek inscription: 'Wash my sins and not my face only'.

LETHERINGSETT † St Andrew
5m/8km S.W. of Sheringham
OS *TG060389* **GPS** *52.9082N, 1.0626E*

This is a mostly early 13th-century church with a round tower, restored by William Butterfield in the 1870s. There are some fragments of old glass in the S. chancel window and a nice carved alabaster reredos, but it is the 19th- and 20th-century glass that commands attention: window after window of unusually good work.

LITCHAM † All Saints
7m/11km N.E. of Swaffham
OS *TF887176* **GPS** *52.7236N, 0.7928E*

The church stands in the middle of a pretty village, its brick tower built by Matthew Halcot, 1669, the rest consecrated in 1412. Inside is a charming W. gallery, with Royal Arms of Victoria and an organ. There are low box pews, a good 15th-century painted screen and old stalls with misericords. The pulpit is Perpendicular, and in the E. window is 15th-century foreign glass.

LITTLE SNORING † St Andrew ★
3m/4km N.E. of Fakenham
OS *TF953325* **GPS** *52.8551N, 0.8994E*

The detached Norman round tower has a conical cap with lucarnes (dormer-type windows). The church is slightly later Norman and Early English: the very pointed S. doorway is made up of Norman materials, and there are two Norman windows, lancets and a Decorated W. window. At the W. end are boards recording the fighter missions from the nearby base during the Second World War.

LODDON † Holy Trinity ★
6m/10km N.W. of Beccles
OS *TM363987* **GPS** *52.5351N, 1.4834E*

A fine late 15th-century church with a battlemented tower of 1500. Inside it is light and lofty, with a hammer-beam roof and a seven-sacrament font, 1487, defaced by one Mr Rochester, a Beccles glazier paid six shillings for his iconoclastic work. Surprisingly the screen – with painted panels including the martyrdom of William of Norwich – survived. Monuments include that to Lady Williamson,

1684; there is a 15th-century painting of Sir James Hobart, who built the church, and his wife, who built St Olave's bridge.

LUDHAM † St Catharine ★

12m/19km N.W. of Great Yarmouth
OS *TG388182* **GPS** *52.7093N, 1.5339E*

A Broads church in a spacious churchyard, it has a fine 14th-century flushwork porch, and very fine Perpendicular and Decorated tracery. The 15th-century font has the Evangelists, lions and wild men, and set into the chancel arch is an exceptional canvas tympanum, with the Royal Arms of Elizabeth I facing the E. end and the rood facing the nave – an unusual Crucifixion group with a grieving Mary in it. Underneath is an equally interesting screen with the four Latin doctors and E. Anglian saints – all finely painted, with gilded buttresses and panel surrounds.

MATTISHALL † All Saints ★

4m/6km E. of Dereham
OS *TG053110* **GPS** *52.6584N, 1.0347E*

This is a restored late Perpendicular church adjacent to a lovely market square. The heavily buttressed tower has a curious 1640 short leaded spire with cupola and weather vane. Inside is a very fine hammer-beam roof, the hammers well carved with angels and saints, and there are four tie-beams across the nave, also painted. The dado of the rood screen survives – a wonderfully painted Creed sequence with two figures to each panel. Note the intricate work in the spandrels. For a traditionalist, the electronic paraphernalia of a very evangelical church – huge screen, mixing desk and bandstand – may be a bit disconcerting.

MATTISHALL BURGH † St Peter

4m/6km E. of Dereham
OS *TG056117* **GPS** *52.6646N, 1.0398E*

This is a charming little 14th-century church, with good open roofs, especially in the chancel, and a surprisingly large N. transept – so large that it has an arcade dividing it from the nave. A lovely, simple screen separates the nave from the chancel, and set by the tower arch is a nice Purbeck marble font on a slender colonnade, with a barrel organ close by.

MERTON † St Peter ★

8m/13km N.W. of Attleborough
OS *TL911980* **GPS** *52.5465N, 0.8183E*

St Peter's stands in the grounds of Merton Park on a sharp rise: it has a Norman round tower, and Decorated nave and chancel that make the tower look as though it has come from another, much smaller church. The 13th-century window tracery is fine and very free-flowing, and the only incongruous note is a hideous 19th-century N. porch – a private entrance for the Walsinghams. Inside is a lovely screen with fluid Reticulated tracery. There is a good Jacobean two-decker pulpit, medieval bench-ends and a good but defaced font.

MORSTON † All Saints ★

1m/2km W. of Blakeney
OS *TG008438* **GPS** *52.9542N, 0.9883E*

The painter Sir Alfred Munnings was inspired by the church: '...nowhere could an artist have found a church in a more peaceful setting...'. Ironically his painting of the church also marked the outbreak of the Second World War. In the W. wall are traces of an earlier Norman fabric, but most here is of the 13th-century, with 18th-century patchwork repairs to the tower and 16th-century work in the nave and aisles.

MUNDFORD † St Leonard ★

5m/8km N. of Brandon
OS *TL800938* **GPS** *52.5124N, 0.6519E*

The tower is a curiosity – a Victorian replacement for the original Norman tower; similarly inside is a dull Victorian restoration of the nave. The chancel is a different matter altogether, though. This is a complete scheme by Sir Ninian Comper, c. 1911, with alabaster gilded and painted reredos, a wonderfully painted ceiling, the screen topped with an organ case, front pews, pulpit and chancel stalls. It is all excellent Comper work, though it was not approved of by Pevsner.

NECTON † All Saints ★

4m/6km E. of Swaffham
OS *TF878097* **GPS** *52.6529N, 0.7757E*

A rebuilding of 1864–5 replaced the old tower and added a lead-covered cupola. The wonderful hammer-beam roof is a result of a

△ **OXBOROUGH: ST JOHN THE EVANGELIST** – *the Beddingfield Chantry houses this amazing 16th-century terracotta canopied tomb, through which one can walk to see further family monuments*

c. 1490 heightening of the nave to include a clerestory. The usual East Anglian angels of the roof were complemented by large niches containing figures; much of the medieval colouring is retained. The reredos is unusually large for so small a chancel, rising up to partly obscure the Perpendicular E. window, and in the S. chapel are two Pugin monuments to the Mason family.

NEWTON † All Saints

4m/6km N. of Swaffham
OS *TF830155* **GPS** *52.7062N, 0.7083E*

This very attractive small church was partly rebuilt in the 14th century, but retains much evidence of Saxon work in the central tower. Of the two tower arches inside, one is pointed, the other Saxon. The old brick floor is still in place, and the church is charming in its simplicity.

NORTH CREAKE † St Mary

7m/11km N.W. of Fakenham
OS *TF854377* **GPS** *52.9050N, 0.7555E*

The massive tower of the 15th century stands by the road and is part of a general rebuilding of that time. The interior is a late and colourful 19th-century restoration, except for the extremely good angel roof in the nave, and a large Easter Sepulchre, sedilia and piscina in the chancel.

NORTH RUNCTON † All Saints

3m/4km S.E. of King's Lynn
OS *TF646159* **GPS** *52.7157N, 0.4361E*

This is one of Norfolk's few Classical churches, built by Henry Bell, 1703–13, delightful inside and out, with tower, a small steeple, painted reredos and early 18th-century monuments.

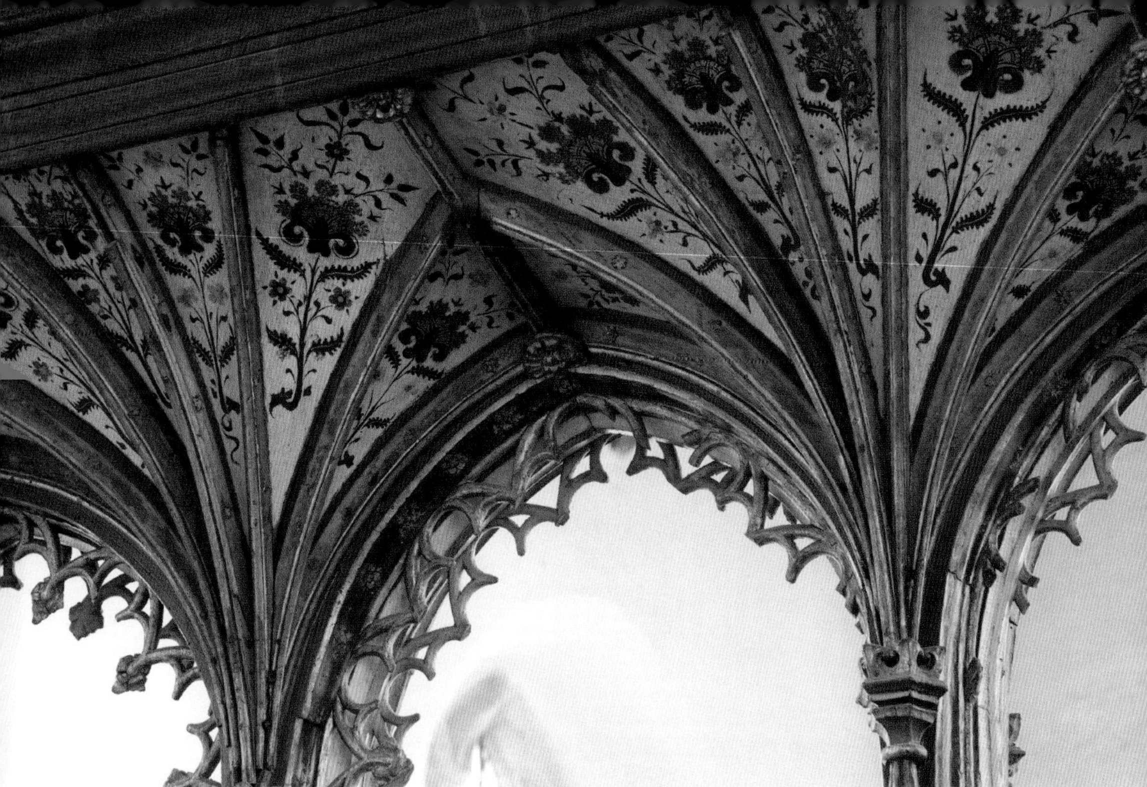

△ **RANWORTH: ST HELEN** – *the decorative paintwork on the rood screen is of exceptional quality and displays a tremendous deftness and brio in the brushwork*

NORTH TUDDENHAM † St Mary ★

10m/16km W. of Norwich
OS *TG055129* **GPS** *52.6753N, 1.0397E*

The church stands with the former rectory in fields among old trees. The interior is amazing. The Rev. Robert Barry, incumbent 1851–1904, lined the whole church from floor to the base of the windows with shiny red and yellow tiles, and had the remaining bits of wall stencilled. Then he was lucky enough to find a hoard of Norwich School 15th-century glass, which he put in the windows; much of it was removed for safety in 1942 and only three panels have returned. They are in the W. window of the tower.

NORTH WALSHAM † St Nicholas ★

14m/22km N. of Norwich
OS *TG283302* **GPS** *52.8216N, 1.3874E*

As at Fakenham, the old houses and alleys of the market-place surround the church. The tower fell in 1742 and remains a picturesque and monolithic ruin at the W. end of the church. Everything about this church is big: the 14th-century porch, the wide interior, noble and spacious with delicate arcades. The absence of a clerestory makes the roof seem low, but this is compensated for by the light admitted through the clear-glazed Perpendicular windows. There is a superb monument to Sir William Paston, 1608, made by John Key but designed by Sir William himself. There is a very tall Perpendicular font cover, impressively restored and painted, and 20 painted but defaced panels spanning the width of the nave – the original dado of the screen.

NORTHWOLD † St Andrew ★

10m/16km S.E. of Downham Market
OS *TL755970* **GPS** *52.5426N, 0.5878E*

From the outside all is Perpendicular; the tower, 'new' in 1470, bears an inscription: 'Pray for the soule of John Stalyng'. Inside are most attractive 13th-century arcades and a very fine Easter Sepulchre. There is a wooden tablet of 1727 to Robert Burhill, friend of Sir Walter Raleigh, who 'took sanctuary' here in 1641; on it is a long inscription that's well worth reading.

NORWICH † St Giles

St Giles Street
OS *TG225085* **GPS** *52.6295N, 1.2873E*

A fine, large Decorated building of c. 1400, of knapped flint with flushwork on the face of the buttresses, it stands at the highest point within the old city walls. The porch is fan-vaulted and impressive, and has a parvise above. The chancel and nave tracery are by R. W. Phipson, 1866. The interior is full of interest: an early hammer-beam roof, fine brasses under the carpets, an 18th-century sword and mace rests, as well as excellent wall tablets.

NORWICH † St Helen ★

Bishopgate
OS *TG237090* **GPS** *52.6328N, 1.3048E*

St Helen's was part of the Great Hospital founded by Walter de Suffield, Bishop of Norwich, in 1249, to shelter all 'poor and decrepit clerks'. At the Reformation, the Corporation turned it into a home for old people, and in Edward VI's reign the church was divided into three: the W. end became two men's wards, and the chancel end two women's wards. At the time, the chancel was new, having been completed in 1383; some 10 years late it was further adorned with a ceiling painted with great black eagles in honour of Anne of Bohemia. In the church there is no high altar; before the blocked chancel arch are box pews and the pulpit. The parochial altar was always in the S. transept, where it stands under a most beautiful vaulted ceiling of 1480. The magnificent Georgian reredos was probably by Thomas Ivory, whose son William built the Gothic pew opposite in 1780. Note the Tudor bench-ends and early hymn boards and numerals.

NORWICH † St John Maddermarket / St John the Baptist

On corner of Maddermarket and Pottergate
OS *TG229086* **GPS** *52.6299N, 1.2928E*
Churches Conservation Trust

A mid-15th-century church, its design was adapted to its cramped site, the original chancel having been demolished to widen the road for a visit by Elizabeth I. Of note is the fine Decorated E. window, and the

△ **RANWORTH: ST HELEN** – *the attendant angel over the Virgin Mary and Christ child on the south parclose screen*

eccentric collection of furnishings by the Rev. Busby, vicar at the beginning of the 20th century: the Gothic Revival reredos is partly obscured by a lowering baldachino, and there is a revolving Italian font and many brasses mounted on the wall nearby.

NORWICH † St Peter Mancroft ★★

Market Place
OS *TG229084* **GPS** *52.6278N, 1.2926E*

This superb 15th-century church dominates the Market Place, and was rebuilt from 1430 onward, though not finished until the eve of Reformation. The interior is tall and open, with no chancel arch and a hammer-beam roof. There is a rare font canopy of 1463, and interesting glass of 1921 by H. Hendrie. The high point, though, is the E. window, which retains much of its original Norwich School glass; take binoculars or a telescope to appreciate the subtle, endearing detail. This survived both gunpowder explosions during the Civil War and a famous 17th-century Puritan congregation, who surely found it very idolatrous. The reredos is by Seddon, 1895, gilded and finished by Comper, 1930.

OUTWELL † St Clement

5m/8km S.E. of Wisbech

OS *TF513036* **GPS** *52.6097N, 0.2341E*

The church sits in an oasis of calm in the Fens, with its ambitious 13th-century W. tower and Decorated bell-stage and mischievous gargoyles all round the church. The whole building is very ornamentally step-buttressed. The S. porch has a second floor, and is vaulted. The N. transeptual chapel, c. 1527, has a very good miniature hammer-beam roof with angels, wall-post figures and a lovely carved frieze.

OXBOROUGH

† St John the Evangelist ★

7m/11km E. of Downham Market

OS *TF744014* **GPS** *52.5829N, 0.5728E*

The tower fell in 1948, destroying the nave, and the ground on which it stood is now an open grassy space, flanked by the derelict pointed N. arcade and clerestory. Only the chancel, N. aisle and chapel survived. The treasure of St John's is the Bedingfield Chantry. The Bedingfield family, who built the moated hall in 1482, also built this beautiful chantry containing two superb early 16th-century canopied tombs of terracotta in Renaissance style.

PULHAM ST MARY

† St Mary the Virgin ★

6m/10km N.E. of Diss

OS *TM212852* **GPS** *52.4207N, 1.2521E*

The church has a most beautiful flushwork two-storeyed 15th-century S. porch with figures for pinnacles and a canopied arcade with windows and niches above a row of shields. There are rows of tracery with angels playing musical instruments. Inside there is a curious wooden staircase at the W. end going up to the ringing chamber. There is much old glass in the window traceries, some difficult to identify, but including the 12 Apostles in the N. aisle. The screen is very good, with a loft by Bodley, who also restored the mid-13th-century chancel very well in 1886. One further detail is the amazing 15th-century font, which has been re-coloured.

RANWORTH † St Helen ★★

7m/11km N.E. of Norwich

OS *TG356147* **GPS** *52.6794N, 1.4840E*

The nave was thatched till it burned in 1963. The W. tower is fine but the really marvellous thing is the 15th-century screen – the best in Norfolk. It extends right across the church with very pretty projecting wings dividing the two aisle altars from the central opening. The painting of the figures in the panels, as well as of the backgrounds and the decoration on the ribs and tracery, is superb. The church also possesses the *Sarum Antiphoner*, an illuminated manuscript of 14th-century East Anglian workmanship.

RINGLAND † St Peter ★

7m/11km N.W. of Norwich

OS *TG133140* **GPS** *52.6823N, 1.1553E*

In the clerestory windows is beautiful Norwich School glass, with large figures, more complete than usual and of wonderful colours. Here is the Blessed Virgin Mary with the Child, an Annunciation, the Trinity, several saints, and some figures of donors. There is also a fine hammer-beam roof with angels and delicate vaulting over the clerestory. The screen is now dismantled, but five defaced panels stand at the W. end, and in the tower are 18th-century canvas commandment boards and hatchments.

SALLE † St Peter and St Paul ★

Village sometimes spelt Sall; 12m/19km N.W. of Norwich

OS *TG110248* **GPS** *52.7803N, 1.1277E*

A wonderful church, whose very tall tower dominates the almost empty countryside. It has the best of everything the 15th century produced. The architecture, of about 1420, is superb, and the W. tower richly decorated – notice the feathered angels in the spandrels. There are two-storeyed porches on the N.E. side; that to the N. has lierne vaulting and bosses, and there are more beautiful bosses in the chancel roof. The nave roof has angels, the transept roofs panelling; there is very good Norwich School glass, and the base of a screen with painting. The pulpit has 15th-century panels and a later, Jacobean tester. The stalls, misericords and bench-ends

◁ **SALLE: ST PETER AND ST PAUL** – *the church houses one of Norfolk's best seven-sacrament fonts*

△ **SALLE: ST PETER AND ST PAUL** – *the misericords are not just superbly carved but also deeply expressive and subtly wrought*

are all excellent. There are many brasses and monuments. The font cover, beam and pulley are all Perpendicular too, and there is a seven-sacrament font.

SALTHOUSE † St Nicholas ★

3m/4km N. of Holt
OS *TG076436* **GPS** *52.9503N, 1.0890E*

This great church, built by Sir Henry Heydon of Baconsthorpe at the end of the 15th century, stands high above the marsh and sea in a village that has suffered many floods. It is a most wonderful Perpendicular church with a very large E. window and unusual, very plain nave windows of two lights only. There are remains of a screen with defaced panels, and impish graffiti of sailing ships on the choir stalls and panels, scratched into the woodwork by bored children. In the E. window of the S. aisle there is a panel of medieval glass.

SANDRINGHAM

† St Mary Magdalene ★
7m/11km N.E. of King's Lynn
OS *TF691285* **GPS** *52.8283N, 0.5088E*

This little church, much rebuilt and restored by Teulon in 1857 and Blomfield in 1890, has been the home church of the Royal Family since 1861. There are many affectionate family monuments to Queen Victoria, Queen Mary, King George VI and others; in a stained-glass representation of St Edward in the tower window one suspects the features of the late Duke of Clarence. The silver altar and reredos were given by an American, Rodman Wanamaker. There is a Greek font of the 9th century, and a very good E. window by W. E. Tower, 1911; part of the restoration of the chancel was in memory of Edward VII. Note the beautiful and unusual stained-glass figures of saints in the N.E. side aisle windows; they were probably made in King's Lynn, c. 1500.

△ **SALTHOUSE: ST NICHOLAS** – *a beautiful interior, sun-drenched on a good day through the abundant clear glass; some of the screen panels have nautical graffiti on their reverse sides*

SAXLINGHAM NETHERGATE
† St Mary the Virgin ★
7m/11km S. of Norwich
OS *TM231972* **GPS** *52.5270N, 1.2880E*

The church stands on a pretty village green with a rectory by J. Soane, 1784, to the W. and an Elizabethan house to the E. This Perpendicular church contains some of the best glass in Norfolk, notably 13th-century roundels of the martyrdom of St Edmund, 14th-century figures of St Philip and St James, and 15th-century representations of the Annunciation and Resurrection. There is also a good font, and Royal Arms of William IV.

SHELTON † St Mary ★★
12m/19km S. of Norwich
OS *TM220910* **GPS** *52.4721N, 1.2686E*

This is a most exciting, surprising and beautiful church. It was built of flint and red brick with diapering in the 1480s in the purest Perpendicular style – apart from the tower, which is earlier. The inside is all one space and is delightful, with white walls and warm stonework. Large figures of donors in 15th-century dress are depicted in the E. windows. In the S. aisle is a monument to Sir Robert Houghton, 1623, and over the chancel is a very good carved Arms of William III.

SNETTISHAM † St Mary ★
4m/6km S. of Hunstanton
OS *TF690342* **GPS** *52.8794N, 0.5107E*

The once central magnificent tower of c. 1340 is now at the E. end, the chancel having fallen down. The W. front has a tripartite porch and six-light Decorated window of great beauty, well described in L. P. Hartley's novel *The Shrimp and the Anemone*. Good brasses included that to John Cremer, d. 1610, with wife and children.

△ **SWAFFHAM: ST PETER AND ST PAUL** – *the ceiling is majestic, a double hammer-beam roof, thronged with angels*

SOUTH CREAKE

† Assumption of St Mary ★

7m/11km N.W. of Fakenham

OS *TF855362* **GPS** *52.8915N, 0.7564E*

A large 14th-century church rebuilt in the 15th century with a restored angel roof, 1950s, over new arcades. It has a surprisingly squat tower. The interior is full of light, colour and objects of piety. There is 14th-century glass with 15th-century angels in tracery, as well as 16th-century Continental panels. A 15th-century wine-glass pulpit, screen, seven-sacrament font, restored altars and shrines give the impression that the Reformation never got this far – until you see what 17th-century vandals did to the font.

SOUTH LOPHAM † St Andrew ★

5m/8km N.W. of Diss

OS *TM039817* **GPS** *52.3958N, 0.9962E*

The superb early Norman central tower is claimed to be the best in Norfolk – a miniature and less ornate version of Tewksbury Abbey in appearance. Pevsner dates it at 1120. Inside there are two plain Norman arches, leading respectively to the choir and chancel, with its large round-headed Decorated window. The late medieval bench-ends are very entertaining: a beaked elephant, a cat with kittens and a blacksmith among them.

SPARHAM † St Mary ★

7m/11km N.E. of Dereham

OS *TG071196* **GPS** *52.7349N, 1.0662E*

A stately church, mainly Perpendicular, with a very tall tower and clerestoried nave. Panels of the screen are preserved in the N. aisle, with three figures from the Dance of Death: one in a shroud; the other two – one male, one female – cadavers with grinning skulls and bony limbs clad in fashionable 15th-century clothes.

STOW BARDOLPH † Holy Trinity ★

2m/3km N. of Downham Market

OS *TF628056* **GPS** *52.6241N, 0.4043E*

The exterior of this church, with rubble and brickwork in need of attention, contrasts markedly with the restored interior by John

Brandon, 1848–9. In the N. chapel are the Hare memorials, the most notable of them being a life-sized wax effigy bust of Sarah Hare, d. 1744, in a mahogany cupboard. It is frankly one of the most alarming items to be found in any church in the land. Her will specified this effigy and the clothes in which it was to be dressed, and the result is as sinister as anything to be found in a travelling showman's caravan.

STRATTON STRAWLESS † St Margaret ★★

8m/12km N. of Norwich
OS *TG221207* **GPS** *52.7389N, 1.2895E*

Little, long and low, the church is set beside a lane under a truncated medieval tower. The S. aisle was rebuilt in brick in the 17th century to house the Marsham monuments, which include rhyme-and-portrait figures of parents and children, 1678; further along is the macabre shrouded figure of Thomas Marsham, 1638, with angels above and skulls and bones beneath. Also in the S. aisle is a 13th-century effigy of a woman in black stone, known as the Black Abbess. A huge 17th–18th-century candelabrum hangs in front of the screen, and on the N. side of the church is an outstanding collection of reset Norwich School glass, including the famous Angel's Head – a piece of 15th-century glass of breathtaking beauty.

SWAFFHAM † St Peter and St Paul ★★

14m/22km S.E. of King's Lynn
OS *TF820089* **GPS** *52.6482N, 0.6902E*

The pretty spirelet, familiar in the country around, was a felicitous addition of 1897. Entering through the fine W. doorway, one is afforded a stunning view of the beautiful double hammer-beam roof with angels, a monument to Katherine Steward, 1590, and a brass to Sir John Audley, c. 1530, unfortunately mounted on a wall. There are scraps of old glass in the tracery of the N. nave windows; otherwise the glass is very horrid. Scattered through the church are fragments of old reset wood carving in the Victorian pews and choir stalls: most notable is the Victorian carving of the legendary Swaffham pedlar, John Chapman. In the S. transept is a fine saints window by Morris & Co, and in the bottom panels very interesting stained glass scenes from the Great War, including a field hospital, Zeebrugge and Mons: wholly suitable for this part of the church, which is dedicated as a memorial to the Great War.

TERRINGTON † St Clement ★

4m/6km W. of King's Lynn
OS *TF552204* **GPS** *52.7592N, 0.2986E*

This priory-like church stands above the marshlands with a detached Perpendicular tower. The W. front with five-light window and canopied niches is very imposing, the aisles flanked by lofty pinnacles. It was intended as a cruciform church with central tower, but realising the softness of the ground, the medieval builders thought better of this and prudently sited the tower to the N.W. There is a wonderful Perpendicular font cover, almost as tall as the arcade, which opens to show paintings of the Life of Christ, and large Decalogue boards of 1635 in the transepts.

THOMPSON † St Martin

11m/18km S.E. of Swaffham
OS *TL929969* **GPS** *52.5362N, 0.8441E*

The church is attractive and assured and little changed since the 14th century, apart from the mid-15th-century S. chapel. The rustic interior is of great charm and a 17th-century air, with a Stuart canopied pulpit, box pew, altar and rails. The poppyhead benches have 17th-century graffiti, and there are medieval choir stalls with misericords. The most notable medieval survival is the stencilled screen, which is rudimentary but totally in character with the church.

THORPE MARKET † St Margaret

4m/6km S. of Cromer
OS *TG244353* **GPS** *52.8690N, 1.3341E*

This is a lovely rural early Gothic Revival church of 1796, with cheerful W. and E. pinnacled porches and octagonal turrets with conical caps. The church could almost be rotated on its axis with little change to the exterior appearance. Inside is homely and welcoming, with a coved ceiling that has ribs and rose bosses, screens at either end of the church, and displays of pictures and the like.

THURNING † St Andrew ★
12m/19km E. of Fakenham
OS *TG080294* **GPS** *52.8224N, 1.0862E*

A rather lonely church of unassuming proportions, it has excellent 17th-century woodwork, most of which came from Corpus Christi College, Cambridge. Panelling, a grand pulpit with tester and altar rails were installed as part of an 1825 restoration by the then rector, a Fellow of Corpus Christi. There are also named farmers' box pews, a squire's pew and pews and benches for the lesser folk too.

THURSFORD † St Andrew ★
5m/8km N.E. of Fakenham
OS *TF983337* **GPS** *52.8651N, 0.9459E*

This is a rare example of a Victorian restoration transforming a dull medieval church into something much more interesting than it was before. W. Lightly restored it in 1862 in accordance with mid-Victorian High Church principles; a model of the period and unharmed by later 'good taste'. Inside are encaustic tiles, well-designed furnishings and stained glass in the E. window by the Rev. Arthur Moore, which Professor Pevsner declared 'one of the most beautiful of its time in England, or indeed in Europe'. The S. transept has an upper level reached by steps containing the family pews for the Chadd family; underneath is the family vault.

THWAITE † All Saints
5m/8km N. of Aylsham
OS *TG192333* **GPS** *52.8533N, 1.2554E*

The church has a Norman round tower, a 15th-century S. aisle and an early 19th-century chancel and Sunday school room N. of the chancel. The school room is of 1824, and has old lettering, texts, original wooden coat pegs and, most importantly, a fireplace.

TIBENHAM † All Saints ★
6m/10km N. of Diss
OS *TM134898* **GPS** *52.4652N, 1.1413E*

The sheer faced chequerwork tower is almost intimidating in its plainness, but inside is a splendid enormous carved and gilded Jacobean pulpit with an outsize tester, and an unusual raised family pew for the Buxtons for which Archbishop Laud himself granted a faculty in 1635; it is reached by a staircase in the S. aisle, and effectively blocks the chancel from the nave. Its dark wood is relieved by a colourful Buxton hatchment and Buxton Arms.

TILNEY † All Saints ★★
4m/6km W. of King's Lynn
OS *TF568179* **GPS** *52.7366N, 0.3216E*

Twelfth-century arcades are unusual in Norfolk, and those of All Saints are very good – seven bays spanning the nave and chancel, with water, stiff-leaf and scalloped capitals. There are good fittings too, including an exceptional Jacobean rood of 1618, with carved foliage and obelisks and balusters at the top. The high, narrow nave with triple lancets seen through the grand W. tower arch gives the church a French atmosphere, offset by the lovely East Anglian hammer-beam angel roof. The view E. to W. is stunning.

TRUNCH † St Botolph ★
3m/4km N. of North Walsham
OS *TG287348* **GPS** *52.8626N, 1.3963E*

This church has many interesting features, including a screen of 1502 with painted panels of 11 Apostles, and return stalls carved with many names and with holes for ink pots, indicating that it served as a school room. There are a few scraps of medieval glass and an Elizabethan monument in the chancel, and a nice 15th-century roof with angels and a ringers' gallery with some original colour. But the church's greatest glory is the celebrated font canopy of c. 1500 – almost unique, and enchanting even in its present state. It has carved panels with traces of colour, flying buttresses and a pinnacled top. It also has splendid carvings of flowers, vines, monkeys and a wild man fighting a dragon. The open stonework at the top is reminiscent of the great Gothic crown spires of Scotland.

TUNSTEAD † St Mary
4m/6km N. of Wroxham
OS *TG308227* **GPS** *52.7527N, 1.4195E*

An unusual church in several ways: outside there is flushwork arcading instead of clerestory windows. In the Perpendicular chancel, behind the high altar, is a mysterious raised

△ **WALPOLE ST ANDREW: ST ANDREW** – *a church of understated beauty but the interior is currently in a parlous state, with salt eating away at the arcade's pillars*

platform with a vaulted chamber beneath – possibly a strong-room for relics which would be exhibited above. There is also a good screen with ogee arches and painted panels.

UPPER SHERINGHAM † All Saints ★

1m/2km S.W. of Sheringham
OS *TG144418* **GPS** *52.9312N, 1.1890E*

The church is full of interesting things, notably the 15th-century rood screen with loft, painted beam with pulley for raising the font cover and very good bench-ends, including a mermaid, nurse with Christ-child and cat with a kitten in its mouth.

UPWELL † St Peter ★

5m/8km S.E. of Wisbech
OS *TF505027* **GPS** *52.6019N, 0.2222E*

This is a watery place, where the River Nene runs straight as an arrow, overlooked by St Peter, a 13th-century and Perpendicular church, marked out by a very distinctive tower with an irregular octagonal 14th-century belfry stage. Inside are very good Georgian furnishings, including two galleries. The N. gallery allows a rare high and close view of the carved beams and traceried spandrels of a fine angel roof. There are some good interesting brasses, and a 15th-century brass eagle lectern with three affable lions at its base.

WALPOLE ST ANDREW † St Andrew

6m/9km N.E. of Wisbech
OS *TF501175* **GPS** *52.7348N, 0.2226E*
Churches Conservation Trust

This important marshland church is somewhat overlooked in favour of its illustrious neighbour at Walpole St Peter, but it is a very good Perpendicular church. The mid-15th-century tower is mostly brick, and inside is a tall nave and arcades, with a fine clerestory. In recent years, there has been extensive salt damage to the pillars. At the time of writing, this erosion was being tackled, along with a complete floor restoration.

△ **WALPOLE ST PETER: ST PETER** – *the carved and pedimented western screen is an unusual and quite theatrical feature, and dates to about 1630*

WALPOLE ST PETER † St Peter ★★

5m/8km N.E. of Wisbech
OS *TF502168* **GPS** *52.7287N, 0.2230E*

The finest of all, the church is known as the 'Queen of the Marshlands'. The exterior is wonderful: the aisles, nave and chancel are all embattled, and the E. nave gable terminates with finely-crocketed spirelets. The aisles have huge Perpendicular windows, and there are very fine porches, especially the two-storeyed one on the S., which has good brasses. Inside, the impression is Jacobean; there is a big screen W. of the pews, a tall font cover, benches, pulpit, and a great chandelier of brass and wrought iron. All this is of the highest quality and looks good in the nave, but the vaulted chancel is such a Gothic masterpiece that it is a pity it has been mutilated and over-crowded with benches and monuments – again, mostly 17th-century. The saints on all that is left of the Perpendicular screen were clearly painted by several different hands; some are rather crude but all are charming. Under the chancel is a tunnel of grand quality – lierne-vaulted with bosses and flagstones. Its purpose is not entirely clear, but it is thought to have been used for processional purposes in medieval times and, in the 17th and 18th centuries, simply for stabling horses.

WALSOKEN † All Saints ★★

N.E. district of Wisbech
OS *TF477105* **GPS** *52.6725N, 0.1833E*

All Saints is late Norman and Early English, with the county's largest Norman nave. The arcading inside is very good and complete, terminating at the W. end in an elegant Early English tower arch. Under this arch is a truly outstanding 1544 seven-sacrament font. The panels more or less survived the iconoclasts, to leave an extraordinary legacy of church art. For some strange reason there are references to Solomon everywhere: a painting of the Judgement of Solomon and 18th-century wooden figures of Solomon over the tower arch, four more in the chancel and a statue of King David with his harp over the chancel arch.

△ **WORSTEAD: ST MARY** – *part of the early 16th-century screen; most of the panels have been restored and overpainted, but there is still much medieval work evident*

WEST WALTON † St Mary ★★

3m/4km N. of Wisbech
OS *TF471133* **GPS** *52.6979N, 0.1756E*
Churches Conservation Trust

The distant view of the grand Perpendicular tower is misleading. It is detached, and only the upper stages are Perpendicular; the lower part is Early English, as is the long, low church itself. It is a fine and interesting work, with a short clerestory that mixes blind arcading and intermittent round arched windows. The aisles are later additions. Huge pinnacles flank a grand entrance, now topped off with a brick-stepped gable; once this must have been a magnificent porch. Inside are exquisite Early English arcades and capitals, and traces of 13th-century wall-paintings.

WEYBOURNE † All Saints

4m/6km N.E. of Holt
OS *TG111430* **GPS** *52.9431N, 1.1414E*

This is a Saxon building taken over by Augustinian canons in the 13th century. The central Saxon tower has characteristic triangular slab heads to the double openings; the Early English doorway has dog-tooth decoration. There is a pillar piscina in the sanctuary.

WICKHAMPTON † St Andrew ★

7m/11km W. of Great Yarmouth
OS *TG427054* **GPS** *52.5928N, 1.5823E*

A very rewarding church, mainly of c. 1300 with a 15th-century tower. It contains superb 14th-century wall-paintings: Seven Works of Mercy and Three Living and Three Dead, and two very fine 13th-century effigies of Sir William Gerbygge and his wife, he with his heart in his hands.

WIGGENHALL ST GERMANS
† St Germaine / St Germans ★

4m/6km S. of King's Lynn
OS *TF596140* **GPS** *52.7003N, 0.3619E*

An Early English and Perpendicular church, with very fine 16th-century bench-ends: Vices in the Jaws of Hell, grotesque monks and Apostles. Also of note is the 17th-century pulpit and clerk's desk.

WIGGENHALL ST MARY

† St Mary the Virgin ★★

5m/8km N. of Downham Market

OS *TF582144* **GPS** *52.7042N, 0.3410E*

Here are remarkable sets of late medieval pews: the bench-ends are outstanding, with free-standing figures and deep-relief carving lower down. Those to the centre of the nave are Victorian reproductions and mostly very good. On the S. side, the bench-ends depict the Seven Deadly Sins, with statues of the Apostles set below, and on the N. side are bench-ends showing the Sacraments, Evangelists and animals. This is a truly outstanding collection, animated and lively, and rather eclipsing the other features of this pleasant church.

WIGGENHALL ST MARY MAGDALEN † St Mary Magdalen ★

5m/8km N. of Downham Market

OS *TF598113* **GPS** *52.6765N, 0.3632E*

The outside of the church shows a liberal use of available materials – brick and freestone – but makes a pleasant composition, with a good porch and fine early Perpendicular tracery. Inside, the enormous chancel arch contributes to the great sense of space. There are simple 15th-century benches and an original roof, with good ceiling figures that you need binoculars to appreciate fully. The chancel has Jacobean panelling. In the N. aisle windows is a large collection of 15th-century stained-glass figures, mostly representing bishops, archbishops and popes.

WIGHTON † All Saints

3m/4km S.E. of Wells

OS *TF940399* **GPS** *52.9219N, 0.8853E*

This is a huge, light church, whose early 15th-century nave roof has fine Norwich School angels and saints in the tracery. The chancel was built from 1440 onward by celebrated mason James Woodrofe, sent from the Cathedral Priory by the rectors. The S. porch of the 1490s has a mermaid boss over one window, and a face of Christ over the other. Inside, the absence of chairs in the aisles makes everything feel very spacious. There is a splendid black and white marble tomb of Elizabeth Bacon, 1686, and many fine ledger slabs. The tower fell in 1965 but, thanks to the generosity of Canadian Mr Leeds Richardson, was rebuilt and rededicated in 1976.

WORSTEAD † St Mary ★

3m/4km S.E. of North Walsham

OS *TG302260* **GPS** *52.7830N, 1.4121E*

St Mary's is considered to be one of the best 14th-century churches in Norfolk. The chancel screen is 1512, with delicate filigree tracery and restored dado panels. Amongst the saints in the panels on the screen are St William of Norwich, holding nails and a dagger, and the wonderful St Uncumber, a lady who grew a beard to escape an undesirable suitor. There are box pews and a ringing gallery over a very good tower screen of 1501; in the dado panels are painted copies of stained glass by Joshua Reynolds at New College in Oxford.

WYMONDHAM

† St Mary and St Thomas of Canterbury ★

9m/15km S.W. of Norwich

OS *TG106014* **GPS** *52.5705N, 1.1075E*

A wonderful church, its setting is mysterious, adjacent to the ruins of the Benedictine Abbey of which it was a part. The monks and townsfolk were a quarrelsome lot, whose disputes were eventually settled by division of the church into two – with the nave and N. aisle going to the town. Much of it is Norman, with splendid arcades and triforium windows, but there is a Perpendicular clerestory and spectacular angel roof. The terracotta Ferrers monument, very like those at Oxborough, is of c. 1525. There are fragments of a 13th-century font, as well as a complete 15th-century one. Sir Ninian Comper did much work here, including the beautiful reredos. In the parvise can be seen the famous Corporal case, used to hold the cloth Corporal upon which the bread and wine are consecrated.

◁ **WORSTEAD: ST MARY** – *the tower screen, with its painted panels replicating the work of Reynolds*

NORTHAMPTONSHIRE

A too little-regarded county, Northamptonshire is marked by an assured and beautiful use of stone – for country houses, farms, cottages, outbuildings and, above all, for churches. The county is on the limestone belt, and the building stone varies from a pale silvery limestone to a deep-brown ironstone, with every shade of yellow and gold between. Medieval masons delighted to arrange the stone to give decorative effects to the outside of walls, as at Finedon and Irthlingborough. Old roofs are tiled, with stones graded from small at the ridge to large at the eaves. Of these stone tiles, the best are those known as Collyweston slates, which come from this county.

If ever the term 'steeple chasing' needed explanation, this is the county to describe what it means, for it abounds in steeples. Broach spires, whose chamfered sides rise to a graceful point, like a sharpened pencil from a tower that seems part of the same design, such as that at Stanwick. There are crocketed spires of immense height, as at Oundle and Higham Ferrers, and dumpy spires, which are almost pyramids. And there are towers and spires in which it is hard to say which lends more grace to which, as at Raunds and King's Sutton. These steeples rise generally out of trees on hills and in valleys, so that not even the pylons and poles of our own age can quite extinguish their effect. There are few eminences in the pastoral parts of this mildly undulating country from which one can see less than three church spires. More times than not one finds clustered about the church an attractive stone-built village.

Norfolk has larger churches and grander woodwork. Somerset has more lace-like towers, but Northampton above all counties has variety and originality and elegance in its architecture, from the Saxon long-and-short work on the tower of Earls Barton to the stone octagonal lantern with its flying buttresses on the top of the late Perpendicular tower of Lowick. Northampton's medieval church builders seem to have been conscious architects and not mere labourers. This quality in their church towers and spires, particularly in the 13th and 14th centuries, together with the fact that Early English and Decorated styles were regarded as pure and perfect respectively, made the spires of the east and north of the county, and of S. Lincs, the model for Victorian church architects. So Northamptonshire spires may be seen rising out of the suburbs of London and other big cities, and even over the rooftops of foreign and dominion capitals where there is an Anglican church.

Naturally, churches so deservedly popular with the Victorians came in for a good deal of 'restoration' at their hands. Many have been ruined internally by having the plaster stripped from their walls and the stone picked out in cement

◁ **EARLS BARTON: ALL SAINTS** – *the Saxon tower is enriched by stripwork, arcades and quoins*

to give an 'ancient' effect; shiny tiles have replaced old stone or brick floors; and cheap pews and church furnishings have completed the devastation. We have listed here those medieval churches which are wholly or comparatively unharmed by Victorians. But there is hardly a medieval church in the county which is without beautiful stonework somewhere, either in the many mouldings of an arch or in a lively piece of carving acting as capital, corbel or water-spout.

The county has suffered more than most in the South Midlands from 19th-century and modern industry. It was never grim, so that factories, pylons and power stations ill-become its gentle landscape. The boot and shoe industry caused a rash of hard, bright brick villas in the 19th century in Northampton itself, and Rushden, Wellingborough and Irthlingborough. But these villas are Midland-looking and have no affinities with London. In the 20th century great harm was done to its loveliest scenery by the former iron and steel industry, whose huge dredgers picked their way like prehistoric animals over the farms, digging up the earth and raising mountains and bringing poles and wires and mineral lines in their trail. Recent legislation, however, has made restoration compulsory, and this has improved matters. Northampton was itself designated a New Town in 1968 and has grown substantially.

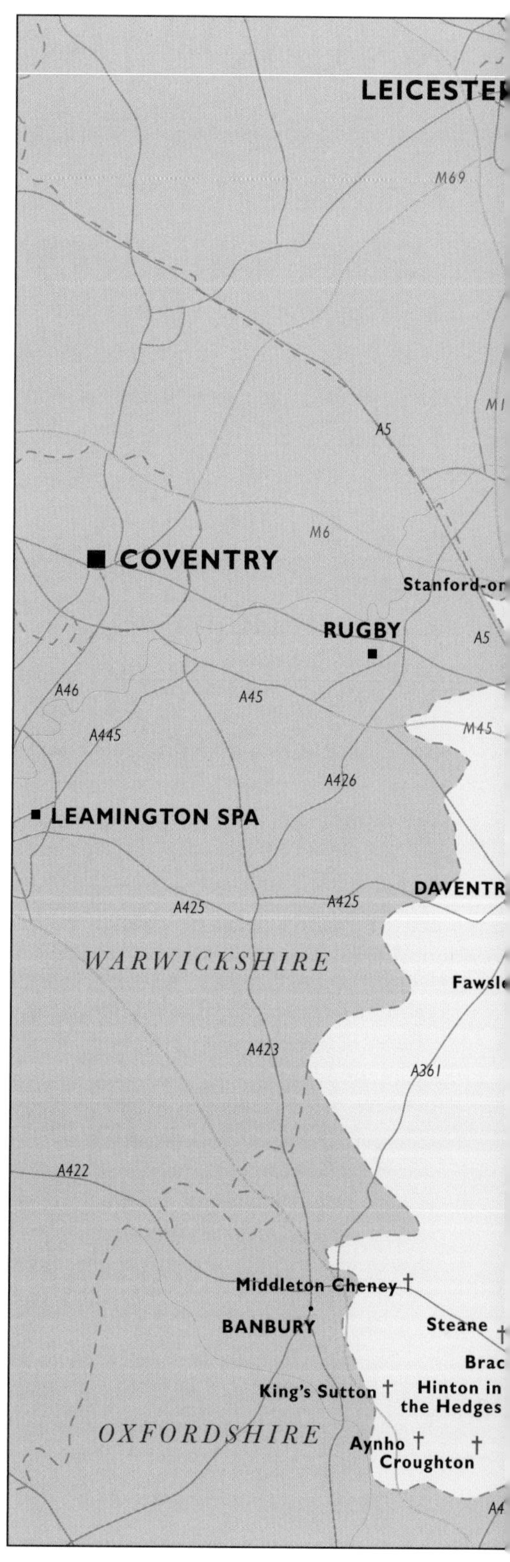

RUTLAND
LEICESTERSHIRE
NORTHAMPTONSHIRE
CAMBRIDGESHIRE
BEDFORDSHIRE
BUCKINGHAMSHIRE
PETERBOROUGH
Wakerley
Gretton
Fotheringhay
Warmington
MARKET HARBOROUGH
CORBY
OUNDLE
Stoke Doyle
Polebrook
Brigstock
Aldwincle
Rothwell
KETTERING
Lowick
Titchmarsh
Cransley
Cottesbrooke
Raunds
Finedon
Stanwick
Irthlingborough
Brixworth
Higham Ferrers
WELLINGBOROUGH
Rushden
Great Brington
Earls Barton
NORTHAMPTON
ch Stowe
Easton Neston
TOWCESTER
Slapton
BEDFORD
Newport Pagnell
Wicken
Passenham
MILTON KEYNES
BUCKINGHAM
0 5 miles
0 5 km
A47
A6121
A6
A6003
A43
A1
A427
A605
A508
A6116
A1(M)
A14
A45
A510
A509
A5199
A428
A6
A421
A5
M1
A413
A600
A422

△ **BRIXWORTH: ALL SAINTS** – *a prodigious 7th-century Saxon church of the first importance that has been extended and written into with the architecture of later centuries*

ALDWINCLE † All Saints ★
4m/6km S.W. of Oundle
OS *TL011815* **GPS** *52.4223N, 0.5144W*
Churches Conservation Trust

Set in meadowland in a stone village with two churches, All Saints is an intriguing church of 12th-century origins, with a pinnacled and delicately moulded 15th-century tower. The body of the church is 13th- and 14th-century, with a late 12th-century N. aisle. The 15th-century Chambre Chantry is of great interest. The whole interior shows how well a medieval church can look without pews, and the exterior string course is adorned with birds, beasts and other fantastical creatures.

AYNHO † St Michael ★
6m/10km S.E. of Banbury
OS *SP514330* **GPS** *51.9936N, 1.2521W*

St Michael's church, situated adjacent to Aynho House, retains a rich Decorated tower, but the rest was transformed in 1723, after the manner of Vanbrugh, by a local carpenter-cum-architect, Edward Wing. Wing's alterations are uncompromisingly domestic in style, with windows in two storeys; an illustration of that phase in the history of English churches which most Victorians tried to pretend had never existed. An unpleasant mid-20th-century ceiling detracts from an otherwise interesting interior.

BRIGSTOCK † St Andrew
4m/6km S.E. of Corby
OS *SP946852* **GPS** *52.4567N, 0.6090W*

There are impressive remains of the original substantial Saxon church in the upper parts of the nave walls, the W. tower and big circular stair turret. The tower has good long-and-short quoins and well-built single-splayed windows. Unusually, the nave extends westward alongside the tower.

BRIXWORTH † All Saints ★★
7m/11km N. of Northampton
OS *SP747712* **GPS** *52.3340N, 0.9044W*

This is one of the most important buildings in England. Originally monastic, the sheer scale of the surviving early fabric of rubble dressed with Roman tiles is fantastic. The church

△ **BRIXWORTH: ALL SAINTS** – *the Saxon round arches are created without the structural knowledge and finesse of Norman arches, but they are appealingly rustic*

was conceived as a huge basilica with lateral porticus and a narthex at the W. end. It was probably damaged during Danish raids in the late 8th or early 9th century, presumably necessitating some later rebuilding; certainly the lower part of the sanctuary, the tower and the circular stair turret were added during the 10th and 11th centuries. Other medieval alterations included the 14th-century belfry and spire, but in the mid-19th century some of the later accretions were removed and the apse restored on its old foundations. A semi-circular subterranean ambulatory may have given a passageway to pilgrims, permitting the viewing of a relic set in a recess. Of later interest is the repainted 15th-century screen to the Verdun Chapel, moved from its original position in front of the apse.

CHURCH STOWE † St Michael

Village also known as Stowe-Nine-Churches
6ml/10km S.E. of Daventry
OS *SP638576* **GPS** *52.2137N, 1.0663W*

Traditionally, the name relates to eight attempts to build the church elsewhere in Saxon times, the Devil removing the stones each night to the present site. Certainly there is a tall Saxon W. tower, though the rest is mainly Perpendicular, much restored inside, but with a beautiful effigy of Lady Carey, d. 1620, by Nicholas Stone, and a sumptuous wall monument to Dr Turner, d. 1714, by Thomas Stayner.

COTTESBROOKE † All Saints

9ml/15km N. of Northampton
OS *SP710735* **GPS** *52.3553N, 0.9588W*

A secluded church of c. 1300, All Saints has been much restored, but retains Georgian fittings, including a three-decker pulpit, box pews and an extraordinary two-storeyed family pew with fireplace. There are many 17th- and 18th-century monuments, principally to the Langham family.

CRANSLEY † St Andrew

3ml/4km S.W. of Kettering
OS *SP828765* **GPS** *52.3805N, 0.7843W*

Adjacent to Cransley Hall, St Andrew's church dates from the 14th and 15th centuries, with a large Perpendicular ashlar tower and recessed spire, Decorated nave and chancel, and an 18th-century baluster font. The E. window is by Kempe. Nineteenth-century restorations were by Slater and Carpenter.

CRICK † St Margaret ★
6ml10km E. of Rugby
OS *SP588724* **GPS** *52.3473N, 1.1378W*

St Margaret's has fine Decorated work, including an enriched broach spire; the exterior has a warm glow, and the tower is of red ironstone. Inside is a Norman font unusually supported on atlantes – columns sculpted in the form of a man.

CROUGHTON † All Saints
4ml6km S.W. of Brackley
OS *SP545335* **GPS** *51.9977N, 1.2064W*

The church is Norman and Early English, with good woodwork and an extensive series of early 14th-century wall-paintings of Marian themes, the Life of Christ and the Last Judgement.

DAVENTRY † Holy Cross ★
12ml19km W. of Northampton
OS *SP575625* **GPS** *52.2583N, 1.1589W*

An impressive town church of 1752–8 by David Hiorn of Warwick, built of ironstone with giant pilasters, Gibbsian surrounds and arched windows. The whole is surmounted by a rusticated tower and obelisk spire. A galleried interior has Tuscan columns supporting plaster groin vaults and retains a Doric reredos and delicately wrought pulpit and reader's desk.

EARLS BARTON † All Saints ★★
4ml6km S.W. of Wellingborough
OS *SP851638* **GPS** *52.2659N, 0.7531W*

The celebrated Saxon tower, with long-and-short quoins and extensive stripwork decoration, overlooks the market square. It is both solid and beautiful, a work redolent of all that is best in the Anglo-Saxon tradition. Here the debate about the purpose of such towers is finely focused: perhaps this was the nave of the early church, as revealed by excavation at Barton on Humber. Later work includes a good Norman S. doorway and a splendid 17th-century pulpit. The 15th-century rood screen was painted by the Northamptonshire artist Henry Bird in the 20th century, the lower panels depicting saints, the fan vaulting rippling with butterflies – a delightful modern touch in this ancient church.

EASTON NESTON † St Mary
½ml1km N.E. of Towcester
OS *SP702491* **GPS** *52.1365N, 0.9755W*

An attractive and secluded church, St Mary's is 13th-century, with a good deal of Perpendicular work. The fittings and monuments are of Classical character: pulpit, communion rail and box pews; there are impressive Fermour hatchments, too, and a Royal Arms of George IV. Adjacent to the rood loft in the N. aisle is a remnant of a medieval wall-painting.

FAWSLEY † St Mary the Virgin
4ml6km S. of Daventry
OS *SP565567* **GPS** *52.2065N, 1.1741W*

The church is set beautifully above a lake in the park where Charles I hunted before riding to Naseby. Remote and unspoiled, it contains Knightley monuments and beautiful carved late medieval bench-ends incorporated into box pews, as well as some old Flemish and heraldic glass.

FINEDON † St Mary the Virgin ★
3ml4km N.E. of Wellingborough
OS *SP912719* **GPS** *52.3382N, 0.6623W*

A stately Decorated church of ironstone with grey-stone dressings, whose handsome chancel has a five-light E. window. There is a strainer arch – the internal version of a flying buttress – across the nave, similar to that at Rushden, and a richly decorated organ case of 1717 by Shrider.

FOTHERINGHAY
† St Mary and All Saints ★★
4ml6km N.E. of Oundle
OS *TL059931* **GPS** *52.5259N, 0.4391W*

The fragments of this great 15th-century collegiate church, of which only the nave and tower remain, are best viewed over the River Nene. They are themselves an impressive landmark to this part of the Nene Valley, with flying buttresses and a great deal of glass. The great octagonal lantern is such as James Wyatt must have dreamed of when working on his tower at Fonthill Abbey in Wiltshire at the turn of the 19th century. The base of the tower at Fotheringhay opens three ways into the body of the church and is fan-vaulted. Inside, the 18th-century fittings include an attractive reredos with Decalogue and creed in gold, after the fashion of the time. The pulpit, a gift from Edward IV who refounded the college, and the Perpendicular font are noteworthy.

GREAT BRINGTON † St Mary ★

6m/10km N.W. of Northampton
OS *SP667652* **GPS** *52.2811N, 1.0234W*

This is a good, sober 13th-century church with conventional arcades and small country clerestory, with a modest 'English type' timber ceiling. The canopied tomb of Sir John Spencer, d. 1522, is therefore of unexpected magnificence, as are all the other Spencer monuments. Lawrence Washington, an ancestor of George Washington, is buried in the churchyard.

GRETTON † St James the Great

4m/6km N. of Corby
OS *SP898944* **GPS** *52.5402N, 0.6766W*

The Perpendicular tower dominates the Welland Valley. There are splendid Norman pillars in the nave, and the aisles and chancel are in Decorated style. The chancel was raised in the late 17th century to accommodate the Hatton vault, and is roofed with Colleyweston slate. The choir stalls have Queen Anne panelling, and matching work can be seen in the communion rails and altar panels.

HIGHAM FERRERS
† St Mary the Virgin ★

4m/6km E. of Wellingborough
OS *SP961685* **GPS** *52.3065N, 0.5913W*

A narrow side street in this old limestone town gives the first view of the rich crocketed steeple of St Mary's, with its pierced parapet, flying buttresses and deep Early English mouldings. The 13th-century W. tower has a carved doorway reminiscent of the style of Westminster Abbey, c. 1260. Internally, the church is a double building: 13th-century on the S.; 14th-century on the N. There is much good carved woodwork, old and modern, the latter by Comper. Henry Chichele, Archbishop of Canterbury and founder of All Souls College, Oxford, was born here in 1362, and gave the stalls and choir screen to the church. He endowed the fine Perpendicular chantry chapel, a detached building to the W., used for centuries as the grammar school. He also built Chichele College here, now in ruins, and the bedehouse on the S. side of the churchyard.

HINTON-IN-THE-HEDGES
† Holy Trinity

2m/3km W. of Brackley
OS *SP558369* **GPS** *52.0281N, 1.1880W*

A tiny medieval church with a Norman W. tower. The N. doorway is early 14th-century, and there is some pretty 16th-century carving round the S. door. Inside there are effigies believed to be of Sir William de Hinton, b. 1284, and his wife. The tub font is a robust piece of rustic stone carving.

IRTHLINGBOROUGH † St Peter

4m/6km N.E. of Wellingborough
OS *SP947706* **GPS** *52.3258N, 0.6106W*

One of the boot and shoe towns of Northants., but wedded to the country tradition, it retains a market cross and a great bridge across the Nene, as well as the medieval church. The 14th-century tower, rebuilt in 1887–93, is practically divorced from the rest of the building and, with octagonal lantern, is reminiscent of a lighthouse.

KETTERING † St Peter and St Paul

Off Market Place
OS *SP867784* **GPS** *52.3969N, 0.7266W*

The steeple, soaring above the busy town, is justly famed. The Perpendicular tower and spire are from the same school of design as Oundle, and while the treatment is more restrained, the silhouette is more satisfying. The body of the church is long and low by comparison. The clean horizontal lines at the eaves, without pinnacles, blend well with the lead roofs and Barnack stone.

KING'S SUTTON † St Peter and St Paul
4m/6km S.E. of Banbury
OS *SP497361* **GPS** *52.0212N, 1.2764W*

The church is famous for its spire, richly ornamented and rising to almost 200 feet above the flying buttresses at its base; it is hardly surpassed in the county in its soaring grace. The screen is by Sir George Gilbert Scott, who restored the church in 1866.

LOWICK † St Peter
5m/8km E. of Kettering
OS *SP977810* **GPS** *52.4183N, 0.5639W*

A small village, its glory evidently departed save for the 15th-century church with pinnacled lantern tower which dominates the group. It has beautiful figured 14th-century glass and remarkable effigies on the 15th-century Greene monument. Among the later sculpture is a Westmacott work of 1843 commemorating the 5th Duke of Dorset.

MIDDLETON CHENEY † All Saints ★
3m/4km E. of Banbury
OS *SP498420* **GPS** *52.0744N, 1.2741W*

The church is mainly Decorated with a Perpendicular spire. The steeply roofed porch is built entirely of interlocking stones; the 15th-century painted ceiling and pulpit were restored with the rest of the church by Sir George Gilbert Scott in 1865. A Victorian rector was connected with the Pre-Raphaelite movement and there are important windows here by Rossetti, Ford Madox Brown and Burne-Jones, as well as Simeon Solomon, Webb and William Morris. These include the original of Burne-Jones's 'Six Days of Creation'.

NORTHAMPTON † Holy Sepulchre ★
Sheep Street
OS *SP753609* **GPS** *52.2415N, 0.8973W*

One of the five surviving round churches in England, it owes its character and dedication to the inspiration of the Crusaders. The early 12th-century round part of the church is the original nave. The present nave was built half a century later and formed the choir, to which aisles were added during the next two centuries. The result is a disjointed exterior, but the interior has a peculiar fascination that belongs to any rarity. The Church of the Holy Sepulchre in Cambridge gives a good impression of the probable original appearance. The festive chancel and outer walls, except the round part and the S. aisle, were added by Sir George Gilbert Scott in 1860–4. An Orthodox congregation also worships here.

NORTHAMPTON † St Giles
St Giles Street
OS *SP759605* **GPS** *52.2382N, 0.8897W*

St Giles's Church is a big, golden ironstone medieval church with a central tower and the only peal of 10 bells in the county. There are chained books and an excellent E. window by Clayton & Bell, 1876.

NORTHAMPTON † St Peter Marefair
Between Marefair and St Peter's Street
OS *SP749603* **GPS** *52.2365N, 0.9034W*
Churches Conservation Trust

Reputed to have been the shrine of St Ragener, nephew to St Edmund, this is a grand Norman church, whose rich arcades have alternating supports of quatrefoil and collared round shafts. The aisles were rebuilt in the 14th century, and the stocky tower, rebuilt in the 17th century, was cut into the symmetrical Norman arcades. The chancel is a weak invention of Sir George Gilbert Scott, in whose time the church was smartened up to suit the conventions of the 19th century. In the S. aisle is a superb late Saxon sepulchral slab.

OUNDLE † St Peter ★
8m/13km E. of Corby
OS *TL041881* **GPS** *52.4817N, 0.4671W*

Set in the heart of a small, unspoilt town of stone and slate, the church is large and opulent. Its chief glory is its Decorated steeple, rebuilt in 1634. This is a true piece of architecture; the massive surfaces of the tower are vertically panelled to carry the eye to the spire above. The interior was spoilt by scraping in the 19th century, but the pulpit and brass eagle lectern are both 15th-century.

△ **STANFORD-ON-AVON: ST NICHOLAS** – *the interior is an exquisite and harmonious balance of ad hoc furnishings, refined wood carving and subtle gradations of stonework bathed in diffuse light*

PASSENHAM † St Guthlac ★

3m/5km W. of Milton Keynes
OS *SP780394* **GPS** *52.0479N, 0.8636W*

The upper part of the Decorated tower and chancel were rebuilt c. 1626. The resulting chancel roof is an architectural oddity – barrel-roofed, with an E. Gothic Revival window, the arch of which struggles with the curve of the roofline above. There are splendid 17th-century fittings that include delicately carved stalls and a W. gallery with Ionic columns. In the 1950s wall-paintings of patriarchs and prophets were uncovered, and the mixture of craftsmanship and amateur intervention in them only serves to enhance the charm of this somewhat eccentric church. There is a good monument to Sir Robert Banastre, d. 1649, who was responsible for the 17th-century reworking of the church.

POLEBROOK † All Saints

2m/3km E. of Oundle
OS *TL068870* **GPS** *52.4710N, 0.4286W*

The church is an example of interesting late 12th- and early 13th-century work, with blank arcading, stiff-leaf capitals, dog-toothing and one of the best 13th-century broach spires in the county. Repositioned grotesques can be seen on the outside, and there are some interesting carved ceiling bosses.

RAUNDS † St Peter

6m/10km N.E. of Wellingborough
OS *TL000730* **GPS** *52.3467N, 0.5328W*

St Peter's greatest assets are the 15th-century wall-paintings on the N. nave wall – including vigorous depictions of the life of St Catherine, the Seven Deadly Sins and St Christopher. The ornate 13th-century W. tower has a good broach spire, and the six-light E. window of c. 1275 is superb.

ROTHWELL † Holy Trinity

4m/6km W. of Kettering
OS *SP816811* **GPS** *52.4222N, 0.8012W*

Holy Trinity is a large cruciform Norman church, now mainly 13th-century, with a famous crypt or charnel-house under the S. aisle containing the bones of some 1,500

△ **STANFORD-ON-AVON: ST NICHOLAS** – *rebuilt on the site of an earlier church, the construction of the tower was interrupted by the Black Death, which took many of the workmen*

people. A recent acquisition is an interesting stained-glass memorial window by Helen Whittaker, whose work can also be seen in Ely Cathedral.

RUSHDEN † St Mary
4m/6km E. of Wellingborough
OS *SP957665* **GPS** *52.2886N, 0.5973W*

A grand Perpendicular church with a prominent strainer arch across the nave (see also Finedon), St Mary's has some good 15th-century figured glass and medieval iron-work on the doors, and a rare 14th-century oak pulpit.

SLAPTON † St Botolph ★
4m/6km W. of Towcester
OS *SP640468* **GPS** *52.1166N, 1.0666W*

Primitive, small and unspoiled, St Botolph's is basically Norman and Early English, the chancel lower than the nave, with good wall-paintings of c. 1400 depicting diverse saints.

STANFORD-ON-AVON
† St Nicholas ★
6m/10km N.E. of Rugby
OS *SP588788* **GPS** *52.4045N, 1.1364W*

A light and spacious 14th-century church, the nave cleared of pews, and hatchments used intelligently as decoration. The delightful 17th-century organ case was turned out of Whitehall by Cromwell, and now perches on Tuscan columns. The 14th-century and later glass is prolific, most of it dated to 1314–26. Of particular note are three lights, one to St Agnes, and the other two to unnamed female saints. Archbishop Laud was once rector here.

STANWICK † St Laurence
2m/3km N.E. of Higham Ferrers
OS *SP980714* **GPS** *52.3325N, 0.5630W*

The church has a distinctive octagonal 13th-century tower with lofty Nene Valley spire; richly composed with excellent mouldings. Inside is a carved 14th-century font, and a good Jacobean altar table in the Lady Chapel.

△ **STANFORD-ON-AVON: ST NICHOLAS** – *for a small and modest church, there remains at St Nicholas an astounding collection of medieval glass, all in beautiful condition*

STEANE † St Peter ★

3m/4km N.W. of Brackley
OS *SP554390* **GPS** *52.0468N, 1.1928W*

This is a little chapel set in a park and was built by Sir Thomas Crewe in 1620, though at first sight it appears completely medieval. The remarkable interior has box pews and a two-decker pulpit left behind by the Age of Reason. There are 17th- and 18th-century Crewe family monuments, including work by the Christmas brothers (Gerard, John and Mathias) of the mid-17th century.

STOKE DOYLE † St Rumbold ★

1m/2km S.W. of Oundle
OS *TL026862* **GPS** *52.4647N, 0.4904W*

A rustic Georgian church of 1722–5 by an unknown artist, St Rumbold's retains its original pulpit, pews and font. Contemporary monuments, including a Rysbrack of c. 1714, sustain the atmosphere of the time.

TITCHMARSH † St Mary the Virgin

8m/13km E. of Kettering
OS *TL022798* **GPS** *52.4073N, 0.4990W*

A quaint unspoilt village church with a celebrated Perpendicular tower, curiously West Country in character, with coupled windows in the upper storey and profuse pinnacles. There are many Pickering family monuments; the parvise was originally the Pickering family pew. The poet John Dryden spent his early childhood here and loved to return in later years: he is commemorated on a painted panel in the N. transept.

TOWCESTER † St Lawrence

8m/12km S.W. of Northampton
OS *SP694487* **GPS** *52.1323N, 0.9874W*

This large ironstone church stands at the centre of the historic market town, a mixture of Early English, Decorated and Perpendicular. A 15th-century chest tomb bears an effigy of Archdeacon Sponne, local benefactor and founder of the town's first grammar school; the head is restored,

S MARK
S LUKE
JUDAH

and underneath there is a particularly unsavoury depiction of his decomposed body – a macabre reminder of mortality. One of the earliest rectors, Benedetto Gaetano, later became Pope Boniface VIII in 1294; a remarkable circumstance.

WAKERLEY † St John the Baptist

8ml/13km N.E. of Corby
OS *SP956992* **GPS** *52.5824N, 0.5894W*
Churches Conservation Trust

An agreeable church on the slopes of the Welland Valley, the church has a prominent Decorated W. tower, with crocketed Perpendicular spire. Although the Perpendicular E. window, clerestories and N. porch suggest a late medieval building, the earlier origins of St John's are revealed in the chancel arch, which is Norman and a wondrous thing of knights and castles, monsters and foliate trails – delightful.

WARMINGTON
† St Mary the Blessed Virgin

3ml/4km N.E. of Oundle
OS *TL077910* **GPS** *52.5064N, 0.4141W*

The church is consistent Early English, and has a justly celebrated Northants. broach spire. The rib-vaulted nave ceiling is in timber throughout, a pleasant medieval conceit and a useful precedent for Victorians who wanted boarded ceilings for cheapness. Perpendicular woodwork includes a rood screen, restored painted pulpit and some bench-ends. There is a good Jacobean screen to the N. aisle.

WELLINGBOROUGH † All Hallows ★

Market place
OS *SP891679* **GPS** *52.3025N, 0.6935W*

A fine old town church, originally Norman – see the S. doorway – but mostly of 13th–15th-century construction. There are good Perpendicular roofs with bosses, screens and stalls with carved misericords. The important modern glass includes work by John Piper, Evie Hone and Patrick Reyntiens.

WELLINGBOROUGH
† St Mary the Virgin

Knox Road
OS *SP901680* **GPS** *52.3031N, 0.6796W*

Ninian Comper's superlative answer to the challenge of the incomparable Nene Valley churches is Perpendicular and fan-vaulted, with a bold tower, contrasting on the skyline with the spire of the medieval church but using the same traditional ironstone. The sumptuous furnishings combine all that is best in Comper's work – colour, scale and proportion – and exemplify his insistence that a church should be timeless and atmospheric. Building went on from 1908 to 1930, and the E. window of the N. chapel is a memorial to Lady Comper.

WICKEN † St John the Evangelist

5ml/8km N.E. of Buckingham
OS *SP745395* **GPS** *52.0489N, 0.9149W*

A remote and pretty village, with a Gothic church designed and built, according to the inscription, by Thomas Prowse, the local squire, in 1758–67. It's an odd design, with Frenchified capitals and plaster fan vaults, but redeemed by Sir Henry Cheere's excellent Rococo monument to the Hosiers, Squire Prowse's parents-in-law.

◁ **WELLINGBOROUGH: ALL HALLOWS** – *one of three John Piper windows in the church, this one in a vigorous figurative modernist style; his others here are more abstract*

NORTHUMBERLAND
AND TYNE & WEAR

The most northerly county of England, Northumberland covers the last seaward miles of the rivers Tyne and Tweed, the Cheviot and Pennine tops, and a 70-mile stretch of coast. Its south-eastern corner – carved out of Northumberland and County Durham as the metropolitan county of Tyne & Wear in 1974 – contains the remnants of a fine shipbuilding tradition and shades of past industrial glory. The conurbation is sullen and soiled, but contains, nevertheless, England's finest industrial city, Newcastle.

The industrial area of Tyne & Wear is less than a tenth of the two counties put together, yet carries 80% of the population. The modern county of Northumberland itself is the least populous county of all in relation to its size. It is by far the largest tract of deeply quiet country in England. There are only four small country towns – Morpeth, Berwick-upon-Tweed, Hexham and Alnwick – and fewer than half a dozen medium-sized villages, while the rest of the population is in scattered small villages, hamlets, farmhouses and isolated cottages.

The Northumberland coastline is lined with golden sands, dunes and basalt cliffs, with rocky islands off-shore. The coastal plain, where the mainline railway goes to Scotland, is stock-rearing and mixed-farming country. The hills (and all over the county you are conscious of the hills) are high, wide and lonely; not whale-backed and heathery (except the Pennines in the south-west) but mostly grassy hills, pitching into individual summits. The richly wooded valley of the Tyne lies in the gap between Cheviots and Pennines, while narrower dales run up into the folds of the hills. It is a very varied county; a very individual county.

Northumberland's history and frontier character are shown, inevitably, in its old buildings. In the Roman wall striding along the top of the crags above the waters of dark loughs; in scores of castles and pele towers, vast like Alnwick, small like Holy Island, ruined like Simonburn; in fortified rectories, as at Corbridge; and in semi-fortified churches, too, as at Edlingham. And in what has gone as well as in what remains. Bolam church, with its Saxon tower, standing in complete solitude where once was a town with a castle and 'two-hundred slated houses enclosing a green'. Bywell, also once a flourishing town, with, now, two churches, a castle, a medieval market cross, a hall, a vicarage, all in a wooded loop of the Tyne, and not another building in sight.

Old, wild, wide, quiet, remote. That is Northumberland beyond the conurbation.

◁ **BYWELL: ST ANDREW** – *the tower dates from c. 850 and is the best example of Saxon work in Northumberland; built for defence, its walls are about 15 feet thick*

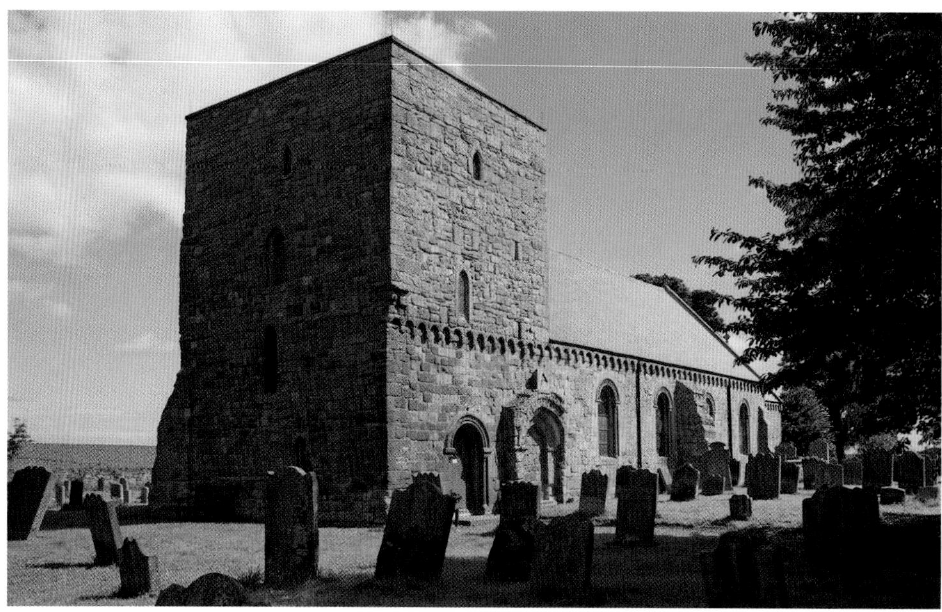

△ **ANCROFT: ST ANNE** – *the 14th-century pele tower was restored in 1886*

ALNWICK † St Michael ★★

Canongate
OS *NU183137* **GPS** *55.4169N, 1.7111W*

Beautifully situated on the top of an outcrop at the edge of this delightful town, the church embodies the most important 15th-century work in Northumberland. Aisles extend to the total length of the chancel, thus forming a plan rather square in character; the window tracery is fine Perpendicular. There are 14th-century effigies of great beauty, and fragments of 15th-century glass, including a delightful example of a Pelican in her Piety, signifying selfless love of one's young. The only intrusion is the suspended ceilings; plagued with rain-water leaks and repaired frequently, they now cut through the apex of the E. windows.

ANCROFT † St Anne

5m/8km S. of Berwick-upon-Tweed
OS *NU002451* **GPS** *55.7001N, 1.9980W*

In a long abandoned village setting, the Norman nave's S. wall with corbel table and decayed but important doorway are the only original parts of the nave and chancel. The remainder is a Victorian Romanesque restoration, save for the fortress-like 14th-century Pele tower, set at the W. end.

BAMBURGH † St Aidan ★

14m/22km N. of Alnwick
OS *NU178349* **GPS** *55.6080N, 1.7182W*

On a windblown coastal site, the church is a 12th- to 14th-century structure, with a 13th-century crypt beneath the chancel, sadly not accessible to the casual visitor. The N. transept was made into a chantry in the 14th century and is now known as St Oswald's Chapel. The reredos was installed at the end of the 19th century and is a fine example of carving in Caen stone, depicting Northumbrian figures, principally St Aidan and St Oswald. The churchyard monument to Grace Darling, a local heroine who in 1838 rescued 13 shipwrecked people, replaces the early effigy, which was moved into the church in 1885.

BERWICK-UPON-TWEED
† Holy Trinity

Off Parade
OS *NU000531* **GPS** *55.7721N, 2.0010W*

A mixed Gothic and Classical building of considerable architectural interest. It was built by mason J. Young of London in 1648–52, a rare piece of church building during the time of Cromwell's Commonwealth. Inside is

Eyemouth
0
10 miles
0
10 km
A6112
A1
A6105
BERWICK-UPON-TWEED
A6105
Norham
Ancroft
A6112
A698
Holy Island
Coldstream
Carham
Ford
A6089
A698
KELSO
Bamburgh
A699
A1
Kirknewton
Wooler
Chillingham
SCOTLAND
Old Bewick
Rock
JEDBURGH
A68
Whittingham
ALNWICK
Edlingham
A1068
A6088
A697
Warkworth
Amble
A68
Rothbury
Brinkburn
A1
A1068
Otterburn
NORTHUMBERLAND
Newbiggin-by-the-Sea
Bothal
Kirkwhelpington
Mitford
MORPETH
Bolam
Bedlington
A189
Blyth
Thockrington
A696
Cramlington
A68
Seaton
Simonburn
Ponteland
A1
Whitley Bay
Cullercoats
A6079
Tynemouth
Heddon-on-the-Wall
Gosforth
NEWCASTLE UPON TYNE
A69
Corbridge
Newburn
HEXHAM
Ovingham
A69
Haltwhistle
Bywell
Jarrow
TYNE & WEAR
Roker
A689
Monkwearmouth
A68
SUNDERLAND
A686
A692
Blanchland
Houghton le Spring
Alston
A691
A1(M)
A182
DURHAM
A68
DURHAM
CUMBRIA
A689
A181

△ **BAMBURGH: ST AIDAN** – *the site has been a place of worship since 635, when King Oswald called St Aidan from Iona here to establish Christianity at the heart of his kingdom of Northumbria*

a 17th-century gallery and pulpit with tester; the reredos is an early design by Lutyens. The lettering on one or two small brass plates of 18th-century date is worth noting.

BLANCHLAND † St Mary the Virgin

9m/15km S. of Hexham
OS *NY966504* **GPS** *54.8484N, 2.0541W*

Set in an 18th-century village of great charm by the River Derwent, the church has a fine tower and an unusual L-plan remodelled from the ruins of a 13th-century Premonstratensian foundation. The 19th-century wooden screens are intrusive, which is a shame, as the whole interior has a stately, spacious feel.

BOLAM † St Andrew ★★

6m/10km S.W. of Morpeth
OS *NZ092826* **GPS** *55.1377N, 1.8565W*

The church is beautifully set in the midst of undulating parkland, near the site of an abandoned village. The Saxon tower is well proportioned, and the Norman nave and S. aisle are very appealing, the S. arcade being formed of late Norman quatrefoil piers. A 14th-century chapel forms the E. end of the S. aisle, in which is the recumbent effigy of a knight, Sir Robert de Reymes of Aydon and Shortflatt, and interesting medieval grave slabs. Extraordinary that such a quiet, secluded and peaceful church should be only a half-hour car journey from Newcastle.

BOTHAL † St Andrew ★

3m/4km E. of Morpeth
OS *NZ239866* **GPS** *55.1733N, 1.6249W*

This is a 13th- to 14th-century church in a most beautiful setting. The nave and S. aisle are plain, but with great charm. There are extensive fragments of medieval glass in situ: one tracery light contains a magnificent rose. There are good 17th-century altar rails and a 16th-century alabaster table-tomb of Ralph, Lord Ogle, and his Lady.

BRINKBURN
† Priory Church of St Peter and St Paul ★★

8m/13km N.W. of Morpeth
OS *NZ115983* **GPS** *55.2789N, 1.8190W*

If it were not for the late Georgian and Victorian remodelling of the former conventual buildings of this Augustinian foundation, one could be forgiven for thinking that one was in France. Set near the banks of the

△ **BOLAM: ST ANDREW** – *the effigy of Sir Robert de Reymes, d. 1324, who fought the Scots*

River Coquet in wooded countryside, this is a complete late 12th-century structure, resurrected from ruin by Cadogan Hodgson Cadogan in 1858. The long round-headed and lancet windows under steep-pitched tiled roofs, the 19th-century wheel window in the gable and tower barely higher than the main parts of the abbey roof have a distinctly Continental feel. The only medieval monuments are a fine cross slab with an inscription to Prior William, suffragan Bishop of Durham, d. 1484, a few plain slabs and the font. The grisaille window, south of the presbytery, is by Austin, incorporating fragments of original glass; other windows are by Wailes and Clayton and Bell.

BYWELL † St Andrew ★

4m/6km S.E. of Corbridge
OS *NZ048614* **GPS** *54.9481N, 1.9260W*
Churches Conservation Trust

Why two parish churches (see also St Peter's below) should be sited within a stone's throw from each other is a mystery, but both churches have an individual charm that complements the other. The setting is exquisite for both, a wooded site on the edge of the River Tyne. St Andrew's tower is Saxon, the best in the county and perhaps beyond; square, unbuttressed, with short-and-long quoins and small round-headed windows. The nave and chancel are 13th-century, and the Victorian restoration was unobtrusive. There is stained glass by Wailes: the Victorian grocer and tea dealer turned stained glass designer is buried nearby, in St Peter's churchyard. Both inside and outside is a collection of medieval grave slabs, thought to be the best in Tynedale.

BYWELL † St Peter ★★

4m/6km S.E. of Corbridge
OS *NZ049614* **GPS** *54.9475N, 1.9246W*

St Peter's is the more complete Saxon of the two churches, with a high narrow nave, and Saxon windows in the N. wall. The tower was improved by the Normans, and was later made defensive, its only access being a small door a ladder's length from the ground. The 13th-century Norman enlargement included the chancel, with three elegant Early English lancet windows at the E. end. The 14th-century chantry chapel has good Reticulated window tracery, and in the churchyard is a multitude of interesting headstones and tombs. 'Life: how short', one of them ruefully reflects.

CARHAM † St Cuthbert

3m/5km S.W. of Coldstream
OS *NT797384* **GPS** *55.6389N, 2.3238W*

Carham, right on the England/Scotland border, is a hamlet contained within a curve of the River Tweed. The church itself is plain – built in the late 18th century in more or less Early English style. The tower was added in 1890. St Cuthbert's is a church to visit for its setting – the broad sweep of meadows running down to the Tweed is the essence of scenes that inspired the Picturesque movement.

BOLAM: ST ANDREW – *the church narrowly missed destruction in the Second World War, when a bomb fell on the chapel without exploding; the German pilot visited 60 years later to apologise* ▷

△ **CARHAM: ST CUTHBERT** – *on the south bank of the Tweed, the 18th-century Carham church is a landmark on the English–Scottish border, near the site of the Battle of Carham, c. 1018*

CHILLINGHAM † St Peter ★

4m/6km E. of Wooler
OS *NU062259* **GPS** *55.5273N, 1.9031W*

Sited on a gentle elevation amongst trees, this is a simple stone church whose origins are in the 12th century. Its chief interest is in the magnificent 15th-century tomb of Sir Ralph Grey, in the S. chapel. The font and cover date from 1670, and there are 19th-century box pews and a 17th-century pulpit. John Smith refurbished the chancel in 1967.

CORBRIDGE † St Andrew ★

3m/4km E. of Hexham
OS *NY988644* **GPS** *54.9745N, 2.0197W*

In the centre of the historic country town, St Andrew's stands alongside a splendidly preserved 14th-century vicar's pele tower, built of Roman stone. The tower is 8th-century Saxon, and the main body of the church is 13th-century, with good lancet windows. The doorway is Norman, and the large tower arch is thought to have come complete from the nearby Roman camp. A 19th-century restoration was harsh and overzealous, however.

CULLERCOATS † St George ★

Between Tynemouth and Whitley Bay
OS *NZ364708* **GPS** *55.0307N, 1.4314W*

A stately and beautiful ashlar church, it was built at the expense of the 6th Duke of Northumberland in French Gothic style by J. L. Pearson, 1882–4. The polygonal apse abuts a lofty tower with broach spire – 180 ft in height – that became an essential landmark for fishermen and major shipping alike. The interior has dignified rib-vaulting and glass by Kempe in a strong range of colours. The marauding north-easterly winter winds ensure a constant struggle to maintain this fine church's fabric.

EDLINGHAM † St John the Baptist

5m/8km S.W. of Alnwick
OS *NU114091* **GPS** *55.3760N, 1.8209W*

In rugged moorland country near the ruined Edlingham Castle, the squat early 14th-century W. tower of St John's gives the church the appearance of a military blockhouse. Within the tower are traces of late Saxon and Early Norman stonework. The nave and chancel dwindle into insignificance in comparison. Inside are plastered walls and

△ **FORD: ST MICHAEL AND ALL ANGELS** – *the typical Northumbrian-pattern bellcote is two-tiered, with paired lancet bell openings on the lower tier and a single lancet opening on the upper tier*

a four-bay Norman arcade. The chancel arch is 12th-century, and the E. window is Romanesque. A tomb recess on the S. wall of the nave holds a fragment of a pre-Conquest cross.

FORD † St Michael and All Angels

7m/11km N.W. of Wooler
OS *NT944374* **GPS** *55.6302N, 2.0894W*

Close to the beautiful grounds of a castle in open countryside with views to the Cheviots, the church is 13th-century, though much overlaid by John Dobson's 1853 restoration. There is a typical Northumbrian-pattern Early English bellcote. Inside, at the back of the church, are some interesting slabs set into the floor. One shows a Northumbrian bagpipe, with the drone worked into the form of a cross.

HALTWHISTLE
† Church of the Holy Cross

14m/22km W. of Hexham
OS *NY707640* **GPS** *54.9700N, 2.4583W*

This is a very complete 13th-century towerless church in a pleasant setting on a slope in the midst of a country town. The plastered interior contains a stepped sedilia and monuments of the Blenkinsopps and Thirwells, and is lit throughout by tall, slender lancet windows. The glass is attributed to Morris & Co., and there is a pleasing carved alabaster reredos of unknown origin.

HEDDON-ON-THE-WALL
† St Andrew ★

7m/11km W. of Newcastle
OS *NZ133668* **GPS** *54.9964N, 1.7923W*

The church is set on a mound in the centre of the village. It is a heavily restored Norman church with late Saxon S.E. nave quoins, an impressive 12th-century vaulted sanctuary and fine zigzag chancel arch.

HEXHAM † St Andrew ★★

Beaumont Street
OS *NY935641* **GPS** *54.9715N, 2.1025W*

Of great historical importance, founded by St Wilfrid in c. 675, the Saxon crypt and apse survive intact; the latter is barrel-vaulted, of great austerity and grandeur, with many re-used stones bearing Roman inscriptions. Sacked by the Danes in 876, Hexham was eventually refounded as an Augustinian

priory in 1113. What can be seen today is the 12th- to 13th-century chancel and transepts and the good nave of 1907 by Temple Moore. The interior is rich in medieval features: the unique monks' night staircase; the Saxon Frith stool; 15th-century wooden pulpit; painted screen of Thomas Smithson, prior in 1491–1524; 15th-century stalls and misericords; a chantry chapel; and many effigies. At the E. end of the N. choir aisle is a chapel to St Wilfrid, created in 1996.

HOLY ISLAND † St Mary the Virgin ★★

Off coast 12m/19km S.E. of Berwick-upon-Tweed
OS *NU125417* **GPS** *55.6693N, 1.8018W*

The church itself is modest, robustly built to withstand the elements on this windswept island; a mix of Norman and Early English, with a long chancel and 18th-century bellcote. The wild setting is all, the heart of early Christianity in Britain. It was here that St Aidan came in 635 at the invitation of King Oswald to found his monastery, and the remains of the re-founded 12th-century Norman priory are next to the church.

JARROW † St Paul

5m/8km E. of Gateshead
OS *NZ338652* **GPS** *54.9804N, 1.4722W*

This is the church where Bede worshipped, preserving a curious flavour of romance as it looks out over the mudflats to the ships passing up and down the River Tyne. Originally it was two churches, joined into one in the late 11th century by the addition of a crossing tower. Above the chancel arch is the dedication stone, dated 685, of the original Saxon basilica, which was destroyed in the 18th century. The smaller Saxon church, built of Roman stone from nearby Wallsend, now forms the chancel. The 19th-century nave by George Gilbert Scott is unremarkeable, and the N. aisle has been turned into a museum. There are good carved stones and a medieval chair in the chancel, a small window with rearranged fragments of Saxon glass, and glass based on the Jarrow Cross – now in the N. aisle – by John Piper. South of the church are the remains of the Benedictine monastery refounded by the Normans in 1074 on the site of Bede's original monastery.

KIRKNEWTON † St Gregory ★

5m/8km W. of Wooler
OS *NT913302* **GPS** *55.5659N, 2.1388W*

This village church is in the centre of Kirknewton, a village set in a traditional shepherds' landscape at the foot of the Cheviots. The chancel and S. transept are late 15th-century. A rustic but beautiful late Saxon stone carving depicting the Adoration of the Magi is set in the N. wall of the chancel arch. In the graveyard are World War II graves of airmen from nearby Milfield, and a mausoleum to the Davidson family, chandlers to Horation Nelson. John Dobson of Newcastle did the restoration in 1860.

KIRKWHELPINGTON
† St Bartholomew

9m/15km S.E. of Otterburn
OS *NY996844* **GPS** *55.1541N, 2.0070W*

Set in a small village at the foot of vast moorland, St Bartholomew's is a lovely old church – long and low, with a squat tower. The chancel and nave are 13th-century, with 15th-century alterations. The blocked tower arch has scalloped capitals and chevron ornamentation. The trefoiled sedilia has slender 13th-century shafts, and there is splendid lettering on 18th-century ledgers in the chancel floor.

MITFORD † St Mary Magdalene ★

2m/3km W. of Morpeth
OS *NZ168856* **GPS** *55.1645N, 1.7363W*

In a valley close by the ruins of Mitford Castle: this a beautiful site, with the 19th-century broach spire of the church standing above the surrounding trees. The 13th-century chancel is long and distinguished with shafted lancets, and the N. arcade is Norman – all rebuilt after destruction by King John in 1215. Fires in the 14th and 18th centuries took their toll, and in the 19th century the church was enlarged and restored under the auspices of the local squire.

MONKWEARMOUTH
† St Peter with St Cuthbert ★

St Peter's Way, 1m/2km N. of Sunderland centre
OS *NZ401577* **GPS** *54.9131N, 1.3749W*

Like St Paul's in Jarrow, this is the church of a Saxon monastery situated at the mouth of

◁ **HEDDON-ON-THE-WALL: ST ANDREW** – *the Saxon foundations of the church date back to c. 680; the sanctuary with its fine zigzag decoration is Norman*

a river, now somewhat stranded in enclosed parkland and walled off from the river by the modern buildings of Sunderland University and a business centre. Nearby lampposts intone automatic warnings about theft for the unwary motorist. Originally built by Benedict Biscop in 674, only the W. wall and the tower remain; the tower was altered and raised many times between the 7th and 11th centuries. In the porch under the tower, Saxon baluster shafts are still in their original position. Inside the church is an exceptionally fine collection of Saxon carved stones.

MORPETH † St Mary ★

Town centre

OS *NZ197850* **GPS** *55.1597N, 1.6922W*

A good example of 13th- and 14th-century work, so little seen in Northumberland, with Early English arcades and fine stone vaulting under the tower – the oldest part. A charming carving of an angelic musician can be seen on the S. side of the chancel. The E. Jesse window is 14th-century and one of the finest features of the church: it was restored by Wailes and is the most complete medieval glazing in the county. Outside is the burial place of Emily Wilding Davidson, heroine of the Suffragette movement who died under the hooves of the King's horse at the 1913 Epsom Derby.

NEWBIGGIN-BY-THE-SEA
† St Bartholomew

1m/2km W. of Blanchland

OS *NZ317880* **GPS** *55.1855N, 1.5023W*

The dramatic headland site at the sea's edge tells of the significance of St Bartholomew's as a maritime landmark and refuge for storm-tossed mariners. Remote from the town, it supersedes an early Anglo-Saxon chapel. Like many coastal Northumberland churches, it is long and low, with a sturdy tower and spire. Mostly early 13th-century – see the E. arcade piers with nail-head decoration – the chancel and spire are Decorated.

NEWBURN † St Michael and All Angels ★

5m/8km W. of Newcastle

OS *NZ166653* **GPS** *54.9826N, 1.7409W*

This is a fine church of rubble stonework that has been stripped of a good deal of 19th-century fussiness, but is still plastered. The tower is Norman, the N. and S. aisles and chancel 13th-century.

NEWCASTLE UPON TYNE
† St Andrew

Newgate Street

OS *NZ245644* **GPS** *54.9738N, 1.6181W*

The S. porch of St Andrew's is early Georgian. Inside is a 12th-century chancel arch and 12th-century nave arcading, and a good Royal Arms of George III. The font cover is 15th-century and of elaborate design.

NEWCASTLE UPON TYNE
† St George ★

Osborne Road, Jesmond

OS *NZ255667* **GPS** *54.9951N, 1.6027W*

By T. R. Spence, 1888: a fascinating blend of 13th-century and Italian Renaissance styles with much high-quality Arts and Crafts decoration. The internal W. wall is entirely covered in Caen stone tracery, with a bronze of St George by Spence. The chancel is lined with mosaic.

NEWCASTLE UPON TYNE
† St John the Baptist

Grainger Street

OS *NZ247640* **GPS** *54.9701N, 1.6157W*

This church is largely 14th- to 15th-century, with a prominent Perpendicular tower. Inside is a 15th-century font cover and impressive 17th-century pulpit. There are fragments of medieval glass, chief among them a 14th-century Shield of Arms of Newcastle.

NORHAM † St Cuthbert ★

7m/11km S.W. of Berwick-upon-Tweed

OS *NT896474* **GPS** *55.7200N, 2.1656W*

St Cuthbert's stands at the far end of the town from the magnificent Norman castle. Of reddish stone, it has a Norman chancel and chancel arch, and a S. arcade with massive stonework for a church of this scale. There is a 14th-century effigy and a Stuart Royal Arms.

JARROW: ST PAUL – *remains of the monastery where the Anglo-Saxon scholar Bede lived until his death in 735 are juxtaposed with the façade of the later tower* ▷

△ **OVINGHAM: ST MARY** – *a slab in the porch commemorates the local engraver Thomas Bewick, d. 1828, whose illustrated books of birds and animals are regarded as the best of their genre*

OLD BEWICK

† Chapel of the Holy Trinity

6ml/10km S.E. of Wooler

OS *NU068221* **GPS** *55.4931N, 1.8939W*

Set in remote and beautiful hill country, the small Norman apsidal chancel and nave are relatively complete in fabric and entirely complete in atmosphere.

OVINGHAM † St Mary the Virgin ★★

10m/16km W. of Newcastle upon Tyne

OS *NZ084637* **GPS** *54.9679N, 1.8688W*

This handsome church near a delightful vicarage has a good pre-Conquest tower and magnificent 13th-century nave, transepts and chancel arch, well carved with zigzags. The chancel is vaulted with tall lancets, giving strong vertical emphasis. It is set in a quiet churchyard screened by trees.

PONTELAND † St Mary the Virgin ★

7m/11km N.W. of Newcastle

OS *NZ165729* **GPS** *55.0508N, 1.7419W*

Although there is 12th-century work in the tower, it is the 13th-century N. transept that commands special attention, with deeply splayed, long lancet windows. The 14th-century windows in the chancel contain many fragments of contemporary glass, chiefly heraldic. The beautiful 14th-century font is undecorated. There is plain lead glazing of great beauty, c. 1861, and Royal Arms of the third Hanoverian period. A most satisfying interior.

ROCK † St Philip & St James

5m/8km N. of Alnwick

OS *NU202202* **GPS** *55.4755N, 1.6817W*

In a parkland setting, this is a good small Norman church with a fine mid-12th-century shafted chancel arch, which has suffered from 19th-century additions.

ROKER † St Andrew

District of Sunderland N. of harbour

OS *NZ404593* **GPS** *54.9275N, 1.3710W*

St Andrew's was built in 1906–7, a massive and original design by E. S. Prior, carried out in local stone. The fittings and ornaments are in Arts and Crafts style, and the Burne-Jones tapestry was woven by William Morris & Co. There is a Morris carpet, and altar ornaments, processional cross, choirstalls, pulpit and lectern by E. W. Gimson. The tablets are by Eric Gill, most of the glass by H. A. Payne. A bold and imaginative experiment which has triumphantly succeeded.

ROTHBURY † All Saints

11m/18km S.W. of Alnwick

OS *NU057016* **GPS** *55.3090N, 1.9106W*

Set in a delightful Northumbrian town amongst hills, All Saints has a medieval 13th-century chancel and transepts, but was much rebuilt in 1850. The font is important, with a bowl of 1664 and shaft made from a splendid carved Saxon cross shaft, c. 800.

SEATON † Our Lady ★★

4m/6km S. of Blyth

OS *NZ321764* **GPS** *55.0812N, 1.4973W*

Set in the grounds of Vanbrugh's house is this small Norman church of great beauty, with zigzag chancel arch and chancel extension of c. 1330. The W. porch was added in 1895; inside are 14th-century effigies and eight medieval stone shields of outstanding merit.

SIMONBURN † St Mungo ★

7m/11km N.W. of Hexham

OS *NY870735* **GPS** *55.0564N, 2.2037W*

St Mungo's is set in a beautiful village in the North Tyne Valley, in an enormous parish containing a vast area of moorland. Mostly 13th-century, the long chancel has a double piscina and windows by Anthony Salvin, 1860. There are numerous fragments of early stonework, and a monument of 1625 to Cuthbert Ridley, rector.

THOCKRINGTON † St Aidan ★

9m/15km N. of Hexham

OS *NY957789* **GPS** *55.1049N, 2.0685W*

St Aidan's stands on a hillock in open, sweeping country, a small Norman church with medieval alterations. Its 13th-century chancel has exquisite proportions and a vaulted ceiling.

TYNEMOUTH † Christ Church ★

6m/10km N.E. of Newcastle upon Tyne

OS *NZ353686* **GPS** *55.0115N, 1.4481W*

This is a fine Classical town church, mainly from 1792; the chancel and apse were added in 1869. Built of ashlar, it has a splendid square tower and a dignified plastered interior with galleries. The wooden font is original, while clear glass of the traditional Northumbrian pattern now replaces some of the 19th-century stained glass. The organ is now in the W. gallery.

WARKWORTH † St Lawrence ★★

6m/10km S.E. of Alnwick

OS *NU246061* **GPS** *55.3491N, 1.6122W*

The church and castle are set at opposite ends of the long, sloping main street of a once strategic coastal town. St Lawrence's is a large and relatively complete Norman building with remarkable vaulted chancel, (regrettably scraped), the ribs enriched with zigzag carving. The chancel arch has shafts and scalloped capitals, and the nave is Norman. The Norman tower supports a 14th-century broach spire, whilst the S. aisle has Perpendicular windows and a Decorated arcade. The porch, with parvise, is 15th-century, and inside are exquisite 17th-century wrought-iron communion rails, fragments of 15th-century glass in the E. window, and Royal Arms of James II.

WHITTINGHAM † St Bartholomew

6m/10km N. of Rothbury

OS *NU066119* **GPS** *55.4014N, 1.8969W*

The tower has Pre-Conquest work and a massive arch leading to the nave. The medieval work elsewhere was much altered by John Green in 1840; the plain lead glazing is his best work.

NOTTINGHAMSHIRE

Nottinghamshire, south of the Trent, along the Fosse Way, is of a piece with Leicestershire, with gentle hills, ridged meadows, and bramble and dog-rose hedges; many of the villages here have shrunk during the past two centuries, and some of the churches have been shorn of aisles. The western part of the county lies on coal and is well populated. Some of the colliery villages are nicely grouped on hill-tops around new or enlarged churches, but in the main the scenery is unattractive, apart from a few square miles in the upper Erewash Valley and the pure medieval landscape that contains the ruins of Beauvale Priory.

On the limestone of the north-west, both buildings and landscape are more austere, with dry-stone walls in the Derbyshire manner and even a quite precipitous gorge at Creswell Crags. The mining settlements to the north of Worksop are scarcely distinguishable from their neighbours in South Yorkshire. The 'Carrs' of the north-east are rich fens. In the east, along the Lincolnshire border, the Trent flows through a fairly rich mixed agricultural landscape, which is dominated by the distant west front of Lincoln Cathedral and traversed by the old Great North Road, now the A1, and its attendant East Coast railway; the houses here are of good brick, and many of them are roofed with pantiles. Enormous power stations have been put here, heated by coal from the west of the county and cooled by Trent water.

The centre of the county, between Mansfield, Worksop and Tuxford, has lost the vitality of the old colliery villages, built to serve the needs of a once-thriving coal-mining industry. In its landscape and in the character and dialect of its people, Nottinghamshire belongs partly to the Midlands and partly to the North. What unity it has comes from the town of Nottingham, whose undisputed supremacy within the county (since the 9th century, when Nottingham was a Danish Viking military district), contrasts markedly with the far shakier authority of its neighbours, Lincoln, Derby and York. The agricultural shows at Wollaton Park have given way now to pop concerts, dog shows and the Nottingham Motor Show, and the annual Goose Fair still brings in folk from wide and far. It was an industrial town, but textiles and lace making have long given way to pharmaceuticals, science, biotechnology and service industries.

North of Nottingham, the small towns of Mansfield, Sutton, Worksop and Retford played a similar role in the life of the county; but they are infinitely poorer than Nottingham, both in their architecture and in their entertainments. Newark, in the south-east, is a wholly admirable town; its castle and its Civil War fortifications are impressive. There are few large churches in the county. Southwell Minster is, of course, in a

◁ **NEWARK: ST MARY MAGDALENE** – *As well as magnificent screens, the panelled and painted ceilings are a particular delight of this church*

DONCASTER
S. YORKSHIRE
Bawtry
Blyth
Carlton-in-Lindrick
Retford
WORKSOP
Clumber Park
Milton
West Markham
East Markham
Staveley
CHESTERFIELD
DERBYSHIRE
Egmanton
Laxton
Ollerton
Ossington
South Scarle
Sutton in Ashfield
MANSFIELD
Holme
Winkburn
Kirkby in Ashfield
NOTTINGHAMSHIRE
Coddington
Southwell
NEWARK-ON-TRENT
Papplewick
Hawton
Hucknall
Elston
Sibthorpe
Lambley
Daybrook
LINCOLNSH
Car Colston
Ilkeston
Strelley
NOTTINGHAM
Stapleford
Beeston
Clifton
Long Eaton
GRANTHAM
Ratcliffe-on-Soar
Kingston-on-Soar
Wysall
Upper Broughton
Willoughby-on-the-Wolds
Rempstone
Normanton-on-Soar
LOUGHBOROUGH
LEICESTERSHIRE
MELTON MOWBRAY
0
5 miles
0
5 km
A614
A161
A159
A631
A1(M)
A156
A620
A57
A1
A60
A1500
A638
A619
A632
A6075
A61
A1133
A46
A616
A38
A617
A17
M1
A611
A612
A608
A52
A453
A606
A6006

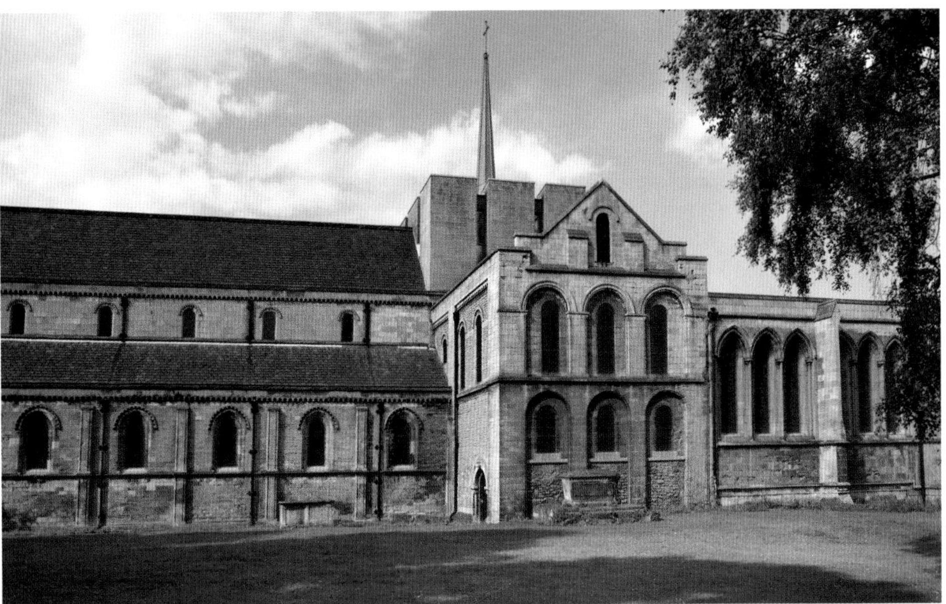

△ **WORKSOP: ST MARY AND ST CUTHBERT** – *an intriguing melding of the centuries*

class of its own, and the only two parish churches of impressive size are St Mary, Nottingham, and St Mary Magdalene, Newark. Worksop and Blyth are in the separate category of 'monastic remains' and are easily the two finest churches in the north of the county.

The small churches are often well-sited, and the Nottinghamshire village of red-brick and pantiled cottages grouped around its grey church makes an attractive picture. Spires punctuate the rolling landscape south of the Trent, but in the North the medieval churches are normally low-towered, squat and rather square. There are no grand and urbane Classical churches of the Derby Cathedral type, merely a few quite good 18th-century rectangles, put up to replace, as modestly as possible, decayed medieval structures. But there are two examples of this period, Papplewick and Ossington, which have a very individual right to attention. Victorian building and rebuilding were extensive; after the grey-brick 'regulation' churches of the early 19th century, red brick was widely used. The new colliery towns grew quickly, and churches were put up quickly to meet the need; few are worthy of attention. Of the famous Victorian architects only three are worthily represented: Pearson by the splendidly lavish St Paul's, Daybrook, Bodley by Clumber and Sneinton at St Alban. Comper's inspired restoration work can be seen in various places. Of 20th-century churches there is a distinguished example at Wollaton Park, Nottingham by Cecil Howitt, the architect who designed parts of the University and the City Hall.

Good fittings are disappointingly meagre. The best fragments of medieval alabaster are now in the Castle Museum in Nottingham. There are few spectacular wall-paintings. In fact the sober 'workaday' atmosphere of the Midlands is faithfully reproduced in its places of worship; and we find, therefore, a homely, unspectacular beauty, which is very appealing.

BLYTH † St Mary and St Martin ★

5m/8km N.E. of Worksop

OS *SK624872* **GPS** *53.3788N, 1.0634W*

A priory fragment, whose once-beautiful village green setting is somewhat marred now by nearby modern housing, is visited principally for its rugged late 11th-century nave. The 15th-century screen acts as reredos for the altar, with painted lower panels depicting various saints. Medieval paintings were uncovered by Bentley on the E. wall. The 1987 restoration of the Last Judgement has revealed a very large and nearly complete medieval mural of great interest. Outside, the extraordinary design of the shortened E. end is due to its having been used as a menagerie for the hall in the 18th century.

CAR COLSTON † St Mary

8m/13km E. of Nottingham

OS *SK720430* **GPS** *52.9798N, 0.9279W*

St Mary's is distinctive for its splendid mid-14th-century chancel, five-light E. window with cusped flowing tracery, grand sedilia and piscina on the Hawton model, with nodding ogee arches. The handsome altar rail of 1732 has a curved central section. There is a plain Norman font, and an early 16th-century wooden pillar alms box. Dr Robert Thoroton, 1623–78, antiquarian, was buried here, and his stone coffin can be seen inside the church.

CARLTON-IN-LINDRICK

† St John the Evangelist ★

3m/4km N. of Worksop

OS *SK588839* **GPS** *53.3487N, 1.1178W*

The church has a fine late Saxon tower with Perpendicular belfry stage. Much Norman work survives, particularly in the chancel and nave arcade. In the Becket Chapel is a small 15th-century Nottingham alabaster reredos.

CLIFTON † St Mary the Virgin

Suburb of Nottingham 2m/3km S. of centre

OS *SK541348* **GPS** *52.9080N, 1.1969W*

The interior of this mostly 14th-century cruciform church has been unfortunately scraped and 'reordered', but in the N. transept is a magnificent collection of tombs of the Clifton family, from the 15th century to the present day. The reredos, formerly at Kelham College, is by Bodley.

CLUMBER PARK † St Mary the Virgin

In grounds of park, 4m/6km S.E. of Worksop

OS *SK626746* **GPS** *53.2648N, 1.0618W*

National Trust

By Bodley, 1886–9, this is a grand work in a sumptuously pious setting. On a cruciform plan and in his favourite flowing Decorated style, it is one of Bodley's best. There is excellent glass by Bodley's friend Kempe, and a superb alabaster altar and chancel screens. The woodwork, alas, was the effort of the Rev. Geldart, commissioned after the 7th Duke of Newcastle fell out with Bodley over the accounts.

CODDINGTON † All Saints

2m/3km E. of Newark-on-Trent

OS *SK834544* **GPS** *53.0811N, 0.7550W*

Bodley's hand can be seen here too: he and William Morris restored the church in the 1860s, which is most notable for the Morris stained glass and painted ceiling panels. Bodley also designed the oak screen.

DAYBROOK † St Paul

3m/5km N. of Nottingham

OS *SK579451* **GPS** *53.0006N, 1.1377W*

Founded by Charles Seely and John Robinson, and opened in 1896, St Paul's is a magnificent example of Neo-Gothic in the Decorated style by J. L. Pearson. Anglo-Catholic in atmosphere, the interior has fine Italian marble mosaics, a carved reredos of the Last Supper and good stained-glass windows, whose angels' faces are modelled on the founders' children.

EAST MARKHAM

† St John the Baptist ★

4m/7km S. of Retford

OS *SK743726* **GPS** *53.2458N, 0.8877W*

This is the county's Thaxted (see Essex chapter), though not so vast, so famous or so complete. It is Perpendicular, clerestoried, and large for a village – so much so that Betjeman referred to it as the 'Cathedral of the Trent Valley'. The Comper E. window and wide high altar are in complete accord; there is a small grey chamber organ, tapers on brackets and enough antiquity in wood, brass and glass to fascinate the historically minded.

EGMANTON † St Mary ★★

7m/11km S. of Retford
OS *SK735689* **GPS** *53.2122N, 0.8994W*

The modest, porchless exterior gives no hint of the pious gaiety within. Here, sponsored by the Duke of Newcastle and executed by Comper, is Anglo-Catholic romanticism at its best. The canopied rood screen dominates the interior, and the colour is repeated on organ casing, font cover and openwork pulpit. Beyond the screen is less colour and more mystery: the candled shrine of Our Lady of Egmanton and, in front of Comper's E. window, a hanging pyx. The antiquarian will admire the Norman doorway and font, the 17th-century altar and the fragments of old glass, but these are commonplace; the Comper shrine is superlative.

ELSTON † Elston Chapel

5m/8km S.W. of Newark-on-Trent
OS *SK761482* **GPS** *53.0259N, 0.8658W*
Churches Conservation Trust

This ancient building, once a chapel of ease for nearby St Oswald's, stands in a field and is approached up a lane. The bulk of the building is 14th- and 15th-century; the Norman doorway has carved zigzag work, and the interior is fitted out with Georgian box pews, pulpit, reader's desk and simple W. gallery. Recent restorations have revealed a series of Georgian wall paintings – animals, texts and Royal Arms.

HAWTON † All Saints ★

2m/3km S. of Newark-on-Trent
OS *SK788511* **GPS** *53.0517N, 0.8254W*

Seen from the W., across the open unhedged fields, this church appears as it must have done 500 years ago. Its 15th-century tower is noble and has an original carved and inscribed door. Within, the simple old pews in the nave are well spaced; but the eye is led to the chancel, with its curvilinear E. window and superb 14th-century stonework. The Easter Sepulchre is one of the best in the country. Its figures are slightly mutilated, but the detailed decorations are magnificently abundant and various. This, and the sedilia, are of a deep golden stone; and the similarity to Southwell, both in material and intricate workmanship, is obvious.

HOLME † St Giles ★

3m/4km N. of Newark-on-Trent
OS *SK802591* **GPS** *53.1231N, 0.8018W*

A small, rather inaccessible church by the Trent, which richly rewards the finder. The fine Perpendicular S. aisle and two-storey porch were built by John Barton, d. 1491, Merchant of the Staple of Calais. There is simple old woodwork in the screen and benches; the altar rails are Jacobean, and the roof 18th-century. The church was rescued in the 1930s by Nevil Truman. He and Barton are both commemorated in the E. window, which contains medieval glass, carefully re-assembled by Nevil Truman.

KINGSTON-ON-SOAR † St Winifrid ★

6m/10km N. of Loughborough
OS *SK501277* **GPS** *52.8449N, 1.2563W*

In an estate village setting, St Winifrid's was originally known as St Wilfrid's. The re-dedication took place after R. Creed's 1900 rebuilding. The most striking feature is the remarkable Babington Chantry of 1540: a bizarre canopied edifice adorned with the family rebus of babes in tuns, a structure so exotic that the architecture critic Sacheverell Sitwell (1897–1988) likened it to a Portuguese Indian temple.

LAMBLEY † Holy Trinity

5m/8km N.E. of Nottingham
OS *SK631454* **GPS** *53.0025N, 1.0609W*

An imposing mid-15th-century Perpendicular church built by Ralph, Lord Cromwell, Lord High Treasurer of England, whose purse, symbol of his office, adorns the E. wall. It is one of the most complete Perpendicular survivals in the county.

LAXTON † St Michael the Archangel

4m/6km E. of Ollerton
OS *SK722670* **GPS** *53.1958N, 0.9207W*

Famous as the village with open fields on the medieval model, Ollerton has a church to match, with a notable late-Perpendicular

△ **NEWARK: ST MARY MAGDALENE** – *the richly carved choir, surrounded by canopied screens*

clerestory, a dated screen of 1532 and, in the chancel, the only medieval wooden effigy left in the county.

MILTON † All Saints / Milton Mausoleum

5m/8km S. of Retford
OS *SK715730* **GPS** *53.2493N, 0.9297W*
Churches Conservation Trust

By Sir Robert Smirke, 1832, the building was designed for the 4th Duke of Newcastle as a mausoleum. The nave is used by the parish, but the E. end and transepts are currently closed to the public. The mausoleum was built to a Latin cross plan, with pedimented roof and Doric pillars, the whole surmounted by a dome resting on an octagonal colonnaded drum. One of Smirke's best buildings, and a striking if incongruous sight from the nearby A1.

NEWARK † St Mary Magdalene ★★

Between Wilson Street and Appleton Gate
OS *SK799539* **GPS** *53.0766N, 0.8081W*

A town church in the grand manner, largely 15th-century, with transepts, aisles, nave and choir, and a splendid landmark of a spire. Within, one sees thick poppy heads up to the black medieval screen, and the pews in the transepts look pulpitward. But all is different beyond the screen. Comper's great gilded reredos of 1937 shines triumphantly above the high altar and gives a needed focus to the whole interior; around it are brassily furnished chantry chapels, and beyond it three good altars. The E. window of the S. aisle is a gay medieval jumble of glass, and the two painted panels of the Dance of Death are alone worth a long journey to see. In the W. wall of the S. transept is the 1939–45 War Memorial, a Pietà by R. Kiddey; good modern work of the post-Eric Gill era. Notice, too, the old library in the S. parvise, and the dim, effective oratory in the N. porch.

NORMANTON-ON-SOAR
† St James the Great

2m/3km N.W. of Loughborough
OS *SK518229* **GPS** *52.8013N, 1.2320W*

Charmingly situated beside the River Soar, and known locally as the boatman's church, this is a splendid, largely 13th-century cruciform church with lofty central broach spire. The interior is scraped but retains a plaster Royal Arms of Charles II and two 17th-century monuments.

NOTTINGHAM † St Mary ★★

High Pavement, by Lace Market
OS *SK576396* **GPS** *52.9512N, 1.1430W*

This is a huge cruciform Perpendicular church in crumbling stone, stifled by the buildings of the Lace Market, in the oldest part of the old town. The splendid bronze doors in the S. porch, by Henry Wilson, 1904, lead one to the vast, quiet, multi-windowed interior. It is all impressively homogeneous in structure and furnishing. The latter is nearly all good Victorian with Bodley as a pervasive influence; the stained glass is encyclopaedic in its range of designers. A large, colourful Prince Consort memorial window of 1863 is partly blocked by the towering gilded Bodley reredos of 1885; and the two wings of this reredos can never be closed because of the English 'four poster' altar erected beneath them! Fragments of old glass and alabaster may be found in the S. choir aisle. Other details are the medieval vestry, the incomplete rood screen, the wall-monuments, as thick as stamps in an album, but less colourful, the rows of tattered flags and the spirited wood-carved Lion and Unicorn of 1710. The S. chapel is by Temple Moore, 1912.

NOTTINGHAM † St Mary Wollaton

Wollaton Park
OS *SK547391* **GPS** *52.9469N, 1.1866W*

Built in 1939 by T. Cecil Howitt, St Mary's is a good red-brick church by Nottingham's most distinguished architect of the inter-war period. Single-cell and tall, it has prominent gables and tall, narrow round-headed windows to the sides. The interior has fair-faced brick with traditional wooden fittings, and a panelled roof with stencilled decoration.

NOTTINGHAM † St Stephen ★

Newark Street, Sneinton
OS *SK584396* **GPS** *52.9510N, 1.1316W*

'Bodleyism' at its most complete, although in fact nearly all by C. G. Hare, 1912, who rebuilt the Rickman church of 1839, retaining the central tower and crossing. The proportions are good, and the main axial vista leads from a tall-canopied font through the coloured rood to the gorgeous Oberammergau high altar – so-named for the florid style of woodcarving and decoration seen at Oberammergau in Bavaria. But not all of St Stephen's beauties are apparent at first glance: each transept is differently and effectively treated; the gold and green organ casing stands on a screen between S. transept and crossing. There are modern Continental statues and a vigorous set of Stations of the Cross, 1926. The 15th-century oak stalls, from St Mary's, Nottingham, are beautifully arranged in the choir; there are eight misericords.

OSSINGTON † Holy Rood

7m/11km N.W. of Newark-on-Trent
OS *SK759651* **GPS** *53.1781N, 0.8657W*

Built by John Carr of York, 1782, Holy Rood is a model of Classical restraint in its W. tower with cupola and triple arches dividing nave and sanctuary. The barrel organ is by Thomas Robson, 1840, and there are elegant Denison statues by Nollekens. The sylvan setting is a delight in itself.

PAPPLEWICK † St James ★

1m/2km N.E. of Hucknall
OS *SK545515* **GPS** *53.0583N, 1.1872W*

This is the county's best example of Georgian Gothic; the tower is 14th-century, otherwise all is of 1795, with Y-traceried windows, battlements, pinnacles and quatrefoils. We enter the light and elegant interior through a porch as tall as the nave. A gallery on slender clustered shafts extends over the N. side of the nave, and the E. window has glowing figures of Hope and Faith by F. Eginton. There is a good walnut pulpit with Gothic panels, a small marble font and Royal Arms of George III.

RATCLIFFE-ON-SOAR † Holy Trinity

6m/10km N.W. of Loughborough
OS *SK494288* **GPS** *52.8553N, 1.2666W*

Menaced by the power station, but mercifully screened by trees, the church has a doughty

13th-century W. tower and a great wealth of 16th–17th-century alabaster Sacheverell tombs.

REMPSTONE † All Saints
4m/6km N.E. of Loughborough
OS *SK575245* **GPS** *52.8150N, 1.1478W*

All Saints is a small church of 1773 – a rare survival in these parts, with big round-headed windows, pinnacled tower and interior retaining two-decker pulpit and box pews. There are good slate tombstones in the churchyard.

SIBTHORPE † St Peter
6m/10km S. of Newark-on-Trent
OS *SK763454* **GPS** *53.0006N, 0.8631W*

St Peter's has a glorious 14th-century chancel with Easter Sepulchre and plain 18th-century nave, with medieval windows re-inserted. There is an impressive alabaster tomb chest of Edward Burnell, d. 1589.

SOUTH SCARLE † St Helen
7m/11km N.E. of Newark-on-Trent
OS *SK848640* **GPS** *53.1666N, 0.7326W*

The church has a splendid 12th-century N. arcade with leaves and scallops, Early English chancel, and Perpendicular W. tower, nave roof and screen. A 'vamping horn' – an 18th-century megaphone – was discovered in the roof space of the N. aisle during conversion works. There are several medieval pews with lozenge finials.

SOUTHWELL † Southwell Minster ★★
6m/10km W. of Newark-on-Trent
OS *SK701538* **GPS** *53.0768N, 0.9540W*

This fine building, both cathedral and parochial, is the jewel of the county and arguably one of England's most outstanding church buildings. Seen from a distance, the twin 'Rhenish' spires of the W. towers give the impression that one is in northern France. Romanesque and Early English are the dominant themes, with a grand Decorated pulpitum and a 13th-century chapter house with 'star' vaulted roof. Finely detailed stone carving features throughout – Green Men and botanically-accurate foliage – and elsewhere in the church can be seen a good collection of masons' marks. Nothing jars at Southwell, and its lofty spaces inspire awe and reverence.

STRELLEY † All Saints
4m/6km W. of Nottingham
OS *SK506420* **GPS** *52.9738N, 1.2472W*

Apart from the base of the tower, 13th-century, and the clerestory, 15th-century, the whole was built by Sir Sampson Strelley in the mid-14th century. His fine alabaster tomb is in the chancel, separated from the nave by the best ancient screen in the county, which doubtless he provided. Strelley Hall, 18th-century, but with the medieval house of the Strelleys incorporated, stands next door.

UPPER BROUGHTON † St Luke ★
6m/10km N.W. of Melton Mowbray
OS *SK683262* **GPS** *52.8293N, 0.9871W*

In a delightful setting, with views over the Vale of Belvoir, St Luke's is a 13th-century and later church of warm sandstone, with a chancel by S. S. Teulon, 1855. In the churchyard is an unusually good collection of early 18th-century slate gravestones.

WEST MARKHAM † All Saints
5m/8km S. of Retford
OS *SK721726* **GPS** *53.2463N, 0.9203W*

All Saints is a charming and simply restored small church with weatherboarded bell-turret and some Saxon masonry. The Transitional S. doorway has its original door; there is an earth floor at the W. end, and a good 12th-century font.

WILLOUGHBY-ON-THE-WOLDS
† St Mary and All Saints ★
8m/12km N.W. of Melton Mowbray
OS *SK633254* **GPS** *52.8226N, 1.0608W*

An impressive 13th- and 14th-century church with broach spire. In the N. transept are the notable 14th–15th-century Willoughby tombs, with effigies wonderfully preserved. A brass plaque commemorates a 'souldier for King Charles the First', killed at the Battle of Willoughby Field, 1648.

WINKBURN † St John of Jerusalem
6m/10km N.W. of Newark-on-Trent
OS *SK711583* **GPS** *53.1172N, 0.9380W*

A 12th–13th-century church with a stocky Norman, diagonally buttressed tower and delightful interior. It contains an almost

△ **WORKSOP: ST MARY AND ST CUTHBERT** – *a new choir and sanctuary for this former priory church was built by Laurence King in 1974*

complete set of 17th–18th-century furnishings: box pews, communion rail, pulpit and a rare 17th-century arched screen with plaster tympanum bearing the Arms of George III. There is a good collection of Burnell family monuments.

WORKSOP † St Mary and St Cuthbert ★

Priorswell Road
OS *SK590789* **GPS** *53.3039N, 1.1157W*

The twin-towered W. front of the former priory with its fine doorway is the feature of the exterior. Within, the long and narrow nine-bay nave is late Norman and has a lofty triforium. Rebuilding has been drastic, continuous and interesting, culminating in the controversial chancel and flèche by Laurence King, 1970–4. Scott's E. window is now in the N. transept, where his coloured reredos looks like an uncomfortable but commodious sedilia. There are many good small objects of devotion, including paintings. The rebuilt Lady Chapel, by Sir Harold Breakspear, 1922, though simple in design, has a mysterious peace, unlike the regretted high altar sanctuary of 1970–4, which is cheap and hideous.

WYSALL † Holy Trinity ★

6m/10km N.E. of Loughborough
OS *SK604271* **GPS** *52.8383N, 1.1044W*

A Norman and late Decorated church, it has important 15th-century fittings of pulpit, screen, stalls and a rare altar canopy in the chancel roof. There is a splendid alabaster monument to Hugh Armstrong, d. 1572, and his wife Marye, and an unusual painted wooden memorial of 1689.

OXFORDSHIRE

Oxfordshire is the most diversified of all inland counties. In the north it is the Midlands, with hints of oncoming Birmingham when one sees the pinkish brick Victorian and Edwardian villas in the Banbury district, bringing a 19th-century industrial atmosphere into the medieval and Georgian brown ironstone of the older groups of buildings. Twentieth-century industry turns Midlands-ward too: the motor industry at Cowley had noisy, long links with Coventry and Brum. In the west, Oxon. is the Cotswolds, with that perfect limestone town of Burford, which strangers fancy is in Gloucestershire.

The City and University are largely a limestone Cotswold town, at any rate in their surviving ancient streets. The south-eastern part of the county, slipped between Berkshire and Buckinghamshire, is Chiltern scenery, near-suburban, with beech woods and steep chalk hills and scenario-writers' hide-outs in valleys, and pleasure-seekers' haunts by the broad Thames. The capital of this part of the county is the old red-brick town of Henley, and Watlington is its isolated poor relation.

There is the flat Upper Thames country of willows, limestone churches and cottages. Around Stanton Harcourt and Eynsham this scenery is full of Matthew Arnold and by Bampton and Kelmscott it is full of William Morris. There is the wide inland marsh of Otmoor, once all aeroplanes and bombs and now a nature reserve, the remote medieval park of Wychwood, and the picturesque planted park of Blenheim, where the palace spreads its curious outline above the lake. There is a remote mid-Oxon. associated with the books of Flora Thompson and with the landscaped village of Great Tew. Then, in the north-west corner, with Northamptonshire and Warwickshire near, is a land that looks like a medieval manuscript scene, with little hills and golden-brown churches and cottages.

The finest old churches are not in the chalky southern end but where the quarries are in the north and west, whence the stone could be floated down the Thames and its tributaries to Oxford and Dorchester.

The great medieval churches of the county – Adderbury, Bloxham, St Mary the Virgin in Oxford, Horley, Thame, Dorchester, Stanton Harcourt, Burford, and Cropredy – are all Midland in character, with the exception of the complete late-Norman church of Iffley, which is on its own. The Gloucestershire masons influenced the Perpendicular work which is abundant in the county. But Oxfordshire is also a county of great houses: Blenheim, Ditchley, Middleton Stoney, Nuneham, Shirburn, Stonor, Thame Park, and smaller stone manor houses like Kelmscott, Yarnton, Chastleton, Garsington. In fact, most

◁ **EWELME: ST MARY THE VIRGIN** – *angels line the stone canopy over the tomb of Alice, Duchess of Suffolk, and throng the remarkable wooden ceiling*

0
5 miles
0
5 km
WARWICKSHIRE
NORTHAMP-
TONSHIRE
OXFORDSHIRE
BUCKINGHAMSHI
BERKSHIRE
WILTSHIRE
Cropredy
Great Bourton
Horley
Hanwell
Shipston-on-Stour
BANBURY
Broughton
Bloxham
Adderbury
Hook Norton
South Newington
BUCKINGHAM
Moreton-in-Marsh
Great Rollright
Little Rollright
Great Tew
Chipping Norton
Stow-on-the-Wold
Bicester
Idbury
Shorthampton
Tackley
Milton-under-Wychwood
Merton
Combe
Charlton on Otmoor
Kidlington
North Leigh
Yarnton
Woodeaton
Burford
Widford
Minster Lovell
Witney
Stanton St John
Carterton
Stanton Harcourt
Forest Hill
OXFORD
Waterperry
Thame
Rycote
Iffley
Cuddesdon
Garsington
Langford
Chinnor
Besselsleigh
Kelmscott
Sunningwell
Wheatfield
Kingston Bagpuize
Tubney
Radley
Nuneham Courteney
Lewknor
ABINGDON
Chalgrove
Faringdon
Charney Bassett
Baulking
Sutton Courtenay
Dorchester
Ewelme
Swyncombe
Shrivenham
Uffington
Sparsholt
Wantage
Wallingford
Didcot
North Moreton
West Hendred
Compton Beauchamp
Childrey
Kingston Lisle
Ashbury
Blewbury
Henley-on-Thames
READING
A423
A361
A3400
A422
A429
A3400
A361
A44
A4260
A43
A413
A436
A4421
M40
A361
A44
A424
A4095
A34
A41
A4095
A40
A418
A361
A40
A412
A40
A4095
A415
A40
A34
A329
A417
A415
A338
A415
A420
A417
A4130
A417
A338
A34
A329
A346
M4
A4

of the stone villages have gabled manor houses. The churches, therefore, often have the look of family chapels, and in some instances, not content with grand Baroque monuments or a new aisle, a tasteful squire would wholly rebuild or refurbish a church in Classical style, such as the case by Rudge at Wheatfield in the 18th century. The best of all private chapels, excluding the college chapels in Oxford itself, is that at Rycote, with its 17th-century furniture.

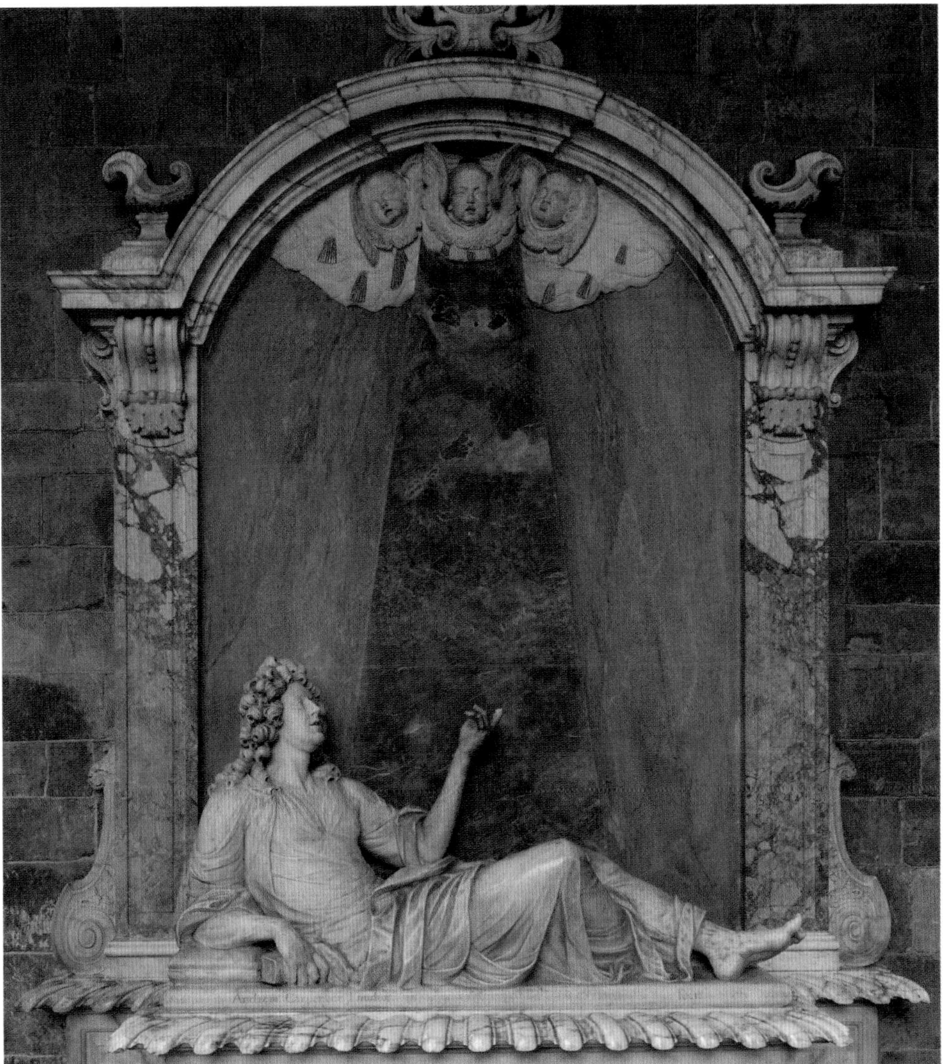

△ **BLOXHAM: ST MARY** – *memorial to Sir John Thornycroft, d. 1725, in the Milcombe Chapel. Sir John angered the Bloxham parishioners when he blocked the E. window with his family memorials; this one was moved to its present position by G. E. Street in the 1860s*

△ **ADDERBURY: ST MARY** – *a Green Man, carved into the bench-end of a pew*

ABINGDON † St Helen

6m/10km S. of Oxford
OS *SU496967* **GPS** *51.6676N, 1.2828W*

Set among 17th- and 18th-century brick almshouses by the Thames, this is a large town church with a spire and four aisles flanking the nave, so that it is broader than it is long. There are decidedly graceful arcades and the whole building is mostly 14th-, 15th- and 16th-century Perpendicular, with an older, 13th-century tower topped off with a rebuilt spire of 1888. In the N. aisle chapel is a distinguished and unique painted roof of the late 14th century. The font cover and pulpit are 17th-century, and there is a Hawkins monument, 1782, by John Hickey. The N.W. corner has a late Georgian stained and enamelled glass window; the reredos is by G. F. Bodley, 1897.

ADDERBURY † St Mary the Virgin ★

3m/4km S. of Banbury
OS *SP470353* **GPS** *52.0148N, 1.3153W*

Adderbury is a large hilly village of golden ironstone Georgian houses and old cottages, with a magnificent Decorated and Perpendicular church to match. The imaginative corbel table of musicians on the N. wall, plus the lovely late Perpendicular chancel in the style of the Divinity Schools at Oxford, and the tower, spire and windows make its exterior about the finest in the county. The inside is rather too restored, but retains a screen and brasses.

ASHBURY † St Mary the Virgin

7m/11km E. of Swindon
OS *SU265849* **GPS** *51.5625N, 1.6186W*

St Mary's is Norman in origin, with good 13th-century work, including fine tracery. The N. door has good dogtooth and chevron carving. The excellent two-storey early 15th-century porch has delicate star vaulting, and inside are Perpendicular arcades and a King-post roof. Three well preserved medieval brasses are set in the chancel floor. The Rev. Thomas Stock held the first Sunday School here in 1777.

BANBURY † St Mary

Off Horse Fair
OS *SP454405* **GPS** *52.0615N, 1.3391W*

The decayed medieval church was blown up with gunpowder in 1790 and replaced by the cool Classicism of S. P. Cockerell. The striking exterior has Tuscan columns, green copper roofs and a round tower. The centrally planned galleried interior was spoiled by the addition of a chancel by Sir A. Blomfield in 1873. The generally good stained glass illustrates the parables on the ground floor and the life of Christ on the gallery level.

BAULKING † St Nicholas

4m/6km S.E. of Faringdon
OS *SU317907* **GPS** *51.6143N, 1.5432W*

Small, rustic and unspoilt, the church overlooks a goose green. It is mainly 13th-century, with a good nave roof, surprisingly dated 1708, and a Jacobean pulpit. In 1988 some 14th-century wall-paintings were uncovered and restored.

BESSELSLEIGH † St Lawrence

4m/6km N.W. of Abingdon
OS *SP456010* **GPS** *51.7065N, 1.3410W*

St Lawrence's is set in a tree-shaded park; Cotswold style and small. It retains all its

△ **BANBURY: ST MARY** *stained glass by an unknown artist to a scheme by Blomfield, c. 1873*

box pews and original seating and ritual arrangements. The mid-17th-century font is interesting, with a garlanded bowl on a rough carved round stem.

BLEWBURY † St Michael and All Angels (St Michael the Archangel)

3m/4km S. of Didcot
OS *SU531859* **GPS** *51.5696N, 1.2346W*

A picturesque village of brick and cob and thatch among willows and orchards at the foot of the Downs, whose large cruciform church with W. tower is in various medieval styles. The church is spacious, light and impressive with pre-Perpendicular work predominating. The 15th-century octagonal font bowl curiously has one blank facet.

BLOXHAM † St Mary ★★

4m/6km S.W. of Banbury
OS *SP430356* **GPS** *52.0179N, 1.3746W*

On a hill above a golden ironstone village with thatched cottages stands this grand church whose 14th-century spire is visible for miles. There is a superb 13th-century W. doorway, with Last Judgement presided over by Christ and the angels. The spacious aisled and clerestoried interior was harshly restored by G. E. Street, but there is a splendid painted 15th-century screen, and the Milcombe

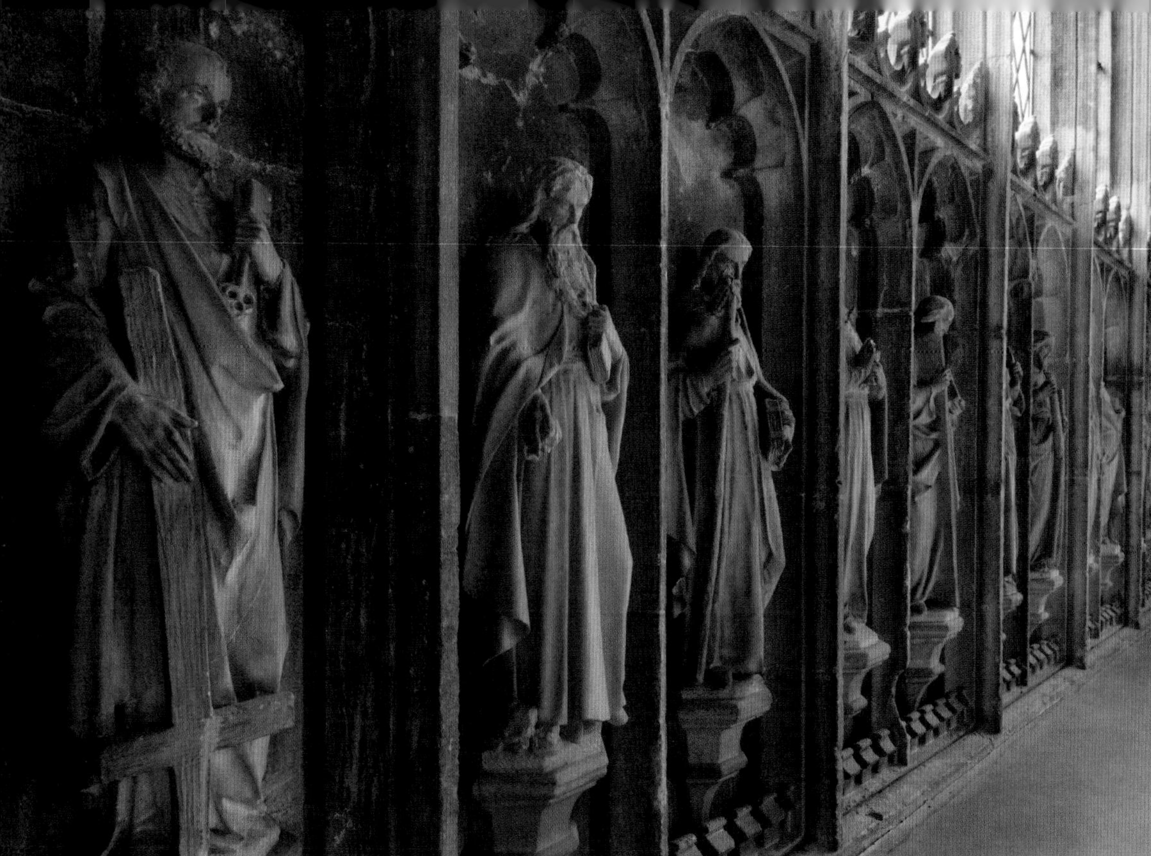

△ **BLOXHAM: ST MARY** – *St Peter, left, holding the keys to Heaven, alongside other saints and their traditional symbols, set into niches in the Milcombe Chapel*

Chapel on the S. side is a delight, with wall-paintings, including one of an unknown saint. The Thornycroft monument of 1725 is by A. Carpenter.

BROUGHTON † St Mary

3m/4km S.W. of Banbury
OS *SP418383* **GPS** *52.0417N, 1.3911W*

In a park setting beside the castle, St Mary's is a high-quality church of c.1300, illustrating well the transition from Early English to Decorated. There is a rare Decorated stone screen, a series of monuments, 14th-century wall-paintings and a Crucifixion on a column.

BURFORD † St John the Baptist ★★

7m/11km W. of Witney
OS *SP253124* **GPS** *51.8097N, 1.6342W*

Burford is a 'model old English town' (J. Piper) of Cotswold stone, whose cathedral-like church, a testament to the wealth of the wool trade, is set at the bottom of the hill beside the River Windrush. The church with spire and tower and parvised porch is cruciform, of various dates with chapels added, the interior effect being largely 15th-century. The Tanfield monument, in St Katherine's Chapel, is a grand affair. The W. window has good glass by Kempe. Edmund Harman, barber and surgeon to Henry VIII, erected his own monument in the church, on which he commemorates, among other things, the 16 children his wife bore him. The churchyard is rich in sculptured table-tombs, Georgian and earlier.

CHALGROVE † St Mary the Virgin ★

9m/14km S.E. of Oxford
OS *SU637965* **GPS** *51.6642N, 1.0802W*

The 14th-century chancel has Reticulated tracery and one of the most extensive series of wall-paintings in the county. Of 14th-century date, they include a Jesse tree, the Resurrection and, particularly noteworthy, the life of the Virgin.

△ **BROUGHTON: ST MARY** – *in the grounds of the Broughton Castle estate, the church was built with soft Northamptonshire marle stone c. 1300 and restored in 1877–80*

CHARLTON-ON-OTMOOR

† St Mary the Virgin

4m/6km S. of Bicester

OS *SP561158* **GPS** *51.8382N, 1.1858W*

The church is mostly Decorated, with a Perpendicular nave roof and clerestory. The sumptuous early 16th-century screen was repainted by the Victorians; there is some 13th-century glass, with Royal and other Arms.

CHILDREY † St Mary the Virgin

2m/3km W. of Wantage

OS *SU360877* **GPS** *51.5879N, 1.4817W*

A low cruciform church of Norman origin, but now mainly Perpendicular and Decorated, St Mary's has a fine relief-carved 12th-century lead font. The screen – greatly restored in the 19th century – and chancel stalls are from the 15th century. Amongst the brasses are two very fine ones to William Fyndene, d. 1444, and his wife. In the S. chantry is a good monument to William Fettiplace, d. 1528, and his wife.

CHINNOR † St Andrew

15m/24km E. of Oxford

OS *SP756008* **GPS** *51.7016N, 0.9063W*

A knapped flint church, almost all 13th- and early 14th-century, St Andrew's has important stained glass in the N. and S. chancel windows. The rood screen is 14th-century, with quatrefoil tracery at the top. The church was restored c. 1858 by E. Banks of Wolverhampton under the supervision of G. E. Street and J. H. Parker.

CHIPPING NORTON † St Mary ★★

13m/21km S.W. of Banbury

OS *SP311273* **GPS** *51.9438N, 1.5479W*

This is a fine Cotswold wool church, mostly 14th-century, pleasantly situated at the lower edge of this hillside town. The vaulted hexagonal S. porch has good ceiling bosses, but the church's chief glory is the nave, rebuilt in the mid-15th-century by John Smyth of Canterbury. Soaring pillars, modelled on those at Canterbury Cathedral, lead up to an almost continuous clerestory that floods the nave with light.

Dorcas

△ **COMPTON BEAUCHAMP: ST SWITHUN** – *a striking example of a church built with chalk*

COMBE † St Lawrence the Martyr
5m/8km N.E. of Witney
OS *SP413158* **GPS** *51.8400N, 1.4007W*

The church is in an unspoiled village adjacent to the Blenheim Estate. It was rebuilt in 1395 and has been little altered since; there is an unusual 14th-century polygonal stone pulpit on a ribbed stem, stained glass and extensive 15th-century wall-paintings, uncovered in 1894. The Doom includes among the damned a wanton offering herself to a devil!

COMPTON BEAUCHAMP
† St Swithun ★
6m/10km E. of Swindon
OS *SU279869* **GPS** *51.5804N, 1.5984W*

A small whitewashed medieval church built of chalk, St Swithun stands at the foot of the Downs and beside a moated manor house, a beautiful situation. The uplifting interior is decorated with vines painted c. 1900 by Lydia Lawrence of the Kyrle Society; Anthony Baynes and T. L. B. Huskinson added the insects, birds and bats in the 1960s. There is a gilded altar, a 15th-century font with a mid-20th-century canopy by Martin Travers, a rich rood and other furnishings, also mostly by Travers.

CROPREDY † St Mary the Virgin
4m/6km N. of Banbury
OS *SP468466* **GPS** *52.1163N, 1.3165W*

The S. aisle of St Mary's has traces of 13th-century work, but most of the church is large, stately Decorated and Perpendicular, and built of warm ironstone. It retains a late 15th-century polygonal pulpit and brass eagle lectern. Over the chancel arch are fragments of a painted Last Judgement.

CUDDESDON † All Saints
6m/10km S.E. of Oxford
OS *SP600030* **GPS** *51.7230N, 1.1316W*

This is a handsome cruciform church of c. 1180. The W. door is particularly fine, with carved lozenges, dogtooth and early stiff-leaf capitals, and the crossing has good chevron carving and water-leaf capitals. Street restored the church in 1851–3, and there is glass by Hardman and Kempe.

◁ **COMPTON BEAUCHAMP: ST SWITHUN** – *the vines were painted on the chancel walls c.1900 by Lydia Lawrence; the birds were added c.1967 by Anthony Baynes and T.L.B. Huskinson*

DORCHESTER † St Peter and St Paul ★

6m/10km S.E. of Abingdon

OS *SU579941* **GPS** *51.6436N, 1.1642W*

The abbey church, approached through a Butterfield lych gate, is splendid in its proportions and detail. Mostly Decorated, it has earlier and later parts. The Jesse window, some of its stonework imitating tree branches, has its original figures in glass and stone, and there is much old glass in other windows too. Among the tombs is the justly celebrated stone effigy of a late 13th-century knight, which has inspired many sculptors. Clayton and Bell restored much of the abbey's medieval wall-painting, and in 2006 a large but rather nebulous painting of St Christopher was uncovered in the S. Birinus Chapel. William Butterfield and Sir George Gilbert Scott carried out major restoration of the roofs and chancel in the mid-19th century.

EWELME † St Mary the Virgin ★

10m/16km S.E. of Abingdon

OS *SU646914* **GPS** *51.6178N, 1.0675W*

In a Chiltern foothills flint and brick village where watercress grows, this is a castellated 15th-century stone and flint church, patched with brick, rising above old almshouses. It is all distinguished late Perpendicular, not village building. Inside, the effect is East Anglian, possibly inspired by Alice de la Pole, 1st Duchess of Suffolk, whose extraordinary tomb is set between the chancel and N. chapel – fine alabaster, with a macabre representation of a cadaver set below. Comper sensitively restored the S. chapel in 1902–3, and Jerome K. Jerome, author of *Three Men in a Boat*, is buried in the churchyard.

FARINGDON † All Saints

15m/24km W. of Abingdon

OS *SU288957* **GPS** *51.6596N, 1.5840W*

All Saints is a large Norman and Early English church with Transitional carvings and iron work on the S. door dating from c.1200. The nave arcades and crossing arches have good stiff-leaf carved capitals. The church has an outstanding collection of funerary monuments: the Pye family in the N. chapel, and in the N. transept a table-top tomb to Sir Thomas Unton, d. 1533, and his wife, and an effigy of an Elizabethan woman, possibly Lady Dorothy Unton, wife of Sir Thomas Unton, d. 1547, whose tomb in the N. transept was partially destroyed during the Civil War.

FOREST HILL † St Nicholas

5m/8km E. of Oxford

OS *SP582075* **GPS** *51.7632N, 1.1576W*

A very pleasantly situated hilltop late Norman church with a massively buttressed W. bellcote: St Nicholas's was remodelled in the 13th century and restored in the 19th by various Victorian architects. Stencilled decoration can be seen in the spandrels of the N. arcade and above the chancel arch. The Tractarian furnishings and glass are by T. Willement. John Milton was married here to Marie Powell.

GARSINGTON † St Mary

5m/8km S.E. of Oxford

OS *SP580020* **GPS** *51.7139N, 1.1610W*

Another hilltop church, with splendid views from the churchyard over the Thames Valley. The W. tower is late Norman, and there is a Perpendicular timber S. porch and 15th-century screen reset in the tower arch. Joseph Clarke over-restored the church in 1849.

GREAT BOURTON † All Saints

3m/4km N. of Banbury

OS *SP456455* **GPS** *52.1062N, 1.3350W*

William White restored and altered this 13th-century church in 1863 after post-Reformation secular use. The chancel and W. wall are medieval, but the arcade, tiled floor and fittings are all White's. But the most important thing is his remarkable lych gate of 1882, replete with tall openwork timber bell-tower.

GREAT ROLLRIGHT † St Andrew ★

3m/4km N. of Chipping Norton

OS *SP326314* **GPS** *51.9810N, 1.5254W*

A small Norman church with Perpendicular tower and screen; the 12th-century S. doorway is enriched with zigzags and beak-heads, and the tympanum is of interest – rustic in execution, with a shrouded figure set among shields and zigzags. The 14th-century font is good, as is the medieval screen – although

△ **DORCHESTER: ST PETER AND ST PAUL** – *the famous 13th-century effigy of a knight in the act of drawing his sword, which is said to have influenced the sculptor Henry Moore*

over-enthusiastically repainted by the Victorians. Against the N. wall is the Batersby Brass, a 16th-century memorial to a former incumbent.

GREAT TEW † St Michael and All Angels

5m/8km E. of Chipping Norton
OS *SP399288* **GPS** *51.9569N, 1.4204W*

In a parkland setting beside a thatched village, St Michael's is a spacious 13th- and 14th-century church with Perpendicular W. tower and clerestory, 15th-century brasses and a nice Chantrey monument of 1829 to Mary Anne Boulton, set against the N. chancel wall.

HANWELL † St Peter

2m/3km N.W. of Banbury
OS *SP435435* **GPS** *52.0888N, 1.3655W*

The church, of orange ironstone, overlooks the site of Hanwell Castle and is best known for its lively rustic bestiary carvings on the corbel frieze outside and carved stone figures on the capitals in the nave. Similar work can be seen at Adderbury.

HOOK NORTON † St Peter

5m/8km N.E. of Chipping Norton
OS *SP355331* **GPS** *51.9955N, 1.4842W*

St Peter's occupies a commanding position at the centre of the village. The spacious interior has an impressive Norman chancel and circular 11th-century font carved with Adam and Eve and Zodiac signs; 15th-century wall-paintings depict St Peter and St Paul. The village's first fire engine, not used since 1896, is housed here.

HORLEY † St Etheldreda ★

3m/4km N.W. of Banbury
OS *SP416439* **GPS** *52.0925N, 1.3930W*

Horley is a north Oxon. ironstone village, whose spacious church of various dates has been made distinguished by sympathetic modern furnishing and restoration; there are 15th-century wall-paintings of St Christopher and St Etheldreda, rather touched up; the rood loft and screen are by T. Lawrence Dale, 1949.

EWELME: ST MARY THE VIRGIN – *the finely carved alabaster figure of Alice de la Pole, d. 1475, her head on a cushion supported by delicate, elfish angels with very large feet* ▷

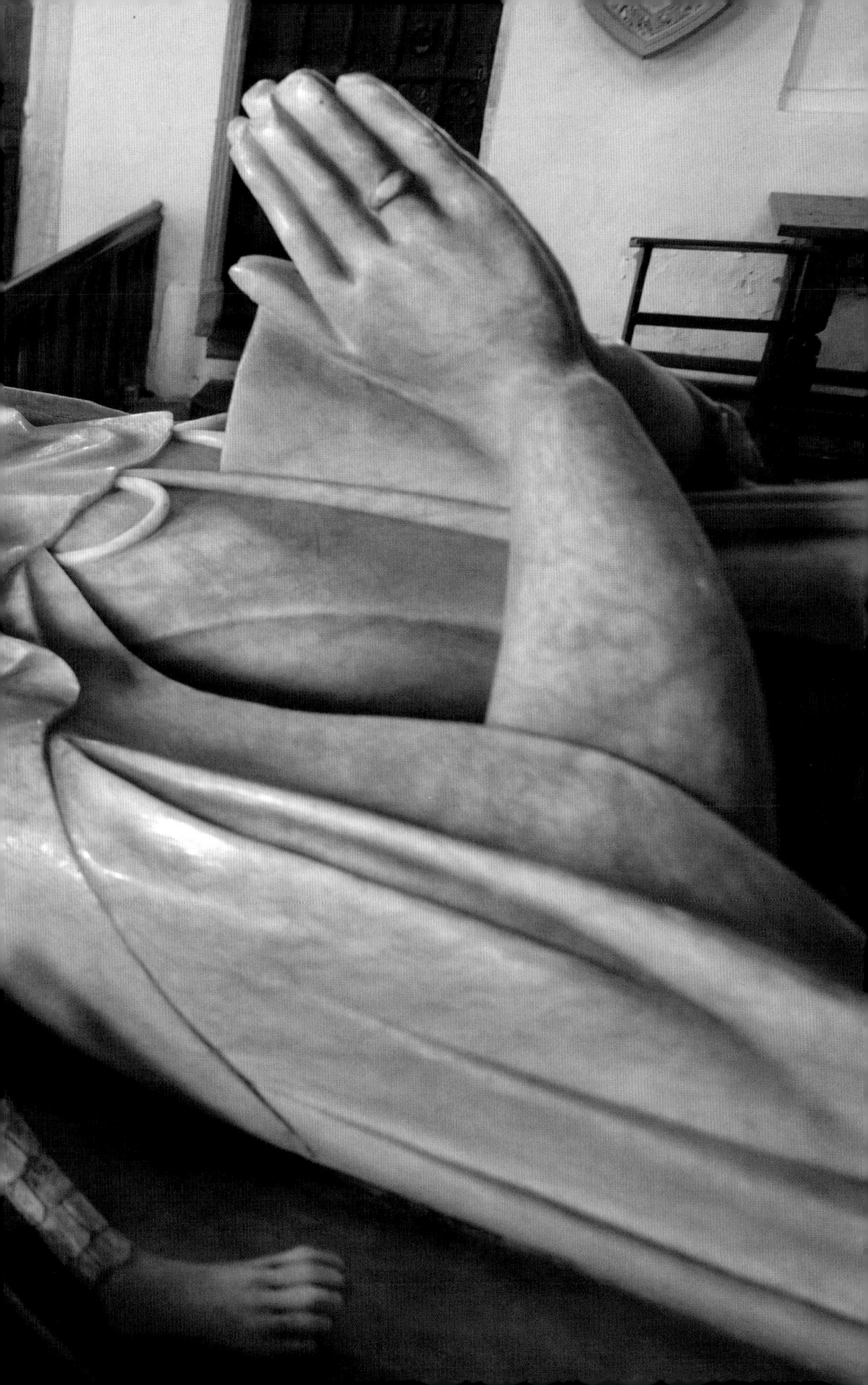

△ **EWELME: ST MARY THE VIRGIN** – *St John's Chapel, with the monogram IHS as a wall pattern, altar by Comper and four-light E. window using fragments of medieval glass*

IDBURY † St Nicholas

5m/8km S.E. of Stow-on-the-Wold

OS *SP236200* **GPS** *51.8784N, 1.6584W*

In a small village with splendid views, St Nicholas's has a fine reset Norman doorway with zigzags, chevrons and scallops; otherwise 14th-century and Perpendicular – but unfortunate Victorian woodwork.

IFFLEY † St Mary ★★

On Mill Lane in S.E. district of Oxford

OS *SP527034* **GPS** *51.7274N, 1.2382W*

A Romanesque, c. 1170, showpiece, and rightly so, within and without. The W. front is rich in beak-head and zigzag carving. The dark aisleless interior shows an E. view of two elaborate Norman arches with vaulting between, leading to a contrastingly light Early English vaulted E. end. Inside the Baptistry is a fine Piper window, inspired by an Elizabethan wall-painting at Shulbrede Abbey.

KELMSCOTT † St George ★

3m/5km N.W. of Faringdon

OS *SU249993* **GPS** *51.6925N, 1.6409W*

This charming rustic Norman and Early English church in the village is associated with William Morris, who did much to preserve the church; his tomb by Philip Webb is in the churchyard. In the N. chapel are fine late 13th-century wall-paintings – the Presentation, Adam and Eve, the Last Judgement and Cain and Abel, all depicted in red ochre.

KIDLINGTON † St Mary the Virgin

5m/8km N. of Oxford

OS *SP497148* **GPS** *51.8297N, 1.2799W*

Early English and Decorated cruciform church with a Perpendicular tower and octagonal spire known locally as 'Our Lady's Needle'. There is much reset medieval stained glass in the E. window and good 15th-century screens. The 13th-century choir stalls have misericords, and the desks in front of the stalls have re-used 14th-century carved oak bench-ends containing designs relating to the Bassett family.

LANGFORD † St Matthew ★★

4m/6km S.W. of Carterton

OS *SP249025* **GPS** *51.7209N, 1.6408W*

A striking example of a late Saxon/early Norman church, St Matthew's stands in a stone village in the flat, willowy Upper Thames region. This is a church on a grand scale, with a typically high Saxon nave and, over the S. porch, a Saxon carving of the Crucifixion. On the porch's E. wall is the Langford rood, a late Saxon carving of Christ in Majesty.

LEWKNOR † St Margaret

14m/22km S.E. of Oxford

OS *SU715976* **GPS** *51.6731N, 0.9664W*

A cruciform church of c. 1200, the chancel was handsomely rebuilt in the 14th century with crocketed canopies and much foliage. There are good 17th- and 18th-century monuments; the glass in the N.E. and S.E. chancel windows is by William Morris and was brought here from Llandaff. Blomfield restored the nave extensively in 1863.

LITTLE ROLLRIGHT † St Philip

2m/3km N.W. of Chipping Norton

OS *SP293301* **GPS** *51.9688N, 1.5741W*

This is a simple rustic church in a delightful and isolated setting. Its small square W. tower dates from 1617. Inside all is plain whitewash, with Perpendicular chancel windows and two good alabaster tombs.

MERTON
† St Swithin, Bishop of Winchester

3m/4km S. of Bicester

OS *SP577178* **GPS** *51.8560N, 1.1631W*

A grand Decorated church with Perpendicular additions and demolitions; the chancel carving is particularly fine, as are the elaborately carved 14th-century roof corbels. The Jacobean stem pulpit, the 17th-century stalls from Exeter College Chapel and the monuments are all interesting.

MILTON-UNDER-WYCHWOOD
† St Simon and St Jude

4m/6km N. of Burford

OS *SP264186* **GPS** *51.8661N, 1.6168W*

By G. E. Street, 1854, this is an imposing village church in the Early Decorated style, with slender bell-turret and octagonal spire. The lofty clerestoried nave has wide arches, white walls and dark-stained roofs. The church was designed as part of a group with lych gate, school and house.

MINSTER LOVELL † St Kenelm

3m/4km W. of Witney

OS *SP324113* **GPS** *51.8000N, 1.5315W*

Delightfully set in the Windrush Valley next to the ruined Minster Lovell Hall, St Kenelm's is a Perpendicular church with cruciform plan, central tower and vaulted crossing. There are good details throughout; 15th-century glass and monuments, and a reredos by J. L. Pearson.

NORTH LEIGH † St Mary

3m/4km N.E. of Witney

OS *SP387136* **GPS** *51.8202N, 1.4394W*

A late Saxon, Early English and later church. There is a small finely fan-vaulted chantry chapel of 1439 with contemporary glass and alabaster effigies, and a good mid-15th-century wall-painted Doom. The unusual early 18th-century N. aisle has Baroque details.

NORTH MORETON † All Saints

2m/3km E. of Didcot

OS *SU562895* **GPS** *51.6022N, 1.1898W*

Attractive brick, cob and timber village with a fair-sized village church, mid-13th-century. The superb late 13th-century chantry chapel of the Stapleton family has Geometrical tracery and spirited carving outside, and an E. window of five lights filled with 13th-century glass, showing the Passion and incidents in the life of Our Lady, St Peter, St Paul and St Nicholas. There are remains of 13th-century glass in other windows.

NUNEHAM COURTENEY † All Saints

5m/8km S.E. of Oxford
OS *SU541982* **GPS** *51.6805N, 1.2181W*
Churches Conservation Trust

All Saints is essentially an ornamental church on a hill in a landscaped park – a domed temple in the Greek taste built in 1764 to designs by the first Earl Harcourt, assisted by 'Athenian' James Stuart. The pedimented Ionic portico fronts a blank E. wall. The interior is cool and impressive: more a view-stopper than a shrine.

OXFORD † St Mary the Virgin ★

High Street
OS *SP516062* **GPS** *51.7528N, 1.2537W*

The soaring spire and eccentric Baroque porch facing the High Street make this the grandest parish church in Oxford, a focus on the skyline and a glory of the High Street. Inside, the clerestoried and aisled nave is rather untidy, though steeped in history. The noblest thing is the chancel, c. 1467, with its old clear glass, 17th-century communion rails and niched E. wall.

RADLEY † St James the Great

3m/5km N.E. of Abingdon
OS *SU521993* **GPS** *51.6907N, 1.2463W*

A simple country church that lost its N. aisle and N. transept in the Civil War, it now has an eccentric lopsided appearance. Separating the nave from the S. aisle is an arcade of five bays of stocky wooden piers, each supporting longitudinal wooden arch braces. A notable feature is the 12th-century font, whose bowl is elaborately carved with a continuous blind arcade.

RYCOTE † St Michael and All Angels ★

In Rycote Park, 3m/4km W. of Thame
OS *SP666046* **GPS** *51.7366N, 1.0355W*
English Heritage

In a park near a lake, this remote mid-15th-century domestic chapel near Thame is of ashlar, with its tower, buttressed nave and chancel clearly the work of an architect. Inside it is remarkable for containing nothing later than Laudian times and all things up till then; sumptuous 15th-century benches and screen base, early 17th-century family and royal pews, one domed and the other of two storeys, a blue ceiling with gold stars, late 17th-century altarpiece and communion rails. Clear old glass. Queen Elizabeth and Charles I worshipped here when on visits.

SHORTHAMPTON † All Saints ★

4m/6km S. of Chipping Norton
OS *SP328201* **GPS** *51.8785N, 1.5246W*

A tiny hamlet church near Charlbury, it is a small and simple building, aisleless and bell-coted, of various dates from Norman to 20th century. It was furnished in carpenter's style with box pews and a high pulpit in 1820. The plaster walls have medieval wall-paintings in various states of repair, and the appeal of the building is its remoteness and feel of rustic worship.

SHRIVENHAM † St Andrew

6m/10km E. of Swindon
OS *SU240890* **GPS** *51.6000N, 1.6538W*

Most of St Andrew's, apart from the late medieval tower, was rebuilt during the reign of Charles I by Lord Craven, in a period of little church building, creating an interesting blend of Perpendicular and Classical in which fine arcades are supported on Tuscan columns.

SOUTH NEWINGTON
† St Peter ad Vincula ★★

6m/10km S.W. of Banbury
OS *SP407333* **GPS** *51.9970N, 1.4079W*

A Norman and later church with an elaborate Perpendicular S. porch, St Peter's contains the finest 14th- and 15th-century wall-paintings in the county – a feast of saints and martyrs. The 15th-century Passion cycle, discovered in the 1930s above the N. aisle arcade, is less skilled

△ **UFFINGTON: ST MARY** – *Betjeman moved to Uffington in 1934 with his wife Penelope and became a warden of this church, which he loved*

than some of the wall-paintings in the N. aisle itself, but is enthusiastically executed in a thoroughly delightful, naive and rustic style.

SPARSHOLT † Holy Cross ★

3m/5km W. of Wantage
OS *SU346875* **GPS** *51.5857N, 1.5008W*

This is a substantial aisleless church, with traces of late 12th-century origins in the nave. The N. door is from this time and the font is earlier – Saxon – from the original church on the site. At the head of the S. transept is one of the county's oldest surviving wood screens, and in the transept are two finely carved 14th-century wooden effigies.

STANTON HARCOURT
† St Michael ★

6m/10km W. of Oxford
OS *SP416056* **GPS** *51.7480N, 1.3977W*

A grand cruciform church stands near a delightful manor house and other old buildings, reflected in ponds; the Early English and Perpendicular details are delicate and well thought-out. The inside is little spoiled and much enhanced by its old stone and marble floor. There is an Early English screen, old glass, and 17th- to 19th-century Harcourt monuments in the Perpendicular S.E. chapel. Crude stone corbels support the roof braces, and the shrine of St Edburg stands in the chancel.

STANTON ST JOHN
† St John the Baptist

5m/8km N.E. of Oxford
OS *SP577093* **GPS** *51.7800N, 1.1643W*

Perched above the village street, the church stands opposite the birthplace of John White, founder of Massachussetts. The fine chancel of c. 1300 has good 13th-century stained glass; there are 15th-century screens and 16th-century benches with carved bench-ends.

SUTTON COURTENAY † All Saints ★

3m/4km N.W. of Didcot
OS *SU504941* **GPS** *51.6443N, 1.2718W*

A show Thames-side village with wide, tree-lined streets and old houses of various dates. The church is of various dates, too, from the 12th century onwards. The 14th- and

△ **WHEATFIELD: ST ANDREW** – *a 14th-century church remodelled c. 1730 for the Rudge family, who added fenestrations, parapet, Classical porch and contemporary furnishing inside*

15th-century woodwork includes some crude misericords, and there is some curious re-use of Norman zigzag motifs inside. Nothing is outstanding, but the general effect outside and within is of gradual growth through the centuries; full of gentle texture and colours. George Orwell and Herbert Asquith are both buried in the churchyard.

SWYNCOMBE † St Botolph

5m/8km E. of Wallingford
OS *SU682901* **GPS** *51.6064N, 1.0159W*

This is a charming church beautifully and remotely set at the gates of Swyncombe House. A small early Norman building with patches of herringbone work, it has a W. bell-cote, and apsidal E. end. The later extensive 19th-century restorations still retain the character. Inside are retouched wall-paintings and a rood screen by W. Tapper.

TACKLEY † St Nicholas

10m/16km N. of Oxford
OS *SP475201* **GPS** *51.8781N, 1.3101W*

A Norman cruciform church on a hillside with 13th-century tower and Perpendicular top stage, St Nicholas's was restored by G. E. Street in 1864; his are the reredos, stalls and benches; there is a good collection of 17th- and 18th-century monuments.

THAME † St Mary the Virgin ★

9m/15km S.W. of Aylesbury
OS *SP703063* **GPS** *51.7511N, 0.9818W*

A fine church of an attractive brick, flint and plaster market town: it is cruciform, and developed from Norman origins in later styles in a consistent manner. Note the S. porch, window tracery, Tudor screen and choir stalls, brasses, and many monuments, especially that of Lord Williams, d. 1599, in the middle of the chancel.

UFFINGTON † St Mary

4m/6km S. of Faringdon
OS *SU302893* **GPS** *51.6019N, 1.5649W*

St Mary's is a large cruciform stone and pebble-dashed church, almost wholly Early English, at a corner of a chalk and thatched vale village, with a 17th-century school-house nearby. The church is quite cathedral-like outside, though the spire fell in 1740 from the octagonal tower, which was subsequently raised a storey in compensation. There are stone porches and transeptal chapels. The interior is rather bare after restoration in 1851, supervised by G. E. Street. Betjeman was a churchwarden here is the 1930s, and insisted on retaining the old oil lamps when electric light was introduced.

WANTAGE † St Peter and St Paul

8m/13km S.W. of Abingdon
OS *SU396879* **GPS** *51.5887N, 1.4285W*

A substantial church, cruciform in plan with a bulky tower, St Peter and St Paul's is 13th-century with Perpendicular additions. Note the hammer-beam roof and corbels, the misericords in the Perpendicular stalls, and the excellent full-length brass of Ivo FitzWarin, d. 1414.

WATERPERRY † St Mary the Virgin ★

7m/11km E. of Oxford
OS *SP629063* **GPS** *51.7521N, 1.0894W*

In a once remote village in meadows, St Mary's is a small 11th–15th-century church close by a former manor house, with a distinctive 'herring-bone' wooden belfry. The delightful interior has a 17th-century pulpit, reader's desk and box pews, old glass of good quality, a monument by Chantrey, hatchments and old stone floors.

WEST HENDRED † Holy Trinity ★

3m/4km E. of Wantage
OS *SU447882* **GPS** *51.5916N, 1.3557W*

West Hendred is not such a show village as its neighbour, East Hendred, but the stream-side church, mostly 14th-century Perpendicular, has a pleasant plastered exterior and lead roofs, with dormer windows set in the nave roof. Neither is the interior a disappointment, with its pieces of old glass, 17th-century woodwork, and stone and tiled floors. The rustic attraction was preserved in the gentle restoration by Philip Johnston, 1929.

WHEATFIELD † St Andrew ★

10m/16km S.E. of Oxford
OS *SU688992* **GPS** *51.6880N, 1.0052W*

A remote place from which the glory has departed – the former manor house burnt down, leaving a stable, park, walled garden and, on a slope of the park, the church. Originally medieval, the church was Classicized c. 1730; inside are hatchments, tombs, a two-decker pulpit, old pews and clear glass with fragments of old stained glass. There is a Peter Scheemakers tomb of 1739, and a rich, Classical altar and rails.

WIDFORD † St Oswald

1m/2km E. of Burford
OS *SP273120* **GPS** *51.8068N, 1.6048W*

The visitor can approach this tiny medieval church by a footpath alongside the River Windrush below Burford. The setting is one of great charm. Inside are 14th- and 15th-century wall-paintings, box pews, clear glass and bits of Roman pavement.

WOODEATON † Holy Rood

4m/6km N.E. of Oxford
OS *SP534118* **GPS** *51.8032N, 1.2257W*

Set on a bank with yews, this is a small 13th-century church of nave and diminutive chancel. The tower is 14th-century, and inside is a wall-painting of St Christopher with a Norman French inscription, hatchments, box pews, an 18th-century pulpit and reader's desk.

YARNTON † St Bartholomew ★

4m/6km N.W. of Oxford
OS *SP477116* **GPS** *51.8017N, 1.3087W*

The manor house, vicarage and church form a group. To the 13th-century church were added by Sir Thomas Spencer in 1611 an ashlar tower with mellifluous bells, a porch and a S.E. chapel – all late Perpendicular. In the church is much old woodwork and a rich Jacobean screen to the Spencer Chapel, which has painted walls and roofs and grand 17th-century monuments. In the chancel is an alabaster 15th-century reredos, and in the aisle a medievalist brass of 1826. There is much reset English and Flemish glass.

RUTLAND

The two stone quarries of Ketton and Clipsham, which have been worked since medieval times and are still in use, and centuries of prosperous agriculture make this – the smallest and most compact county of England – the richest in old stone buildings, whether churches, barns, country houses, farms or cottages.

The scenery is hilly, and its wide uplands are thus described by the 20th-century historian Dr W. G. Hoskins in his guide to Rutland: '...limestone walls shining from afar in the clear winter sun and the rows of stacks in the corners of the great ploughed fields; fields that themselves gleam like a rich, brown velvet, ready for the barley and the wheat. It is very like the Cotswold country – indeed it is the same stone underneath – but without the self-consciousness of so much of that well-known land.' The stone varies from what he aptly calls 'sheep-grey' limestone in the east of the county around Ketton and Clipsham, where the finest churches are, to golden-brown, yellow and orange in the west. Between 1150 and 1350, the villages of Rutland seemed to have vied with each other as to which could build the finest church, and, as Dr Hoskins says, 'no county in England can show so many fine churches in such a small area, except perhaps the neighbouring area of South Lincolnshire . . .'

In later centuries most of Rutland was parcelled out among four great landlords, the Finches at Burley-on-the-Hill, the Noels at Exton, the Heathcotes at Normanton (only the Classical church remains, with its 1911 nave and chancel by Romaine Walker), and the Cecil family, who are still associated with the splendid Elizabethan Burghley House, just over the border by Stamford town. There were also smaller squires with their houses and modest parks. In the past century the county became popular with hunting people, who like the old way of life, good inns and ample stables. Thus Rutland today still retains an atmosphere of having been cared for by landlords. The two chief towns of Oakham and Uppingham are small enough to be what old-fashioned landowners would describe as 'the village'; once more to quote Dr Hoskins, 'Everywhere in the villages one sees the hand of the same benevolent despotism, and one sees too frequently also the impact of a new form of society in the broken-down stone walls which no one can afford to put up again, in the Colly Weston roofs patched with corrugated iron, in the big house which is more often than not a hospital or a school.' There is really only one blemish on the face of Rutland, and that is the strings of overhead wires which bedevil every village in profusion.

The formation of Rutland Water, the largest man-made lake in Europe, has transformed much of Rutland in an astonishing and spectacular way. Views of the Water can be had from many unexpected locations, but the biggest change has been the influx of sailing enthusiasts, walkers and cyclists, who now flock to this once quiet place.

◁ **KETTON: ST MARY THE VIRGIN** – *the chancel was rebuilt in 1863 by T. G. Jackson; its roof with angels was colourfully painted in 1950 by Charles Nicholson*

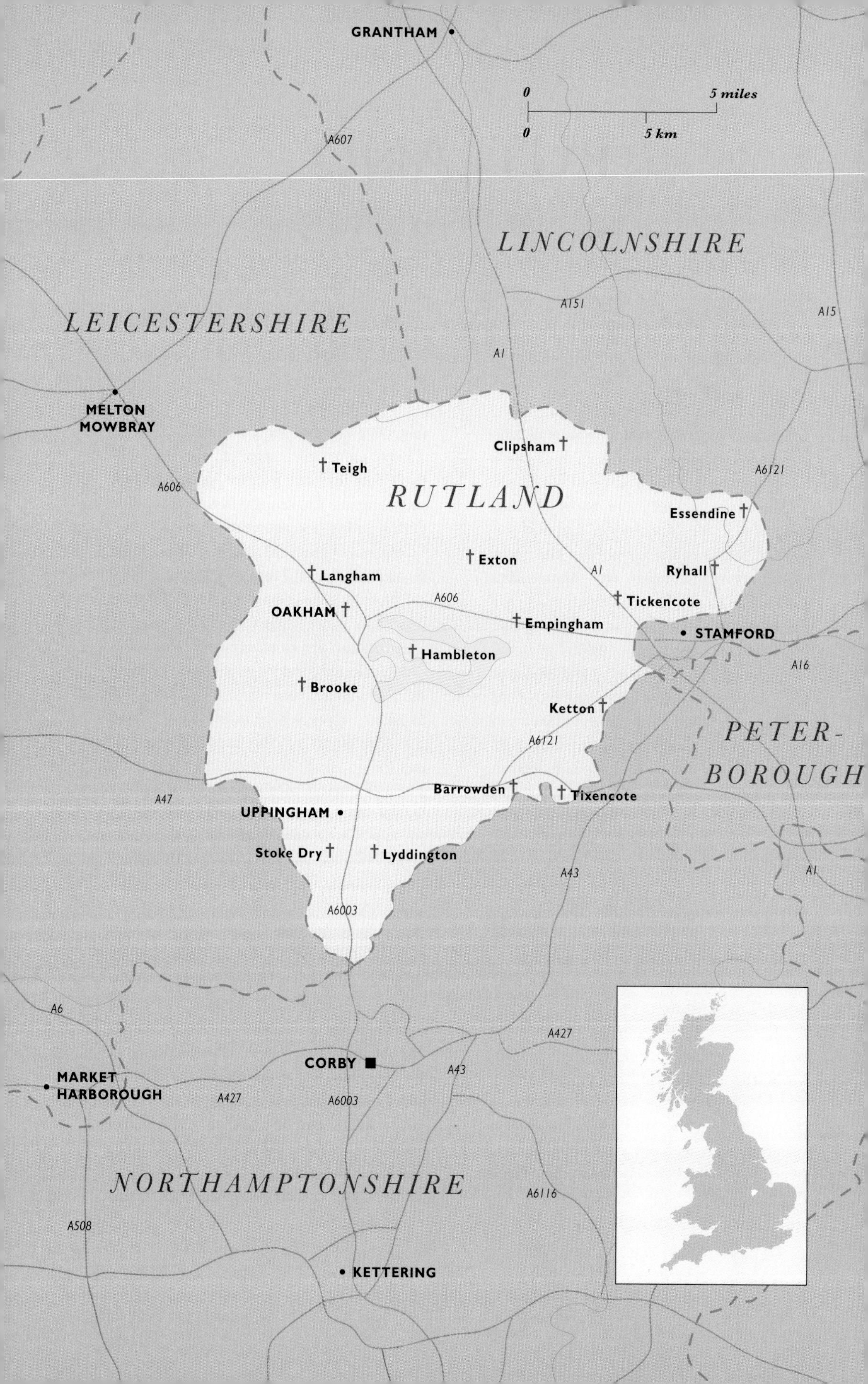

GRANTHAM
0
5 miles
0
5 km
A607
LINCOLNSHIRE
A151
A15
LEICESTERSHIRE
A1
MELTON
MOWBRAY
Clipsham
Teigh
A6121
A606
RUTLAND
Essendine
Exton
Langham
A1
Ryhall
A606
Tickencote
OAKHAM
Empingham
STAMFORD
Hambleton
A16
Brooke
Ketton
PETER-
BOROUGH
A6121
Barrowden
Tixencote
A47
UPPINGHAM
Stoke Dry
Lyddington
A43
A1
A6003
A6
A427
CORBY
A43
MARKET
HARBOROUGH
A427
A6003
NORTHAMPTONSHIRE
A6116
A508
KETTERING

△ **EMPINGHAM: ST PETER** – *looking towards the Early English chancel from the nave*

BARROWDEN † St Peter
5m/8km E. of Uppingham
OS *SP944999* **GPS** *52.5888N, 0.6066W*

St Peter's stands on a slope above the River Welland, the graceful tower and spire rising over a church whose earliest parts are Norman and remarkably wide, even by Rutland standards, where wide churches are common. The clerestory and E. window are 15th-century. A fine scrolly Renaissance monument to Rowland Durant, d. 1588, is set on the N. wall.

BROOKE † St Peter
2m/3km S. of Oakham
OS *SK849057* **GPS** *52.6426N, 0.7455W*

Remote in a gentle valley S. of Braunston, with sweeping limestone uplands all around, the church is 12th-century, but with a 13th-century tower. There is Norman work inside and a well-carved late Norman doorway, but the church was much rebuilt in about 1579. It looks as though nothing has changed since then, with a complete Elizabethan screen, benches and stalls, and a beautiful Renaissance tomb of Charles Noel, 1619, which retains its original colouring.

CLIPSHAM † St Mary
7m/11km N.W. of Stamford
OS *SK970163* **GPS** *52.7362N, 0.5645W*

There is much excellent 16th–19th-century village building in limestone here, and a large, beautiful church on the edge of a small, tree-rich park. The fine tower, c. 1300, has a broach spire of unusual design. The interior was originally Norman, and the N. arcade has massive 12th-century capitals. The S. arcade is 13th-century, and there is much 14th-century reconstruction, including the window tracery and the usual Perpendicular clerestory. But the most striking feature of Clipsham is the exterior view from the S.

EMPINGHAM † St Peter ★
5m/8km W. of Stamford
OS *SK950084* **GPS** *52.6656N, 0.5957W*

Rutland at its best: a large, attractive limestone village above the Gwash Valley, now Rutland Water, and a splendid church overall. The three adjacent churches of Empingham, Exton and Ketton are as hard to beat as a trio anywhere in England. Empingham is nobly proportioned: note the W. tower, crocketed spire and W. front, all 14th-century.

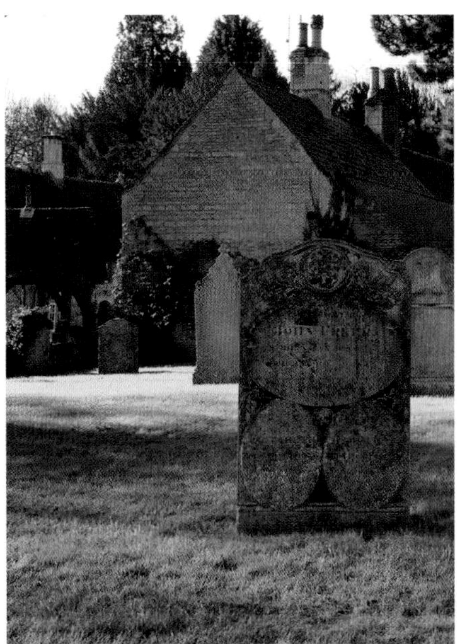

△ **KETTON: ST MARY THE VIRGIN** – *one of the elegantly carved limestone headstones*

Internally, nearly all is Early English; both arcades and especially the S. transept are almost in original condition with some medieval colouring. The Early English chancel has beautiful double piscinas and triple sedilia. There are substantial 15th-century changes: new windows, roofs and clerestory.

ESSENDINE † St Mary the Virgin ★

4m/6km N. of Stamford
OS *TF049127* **GPS** *52.7026N, 0.4489W*

St Mary's stands on the site of a Norman castle, of which it was the chapel, with trees and earthworks all around. Considerably repaired and rebuilt, but it remains substantially a Norman building still, remodelled in the 13th century. The striking S. doorway of c. 1140 has a tympanum of Christ attended by angels.

EXTON † St Peter and St Paul ★

4m/6km E. of Oakham
OS *SK920111* **GPS** *52.6906N, 0.6395W*

Another noble church, in the park of one of Rutland's great houses, by an excellent limestone village. There was a drastic rebuilding of the church after damage by lightning in the 1850s, which explains the incongruity of details, but the general effect is still fine. The tower and spire are especially notable. But the monuments to the Noels, Haringtons and others connected with them are the really splendid thing about the church. Notice especially the table-tomb with alabaster effigies of John Harington, d. 1524, and wife, the appealing monument to Sir James Harington, d. 1591, and wife in the chancel, the splendid tomb of Robert Kelway, d. 1580, and the Noel monuments and sculpture by Grinling Gibbons and Nollekens; and read the gorgeous, rolling epitaphs aloud. Exton is intoxicating.

HAMBLETON † St Andrew

By Rutland Water
OS *SK899075* **GPS** *52.6585N, 0.6712W*

All delightful, with views over Rutland Water. The original Saxon and Norman fabric is now largely obscured by Victorian work, including a Burne-Jones window, but this is chiefly worthy of a visit for its setting.

KETTON † St Mary the Virgin

4m/6km S.W. of Stamford
OS *SK981042* **GPS** *52.6276N, 0.5508W*

The church stands in a large, attractive village built of local honey-coloured limestone, its fine tower and spire rising above the trees and the sepia Colly Weston slate roofs. The W. front is a fine example of late 12th-century work, Norman evolving into Early English; the rest of the church is almost entirely 13th-century, with very lofty and dignified arcades. The spacious chancel was practically rebuilt in 1863, but is still striking because of its great size; the panelled roof painted in medieval colours and the E. window and altar by Comper, 1907. There is a notable collection of carved Ketton headstones in churchyard – a local art now dead.

LANGHAM † St Peter and St Paul ★

2m / 3km N. of Oakham
OS *SK843112* **GPS** *52.6920N, 0.7532W*

Dating from the 13th century, the church is one of Rutland's largest, with a 14th-century nave, aisles and chancel arch, and imposing 15th-century transepts with fine Perpendicular windows. Carved faces are clustered around

△ **TICKENCOTE: ST PETER** – *the exceptional large Norman chancel arch with its orders of grotesques, zigzag, billets, beakheads and roll moulding*

the church, and in the vestry are two oriental carved elephant heads. A scroll in the S. transept commemorates Simon de Langham, b. 1330, who became Archbishop of Canterbury and Lord High Treasurer to Edward III. The churchyard is lovely with its rose shrubs, flower beds, meadow grass and flowers.

LYDDINGTON † St Andrew ★

2m/3km S. of Uppingham
OS *SP876969* **GPS** *52.5637N, 0.7089W*

A grand church in a village of good buildings in ironstone, Lyddington belonged to the medieval bishops of Lincoln, who had a palace here of which one 15th-century range remains. Although mostly Perpendicular, the tower and chancel of the church belong to an older building, 1320–40: the nave and aisles were rebuilt c. 1500 by one of the bishops. The height and symmetry of this work make it of great beauty, although it was severely scraped by Ewan Christian, 1890. Note the 15th-century wall-paintings, and especially the 17th-century arrangement of the sanctuary, with altar enclosed by Laudian rails on all sides. Small cavities for acoustic jars are set high in the side walls of the chancel, a rare feature.

OAKHAM † All Saints ★

Church Street
OS *SK860089* **GPS** *52.6710N, 0.7286W*

An attractive little country town with a magnificent church, which rises like a central jewel in all distant views of the Vale of Catmose. The noble 14th-century tower and spire are of ashlar limestone. A lofty interior of the same date has notable sculptured capitals, including the Coronation of the Virgin, Man's Redemption and Fall. There are the

△ **TIXOVER: ST LUKE** – *the church is reached via a long farm track, and is worth the trek for the Norman carving, fine Jacobean marble monument and Tudor windows of the interior (above right)*

usual enlargements of the 15th century – the clerestory and good Perpendicular windows. Excellent parclose screens date from Sir George Gilbert Scott's overenthusiastic restoration of 1857–8.

RYHALL † St John the Evangelist

2m/3km N. of Stamford
OS *TF036108* **GPS** *52.6852N, 0.4685W*

A pleasant village by Rutland Water, it has one of the best churches in the county, with an exquisite 13th-century tower and spire. The nave and aisles are broad and generous with a c. 1200 N. arcade and a S. arcade of a little later. The chancel was rebuilt in the 15th century and is lined with wall memorials, including a tablet of 1696 to an infant genius, aged two. St Tibba, patron saint of falconers, lived and died here c. 690. By the W. wall of the N. aisle are remains of a medieval hermitage associated with her cult – possibly the burial place of the saint – against which the first church was built.

STOKE DRY † St Andrew

2m/3km S. of Uppingham
OS *SP855967* **GPS** *52.5620N, 0.7394W*

Setting aside the contentious claims that St Andrew's is where the Gunpowder Plot was hatched, it is the surviving Norman stonework and wall-paintings that draw attention here. Note the finely carved chancel arch columns and capitals: birds, beasts, even a figure tugging on a rope bell, and, off the chancel, the Digby Chapel. On the S. wall of the chapel are 13th-century paintings depicting St Christopher and the infant Christ, and the Martyrdom of St Edmund.

TEIGH † Holy Trinity

4m/7km N. of Oakham
OS *SK864160* **GPS** *52.7348N, 0.7206W*

A pleasant church of the 13th–14th century in a tiny village, whose finialed tower has a Somerset look to it. The interior is entirely Georgian, with collegiate pews, and two of the three E. windows are filled with text boards. The pulpit, flanked by two reader's desks, stands above the W. door, so that the congregation has to incline from E. to W., depending on the emphasis of the service. The interior is painted in pastel colours, and there is a lovely Georgian mahogany font.

TICKENCOTE † St Peter ★★

3m/4km N.W. of Stamford
OS *SK990094* **GPS** *52.6741N, 0.5366W*

Just off the A1, St Peter's treasure is the Norman chancel arch, a staggering thing in six intricate orders, each carved differently. There are muzzled bears, cats, a fox holding a monk's hood, other faces and grotesques jostling with zigzags, beakheads and billets, all mercifully left intact when S. P. Cockerell rebuilt the church in 1792 in romantic Norman style. The chancel was left largely unaltered and has fine sexpartite carved vaulting and a very rare carved stone boss.

TIXOVER † St Luke ★

5m/8km S.W. of Stamford
OS *SP970997* **GPS** *52.5871N, 0.5685W*

A happy surprise in the meadows of the Welland Valley, far from the village and everything except grass, buttercups and bullrushes. Mostly Norman, it has a magnificently solid, untouched tower, and inside is an imposing tower arch, all c. 1140. The rest of the church is mostly 13th-century, with Tudor windows, and original medieval stone seats along the chancel walls. In the S. aisle is 16th-century glass. There is a marble monument to Roger Dale, d. 1623.

SHROPSHIRE

There is not one sort of scenery that can be called characteristic of the varied and beautiful landscape of Shropshire. This agricultural county, comparatively free from modern factories, is bisected by the Severn. Shrewsbury, the capital, and Ludlow, Bridgnorth and Whitchurch are its attractive old towns. Its Cheshire borders are flat and pitted with ponds: Wenlock Edge with its 'forest fleece' and the Clee Hills give wonderful outline to the pastoral country south of the spires and towers of Shrewsbury.

Wooded combes like those of Devon descend to orchard-land on the borders of Worcestershire; the north-west corner of the county round Oswestry has a Welsh quality. The Long Mynd, Stiperstones and Clun Hills on the edges of Montgomery and Radnor, to the west, have the grand and under-populated look of border country, and there the few old churches are fortress-like. Scenery is more memorable in Shropshire than buildings; castles are prominent and, if a generalisation is possible about the medieval churches, it is that most of them are small (with the exception of St Mary, Shrewsbury, and Ludlow), and show the gradual growth of ages. The prevailing materials are a good sharp pink sandstone and half-timber. Timber-framed churches have been much repaired, and the most complete example, Melverley, does not look as old as its origin.

'Fear God and honour the Corbets' is said to be a Shropshire motto, and the non-Welsh half of the county is diversified, with the seats of hunting squires who did much church rebuilding and repair in the 18th century. The Myttons, Clives, Hills, Cottons, Hebers: they do not seem to have been markedly Puritan, but either old-fashioned High Church, before becoming Tractarian in Victorian times, or Roman Catholic. Two-bottle squires hung on in the Newport neighbourhood until this century.

To this remote county, in late Georgian times, came that early industrialisation of pottery at Coalport and iron at Coalbrookdale, which turned the chasm-like Severn Valley north of Bridgnorth into a brick semblance of the Stroud Valley in Gloucestershire. Ironbridge, Broseley and Madeley are its romantic survivals. The industrial churches here are either severe Classical by Telford or starved-looking 'Early Pointed' in brick. Methodism flourished.

In Victorian times, iron-masters from Wolverhampton and manufacturers from Kidderminster, Birmingham and Manchester discovered Shropshire, much as London discovered Surrey and Sussex. Norman Shaw and Eden Nesfield built them houses; Street, Pearson and Scott 'restored' the old churches or built new ones. Shropshire more than most English agricultural counties is remarkable for its 18th-century and Victorian churches. But although its older churches are more impressive for their fittings, monuments, hatchments and liturgical arrangements than for their architecture, Norman and medieval architecture abounds in a charming rural context. Here scenery, rural settings and church architecture combine in a delightful way.

◁ **BURFORD: ST MARY** – *standing in a beautiful setting, with a fine 14th-century ashlar-faced tower that was restored, along with the nave, by Sir Aston Webb in 1889*

△ **ASTON EYRE** – *a small Norman church with Norman tympanum and Transitional chancel arch*

ACTON BURNELL † St Mary

7ml11km S. of Shrewsbury
OS *SJ533019* **GPS** *52.6132N, 2.6904W*

Adjacent to a ruined manor is this good-quality but heavily restored late 13th-century church. There is a brass, 1382, of Nicholas Burnell, 1st Lord Burnell, and a fine alabaster monument to Sir Richard Lee, d.1591. In the N. transept are medieval tiles, and traces of possibly medieval wall decoration in the S. transept.

ADDERLEY † St Peter ★

4ml6km N. of Market Drayton
OS *SJ661395* **GPS** *52.9522N, 2.5059W*
Churches Conservation Trust

Mostly Gothic of 1801 by Richard Baker, the church is large and cruciform with a N. transept of 1635–7 furnished as a manorial pew with a very fine screen and panelling; the sturdy Classical W. tower is 1712. The windows are pointed and most of the panes are clear crown glass. The Gothic iron window tracery is typical of this part of Shropshire at the date. The chancel and transepts are in the care of the CCT; the nave and tower are partitioned off and are used by the parish.

ALBERBURY † St Michael

10ml16km W of Shrewsbury
OS *SJ358144* **GPS** *52.7238N, 2.9511W*

Close by the remains of Alberbury Castle, St Michael's is Saxon in origin but with work of all medieval periods; of note is the massive 13th-century saddleback tower at the N.E. of the nave. The 14th-century S. chapel is very fine and there are handsome 15th-century roofs. There was much rebuilding and embellishment in the 1840s, and a complete restoration in 1902. The splendid Art Nouveau window is by Barbara Leighton, 1897, and throughout is a great array of Leighton and Lyster monuments.

ALVELEY † St Mary ★★

6ml10km S.E. of Bridgnorth
OS *SO759845* **GPS** *52.4583N, 2.3552W*

This is a large aisled Norman and later church with a 15th-century clerestory and roof, and a Georgian top to the tower. There is much Early English character inside in the S. arcade and chancel, which has a 15th-century altar frontal. The faded 14th-century wall-painting in the S. chapel is noteworthy, as is the S. chapel reredos, painted on zinc, by Kempe, 1887. A. W. Blomfield's extensive 1879 restoration complements the many fine features of this interesting church.

ASTON EYRE
† Dedication unknown ★★

4ml6km W. of Bridgnorth
OS *SO653940* **GPS** *52.5435N, 2.5129W*

A delightful rural hamlet setting for a diminutive two-cell Norman church with

WALES
CHESHIRE
STAFFORDSHIRE
SHROPSHIRE
WORCESTERSHIRE
HEREFORDSHIRE
WREXHAM
NEWCASTLE-UNDER-LYME
WHITCHURCH
Adderley
ELLESMERE
MARKET DRAYTON
Cheswardine
OSWESTRY
Wem
Llanyblodwell
Llanymynech
Clive
Battlefield
Newport
Melverley
Alberbury
Berwick
SHREWSBURY
Meole Brace
Wroxeter
TELFORD
Tong
Minsterley
Pitchford
Madeley
Acton Burnell
Langley Chapel
Much Wenlock
Leebotwood
Chirbury
Aston Eyre
Claverley
Church Stretton
Eaton-under-Heywood
BRIDGNORTH
More
Holdgate
Bishop's Castle
Cleobury North
Heath
Lydbury North
Stottesdon
Alveley
Hopesay
Craven Arms
Stoke St Milborough
Kinlet
Clun
Stokesay
Onibury
Stanton Lacy
KIDDERMINSTER
Bromfield
LUDLOW
KNIGHTON
Richards Castle
Burford
LEOMINSTER
Kington
WORCESTER
0 5 miles
0 5 km
A41
A49
A530
A525
A483
A539
A528
A495
A5
A51
A53
A529
A519
A518
A458
A488
A464
A4169
A490
A454
A489
A442
A4113
A4117
A456
A4112
A443
A44
M54

△ **BATTLEFIELD: ST MARY MAGDALENE** – *the limestone walls rise up to a parapet pierced with quatrefoils and crocketed pinnacles; the roofs are of Welsh slate*

reputedly the best piece of Norman sculpture in the county – a tympanum over the S. door depicting Christ's Entry into Jerusalem. This is a powerful carving of the Herefordshire School.

BATTLEFIELD † St Mary Magdalene ★
3m/4km N. of Shrewsbury
OS *SJ512172* **GPS** *52.7507N, 2.7236W*
Churches Conservation Trust

Standing in open Shropshire countryside, this is the church of a chantry college founded in 1406 for the many souls of those slain in the Battle of Shrewsbury, 1403, between Henry IV and Harry Hotspur. The tower was finished c. 1500. Inside is a mid-15th-century Pietà. The building was rescued from ruin by S. Pountney Smith in 1861 and given a spectacular hammer-beam roof, screen, reredos, stained glass and Maw's tiles.

BERWICK † Berwick Chapel
2m/3km N.W. of Shrewsbury
OS *SJ473148* **GPS** *52.7285N, 2.7815W*

Set in the grounds of Berwick House, the chapel was built in 1670 with a tower and S. porch of c. 1735. There is much furnishing of both periods, though the 18th-century reredos is preserved in the house. The newer E. end, 1892–4, is by Walker, and there is a monument to two Powys daughters by Chantrey.

BRIDGNORTH † St Leonard
St Leonard's Close
OS *SO716933* **GPS** *52.5371N, 2.4187W*
Churches Conservation Trust

Standing at the top of the town in a close surrounded by old brick houses, St Leonard's is an imposing church whose tower is a landmark for miles around. Largely a Victorian rebuilding by William Slater, it is attractive and interesting, with a 17th-century hammer-beam roof over the extraordinarily wide nave and aisles. There are fine vistas in the S. aisle and some Arts and Crafts metalwork.

BRIDGNORTH † St Mary Magdalene ★
East Castle Street
OS *SO716928* **GPS** *52.5325N, 2.4187W*

The imposing façade of Thomas Telford's church provides a dramatic termination for a street of elegant Georgian town houses. It is a bold Classical design with fine tower, lit inside by two-storey round-headed windows. The chancel was added by Blomfield, 1876. There are fine views over the low town from the E. side.

BROMFIELD † St Mary the Virgin ★

3m/4km N. of Ludlow

OS *SO481768* **GPS** *52.3868N, 2.7625W*

The glory of this remnant of a small Benedictine priory church of the 12th and 13th century is the painted chancel roof by Thomas Francis, 1672, which has clouds, angels and biblical texts, and the symbol of the Trinity in the centre. It was restored in 1889–90 by C. Hodgson Fowler.

BURFORD † St Mary

5m/8km S.E. of Ludlow

OS *SO583680* **GPS** *52.3088N, 2.6127W*

Delightfully set by Burford House and gardens, this is a splendid medieval church with outstanding monuments and effigies to the Cornewall family. It is also remarkable for a gorgeous Arts and Crafts ensemble of 1889 onward by Sir Aston Webb and collaborators. The ornamental barrel-vaulted chancel ceiling has endearing carved angels, and the immense triptych is to Richard Cornewall, d. 1568, Janet his wife, d.1547, and their son Edmund, d.1585, by Melchior Salabuss, 1588. A church of infinite interest.

CHESWARDINE † St Swithun ★

4m/6km S.E. of Market Drayton

OS *SJ719299* **GPS** *52.8659N, 2.4184W*

This is a good work by J. L. Pearson, 1888–9, in the Early English style – very fine, retaining the big 15th-century tower and 13th-century N. chapel. Fittings by Pearson include a panelled wooden altar, stone reredos with marble top and a painted and carved wooden triptych. There is also some early Kempe glass.

CHIRBURY † St Michael

3m/4km N. of Church Stoke

OS *SO261985* **GPS** *52.5794N, 3.0915W*

The post-Reformation remains of an Augustinian church, St Michael's has a big parochial nave and aisles, and a W. tower. The

△ **CLAVERLEY: ALL SAINTS** – *wall-painting showing mounted knights in battle*

choir stalls, screen and rood loft were removed to Montgomery after the Dissolution. The small brick chancel is of 1733 with a mosaic reredos by Blomfield. A fine 18th-century candelabrum hangs in the nave. There are interesting monuments, and glass by Kempe in the S. aisle.

CLAVERLEY † All Saints ★★

5m/8km E. of Bridgnorth

OS *SO792934* **GPS** *52.5383N, 2.3071W*

A lovely sandstone church set in an attractive hilltop village with black and white houses, All Saints is of Norman origin, as shown by the tower base and N. arcade; the rest is Decorated and Perpendicular. Impressive wall-paintings of c. 1200 over the N. arcade are reminiscent of the Bayeux Tapestry. The nave is good Perpendicular, and there are 15th–16th-century monuments – note the alabaster effigies of Sir Robert Broke, his wives and 16 children. This church is full of interest.

CLEOBURY NORTH

† St Peter & St Paul ★

7m/11km S.W. of Bridgnorth

OS *SO623870* **GPS** *52.4796N, 2.5562W*

A distinctive short Norman N.W. tower with pyramidal roof marks out the church,

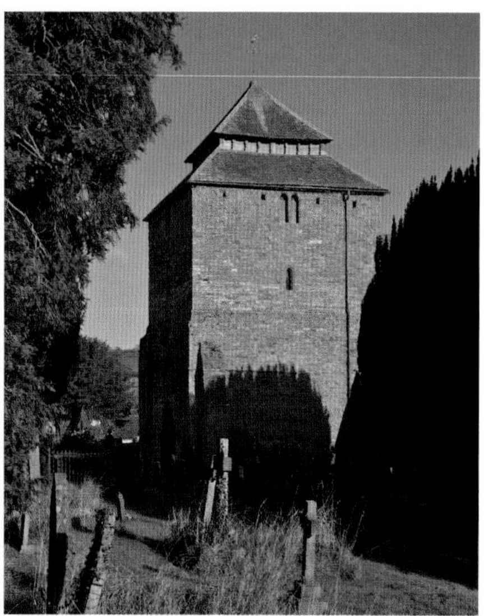

△ **CLUN: ST GEORGE** – *the squat tower of coursed limestone and sandstone rubble*

whose whitewashed interior is intimate and largely unspoilt. The chancel was rebuilt in 1890. There is a good 16th-century hammer-beam roof in the nave and medieval parclose screens in the aisle.

CLIVE † All Saints

3m/4km of Wem
OS *SJ514240* **GPS** *52.8116N, 2.7213W*

Set on a steep timbered hillside, All Saints is by C. J. Ferguson, 1885–94, who enclosed the medieval core. The church has a spectacular tower and spire, and rich Arts and Crafts Gothic furnishings.

CLUN † St George ★

5m/8km N. of Knighton
OS *SO300805* **GPS** *52.4185N, 3.0301W*

The church is basically Norman, with a characteristically squat border tower. Inside, it is large and aisled; later alterations include noble 15th-century collar-braced roofs. The church was restored and partly rebuilt by Street, 1877; a fine 15th-century carved wood canopy is set over the altar. The lych gate has fine open timber-work.

EATON-UNDER-HEYWOOD
† St Edith ★

4m/6km S.E. of Church Stretton
OS *SO499900* **GPS** *52.5056N, 2.7383W*

With a prominent S. tower, the church is of Norman origins, with a 13th-century chancel; the roofs and battlements are Perpendicular. Inside, the six-bay nave roof of arch-braced collar trusses has carved bosses. The church was sympathetically restored in 1868.

HEATH † Dedication unknown ★★

6m/10km N.W. of Ludlow
OS *SO557856* **GPS** *52.4667N, 2.6531W*

A perfect, small Norman two-cell chapel with largely 17th-century furnishings – box pews, two-decker pulpit and three-sided altar rails. There is good carving on the S. door and chancel arches. The interior is dark, lit by the narrowest of windows, all giving an authentic feel of the original chapel. The isolated setting in the hills with earthworks of the deserted village nearby is superb.

HOLDGATE † Holy Trinity ★

10m/16km W. of Bridgnorth
OS *SO561895* **GPS** *52.5024N, 2.6472W*

Next to a massive tree-covered motte of a long-gone Norman castle, this is a church of the 12th century or earlier, with a 13th-century chancel. The tower is 13th-century with a 15th-century upper stage. The richly carved S. doorway and font may well be the work of the famous Herefordshire School. Inside are late medieval benches and misericords. On the external S. wall a Sheela-na-Gig is set below the eaves.

HOPESAY † St Mary

3m/4km W. of Craven Arms
OS *SO389832* **GPS** *52.4441N, 2.9000W*

Ringed by hills in this Marches region, this is a 12th- and 13th-century church restored in 1880. The massive, thickset W. tower has a 17th-century double pyramidal roof similar to that at Clun. Another typical local feature is the impressive 15th-century arch-braced collar-beam roof with quatrefoil wind-braces. Some 17th-century decorative panelling has been reused in the 19th-century pews, as well as in wainscotting and the choir stalls.

△ **EATON-UNDER-HEYWOOD: ST EDITH** – *on the lower slopes of Wenlock Edge, this is a church to visit for its remote and peaceful setting*

KINLET † St John the Baptist ★

7m/12km S. of Bridgnorth
OS *SO710810* **GPS** *52.4265N, 2.4269W*

The church stands in parkland by a hall of 1729, and is formed of a 12th-century core, aisled and cruciform, with good detail. It was restored, scraped and painted in 1892–3 by J. Oldrid Scott; he also rescued the c. 1500 timber-framed Perpendicular clerestory. The E. window has beautiful and well-restored 14th-century glass, and there is an extensive collection of monuments – next best in the county after Tong – from the 14th-century onward, to the Blount, Childe and Baldwin families. Note particularly the fine alabaster Blount tomb of 1584 with kneeling figures.

LANGLEY CHAPEL † Dedication unknown ★★

7m/12km S.E. of Shrewsbury
OS *SJ538000* **GPS** *52.5966N, 2.6829W*
English Heritage

An atmospheric and charming chapel of the utmost simplicity, standing in a field in quiet countryside near the site of the old manor house. The furnishings of the whitewashed interior are almost all of the 17th century – pews with turned knobs and doors; musicians' seats; benches for the poor at the back; a pulpit and canopied reading pew; and holy table away from the E. wall, with kneelers around it. This is a very early example of a building being taken into care by the State – the Ministry of Works, 1914.

LEEBOTWOOD † St Mary the Virgin ★

7m/12km S. of Shrewsbury
OS *SO470986* **GPS** *52.5833N, 2.7827W*

This small single-cell church is situated in the foothills of the Long Mynd. Although there are medieval details in the walls and roof, everything is of the 18th-century, and little changed. It has clear glass except for the bright early Victorian E. window. The box pews have iron hat-pegs; there is a two-decker pulpit, a sort of chancel screen, wall tablets in the chancel, remains of a wall-painting and a W. gallery. The interior is spoiled only by the unhappily match-boarded roof.

LLANYBLODWELL † St Michael ★

5m/8km S.W. of Oswestry
OS *SJ239228* **GPS** *52.7982N, 3.1295W*

Beautifully sited on the edge of Wales, the church was largely rebuilt and redecorated between 1845 and 1860 by a 19th-century incumbent, the Rev. John Parker. The octagonal tower has a curious convex spire. Inside, all is colour – red, blue and gilt. The screen is 15th-century, repainted. The altar is copied from an Italian model. Black letter texts adorn the walls, and the overall effect is rich and pleasing, but not to those who dislike decoration laid over architecture.

LLANYMYNECH † St Agatha

6m/10km S. of Oswestry
OS *SJ267207* **GPS** *52.7798N, 3.0875W*

Straddling the English/Welsh border, this is a good church by Thomas Penson, 1843–5, in the neo-Norman style of grey limestone with yellow terracotta mouldings, and festive E. and W. fronts. The N.W. tower has a porch, large angle buttresses and pyramidal roof. The interior was refitted in 1879, but retains glass by Wailes, 1855.

LUDLOW † St Lawrence ★★

24m/38km S. of Shrewsbury
OS *SO511747* **GPS** *52.3682N, 2.7187W*

This is a large and well-known Perpendicular cruciform church at the centre and summit of the town, with Norman, Early English and Decorated features. Of note is the hexagonal S. porch, and the soaring wooden vaulted crossing tower. The nave and chancel are of equal size, further enhancing the sense of a very spacious building. The interior is generally rich in screens and other woodwork, particularly the splendid choir stalls of 1447 with misericords: there is a good patchwork of 15th-century glass in the S. transept, but the best original glass is in St John's Chapel. The Lady Chapel, once used to house the town fire engine, has a much-restored fine Jesse window. The Victorian restorations were by Sir George Gilbert Scott and Blomfield. A. E. Housman's ashes were scattered in the churchyard, and he is remembered by a plaque.

△ **LUDLOW: ST LAWRENCE** – *detail from a 15th-century misericord*

LYDBURY NORTH † St Michael

3m/4km S.E. of Bishop's Castle
OS *SO352860* **GPS** *52.4683N, 2.9551W*

This picturesque long, low 12th-century cruciform church, plastered inside and out, was well restored by J. T. Micklethwaite, 1901. The 13th-century tower is heavily buttressed, with a one-handed clock set in the S. buttress. The transepts are 14th- and 17th-century, and the 12th-century nave has a fine 15th-century roof with typical regional arch-braced collar trusses. The rood screen has pierced tracery with a plastered tympanum of 1615 above, on which are painted the Commandments and Creed.

MADELEY † St Michael

Adjoins Telford to the S.
OS *SJ696040* **GPS** *52.6337N, 2.4502W*

This is a severe but pleasing Greek-style octagonal, galleried Evangelical Revival church by Thomas Telford, 1794–6. Sadly the central pulpit and all of Telford's other furnishings have gone, but the interior is still pleasing, light and bright, with extensive galleries. The E. end was added in 1910. Outside is the cast-iron Fletcher tomb, and the tragic grave of the 'Nine Men of Madeley'.

MELVERLEY † St Peter ★
10m/16km W. of Shrewsbury
OS *SJ332165* **GPS** *52.7425N, 2.9902W*

This may be the earliest timber-framed church in the county, with wattle and daub infill. It stands picturesquely on the banks the River Vyrnwy with fine distant views. Inside, a frame of the building divides chancel from nave, and another makes a W. division with a gallery of 1718. Of the three divisions, the chancel is the largest, and the frame, looking like a chancel screen, produces an odd effect. There is a Jacobean pulpit and panelling and a chained bible.

MEOLE BRACE † Holy Trinity ★
S. district of Shrewsbury
OS *SJ486105* **GPS** *52.6902N, 2.7616W*

Set in a historic village on the edge of Shrewsbury, this is an ambitious work by E. Haycock Jnr, 1867–8. The focal point of the church is the glorious feast of stained glass in the apse, 1869–70. This is some of the best ever designed by William Morris, Ford Madox Brown and Sir Edward Burne-Jones: rich clear panels of the Crucifixion, kings, martyrs and apostles. There is glass by Kempe in the E. window of the S. aisle, 1894.

MINSTERLEY † Holy Trinity
9m/15km S.W. of Shrewsbury
OS *SJ373050* **GPS** *52.6397N, 2.9266W*

By William Taylor of London, 1689, the church was built in a strange brick and stone Baroque style with fantastic details. The W. front has a barrel gable topped by a tiled and louvered bell tower, and a grand domestic appearance. The interior is plastered, with lively carving on the screen.

MORE † St Peter ★
2m/3km N.E. of Bishop's Castle
OS *SO342915* **GPS** *52.5176N, 2.9697W*

Among black and white houses in remote, flat landscapes between the hills of the Welsh border, the church was rebuilt in 1845 in a countrified Gothic style, apart from the massive tower of local type. The interior was not much disturbed by the rebuilding, retaining the W. gallery and remarkable More Chapel pew.

MUCH WENLOCK † Holy Trinity
8m/13km S.W. of Telford
OS *SO623999* **GPS** *52.5964N, 2.5570W*

A 12th-century Cluniac church prettily set in a market town, the tower obscures the original ornate W. front, and now serves as the main entrance to the church. The nave is principally Norman, with a fine chancel arch, and the S. aisle and Lady Chapel are late 13th-century. The 14th-century porch has a parvise. Recent interior changes – a meeting room cum kitchen et al – are not too intrusive.

ONIBURY † St Michael ★
3m/4km S.E. of Craven Arms
OS *SO455791* **GPS** *52.4077N, 2.8014W*

This small Norman church was sensitively restored by Detmar Blow in 1902–3 on sound anti-scrape principles. The interior has rough whitened plaster, a rough-hewn oak W. gallery with square front and vivid Edward VII carved Arms. Rough-hewn oak pews with oak posts support iron lanterns for electric lights; there are 1902 commandment boards and box pews at the W. end. An affectionate pastiche of village simplicity.

PITCHFORD † St Michael ★
6m/10km S. of Shrewsbury
OS *SJ527042* **GPS** *52.6343N, 2.6995W*

The church forms a group with the nearby timbered-framed manor house. It is early Norman and later, small and little-restored, with 17th- and 18th-century furnishings, including box pews and pulpit. Of note are the wooden effigy of a knight in chain mail, c. 1230, fragments of 14th- and 18th-century armourial glass, Tudor incised slabs and hatchments.

RICHARDS CASTLE † All Saints
3m/4km S. of Ludlow
OS *SO494706* **GPS** *52.3316N, 2.7435W*

R. Norman Shaw built this impressive hillside church, 1891–2. Its cliff-like walls and big, austere S. tower are unmistakable. The interior is also on the grand scale, ashlar-faced, but lacking the decoration Shaw intended; the main features are the sumptuous triptych painted by C. E. Buckeridge and Shaw's own organ case and chancel fittings. There are evocative paintings of the angels at the sepulchre.

SHREWSBURY † St Chad

Between St Chad's Terrace and Claremont Hill
OS *SJ488124* **GPS** *52.7073N, 2.7589W*

This large Georgian church by George Steuart, 1790–2, replaced a large collegiate church that had been allowed to fall down; its churchyard and side chapel survive in the town centre. The new church, a carefree blend of Doric, Corinthian and Ionic styles, has a circular galleried nave built for a central pulpit, replaced by an Art Nouveau copper and brass one at the side. The sweeping staircase to the galleries is very grand.

SHREWSBURY † Holy Cross

Abbey Foregate
OS *SJ498124* **GPS** *52.7076N, 2.7438W*

This is the parochial nave of the former abbey church of St Peter and St Paul, founded in 1083. The E. part of the spacious aisled nave was built soon after, and the W. end is late 14th-century with a massive tower. The abbey was the setting in 1398 for the summoning of the Great Parliament by Richard II. The monastic E. end was rebuilt on a smaller scale by J. L. Pearson, partly vaulted and with a fine triptych, 1886–7. The organ case is by Charles Nicholson. There is an extensive assortment of monuments, mostly from elsewhere.

SHREWSBURY † St Mary ★★

St Mary's Place
OS *SJ493126* **GPS** *52.7087N, 2.7513W*
Churches Conservation Trust

St Mary's is an exquisite former collegiate church of many periods and high architectural quality, standing at the top of the town. Its fine arcades, excellent 15th-century oak roofs with angels, birds and animals, a finely carved early medieval font and vividly coloured Victorian floor tiles all combine to make a splendid impression. There is also remarkable glass, late medieval and imported from Germany and the Netherlands in the 19th century, and a very fine 14th-century English Jesse E. window, possibly transferred from a friars' church in the town. There is little old furniture but many interesting monuments. The interior is scraped but still splendid and welcoming.

STANTON LACY † St Peter ★★

3m/4km N. of Ludlow
OS *SO495788* **GPS** *52.4051N, 2.7430W*

One of the best Saxon churches in Shropshire, cruciform with late 11th-century work in the nave and N. transept; outside is pilaster strip decoration and a fine blocked N. doorway. There was much rebuilding in the early 14th century, and an 1850s restoration by Wyatt. The setting is romantic – tree-shrouded and overgrown.

STOKE ST MILBOROUGH
† St Milburga

6m/10km N.E. of Ludlow
OS *SO566822* **GPS** *52.4369N, 2.6393W*

In a remote village in the Clee hills, this is a spacious, aisle-less Early English and later church full of sunlight. Left unscraped by the Victorians, it has barn-like roofs and a timber porch with brick nogging.

STOKESAY † St John the Baptist ★★

1m/2km S. of Craven Arms
OS *SO435817* **GPS** *52.4307N, 2.8311W*

Two very special buildings form an outstanding group in the pastoral Onny Valley; the incredible 13th-century fortified manor house and a small, basically Norman church, nearly demolished in the Civil War. The nave and tower were rebuilt in 1654 and the chancel in 1664. The furnishings are nearly complete: box pews, an elegant two-decker canopied family pew, wall-texts and an 18th-century W. gallery. The rebuilding was one of a very few that date from the time of the Commonwealth. The churchyard is managed as a wildflower meadow.

STOTTESDON † St Mary ★

7m/12km S.W. of Bridgnorth
OS *SO672828* **GPS** *52.4429N, 2.4833W*

A substantial church with some Saxon and Norman work but mainly 14th-century with good details and glass. The elaborate Norman font, carved with medallions, scrolls

△ **STOKESAY: ST JOHN THE BAPTIST** – *next to a fortified manor house built in the 1390s, the church was rebuilt after the Civil War and is a rare example of Commonwealth church building*

and leaves, is one of the county's best. Of note, too, is the carved tympanum over the W. door.

TONG † St Bartholomew ★

5m/8km E. of Telford
OS *SJ795073* **GPS** *52.6638N, 2.3035W*

Sometimes referred to as Britain's smallest cathedral, the church was collegiate and rebuilt in 1410. Although not large, it is rather spectacular, with a remarkable array of medieval furnishings and monuments, screens, stalls, seating, altar tombs and effigies, many to the Pembrugge and Vernon families. The fan-vaulted chantry chapel was added in 1515; it has traces of colour and the original altar-slab. Fairly restrained restorations were by Street and Christian.

WHITCHURCH † St Alkmund ★

18m/29km N. of Shrewsbury
OS *SJ540417* **GPS** *52.9708N, 2.6850W*

This is a very fine large town church of 1712–13 by William Smith of Warwick, according to a design by John Barker. The handsome exterior is marked by a splendid red sandstone tower. The interior is late Victorian, when it was lined with dark red sandstone, rearranged and sumptuously refurnished using some of the old woodwork and introducing fine Tuscan arcades to the nave. The interior has benefited from the removal of some very gloomy Victorian stained glass.

WROXETER † St Andrew

5m/8km S.E. of Shrewsbury
OS *SJ563082* **GPS** *52.6702N, 2.6472W*
Churches Conservation Trust

On the site of the Roman town of Viroconiumoman, St Andrew's churchyard entrance is flanked by two Roman columns at the gate. Much use was made of Roman building materials throughout, including a font made from a Roman capital and the re-use of more Roman materials in the Saxon nave. The rest of the church is medieval of various dates, altered in the 18th century. The interior has remained unchanged since early in the 19th century, with brick floors, a W. gallery with Gothic organ and seating. Very good 16th-century monuments include those to the Bromleys and Newports.

SOMERSET
& BRISTOL

No county really comes up to Somerset for medieval churches, and of these three-quarters are Perpendicular (15th-century). As A. K. Wickham said in *The Villages of England*, 1932: 'Those boundaries are natural, and have from very early times also been those of the diocese... It is not of course suggested that the local style ceased at the county borders, or even that the medieval builders were conscious of them, but merely that they provide today a casket, as it were, in which these jewels can most easily be compared and admired.'

Churches are mentioned first here because they are the most prominent sights in Somerset, despite the wide variety of its scenery. This variety contains: sea coast along the Bristol Channel; heathery hills on Exmoor; rich valleys in the south-west, full of orchards; wooded steel combes round Bruton and Shepton Mallet; a bare and comparatively churchless area on the west where the Bredons rise nearly as high between Bridgwater and Taunton; a silvery gorge like Cheddar in the Mendips; on the east, Radstock, where coal is quarried; and in the middle of the county the flat alluvial basin providing a fen district where Axe, Brue and Parrett flow into the Bristol Channel and hills rise like blue islands from the flat.

Nor are the towns less varied: Bath so 18th-century with its limestone crescents and terraces and squares; Wells, whose towers rise from a hollow in the Mendips, a city where the cathedral predominates and the atmosphere is medieval in the sound of bells; Taunton, Yeovil and Bridgwater, chain-stored and industrialised; Ilminster, Crewkerne and Axbridge, old-fashioned market towns with grand Perpendicular churches.

Over orchards and willows, wherever you are in Somerset, you can hear the church bells, for few towers contain less than six of them and this is the chief county of ringers.

The variety of stones gives the county a colour. Bath quarries provide pale-yellow stone. Doulting stone, from which Wells and the Mendip churches are built, is silvery-grey; around Somerton and the Polden Hills the quarries yield Blue Lias, which looks particularly good with the old red curly tiles on cottages; and in the west is red sandstone. Finest of all stone is that from Ham Hill in the south. On the Dorset border the old cottages and churches are a rich golden-yellow.

It was after the Black Death and at the end of the 14th century that the great rebuilding of Somerset churches started, and there is no better summary of these buildings than that of the Victorian antiquarian Freeman: 'The typical form is a lofty and elaborate west tower, disengaged from the aisles, often vaulted within, and nave and aisles with or without clerestory;

◁ **BATH: ST PETER AND ST PAUL (BATH ABBEY)** – *the decorative scheme on the west front is based on the biblical story of Jacob's ladder, with angels climbing the rungs heavenward*

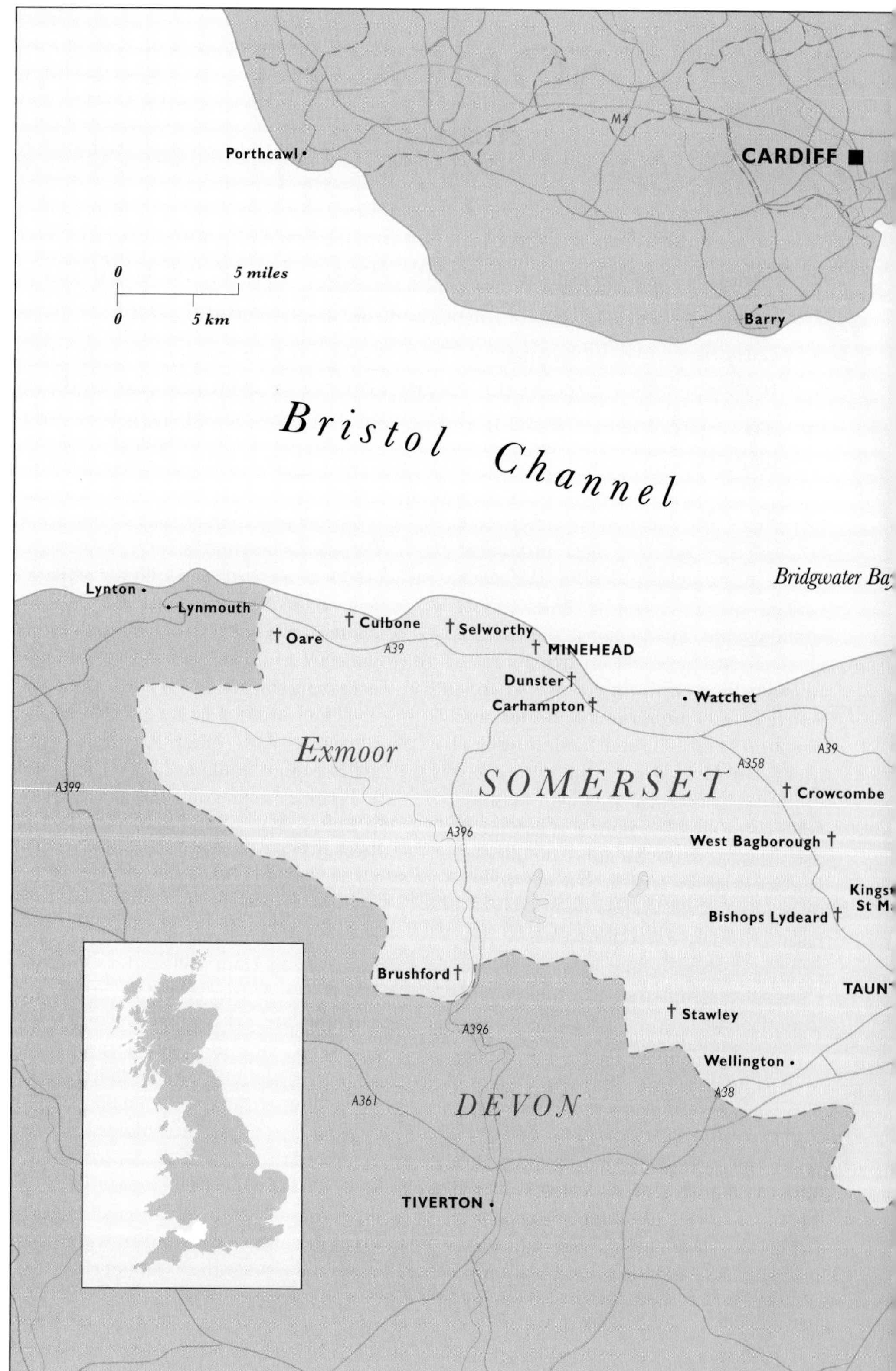

Porthcawl
M4
CARDIFF
0
5 miles
0
5 km
Barry
Bristol Channel
Bridgwater Ba
Lynton
Lynmouth
Culbone
Selworthy
Oare
A39
MINEHEAD
Dunster
Carhampton
Watchet
Exmoor
A358
A39
A399
SOMERSET
Crowcombe
A396
West Bagborough
Kings
St M
Bishops Lydeard
Brushford
TAUN
Stawley
A396
Wellington
A38
A361
DEVON
TIVERTON

GLOUCESTERSHIRE
M49
M4
M5
A4
A420
A46
Avonmouth
Henbury
Westbury-on-Trym
Horfield
Stapleton
Redland
BRISTOL
Clevedon
Backwell
A370
Yatton
Congresbury
Puxton
A37
A4
BATH
A363
WESTON-SUPER-MARE
Wrington
A38
A36
A368
Banwell
Cameley
A367
Wellow
Winscombe
Compton Martin
Hinton Blewitt
Trowbridge
Charterhouse-on-Mendip
A370
Axbridge
A366
Cheddar
Chewton Mendip
A38
A367
Babington
East Brent
A371
A362
Brent Knoll
A37
Holcombe
Mells
Burnham-on-Sea
Wedmore
Leigh-upon-Mendip
A36
FROME
WELLS
A371
Croscombe
A361
Pawlett
SHEPTON MALLET
A39
Witham Friary
Pilton
A361
Glastonbury
Evercreech
Batcombe
West Pennard
Chedzoy
A39
RIDGWATER
Street
A359
A371
WILTSHIRE
Westonzoyland
Bruton
Hornblotton
orth Petherton
A37
High Ham
Low Ham
Wincanton
A361
A372
Somerton
Huish Episcopi
North Cadbury
Langport
North Curry
Curry Rivel
Long Sutton
A303
Queen Camel
A378
Swell
A357
A30
Isle Abbotts
Kingsbury Episcopi
Martock
A37
A359
A358
Brympton
YEOVIL
Sherborne
Norton-sub-Hamdon
Ilminster
A303
A356
A357
Hinton St George
A30
DORSET
A358
Crewkerne
Chard
A358
A356

very commonly a S. porch as high as the aisles, a high roof, and a comparatively insignificant chancel of earlier work, with Perpendicular chapels on each side. Polygonal turrets are frequent. The roofs are various, but different forms of the coved roof are typical. The interiors are rich in screens and other woodwork. The work is generally superior in the North to that in the South part of the county, owing to the superior quality of the stones admitting more delicate chiselling. The towers, which are the great glory of the county, may be ranked under three typical forms. (1) The Taunton type with a staircase turret at one corner and double buttresses at the others, all the pinnacles being of equal height, the tower being divided into stages by horizontal string courses: e.g. St Mary Magdalene and St James, Taunton; Isle Abbots; Bishops Lydeard; and Huish. (2) The Bristol type, with a prominent turret, crowned with a single spirelet rising above the rest. (3) The Wrington type, which dispenses with staircase turret and horizontal divisions and is panelled with two enormous lofty belfry windows, with pinnacled turrets of the same height; Wrington; St Cuthbert's, Wells; St John's, Glastonbury; and North Petherton. Spires are very unfrequent and where they exist are sometimes imperfect… .'

To these glorious towers, built by Somerset people for themselves and essentially non-monastic, the Victorians did little harm. They seem to have been over-awed into leaving them alone and confined their attentions to interiors, though even such 'restorations' were generally mild. Would it be slightly unfair to comment that with such a wealth of Perpendicular architecture, the only lack in the county's churches is one of diversity?

Among all our provincial cities Bristol has few rivals in the matter of old parish churches; some of its best are buildings that once served villages now engulfed in the city's suburbs or outer 'neighbourhoods'. York and Norwich may both beat Bristol in the actual numbers of their parish churches, which have outlasted both the Reformation and later, more insidious, nibblings by demolition gangs, bombs, and the amalgamators of livings. But Bristol's surviving medieval churches and church ruins make up a group whose sheer architectural quality is hard to beat, and after them come several which are good Georgian, and a few worth mentioning among the myriads of the Victorian host.

Too many Bristol churches, alas, have themselves fallen victims to bombs and deliberate demolition; the latter process has been going on at intervals ever since St Lawrence's was pulled down in about 1580. Bristol has been too zealous a 'beautifier' for any parish church interior to be left untouched by the inroads of church furnishers of various dates. So one finds many Bristol churches whose contents include good monuments, ironwork, or other curios, but not one that can show a complete 'period' interior, whether medieval, 17th-century in the manner of Staunton Harold, or even Georgian. To see exactly how Bristol's churches looked inside in the days of high pews and parson and clerk, one must go to the City Art Gallery and look through the unique collection of Braikenridge drawings and watercolours – a perfect record, nearly 1,500 drawings strong – of how Bristol appeared at the tail end of her great Georgian phase.

△ **AXBRIDGE: ST JOHN THE BAPTIST** – *in the Lady Chapel is this monument of 1668 to Anne Prowse, which was overpainted at a later date in chalky hues to pick out the figures*

AXBRIDGE † St John the Baptist ★
2m/3km W. of Cheddar
OS *ST431546* **GPS** *51.2878N, 2.8166W*

An impressive 15th-century town church with central tower, it is approached up a flight of steps from the corner of the market square. The interior is spacious and airy, with a huge plaster ceiling dated 1636 over the nave, and 15th-century fan vaulting over the crossing. There are good memorials, a brass of 1493 and an altar frontal of 1720.

BABINGTON † St Margaret ★
6m/10km N.W. of Frome
OS *ST704510* **GPS** *51.2577N, 2.4243W*

The church of 1750 and manor house form a charming group away from all other habitations. The church is the best Georgian example in Somerset, matched only by Bristol's Redland Chapel. It has an apsidal sanctuary and small W. tower with octagonal cupola. The interior has good moulded plasterwork on its roof and apse. There are box pews, a curved holy table, gated altar rails, two-decker pulpit, a pedestal font and clear glass.

BACKWELL † St Andrew ★
6m/10km S.W. of Bristol
OS *ST493683* **GPS** *51.4117N, 2.7302W*

The fine 15th-century tower of this 12th–17th-century church, repaired in the 20th century, is comparable to those at Portishead and Winford. The N. chancel chapel appears to have been rebuilt in the 16th century and contains an elaborate monument to Sir Walter Rodney, 1466. A brass to Rice Davis, 1638, shows him kneeling with his wife on cushions with their children behind. The screen is from the early 1500s.

BANWELL † St Andrew ★★
5m/8km E. of Weston-super-Mare
OS *ST399591* **GPS** *51.3281N, 2.8632W*

Largely rebuilt in the 15th century, the church has a good W. tower and impressive interior. It contains the finest rood screen in the area, 1522 – seven bays with linenfold panelled dado and Perpendicular tracery, the fans rising to a multi-frieze cornice. In the wider central bay is a pair of doors. The ribbed wagon roof has carved angels. An unusual survival is a

fragment of the rood loft. The W. gallery is partly Elizabethan and apparently made up from a manorial pew. Bench-ends have simple poppyheads, and there are civilian brasses of c. 1480. Eight fine 16th-century Flemish glass panels, restored in 1984, illustrate biblical scenes and the bearded St Louis of France. Particularly attractive is that showing the betrothal of Tobias and Sarah.

BATCOMBE † St Mary

5ml/8km S.E. of Shepton Mallet
OS *ST690390* **GPS** *51.1497N, 2.4444W*

The church is set on the flank of a secluded valley N. of Bruton. Its tower, built in 1540, is a massive example of the E. Mendip type. The chancel is 14th-century with a 17th-century E. window, and to the N. is a picturesque 18th-century vestry. There are pierced parapets without and, within, good aisle roofs, fan vaulting to the tower and 17th-century altar rails.

BATH

† Bath Abbey (St Peter and St Paul) ★★

Between Cheap Street and York Street
OS *ST751647* **GPS** *51.3814N, 2.3588W*

One of the last big Perpendicular monastic churches to be built, it was begun in 1499 on the site of an earlier building, but still not completed by the time of the Dissolution, when the glass and lead of the nave were sold and the building became the mother church of Bath. The nave was finally completed in the 17th century by public subscription and the windows glazed. The W. door was given by Sir Henry Montague in 1617, carved with Arms, drapery and cartouches. On each side are original early 16th-century figures. The famous W. front depicts ladders on which angels ascend and descend. A number of monuments can be seen inside, including a fine one to Sir Philip Frowde, 1674.

BISHOPS LYDEARD † St Mary ★

5ml/8km N.W. of Taunton
OS *ST167297* **GPS** *51.0611N, 3.1887W*

This is a magnificent 15th-century church on the edge of a village at the foot of the Quantocks. The Quantock group of churches includes St Mary's, Huish Episcopi, and St Martin's, Kingsbury Episcopi. Sir Ninian Comper repaired the rood screen that spans the S. aisle and nave, and fitted out the chancel in his own distinctive style in 1923–5. The Jacobean pulpit is well carved and coloured, and the late 15th-century bench-ends are of great interest, among them a carved stag, windmill and ship.

BRENT KNOLL † St Michael ★★

2ml/3km N.E. of Burnham-on-Sea
OS *ST335507* **GPS** *51.2520N, 2.9536W*

On the lower slopes of Brent Knoll, the church stands on an isolated hill rising out of the Somerset flats. There is a Norman S. doorway and some 13th–14th-century work, including the S. chapel, but the fabric is mostly Perpendicular. The carved medieval bench-ends are of great interest: three tell the allegorical tale of an avaricious abbot, represented by a fox. Others depict a Pelican in her Piety and Green Men. Fine carving can be seen too on the Jacobean pulpit. John Somerset, d. 1663, is commemorated in a stately effigy, brightly coloured, under a relief panel showing his family at prayer.

BRISTOL – CITY CENTRE

† All Saints ★

Corn Street
OS *ST588730* **GPS** *51.4548N, 2.5932W*

A very old foundation and a truly lovely English town church. Half the nave is late Norman, the rest particularly graceful Perpendicular, with the mullions of some windows continued down the wall. The simple N. tower is early Georgian, with a delightful Corinthian cupola of 1807. The church is full of monuments to commercial families, the best being to the Colstons. One Colston mural, set up soon after 1701, is a brilliant little Baroque work, probably by some London sculptor such as Richard Crutcher. The one to Bristol's famous philanthropist Edward Colston is an Ionic composition by Gibbs, erected in 1729 by the local mason, Daniel Sidnell. The magnificent reclining figure is by Rysbrack and is worth coming a long way to see. The church is now in use as a Diocesan Education Centre.

◁ **AXBRIDGE: ST JOHN THE BAPTIST** – *a monument of 1670 to William Prouse in the north-east chapel, which is now used as the vestry*

△ **BATH: ST PETER AND ST PAUL (BATH ABBEY)** – *the very worn early 16th-century figures of the church's patron saints, Peter and Paul, on the west façade*

BRISTOL – CITY CENTRE

† St John the Baptist ★

Corner of Broad St, Nelson St and Quay St
OS *ST587731* **GPS** *51.4560N, 2.5950W*
Churches Conservation Trust

The tower and spire of this lovely little unaisled church are specially picturesque, rising above the Gothic city gates. Under the chancel is an early Perpendicular vaulted crypt with a good alabaster tomb of a merchant and his wife, their ten children shown in lower panels. Above, in the chancel, a fine tomb chest with effigy commemorates Walter Frampton, 1388, the founder of the church. The gallery, font and other fittings are of the 17th century, and the Holy Table, 1635, is perhaps England's finest of its kind. This is a church of great character, not much Victorianized.

BRISTOL – CITY CENTRE

† St Mark (The Lord Mayor's Chapel) ★★

College Green
OS *ST583728* **GPS** *51.4530N, 2.6002W*

In the Middle Ages this was the chapel of St Mark's Hospital, and it has never been a parish church. At the Dissolution it passed into civic hands, and is the only church in England owned by a city council. Some of the building is of the 13th century; there are interesting 'Decorated' portions; the Perpendicular tower is of 1487; and the early 16th-century architecture, including the delightful little fan-vaulted Poyntz chantry with Spanish floor tiles, is really brilliant late Perpendicular. This chapel is one of the most important sepulchral churches in England. Many tombs are of civic magnates, but they include a Bishop of Llandaff and the mail-clad effigies of the Berkeley founders. Generally speaking, this is a complete church-trotter's paradise: hatchments, Baroque ironwork by William Edney, Charles II's Arms, and a specially magnificent collection of glass, some of it always having resided in St Mark's, the rest foreign from the Bagot collection and that of William Beckford of Fonthill. For its size, it is one of the very best churches in England.

BRISTOL – CITY CENTRE

† St Mary Redcliffe ★

Redcliffe Way
OS *ST591723* **GPS** *51.4483N, 2.5895W*

The most splendid parochial church in England, its main distinction is its abbey-like size and plan, with double-aisled transepts, ambulatory and E. Lady Chapel. One must spend hours admiring it, not overlooking the important work of about 1200 and the glorious hexagonal N. porch of the early 14th century with fine tierceron vaulting, and the poet Chatterton's muniment room above it. Otherwise it is mostly early Perpendicular, with stone vaults and hundreds of bosses, but the Renaissance monuments are disappointing. There is a brass eagle lectern of 1638 and a fine Baroque iron screen by William Edney, and three fonts, one medieval, one Georgian, one Victorian. There is quite good Victorian furniture, and a stone to The Church Cat, 1912–27, in the churchyard.

BRISTOL – HENBURY

† St Mary the Virgin ★

Church Lane, 4ml6km N.W. of city centre
OS *ST563787* **GPS** *51.5063N, 2.6306W*

The nave and lower tower are the Norman survivors of this village church: the upper tower, S. chapel, chancel and arcades are all Early English. Thomas Rickman restored the church and built the N. chapel in 1836, and in 1875–7 there was further restoration by Street and some very queer Victorian grisaille glass. Inside is an unusual wealth of mural monuments, of the Baroque and later schools, to 18th-century businessmen who had country residences at Henbury. Best of all is the gravestone to Scipio Africanus, a slave to the Earl of Suffolk, who died in 1720 aged 18.

BRISTOL – HORFIELD

† St Gregory the Great ★

Filton Road, 3ml5km N.E. of city centre
OS *ST598778* **GPS** *51.4982N, 2.5797W*

This is a relatively unknown good red-brick neo-Byzantine church of 1934 by A. R. Gough, with a distinctive low octagonal tower.

BRISTOL: ST MARY REDCLIFFE – *the nave is stunning, the delineation of its slender Perpendicular columns emphasizing the vertical dynamism of the space* ▷

The interior is attractive, with soft tones of brick and plaster, noble arcades and chancel arch – delightful and unexpected. Furnishings are by Martin Travis.

BRISTOL – REDLAND
† Redland Chapel

Redland Green Road, 2m/3km N. of city centre
OS *ST579749* **GPS** *51.4722N, 2.6063W*

Built as a private chapel of ease in Westbury parish, the church is a delightful Classical building, with W. cupola and Ionic façade. It is a construction of 1740–3, possibly by John Strahan, and was finished by William Halfpenny for the Cossins family. It became parochial in the 1940s, when the parish of Redland was created. There is fine Georgian woodwork inside, and some busts by Rysbrack. Although the pews are Victorian, the general feeling is still Georgian.

BRISTOL – STAPLETON
† Holy Trinity ★

Corner of Bell Hill and Colston Hill, 3m/5km N.E. of city centre
OS *ST615759* **GPS** *51.4815N, 2.5549W*

Another replacement of an older building, the present church dates from 1856–7. It is Victorian Decorated in the manner of Pugin – the architect was John Norton, a pupil of Benjamin Ferrey, who himself studied under Pugin. The fabric is an opulent composition and Bristol's best Victorian church, a mixture of carved stone and polished marble, with a really fine crocketed spire in the manner of the East Midlands. This church would be at home in Lincolnshire.

BRISTOL – WESTBURY-ON-TRYM
† Holy Trinity ★

Church Road, 3m/5km N. of city centre
OS *ST573774* **GPS** *51.4940N, 2.6160W*

The best of Bristol's outlying churches, it was once partly collegiate, partly parochial. Much of it is of the 13th century, including the 'collegiate' sedilia in the S. aisle. The chancel, once the college choir, has graceful 15th-century architecture and the rarity of a Perpendicular apse. The tower is of that delicate beauty evolved by late 15th-century local designers who made one pinnacle rise like a needle above the rest. Inside is the Victorian tomb of Bishop Carpenter of Worcester, d. 1476, and many Georgian monuments to wealthy Bristolians who came to live in what was then a country parish.

BRUSHFORD † St Nicholas

17m/27km W. of Taunton
OS *SS919257* **GPS** *51.0208N, 3.5419W*

This is a pleasant medieval church with N. chapel by Sir Edwin Lutyens, 1926. The exterior has banded stonework and small round-headed windows; in the E. gable is a cross-shaped light. Inside is Geometrical decoration, a 13th-century screen and a canopied tomb to Aubrey Herbert, d. 1923, with a recumbent effigy.

BRUTON † St Mary ★

7m/11km S.E. of Shepton Mallet
OS *ST684347* **GPS** *51.1116N, 2.4520W*

The stately church stands on the S. edge of the town, adjacent to a playing field that is the site of a former Augustinian abbey. The N. porch has a miniature tower, dwarfed by the splendid 15th-century W. tower. Inside, the nave has a highly decorated tie-beam roof and Jacobean screen, benches and pulpit. The chancel was rebuilt in 1743 and, apart from the screen of 1938, preserves much of its original furniture.

BRYMPTON † St Andrew

2m/3km W. of Yeovil
OS ST519153 **GPS** 50.9359N, 2.6856W

This cruciform church dates from the 13th century, and has a N. porch, N.E. chapel and W. bell turret. It was lightly restored at the turn of the 19th–20th century, and is notable for a fine canopied tomb to John Sydenham, d. 1626, and effigies of a knight, c. 1275, and a larger-than-life lady, c. 1440, in the N transept. There is also a canopied memorial to a priest, c. 1348, and a large assembly of brasses and wall plaques. Note too the good 18th-century brass chandeliers, possibly Dutch.

△ **BRISTOL: REDLAND CHAPEL** – *the church has a refined Georgian interior, the walls lined by winged cherub corbels mounted on dark wood panelling*

CAMELEY † St James ★★

8m/13km S. of Bristol
OS *ST610575* **GPS** *51.3159N, 2.5606W*
Churches Conservation Trust

A small church with good decoration and furnishings, it is beautifully situated in the Mendip Hills. The 12th-century nave, chancel and S. porch are built of Blue Lias limestone, and the W. tower, refashioned in the 15th century, is of contrasting red sandstone. The interior is one of the most attractive in the county, an interesting blend of medieval and Georgian. Medieval wall-paintings show a jester and decorative motifs, and over the chancel arch is an early painting of the Ten Commandments. The good 15th-century box pews have their original door furniture. There is a Jacobean pulpit, reader's desk and balustraded communion rail; the reredos, coat hooks, pews and gallery are all Georgian. The S. gallery, 1819, is entered by an external stair and inscribed, 'For the free use of the inhabitants'.

CARHAMPTON † St John the Baptist

4m/7km S.E. of Minehead
OS *ST009426* **GPS** *51.1746N, 3.4185W*

This is a modest 15th-century Perpendicular church close to a busy main road, whose glory is a fine Perpendicular rood screen, restored and painted by spirited Victorians. The wagon roof and carved roof bosses are original, and there is a good carved 18th-century pulpit.

CHARTERHOUSE-ON-MENDIP
† St Hugh

3m/4km N.E. of Cheddar
OS *ST501556* **GPS** *51.2979N, 2.7166W*

By W. D. Caroe, 1908, this is a tiny, rustic Arts and Crafts mission church with cat-slide roof over the entrance, panelled inside with limed oak, and a delightful carved reredos, altar and screen. Plain but very charming, it overlooks the old Roman lead mines of Charterhouse.

△ **BRISTOL, WESTBURY-ON-TRYM: HOLY TRINITY** – *the roof trusses are supported on a delightful group of corbel heads, each distinct and decidedly characterful*

CHEDZOY † St Mary
3m/4km E. of Bridgwater
OS *ST341376* **GPS** *51.1345N, 2.9430W*

A fine 15th–16th-century rebuilding preserves the 13th-century nave arcades and N. aisle, with further alterations to the chancel in 1885 by William Butterfield. From the tower Royalist troops were first seen closing on Monmouth's army prior to the Battle of Sedgemoor, 1685.

CHEWTON MENDIP
† St Mary Magdalene ★★
6m/10km N.E. of Wells
OS *ST596531* **GPS** *51.2761N, 2.5800W*

The original church was Norman, substantially rebuilt every century from the 14th to the 16th, with a mediocre Victorian restoration of 1865. The glorious 16th-century tower of E. Mendip type is regarded as one of the best of its kind: it has an elaborate parapet and panelled middle stage with original sculpture on the W. front. The N. doorway is late 12th-century; there are 16th-century bench-ends and a 17th-century lectern and holy table. In the chancel is a 'frid-stool', a seat of Anglo-Saxon origin offering sanctuary to those who sat on it. Concealed by the 19th-century porch is part of a corbel table, and outside is a complete medieval churchyard cross with canopied crucifix.

COMPTON MARTIN † St Michael ★
9m/14km S.W of Bristol
OS *ST544569* **GPS** *51.3102N, 2.6542W*

Musty and dark, nevertheless this is probably the best Norman village church in the area. Norman work includes the nave arcades, clerestory and chancel. The arcades have circular piers with scalloped capitals; one pier is spirally fluted. The good corbel table on the N. side has monsters and heads, and the low rib-vaulted chancel is impressive: it has a disused columbarium above. The circular Norman font has a zigzag frieze, and in the N. aisle are interesting monuments.

CREWKERNE † St Bartholomew ★★
8m/12km S.W. of Yeovil
OS *ST439098* **GPS** *50.8850N, 2.7980W*

This is a magnificent 15th-century cruciform church with central tower, all of glowing Ham Hill stone, with breathtaking Perpendicular tracery. The imposing W.

façade, with flanking octagonal turrets, is very fine: the detailing of the turrets is particularly good, and similar detailing can be seen on the S. porch, which has good fan-vaulting. The heavy crossing piers are an indication that the present building is a grand remodelling of an earlier 13th-century cruciform church. The six-light Perpendicular windows in the aisles are very fine, as is the collection of Tudor and later chapels to the N.E. The W. galleries were added in the early 19th century to provide further room in an already spacious interior.

CROSCOMBE † St Mary the Virgin ★

3m/4km E. of Wells
OS *ST590444* **GPS** *51.1975N, 2.5873W*

The wagon roof is notable and there is a good series of late medieval poppyheaded benches, but it is the Jacobean woodwork that makes the church so remarkable. This includes a two-tiered arcaded screen with obelisk finials, strapwork, heraldic shields and Stuart Arms; box pews and medieval pews with poppyheads converted into box pews, and a towering pulpit together with an elaborate tie-beam chancel roof set on carved angels.

CROWCOMBE † Holy Ghost ★

9m/14km N.W. of Taunton
OS *ST140367* **GPS** *51.1232N, 3.2292W*

The top section of the 14th-century spire, hit by lightning in 1724, is now planted in the churchyard. The main fabric of this attractive red sandstone church is 15th-century. But it is the 16th-century bench-ends that draw attention: two men spearing a dragon, a Green Man and Coats of Arms are among these richly carved treasures from 1534. The same sculptors are believed to have carved the octagonal sandstone font with a mitred bishop, an early church father, a nun and knight at prayer, St Anne and the Virgin Mary, and the Virgin Mary crowned.

CULBONE † St Bueno ★

On coast path between Porlock Weir and County Gate, 7m/11km W. of Minehead
OS *SS842482* **GPS** *51.2215N, 3.6593W*

Reputedly the smallest parish church in England, the church is set in a secluded wooded valley inaccessible by public roads, but well worth the two-mile walk from the Culbone Inn. The nave and chancel are probably Norman, with all but one window replaced in the 15th century or later. The survivor is a single stone, carved outside with the head of a biting beast. The large tub font is also early. Small-scale pre-Reformation benches have linenfold panels; the rood screen is 16th-century, and there is a 17th-century manorial pew.

CURRY RIVEL † St Andrew ★

9m/14km E. of Taunton
OS *ST391253* **GPS** *51.0247N, 2.8687W*

The church is mainly Perpendicular, and the exterior is decorated with a variety of grotesques ('hunky punks' in local parlance), among which are a bagpiper, a fiddler and a dog. The S. porch is good – two storey with a parvise, and inside are fine slender arcade columns, good 15th-century parclose screens to the N. and S. aisles, and carved bench-ends. In the N. chapel, the oldest part of the church, is a 13th-century recessed tomb, thought to be of the chapel's founder Sabina de Lorty. And between the chapel and the chancel is the fine canopied monument to Marmaduke Jennings, d. 1625, and his son Robert, d. 1630. The two effigies are attired as troopers.

DUNSTER † St George ★

2m/3km S.E. of Minehead
OS *SS990436* **GPS** *51.1832N, 3.4459W*

The church is hidden away behind the top end of a picturesque market town. Although remodelled in the 15th century, the form of the Norman church survives, the Benedictine monastic choir separated from the parish church by a massive central tower. The huge 15th-century rood screen runs right across the nave and aisles. The former monastic choir houses impressive 14th–18th-century Luttrell monuments.

EAST BRENT † St Mary

3m/4km N.E. of Burnham-on-Sea
OS *ST343519* **GPS** *51.2626N, 2.9417W*

This is a large 15th-century church with a tall stepped tower and slender spire. The sumptuous plaster ceiling, pulpit and chancel screen, now at the W. end, are additions of the 1630s. Note the medieval eagle lectern, 15th-century bench-ends, restored Passion window and Victorian stencilling in the chancel.

EVERCREECH † St Peter

4m/6km S.E. of Shepton Mallet
OS *ST649386* **GPS** *51.1463N, 2.5026W*

The slender yet imposing 15th-century tower of the church, which dominates the village, is a typical E. Mendip type, with belfry windows carried down into long panels. Note the corner and intermediate pinnacles. The rest of the church is, disappointingly, much restored from the 19th century, and full of furnishings of the same period.

GLASTONBURY
† St John the Baptist ★★

13m/21km E. of Bridgwater
OS *ST500390* **GPS** *51.1482N, 2.7162W*

This spacious Perpendicular town church, mostly mid-15th-century, has one of the finest towers in Somerset; the elaborate parapet and panelled middle stage are more characteristic of Gloucestershire than Somerset. The church has a handsome two-storeyed lierne-vaulted porch. The late 15th-century tie-beam nave roof is sumptuous, stout oak with moulding, bosses and tracery. The tower is vaulted, and underneath the Scott pulpit is the alabaster tomb of John Cammell, d. 1487, with an effigy and carved camels below. In the centre of the N. transept is an early 15th-century tomb/shrine, said to be that of Joseph of Arimathea, originally from the abbey.

HIGH HAM † St Andrew ★

8m/13km S.E. of Bridgwater
OS *ST425310* **GPS** *51.0760N, 2.8217W*

The churchyard forms the N. side of an attractive group of buildings around the green. With the exception of its 14th-century tower, the building was erected c. 1476. The timberwork is particularly complete: the rood screen with rood beam over is of a type native to Devon, with a very fine elaborate fan-vaulted overthrow. The roofs are splendid examples of the Somerset type: the nave and aisle roofs have moulded ribs and panels with rose bosses; the chancel roof has fine moulded king-post trusses, arched-braced ties and a wealth of rosettes, angels and other carvings.

△ **CREWKERNE: ST BARTHOLOMEW** – *built of Ham Hill stone, the detail of the exterior carving has weathered badly but is still a delight in its tonal variations and sculptural traces*

HINTON BLEWETT

† St Andrew Margaret ★

9m/14km S. of Bristol

OS *ST594569* **GPS** *51.3104N, 2.5834W*

The church stands behind a row of cottages and a pub which front the pretty village green. Mainly 15th-century, the interior is light and airy, with stone floors. There is a timber roof with bosses in the nave and N. aisle, a Norman font, 15th-century square-headed bench-ends and a canopied pulpit of 1638. Windows on the N. side have some 16th-century glass.

HINTON ST GEORGE † St George

2m/3km N.W. of Crewkerne

OS *ST418126* **GPS** *50.9107N, 2.8286W*

A good Perpendicular church with very nice W. tower of 1494, it has a notable series of 16th–19th-century Poulett monuments, including a bizarre Baroque structure to John Baron Poulett, d. 1649; decidedly un-English. The W. façade has an ornate pointed arched doorway with hood mould and a mullioned window above. There are some 15th-century traceried bench-ends and a cushion bowl Norman font in the nave.

HOLCOMBE † St Andrew

6m/10km N.E. of Shepton Mallet

OS *ST668507* **GPS** *51.2548N, 2.4760W*

Churches Conservation Trust

St Andrew's stands alone in the fields, its village now a mile away to the S. It is a plain and simple church of great charm – 12th-century refashioned in the 16th and later. The S. porch has a very good re-set Norman doorway. The

△ **CROSCOMBE: ST MARY THE VIRGIN** – *a triumph of mostly Jacobean wood carving, including box pews, pulpit and tester, and two-stage screen*

early 19th-century interior is atmospheric, with box pews, hat pegs, two-decker pulpit, gallery and clear glass.

HORNBLOTTON † St Peter ★★

6m/10km S.E. of Shepton Mallet
OS *ST591341* **GPS** *51.1052N, 2.5848W*

By Sir T. G. Jackson, 1872–4, under the influence of R. Norman Shaw, with tile-hung belfry and shingled broach spire in the Home Counties taste. Within are tall cream walls with delightful strawberry sgraffito, enriched with aesthetic sunflowers, all complemented by tasteful inlaid hardwood furnishings, agreeable mosaic, and a reredos by Powell & Sons, who also made the glass. Completely enchanting.

HUISH EPISCOPI † St Mary the Virgin ★

E. side of Langport, 8m/13km S.E. of Bridgwater
OS *ST427266* **GPS** *51.0361N, 2.8183W*

The tower is a renowned example of the Taunton type, sumptuously decorated, a companion to that of St Martin's in Kingsbury Episcopi. The church is a pleasant mix of Blue Lias limestone and Ham stone. Note the elaborate 12th-century S. doorway and tall panelled tower arch, filled by a fine 15th-century timber screen from Enmore in 1873, and the Burne-Jones window by Morris & Co. in the S. chapel.

ILMINSTER † St Mary

10m/16km S.E. of Taunton
OS *ST360145* **GPS** *50.9271N, 2.9117W*

This is one of the great Perpendicular Somerset cruciform churches; the early 17th-century tower is impressive – open stone tracery to the top section, good crocketed finials and a finely proportioned stair turret. The nave was remodelled to take galleries in 1825. There are good 15th- and 17th-century Wadham memorials in the N. transept.

ISLE ABBOTS † St Mary

7m/11km S.E. of Taunton
OS *ST352209* **GPS** *50.9843N, 2.9236W*

Another church with a fine 15th-century Somerset tower that retains several original medieval sculptures, some still with traces of colour: among them the risen Christ, St Peter and St Paul, St Margaret, St Michael, and the Virgin and Child. Inside is a simple 15th-century screen with some original paintwork, Jacobean fittings and furnishings, a carved Norman font and three-seat sedilia of the 1300s.

KINGSBURY EPISCOPI † St Martin ★
7ml/11km N.W. of Yeovil
OS *ST436210* **GPS** *50.9865N, 2.8042W*

In a large village of Ham stone in the marshy basin of the River Parrett, set about with willows, the imposing church is mainly 14th- and 15th-century, with one of the most satisfying of the great Somerset towers. The lofty chancel has splendid transomed windows and an E. sacristy. There is a fine fan-vaulted tower base, a 15th-century screen and fragments of old glass.

KINGSTON ST MARY † St Mary
3ml/5km N. of Taunton
OS *ST222297* **GPS** *51.0615N, 3.1103W*

Set at the southern end of the Quantock Hills, St Mary's is another church with a grand 16th-century tower, all pinnacled, with Somerset tracery and grotesques at each corner. Inside is good woodwork, particularly the 16th-century bench-ends in the nave.

LEIGH-ON-MENDIP † St Giles
5ml/8km W. of Frome
OS *ST692472* **GPS** *51.2239N, 2.4417W*

The huge W. tower, with complex pinnacles and pierced parapets, dominates this splendid 15th-century Somerset church. The scraped but still splendid Somerset nave has slender arcade piers: the nave and chancel roofs are tie-beamed with carved angels and bosses. There is some early glass and a remarkably complete set of traceried benches. On the sill of the S.E. window is a 12th-century stone figure of St Catherine.

LONG SUTTON † Holy Trinity ★
9ml/14km N.W. of Yeovil
OS *ST469253* **GPS** *51.0247N, 2.7577W*

The lofty late 15th-century tower looms over the spacious village green surrounded by Blue Lias-stone houses of many periods. The church is a spacious and impressive fabric in the best Somerset manner, with clerestoried nave and magnificent tie-beam roof of local type; the 15th-century pulpit and rood screen both have vivid Victorian colouring.

LOW HAM † Dedication unknown
9ml/14km S.E. of Bridgwater
OS *ST432291* **GPS** *51.0584N, 2.8113W*

This is a remarkable church built 1629–69 on a green-field site below the terraces of a failed scheme for a great house. Now it stands surrounded by farm machinery. The innovative window tracery in particular led Pevsner to describe it as 'one of the most instructive cases of early Gothicism in England'. Inside are effigies of the founder, Sir Edward Hext, and his wife; the monument to Sir George Stawell in the S. aisle has superb iron railings. The benches, screen, pulpit, communion rails and glass in the E. window are all contemporary, and the elaborate stone entrance screen was removed from the Lord Mayor's Chapel in Bristol.

MARTOCK † All Saints ★
6ml/10km N.W. of Yeovil
OS *ST461191* **GPS** *50.9693N, 2.7687W*

Martock is not far from the famous Ham Hill quarries, which provided the stone for this noble church and many interesting houses. The church has a 13th-century chancel, but the rest is good Somerset Perpendicular. Inside is a superb roof of 1513, made when the nave was heightened; it is one of the finest tie-beam roofs in the country. Canopied niches in the clerestory have 17th-century paintings of the Apostles. Restored successively by Ferry and Scott, 1860, and Ewan Christian, 1883–4.

MELLS † St Andrew ★★
3ml/4km W. of Frome
OS *ST727492* **GPS** *51.2420N, 2.3912W*

One of the best villages in Somerset, which is saying a good deal, it has a stately church, mellow Tudor manor house, and many charming cottages and farmsteads. The church was rebuilt in the 15th century with a noble tower and a profusion of carved detail.

△ **HOLCOMBE: ST ANDREW** – *left alone in the corner of a field when its village moved south, St Andrew's is a neat little church with an early 19th-century interior*

The beautiful though restored interior has a fine nave and chapel roofs, and the 1930s E. window is by Charles Nicholson. There are some very good monuments here, such as the equine memorial to the Horner family by A. Munnings, 1920, on a Lutyens base. Under the tower is a gesso plaque of a peacock by Burne-Jones to Laura Lyttleton, 1886, and nearby is incised lettering by Eric Gill, 1916, to Raymond Asquith, with a Lutyens bronze wreath above. The Horner manor house nearby was something of a gathering place for leading artists of the time. Outside are more interesting memorials to Horners and Asquiths, and most notably Seigfreid Sassoon, who is buried close to his friend Ronald Knox, the Catholic theologian.

MINEHEAD † St Michael

St Michael's Road
OS *SS966467* **GPS** *51.2109N, 3.4805W*

In the old town, perched in the lee of a huge whale-backed hill, is an imposing and spacious, mostly Perpendicular church set in a graveyard with stones commemorating the human cost of the town's dependence on the sea. There are interesting fittings of good quality: 15th-century screens, a brass of a lady, an effigy of a priest, a superb 16th-century communion table, 17th-century pulpit, Royal Arms and texts.

NORTH CADBURY † St Michael ★★

9m/14km N.E. of Yeovil
OS *ST635270* **GPS** *51.0417N, 2.5214W*

This is a splendid Somerset Perpendicular church adjacent to North Cadbury Court. The tall panelled collegiate chancel is particularly impressive, with a traceried king-post trussed roof and good windows. The nave also has a traceried king-post roof, more ornate than the chancel, with leaf bosses and angel corbels. There are numerous fragments of 15th-century painted glass, particularly in the W. window. There is a good collection of 16th-century carved bench-ends – note the one of a kissing couple.

△ **NORTON-SUB-HAMDON: ST MARY** – *a light and spacious interior, with clear glass, large window openings and only a delicate screen to separate nave from chancel*

NORTH CURRY
† St Peter and St Paul ★

6m/10km E. of Taunton
OS *ST319255* **GPS** *51.0254N, 2.9717W*

This large cruciform Perpendicular church is set on a slight rise with fine views over the Somerset Levels. The church is Norman in origin, with Early English transepts and nave. The octagonal lantern over the crossing is particularly striking. It was scraped and re-ordered by J. Oldrid Scott in 1881; Scott also built the vestry.

NORTH PETHERTON † St Mary ★

2m/3km S. of Bridgwater
OS *ST290330* **GPS** *51.0921N, 3.0148W*

In a large village near the edge of Sedgemoor, this is a fine, mainly 15th-century church with a superb W. tower retaining most of the original figure sculpture and crowned by a richly pinnacled parapet. There is an E. sacristy as in several other important Somerset churches. The nave and aisles have good roofs; there is a 14th-century font and Perpendicular pulpit with traceried panels. From the upper stage of the porch a balcony opens onto the S. aisle.

NORTON-SUB-HAMDON † St Mary ★

5m/8km W. of Yeovil
OS *ST470159* **GPS** *50.9407N, 2.7548W*

This delightful church of c. 1500–10 is set on a hill with a wonderful W. tower, having tall belfry openings and big gargoyles. There is little differentiation between the nave and the chancel, giving a fine impression of a lofty, airy space, with a ribbed wagon-vault ceiling over. The Art Nouveau screen across the tower is by Henry Wilson, 1894, who also designed the glorious but incongruous alabaster font, a circular tub on a square base with large fish at each corner, and a wooden octagonal cupola lid. There are some unexpected traces of Wilson's Art Nouveau touches near the W. window. More appropriate to a Perpendicular church is Wilson's glass of 1904 in the S. chapel.

OARE † St Mary ★
10m/16km W. of Minehead
OS *SS802473* **GPS** *51.2124N, 3.7164W*

A charming church, small and neat: it was immortalised by R. D. Blackmore as the scene of the marriage of Jan Ridd in *Lorna Doone*. It is formed of a modest W. tower, scaled nave, inner and outer chancel (added in the late 19th century), all under separate slate roofs. The interior character of the church is pleasingly rustic, with box pews and 18th-century painted slate slabs to the Spurry family. The painted wooden panel is believed to be a representation of Moses. Of note is the unusual piscina in the form of a man's head clasped between his hands.

PAWLETT † St John the Baptist ★
4m/6km N. of Bridgwater
OS *ST300426* **GPS** *51.1788N, 3.0016W*

The church stands on high ground above the rich pastures of Pawlett Hams. It is medieval, with a good atmospheric interior. The 12th-century core was refashioned and enlarged in the 13th and 15th centuries. There is a good 12th-century font, 15th-century screen and a fine display of 17th-century fittings, including three-sided altar rails, box pews, font cover, pulpit and reading desk. The windows mostly have clear glass in rectangular leading.

PILTON † St John the Baptist ★
2m/3km S.W. of Shepton Mallet
OS *ST588408* **GPS** *51.1651N, 2.5898W*

In a pleasant, rambling village on a hillside with a great 14th-century tithe barn on the opposite slope, this is a 12th-century church refashioned and enlarged in the 15th century, with clerestoried nave and chancel, a late 12th-century arcade and splendid 15th-century roofs. There are good parclose screens, fragments of glass and part of a 15th-century cope.

PUXTON † St Saviour
4m/6km N.E. of Weston-super-Mare
OS *ST406632* **GPS** *51.3653N, 2.8536W*
Churches Conservation Trust

This is a small isolated church on the Somerset Levels with a short, 15th-century W. tower whose lean to the W. almost rivals that of St Martin in the Black Mountains. The simple whitewashed interior retains Jacobean furnishings: reader's desk, altar rails, pulpit and some fine 18th-century oak box pews. The floor is flagstoned with ledger slabs inset, and the rood beam is still visible, cut off flush with the walls.

QUEEN CAMEL † St Barnabas ★
6m/10km N.E. of Yeovil
OS *ST597249* **GPS** *51.0225N, 2.5754W*

Up a side street at the N. end of this large Lias-stone village is the impressive 14th- and 15th-century church; its charming 18th-century portico somehow escaped the Victorian 'restorers'. Although scraped inside, it is still interesting on account of the fine tie-beam nave roof, lofty vaulted screen and early Perpendicular font unusually enriched with figures. Of note too are the 15th-century bench-ends and pulpit, and the Mildmay monuments and hatchments.

SELWORTHY † All Saints ★★
3m/5km W. of Minehead
OS *SS919468* **GPS** *51.2102N, 3.5477W*

The dazzling whitewashed exterior of the church is visible for miles, and from the churchyard are wonderful views over the Vale of Porlock to the moors beyond. The crenellations on the S. and on the tower, and the contrast between the stone tracery of the windows and the white exterior, give this delightful little church a slight dolls' house appearance, an effect enhanced by the cheerfully painted and fascinating ceiling bosses that decorate the wagon roofs. Elsewhere inside is much of interest: Comper glass, the fine E. window glass by Clayton & Bell, the early 19th-century Gothic manorial pew over the S. door, a delightful painted reredos by Philip Burgess of West Porlock, 1900, and a good assembly of monuments.

SHEPTON MALLET
† St Peter and St Paul
Between Peter Street and Paul Street
OS *ST619436* **GPS** *51.1910N, 2.5455W*

Hidden behind a large concrete theatre is the town church, whose 14th-century tower with

△ **WESTONZOYLAND: ST MARY** – *a beautifully balanced interior, with a fine medieval roof, good bench-ends and a rood and screen by Caroe, part of late 19th- and early 20th-century restorations*

its unfinished spire is one of the earliest of the 'Somerset Perpendiculars'. Inside, above the 12th-century arcades, is the most intricate wagon roof in the county, with 350 individual hand-carved panels. The church was much altered in the mid-19th-century, when the side chapels and transepts were demolished.

SOMERTON

† St Michael and All Angels ★

8m/13km N.W. of Yeovil

OS *ST490286* **GPS** *51.0546N, 2.7284W*

This is a large 13th–14th-century church set back from the market-place. The square 13th-century tower has rough broaches under an octagonal upper stage with external staircase turret, and from the outside is rather plain. Inside is a fine and richly ornamented panelled late Perpendicular nave roof, with pig's head, foliate and barrel bosses separating the finely carved quatrefoil panels. There is a well carved octagonal Jacobean pulpit on a narrow stem, still with traces of original colouring, a reredos with 17th-century panelling, communion table of 1626 and much reuse of 15th-century woodwork. Betjeman always claimed that the inscription on one of Somerton's chandelier roundels inspired his *Collins Pocket Guide to England's Parish Churches* (the original edition of the book you are reading). The inscription reads: 'To God's Glory & the Honor of the Church of England, 1782.' (See the essay at the front of this book for Betjeman's introduction in full.)

STAWLEY † St Michael

9m/14km W. of Taunton

OS *ST060226* **GPS** *50.9954N, 3.3404W*

A little church of the 11th, 13th and 16th centuries in lovely remote hilly country near the Devon border, it is unusual for the absence of 19th-century changes. The atmospheric interior has most of the 18th-century furnishings: box pews, pulpit with ogee tester, baluster altar rails, Commandment boards in the tower and the Lord's Prayer and Creed on painted boards on the N. wall.

SWELL † St Catherine
7ml11km E. of Taunton
OS *ST369235* **GPS** *51.0082N, 2.9003W*

Visit this delightful little church for its setting and simplicity. The Norman doorway is protected by the S. porch, in which there is a stone bench and early graffiti. The interior is plastered with flagstone floors, all under wagon roofs with bosses. There is an excellent Jacobean carved pulpit of 1634.

TAUNTON † St Mary Magdalene ★
Magdalene Street
OS *ST228246* **GPS** *51.0157N, 3.1007W*

A stately and noble 15th–16th-century Ham stone town church, it forms an important group with Hammett Street and Church Square. The double aisles to the nave have created an almost square plan and a forest of pillars. The elaborate tower, with its pierced parapets and soaring crocketed finials, is one of the tallest and finest in the county, rebuilt in 1862 by Ferrey and Scott. The nave has a handsome cusped tie-beam roof with gilded angels, and the elaborate S. porch is of 1508. Repeated restorations have left little original furnishing.

WEDMORE † St Mary the Virgin
4ml6km S. of Cheddar
OS *ST434479* **GPS** *51.2277N, 2.8110W*

This is a huge Perpendicular church with tall central tower. The N.E. chapel has a good 15th-century painted and panelled ceiling; here are the brasses of Thomas Hodges, killed at the siege of Antwerp, 1583, and George Hodges, 1684. A robust wall-painting of c. 1520 above the pulpit depicts St Christopher with mermaid and ships.

WELLOW † St Julian ★
4ml6km S. of Bath
OS *ST741583* **GPS** *51.3241N, 2.3718W*

Founded before the 12th century, the present fabric of this large church dates from the 14th. The chancel is by Bodley and Garner, 1890, and Caroe & Partners completed restorations in 1952. There are fine 15th-century roofs in the nave and Hungerford Chapel, which also contains wall-paintings of Christ and the 12 Apostles – a rare subject. There are bench-ends with poppy heads, an effigy of a priest in Mass vestments, c. 1400, and 12 small carved heads, probably 14th-century, reset in the chancel. The Perpendicular rood screen of c. 1430 is finely carved, with the loft and rood by Caroe & Partners, 1952.

WELLS † St Cuthbert ★★
St Cuthbert Street
OS *ST546456* **GPS** *51.2083N, 2.6503W*

Seen from afar, the superb W. tower of this fine Perpendicular church counterbalances the Cathedral. The impressive 13th-century cruciform interior was beautifully enhanced in the 15th century; the many chapels afford great spaciousness. There are fine roofs, especially the exquisitely carved ceiling over the S.W. chapel and the nave roof, which was fully coloured after a 1963 restoration by Alan Rowe. St Catherine's Chapel has the remains of a 13th-century reredos on the wall, and in the Lady Chapel is another stone reredos – a Tree of Jesse by John Stowell, 1470. The resplendent pulpit of 1636 has scenes from the Old Testament, including Jonah and the Whale, and Daniel in the Lions' Den.

WEST BAGBOROUGH † St Pancras ★
7ml11km N.W. of Taunton
OS *ST168337* **GPS** *51.0966N, 3.1888W*

The little 15th-century church stands on the lower slope of a wooded hill hard by the late Georgian manor house. The interior is rich in Comper fittings and glass, and has a fine display of the early 16th-century bench-ends so characteristic of the Quantocks. The genius of Sir Ninian Comper has made it an ideal village church.

WEST PENNARD † St Nicholas
3ml4km E. of Glastonbury
OS *ST552382* **GPS** *51.1419N, 2.6415W*

In a large Lias-stone village with a network of lanes, almost in the shadow of Glastonbury Tor, the handsome church was completely rebuilt in the second half of the 15th century. The W. tower has a timber and lead spire, and there are fine and richly carved roofs throughout. There is a late 15th-century restored rood screen and glass, including the Coronation of the Virgin. The churchyard cross has emblems of the Passion on the base.

WESTONZOYLAND † St Mary ★
4m/6km E. of Bridgwater
OS *ST351347* **GPS** *51.1087N, 2.9274W*

A stately 14th–15th-century church overlooking Sedgemoor, its history is intertwined with the 1685 Battle of Sedgemoor; it was used to house some 500 prisoners overnight after the battle. Robust tie beams with king posts support the nave roof, with angel busts and corbels. In the S. transept are the initials of a Glastonbury abbot, Richard Beere, and an incised pelican. There is much of Caroe's work here too: the organ case, rood screen, loft and polygonal rood stair. Built under the patronage of the abbots of Glastonbury, it is a good Somerset Perpendicular church.

WINSCOMBE † St James
5m/8km S.E. of Weston-Super-Mare
OS *ST411566* **GPS** *51.3059N, 2.8456W*

A fine 15th-century church set on a hill above the village, it has a good W. tower and original roofs to the aisles and chapel, and exceptionally good stained glass. The N. chapel has a 15th-century Crucifixion, saints and donors; a window of 1535 depicts the three St Peters and the chancel's E. lancets have excellent Pre-Raphaelite-style glass of 1863 by W. G. Saunder.

WITHAM FRIARY † St Mary, St John the Baptist and All Saints ★
6m/10km N.E. of Bruton
OS *ST744411* **GPS** *51.1686N, 2.3675W*

The first English Carthusian house was founded here in 1178–9 by Henry II. St Hugh, the Burgundian prior, third prior of the foundation and later Bishop of Lincoln, probably erected the first stone buildings here in the French style with which he was familiar. The priory was disbanded during the 16th-century Dissolution of the Monasteries, but part was retained for use as a parish church. The current church was created in 1875 by William White, who rebuilt and extended a portion of the original buildings in 'Muscular Gothic' style.

WRINGTON † All Saints
8m/13km E. of Weston-super-Mare
OS *ST467627* **GPS** *51.3610N, 2.7657W*

Pleasantly situated in the Yeo Valley, the church was substantially rebuilt in the 15th century, with yet again a fine Somerset tower, not dissimilar to that at Evercreech. The shortness of the nave is offset by its height, and the full-width rood screen is very fine, though sadly lacking its original colouring, stripped in 1859. The 1832 Caen stone reredos was designed by Sir Charles Barry.

YATTON † St Mary ★
4m/6km S. of Clevedon
OS *ST431654* **GPS** *51.3850N, 2.8186W*

The central tower of this impressive church is topped by a truncated spire abandoned before completion. Of 13th-century origins, the nave, aisles and chancel were rebuilt in the 15th century, and the highly decorated S. porch and N. chancel chapel added by Isobel of Cheddar, d. 1498. There is very good Y-tracery in the N. aisle and tower, and the S. transept has good Intersecting tracery too. The wagon nave roof has carved bosses and angels, and there are interesting 15th-century Newton effigies. Outside is the medieval Yatton Cross.

YEOVIL † St John the Baptist ★
Silver Street
OS *ST556160* **GPS** *50.9422N, 2.6322W*

A large town church, it was entirely rebuilt c. 1382, apart from the vaulted crypt, which is slightly earlier. The pioneering and sophisticated Perpendicular design is attributed to William Wynford, master mason at Wells Cathedral. The exterior, though closely hemmed in by other buildings, is majestic. The remarkable, elegant 'hall church' interior has aisles rising to the same height as the nave, chancel and transepts. Most of the furnishings are Victorian, but there is an Easter Sepulchre, a brass lectern of c. 1450 and a fine series of monuments.

OREMUS IN AETERNUM SANCTISSIMUM

STAFFORDSHIRE

Staffordshire is believed by many people to be 'just the Black Country and Potteries', which only proves how unknown the county is. If it were not famous for heavy engineering, pottery and coal, it would still deserve a measure of fame for the charm and variety of its landscape and architecture. Four centuries ago, William Camden's *Britannia* (published 1586) described the county in terms still fairly relevant: 'The north part is mountainous and less fertile; but the middle, which is watered by the Trent, is fruitful, woody and pleasant, by an equal mixture of arable and meadow grounds; so is also the south, which has much pit-coal and mines of iron; but whether to their loss or advantage, the natives themselves are the best judges ...'

Few people apart from the natives realize that there is a large part of the Peak District in the county. In fact, it is said that 'the best parts of Derbyshire are in Staffordshire' – the hundred square miles between Dovedale and the Dane Valley, across the Leek moors. To the west, the crag of Mow Cop, the birthplace of Primitive Methodism, overlooks the Cheshire plain; in the north, the Weaver Hills overlook Alton Towers and Castle with their exciting Pugin skylines. In the centre and south there are the old royal forests of Cannock Chase and Kinver, and to the east is Needwood Forest, with its great estates – and Bodley's masterpiece at Hoar Cross. In the central undulating lowlands lies Lichfield, and the Cathedral of St Chad.

A county for over a thousand years, Staffordshire still forms a rather separate and independent region, across which runs the Watling Street, leading the Romans and everyone else since through the county rather than into it.

Culturally conservative, the county seems to have woken late but vigorous to its tasks; witness the notable architecture of the 19th-century churches, especially the outstanding work of Bodley, Norman Shaw, Pugin and Street. Street's personal favourite design is at Denstone, while among Pugin's 10 churches in the county is the Roman Catholic St Giles in Cheadle, with its fabulously coloured interior, patterns covering every surface.

But to begin at the beginning, there is fine Norman work at Stafford and Tutbury, besides less considerable remains in 17 other churches; good 13th-century at Brewood and Coppenhall, and, of course, the nave of Lichfield Cathedral; much fine Decorated, notably in the Lichfield Lady Chapel, and at Clifton Campville and Checkley; and the usual amount of 15th-century work, the most complete example being in Penkridge. Very late Gothic occurs at Broughton (1633) – small, isolated and one of the most charming churches. The building

◁ **CHEADLE: ST GILES** – *the gateway between the chancel and Blessed Sacrament Chapel*

materials are usually local stone and tiles, though timber arcades are found at Betley and Rushton. Towers are the rule, though a few good spires exist.

Among the Renaissance churches are Ingestre by Wren, Patshull by Gibbs and Burton upon Trent by Francis Smith.

This is no place for too archaeological or historical an approach, whether to churches or the architecture of the county – the guidebooks can tell about the ancient forts, castles, abbey ruins, the great houses set in their parkland and the architectural details of churches, such as tracery, screens, woodwork and the characteristic Staffordshire incised stone tomb-slabs. But if a list were made of the significant details to make a pilgrimage to see, it should include All Saints, Leek, the Gerard tomb at Ashley and the great figure of Christ at Swynnerton.

In landscape and architecture, Staffordshire is a good average, with numerous high spots. There is quiet, remote country, especially in the centre and north; there is much industrial building in certain parts; and both in the towns and the countryside there are many churches which well deserve to be loved more widely.

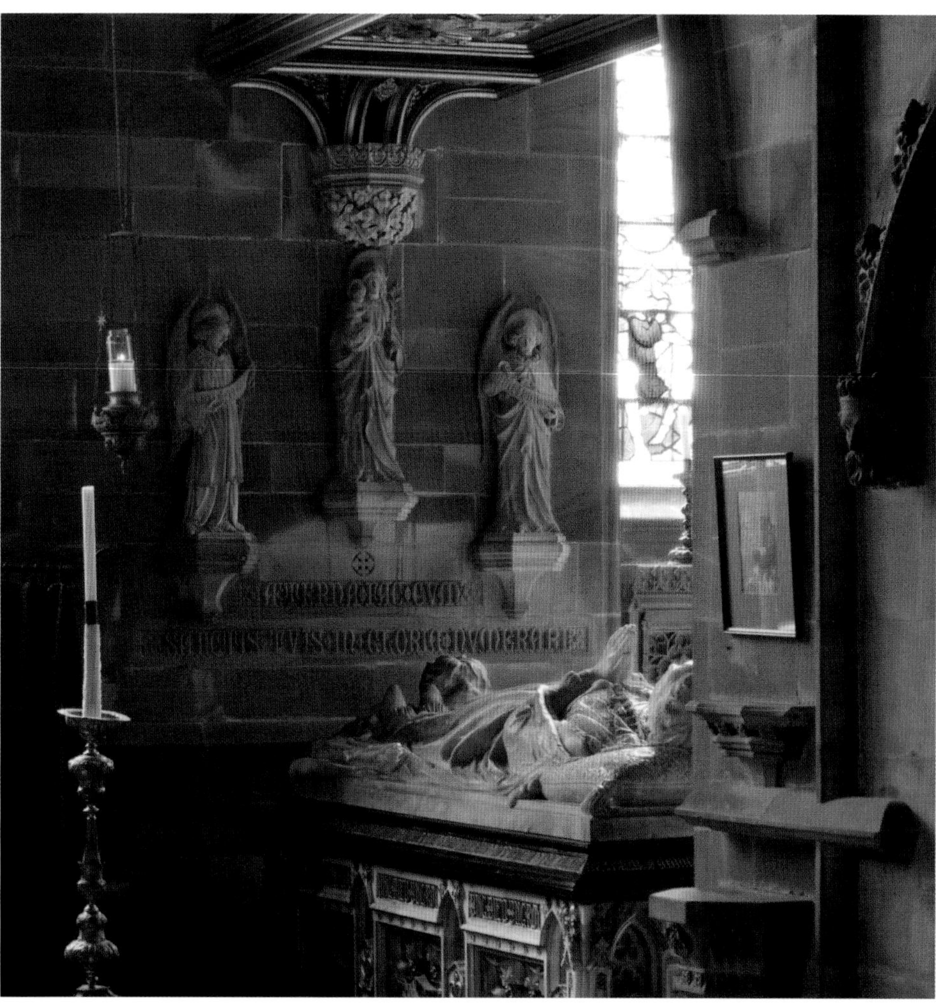

△ **HOAR CROSS: HOLY ANGELS** – *the tomb of Emily Charlotte Meynell-Ingram in the Chantry Chapel; she had the church built to honour her husband Hugo, who also lies in this chapel*

CHESHIRE
STAFFORDSHIRE
DERBYSHIRE
SHROPSHIRE
WEST MIDLANDS
WORCESTERSHIRE
0 5 miles
0 5 km
Congleton
Rushton Spencer
Warslow
Matlock
Biddulph
CREWE
LEEK
Alstonefield
Kidsgrove
Cheddleton
Wirksworth
STOKE-ON-TRENT
Betley
Ashbourne
Mayfield
NEWCASTLE-UNDER-LYME
Cheadle
Trentham
Denstone
Checkley
Ashley
Church Leigh
Swynnerton
Uttoxeter
Broughton
Stone
Market Drayton
Slindon
Sandon
Eccleshall
Tutbury
Hanbury
Stretton
Newborough
Seighford
Ingestre
Norbury
Blithfield
Hoar Cross
STAFFORD
BURTON UPON TRENT
Forton
Gnosall
Hamstall Ridware
Coppenhall
Church Eaton
Bradley
Rugeley
Mavesyn Ridware
Wychnor
Newport
Alrewas
Penkridge
Blymhill
CANNOCK
Elford
Brewood
TELFORD
LICHFIELD
Brownhills
TAMWORTH
Patshull
WOLVERHAMPTON
Pattingham
Bridgnorth
Himley
Enville
BIRMINGHAM
STOURBRIDGE
Kinver
KIDDERMINSTER
A535
A34
A52
A54
A53
A534
A530
A523
A5012
A500
A515
A517
A525
A52
A51
A50
A520
A519
A529
A511
A518
A513
M6
A460
A444
A41
A5
A38
M42
M6 TOLL
A449
A464
M54
A454
A458
A442
A456
A491
M5

ALREWAS † All Saints ★

5m/8km N.E. of Lichfield
OS *SK167152* **GPS** *52.7348N, 1.7531W*

The tower and exterior are mainly Perpendicular, the clerestory being raised directly over the aisle and chancel walls. The chancel is lofty Early English, with a sedilia. Overall the interior is high and spacious, with good 16th-century roofs. Interesting fittings include a Perpendicular font, pulpit of 1639 and stalls. The W. door dates from 1622, with appropriate ironwork. The old W. doorway of c. 1200 has been reset in the tower. Basil Champneys built the N. aisle in 1891, and there is glass by Kempe in the N. aisle windows.

ALSTONEFIELD † St Peter ★

11m/18km E. of Leek
OS *SK132553* **GPS** *53.0952N, 1.8031W*

This is a pleasant setting in the Peak limestone country near Dovedale. The church has outer walls of attractive chequered sandstone and limestone. Inside all is plain and serene: Norman, Decorated and Perpendicular. Much good woodwork of 1637–9 includes excellent box pews, a two-decker pulpit and the handsome Cotton pew.

ASHLEY † St John the Baptist ★

6m/10km E. of Market Drayton
OS *SJ762364* **GPS** *52.9248N, 2.3541W*

An early 17th-century Gothic Survival W. tower is the redeeming external feature of St John's – the rest a pedestrian exterior of 1861. But the interior, completed by Bodley & Hare in 1910, is surprisingly good. The chancel is divided from the nave by a rood screen after only two bays. The reredos is good, and the altar well lit; the whole effect is enlivened by many brass candelabra. There is a magnificent alabaster tomb to Sir Gilbert Gerard, d. 1592, and impressive 19th-century marble monuments to the Kinnersleys and Meynells.

BETLEY † St Margaret

6m/10km W. of Newcastle-under-Lyme
OS *SJ755484* **GPS** *53.0328N, 2.3658W*

St Margaret's has an early 16th-century stone tower, timber-framed nave, clerestory and porches. There is unusual and impressive work inside, with heavy late 15th-century timber arcades and trusses to the nave, and an early 16th-century parclose screen. The Gothic chancel of 1610 has an open timber roof, and there is a good monument to Ralph Egerton, d. 1610, whose son built the chancel.

BLITHFIELD † St Leonard ★

4m/6km N. of Rugeley
OS *SK044239* **GPS** *52.8134N, 1.9359W*

In an isolated setting by the manorial hall, home of the Bagots since the 1300s, the church has a simple 14th-century tower; the lofty nave has Early English arcades and a later clerestory. There is a good Perpendicular screen and many traceried bench-ends, as well as a fine collection of 16th–18th-century Bagot tombs and memorials, including one of 1695 by William Stanton.

BLYMHILL † St Mary ★

7m/11km E. of Telford
OS *SJ808122* **GPS** *52.7074N, 2.2848W*

Almost rebuilt by G. E. Street, 1856–9, St Mary's is of great originality and interest, with some old work left, including the tower and Decorated chancel. The nave has striking clerestory dormers and bold Plate tracery in the lower windows, and there is a huge gargoyle at the E. end of the S. aisle. Inside, the roof is tall and arch-braced, and there are good Street fittings and furnishings. The glass is by Burlison & Grylls, Wailes and Hardman.

BRADLEY † St Mary and All Saints ★

4m/6km S.W. of Stafford
OS *SJ879180* **GPS** *52.7599N, 2.1799W*

The church is mostly Perpendicular outside, including the W. tower and generous windows on the S. side. The Early English nave arcades have slender clustered shafts. There is a late 13th-century chancel, N. arcade and Decorated E. window with flowing tracery; below is a contemporary reredos. Of note is an alabaster tomb with kneeling figures for Thomas Browne, d. 1633, and his wife. At the time of writing the church was undergoing major restoration work.

△ **CHEADLE: ST GILES** – *the Easter Sepulcre on the north wall and high altar on the east in Pugin's fabulously decorated chancel*

BREWOOD † St Mary ★

7ml/11km N. of Wolverhampton

OS *SJ883086* **GPS** *52.6755N, 2.1737W*

In an attractive small town in romantic Charles II countryside, this largish church with Perpendicular tower and early 16th-century recessed spire has a 14th-century nave with Decorated windows in the N. aisle. The S. aisle is by Street, 1878–80. The early 13th-century chancel is handsome – long and low with a full complement of lancets – and the excellent 16th–17th-century Giffard tombs have 10 recumbent alabaster effigies; the Giffards have lived at Chillington since 1178, and Sir John, d. 1556, was Henry VIII's standard-bearer. There is also a tablet to Colonel Carliss, who accompanied Charles II in the Royal Oak at Boscobel, 1651.

BROUGHTON † St Peter ★

6ml/10km E. of Market Drayton

OS *SJ766337* **GPS** *52.9004N, 2.3491W*

In a solitary position opposite the big timber-framed Elizabethan Hall, this is a little Gothic Survival gem of 1630–40, its unspoiled interior with high box pews, Georgian altar rail, good 17th-century armorial glass and other fittings. In the chancel are wonderful reset 15th-century quarries depicting members of the Broughton family. The small font protrudes from the wall like a stoup. Good 17th–18th-century monuments to the Broughton baronets and their families.

BURTON UPON TRENT † St Chad

Hunter Street

OS *SK246244* **GPS** *52.8173N, 1.6362W*

This is Bodley's last church, completed by C. G. Hare after Bodley's death in 1910. It is a grand Decorated church with tall tower and good massing. The tower has pierced screens to the elegant bell-openings and a low leaded spire. It is attached to the church by a vaulted passage and forms a perfect foil to the austere and dignified interior. With slender columns and a wooden barrel vault, the chancel is defined only by a projecting fringe of pierced woodwork. All is well-detailed, with no memorials to disturb the serenity. St Chad's was the gift of Michael Arthur Bass, the 1st Lord Burton.

△ **CLIFTON CAMPVILLE: ST ANDREW** – *the spacious and light-filled nave is helped by the low, open benches and the largely clear windows that let sunlight flood in through the wide arcade*

BURTON UPON TRENT † St Modwen

Between High Street and river
OS *SK250227* **GPS** *52.8014N, 1.6291W*

By William & Richard Smith of Tettenhall and finished by Francis Smith, 1719–26, this is a handsome Classical church by the river, with large windows, a bold W. tower with urns and balustrade, and felicitous interior with Tuscan columns, woodwork and monuments.

CHEADLE † St Giles RC ★★

7m/11km E. of Newcastle-under-Lyme
OS *SK008431* **GPS** *52.9860N, 1.9890W*

This is considered one of A. W. N. Pugin's best churches, the 200-ft spire of which dominates the town and surrounding countryside. The church conforms to Pugin's strict ideas of Gothic Revival – architecture combined with medieval liturgy. Dazzling colour greets the visitor: stencilled chevrons on pillars and motifs on walls, rich gilding on the rood screen and ornate reredos behind the High Altar, focal point for the whole church. The reredos is by Thomas Roddis, who also made the alabaster altar in the Blessed Sacrament Chapel. The rood screen to the chapel comprises panels of Minton tiles, whereas the rood screen and rood in the nave – very grand and colourful affairs – were carved from Alton oak: above is a Doom painted on canvas in Rome and shipped to Cheadle.

CHECKLEY † St Mary and All Saints ★

5m/8km N.W. of Uttoxeter
OS *SK027378* **GPS** *52.9384N, 1.9598W*

The best medieval church in N. Staffs., St Mary and All Saints has a bold Norman and Perpendicular tower, embattled nave and chancel, and N. and S. porches. The lofty early 13th-century nave has a clerestory and 17th-century roof. The excellent raised Decorated chancel has 16th-century stalls and much contemporary glass. The E. window is an elegant example of Intersecting Y-tracery. The Romanesque font has a low-relief Agnus Dei carving. The parclose screen, glass and English altar are by Comper, 1922, and outside are Saxon cross shafts in the churchyard.

CHEDDLETON
† St Edward the Confessor ★

3m/4km S. of Leek

OS *SJ970524* **GPS** *53.0689N, 2.0448W*

Set in grand moorland country, the church has a Perpendicular tower, broad Early English nave and Decorated chancel. It was impressively restored by George Gilbert Scott Jnr in 1863–4. The sanctuary has painted decoration and important glass by Morris, Ford Madox Brown, Rossetti and Burne-Jones. The 15th-century Flemish triptych has wings added by Morris, who was friendly with the incumbent here, Edward Wardle, which may explain the particularly high standard of the restorations.

CHURCH EATON † St Editha ★

6m/10km S.W. of Stafford

OS *SJ848176* **GPS** *52.7560N, 2.2256W*

St Editha's has a Transitional tower with slender 15th-century spire and a simple, long roof-line. The E. end is dominated by a seven-light Perpendicular window spanning the full width of the chancel. The interior is a good mixture of late Norman and Perpendicular, with pleasant late 19th-century glass. There is a good Street-ish font and pulpit, and the glass in the huge E. window by Kempe is said to have come from Old St Paul's.

CHURCH LEIGH † All Saints ★

5m/8km N.W. of Uttoxeter

OS *SK023358* **GPS** *52.9199N, 1.9659W*

By Thomas Johnson of Lichfield, 1845–6, this is a remarkable cruciform church in the Decorated style by an obscure architect, with bold central tower and good details. The interior is simple and very good, with a rib-vaulted tower and chancel; there is much excellent Victorian glass by Burne-Jones and Morris & Co. The rich tiles on the chancel floor were designed by Pugin, who also designed the E. window, chancel screen and stalls.

CLIFTON CAMPVILLE † St Andrew ★

5m/8km N.E. of Tamworth

OS *SK252107* **GPS** *52.6941N, 1.6272W*

Perhaps the best medieval parish church in the county. It is mainly 13th- and 14th-century, with a small vaulted N. transept, originally balanced to the tall S. spire, the tower pierced at the base with large windows. The light and spacious nave has a 14th-century collar-rafter roof, and there are 14th-century stalls with misericords in the chancel, set beside some new choir stalls. A painting of the Coronation of the Virgin is in the S. aisle. The rood screen is good Perpendicular, and there are notable monuments by J. M. Rysbrack and a 16th-century alabaster tomb.

COPPENHALL † St Lawrence

2m/3km S. of Stafford

OS *SJ907194* **GPS** *52.7722N, 2.1382W*

This is a perfect village church of c. 1220, restored c. 1866 – small, complete and almost unspoilt Early English. Its 3-bay nave and 2-bay chancel are pierced with copious lancet windows, and topping the W. wall is a weather-boarded Victorian bellcote.

DENSTONE † All Saints ★

5m/8km N. of Uttoxeter

OS *SK100409* **GPS** *52.9654N, 1.8520W*

By G. E. Street, 1860–2, an original and dramatic composition in the Middle Pointed style, especially when seen from the N.; the round turret and high chancel are very well composed. The stonework, iron, brass, marble, stained glass, light-fittings and lettering are all designed with great skill and verve. The church forms part of a very pleasing Street group that includes the school, church hall and coach house with stables.

ECCLESHALL † Holy Trinity ★

7m/11km N.W. of Stafford

OS *SJ827291* **GPS** *52.8598N, 2.2575W*

Sited at the end of a pleasant market town, the W. tower has an Early English base and fine Perpendicular top with pinnacles. The spacious nave, mostly late 15th-century, is entered by a large vaulted porch; the chancel is 13th-century. There are tombs of four bishops of Lichfield; Eccleshall Castle was their palace until the 19th century. Bishop Overton's effigy of 1609 is especially good. The gloomy N. chancel chapel was transformed in the 1920s by W. D. Caroe, who also designed the casing for the new organ, using limed-oak panels and carvings: Basil Champneys designed the reredos.

ELFORD † St Peter ★

4m/6km N. of Tamworth

OS *SK185106* **GPS** *52.6929N, 1.7274W*

At the end of an avenue, close to the site of the big Georgian hall, is Salvin's 1843–9 essay in the Tudor taste. The tower is genuinely 1598; the S. aisle and chapel were added by Street in 1870. Rich detail decorates the side which faced the hall. The church is usually visited for the tombs, including the charming child effigy with tennis ball, c. 1460, but is also architecturally interesting. The roof has angelic and heraldic corbels; there are carved, coloured and gilded capitals, red and blue lettering round the arches – harmoniously done for once – an altar rail with brassy angels and good ironwork on the door.

ENVILLE † St Mary the Blessed Virgin

5m/8km W. of Stourbridge

OS *SO823868* **GPS** *52.4792N, 2.2610W*

In a grand position, presiding over the patriarchal village and great house, this is a pink sandstone church, the Somerset tower a rebuilding by George Gilbert Scott Jnr, 1872–5, with Norman and Early English arcades, and windows that were replaced by Scott. There is a good alabaster tomb of Thomas Grey, 1559, and many later monuments to the family, later earls of Stamford and Warrington. There are also some late 15th-century stalls with misericords and a nice figured bench-end.

FORTON † All Saints ★

7m/11km N.E. of Telford

OS *SJ755211* **GPS** *52.7877N, 2.3644W*

This is a nicely handled association of Georgian and medieval, and Caroe restored the church in 1910. The stocky but handsome 15th-century tower and the Decorated E. end are linked by the S. wall and nave of 1723. The N. aisle is medieval, but with a Tuscan arcade. There are good 17th-century monuments to the Skrymsher family.

GNOSALL

† Collegiate Church of St Lawrence ★

6m/10km W. of Stafford

OS *SJ830208* **GPS** *52.7853N, 2.2533W*

One of the county's most important Romanesque churches, it is cruciform, possibly collegiate originally, and stands on the fringe of a scattered village. The Norman crossing arches are impressive, rising from clustered half-shafts, and decorated with carved chevrons, symmetrical foliage and patterned blind arcading. The S. transept has a triforium, and there are traces of Norman work all through the church; otherwise everything is mainly 13th–15th-century. The Decorated E. window has good flowing tracery.

HAMSTALL RIDWARE

† St Michael and All Angels ★

4m/6km E. of Rugeley

OS *SK105193* **GPS** *52.7717N, 1.8448W*

An isolated village church of supremely simple silhouette, with 14th-century spire, in a wonderful setting of ruined tower, gatehouse and dovecotes of the old manor house nearby; the church is mainly 16th-century. An airy Norman nave flows straight into the chancel without a break; a perfect setting for the old glass, parclose screens, tombs, memorials and medieval painted panels in the reredos.

HANBURY † St Werburgh

5m/8km N.W. of Burton upon Trent

OS *SK170279* **GPS** *52.8485N, 1.7478W*

In a fine hill-top setting on the site of a 7th-century nunnery, this impressive 13th-century and later church was much restored in the 19th century by Hine and Evans. It has good arcades, a 17th-century nave roof, and handsome Victorian chancel of 1862, replete with murals, tiles and glass. The excellent 17th-century alabaster effigies include two prim Puritan ladies, Katherine Agard, d.1628, and Ann Woodlocke, d. 1657, above the vicar's stall.

HIMLEY † St Michael and All Angels

5m/8km S. of Wolverhampton

OS *SO882911* **GPS** *52.5177N, 2.1739W*

This is a wonderful oasis in the Black Country landscape, with a restrained stuccoed church of 1764, that has a W. tower, nave and apsidal chancel. The pulpit is Georgian and there is an elegant curved W. gallery on slender iron columns. The private Garden of Remembrance of the Earls of Dudley has four 1930s gravestones by Eric Gill; it is

△ **HOAR CROSS: HOLY ANGELS** – *the intricately carved and decorated font cover*

approached by a high-walled orchard, and watered by a stream.

HOAR CROSS † Holy Angels ★

7m/11km W. of Burton upon Trent
OS *SK124230* **GPS** *52.8049N, 1.8162W*

This red sandstone church is by G. F. Bodley, 1872–6, and the architecture is splendid. Like Broughton, Patshull and Ingestre, the family church stands near the manor house and architecturally is all of a piece. Lavish and original design in the Decorated style, well-massed and detailed, it is a perfect association of splendour and intimacy. The tower is deeply buttressed, the nave outside is severe, while the chancel is high and richly done – all perfectly handled contrasts within, from the chancel sculptures and the rood to the font – good workmanship everywhere. Bodley even recommended a style for gravestones in the churchyard.

INGESTRE † St Mary

4m/6km E. of Stafford
OS *SJ976246* **GPS** *52.8198N, 2.0360W*

This was probably by Sir Christopher Wren, 1676, and originally the hall chapel. The chaste ashlar exterior has rusticated quoins, keyed round-headed windows, oculi and a modest W. tower. The plan is square (plus the chancel), articulated by engaged Tuscan columns with a single abacus. Described, perhaps by Wren himself, as: 'not great, but uniform and elegant … The Chancel within paved throughout with Black and White marble, the Windows illustrated with Armes and matches of the Chetwynds in painted glass; and the Ceilings with the same in Fretwork … an elegant skreen of Flanders Oak, garnisht with the Kings Armes … the Ironwork about it curiously painted and guilt …' It contains a gallery of monuments to Chetwynds, Talbots, Chetwynd-Talbots and earls of Shrewsbury, with woodwork by Gibbons and glass by Burne-Jones.

KINVER † St Peter

4m/6km W. of Stourbridge
OS *SO846830* **GPS** *52.4452N, 2.2278W*

A dramatic position, in magnificent isolation, on Kinver Edge; the 14th–15th-century church has a Decorated tower and font, a remarkable brass to Sir Edward Grey, d.

DAVID
PROFETA
hodie

1528, with wives and children, and a handsome Doric monument of 1789.

LEEK † All Saints ★
Compton (A520), 10m/16km N.E. of Stoke-on-Trent
OS *SJ984561* **GPS** *53.1023N, 2.0239W*

By R. Norman Shaw, 1885–7, this is an Arts and Crafts church – large and squat-towered, and reminiscent of a North Yorks. church. The interior is surprisingly light and airy: there is a nice contrast between the intimate scale and the great arches. The splendid font is of green marble; the chancel panelling and reredos by Lethaby, painted by F. Hamilton Jackson. The chancel murals are by Gerald Horsley and the glass by Morris – all done to good Tractarian principles.

LICHFIELD † St Chad ★
St Chad's Road, Stowe district
OS *SK122102* **GPS** *52.6894N, 1.8209W*

Close to Stowe Pool, and best viewed from the other side of the pool, here St Chad had his hermitage and well. The Early English nave has a fine doorway and five-bay S. arcade. The E. window and tower are Decorated, and the ceiling and clerestory are c. 1800. There is glass by Morris & Co., Whall and Hardman.

MAVESYN RIDWARE † St Nicholas
3m/4km E. of Rugeley
OS *SK081168* **GPS** *52.7494N, 1.8805W*

An unusual composition of medieval tower and N. aisle, called the Trinity Chapel, and a brick Gothic nave, 1782. The interior is also interesting; the N. aisle has two knights' effigies and 16 incised slabs with figures and heraldry – mostly late 18th-century conceits. There are 10 hatchments and a good heraldic window of 1870, cast-iron altar rails and a Norman font; all very odd.

MAYFIELD † St John the Baptist ★
2m/3km W. of Ashbourne
OS *SK154447* **GPS** *52.9999N, 1.7716W*

In a pleasant setting in the Dove Valley, though now surrounded by modern housing, the church has a good tower of 1515 and a 14th-century tower with a jolly scalloped parapet. The late Gothic porch and Norman doorway lead into a spacious Norman nave. The pews, pulpit and three-sided communion rail are all 1633; there are two nice 18th-century memorials and a font of 1514.

NEWBOROUGH † All Saints
6m/10km W. of Burton upon Trent
OS *SK135254* **GPS** *52.8260N, 1.8007W*

By J. Oldrid Scott, 1899–1901, the church has a slender octagonal pinnacled tower with a spire of great beauty and originality. The rest is simple and serene.

NORBURY † St Peter ★
8m/13km W. of Stafford
OS *SJ786234* **GPS** *52.8084N, 2.3184W*

An excellent nave and chancel of c. 1340 with original roof to which a brick Gothic tower was added by William Baker, 1759. But it is the Decorated work that claims our attention: four sedilia, a founder's tomb with painted figure and exciting carvings, and a lovely brass to Lady Hawys Botiller.

PATSHULL † St Mary ★
7m/11km W. of Wolverhampton
OS *SJ800006* **GPS** *52.6034N, 2.2957W*
Churches Conservation Trust

The church is by James Gibbs, 1744, the N. aisle and tower altered in 1874. It is a simple composition in parkland beside a lake. The square tower is topped by an octagonal cupola, and the S. nave front has a Tuscan porch, the E. window being Venician in style. The interior is a little coarse: an 18th-century font and gilded screen by W. C. Banks, 1893; and 16th–18th-century Astley tombs and monuments, which include an alabaster tomb chest of c. 1532 and a composition of 1687 with standing figure.

PATTINGHAM † St Chad
6m/10km W. of Wolverhampton
OS *SO820991* **GPS** *52.5898N, 2.2657W*

A Norman, Early English and Decorated church with a spire of 1871, whose high nave has a Norman arcade. The N. aisle is a double, and the beautiful 13th-century chancel has lancets.

◁ **HOAR CROSS: HOLY ANGELS** – *Neo-Gothic stained glass in the south aisle west window, the work of Burlison & Grylls*

PENKRIDGE
† St Michael and All Angels ★
6m/10km S. of Stafford
OS *SJ921141* **GPS** *52.7250N, 2.1177W*

This was once a collegiate church with dean and four canons, and is mostly 16th-century Perpendicular outside, including the top of the Decorated tower. The interior is high and spacious, with 13th-century arcades. The Dutch wrought-iron screen is from 1778. There are two splendid table-tombs and one 16th–17th-century two-storeyed tomb; others include recumbent effigies to the Littleton family of Pillaton, and there are two 15th- and 16th-century incised slabs with figures.

RUSHTON SPENCER † St Lawrence ★
5m/8km N.W. of Leek
OS *SJ934620* **GPS** *53.1557N, 2.0996W*

In isolation on a ridge, with a view of the fringes of the Peak District, this is a church of rare interest and individuality, mostly 17th- and 19th-century outside, with a weatherboarded bell-turret and high-gabled dormers. Inside, the original timber nave of c. 1200 is spanned by low beams with a text in good Georgian lettering. The hefty posts and struts are like low, spreading trees. The arched ceiling is Gothic, and there is a Georgian minstrels' gallery, a Jacobean pulpit, squire's pew with hatchments above, big Tables of the Law and oil lamps. Everything is friendly and domestic – clearly the House of God.

SANDON † All Saints ★
4m/6km N.E. of Stafford
OS *SJ954294* **GPS** *52.8629N, 2.0696W*

On a hill in Sandon Park, the church is mostly 14th-century, the tower massing and fenestration generally intriguing and full of interest. The interior is dominated by the screen supporting the family pew of the Harrowbys. In the chancel are the Erdeswick tombs, notably that of Staffordshire historian Sampson Erdeswick, 1601, to his own design. There are also wall-paintings of heraldic shields hung on family trees. The beautifully furnished interior has 17th-century pews, many Harrowby hatchments and monuments, and a Stuart Royal Arms.

SEIGHFORD † St Chad ★
3m/4km N.W. of Stafford
OS *SJ882249* **GPS** *52.8224N, 2.1759W*

This is a church of much antiquarian interest with some architectural detective problems. Seen from the road it appears mostly brick Gothic, with a 17th-century W. tower tricked out in 1748. But the chancel and N. side are medieval, and the interior mostly early Norman. Inside is a good Jacobean pulpit, tomb with effigies of c. 1593, hatchments, scraps of old glass and some wall-painting.

SLINDON † St Chad
8m/13km N.W. of Stafford
OS *SJ827322* **GPS** *52.8871N, 2.2576W*

By Basil Champneys, 1894. A delightful, small, late Victorian church, its quirky details loosely based on the low 14th-century tower. The choir and sanctuary are vaulted, and there is a richly carved reredos and stained-glass by Kempe.

STAFFORD † St Chad ★
Between Greengate Street and St Chad's Place
OS *SJ922231* **GPS** *52.8062N, 2.1163W*

St Chad's was restored and refaced by Sir George Gilbert Scott, 1874. Almost all the interior is grand Norman work with an unusually rich chancel arch. The chancel and crossing are longer than the nave, and there is a fine fake-Norman font, c. 1850.

STAFFORD † St Mary
Between Earl Street and Greengate Street
OS *SJ921232* **GPS** *52.8063N, 2.1181W*

Cruciform with a central octagonal tower, the church was originally Early English, but thoroughly overhauled by Sir George Gilbert Scott in 1841–4. The generally fine interior has 13th-century arcades, a Decorated N. transept, a Tudor nave roof, inscribed Norman font and alabaster tomb effigies. It is built on the site of St Bertelin's shrine.

STRETTON † St Mary
2m/3km N.E. of Burton upon Trent
OS *SK253263* **GPS** *52.8341N, 1.6248W*

By Micklethwaite and Somers Clarke, 1897, this is a large and handsome brewer's church in the Decorated style. The nave and chancel are of equal height and separated by a boldly buttressed tower with pyramidal roof. The light and assured interior has much pretty painting, good woodwork and a marble font; the fine glass was made by Powell & Sons.

SWYNNERTON † St Mary

5m/8km S. of Newcastle-under-Lyme
OS *SJ852355* **GPS** *52.9167N, 2.2211W*

St Mary's is a 12th–15th-century church with good Norman doorways in the tower, an Early English chancel and arcades, and a good Perpendicular screen. However, in the S.E. chapel is a huge and celebrated figure of Christ. Of cathedral-like quality and proportions, and dating to 1260–80, it was found beneath the chancel floor, perhaps buried at the time of the Reformation; but what is it doing here?

TAMWORTH
† Collegiate Church of St Editha

Church Street 14m/22km N.E. of Birmingham
OS *SK207040* **GPS** *52.6342N, 1.6943W*

The pinnacled church tower and castle dominate the silhouette of this largely Georgian town, only marred by hideous 1960s flats. The effect inside the W. door beneath the tower is grand and immediate. The church is generally of 'noble and ample proportions', mostly late 14th-century with a Perpendicular clerestory and roofs. There is unexpected Norman work in the choir, an elegant 18th-century wrought-iron screen, good Pre-Raphaelite glass and a unique double spiral staircase in the tower.

TRENTHAM † St Mary and All Saints

3m/4km S. of Stoke-on-Trent
OS *SJ865409* **GPS** *52.9654N, 2.2018W*

Close to the magnificent gardens of Trentham House – demolished in 1910 and once a home of the Dukes of Sutherland – stands the church of 1844 by Sir Charles Barry. It is a large ashlar building with re-used late-Norman arcades, a screen of 1633 and a Georgian W. gallery. Good 16th-century and later monuments include work by Chantrey and Matthew Noble. Nearby is Charles Heathcote Tatham's awesome mausoleum of 1807 on the roadside.

TUTBURY † Priory Church of St Mary ★

4m/6km N.W. of Burton upon Trent
OS *SK211291* **GPS** *52.8590N, 1.6878W*

Near the castle and overlooking the town, this is an important Norman church, the outside of which belies the excellent interior. It has a rich W. front and fine doorway of seven orders, including the earliest English alabaster work. Inside, the splendid Norman nave happily terminates in Street's apsidal E. end of 1866. The arcades of c. 1100 are tall and hefty, the old triforium now serving as a clerestory. Fine Street fittings and good ironwork on the doors complete the church.

WARSLOW † St Lawrence

7m/11km E. of Leek
OS *SK086586* **GPS** *53.1249N, 1.8724W*

A church of 1820 in a Peakland estate village, with handsome chancel added by Charles Lynam in 1908. There are good original fittings of a two-decker pulpit, box pews and a squire's pew; the stained glass is by Morris, and there are good Art Nouveau mosaics in the chancel.

WYCHNOR † St Leonard

5m/8km N.E. of Lichfield
OS *SK176160* **GPS** *52.7420N, 1.7394W*

Isolated St Leonard's takes in a wonderful wide panorama across the plain – Alrewas Church, Lichfield Cathedral and Cannock Chase are all visible on a clear day. It is mostly 14th-century Decorated, with a late 16th-century brick top to the tower. A bold and friendly building, with good, large square-headed traceried windows, and richly coloured and textured stone. A little heraldic glass.

SUFFOLK

South Norfolk glides almost imperceptibly into Suffolk. Beginning with the leafy countryside just south of Norwich, where the Romantic landscape painter John Crome painted that king among trees, *The Poringland Oak*, c. 1818–20, and proceeding down the valley of the Tas, the whitewashed cottages and farms, timber-framed with wattle and daub and high-pitched roofs, become more and more frequent. Villages begin to have wide greens, like that of Saxlingham Nethergate, with cottages dotted about round the edge; this is typical of so many villages in Suffolk.

Little towns like Loddon, Long Stratton and Pulham Market are similar places to Debenham, Stradbroke and Laxfield; and though Harleston and Diss are on the Norfolk side of the Waveney Valley, they are but smaller versions of their Suffolk, though more northerly, neighbours, Bungay and Beccles.

Then as one proceeds farther into the Suffolk countryside the villages appear more remote. There are few main roads and, now that so many branch lines have been abandoned, fewer railways. At best the villages are lucky if they have a bus service.

The brick and flint give way to colourwash and thatch, the villages have a softer appearance, the fields are smaller, the woodlands thicker and the trees larger, so that by the time one has left Harleston and Fressingfield behind, or penetrated into the quiet villages just inland from the coast at Southwold or Aldeburgh, one has the feeling of being in the depths of the country as nowhere else in East Anglia.

What may be said of the villages may also be said of the towns. They are more compact, quieter and more retired. No 'A' road runs into Framlingham or Eye, and those which are on some important line of communication seem to have kept themselves apart from the main stream of traffic, like Woodbridge, where the bypass helps it to remain as a perfect example of an old country town, spreading along the main street and thickening about the market-place in the middle.

As for the towns, so for the capital. Whereas Norwich is an industrial city and county capital all in one, Suffolk has intensified both but kept them well apart. Ipswich is its industrial capital, with the result that the parochial distinctions of the old medieval city are less evident; Bury is the county market town, where the industries are kept in the background.

So also for the coast. Like Norfolk's Yarmouth, Lowestoft is both a pleasure resort and a fishing-town, but smaller, quieter and more restrained, and the same sort of comparison could be made between Cromer and Southwold, Sheringham and Aldeburgh, and between Hunstanton and Felixstowe.

The Suffolk rivers are smaller but they have longer estuaries which penetrate for a long distance inland. The Ore follows the coast for ten miles and more before

◁ **SOUTHWOLD: ST EDMUND** – *a gloriously painted and gilded section of the roof, an angel watching over the church from one of the hammer-beams*

0
5 miles
0
5 km
A10
A11
A134
Santon Downham
Brandon
A1075
A1065
THETFORD
Lakenheath
A1066
Elveden
Euston
A1101
A11
A1088
MILDENHALL
A134
Rickinghall
A143
Bardwell
A142
Icklingham
Walsham le Willows
Gislinghar
Ampton
Ixworth
A1101
A11
Westhorpe
Stowlangtoft
Landwade
Bacton
Risby
Great Barton
A14
BURY ST EDMUNDS
NEWMARKET
Little Saxham
A14
Elmswell
Dalham
Rushbrooke
Hessett
Rougham
A14
Shelland
A143
Hawstead
Rattlesden
STOWMARKET
SUFFOLK
Combs
Cowlinge
Great Bradley
Cockfield
Denston
Boxted
A134
Kettlebaston
Great Bricett
Lavenham
Kedington
A1092
A1307
Cavendish
Clare
Long Melford
A1141
HAVERHILL
Great Waldingfield
Kerse
SUDBURY
HADLE
Boxford
A1071
A1017
A131
Polstead
ESSEX
Stoke-by-Nayland
Nayland
Bures
Wissington
A134
Halstead

NORFOLK
Lound
Herringfleet
LOWESTOFT
Bungay
Barsham
BECCLES
North Cove
A140
A143
A144
A145
Kessingland
A12
Covehithe
Rumburgh
Westhall
Withersdale
Metfield
SS
Halesworth
SOUTHWOLD
Wingfield
Wenhaston
Cratfield
Blythburgh
Bramfield
EYE
Laxfield
rnham
va
Brundish
Tannington
Badingham
Dennington
Monk
Soham
dlesham
A12
Framlingham
SAXMUNDHAM
Leiston
A1120
Hoo
Stonham
A1094
Helmingham
Iken
ALDEBURGH
HAM MARKET
WICKHAM MARKET
Swilland
Ufford
A12
Orford
A14
WOODBRIDGE
Bramford
IPSWICH
Brightwell
A14
A137
A14
FELIXSTOWE
anningtree
HARWICH

it decides to turn inland as the Alde; Woodbridge is on the tidal estuary of the Deben, but it is a long way from the sea. The Gipping is a quiet little stream until at Gippeswick (Ipswich – the creek of the Gipping) it becomes the long estuary of the Orwell; and the same may be said of the Stour, which Suffolk shares with Essex on its southern border.

It is to the Stour Valley that one comes after the remote country of East Suffolk and, though it is apparent at once that Constable's country is near enough to London to have been discovered by the weekender, it is a lovely district with a character that is all its own and with its own capital – a collection of medieval villages that have coalesced into the town of Sudbury, with a statue of Gainsborough in the Market Place.

Gainsborough and Constable. How often did those painters set their figures against the background of a landscape park, for that is exactly what the Stour Valley is as you see it spread out beneath the high ground at Stoke-by-Nayland or at Bures. A park continues right on through Sudbury to that wonderful village of parks and halls, Long Melford.

West of Long Melford, Suffolk becomes Essex and, though Clare is on the Suffolk side of the Stour, it is essentially an Essex country town, with the houses rich in pargetry work. But north and east of Melford one is back again in the heart of Suffolk. Even 'B' roads are few and far between, so that, with no map and with all the signposts destroyed (as patriotic East Anglians both in Norfolk and Suffolk were most insistent on doing in the early days of the Second World War), 'the man in the moon who came down too soon' to Shimpling or to Hawkedon, Thorpe Morieux, Nedging Tye or Kettlebaston, would find it difficult 'to find his way to Norwich', as the saying goes, and would be more likely to get hopelessly lost in the maze of lanes and footpaths. But it is a county in which one would be quite content to get lost, for sometime or another all the roads lead to the local metropolis, which is not only the most lovely town in Suffolk, but one of the most beautiful in all England – Lavenham.

To enter into the spirit of the country the traveller in East Suffolk will find it almost essential to be equipped with the poems of George Crabbe (1754–1832), and for the highlands of West Suffolk he will be well advised to seek out some faded copy of the works of the contemporary Robert Bloomfield (1766–1823), who, though a more pedestrian poet, could at times describe the spirit of a place even better than Crabbe himself. He depicts the rolling grassland of Euston Park and the wide upland fields of Honington, of Troston, and of Sapiston, around which he had plodded as a 'Farmer's Boy', and with the foliage of spring, the shimmering heat of summer, the falling leaves of autumn, and the hard cold of winter, with the accuracy of a steel engraving.

West Suffolk, too, has a distinct character, but the various districts are not so sharply distinguished from one another as they are in Norfolk. If Suffolk melts into Norfolk along the Tas, and into Essex in the valley of the Stour, so also the chalky heights of West Suffolk blend into the white chalk of Cambridgeshire; the cottages, and the churches too, are built of hard chalk or clunch, and one can make one's way over the Gog Magogs into the Midlands without meeting the barrier of the Fens.

△ **BLYTHBURGH: HOLY TRINITY** – *Perpendicular perfection in the large south aisle windows with delicate quatrefoil parapet above and then the exquisite run of 18 clerestory windows*

ALDEBURGH † St Peter and St Paul ★
6ml10km S.E. of Saxmundham
OS *TM463568* **GPS** *52.1549N, 1.6000E*

The oldest part of the church is the 14th-century tower with its external stair turret: in the sides of the S. porch are arches to permit processions to pass on consecrated ground. Generally, the church was much restored in the 18th century, and inside are many Victorian touches. Most notable, though, is the three-light window by John Piper in memory of Benjamin Britten, who is buried in the churchyard: the three sections depict *The Prodigal Son*, *Curlew River* and *The Burning Fiery Furnace*. In the churchyard are the graves of many other musicians, including Imogen Holst.

AMPTON † St Peter ★
4ml6km N. of Bury St Edmunds
OS *TL866711* **GPS** *52.3070N, 0.7359E*

In the church is the chantry chapel of John Coket, d. 1479. The Calthorpe monument in the chancel is by the E. Anglian sculptors John and Mathias Christmas, who did much of the embellishing of Charles I's great ship 'The Sovereign of the Seas'. There is also a kneeling effigy of Dorothy Calthorpe, 'a virgin votary oft in snares', who 'troubles no man's dust'. She gave the handsome row of almshouses E. of the church. A great treasure of this church is a 'sealed book' of Common Prayer, of which neither the British Museum nor the Bodleian Library possess a copy.

BACTON † St Mary
5ml8km N. of Stowmarket
OS *TM053671* **GPS** *52.2646N, 1.0074E*

The church has one of Suffolk's best double hammer-beam roofs. The front part nearest the chancel is now repainted. This is how these fine roofs first were. Above the chancel are the tantalising remains of a Doom. Butterfield did the 19th-century restoration – not one of his best perhaps.

BADINGHAM † St John the Baptist ★
3ml4km N.E. of Framlingham
OS *TM305683* **GPS** *52.2647N, 1.3775E*

There are remains of Norman work in the lower part of the tower and at the W. end of the nave. The hammer-beam roof is distinguished, and the church has one of the finest and best preserved seven-sacrament fonts in E. Anglia. In the panel representing Penance, evil is vigorously portrayed as a devil with horns, and in the Last Rites panel can be seen the dying man's chamber pot and shoes under the bed.

BADLEY † St Mary ★★

2m/3km S.E. of Stowmarket
OS *TM062559* **GPS** *52.1630N, 1.0140E*
Churches Conservation Trust

This is a remote and unspoilt gem in a meadow, grouped with an old farmhouse and reached only by a track: the setting is superb, though the Puritan iconoclast William Dowsing did his worst in 1644, destroying the glass and high chancel steps. The rectangular tower has a Tudor brick top and a great Perpendicular W. window. The 15th-century benches, 17th-century box pews and pulpit have all weathered to a silvery grey. The church is unforgettable, rustic and well worth visiting.

BARDWELL † St Peter and St Paul

2m/3km N. of Ixworth
OS *TL941736* **GPS** *52.3263N, 0.8470E*

The church is unexpectedly grand for its rural setting – high and lofty, with its aisleless nave and single hammer-beam roof, dated 1421. The 15th-century glass is in memory of William de Bardwell, all reset on the N. side of the nave. The chancel was remodelled in the 19th century by Bacon and Bell and contains a very fine late 17th-century memorial to Thomas Reade and his wife Bridget. It retains some original colour, and shown under the kneeling couple are their children, some holding skulls to indicate that they predeceased their parents.

BARSHAM † Holy Trinity

2m/3km W. of Beccles
OS *TM396896* **GPS** *52.4520N, 1.5263E*

This little shrine has a delightful setting in a meadow. It has a Saxon round tower and unique E. window with lozenge trellis-work. Inside is much 17th-century woodwork, including the screen. There was a remarkably sensitive early 20th-century restoration by Charles Kempe and F. C. Eden, with much glass by them. They created an Anglo-Catholic interior; tasteful, colourful and with great character, wonderfully made to live again after a fire in 1979.

△ **BLYTHBURGH: HOLY TRINITY** – *a Jack-o'-the-clock ready to strike his bell on the hour*

BECCLES † St Michael

8m/12km W. of Lowestoft
OS *TM420904* **GPS** *52.4586N, 1.5621E*

In a commanding position in the town centre, this great barn of a church has a massive detached 16th-century bell-tower. The church has two superb porches of the 15th century, and a vast but well-proportioned interior, restored by J. H. Hakewill, 1857–66.

BLYTHBURGH † Holy Trinity ★★

4m/6km W. of Southwold
OS *TM450753* **GPS** *52.3212N, 1.5948E*

The glorious exterior of this ship-like church juts out into heathland and the Blyth marshes. It is one of the county's Perpendicular treasures, with fine windows, superb clerestory and parapets, and 15th-century doors. The interior is lofty and glitters with light that pours in through the clear glass. In every direction there are fine vistas. William Dowsing rampaged through here at the time of the Civil War, ordering the removal of angels from the roof, mutilating the large font and taking down the porch and tower crosses. He was less successful in getting down all the roof angels, and in the long, unbroken roof there is still medieval colour, and angels fly regardless of the iconoclasts. There are intriguing bench-ends with the Seven Deadly Sins and the Seasons of the Year, stalls with carved fronts, original screenwork and much else in this unforgettable church.

BOXFORD † St Mary
4m/6km W. of Hadleigh
OS *TL962404* **GPS** *52.0281N, 0.8594E*

In the middle of a pretty village is a church with a 14th-century timber N. porch, beautiful vaulting and a stone S. porch with a representation of the Annunciation. The tower is 14th-century, with a tiny wood and lead spire atop. The main fabric is 15th-century. There is a 17th-century font cover with doors that fold back to reveal texts painted on scrolls. The lovely glass in the E. window, representing the Transfiguration, is by Rosemary Rutherford, 1973.

BOXTED † All Saints ★
4m/6km N.W. of Long Melford
OS *TL824504* **GPS** *52.1224N, 0.6642E*

Ornate Poley family pews fill the N. aisle, with partitions separating the family places from those of their retainers. There is good 17th-century woodwork and fine monuments, particularly the alabaster figure of Sir John Poley, d. 1638, in elaborate armour.

BRAMFIELD † St Andrew ★
3m/4km S. of Halesworth
OS *TM398737* **GPS** *52.3098N, 1.5179E*

This little church has a very early circular tower standing by itself to the S.W. Inside is a beautiful screen with vaulting, the best of its kind in Suffolk. In the chancel is Nicholas Stone's exquisite effigy of Elizabeth Coke, who died in childbirth in 1627.

BRAMFORD † St Mary ★
3m/4km N.W. of Ipswich
OS *TM127463* **GPS** *52.0742N, 1.1028E*

This 13th–15th-century church must have been aglow with the most wonderful glass before 1644, when the iconoclast William Dowsing destroyed '841 superstitious pictures'. Yet there are many things remaining, including a good hammer-beam roof in the nave and chancel, a stone rood screen, c. 1300, and an early 16th-century font cover like that at Boxford, but more elaborate. The sturdy Decorated tower has an 18th-century lead spire.

BRIGHTWELL † St John the Baptist
6m/10km E. of Ipswich
OS *TM249435* **GPS** *52.0445N, 1.2792E*

A tiny church in an idyllic setting: it is mostly c. 1300, but was remodelled in 1656–7 and given its brick tower, which rests upon a massive Tuscan arch. The 14th-century door still has its sanctuary ring, and inside is an exquisitely carved early 14th-century font and moving memorials, especially to the five-year-old son of Thomas Essington, who was responsible for the tower and Tuscan arch.

BRUNDISH † St Lawrence
4m/6km N. of Framlingham
OS *TM271695* **GPS** *52.2771N, 1.3283E*

The church is worth visiting for its high and lonely setting. The lower part of the tower is Norman, the upper part 14th-century. The interior is atmospheric, with old bench ends, box pews and plain brick flooring.

BUNGAY † Holy Trinity
12m/20km W. of Lowestoft; Trinity Street
OS *TM338897* **GPS** *52.4553N, 1.4400E*

This is a charming town with a lovely church – one of four in the town. It has an 11th-century round tower with later castellated parapet, and inside a very fine traceried pulpit of 1558, near to which is a Scheemakers monument to Thomas Wilson and his wife Catherine.

BUNGAY † St Mary ★
12m/20km W. of Lowestoft, St Mary Street
OS *TM336897* **GPS** *52.4555N, 1.4380E*
Churches Conservation Trust

The former nave of a Benedictine nunnery, the church has a stately 15th-century tower and vast W. window with clear glass. This floods the interior with light. In the roof are some good carved bosses, among them a bat, a lion and two-headed eagles. Note the wooden dole cupboard with a rat carved on the door.

BURES † St Mary
6m/10km S. of Sudbury
OS *TL906340* **GPS** *51.9719N, 0.7747E*

The church has remarkable porches, one of timber, one of Tudor brick with crude chevroning. The chancel must once have been fine, a sort of Wingfield. Monuments include an early 14th-century worm-eaten wooden effigy of a Cornard and a monumental pile in alabaster to Sir William and Dame Elizabeth Waldegrave and their 10 children, 1613.

BURES † St Stephen's Chapel ★
1m/2km N.E. of Bures
OS *TL917344* **GPS** *51.9753N, 0.7907E*

This is a remote, thatched, Early English building, more like a barn (it was used as one until 1940) than a church, with a ship-lapped timber N.W. wall. It was originally dedicated in 1218 and is on the reputed spot where St Edmund was crowned. It contains the superb 14th-century monuments of the De Veres, brought here from Earls Colne Priory.

BURY ST EDMUNDS † St John ★★
St John's Street
OS *TL852646* **GPS** *52.2491N, 0.7128E*

St John's is a dignified Early English Gothic Revival building in weathered brick, by William Ranger, constructed in 1841, with 1870s modifications by J. D. Wyatt. The tower is a notable town landmark, topped with tall pinnacles and flying buttresses that support a tall tapering octagonal spire. Its Tractarian interior owes much to Fr. Holland, an enthusiastic supporter of the Oxford Movement.

BURY ST EDMUNDS † St Mary ★★
Crown Street
OS *TL856639* **GPS** *52.2424N, 0.7171E*

A noble church with a grand exterior and sturdy N. tower, St Mary's stands next to the Cathedral of St James. The 15th-century N. 'Notyngham' porch has a fine wheel vault. The interior is breathtaking: the 10-bay nave, with grand, slender arcades, has a superb late 15th-century angel roof, and there is a panelled and painted wagon roof in the chancel. The Victorian choir stalls have re-used good medieval bench-ends. The many memorials include the simple tomb of Mary Tudor, and John Boret's monument in the S. chapel, 1467, which has a grim cadaver effigy and his motto, 'Grace me Governe', in the wonderfully painted roof.

CAVENDISH † St Mary ★
4m/6km W. of Long Melford
OS *TL805465* **GPS** *52.0878N, 0.6334E*

An unusual open bell-frame crowns the stair turret of this pleasantly situated church. The clerestory and chancel have beautiful 15th-century flushwork. The treasure here is a sumptuous 15th-century Flemish reredos set in a fine Comper frame – all imperial blues and gilding.

CLARE † St Peter and St Paul
7m/11km N.W. of Sudbury
OS *TL769454* **GPS** *52.0792N, 0.5811E*

This is one of Suffolk's biggest churches, with a grand embattled nave and aisles of c. 1460, with rood stair turrets topped by crocketed finials. The chancel was restored in 1617. Dowsing got most of the glass; the remnants are in the E. window, all 1617. In the S. porch is a Green Man boss, and the sundial outside says 'Go about your business'!

COCKFIELD † St Peter
4m/6km N. of Lavenham
OS *TL903549* **GPS** *52.1603N, 0.7822E*

There is some lovely flint and flushwork on the porch, tower parapet and buttresses of this church, which dates from the 14th century. The interior is tall and light, with lofty arcade arches. In the N. aisle is a 14th-century canopied tomb, and in the chancel a sizeable Easter Sepulchre recut by the Victorians.

BLYTHBURGH: HOLY TRINITY – *showing signs of studious late 20th-century repair, the angels, with outstretched wings, are the crowning glory of a fabulous nave* ▷

COMBS † St Mary ★

1m/2km S. of Stowmarket

OS *TM051569* **GPS** *52.1724N, 0.9982E*

Amidst fields and as yet untouched by the southern growth of Stowmarket, there is much of interest in this church, but best of all is the beautiful glass in the S. aisle representing Old Testament Kings and Prophets in the genealogy of Christ, the Works of Mercy and, most vivid of all, scenes from the Life of St Margaret of Antioch. She is represented as a shepherdess cast into prison, swallowed up by the Devil, and stepping light-heartedly into a cauldron of boiling oil.

COVEHITHE † St Andrew ★

4m/6km N. of Southwold

OS *TM523818* **GPS** *52.3768N, 1.7056E*

Churches Conservation Trust

This tiny thatched church of 1672 was built inside the ruins of a great 15th-century church, against the tall 14th-century tower, which was preserved as a mariner's landmark. The tower and ruins are in the care of the Churches Conservation Trust. It can only be hoped that the rapidly encroaching sea leaves both ruins and remains intact over the coming years.

COWLINGE † St Margaret

6m/10km N.E. of Haverhill

OS *TL718549* **GPS** *52.1659N, 0.5112E*

A largely Decorated church with brick tower of 1733, it has an unspoilt interior, with 14th-century crown-post roof, a handsome rood screen of c. 1400, a beautiful 15th-century parclose screen and 18th-century W. gallery, pulpit, rails and seating. There is an old Doom painting over the chancel arch, and a good window by Christopher Webb, 1931. In the chancel is a large and urban monument by Scheemakers to Francis Dickins, lawyer at the Temple, d. 1747.

CRATFIELD † St Mary ★

5m/8km W. of Halesworth

OS *TM313748* **GPS** *52.3227N, 1.3939E*

The church retains a good amount of Decorated detail. Above the porch archway there are two animated carvings, one of a dragon, and the other of a wild man with club and shield. Inside is one of the finest of the county's seven-sacrament fonts. All but two of the panels survived centuries under plaster: those that survived have managed to retain much of their original colour.

DALHAM † St Mary ★

5m/8km E. of Newmarket

OS *TL724625* **GPS** *52.2342N, 0.5236E*

Standing behind the hall that was home to the Rhodes family, this is a spacious 14th–15th-century building with Perpendicular roof and screen. The tower is interesting, having been rebuilt in the 17th century, with texts set into the flushwork parapet: 'Keep my Sabbaths', 'Deo Trin Unum Sacrum', and 'Reverence my Sanctuary'. Traces of medieval painting remain on the N. arcade and chancel arch, and there are many memorials to the Affleck family.

DENNINGTON † St Mary ★

2m/3km N. of Framlingham

OS *TM281669* **GPS** *52.2535N, 1.3414E*

The dignified exterior has a Perpendicular nave, aisles and porch, a 14th-century chancel with handsome Reticulated windows, and a sturdy tower, c. 1383. The view from the W. end is splendid and unhindered. Seven medieval doors remain, and the unforgettable interior has 76 15th-century bench-ends and many parclose screens, complete with their original lofts. The Decorated chancel has exquisitely carved corbels and capitals, and a rare pyx canopy of c. 1500 over the altar. In the S. chapel is the superb alabaster tomb of Lord and Lady Bardolph, 1441.

DENSTON † St Nicholas ★★

5m/8km N. of Clare

OS *TL760529* **GPS** *52.1468N, 0.5711E*

This is a lovely bright church with aisles as wide as the nave, separated by fine arcades. It is all late 15th-century with an interior little changed since the 17th century. The roof is a fine piece of arch-bracing with cambered tie-beams, all faded with age as at Blythburgh, together with very good choir stalls and an excellent seven-sacrament font. The bench ends are all animals, with a preponderance of rabbits, echoed in the animated animal carvings of the wall plates. Here, more than

△ **FRAMLINGHAM: ST MICHAEL** – *the chancel end is open and, with its aisles, extremely wide; in the south aisle at the far east end is the tomb of Thomas Howard, the 3rd Duke of Norfolk*

anywhere else in the county, we get the feeling of what this Suffolk type of late 15th-century church was like in its original splendour.

EARL STONHAM † St Mary ★★

4m/6km E. of Stowmarket
OS *TM107588* **GPS** *52.1875N, 1.0821E*

Here is one of Suffolk's finest oak roofs, well lit by the clerestory. It is double hammer-beam, and all the timbers, from the wall plate to the rafters, are richly carved with winged angels, pendant pineapples, figures holding shields and Green Men, and in the spandrels a multitude of animals. The original 15th-century benches are of interest too, with poppyheads – look for the bagpiper and the monster – and the 17th-century pulpit has four hour-glasses for each quarter of the hour.

ELMSWELL † St John the Divine

5m/8km N.W. of Stowmarket
OS *TL982635* **GPS** *52.2349N, 0.9011E*

This is a lovely hilltop church with a fine flint and stone tower. Most of the fabric is 19th-century; the S. aisle, 1862, is by E. C. Hakewill, the 1867 N. aisle by Wyatt and the chancel by Wither, 1872. In the S. aisle is a monument said to be by Maximilian Colt for Sir Robert Gardener, Lord Chief Justice, 1619.

ELVEDEN
† St Andrew and St Patrick ★★

4m/6km S.W. of Thetford
OS *TL822799* **GPS** *52.3872N, 0.6772E*

Situated at the edge of a park in an estate village, this church has an extraordinary story: it was restored by Maharaja Duleep Singh, a Christian convert and victim of British subjugation of India, who had been granted a lease on the derelict Elveden Hall. After the Maharajah's death, under the Guinness family, the estate's new owners, the old church became the S. aisle of a new church, which was given a sumptuous new nave and chancel on the N. side by W. D. Caroe, 1904–6. It contains magnificent woodwork in roofs and benches and a glorious alabaster reredos. To

the S. is Caroe's cloister and noble bell-tower of 1922, and there is good glass by Kempe, Hugh Easton and F. Brangwyn.

EUSTON † St Genevieve

3m/4km S.E. of Thetford
OS *TL900784* **GPS** *52.3714N, 0.7901E*

Set amid the rolling grassland of Euston Park, this is one of the few examples in E. Anglia of a fine 17th-century church. Built by Lord Arlington in 1676, it is an interesting combination of the E. Anglian medieval and Renaissance. Inside it is embellished with beautiful panelling and a magnificent reredos, possibly by Grinling Gibbons.

EYE † St Peter and St Paul ★

4m/6km S.E. of Diss
OS *TM148737* **GPS** *52.3202N, 1.1516E*

The flushwork of the church's magnificent tall tower is breathtaking, with clusters of vertical panels soaring upwards to the fine carved parapets. There is an imposing Anglo-Catholic interior, dominated by a glorious screen of c. 1480 with 15 painted figures. The rood loft, rood, font cover, sanctuary lamps and E. window are all by Comper.

FRAMLINGHAM † St Michael ★★

9m/15km N. of Woodbridge
OS *TM285635* **GPS** *52.2223N, 1.3446E*

This is a dignified and rambling town church with a sturdy Perpendicular W. tower and fine clerestory completed in 1520; the chancel and E. chapels were not finished until c. 1553. The spacious interior has a handsome nave roof, the hammer-beams concealed by vaulted coving. The church is noted for the splendid monuments to the Howards, Dukes of Norfolk, including the outstanding tomb of Thomas, 3rd Duke, c. 1554, and the tomb of Sir Robert Hitcham, d. 1636.

GIPPING † St Nicholas ★

3m/4km N.E. of Stowmarket
OS *TM072635* **GPS** *52.2314N, 1.0328E*

This exquisite 15th-century chapel of the Tyrell family is extra-parochial and stands in an idyllic setting next to the site of Gitting Hall. The flushwork is striking, and the whole exterior with the exception of the tower features glittering flintwork and very large elegant Perpendicular windows: the flushwork bears devices of the Tyrell family. The interior is very bright, with 15th- and 18th-century benches: the great E. window is filled with re-set glass of c. 1494–1513, and has flanking pillars ornamented with swags of fabric. Note the old chaplain's quarters grafted onto the N. side of the chapel.

GISLINGHAM † St Mary ★

6m/10km S.W. of Diss
OS *TM076717* **GPS** *52.3050N, 1.0441E*

St Mary's is a large church of simple plan with a superb double hammer-beam nave roof, a sturdy brick tower of 1639 and embattled 15th-century porch. The excellent interior has a 15th-century font with 17th-century cover, an 18th-century W. gallery, medieval benches and 18th-century numbered box pews around a three-decker pulpit in its original position. The 15th-century glass includes early pictures of wild flowers.

GREAT BARTON † Holy Innocents

2m/3km E. of Bury St Edmunds
OS *TL889660* **GPS** *52.2601N, 0.7678E*

The church tower is Perpendicular, with very good flushwork to the parapets. The aisles are terminated by octagonal and embattled flushwork turrets. The 13th-century chancel is very spacious, and the tall clerestoried nave has a 15th-century hammer-beam roof. The church was restored in the 1850s.

GREAT BRADLEY † St Mary

5m/8km N. of Haverhill
OS *TL674531* **GPS** *52.1514N, 0.4458E*

The stair turret of the church's tower rises above the battlements of this very pleasant and out-of-the-way church. Of the S. and N. Norman doorways, the S. is the more interesting, with zigzag carving on the arch and a flint-infilled tympanum. The doorway is protected by a step-gabled Tudor brick porch. Inside there is a light, bright atmosphere, simple furnishings and, under the tower, a fireplace. The sedilia in the chancel is hard up against the E. end, suggesting that the chancel has been shortened.

◁ **LITTLE SAXHAM: ST NICHOLAS** – *a delightful church with a refined Norman round tower of flint*

GREAT BRICETT
† St Mary and St Lawrence
5m/8km N. of Hadleigh
OS *TM038506* **GPS** *52.1168N, 0.9762E*

This towerless and remarkably long church of Augustinian canons was founded c. 1110, with a nave and chancel all one space. The predominant style of the windows is simple Y-tracery, and the restored 14th-century glass gives a fine coloured effect inside. The late 12th-century font is very interesting, with chunky interlaced arcading.

GREAT WALDINGFIELD † St Lawrence
3m/4km N.E. of Sudbury
OS *TL912439* **GPS** *52.0606N, 0.7877E*

The overall impression of St Lawrence's from the outside is one of battlements, tower, aisles, porch and clerestory. The only exception is Butterfield's 1867 chancel. The sanctuary here is of great interest, with the Gibbs stained glass E. window depicting the Nativity, and walls set with ancient stones taken from archeological sites in Rome and Egypt, all polished and set into decorated panels.

HADLEIGH † St Mary ★
8m/12km W. of Ipswich
OS *TM025424* **GPS** *52.0436N, 0.9526E*

The 15th-century Guildhall, Tudor brick Deanery Tower and massive flint church make a picturesque group. It's a big-boned church, with a wide, spacious interior, mostly 15th-century Perpendicular, and a bold S. doorway with very finely carved doors. The tall, lead-covered broach spire is c. 1300 and contains a 13th-century clock-bell. Of note are the chancel roof, a 14th-century font with tall cover of 1925 by Charles Spooner, 15th-century chapel screens and a bench-end with a wolf guarding St Edmund's head. Rowland Taylor, martyred in 1555 in the Counter-Reformation, is commemorated in a S. aisle window.

HAWSTEAD † All Saints
3m/4km S. of Bury St Edmunds
OS *TL855592* **GPS** *52.2003N, 0.7141E*

A rich and extensive collection of monuments and tablets fill this church, notably a late 13th-century military effigy of Sir Eustace Fitz-Eustace, a marble monument by Nicholas Stone, 1615, a recumbent figure of the Viscountess Carleton, the brilliantly coloured memorial to Sir Thomas Cullum and a graceful marble memorial to Elizabeth Drury. Also of great appeal is the stained glass, the most notable examples being by Henry Holiday – lovely and reflective Pre-Raphaelite work.

HELMINGHAM † St Mary ★
4m/6km S. of Debenham
OS *TM190576* **GPS** *52.1735N, 1.2025E*

This is a beautiful setting, by the edge of Helmingham Hall, close to a lake. The church is the estate church of the Tollemache family. The late 15th-century tower bears their Arms. The interior is completely dominated by tombs and memorials to the Tollemache family. The memorial to four Lionel Tollemaches reaches the dormer window above: perhaps the dormer was built to accommodate it. Scriptural texts fill every available wall space too, the work of John Charles Ryle, rector here and later the first Bishop of Liverpool.

HERRINGFLEET † St Margaret
6m/10km N.W. of Lowestoft
OS *TM476978* **GPS** *52.5219N, 1.6493E*

This little church retains its charming thatched nave and S. porch, and the ancient round tower with slab-headed Saxon upper openings. An early 19th-century restoration saw the installation of window tracery from the nearby priory, in which is set some very interesting Flemish and French medieval glass.

HESSETT † St Ethelbert ★
5m/8km E. of Bury St Edmunds
OS *TL936618* **GPS** *52.2207N, 0.8342E*

Castellated, buttressed and graced by fine 15th-century stonework with a splendid S. porch, this is a lovely Suffolk church. Inside there are many wall-paintings including St Christopher, the Seven Deadly Sins, Christ of the Trades (these latter two being of special interest), and grand glass – saints in the S. aisle, the life of Christ in the W. window and the Passion in the N. aisle.

HOO † St Andrew and St Eustachius

4m/6km N.W. of Wickham Market
OS *TM256592* **GPS** *52.1855N, 1.2993E*

A humble, rustic, isolated and endearing church, mostly of c. 1300–30, with an early 16th-century Tudor brick tower. Inside everything is atmospheric and homely, with brick floors, a plaster ceiling and 18th-century pulpit, altar table and rails. The octagonal 15th-century font has four lions and angels with interlacing wings and roses below the bowl.

ICKLINGHAM † All Saints

7m/11km N.W. of Bury St Edmunds
OS *TL775726* **GPS** *52.3228N, 0.6042E*
Churches Conservation Trust

A recently re-thatched and largely unspoilt church, it has Norman work in the nave and Decorated windows, font and niches in the S. aisle; the benches and screen base are 15th-century, and there is a 17th-century pulpit, rails and box pew. In the chancel is a remarkable array of rare medieval floor tiles.

IKEN † St Botolph ★

4m/6km N. of Orford
OS *TM412566* **GPS** *52.1553N, 1.5248E*

This is an incomparable setting beside the Alde estuary, and possibly the site of St Botolph's 7th-century monastery. The nave is Norman and for many years was roofless after a fire in 1968. It has now been re-thatched under a nice wagon roof. The interior is simple, quiet and peaceful – a real delight. The ragstone chancel of 1853 by S. Whichcord has in it a Saxon cross shaft found embedded in the wall.

IPSWICH † St Mary at Quay

Foundation Street
OS *TM165440* **GPS** *52.0529N, 1.1565E*
Churches Conservation Trust

Surrounded by busy roads and industrial estates, the exterior of this 1450s church has the sooty appearance of a city church, but inside is clear of furnishing, with a modest hammer-beam nave roof. The wealth of memorials has now been moved to the town museum, but there are reproductions of the brasses to Thomas Pounder, one of the town's many wealthy merchants.

KEDINGTON † St Peter and St Paul ★★

2m/3km E. of Haverhill
OS *TL705470* **GPS** *52.0953N, 0.4876E*

The church is memorable for its atmospheric interior and furnishings, untouched by Victorian alteration, with a 16th-century hammer-beam roof, medieval benches and 17th–19th-century box pews with children's seats in tiers either side of the 1750 singers' gallery. The Barnardiston family pew dominates the church and is built of panels and tracery from the medieval rood screen. There is a superb array of 16th–18th-century Barnardiston monuments, and hatchments on the arcades. Betjeman called this church 'a village Westminster Abbey'.

KERSEY † St Mary

2m/3km N.W. of Hadleigh
OS *TM002439* **GPS** *52.0577N, 0.9189E*

Set above the village, the church has a good 'wool' tower, porches and 14th-century N. aisle, in which are the remains of medieval wall-paintings, and an eclectic assortment of medieval bits and pieces – stonework, corbels and the like. There are six painted screen panels, one of which has the county's best portrayal of St Edmund.

KESSINGLAND † St Edmund

4m/6km S. of Lowestoft
OS *TM527862* **GPS** *52.4159N, 1.7157E*

The tower of this coastal church served as a landmark for mariners: it has good flushwork panelling. Inside there are reminders of the church's maritime role: pilot tights, ships' wheels and anchors abound. On the S. side of the church is the window by Nicola Kantorowicz, 2007, in memory of the Kessingland driftmen.

KETTLEBASTON † St Mary ★

3m/4km E. of Lavenham
OS *TL965502* **GPS** *52.1159N, 0.8697E*

Simply finding this endearing and atmospheric church, set on a tiny hill at the end of a maze of country lanes, is an adventure. The nave is Norman and lit with oil lanterns. The most striking features inside are the colourful high altar reredos, designed by Fr. Ernest Geldart and painted in 1948 by Patrick

△ **LAVENHAM: ST PETER AND ST PAUL** – *St Catherine carved on the Spryng Parclose*

Osborne, and the rood screen, also designed by Geldart and painted by Osbourne. Enid Chadwick added the figures in 1954. At the W. end is a big, square, rustic Norman font, and, close by, reproductions of the 14th-century Kettlebaston Alabasters, now in the British Museum.

LAKENHEATH † St Mary ★

5m/8km S.W. of Brandon
OS *TL714827* **GPS** *52.4158N, 0.5196E*

This is an interesting church of several periods; the tower is 13th-century, and the main body of the church is built round a Norman core. The cambered tie-beam roof is early 15th-century and similar to that at Mildenhall, but lower and thus more easily damaged by the Puritans. There is an elaborate 13th-century font and a complete set of carved benches with poppyheads; these are some of the best in the county. Among the most interesting of the carvings are wrestlers and the Lakenheath Tigress. On the N. arcade there are traces of wall-paintings of different ages; they include the figure of St Edmund, a Tree of Life and, above, an Annunciation. To the S. of the chancel arch is a Christ in Majesty.

LANDWADE † St Nicholas

3m/4km N.W. of Newmarket
OS *TL623680* **GPS** *52.2870N, 0.3785E*

A pocket parish of a hundred acres or so has a delightfully situated church built by Sir Walter and Joan Cotton, c. 1445, as a private chapel, in which a number of attractive medieval fittings and monuments for members of the Cotton family can be found; the place takes a little finding but should not be missed.

LAVENHAM † St Peter and St Paul ★★

6m/10km N.E. of Sudbury
OS *TL912490* **GPS** *52.1064N, 0.7917E*

One of England's best-known and last of the parish wool churches – its massive 141-foot tower dominates the countryside and the unforgettable village beneath it. The chancel is Decorated, c. 1340; the aisles, E. chapels, tall clerestory, tower and porch are masterpieces of the 15th-century stonemason's craft – lavish and stately with stone panelling above. The rood screen is 14th-century, and there are 15th-century parclose screens to the E. chapels, and the superb Renaissance Spryng Parclose of c. 1525. The misericords, though few, are delightful, particularly the depiction of a man squeezing a pig.

LAXFIELD † All Saints ★

6m/10km N. of Framlingham
OS *TM296724* **GPS** *52.3021N, 1.3664E*

One of Suffolk's finest towers, it is a rare example of stone-facing in the county. The mid-15th-century seven-sacrament font is enormous, set on a great raised stone cross. Raked box pews for schoolchildren are set in the nave. There are 15th-century benches, box pews, a 17th-century pulpit and a very

△ **LONG MELFORD: HOLY TRINITY** – *damaged yet still magnificent, the 15th-century glass honouring Sir Thomas Clopton, his wife Catherine (right) and Elizabeth (left), wife of Walter Clopton*

fine reading desk with two carved and very obviously female supporting figures. The iconoclast William Dowsing is thought to have come from Laxfield.

LITTLE SAXHAM † St Nicholas ★★

4m/6km W. of Bury St Edmunds
OS *TL799637* **GPS** *52.2422N, 0.6339E*

The church has one of the county's and perhaps the country's best Norman round towers. The lower stage is possibly Saxon. The Norman S. doorway with tympanum, though plain, is very well preserved. Inside, the tower arch is stupendous, high and narrow. There are some very attractive bench-ends, including a rather irritated-looking monkey and a barking terrier. The Lucas Chapel is now the vestry and contains a Baroque monument to William, Baron Crofts, whose wife Elizabeth, Lady Crofts, is portrayed below in a considerable state of déshabillé, gazing up at him in adoration.

LONG MELFORD † Holy Trinity ★★

3m/4km N. of Sudbury
OS *TL865467* **GPS** *52.0878N, 0.7209E*

This is a regal church of cathedral proportions, a giant amongst churches, 250 feet long, and shows Suffolk Perpendicular at its very best. The exterior is a mass of flushwork panelling and great windows, with a large three-gabled E. Lady Chapel. The old flint-encased brick tower is by G. F. Bodley, 1903. The interior is vast, light, airy and spacious, with a long, unbroken 15th-century arch-braced cambered tie-beam roof and a remarkable array of 15th-century glass in the N. aisle windows. The grand reredos is by Farmer and Brindley, 1877, to the S. of which is William Cordell's splendid monument, 1580. The tiny, intimate Clopton Chapel has a remarkable painted roof, fine sedilia, canopied niches and a Lily crucifix in the 15th-century glass.

LONG MELFORD: HOLY TRINITY – *a massive form, with solid battlements on the nave and tower, and at this, the east end, a three-gabled Lady Chapel with extensive flushwork* ▷

LOUND † St John the Baptist ★★

5m/8km N.W. of Lowestoft

OS *TM506989* **GPS** *52.5311N, 1.6939E*

A Norman round tower graces a lovely church, exquisitely restored. The screen, loft and rood, and the wonderful organ case and font cover, are all the work of Sir Ninian Comper between 1912 and 1914. He produced wall-paintings for this church, with modern elements such as a self-portrait of himself in his Rolls Royce, down near the feet of a giant St Christopher. This was all completed at the outbreak of war, and when Comper returned to the church in 1920 it was to design the war memorial on the exterior of the S. wall. An airliner flying over the shoulder of St Christopher was added to Comper's wall-painting in the 1960s when it underwent restoration.

LOWESTOFT † St Margaret ★

OS *TM541941* **GPS** *52.4864N, 1.7420E*

This large and handsome building is set in a superb position slightly above and apart from the old fishing-port. The porch, one of Suffolk's largest, has an upper story that was once an anchorite's cell, and the vaulting of the lower chamber has a fine medieval Trinity boss. The S. chancel window has glass by Robert Allen, 1819, of the Lowestoft china factory. The proportions here are superb. Sir Ninian Comper designed the elegant font cover of 1940.

MENDLESHAM † St Mary ★

6m/10km N.E. of Stowmarket

OS *TM105657* **GPS** *52.2500N, 1.0832E*

The porches of this large church are exceptional. That to the S. is closed up, but the open N. porch is enormous, decorated with gigantic grotesques, and in the upper storey is a fine collection of village armour dating between the 15th and 17th centuries. This can be visited by appointment. The interior, restored by Ewan Christian, 1860, is mysterious, with flickering candles and icons everywhere, and five altars. The furnishing is beautiful: 17th-century woodwork, and the pulpit, reading desk and font cover all made by John Turner of Mendlesham in 1630.

METFIELD † St John the Baptist ★

4m/6km S.E. of Harleston

OS *TM294803* **GPS** *52.3729N, 1.3691E*

The two-storey porch is a lovely example of flint flushwork, studded with Tudor roses, and with wooden vaulting inside with face bosses staring down: much appreciated by the nesting swallows. Inside is one of the best surviving canopies of honour in the county. It originally stood above the rood, and is formed by the decoration of the easternmost bay of the nave roof; the original painted scheme of the IHS Christogram.

MILDENHALL † St Mary ★★

8m/12km N.E. of Newmarket

OS *TL710745* **GPS** *52.3428N, 0.5092E*

This enormous church has high-quality work of many periods from the 13th century onward. The great W. tower is one of the legendary landmarks of the Fens. The nave roof is a splendid example of cambered tie-beam construction, interspersed with arch-braced hammer-beams on which are angels with spread wings, poised as if to swoop onto the congregation below. In the aisles there are hammer-beam roofs too. The wealth of carving on the N. aisle roof in particular is unsurpassed, with saints on the wall posts and biblical scenes cut into the spandrels.

MONK SOHAM † St Peter

3m/4km N.E. of Debenham

OS *TM213650* **GPS** *52.2394N, 1.2407E*

The font is the main attraction at St Peter's. It is one of the county's seven-sacrament fonts, and some of its details reflect the monastic life here in the 15th century, particularly the cowled monks seated round the base of the font stem: the parish was used for retreats by the monks at Bury Abbey.

NAYLAND † St James ★

6m/10km N. of Colchester

OS *TL975342* **GPS** *51.9714N, 0.8748E*

William Abell's vaulted S.W. porch of 1525 is a masterpiece, although no longer used. Though much Victorianised, the inside is very good, with a tall nave leading to a chancel with a lovely Reticulated E. window, under which stands one of the church's great

MILDENHALL: ST MARY – *the angels here seem to loom over the narrow nave* ▷

△ **MILDENHALL: ST MARY** – *poppyheads carved in a variety of forms*

treasures – John Constable's c. 1809 altar-piece depicting Christ blessing the bread and wine. In the S. aisle are some panels that form the medieval rood screen.

NEEDHAM MARKET
† St John the Baptist ★

3m/4km S.E. of Stowmarket
OS *TM087551* **GPS** *52.1554N, 1.0506E*

This was the chapel of ease to Barking, not parochial until 1901, hence the absence of a churchyard. The towerless exterior is late 15th-century, with good Perpendicular windows, but the fabric is generally unremarkable. From the outside the clerestory is ugly, as is the rather silly S. porch and spirelet by H. W. Hayward, 1883. However, the hammer-beam angel roof is of a unique and remarkable construction, and simply enormous and exquisite in its beauty.

NEWMARKET † St Agnes

13m/21km E. of Cambridge
OS *TL650640* **GPS** *52.2495N, 0.4159E*

R. H. Carpenter built this small, flamboyant and beautiful red-brick Gothic Revival church in 1886. The interior is magnificent, with an elaborate use of tiles and mosaic, culminating in Boehm's superb marble reredos showing the Assumption of St Agnes.

NORTH COVE † St Botolph

3m/4km E. of Beccles
OS *TM461893* **GPS** *52.4470N, 1.6210E*

This is an unassuming thatched church with Norman, Early English and Decorated work, and outstanding 14th-century wall-paintings of the Life of Christ in the chancel. These were painstakingly restored in the 1990s, having been clumsily 'medievalised' in oil paints by the Victorians. This recent restoration also highlighted a minute figure in a coffin, scroll in hand: he was the donor of the paintings.

ORFORD † St Bartholomew ★

9m/15km E. of Woodbridge
OS *TM422499* **GPS** *52.0952N, 1.5349E*

Orford has two landmarks: the massive keep of the Norman Castle, and the more modest tower of St. Bartholomews, the upper parts of which were somewhat uneasily rebuilt in the 1960s after a spectacular failure of the buttresses in the 19th century. In the ruined chancel are remains of the Norman arcades that formed the crossing. The Decorated nave and aisles are the only surviving parts of the 14th-century work of the church, but there is a lovely 15th-century octagonal font with carved panels, one of which depicts a rare Pietà. Through the church is scattered a good collection of brasses. There is a roundel in the nave to Benjamin Britten: he had a soft spot for St Bartholomew's: it was the setting for his musical adaptation of the Chester mystery play *Noyes Fludde*.

POLSTEAD † St Mary ★

4m/6km S.W. of Hadleigh
OS *TL989380* **GPS** *52.0054N, 0.8965E*

Set on a hill in the grounds of Polstead Hall, the church has Suffolk's only medieval 14th-century stone spire and is unusual in the county for the extent and materials of the remaining Norman fabric; a good Norman doorway with zigzags, and remarkable Norman arcades and clerestory windows incorporating late 12th-century brickwork. The font is brick too, but of undetermined age. The atmospheric interior has a handsome king-post roof and some good 17th-century woodwork.

RATTLESDEN † St Nicholas ★
5m/8km W. of Stowmarket
OS *TL978590* **GPS** *52.1942N, 0.8927E*

This is a stately church, whose early 14th-century tower has an octagonal shingled broach spire. The rest of the fabric is Perpendicular, with a good clerestory and superb porch of c. 1476, 15th-century benches and stalls, a 17th-century pulpit, and two sets of rails, one from Kettlebaston. The most remarkable aspect of the church is the rood, reconstructed by G. H. Fellowes Prynne incorporating an earlier medieval fragment and the original stairs. It is not so much an attempt to recreate the medieval patina, but more to show how such structures work from a practical point of view.

RICKINGHALL INFERIOR † St Mary
6m/10km S.W. of Diss
OS *TM038751* **GPS** *52.3363N, 0.9911E*
Churches Conservation Trust

Here is an early round tower extended, as often happened, into a pleasing 15th-century octagonal belfry. The interior was restored quite heavily by J. C. Wyatt in the 19th century, but the church is still attractive inside, with a beautiful S. aisle of c. 1300 with remarkable Geometrical window tracery and carved foliage in the S.E. window.

RISBY † St Giles ★
4m/6km N.W. of Bury St Edmunds
OS *TL802663* **GPS** *52.2660N, 0.6396E*

The Norman round tower sits well with the 14th-century church. Inside are two good rustic Norman arches, one to the chancel and one to the tower. The little rood screen is a treasure, restored very well in the 1960s, and indistinct wall-paintings of c. 1200 depict the Nativity and Lives of the Saints.

ROUGHAM † St Mary ★
4m/6km S.E. of Bury St Edmunds
OS *TL912625* **GPS** *52.2284N, 0.7982E*

This well-proportioned 14th–15th-century building has an early 16th-century N. aisle, the buttresses inscribed with the names of donors and dated 1514, and a well-proportioned tower of the 15th-century. Here the iconoclasts really went to work on the medieval benches, chopping off bench-end figures entirely. Oddly, the angel hammer-beam roof survived relatively intact, though the angels have lost their heads and wings.

RUMBURGH † St Michael ★
4m/6km N.W. of Halesworth
OS *TM346818* **GPS** *52.3846N, 1.4466E*

This is a former Benedictine 13th-century priory church. It has a massively broad rectangular tower, with three W. lancet windows and an unusual tiled and timbered belfry stage topped by a hipped roof. Inside is a lovely screen on which some of the original colour remains; also a medieval roof, a few old benches and a 17th-century pulpit.

RUSHBROOKE † St Nicholas ★
3m/4km S.E. of Bury St Edmunds
OS *TL893615* **GPS** *52.2193N, 0.7704E*

Lovely and lonely on a ridge, the 14th-century tower can be seen for miles around. The church is mostly 1540, with an excellent Tudor roof and brilliant glass by a Bury glazier. The interior is a Gothic fantasy created by the very eccentric Colonel Rushbrooke – a keen amateur joiner – in the 19th century. He rebuilt the nave in collegiate choir style, with seating facing N. and S. across a central aisle. He also placed, in the tympanum above the chancel arch, a unique Royal Arms of Henry VIII.

SANTON DOWNHAM † St Mary ★
2m/3km N.E. of Brandon
OS *TL816876* **GPS** *52.4563N, 0.6716E*

A tranquil forest provides the background for St Mary's, with its Norman nave, 13th-century chancel and 15th-century W. tower with donors' names in the base-course. The interior is well cared for, with a 14th-century screen, 17th-century pulpit, font cover and chest; in the N. wall are three lancet windows with lovely glass by C. E. Kempe.

SHELLAND † King Charles the Martyr ★

3m/4km N.W. of Stowmarket

OS *TM003602* **GPS** *52.2038N, 0.9306E*

Charming outside and in, and much rebuilt in 1767, the interior is a period piece, with box pews, two-decker pulpit and altar rails. There is a 14th-century font and, in the W. gallery, a barrel organ of c. 1820.

SOUTHWOLD † St Edmund ★★

8m/12km E. of Halesworth

OS *TM507763* **GPS** *52.3282N, 1.6787E*

This is a glorious Perpendicular church, built in one piece c. 1450–1500, with a distinctive copper nave roof and sanctus belfry. The lofty W. tower has richly panelled flushwork and diapering on the W. front: the superb two-storey vaulted S. porch has diapering outside, and grand flushwork angled buttresses. The colourful interior is entered through traceried doors. The sumptuous painted screen stretches the full width of the church, effectively forming three screens for the chancel arch and aisles. The dado figures in the centre are original, though restored – 11 disciples. The S. chancel section has the Old Testament prophets, and the N. section is painted with all the hierarchy of angels. Later work includes a lofty 1930s font cover, a reredos by F. E. Howard and Comper glass in the E. window.

STOKE-BY-NAYLAND † St Mary ★

8m/12km S.E. of Sudbury

OS *TL986362* **GPS** *51.9895N, 0.8915E*

Here is the tower so loved by John Constable, simply massive with stepped angled buttresses and stout finials at the corners of the parapet. The S. porch was a Victorian restoration, but the corbels and bosses are 14th-century. The church is entered through traceried S. doors that rank among the county's best. The well-proportioned interior has an impressive tower arch, 14th-century misericords, a fine font, and 15th-century nave roof and chapel screens. Good monuments include that of Sir Francis Mannock, 1634, and Lady Anne Windsor, 1615; amongst the brasses is the six-foot effigy of Sir William de Tendring, 1408.

STOWLANGTOFT † St George ★

2m/3km S.E. of Ixworth

OS *TL957682* **GPS** *52.2771N, 0.8684E*

Simple in plan but lofty and impressive in stature, the church was all built c. 1370–1400. The exterior has tall windows, fine gargoyles, an elegant tower and flushwork porch. Inside there are original 15th-century benches, among which are some bench-ends restored and replicated by the noted Ipswich woodcarver Henry Ringham. There is a canopy of honour over the rood: the stalls in the chancel are complete – probably the best in E. Anglia with some fine misericords.

SUDBURY † All Saints

Friars Street

OS *TL868409* **GPS** *52.0357, 0.7230*

The church is chiefly notable for its 15th-century pulpit, parclose screens in the chancel and an unusual 17th-century painting representing the pedigree of the Eden and Waldegrave families.

SUDBURY † St Gregory

The Green, by The Croft

OS *TL870414* **GPS** *52.0402N, 0.7259E*

The S. porch here forms one of the county's most imposing entrances to a fine town church. Inside is a magnificent font cover and 15th-century roof with canopy of honour for the rood. The 14th-century chancel is very collegiate in atmosphere: the stalls have misericords. It was built by Simon de Sudbury, Archbishop of Canterbury and instigator of the hated Poll Tax; he was murdered at the time of the Peasants' Revolt in 1381. His skull is in a glass case, viewable by appointment.

SUDBURY † St Peter

Marketplace

OS *TL874413* **GPS** *52.0386N, 0.7314E*

Churches Conservation Trust

A former chapel of ease to St Gregory's, it is in an imposing setting by the market-place. In the chancel are interesting paintings of Moses and Aaron, part of a Classical reredos of c. 1730, by Robert Cardinal. William Butterfield painted the canopy of honour in blues and golds during his extensive restoration of the chancel and the S. aisle, 1854–8.

△ **SOUTHWOLD: ST EDMUND** – *despite severe damage to most of the figures, the screen here still possesses a profound beauty, and it is clear that the medieval painting is of a superb quality*

SWILLAND † St Mary ★

5m/8km N. of Ipswich
OS *TM187529* **GPS** *52.1317N, 1.1952E*

This small church looks from a distance like a folly: its character comes largely from the extraordinary Tudor brick tower, with a Bavarian fairytale brick and timber-framed top stage, complete with dormer windows and spirelet, by J. S. Corder in 1895. Inside is a large Comper-like gilded reredos, with ranks of saints in the niches to either side of the central Crucifixion. At the back of the church is a very good and rare carved Royal Arms of Queen Anne. Of note from the earlier fabric is a fine Norman doorway.

TANNINGTON † St Ethelbert

4m/6km N.W. of Framlingham
OS *TM242674* **GPS** *52.2599N, 1.2844E*

A long, low church of the 14th century with a stocky tower and flushwork S. porch, it has a charming irregular run of windows from the 13th to 15th centuries. The E. window has particularly nice Intersecting tracery. Inside there are good bench-ends (sadly much mutilated), part of a series depicting the Sacraments. The canted wagon nave roof has a canopy of honour, and there is a delightful memorial window to a churchwarden – all rural local scenes.

THORNHAM PARVA † St Mary ★★

3m/4km S.W. of Eye
OS *TM109726* **GPS** *52.3114N, 1.0926E*

This is a thatched gem in a meadow – even the truncated tower is thatched – showing work of most periods from Saxon onward. Inside, the fine interior has wall-paintings, some of the best in the county, a 15th-century screen, and above all the celebrated retable of c. 1300 with its exquisite painted figures. There is also a lovely piece of engraved memorial glass by Laurence Whistler. Sir Basil Spence is buried in the churchyard.

△ **THORNHAM PARVA: ST MARY** – *a rare church with thatching to the nave and tower roofs; the setting and quaintness are not all though, and the church has a fine interior with much to see*

UFFORD † St Mary ★

3m/4km N.E. of Woodbridge

OS *TM298521* **GPS** *52.1202N, 1.3562E*

The 11th-century herringbone masonry in the N. nave wall reveals the Saxon origins of St Mary's, whose greatest treasure is the colossal carved and crocketed 15th-century font cover. It stands over 18 feet high and is topped by a Pelican in her Piety. The reredos and war memorial window in the S. chapel are by J. N. Comper.

WALSHAM-LE-WILLOWS

† St Mary ★

5m/8km E. of Ixworth

OS *TL999711* **GPS** *52.3017N, 0.9315E*

This is a grand, spacious Perpendicular 15th-century church: outside is good diapering and some flushwork, whilst over the clerestory window arches is a decorative brick pattern. The interior is very light, with a remarkable Suffolk-type tie-beam and hammer-beam roof with some original colour, and a sensitively restored and re-gilded screen. A maiden's garland hangs in the nave, 'For Mary Boyce 1685', and in the N. wall of the chancel is a memorial window to the noted 20th-century stained-glass artist Rosemary Rutherford, sister of the vicar in the 1950s and 60s.

WENHASTON † St Peter ★

3m/4km S.E. of Halesworth

OS *TM424754* **GPS** *52.3238N, 1.5571E*

The great feature of this church is the spirited Doom painting, discovered on a wooden tympanum of c. 1520 when the Victorians left it out in the rain in 1892: the overnight rain washed away the covering whitewash. Originally the tympanum filled the space above the chancel arch, but it now rests against the N. nave wall. The colours are fresh-looking and the images vivid; it's also clear to see where the rood would once have been attached directly to the panels.

WESTHALL † St Andrew ★★
3m/4km N.E. of Halesworth
OS *TM423804* **GPS** *52.3683N, 1.5582E*

There is so much to see and admire in this secretive and wonderful church, which is well worth visiting, even if only for its setting. The original and superb Norman W. portal is seen from the base of the tower, c. 1300. There are fine Decorated windows in the chancel, and a seven-sacrament font with a great deal of original colour, and the base of the screen with 16 painted panels, three of which have a rare portrayal of the Transfiguration.

WESTHORPE † St Margaret
7m/11km N. of Stowmarket
OS *TM043692* **GPS** *52.2832N, 0.9948E*

The great buttresses on the 15th-century tower of this delightful church look like pendulous ears. Of the 14th century is the exquisite parclose screen, the sanctuary piscina and the fine tracery in the S. aisle. The 15th century provided the tie-beam and hammer-beam nave roof, the tiny pulpit and bench-ends. There is a good monument of 1613 to William Barrow in the chancel, and a vast marble edifice to Maurice Barrow, 1666.

WINGFIELD † St Andrew ★
2m/3km N. of Stradbroke
OS *TM230768* **GPS** *52.3440N, 1.2725E*

This is a large, light and airy formerly collegiate church of the de la Poles, noted mainly for the superb monuments, most of which can be found in the chancel and adjacent N. and S. chapels. The best are in the chancel: to the S. is the tomb of the 2nd Earl of Suffolk, d. 1415, and on the N. wall is the tomb of John de la Pole, Duke of Suffolk, d. 1491, represented in exquisitely well-detailed armour, next to his wife Elizabeth Plantagenet. In the N. chapel is the tomb of Sir Richard Wingfield, d. 1361, and above the chapel is a priest's room.

WISSINGTON † St Mary ★
1m/2km S.W. of Nayland
OS *TL954332* **GPS** *51.9635N, 0.8437E*

An 1853 restoration rebuilt the apse of this small early Norman church set on the Wissington Hall estate: the church was filled with rather silly faux-Norman furnishings, as if it was not quite Norman enough for the restorers. But there really is plenty of Norman work here, including fine 12th-century doorways, a chancel arch, cross vaulting in the chancel and a well-carved E. window. There is other interesting old work here too: on the walls are early wall-paintings in two rows. The complete set survives, though some of the paintings are incomplete. For the most part, they illustrate the life of Christ from the Annunciation to the Ascension. There is also an early image of St Francis, possibly contemporary with the saint himself.

WITHERSDALE † St Mary Magdalene ★
2m/3km S.E. of Harleston
OS *TM283807* **GPS** *52.3774N, 1.3539E*

This tiny, rustic Norman church has a lovely 17th-century interior, complete with pews, pulpit with tester, altar table and rails; a perfect example of an unspoilt village church of the period. The font is very ancient, possibly pre-Conquest; it stands on a brick base.

WOODBRIDGE † St Mary ★★
8m/12km N.E. of Ipswich
OS *TM270490* **GPS** *52.0935, 1.3135*

A well-proportioned Perpendicular town church of the 15th century, it has a superb tower, covered with good flushwork, and four types of buttress. The N. porch is one of Suffolk's finest flushwork porches. It is remarkably detailed, with many inset monograms and heraldic devices. The interior is for the most part a very good Victorian restoration by R. M. Phipson. It does, though, contain a seven-sacrament font, whose damaged but recognisable panels have a curious fanned-out background. The surviving panels of the rood are placed near the font on the W. and S. walls.

W
E

SURREY

For centuries the small area of Surrey was little regarded. It was an unattractive district to the Romans, and it has few extensive medieval remains. The 17th century found profit from its rich meadows in the Thames Valley, and there were once fields round Mitcham and Carshalton, redolent with lavender, mint, camomile, penny royal and other herbs for supplying London herb-sellers. Battersea, now part of London, was famous for asparagus, and Chertsey for carrots. In the 18th century the heights of Richmond Hill, Cooper's Hill and St Anne's, looking over the winding Thames, were favoured for country seats by the nobility.

As Denham said of Cooper's Hill, the view was: 'Though deep, yet clear; though gentle, yet not dull; Strong, without rage; without o'erflowing, full.'

This, of course, was the Surrey of the past. Twentieth-century boundary changes took away Battersea, Richmond, Mitcham, Carshalton, Croydon and other districts, and these are now dealt with in this book as part of Greater London.

Through the middle of the county on an east-west axis runs a narrow, high ridge of chalk, the North Downs, which continues east into Kent. The views from the Hog's Back and Box Hill have long been famous. Leith Hill, on the Greensand Ridge, is 965 feet, the highest eminence in this part of England. But for the most part Surrey was regarded in polite circles as a barren county of heaths, firs and unprofitable soil. It was not until Victorian times that its scenery came to be much admired, except by a few Romantics in advance of public taste.

When it was admired, however, much happened to Surrey. Rich city gentlemen built themselves houses on its heights, and less affluent citizens built themselves villas. As land was cheap and infertile, Government departments found it desirable for barracks, orphanages and asylums. Schools, too, were built on its sandy commons among the conifers. Although now a desirable and populous place for commuters, there is still much of the county that retains a rural feel – the slopes and the woods of the North Downs offering a haven of peace to the harassed commuter. The county has great natural beauty, and the outline of its hills, the wide views, the safe wildness – safe now from the footpads and highwaymen of two centuries ago – the ponds, the timbered cottages, and the newer villas with their lovingly tended gardens, the gorse, bracken and heather, the sheepy valleys still to be found on the southern slopes of the Downs, make one wish one had known it before it was discovered.

Several old towns of real beauty survive, including Guildford, Dorking, Farnham and Reigate. And the rural charm of the county has been safeguarded by protection to ancient routes such as the Pilgrim's Way (a footpath to Canterbury) and the North Downs Way, while the Surrey Hills has been designated as an area of outstanding natural beauty.

◁ **DUNSFOLD: ST MARY AND ALL SAINTS** – *a church much admired by William Morris*

SLOUGH
M25
GREATER LONDON
BERKSHIRE
Windsor
RICHMON
M4
STAINES
Englefield Green
Egham
KINGSTON UPON THAMES
BRACKNELL
Laleham
Littleton
A30
M3
A322
Esher
SURREY
A319
A3
CAMBERLEY
EP
M25
WOKING
Stoke D'Abernon
A24
Ockham
LEATHERHEAD
A322
A3
A331
Great Bookham
A320
Worplesdon
A246
Mickleham
West Horsley
Aldershot
GUILDFORD
Betchw
Ranmore
DORKING
A31
Shere
Wotton
Compton
A248
Albury
A25
A24
FARNHAM
Blackheath
Wonersh
Holmbury St Mary
Shackleford
GODALMING
Peper Harow
Busbridge
A287
Grafham
Ewhurst
A3
Cranleigh
Thursley
Witley
Hascombe
A29
Dunsfold
A286
A281
Alfold
A3
Haslemere
HORSHAM
WEST SUSSEX
A283
A24
A286
Billingshurst

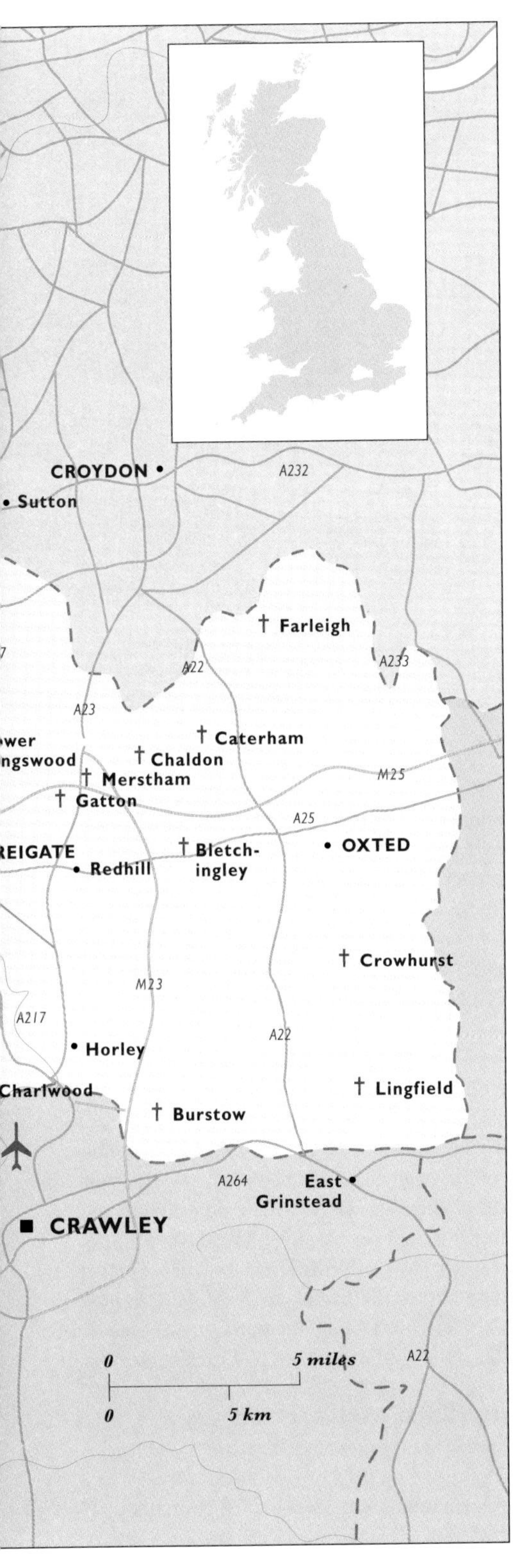

There is more to Surrey than is generally thought. The story of the county's churches is mostly one of heavy restoration, of unpretentious fabrics or of new Victorian buildings. But there was a wide variety of local stone, such as Bargate, which gives the older churches delightful texture. Most of the finest churches are 19th-century, for here lived the great Victorian church architects, Woodyer and G. E. Street, and between them they left their mark upon Surrey churches, and their imitators and pupils did not let them down.

For eccentric church architecture, the Watts Cemetery Chapel at Compton – a testament to the Home Arts and Industries Association, and stylistically all Art Nouveau, Romanesque, Celtic and Egyptian – rivals the flourishing pastiche of architectural styles at St Conan's, on the shores of Loch Awe. And although not referred to in detail here, it would be remiss not to make passing reference to the great legacy of vernacular Arts and Crafts architecture through the county – Lutyens' great collaborations with Gertrude Jekyll, Baillie Scott and C. F. A. Voysey among the leading exponents. Lutyens also left his mark on some of the county's churches, among them a war memorial and surround to Gertrude Jekyll's tomb in Busbridge churchyard, and a lych gate at St James's in Shere.

△ **ALBURY: ST PETER AND ST PAUL OLD CHURCH** – *charmingly crooked in a parkland setting*

ALBURY
† St Peter and St Paul Old Church ★
Albury Park, 4m/6km E. of Guildford
OS *TQ063478* **GPS** *51.2199N, 0.47891W*
Churches Conservation Trust

Henry Drummond, one of the apostles of the Catholic Apostolic Church, built a new parish church of the same name outside Albury Park, and hence the old church, though set beautifully within the park, has been disused since 1848: the chancel became a ruin. It was of Norman nave-tower-chancel plan, with a late 13th-century S. aisle, and chancel now Perpendicular. The S. transept was added in 1290 and lavishly decorated by Pugin, 1839, in red, blue and gold. The tower, originally the Saxon chancel, was heightened c. 1140, and in the 18th century given a shingled cupola.

ALFOLD † St Nicholas
4m/6km S.W. of Cranleigh
OS *TQ037339* **GPS** *51.09565N, 0.52015W*

Attractively approached between tile-hung cottages on a tiny triangular green, this is a church of 12th-century origins and many later additions – an Early English N. aisle, a chancel and chancel arch of the early 1400s, and a timber belfry of the 15th century supported internally on massive timbers. The Norman font has cable moulding around the lower rim, and panels with carved Maltese crosses. The N. aisle was rebuilt by Woodyer in 1845.

BETCHWORTH † St Michael
3m/4km E. of Dorking
OS *TQ210496* **GPS** *51.23354N, 0.26722W*

Mostly 13th-century, with an early Norman tower, originally central; the N. windows of the chancel are also Norman. The church was much rebuilt on the S. in 1851, when the S. transept was added. The Goulburn Chapel dates from 1879, and at the E. end of the nave are interesting memorials and brasses. The 1951 font was carved by Eric Kennington.

BLACKHEATH † St Martin ★
3m/4km S.E. of Guildford
OS *TQ031462* **GPS** *51.205888N, 0.525133W*

A charming Arts and Crafts church by C. Harrison Townsend, 1893, set in a pretty village; the church is exactly suited to such a place. It is Italianate-looking outside – possibly inspired by an Italian wayside chapel – with deep eaves and very low walls. The interior is a charming little barrel-vaulted chapel made mysterious by a screen and hidden lighting behind the wide and rounded arch of the marble sanctuary. There is a sparing and wise use of illustrative decoration, using soluble silicate paints, by the American artist Anna Lea Merritt, famous for her picture *Love Locked Out.*

BLETCHINGLEY † St Mary
3m/4km E. of Redhill
OS *TQ327508* **GPS** *51.24127N, 0.09948W*

An interesting church, with an early Norman tower; the fabric is now mainly 15th-century. The fine reredos by G. E. Street shows Samuel Wilberforce with apostles and saints flanking the Crucifixion. The two-storey porch and oak door date from 1460, and from the same date are the S. arcade and chancel arch. The sumptuous Sir Robert Clayton monument is by Richard Crutcher, 1707, in majestic Corinthian taste.

BURSTOW † St Bartholomew
2m/3km S.E. of Horley
OS *TQ312412* **GPS** *51.15582N, 0.12479W*

In a quiet tree-lined lane, this is an early Norman church with traces of Saxon herringbone stonework in the N. nave wall. The tower, S. aisle and E. end of the chancel are all 15th-century. At the W. end is a most remarkable handsome shingled belfry, medieval in origin but tricked out in the 18th century. John Flamsteed, Astronomer Royal to Charles II, 1675–1719, held the living and is buried in the chancel.

BUSBRIDGE † St John Baptist ★
1m/2km S.E. of Godalming
OS *SU978429* **GPS** *51.17706N, 0.60163W*

By G. G. Scott Jnr, 1865–7, this is an essay in Surrey-style Early English Gothic Revival, with Bargate stone and shingles. The celebrated ironwork rood was made by J. Starkie Gardner to designs by Lutyens; dark and almost holy. The very good stained glass in the sanctuary, chancel and W. end is by Burne-Jones, 1899. Lutyens designed the war memorial outside, and Gertrude Jekyll's tomb surround.

CATERHAM † St Lawrence
5m/8km S. of Croydon
OS *TQ335553* **GPS** *51.2821N, 0.0860W*

This is an apsed 12th-century church whose S. chancel chapel was destroyed. The remaining fabric comprises the nave, N. aisle and vestry, and chancel with 13th-century restorations to the chancel arch. Remains of medieval wall-paintings can be seen in the chancel arch spandrels and on the N. wall.

CHALDON † St Peter and St Paul ★★
2m/3km W. of Caterham
OS *TQ308556* **GPS** *51.28539N, 0.12448W*

The church stands almost alone on the high downland: Norman, enlarged later, with a W. tower and spire of 1843. The wall-painting of c. 1200 on the W. wall is one of the most important and complete early schemes in England. This is an astounding vision of the Last Judgement, alive with imps, devils and serene angels, all against an entirely suitable background of blood-red ochre. On the N. side of the chancel is a 15th-century Easter Sepulchre with quatrefoils and blank shields.

CHARLWOOD † St Nicholas ★
3m/4km N. of Crawley, on W. side of Gatwick Airport
OS *TQ240411* **GPS** *51.15573N, 0.22739W*

Set among picturesque tile-hung cottages, the golden sandstone church has an 11th-century nave, central tower and chancel. The 15th-century screen at the W. end of the S. chapel (now the chancel) was embellished by William Burgess during his restoration of 1858, and the frieze repainted in 1973. The 13th-century wall-paintings depict the life of St Margaret of Antioch and St Nicholas, and were partly overpainted in the 15th century.

COMPTON † St Nicholas ★★
3m/4km S.W. of Guildford
OS *SU954470* **GPS** *51.2143N, 0.6347W*

Pleasantly set in a pretty Surrey village, this is one of the county's best Norman churches: the tower and parts of the walls are 11th-century, the chancel arch and tower even earlier. The arcades and aisles date from c. 1170. The late 12th-century two-storey sanctuary, .set into the existing chancel, is the only one remaining in England. The lower stage of the sanctuary is groined; the upper has a late 12th-century carved wooden balustrade.

COMPTON † Watts Cemetery Chapel ★

3m/4km S.W. of Guildford

OS *SU956473* **GPS** *51.2178N, 0.6321W*

A wonderful and eclectic example of architecture by Mary Watts, espousing Celtic, Art Nouveau, Romanesque and Egyptian themes and motifs, the whole thing was inspired by the aspirations of the Home Arts and Industries Association. The chapel peers over the trees like a miniature Byzantine basilica – most unexpected. The outside is decorated with mournful faces, swirls of foliage, Celtic knots and dragons' tails. Inside is a wonderful gesso decorative scheme of angels, a tree of life, medallions and mystical symbols.

CROWHURST † St George

3m/4km S. of Oxted

OS *TQ390474* **GPS** *51.20929N, 0.01066W*

A simple 12th–13th-century church of Wealden sandstone, whose timber tower has a distinctive sharp spire. Monuments include a rare 16th-century cast-iron ledger slab. The E. walls of the chancel are painted in a Pre-Raphaelite style. Outside is a vast yew tree claimed to be 4000 years old, hollowed out in 1820 to make a room with a padlocked door and circular benches inside.

DORKING † St Martin

11m/18km E. of Guildford

OS *TQ165494* **GPS** *51.23268N, 0.33231W*

Rebuilt in 1868–77 by Henry Woodyer, this is one of his best works – a really grand church, with tall and graceful W. tower and spire. The well-proportioned interior has triplets of clerestory windows and good contemporary fittings. Over the chancel arch is a mosaic by Arthur Powell depicting the Crucifixion, c. 1890.

DUNSFOLD † St Mary and All Saints ★

4m/6km S.W. of Cranleigh

OS *SU998363* **GPS** *51.11763N, 0.57502W*

For William Morris, this church was 'the most beautiful country church in all England'. Approached through tunnels of clipped yews, this notably complete late 13th-century village church has good details, including the late Geometrical windows, rare surviving pews and a 15th-century timber belfry. The timber porch, renewed in the 16th century, shelters the original door with its ironwork still intact.

ENGLEFIELD GREEN
† St Simon and St Jude

2m/3km W. of Staines

OS *SU992708* **GPS** *51.4279N, 0.5733W*

Very prettily set, this is a rather odd Victorian church by Edward Buckton Lamb, 1859, of Kentish rag with Bath stone dressing, with a polychromatic brickwork interior. The cruciform structure is somewhat off-balanced by Lamb's placing of the tower over the S. transept. The two small mausolea at the entrance – fish-scale tiled steep roofs with pronounced overhanging eaves – look as if a Thai temple has landed on banded Victorian brickwork.

ESHER † St George ★

4m/6km S.W. of Kingston

OS *TQ139646* **GPS** *51.3692N, 0.3645W*

Churches Conservation Trust

A most loveable, unrestored church; basically 16th-century with a jaunty lop-sided wooden belfry. The brick transept with gallery pew for the Duke of Newcastle was built in 1725–6 by Sir John Vanbrugh, with a front towards the nave like a little garden temple with Corinthian columns. The upper W. gallery is 1840–2. The picture of the Apotheosis of Princess Charlotte is by A. W. Devis, and there is a Greek-style marble monument to her by F. J. Williamson.

EWHURST † St Peter and St Paul

2m/3km E. of Cranleigh

OS *TQ091404* **GPS** *51.1531N, 0.4409W*

Delightfully set in a hill-top village, the church is cruciform, largely 13th-century and partly rebuilt by Robert Ebbels after the fall of the tower in 1837. The massive S. doorway is

△ **BLACKHEATH: ST MARTIN** – *a barrel-vaulted chapel, with wall-paintings by Lea Merritt*

early 12th-century, with powerful roll mouldings and cabled imposts, the best in Surrey. Inside there are fine late 17th-century altar rails and a Jacobean pulpit.

FARLEIGH † St Mary

4m/7km S.E. of Croydon
OS *TQ372600* **GPS** *51.32318N, 0.03176W*

This is a simple Norman church in a hamlet. Largely 11th-century, with a nave and chancel, it has been gently restored, with some 13th-century alterations. There is a memorial brass to John Brock, a London merchant, and his wife and five children, 1495. One of the county's lesser-known gems.

GATTON † St Andrew ★★

Gatton Park, 2m/3km N. of Redhill
OS *TQ275528* **GPS** *51.2608N, 0.1736W*

The church is situated in the grounds of the Royal Alexandra and Albert School. Its 1834 restoration by E. Webb created the finely furnished interior that has carved stalls with misericords from Ghent and wainscotting and canopies from Louvain. The result is like an Oxford college chapel. The N. transept is a parlour pew with fireplace and chairs; the S. transept has a gallery from which the pulpit is suspended. The interior is a remarkable example of a church furnished by an antiquarian traveller and collector. Outside is the burial place of the Coleman family – kings of mustard.

GODALMING † St Peter and St Paul ★

4m/6km S.W. of Guildford
OS *SU968440* **GPS** *51.1870N, 0.6161W*

The church dominates Church Street with its twisted lead-clad 14th-century spire. Although there are some pre-Conquest remains, the central tower, chancel and transepts are Norman. Aisles were added in the 13th century, and the chancel aisles rebuilt in the 14th. Interesting internal features include Anglo-Saxon carved stones in the S. chapel, which also contains 13th-century paintings of saints on the window jambs, one of which was only uncovered in 1992. It was restored in 1840 by John Perry of Godalming, who gathered all the carved roof bosses and re-used them in the nave. There was a further restoration by Sir George Gilbert Scott, completed after his death in 1879.

HASCOMBE: ST PETER – *a 15th-century screen was redecorated by Hardman and Powell in 1864 and used across the chancel in Woodyer's ebullient church* ▷

Lord God of
Mary the Mother of Jesus
Ruth
Rebekah

△ **COMPTON: ST NICHOLAS** – *the nave is flanked by hefty Norman arcades, while beyond the chancel arch is a unique Sanctuary (above right) built into the chancel with a gallery above*

GRAFHAM † St Andrew

3m/4km N.W. of Cranleigh
OS *TQ023416* **GPS** *51.16492N, 0.53812W*

This was H. Woodyer's 1864 parish church, paid for by him as a memorial to his wife. It is built of Bargate stone in the Early English style. Woodyer is buried in the churchyard. The solid screen supports the roof and was put there by Woodyer because Sumner, then Bishop of Winchester, refused to consecrate churches with screens – Woodyer made this one structural, so got his way. A series of seven restored silk embroidered panels by Thomas Gambier Parry and Woodyer hang on the nave wall.

GREAT BOOKHAM † St Nicholas

2m/3km S.W. of Leatherhead
OS *TQ134546* **GPS** *51.27984N, 0.37416W*

An inscription records the rebuilding of the chancel by John Rutherwyke, Abbot of Chertsey, in 1341. The 12th-century arcades are of differing dates, and the church has a delightful weather-boarded W. tower with shingled spire, all on a flint base. The restoration was by Carpenter, 1845, and Butterfield, 1885. The E. window has reused 15th-century glass, possibly Flemish. There is a good collection of brasses, ledger slabs and memorials.

GUILDFORD † Holy Trinity ★

High Street, central Guildford
OS *SU998494* **GPS** *51.23594N, 0.57082W*

The tower fell in 1740 and wrecked the old church. The new church, opened in 1763, was designed by James Horne, architect of St Catherine Coleman and Christchurch in Southwark. It is a solid red-brick church in the Palladian style with battlemented tower. The oldest part of the church, 1540, is the Weston Chantry Chapel in the S.W. corner. As in all Horne's churches, the ironwork and joinery are very good. The chancel was added by A. W. Blomfield in 1888. He also conceived the painted scheme for the apse. Monuments include that to Archbishop Abbot, d. 1633. Made of alabaster with columns resting on piled books, it survived the collapse of the original church.

GUILDFORD † St Mary ★
Quarry Street, central Guildford
OS *SU995493* **GPS** *51.23457N, 0.57477W*

Built on the slope above the river, the central tower is late Saxon. Transepts were added and the chancel rebuilt in the late 11th century. The nave, aisles, apsidal chapels and the chancel were remodelled in Early English style, c. 1160. The apse was lost when the chancel was shortened in 1825. The interior is attractive (apart from some rather strident purple chairs) and is steeply stepped up from W. to E.; there are traces of 13th-century wall-paintings in St John's Chapel. Lewis Carroll's funeral was held at the church, in which he preached several times.

HASCOMBE † St Peter ★★
3ml/4km S.E. of Godalming
OS *TQ001395* **GPS** *51.1464N, 0.56925W*

In one of the prettiest villages in Surrey, this is another church by H. Woodyer, 1864 – a Tractarian work of art. The exterior is plain, and the richness of the interior effect is gained by gilding and painting on the roofs and the reredos, and by the richly moulded interior arches of coupled windows. There is good dark Hardman glass throughout, except for the E. window by Clayton & Bell. The nave walls are painted all around with the 153 fishes caught in St Peter's net, and the 15th-century screen is redecorated in green, gold, brown and red.

HOLMBURY ST MARY † St Mary ★★
5ml/8km S.W. of Dorking
OS *TQ109444* **GPS** *51.1883N, 0.4132W*

This is a model village church by G. E. Street, 1879, beautifully set against the wooded hillside of Holmbury Hill. Street lived here and built it of local stone in memory of his wife. The whole building has great charm and appeal, fashioned from the sandstone on which it stands in Early English style, with a shingled belfry, two-storey chancel and aisles under distinctive cat-slide roofs. Interesting paintings include the reredos – the Infant Saviour and Virgin – attributed to Spinello Aretino, and donated by Street. In the N. chapel is a painting, possibly by Jacopo de Sellaio (1442–93), and a Limoges enamel 12th-century crucifix, also given by Street. In the narthex is a roundel by Luca della Robbia (1400–81) in majolica work, depicting the Madonna and

Child: a gift by J. R. Clayton, who also made the vivid stained glass to Street's designs.

LALEHAM † All Saints

2m/3km S.E. of Staines

OS *TQ051688* **GPS** *51.40917N, 0.48979W*

A 12th-century village church in a country and river setting, with a brick W. tower of 1732 and sturdy Norman arcades of clunch. A medieval altar slab stands against the W. wall, and there is interesting medieval graffiti throughout. On the N. end of the W. wall is a painting of Christ walking on water, by G. H. Harlow. The Tudor Lucan Chapel is on the N. side, and the 3rd Earl of Lucan is buried in the churchyard, as is the 19th-century poet Matthew Arnold.

LINGFIELD † St Peter and St Paul ★★

4m/6km N. of East Grinstead

OS *TQ388437* **GPS** *51.17634N, 0.01489W*

With traces of its late Saxon origin only in the W. wall, the church was made collegiate in 1431 by Sir Reginald Cobham, when the church was largely rebuilt. It is a pleasing statement of restrained Perpendicular, with contemporary stalls – some with misericords – screen and lectern with chained Bible. The main feature of the church is the excellent assembly of Cobham family monuments, principal among which is the brightly coloured effigy of the 1st Lord Cobham, d. 1361, his feet resting on a mournful Saracen. The brasses are the best in the county.

LITTLETON † St Mary Magdalene

3m/5km S.E. of Staines

OS *TQ070686* **GPS** *51.40673N, 0.46203W*

This medieval church in a tiny village is now almost overshadowed by a gigantic reservoir. There is some 12th-century work, with a 16th-century brick clerestory and W. tower. On the N. side is a mausoleum of 1705, and the tower has a top stage of the same date. Inside are good old pews, stalls, screens, Flemish altar rails, c. 1700, pulpit and 24 colours of the Grenadier Guards hanging in the nave. The church was restored in the 20th century by Martin Travers.

LOWER KINGSWOOD
† Wisdom of God

2m/3km N. of Reigate

OS *TQ248537* **GPS** *51.26928N, 0.21183W*

A replica of a Balkan church, with narthex and apse, and much material brought from Balkan ruins. It is by Sidney H. Barnsley and was completed in 1892; Barnsley painted the pretty wagon roof himself. The church is unique in England in its thoroughgoing Byzantine spirit.

MERSTHAM † St Katharine

2m/3km N. of Redhill

OS *TQ290537* **GPS** *51.2687N, 0.1520W*

A pretty 13th-century church, with a nicely proportioned lime-washed tower and broach spire. The chancel chapels are Perpendicular, and there is good late medieval roof work. The S. aisle, rebuilt in the 19th century, has good quirky tracery in square-headed windows. Inside is a mutilated stone effigy of the 1420s, which is thought to be of Nicholas Jamys.

MICKLEHAM † St Michael

2m/3km S. of Leatherhead

OS *TQ170533* **GPS** *51.26754N, 0.32337W*

The massive 12th-century tower of this heavily restored church is topped with a steeply angled broach spire. The best Norman feature is the broad chancel arch carved with chevrons and dog-tooth patterns. After a fairly disastrous restoration in 1822 by P. F. Robinson, the church was partly rebuilt by Ewan Christian in 1872; he gave it a new E. end, with good neo-Norman windows and a chubby round tower to the S. The Norbury Chapel dates from the 1300s and contains an interesting stone tomb and brasses.

OCKHAM † All Saints ★

5m/8km E. of Woking

OS *TQ066565* **GPS** *51.29807N, 0.47183W*

Set among the trees in Ockham Park, the church fabric illustrates the classic changes of style of English parish churches: it is 12th-century, with a 13th-century chancel and N. aisle; the S. nave wall is 14th-century, and the tower and N. aisle are 15th-century. There is also an early 18th-century chapel – a mausoleum chapel containing monuments by

△ **HASCOMBE: ST PETER** – *153 fish caught in St Peter's net line the nave walls*

Rysbrack, R. Westmacott Jnr and, in strange contrast, a Voysey casket with lettering by Eric Gill. Of note is the fine E. window of seven stepped lancets, possibly brought here from another church.

PEPER HAROW † St Nicholas ★

2m/3km W. of Godalming
OS *SU934440* **GPS** *51.18803N, 0.66394W*

Originally Norman but boldly and well restored by Pugin, 1844, in Early English and Decorated styles, and, unusually for Pugin, an ornate Romanesque chancel arch. There are some attractive memorials, notably the reclining effigy in the nave to Viscount Midleton. The 17th-century memorial to Vice Admiral Thomas Broderick on the chancel wall in the nave was lost in a fire in 2007. The fire caused much damage, but restoration is underway, and this pleasant church will soon be open again, with the wonderful Pugin ceilings returned to their original glory.

RANMORE † St Barnabas ★

1m/2km W. of Dorking
OS *TQ145504* **GPS** *51.24174N, 0.36W*

The church stands high on Ranmore Common – a delightful setting for this bold piece of Gothic Revival by Sir George Gilbert Scott, 1859. An estate church of stately dimensions built for the Cubitt family, the prominent octagonal spire and tower is known locally as 'Cubitt's finger'. The exterior is faced with rounded flints, and the interior contains much fine marble and alabaster.

SHACKLEFORD † St Mary

Norney, 3m/4km N.W. of Godalming
OS *SU940448* **GPS** *51.19508N, 0.65511W*

Another good church by Sir George Gilbert Scott, 1865-6, it stands in a pleasant village. The style is Early English in Bargate stone. The central tower with its wood-shingled broach spire is impressive, and the apsidal chancel, with five lancet windows and corbelled eaves, is simply but well detailed.

SHERE † St James ★★

5m/8km E. of Guildford
OS *TQ074477* **GPS** *51.21909N, 0.46288W*

A beautiful village on the Tillingbourne, discovered by cyclists in 1900 and its praises sung in guidebooks of the time. The cruciform 12th-century church stands on the banks of the River Tillingbourne, approached past a timber and plaster cottage and through a Lutyens lych

△ **SHERE: ST JAMES** – *the Norman tower at the church's centre was aggrandized in the 13th century*

gate. The lower stage of the tower is Norman; the top stage and S. aisle are good 13th-century work. The 15th-century N. window has nice Curvilinear tracery, and there is Perpendicular work in the S. aisle. The quatrefoil window and squint in the N. chancel wall formerly led to the cell of the 14th-century anchoress Christine Carpenter, who spent a lonely three years enclosed within. The church was sensitively restored by S. Weatherley in 1895 and again, brightly, by Louis Osman in 1957.

STOKE D'ABERNON † St Mary ★★

3m/4km N.W. of Leatherhead
OS *TQ129584* **GPS** *51.31382N, 0.38113W*

Reputed to be one of the county's oldest churches, St Mary's has a Saxon S. wall, with a blocked doorway 12 feet from the ground. Traces of re-used Roman bricks can be seen in both the S. nave and chancel walls. The N. aisle is late 12th-century and the chancel was remodelled and vaulted in the 13th. The 15th-century Norbury Chapel is entered through a fine pair of 17th-century Italian wrought iron gates, and contains much of interest: a kneeling figure of a knight; a 15th-century funerary helm; a stone Roman cinerary coffer from the 2nd century, set in the E. wall; and the tomb of Lady Sarah Vincent, d. 1608. A disastrous 'restoration' by Ford and Hesketh in 1866 saw the removal of the original Saxon chancel arch, but much has been done since to reverse the many ill-informed changes they wrought. In the chancel are the magnificent D'Abernon brasses. That of Sir John D'Abernon, dated 1277, is the earliest surviving brass in England and is unique for showing a lance. There is also a brass for his son, Sir John, of 1327. Note too the very fine 17th-century heptagonal pulpit of walnut.

THURSLEY
† St Michael and All Angels ★

5m/8km S.W. of Godalming
OS *SU901393* **GPS** *51.1466N, 0.7133W*

The Saxon origins of this church were uncovered during restoration by Benjamin Ferrey in 1860; a triangular recess in the chancel has been interpreted as a Saxon oven for baking wafers. Two Saxon lancets were rediscovered in 1927 on the N. chancel wall, and the tub font is possibly Saxon too. The nave is dominated by a massive free-standing timber cage supporting an impressive 15th-century wooden bell-turret. On the S. wall is a good monument to Katherine Woods, 1793, using polychromatic marble, with a Grecian urn on the top.

WEST HORSLEY † St Mary

6m/10km E. of Guildford
OS *TQ088526* **GPS** *51.2626N, 0.4416W*

A church of Norman and later work, but mainly of the 13th century, with stone W. tower and shingled spire, timber W. porch and limewashed exterior to the S. aisle. There are 13th-century wall-paintings, including a good St Christopher, on the W. wall of the nave to the side of the tower arch.

WITLEY † All Saints ★

3m/5km S. of Godalming
OS *SU946396* **GPS** *51.14864N, 0.64781W*

Uncannily pretty, like all Witley: the crossing tower has an octagonal shingled spire, and the large nave, part of the original Saxon church, was extended by the Normans. The rest is largely 13th-century with a font and piscina of that time. The 12th-century frescoes on the S. wall of the nave depict scenes from the New Testament, and continuing restoration works of the late 20th century have revealed further paintings on the W. wall and the return of the N. arcade. In the Manor Chapel are fragments of early glass and some interesting monuments and inscriptions.

WOKING † St Peter

6m/10km N. of Guildford
OS *TQ020568* **GPS** *51.30151N, 0.53707W*

This late 11th-century church stands between tall 18th-century houses and the River Wey, in the old town. The W. doorway in the 15th-century tower is interesting – dating from 1100, or thereabouts, of oak and with large iron C straps. The chancel is 13th-century, and the arcaded gallery was presented to the church by Sir Edward Zouch in 1622. The church retains a good medieval atmosphere, despite some of the pews being copies of medieval originals.

WONERSH † St John the Baptist

3m/4km S.E. of Guildford
OS *TQ014450* **GPS** *51.19599N, 0.54921W*

Although probably of Saxon origin with Norman enlargements, what is seen today is mostly from the rebuilding of 1793–4 after a fire, and the sensitive and informed restoration in 1901–2 by Sir Charles Nicholson. He used old paintings to reinstate, as far as possible, the church to its earlier plan. Carved screens discovered in the walls were used to form a parclose screen; 14th-century encaustic tiles were re-set in the altar step, and fragments of buried carved stone and the old Norman font were unearthed and made use of.

WORPLESDON † St Mary

3m/4km N.W. of Guildford
OS *SU972535* **GPS** *51.27299N, 0.6068W*

The N. chapel is the oldest part of this pleasantly situated church. Most of the fabric is 13th–14th-century, with a good Perpendicular tower capped with a rather flippant cupola taken from the rectory stables, 1766. Fittings include 18th-century altar rails, a 17th-century pulpit and font from Eton College and 14th-century figured glass in the E. window of the N. aisle.

WOTTON † St John the Evangelist

3m/4km W. of Dorking
OS *TQ125479* **GPS** *51.21979N, 0.38952W*

Beautifully situated among large trees facing the Downs, the church has an 11th-century tower and chancel. The rest is mainly 13th-century, apart from the late 17th-century Evelyn Mortuary Chapel, the burial-place of the Evelyn family of Wotton House. John Evelyn, the diarist, d. 1706, lies here with his wife. The screen separating the chapel from the N. aisle is from 1623 – a rare survival in the county. Restoration in the 19th century added a S. porch and vestry.

INRI

SUSSEX – EAST

The ancient kingdom of Sussex stretched along the English Channel from Rye in the east to Thorney Island in the west. This area still retains its identity as Sussex, though administratively it has been split into East and West for at least 500 years. The coastline itself has been built up from end to end by the desire of London's overspill to have a house by the sea, or at least to spend the weekend there. The only unspoilt part is between Eastbourne and Seaford, which belongs to the National Trust and is therefore immune.

East Sussex contains the majority of the lower-lying marshy lands near the coast – the Walland Marsh, part of the extensive Romney Marshes, and, beyond Hastings, the Pett Levels, at the end of the Royal Military Canal. The Pevensey Levels are the largest tract of marshy land in East Sussex and are administered as a national nature reserve. As in West Sussex, the sea has been a constant adversary, stranding New Winchelsea and Pevensey. Brighton, which was all but destroyed by the great storms of the 18th century, prospered under royal patronage.

Parallel with the coastline run the South Downs, referred to in Sussex villages as 'the hill'. They begin dramatically in East Sussex at the Devil's Dyke and run almost unbroken to Beachy Head, with the highest point in the county at Ditchling Beacon. Compared to the lower Downs of West Sussex they are relatively treeless through East Sussex. Although agriculture is still a feature of the county's economy, the numbers of sheep that traditionally graze the chalk downlands has significantly declined, which has allowed a cloak of wild shrubs to encroach. The remnants of Ashdown Forest, whose cattle so excited the attention of the radical anti-Corn Law campaigner William Cobbett in his *Rural Rides*, published 1830, is now a nature reserve.

Behind the Downs is the Weald – a belt of heavy clay which in early medieval times was dense forest, in which the Wealden iron industries thrived. In the early 20th century the clay industry thrived in Sussex, particularly around Burgess Hill. Sussex bricks and tiles were in demand throughout the country: now only one tileworks remains.

There are many striking historical landmarks in East Sussex, notably at Herstmonceux, Bodiam, Battle, Lewes and Pevensey. Prosperous former market towns include Crowborough, Uckfield, Heathfield, Hailsham and the Cinque Port of Hastings. East Sussex was generally more prosperous than West; several feudal lords, the dukes of Norfolk and Richmond, and Lord Leconfield owned (and some still own) large tracts of country, while many villages were small hamlets, with no squires or people of any standing. Consequently the churches of E. Sussex are for the most part grander than those of its western neighbour, although, like W. Sussex, there is only

◁ **BRIGHTON: ST MICHAEL AND ALL ANGELS** – *Burges's nave and chancel*

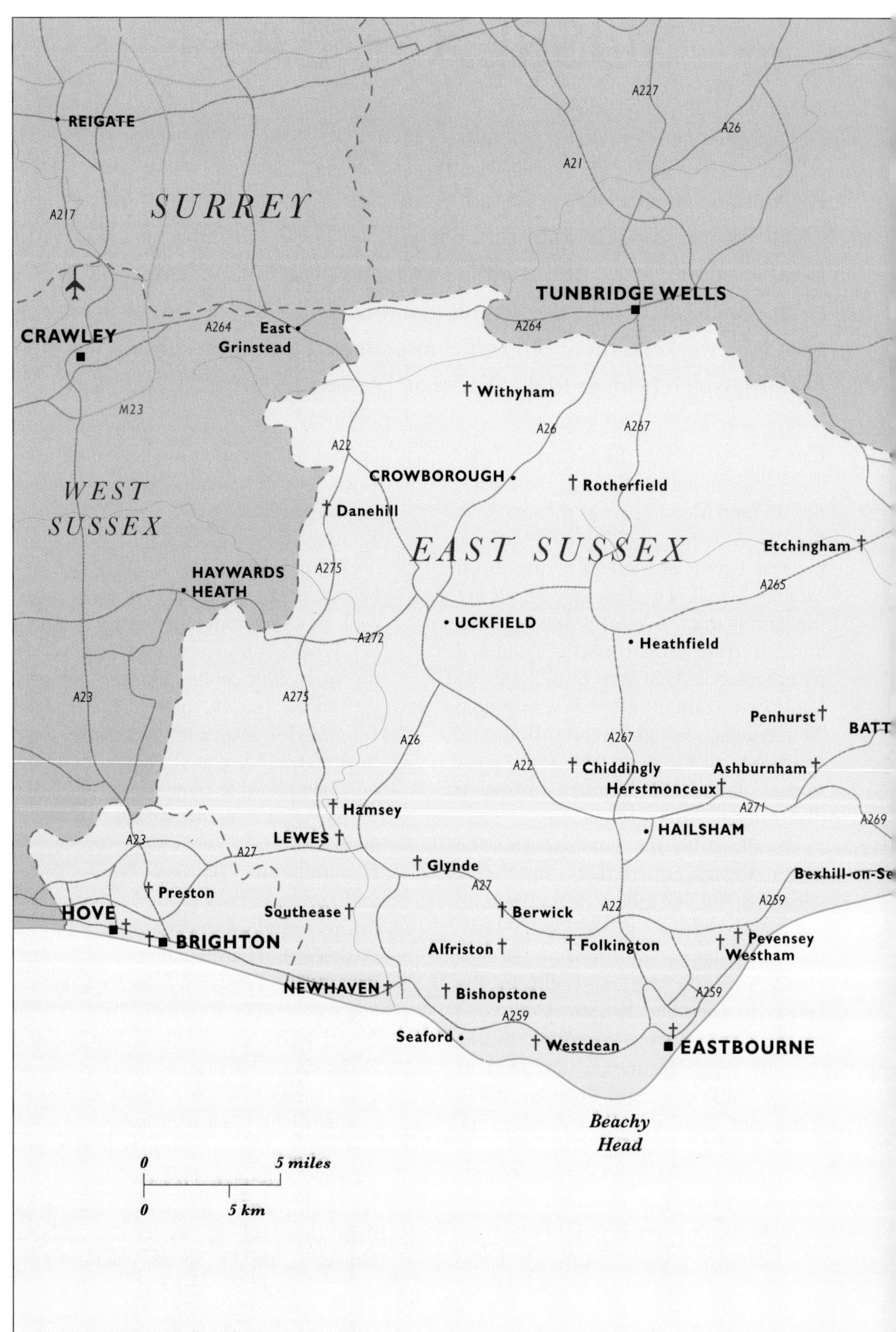

REIGATE
SURREY
A217
A227
A26
A21
TUNBRIDGE WELLS
A264
CRAWLEY
A264
East Grinstead
M23
Withyham
A26
A267
A22
CROWBOROUGH
Rotherfield
WEST SUSSEX
Danehill
EAST SUSSEX
Etchingham
HAYWARDS HEATH
A275
A265
UCKFIELD
A272
Heathfield
A23
A275
Penhurst
BATT
A26
A267
A22
Chiddingly
Ashburnham
Herstmonceux
A271
Hamsey
A269
HAILSHAM
A23
LEWES
A27
Glynde
Bexhill-on-Se
Preston
A27
A259
HOVE
Southease
Berwick
A22
BRIGHTON
Alfriston
Folkington
Pevensey
Westham
NEWHAVEN
Bishopstone
A259
A259
Seaford
Westdean
EASTBOURNE
Beachy Head
0
5 miles
0
5 km

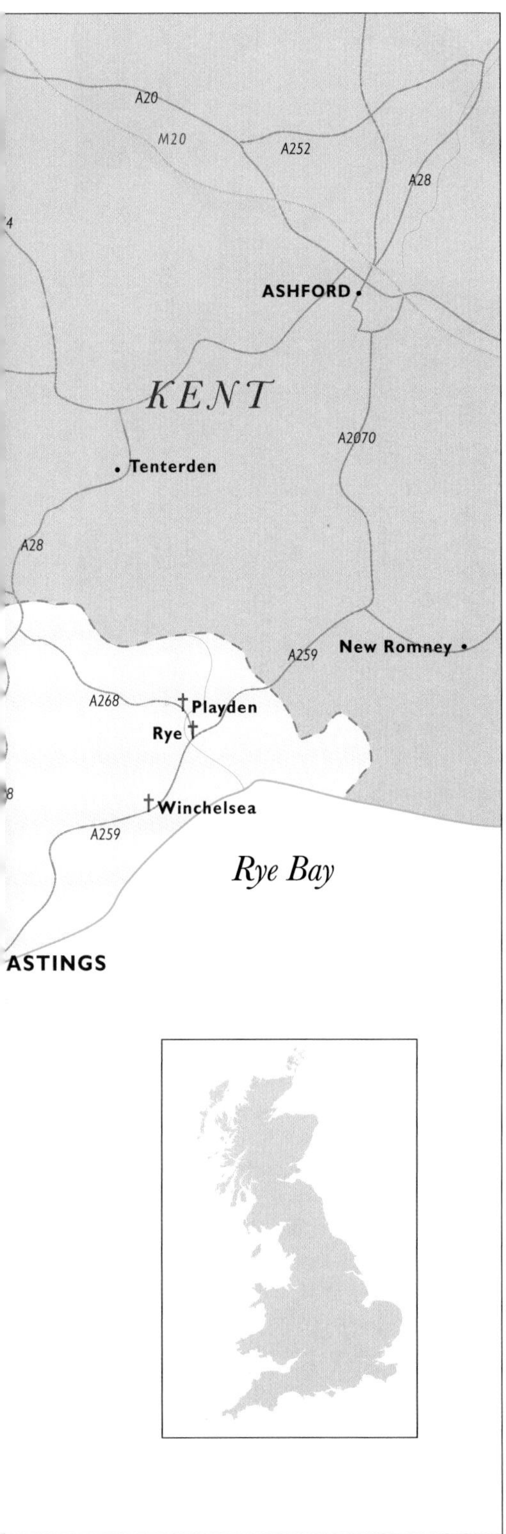

one significant piece of ironwork, the iron screen at Ashburnham. Very few churches were rebuilt in the 18th century; Glynde is the one of most architectural interest. Most were scraped, refurnished and mercilessly 'cleaned up' in the 19th century; there is a certain amount of medieval church furniture still surviving, but very few 18th-century box pews.

Oak shingling (thin 'slates' of cleft wood) is a distinguishing feature of many E. Sussex churches – Playden and Herstmonceux being good examples of Sussex oak-shingled spires. Fine frescoes of the Lewes School can be seen at Hardham, and flint and chalk are characteristic of many churches, notably at Alfriston. Of the very few round towers, Lewes has one, Southease another. There are some exquisite settings too, from the picture-postcard village and church at Penshurst, and the charming river valley setting of Folkington, to the grander town setting of Rye. And there is a rare stone spire at Chiddingly.

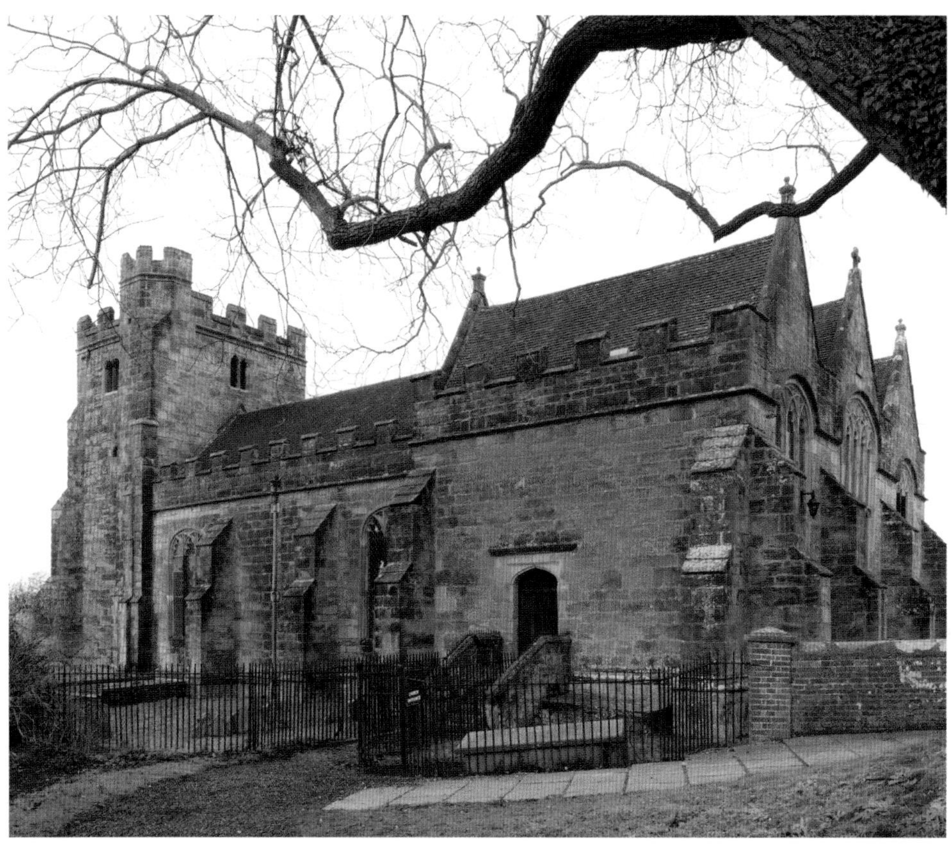

△ **ASHBURNHAM: ST PETER** – *the 15th-century tower was kept during the 17th-century rebuilding*

ALFRISTON † St Andrew ★★
4m/6km N.E. of Newhaven
OS *TQ521030* **GPS** *50.8066N, 0.1581E*

A handsome cruciform church of knapped flint, c. 1370, with a central tower and shingled broach spire, St Andrew's is interesting as an obvious example of the transition in Gothic style from Decorated to Perpendicular. It stands picturesquely in meadowland between the village and the river in the Cuckmere Valley, adjacent to a 14th-century thatched clergy house now in the ownership of the National Trust. The inside is refurnished, but of fine proportions, with unusually high arches at the crossing. The piscina and sedilia are of unusual design, and there is an Easter Sepulchre on the N. wall of the chancel. Kempe did the glass for the Jesse Tree window in the S. transept.

ASHBURNHAM † St Peter ★
7m/11km N.W. of Hastings
OS *TQ689145* **GPS** *50.9057N, 0.4016E*

In the park, next to the remains of the house of the Ashburnhams, St Peter's was rebuilt in 1665–7 as Gothic Survival, except for the Tudor tower, by John Ashburnham. It is a rare survival of the 17th century. Happily the furnishings remain – box pews, gallery, pulpit, font, tower staircase and, on the S. nave wall, an elaborate painting of the Commandments in a gilded frame with putti and doves. There is also armour, and the tombs of Ashburnhams – John, 1671, and William, 1675.

BATTLE † St Mary ★
6m/10km N.W. of Hastings
OS *TQ750157* **GPS** *50.9151N, 0.4885E*

Inside is a magnificent 12th-century nave and arcades, and on the N. wall a rare

△ **ASHBURNHAM: ST PETER** – *Commandments painting in a gilded frame with putti and doves*

series of wall-paintings depicting the life of St Margaret of Antioch, c. 1300. Over the chancel arch and to its N. and S. is a fine Doom. Although somewhat faded, these restored wall-paintings are some of the best medieval examples in the county. Set between the chancel and the Lady Chapel is the gilded and painted alabaster tomb of Sir Anthony Browne, d. 1548, and his wife Alice. He was granted the abbey and its lands by Henry VIII in 1539, after the Dissolution. There are also three brasses of note dating from 1426.

BERWICK † St Michael and All Angels ★

7m/11km N.W. of Eastbourne

OS *TQ518049* **GPS** *50.8239N, 0.1551E*

This simple 13th-century church stands in a hamlet at the foot of the Downs. The nave roof has a strikingly high pitch, reaching up to the base of the shingled broach spire. H. Woodyer's 1855–6 restoration shaped much of the fabric as it appears today, but the most striking feature is the wall-painting of 1941–3 by Bloomsbury artists Vanessa Bell, Duncan Grant and Quentin Bell. It's not to everyone's taste, but an admirable attempt to revive the custom of wall-painting in rural Sussex churches.

BISHOPSTONE † St Andrew ★

1m/2km N. of Seaford

OS *TQ472009* **GPS** *50.7897N, 0.0877E*

Built between 600 and 800 AD, this is one of Sussex's earliest surviving churches. Recent restoration work has found many Saxon and Norman details under the 19th-century plaster. The tall S. porch was a porticus, later pierced by a Norman doorway, above which is a Saxon sundial inscribed 'EADRIC'. The four-stage tower with 'Rhenish' pyramidal cap is Norman, and the steep cat-slide roof is impressive. Inside is a Romanesque coffin lid carved with a cross and Agnus Dei.

BRIGHTON
† St Michael and All Angels ★
Victoria Road
OS *TQ304047* **GPS** *50.8275N, 0.1498W*

G. F. Bodley's original modest brick church, 1858–62, was built to serve the smart houses of Brighton's Montpelier and Clifton Hill districts. The distinctive banded exterior brickwork and steep-pitched roof was in the Italianate style. W. Burges built a parallel church in 1893–5 in the same external style: the original building's N. aisle was demolished, and what was left became the S. aisle of the expanded church. Burges had planned a complete set of Italianate furnishings, including reredos, predella and baldacchino: these never materialised, but c.1900 W. H. Romaine-Walker installed a marble wall between the chancel and nave in Cosmatesque style, as well as a new chancel screen, marble altar and reredos. In the Bodley part of the church there is Pre-Raphaelite glass designed by Burne-Jones, Ford Madox Brown, Morris and Philip Webb. The roof was painted by Morris and Webb too. A 16th-century Flemish triptych is in need of restoration and currently not on display.

CHIDDINGLY † Dedication unknown
10m/16km N.W. of Eastbourne
OS *TQ544141* **GPS** *50.9062N, 0.1956E*

The church's origins are 12th-century with medieval and 19th-century alterations. The tall stone spire, one of four in Sussex, is delightful: octagonal and flanked by four polygonal pinnacles. Inside the S. transept is a monolithic monument to Sir John Jefferay, d. 1612, and family; the standing effigies are unique in English monuments of the pre-Civil War period. There is one window of note and character: the E. window of 1875, commemorating the Reverend James Vidal and his wife.

DANEHILL † All Saints
5m/8km N.E. of Haywards Heath
OS *TQ402274* **GPS** *51.0297N, 0.0018W*

In a commanding position on the edge of the Ashdown Forest, this is a handsome and elegant Decorated church by Bodley and Garner, 1892. The reredos is by Comper, and there are windows by Kempe.

EASTBOURNE † St Mary
Church Street
OS *TV598994* **GPS** *50.7727N, 0.2659E*

The church, timber-framed Lamb Inn, medieval rectory and a few Georgian houses are all that remain of the small town that gave its name to the modern seaside resort. The church has a large Perpendicular tower and admirable arcades, like those on the N. of New Shoreham (see Shoreham-by-Sea in W. Sussex chapter). The fabric is c. 1170 onward, with aisles rebuilt in the 14th century. In the chancel is a triple sedilia, and 14th-century parclose screens fill the choir arcades.

ETCHINGHAM
† Assumption and St Nicholas ★
7m/11km N. of Battle
OS *TQ713262* **GPS** *51.0097N, 0.4413E*

This once collegiate stately church stands on low ground near the Rother, distinguished for is monumental central tile-capped tower separating the nave and chancel; the site was once surrounded by a moat. The church was built by Sir William de Echyngham, d. 1389, whose brass is here. It is an unusual church, with some of the best 14th-century work in Sussex, particularly in the chancel and flamboyant E. window. There are many fragments of old glass, a screen, carved stalls, misericords and brasses to the Echyngham family. The pulpit was designed by Clayton, of Clayton & Bell, 1857, and executed by James Forsyth. The Minton tiles in the chancel are copies of surviving medieval originals.

FOLKINGTON † St Peter
5m/8km N.W. of Eastbourne
OS *TQ559038* **GPS** *50.8128N, 0.2121E*

Ancient and rustic, this lovely church nestles at the foot of the Downs, surrounded by woodland. Its ship-lapped wooden bellcote is topped by a tiny broad spirelet. Inside are high 18th-century box pews oriented towards the pulpit. The two striking monuments in the chancel are to Lady Barbara Thomas, d. 1697, and her husband Sir William Thomas,

△ **BRIGHTON: ST MICHAEL AND ALL ANGELS** – *a whimsical misericord in the Burges choir depicting one frog shaving another*

d. 1720. In the churchyard is a delightful stone carved with vegetables and a saucepan to the renowned cookery writer Elizabeth David, d. 1992.

GLYNDE † St Mary ★

3m/4km E. of Lewes
OS *TQ456092* **GPS** *50.8646N, 0.0683E*

A fine classical church of dressed flint and Portland stone, it was designed by Sir Thomas Robinson for Bishop Trevor and built in 1763–5. It groups well with the 18th-century stables of Glynde Place. The interior is all complete, with box pews, pulpit, W. gallery and altar rail. Later additions include a neo-Renaissance E. window attributed to Kempe (but not at all like his typical work) and a magnificent brass gasolier, probably by Hardman of Birmingham.

HAMSEY † (Old) St Peter ★

2m/3km N. of Lewes
OS *TQ414121* **GPS** *50.8912N, 0.0095E*

Alone on a hill in a loop of the Ouse, the church fell into disuse in 1860, when it became first a chapel of ease, then a mortuary chapel. It has a Norman chancel arch and stout Perpendicular tower. It was spared by the Victorians and has been carefully repaired since. Inside there are hatchments, Arms of George II, Commandments and a few ancient pews. Black-letter texts adorn the walls.

HERSTMONCEUX † All Saints ★

8m/13km N. of Eastbourne
OS *TQ642101* **GPS** *50.8678N, 0.3331E*

Near the castle and with splendid views of the Downs, this is a 12th–15th-century church whose good, lightly restored interior has attractive 19th-century dormer windows. The 12th-century tower is set to the N.E. of the church, forming part of the W. end of the nave, and has a shingled broach spire. Inside is a 'Pardon' brass to Sir William Fiennes, d. 1402, with an inscription offering 120 days' pardon of sins for those who pray for his soul. Between the chancel and chapel is a striking monument to Thomas, Lord Dacre, d. 1533, and his son, vividly but perhaps over enthusiastically repainted in the 1960s.

△ **BRIGHTON: ST MICHAEL AND ALL ANGELS** – *Pre-Raphaelite glass designed by Burne-Jones in the Bodley side of the 19th-century church*

HOVE † St Andrew
Waterloo Street
OS *TQ299042* **GPS** *50.8235N, 0.1568W*
Churches Conservation Trust

A Regency church of 1827–8, built to serve the fine houses of the surrounding area, it is by Sir Charles Barry; the E. parts were reconstructed by his son. It is of considerable interest as one of the earliest examples of the revived Italian Quattrocento style. The attractive interior is enhanced by W. Randoll Blacking's pulpit, font, stalls, altar rails and baldacchinos, all added c. 1925 at the behest of the vicar, who wanted the church to be 'a little bit of Italy in Waterloo Street'.

LEWES † St Michael ★
High Street
OS *TQ413100* **GPS** *50.8722N, 0.0072E*

A church with a highly unusual 13th-century round tower, it was rebuilt in 1748, after much damage inflicted by the local populace in the post-Reformation period. The S. arcade was extended, for no apparent reason, with wood. A further restoration of 1884 restored a pre-Georgian Gothic look to the church. There are many monuments inside, and a reredos by J. L. Pearson.

NEWHAVEN † St Michael
9m/15km E. of Brighton
OS *TQ442011* **GPS** *50.7918N, 0.0454E*

The interesting E. Norman tower and apsidal chancel give this church a French appearance. Their quality is not matched by a poor 1819 extension of the nave.

PENHURST † St Michael ★
4m/6km W. of Battle
OS *TQ694165* **GPS** *50.9236N, 0.4093E*

This is the idyll of Sussex settings: manor house, farm buildings and church all grouped perfectly. The 14th-century church stands high and alone by a farmhouse, overlooking

Ashburnham Park. Inside, despite the scraped walls, the old fittings remain untouched, including Perpendicular screen, 17th-century pulpit, lectern, altar rails and elegant font cover. The nave has oak seating with doors and panelled walls, and a 14th-century rood screen. At the base of the tower is a 'fitting out' stone, which was used as a template by masons to ensure uniformity of design and shape in their windows.

PEVENSEY † St Nicholas

4m/6km N.E. of Eastbourne
OS *TQ646048* **GPS** *50.8196N, 0.3368E*

Now a shrunken inland village, Pevensey was once a thriving seaport. The church, mostly 13th-century, looks seaward, a few hundred yards E. of the castle. The attractive tower is of three stages, the third stage being built by George Gilbert Scott Jnr, 1893, who retained the fine design of the original broach spire. Inside it is spacious and dignified, and built of green sandstone, which casts a grey-green light over all. There is good Early English work in the arcades, whose piers alternate between clustered and octagonal, and a fine crown-post roof. The very good 17th-century alabaster monument with recumbent figure in the S. aisle is to John Wheatley, d. 1616.

PLAYDEN † St Michael ★

1m/2km N. of Rye
OS *TQ920216* **GPS** *50.9625N, 0.7331E*

The graceful shingled spire of this pleasing church is a landmark for miles across marshes. The high nave and S. aisle are roofed with golden-red tiles. The arcades are Norman, and the aisles run either side of the E. tower. Access to the tower is via a rickety 17th-century ladder. The two screens are notable: an exuberant Decorated screen with ogee work separates the N. aisle from the choir, and in front of the chancel is a Perpendicular screen.

PRESTON † St Peter ★

1m/2km N. of Brighton
OS *TQ303063* **GPS** *50.8423N, 0.1494W*
Churches Conservation Trust

This is a 13th-century two-cell church, the tower of which butts into the garden of Preston Manor (now the Brighton Museum). The interior has early 14th-century wall-paintings of the Murder of Becket, the Weighing of Souls, the Nativity and the Last Supper. The nave fared poorly with a scraping by James Woodman in 1872, but Ewan Christian's restoration of the chancel in 1878 has left attractive stencilling and well-carved choir-stalls.

ROTHERFIELD † St Denys ★★

3m/4km E. of Crowborough
OS *TQ556297* **GPS** *51.0460N, 0.2184E*

The church stands in the centre of this hill-top Wealden village. The fabric is mostly Early English, and two restorations have left the interior unspoiled. There is much of interest here: a fine 13th-century Doom over the chancel arch and, in the Neville Chapel, traces of 14th-century paintings of St Gabriel and Adam and Eve. Over the N. door is a good painted Royal Arms of George I. The elaborate carved and canopied pulpit, 1632, came here from the Archbishop of York's private chapel, and the carved font cover, 1533, has Arms of the Nevills. The 14th-century E. window is very good – the glass is Burne-Jones' representation of the Te Deum: the figures in the five main lights stand amidst a swirling pattern of intricate foliage, all arising from a single root.

RYE † St Mary ★★

9m/15km N.E. of Hastings
OS *TQ921203* **GPS** *50.9501N, 0.7342E*

This is a large cruciform church of Norman origin, standing in a prominent position on the hilltop with the town below. It is approached by ancient, narrow streets, some still cobbled. Its grand proportions reflect the town's historic status as one of the Cinque Ports. The French stole the bells in 1377, and the men from Rye took them back a year later. Although the church dates from c. 1150, the fabric is mostly 13th–15th-century, with two fine E. Perpendicular windows. The tower clock is very old; its long gilt pendulum swings under the tower, and it strikes on the quarter hour. Inside is a tie-beam and king-post roof, and an early

△ **WINCHELSEA: ST THOMAS THE APOSTLE** – *preacher John Wesley referred to 'that poor skeleton of Ancient Winchelsea with its large church now in ruins'*

16th-century pulpit with linenfold panels, the only example of its date in Sussex.

SOUTHEASE † St Peter ★

3m/4km S. of Lewes
OS *TQ423052* **GPS** *50.8295N, 0.0192E*

A very small, charming church in a lovely Ouse Valley setting, its walls are pleasantly textured flint rubble, with large brick buttresses. It has a hipped roof and one of the county's three round towers, with a shingled spire. Possibly through neglect, the church lost its chancel and aisles in the 16th century, but the inside is characterful with its surviving plasterwork and remains of wall-paintings of the 13th and 14th centuries. Note the curious wooden chancel arch, which replaces the 15th-century rood screen.

WESTDEAN † All Saints

2m/3km S. of Alfriston
OS *TV525996* **GPS** *50.7768N, 0.1617E*

Adjacent to the South Downs Way, this is a little Norman church with 14th-century alterations. The tower is charming: Norman and later, it has a tiled gable roof reminiscent of a nun's wimple. There are two medieval monuments in the chancel, two 17th-century monuments, a bronze bust of Sir Oswald Birley, d. 1952, by Clare Sheridan, and a bust of Lord Waverley by Epstein, 1960.

WESTHAM † St Mary

4m/6km N.E. of Eastbourne
OS *TQ641045* **GPS** *50.8176N, 0.3291E*

The S. wall and transepts reveal the early Norman origins of this church, which stands just W. of Pevensey Castle. The tower is early 14th-century, and the N. aisle was also added in the 14th century. The inside is scraped, but has a Perpendicular screen to the Lady Chapel, and 13 small panels of 15th-century glass in the E. window.

WINCHELSEA
† St Thomas the Apostle ★★

2m/3km S.W. of Rye
OS *TQ904173* **GPS** *50.9242N, 0.7092E*

The 'new' town of Winchelsea was laid out in 1288 after the original town was flooded in the previous year. Formerly one of the Cinque Ports, it is now an inland village of

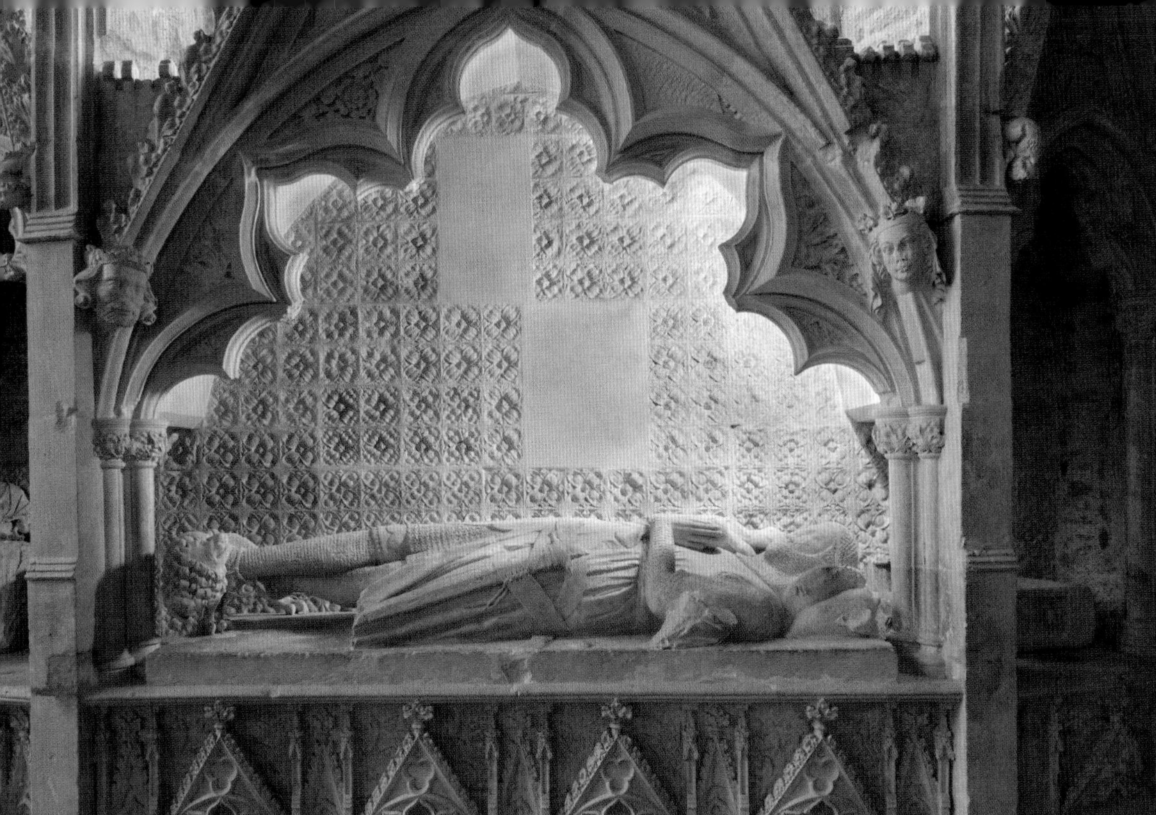

△ **WINCHELSEA: ST THOMAS THE APOSTLE** – *the 13th-century tomb of Gervase Alard, which features in the background of a painting by the Pre-Raphaelite painter Millais*

brick cottages, guarded by three grey medieval gateways, with houses grouped around a large, open churchyard and weathered fragment of the church, completed early in the 14th century. The choir and aisles remain, magnificent in themselves. The rest was destroyed in raids by the French, or never completed; nevertheless it is intriguing as a blend of abandonment and use. There is Purbeck stone in the piers and window shafts, richly canopied sedilia and piscina with crocketed gables in the sanctuary, and outstanding medieval tombs in both aisles. To the S. are two canopied 14th-century tombs of the Alards, and to the N. recumbent figures of a man and woman and a knight, all under rich Decorated canopies. The windows are dramatic, filled with glass by Strachan, highly coloured and heavily leaded. In the 18th century John Wesley, founder of the Methodist movement, preached his last open-air sermon here, under an ash tree in the churchyard.

WITHYHAM † St Michael ★

6m/10km S.W. of Tunbridge Wells
OS *TQ493355* **GPS** *51.0999N, 0.1323E*

The church was struck by lightning in 1663 and rebuilt re-using bits of the 14th-century fabric. Over the chancel arch is a Doom, c. 1856, by the then rector, Earl de la Warr, and there is 14th- and 15th-century Italian painting in the S. aisle. There are good monuments too: the best is that of Richard, Earl of Dorset, and his son Thomas, by C. G. Cibber; it is a table-tomb, with an effigy of the boy and his two parents kneeling either side of him.

SUSSEX – WEST

West Sussex contains part of the Weald, and a more wooded and lower part of the Downs than in East Sussex. The coastal area is low-lying and in places marshy, mostly between Pagham and Chichester harbours, though not to the same extent as East Sussex. Through the county run the rivers Adur, Arun and West Rother. Silting at the head of Chichester Harbour has left the old ports of Steyning and Bramber high and dry, as well as restricting maritime access to Bosham, Old Shoreham, Dell Quay and Fishbourne.

Among the prehistoric tumuli that dot the west Downs are reminders of vanished communities and their churches. St Peter's at Treyford, built by Benjamin Ferrey of inferior local stone, lasted little more than 100 years; happily the church it replaced, the old church of St Mary, Treyford, is in the process of being restored. Agriculture still plays a part in the county, though the emphasis now is on arable farming, especially towards the coast. New towns have gobbled up much former countryside – Crawley, East Grinstead and Burgess Hill saw massive growth through the second half of the 20th century. Much of the county is blighted by the noise of aircraft using Gatwick Airport, and on the coast Worthing saw an explosion of dreary retirement bungalows.

The churches of Sussex are many and varied, including some lovely examples, although they are not generally among the most magnificent. There are two main reasons for this: unlike the case in East Anglia and Gloucestershire, there was no flourishing local industry here when Gothic architecture reached its zenith in the 15th century; and of the many religious foundations with churches or chapels only the great Priory Church of Boxgrove survived the Dissolution. It is true that throughout all the Middle Ages and up to 1811, when Ashbourn Forge closed down, Sussex was the centre of the iron industry; but disappointingly little evidence is to be found in the churches, and the iron grille at Arundel is the only important example of iron-work in West Sussex's church furniture. The craft of oak shingling – very typical of many Sussex churches – can be seen at Cuckfield. There is a great deal of Norman and Early English architecture, very little Decorated and not much Perpendicular. Of the many churches with fresco decoration, West Chiltington is a good example, while Roman brick-work occurs at Chichester and Bosham. Another local feature is Horsham stone. These large, thin slabs are used for roofing on many of the larger churches, and charmingly on some small churches – see Coombes. They are not generally found in the extreme west or east where tiles take their place.

West Sussex churches are, on the whole, smaller and more rustic than those in East Sussex, with the notable exceptions of Boxgrove Priory and Chichester Cathedral.

◁ **BOSHAM: HOLY TRINITY** – *the shingled broach spire tops a part-Saxon tower in this church of ancient foundation, which has been identified in the Bayeux Tapestry*

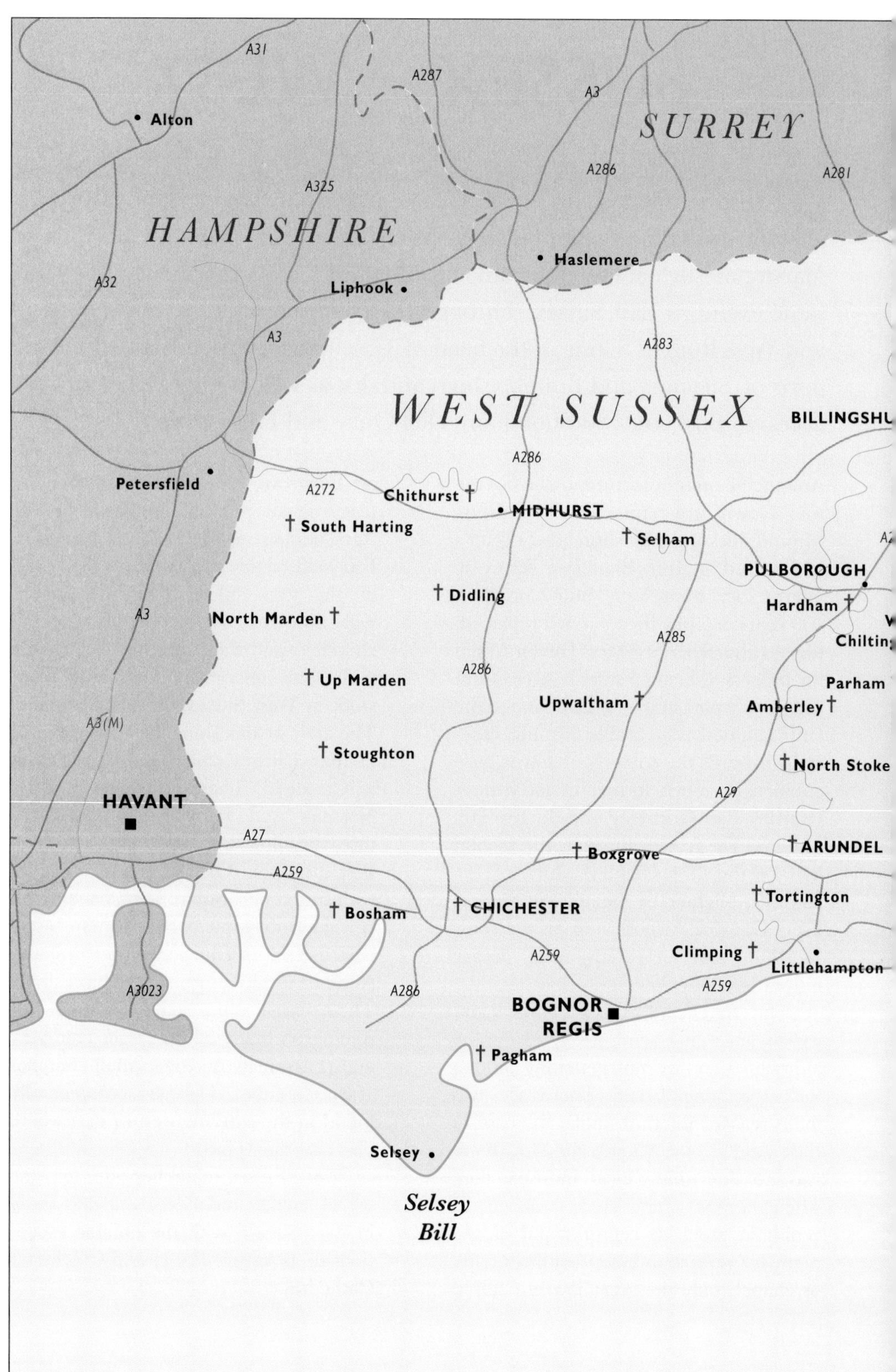
A31
A287
A3
Alton
SURREY
A286
A281
A325
HAMPSHIRE
Haslemere
A32
Liphook
A3
A283
WEST SUSSEX
BILLINGSHU
A286
Petersfield
A272
Chithurst
MIDHURST
South Harting
Selham
PULBOROUGH
Didling
Hardham
North Marden
A3
A285
Chilting
A286
Up Marden
Parham
Upwaltham
Amberley
A3(M)
Stoughton
North Stoke
HAVANT
A29
A27
Boxgrove
ARUNDEL
A259
Tortington
Bosham
CHICHESTER
A259
Climping
Littlehampton
A3023
A286
A259
BOGNOR REGIS
Pagham
Selsey
Selsey Bill

A29
Lowfield Heath
A264
EAST
GRINSTEAD
CRAWLEY
Worth
A264
A22
HORSHAM
Crowborough
A24
A281
A26
A275
Cuckfield
HAYWARDS
HEATH
A272
Uckfield
A272
West Grinstead
Shermanbury
rminghurst
A281
A23
A275
Hurstpierpoint
A26
Buncton
Clayton
EAST
SUSSEX
A283
Steyning
A23
Coombes
A27
A27
Botolphs
Sompting
HOVE
Shoreham-
by-Sea
BRIGHTON
Broadwater
WORTHING
0
5 miles
0
5 km

△ **BOXGROVE: ST MARY AND ST BLAISE** – *the richly decorated chantry built by Thomas de la Warre in 1532; the building of such chantries was abolished in 1547*

AMBERLEY † St Michael ★
4m/6km N. of Arundel
OS *TQ027131* **GPS** *50.9090N, 0.5394W*

The church forms a medieval group with the castle, which was the former palace of the bishops of Chichester – all very picture-postcard Sussex. The nave and chancel arch are Norman, the fine arch with double and triple chevron mouldings; the chancel, aisle and tower are 13th-century. The 14th-century S. porch has a doorway with capitals of vine and oak leaves. Inside there are medieval wall-paintings on the S. side of the chancel arch, including a Crucifixion. The Minton tiled floor was designed by the Rev. Lord Alwyne Compton, c. 1864–5.

ARUNDEL † St Nicholas ★
London Road
OS *TQ016072* **GPS** *50.8559N, 0.5574W*

A cruciform, late 14th-century church, it has wall-paintings and a good medieval wrought-iron grille of Sussex ironwork, which separates the Fitzalan Chapel, the property of the Duke of Norfolk, from the rest of the church. On the N. wall there are 14th-century wall-paintings of the Seven Deadly Sins and Seven Works of Mercy. The canopied carved stone pulpit is a rare pre-Reformation survivor in the county, and the octagonal font of Sussex marble is also of interest.

BOSHAM † Holy Trinity ★★
4m/6km W. of Chichester
OS *SU804038* **GPS** *50.8289N, 0.8594W*

This is a breezy seafaring place overlooking the mud creeks of Chichester Harbour. A small Irish monastery was here before the mission of St Wilfrid in the 7th century, and the visit by Harold II to the church is depicted in the Bayeux Tapestry. The partly Saxon tower now has a shingled broach spire, and the high Saxon nave has a fine 11th-century chancel arch. The E. window of five lancets and the aisles are 13th-century. Underneath All Hallows Chapel is a 14th-century crypt – once the charnel house – and in the Fishbourne Chantry is a 12th-century piscina drained by a hollow column. An intriguing carved serpentine figure with four fanged heads curls round the base of one of the N. arcade piers.

BOTOLPHS † St Botolph ★

5m/8km N. of Shoreham-by-Sea
OS *TQ193092* **GPS** *50.8705N, 0.3051W*

Lovely, lonely and simple, the church has an interesting blocked 13th-century N. arcade, showing evidence of rural decline. Nearby mounds mark the site of long-vanished dwellings. The interior, as plain as can be, has a Jacobean pulpit and Charles II Royal Arms. The nave is lit by converted oil lamps and candles. The whole church and its setting is a world away from the 21st century.

BOXGROVE † St Mary and St Blaise ★★

3m/4km N.E. of Chichester
OS *SU908075* **GPS** *50.8600N, 0.7109W*

This is the stately relic of a Benedictine priory church; the adjacent conventual buildings are in the care of English Heritage. Considering what was lost, the surviving parts are very fine. The transepts with oak galleries and tower are 12th-century; the choir is early 13th-century. There is a vaulted roof, clerestory with Purbeck marble shafts and rich arcades, each pair within a large, round containing arch. The 16th-century painted decoration on the vaulting is by Lambert Barnard, 1520s. A splendid chantry was built by Thomas de la Warre, 1532 – a mix of late Gothic and Renaissance. There is a monument to Mary, Countess of Derby, d. 1752, in the chancel. Above George Gilbert Scott's carved reredos is good Victorian stained glass set in the three elegant lancet windows, and in the S. aisle is fine Arts and Crafts stained glass, by the painter and cartoonist Mary Lowndes, a founder of the Artist's Suffrage League. At the W. end, Nicola Kantorowrcz's 'Creation' stained glass floods the crossing with rich colour.

BROADWATER † St Mary

District of Worthing 1m/2km N. of centre
OS *TQ146043* **GPS** *50.8278N, 0.3733W*

This is a handsome, spacious cruciform church in a N. suburb of Worthing, and mostly 12th- and 13th-century. The tower arches have rich chevron mouldings, and the vaulted 13th-century chancel has carved stalls and misericords. There are two 16th-century tombs to members of the de la Warre family.

BUNCTON † All Saints

8m/13km N. of Worthing
OS *TQ145139* **GPS** *50.9133N, 0.3726W*

The church is approached through a wooded dell and noted for its mostly unrestored Norman interior. Lots of oddities here, most notably the miscellany of blind arches around the outside of the chancel, perhaps recycled from a nearby priory in the 14th century. The work of an enthusiastic but not very talented 14th-century builder, the chancel is curious but entertaining. Inside is simple, with a Norman nave and chancel rebuilt in the 14th century, the nave having yet more odd blind arches and rusticated Norman carving on the chancel arch. There are fragments of medieval wall-paintings.

CHICHESTER † St John the Evangelist ★

John's Street
OS *SU863047* **GPS** *50.8354N, 0.7747W*
Churches Conservation Trust

This is James Elmes's Greek Revival style evangelical preaching house, built 1812–13. And very severe it is too – an interesting example of the 'no-frills' ethos of the evangelical movement of the time. The galleried interior focuses on a three-decker pulpit, which blocks the diminutive chancel and towers over the nave, reminiscent of post-Reformation Scottish churches, where the Word takes precedence over the Sacramental. Built as a proprietary chapel, it is a unique survival of a plan once common but now very rare.

CHITHURST † St Mary

3m/4km W. of Midhurst
OS *SU842230* **GPS** *51.0010N, 0.8007W*

A tiny 11th-century church in a remote and attractive setting, it is aisleless, and has never been extended. There is an organic rough, irregular texture to the outside walls. Inside, the plain chancel arch and some simple old seating reflect the rural poverty of the time.

CLAYTON † St John the Baptist ★

6m/10km N. of Brighton
OS *TQ299139* **GPS** *50.9105N, 0.1534W*

This church of Saxon and Norman origins has superb 12th-century wall-paintings around the chancel arch and on the nave walls: they are believed to be the work of the

BOXGROVE: ST MARY AND ST BLAISE – *Thomas de la Warre commissioned a local artist, Lambert Barnard, to paint the ceiling of the nave with his family crests, entwined with flowers and foliage* ▷

Lewes Group (see also Hardham), who were Burgundian artists employed by the Cluniac monks of Lewes Priory. The paintings were discovered in 1893 and 1917–19.

CLIMPING † St Mary

2m/3km W. of Littlehampton
OS *TQ002025* **GPS** *50.8138N, 0.5778W*

The church stands out for its solid Transitional tower on the S. The rest is 13th-century, with a pre-Reformation stone pulpit and one of the finest 13th-century chests in England. There are some medieval benches, and in the N. transept is a series of paintings by Heywood Harty, 1925–6; very much period pieces, one shows Christ preaching to villagers in typical Arun scenery.

COOMBES † Dedication unknown ★★

2m/3km S.E. of Steyning
OS *TQ190081* **GPS** *50.8607N, 0.3097W*

Hidden up a combe by a farm in the Adur Valley, this low and humble church is a delight. The tower and part of the church were 'lately fallen' in 1724. Inside are extensive remains of duotone Romanesque wall-paintings, discovered in 1949. They date from c. 1080–1120 and depict scenes from the Gospels, as well as St Mark's lion and a very uncomfortable-looking monster. These are attributed to the Lewes Group. Outside is an amusing tombstone in the churchyard to Henry Daniel, d. 1860; his dying words were, 'I shall not be here long, Mother'.

CUCKFIELD † Holy Trinity ★

2m/3km W. of Haywards Heath
OS *TQ303244* **GPS** *51.0049N, 0.1434W*

This is a spacious 13th-century village church, with a graceful shingled spire. The unusual 15th-century roof was painted by Kempe, with roses and foliage, singing angels on the corbels: all very cheerful but sensitive. The screen and pulpit are by Bodley, and there is much early Kempe stained glass.

DIDLING † St Andrew ★

4m/6km S.W. of Midhurst
OS *SU835181* **GPS** *50.9565N, 0.8124W*

This is another Sussex church whose once ample village disappeared after the ravages of the plague. Now it is small and lonely in a field beneath the Downs – the 'Shepherd's Church', still with hooks for the sheepdogs' leashes. Inside is rough-hewn old seating, a 17th-century pulpit, and a small tub-shaped Norman font, all lit by candles. A delightful and unspoiled little church.

HARDHAM † St Botolph ★★

1m/2km S.W. of Pulborough
OS *TQ038176* **GPS** *50.9486N, 0.5227W*

This small church, probably 11th-century, stands on the Arun flats near Pulborough, and is chiefly known for its series of Lewes Group wall-paintings in the nave and chancel, showing Adam and Eve, episodes in the life of Christ, the Apostles, the story of St George, and Heaven and Hell. They date from c. 1080–1120, were discovered in 1866, and represent the most highly integrated scheme of all-over church decoration still to survive.

HORSHAM † St Mary

8m/12km S.W. of Crawley
OS *TQ170302* **GPS** *51.0597N, 0.3309W*

St Mary's is a large, mostly 13th-century, church with a tall shingled spire, pleasantly situated at the end of a causeway. The stained glass is a complete summary of 19th-century work: there is a 15th-century brass and various monuments, the best by Edward Marshall, 1654.

LOWFIELD HEATH
† St Michael and All Angels

1m/2km N. of Crawley
OS *TQ274401* **GPS** *51.1460N, 0.1798W*

A William Burges French Gothic church of 1867, it consists of nave, beautiful little chancel and S.W. tower. The E. window is filled with Art Nouveau glass. The church escaped demolition during the 1970s Gatwick Airport expansion, but is now overwhelmed by airport buildings: how nice it would be to move it.

NORTH MARDEN † St Mary ★

6m/10km S.E. of Petersfield
OS *SU807161* **GPS** *50.9390N, 0.8526W*

One of a group of tiny churches in this area, St Mary's is a Norman building of nave and apse, approached through a farmyard. Dark and mysterious inside, it has a good

△ **SHOREHAM-BY-SEA: ST MARY DE HAURA** – *it was funded from port fees in the 12th century*

18th-century altarpiece consisting of Creed, Decalogue and Lord's Prayer, now in the nave. The church is still lit by candles.

NORTH STOKE † St Mary the Virgin

2m/3km N. of Arundel
OS *TQ019107* **GPS** *50.8874N, 0.5514W*
Churches Conservation Trust

A very attractive simple cruciform church of local sandstone. The nave is 12th-century, the chancel 13th-century; there is no tower, just a timid dormer belfry. Inside is bright, due to much clear glass, although there are two stained-glass panels of the Coronation of the Virgin, c. 1290–1300. There is a nice sheep's head corbel in the S. transept and fragments of a medieval wall-painting.

PAGHAM † St Thomas of Canterbury

4m/6km W. of Bognor Regis
OS *SZ883974* **GPS** *50.7702N, 0.7482W*

Traces of the original Saxon church were discovered during work on the church floor in 1976, but most of the church is Early

△ **SHOREHAM-BY-SEA: ST MARY DE HAURA** – *alternate octagonal and round pillars on the near arcade; on the other side of the nave, the arcade is formed with clustered piers*

English and notable for a remarkable wheel window, by J. Elliott of Chichester, 1837, and an interesting square Norman font of Sussex marble with carved arcades. The glass in the E. lancet windows is mostly 16th-century French, rearranged by M. Travis, 1939.

PARHAM † St Peter ★

3m/5km S. of Pulborough
OS *TQ059140* **GPS** *50.9165N, 0.4940W*

This small Perpendicular church stands in a park near the Elizabethan house. It was remodelled in the early 19th century and has Georgian box pews, pulpit and screen. Note the squire's pew with its fireplace. The chancel has Strawberry Hill Gothic vaulting, and there is a rare lead font, 14th-century, with Lombardic lettering.

SELHAM † St James ★

3m/4km E. of Midhurst
OS *SU932206* **GPS** *50.9780N, 0.6727W*

Set in beautiful countryside, this is an attractive little 11th-century church whose much-restored walls are a jumble of herringbone stonework. The chancel arch has remarkable carved capitals, one carved with interlace and foliage, the other with a monstrous head. There is also a capacious plain Norman tub font.

SHERMANBURY † St Giles ★

9m/14km N.W. of Brighton
OS *TQ214188* **GPS** *50.9562N, 0.2726W*

Rather dilapidated outside, the church stands in the former grounds of Shermanbury Place. It was repaired in 1710 in countrified Georgian. The inside is unspoiled and interesting: Royal Arms of Queen Anne, pews with the names and farms of the former occupants painted on them, and, in a glass case, the recorders and viol used by the gallery minstrels. There are also some carved Norman corbel heads set into the W. wall of the nave.

SHOREHAM-BY-SEA
† St Mary de Haura ★★

In New Shoreham, 6m/10km W. of Brighton
OS *TQ216051* **GPS** *50.8329N, 0.2745W*

This very fine Romanesque church of Caen stone is set in a former seaport. Its scale and form give it a monastic appearance, but it was always parochial. Only the tower, transepts and unusually long chancel, choir and aisles remain. The nave fell into ruin from late medieval times. The E. bay of the nave is built up as a porch, the transepts and lower part of the tower are c. 1130; the rest is from about 1175 to the beginning of the 13th century. The N. arcade is rich in carving. Note the difference in the arcades, the N. being alternate round and octagonal, with richly carved capitals and arches, the S. being more complex, with clustered piers whose capitals are also rich in carved foliage. A clerestory and triforium are all set under fine vaulted roofs. In the 1876–9 restoration, lancet windows were re-opened and repaired, and have some good Willement glass. The De Braose window by Diane Smart, 1953, shows a Norman knight in chain mail, with the old church behind: very pleasing.

SHOREHAM-BY-SEA † St Nicolas ★
St Nicolas Lane, in Old Shoreham, ½m/1km N. of New Shoreham
OS *TQ208059* **GPS** *50.8408N, 0.2856W*

The church looks across the River Adur to Lancing College. There is pre-Conquest work in the nave, which the Normans extended, at the same time building the central tower and chancel. The tower has arcading and round openings, and the arches are richly chevroned. The choir, complete with clerestory, triforium and flying buttresses, is outstanding: splendid Transitional and Early English work. There is an early 14th-century screen, and a painted chancel roof from the 1841 Cambridge Camden Society restoration. Before its restoration, J. M. Neale rather cryptically described it as resembling 'the dungeon of a criminal rather than the house of the Lord'.

SOMPTING † St Mary ★
2m/3km N.E. of Worthing
OS *TQ161056* **GPS** *50.8386N, 0.3519W*

This intriguing Saxon church overlooks Worthing from a S. slope of the Downs. It is famous for its tower, the lower stage Saxon, the upper stage late 11th-century, and the ungainly 'Rhenish helm' spire early

△ **SOMPTING: ST MARY** – *the unusual tower, of Saxon origin and later 'Rhenish helm'*

14th-century. The tower arch is carved with crude acanthus capitals and volutes. The rest of the church was rebuilt in the late 12th century. The N. transept has two E. chapels, stone-vaulted; the S. transept is the Templars' Chapel, originally separate from church, and there is a ruined 14th-century chapel at the N.W. built by the Knights Hospitallers.

SOUTH HARTING
† St Mary & St Gabriel ★
3m/4km S.E. of Petersfield
OS *SU784194* **GPS** *50.9688N, 0.8845W*

The cruciform church stands overlooking the main street of the village, at the extreme W. of the Downs; its verdigris copper spire is unmistakable. It was rebuilt and enlarged about the beginning of the 14th century, with plain nave arcades. After a fire in 1576, the church was repaired with new roofs, the most elaborate of which is that of the chancel. The S. transept has a very good monument to the Cowper and Coles families, with painted recumbent figures, one above the other; a third kneels in prayer, and there is a wall monument by Westmacott to Sir Henry Fetherstonhaugh of Uppark. Outside there are the village stocks and whipping post, and a striking Great War memorial by Eric Gill.

STEYNING † St Andrew

5m/8km N.W. of Shoreham-by-Sea
OS *TQ179114* **GPS** *50.8901N, 0.3250W*

Set back behind a long street with tile-hung and half-timbered houses, the church is 12th-century, lofty, spacious and massive; the chancel arch is 38 feet high. The arcades and clerestory have rich carving – chevron and dog-tooth – which gives a very powerful impression. The huge tile-capped tower of flint and stone chequerwork was built after 1577 in place of a central tower. Behind the altar is fine 16th-century panelling, originally in the vicarage.

STOUGHTON † St Mary ★★

6m/10km N.W. of Chichester
OS *SU800115* **GPS** *50.8980N, 0.8624W*

A wonderful church surrounded by trees on a chalky slope, it retains much of its Anglo-Saxon origins and is remarkably complete. The plan is clear: a high Saxon nave, with porticos to the N. and S., that to the S. built up as a tower in the 14th century. The chancel arch is magnificent, and in the chancel can be seen results of the 16th-century repairs, with the upper sections of the old N. and S. windows disappearing behind a much-lowered roofline. St Mary's is an outstanding example of a well-loved country church.

TORTINGTON † St Mary Magdalene

2m/3km S.W. of Arundel
OS *TQ003049* **GPS** *50.8357N, 0.5768W*
Churches Conservation Trust

Small and rustic, with flint walls and a white wooden turret, the church sits among farm buildings by a mellow Georgian house. There is a richly carved Norman S. doorway, a chancel arch of hard chalk with beak-heads and grotesques, and a Norman font with arcading and cable moulding. Despite an over-enthusiastic restoration of 1867–8, the church retains a pleasing atmosphere.

UP MARDEN † St Michael ★★

6m/10km S.E. of Petersfield
OS *SU795141* **GPS** *50.9210N, 0.8699W*

This beautiful little 13th-century church is surrounded by trees behind a farm, in a remote part of the W. Downs. It is of the greatest simplicity and unrestored; walls plastered, in and out, brick floors and a few box pews. Though not used, it is looked after, and there is no feeling of dereliction. Still lit by candles, this is one of those churches in which everything is just right.

UPWALTHAM † St Mary the Virgin ★

7m/11km N.E. of Chichester
OS *SU943138* **GPS** *50.9165N, 0.6598W*

Known locally as the church in the field, it sits in a fold of the Downs, small and rustic with a Norman nave and apse, and later windows. Inside is candle-lit, with plain solid oak seating. It is one of only a few apsidal churches in the county.

WARMINGHURST † Holy Sepulchre

4m/6km E. of Pulborough
OS *TQ117168* **GPS** *50.9403N, 0.4114W*
Churches Conservation Trust

The small 13th-century church stands at the end of a lane with fine views to the Iron Age fort on the Downs. Pleasing from the outside, its treasures are kept for those who venture in: a complete set of 18th-century deal furnishings, including handsome triple-arched screen, pulpit and box pews. A colourful Queen Anne Royal Arms with swags is painted on plaster above the triple-arched screen. There are hatchments, a wonderful wrought-iron crane for the font canopy, two 18th-century monuments and a good 17th-century brass to the Shelley family. Note the clerk's chair, made for a gentleman of ample proportions.

WEST CHILTINGTON † St Mary ★

3m/4km E. of Pulborough
OS *TQ090183* **GPS** *50.9542N, 0.4493W*

A largely unspoiled 11th- and 12th-century church of nave and S. aisle, with shingled belfry and spire. Note the chevroned N. doorway and massive Transitional S. arcade with scalloped capitals. The chancel arch is curious, high, narrow and recessed. At

△ **STOUGHTON: ST MARY** – *despite its cement render, the church is attractive and pleasantly sited; its Anglo-Saxon origins are evident in the form of the high nave*

the E. end of the S. aisle are 12th-century wall-paintings; in the nave are 13th-century murals of the Life of Christ. In a window splay is a rare 15th-century scene of Christ of the Trades; the Saviour's flesh is ripped by tools used on the Sabbath.

WEST GRINSTEAD † St George

5m/8km S. of Horsham
OS *TQ170206* **GPS** *50.9737N, 0.3337W*

By the River Adur, and 'all alone since the disappearance of its village. The roofs are stone-slabbed, and it has a low shingled spire. The N. side is early Norman, the aisle and tower are 13th-century, and there is a 15th-century timber porch. Inside is old, solid seating, painted with house names. Interesting monuments include that to William Powlett, 1746, by Rysbrack, Sir Merrik Burrell, 1787, by N. Smith and Sir William Burrell, 1796, by Flaxman.

WORTH † St Nicholas ★

2m/3km E. of Crawley
OS *TQ301361* **GPS** *51.1103N, 0.1415W*

The church forms a secluded group with the old rectory and is cruciform, with an untouched pre-Conquest ground plan, except for the tower added in 1871. The outside walls have a string course round the nave and apsidal chancel, and inside, the 22-foot-high chancel arch, one of the largest Saxon arches in England, has a rugged dignity. The arches to the transepts, 15 feet high, are similarly impressive. The nave is lit by very distinctive two-light windows with baluster shafts. The church was damaged by fire in 1986, and despite an extensive and expensive restoration, one gets a better impression of this fine Saxon church from outside, as the patina of the old interior has gone.

WORTHING † St Andrew

Between Clifton Road and Victoria Road
OS *TQ143030* **GPS** *50.8153N, 0.3776W*

By Sir Arthur Blomfield, 1885–8, this is a Gothic Revival in Early English with French overtones, with an apsidal baptistry. Inside is some interesting wood carving – the choir screen and reredos – but it is particularly worth visiting to see the excellent collection of Kempe glass, most of which was originally in All Souls, Brighton.

WARWICKSHIRE & WEST MIDLANDS

Leafy Warwickshire the guidebooks call it, though no one has planted trees in Warwickshire for generations and one day, probably, the oaks of Arden will die out. The county was once split between Arden, the woodland of the north, and Feldon, the corn valley of the south. Across the 'sandy grownde' of Arden, 'betar wooded than fertile of corne', now creep the suburban tentacles of Birmingham: out beyond Sutton, Castle Bromwich and Solihull. Respectable Leamington is still in favour, despite a genteel shabbiness hanging over the Regency squares.

The greater part of the county is quite practical and down-to-earth, and has fewer great estates than other counties. The former mining districts of the north-east retain their own character, with their blue brick, mellowing after more than a century, and their man-made landscapes of pit mounds and power stations, the former encountered by surprise among the woods and lanes of a still rural countryside. We find no great churches in north Warwickshire, where, in the Middle Ages, there was poverty and meagre population, but some steeples of a local red sandstone pierce the gentle rise and fall of the horizon.

The Bard reigns in the Avon Valley, and the Shakespearean villages and their churches benefit from a constant stream of tourists from all corners of the world. The remoter villages of the south, with no Shakespearean links, are the poor relations of modern Warwickshire, for here the drift from the land has left the countryside still and quiet. The towns and large villages – Shipston, Alcester, Henley – dream through the weekdays but are shocked into a parody of their ancient bustling life by the internal combustion engine, which invades at weekends, when the ice-cream flows as freely as the water of the River Avon.

If the roads are crowded, the canals and some of the railways of Warwickshire are tranquil now – and somewhat seedy and nostalgic. Here, and in the villages that are not on the road to anywhere, is a wistful, apprehensive calm; the atmosphere perhaps in any of the hundred Warwickshire villages before they died in the enclosures of Tudor days – leaving sometimes a dusty, ruined church behind them.

And in 1972 a new region entered the area, the West Midlands – an urban county including the conurbations of the City of Birmingham, the City of Coventry and the City of Wolverhampton, as well as Dudley, Sandwell, Solihull and Walsall. The only rural stretch here is the Meridian Gap, a strip of green belt separating Coventry from the rest.

◁ **WOOTON WAWEN: ST PETER** – *fragments of 14th- and 15th-century glass, artfully reset into the chancel's east window*

CANNOCK
LICHFIELD
STAFFORDSHIRE
TAMWORTH
Brownhills
LEICESTERSHIRE
WOLVERHAMPTON
WALSALL
SUTTON COLDFIELD
Merevale
Mancetta
HINCKLEY
WEST BROMWICH
WEST MIDLANDS
NUNEATON
DUDLEY
Coleshill
Astley
BIRMINGHAM
Bedworth
HALESOWEN
STOURBRIDGE
Sparkbrook
Great Packington
Monks Kirb
Hall Green
COVENTRY
SOLIHULL
King's Norton
Berkswell
Binley
Knowle
RUGBY
Stoneleigh
Honiley
Kenilworth
Bromsgrove
Lapworth
Wroxall
Ashow
Rowington
LEAMINGTON SPA
REDDITCH
Beaudesert
Henley-in-Arden
WARWICK
WARWICKSHIRE
Studley
Droitwich
Wootton Wawen
Coughton
Sherbourne
Aston Cantlow
Snitterfield
Wilmcote
Alcester
Billesley
Hampton Lucy
Chesterton
Priors Har
Wormleighton
STRATFORD-UPON-AVON
NORTHA TONSH
Welford-on-Avon
Burton Dassett
Preston on Stour
WORCESTERSHIRE
Halford
Ilmington
Tredington
Honington
Evesham
Shipston-on-Stour
BANBURY
Barcheston
Brailes
OXFORDSHIRE
Moreton-in-Marsh
GLOUCESTER-SHIRE
Chipping Norton
Stow-on-the-Wold
0
5 miles
0
5 km
Kidlington
A38
A5
A449
M54
M6 TOLL
A34
M42
A447
M1
A444
A47
M6
M69
A5
A444
M6
A45
A38
M5
M42
A491
A452
A435
A4141
M42
A46
A45
A448
A445
A3400
A423
A426
A441
A425
A425
A435
A46
M5
A46
A422
M40
A423
A429
A44
A46
A3400
A422
M5
A422
A361
A3400
M4
A4260
A44
A429

ALCESTER † St Nicholas
7m/11km W. of Stratford-upon-Avon
OS *SP090574* **GPS** *52.2154N, 1.8689W*

Only the medieval tower remains, a mix of 13th- and 15th-century fabric. The nave and aisles were rebuilt by Edward and Thomas Woodward, 1729–30. The Gothic exterior is deceptive, as inside is Classical, with colonnades of Tuscan columns. Of interest is the tomb of Sir Fulke Greville, d. 1599, and his wife: their effigies have remains of colouring.

ASHOW † Assumption of Our Lady
2m/3km S.E. of Kenilworth
OS *SP312702* **GPS** *52.3291N, 1.5431W*

Delightfully and peacefully set beside the Avon, this is a Norman and Early English church, with a Perpendicular tower. A fine 16th-century nave roof with bosses was revealed in 1957, and there are good oak box pews, an 18th-century pulpit, chancel dado and reading desk. Over the altar hangs a modest 16th-century Dutch painting of the Crucifixion, and on the S. wall are Royal Arms of George III.

ASTLEY † St Mary the Virgin ★★
4m/6km S.W. of Nuneaton
OS *SP311894* **GPS** *52.5019N, 1.5432W*

The village is a cluster of cottage gardens and trees on the fringe of the N. Warwickshire coalfield. The church was concocted in 1608 from the 14th-century chancel of the old cruciform collegiate church. It was vandalised in the mid 1500s; the spire was stripped of its lead and collapsed in 1600. Sir Richard Chamberlayne subsequently demolished the whole W. part, rebuilding the tower, converting the old chancel into a nave and building a new low chancel at the E., all in the old Perpendicular tradition. Over the chancel arch is the Perpendicular tracery of the old E. window, now filled with plaster. The fine early 15th-century choir stalls, painted with figures of the Apostles, now stand in the chancel. A recent restoration of the many interesting painted wall texts has restored them to their former glory.

ASTON CANTLOW
† St John the Baptist
5m/8km N.W. of Stratford-upon-Avon
OS *SP137598* **GPS** *52.2368N, 1.7998W*

A medieval church in 'leafy Warwickshire's' Shakespeare country – Early English and Decorated, with a Perpendicular font, and rumoured to be the church where William Shakespeare's parents were married. The tower has an unusual hexagonal external stair turret, and the niche above the N. doorway has the remains of a medieval carving of the Nativity. Inside is a 17th-century pulpit and good glass by Kempe. Butterfield built the porch and restored the church in 1850.

BARCHESTON † St Martin
½ m/1km S.E. of Shipston-on-Stour
OS *SP264399* **GPS** *52.0573N, 1.6151W*

Once a church at the heart of England's first tapestry-weaving industry, it is known for the leaning tower, a prominent landmark of the area. The church is mainly late 13th- and 14th-century, with a Perpendicular clerestory. Inside is a fine tomb dedicated to a wealthy wool producer, William Willington, d. 1555, along with his first wife Anne and their seven daughters.

BEAUDESERT † St Nicholas ★
adjoins Henley-in-Arden, 7m/11km E. of Redditch
OS *SP152660* **GPS** *52.2923N, 1.7772W*

Both the hamlet and church lie hidden down a narrow lane off Henley High Street, with a medieval castle mound next to the churchyard. With a narrow nave and chancel, St Nicholas's is typical of a number of Norman churches in the county. There are good chancel arches and a later tower at the W. end. The handsome Norman chancel was given a good pseudo-Norman vault by Thomas Garner in 1865.

BERKSWELL † St John the Baptist ★
6m/10km W. of Coventry
OS *SP243791* **GPS** *52.4099N, 1.6429W*

A secluded black, white and red village with stocks, pump and smithy. This is the richest Norman church in the county, with a vaulted crypt beneath the chancel extending into an octagonal bay under part of the nave. The

△ **BILLESLEY: ALL SAINTS** – *a charming touch of late 17th-century Classicism applied to an ancient building in a rustic setting*

black and white of the two-storey 16th-century timber porch enlivens the masonry.

BILLESLEY † All Saints ★★

4m/6km W. of Stratford-upon-Avon
OS *SP147568* **GPS** *52.2094N, 1.7854W*
Churches Conservation Trust

This delightful, tiny church is approached down an avenue of lime trees. At first sight it resembles an odd Georgian cottage more than a church, but its origins are much earlier, going back to the 11th century. Two pieces of stone carving remain from the earlier church: a section of stone cross with the carved figure of Christ, and a tympanum with snake bird and dragon, and, most oddly, a kilted soldier. The interior is of the 1692 rebuilding but re-using some earlier fabric – see the blocked N. door. There is a tiny W. gallery and, in the S. transept, a family pew with a fireplace. Regrettably there is no evidence to support the local story that William Shakespeare and Anne Hathaway were married here.

BINLEY † St Bartholomew

3m/5km E. of Coventry
OS *SP377784* **GPS** *52.4032N, 1.4468W*

A surprising Classical church of 1773, said to be from the hand of Robert Adam, and sufficiently like his work at Mistley in Essex to make this seem likely. It has a sober exterior with an elegant octagonal cupola at the W. to break the skyline. Inside it is picked out in Adamesque plaster to resemble a saloon of the period. The chancel is a shallow apse with Grecian altar rails in iron and coloured windows painted naturalistically.

BIRMINGHAM – CITY CENTRE
† St Martin in the Bullring
Next to the Bull Ring
OS *SP073865* **GPS** *52.4770N, 1.8932W*

The old parish church of Birmingham, it was cased in brick in 1690, and altered and enlarged several times in the 18th century. The tower and spire, restored by P. C. Hardwick in 1853–5, show scarcely a trace of old work. The rest of the church was entirely rebuilt by J. A. Chatwin in 1873–5. Four medieval monuments remain, and one Burne-Jones window that survived Second World War bomb damage.

BIRMINGHAM – HALL GREEN
† Church of the Ascension ★
Corner of School Road and Fox Hollies Road
OS *SP109817* **GPS** *52.4340N, 1.8397W*

The earliest surviving Classical church in the city, this is an elegant little Queen Anne building, dated 1704, with Doric pilasters and distinctive balustrades, and set in attractive, leafy suburban surroundings. Its octagonal W. tower is capped by a copper cupola. The matching chancel and transepts were added in 1860.

BIRMINGHAM – KINGS NORTON
† St Nicolas ★
Corner of Pershore Road South and Back Road
OS *SP049789* **GPS** *52.4086N, 1.9289W*

A large medieval church, St Nicholas's is set in a green in a delightful grouping of restored late medieval grammar school and manor house. The church has a fine diagonally buttressed 15th-century tower with finialled parapets and a crocketed spire, and in the niches above the clock face are set Victorian carvings of St John, Jesus and the Virgin. Inside there are late 13th-century arcades and a good Decorated chancel arch with ballflowers. Although severely scraped by W. J. Hopkins during the 1872 renovations, there is much of interest: two Norman windows in the N.E. corner with good Hardman & Co. glass; Kempe glass in the E. window; a ledger stone to Humphrey Toye, chantry priest, d. 1514, underneath the altar in the S. aisle; a table tomb to Humphrey and Martha Lyttleton, c.1700, and an alabaster memorial to Sir Richard Grevis and his wife Dame Anne.

BIRMINGHAM – SPARKBROOK
† St Agatha ★
Stratford Road
OS *SP086847* **GPS** *52.4609N, 1.8739W*

A striking and successful church, bravely overshadowing a dreary industrial estate and petrol station, St Agatha's was built by W. H. Bidlake, 1899–1901. The imposing red brick W. tower has a sculptured front, a projecting baptistry and porches on each side with carved tympana. The string courses, mullions, parapet and corner finials are in contrasting light stone. All here is Perpendicular Revival with an Arts and Crafts flourish. The nave has piers without capitals, a rather tall clerestory and a simple painted roof; the aisles broaden out into chapels. The chancel was completely wrecked by bombing, and the interior was damaged by fire in 1957. The surviving fabric shows the excellent quality of Bidlake's carving and moulding detail.

BRAILES † St George ★
3m/4km E. of Shipston-on-Stour
OS *SP315393* **GPS** *52.0514N, 1.5416W*

The village never recovered from a body-blow dealt by enclosures in the 16th century. The church, known as 'The Cathedral of the Feldon', is left as a memorial to its medieval greatness. The Perpendicular steeple is a good example of those of the Cotswold fringe, and the nave and aisles are good Decorated work. The interior was altered in 1649, and would have been a Commonwealth rarity but for Gothic facelifting in 1879. There is a good 14th-century font and a 15th-century carved chest.

BURTON DASSETT † All Saints ★★
8m/13km N.W. of Banbury
OS *SP398514* **GPS** *52.1598N, 1.4189W*

Built into a hillside, the church rises some 15 feet from the W. tower to the chancel. It is a rare opportunity to see an old church almost devoid of furniture and largely unaltered – simple Early English with Y-tracery to the E. window, a medieval altar stone in the Lady Chapel, some interesting rustic carving on

COVENTRY: HOLY TRINITY – *the painted roofs at the crossing displaying the exquisite Coventry blue, a medieval pigment that has thus far proved impossible to emulate* ▷

the piers and responds of the N. arcade, and restored 13th-, 14th- and 17th-century wall-paintings and cartouches. The wealth of architectural details also includes reset Romanesque doorways, a fine oak door with original strap hinges, medieval piscina and aumbrey, and 14th-century floor tiles.

CHESTERTON † St Giles ★

5m/8km S.E. of Leamington Spa
OS *SP357582* **GPS** *52.2212N, 1.4787W*

Lovely and lonely, this long, low, embattled church stands apart, its plague-blighted village long disappeared. A mix of Perpendicular and Decorated, the inside, with little differentiation between the chancel and nave, has a tunnel-like feel. Of great interest are the monuments to the Peyto family: a painted chest tomb, alabaster busts, cartouches and a floor slab – all very fine. Their long vanished mansion stood to the N. of the church. Above the porch is an early 15th-century sculptured panel depicting the Adoration of the Magi.

COLESHILL † St Peter & St Paul ★★

9m/15km E. of Birmingham
OS *SP201890* **GPS** *52.4991N, 1.7050W*

This is a predominantly Georgian town in Warwickshire red brick. The church crowns the steep hill, its red sandstone blending well with the surrounding work. The church was violently restored and vigorously scraped by the Victorians, but is still essentially a fine 14th- and 15th-century town church. The steeple is the best of a group probably by the same local mason. The late Norman drum-shaped font is a work of art: Caen stone, with semi-circular compartments containing carved representations of the Crucifixion, St Peter, St Paul, Mary Magdalene and a cleric. There is a very curious brass of a cleric with six fingers, and many interesting monuments to the Digby family.

COUGHTON † St Peter

2m/3km N. of Alcester
OS *SP083605* **GPS** *52.2432N, 1.8792W*

In the grounds of Coughton Court, home of the recusant Throckmorton family, the church is a very complete 16th-century Perpendicular church, whose W. doorway has original double-leaf oak doors, and a Gothic S. porch of c. 1780. Inside there is much re-used Perpendicular woodwork, and in the S. aisle an old bread dole board. The church's most prominent feature is the large collection of Throckmorton monuments – finely carved tomb chests with marble tops. Of particular note is the tomb chest in the nave to Sir Robert Throckmorton, d. 1518, and to the S. a large canopied alabaster monument with panelled base and Corinthian columns with effigies of Sir John Throckmorton, d. 1580, and his wife.

COVENTRY † Holy Trinity ★★

Trinity Lane, opposite old and new cathedrals
OS *SP335790* **GPS** *52.4085N, 1.5088W*

A splendid town church, the spire grouping well with the ruins of the old cathedral and Basil Spence's new cathedral of 1962 nearby. It is a large Perpendicular church which contains stalls with misericords and a high stately 15th-century stone pulpit. The interior was restored by Sir George Gilbert Scott in 1854–6. The W. and E. windows are very fine: the former with glass by Hugh Easton, 1955; the latter by Sir Ninian Comper. The ceiling still has vivid traces of its original medieval Coventry blue paint and gold leaf, and over the high crossing archway is an outstanding Doom painting of 1430; it was rediscovered and cleaned in 2004, and is thought to be the finest of its kind in the country.

COVENTRY † St John the Baptist

Corner of Corporation Street and Spon Street
OS *SP330790* **GPS** *52.4088N, 1.5154W*

Founded as a guild church in 1342, the remaining fabric is mostly Perpendicular, and built of red sandstone with a central tower and tall clerestory lights. Due to its unconventional foundations – oak piles sunk into a lake bed – and the lowering of the floor by Sir George Gilbert Scott in his 1877 restoration, the building suffered intermittent flooding. This has now been resolved, with the floor being raised, the bases of the columns covered, along with the lower parts of some windows.

△ **COVENTRY: HOLY TRINITY** – *the sanctuary as it is today owes much to 19th-century restorations, which introduced the Minton floor tiles, wall-paintings and the Caen stone reredos*

GREAT PACKINGTON † St James ★★

11m/18km E. of Birmingham
OS *SP229840* **GPS** *52.4541N, 1.6630W*

This is an outstanding church by Joseph Bonomi, 1789–90, in the grounds of Packington Hall, built for the 4th Earl of Aylesford. The plan is an inscribed cross, with a square centre, four short arms and four lower rooms. The exterior is somewhat austere, the four corner towers with semi-circular lunettes and shallow lead domes. The interior is boldly executed in the gargantuan manner, with heavy Greek Doric columns and painted ashlar. Inside are the original altarpiece and balustraded marble rails, and two charming painted recumbent figures of John Fisher and his wife, d. 1570, with two mythical animals at their feet. The organ, of an earlier date than the church, is said to have been used by Handel.

HALFORD † St Mary

3m/4km N. of Shipston-on-Stour
OS *SP258456* **GPS** *52.1083N, 1.6235W*

Standing in a pleasant rural setting, this is a much restored 12th- and 13th-century church. The S. doorway is Romanesque, but badly weathered. The handsome Romanesque N. doorway, the best in the region, has an early tympanum showing the half-figure of an angel. The rustic Norman chancel arch has a zigzag string course running through it.

HAMPTON LUCY
† St Peter ad Vincula ★★

4m/6km E. of Stratford-upon-Avon
OS *SP256570* **GPS** *52.2108N, 1.6261W*

A good 19th-century hybrid Gothic church, it is best seen in sunlight across the Avon from Charlecote Park. The tower is by Thomas Rickman, 1825; the nave and aisles by his partner, Henry Hutchinson. The choir and apsidal sanctuary were added by Sir George Gilbert Scott in 1858. The nave, lofty in proportion to its width, with

△ **HAMPTON LUCY: ST PETER AD VINCULA** – *the interior is beautifully delineated with clustered columns and simple vaults, and the relative height of the nave gives it tremendous grandeur*

a sensitive plaster vault, gives an impression of a cathedral in miniature. Of note is the cast-iron tracery in Rickman's windows and the splendid Life of St Peter by Willement, 1826, in the W. window.

HENLEY-IN-ARDEN
† St John the Baptist

7m/11km E. of Redditch
OS *SP151660* **GPS** *52.2921N, 1.7798W*

A mid-15th-century Perpendicular church, the W. tower just protruding into the High Street. The interior is an undivided nave and chancel, and retains the original queen-post roof and 16th-century linenfold panelled pulpit. The good S. porch has corbels of Henry VI and his consort, and there are some entertaining corbels in the N. aisle.

HONILEY † St John the Baptist

3m/4km W. of Kenilworth
OS *SP244722* **GPS** *52.3476N, 1.6419W*

Originally the private chapel of Honiley Hall, this is a pretty Baroque church of 1723, with a bold W. tower, arched windows and pilasters. Inside, the apse has marble pillars and there are good original fittings, including box pews, altar rails, a three-decker pulpit and a W. gallery.

HONINGTON † All Saints

1m/2km N. of Shipston-on-Stour
OS *SP261426* **GPS** *52.0818N, 1.6200W*

Near a hall, this is a curious assembly of late 13th-century W. tower, and c. 1680–85 Georgian. The arched windows of the nave extend round the apse, and formal vases decorate the parapet. Inside are Tuscan arcades and a shallow plaster vault to the nave. There are good 17th-century stalls and fine 18th-century monuments.

ILMINGTON † St Mary the Virgin

4m/6km N.W. of Shipston-on-Stour
OS *SP209434* **GPS** *52.0892N, 1.6955W*

On the fringes of the Cotswolds, this is basically a Norman church with an Early English chancel. The 12th-century tower arch is of note, with four orders of plain stonework; see also the N. and S. doorways and chancel arch.

Inside is pleasing wooden furniture carved by Robert 'Mouseman' Thomson, installed in the 1930s, and a locally created apple map, showing the many varieties of apple that once grew in the district.

KNOWLE † St John the Baptist, St Lawrence & St Anne ★

3m/4km S.E. of Solihull
OS *SP182767* **GPS** *52.3883N, 1.7334W*

A substantial Decorated and Perpendicular church, it is part of an attractive cluster of medieval buildings that includes the guild house and cottage, the whole group being used for church purposes. Externally, the nave and aisles are stoutly embattled, with intermittent finials, and there are generous three-light windows on the S. side of the chancel. Inside is a tall 15th-century vaulted screen and stalls with carved misericords.

LAPWORTH † St Mary

5m/8km S. of Solihull
OS *SP163711* **GPS** *52.3377N, 1.7620W*

In a secluded village in undulating wooded country, the largely 13th- and 14th-century church is remarkable for its detached tower and steeple connected by a passage with the N. aisle. The tower is built sheer, without string courses, and with a projecting stair, both unusual features for Warwickshire. The double-storey porch, with its two staircases at the W. end, is another curiosity; perhaps the upper room was for the display of relics. The chancel is mostly 19th-century, and there is a good mixture of Perpendicular window tracery. In the N. chantry chapel are fragments of wall-painting and an Eric Gill memorial to Florence Bradshaw, 1928.

LEAMINGTON SPA † All Saints ★

Corner of Victoria Terrace, Priory Terrace and Church Street
OS *SP320654* **GPS** *52.2861N, 1.5323W*

A fine church, though alien to the Regency character of the town, All Saints was designed by the Reverend John Craig and built between 1843 and 1869 in a French Gothic style. An English tower and W. end were perversely added by Sir Arthur Blomfield in 1898. The scale of the work is gigantic throughout, particularly in the two transepts. Internally the church suffers the lack of a vault such as Pearson might have given it, and the glass and fittings detract from the serenity of the design.

MANCETTER † St Peter

5m/8km N.W. of Nuneaton, adjoining Atherstone
OS *SP320966* **GPS** *52.5671N, 1.5288W*

A squat tower announces the presence of St Peter's in this pleasant, leafy setting with timber-framed almshouses and the old manor. It is mainly 13th- and 14th-century, with a Perpendicular upper stage to the tower. There is a 15th-century roof, and much fine 14th-century glass in the chancel. The Reticulated tracery of the E. window is very good. Two Protestant martyrs are commemorated inside: Robert Glover, who was burnt at the stake in Coventry in 1555 and Joyce Lewes, who suffered the same fate at Lichfield in 1557.

MEREVALE † St Mary / Our Lady

6m/10km S.E. of Tamworth
OS *SP290977* **GPS** *52.5766N, 1.5728W*

This is a remnant of the old Cistercian Abbey – the Chapel of Our Lady at the Gate, and it is mainly 14th- and 15th-century. A considerable amount of high-quality 14th–16th-century glass remains, including an incomplete but fine 14th-century Jesse Tree in the E. window. There is a medieval screen from the old abbey church, a 13th-century effigy of a knight and lady, and 15th-century brasses.

MONKS KIRBY † St Edith

6m/10km N.W. of Rugby
OS *SP463831* **GPS** *52.4443N, 1.3198W*

An imposing priory church with a 13th-century chancel and the rest from the 14th century, apart from the late 15th-century upper section of the tower. The tower is vaulted and has an elaborate 18th-century Gothic parapet, erected after the fall of the spire; a large, two-storey Decorated porch abuts the tower. Inside, in the chancel, are two alabaster 16th-century Fielding tomb monuments.

△ **STRATFORD-UPON-AVON: HOLY TRINITY** – *the inner doors are late 15th-century and original; the sanctuary ring is 13th-century*

PRESTON ON STOUR † St Mary ★★

3m/4km S. of Stratford-upon-Avon
OS *SP203499* **GPS** *52.1473N, 1.7042W*

An unspoilt village mixing well the characteristics of the brick, timber and Cotswold stone districts. The church is a collector's piece, partly rebuilt in fanciful 18th-century Gothic by Edward and Thomas Woodward of Chipping Campden for the antiquary James West in 1752–7. The building is set about with yews, and much occupied with the then fashionable idea of sublime melancholy. Inside there is a deal of 17th- and 18th-century glass given over to the 'universal dominion of death'. Death is also recorded in monuments carved by Thomas Scheemakers and the Westmacotts, father and son. There is an interesting Gothic gilded ceiling.

PRIORS HARDWICK † St Mary

11m/18km S.E. of Leamington Spa
OS *SP471561* **GPS** *52.2020N, 1.3112W*

This is very much a traditional country church, with a splendid late 13th-century chancel and triple sedilia carved with foliage. The nave was decently rebuilt in 1868, with an elaborate Early English style chancel arch with naturalistic carving. The altar rails are late 17th-century, and there is a fine 13th-century piscina, and double sedilia decorated with carved naturalistic work.

ROWINGTON † St Lawrence

6m/10km N.W. of Warwick
OS *SP204692* **GPS** *52.3211N, 1.7021W*

The dominant feature of this Norman church is its large 13th-century central tower. Inside is a 15th-century screen and pulpit, early glass, and the remnants of Bodley's painstaking 1872 restoration – the painted ceiling in the N. aisle, the lecterns, vestry and altar crosses.

SHERBOURNE † All Saints

3m/4km S.W. of Warwick
OS *SP262611* **GPS** *52.2482N, 1.6173W*

Built by Sir George Gilbert Scott, 1862–4, for Miss Louisa Ann Ryland, All Saints is an expensive estate church, with a soaring steeple reflected in a lake. The elegant interior has marble-shafted arcades, an impressive alabaster reredos, and stained glass by Clayton & Bell. The monument of 1843 in the Ryland Chapel is by A. W. N. Pugin, and there is a memorial to Henry Eric Maudslay DFC, one of the 'Dambuster' aviators.

SNITTERFIELD † St James the Great

3m/4km N. of Stratford-upon-Avon
OS *SP218600* **GPS** *52.2386N, 1.6815W*

A handsome church, much restored and scraped in 1852, it is mostly 13th–15th-century. The shafted Decorated nave piers to the S. arcade have unusual capitals, and there are some finely carved stalls of c. 1530. The early 14th-century font has carved heads coming from the underside. William Shakespeare's grandfather, Richard, was a churchwarden here, and his uncle Henry was excommunicated from the church in 1581 for non-payment of tithes.

SOLIHULL † St Alphege ★★

Between New Road and St Alphege Close
OS *SP153792* **GPS** *52.4112N, 1.7760W*

This is a good, mostly 13th- and 14th-century cruciform church of red sandstone with spire.

△ **WARWICK: ST MARY** – *a masterpiece of refinement, the mid-15th-century Beauchamp Chapel; the Doom is contemporaneous, but was overpainted in 1678 in a more Italian Renaissance style*

In the reredos of the Thomas à Becket Chapel is a copy of an Anthony Van Dyke Crucifixion painting by Gaspar de Crayer (1584–1669). The chantry chapel has a delightful Arts and Crafts E. window, rich with flora and fauna, by Bertram Lamplugh, 1908, and in the vaulted Chapel of St Francis is a medieval altar. The Decorated chancel is very fine, with glass by Wailes in the E. window. There is good Kempe glass too, 1898, in the square-headed window in the St Antony Chapel. Of note in the nave is the arch-trussed rafter roof: this was revealed as a beneficial side-effect of a thorough Victorian scraping.

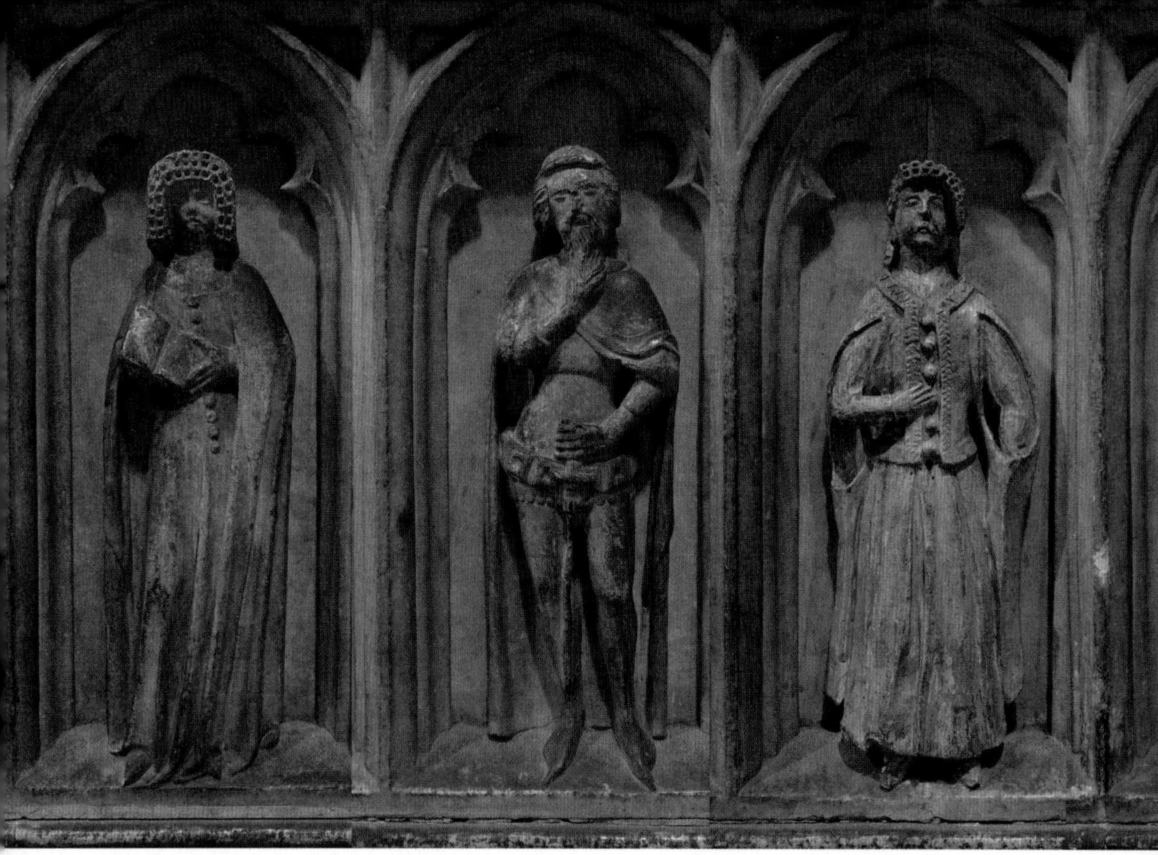

△ **WARWICK: ST MARY** – *carved in alabaster with great character, a selection of the 36 mourning relatives that surround the base of the tomb of Earl Thomas Beauchamp and his wife Katherine*

STONELEIGH † St Mary

3m/4km E. of Kenilworth

OS *SP330725* **GPS** *52.3504N, 1.5164W*

A Norman church of red sandstone, with a rich chancel arch rejoicing in zigzags and stylised beak-heads; note the 12th-century font with Apostles in the arcades, and very good early 19th-century furnishings, such as the high oak box pews and W. gallery. In the N.E. of the chancel is an ornate black and white marble memorial to Alice Leigh, Duchess Dudley and her daughter, erected in 1668 with two recumbent figures under a canopy supported on Ionic columns.

STRATFORD-UPON-AVON

† Holy Trinity ★★

Mill Lane

OS *SP201543* **GPS** *52.1866N, 1.7074W*

An estimable former collegiate town church of the 15th century; rarely visited for its own sake, the setting and approach is tidied up for the reception of Shakespeare-worshippers. The chancel is brilliant when seen through the dark arches of the central tower (crossing towers are the exception in Warwickshire). Externally, the church is best viewed romantically from across the Avon. The steeple is actually a Georgian pastiche by William Hiorn of Warwick, 1763. In the Clopton Chapel is a striking Renaissance tomb to George Carew, d. 1629, and his wife Joyce, and in the chancel are 26 carved misericords dating from the 15th-century collegiate period of the church. The Bard is buried in the sanctuary, where there is also a wall monument to him.

STUDLEY † The Nativity of the Blessed Virgin Mary

4m/6km S.E. of Redditch

OS *SP081637* **GPS** *52.2719N, 1.8822W*

A little apart from the noise of the town in a valley setting, the church is chiefly Decorated with a Norman N. doorway. Apart from the rood stair and 17th-century fittings, there is a superb 13th-century coffin lid with exquisite foliated cross, a monument to a prior of the vanished monastery. King Henry's own commissioners described the monks here as 'good men', but it didn't save them.

TREDINGTON † St Gregory ★★

2m/3km N. of Shipston-on-Stour
OS *SP259435* **GPS** *52.0899N, 1.6231W*

A delightful church – all of a hotchpotch outside, with Saxon nave walls, a 14th-century tower, 15th-century octagonal spire, nave of 11th- to 12th-century and 17th-, 18th- and 19th-century alterations. Note the double-splayed Anglo-Danish windows above the later arcades. There are Decorated benches throughout the nave, a carved 17th-century screen, a splendid Jacobean pulpit, painted arcade arches and fragmentary medieval wall-paintings.

WARWICK † St Mary ★★

Corner of North Gate Street and Church Street
OS *SP281649* **GPS** *52.2822N, 1.5881W*

This is the most interesting of the Warwickshire town churches. The W. tower over the roadway frames pleasant views of surrounding Georgian houses. Medieval work is restricted to the celebrated Beauchamp Chapel and the choir with its flying vault. The rest was destroyed by fire in 1694 and rebuilt in a Gothic Survival manner by Sir William Wilson, with some interference by Wren. The nave and tower are out of scale with the older work, but Wilson's interior is noble and his vaults and arcades a tour de force; there is no clerestory. A fine Baroque organ case stands over the W. lobby. The Beauchamp Chapel, a most accomplished and robust example of 15th-century work, contains the delectable shrine of Richard, Earl of Warwick, d. 1439. Notice how the eyes of the effigy gaze in wonder at the tiny figure of God the Father above the E. window. Other good monuments include that of Earl Thomas Beauchamp and his wife, in the centre of the chancel.

WELFORD-ON-AVON † St Peter

4m/6km W. of Stratford-upon-Avon
OS *SP145522* **GPS** *52.1681N, 1.7882W*

This small, mainly Norman and Perpendicular church stands in a pleasant thatched village. The W. tower is 12th-century, and inside are robust arcades with scalloped capitals. The Decorated chancel was restored by Sir George Gilbert Scott in 1866–7. Joseph Northcott copied a Benedictine screen for the church in the 1920s.

△ **WARWICK: ST MARY** – *at rest in the chancel, the effigies of Thomas Beauchamp and his wife Katherine Mortimer, a beautifully realised and touching monument*

WILMCOTE † St Andrew ★

3m/4km N.W. of Stratford-upon-Avon
OS *SP163578* **GPS** *52.2190N, 1.7616W*

The village is of little interest but for Mary Arden's Farm, mistakenly preserved as the childhood home of Shakespeare's mother. Of importance in the history of the Oxford Movement, however, is the church, school and vicarage, built as a group in the 1840s, and attributed to W. Butterfield before his individual style developed. Inside, the church is very dimly lit and mysterious, to such an extent that the wall decoration – including a good deal of blue and gold wallpaper – is barely discernible. Everything is according to Tractarian principles, from the stencilling above the chancel arch, the gilding, wall and ceiling painting to the triple lancets in the chancel.

WOLVERHAMPTON † Collegiate Church of St Peter

Between Wulfruna Street and Lichfield Street
OS *SO914987* **GPS** *52.5868N, 2.1280W*

The church is well sited on a hill, a large and well-massed composition of c. 1480, with a tall central tower, two-storey vaulted porch, high transepts and a good chancel by Ewan Christian, 1852–65. It is spacious and lofty inside; integral to the main structure is a very fine stone pulpit, with a jolly lion on the balustrade. The woodwork is good too: a W. gallery of 1610, choir stalls and a parclose screen. There are also some excellent monuments, especially the bronze standing figure of Sir Richard Leveson by Le Sueur, c. 1634, and in the churchyard a splendid 9th-century carved circular cross shaft.

WOOTON WAWEN † St Peter ★★

7m/11km N.W. of Stratford-upon-Avon
OS *SP153632* **GPS** *52.2674N, 1.7771W*

The village retains old brick and timber cottages. The church has a very strong and authentic atmosphere of the past. Built in stages about its early 11th-century central tower, St Peter's is a rare instance of Saxon work in the county, with the Saxon sanctuary at its core. Each generation has made its own contribution, so that the building now appears as three churches in one. There are

△ **WOOTON WAWEN: ST PETER** – *the chancel, with its rustic oak roof, large Perpendicular window and blocked up south window, a result of the addition of a Lady Chapel in the 14th century*

recognisable fragments of 14th-century medieval wall-paintings, a Perpendicular pulpit and 15th-century parclose screens in the E. of the nave. In the chancel and Lady Chapel are many very good monuments from the 15th century onwards and odd fragments of 13th- and 14th-century glass set into otherwise clear panes. A permanent exhibition in the church draws out the church's history, particularly in the Saxon period.

WORMLEIGHTON † St Peter

10m/16km S.E. of Leamington Spa
OS *SP447539* **GPS** *52.1817N, 1.3466W*

Set in a charming hill-top village, this is a largely 13th-century church, the chief glory of which is a 15th-century screen – lofty, richly carved and with a beautiful vaulted canopy (possibly 19th-century). There are also well carved bench-ends in the chancel, Royal Arms of 1826 and Spencer Arms on the W. wall.

WROXALL † St Leonard / Wren's Chapel

6m/10km N.W. of Warwick
OS *SP221707* **GPS** *52.3342N, 1.6757W*

In the grounds of Wroxall Abbey estate, opposite a luxury hotel and spa: the church is mainly early 14th-century, and is a relic of a Benedictine nunnery, the brick W. tower added in 1663–4. There is a good collection of 14th–15th-century glass and the Wren family tombs; Sir Christopher moved here from London after completing St Paul's.

WILTSHIRE

This large, oblong county is simple to describe. Two-thirds of it is chalk, one-third is 'cheese'. The chalk runs across the county from east to west. The vale of Pewsey, all trees and flint, and brick and cob cottages and thatch and clear streams, divides the areas of chalk into two. The northern half of the chalk is the Marlborough Downs, where Avebury stands, a prehistoric site as impressive as the more monolithic Stonehenge. The southern half is Salisbury Plain, whose cathedral spire gathers the rolling downs around it.

The plain is 'like the ocean after a storm, it is continually heaving in large swells. Through all this vast district, scarce a cottage or even a bush appears.' (Rev. W. Gilpin, 1808.) But the valleys in Salisbury Plain, particularly the Wylye and the Ebble, contain charming thatched villages with flint and limestone churches and small manor houses among beeches under the smooth, chalky hills. The plain itself is now much scarred with military camps and manoeuvre grounds, and Stonehenge does not seem as remote as it did when Constable painted it. The Marlborough Downs, associated with Richard Jefferies, naturalist and writer on English rural life, are bolder, with great hills like Martinsell rising like cliffs, and, at their feet, the thatched habitations of man. Devizes is the capital of the north, Salisbury of the south.

The 'cheese' is a flat limestone dairy country in the north of the county on the banks of the Bristol Avon, and the pull of Bristol is felt in it. Cricklade, Malmesbury, Bradford-on-Avon and Corsham are its most attractive grey-stone towns. Here are grand parish churches, like Malmesbury Abbey, Steeple Ashton and Edington. All the great houses of Wiltshire are below the edges of the downs, except for Wilton and Trafalgar, Littlecote and Ramsbury, which are in downland valleys.

The 17th-century antiquarian John Aubrey summed up the people of his birth county in a description that seems laughably absurd today: 'According to the several sorts of earth in England (and so all the world over) the indigenae are respectively witty or dull, good or bad. In North Wiltshire (a dirty clayey country) the indigenae or aborigines speake drawlinge; they are phlegmatique, skins pale and livid, slow and dull, heavy of spirit; hereabout is but little tillage or hard labour; they only milk the cowes and make cheese; they feed chiefly on milke meats, which cools their braines too much and hurts their inventions. These circumstances make them melancholy, contemplative and malicious … Contrariwise on the Downes, & c, the south part, there 'tis all upon tillage, and where the shepherds labour hard, their flesh is hard, their bodies strong. Being weary after hard labour, they have not leisure to read on or contemplate religion, but goe to bed to their rest to rise betimes the next morning to their labour.'

In the past century many square miles of grassy down have been ploughed; only the army and racehorse trainers have

◁ **WILTON: ST MARY AND ST NICHOLAS** – *the short cloister joining the campanile to the main body of the church contains some of the building's best Italian Romanesque carving*

saved some of them. Swindon has grown to be the largest town in the county and factories have transformed the characters of Chippenham and Calne.

The churches of Wiltshire, except those listed below, were never remarkable as architecture, and the county was unlucky in having, in the 19th century, one of the dullest Victorian architects, Mr T. H. Wyatt, as its chief restorer. His hand is heavy on many a once-old flint church, and for the only interesting new church he built, the Lombardic one at Wilton, he had to have the assistance of David Brandon, an architect of more talent and originality.

△ **ALTON PRIORS: ALL SAINTS** – *beautifully set in the undulating Wiltshire countryside, the church is no less impressive on the inside, with lime-washed walls and Jacobean stalls*

GLOUCESTERSHIRE
OXFORDSHIRE
BERKSHIRE
WILTSHIRE
HAMPSHIRE
DORSET
MERSET
STROUD
CIRENCESTER
Lechlade
Inglesham
Tetbury
Oaksey
Cricklade
MALMESBURY
Purton
SWINDON
Wanborough
Dauntsey
Chipping Sodbury
Castle Combe
Winterbourne Bassett
Aldbourne
Hardenhuish
Biddestone
CHIPPENHAM
Compton Bassett
Corsham
Calne
Avebury
Mildenhall
Lacock
MARLBOROUGH
HUNGERFORD
BATH
Bromham
Melksham
Bishops Cannings
DEVIZES
Alton Barnes / Alton Priors
Bradford-on-Avon
Potterne
Manningford Bruce
TROWBRIDGE
Steeple Ashton
Urchfont
Edington
WESTBURY
Old Dilton
Netheravon
FROME
South Tidworth
ANDOVER
WARMINSTER
Heytesbury
AMESBURY
Stockton
Durnford
Mere
East Knoyle
Wilton
Tisbury
Fugglestone
SALISBURY
Farley
Bishopstone
Stratford Tony
Broad Chalke
Vincanton
Shaftesbury
Sturminster Newton
BLANDFORD FORUM
SOUTHAMPTON
0
5 miles
0
5 km
M5
A46
A417
A429
A361
A419
A4135
A433
M4
A3102
A350
A4361
A338
A420
A346
A4
A342
A365
A345
A363
A36
A360
A366
A343
A303
A30
A3057
A354
A27
A31
A35

ALDBOURNE † St Michael ★
6m/10km N.E. of Marlborough
OS *SU263758* **GPS** *51.4808N, 1.6214W*

The church is prettily set at the top of an attractive village green. It is 12th-century, but was much enlarged in the 14th and 15th centuries to a cruciform plan, with a crossing tower, aisled nave, chantry chapels and clerestory. There are interesting monuments to the Walronds and the Goddards. The Butterfield restoration saw a new, steeper pitched roof constructed over the 15th-century one, which was retained as the ceiling. Inside, the church is spacious and airy, with a refreshing absence of superfluous furnishing: note the carving on the S. arcade arches, the painted chancel arch and fine Norman S. door.

ALTON BARNES † St Mary the Virgin ★
7m/12km S.W. of Marlborough
OS *SU107620* **GPS** *51.3572, -1.8467*

Altogether a delightful little rural church, it combines a Saxon nave with shallow pilasters and Georgian furnishings; the chancel was rebuilt in 1748. Inside is Georgian: pews, triple-decker pulpit, panelling and a W. gallery with texts, all under a rustic roof. By contrast, the chancel ceiling is bright blue.

ALTON PRIORS † All Saints ★
7m/12km S.W. of Marlborough
OS *SU109621* **GPS** *51.3580N, 1.8446W*
Churches Conservation Trust

A stone's throw eastward of Alton Barnes is a disused but loved church in the middle of a field criss-crossed by cobbled footpaths. The limestone square tower is Perpendicular, and inside the church is lime-washed, with a rustic open-timbered roof. The chancel arch is Norman, though the chancel itself was rebuilt in the 19th century; it contains nicely carved Jacobean choir stalls.

AMESBURY † St Mary and St Melor
7m/11km N. of Salisbury
OS *SU151414* **GPS** *51.1719N, 1.7843W*

Proudly detached from the mundane town, this former abbey church is 13th-century and cruciform in plan, though refashioned in the 15th century with fine timber roofs. Inside is a stone-vaulted chapel off the N. transept, a Norman font, a 15th-century screen and the remains of medieval painted glass. It was heavily restored by William Butterfield in 1853.

AVEBURY † St James ★
6m/10km W. of Marlborough
OS *SU099699* **GPS** *51.4286N, 1.8579W*

St James's is beautifully grouped with the manor house and village, adjoining the extensive prehistoric site. The notable Saxon nave had aisles added in the 12th century. The arcades were replaced in 1812 and the chancel rebuilt in 1879, retaining the 13th-century chancel arch. The Perpendicular screen supports a fine traceried rood loft, and was restored with good care in the 20th century. Of interest too is an early Norman font.

BIDDESTONE † St Nicholas
4m/6km W. of Chippenham
OS *ST861735* **GPS** *51.4607N, 2.2003W*

There is a remarkable Norman doorway here with a Byzantine cross. The conical capped 15th-century bell-turret over the E. gable is also of great interest – built to house a sanctus bell. One of the lever-operated bells was discovered in a nearby farmyard in the 1920s. The furnishings are mostly 18th-century.

BISHOP'S CANNINGS
† St Mary the Virgin ★★
3m/4km N.E. of Devizes
OS *SU037641* **GPS** *51.3766N, 1.9472W*

This is a magnificent 13th-century cruciform church, with later, mostly Perpendicular additions. Inside there is fine Early English arcading in the nave, with lightly pointed arches on round columns and two orders of capitals. The clerestory is Perpendicular; the king-post roof of 1670. There are recessed altars in the transepts and, adjoining the S. transept, the Chapel of Our Lady of the Bower, with a fine Ernli monument of 1571. Close to the crossing is a rare 17th-century penitential 'carrel', or confessional chair, on the back of which is painted a hand inscribed with various admonitory warnings.

△ **BRADFORD-ON-AVON: ST LAURENCE** – *the nave is small but lofty, and those narrow proportions are echoed in the chancel arch that leads through to the altar*

BISHOPSTONE † St John Baptist ★

4m/6km S.W. of Salisbury

OS *SU084265* **GPS** *51.0380N, 1.8810W*

A church left behind after the disappearance of its village following the Plague; it is cruciform, and was entirely remodelled in the 14th century. The chancel and N. transept have lovely and varied windows of late, 'flowing' Decorated work. The S. transept has fine Reticulated tracery. The N. transept, known as the 'Farmers' aisle, was set aside for tithe-paying farmers. The chancel is very good – stone-vaulted with carved bosses and corbels, and excellent sedilia, set in canopied niches. The pulpit is made from reset old imported Renaissance panels. Glass by Wailes commemorates George Augustus Montgomery, the rector who brought this Renaissance woodwork to the church. The rector's canopied memorial – the work of A. W. N. Pugin – is in the S. transept.

BRADFORD-ON-AVON † Holy Trinity

3m/4km N.W. of Trowbridge

OS *ST824608* **GPS** *51.3467N, 2.2539W*

The little town rises steeply from the Avon, full of beautiful buildings and picturesque corners. The parish church near the river has a sturdy 15th-century tower and short spire; it is a 12th-century fabric, enlarged and refashioned in the 14th, 15th and early 16th centuries. The over-restored interior has 14th-century recessed and canopied tombs either side of the chancel arch, and a charming early 14th-century sculpted female head.

BRADFORD-ON-AVON

† St Laurence ★

3m/4km N.W. of Trowbridge

OS *ST824609* **GPS** *51.3470N, 2.2538W*

One of England's most ancient Saxon churches, if not the largest, it is believed to have been built originally by St Aldhelm c. 700, and possibly rebuilt c. 1000. The building was rediscovered by chance in 1856

△ **BRADFORD-ON-AVON: ST LAWRENCE** – *the south wall has original blind arcading incised into the stonework; the buttresses and west wall were necessary additions of the 19th century*

after having been used as a school, warehouse and private dwelling. The church now stands as one of the oldest, smallest churches in the land. Except for some blind arcading, the interior is stark save for two ministering angels above the chancel arch, attendants to a vanished rood.

BROAD CHALKE † All Saints

6m/10km S.W. of Salisbury
OS *SU040253* **GPS** *51.0275N, 1.9432W*

This is a fine cruciform church in the Chalke Valley, where the willow-fringed Ebble flows lazily through water meadows. The 13th-century arcades were removed in the 15th century and the whole put beneath one king-post roof. The external treatment of the W. end is similar to Edington and Bishopstone, and the embattled parapet runs, unusually, in front of the E. end gable. The chancel is late 13th-century, the N. transept 14th-century. The 17th-century antiquarian John Aubrey, once churchwarden here, described the bells as 'one of the tuneablest rings in Wiltshire'.

BROMHAM † St Nicholas

3m/4km E. of Melksham
OS *ST963651* **GPS** *51.3857N, 2.0544W*

Of 12th-century origins, the outstanding feature of this church is the rich Perpendicular S. chapel, begun in 1492, complete in all its details including the painted roof. In the centre is the alabaster effigy of Sir Richard Tocotes, d. 1457, and at the E. end two lovely canopied tomb chests of c. 1492 and 1593. There is an excellent E. window, designed by Burne-Jones and executed by Morris & Co.

CASTLE COMBE † St Andrew

5m/8km N.W. of Chippenham
OS *ST841771* **GPS** *51.4934N, 2.2297W*

The church stands at the heart of one of the prettiest villages in Wiltshire, the 15th-century market cross reflecting its medieval wealth. It has a proud 'wool' tower of 1436, with a 16th-century relief panel depicting the tools of the cloth trade: a comb, shears and a shuttle. The interior is delicately carved Perpendicular, the chancel arch with canopied statues. The 13th-century chancel contains an effigy of a knight. In the mid-19th century the whole building, tower excepted, was taken down and rebuilt to the original plan.

COMPTON BASSETT † St Swithin ★

3ml4km E. of Calne
OS *SU030715* **GPS** *51.4434N, 1.9570W*

Set in a commanding position on a hill-side above the town, the church is largely Perpendicular with a 12th-century N. arcade, and chancel and side chapels of 1866 by Woodyer. Its main interest is the very fine early 15th-century vaulted stone screen, with intricately carved decoration and statues of the Apostles, all set under an equally interesting fine 14th-century moulded chancel arch.

CRICKLADE † St Sampson ★★

7ml11km N.W. of Swindon
OS *SU099935* **GPS** *51.6406N, 1.8579W*

This is one of the glories of Wiltshire, the church's great Tudor central tower dominating the little town. The fabric is 12th–16th-century, with Saxon carvings and a late 15th-century S. chapel; there is good painted glass, altars, and other fittings by Martin Travers. The lierne vaulting under the tower has remarkable bosses depicting the Arms of the Duke of Northumberland.

DAUNTSEY † St James

4ml6km S.E. of Malmesbury
OS *ST979824* **GPS** *51.5411N, 2.0303W*

Apart from the Norman N. and S. doorways, the rest of St James's is mainly 14th- and 15th-century, with a good Gothic Survival tower rebuilt in 1630. Important contents include a 14th-century screen, 16th-century wooden tympanum with Doom painting now moved from the chancel arch to the W. end of the N. aisle, and painted glass of 1525 in the N.E. chapel. There is also a fine array of 16th-century and later Danvers monuments.

DEVIZES † St John ★★

Long Street
OS *SU004612* **GPS** *51.3503N, 1.9946W*

This is an important Norman church with a 12th-century central tower and vaulted chancel replete with astonishing zigzag wall arcading and excellent stone vaulting. The contrast between the Norman chancel and Perpendicular nave is striking. The S. or Beauchamp Chapel is very fine, battlemented and pinnacled, with carved angels inside and out, a rich panelled roof and grimacing corbels that came from the outside of the old church. The monolithic crossing tower commands attention, and has an unusual circular external stair turret.

DEVIZES † St Mary

Commercial Road
OS *SU005616* **GPS** *51.3536N, 1.9928W*

Although on a smaller scale than its neighbour St John's, the church is very distinctive, with its embattled aisles, porch and clerestory with exaggerated pinnacles. The chancel is 12th-century and stone-vaulted, and the rest is mainly Perpendicular work of before 1436, with a good tower and nave roof.

DURNFORD † St Andrew ★

5ml8km N. of Salisbury
OS *SU136383* **GPS** *51.1440N, 1.8064W*

This unspoilt church stands amidst the willows on the E. bank of the Avon. The church is very ancient; the 12th-century nave walls with original doorways encase yet earlier fabric. The W. tower is a fine example of 13th-century work, and the chancel, partially rebuilt c. 1890, has a floral painted motif on the E. wall. There are further indistinct medieval wall-paintings in the nave and over the chancel arch. The furnishings are very good, and include a pulpit of 1619, and lectern with a chained copy of *Jewel's Apology*, 1562. At the W. end are medieval benches, and at the chancel elaborate traceried communion rails of the late 17th century. A delightful Wiltshire church, with a good collection of monuments too.

EAST KNOYLE † St Mary

5ml8km N. of Shaftesbury
OS *ST880305* **GPS** *51.0740N, 2.1723W*

There is some Norman work here, but the church is mostly Early English with a Perpendicular tower. The chancel walls are completely covered in wonderful plasterwork, c. 1640, by Robert Brockway; the strapwork panels have Biblical inscriptions, a decorated frieze and a vividly executed story of Jacob's

Dream, with the ladder rising up the E. wall. Sir Christopher Wren was born in the village and his father, as rector, was responsible for this plasterwork; he was ejected from his living during the Civil War, and this lovely decoration was cited against him at his trial.

EDINGTON † Blessed Virgin Mary, St Katharine and All Saints ★★

4ml6km E. of Westbury

OS *ST926533* **GPS** *51.2789N, 2.1069W*

Grey, flecked with golden lichen and standing below the steep northern escarpment of the plain, this is not only the best example of a 14th-century collegiate church in S. England but, excepting Salisbury Cathedral, the most perfectly proportioned church in the county. It was built in 1352–61 by William of Edington. Cruciform, with central tower, the three-bay chancel formed the monastic choir, the nave serving as the parish church. Nothing now remains of the monastery, but the S. walk of the cloisters was against the N. aisle, where the window sills are higher. In the choir are rich mouldings – plainer masonry in the parochial part. Four canopied niches in the chancel have mutilated figures of the Evangelists, the drapery of great refinement. Here too is a multitude of carved heads, forming a fascinating portrait gallery of people from all walks of medieval life. The tracery in the chancel is Reticulated, whilst that in the nave is Perpendicular. There is a fine restored 15th-century oak screen with loft, and a pulpitum. The nave ceiling is 17th-century panelled plaster. The sedilia were much mutilated by the erection of the beautiful Lewys monument, 1630, now moved farther W. In the S. transept is a magnificent tomb and effigy of an Austin canon with much of its original colour.

FARLEY † All Saints

5ml8km E. of Salisbury

OS *SU224295* **GPS** *51.0652N, 1.6811W*

An assured red brick church of 1688, it was possibly built to designs by Sir Christopher Wren for Sir Stephen Fox, with whom he was working to build the Chelsea Hospital for pensioners. The Victorians referred to the church as 'Little St Paul's in the country', although the rustic interior of All Saints could not contrast more sharply with Wren's interior of the cathedral. The plan is that of a Greek Cross with some original fittings and handsome Fox monuments in the N. transept. The church and almshouses opposite make a splendid late 17th-century group.

FUGGLESTONE † St Peter

½ml1km E. of Wilton

OS *SU102313* **GPS** *51.0815N, 1.8554W*

This is a small church of Norman origin, although none of the Norman work remains. The fabric that remains is mainly Early English, including the chancel, with its stepped lancet windows. There is a 15th-century octagonal belfry, early 19th-century Gothic fittings and a Georgian baluster font.

HARDENHUISH † St Nicholas

N.W. neighbourhood of Chippenham

OS *ST909747* **GPS** *51.4716N, 2.1314W*

Completely rebuilt on a new site in 1779 by John Wood the Younger of Bath, this is a little Georgian gem set on a green hill, with an apsidal sanctuary, balustraded parapets, Venetian windows and a small domed tower. The windows are filled with clear glass. The quixotic diarist of rural life Francis Kilvert was born in the vicarage opposite in 1840.

HEYTESBURY † St Peter and St Paul

3ml5km S.E. of Warminster

OS *ST925425* **GPS** *51.1822N, 2.1086W*

A noble, formerly collegiate cruciform church with central tower, it has features of the late 12th, 13th and 15th centuries. It was over-restored by Butterfield, 1865–7. The earliest surviving parts are the chancel arcades, c. 1185. The glass by Alexander Gibbs in the immense E. lancet window is some of his best. The impressive interior has an immense single E. lancet and a vaulted 16th-century stone screen. A 1967 restoration gave cheerful colour to the many carved roof bosses and a sky-blue hue to the nave ceiling.

LACOCK: ST CYRIAC – *the Sharington tomb, an early Renaissance work of 1566 with dusty traces of the original colour* ▷

INGLESHAM † St John the Baptist ★
1m/2km S.W. of Lechlade
OS *SU205984* **GPS** *51.6843N, 1.7044W*
Churches Conservation Trust

Two houses, this towerless church and a farm adjoining, all of golden-grey Cotswold stone, stand among the wide meadows of the upper Thames. William Morris, who lived in nearby Kelmscott, saved this church from excessive Victorian restoration. Inside there are medieval wall-paintings with 17th-century paintings on top, remnants of old glass, remains of painted screens, high pews of differing depths, old, uneven floors and clear glass. The wonderful late Saxon carving of the Virgin and Child is set in the S. wall – it was saved from use as a sundial on the outside in 1910.

LACOCK † St Cyriac ★★
3m/4km S. of Chippenham
OS *ST917685* **GPS** *51.4161N, 2.1206W*

This is a beautiful church in a village with extensive monastic remains and houses from the 14th century onward. The cruciform church is mainly 14th–15th-century with a W. tower and spire. The chancel is Arts and Crafts – remodelled by Sir Harold Brakspear as a memorial to the pioneering photographer William Fox Talbot, who lived at Lacock Abbey. The pièce de résistance is the late 15th-century N. chapel – the intricate lierne vault has richly carved bosses and centre pendants retaining their original colour. Sir W. Sharington's tomb of 1566 is one of the best English examples of early Renaissance work, carved with putti, dolphins and cartouches. The brass to Robert Baynard, d. 1501, and his wife Elizabeth, is a surprisingly flowing example; the couple, respectively in armour and gown, stand above their 13 children.

MALMESBURY † St Mary ★★
10m/16km N. of Chippenham
OS *ST932873* **GPS** *51.5846N, 2.0984W*

Little else remains of this vast cruciform monastic church other than the massive nave and aisles; even the W. end is in ruins. It is Norman, refashioned in the 14th century. The S. porch has some of the finest Romanesque sculpture in the country. Inside, the admirably sturdy 12th-century arcades and elegant 14th-century clerestory are most impressive. The present E. wall rests on the 15th-century stone pulpitum which formerly closed off the monastic choir. In the aisles are sections of the stone rood screen, and a 15th-century table tomb with recumbent effigy, said to commemorate King Athelstan, who was certainly buried here. To the S. is a tower with spire, sole remnant of the former parish church of St Paul. The little town has much of interest, including the fine, late medieval market cross.

MANNINGFORD BRUCE † St Peter
10m/16km S. of Marlborough
OS *SU139580* **GPS** *51.3211N, 1.8010W*

A remarkably unspoilt Norman church, it was built on top of a Roman building. Outside is coursed herringbone flint work with limestone quoins, an apsidal chancel and leaded W. bell-tower. Inside the church is a simple two-cell structure with a plain arch between the nave and chancel. It was restored by Pearson in 1882, and his designs for the painting scheme, fittings and reredos (much of which was executed by Clayton & Bell) harmonises well with the Norman structure.

MERE † St Michael ★
7m/11km N.W. of Shaftesbury
OS *ST811322* **GPS** *51.0893N, 2.2711W*

St Michael's is one of Wiltshire's best town churches, with work and fabric of many dates – the core may be 12th-century, the chancel is Early English, and the rest was almost entirely rebuilt in the 14th century when two chantry chapels were also added. The handsome Perpendicular W. tower stands on Norman footings. The fine interior has seven old screens of various types, and the Perpendicular rood loft was restored by local antiquarians in the 1880s. There are good 14th–15th-century brasses, 15th-century painted glass and complete 17th-century nave seating with shell-headed bench-ends.

MILDENHALL † St John Baptist ★★
1m/2km E. of Marlborough
OS *SU209694* **GPS** *51.4239N, 1.6994W*

The pleasant plastered exterior with Perpendicular tower, aisles and clerestory

△ **MALMESBURY: ST MARY** – *the robust 12th-century arcade; the triforium is now bricked up beyond the triple arcades but would once have been open to a walkway for the inhabitant monks*

gives no hint of the glories within. Transitional white plastered arcades rise from a forest of dark oak box pews; the pulpit and reading desk are twin forms flanking the chancel arch, behind and above each is a tall back-board and delicately carved tester. All this rich woodwork, along with panelling, a fine reredos, altar rails, choir stalls and a W. gallery, resulted from a refitting of the church, c. 1816, paid for and executed by the local parishioners. Betjeman visiting the church described 'walking into a church of a Jane Austen novel'.

NETHERAVON † All Saints ★

5m/8km N. of Amesbury
OS *SU147483* **GPS** *51.2346N, 1.7896W*

The church has a rather dumpy profile, but is of great interest. The impressive tower is largely late Saxon, with an upper stage added at a later date in the 12th or 13th century. Even without this addition, the tower still represents a rare instance of pre-Conquest work on a monumental scale. The entrance to the church is through an 11th-century W. doorway at the foot of the tower. The round arch of the doorway is supported by paired pilasters either side, topped off with capitals nicely carved with flora and fauna motifs. Inside is an Early English nave and chancel with lancets and a corbel table.

OAKSEY † All Saints

5m/8km N.E. of Malmesbury
OS *ST990936* **GPS** *51.6415N, 2.0145W*

A good example of a Wiltshire village church, it was built in the 13th century, with 14th- and 15th-century additions. The nave has a clere-story but only a S. aisle, so that there are two stages of windows on the N. side. There is 15th-century glass in the N.E. nave window, and on the S. aisle wall are some extremely good early 15th-century wall-paintings showing St Christopher and Christ of the Trades.

OLD DILTON † St Mary

1m/2km S.W. of Westbury, just S. of Dilton Marsh
OS *ST858490* **GPS** *51.2404N, 2.2039W*
Churches Conservation Trust

Down a pretty lane and through the railway arch, St Mary's is a lovely little church – Perpendicular with a spired stone bellcote.

△ **MALMESBURY: ST MARY** – *characterful ceiling bosses look down upon the east end of the nave; they were repainted in the original colours in 1935*

Its glory is the unrestored 18th-century interior, with box pews, gallery, three-decker pulpit with tester, and clear glass. There is a plastered tympanum between the nave and chancel, and the upper storey of the vestry was once a school.

POTTERNE † St Mary *

2m/3km S. of Devizes
OS *ST995585* **GPS** *51.3260N, 2.0079W*

The cruciform church stands above a row of medieval cottages, and is remarkable for being entirely of the 13th century apart from the top of the tower. The 13th-century work is beautiful in its simple austerity and worthy to rank with Salisbury Cathedral, the similarity probably due to Potterne being a manor of the bishops of Salisbury. An Anglo-Saxon tub font with Latin inscription stands under the W. window.

PURTON † St Mary the Virgin

4m/7km N.W. of Swindon
OS *SU096871* **GPS** *51.5833N, 1.8616W*

This sandstone church is situated next to a lovely Elizabethan mansion. Like Wanborough, there is a central spire as well as a W. tower, though here the spire rises from another tall tower. Building and rebuilding went on from the 13th century until the completion of the W. tower in the 15th century. With its decoratively painted nave arcade arches, 14th-century Lady Chapel wall-painting and fragment of painting over the chancel arch, the place is one of the most worshipful in Wiltshire. Over the altar is a much travelled 17th-century Dutch painting of the Last Supper, stolen in 1994, recovered in the USA in 2001 and returned to the church in 2004.

SALISBURY
† St Thomas of Canterbury **

Off High Street, N. of cathedral
OS *SU143299* **GPS** *51.0690N, 1.7968W*

A fine town church founded in the first half of the 13th century, it was progressively rebuilt on a spacious plan during the 15th century, with a clerestoried nave and chancel with S. tower, and three-storeyed vestry. The interior is very fine Perpendicular, with resplendent roofs, particularly in the nave. Over the chancel arch is a splendid Doom painting with unusual scenes such as the damned miser still clutching his money bags, and bishops being swallowed up by the jaws of death. The Doom was painted over in 1593, and, after its re-discovery in 1881, was restored and repainted.

△ **MALMESBURY: ST MARY** – *at the east end of what remains of the church, the vast arches of the original crossing can be seen, with fragmentary remains of the transepts*

SOUTH TIDWORTH † St Mary
9m/15km W. of Andover
OS *SU235476* **GPS** *51.2279N, 1.6642W*
Churches Conservation Trust

By John Johnson, 1879–80, St Mary's is a lavish estate church in Early English style. The lofty interior has rich carving, a sculptured reredos by James Forsyth, and glass by Heaton, Buder & Bayne, and Clayton & Bell.

STEEPLE ASHTON
† St Mary the Virgin ★★
3m/4km E. of Trowbridge
OS *ST906571* **GPS** *51.3131N, 2.1356W*

Betjeman likened the church to 'a silvery battleship', and so it is, especially if you approach across the clay lands from Edington. A great church built at the height of the cloth-weaving prosperity of the 15th century, it presents a fantasy-like profile, with turrets, pinnacles and crenellations. Rebuilt between 1480–1500, this was the last flowering of medieval church building in the county. The steeple was blown down in 1670 and had to be rebuilt twice, together with parts of the nave; a brass at the W. end records the rebuilding and loss of two workmen's lives. The vaults are very fine: there is lierne vaulting in the chancel, aisles, chapels and S. porch; it was clearly intended to vault the nave in similar fashion, but instead there is a rich plaster ceiling with pendants and bosses, all originally coloured. Much carving adorns the vaults, all very bold and virile.

STOCKTON † St John Baptist
12m/18km S.E. of Warminster
OS *ST981382* **GPS** *51.1433N, 2.0272W*

St John's is a 14th-century church set in a little close in a lovely village of thatched buildings. Of great interest is the solid wall which, save for a central doorway and two squints, completely shuts off the chancel. Though apparently 15th-century, the arrangement is curiously like that in an Eastern church. A rood loft supported on corbels once existed on the W. side of the wall.

OPEN

STRATFORD TONY † St Mary and St Lawrence

3m/4km S. of Wilton
OS *SU091263* **GPS** *51.0368N, 1.8704W*
Churches Conservation Trust

Simply getting to this delightful church is a pleasure – a narrow lane leading to a footbridge over the stream, and then up to the village church, charmingly set on a mound above the Ebble. The 14th-century chancel has lovely Kempe glass in the Reticulated E. window. The brick and flint nave walls were rebuilt and fenestrated in the 18th century owing to the instability of the sloping site. The unrestored interior has 17th-century pews, screen and dado panelling with colonnaded tops.

TISBURY † St John Baptist

6m/10km N.E. of Shaftesbury
OS *ST944291* **GPS** *51.0614, -2.0812*

An important cruciform church, it is pleasantly situated below the small town on the River Nadder. It is mostly 14th–15th-century, with a fine 13th-century N. porch with parvise, and some 12th-century features; the medieval crossing tower was replaced after it fell in 1762. Inside, the Lady Chapel of 1299 has richly carved niches. There are good 17th-century aisle roofs with names of donors, and Jacobean pews and a pulpit. Many of the Arundells of Wardour are buried in the chancel, including Lady Blanche, heroic defender of Wardour Castle in the Civil War.

URCHFONT † St Michael

4m/6km S.E. of Devizes
OS *SU040573* **GPS** *51.3148N, 1.9429W*

A mainly 14th-century church with Perpendicular additions, it is distinctive for the excellent Reticulated tracery in the S. transept. The notable Decorated chancel with gabled buttresses and stone vaulting enriched with carved bosses is of great interest, as is a good 18th-century monument to Robert Tothill by Scheemakers on the S. wall of the chancel.

WANBOROUGH † St Andrew

3m/5km E. of Swindon
OS *SU207825* **GPS** *51.5416N, 1.7019W*

A lovely russet and golden church on high ground, it has a fine Perpendicular W. tower and very unusual octagonal E. tower and spire over the crossing. Inside are 14th-century aisles and nave. The S. porch contains two gisants (figures depicted at the point of death) of a man and woman, 13th-century.

WILTON † St Mary and St Nicholas ★

3m/4km W. of Salisbury
OS *SU094312* **GPS** *51.0809N, 1.8660W*

'Lombardy in Wiltshire.' An aggressive, uncompromising and extremely expensive design in Italian Romanesque style by T. H. Wyatt and David Brandon, 1841–5, it was in complete contradiction to the Gothic Revival principles of the time. The outside is domineering and rather off-putting. Inside, passing quickly by the intimidating scale of the arcades, the black marble draws one's attention. The columns supporting the chancel aisle arcades came from a 2nd-century B.C. Roman temple; the font, also of black marble, is a reproduction of a Baroque original. There is remarkable imported late medieval glass from the Netherlands and Germany, and yet earlier, 12th- and 13th-century glass from France – the Abbey of St Dennis and La Sainte-Chapelle – in the apse windows.

WINTERBOURNE BASSETT † St Katharine and St Peter ★

3m/4km N. of Avebury
OS *SU101749* **GPS** *51.4730N, 1.8554W*

An architectural gem near to the headwaters of the River Kennett, the nave, N. aisle with N. transeptal chapel, chancel and S. porch are all purest Decorated; only the W. tower and a few minor features are later. In the transept is a beautiful window and recessed tomb, beneath which is a touching 13th-century tomb slab with a man and wife hand-in-hand. The late Norman font has a 17th-century cover and there is much other 17th-century furniture, good monuments and hatchments.

◁ **WILTON: ST MARY AND ST NICHOLAS** – *although designed by T. H. Wyatt and David Brandon, the motivation for the Italian Romanesque style of the building came from the benefactor, Sidney Herbert*

WORCESTERSHIRE

Worcestershire is a small and richly varied county. It is, if the simile will be forgiven, like a fruit tart. The centre, containing the Severn and Avon valleys with their tributaries, is mostly orchards and miraculously beautiful in spring. The edges of the tart are the hills that surround Worcestershire on all sides. Wherever you are in the county you can see hills not far off; they are usually flanked with, or crowned by, trees.

The northernmost corner of the fruit tart is burned black; it is part of the Black Country and extends northward from Kidderminster towards Birmingham, which now extends into Worcestershire. The old industrial towns of the county were devoted to ironworking, from founding and engineering through chains down to needles and fish-hooks. In this industrial corner, pinkish brick houses and mills stretch over hills and valleys, peppered with undistinguished Victorian towers, spires and bellcotes, and the occasional weathered stone tower of some medieval church, such as the fine ones of Kidderminster and Bromsgrove. Now the northern parts of the county are an urban sprawl.

The rest of the county is a marked contrast. What Surrey is to London, Worcestershire has become to Birmingham and the Black Country, and many an old timber-framed cottage set among orchards or at the foot of steep pastoral hills may be seen on closer inspection to have been saved from destruction by some incomer who uses it as a weekend hide-out or as a commuter base. His or her forebears would have lived on the outskirts of Kidderminster, Dudley or Redditch in some heavy Victorian mansion now divided into flats. The building materials of houses and churches are as varied as the scenery. Only the big abbeys and priories, in which Worcester was richer than any other county, could afford impressive architecture. Worcester Cathedral (severely but impressively restored by Sir George Gilbert Scott), Great Malvern Priory, with its many windows of late medieval and 18th-century glass, Pershore Abbey, which is now only a huge choir with tower crossing, and the stately Perpendicular bell-tower of Evesham are the chief survivors.

In the fruit districts, and where building stones were not easily obtained, the churches were like the old cottages, partly of timber construction, often with timber-framed towers or bellcotes. At the east of the county, where the Cotswold hills rise, churches such as Broadway are of a local golden limestone, like their villages. In the west of the county, south of the Malvern Hills, churches are of red sandstone, and the tower of Martley church is of a brilliant scarlet sandstone which has to be seen to be believed. The church at Shelsley Walsh is of limestone tufa, a pale-pink stone, which was also used in ancient Rome.

As in all Midland counties where an industrial life started in the 18th century, there is much 18th-century church

◁ **LITTLE MALVERN: ST GILES** – *formerly a monastery founded in 1125, it was dissolved in 1534 and only the presbytery and crossing were retained for worship by the local parishioners*

building. Not all of it was swept away by disgusted Victorians – indeed they did well by Great Witley, which is the most sumptuous classic interior in England – and there is a Worcestershire Baroque style and a Worcestershire Strawberry Hill Gothic style, both of which are individual and charming. Some of the Victorian work in the county is poor, all style and mock construction, and this applies to larger villas as well as churches. However, there are some, such as the bold church by W. J. Hopkins at Hallow, that are distinguished.

△ **BESFORD: ST PETER** – *the 14th-century timber-framed building is unique in the county*

Bridgnorth
A454
M6
WEST BROMWICH
DUDLEY
BIRMINGHAM
SHROPSHIRE
A458
HALESOWEN
STOURBRIDGE
WEST MIDLANDS
A442
A449
A38
M5
SOLIHULL
KIDDERMINSTER
A456
A491
A4117
A435
Chaddesley Corbett
M42
Dodford
A448
Rock
Stourport-on-Severn
BROMSGROVE
Knighton-on-Teme
A442
A456
A443
Stockton-on-Teme
Stoke Prior
A451
A449
A448
Tenbury Wells
REDDITCH
Great Witley
Shelsley Walsh
A443
Holt
DROITWICH
Ombersley
A441
WARWICK-SHIRE
Martley
A38
M5
Hallow
Dormston
A44
Warndon
WORCESTER
A422
A46
Bromyard
Spetchley
A44
A465
A449
WORCESTERSHIRE
A46
Newland
A4103
Croome D'Abitot
Besford
Pershore
Cropthorne
HEREFORDSHIRE
GREAT MALVERN
EVESHAM
A4103
M5
A438
Strensham
Elmley Castle
Little Malvern
A4104
Ripple
Ledbury
Queenhill
Bredon
A46
Broadway
Beckford
A44
Birtsmorton
A438
A417
M50
TEWKESBURY
A417
A38
A449
GLOUCESTERSHIRE
Ross-on-Wye
CHELTENHAM
A40
M5
GLOUCESTER
0
5 miles
0
5 km
A417

△ **BROADWAY: ST EADBURGHA** – *set in woodland near a popular village, it was built c. 1400 and restored in 1866*

BECKFORD † St John the Baptist

6ml10km E. of Tewkesbury

OS *SO976358* **GPS** *52.0210N, 2.0362W*

A 12th-century church of nave, central tower and chancel, it has interesting carved N. and S. nave doorways: the S. doorway is particularly richly carved, with a tympanum. The N. doorway is more worn – the tympanum above represents the Harrowing of Hell. The W. tower arch, formerly the chancel arch, has zigzags and a centaur. The chancel is pleasing Early English with a queen-post roof.

BESFORD † St Peter ★

7ml11km S.E. of Worcester

OS *SO910447* **GPS** *Bes*

This 14th-century timber-framed church is the only one of its kind in the county, and was heavily restored in 1880. There is a complete Decorated rood loft, and Jacobean communion rail and panelling. Good 16th-century monuments include a remarkable triptych with painted figures and heraldry, probably by Michael Salabos, 1588.

BIRTSMORTON

† St Peter and St Paul ★

6ml10km W. of Tewkesbury

OS *SO801355* **GPS** *52.0176N, 2.2912W*

The church is next to Birtsmorton Court, a handsome moated house. A charming little Decorated cruciform church with a Perpendicular tower, it has interesting monuments, including a marble monument on the N. chancel wall to Admiral William Caldwell, who died at Birtsmorton Court in 1718. The reredos is very unusual: the background has carvings of navigational instruments; above are flaming lamps and a cartouche with military trophies.

BREDON † St Giles ★★

3ml4km N. of Tewkesbury

OS *SO920369* **GPS** *52.0311N, 2.1179W*

The village, on the banks of the Avon, forms a delightful group, with its street of old houses leading to the church, the rectory as large and stately as a manor house, and the 14th-century tithe barn one of the finest in the country. The great church, much of it of the 12th century, with central tower and spire,

△ **CHADDESLEY CORBETT: ST CASSIAN** – *one of four dragons carved by the Herefordshire School on the bowl of the goblet-shaped Norman font*

dominates the scene. It is full of interest: a wonderfully carved and painted pulpit, old glass, medieval tiles in the sanctuary and a fine colourful memorial in the N. aisle to Sir Giles Reed, d. 1611, recumbent with his wife beside him. In the sanctuary is the 14th-century tomb of a couple and their daughter, and an exquisitely carved 14th-century stone coffin lid. In a recess on the N. chancel wall is the burial place of a crusader's heart. Altogether a most satisfying church to visit.

BROADWAY † St Eadburgha ★★

5m/8km S.E. of Evesham
OS *SP097362* **GPS** *52.0247N, 1.8600W*

The church is in a fine wooded setting, overlooking a gentle valley a short distance away from the frantic tourism of nearby Broadway. It is cruciform with a central tower, externally mainly Perpendicular, but with Early English arcades. The interior is almost stark in its lack of adornment, but the effect is of a devout and quiet space – almost monastic. The atmosphere is complemented by the lime-washed contemporary pews, all excellently thought out.

BROMSGROVE † St John the Baptist

12m/19km S.W. of Birmingham
OS *SO956706* **GPS** *52.3342N, 2.0646W*

This, the third church on the site, is mainly Perpendicular, built in red sandstone, with a mid-14th-century tower with panelled parapet and crocketed octagonal spire. At the E. end of the N. aisle are good Talbot and Stafford tombs with alabaster effigies; one furnished evidence that established Lord Talbot of Ingestre's claim to the Earldom of Shrewsbury in 1856. In the S. aisle is a carved organ screen from 1969, made by Robert Pancheri of the Bromsgrove Guild. His work can be seen in several churches in the region – St Agnes, Moseley, and St Augustine, Edgbaston.

CHADDESLEY CORBETT
† St Cassian ★

4m/6km S.E. of Kidderminster
OS *SO891735* **GPS** *52.3603N, 2.1610W*

The chancel of this church is the best example of Decorated work in the county. At the W. end is a celebrated Norman font with intertwined dragons, an outlier of the Herefordshire School. There is also a very good collection of monuments: of particular note is the tablet to Humphrey Packington, d. 1631, in black and white marble, and, in the N. chapel, a recumbent stone effigy of a 13th-century priest.

CROOME D'ABITOT

† St Mary Magdalene ★★

7ml11km S. of Worcester
OS *SO886450* **GPS** *52.1035N, 2.1672W*
Churches Conservation Trust

The church was built in 1758–63 by Robert Adam and Capability Brown as a feature of Croome Park, balancing a Classical temple that still exists, though the park has been ploughed up. It is an important instance of Gothic Survival, or rather of the logical development of the Perpendicular style. Inside it is spacious, dignified and airy, the piers being so slender as to foreshadow cast iron. The detail is beautifully executed, especially the carved wooden font by Adam, and the Rococo Gothic pulpit. The church has many Coventry monuments; note especially that of a Lord Keeper of the Great Seal, d. 1639, attributed to the workshop of Nicholas Stone.

CROPTHORNE † St Michael

3ml4km W. of Evesham
OS *SP000451* **GPS** *52.1045N, 2.0012W*

This 12th-century church contains a celebrated equal-armed stone cross of c. 800, the best piece of Anglo-Saxon art in the county. There is a delightful and colourful Comperesque reredos of 1932 by W. E. Ellery Anderson. There are also fragments of wall-painting over the arcade.

DODFORD † Holy Trinity and St Mary ★

2ml3km N.W. of Bromsgrove
OS *SO932724* **GPS** *52.3503N, 2.1010W*

This is a good church in Arts and Crafts Gothic by Arthur Bartlett, 1907–8. The decorative work was by the Bromsgrove Guild, particularly Celestino Panchini, who carved the organ case, pulpit and altar rails. There are gilded details on the rood screen, which supports an ornately decorated cross. This is an excellent church of its type.

DORMSTON † St Nicholas

8ml13km E. of Worcester
OS *SO987575* **GPS** *52.2164N, 2.0201W*

Remotely situated in Worcestershire countryside, this is a mainly 15th-century church with Early English origins. It has a delightful 15th-century timber-framed and gable-roofed W. tower, and a 14th-century S. porch. Inside are old pews, Jacobean altar rails and an old stone crucifix built into the S. wall near the altar.

ELMLEY CASTLE † St Mary ★★

4ml6km S.W. of Evesham
OS *SO981410* **GPS** *52.0674N, 2.0278W*

The village forms a very beautiful group at the foot of Bredon Hill, its wide street of pleasant houses leading directly to the church. This is a charming medieval building, with an 11th-century chancel and dominated by a 13th-century tower. The unusual font of c. 1200 has a 15th-century bowl supported on writhing dragons. There are two excellent 17th-century monuments: the first of c. 1631 has effigies of Giles Savage, his father, and his wife holding a closely wrapped infant. The second commemorates the first Earl of Coventry, d. 1699: a huge marble erection designed by William Stanton, the earl taking his ease beneath a pedimented arch. It was intended for Croome, but owing to a family row was placed here instead. It would have been a fine thing at Croome, and Elmley could well have been spared it. The only jarring feature of this interior is the aggressively scraped walls.

EVESHAM † All Saints

Between Abbey Mews and Market Place
OS *SP037436* **GPS** *52.0916N, 1.9469W*

This church forms a striking group with its neighbour St Lawrence and the old abbey Perpendicular bell-tower. All Saints is mainly Early English and Perpendicular, although there are traces of Norman origin. There is a fine mortuary chapel of c. 1513 for Clement Lichfield, Abbot of Evesham, with fan vaulting and pinnacles. The good Arts and Crafts chancel gates are from 1910, and the ornate Perpendicular W. porch is of note.

EVESHAM † St Lawrence ★

Abbey Mews
OS *SP036436* **GPS** *52.0914N, 1.9476W*
Churches Conservation Trust

Part of Evesham Abbey precincts group, this is a Perpendicular building, sympathetically altered in 1836 by H. Eginton, who added a N. aisle in similar style to the original S. aisle. The S. chapel, c. 1520, is a chantry chapel to St Clement, with good panelling and fan vaulting. In the W. tower is a striking tierceron star vault. The E. end has a fine six-light window with intricate tracery.

GREAT MALVERN † Great Malvern Priory (St Mary and St Michael) ★★

Between Abbey Rd, Grange Rd and Church St
OS *SO775458* **GPS** *52.1105N, 2.3286W*

A very imposing church set at the top of this genteel Victorian town, the priory is a Norman building extensively enlarged in the 15th century. This great priory is well known for its choir stalls, 22 misericords depicting everything from animals, sea monsters, hunting and angels, to some rather painful looking medical procedures! But above all is the priory's glass, which is of the highest interest. The intricate Perpendicular E. window has reset medieval glass, and of great interest is the 'Magnificat' window in the N. transept. The glass all dates from c. 1440–1506, and is the most complete set in England. Similarly striking are the unique and attractive 15th-century tiles on the screen walls of the chancel, which were made here and form the most complete scheme in England. There are many interesting monuments, particularly the one to Prior Walcher, d. 1135, and the fine altar tomb to John Knutsford and his wife, which shows their daughter in pious prayer at their feet.

GREAT WITLEY † St Michael ★★

8ml13km N.W. of Worcester
OS *SO769649* **GPS** *52.2825N, 2.3392W*

One of the finest Baroque churches in the country, it was built for the Foleys, perhaps by James Gibbs. Set in the midst of a park among Italianate gardens, the outside suggests southern Europe, and on entering the building one is taken straight there. Walls and ceiling are adorned with superb Baroque papier-mâché work by Bagutti, and on the ceiling are three paintings by Antonio Bellucci which, together with ten windows by Joshua Price, were taken from the Duke of Chandos's palace at Canons. All is exceedingly rich and of great beauty. The harmonious seating and other 19th-century furnishings in the Gothic style were introduced by Lord Dudley.

△ **HOLT: ST MARTIN** – *wonderful carving dating from the mid-12th century*

HALLOW † St Philip and St James

3ml4km N.W. of Worcester
OS *SO828579* **GPS** *52.2193N, 2.2524W*

By W. J. Hopkins, 1867–9, an ambitious Gothic essay in red and white stone with the nave roof supported on transverse arches. The flying buttresses supporting the nave roof are an interesting feature of this church, whose lofty steeple was only completed in 1900. The canopied alabaster and marble reredos is by local sculptor R. Boulton. The memorials are mostly from the old church, and of interest is that for Sir Charles Bell, d. 1842, whose work on the human nervous system gave rise to the naming of the condition of Bell's palsy.

△ **KNIGHTON-ON-TEME: ST MICHAEL** – *built with sandstone and tufa, the church has a Norman core, with Decorated and Perpendicular additions and alterations*

HOLT † St Martin ★

5m/8km N. of Worcester
OS *SO829625* **GPS** *52.2609N, 2.2511W*

A pleasing group of 12th-century church and 14th-century castle, remote from other buildings. Of great interest are the richly carved mid-12th-century doorways and chancel arch – the finest in the county. The tower is 15th-century, and the nave is fine Norman. In the S. chapel is a delicate stained-glass Annunciation of 1450. An incongruous feature is the 19th-century mosaic placed over the chancel arch – a copy of the 5th-century mosaic in Ravenna's Mausoleum of Galla Placidia. This was obtained by Mrs Sales, wife of the incumbent of the time. She was a lady of artistic inclinations, who also acquired old glass from Nuremberg for the church and carved the pulpit and stone reading desk.

KIDDERMINSTER
† St Mary and All Saints

Between St Mary's Ringway, Glensmore Street and the river
OS *SO830769* **GPS** *52.3902N, 2.2510W*

Best seen from the nearby canal, this is a very large 16th-century town church of red sandstone with much Victorian and later restoration, notably the Whittall Chapel by Sir Giles Gilbert Scott, 1922. There is a good screen carved by Robert Pancheri of the Bromsgrove Guild, a well-carved reredos of the Last Supper under an elaborate ogee canopy by Hopkins and Boulton, and good medieval brasses and tombs.

KNIGHTON-ON-TEME † St Michael ★

13m/21km S.W. of Kidderminster
OS *SO633699* **GPS** *52.3261N, 2.5394W*

A venerable and simple old church in a remote rural setting, it is mainly 12th-century, with a good S. doorway set in a projection with a blind arcade of four arches over it. The chancel arch is also Norman and flanked by blind arcades. The W. bell-tower is supported on huge timbers internally and separated from the nave by a 15th-century timber screen; the bell-turret above is a 20th-century replacement. The good nave roof is of the same date with collar and tie-beam trusses.

LITTLE MALVERN † St Giles ★

4m/6km S. of Great Malvern
OS *SO770403* **GPS** *52.0614N, 2.3364W*

The presbytery and crossing, surmounted by a tower, are all that remain of this monastic church. Seen in conjunction with the adjoining court, which incorporates parts of the domestic range of the monastery, against the background of the hills, it forms a very pleasing picture. Bishop Alcock rebuilt most of the priory, including the church, at the end of the 15th century. Inside are interesting late 15th-century glass and floor tiles.

△ **RIPPLE: ST MARY** – *a 15th-century misericord depicting one of the labours of the months, possibly the month of December, the time for killing the pig*

MARTLEY † St Peter ★★

7m/11km N.W. of Worcester
OS *SO756598* **GPS** *52.2360N, 2.3582W*

One of Betjeman's favourites, the red sandstone church is just off the village street in quiet, lush countryside between the Severn and Teme, and should be seen when the fruit blossom is clothing all the hills and filling all the valleys with its beauty: there is nothing in England to compare with west Worcestershire in the spring. The 12th–15th-century church has good 13th-century curtain pattern wall-paintings in the chancel and 15th-century scenes on the N. side of the nave, together with the Arms of Mortimer and Despenser. The last restoration was by Sir Charles Nicholson in 1909, when the simple and appropriate screen was installed. This is a church of simple dignity and should not be missed.

NEWLAND † St Leonard ★

2m/3km N. of Great Malvern
OS *SO795484* **GPS** *52.1343N, 2.2995W*

By P. C. Hardwick, 1862–4, this is a grouping of a stone church and brick almshouses, all in French Gothic style. The interior of the church is richly decorated, walls covered with mural paintings in a style known as spirit fresco. Everywhere are coloured marbles and mouldings, the windows filled with good stained glass by Clayton & Bell and Hardman. Of note are the sedilia, with slender marble columns rising to ornate crocketed pinnacles, the reredos by Boulton and the Bath-stone pulpit, but the church's most striking internal feature is the chancel's S. arcade: four richly veined Levantine marble pillars rising to frescoed arches.

OMBERSLEY † St Andrew ★

4m/6km W. of Droitwich
OS *SO844635* **GPS** *52.2699N, 2.2294W*

Thomas Rickman, self-taught architect, amateur antiquarian and leading figure of the Gothic Revival movement, built the church in 1825–9, and it is considered to be one of his best. It is set back from the village street, a well-found estate church in the Decorated style. It has an agreeable exterior with handsome W. tower and well-proportioned recessed spire. Tall and spacious inside, the nave has a very pleasing vaulted ceiling. From Rickman's studies came the terms Early English, Decorated English and Perpendicular English.

PERSHORE
† Pershore Abbey (Holy Cross) ★

9m/13km S.E. of Worcester
OS *SO947457* **GPS** *52.1104N, 2.0776W*

All that remains of the great abbey church is the presbytery, one transept and the

△ **ROCK: ST PETER AND ST PAUL** – *Norman carving round the north doorway*

central tower. There is beautiful 13th-century arcading on the presbytery and copious ball-flowers on the 14th-century tower. The chancel (now the nave) has excellent Gothic arcades, and the lierne vaulting is breathtaking – a study in itself. The aisles are finely rib-vaulted, and there are some lovely carved stone bosses, some with Green Men. The 19th-century apse does not adequately match the fine architecture seen here.

QUEENHILL † St Nicholas

3m/4km N.W. of Tewkesbury
OS *SO860366* **GPS** *52.0281N, 2.2044W*

Although close to the hum of the M50, St Nicholas is an isolated and beautifully situated field church. Dating from the 11th century, the modestly proportioned W. tower (with 1855 saddleback roof), nave and chancel form a charming building, enhanced by the 19th-century timber S. porch. There are fragments of 14th-century glass in the N. nave window. The church is worth visiting for its setting alone.

RIPPLE † St Mary ★

3m/4km N. of Tewkesbury
OS *SO876377* **GPS** *52.0379N, 2.1819W*

This is an almost unaltered late 12th-century church of chancel, central tower with 18th-century top, transepts and aisled nave. There is some 15th-century glass and a fine set of 15th-century misericords showing the labours of the months. A charming place with a sense of continuity and abiding peace.

ROCK † St Peter and St Paul

7m/11km S.W. of Kidderminster
OS *SO731711* **GPS** *52.3379N, 2.3954W*

Visible from miles around, the church is a grand 12th-century fabric, with excellent Norman stone carving, notably on the lofty chancel arch and the N. doorway. The 12th-century font tub has low relief strapwork and is set on 19th-century shafts. The Perpendicular tower is dated 1510.

SHELSLEY WALSH † St Andrew ★★

10m/16km N.W. of Worcester
OS *SO721629* **GPS** *52.2641N, 2.4094W*

This is a very charming church set on the slopes of the Teme Valley. St Andrew's is of the 12th–13th centuries, built of local tufa, and was sensitively restored by George Truefitt in 1859. The N. door arch has deep zigzags and a plain tympanum. The nave and chancel form one space, and the nave roof is fine tie- and collar-beam. The late 15th-century screen – one of the finest in the county – has linenfold lower panels and open traceried upper panels; at the S. the screen returns to form a parclosed chapel. There is an unusual wooden table-tomb to Francis Walsh, d. 1596, with pilasters and heraldic panels, and some 15th-century floor tiles in the chancel. The unfortunate proximity of a hill-climbing motor racetrack makes it imperative to choose a quiet time to visit.

SPETCHLEY † All Saints

3m/4km E. of Worcester
OS *SO895539* **GPS** *52.1837N, 2.1540W*
Churches Conservation Trust

Adjoining Spetchley Park, the church is a small, mainly 14th-century building: its principal feature is a fine S. chapel of 1629,

SHELSLEY WALSH: ST ANDREW – *built in the 12th–13th centuries with coursed and squared tufa blocks, and with a timber bell-turret added in 1859* ▷

△ **STOCKTON-ON-TEME: ST ANDREW** – *its leaning weatherboarded bell-turret with slate roof and timber-framed south porch give great character to the mid-12th-century sandstone core*

crowded with a series of Berkeley monuments and heraldry. Of particular note is the flamboyant coloured central chest tomb to Sir Rowland Berkeley, d. 1611, and his wife, whose effigies lie under an arched canopy supported by Ionic columns and flanked by obelisks at each corner.

STOCKTON-ON-TEME † St Andrew ★

12m/19km N.W. of Worcester
OS *SO716673* **GPS** *52.3034N, 2.4177W*

St Andrew's stands in a hamlet on the slopes of the Teme Valley – a small 12th-century church with 18th-century additions. It is a simple fabric, with an engaging tipsy wooden bell-turret. There is interesting Norman work here: the S. doorway, protected by the 15th-century timber porch, has a rustic stone panel above with a much eroded relief of a winged figure and a tree; and a good simple chancel arch, on either side of which are two stone carved panels showing a lion and the Angus Dei. There is a squint on the S. side of the chancel arch, and in the chancel is a restored late 16th-century painted wooden tomb to Thomas Walsh, d. 1693, and a 13th-century ledger stone to Redulphius, the first known rector of the church, 1284.

STOKE PRIOR † St Michael ★

2m/3km S. of Bromsgrove
OS *SO949676* **GPS** *52.3074N, 2.0757W*

A fine church of c. 1200, with a big Early English tower topped by a modern shingled spire. The whole building is an interesting early group with its chapel, chancel and sacristy. The N. arcade is Norman, the S. arcade is Early English. There are some early monuments within, and of interest is the stained glass: the E. window by S. Evans, 1860, commemorates the decision by the philanthropical 'Salt King' John Corbett to cease employing women and children in the local salt pans (he raised the mens' wages in compensation). Corbett also paid for J. L. Pearson's restoration of 1894–5.

STRENSHAM † St John the Baptist ★

5m/8km N. of Tewkesbury

OS *SO910406* **GPS** *52.0640N, 2.1315W*

Churches Conservation Trust

Another church hard by the M50, St John's enjoys a surprisingly quiet rural elevated setting with views E. over the Avon to Bredon Hill, and W. to the rampart of the Malvern Hills. Its rendered tower is unmistakable, and inside are many monuments to the Russell family dating from the 14th to 19th centuries, Tudor pews in the broad nave, and a W. gallery that incorporates most of the 15th-century rood screen, including more than 20 painted panels.

TENBURY WELLS

† St Michael and all Angels

8m/12km N.E. of Leominster

OS *SO582657* **GPS** *52.2883N, 2.6132W*

By Henry Woodyer, 1854–8, the church was built for the college founded by the composer Sir Frederick Gore Ouseley. Since 1985 it has served as the parish church of Tenbury. It is a marvellous, steeply roofed cruciform church with a polygonal apse. There is beautiful tracery and, inside, ornate carvings to the capitals. The High Victorian interior has sanctuary glass by Hardman. The church is linked to the college buildings, also by Woodyer, by a timber cloister.

WARNDON † St Nicholas ★

3m/4km N.E. of Worcester

OS *SO887568* **GPS** *52.2101N, 2.1656W*

A small field church in a parish with no village, now near Worcester's outskirts and bypass. Close to farm buildings, this is a very simple little 12th-century church with a delightful 15th-century half-timbered tower with single-gable roof. The unspoiled interior has some 14th-century glass, a 17th-century communion rail, a sanctuary floor with 15th-century Malvern School tiles and box pews – very charming and untouched by the Victorians.

WORCESTER † All Saints ★

Deansway

OS *SO847548* **GPS** *52.1919N, 2.2240W*

This large and spacious mid-18th-century church was possibly built by Thomas White in the Classical manner on an earlier foundation: it has dignity, space and light to an unusual degree, with fine tunnel vaulting to the nave roof. The lower part of the tower is 15th-century; the upper storeys 18th-century in the style of Wren. The E. end is what Pevsner describes as the 'real' façade. Inside are fine Doric columns, and a reredos painted by Josiah Rushton of the Royal Worcester Porcelain Works, 1867. The interior is a world away from the horrible swirl of traffic in the adjacent 1960s road 'improvement' scheme.

WORCESTER † St Swithun

Church Street

OS *SO850549* **GPS** *52.1926N, 2.2202W*

Churches Conservation Trust

By E. and T. Woodward, 1734–6, St Swithun's is a perfectly preserved example of an 18th-century church with all its furnishings intact – one of a group of significant Georgian Worcester churches that also includes All Saints. The only remnant of the earlier church is the Perpendicular W. tower. The elegant E. elevation has a Venetian window, pilasters and urns, and the marvellous interior has a Gothic plaster ceiling and Roman Doric screen walls to the chancel. Above the fine three-decker pulpit and tester is a gilded Pelican in her Piety.

YORKSHIRE – EAST RIDING

Here lie the broad acres of Yorkshire. With the Wolds as backbone, the Riding stretches from Flamborough in the north to Spurn Head in the south, and westward towards Malton and York. There are three distinct regions. The first is the gently undulating Plain of Holderness, a peninsula of distant views and wide skies, whose winding lanes reflect the strong light from the sea.

The indigenous cobbles, laboriously gathered from the boulder clay, form the material for its trim churches and old farmsteads. The former culminate in the Gothic splendours of Humberside, where medieval wealth and proximity to navigable water are seen in the village churches of the 'Saxon Line', and in the city of Kingston upon Hull.

The medieval city was small, and concentrated around the docks and along the River Hull. It has a memorable church in Holy Trinity, one of the largest parish churches in England, with a tower which is still one of the city's chief landmarks. The 19th century saw rapid expansion to the north and new churches by Street and Temple Moore. The 20th century has pushed big housing estates out into the countryside, but little in the way of memorable church architecture has resulted.

The second region is the area that forms the dry valleys, ancient barrows and protective belts of trees in the landscape of the Wolds. Except in the Bayle and north-west tower at Bridlington, chalk is principally confined to domestic work. Norman fonts abound in the sturdy churches, evidence of rebuilding after the Harrying of the North in the 11th century. Beverley and Driffield grace the eastern slopes, whilst the churches of the central Wolds bear the indelible mark of the inveterate 19th-century church restorer Sir Tatton Sykes, 5th Bart.

The third region is the Vale of York, watered by the Derwent, which takes on the aspect of the Low Countries. Here, tree-lined lanes lead to remote villages, like Aughton with its melancholy atmosphere. The towers, especially the upstanding one at Holme-upon-Spalding Moor and Bishop Skirlaw's at Howden, are marked features in the plain.

◁ **PATRINGTON: ST PATRICK** – *the many pinnacled and crocketed 'Queen of Holderness'*

ALDBROUGH † St Bartholomew

11m/19km N.E. of Kingston upon Hull

OS *TA244387* **GPS** *53.8298N, 0.1110W*

The stout tower is the clearest sign of St Bartholomew's Norman origins, although a circular inscribed 11th-century sundial in the S. aisle records an earlier founding of the church: 'Ulf who ordered this church to be built for his own and Gunware's souls'. The church was extensively rebuilt in the 19th century – note the 19th-century arcades and E. window. In the N. chancel chapel is a fine 14th-century alabaster effigy of Sir John de Mulsa, d. 1377.

ATWICK † St Lawrence

15m/25km N.E. of Beverley

OS *TA184507* **GPS** *53.9397N, 0.1968W*

This is an eccentric 1876 French Gothic Revival church in red brick by H. R. Gough, who is noted for his collaborations with Seddon and the Gothic Revival masterpiece of St Cuthbert, in London. The church has a distinctive saddleback tower and tall, narrow, round-headed windows, and the inside is all exposed red brickwork under a wagon roof, with oak and pitch pine furnishings.

AUGHTON † All Saints ★

11m/18km W. of Market Weighton

OS *SE701386* **GPS** *53.8394N, 0.9352W*

Remote and attractively situated in water meadows between the River Derwent and earthworks of the former Aske residence, the sturdy 1536 tower displays several shields under which is a carved inscription that translates as 'Christopher the second son of Robert Aske Knight ought not to forget AD 1536'. Among several pieces of graffiti is a carved newt or 'Asker' (Old English for newt) – a rebus on the family name. The interior is largely unspoilt: the broad Norman chancel arch of three orders with chevrons is very good, as is the tall arcaded Norman tub font. In the chancel is a brass to Sir Richard Aske and his wife Margaret, d. 1460.

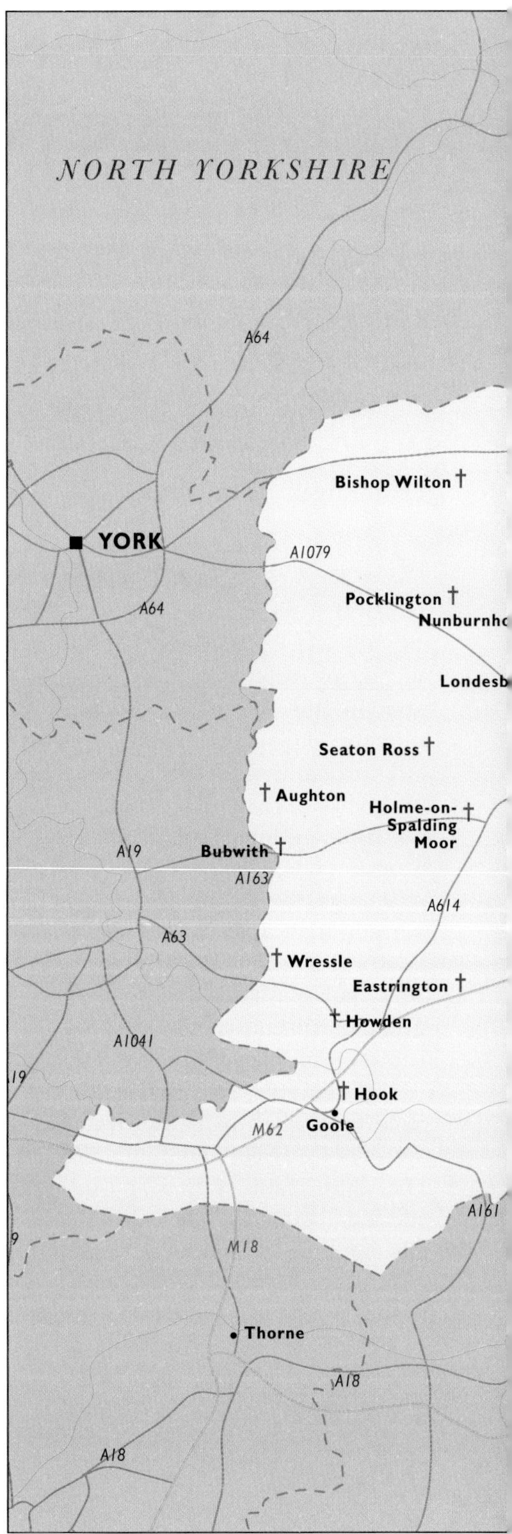

BEVERLEY: ST JOHN OF BEVERLEY – *one of the finest Gothic churches in Europe* ▷

△ **BEVERLEY: ST JOHN** – *finely carved figure of a medieval musician*

BAINTON † St Andrew

5m/8km S.W. of Driffield
OS *SE965523* **GPS** *53.9583N, 0.5305W*

The church, known as the 'Cathedral of the Wolds', dominates a pretty village, and is almost purely 14th-century Curvilinear. The nave and aisles have lofty arcades, the chancel is spacious, and the W. tower was once crowned by an octagonal spire. In the chancel is a worn brass to Roger Godeale, priest, d. 1429. There is a coloured wall monument to Robert Faucon, an ejected rector, dated 1661, and in the S. aisle a large niche tomb to the Mauley family: note the wyvern tugging at the shield.

BESSINGBY † St Magnus

1m/2km S.W. of Bridlington
OS *TA159659* **GPS** *54.0764N, 0.2301W*

Rebuilt almost completely in 1893–5 by Temple Moore, the church is charmingly situated in a village amongst trees on a flank of the Wolds. The dominant feature is the strong central tower and recessed spire. This is a successful 19th-century version of a late 14th-century church, preserving a fine Norman font and several good monuments, one to Lady Ann Hudson by R. J. Wyatt, 1818.

BEVERLEY † St John of Beverley, the Minster ★★

Between Minster Moorgate, St John Street and Minster Yard South
OS *TA037392* **GPS** *53.8392N, 0.4246W*

This is a superb building exhibiting work of all periods, and stands with the finest Gothic churches in Europe. Formerly collegiate, it has double transepts, a choir and main transepts with double aisles, all Early English. These merge almost imperceptibly into a Decorated nave, with an elegant Perpendicular W. front and twin towers as the crowning glory. The vaulting is breathtaking, spanning the entire length of the building, only briefly interrupted by the stately crossing arches. In the chancel is a 14th-century altar screen with a platform above, and to the N. is the superb Decorated Percy tomb. The choir stalls have canopies and misericords by local carvers – one depicts a fox with a rosary (representing a Dominican friar) preaching to a gaggle of geese (the congregation). Stone carved minstrels decorate the capitals, eaves and corners of the nave – a veritable visual encyclopaedia of early instruments. Hawksmoor designed the great W. door with Evangelists and their symbols; the font cover was also designed by him.

BEVERLEY † St Mary ★★

Hengate
OS *TA031397* **GPS** *53.8442N, 0.4337W*

How lucky Beverley is to have not only its outstanding minster but also St Mary's, one of the most beautiful parish churches in England. Cruciform, with a rich exterior, the nave and tower were rebuilt after the fall of the old 12th-century tower in 1520, and the W. front, with its beautiful window, stone panelling and polygonal turrets with open tracery, is simply breathtaking. The interior is spacious, the arcade piers and small capitals recalling those at Hull, but here the bases are exaggerated. The choir is in the pre-collapse part of the church, and the 14th-century stalls with misericords include hunting scenes and a tusked elephant. Whoever the carvers were, they certainly celebrated country pursuits here. A pier on the N. side has a delightfully coloured group of five minstrels – 1530 benefactors of the rebuilding, the Northern Guild of Musicians. On the pillar

BEVERLEY: ST JOHN OF BEVERLEY – *the vaulting throughout the church is especially noteworthy* ▷

is inscribed 'Thys Pyllor made the meynstyrls [sic]'. The original roofs were repainted under Leslie Moore, and 19th-century restorations were by A. W. N. and E. W. Pugin.

BISHOP WILTON † St Edith ★

5m/8km E. of Stamford Bridge
OS *SE798552* **GPS** *53.9868N, 0.7841W*

The church lies behind the main street, which follows a stream down the chalk scarp of the Wolds. Pearson did a wonderful job in his restoration of 1858–9, such as few Victorian architects could have achieved. The chancel arch has original beak-heads and scrolls. The S. doorway is a successful reconstruction from old materials, with animals, faces, beak-heads and human forms. The Norman chancel is separated from the nave by a good ironwork screen by George Street, and the fine black-and-white mosaic floor in the chancel is by Salviati, based on a design in the Vatican.

BOYNTON † St Andrew

3m/4km W. of Bridlington
OS *TA136679* **GPS** *54.0951N, 0.2635W*

Situated close to the gates of Boyton Hall Manor, at the end of a village street of white-washed chalk cottages, is a delightful Georgian church with a late 14th-century tower. The classical nave and chancel were rebuilt in brick by John Carr, 1768, with 'Gothick' details by Batty Langley, an eccentric garden designer and self-appointed expert on 'ancient architecture'. Until the restoration, 1910, by J. Bilson, the altar stood beneath an architectural baldacchino. Beyond lies the Strickland mortuary chapel containing family monuments, one of which is a cenotaph attributed to William Kent. The tower has a Gothic plaster vault and gallery, formerly the squire's pew. The unusual turkey lectern and font cover were designed by Francis Johnson – Sir William Strickland introduced wild turkeys to England in the 16th century.

BRIDLINGTON † St Mary

5m/8km S.W. of Flamborough Head
OS *TA177679* **GPS** *54.0943N, 0.2018W*

This is another glorious E. Riding town church, the nave of a former Augustinian priory. It forms a group with the 14th-century Bayle Gate. In 1876–80 George Gilbert Scott Jnr completed the W. towers, left unfinished at the Dissolution, between which is set one of the grandest Perpendicular windows in Yorkshire. Inside, fine 13th- and 14th-century arcades support a triforium and clerestory; the space is unified, with only the style of roof construction, from hammer-beam in the W. to arch-braced tie-beam in the E., marking the transition from the nave to the chancel, in which is a fine Jesse Tree window by Wailes. Behind the choir stalls is a carved group of angelic musicians, one of whom appears to be playing a tenor saxophone. At the W. end is a black marble tomb slab commemorating Walter de Gant, the founder of the priory.

BUBWITH † All Saints

5m/8km N.W. of Howden
OS *SE711361* **GPS** *53.8170N, 0.9205W*

A fine church beside the River Derwent at the end of the village street, its early 15th-century tower, S. aisle and clerestory were built with a bequest by Nicholas de Bubwith. A Norman chancel arch leads from the 13th-century nave to the chancel of the same period, in the N. side of which is a funeral helm and sword. The pews have good Jacobean fronts.

BURTON AGNES † St Martin

5m/8km S.W. of Bridlington
OS *TA102632* **GPS** *54.0535N, 0.3180W*

The church forms a pleasant group with a medieval manor house and Jacobean hall. It is Norman, with 13th- and 14th-century alterations and a fine late 15th-century W. tower. The chancel was restored c. 1840 by Archdeacon Wilberforce, son of the great Victorian social reformer, whose likeness appears on a corbel, and in the N. arcade are the mutilated remains of a Georgian Doric squire's pew. There are many Somerville and Griffith monuments in the Boyton Chapel, one with three coffins in place of effigies and two grisly panels of skulls and bones.

BURTON PIDSEA † St Peter

Anciently St Peter and St Paul; 5m/8km E. of Hull
OS *TA251311* **GPS** *53.7612N, 0.1023W*

A pleasant, small Holderness church, it is built of cobbles with freestone dressings, and is mainly Decorated and Perpendicular.

HOLME-UPON-SPALDING MOOR: ALL SAINTS – *the pierced, battlemented tower of many periods is a landmark for miles around* ▷

△ **HOWDEN: ST PETER AND ST PAUL** – *a canopied tomb in the Saltmarshe Chantry*

The S. doorway has traceried spandrels, and the brick E. end of the chancel dates from 1838.

DRIFFIELD † All Saints

11m/18km S.W. of Bridlington
OS *TA022579* **GPS** *54.0078N, 0.4420W*

A handsome, many-pinnacled 15th-century W. tower announces this Norman church, with 14th-century S. aisle and 15th-century N. aisle. It was restored by George Gilbert Scott Jnr who rebuilt the chancel and the N. aisle and added the S. porch, 1879–80. The chancel and Lady Chapel Gothic Revival screens are by Temple Moore, 1904 and 1909, and the Lady Chapel contains a delightful collection of architectural bits and pieces – mouldings and capitals with water-leaf carving.

EASTRINGTON † St Michael ★

3m/4km N.E. of Howden
OS *SE796299* **GPS** *53.7601N, 0.7933W*

This fine church has a Norman core with 12th- and 13th-century work in the nave and chancel. The battlemented W. tower and clerestories were added in the 15th century. There is interesting patching to the N. chancel arcade following a collapse in 1632; it was largely rebuilt with a square central pier and oak timber framing. The altar tomb in the N. chapel is of Judge Portington, d. 1456, shown wearing a pigtail. In the S. porch is a large Norman stone carved with eight fantastic beasts.

FLAMBOROUGH † St Oswald

4m/6km N.E. of Bridlington
OS *TA226701* **GPS** *54.1127N, 0.1258W*

The church stands rather squat and sentinel-like at the approach to the village. Its W. tower is by C. Hodgson Fowler, 1897. Generally the church is much restored but rich in atmosphere, with an early 16th-century rood screen and loft retaining considerable traces of original colour, the work of Ripon carvers. There is an altar tomb to Marmaduke Constable, d. 1520, who fought at Flodden Field, and a monument to 'Wild' Walter Strickland, 1671, whose pardon granted by Charles II is framed in the nave. In the vestry is an intriguing curiosity – a pair of white paper gloves used at the funerals of maidens.

GOXHILL † St Giles ★

12m/19km N.E. of Hull
OS *TA185448* **GPS** *53.8860N, 0.1981W*

This is a charming and unusual church of cobble and brick – late Georgian, with an overhanging pyramidal roof on its tower, which imparts a Mediterranean look. Note the overhanging eaves over the chancel, almost like a bonnet. The pointed Y-tracery windows are from 1849, and the church is lit by oil lamps. Set into the chancel floor is a finely detailed 14th-century effigy of Johanna de Lellay.

HARPHAM † St John of Beverley ★

5m/8km N.E. of Driffield
OS *TA092615* **GPS** *54.0387N, 0.3336W*

A delightful and interesting church with a Norman core, it was extensively remodelled in the 14th century, when it acquired its bold W. tower that rises above the village. The E. end of the chancel was rebuilt in brick, 1827, and a conservative restoration by Temple Moore, 1908–14, retained the Georgian fittings. There is a fine collection of medieval and 18th-century monuments to the St Quintin family in the N. chapel, including two brasses: the monument N. of the sanctuary is to Charlotte St Quintin, 1762. The N. chapel windows have excellent 18th-century heraldic glass, by William Peckitt of York.

HEDON † St Augustine ★

6m/10km E. of Hull
OS *TA188287* **GPS** *53.7415N, 0.1997W*

The church is known as the 'King of Holderness' and is the focal point of the small market town of Hedon. The great 15th-century central tower has fine traceried windows, pierced parapets and distinctive crocketed finials. The transepts and chancel are Early English, and there is a Perpendicular E. window. The N. transept has a fine elevation, with grouped lancets and recessed doorway, and much dog-tooth carving – this has a Continental look to it. The S. transept was all restored and rebuilt by G. E. Street, 1866–8. Of great interest inside are the 14th-century octagonal font, a 13th-century marble ledger stone, a Baroque cartouche in the N. transept and a 14th-century effigy of a knight in the chancel.

HOLME-UPON-SPALDING MOOR † All Saints

5m/8km S.W. of Market Weighton
OS *SE820389* **GPS** *53.8402N, 0.7538W*

Unmistakable on the crest of an island hill rising from the flat plain four miles W. of the Wold scarp: the pierced, battlemented 15th-century tower emerges from tufted tree-tops and provides a landmark for the surrounding area. It is mainly 13th- and 15th-century with early 18th-century brick parapets and porch. The charming unspoilt interior has considerable remains of a medieval screen, a Jacobean pulpit with tester, an 18th-century gallery housing a 17th-century barrel organ by J. Hunton of York, and early 19th-century Gothic box pews.

HOOK † St Mary

1m/2km N.E. of Goole
OS *SE759255* **GPS** *53.7204N, 0.8511W*

This small, intimate church stands in a picturesque churchyard and dates mostly from the 14th and 15th centuries, though with considerable restoration in the 19th. A chancel window shows Queen Victoria visiting the Boer War wounded. Recent renovation has revealed a medieval wall-painting of Christ in Majesty. Outside are many marked cholera graves from the locality.

HOWDEN † St Peter and St Paul ★★

3m/4km N. of Goole across R. Ouse
OS *SE748282* **GPS** *53.7453N, 0.8672W*
English Heritage

At the building's core is a large cruciform collegiate church of the late 13th and 14th centuries. After the Reformation, the parishioners retained the nave, while the E. end fell into disrepair. The choir collapsed in 1696, and remains a ruin to this day; together with the chapter house, it is now in the care of English Heritage. The Perpendicular crossing tower is very good, as is the Decorated W. front, whose buttresses terminate with little open-traceried turrets. The S. transept contains the Saltmarshe Chantry, housing several medieval tombs and effigies, including a notable early 14th-century effigy of a knight in chainmail. A very rare 15th-century stone pulpitum, its niches containing salvaged statues from the ruined portions of the church, now serves as an imposing reredos. And in front of the reredos is a delightful altar by Robert 'Mouseman' Thomas, 1929.

KINGSTON-UPON-HULL
† Holy Trinity ★★

Market Place
OS *TA099285* **GPS** *53.7418N, 0.3344W*

The largely intact old town surrounding Holy Trinity has sheltered it from some of the excessive and dreary modern surroundings. The W. front of this imposing cruciform town church overlooks a market square. The earliest medieval brickwork is in the Decorated choir and transepts, while the central tower and nave are 15th-century. Inside, the walls are mere screens for glass: the tracery is outstanding, from the Decorated tulip tracery in the E. window to the Perpendicular work further W. Look up in the crossing, and there are good painted ceiling panels and lierne vaulting. At the W. end is a fine 14th-century marble carved font where William Wilberforce, leader of the anti-slave trade movement, was baptised. The De la Pole family is commemorated particularly well in the S. choir aisle by 14th-century alabaster effigies.

LANGTOFT † St Peter

6m/10km N. of Driffield
OS *TA008670* **GPS** *54.0892N, 0.4599W*

Very thoroughly over-restored in 1900 by Hodgson Fowler – he added a N. aisle – the church nevertheless managed to retain the original Norman tower, S. porch and a portion of the S. aisle. The wonderful Norman font is from the lost village of Cottam, with Adam and Eve, St Margaret and the Dragon and St Laurence, all rudely carved.

LOCKINGTON † St Mary ★

5m/8km N. of Beverley
OS *SE997468* **GPS** *53.9083N, 0.4835W*

In a well-kept, unspoilt village to the N. of Beverley is a stone church, much patched with brickwork, in which are the mutilated remains of a Norman chancel arch – the space above filled with screenwork by Temple Moore, 1893. The Estoft Chapel to the S. is a testament to two feuding families, the Estofts and the Moysers. In the centre is a tomb chest with the reclining effigy of Mary Moyser, d. 1633. But the Estofts dominate, the painted panelling of 1634 emblazoned with Estoft Arms and those of family alliances.

LONDESBOROUGH † All Saints ★

2m/3km N. of Market Weighton
OS *SE868453* **GPS** *53.8974, -0.6796*

The church stands in a pretty estate village: it is 12th- and 13th-century, and over the Norman S. doorway is a celebrated 11th-century Anglo-Danish cross head. Inside are funeral banners and brasses to the Earls of Burlington, including one to the celebrated Palladian architect Richard Burlington, who designed Chiswick House and the York Assembly Rooms. At the W. end of the S. aisle is the funeral helm of the lst Earl of Burlington, 1698.

NORTH DALTON † All Saints

6m/10km S.W. of Driffield
OS *SE934522* **GPS** *53.9575N, 0.5770W*

A pretty, modest church, it stands on a knoll above the village with its pond. There is much Norman work: the S. door, with carved capitals, the font and the chancel arch, carved with zigzags. The tower is a Perpendicular addition, and the E. window glass is by Morris & Co. to a Burne-Jones design, 1892, and depicts the Crucifixion.

NORTH NEWBALD † St Nicholas ★

4m/6km S.E. of Market Weighton
OS *SE911365* **GPS** *53.8175, -0.6164*

This austere, aisleless 12th-century church is

△ **NUNBURNHOLME: ST JAMES** – *the castellated tower and south porch were Temple Moore's additions in the early 20th century to a Norman core*

very fine – perhaps the finest Norman church in the E. Riding. The lower part of the tower with its round arches is Norman. Above is an Early English bell stage, surmounted by 15th-century battlements. There is a well-preserved corbel table, and three Norman doorways, the best of which is the S. doorway, elaborately carved, with a carved seated figure of Christ above. The late 12th-century circular font has conventional carved foliage and a 17th-century cover, and the crossing has excellent Norman archways. The various wall monuments include one to the Royalist Philip Monckton, who served with distinction in the Civil War.

NUNBURNHOLME † St James

3m/4km E. of Pocklington
OS *SE847477* **GPS** *53.9193N, 0.7107W*

This little Norman church contains features and items of great interest. The reset tower arch, formerly the Norman chancel arch, is carved with fantastic and bizarre faces, but of the greatest interest is the celebrated 10th-century Anglo-Norse cross shaft under the tower, with carved figures, foliage and beasts. The tower itself is of 1901–2, by Temple Moore.

PATRINGTON † St Patrick ★★

4m/6km S.W. of Withernsea
OS *TA315225* **GPS** *53.6828N, 0.0096W*

The 'Queen of Holderness' is celebrated as a church of exceptional Decorated Gothic. The church is cruciform with double-aisled transepts, the central tower being crowned by an open corona from which rises a lofty spire. Free-flowing Curvilinear tracery predominates throughout, and in the nave there are sophisticated carved foliated capitals. In the crossing are animated corbels depicting villagers, monks and animals. The splendid Easter Sepulchre – unusual in that it still has its slumbering soldiers and figure of Christ – combines with the sedilia and piscina to make a unified group in the chancel. Of the relatively modern age is a very good 1936 gilded reredos by Harold Gibbons, in memory of King George V, who held the Lordship of the Manor.

△ **RUSTON PARVA: ST NICHOLAS** – *the little leaning tower adds to the character of this quaint rustic church of 1832, given an elegant dash by its Y-tracery windows*

PAULL † St Andrew and St Mary

2m/3km S.W. of Hedon

OS *TA172257* **GPS** *53.7149N, 0.2252W*

This is a strange landscape close to the Humber, with masts and funnels passing along the S. horizon. A lighthouse tower rises from the village, but the church is on a knoll apart, its high, bare crossing tower a landmark. The Perpendicular church is cruciform, and was extensively restored by J. T. Webster in 1877–9. Of interest inside is a stone lectern in the chancel wall and some 14th-century glass in the E. window.

POCKLINGTON † All Saints ★

7m/11km N.W. of Market Weighton

OS *SE802489* **GPS** *53.9307N, 0.7795W*

A tall Perpendicular tower marks out this large market town church, which is all of the 12th to 15th centuries. The tower has richly carved corbels, and the late 12th-century N. arcade capitals are intricately ornamented with beasts, foliage and humans, in contrast to those of the more restrained 13th-century S. arcade. The high pointed tower arch is also carved with grotesques and foliage. Outside is the burial place of one Thomas Pelling, a travelling showman whose set piece was flying by rope between two fixed points. Sadly at All Saints things did not go according to plan.

RUSTON PARVA † St Nicholas ★

4m/6km N.E. of Driffield

OS *TA064616* **GPS** *54.0395N, 0.3758W*

A delightful surprise awaits those who follow a grassy path uphill from the pantiled farms and cottages of the tiny village: all by itself in a field stands a minute Gothic church of pale brick with a bell-turret slightly awry. The cast-iron pillars inside are dated 1832, and the Norman font, two-decker pulpit and box pews all make the interior rather special. The walls and chancel arch are whitewashed, and the communion rails painted white.

SCORBOROUGH † St Leonard ★

4m/6km N. of Beverley

OS *TA015453* **GPS** *53.8942N, 0.4558W*

J. L. Pearson lavishly rebuilt this estate church in 1859 for Lord Hotham – a pleasing work of Geometric Gothic Revival. The octagonal spire is very distinctive; turrets with hexagonal caps at its base. The interior is unified by Pearson's use of marble shafts everywhere, and by the constructional polychromy. The medieval age is recalled here by the 16th-century effigy of a priest in the chancel.

SEATON ROSS † St Edmund

6m/10km W. of Market Weighton

OS *SE781413* **GPS** *53.8623N, 0.8135W*

An 18th-century Classical brick church, it was well restored by Temple Moore, 1908. The W. tower is dated 1788. The Venetian E. window contains bold glass by Stammers, 1953, and William Watson (1784–1857), painter of sundials, is buried in the churchyard; one of his sundials, dated 1825, can be seen over the entrance to the church.

SKIRLAUGH † St Augustine ★

7m/11km N.E. of Hull

OS *TA141397* **GPS** *53.8410N, 0.2663W*

A lavish Perpendicular church replete with parapets, pinnacles and buttresses, it was built in his native village in 1401 by Bishop Skirlaw. The exterior is unchanged from its original plan, and is exemplary Perpendicular. It featured in A. W. N. Pugin's *Contrasts*, his publication of building comparisons extolling the virtues of medieval architecture.

SLEDMERE † St Mary ★

7m/11km N.W. of Driffield

OS *SE930645* **GPS** *54.0685N, 0.5803W*

Built in the Decorated style by Temple Moore in 1898 for Sir Tatton Sykes, 5th Bart and inveterate church rebuilder, this is one of the best village churches in the county. There are medieval origins to the church, however, and Moore made use of the existing 14th-century tower base. The Sykes family monuments are from the former church.

SWINE † St Mary ★

5m/8km N.E. of Hull

OS *TA134358* **GPS** *53.8063N, 0.2791W*

The church is formed from a lovely E. fragment of a Cistercian nunnery; the chancel, nave and choir are 12th-century, and the tower was added in 1787. The arcades are Transitional, the aisles have square-headed 14th-century windows, and the seven-light Perpendicular E. window is outstanding. But most interesting of all is a grand set of misericords, whose carvings include a man looking through his legs, and a griffin. The alabaster altar tombs with seven effigies are of note too, mostly to the Hilton family.

WELTON † St Helen

1m/2km E. of Brough

OS *SE958273* **GPS** *53.7333N, 0.5478W*

Set in a village centre, overlooking a duck pond, this is a church almost entirely rebuilt by Sir George Gilbert Scott in his favourite Middle Pointed style in 1863. There is a very good collection of Morris glass, and in the S. aisle a late 12th- or early 13th-century effigy of a cross-legged knight in chain mail, and a startlingly coloured window by the French stained-glass artist J. B. Capronnier. In the churchyard is an amusing stone to the much-married Jeremiah Simpson.

WINESTEAD † St Germain

1m/2km N.W. of Patrington

OS *TA298237* **GPS** *53.6940N, 0.0346W*

Prettily situated amidst meadows in a secluded position away from the road and village, this tiny 12th-century church of nave and chancel has the remains of a corbel table on the S. side. The Hildyard Chapel was added c. 1602 and rebuilt by Temple Moore in around 1890 re-using Italianate panels bearing trophies of Arms. Inside is an 18th-century pulpit, restored medieval screen and a good collection of Hildyard monuments.

WRESSLE † St John of Beverley

3m/4km N.W. of Howden

OS *SE707312* **GPS** *53.7729N, 0.9276W*

This delightful Gothic brick church was built in 1799 to replace a chapel previously used by the parish in the E. tower of Wressle Castle. It has a rather charming but disproportionately small W. tower. The interior was refurbished and the round windows were Gothicised in 1873.

YORKSHIRE – NORTH

North Yorkshire is the largest modern county in England, covering not only most of the historic North Riding but also parts of the old West Riding and East Riding, and the borough of York. Its landscape includes a central plain, bounded on either side by moorland sloping off into dales. Here is some of Yorkshire's noblest scenery. The western dales, Wensleydale and Swaledale, each have their own ruined abbey, castle and group of waterfalls. On the opposite side, the moorland runs to the coast, with villages few and far between. The churches are isolated, and so often locked that the visitor needs to be adept at hunting for the key.

Industry was largely confined to the area on the north by the Tees, where the extensive ship-building and iron and steel industries spawned during the 19th century have now greatly declined, to be replaced by petro-chemical and service industries. Mining reached into the North York Moors, now a national park: the industrial archeological remains are gently being reclaimed by nature. Mining reshaped parts of the coastline too, and the Victorians came to build coastal spa towns, notably at Scarborough.

In North Yorkshire generally there is much pre-Conquest work. Kirkdale has a Saxon nave and sundial. Many churches possess sculpted crosses, complete or fragmentary. Norman doorways and chancel arches have survived many a later reconstruction. Lastingham is a place of pilgrimage because of its Norman crypt and links with saints Cedd and Chad.

For grandeur, though, it is the town churches which score – such as Bedale and Thirsk. There are few brasses (Wensley has a Flemish one), but an abundance of 14th-century stone effigies. Admirers of 18th-century 'churchwarden' will enjoy themselves in Cleveland; Ingleby Arncliffe has been tidied up, and of course Whitby must be allowed to stand as a museum-piece.

The Victorian builders had their fling on Teesside, with happier results than in Leeds or Sheffield. Also, in the country estates interesting new churches were built. Thanks to Viscount Downe, Butterfield was commissioned to build an entire village, consisting of church, vicarage, schools and cottages, at Baldersby; Pearson studied in a French mood at Appleton-le-Moors. His friend and admirer Temple Moore did scholarly restoration work throughout the North Riding, and new building in and around Middlesbrough.

In York itself, 20 old churches survive from a 16th-century total of 41, and some of these have now been converted to non-ecclesiastical use: St Martin-cum-Gregory, for example, is now a national stained-glass centre. For size they have nothing to compare with St Margaret's and St Nicholas', King's Lynn, or even with St

◁ **ARNCLIFFE: ST OSWALD** – *beautifully set by the River Skirfare in the heart of the dales*

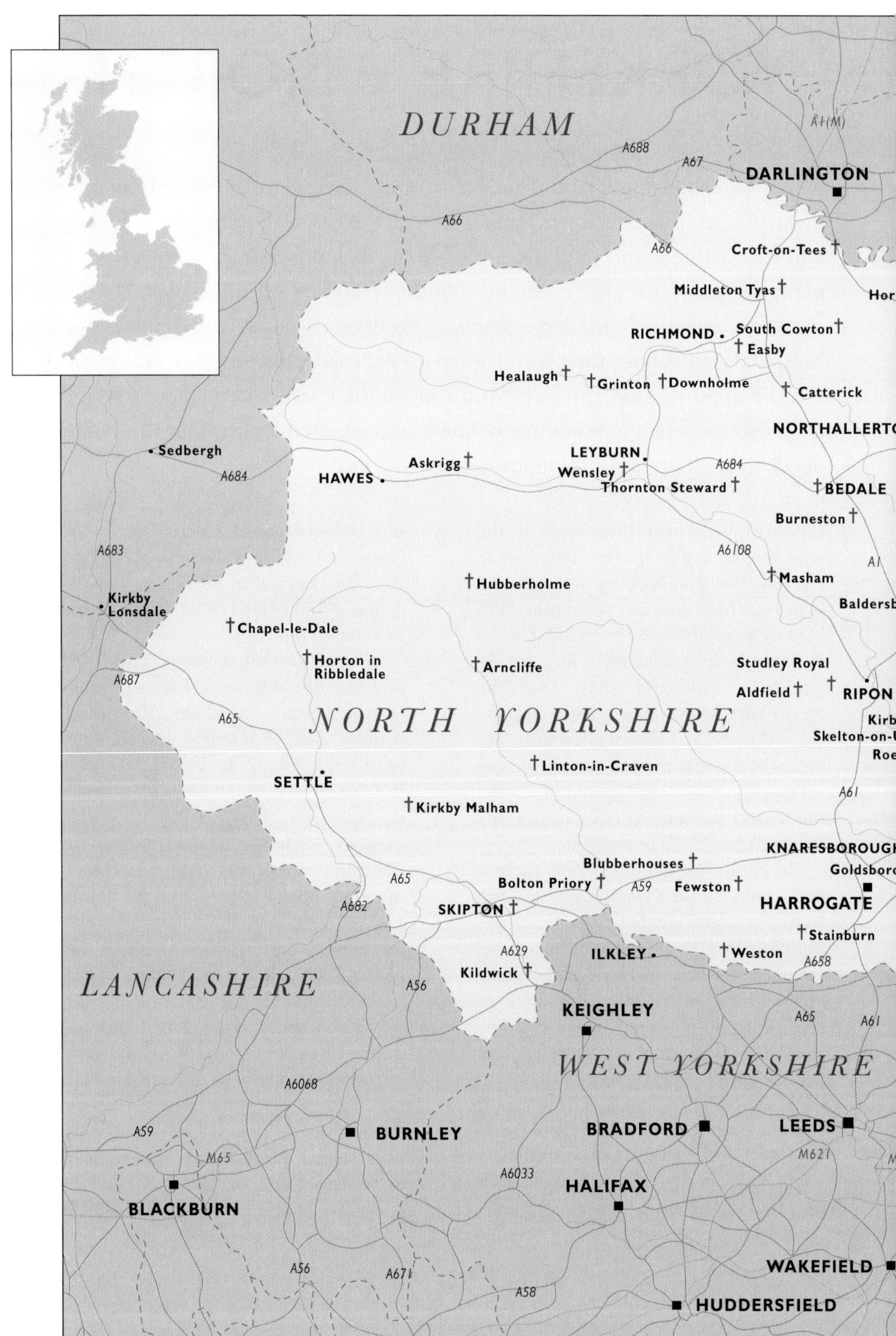
DURHAM
A688
A67
A1(M)
DARLINGTON
A66
A66
Croft-on-Tees
Middleton Tyas
RICHMOND
South Cowton
Easby
Healaugh
Grinton
Downholme
Catterick
NORTHALLERT
Sedbergh
A684
HAWES
Askrigg
LEYBURN
Wensley
A684
Thornton Steward
BEDALE
Burneston
A683
A6108
A1
Masham
Hubberholme
Kirkby Lonsdale
Baldersb
Chapel-le-Dale
Horton in Ribbledale
Arncliffe
Studley Royal
Aldfield
RIPON
A687
A65
NORTH YORKSHIRE
Kirb
Skelton-on-
Roe
Linton-in-Craven
SETTLE
A61
Kirkby Malham
KNARESBOROUGH
Blubberhouses
Goldsboro
A65
Bolton Priory
A59
Fewston
HARROGATE
A682
SKIPTON
Stainburn
A629
ILKLEY
Weston
A658
Kildwick
LANCASHIRE
A56
KEIGHLEY
A65
A61
WEST YORKSHIRE
A6068
BRADFORD
LEEDS
A59
BURNLEY
M621
M65
A6033
HALIFAX
BLACKBURN
A56
A671
WAKEFIELD
A58
HUDDERSFIELD

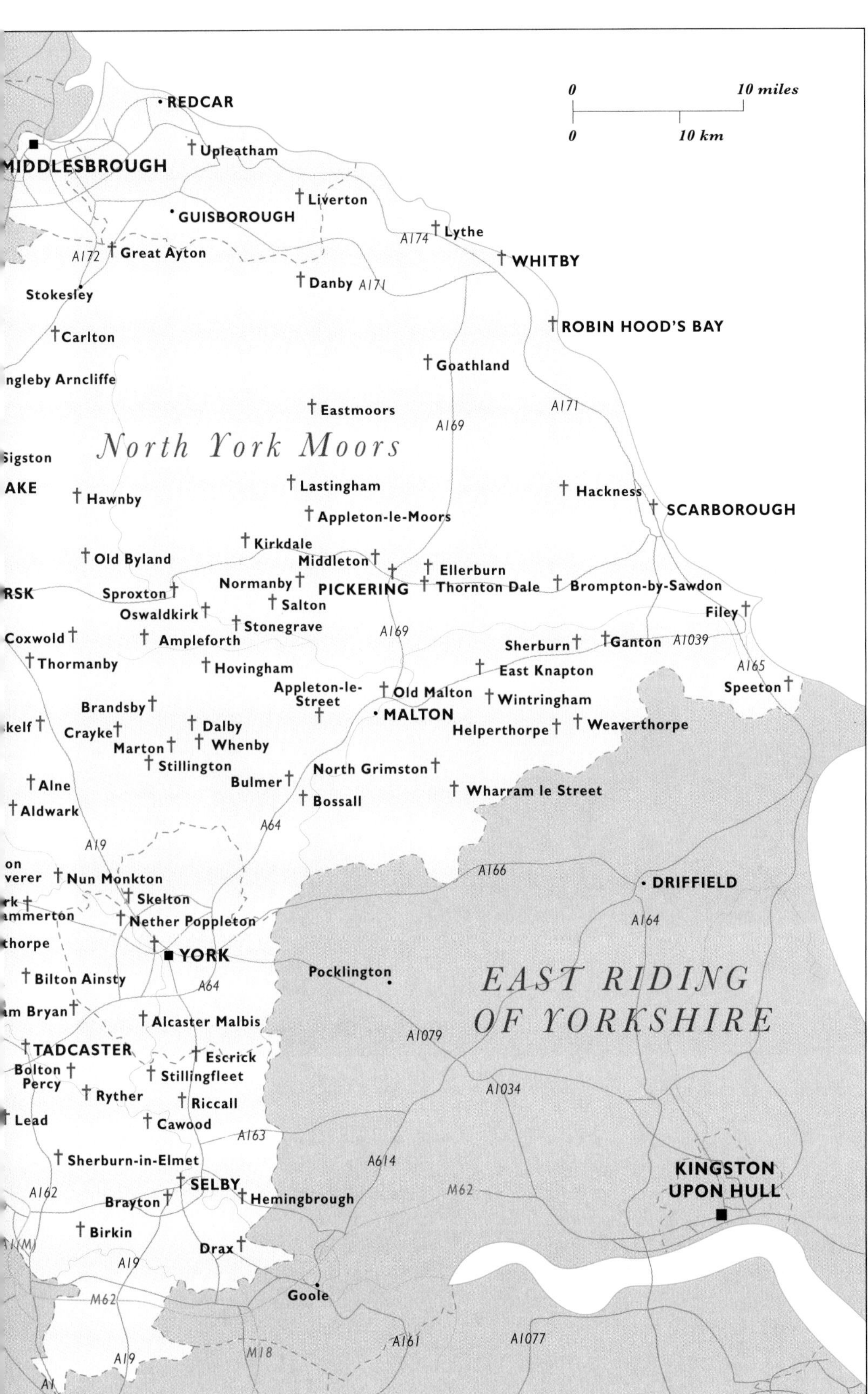
0
10 miles
0
10 km
REDCAR
MIDDLESBROUGH
Upleatham
Liverton
GUISBOROUGH
Lythe
A174
WHITBY
A172
Great Ayton
Danby
A171
Stokesley
ROBIN HOOD'S BAY
Carlton
Goathland
Eastmoors
A171
A169
North York Moors
Lastingham
Hackness
Hawnby
SCARBOROUGH
Appleton-le-Moors
Kirkdale
Old Byland
Middleton
Ellerburn
Normanby
Thornton Dale
Brompton-by-Sawdon
Sproxton
PICKERING
Salton
Filey
Oswaldkirk
Stonegrave
A169
Coxwold
Ampleforth
Sherburn
Ganton
A1039
Thormanby
Hovingham
East Knapton
A165
Appleton-le-Street
Old Malton
Speeton
Brandsby
Wintringham
MALTON
Crayke
Dalby
Helperthorpe
Weaverthorpe
Marton
Whenby
Stillington
North Grimston
Alne
Bulmer
Wharram le Street
Aldwark
Bossall
A64
A19
A166
Nun Monkton
DRIFFIELD
Skelton
Nether Poppleton
A164
YORK
Pocklington
EAST RIDING OF YORKSHIRE
Bilton Ainsty
A64
Alcaster Malbis
A1079
TADCASTER
Escrick
Bolton Percy
Stillingfleet
A1034
Ryther
Riccall
Lead
Cawood
A163
Sherburn-in-Elmet
A614
KINGSTON UPON HULL
SELBY
A162
Brayton
Hemingbrough
M62
Birkin
Drax
A19
Goole
M62
A161
A1077
A19
M18
A1

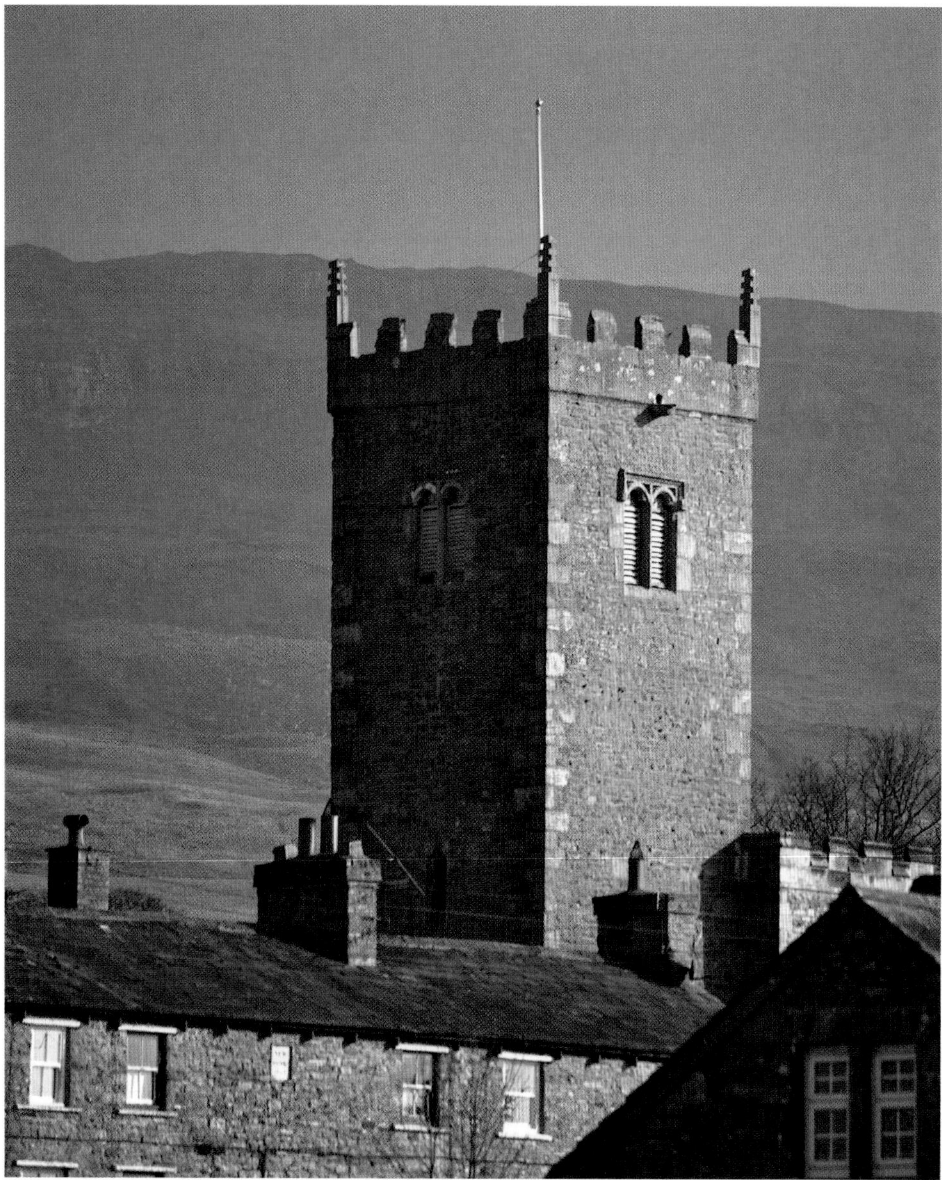

△ **ASKRIGG: ST OSWALD** – *an imposing church in Wensleydale*

Peter Mancroft, Norwich, so completely is York overshadowed by the Minster. They are all worth seeing, not least for their glass, which escaped destruction in the Civil War through the decency of Fairfax. In design, the city churches show a certain uniformity; most are rectangular with towers engaged inside the aisles.

Here and there the old crafts are still encouraged – at St Mary's Priory in Old Malton 20th-century misericords complement those of the 15th century. The best reconstruction of a medieval interior is at All Saints, North Street in York; no other church in Yorkshire so vividly preserves the spirit of medieval England.

ACASTER MALBIS † Holy Trinity

4m/6km S. of York
OS *SE593458* **GPS** *53.9053N, 1.0977W*

Standing by the River Ouse, Holy Trinity is a small early 14th-century cruciform church of high architectural quality. On the N. side of the nave are remains of medieval wall-paintings. The 17th-century pulpit is of Continental origin and has finely carved Geometrical panelling. The shingled bell-tower and spirelet were added as part of a restoration by Hodgson Fowler, 1886.

ALDFIELD † St Lawrence ★

3m/4km W. of Ripon
OS *SE265694* **GPS** *54.1204N, 1.5948W*

Just up the hill from Fountains Abbey is a tiny church that could easily be mistaken for an independent chapel. It replaced an earlier foundation and has a modest Georgian Gothic exterior of 1782. Inside is a delightful ribbed plaster vault, box pews, a three-decker pulpit and Gothic Commandment boards: all is rustic and plain Protestantism.

ALDWARK † St Stephen ★

12m/18km N.W. of York
OS *SE467633* **GPS** *54.0638N, 1.2873W*

This is a lovely and underrated church by E. B. Lamb, 1846–53, all herringbone brick-work and cobbles. The design emphasises the centre of the church with a wide, square crossing. The diamond patterning on the roofs is created by plain and fish-scale tiles. The E. window is a hybrid of the wheel and rose pattern. Inside, the elaborate wooden roof rises from stone corbels, arch-braced with king-posts and tie-beams. The W. window is neo-Perpendicular and has glass by Kempe.

ALLERTON MAULEVERER † St Martin

13m/19km N.W. of York
OS *SE415579* **GPS** *54.0159N, 1.3669W*
Churches Conservation Trust

The Mauleverers were here for 600 years. The present church was founded by their successor, Richard Arundell, a Surveyor of the King's Works. It is a romantic 18th-century Classical design with Romanesque overtones, particularly evident on the W. front. The inside is very atmospheric, with dilapidated medieval monuments, including two stunning oak effigies of knights. The pulpit, pews and hammer-beam roof are all part of the 1745 design, as is the large painting of Moses and Aaron over the chancel arch.

ALNE † St Mary ★

12m/18km N.W. of York
OS *SE495653* **GPS** *54.0816N, 1.2447W*

The tower has a medieval ground stage and Georgian upper stages of brick finished with obelisks at the angles of the parapet. The Norman S. doorway has two orders of bestiary medallions, and the inner orders have medallions depicting the Zodiac, Labours of the Month and an Agnus Dei. The font, with a broad pattern of leaf scrolls, is also good Norman work. The nave and N. aisle are mostly 15th-century and of 'typical Yorkshire' proportions, low and wide. The pale washed plastered walls of the church interior form a good background to the Norman tower arch and the Jacobean pulpit. The ground stage of the tower, shut off behind an indifferent 20th-century Gothic screen, contains pleasant 18th-century panelling, a homely brick floor and an exquisite cartouche, 1695.

AMPLEFORTH † St Hilda

10m/16km E. of Thirsk
OS *SE582786* **GPS** *54.2002N, 1.1079W*

Sited on a steep hillock with a fine view of the Vale of Pickering, the church has Norman origins, a 13th-century chancel and 15th-century tower. There was a thorough restoration in 1868 by T. H. and F. Healey, when the N. aisle was added. The Norman N. doorway has rustic carvings of the Zodiac. Inside, by the W. wall of the tower, is an effigy of a bearded man of c. 1330: a lady wearing a wimple peers over his shoulder. In the N. aisle is a priest's tomb slab.

APPLETON-LE-MOORS
† Christ Church ★★

5m/8km N.W. of Pickering
OS *SE734880* **GPS** *54.2832N, 0.8728W*

This finely conceived church by J. L. Pearson, 1863, has been described as a 'little gem among moorland churches'. The external highlights are the W. front, an almost detached tower and spire, and the apsidal chancel, all Gothic in the French style. Inside, bold sgraffito decorates the apse and pulpit, and polychromatic stone is used to great effect. Above the narthex is a bold wheel window illustrating the Christian virtues.

APPLETON-LE-STREET † All Saints ★
4m/6km W. of Malton
OS *SE734735* **GPS** *54.1528N, 0.8771W*

Rising above the village like some church in the Dordogne, the pre-Conquest tower is one of the best in Northern England. The lower stages are Saxon, the upper is Norman. The N. aisle is late 12th-century, with a pleasing Early English arcade, and the nave retains the Norman tower arch. The S. aisle is early 14th-century, and has in it a very early crude tub font with later conical cover. In the sanctuary are two 14th-century female effigies of the Bolton family, Lords of Appleby.

ARNCLIFFE † St Oswald ★★
in Littondale 7m/11km N.W. of Grassington
OS *SD933719* **GPS** *54.1437N, 2.1038W*

This church should be visited for no other reason than its breathtakingly beautiful dales setting beside the River Skirfare. The building itself, with the exception of the Perpendicular tower, was demolished at the end of the 18th century and rebuilt very harmoniously in 1841 by Salvin. Charles Kingsley found inspiration for *The Water Babies* here.

ASKHAM BRYAN † St Nicholas
4m/6km S.W. of York
OS *SE553484* **GPS** *53.9294N, 1.1581W*

St Nicholas is charming and small, a late Norman church with undivided nave and chancel, and Roman tiles in the walls. The S. entrance has water leaf and ram's head capitals and zigzags. The inside is plain whitewash, and at the E. end is a *vesica piscis* (or fish) window.

ASKRIGG † St Oswald
5m/8km E. of Hawes
OS *SD947910* **GPS** *54.3147N, 2.0820W*

Wensleydale's largest and most stately church is in a suitably commanding position in this small market town. It is mainly 15th- and early 16th-century, with a unified nave and chancel space under a fine moulded Tudor ceiling. The W. end tower space is curious – tunnel vaulted with stone ribs.

BALDERSBY † St James ★
5m/8km S.W. of Thirsk
OS *SE366769* **GPS** *54.1871N, 1.4403W*

The first sight of Baldersby is of the 160-foot tower and spire rising over the York plain. The whole hamlet of church, school and cottages is the work of William Butterfield, 1857 – an outstanding composition. The warm and beautiful interior has red brick and ashlar banded walls, with inlaid patterns. The font of inlaid marble and its spire-like cover, the pews, the dwarf wall at the entrance to the chancel, the clock face and the alabaster reredos are all to Butterfield's designs. In the impressive chancel floor is set the brass cross of the founder's memorial. The glass is by O'Connor, Wailes and Preedy of Worcester.

BEDALE † St Gregory ★★
7m/11km S.W. of Northallerton
OS *SE265884* **GPS** *54.2910N, 1.5935W*

The great semi-fortified W. tower of the church was built in 1330, as a refuge against the Scots after the Battle of Bannockburn. Inside are refuge rooms and the remains of a portcullis on the stairs. The S. porch has a pointed ribbed barrel vault, covered externally with stone slabs. In the main body of the church are windows of every type from Decorated and Perpendicular to Victorian Gothic. Of particular interest is the E. window, believed to have come from Jervaulx Abbey. There are monuments to the Fitzalan family, the most notable being that of Sir Brian Fitzalan, d. 1306, a very early example of an alabaster effigy; and on the N . wall is a recently restored mural painting of St George and the Dragon.

BILTON AINSTY † St Helen ★
5m/8km E. of Wetherby
OS *SE476503* **GPS** *53.9474N, 1.2762W*

This is a very typical Vale of York church: little, late Norman, with good W. front windows and a 13th-century bellcote. The chancel arch is Norman, carved with oversized zigzags, and the arcades have circular piers. In the E. end are some interesting corbels of animals,

△ **BEDALE: ST GREGORY** – *the 14th-century tower was built like a fortress*

human faces and birds. A remnant of a carved Saxon cross stands against the W. wall, and in the S. chapel are fragments of 10th-century Anglo-Norse crosses. In the N. chancel aisle is a delightful detailed c. 1400 monument of a woman with plaited hair resting her feet on a dog and holding a bird in her hands.

BIRKIN † St Mary ★

6m/10km S.W. of Selby
OS *SE530265* **GPS** *53.7324N, 1.1976W*

Viewed from the S., the 14th-century S. aisle and upper tower of this pretty church conceal its very complete Norman features. The rounded Norman apse is unusually impressive and richly decorated. The nave, chancel and vaulted apse retain the original corbel tables, chevron moulding, beak-heads and medallions. A timbered 19th-century porch shelters a well-carved Norman doorway of four orders.

BLUBBERHOUSES † St Andrew

10m/16km W. of Harrogate
OS *SE167552* **GPS** *53.9932N, 1.7453W*

This is a tiny church in a steep moorland setting by E. B. Lamb, 1849–51. The style is simple Early English with an assertive tower and imaginative coarse detailing; the dark interior has a hammer-beam roof in the nave, and in the chancel is an arch-braced roof. The triple lancet E. window is very elegant.

BOLTON PERCY † All Saints

3m/4km S.E. of Tadcaster
OS *SE531412* **GPS** *53.8650N, 1.1929W*

A strikingly handsome limestone church in a remote village near the River Wharfe, it was built by Thomas Parker, its rector in 1411–23, and consecrated in 1424. There is some good woodwork, notably the Jacobean box pews and the two pews, one 17th-century and the other, more ornate, 18th-century. The E. window is the most interesting feature, with medieval glass showing bishops and saints, and in the centre is a rare survival of the Reformation, the Virgin Mary. John Turner's millennium window is a striking piece of contemporary glass – intense blues, greens and yellows.

BOLTON PRIORY
† Blessed Virgin and St Cuthbert ★★

5m/8km N.W. of Ilkley
OS *SE073542* **GPS** *53.9838N, 1.8887W*

This grand setting by the Wharfe was much painted by Turner and other Romantic artists. The former monastic 13th-century nave survived the Dissolution as a parochial space. In the S. wall is an impressive series of six lancet windows with stained glass by A. W. N. Pugin, 1853, depicting 36 scenes from the life of Christ. An exquisite Early English W. front is hidden behind the ostentatious unfinished W. tower started just before the Dissolution. It was roofed as part of the church restoration in 1983.

BOSSALL † St Botolph ★

9m/15km N.E. of York
OS *SE718607* **GPS** *54.0377N, 0.9046W*

A mostly 12th-century cruciform church, it stands on its own near the moat of a hall. It has a sturdy central tower with fine Transitional stonework in the crossing, and a chancel rebuilt in the 13th century. Around the nave and transepts is a fine corbel table; an early 19th-century S. porch floored with brick shelters a superb 13th-century doorway, with stiff-leaf capitals. The late 12th-century font has a fine Jacobean corona font cover, and on the N. wall is a colourful Queen Anne Royal Arms in a marbled wood frame. There is good glass by Kempe in the chancel.

BRANDSBY † All Saints

15m/24km N. of York
OS *SE598719* **GPS** *54.1398N, 1.0856W*

The church, which stands in undulating and well-wooded country, was built by Thomas Atkinson in 1767–70. Outside, the Classical detail is a trifle heavy, excepting the stone cupola poised imaginatively over the body of the church. The church is entered through a narthex in which stands an 18th-century baluster font. The door to the nave is protected by a wrought-iron grille. In the body of the church are four Roman Doric columns connected by plaster cross vaults which form the base supports of the cupola. There is plenty of free floor space, a well-detailed W. gallery and good early 20th-century furniture.

BRAYTON † St Wilfrid ★

1m/2km S.W. of Selby
OS *SE604309* **GPS** *53.7718N, 1.0848W*

The superb Norman tower with octagonal Perpendicular lantern and spire dominates the surrounding countryside. Of particular note is the sumptuous Norman S. door of the York Romanesque school, with beakheads, medallions and chevrons. The Reticulated E. window is very fine, and in the long Decorated chancel is a chest tomb to Lord Darcy, d. 1558, and his wife Dorothea with a mixture of Gothic and early Renaissance details.

BROMPTON-BY-SAWDON † All Saints ★

7m/11km S.W. of Scarborough
OS *SE942821* **GPS** *54.2262N, 0.5552W*

Poised above a lake at the centre of the village, All Saints is a church of the 14th–15th centuries, with an octagonal broach spire with lucarnes (small dormer windows). The porch was added in 1895 as a memorial to George Cayley, an early pioneer of aviation. Inside is a brightly painted organ case and W. gallery by Temple Moore, a 13th-century font with cable moulding and many monuments to the Cayley family. In the S. wall of the chancel is a window with a reproduction of Raphael's *Sermon of St Paul at Athens* from his design for the Sistine Chapel tapestries. Wordsworth married Mary Hutchinson here in 1802.

BULMER † St Martin

6m/10km S.W. of Malton
OS *SE699676* **GPS** *54.0998N, 0.9320W*

The simple small village church has a late 11th-century core; note the herringbone masonry in the N. wall. There is the head of a Saxon wheel cross above the blocked N. doorway, and on an outer wall of the S. porch a slab with a Greek key border decoration to Christopher Thompson, d. 1748, who 'wrought in brass and iron for 45 years for the third and fourth Earls of Carlisle' at Castle Howard.

BURNESTON † St Lambert

3m/4km S.E. of Bedale
OS *SE308849* **GPS** *54.2592N, 1.5277W*

St Lambert's has a 15th-century exterior busy with pinnacles, crocketed finials, battlements and good buttresses. Inside the church are fine c. 1625 oak pews, that of the Robinson family being a two-tiered pew dominating the N. aisle. The altar and its surrounding woodwork were given in 1908 by the vicar, Canon John Hartley, the only priest to win the Wimbledon Lawn Tennis Championship – twice, in 1879 and 1880. He is buried in the churchyard.

CARLTON † St Botolph ★

10m/16km S. of Middlesbrough
OS *NZ506045* **GPS** *54.4337N, 1.2203W*

The church stands on a knoll at the N. of this village below the Cleveland Hills, a distinguished building of warm-coloured stone by Temple Moore, 1896–7. He was an architect alive to the needs of a small village church and sensitive to the local medieval regional characteristics, yet there is plenty of originality. From the doorway a tunnel-vaulted passage leads to a baptistry, a stone-vaulted space carrying a gallery above; an exciting composition. The E. window is excellent and filled with rich glass. Small rectangular plain windows at the head of each sedilia also add a nice touch.

CATTERICK † St Anne

5m/8km S.E. of Richmond
OS *SE240979* **GPS** *54.3767N, 1.6318W*

Fortunately the A1 now bypasses the village and the army camp is at some distance, so the village remains a pleasant surprise with a green and a stream. The church is quite large, with a strong W. tower; it is mostly of c. 1412, the master mason being Richard of Crakehall, whose contract still survives. Inside are three 15th-century Burgh brasses, a fine black marble font, also 15th-century, and hatchments over the arcades and chancel arch.

CAWOOD † All Saints

4m/6km N.W. of Selby
OS *SE577377* **GPS** *53.8332N, 1.1235W*

Notable for its setting on a sweep of the River Ouse, the church is Transitional and Early English with Perpendicular additions including a lively W. tower of three stages; in the first stage is set an ogee niche with a 20th-century statue of the Virgin. Inside is a graceful Early English S. arcade and a monument to George Mountain, who rose from poverty to become Archbishop, but died within hours of his enthronement in 1628.

CHAPEL-LE-DALE † St Leonard ★★

11m/17km N.W. of Settle
OS *SD737771* **GPS** *54.1898N, 2.4033W*

Utterly remote, peaceful, simple and charming: this is a little 17th century building with mullioned windows, partly rebuilt in 1869. A wall-plaque commemorates those who died building the Settle–Carlisle railway, completed 1876. For those who like churches for their settings, St Leonard's is unmissable.

COWTHORPE † St Michael

3m/4km N.E. of Wetherby
OS *SE427526* **GPS** *53.9685N, 1.3506W*
Churches Conservation Trust

Built by Bryan Roucliff, a Baron of the Exchequer in the reign of Henry VI, the church has the oddest tower, more like a guard post. The building is all simple Perpendicular, and in the chancel are the remains of the founder's brass, 1494, fragments of heraldic glass, a very good Easter Sepulchre and lovely Perpendicular font incised with the Arms of Lord de Ross, the Plumptons and the Hammerton families.

COXWOLD † St Michael ★

8m/13km S.E. of Thirsk
OS *SE533772* **GPS** *54.1878N, 1.1846W*

The village street climbs a steep hill to the church at its summit. With the exception of the chancel, rebuilt in 1777, the stately exterior is of the 15th century. The tower is octagonal, and the buttresses and pinnacles display an effortless subtlety in design. Inside, the 17th and 18th centuries have left their delightful mark on the W. gallery, the plaster-work on the E. wall of the nave, the box pews, pulpit and the monuments in the chancel. The communion rail is extended down the length of the narrow chancel, leaving room on either side for the enormous Fauconberg tombs. The novelist and clergyman Lawrence Sterne was reburied in the churchyard two centuries after his death in London in 1768.

CRAYKE † St Cuthbert

14m/23km N. of York
OS *SE560706* **GPS** *54.1287N, 1.1440W*

The church is dedicated to St Cuthbert, who often stayed here on his visits to and from York; his body also rested here for a brief period in the 9th century. The church and castle stand at the top of a hill overlooking the plain of York. The structure is mostly of 15th-century date. The wide and squat nave and N. aisle should be compared with St Mary in Alne. Both nave and chancel have heavily timbered 15th-century roofs, and inside are excellent pews with bobbin-ends, a clerk's desk, churchwardens' seats and a pulpit of 1637.

CROFT-ON-TEES † St Peter ★★

3m/4km S. of Darlington
OS *NZ288098* **GPS** *54.4831N, 1.5557W*

Standing near the bank of the Tees, close to the great medieval bridge that leads into County Durham, this is the childhood home of Lewis Carroll; his father was rector here from 1843 to 1868. It is a long, low building of colourful pink stone of varied texture, and well weathered. The 14th-century chancel has

CHAPEL-LE-DALE: ST LEONARD – *one of the loveliest settings in all of England* ▷

good buttresses and tracery. Built into the S. wall is a piece of Romano-British sculpture representing a local deity. The ostentatious elevated Restoration Milbanke pew should not be missed. It stands on Doric columns, and has upholstered furnishing and curtains to conceal its occupants from the common gaze.

DALBY † St Peter

13m/20km W. of Malton
OS *SE637712* **GPS** *54.1328N, 1.0263W*

The church enjoys a remote setting in the Howardian Hills, and has features of the 12th, 15th and 16th centuries. The Norman S. doorway and chancel arch are all that remain from the early church. Inside are several memorials, the most notable being that to Alan Ascough, Armiger, d. 1675, on the S. nave wall. The 15th-century chancel is attractively barrel-vaulted; from outside it is all at odds with the gabled nave – embattled, and with the look of a miniature Pele tower.

DANBY † St Hilda

12m/19km W. of Whitby
OS *NZ696063* **GPS** *54.4474N, 0.9279W*

The church stands in an isolated position in a valley below the moors. The detached 15th-century tower of warm stone is placed on the S. side. Its ground stage is a porch entered through an elegant wooden gate of early 19th-century date. The nave was classicized in the 18th century and given 13th-century-looking arcades by Temple Moore in 1903. The 18th-century W. gallery has been retained and is approached by external stone steps. Butterfield built the chancel in 1848. The spacious interior has a large, bright Kempe window of the Good Shepherd and much clear glass. There is a Royal Arms of George IV, 1829, and a good series of 17th- and 18th-century monuments in the churchyard.

DOWNHOLME
† St Michael and All Angels ★

4m/6km S.W. of Richmond
OS *SE110983* **GPS** *54.3804N, 1.8311W*

This sturdy small church of Norman origin was left perched all on its own high up on the S. side of Swaledale, when the village moved south. There is a stone barn in the corner of the churchyard that may have been for stabling worshippers' horses. Good tombstones lie at all angles. In the small bell turret is a pre-Reformation bell. The interior is pleasingly painted cream, and there is a three-bay Early English arcade, Royal Arms of George III and Hutton hatchments. Clear glass in the windows gives views of sheep grazing on the surrounding fells.

DRAX † St Peter and St Paul

5m/8km S.E. of Selby
OS *SE675263* **GPS** *53.7294N, 0.9770W*

Built on the site of an Augustinian foundation, the church has a fine Transitional tower with a 15th-century spire and a large Early English chancel. In the S. porch are several reset corbel heads. The N. arcade is 12th-century, and the S. arcade is 14th-century: the Perpendicular clerestory is very grand, with eight arcades of windows and a fine range of small medieval figures, and sumptuous coloured nave roofs by Sir Charles Nicholson.

EASBY † St Agatha ★★

1m/2km S.E. of Richmond
OS *NZ185002* **GPS** *54.3976N, 1.7158W*

The church is close to the ruins of the abbey, by the River Swale below Richmond Castle. It is long and low and of beautiful weathered stone, with a double bellcote and a tunnel-like two-storey S. porch with colour-washed barrel vault and walls. The arcade arches are boldly painted with chevrons, and on the walls are the famous murals: on the N. wall scenes from the Old Testament, and on the S. wall scenes from the New Testament. They were restored by Burlison & Grylls during Sir George Gilbert Scott's 1869 general restoration. In the chancel is a facsimile of the 8th-century Saxon Easby Cross – a copy of the original now in the V&A museum in London.

EAST KNAPTON † St Edmund ★

7m/11km N.E. of Malton
OS *SE880756* **GPS** *54.1691N, 0.6530W*

A most enjoyable church in the quiet park of a hall, it was mostly built in the 1870s by John Gibson & Son of Malton. The entry leads to a polygonal baptistry with painted ceiling

△ **EASBY: ST AGATHA** – *one of the celebrated 13th-century wall-paintings*

showing a multitude of storks and fish. The nave and chancel are all one, the nave with an arcade and N. aisle and a prettily stencilled hammer-beam roof. The chancel has stencilled walls with bishops' shields on the ceiling. The S. vestry is like a little chapter-house, and a squire's pew is at the head of the N. aisle.

EAST MOORS † St Mary Magdalene ★

15m/24km N.E. of Thirsk
OS *SE609903* **GPS** *54.3051N, 1.0645W*

The W. bell-turret rises among rhododendron bushes. It is a memorable small church by Temple Moore – his first church and one that is handled with much skill and originality, adapting George Gilbert Scott Jnr's earlier design. The nave and chancel are all in one, with a painted ceiling in hues of red, white and green. The beautifully simple circular font is by Temple Moore. The S. aisle can be shuttered off to form a classroom or bedroom for a snow-bound incumbent!

ESCRICK † St Helen ★
6m/10km S. of York
OS *SE628431* **GPS** *53.8805N, 1.0461W*

A Gothic Revival church by F. C. Penrose, 1856–7, it stands in the centre of the village. The long, mysterious nave and chancel terminate at each end in semi-hexagonal apses. At the W. this forms a baptistry, the vault of which is supported on red Devonshire marble. Inside is a delicate white marble font, whose bowl is held by two cherubs, male and female, back to back, carved by Gio Tognolt of Rome. The baptistry also houses monuments, including one by Eric Gill. The vistas in this finely proportioned church are inspiring. Following a devastating fire of 1923, the church was sensitively restored by John Bilson, 1925.

ELLERBURNE † St Hilda
3m/4km E. of Pickering
OS *SE841842* **GPS** *54.2467N, 0.7102W*

Hidden away in a valley behind Thornton Dale is a church of simple beauty, originally 11th-century with 17th–18th-century fittings. A careful restoration by W. D. Caroe, 1905–11, kept its unassuming character while adding a new porch and vestry. There are several Anglo-Norse stones set into the fabric.

FEWSTON † St Michael and St Lawrence
8m/13km W. of Harrogate
OS *SE194541* **GPS** *53.9826N, 1.7044W*

The church stands beside Fewston reservoir, pleasantly remodelled in 1697 after a fire which left only the 14th-century tower standing. The S. porch has a shallow arch flanked by pilasters, and the massive door is most likely from the old church. Inside is a Tuscan arcade, with a similarly styled chancel arch. The 17th-century octagonal stone font is suspended from iron brackets.

FILEY † St Oswald ★
7m/11km S.E. of Scarborough
OS *TA117810* **GPS** *54.2132N, 0.2874W*

In a wooded position overlooking a ravine away from the town there is a grand cruciform church, mainly 12th- and 13th-century with 19th- and early 20th-century restoration and rebuilding. The central tower, transepts and chancel are monolithic, built to withstand wild North Sea weather. They retain a good set of round arched and tall lancet windows. In the S. aisle is a rough carved figure of a boy bishop – a relic of the mock festivities at the feast of St Nicholas.

GANTON † St Nicholas
8m/12km W. of Filey
OS *SE989775* **GPS** *54.1846N, 0.4846W*

The church is set near the foot of the N. scarp of the Wolds, at the top of a pretty village street of whitewashed cottages, along which a chalk stream flows. It is mainly 13th- and 14th-century with a S. transept, formerly the Legard mortuary chapel, in which there is a very fine mid-17th-century monument to John Legard. There are several monuments to the Legard family in the church, and one to William Wilson, d. 1792, 'an honest, industrious, sober ploughman', gardener of the Legard family. The 15th-century W. tower has a small recessed octagonal spire, and the belfry string course is decorated with masks, fleurons and grotesques. There is also good glass by Capronnier and Wailes.

GOATHLAND † St Mary ★
7m/11km S.W. of Whitby
OS *NZ827007* **GPS** *54.3951N, 0.7266W*

Originally intended to stand out starkly against the moorland, today the church, a powerful work of W. H. Brierley, 1894–6, is almost hidden by a churchyard of trees and shrubs. Norman Shaw's influence can be felt in this modern Perpendicular-style building whose broad central tower is as wide as the church itself. Two round tower arches inside lead the eye to the short chancel. Every detail of wood and stone is straightforward and honest. The pews are green-stained, very much in the Arts and Crafts tradition.

GOLDSBOROUGH † St Mary
2m/3km E. of Knaresborough
OS *SE384560* **GPS** *53.9995N, 1.4151W*

This is a pleasant village church of the 13th and 14th centuries, with 12th-century S. doorway, heraldic glass of 1696 and a fine series of monuments, including two 14th-century knights, one in a canopied

HACKNESS: ST PETER – *a fine church with two great treasures – a carved Saxon cross and this pearwood Oberammergau carving against the 15th-century font cover* ▷

niche to Sir Richard Goldsborough, c. 1333, and a delightful 18th-century piece by Joseph Wilton with figures of Faith and Charity.

GREAT AYTON † All Saints

5m/8km S.W. of Guisborough

OS *NZ556108* **GPS** *54.4897N, 1.1429W*

The church stands quietly behind the more prominent (and less interesting) Christ Church of 1876 by Ross & Lamb. The stonework of the old church is of the warm local stone, beautifully textured and weathered. The tower was demolished c. 1880. There is an altogether delightful mixture of Norman, Early English and late 18th-century churchwarden Classical so popular in the region. The furniture of 1790 includes a three-decker pulpit complete with sounding board. Captain Cook's mother and five of her children are buried in the churchyard.

GRINTON † St Andrew ★

½m/1km S.E. of Reeth, 6m/10km S.W. of Richmond

OS *SE046984* **GPS** *54.3813N, 1.9305W*

A great, long, grey church, it seems almost to have been extruded out of the ground in this wonderful Swaledale setting, all at one with the wandering drystone walls. The exterior is chiefly remarkable for its austerity and the almost domestic character of its windows. The arcades are mostly of the 15th-century; there is a pulpit with tester, 1718; 15th-century parclose screens; a painted wood tablet to Dorothy Darcy, 1698; and an oval-framed Royal Arms. In the Blackburn Chapel is the tombstone of Elizabeth Blackburn, c. 1688, and some fragments of medieval glass in the E. window, all enclosed by a homely 17th-century parclose screen.

HACKNESS † St Peter ★★

5m/8km W. of Scarborough

OS *SE969905* **GPS** *54.3014N, 0.5123W*

A romantically set church in a deep wooded valley, it stands beside the River Derwent. Inside is a very good Norman S. arcade and an Early English N. arcade. The chancel arch dates from the late 1200s and is very finely proportioned, with Norse patterning on one of the imposts. The choir has some good misericords, said to have come from Whitby Abbey, and in the S. aisle is a grand Saxon cross shaft, with inscriptions in Latin, Ogham, Norse Anglo-Saxon runic and an as yet undeciphered runic inscription looking for all the world like pine needles. This was rescued from use as a gatepost. At the other end of the aisle is a fine font with an intricately carved 15th-century font cover.

HAWNBY † All Saints

10m/16km N.E. of Thirsk

OS *SE536896* **GPS** *54.2999N, 1.1771W*

On the banks of the River Rye, this is a church in a beautiful and isolated setting, basically 12th-century with medieval alterations and a 19th-century restoration. It is simple and humble, with a twin bellcote and 17th-century Tankard monuments, a church that the Hawnby Dreamers – the first Methodists in Rydale – turned their backs on.

HEALAUGH † St John the Baptist

3m/4km N. of Tadcaster

OS *SE498479* **GPS** *53.9250N, 1.2424W*

A Norman church, whose fine S. door has beak-heads and plain roll moulding. The nave retains its corbel tables outside, and, inside, the arcades have clustered responds and waterleaf capitals. The chancel arch shafts are carved with interlaced bands and small animals, and in the N. chapel is the imposing tomb of Lord Wharton, shown in full armour with his two wives and children set below.

HELPERTHORPE † St Peter ★

11m/18km E. of Malton

OS *SE952704* **GPS** *54.1207N, 0.5437W*

Set on the Wold-side above the village, the church was built in 1872–5 by G. E. Street for Sir Tatton Sykes. It is perhaps the most original of G. E. Street's churches, with its individual stair turret a feature of the exterior. Inside are fine painted roofs, a gaily painted iron chancel screen, a beautiful font cover and Burlison & Grylls stained glass. The N. aisle by Temple Moore, 1893, was a gentle addition.

HEMINGBROUGH † St Mary the Virgin

4m/6km E. of Selby

OS *SE673306* **GPS** *53.7676N, 0.9797W*

The lofty 15th-century Tadcaster stone

◁ **HORTON-IN-RIBBLESDALE: ST OSWALD** – *a rugged edifice built to withstand the elements*

octagonal spire of the church dominates the village and can be seen for miles around. It is set on a 13th-century tower. The church was once collegiate, and has fabric from the 13th to the 15th centuries. The chancel is Decorated, while the Tudor S. aisle has clustered shafts and four-centred arches to the arcades. Inside are medieval parclose screens in the N. chancel aisle, 16th-century bench-ends and misericords dating from c. 1200. Among the memorials are the jousting helmet and gauntlets of Sir Roger Pilkington, c. 1750.

HORNBY † St Mary

8m/12km N. of Northallerton

OS *SE222937* **GPS** *54.3389N, 1.6594W*

The attractive exterior owes much to the varying colour and textures of local stone used in its building. The campanile-type tower contains 11th-century bell openings to which a new belfry was added in the 15th century. The E. wall of the chancel is 19th-century neo-Norman by J. L. Pearson, 1878–9. Inside there is a Norman arcade, a 19th-century decorated font, mosaic chancel floor, medieval and later monuments, brasses and early 16th-century painted panels with birds and foliage on a parclose screen.

HORTON-IN-RIBBLESDALE
† St Oswald ★

5m/8km N. of Settle

OS *SD810721* **GPS** *54.1445N, 2.2922W*

This is a rugged no-nonsense fell-side church under the heights of Pen-y-ghent. The rough battlements and stocky angled buttresses of the Perpendicular tower, together with the low nave mark this out as a church built to withstand wild weather, huddled together with a group of stone cottages. The churchyard is entered under a low, stone slab-covered lych gate, and a timber roofed stone porch protects the delightful rustic Norman doorway. The shallow king-post roof was restored c. 1879.

HOVINGHAM † All Saints ★

8m/12km W. of Malton

OS *SE666757* **GPS** *54.1730N, 0.9803W*

In a beautifully kept estate village with the great house of the Worsley family adjacent, the church has a pre-Conquest unbuttressed W. tower whose mighty stonework is visible inside the nave. High on the S. face of the tower is a 10th-century Norse wheel cross, whilst on the W. face, above an old Saxon doorway, is an Anglian cross, possibly of the 9th century. Otherwise it is mostly Victorian, the nave and chancel of 1860 by Rhode Hawkins incorporating medieval features. A weathered but very fine Saxon carving serves as the reredos in the S. chapel, and behind the high altar is a carved 10th-century cross with knotted strapwork.

HUBBERHOLME
† St Michael and All Angels ★

In Langstrothdale, 8m/13km S.E. of Hawes

OS *SD926782* **GPS** *54.2001N, 2.1147W*

This is a lovely setting in a Pennine valley. The church was altered in the 14th century, retaining its stubby Norman tower. The nave and aisles are low and broad, and inside is a late rood screen of 1558 retaining some painted decoration as well as its rood loft, one of only two in Yorkshire. The pews are by 'Mouseman' Thomas, and the writer J. B. Priestley is buried here.

INGLEBY ARNCLIFFE † All Saints

7m/11km N.E. of Northallerton

OS *NZ452002* **GPS** *54.3959N, 1.3042W*

The little church stands below tree-covered slopes of the Cleveland Hills and adjacent to the 18th-century hall built by John Carr. It was largely rebuilt in 1821 in Cleveland churchwarden Classical. The light interior has sash windows, white walls and box pews painted a deep red with their original painted numbers. A Scandinavian ship sits on a ledge above the door. There are some 14th-century glass fragments from Mount Grace Priory and two effigies, also 14th-century, in the chancel.

KILDWICK † St Andrew ★

4m/6km N.W. of Keighley

OS *SE011458* **GPS** *53.9092N, 1.9841W*

The 'Lang Kirk' of Craven has an enormous weather vane on the tower turret, and is 14th-century with Tudor elongation. There are reset 16th-century screens with linenfold

△ **KIRKDALE: ST GREGORY** – *an ancient church of Saxon foundation, added to and restored in the 19th and 20th centuries*

panelling, and 17th-century pews, including the grand Eltoft family pew of 1633, with turned baluster and cock's head hinges. The W. end was restored in 1868–75, the E. end in 1901–03, when 10th-century cross fragments were discovered. These are displayed in the S. aisle. There is a 15th-century octagonal bowl with carved symbols of the Crucifixion; the finely carved 19th-century three-tier cover is probably a replica of the 14th-century original, which was broken up to make dining chairs.

KIRBY HILL (KIRBY-ON-THE-MOOR)
† All Saints

11m/17km N.E. of Harrogate
OS *SE393685* **GPS** *54.1117N, 1.4000W*

The church stands away from the village, and has some pre-Conquest work as evidenced in Saxon cross shafts and tomb slabs. The S. door is 12th-century with contemporary hinges, and inside are benches with poppyheads. The tower was remodelled in 1870 by Sir George Gilbert Scott as part of a more general restoration.

KIRBY SIGSTON † St Lawrence

3m/4km E. of Northallerton
OS *SE416946* **GPS** *54.3458N, 1.3606W*

Standing beside a small lake, the church has a Georgian W. tower of doll's house proportions – the top is the same height as the nave roof. The nave and chancel are Transitional with a Perpendicular E. window. The limewashed interior is very characterful, well restored by Temple Moore, 1890, with a gilded and coloured rood beam and cross. The N. aisle, lower than the nave, contains a font of 1662, and the narrow chancel arch has a good 20th-century screen. In the chancel the 14th-century arches have good carved capitals.

KIRKBY MALHAM
† St Michael or St James

5m/8km E. of Settle
OS *SD894609* **GPS** *54.0448N, 2.1633W*

The church, known as the 'Cathedral of the Dales', is in a beautiful village setting – typical Craven regional Perpendicular with a long, low, rugged exterior. There are benefactors' Arms on the S.W. tower buttress. The inside is filled with 17th–19th-century pews; the 17th-century altar rails compare favourably with the pretentious woodwork of 1923 in the chancel.

KIRK HAMMERTON
† St John the Baptist ★

9m/15km W. of York
OS *SE465555* **GPS** *53.9937N, 1.2918W*

The original small Saxon church forms the S. aisle of a church by C. Hodgson Fowler, 1891, advised by the Society for the Protection of Ancient Buildings. The slender Saxon tower has paired belfry openings – exquisite in its simplicity.

KIRKDALE † St Gregory ★

8m/13km W. of Pickering
OS *SE676857* **GPS** *54.2632N, 0.9623W*

This is a small church of Saxon origin all on its own by a stream in a wooded valley. The porch and tower were added in the early to mid-19th century and the chancel was rebuilt in the late 19th century – all restored by Temple Moore in 1907–09. It is chiefly remarkable for the pre-Conquest sundial set above the S. doorway and a centre panel signed by the makers, Haward and Brand, priests: the inscription records that 'Orm Gamal's son bought St Gregory's Minster when it was all broken down and fallen and let it be made anew from the ground to Christ and St Gregory in Edward's days, the King and Tosti's days…'. The King was Edward the Confessor and Earl Tosti was brother to King Harold; this church can thus be dated to about 1060. Inside are two carved Anglo-Saxon tomb slabs and stone benches around the walls.

KNARESBOROUGH
† St John the Baptist ★★

3m/4km N.E. of Harrogate
OS *SE347571* **GPS** *54.0095N, 1.4718W*

The church occupies a prominent position above cobbled streets in this picturesque riverside town. The Transitional central tower has a 'candle-snuffer' spirelet. There is 13th–14th-century work in the chapels and chancel, although the lovely Reticulated E. window is a Victorian reproduction. In the N. Slingsby Chapel are several family monuments: of note is the standing effigy of Sir William Slingsby, d. 1634. In the S. aisle is lovely window glass by Morris & Co., to designs by Ford Madox Brown.

LASTINGHAM † St Mary ★★

6m/10km N.W. of Pickering
OS *SE728904* **GPS** *54.3045N, 0.8826W*

The village is set in a fold of the moors. Viewed from Spaunton Bank, the basically 11th-century monastic church makes an unusual and very effective silhouette. At the W. end there is a thin 14th-century campanile-type tower. The design of the interior is on a grand but simple scale, crowned with massive ribless groined vaults in stone by J. L. Pearson, 1879, who added the clerestory. The presbytery, crossing and first bay of the nave survive from an unfinished monastic church built 1078–86 by a group of Whitby monks. The church ends in an apse. Abbot Stephen's crypt is entered from a staircase in the centre of the nave and contains good fragments of Anglo-Saxon sculpture and the parish bier. A complete church in itself, apsed, aisled and vaulted, it is unforgettable and one of the most moving places in England.

LEAD † St Mary ★

½m/1km W. of Saxton; 4m/6km S. of Tadcaster
OS *SE464368* **GPS** *53.8263N, 1.2961W*
Churches Conservation Trust

Well known to cyclists and ramblers, whose enthusiasm saved it, this is a tiny 13th-century chapel with a bellcote, standing alone in a field. There are massive ledger stones to the Tyas family set in the floor – richly carved with heraldry. All in all a very atmospheric interior, with 18th-century rustic benches, pulpit, clerk's and reader's desks, and painted texts.

LEAKE † St Mary ★

5m/8km N. of Thirsk
OS *SE433906* **GPS** *54.3094N, 1.3357W*

St Mary's is a village church whose village has long since gone, either lost to the Black Death or Scots raiders. The church has a good stout Norman three-stage W. tower. On each face of the upper stage is triple arcading with twin bell openings set within the middle arch of each face. Built into the W. face of

LASTINGHAM: ST MARY – *Abbot Stephen's crypt* ▷

the tower is a Saxon cross. There is a three-light pointed arch window of a later period at the base of the tower, flanked by Y-traceried windows at the W. ends of the aisles. In the nave are two splendid 15th-century stall-ends from Bridlington Priory, possibly of the Ripon School, carved with poppyheads and little beasts on detached shafts.

LINTON-IN-CRAVEN † St Michael

9m/15km N. of Skipton
OS *SE005632* **GPS** *54.0650N, 1.9937W*

Pleasantly set on the banks of the River Wharfe, this is a low, spreading church with a little cantilevered belfry – a very rewarding example of medieval rural architecture. The nave was rebuilt in the 14th century, but the church still retains a late Norman arcade and font.

LIVERTON † St Michael

8m/13km S.E. of Redcar
OS *NZ711163* **GPS** *54.5370N, 0.9025W*

A modest 12th-century church at the end of a farm track, St Michael's glory is inside: a magnificent chancel arch of three chevron-carved orders and lively capitals showing a boar hunt, birds, a lion, a dragon and much more.

LYTHE † St Oswald ★

4m/6km N.W. of Whitby
OS *NZ850131* **GPS** *54.5067N, 0.6885W*

This hill-top church with its grand tower and octagonal short stone spire forms a prominent landmark near the sea. Of 13th-century origins, it was largely rebuilt in 1910–11 by Walter Tapper. Most here is from Tapper's rebuilding; the 1910 screen, with Curvilinear tracery and fan vaulting, supports a delightful painted organ case. Under the W. gallery is a collection of Saxon stone carving.

MARTON-IN-THE-FOREST † St Mary ★

13m/19km N. of York
OS *SE602682* **GPS** *54.1066N, 1.0807W*

The astonishing exterior with its knobbly crow-stepped gables is due to a rebuilding, probably in 1540, using ashlar and worked stone from the Priory nearby. The form was determined by the stone available. The N. wall, built of river stones, remains in its 12th-century form. The S. door with tracery is 15th-century. The interior boasts an early chancel arch, 17th-century altar rails and benches, 13th-century font and fragments of 15th-century glass.

MASHAM † St Mary the Virgin

8m/12km N.W. of Ripon
OS *SE226806* **GPS** *54.2213N, 1.6537W*

The pleasant town with its square and market cross stands on the bank of the Ure. Hidden off one corner of the great marketplace, the lower part of the church tower is 11th-century work, without buttresses, and carries a 15th-century octagonal stage surmounted by a spire. In c. 1328 the body of the church was rebuilt with aisles and a N. chapel by Sir Geoffrey le Scrope. Renaissance monuments abound, including a fine alabaster monument under a shallow arch with flanking columns to Sir Marmaduke Wyvill and his wife, d. 1613 – reclining effigies propped on their elbows, with child weepers below.

MIDDLETON † St Andrew ★

1m/2km N.W. of Pickering
OS *SE782854* **GPS** *54.2587N, 0.8008W*

This is a church with much Saxon interest, including the Saxon W. tower with a 13th-century bell stage, and a blocked up Saxon doorway with vesica window cut into the arch. Set into the stonework above is an Anglian cross of the 8th-century. The S. doorway is charming – trefoil, with a stout 15th-century panelled door. Inside are 12th–13th-century arcades in the nave. The chancel was rebuilt by Hodgson Fowler, 1884–6, and has a fine Curvilinear E. window. There is an excellent collection of Saxon crosses, including one depicting a warrior with spear, axe, sword and shield.

MIDDLETON TYAS † St Michael and all Angels

5m/8km N.E. of Richmond
OS *NZ235055* **GPS** *54.4450N, 1.6388W*

A Norman church with majestic arcades, it was enlarged in the late 13th to early 14th centuries by the addition of a S. aisle. There is good Plate tracery in the aisle windows and many Early English details. A very beautiful late 13th-century coffin lid with an ornate foliate cross is set into a recess in the S. aisle, and on the S. wall of the chancel is a brass of 1763 to the multilingual Rev. John Mawer.

NETHER POPPLETON † St Everilda

3m/4km N.W. of York

OS *SE564550* **GPS** *53.9884N, 1.1406W*

Set behind a farm at the end of the village, this pleasantly rural church of Norman origin has a central gabled double bellcote. The windows are all set in square-headed frames. The three-light E. window was restored and re-leaded in 1956, and contains early 14th-century window glass depicting composite figures against architectural backgrounds. The central light has later 14th-century material depicting a crowned female and mitred bishop. In the chancel are some good canopied wall monuments to the Hutton family, and there are 18th-century galleries to the N. and W. of the nave.

NORMANBY † St Andrew

3m/4km S.W. of Pickering

OS *SE734816* **GPS** *54.2254N, 0.8744W*

Another delightful small church with a gabled twin bellcote, this is a Georgian rebuilding, all completely refashioned by Temple Moore in 1893–5. The N. arcade is Norman, the chancel arch is c. 1300, and the S. porch has a rebuilt doorway incorporating 12th-century stonework, and a stone coffin lid set in the wall. Inside is a barrel-vaulted roof with fine carved bosses and an unusual poor box formed from a turned baluster.

NORTH GRIMSTON † St Nicholas ★

4m/6km S.E. of Malton

OS *SE841677* **GPS** *54.0990N, 0.7148W*

A gentle, retiring building, all 12th- and 13th-century on the outside, and, inside, a Norman chancel arch and, best of all, a prodigious Norman drum font robustly carved with the Last Supper, Descent from the Cross, and St Nicholas. The flagons, platters and utensils on the Last Supper table are an intriguing cameo of 11th-century eating habits.

NUN MONKTON † St Mary ★★

8m/13km N.W. of York

OS *SE511579* **GPS** *54.0148N, 1.2208W*

This exquisite building in a delightful setting by a late 17th-century manor is a relic of an old Benedictine nunnery. Only the Early English nave survives. The W. front has an outstanding Transitional doorway flanked by niches, in one of which is a fragment of 13th-century sculpture. A tall hood mould stands over the doorway, above which are three elegant tall lancets and a little square pyramid-topped tower, supported inside on a lofty arch. The treatment of the internal walls is superb: set into elevated passages and triforia are deeply-splayed lancet windows separated by tall open arcading. In the restored and rebuilt E. end, 1873, is superb glass by Morris & Co., to designs by Burne-Jones.

OLD BYLAND † All Saints

9m/15km E. of Thirsk

OS *SE550859* **GPS** *54.2663N, 1.1558W*

Behind cottages on the village green, the small, low church is half hidden from view. The nave and S. porch tower are Norman, as is the chancel arch with its rams' head capitals. There is a plain Norman tub font, and on the chancel floor are some medieval tiles. The S. doorway has reset Norman capitals with carvings of dragons. The Anglo-Danish sundial in the tower's E. wall has an inscription that reads *'Sumar-Ledan Huscarl me facit'*.

OLD MALTON

† St Mary the Virgin / St Mary's Priory

17m/27km N.E. of York

OS *SE798725* **GPS** *54.1426N, 0.7790W*

The present parish church is a fragment of a Gilbertine priory church founded c. 1150. The W. front, lacking the N. tower and with part of the great 15th-century window bricked up, would have delighted that great painter of Romantic ruins John Sell Cotman. The W. doorway displays good late 12th-century detail. The interior is full of interest, such as the late 11th-century work at the base of the S.W. tower and in the triforium, and the misericords, some 15th-century, others 20th-century. The stalls and organ case are by Temple Moore, 1887–8.

△ **PICKERING: ST PETER AND ST PAUL** – *the lofty spire dominates the town*

OSWALDKIRK † St Oswald

13m/19km E. of Thirsk
OS *SE620789* **GPS** *54.2023N, 1.0497W*

The church stands on the hillside with fine views over the Howardian Hills. Amongst the massive quoins of the W. front is a re-used section of a Saxon cross shaft. The S. porch, which contains fragments of Viking hogsback stones, shelters an early doorway with finely beaded capitals, and on the N. side is a blocked-up early Norman doorway. The nave is Norman, the simple S. windows are 13th-century. The chancel is an 1886 rebuilding and has a lovely painted ceiling.

PICKERING † St Peter and St Paul ★★

16m/25km W. of Scarborough
OS *SE798840* **GPS** *54.2457N, 0.7755W*

Seen from a distance, the tower and spire rise above the red pantiled roofs of the market town. This is an impressive and sizeable church of the 12th to 15th centuries. The church's glory is on the nave arcades – an arresting long array of 15th-century wall-paintings much repainted in the 1880s, but lively and very enjoyable. Here are shown the Martyrdom of John the Baptist and St Edmund, St George and the Dragon, the Passion and the Resurrection – a remarkable '*Biblia Pauperum*' (poor man's Bible) used to educate the illiterate congregation.

RASKELF † St Mary ★

8m/13km S.E. of Thirsk
OS *SE489707* **GPS** *54.1304N, 1.2524W*

The church is largely a 19th-century rebuilding around a delightful 15th-century weather-boarded timber tower and pyramid cap, unique in N. Yorkshire. The N. arcade is late 12th-century, and the Norman tub font has an elegant 17th-century cover. The renewed oak chancel arch and the oak arcades to the N. chapel are a reminder of the Forest of Galtres, once the hunting ground of the Neville family, at one time Lords of the Manor of Raskelf. Their Arms can be seen in one of the windows. The E. and W. windows have Reticulated tracery, and the S. aisle windows are 19th-century Gothic.

RICCALL † St Mary ★

4m/6km N. of Selby
OS *SE619378* **GPS** *53.8331N, 1.0600W*

J. L. Pearson rebuilt the Norman tower and added a S. porch as part of a sensitive 1864–5 restoration. Chiefly of the 12th and 14th centuries, the church has an exceptional 1160 Norman S. doorway of three recessed orders with fine carving including beakheads. The door is also 12th-century, nail-studded with fine strapwork C-hinges.

ROBIN HOOD'S BAY
† St Stephen (New Church) ★

5m/8km S.E. of Whitby; parish of Fylingdales
OS *NZ948052* **GPS** *54.4341N, 0.5390W*

This is an important work by G. E. Street, 1870. A big and earnest church of French Early Gothic style with a very tall saddleback tower, it has lovely external detailing: decorated covers to rainwater hoppers, decorative ridges on the clay-tiled roof and ornamental terminating finials on the nave and apse roofs. The chancel and apse are rib-vaulted, and the Plate-traceried apse windows have stained-glass images of saints. In the nave is characteristic openwork – scissor beams and collared rafters. On the N. nave wall there are two bronze relief panels, one dedicated to drowned mariners, 1912. Good glass by Henry Holiday includes a dramatic scene with fishermen and nets.

ROBIN HOOD'S BAY
† St Stephen (Old Church)

5m/8km S.E. of Whitby
OS *NZ941059* **GPS** *54.4401N, 0.5496W*
Churches Conservation Trust

The old church of 1821–2, with its cupola and long Gothic windows, stands isolated high up on the hills looking down towards Street's Victorian church and the wide curve of the bay beyond. In spirit it is nearest to Whitby St Mary's with its untouched interior of box pews and three-decker pulpit towering in the middle of the S. side. A gallery runs the length of the N. and W. sides. There are memorials to shipwrecked sailors, and maidens' garlands, recently conserved; and in the churchyard is a list of rescues by the local lifeboat.

ROECLIFFE † St Mary

5m/8km S.E. of Ripon
OS *SE375660* **GPS** *54.0887N, 1.4272W*
Churches Conservation Trust

By R. H. Sharp, 1843, this is an idiosyncratic neo-Norman church with a great barrel-vaulted interior, full of woodwork garnered from other churches: a vestry door from York Minster, a splendid Jacobean pulpit and altar rails, perspective panels dated 1619 and a vestry wall covered with numerous small panels.

RYTHER † All Saints

8m/13km S.W. of York
OS *SE555394* **GPS** *53.8480N, 1.1579W*

In a rural setting, the church has an early Norman chancel arch, a 13th-century nave and Decorated S. aisle with a remarkable group of 14th–15th-century Ryther family monuments and altar tombs, one to Sir Robert Ryther, d. 1327, with very finely detailed armour. Five 11th-century stone altars have incised and stylised symbols of the wounds of Christ. The bell-turret was added by C. Hodgson Fowler when he restored the church in 1898.

SALTON † St John de Beverley

7m/12km S.W. of Pickering
OS *SE716799* **GPS** *54.2105N, 0.9030W*

The church stands by the green of this small village in the Vale of Pickering, close to the confluence of the River Dove and the River Rye. It is a quite large Norman church with plenty of zigzag mouldings and windows like narrow black fingers. There is a very weathered corbel table and a S. door with outer ring of faces, inner of beakheads.

SCARBOROUGH † St Mary ★★

OS *TA046890* **GPS** *54.2865N, 0.3934W*

Perched high above the fishing village and under the lee of the castle, the church lost its great chancel and two W. towers during the Civil War siege of the town castle. The E. tower of 1669 was built on the site of the former central tower, now the new E. end of the church. The interior has good 12th–13th-century piers, arcades and clerestory; the wall shafts in the nave are comparable with Bolton Abbey. A series of 14th-century stone barrel-vaulted chapels opens off the S. aisle; these have fine free-flowing Geometrical tracery in the windows. The walls are crowded with good 18th- and 19th-century monuments, notable among which is one by Roubiliac to Elizabeth Craven, and the churchyard is full of tombs and headstones: the grave of Anne Brontë, 1849, is near the E. end.

SELBY † St Mary and St Germain ★★

13m/21km S. of York
OS *SE615323* **GPS** *53.7841N, 1.0671W*

This former abbey church was one of the earliest and most important Benedictine foundations in England. It is a remarkable survivor of several mishaps: owing to unstable foundations, the tower and central parts of the abbey

collapsed in 1690, and, following two restorations, one in 1871–3 by Sir George Gilbert Scott, and another by J. Oldrid Scott in 1889–90, a fire in the early 20th century destroyed the roof. A further and drastic restoration, again begun by J. Oldrid Scott, included a new crossing tower, 1908, the S. transept, c. 1912, and W. towers, 1935. The result is a splendid church. The exquisite Decorated choir has the restored original Jesse Tree glass in the E. window, itself a masterpiece of Decorated tracery. The mighty interior is Norman and Early English, with very similar piers to those at Durham Cathedral.

SHERBURN † St Hilda ★

11m/18km E. of Malton
OS *SE959774* **GPS** *54.1837N, 0.5312W*

Hodgson Fowler restored the church for Sir Tatton Sykes in 1910, retaining much of the church's early character in the lower 12th-century stage of the tower, an impressive early 12th-century chancel arch, with chevrons and carved symbols to the capitals, and the 14th-century chancel. The N. arcade is late 13th-century; there are traces of painted decoration on some piers and a piscina on the easternmost pier. The S. arcade is a lively Hodgson Fowler recreation, with moulded capitals and a continuous corbelled hood-mould. Much of the furniture was donated by Sir Tatton Sykes, including a fine rood screen and carved choir stalls.

SHERBURN-IN-ELMET † All Saints ★★

6m/10km S. of Tadcaster
OS *SE488335* **GPS** *53.7958N, 1.2606W*

The church occupies a hill-top site, and is visible for miles around. The tower is very distinctive, with overhanging parapets on a corbel table, and crocketed pinnacles at each corner; the W. window is filled with fine heraldic glass. At the church's core is a fine Norman building with stately nave arcades and two fine round-headed arches to the chancel and the tower. The 14th-century S. aisle and alterations to the N. aisle have given the church some good Perpendicular windows and form an interesting contrast to the austere but pleasing Early English chancel, restored by Salvin in 1857. On the E. and S. walls of the S. aisle are the two faces of the famous and recently restored Janus Cross – a 15th-century double-sided crucifix. It was split into two halves to resolve a disagreement about ownership between the vicar and a churchwarden.

SKELTON † St Giles ★★

4m/6km N.W. of York
OS *SE568565* **GPS** *54.0019N, 1.1342W*

'Few ecclesiastical buildings of like dimensions will, I think, be found more perfect in harmony of parts, unity of design and purity of style', said the 19th-century architect Ewan Christian. The church was completed prior to 1247, and is all of an Early English style close to that of the S. transept of York Minster. The great S. doorway was renewed by Henry Graham, 1814–18, and although already weathering, is extremely beautiful with its wind-blown leaf capitals. The font is an octagonal faceted bowl, the chancel piscina has fine leaf decoration, and every detail right up to the stiff-leaf cross on the gable is a joy.

SKELTON-ON-URE
† Christ the Consoler ★

4m/7km S.E. of Ripon
OS *SE359679* **GPS** *54.1062N, 1.4510W*
Churches Conservation Trust

A lavish creation of William Burges, the church was built as a memorial in 1871–6 by Lady Mary Vyner to her son, killed by brigands in Greece. There is a mournful air here, resonant of the church's origins. The theme of the fabric is French Gothic, with a rose window and much Plate tracery. The interior of the nave is muted, with walls and arcades of white stone, and black marble columns. The colour here is in the Ascension sculptures over the chancel arch. In marked contrast the chancel is all coloured marble, rich stone carving and paintwork. The jewelled altar frontal was made by Lady Vyner to Burges's design.

SKIPTON † Holy Trinity ★

16m/25km N.W. of Bradford
OS *SD990519* **GPS** *53.9633N, 2.0161W*

Damaged in the Civil War, the church was restored by Lady Anne Clifford in 1659 and

◁ **PICKERING: ST PETER AND ST PAUL** – *15th-century wall-painting of St George and the Dragon*

is picturesquely set next to the castle. The style is predominantly regional Perpendicular, incorporating some Decorated work. The magnificent tomb of the 3rd Earl George Clifford in the Lady Chapel – which has colourful glass by Capronnier – is a reminder of the links between the church and castle. The Tudor roof and screen are very fine, and there is an excellent Jacobean font cover to the 12th-century font. In the chancel is a startlingly vivid reredos by George Gilbert Scott.

SOUTH COWTON † St Mary

8m/12km S. of Darlington
OS *NZ293026* **GPS** *54.4186N, 1.5497W*
Churches Conservation Trust

A fine late medieval church close to the remains of the castle that belonged to Sir Richard Conyers: the outside is stern, with a bulky external stair turret to the tower, and square-headed mullion windows along the nave and chancel. The Perpendicular S. porch is barrel-vaulted with a room above. The interior is much lighter, with a fine screen, a wall-painting above the chancel arch and a lovely roof. Also of interest are the alabaster effigies of Sir Christopher Boynton and his two wives, and the Conyers and Boynton Arms in the central bay of the nave.

SPEETON † St Leonard

4m/6km S.E. of Filey
OS *TA151746* **GPS** *54.1552N, 0.2384W*

This is a small church of modest charm, set apart in the middle of a field near the edge of high chalk cliffs. The whitewashed interior has a Norman chancel arch and font, and set in the N. wall is a 12th-century Agnus Dei. The church was beautifully restored by Francis Johnson, 1976–7, who replaced the pine furnishings with ones of oak.

SPROXTON † St Chad ★

12m/19km E. of Thirsk
OS *SE613815* **GPS** *54.2264N, 1.0598W*

In the mid-19th century the church was saved from being used as a barn at West Newton Grange, and then in 1879 was moved here, stone by stone, by George Gilbert Scott Jnr and Temple Moore. It has a domestic Jacobean exterior with pleasant windows, grey stone roof, and good gate piers. The interior is even better, with a simple altar table and reredos, part of a fine 15th-century glass Crucifixion in the nave window and a chancel screen by Temple Moore.

STAINBURN † St Mary the Virgin

7m/11km S.W. of Harrogate
OS *SE247485* **GPS** *53.9325N, 1.6246W*
Churches Conservation Trust

On lonely moors, the church has wonderful views over Wharfedale: its stone roof and sandstone walls are almost a part of the natural landscape. Inside is a Norman arcaded polygonal font and a splendid chancel arch, which leads to a narrower chancel on a lower level. Furnishings include a 17th-century pulpit and Jacobean pews.

STILLINGFLEET † St Helen

7m/12km S. of York
OS *SE593410* **GPS** *53.8619N, 1.0994W*

St Helen's has a handsome Norman S. doorway of five recessed orders with similar carvings to Riccall; very early decorative ironwork on the door depicts a Viking-style ship. The Moreby Chapel contains an effigy of a cross-legged knight, Sir Robert Moreby, reputedly c. 1337. The Jacobean screen has decorated panelling surmounted by bulb-on-vase balusters. Outside in the churchyard is a touching monument to 11 choristers who drowned in the River Ouse when the boat bringing them from carol-singing capsized on Boxing Day 1833.

STILLINGTON † St Nicholas

12m/19km N. of York
OS *SE583678* **GPS** *54.1031N, 1.1098W*

The church forms a welcome break in the long village street with its well-kept grass banks covered with bulbs in the spring. The local warm stone is used for the walls and the windows are of a local Perpendicular type. The author Laurence Sterne was vicar here from 1744 to 1768. The atmospheric cream-washed interior has late box pews, arcades with mouldings dying into octagonal piers, red-brick floors and clear glazing. There is a charming little memorial window to a local headmaster, whose love of cricket and gardening are depicted by three colourful chrysanthemums and a silhouette of the Lord's Cricket Ground weathervane.

STONEGRAVE † Holy Trinity

11m/18km N.W. of Malton
OS *SE655778* **GPS** *54.1925N, 0.9965W*

Set on a gentle hillside with wide views over the Howardian Hills, the church is plain but dignified – the smallest former Minster church in the county. Apart from the 12th-century tower, the exterior is all G. Fowler Jones, 1863. The interior is rewarding, with an early Norman N. arcade and a S. arcade only a little later. The Jacobean screen is especially attractive, and the pulpit is Jacobean too. Amongst early sculptural fragments is a fine 10th-century cross with wheel head and close interlace, and over the priest's door hangs a painted memorial to William Thornton, d. 1668, painted on canvas.

STUDLEY ROYAL
† St Mary the Virgin ★★

2m/3km W. of Ripon
OS *SE275692* **GPS** *54.1187N, 1.5801W*
English Heritage

This is William Burges' exotic sister church to Skelton-on-Ure's Christ the Consoler, strikingly set in a deer park at the head of a long avenue, on the Fountains Abbey estate. The rich and exotic exterior is in picturesque style, with a commanding octagonal steeple and elaborate E. end. The cream and grey nave contains the founder's tomb of 1909 and an organ case with overset upper storeys reached by a spiral staircase. Colour here is from the glass rather than the decoration. The chancel is a different matter: a riot of colour and decoration based on the Book of the Revelation; the ceiling has angelic choirs, the floor depicts the four rivers round the Garden of Eden, and there is an Assyrian lion over the sedilia. Set over all this is a fine rose window. As a composition it is a masterpiece.

TADCASTER † St Mary

9m/15km S.W. of York
OS *SE485435* **GPS** *53.8855N, 1.2622W*

The present church is a rebuild of 1875–7, when it was raised about five feet above its original base to preserve it against floods. The church is of light limestone, largely Perpendicular, with many of the Norman features reset, including the chancel arch, now at the W. end of the S. aisle, and the 13th-century N. arcade. In one of the S. aisle windows is a delightful medieval roundel of St Catherine, patron saint of linen weavers. The E. window is by Morris & Co., and there is exceptionally fine early 20th-century woodwork.

THIRSK † St Mary ★★

8m/12km S.E. of Northallerton
OS *SE427823* **GPS** *54.2348N, 1.3458W*

From the market-place a fine 18th-century street, Kirkgate, leads past the hall to the S. side of the 15th-century Perpendicular church. The rather chunky tower has a lovely openwork stone parapet, echoed on the clerestory and aisles, and a very fine, large stone porch with parvise and an outstanding Perpendicular door. The body of the church is an essay in fully developed Perpendicular, and was built in 1420. The nave arcades are tall, interspersed with hatchments of local families. The chancel followed in 1470. The wagon roof is carved, like that in the nave, with heraldic devices, faces and scenes of domestic life. At the W. end of the S. aisle is the 'Happy Warrior' window by Douglas Strachan, 1932. It shows Sir Robert Bower, a soldier from an old Yorkshire family (and later Chief Constable of the North Riding Constabulary) as a mounted knight in armour, with smaller panels illustrating his military exploits. At the W. end is the Victorian font with a 21-foot tall, spire-like font cover, partly 15th-century. The suspension cable that lifts it snapped in 2008, and is now happily renewed.

THORMANBY † St Mary Magdalene

8m.13km S.E. of Thirsk
OS *SE495749* **GPS** *54.1681N, 1.2419W*

This isolated church of 12th-century origin has a domesticated S. porch and squat brick tower of 1822. The external stonework varies much in size, texture and colour, and is most attractive. The homely nave has benches, a simple font cover and lime-washed walls, a contrast with the good early 20th-century

△ **WENSLEY: HOLY TRINITY** – *a winter morning sun brings glory to this Yorkshire church, picking out the east walls and each headstone in sharp relief*

furnishing and glass in the chancel. The E. window is by Kempe, and a window in the S. wall has some 15th-century glass.

THORNTON DALE † All Saints

3m/4km E. of Pickering
OS *SE838831* **GPS** *54.2370N, 0.7153W*

The church tower looks down the hill towards the stream and main street. The whole fabric of the church is Decorated. The S. doorway has lively heads as hood-mould stops. The chancel has an interesting monument: the effigy of Lady Beatrice Hastings lies in a recessed wall tomb, and Sir Richard Cholmley, the 'Black Knight of the North', is buried in the chancel. Outside in the churchyard is the grave of Private Matthew Grimes, who guarded Napoleon on the Isle of St Helena.

THORNTON STEWARD † St Oswald

6m/10km W. of Bedale
OS *SE170869* **GPS** *54.2778N, 1.7396W*

A path leads down through the fields towards the Ure and at the end is a small, unassuming building, but one of great age, for there are Anglo-Saxon or very early Norman quoins at the E. and W. ends, and the remains of a previous arch above the present pointed chancel arch may also be pre-Conquest. The nave, its windows and S. door are Norman, and the chancel is c. 1200. A 14th-century addition is a large tomb recess in the chancel with fine mouldings – probably an Easter Sepulchre.

UPLEATHAM † St Andrew (Old Church)

4m/7km S.E. of Redcar
OS *NZ637193* **GPS** *54.5655N, 1.0161W*

This puzzlingly small church, the subject of much historical conjecture, consists of the W. part of the nave – 18 by 12 feet – of a larger Norman church, and a tiny tower of 1684. The N. wall has 10 corbel heads set at the top. Archaeology has revealed the existence of a larger (but not much larger) church of the 12th century, and among the significant finds were a 14th-century stone effigy of a knight, two pre-Conquest cross fragments, and an 11th-century child's gable-ended grave slab. The setting is delightful, on a valley side looking out towards Skelton and the wooded castle grounds.

△ **WENSLEY: HOLY TRINITY** – *the Scrope family pew, with its 17th-century pendant round arches at the front and early 16th-century parclose screen at the back*

WEAVERTHORPE † St Andrew
13m/19km S.W. of Scarborough
OS *SE966711* **GPS** *54.1267N, 0.5222W*

St Andrew's stands in farmland above the little wolds village. The tall early Norman W. tower is of a type more usually seen in Northumberland; the nave and chancel are Norman too, with a 12th-century sundial over the S. door with a Latin inscription. The Norman drum font has a motif of low relief circles and octagons, some enclosing saltire crosses. Restoration was by G. E. Street, 1871–2, with a brass chancel screen by T. Potter, and glass and polyptych by Clayton & Bell. The nave was given a delightful painted roof.

WENSLEY † Holy Trinity ★★
1m/2km W. of Leyburn
OS *SE092895* **GPS** *54.3013N, 1.8600W*

Set by the River Ure below Leyburn and opposite the entrance to Bolton Hall, the external appearance of Holy Trinity is pleasant but unremarkable. The interior is a different matter, with richly carved early benches, box pews, a fine Early English chancel with dogtooth carving and a Flemish priest's brass of 1395. In the nave is the extraordinary Scrope family pew, with its 17th-century classical front with pendant round arches. The back of the pew is formed from the fine carved early 16th-century parclose screen from the Scrope Chantry at Easby Abbey. The whole assembly must have been very intimidating for the vicar and congregation.

WESTON † All Saints ★
5m/8km E. of Ilkley
OS *SE177466* **GPS** *53.9155N, 1.7313W*

This is a charming jumble of a church, whose W. end is supported to the S. by a narrow stepped buttress, and to the W. by a much bulkier stepped buttress. These have the hallmark of urgent repairs: the whole building has a charming feeling of afterthought about it, with a miscellany of square-headed mullioned windows, Perpendicular and Geometrical tracery and lancets. The curious stone bellcote with its finialled top is a feature more commonly seen on Scottish churches. The chancel gable is higher than the nave, and at a much steeper pitch, all raised in 1819. A vestry with stone chimney stack has been tacked onto the N. side, introducing

△ **WHITBY: ST MARY** – *a squat, weather-resistant church overlooking Whitby Bay, crammed with 18th-century furnishings*

a domestic element to the building. The delightful plastered interior has late Georgian box pews and a three-decker pulpit. A family pew, complete with fireplace, contains the tomb of Sir William Stopham, d. 1317, and in the chancel N. wall is an ogee-arched recess with the tomb of William Vasavour, d. 1587; nearby, three pieces of an Anglo-Saxon cross are built into the wall.

WHARRAM-LE-STREET † St Mary

6ml10km S.E. of Malton
OS *SE863659* **GPS** *54.0820N, 0.6809W*

Reached by a narrow wooded pathway, the church stands in a lovely setting on a Wold hillside, next to an old Roman road, with wide views towards the plain and the Yorkshire Moors on the skyline. The nave and tower are Anglo-Saxon in origin, though the blocked W. doorway is probably very early Norman, as is the top section of the tower. The 19th-century porch shelters a fine Norman doorway with billets and zigzags. The chancel and part of the nave were rebuilt c. 1863, and the N. aisle is 14th-century.

WHENBY † St Martin

10ml16km N. of York
OS *SE630698* **GPS** *54.1204N, 1.0364W*
Churches Conservation Trust

Close to Castle Howard, the church is at its best in Spring, when the churchyard is full of snowdrops and daffodils. Prominent battlements on the tower, nave and chancel suggest that all is Perpendicular, but inside there are hints of a 13th-century church in the offsetting of the tower to the N. The 15th-century chancel screen has some remnants of colour, and the Jacobean screen to the N. chapel has the original door latch and hinges.

WHITBY † St Mary ★★

17ml27km N.W. of Scarborough
OS *NZ901112* **GPS** *54.4889N, 0.6098W*

Near the abbey ruins on a hill high above the old town, St Mary's looks down on the harbour. The church was built to resist coastal storms, and looks like it, with a squat tower, heavy dark walls and an assembly of external stairs and extensions. The interest is mainly inside, in the splendid interior remodelled in the 18th century. The great rectangular nave is filled with box pews and galleries rising almost to the roof, all centred on the high pulpit and reading desk, attached to which are two enormous ear trumpets for a Georgian incumbent's wife. The nave appears light against the murk of the unspoilt 12th-century chancel. Most extraordinary is the Cholmley Pew, supported by barley-twist Corinthian columns. This straddles the chancel arch, imperiously turning its back on the altar, looking W. onto the back of the pulpit.

WINTRINGHAM † St Peter

6ml/10km E. of Malton
OS *SE887731* **GPS** *54.1468N, 0.6431W*
Churches Conservation Trust

Set in a dell of the Wolds away from a village of whitewashed cottages, this is a fine medieval church of Norman origins, restored by Oldrid Scott, 1887, and with fine oak fittings added to the chancel in 1889–91 by Temple Moore. The chancel, with corbel tables, is where most Norman work can be seen. The nave and aisles are Perpendicular, and the W. tower has a slender recessed octagonal spire. The inside has great faded charm, with Perpendicular screens, Jacobean pews and a two-decker pulpit. In 2004 the church was vested in the Churches Conservation Trust, who carried out major repairs and comprehensive restorations in 2005–7.

YORK † All Saints ★★

North Street
OS *SE600517* **GPS** *53.9584N, 1.0863W*

The tower and spire are one of the city's landmarks, and rise from within the body of the church, as is usual here, with a graceful two-stage octagon at the top. The early 20th-century anchorage of reinforced concrete with timber cladding is ingenious. Inside, the church has been restored and re-arranged so that former clutter has given way to clarity and a freshness of detail; it still possesses great beauty. The 13th- and 14th-century arcades run unbroken from the W. to the E. end, and in the E. bays there are lovely traceried parclose screens. The moulded ribs of the ceilings were delightfully painted in 1977: the angels now have gilded wings. The hexagonal 17th-century pulpit is painted too – each panel depicting one of the Virtues. There is medieval painted glass of outstanding interest: two windows of note depict 'Corporal Acts of Mercy', and the 'Pricke of Conscience'. There was extensive restoration here after a 1997 fire.

YORK † Holy Trinity ★

Goodramgate
OS *SE604520* **GPS** *53.9610N, 1.0804W*
Churches Conservation Trust

At the edge of Goodramgate, a brick gateway of 1786 affords a glimpse of the churchyard with weeping ash and ledger stone; by far the most satisfactory entry to any York church. The exterior is a delightful medley of different materials, colours and textures, and pleasant 14th-century windows with Reticulated tracery. Internally, the church, with its different levels, is one of the most picturesque in York. The effect is produced by the pews, of many dates, which weave and flow in waves around the two-decker pulpit, 1785. The arcades spring from very stumpy columns. Excellent 15th-century stained glass includes St George and the Dragon, St John the Baptist with a camel skin, and the Virgin in a brilliant mandorla.

YORK † St Olave

Marygate
OS *SE598521* **GPS** *53.9623N, 1.0890W*

Behind St Olave's is the ruined N. aisle of St Mary's Abbey, linked at the W. end to other abbey buildings, and attached at the E. end to a superb medieval wall. The church has pre-Conquest origins but is largely 15th-century in its present form, the N. side of the church being particularly good. The nave arcades were rebuilt in the 18th century and the columns are a curious hybrid of Gothic Roman Doric. The chancel was added in the 1880s and extended in 1908, when the S. chapel was built by J. F. Doyle – a rich and effective High Church period piece. There is fine 15th-century glass in the E. window of the chancel.

YORKSHIRE – SOUTH

Only created as a county in 1974, South Yorkshire is bounded to the west by the Pennines, and borders Derbyshire, North Yorkshire, the East Riding of Yorkshire, Nottinghamshire and Lincolnshire. Over half the county's population is concentrated in the Sheffield area, the ninth most populous urban area in Britain and once the heart of the steel industry: here there is some monstrous 1960s architecture. Sheffield's churches, many of which were lost during the bombing of the Second World War, were a response to both the city's great industrial wealth and the slum conditions of many of its workers.

One of Sheffield's most notable Victorian buildings is E. W. Mountford's town hall, on top of which stands a statue of Vulcan, the God of Fire, a fitting symbol of the city's heyday of steel. The county's churches are for the most part soot-stained millstone grit and limestone, though notable exceptions can be seen in such churches as St Peter, Barnburgh, with its cream limestone.

To the N.E. of Sheffield is a flatter landscape, with another former industrial centre – Doncaster, a wealthy town well placed on the Great North Road. Later wealth was built on deep seam coal and the availability of good navigable waterways, the River Don and the Don Navigation. This is an area of great country houses, Broderick Hall and Cusworth Hall among them. The railways brought great expansion to Doncaster, with easy transport for the town's foundries to other industrial centres, and the famous GNR Locomotive and Carriage Building Works rivalled the great Midland Railway locomotive works of Derby. The town has suffered from hideous 20th-century building, but its most striking landmark, St Gregory's Minster, is an outstanding piece of Victorian Gothic Revival. Of the county's other main centres, Barnsley had its heart ripped out in a frenzy of awful post-war building, and Rotherham is more or less continuous with Sheffield, only separated from it by the MI. All Saints Church, one of the county's finest, struggles to keep its dignity in the remnants of Rotherham Old Town.

The great coal mines were for the most part concentrated in the N. and E. of the county, as was iron ore extraction. Though almost entirely lost now, their impact on the landscapes was dramatic, and parts of the county remain studded with power stations, and criss-crossed with the overhead lines of the National Grid. Only W. of Sheffield, where the millstone grit moors meet the northern parts of the Derbyshire High Peak, does one get a true sense of solitude.

◁ **SILKSTONE: ALL SAINTS** – *a church for a coalmining community, whose memorials include tributes to children who lost their lives in the mines in the 1830s*

ADWICK-UPON-DEARNE † St John

8ml/13km W. of Doncaster

OS *SE470014* **GPS** *53.5080N, 1.2924W*

This is a small, rustic 12th–13th-century church of sandstone coated with pebble-dash; the vestry was added and chancel arch replaced in 1910 by A. C. Martin. It still retains the Norman nave and chancel, with a mixture of deep splayed square-headed mullion windows and simple pointed windows with Y-tracery. The atmosphere inside is very pleasing, lit by clear glass. On the nave wall is a Royal Arms of 1727. At the W. end is a rare Norman double bellcote, set slightly proud of the W. end wall.

ARKSEY † All Saints ★

Suburb 2ml/3km N. of Doncaster

OS *SE579069* **GPS** *53.5557N, 1.1271W*

The church is close to the almshouses and school built by Sir Bryan Cooke in the late 17th century. It is well-proportioned, cruciform with a central tower and octagonal spire. The stocky tower parapets are repeated around the aisles and porch. Although the exterior is largely Perpendicular, the church has a Norman and Early English core. Good furnishings include the 17th-century pulpit, font cover and a bust of Sir George Cooke in the N. transept.

AUSTERFIELD † St Helena

1ml/2km N.E. of Bawtry

OS *SK661946* **GPS** *53.4448N, 1.0053W*

Set back a churchyard's length from a straggling village street, the church was restored by Hodgson Fowler in 1897–8. There is much of interest from the church's Norman origins: the tympanum of the S. door carved with a dragon and a well-preserved 12th-century N. arcade exposed during the restoration. Carved into the central pier is a Sheila-na-Gig. The Norman chancel arch has zigzag and roll moulding. The N. aisle was built in 1897 in memory of William Bradford, baptised in the church in 1589: he later became Governor of the Plymouth Colony in 1621.

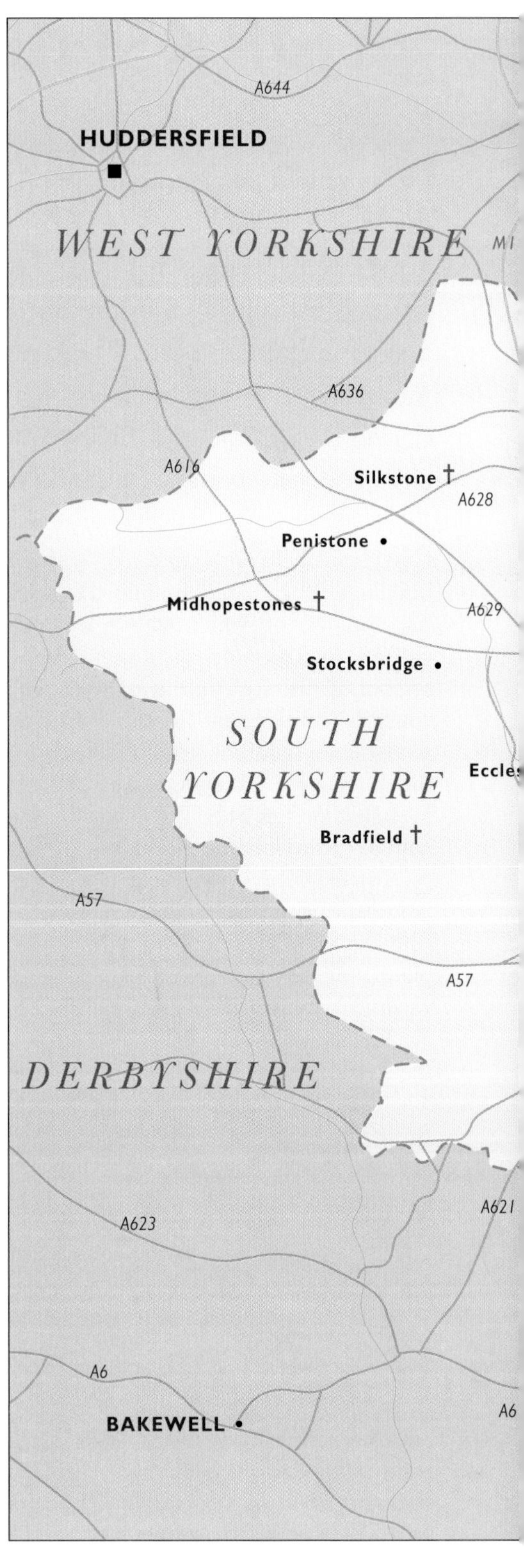

A19
M18
A1
Campsall
Fishlake
Hemsworth
Kirk
Bramwith
Thorne
Burghwallis
Royston
Hatfield
A18
Frickley
Hooton Pagnell
Kirk Sandall
Brodsworth
Great Houghton
Arksea
A18
RNSLEY
Darfield
Hickleton
Marr
Barnburgh
Sprotborough
High Melton
DONCASTER
Cantley
Adwick-
upon-
Dearne
A614
Wentworth
Ravenfield
Braithwell
Austerfield
Tickhill
Bawtry
ROTHERHAM
Maltby
A631
A631
A1(M)
A631
M1
A634
NOTTINGHAM-
SHIRE
Laughton-en-
le-Morthen
Firbeck
SHEFFIELD
A618
A60
A620
M1
A57
Thorpe Salvin
WORKSOP
A619
0
5 miles
CHESTERFIELD
0
5 km
A61

△ **BRADFIELD: ST NICHOLAS** – *originally a chapel of ease to Ecclesfield's St Mary, Bradfield became a parish in its own right in 1868*

BARNBURGH † St Peter ★

7ml/12km W. of Doncaster
OS *SE484032* **GPS** *53.5233N, 1.2712W*

A church of creamy stone in a church-yard grazed by goats, it is Transitional with a 14th-century chancel, S. aisle arcade and Perpendicular top stage to the tower. The N. arcade is Norman. A fine carved Norman cross shaft stands in the nave, and in the Cresacre Chapel is an outstanding oak effigy to Sir Thomas Cresacre, d. 1348, in full armour, with his feet resting upon a cat. Legend tells that he and a wild cat killed each other in the church porch (mentioned by Ted Hughes in his poem *Esther's Tomcat*). A cat appears on the family crest, and in a stone on the tower.

BRADFIELD † St Nicholas ★

8ml/13km N.W. of Sheffield
OS *SK267925* **GPS** *53.4290N, 1.5993W*

There are wonderful views from here, looking over the valley to the surrounding hills. The gritstone church is mostly Perpendicular, but with arcade piers, a chancel arch and font from the original Norman church. A Saxon cross, brought from the lower village, is built into the N. wall. There is a wide array of Victorian glass including a very good E. window by Hardman, installed in the 1886 restoration, and oak medieval panelling from France in the sanctuary.

BRAITHWELL † St James

2ml/3km N. of Maltby
OS *SK529946* **GPS** *53.4464N, 1.2036W*

There are signs of an early proposed central tower: an Early English arch opens into the crossing space from the nave. A plain Norman arch stands at the E. of the crossing space, leading to the Tudor chancel. The S. aisle was added in the 14th century. The interior has pronounced atmosphere, with some re-used Elizabethan panels in the pulpit, and woodwork by Robert 'Mouseman' Thompson, 1947.

BRODSWORTH † St Michael

5ml/8km N.W. of Doncaster
OS *SE506072* **GPS** *53.5593N, 1.2365W*

Approached up a leafy hillside, the church has a Norman core and N. arcade. There are signs of earlier 11th-century work in the tower and chancel arch. The E. end has

Early English lancets, the N. aisle is c. 1200. The S. aisle and chapel are additions by the Thellussons of the great Victorian mansion close by. Inside is a well-carved pulpit of 1696, with marquetry, garland swags and cherubs' heads. There are many early incised ledger stones at the E. end, and monuments to the Thellussons in the S. chapel.

BURGHWALLIS † St Helen

6m/10km N. of Doncaster

OS *SE536120* **GPS** *53.6021N, 1.1900W*

In gaunt countryside festooned with overhead power-lines outside Doncaster stands an unspoilt aisleless church of the 10th–12th-centuries, with Perpendicular alterations. The chancel has herringbone stonework on the S. side and on the N. wall, and in the Perpendicular porch is a restored Saxon doorway. Inside, the tower arch has 12th- and 13th-century stonework, with a Gothic Revival gallery running across. There are many medieval ledger stones, and S. of the altar a slab incised with a jewelled cross, book and chalice – the inscription round the rim is to Richard Lyndall, rector, d. 1460.

CAMPSALL † St Mary Magdalene

7m/11km N. of Doncaster

OS *SE544140* **GPS** *53.6204N, 1.1779W*

This is a Norman cruciform church, extended in the 15th century, close to the site of Campsall Hall. The W. Norman tower is very fine, with a good set of Romanesque windows and blind arcading above the ornate W. door. The magnificent 15th-century rood screen has a long rhyming inscription at the top of the dado, and in the S. chapel there is a carved and painted stone altar by A. W. N. Pugin, brought from Ackworth Grange Chapel. The fine Yarborough monument is by John Flaxman R.A., 1803.

CANTLEY † St Wilfrid ★★

2m/3km E. of Doncaster

OS *SE618014* **GPS** *53.5060N, 1.0689W*

Although Early English with a Perpendicular W. tower, this is principally the recreation of a medieval parish church by Comper in 1894. The interior is a treasury of his work: the beautiful coloured rood screen and rood, the painted and stencilled parcloses and chancel arcades, seating, organ case, statues and font cover; every window except one has his glass; the two altars have wonderful testers set above. The N. side of the church was extended in 1989 by Donald Buttress, an acknowledged expert on Comper and Surveyor of the Fabric to Westminster Abbey.

DARFIELD † All Saints

5m/8km E. of Barnsley

OS *SE418043* **GPS** *53.5338N, 1.3696W*

There is 11th-, 12th- and 15th-century work in the tower of this Norman and Decorated church. The nave and chancel date from the earlier part of the 14th century, the S. aisle from the latter part. Mining subsidence necessitated further restoration in the 20th century. The font has a stout Jacobean corona cover, very similar to that over the pulpit tester, and in the S. aisle is a good carved pew with the Arms of the Boswells. Above, the roof is painted with unicorns, the emblem of the Wombwell family, now rather faint and dilapidated. In the churchyard is a monument to 189 miners killed in a colliery disaster in 1857.

DONCASTER † St George ★★

OS *SE574035* **GPS** *53.5256N, 1.1354W*

This is one of Sir George Gilbert Scott's largest town churches, replacing a 12th-century church that burnt down in 1853. It disdains the adjacent dual-carriageway (incredibly named Church Way) and dismal urban encroachment like a stately ship. Although Scott admirably replaced the old Perpendicular central tower with great accuracy, he reverted to his favourite Geometrical/Decorated style for the rest. The detailing in the finials, buttresses and tracery is outstanding, and the great seven-light W. window with glass by Ward & Hughes, and the equally fine E. window with glass by Hardman, are masterpieces. Inside is very grand and spacious, particularly the S. aisle, with a lovely and very large font of Cornish serpentine, and behind the altar is a sumptuous and richly painted reredos that runs right round the chancel. St George's was dedicated as a minster in 2004.

ECCLESFIELD † St Mary ★

4m/6km N. of Sheffield

OS *SK353942* **GPS** *53.4436N, 1.4700W*

Set on a hillside with a wide churchyard and views across Pennine moorland, this a very fine cruciform church with central tower, rebuilt in the late 15th century, with aisles running the length of the nave and chancel. At the W. end is an octagonal Perpendicular font, with carved panels, and in the chancel, behind an excellent rood screen, are interesting carved stall ends and misericords. In 1858 the blocked up chancel was reopened, and in 1897 any remaining galleries were removed. Colours, swords and bugles of the Ecclesfield Volunteers, raised as a defence force against Napoleon, stand along the N. wall.

FIRBECK † St Martin

6m/10km N. of Worksop

OS *SK562884* **GPS** *53.3900N, 1.1562W*

The old church was demolished in the early 19th century, and a new one built to a design by William Hurst, 1820, in neo-Norman style. A N. aisle was added in 1844, the chancel was rebuilt in apsidal form in 1887, and the 1820 tower was rebuilt in 1900. Considering the number of additions, the church has a distinguished unity of Continental Romanesque. Devotees of the turf will find inside memorials to the famous St Ledger horse racing family.

FISHLAKE † St Cuthbert ★★

3m/4km N. of Hatfield

OS *SE656131* **GPS** *53.6110N, 1.0095W*

A little forlorn in the low lying and marshy pastureland, from a distance the church conveys an impression of Perpendicular. However, the entrance is through a superb Norman S. doorway, richly carved and one of the best in Yorkshire with its large medallions with sitting figures, heads framed in foliage and battling angels. Inside, the arcades with handsome W. responds are 13th-century. So is the base of the tower, raised to its present noble proportions in the 15th century, when the clerestory was added. The spacious interior, wickedly scraped, has fine Decorated work in the chancel, especially in the E. window. The Decorated font with statuettes in niches is a work of great beauty.

FRICKLEY † All Saints

12m/19km N.W. of Doncaster

OS *SE468078* **GPS** *53.5655N, 1.2941W*

The church's isolated setting, approached across fields, is due to the disappearance of its hamlet, said to result from the Great Plague. The little 13th-century unbuttressed tower has a recessed stone spirelet, and inside is a Norman chancel arch and N. aisle. The S. chapel has a lovely Geometrical window. There is a delightful gilded organ case and glass in the E. window by Comper.

GREAT HOUGHTON

† St Michael and All Saints

6m/10km E. of Barnsley

OS *SE430065* **GPS** *53.5537N, 1.3518W*

This interesting chapel of c. 1650 is one of few churches built during the Commonwealth. It has great charm, with sooty Gothic Survival crow-step gables and battlemented parapets with round-headed merlons. The interior has a king-post roof, the original pulpit with tester, and box pews restored by G. G. Pace.

HATFIELD † St Lawrence ★

7m/11km N.E. of Doncaster

OS *SE663095* **GPS** *53.5787N, 1.0001W*

A large cruciform church with much Norman work and fine Perpendicular central tower that rises over the surrounding flat countryside. The tower bears the Arms of the Savage family, as does the commanding interior of the tower. The Norman W. front has lancet windows, the arcades are 13th-century, and the lofty transepts are Perpendicular. The chancel and chapel roofs have many fine carved bosses, and there is also a good 15th-century screen. The S. transept contains a curious memorial to William Oughtibridge, with angels above and large flowers below.

HICKLETON † St Wilfrid

6m/10km W. of Doncaster

OS *SE483053* **GPS** *53.5422N, 1.2726W*

The 2nd Viscount Halifax restored and furnished this late Perpendicular church, pleasantly set by the hall. The interior is enriched by ornate collected furnishings, sculptures and fitments of many dates from all over Europe. Coalmining subsidence led

ECCLESFIELD: ST MARY – *sparkling in the sunshine after rain, Ecclesfield's fine Perpendicular church stands on a knoll in the Pennine moorlands* ▷

△ **FISHLAKE: ST CUTHBERT** – *the south doorway is a rugged survival of bold Norman carving*

to an extensive 1985 restoration. The church is as well known for its lych gate containing three skulls as it is for its exotic contents.

HIGH MELTON

† All Saints or St James ★

4m/6km W. of Doncaster

OS *SE509018* **GPS** *53.5105N, 1.2337W*

The church has a Transitional nave and S. aisle, Perpendicular S. chapel and a good tower with proud crocketed finials. Amid much fine furniture and many monuments, the rood screen and reredos by Comper stands supreme. He also was responsible for the stained glass above the 12th-century font. There is a range of glass in the church, from medieval fragments to glass by Kempe.

HOOTON PAGNELL † All Saints

7m/11km N.W. of Doncaster

OS *SE485079* **GPS** *53.5659N, 1.2685W*

The porch walls of this interesting church contain fragments of ancient stone coffins, and the seats are formed from stone coffin slabs. The doorway is Norman, with original iron-work, as is the chancel arch and tower arch: the W. tower has an upper string course with gargoyles and an embattled and pinnacled parapet. The nave has a pleasing symmetry, with simple Y-tracery windows. The narrower chancel has Y-tracery and lancets. Furnishings include an 18th-century pulpit with marquetry panels, late medieval oak panels and benefaction boards. The church was well restored by J. L. Pearson in 1876.

KIRK BRAMWITH † St Mary

6m/10km N.E. of Doncaster

OS *SE619117* **GPS** *53.5984N, 1.0647W*

Known for the carpet of daffodils and the snowdrops that cover the churchyard in early spring, the church has a fine Norman doorway with scalloped capitals, zigzags and beakheads. This and the chancel arch are the sole Norman remnants: the rest is 14th- and 15th-century. It contains 20th-century heraldic glass, good oak furnishings by Robert 'Mouseman' Thompson, and a nave ceiling with Duchy of Lancaster Arms by G. G. Pace.

KIRK SANDALL † St Oswald ★

4m/6km N.E. of Doncaster
OS *SE609081* **GPS** *53.5663N, 1.0815W*
Churches Conservation Trust

The church stands in a spacious churchyard surrounded by railways, a canal, enormous cooling towers and an industrial estate – David and Goliath in stone and concrete respectively. Traces of the Saxon fabric can be seen in the W. gable, but the church is mostly Early English additions to a Norman core. The most interesting feature in the charming interior is the huge Perpendicular Rokeby Chapel, chantry to Archbishop Rokeby of Dublin and former vicar, commemorated in a very grand monument in the nave. Another ornate Rokeby monument is situated by the organ. There are lovely 15th-century screens, and some early 16th-century glass.

LAUGHTON-EN-LE-MORTHEN
† All Saints

8m/13km N.W. of Worksop
OS *SK517882* **GPS** *53.3882N, 1.2241W*

The distinguishing feature of All Saints is its magnificent Perpendicular tower with a Saxon N. porticus and octagonal spire that soars 185 feet high. Ingenious flying buttresses in two diminishing sizes support the spire – a beautiful piece of design. Inside, the church is unremarkable Perpendicular, restored by Sir George Gilbert Scott.

MALTBY † St Bartholomew

6m/10km E. of Rotherham
OS *SK527918* **GPS** *53.4211N, 1.2074W*

St Bartholomew's has a Saxon-Norman tower of three stages, with a small recessed Perpendicular octagonal stone spire. The remainder was pulled down in 1859 and pleasantly rebuilt in Early English style by P. Boyce.

MARR † St Helen

4m/6km N.W. of Doncaster
OS *SE514053* **GPS** *53.5422N, 1.2250W*

The church is set in a beautiful village and has traces of Saxon herringbone masonry in the N. wall. The nave is Norman, and the W. tower is Early English with a Perpendicular parapet and recessed octagonal spire. The porch has stone rib-vaulting. Inside is a Tudor brass of John Lewis and family, 1579, an Elizabethan font and several pieces of funeral armour. The windows are mainly Tudor arched lights, with a set of paired lancets and Decorated tracery in the N. wall.

MIDHOPESTONES
† St James the Less ★

3m/4km S. of Penistone
OS *SK235995* **GPS** *53.4920N, 1.6473W*

Just inside the northern limits of Sheffield stands a delightful little building with mullioned windows and a bell-turret. A plaque over the porch door bears the Arms of Godfrey Bosville, who rescued the church in 1705. Inside is a W. gallery with a pronounced sag to the centre, a Jacobean pulpit and low box pews. It is very charming.

RAVENFIELD † St James

4m/6km N.E. of Rotherham
OS *SK485954* **GPS** *53.4536N, 1.2698W*

This tiny Gothic Survival church stands in the grounds of the now demolished Ravenfield Hall. It was designed by the celebrated John Carr in 1756. The exterior is delightful, with a canted apse, obelisk finials by the tower and obelisks at the corners of the coped parapets. Inside there is a W. gallery, panelling to the nave dado and twisted baluster communion rails. Thomas Bosville is commemorated by a N. wall monument with a pelican on a sarcophagus, by Fisher of York.

ROTHERHAM † All Saints ★★

Between Bridge Gate and Church Street
OS *SK428928* **GPS** *53.4309N, 1.3567W*

This fine cruciform Perpendicular church stands in the remnants of the old town, a grand architectural statement in a sea of 20th-century mediocrity. The central tower and spire rise 180 feet. The crossing from inside is equally impressive, with a large and lofty 15th-century fan vault. There are charming 15th-century return stalls with poppyheads and misericords, and sedilia with ogee arches, and throughout the church are more than 30 carved Green Men. In the S. transept is the sad memorial to the Masbrough Boat Accident of 1841, when over 50 young people died at the launch of a vessel. The octagonal pulpit of 1604 is excellent: its 18th-century sounding board has cherubs and a corona with dove, and the 1777 Snetzler organ still has the original case, gilded and black. The Perpendicular tracery throughout the building is simply magnificent. As with St George's in Doncaster, the church was re-dedicated as a minster in 2004.

ROYSTON † St John the Baptist ★

3m/4km N. of Barnsley
OS *SE364112* **GPS** *53.5965N, 1.4511W*

A fragment of an Anglo-Saxon cross by the high altar is the only indication of the early origins of the church: the present fabric is mid-13th-century, with a 15th-century nave, clerestory, roof and W. tower. The tall Perpendicular tower has an unusual oriel window on its W. face. In the N. aisle there is Y-tracery, and the chancel has a good Decorated E. window. The nave and aisle roofs have some very good carved bosses – a head of St John the Baptist, the Agnus Dei, a Pelican in her Piety, sacred monograms, a Green Man and, in the N. aisle, an unusual synod of bishops. J. L. Pearson restored the church in 1867–9.

SHEFFIELD † St Matthew

Carver Street
OS *SK351871* **GPS** *53.3797N, 1.4732W*

This is a pleasing missionary church by Flockton & Son, 1854–5, reminiscent of medieval churches in York, but the principal interest is in the fittings: a gilded reredos and high altar by J. D. Sedding, who also designed the E. window; magnificent carved choir stalls by Charles Nicholson; and a font and pulpit with inlaid beaten copper panels added by H. J. Potter in the early 1900s.

SILKSTONE † All Saints ★★

4m/6km W. of Barnsley
OS *SE290058* **GPS** *53.5484N, 1.5625W*

The peaceful Perpendicular church stands on a knoll in this former coalmining community. The tower was moved from the centre crossing to the W. end of the church in the late 15th century, when it acquired its elaborate display of pinnacles, tiny flying buttresses and gargoyles. The arcades are Early English, and the chancel was rebuilt in 1852–8. The 14th-century rood screen is well carved, as are the intricate bosses that stud the Tudor roofs. In the S. Bretton Chapel are several Wentworth memorials, the most striking being that to Sir Thomas Wentworth, d. 1675 and his wife Grace, d. 1698 – fine alabaster effigies on a marble tomb with alabaster panels. On the S. wall is a memorial plaque to Joseph Bramah, whose inventions included the beer pump. Outside, adjacent to the tower, is the Huskar Memorial to 26 boys and girls drowned in a mine in 1838. The incident led to the passing of Lord Shaftesbury's 1842 Mines Act, prohibiting women and children from working underground.

SPROTBROUGH † St Mary

3m/4km W. of Doncaster
OS *SE539020* **GPS** *53.5122N, 1.1878W*

The 13th-century church has a notable Decorated tower, with an added Perpendicular upper stage. The S. porch is very pretty, with a half-timbered gable end. Inside there are Perpendicular arcades and a chancel arch with Royal Arms of George I above. The characterful interior has a rood screen with Decorated tracery, adjacent to two stalls with misericords. In the chancel is a strange stone seat with a caryatid bust of a man; it is thought to be a frith stool – a seat that offered sanctuary to its occupant. Set in the chancel floor is a ledger stone to Thomas Fitzwilliam, d. 1482, a former rector, shown in mass vestments holding a chalice.

THORPE SALVIN † St Peter ★

4m/6km W. of Worksop
OS *SK520811* **GPS** *53.3247N, 1.2201W*

An interesting pastoral setting unites this welcoming church with the ruins of an Elizabethan manor house built by Henry

△ **WENTWORTH: HOLY TRINITY** – *the shortened west tower and windowless south wall of the old church; Pearson's new church stands nearby in this pretty village*

Sandford. Sheltered by a Tudor half-timbered porch is a sumptuous Norman S. door with hollow chevrons, zigzags and lozenges, and inside is the celebrated Norman font with wonderful carvings of the four seasons. An old man warming himself before a fireplace represents Winter; Spring is shown by a figure riding out hawking; a figure harvesting corn represents Summer; and Autumn is shown by a farmer sowing seed. Additional panels depict the Sacrament of Baptism. Of additional interest are a chained Bible, the Sandford Chantry Chapel of 1380 and various Sandford memorials.

TICKHILL † St Mary ★★

6m/10km S. of Doncaster
OS *SK591930* **GPS** *53.4312N, 1.1108W*

Built in whitish-grey magnesian limestone, this is a fine medieval Yorkshire church. The splendid 13th-century W. tower has an early 15th-century top with graceful corona parapets and tall crocketed finials. It is best viewed from over the nearby millpond. The Early English doorway is decorated with nailheads, and the rest of the church was rebuilt during the second half of the 15th century. Inside is a great sense of space, lit well by the large array of windows in the nave, chancel and clerestory. The tomb of Sir Thomas Fitzwilliam is the most important item inside: it came from the nearby friary at the Dissolution. The tomb chest has putti and wreaths in Classical style, whilst the reclining effigies on top are medieval.

WENTWORTH

† Holy Trinity / Old Church ★

4m/6km N.W. of Rotherham
OS *SK383982* **GPS** *53.4799N, 1.4231W*
Churches Conservation Trust

Set in a picturesque village is an extraordinary church. The small Decorated W. tower and ruined 1684 nave form a picturesque group. The tower has lost its two upper stages, and the derelict S. wall of the 17th-century nave still has its ornate Classical porch, with Ionic pilasters and pediment. The chancel and N. chapel were created by Thomas Wentworth, 1st Earl of Strafford: his monument is inside on the N. wall, as well as a fine series of 16th- and 17th-century monuments including one to Charles I's close adviser, the first Earl of Strafford, 'Black Tom Tyrant', who was beheaded by the Long Parliament in 1641.

YORKSHIRE – WEST

The modern county of West Yorkshire is but a small part of the old West Riding; in the mid-1970s its southern end became South Yorkshire, while its northern end and ancient administrative centre of York were absorbed into North Yorkshire, and other bits were handed over to Cumbria, Lancashire, Greater Manchester and, in the east, to the East Riding. What is left of the West, barely a third of the original, is largely a series of conurbations around Leeds, Bradford, Halifax, Huddersfield and Wakefield.

Leeds straddles the Aire Gap – a navigable corridor through the Pennines connecting Yorkshire and Lancashire – and its position made it a city of strategic importance. Once a centre of manufacturing, it is now an important financial services centre, but its Victorian past is proudly proclaimed in the magnificent town hall.

Further south, Dewsbury, Bradford and Halifax are urban landscapes that originally followed the winding valleys of the South Pennines, still dotted with the former textile mills that brought prosperity to the region. To the west is Brontë country, gaunt Pennine uplands, with dark millstone grit outcrops and bare moorland. To the east the landscapes are flatter and lower.

The churches in West Yorkshire are for the most part modest and more dispersed in the Pennines, where the combination of church and setting can be dramatic. The two churches at Heptonstall, one ruined, the other Victorian, are fine examples of an atmospheric setting in the hills above Hebden Bridge. Some lovely small and ancient churches can be found in unpromising suburban surroundings too – one of the finest being at Adel in the northern suburbs of Leeds. In Wakefield, St John's forms a part of a group of outstanding Georgian town buildings. The grand churches are in the towns: the medieval Halifax Minster and St Peter Kirkgate in Leeds, a fine Tractarian missionary building of the 19th century.

◁ **BARDSEY: ALL HALLOWS** – *sunset accentuates the unusual shape of Bardsey's west end, the base of the Saxon tower enclosed by flanking aisles*

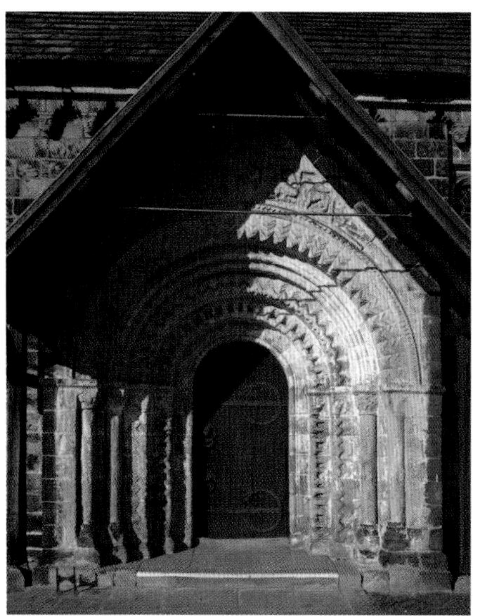

△ **ADEL: ST JOHN** – *Norman porch with four contrasting orders*

ADEL † St John the Baptist ★★

4m/6km N. of Leeds city centre
OS *SE274402* **GPS** *53.8576N, 1.5840W*

This sooty millstone grit church is one of the county's most celebrated Norman churches – astonishingly complete and untouched. An unbroken corbel table runs round the whole church; some of the corbels are Victorian re-cuts but many are original. The doorway, now protected by a canopy, is exemplary: four orders with roll moulding, zigzags and beakheads, with a gabled hood mould on which are carved the Evangelists and an Agnus Dei. The sanctuary ring on the door is a reproduction of the bronze original, stolen in 2002. The chancel arch is outstanding, with three orders towards the nave and two towards the chancel. The voussoirs have an intriguing range of carvings – owls, fish and an array of masks combining human and bestial features – some are very entertaining and some are rather sinister, but all show a great creative energy.

ALMONDBURY † All Saints Hallows ★

2m/3km S.E. of Huddersfield town centre
OS *SE168150* **GPS** *53.6318N, 1.7469W*

A Perpendicular church of dark stained stone, it has an Early English chancel

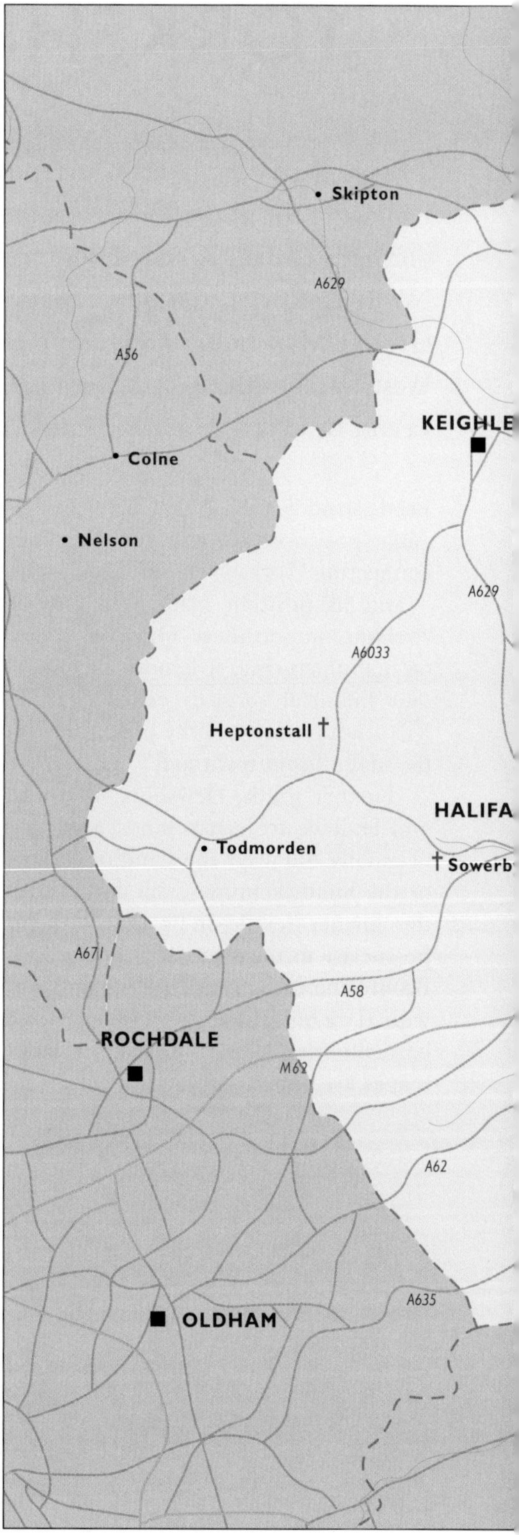

Knaresborough
HARROGATE
A658
NORTH YORKSHIRE
A661
Wetherby
A658
Otley
Collingham
A659
A659
Bardsey
A65
A1
Guiseley
A58
Yeadon
A61
Adel
A6120
A64
A162
Shipley
WEST YORKSHIRE
M1
Garforth
BRADFORD
LEEDS
A64
Kippax
Ledsham
M621
A63
A642
Methley
Castleford
A19
M62
Brighouse
Batley
A642
Dewsbury
WAKEFIELD
Pontefract
A644
Thornhill
Darrington
Horbury
UDDERSFIELD
A19
Almondbury
Netherton
A1
A637
A61
Hemsworth
A629
A628
A636
M1
A616
BARNSLEY
A628
Penistone
SOUTH YORKSHIRE

△ **BARDSEY: ALL HALLOWS** – *interior with Saxon nave and later north and south aisles*

and 14th-century aisles. The nave has a particularly fine ceiling: the long rhymed inscription round the cornice names Geferay Daystre as the joiner, and 1522 as the date of construction. The bosses are very well carved. The chancel roof is Victorian hammer-beam. Fittings include an early Georgian lectern, and a fine Perpendicular font cover. In the N. chapel there is good 15th-century stained glass, restored and possibly reset by the 5th Earl of Dartmouth in 1879.

BARDSEY † All Hallows ★★

7m/11km N.E. of Leeds
OS *SE365431* **GPS** *53.8830N, 1.4453W*

The church is special for its 9th-century Saxon tower, whose slender dimensions are accentuated by the flanking wide aisle gables. At the base is the outline of a blocked-up gabled Saxon doorway: this is a rare example of a Saxon church with a W. entrance, and long-and-short quoins can be seen on the W. face of the tower. The parapet is a 20th-century addition, and not a particularly welcome one. The N. and S. aisles were added between the 12th and 15th centuries, and the Norman doorway, with rustic beakheads and zigzags, was moved to its present position on the S. in the 16th century. Inside it is still possible to trace the outline of the Saxon nave.

COLLINGHAM † St Oswald

2m/3km S.W. of Wetherby
OS *SE390460* **GPS** *53.9096N, 1.4076W*

Although there is Saxon stonework in the nave and chancel, St Oswald's was heavily restored and rebuilt in 1840; happily it has retained the air of a small country church. Inside there are substantial fragmentary remains of two superb Saxon crosses: the Apostle's Cross dates from between the 8th and 10th centuries, and the Runic Cross, carved with intertwining dragons, is believed to be c. 900.

DARRINGTON † St Luke and All Saints

2m/3km S.E. of Pontefract
OS *SE485201* **GPS** *53.6758N, 1.2672W*

This is a very pleasing modest church of Tadcaster limestone set in a well-maintained churchyard away from the A1, whose Norman tower is enclosed by the aisled nave. The medieval interior is full of character, with a vast 15th-century rood stair-turret and little arcaded gallery carried over the N. aisle. There are some traceried Perpendicular bench-ends, four chancel stalls with misericords and, in the N. chapel, some 15th-century stained glass.

GUISELEY † St Oswald

8m/12km N.W. of Leeds
OS *SE194421* **GPS** *53.8751N, 1.7062W*

The original Norman St Oswald's acquired its tower and N. aisle c. 1480. Externally the fabric is complicated, largely due to an excellent rebuilding and extending in 1910 by Sir Charles Nicholson, who added the present nave, chancel, N. aisle and vestries. The 13th-century S. transept is a prominent feature of the older church. Patrick Brontë married Maria Branwell here in 1812.

ADEL: ST JOHN – *a delightful detail of the church is its sanctuary ring on the door, a reproduction of the bronze original* ▷

△ **HEPTONSTALL: ST THOMAS THE APOSTLE** – *a site with two churches, best seen in the rain*

HALIFAX

† St John the Baptist (Halifax Minster) ★★

Church Street

OS *SE097252* **GPS** *53.7232N, 1.8538W*

The large, soot-blackened, Perpendicular church stands at the bottom of the town in a tree-filled churchyard that mercifully screens it from vast areas of car parking. A dignified tower stands 118 feet high, and around the porch are some interesting gargoyles, particularly that of a bagpiper. Inside, near the entrance, is the statue of 'Old Tristam', a life-size figure holding an alms box, 1701. He was well known for begging in the church precincts. The sedilia is unusual, made of wood with three misericords, and more can be seen on the return stalls in the chancel. The nave has extensive Jacobean pews and splendid altar rails of 1698, with fine spiral carving. A grand series of painted panels on the nave and chancel roofs, 1695 to 1703, records the heraldry of various vicars of the church and local families of note. The church also has one of the 'Rolls Royces' of organs – a 1763 Snetzler. Among the inaugural pieces played on it was Handel's oratorio *The Messiah*.

HEPTONSTALL

† St Thomas the Apostle ★★

7ml/12km N.W. of Halifax

OS *SD986280* **GPS** *53.7484N, 2.0220W*

Heptonstall's extensive site with two churches is romantic and atmospheric, paved with mossy grave slabs and flagstones, all high in a valley that runs out to moorland. The old church, St Thomas à Becket, was badly damaged by a storm in 1847, and is now a roofless ruin, with the exception of the moss and lichen-covered tower. The poet Sylvia Plath, wife of Ted Hughes, is buried here. Near the old porch is the gravestone of David Hartley, executed in 1770 for counterfeiting coins. The old church was replaced in 1854 with a grand Gothic Revival church by Mallinson & Healey. The church is neo-Perpendicular, with a high W. tower, nave, aisles, chancel, chapels and N. and S. porch of pleasingly consistent style. The nave is divided in two by a large organ screen, behind which is the unusual 11-sided font from the old church. This is a church to be visited for its site and setting, especially in the rain, when the moss glows, and the pathways of grave slabs glisten.

◁ **GUISELEY: ST OSWALD** – *Sir Charles Nicholson added the nave and vestries in 1910 while keeping the 15th-century tower and north aisle*

HORBURY
† St Peter and St Leonard ★
3m/4km S.W. of Wakefield
OS *SE295183* **GPS** *53.6610N, 1.5548W*

A large and splendid church of 1791–3 in Adam style, it was designed and paid for by the stonemason and architect John Carr, who was born in Horbury and is buried in the crypt. The elegant rectangular tower spire diminishes in stages to a colonnaded rotunda with conical spire, and the projecting Ionic portico makes a fine entrance. The interior is very pretty, with a pastel-coloured plastered Georgian ceiling, a gently domed apse with gilded pilasters, and lovely Corinthian pillars to the nave, with gilded capitals. This was where the hymn *Onward Christian Soldiers* was written.

KIPPAX † St Mary
2m/3km S.E. of Garforth
OS *SE416303* **GPS** *53.7677N, 1.3691W*

A spacious, aisleless Norman church with dramatic herringbone masonry in the tower, its plan is much as it was when the church was first built in the early 1100s. Medieval work was mostly confined to windows in the Early English and Decorated chancel, the S. side of the nave and the re-roofing of the nave. Part of an Anglian cross, now in the nave, was discovered in 1876, set into the high-level doorway on the W. face of the tower. G. H. Fowler Jones undertook a thorough restoration in 1894.

LEDSHAM
† All Saints ★★
3m/5km N.E. of Castleford
OS *SE456297* **GPS** *53.7623N, 1.3090W*

In a village setting on a slight rise, the church has a Saxon nave, chancel arch and lower tower stage, in which is a fine Saxon doorway with lovely interlaced carving. Inside there are also traces of Saxon work in the chancel arch and high-level window openings. In the N. chapel are some very good 17th- and 18th-century monuments with effigies, including one to Sir John and Lady Lewis reclining on a sarcophagus on two levels, 1677, by Thomas Cartwright, and another by Peter Scheemakers to Lady Elizabeth Hastings, benefactor of Queen's College, Oxford, 'whom to love,' declared Steele, 'was a liberal education'.

LEEDS † St Aidan ★
Roundhay Road
OS *SE316352* **GPS** *53.8126N, 1.5207W*

A wonderful red-brick Romanesque basilica by R. J. Johnson and A. Crawford-Hick, 1891–4: the apsidal E. end is particularly good, with blind arcades over the arched apse windows, and flanking buttresses topped by round brick turrets with conical caps. There are great treasures inside, particularly Frank Brangwyn's celebrated mosaic in the apse illustrating the life of St Aidan, and the superb Caen and Bath stone pulpit with spiral steps supported on marble columns. The confessional, an unusual feature in an Anglican church, was carved by Robert 'Mouseman' Thompson: he also carved the oak lectern in the Resurrection chapel. The font is incredible: an imperial piece of Mexican onyx and polychromatic marble.

LEEDS † St Michael ★
Headingley
OS *SE280359* **GPS** *53.8191N, 1.5760W*

Better known for its cricket ground, Headingley also has a fine church with magnificent spire by J. L. Pearson, 1884–5, using much material from the previous church on the site. The impressive stone-vaulted interior has many of Pearson's hallmark features – Early English and Geometrical windows, a fine ironwork screen to the chancel, the triptych in the Lady Chapel and an unusual brass lectern set on the four Archangels. Temple Moore designed the magnificent reredos, a fine composition of some 21 figures spanning the width of the chancel, and throughout the church there is good glass by Powell.

LEEDS † St Peter ★
Kirkgate
OS *SE306333* **GPS** *53.7951N, 1.5361W*

The canalside setting described by Betjeman as 'drab' and by Pevsner as a 'dead end' is now on the rise, with restaurants, museums

HORBURY: ST PETER AND ST LEONARD – *Georgian outside and in, with a stately four-stage tower topped with rotunda and spire* ▷

△ **OTLEY: ALL SAINTS** – *the west tower and aisles enclose a Norman core*

and the formerly deserted railway arches now busily occupied by local traders. This is a Gothic Revival church based uncompromisingly on Tractarian principles by R. D. Chantrell, 1837–41. In Perpendicular style, the planning reflected Dean Hook's uncompromising High Church views in the face of flourishing non-Conformism in the town. There is room for a very large congregation on the floor and in the galleries, and the long elevated E. arm provided space for the first surpliced choir (enrobed choristers) in any Anglican church. To the E. of the choir stalls is a space for the congregation to draw near, and the altar rails will hold 40 people at a time, facing the chancel with its colourful mosaics of the apostles by Salviati. This atmospheric building also has furnishings by Street, Butterfield and Eden.

METHLEY † St Oswald ★

5m/8km N.E. of Wakefield
OS *SE391266* **GPS** *53.7345N, 1.4086W*

Once part of a busy coalmining centre, the old village is clustered round the church, a good Decorated and Perpendicular structure, much restored in 1876. Inside, the arch-bracing of the roof rises from stone carved corbels whose strange devil heads and grimacing features were drawn by the sculptor Henry Moore when he was a young boy: he later commented of these corbels that they had a great effect on his passion for sculpture. Furnishings include a fine early 16th-century lectern, probably from the Netherlands; an Elizabethan font cover; a 17th-century screen and an early Georgian pulpit. Later ones include John Savile, d. 1778, by Wilton, and others by Scheemakers and Westmacott.

OTLEY † All Saints

10m/16km N.W. of Leeds
OS *SE201453* **GPS** *53.9040N, 1.6947W*

The present chancel is Norman, as are the remnants of a reset N. door. The spacious nave has 14th- and 15th-century aisles with Perpendicular windows. In the N. aisle is an outstanding group of Saxon cross fragments, as well as a medieval ledger stone. The Georgian work is not particularly memorable, but there is an altar tomb with recumbent effigies of the grandparents of Thomas Lord Fairfax, commander of the Parliamentary army in the Civil War, and other interesting memorials. In the churchyard is a monument to 23 workmen killed while constructing the Bramhope Tunnel, 1845–9.

SOWERBY † St Peter

2m/3km S.W. of Halifax
OS *SE042232* **GPS** *53.7052N, 1.9365W*

A delightful Classical building of 1763–6 with Gibbsian surrounds, Tuscan columns, parapet and balustrades, and a tower with lancets added in 1781. The stately Corinthian interior has galleries, superb plasterwork on the E. wall, an apsidal E. end and a towering pulpit set on marble columns.

THORNHILL † St Michael ★

2m/3km S. of Dewsbury
OS *SE253188* **GPS** *53.6656N, 1.6180W*

A sooty but interesting Perpendicular parish church, it was restored in 1879 by G. E. Street, who replaced the Georgian nave but left the handsome W. tower engaged with the flanking aisles. The Savile Chapel of 1447 has its original roof, some very good Flemish glass of donors, and a rich series of monuments from 1322 on, both medieval and Renaissance, including a tomb to Sir George Savile, d. 1622, by Maximilian Colt, a good effigy of John Thornhill in full armour, and a wooden effigy of Sir John Savile, d. 1503, and his two wives, Alice Vernon and Elizabeth Paston. The E. window is very fine, with Jesse Tree glass dating from 1499.

WAKEFIELD † St John

St John's Square
OS *SE327214* **GPS** *53.6884N, 1.5055W*

This is a beautiful Georgian church in the middle of a Georgian square surrounded by good town houses. The whole group is very pleasant. Built in 1791–5 by Charles Watson, it was gently re-ordered by James Micklethwaite at the end of the 19th century; Micklethwaite also added the E. end in 1905. The four-stage tower supports an octagonal bell-tower with cupola.

WALES

The change in the church landscape between England and Wales is dramatic. From English towns and villages with their churches proudly displayed, one enters a hilly country, much less populated for the most part, many of whose churches are hidden away modestly in the hills, set in secluded valleys, on remote seashore or in fields apart from their villages. Wales is distinctive with its tongue-twisting place-names, the musical accents of the English-speaking people, and, especially in the west and north of the country, the lilting cadence of the Welsh language. The Welsh are a Celtic people of different origin from the Anglo-Saxon, and with a noble and ancient history of independence, law-making and culture.

For centuries after the Roman occupation, the hills and mountains of Wales were a barrier to invasion by Anglo-Saxon and Norman alike. It was not until 1284 that Edward I finally conquered the whole country, and sporadic revolts against English rule lasted for more than another century.

The Cambrian Mountains, rising to over 3,000 ft, divide Wales down the centre. Here, slopes are steep and the soil is poor; consequently much of the area is moorland or forest, the farming confined to sheep- and cattle-rearing. All the main rivers, such as the Dee, Severn, Usk, Wye, Teifi, Tawe, Dyfi and Conwy, rise in this central core, eventually meeting the 700 miles of Welsh coastline or flowing south-east through Shropshire, Worcestershire and Herefordshire. To the east lie the flatter lands of Flintshire and the rolling pastoral borderland of Powys and Monmouthshire; to the south, the old coalfields, with narrow, steep-sided valleys where Victorian heavy industry has given way to modern high-tech manufacturing, and the highly productive agricultural land of the Vale of Glamorgan; to the west, the dairying pastures of Pembrokeshire. North of Dyfi, except in Lleyn (or Llyn), the mountains reach right down to the sea, culminating in Snowdonia in the north-west and the almost flat isle of Anglesey. The beautiful vales of Conwy and Clwyd penetrate the highlands of the north.

Except in the more prosperous farming areas, most of the churches are small, sturdy and of great simplicity, often isolated from habitation and approached by winding, narrow lanes. In the border marches, bellcotes substitute for towers, though fine ones are to be found in the northern and southern coastal areas, and some of Somerset type in the south. A peculiarity, particularly in the north-east, is the double-naved church, and sometimes triple-naved, a less expensive method of enlargement than the addition of aisles to a single nave.

The predominance of the small nave and chancel church, however, does not mean that grander medieval churches are absent; Flint and Denbigh

◁ **LLANFILO: ST BILO** – *the splendid tower and shingled spire of this Norman church were rebuilt in the mid-19th century*

have a splendid group of Perpendicular churches built by Henry VIII's mother, Lady Margaret Beaufort, comprising Wrexham, Gresford, Mold and Holt, and others of all periods are to be found elsewhere.

A notable feature of Welsh churches is the number of gloriously carved medieval rood screens and lofts that have survived, and 18th-century box pews, pulpits and communion tables are widespread in the remoter rural areas.

A few Georgian churches are to be found, as at Worthenbury, Marchwiel, and Llanfyllin, and Henry Wilson's Art Nouveau tour de force at Brithdir cannot fail to please. But it is to the Victorian period, consequent upon the population explosion which occurred, that we must look for a new flowering of church architecture. All the best English architects are represented: the Scotts, Street, Bodley, Pearson and more. Good local architects like John Prichard, John Douglas, Arthur Baker, Henry Kennedy, and J. D. Sedding produced buildings that have stood the test of time.

The past century has been mainly that of repair, renovation and beautification. Only two churches of any note have been built since the early 20th century: Llandeloy, by J. Coates Carter, and Llangammarch Wells, by W. D. Caroe, who was also a restorer with a highly sensitive touch.

Independent for centuries, the Celtic Church became subject to the rule of Canterbury from the time of the Normans, but in 1921 the Anglican Church in Wales was disestablished, thus regaining its independence as the Church in Wales after an interval of nearly 1,000 years. The price paid was the loss of most of its ancient endowments. The archbishop is now elected by an electoral college, and he retains his bishopric, while the Church is governed by a body of bishops, priests and laity.

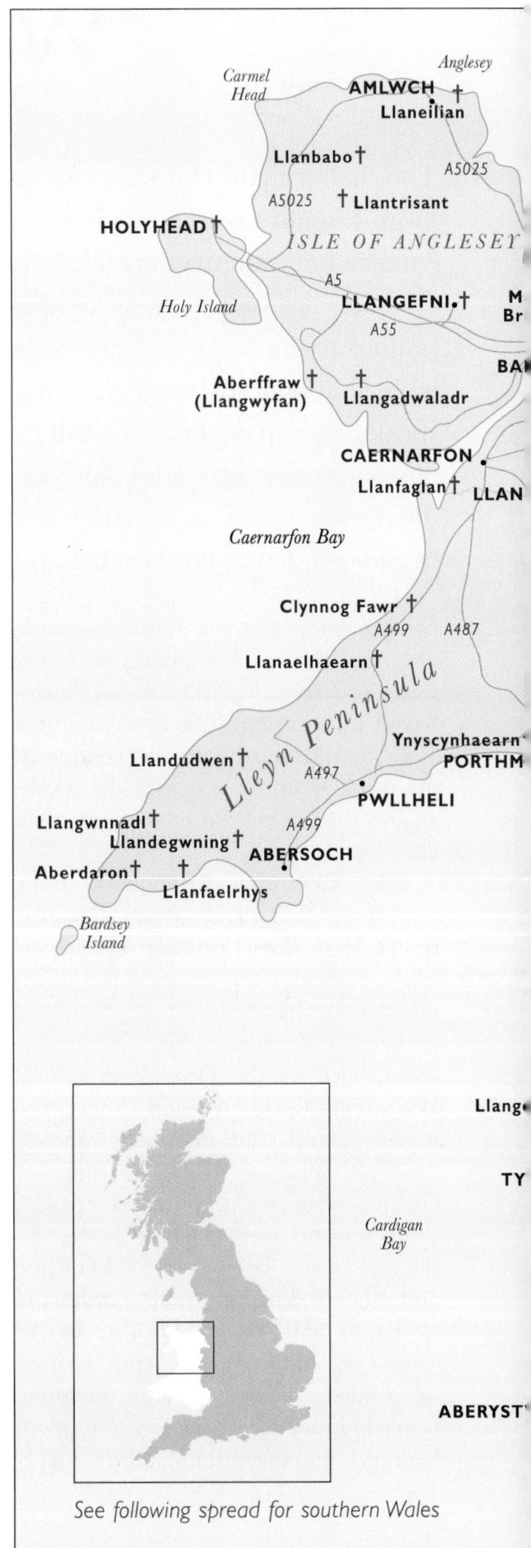

See following spread for southern Wales

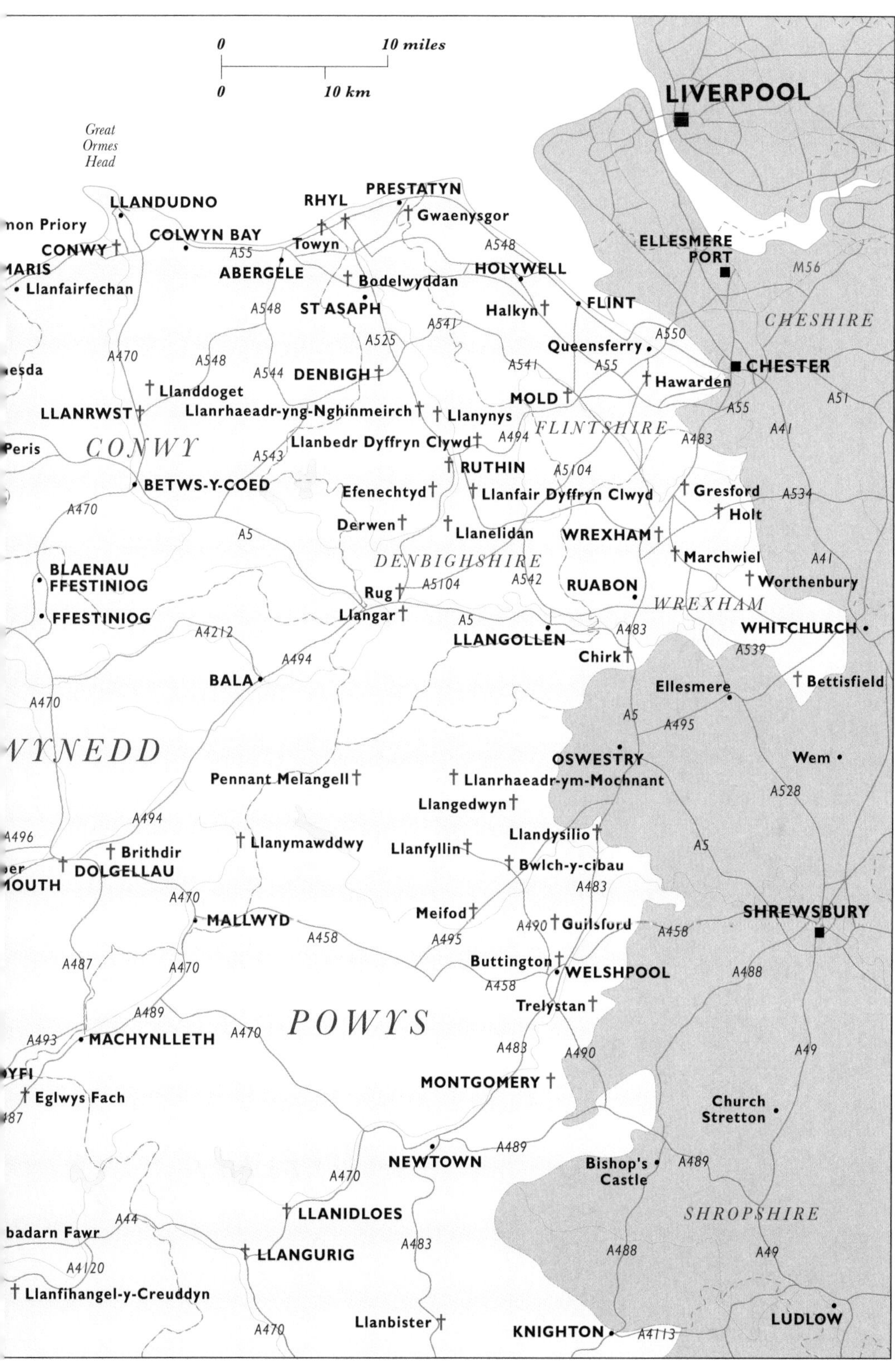
0
10 miles
0
10 km
Great Ormes Head
LIVERPOOL
LLANDUDNO
RHYL
PRESTATYN
Gwaenysgor
COLWYN BAY
CONWY
Towyn
A548
A55
ABERGELE
HOLYWELL
ELLESMERE PORT
M56
Llanfairfechan
Bodelwyddan
ST ASAPH
Halkyn
FLINT
CHESHIRE
A548
A541
A470
A525
Queensferry
A550
A548
A544
DENBIGH
A541
A55
Hawarden
CHESTER
Llanddoget
MOLD
A55
A51
LLANRWST
Llanrhaeadr-yng-Nghinmeirch
Llanynys
FLINTSHIRE
A41
CONWY
Llanbedr Dyffryn Clywd
A494
A483
A543
RUTHIN
A5104
BETWS-Y-COED
Efenechtyd
Llanfair Dyffryn Clwyd
Gresford
A534
A470
Holt
Derwen
Llanelidan
A5
WREXHAM
BLAENAU FFESTINIOG
DENBIGHSHIRE
Marchwiel
A41
A5104
A542
Worthenbury
Rug
RUABON
FFESTINIOG
Llangar
WREXHAM
A5
A4212
A483
WHITCHURCH
LLANGOLLEN
Chirk
A539
A494
BALA
Bettisfield
Ellesmere
A470
A5
A495
OSWESTRY
Wem
Pennant Melangell
Llanrhaeadr-ym-Mochnant
A528
Llangedwyn
A494
Llandysilio
Brithdir
Llanymawddwy
Llanfyllin
A5
DOLGELLAU
Bwlch-y-cibau
A483
A470
Meifod
SHREWSBURY
MALLWYD
A490
Guilsfurd
A458
A458
A495
A487
A470
Buttington
WELSHPOOL
A488
A458
A489
Trelystan
POWYS
A493
MACHYNLLETH
A470
A483
A490
A49
MONTGOMERY
Eglwys Fach
Church Stretton
A489
NEWTOWN
Bishop's Castle
A489
A470
SHROPSHIRE
A44
LLANIDLOES
A483
A488
A49
LLANGURIG
A4120
Llanfihangel-y-Creuddyn
LUDLOW
Llanbister
A470
KNIGHTON
A4113

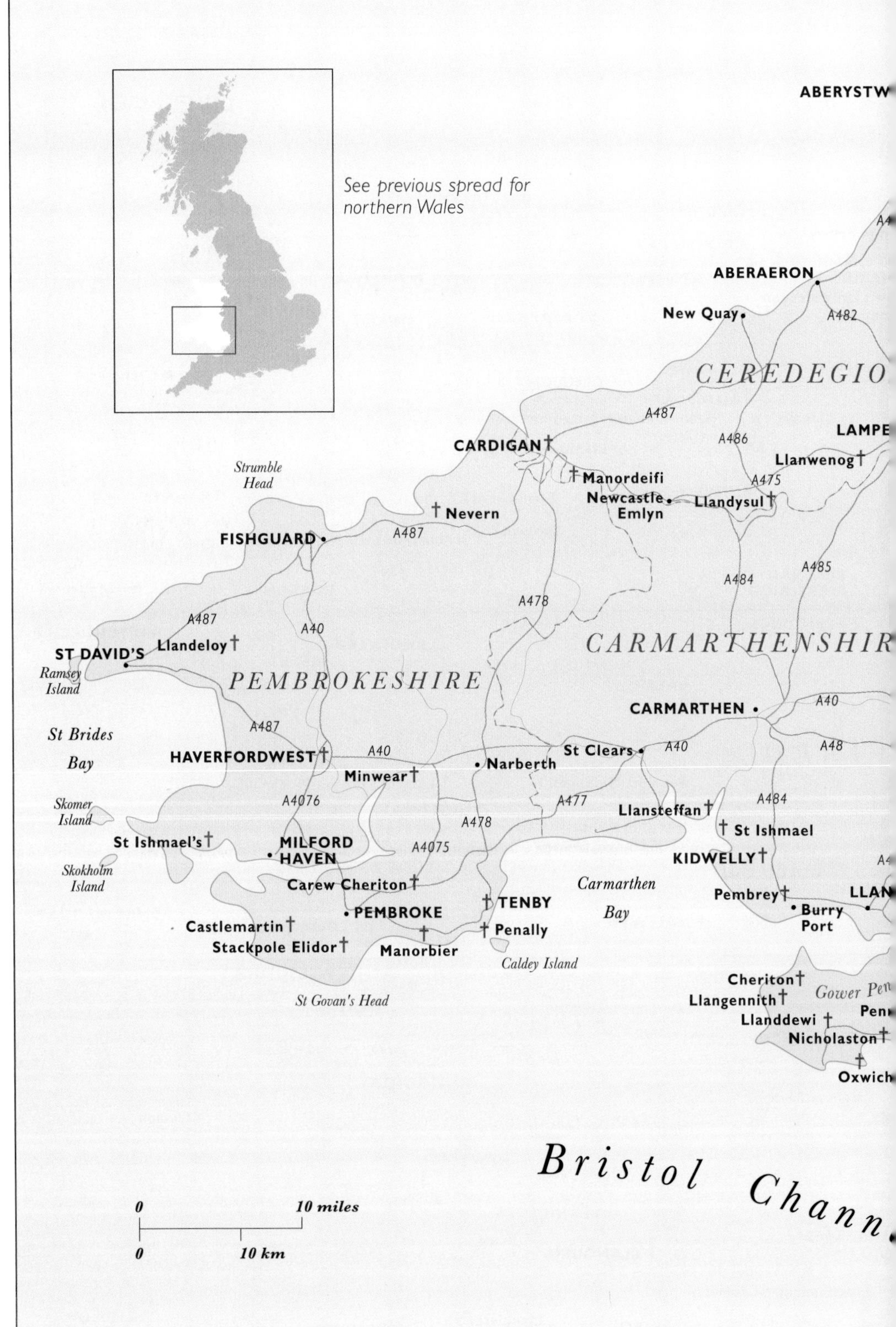

See previous spread for northern Wales
ABERAERON
New Quay
A482
A487
A486
CARDIGAN
Strumble Head
Manordeifi
Newcastle Emlyn
Llandysul
Llanwenog
A475
Nevern
FISHGUARD
A487
A478
A484
A485
A487
A40
ST DAVID'S
Llandeloy
Ramsey Island
PEMBROKESHIRE
CARMARTHEN
A40
A48
St Brides Bay
A487
HAVERFORDWEST
A40
Minwear
Narberth
St Clears
A40
Skomer Island
A4076
A477
Llansteffan
A484
A478
St Ishmael
St Ishmael's
MILFORD HAVEN
A4075
KIDWELLY
Skokholm Island
Carew Cheriton
Carmarthen Bay
Pembrey
Burry Port
PEMBROKE
TENBY
Castlemartin
Penally
Stackpole Elidor
Manorbier
Caldey Island
St Govan's Head
Cheriton
Llangennith
Llanddewi
Nicholaston
Oxwich
Bristol Chann
0 10 miles
0 10 km

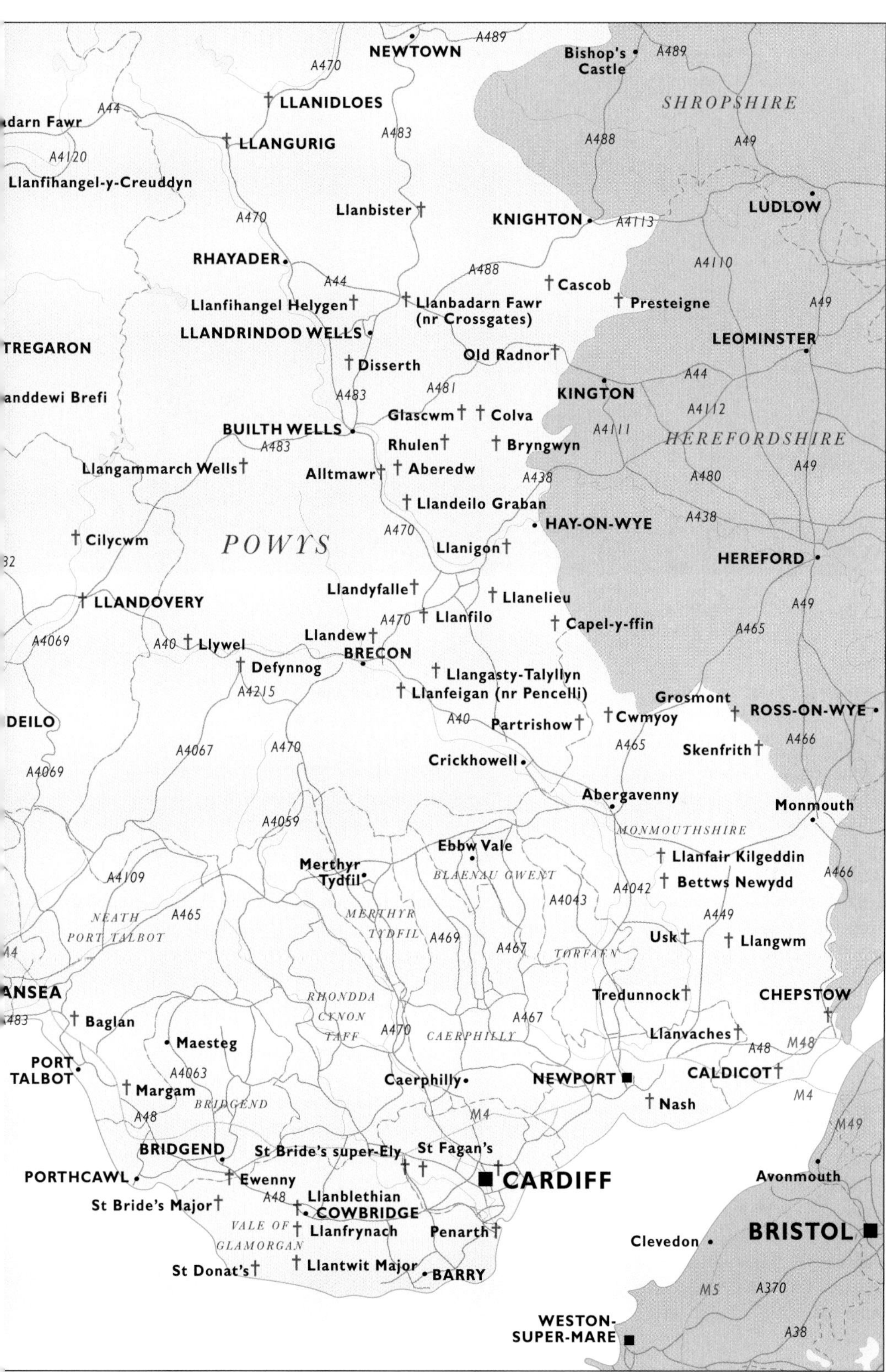
NEWTOWN
Bishop's Castle
SHROPSHIRE
LLANIDLOES
LLANGURIG
Llanfihangel-y-Creuddyn
Llanbister
KNIGHTON
LUDLOW
RHAYADER
Cascob
Presteigne
Llanfihangel Helygen
Llanbadarn Fawr (nr Crossgates)
LLANDRINDOD WELLS
TREGARON
LEOMINSTER
Disserth
Old Radnor
KINGTON
Glascwm
Colva
BUILTH WELLS
Rhulen
Bryngwyn
HEREFORDSHIRE
Llangammarch Wells
Alltmawr
Aberedw
Llandeilo Graban
HAY-ON-WYE
Cilycwm
POWYS
Llanigon
HEREFORD
Llandyfalle
Llanelieu
LLANDOVERY
Llanfilo
Capel-y-ffin
Llandew
Llywel
BRECON
Defynnog
Llangasty-Talyllyn
Llanfeigan (nr Pencelli)
Grosmont
Cwmyoy
ROSS-ON-WYE
Partrishow
Skenfrith
Crickhowell
Abergavenny
Monmouth
MONMOUTHSHIRE
Ebbw Vale
Llanfair Kilgeddin
Merthyr Tydfil
BLAENAU GWENT
Bettws Newydd
NEATH PORT TALBOT
MERTHYR TYDFIL
Usk
Llangwm
TORFAEN
Tredunnock
CHEPSTOW
RHONDDA CYNON TAFF
Baglan
Maesteg
CAERPHILLY
Llanvaches
PORT TALBOT
Caerphilly
NEWPORT
CALDICOT
Margam
BRIDGEND
Nash
BRIDGEND
St Bride's super-Ely
St Fagan's
PORTHCAWL
Ewenny
CARDIFF
Avonmouth
St Bride's Major
Llanblethian
COWBRIDGE
VALE OF GLAMORGAN
Llanfrynach
Penarth
BRISTOL
Clevedon
St Donat's
Llantwit Major
BARRY
WESTON-SUPER-MARE

△ **ABERFFRAW: ST CWYFAN** – *the small tidal island of Cribinau on which the church stands is only accessible by foot at low tide*

ABERDARON † St Hywyn ★

Lleyn Peninsula

OS *SH173263* **GPS** *52.80385N, 4.7114W*

An important seashore clas church (a church with monastic buildings) in a lovely setting, it was built at a point of embarkation for pilgrims to nearby Bardsey Island. Of 12th-, 14th- and 16th-century work with twin gables and a late Norman doorway; inside, two simple spaces are linked by an airy five-bay arcade. Abandoned in 1841, it was restored by Henry Kennedy, 1860.

ABEREDW † St Cewydd

3m/4km S.E. of Builth Wells, Powys

OS *SO080473* **GPS** *52.1165N, 3.3447W*

On a tranquil site above the River Edw, a tributary of the nearby Wye, stands a 14th- and 16th-century church fiercely restored in 1888 by S. W. Williams. Inside are a Perpendicular king-post roof with arch braces, a fine Perpendicular open screen, cast-iron communion rails, commandment boards and, in the porch, a 17th-century memorial.

ABERFFRAW (Llangwyfan)
† St Cwyfan ★★

12m/19km W. of Menai Bridge, Isle of Anglesey

OS *SH335682* **GPS** *53.18552N, 4.49188W*

A church in a breathtaking setting on a small island, only accessible at low tide. St Cwyfan's is now single-cell, dating from 12th century; the nave was extended in the late 14th-century, and the N. wall contains remains of a late 15th-century arcade. The N. aisle was demolished in the early part of the 19th century – presumably a lost battle against the elements.

ALLTMAWR † St Mauritius

3m/4km S.E. of Builth Wells, Powys

OS *SO073468* **GPS** *52.11243N, 3.35462W*

A tiny 13th-century church with a late 19th-century three-sided apse; inside are 18th-century wooden windows, a pulpit, some box pews at the back and a touching monument by Gillick, 1936.

BAGLAN † St Catherine ★

2m/3km N.W. of Port Talbot

OS *SS752922* **GPS** *51.61503N, 3.80289W*

With its elegant pinnacled spire, this is

probably John Prichard's masterpiece, built at the end of his life and consecrated in 1882. Everything is rich, colourful and well done. Inside, pink alabaster contrasts with different shades of grey stone. The floors are of mosaic, the striking reredos of incised marble, and there is glass by Burne-Jones and Morris.

BEAUMARIS
† St Mary and St Nicholas ★

on E. side of Conwy Bay, Isle of Anglesey
OS *SH604761* **GPS** *53.26373N, 4.09427W*

An early 14th-century garrison church for the English, St Mary's has an early 16th-century chancel, 17th-century S. chapel, 18th-century plank pews and communion rails. It was restored by Bodley, 1902. Of note are early 16th-century bench-ends and misericords, one depicting a bearded pope, a 15th-century stone altar tomb of Princess Siwan and effigies of William Bulkeley, d. 1490, and his wife Elin.

BETTISFIELD † St John the Baptist

4m/6km E. of Ellesmere, Wrexham
OS *SJ461360* **GPS** *52.91892N, 2.80255W*

A good Gothic Revival church drawing on an early Decorated style by G. E. Street, 1872–4. It has an elegant octagonal spire and a well detailed interior, with dado on the E. wall of superb Minton tiles, and fine 19th-century glass by Clayton and Bell.

BETWS NEWYDD
† Dedication unknown

3m/4km W. of Raglan, Monmouthshire
OS *SO362058* **GPS** *51.74795N, 2.92527W*

A humble rural church, it is known for the remarkable Perpendicular oak rood screen and loft, richly carved and reaching right up to the roof.

BODELWYDDAN † St Margaret ★★

2m/3km W. of St Asaph, Denbighshire
OS *SJ003754* **GPS** *53.26678N, 3.49497W*

This is a lavish and ornate church by John Gibson, 1856–60, with a tall and richly ornamented W. spire. The luminous white exterior is of local limestone, and inside is a feast of rich details: an Anglesey marble nave entrance, Belgian red marble nave piers, with

△ **BODELWYDDAN: ST MARGARET** – *the richly carved chancel end*

much good detail on the arch springs and richly carved pulpit. The chancel is remarkable, with a motif of red marble and stone carving uniting the choir and E. end.

BRITHDIR † St Mark ★★

1m/2km E. of Dolgellau, Gwynedd
OS *SH763183* **GPS** *52.7487N, 3.83328W*

Henry Wilson built this notable Arts and Crafts church in 1895–8, using local granite and slate. The exterior has a cat-slide roof and rough-hewn stonework. The interior is a Mediterranean riot of colour: red ochre, luminous blue, terracotta and cream transport the visitor to the Italy of the Rev. Charles Tooth, founder of St Mark's English Church in Florence, in whose memory this church was erected. The detail is incomparable – the pews have delightful carvings of woodland creatures, birds and a dolphin, the pulpit and altar have beaten copper relief fronts, and the doors are inlaid with mother of pearl.

BRYNGWYN † St Michael

5m/8km N.W. of Hay-on-Wye, Powys
OS *SO186494* **GPS** *52.13771N, 3.18996W*

Set high on a hill at 1,140 feet, this is a largely

△ **CAPEL-Y-FFIN: ST MARY** – *an 'owl-like' cottage church, according to diarist Francis Kilvert*

13th-century church with 14th-century chancel arch and single-light window. The 19th-century woodwork to the roof is not of the best, but there is a medieval carved stone coffin lid on the E. wall, and outside some interesting grave slabs.

BUTTINGTON † All Saints

2m/3km N.E. of Welshpool, Powys
OS *SJ249088* **GPS** *52.67206N, 3.11079W*

A plain roughcast and whitewashed church with a fine 15th-century arch-braced roof, it is set close to Offa's Dyke and the River Severn. The unusual font is carved from an Early English capital that had been at Strata Marcella Abbey, the remains of which lie half a mile to the N.

BWLCH-Y-CIBAU † Christ Church ★

3m/4km S.E. of Llanfyllin, Powys
OS *SJ178174* **GPS** *52.7485N, 3.21796W*

Admirably suited to its sheltered upland site, the church shows how sensitive Sir George Gilbert Scott could be to the genius loci. It is an excellent little building of 1862–5, in Early English style, small and apsed, with a bellcote. The glass in the chancel is by Wailes and at the W. end by Powell & Sons.

CALDICOT † St Mary the Virgin

5m/8km S.W. of Chepstow, Monmouthshire
OS *ST483886* **GPS** *51.5941N, 2.74737W*

The fine church is medieval and unspoilt, with central tower, rich S. porch and unusual window tracery. It was restored in 1858 by Henry Woodyer, who also built the vicarage; most of his characteristic fittings survive.

CAPEL-Y-FFIN † St Mary ★

3m/4km N.W. of Llanthony, Powys
OS *SO254315* **GPS** *51.97719N, 3.08638W*

This charming little church, one of the smallest in Wales, stands in beautiful surroundings on a bend of the mountain road between Llanthony and Hay-on-Wye, in the Black Mountains. It was described by the 19th-century diarist Francis Kilvert as 'the old chapel, short, stout and boxy, with its little bell turret (the whole building reminded one of an owl), the quiet peaceful chapel yard sheltered by seven great solemn yews'. It was built in 1762 and retains its W. and S. galleries. In the graveyard is a memorial to a carpenter by Eric Gill, 1935.

◁ **BRITHDIR: ST MARK** – *a remarkable Arts and Crafts church with Italian overtones, it was inspired by St Mark's English Church in Florence*

△ **CHERITON: ST CADOG** – *stout and fortress-like, this church of the late 13th century has good Early English details inside*

CARDIFF † St John ★

Between Trinity St, Church St & Working St, Cardiff
OS *ST182764* **GPS** *51.48073N, 3.1784W*

Cardiff's only remaining medieval church, its glory is the tower of 1473 with an elaborate West Country Perpendicular spire. The rest of the church is partly 13th-century, mostly mid-15th, but greatly rebuilt and extended in 1852–3 and again in 1887–91 by Kempson and Fowler, when the outer aisles were added. The high altar reredos is by W. Goscombe John; the S. aisle reredos is by Sir Ninian Comper, who also did the E. window glass. Other glass is by Morris and Co.

CARDIGAN † St Mary

Ceredigion
OS *SN181460* **GPS** *52.08273N, 4.65609W*

St Mary's stands beside the River Teify, a much rebuilt church of the 12th century. The tower and nave were rebuilt c. 1705. Inside, it is grandly spacious and uncluttered; sensitive restorers included R. J. Withers and W. D. Caroe. The Perpendicular E. window has remnants of its medieval glass, and some fine Tudor carving survives.

CAREW CHERITON † St Mary

4m/6km E. of Pembroke, Pembrokeshire
OS *SN045028* **GPS** *51.6899N, 4.829W*

The church forms an attractive group with medieval charnel-house, chapel, old rectory and cottages. It is mainly c. 1400 with Perpendicular and Decorated windows, and was restored by Sir George Gilbert Scott, 1855. The building has a cruciform plan with deep chancel, two aisles, and a barrel-vaulted W. tower with angle buttresses. There are interesting tombs and medieval floor tiles in the chancel.

CASCOB † St Michael

5m/8km S.W. of Knighton, Powys
OS *SO238664* **GPS** *52.29049N, 3.11722W*

In hilly country S. of the Lugg Valley, this is a small but doughtily built church with thick walls; the top part of the tower and the porch are half-timbered. The 14th-century oak screen is elegantly proportioned and has a plain panelled loft.

CASTLEMARTIN

† St Michael and All Angels

5m/8km S.W. of Pembroke, Pembrokeshire

OS *SR910988* **GPS** *51.64982N, 5.02166W*

This double-nave church with tower and high porch makes a pleasing composition in a sheltered site. The Early English limestone arcade is cut by the chancel arch.

CHEPSTOW † St Mary ★

Between Church Rd and A48, Monmouthshire

OS *ST535939* **GPS** *51.64272N, 2.67226W*

A substantial former Benedictine priory church, St Mary's is the earliest Norman foundation in Wales, 1070. The 11th-century W. doorway, flanked by two blind arcades, is very sophisticated, its ornate orders possibly re-carved in the 12th century, and was reset in the 1706 tower. The nave has a grand Norman arcade and triforium. The chancel and transepts were rebuilt in 1834–40, and again in 1890–1904 by J. Seddon and J. Coates Carter. There are good tombs and memorials, including for Henry Somerset, 2nd Earl of Worcester, and two fonts, Norman and 15th-century.

CHERITON † St Cadog

2m/3km S. of Whitford Pt, Gower Peninsula

OS *S450931* **GPS** *51.61614N, 4.23942W*

A late 13th-century church in a combe, with a sturdy, central tower and gabled roof behind battlements. There is a good Early English archway to the S. door, and the chancel choir and nave roofs have decorative painting.

CHIRK † St Mary

5m/8km N. of Oswestry, Wrexham

OS *SJ291376* **GPS** *52.93148N, 3.05576W*

Originally 12th-century, St Mary's was built on the site of a *llan* (the Welsh word for an old place of worship, seen in many placenames). Traces of the Norman structure can be seen in the S. wall, a blocked up doorway. The N. aisle and tower are 15th-century, and there are many 17th- and 18th-century monuments to the Myddleton family, of note being the Robert Wynne memorial to Sir Richard Myddelton, d. 1716, and his wife Dame Frances. Of interest too is the Trevor Mausoleum in the churchyard.

CILYCWM † St Michael

4m/6km N. of Llandovery, Carmarthenshire

OS *SN753400* **GPS** *52.04461N, 3.8192W*

A medieval church with 15th- to 17th-century roofs and remarkable early 17th-century wall-paintings of a skeleton and Royal Arms that were, incredibly, over-painted in 1986 during an ill-conceived local authority youth employment scheme! Good arch-braced and wagon roofs cover the double naves, and the church was sympathetically restored by W. D. Caroe, 1906.

CLYNNOG FAWR † St Beuno ★★

9m/15km S.W. of Caernarfon, Gwynedd

OS *SH414496* **GPS** *53.021N, 4.36542W*

A gracious and imposing church on the coast, it reflects its importance as a shrine on the pilgrim route to Bardsey Island. The Perpendicular rebuilding of cruciform plan began with the transepts and chancel, 1480, and continued into the early 16th century. The passage to St Beuno's Chapel is early 17th-century. Outside, apart from the sturdy W. tower, all is Perpendicular glass, pinnacles and battlements. It is a generous, spreading building; even the vestry has three storeys, and the porch two. The nave, over 30 feet wide, has a handsome oak roof, carved and panelled. The chancel, cut off by a well-restored screen, has Tudor stalls with misericords, a double-headed eagle bench-end of c. 1500, and very attractive sedilia of c. 1480. On a wall memorial of 1609, ten daughters and two sons kneel beside the deceased. St Beuno's stone is in the chapel. At the time of writing the church is closed in the winter.

COLVA † St David

7m/11km S.W. of Kington, Powys

OS *SO199531* **GPS** *52.17065N, 3.17162W*

High in the Radnor hills, sheltered by surrounding yews, stands this remote and likeable church, c. 13th century, and typical of the area. The late 15th-century deep porch and low door make a rather tunnel-like entrance to a single cell, and the deeply splayed windows make the walls seem even thicker. The open roof is arch-braced, and school benches do for the pews. Fragmentary

△ **CWMYOY: ST MARTIN** – *dating mostly from the 13th century, the church has been on the move for centuries, the tower tilting uphill, the chancel sloping downwards*

wall-paintings were uncovered in the 1980s. The little wooden bell turret has a pyramidal slate roof.

CONWY † St Mary ★

Between High St and Rose Hill St, Conwy
OS *SH781775* **GPS** *53.28062N, 3.82895W*

Though right in the middle of town, it is nicely withdrawn in a close surrounded by old houses. Originally the abbey church, its oldest parts are the E. and W. walls; the three lancets in the tower lit the nave. The fine moulded doorway below, of c. 1235, probably came from the chapter house. The rest of the church is of various dates; it was restored in 1872 by Sir George Gilbert Scott. It contains a magnificent rood screen of c. 1500; the loft is supported by fan vaulting on either side. The contemporary stalls have carved ends. There are numerous monuments and a bust of John Gibson, sculptor, by Wm. Theed.

CWMYOY † St Martin ★★

6m/10km N. of Abergavenny, Monmouthshire
OS *SO299233* **GPS** *51.90431N, 3.02033W*

Splendidly sited on a hillside above the River Honddhu, and just N. of Llanthony Abbey, St Martin's was inadvertently built on a glacial landslip. It is memorable for being so utterly drunk: the tower, propped by massive external buttresses, has sunk and leans distinctly N., while the chancel tilts in the opposite direction. There are numerous good things in it: curious plaster panels in the porch, a 13th-century cross, and many memorial tablets. All delightful.

DEFYNNOG † St Cynog

10m/17km E. of Llandovery, Powys
OS *SN925279* **GPS** *51.93942N, 3.56478W*

This double-nave church is in a quiet village setting next to a line of stone cottages. Its tall Perpendicular tower is distinctive and has an external stair turret. The church is 15th- and 16th-century, but here are signs of pre-Conquest work in the stoup, the N. wall and an intriguing early 11th-century font with runic inscriptions.

DENBIGH † St Marcella

1m/2km E. of Denbigh, Whitchurch Rd, Denbighshire
OS *SJ071662* **GPS** *53.18505N, 3.39133W*

Denbigh's parish church, though over a mile

△ **CWMYOY: ST MARTIN** – *if anything, the twisting form of the church is even more pronounced from the inside, the chancel and nave clearly singing from different hymn sheets*

away from the town, is a fine double-aisled remodelling of an earlier building, restored in 1908 by C. Hodgson Fowler. There is an excellent Renaissance alabaster table-tomb with coloured recumbent effigies of Sir John Salisbury, d. 1578, and his wife, with exquisite little weepers on the base, and a 17th-century communion table with contemporary rails on three sides, pulpit and tester. Good 18th-century memorials include work by Sir Richard Westmacott and Edward Stanton.

DERWEN † St Mary ★

5m/8km N. of Corwen, Denbighshire
OS *SJ070507* **GPS** *53.04574N, 3.38826W*
Friends of Friendless Churches

A single-cell sandstone church, St Mary's has an exceptional 15th-century rood screen and loft. The stone carved preaching cross in the churchyard is very fine – an octagonal shaft supporting an intricately carved set of panels depicting the Crucifixion, the Virgin and Child, the Coronation of the Virgin, and St Michael the Archangel.

DISSERTH † St Cewydd ★

2m/3km S.W. of Llandrindod Wells, Powys
OS *SO034583* **GPS** *52.21511N, 3.41437W*

The church stands in a hollow by a white-washed farm and yew trees beside the River Ithon. Largely mid-15th-century with square-headed windows, it has earlier details incorporated. The sturdy tower dates from c. 1400. The nave has a handsome open roof with patterned braces and flagged floor. The 17th-century box pews, rising towards the back of the church, are carved with the owners' initials and dates. There is a three-decker pulpit.

DOLGELLAU † St Mary ★

17m/27km S.W. of Bala, Gwynedd
OS *SH727178* **GPS** *52.74317N, 3.88658W*

In its simple way, this is a virtuoso performance in the use of local stone. The nave was built in 1716 and there is a handsome tower and a neo-Norman apse of 1854. The wide nave has an extraordinary roof, supported on wooden columns. The only medieval survival inside is a 14th-century effigy. The huge windows contain a most remarkable assemblage of Victorian glass.

△ **DERWEN: ST MARY** – *redundant since 2002, it is now under the wing of the Friends of Friendless Churches; it has a wonderful rood screen and some excellent 19th-century glass*

EFENECHTYD † St Michael

2m/3km S. of Ruthin, Denbighshire
OS *SJ111557* **GPS** *53.09182N, 3.32812W*

A tiny church set in a remote valley, it was well restored in 1873 by Arthur Baker. The font is rare, of medieval carved oak, 14-faceted and with a beaded base. The E. window is 14th-century, and there is a remnant of the old rood screen. Also of interest are a painted commandment board and a painted timber monument to Catherine Lloyd, d. 1810.

EGLWYS FACH † St Michael

5m/8km S.W. of Machynlleth, Ceredigion
OS *SN685955* **GPS** *52.54174N, 3.93952W*

In a pretty churchyard, this is a simple church of 1833 built of local grey stone with many original fittings. The E. end is an addition of 1913. There is a plaque to the poet R. S. Thomas in the porch – he was rector here from 1954–67.

EWENNY † St Michael ★★

2m/3km S. of Bridgend
OS *SS912778* **GPS** *51.4888N, 3.56775W*

A delightful place, quiet and rural, a mixture of medieval church and fortification, great house and farmyard. The church was founded c. 1120, the Benedictine priory in 1141, and building went on until c. 1300. The nave (which today constitutes the parish church) and the N. arcade were heightened in the late 12th century, the same time as the chancel, crossing, transepts and W. wall were added. The nave was originally longer; the W. wall is 19th-century. The present aisle and porch are 16th-century, rebuilt in 1895. The font is c. 1200. There is a 14th-century wooden screen with 16th-century linenfold panels. In the S. transept is an interesting collection of monuments.

GLASCWM † St David

8m/12km E. of Builth Wells, Powys
OS *SO155531* **GPS** *52.17022N, 3.23562W*

Founded in the 6th century, nothing remains of the original clas church. The present-day church is big, mostly 13th-century with a 15th-century timber bellcote. There is a massive Perpendicular timber nave roof and some fine Perpendicular windows. The chancel ceiling is 15th-century barrel-vaulted, and there is a memorial to two German airman shot down in the Second World War.

GRESFORD † All Saints ★

3m/4km N. of Wrexham town, Wrexham

OS *SJ346549* **GPS** *53.08801N, 2.97731W*

This is a stately church well set in an iron-railed churchyard full of big yews and good tombs. It was almost entirely rebuilt in the late 15th century and sympathetically restored by G. E. Street in 1865–7. The pinnacled tower contains eight bells, two cast in 1623. The light and spacious interior contains exceptional glass of c. 1500, including the E. window. There are oak misericords, fine medieval and later monuments, including work by Chantrey, Westmacott and Theed, and a Perpendicular font. The pulpit is by Street.

GROSMONT † St Nicholas ★

2m/3km S. of Pontrilas, Monmouthshire

OS *SO404243* **GPS** *51.91408N, 2.86676W*

The church is of remarkable size and grandeur, bearing witness to the former importance of the place. Mostly Early English, it has an octagonal central tower and spire. The interior comes as a great surprise – the great aisles have steeply pitched roofs and elegant arcades. In the nave are the 'Grosmont Hutch' chest and an extraordinarily large unfinished effigy of a knight. The chancel and transepts are cut off from the nave by a great glazed screen, installed during J. P. Seddon's restoration of 1869. There are rich Victorian fittings and some 17th- and 18th-century inscribed stone slabs.

GUILSFIELD † St Aelhaiarn

3m/4km N. of Welshpool, Powys

OS *SJ219116* **GPS** *52.6969, 3.1568W*

A church of the 14th- and 15th-century, mostly Perpendicular, with a 15th-century arch-braced nave roof and Tudor panelled ceiling in the chancel. There are fragmentary remains of the old rood screen, an early font, and good 18th- and 19th-century wall monuments.

GWAENYSGOR † St Mary

1m/2km S. of Prestatyn, Flintshire

OS *SJ075810* **GPS** *53.31808N, 3.38977W*

Feeling relatively remote, high above nearby coastal resorts, this is a small, 13th-century single-cell church with a deep late 15th-century S. porch. The enclosed S. doorway has a massive studded wooden arch, 16th-century. It is crudely and interestingly carved. There are two medieval stone grave slabs in the chancel.

HALKYN † St Mary the Virgin

3m/4km S.E. of Holywell, Flintshire

OS *SJ209711* **GPS** *53.23168N, 3.18621W*

This is a fine Victorian Gothic Revival church with grand views over the Dee estuary, built by John Douglas in 1878. Inside are very striking pillars, formed of polished, fossil-bearing limestone. There is some unusual monochrome glass by Heaton, Butler & Bayne, and Douglas's characteristic furnishings.

HAVERFORDWEST † St Mary

Between St Mary's St, High St and Tower Hill

OS *SM951155* **GPS** *51.80119N, 4.97187W*

The church has a fine interior: graceful, light and carefully detailed. Standing on the steps, which run right across the W. end of the nave, you are looking down into an Early English church, enlarged and improved c. 1500. It has a lovely Early English arcade of clustered columns and capitals carved with medieval vigour. The portraits on the chancel arch are of the Earl of Pembroke and his wife. The E. window has cinquefoil lights in Plate tracery above three-lancet lights. In the late 15th century, clerestories were added to the nave and chancel. There is a very good Tudor oak panelled ceiling, with carved bosses and corbels. There are some good memorials, a 15th-century effigy of a pilgrim, a boldly carved mayor's pew and bench, and an 18th-century organ. W. D. Caroe restored the church between 1901 and 1903.

HAWARDEN † St Deiniol

6m/10km W. of Chester, Flintshire

OS *SJ315659* **GPS** *53.18593N, 3.02591W*

The church was restored in 1855–6 by James Harrison, burnt out in 1857, rebuilt by Sir George Gilbert Scott, and has additions by John Douglas. The Gladstone monument – nice Arts and Crafts – in the chapel is by Sir William Richmond. There is some glass by Wailes, a Burne-Jones Nativity window and a rood by Scott.

HOLT † St Chad

5m/8km E. of Wrexham town, Wrexham
OS *SJ411541* **GPS** *53.08091N, 2.87934W*

Basically 13th-century of red sandstone, the church stands on the banks of the River Dee. Much of the present building dates from 1500, when the aisles were added. The nave arcades are Decorated, and most of the rest is Perpendicular. The octagonal font bears the Arms of Richard III. Ewan Christian and John Douglas restored the church in 1871–97 and installed the screens between the chancel and chapels.

HOLYHEAD † St Cybi ★

on Holy Island, Isle of Anglesey
OS *SH247826* **GPS** *53.31147N, 4.63256W*

The church overlooks Holyhead harbour, and was originally a clas built on the site of the Roman fort. It was largely rebuilt, apart from the 13th-century chancel, in 1480–1520; the tower is 17th-century with internal spiral stairs. The result is a light arcaded building, with a low-pitched, battlemented and pinnacled roof and some intricate carving, particularly on the S. porch and parapet. Note the winged heart by the S. doorway. It was restored first by Sir George Gilbert Scott and later, in 1877–9, by Arthur Baker, who added the S. aisle. The glowing pomegranate window is by William Morris, and Burne-Jones designed the Pre-Raphaelite figures. The organ is from Eaton Hall Library; the Stanley tomb is by Hamo Thornycroft, 1897.

KIDWELLY † St Mary ★

7m/11km N.W. of Llanelli, Carmarthenshire
OS *SN408067* **GPS** *51.73684N, 4.30649W*

The church, topped by a graceful broach spire, is on the site of a Benedictine priory, and beautifully situated on the River Gwendraeth, with the ruined castle on a nearby bluff. The present building has a broad aisle-less nave with a barrel roof, short transepts, and a sweeping, broad pointed arch leading to the chancel. It is light and spacious and dates from the early 14th century, restored by G. G. Scott Jnr in 1884. Of note are the sedilia and piscina, but the 14th-century alabaster figure of the Virgin above the altar is the church's chief treasure. The organ is by Thomas Warne, 1762.

LLANABER † St Mary and St Bodfan ★★

2m/3km N.W. of Barmouth, Gwynedd
OS *SH599180* **GPS** *52.74168N, 4.07634W*

This is a very satisfying church, beautifully sited above the sea in a large churchyard packed with tombs. All Early English, but with the W. front rebuilt in the mid-19th century. The whitewashed interior has narrow aisles, clerestory and a large raised chancel. The S. door is particularly fine, with four orders of arches and fine foliate carving on the clustered columns, echoed on the capitals of the nave arcades. There are two very early carved stones in the church.

LLANAELHAEARN † St Aelhaearn

6m/10km N. of Pwllheli, Gwynedd
OS *SH387448* **GPS** *52.97635N, 4.40372W*

Another Bardsey Island pilgrim church, with a stocky stone W. belfry. It is 12th-century with 16th- and 17th-century transepts, a16th-century screen and an 1892 chancel.

LLANBABO † St Pabo ★

1m/2km N. of Lly Alaw Reservoir, Isle of Anglesey
OS *SH378867* **GPS** *53.35291N, 4.43835W*

This is a typical rural Welsh church – small, long and low – dating from the 12th century. Inside are an aisle-less nave and a very interesting 14th-century stone slab low-relief carving of St Pabo with crown and sceptre, more like a brass in style. Over the door are set some chevron-cut voussoirs and three stone heads, probably reset from a former chancel arch.

LLANBADARN FAWR (nr Aberystwyth) † St Padarn ★

E. suburb of Aberystwyth, Ceredigion
OS *SN599810* **GPS** *52.40911N, 4.06101W*

The size and grandeur of the church, set in a large churchyard on the side of the valley, recall the fame of the clas founded here by St Padarn in the 6th century. The present church, apart from the Perpendicular chancel, was built c. 1200. Big, solid and severe, it is cruciform with a low tower and spire at the crossing. The thick walls are pierced with lancets, except at the E. end, where three large windows were inserted in the 15th century. J. P. Seddon restored it from 1868, leaving

△ **LLANDELOY: ST ELOI** – *a subtle work by J. Coates Carter of the early 20th century that fits into the best Welsh traditions of church building*

the severity of the structure unimpaired, but adding the handsome boarded chancel roof and good fittings, which include a tiled floor and marble reredos. The modern glass is by John Pests. The chancel contains several good monuments, including one of 1813 by John Flaxman.

LLANBADARN FAWR (nr Crossgates) † St Padarn

3m/4km N. of Llandrindod Wells, Powys
OS *SO086643* **GPS** *52.2693N, 3.33946W*

The church was very pleasantly rebuilt in 1878 by S. W. Williams, in a French Norman revival style. The 12th-century Norman S. doorway of the old church has a tympanum with rampant beasts.

LLANBEDR DYFFRYN CLWYD † St Peter

1m/2km N.E. of Ruthin, Denbighshire
OS *SJ144594* **GPS** *53.12492N, 3.28012W*

This is one of Poundley and Walker's best churches, 1863, with vigorously patterned walls and roof. The robust carving includes gargoyles round the apse, and there is a portrait tablet by Gibson and good glass.

LLANBISTER † St Cynllo ★★

8m/12km N. of Llandrindod Wells, Powys
OS *SO109733* **GPS** *52.35062N, 3.3082W*

Founded in the 6th century, the largely 13th-century church juts out of the hillside and makes stunning use of the slope. It was restored by H. Passmore and W. D. Caroe, who built the baptismal pool at the W. end in 1908. The W. gable is windowless and mysterious, and the 16th-century tower is at the E. end, so that is windowless too. A great open roof, largely renewed, runs right through to the E. end. The nave and chancel are separated by a sturdy Perpendicular screen. The musicians' gallery of 1716 across the W. end is pleasantly light and open, with turned balusters. The communion rails are of 1828, and the oil lamps have been well adapted to electricity. Note the attractive and unusual 18th- and 19th-century gravestones.

LLANBLETHIAN † St John the Baptist (formerly St Bleddian)

Adjoining Cowbridge, Vale of Glamorgan
OS *SS984740* **GPS** *51.45612N, 3.46233W*

Set in an attractive valley village, this is a large medieval church with pinnacled Perpendicular tower extensively restored in 1907. Decorated and Perpendicular features predominate. The nave roof is late medieval arch-braced, and underneath the S. chapel is a vaulted crypt.

LLANDDEW † Holy Trinity / St David

1m/2km N.E. of Brecon, Powys

OS *SO054307* **GPS** *51.96713N, 3.37714W*

On the site of a clas church, this is a large cruciform church with a central tower and a remarkably uniform Early English exterior. The tower, rebuilt in 1620, has a pyramidal roof of 1780. The interior is disappointing though – thoroughly scraped – but there are remains of a late medieval wall-painting under the cornice on the N. nave wall. Giraldus Cambrensis lived in the nearby bishop's palace in the 12th century.

LLANDDEWI † St David

3m/4km N. of Port Eynon Pt, Gower Peninsula

OS *SS460890* **GPS** *51.57924N, 4.22393W*

The approach by a grassy farmyard is in character with this most attractive, primitive building, restored in 1876, with a low saddle-back tower. The bright polished interior has a planked floor; there is a clear E. window; barley-sugar communion rails; a painted altar table with Gothic arcading; and a huge flow-erpot font.

LLANDDEWI BREFI † St David ★★

3m/4km S.W. of Tregaron, Ceredigion

OS *SN663553* **GPS** *52.17986N, 3.95566W*

The big, square, late 12th-century tower rests on what was the vaulted crossing of the nave, rebuilt 1874. The long chancel has transepts which collapsed in the 18th century, hence the attractive pointed sash windows. The walls are whitewashed, the floors of polished slate, and there are ceiled wagon roofs in the nave and chancel. The pews are simple early 19th-century pine. Several important 7th- to 10th-century stones, including an Ogham inscription, have been placed in the church. A 7th-century stone, now built into the N.W. corner of the nave, contains the earliest known reference to St David.

LLANDDOGET † St Doged ★

1m/2km N. of Llanrwst, Conwy

OS *SH805637* **GPS** *53.15702N, 3.78726W*

A rebuilding in 1839 by the rector resulted in a delightful double-nave building of domestic feel and proportions, bargeboards, lattice windows, and all. Inside is the original arrangement of tall pews facing the three-decker pulpit on the N. wall. Behind the pulpit is a plaster putto's head, flanked by oil paintings of Moses with the Commandments, and the Royal Arms. The pulpit is lit by a round skylight with coloured glass.

LLANDEGWNING † St Ieslyn ★

3m/4km N.W. of Abersoch, Lleyn Peninsula

OS *SH266300* **GPS** *52.83995N, 4.57563W*

A most engaging dolls' house church by John Welch, 1840, it has a two-stage octagonal and round W. tower, slate sundial and conical spire. Inside all is painted white except the green-grained box pews. There is a Gothic communion rail and a fine tablet of 1721.

LLANDEILO GRABAN † St Teilo

5m/8km S.E. of Builth Wells, Powys

OS *SO093446* **GPS** *52.0931, 3.32434W*

Set in a hamlet above the Wye Valley, the church is largely 14th-century with Perpendicular windows; it was restored by E. V. Collier in 1897. The broad nave is ceiled by a boarded barrel vault and open-roofed chancel; there are 17th-century altar rails and a 14th-century font. The tower may be Norman.

LLANDELOY † St Eloi ★★

7m/11km E. of St David's, Pembrokeshire

OS *SM856266* **GPS** *51.89752N, 5.11631W*

Friends of Friendless Churches

A charming and unusual church by J. Coates Carter of Cheltenham, 1924 – rough stone, with a fine rood screen and loft. All is dark inside, but not gloomy. The elevated chancel is mysterious and moving, with a gesso and tempera reredos. At the W. end is a medi-eval stone font, above which a small coloured window admits a shaft of golden light.

LLANDELOY: ST ELOI – *ancient in mood if not date, the church was built in 1924; the font, though, is genuinely medieval* ▷

△ **LLANEILIAN: ST EILIAN** – *the rood screen is exceptional, with a painted skeleton on the underside and the rickety balustrade of a loft above*

LLANDOVERY (Llanfair-ar-y-bryn)
† St Mary ★
17m/27km W. of Brecon, Carmarthenshire
OS *SN769351* **GPS** *52.00139N, 3.79343W*

Built on the site of a Roman fort, it is like a great tithe barn with a sturdy embattled 13th-century tower with external turreted staircase. The parapets and gargoyles were added c. 1500 but, despite these and its size, the whole gives a sense of humility. Inside are rough plastered walls, and the clear W. window lets in a flood of light. It was restored by W. D. Caroe, 1913. The E. window is by Kempe, and others by John Peters. The great Welsh hymn writer William Williams of Pant-y-celyn, d. 1791, is buried here.

LLANDUDWEN † St Tudno ★
Lleyn Peninsula
OS *SH274368* **GPS** *52.90144N, 4.5676W*

A Lleyn Peninsula church with an enticing approach – a straight path leads down through a massive lych gate to the door in the W. gable, which is capped by a bellcote with jaunty bell, all slightly off-centre. The nave plan is a T, now with no chancel. The nave is thought to be a rebuilding on medieval foundations of 1595; the N. and S. transepts are 17th-century additions. In the nave, there are 18th-century benches with backs, and the oil lamps have been converted to gas.

LLANDYFALLE † St Matthew / St Maelog
Village also spelt Llandefalle; 3m/4km W. of Talgarth, Powys
OS *SO107355* **GPS** *52.01141N, 3.30171W*

Isolated from the village, this is a long Perpendicular church with three-stage tower of Norman origin, and slate-hung pyramidal roof. On each end of the simple c. 1500 rood screen are two carved dragons. Two wall-paintings depict a floral motif and St Christopher (possibly).

LLANDYSILIO † St Tysilio
7m/11km S. of Oswestry, Powys
OS *SJ267193* **GPS** *52.76647N, 3.08664W*

G. E. Street built this superb church in

△ **LLANFAIR KILGEDDIN: ST MARY THE VIRGIN** – *Seddon's interior is lined with sgraffito murals, mostly pastoral in theme, by Heywood Summer*

1867–8, in Early English and Decorated style. The little circular turret has glazed windows set below the conical roof. The nave rises by steps to the chancel, with further steps leading to the altar, behind which is a Caen stone reredos. The excellent E. window by Clayton & Bell was designed by Street. On the S. side is a richly coloured window of the sea giving up its dead.

LLANDYSUL † St Tysul ★

12m/19km N. of Carmarthen, Ceredigion
OS *SN418406* **GPS** *52.04204N, 4.3068W*

Of ancient foundation, the church is mostly 13th-century, including the handsome tower, still being improved in the late 15th century. There is a grand, ancient altar stone, incised with cross patterns, found locally, now in the Lady Chapel, as is the Crucifixion, which includes the Virgin Mary and St John, once on the W. face of the tower.

LLANEILIAN † St Eilian ★

2m/3km E. of Amlwch, Isle of Anglesey
OS *SH469928* **GPS** *53.41063N, 4.3037W*

Do not be deterred by the rather horrid rendering on the 12th-century pyramidal topped tower. The broad nave and square chancel were rebuilt in the late 15th century with low-pitched roofs and battlemented parapets. There are splendid fittings, mostly c. 1500: a sturdy rood screen and loft with painted skeleton, and musicians carved on the corbels of the roof beams. The 14th-century St Eilian's Chapel, with part of his 15th-century shrine, is set at 45 degrees to the chancel and linked to it by a sunny passage.

LLANELIDAN † St Elidan

5m/8km S. of Ruthin, Denbighshire
OS *SJ109505* **GPS** *53.04471N, 3.32921W*

A rural hamlet setting near a tributary of the River Clwyd, this is a well-restored 15th-century double-naved church with good carved woodwork on the rood screen – horses and vines – and a well-carved Jacobean

△ **LLANFAIR KILGEDDIN: ST MARY THE VIRGIN** – *one of Summer's sgraffito panels, said to be inspired by the surrounding Monmouthshire countryside*

pulpit. There are old box pews, 17th- to 18th-century monuments and a portrait of the Roman Catholic martyr Edward Jones.

LLANELIEU † St Ellyw ★★

2m/3km E. of Talgarth, Powys
OS *SO184341* **GPS** *52.00006N, 3.18884W*
Friends of Friendless Churches

This lovely old church stands in a field in the hills above Talgarth. It is 13th-century, small, simple and very atmospheric. A large red-ochre painted 14th-century rood screen dominates the church loft, and there are interesting monuments. The church is a frequent setting for concerts. Exceptional in its simplicity.

LLANFAELRHYS † St Maelrhys

Lleyn Peninsula
OS *SH210268* **GPS** *52.80932N, 4.65704W*

The church is in a lovely setting close to the sea – another Bardsey Island pilgrim route church. It is a long, narrow, medieval church with mid-19th-century box pews and a 15th-century font.

LLANFAGLAN † St Baglan ★

2m/3km S.W. of Caernarfon, Gwynedd
OS *SH455606* **GPS** *53.12099N, 4.30956W*
Friends of Friendless Churches

A rare example of a small, largely unrestored medieval church, with a c.1800 chancel, St Baglan stands in a field overlooking Caernarfon Bay. The E. wall of the porch has some fragments of re-used 5th- to 6th-century stone carving, and the inner doorway has a lintel stone of the same date. The unrestored interior retains 18th-century furnishings, including benches, box pews, a pulpit with sounding board, and a reading desk.

LLANFAIR DYFFRYN CLWYD

† St Cynfarch and St Mary

2m/3km S. of Ruthin, Denbighshire
OS *SJ134554* **GPS** *53.08944N, 3.29405W*

A typical Vale of Clwyd double-naved church with stout tower, it was well restored in 1872 by J. D. Sedding. There is part of the original rood screen, and a 14th-century Welsh Knight's memorial, and some good stained glass by Kempe.

LLANFAIR KILGEDDIN

† St Mary the Virgin ★★

4m/7km SE of Abergavenny, Monmouthshire
OS *SO355086* **GPS** *51.77313N, 2.93502W*
Friends of Friendless Churches

Another deeply rural church, St Mary the Virgin is situated in Monmouthshire farmland in the Usk Valley, tucked away in a patchwork of fields close to the River Usk. A rebuilding by Seddon of an earlier church, St Mary's real treasure is inside – a decorative scheme of 16 sgraffito memorial panels by Heywood Summer, drawing much of their inspiration from the surrounding landscape and the 'Benedicite'.

LLANFEIGAN (nr Pencelli) † St Meugan

Also spelt Llanfeugan; ½m/1km W. of Pencelli, Powys
OS *SO086245* **GPS** *51.91186N, 3.32916W*

On a spur between two tributary streams of the River Usk, this is a church of the 13th- to 15th-centuries with a good tower. The S. W. Williams 1891 restoration revealed remains of the medieval rood screen. Outside is the stump of an octagonal shaft – possibly a preaching cross shaft.

LLANFIHANGEL HELYGEN

† St Michael ★

2m/3km N.W. of Llandrindod Wells, Powys
OS *SO045643* **GPS** *52.26937N, 3.39996W*

The sturdy little church stands like a cottage in a clearing and was mostly rebuilt in 1812. Its brown-stone walls and slate roofs with green moss and a low, white-timber bellcote were sympathetically restored in 1956. The vestry floor is cobbled, the main church paved and the walls lime-washed. The open roof has carved arch braces; the windows are domestic. 17th-century box pews face a two-decker pulpit, and there are some simple diamond-shaped early 19th-century slate memorials: very atmospheric.

LLANFIHANGEL-Y-CREUDDYN

† St Michael

5m/8km W. of Devil's Bridge, Ceredigion
OS *SN665760* **GPS** *52.36623N, 3.96199W*

A 13th-century church with a very grand central tower, it was well restored by Withers in 1871. The plain whitewashed interior has 16th-century wagon roofs, and there is a carved oak reredos, 1919, by Jules Bernaerts, a Belgian sculptor, metalworker and painter.

LLANFILO † St Bilo / St Milburgh ★★

5m/7km N.E. of Brecon, Powys
OS *SO118332* **GPS** *51.99069N, 3.2845W*

The partly Norman church has been most fortunate since the mid-19th century. In 1851 the excellent tower and shingled spire were rebuilt, emulating a previous structure. Then, in 1913, W. D. Caroe began a restoration that was only finally completed in 1951, some 13 years after his death. Outside and inside are whitewashed; the chancel retains its plaster ceiling of 1709. The splendid rood screen was superbly restored with new figures by Nathaniel Hitch. Many old pews remain, as does the 18th-century pulpit. Caroe put in some new windows, basing their design on one in the chancel. The atmosphere is unusually light and bright.

LLANFRYNACH

† St Brynach ★

adjoining Cowbridge, Vale of Glamorgan
OS *SS979746* **GPS** *51.46122N, 3.47032W*

An extraordinary bulky 12th-century and Early English church in a field, whose massive tower, rebuilt in 2002, has a saddleback roof. Inside is an earth floor and stone benches along the walls. The isolation of the church can be explained by the disappearance of the village of Llanfrynach in the 14th-century plague. It has a lovely simple interior without electricity.

LLANFYLLIN St Myllin ★
10m/16km N.W. of Welshpool, Powys
OS *SJ142195* **GPS** *52.7665N, 3.2721W*

A cheerful, embattled, red-brick Georgian church of 1706, it replaced a substantial earlier church. The interior is lit well by tall, round-headed windows. The nave walls are painted pink above the wainscotting, and the ceiling is plastered and coved. Dog-leg stairs lead up to the 18th-century gallery. Walter Scott attempted to 'Normanize' the church in 1863, but much of this was removed in 1959.

LLANGADWALADR † St Cadwaladr ★
2m/3km E. of Aberffraw, Isle of Anglesey
OS *SH383692* **GPS** *53.19588N, 4.42098W*

The church, under the royal patronage of Cadfan, d. 625, and Cadwaladr, his grandson, was a meeting-place of the chieftains. Cadfan's grave slab is reset in the present nave, which dates from the 12th century; the chancel from the 14th. The fine, though reset, E. window is late 15th-century. The interior is lit by lovely brass chandeliers. The N. chapel has a full-blooded Gothic memorial of 1857; the charming mid-17th-century S. chapel is separated from the nave by a daringly flat arch.

LLANGAMMARCH WELLS
† St Cadmarch
7m/12km W. of Builth Wells
OS SN936472 GPS 52.1136N, 3.5552W

W. D. Caroe's 1913–16 building, with its rough masonry and highly finished fittings, sets the Arts and Crafts tone, for which the date is rather late. The tower was added in 1927. Caroe's regard for local character is evident in the plan and Perpendicular details.

LLANGAR † All Saints ★
1m/2km S. of Corwen, Denbighshire
OS *SJ063424* **GPS** *52.97123N, 3.39596W*
CADW

The church is set beautifully on a hillside overlooking the confluence of the Rivers Dee and Alwen. It is a modest whitewashed medieval church with a deep S. porch. It has all its Georgian fittings, box pews, three-decker pulpit and rough benches for the common folk. There is a fine medieval roof with barrel-vaulting over the chancel, and a very good range of wall-paintings – eight layers in all were uncovered and restored.

LLANGASTY-TALYLLYN
† St Gastayn ★
5m/7km E. of Brecon, S. of Llangorse Lake, Powys
OS *SO133261* **GPS** *51.92689N, 3.26226W*

The S. approach to Llangorse Lake runs past the marvellous group of church, mansion and school. The church was almost wholly rebuilt alongside the school in 1848–50, to the design of J. L. Pearson. Now most sympathetically restored, the church is notable for its simplicity and characteristic Tractarian arrangement, stencilled texts and all.

LLANGEDWYN † St Cedwyn
3m/4km S. of Llansilin, Powys
OS *SJ188241* **GPS** *52.80874N, 3.20574W*

Rebuilt in 1869–70 by Benjamin Ferrey, the church has a neo-Norman N. porch with elaborate terracotta decoration by H. L. North, c. 1840. Inside are remarkable altar rails of wood, copper and enamel, probably by John Bonnor, d. 1916, as well as a 14th-century priest's effigy in the chancel and good 18th-century monuments.

LLANGEFNI † St Cyngar
7m/11km W. of Menai Bridge, Isle of Anglesey
OS *SH458759* **GPS** *53.25788N, 4.31303W*

An unusual 1824 church, it is in a market town in the centre of the island. The nave roof is supported by shallow arched beams. There is a W. gallery, and green-grained pews inside. The chancel, an unfortunate addition, was built in 1898.

LLANGELYNIN
† St Celynin Old Church ★
4m/6km N.W. of Tywyn, Gwynedd
OS *SH571072* **GPS** *52.64373N, 4.11311W*

This is a lonely hillside setting, on the site of an ancient settlement. It is Norman in origin with a 14th-century chancel, 15th-century porch and N. transept known as the 'Capel Meibion' (the Mens' Chapel). The S. transept is possibly 16th-century; the altar screen and barley-twist communion rails are 17th-century. Restoration uncovered Welsh

LLANTWIT MAJOR: ST ILLTUD – *through the chancel arch can be seen the elaborately carved 14th-century reredos* ▷

△ **LLANTWIT MAJOR: ST ILLTUD** – *the 'west' tower is almost central, with the collegiate church to the right and the parochial church to the left*

texts painted on the E. chancel wall. On the S. wall of the nave hangs a wooden bier. Outside in the S.E. corner of the churchyard is a holy well.

LLANGENNITH † St Cenydd ★

2m/3km E. of Burry Holms, Gower Peninsula
OS *SS428914* **GPS** *51.59968N, 4.27013W*

A strong, daring, early medieval church with a prodigious saddleback-roofed tower set N. of the nave, this is the Gower's largest church. Inside is a fragment of a carved Celtic wheel cross. Inside the church is a carved effigy of a 13th-century knight.

LLANGURIG † St Curig ★

4m/6km S.W. of Llanidloes, Powys
OS *SN907799* **GPS** *52.40628N, 3.60699W*

This grand church is set in a sloping churchyard on the site of a clas, below the main road and close to the River Wye. The 15th-century tower has a most effective shingled spire, now clad in copper, added at the time of the restoration of 1877–8 by Sir George Gilbert Scott and Arthur Baker. The stained-glass windows by Burlison & Grylls are superbly executed. The rood screen was re-created from 1828 drawings of the original 15th-century screen; together with the stalls and rich chancel fittings, it forms an outstanding ensemble.

LLANGWNNADL
† St Gwynhoedl

Lleyn Peninsula, Gwynedd
OS *SH208332* **GPS** *52.86674N, 4.66241W*

This is a curious 16th-century pilgrim route church, with three broad aisles separated by light three-bay arcades, and a width that's greater than its length. The N. aisle was added in 1520, that to the S. ten years later. The windows in the N. wall date from H. Kennedy's restoration of 1850, at which time the old screen was removed. The inscriptions on the arcade pier record the erection of this aisle over the burialplace of the patron saint. The E. windows are all contemporary. The octagonal font, with its unusual carvings, probably dates from the 1520 restoration.

LLANGWM † St Jerome ★

7m/12km NW of Chepstow, Monmouthshire
OS *SO432005* **GPS** *51.70089N, 2.82197W*

An idyllic setting for this Early English church with a grand tower on the N. side of the chancel. It was restored by J. P. Seddon and Ewan Christian in 1870. Inside is a magnificent Perpendicular rood screen and loft, elaborately carved.

LLANIDLOES † St Idloes ★★

Powys

OS *SN953846* **GPS** *52.45007N, 3.541W*

A very pleasing church dedicated to an obscure saint, on the S. bank of the River Severn. The 14th-century tower is unusual, with a short pyramidal roof set on top of a two-tier stepped wooden belfry. Inside is a fine hammer-beam roof from the former Cistercian monastery at Cwmhir, with gilded carved angels. From the same source is a dignified S. arcade, with stiff-leaf carving to the capitals. G. E. Street restored the church in 1880–82.

LLANIGON † St Eigen

2m/3km S.W. of Hay-on-Wye, Powys

OS *SO213399* **GPS** *52.05218N, 3.14795W*

The 14th-century two-storey porch gives the church the appearance of a tithe barn. The upper floor of the porch houses the bells. Inside is a wide-eaved roof, numbered box pews raised on wooden plinths and a pretty Gothic barrel organ.

LLANRHAEADR-YM-MOCHNANT
† St Dogfan

4m/6km N. of Llanfyllin, Powys

OS *SJ123260* **GPS** *52.8246N, 3.30168W*

Set in a churchyard sloping down to the river, the church was the place where Bishop William Morgan first translated the Bible into Welsh in 1588. Mostly renewed by Spaull, 1882, it has a good plastered barrel-vault ceiling to the nave. In the S. aisle is the Cwgan Stone – a 9th-century inscribed tombstone – and fragments of a Romanesque shrine.

LLANRHAEADR-YNG-NGHINMEIRCH † St Dyfnog ★★

2m/3km N. of Ruthin, Denbighshire

OS *SJ081633* **GPS** *53.15962N, 3.37493W*

Set among trees with a holy well behind the churchyard, this is a late medieval double-nave church, restored by Baker, 1879–80. The timber porch has good wood carving, and the nave roofs are double hammer-beamed. Above the altar is a carved barrel-vault 'canopy of honour' ceiling. The treasure here is the fine Jesse window, 1533. In the window over the vestry are recovered medieval glass fragments.

LLANRWST † St Grwst ★

11m/18km S. of Colwyn Bay, Conwy

OS *SH797616* **GPS** *53.13809N, 3.79923W*

On the banks of the River Conwy, this is a church of the 12th and 15th centuries, rebuilt in 1882–4 by Paley & Austin, with a magnificent rood screen and loft. The carved tracery of the screen has a fine depiction of the instruments of the Crucifixion. The Gwydir Chapel of 1633–4 contains the stone coffin of Llywelyn the Great (Llywelyn ap Iorwerth), with an accompanying knight's effigy, and excellent brasses and other memorials.

LLANSTEFFAN † St Stephen

10m/14km S.W. of Carmarthen, Carmarthenshire

OS *SN350107* **GPS** *51.77067N, 4.39273W*

A village church on the Twyi estuary; the extensive stone lych gate has an entrance for carts and an attached stable for the rector's horse. The church is cruciform, with an embattled 13th-century tower. The scraped interior has a Victorian arch-braced nave roof and wagon-roof in the chancel. Good monuments include that to the Rev. Wm. Lloyd, d. 1706, 'In doeing good who was imploy'd'.

LLANTRISANT
† St Ieuan, St Afran and St Sannan

1m/2km S.E. of Llanddeusant, Isle of Anglesey

OS *SH349840* **GPS** *53.32767N, 4.47984W*

Friends of Friendless Churches

In a remote rural setting near a farm, this is late 14th-century with a 17th-century S. chapel – one of the first Welsh churches to be acquired and rescued by the Friends of Friendless Churches. It retains its 18th-century box pews and a good monument to Hugo Williams. The 12th-century font comes from Buckinghamshire.

LLANYMAWDDWY: ST TYDECHO – *the church seems as much a part of the landscape as the Berwyn Hills that surround it* ▷

LLANTWIT MAJOR † St Illtud ★★

4m/6km S.W. of Cowbridge, Vale of Glamorgan
OS *SS966687* **GPS** *51.40804N, 3.48781W*

This is the site of St Illtud's Celtic monastery. The church is an amazing building of enormous length, consisting of four linked sections: the chancel and nave with aisles and W. tower, which formed the collegiate church; the 'western' or parochial church; and, at the extreme W., the ruined Galilee Chapel. It was restored in 1888–1905 by Halliday. The E. church has a large and elaborate 14th-century reredos, much restored. In the S. aisle is a 13th-century niche, richly carved with a Jesse tree. There are 13th- to 15th-century wall-paintings. The W. church has a splendid timber roof and contains a fine collection of Celtic crosses and medieval tombs. The only jarring note is the glass screen separating the collegiate church from the rest.

LLANVACHES † St Dyfrig

10m/16km E. of Newport
OS *ST433917* **GPS** *51.62177N, 2.81905W*

The integral doughty saddleback tower of the church is unmissable. With Norman origins, most of the church dates from the 14th century, restored in 1863. The interior was charmingly done up by Groves in Arts and Crafts style, 1908 – whitewash, a carved screen and coloured glass. He also did the delightful church room.

LLANWENOG † St Gwenog ★

6m/10km W. of Lampeter, Ceredigion
OS *SN493455* **GPS** *52.08754N, 4.19981W*

An unusual 13th-century church with a big, restored Perpendicular tower. The church is entered through a small door under the tower, down a broad flight of steps and into the pleasantly proportioned nave, barrel-ceiled in the 18th century. In the small S. chapel stands a huge, rustically carved late Norman font, with apostles' heads. A local family transformed the church during World War I, adding carved benches, chancel screen and glass. Interesting memorials include that to Anne Evans, d. 1807, who provided poor relief by 'giving employment in the cultivation of an extensive tract of land'. There was a 1998 restoration by Roger Clive-Powell.

LLANYMAWDDWY † St Tydecho ★

5m/8km N.E. of Mallwyd, Gwynedd
OS *SH903190* **GPS** *52.75793N, 3.62676W*

Deeply remote in the Berwyn Hills, this is a delightful plain church with black and white interior. The E. window of c. 1863 is by Heaton, Butler & Bayne. A wonderful and tranquil setting.

LLANYNYS † St Saeran ★★

3m/4km N. of Ruthin, Denbyshire
OS *SJ103626* **GPS** *53.15359N, 3.34268W*

On the Cistercian Way, this is a big, typical Denbighshire double-naved building, the naves separated by 18th-century fluted wooden columns. It has richly carved hammer-beams, and a 1637 altar table supported by lions. A splendid great wall-painting of St Christopher faces the door, which is sheltered by a pleasing and intricately carved Tudor porch. In the nave is a remarkable hexagonal sepulchral cross, probably 14th-century. On one side is a figure of a bishop, and on the other a Crucifixion. There are very interesting carved Tudor panels near the altar too, from the home of Col. 'Old Blue Stockings' William Salesbury, who was responsible for the riot of carving at Rug Chapel. And for unruly dogs, a rare set of telescopic dog-tongs.

LLYWEL † St David

1m/2km N.W. of Trecastle, Powys
OS *SN869300* **GPS** *51.95746N, 3.64681W*

The 14th- and 15th-century church is sited close to the Usk Valley, with good Perpendicular features excellently restored in 1869 by Sir George Gilbert Scott. The tower has an external stone stair turret, and a string course with gargoyles. The 1925 chancel screen is by Harry Hems.

MANORBIER † St James ★★

4m/6km S.W. of Tenby, Pembrokeshire
OS *SS065976* **GPS** *51.64425N, 4.79805W*

The church where the medieval Welsh-Anglo-Norman chronicler Giraldus Cambrensis worshipped when a boy; he grew up in the castle across the valley in the mid-12th century. Steps lead down through a vaulted porch – note the medieval painting – as into a crypt. The huge walls of the Norman nave give the impression of being carved out to form arcades to the 14th-century aisles. The transept vaults cut the main vault of the nave at different levels. This sculptural character must have been even stronger before the 1865 restoration, when a much larger arch was cut in the chancel wall. Then the old rood screen and the Royal Arms were removed, and the Perpendicular E. window changed for the present three-light one. The tower has an unusual position in the angle between the 13th-century chancel and the N. transept, and is rather startlingly lime-washed.

MANORDEIFI † St David ★
4m/6km S.E. of Cardigan, Pembrokeshire
OS *SN228431* **GPS** *52.05849N, 4.58561W*
Friends of Friendless Churches

On the banks of the Teifi – note the traditional coracle in the porch – the church fabric dates from the 13th and 14th centuries. Inside are charming 19th-century fittings: to the E. are box pews with fireplaces; to the W. raised box pews with fluted columns; Georgian glazing; and a mid-19th-century monument to Charles Colby, d. 1852, killed by a tiger in India.

MARCHWIEL St Marcella
2m/3km S.E. of Wrexham
OS *SJ358476* **GPS** *53.0226N, 2.9584W*

The church has close links with the Yorke family, who bequeathed nearby Erddig Hall to the National Trust. It was built in 1778, with a slightly later N. transept, and a polygonal apse added in the 19th century. The apse is painted in cream and pink. Inside are a painted decalogue and creed board, good memorials and a 20th-century carved reredos with putto. There is a stained-glass window depicting the lineage of the Yorke family.

MARGAM † St Mary
S.E. district of Port Talbot
OS *SS801862* **GPS** *51.56277N, 3.73056W*

The Norman nave of a once-great Cistercian abbey survives as a parish church. The Italianate W. font is of 1805–10; the W. windows, 1873, by Burne-Jones. Note the fine 16th-, 17th- and 19th-century tombs.

MEIFOD † St Tysilio and St Mary ★
4m/6km S. of Llanfyllin, Powys
OS *SJ155131* **GPS** *52.70971N, 3.25173W*

Set in a nine-acre churchyard, the site of a Celtic clas, the church is of Romanesque origin; the W. end of a 12th-century church can be seen in the nave. The tower is 15th-century; there is a 17th-century octagonal font and 19th-century pews incorporating panels from the 17th-century screen. During Benjamin Ferrey's 1871–2 restoration Romanesque arches were uncovered in the S.W. wall. Against the W. wall is a carved Celtic stone slab.

MENAI BRIDGE † St Tysilio ★
Off the A5 on an island in the Strait, reached by a causeway, 1m/2km W. of Bangor, Isle of Anglesey
OS *SH551716* **GPS** *53.22243N, 4.17126W*

In a timeless and secluded atmosphere, this is the simplest of 15th-century churches with medieval roof trusses; outside are touching slate memorials. The setting is all.

MINWEAR † St Womar ★
9m/15km N.W. of Tenby, Pembrokeshire
OS *SN039130* **GPS** *51.78133N, 4.84334W*

Another lovely secluded site near a farm above E. Cleddau; a small, simple Norman and later church.

MOLD † St Mary ★★
11m/17km N.W. of Wrexham town, Flintshire
OS *SJ236641* **GPS** *53.16918N, 3.14304W*

A splendid Tudor church that dominates the main street and much of the Alun Valley, it has a sizeable aisled nave, all 15th- to early 16th-century Perpendicular. The tower was added in 1768–73 by Joseph Turner and the chancel with a canted apse by Sir George Gilbert Scott, 1856. The roofs are very good Tudor and there is plenty of rich stone carving, especially in the springs of the arcade arches and the stonework below the clerestory. The chancel glass is by Wailes; the understated 1878 reredos by Douglas. There is some 15th- and 16th-century glass. The 1921 War Memorial Chapel by Sir T. G. Jackson has a curious Art Deco floor, and there are monuments by Cheere and Rysbrack.

△ **NANT PERIS: ST PERIS** – *Low-lying to battle the elements, the church was extended in sections between the 14th and 17th centuries, then restored in the mid-19th*

MONTGOMERY † St Nicholas ★★

Powys
OS *SO223965* **GPS** *52.56097N, 3.14667W*

A church of great charm in a delightful and unspoilt border town on a hill, with grand views E., St Nicholas's is mostly 13th-century, the tower rebuilt in 1816. Restoration was by G. Beadnell in 1863–8, and the N. arcade by Haycock in 1877–8. The nave has a splendid roof, open in the W. and panelled in the E. The part-restored and intricately carved Perpendicular screen is a delight, and in the chancel is an elaborate reredos designed by R. C. Carpenter, with figures by Earp and mosaics by Clayton & Bell. The S. transept contains a magnificent tomb of 1600 to Richard Herbert of Montgomery Castle, canopied with effigies of Herbert, d. 1596, and his wife Magdalen, and ornamented with skulls, cross-bones, fruit, flowers, Coats of Arms and carvings of their eight children. There are also two much-restored medieval effigies. In the churchyard is the famous Robber's Grave.

NANT PERIS † St Peris ★

2m/3km S.E. of Llanberis, Gwynedd
OS *SH606582* **GPS** *53.10356N, 4.08295W*

St Peris stands in a wild, magnificent mountain setting at the foot of the Llanberis pass. It is a rustic cruciform building with 14th-century nave, 16th-century N. and S. transepts, and 17th-century chancel with contemporary N. and S. chapels. It was restored in 1848 by Henry Kennedy, and the 17th-century fittings and rood screen were removed to the W. end.

NASH † St Mary

4m/6km S.E. of Newport
OS *ST343836* **GPS** *51.54802N, 2.94882W*

Known as the 'Cathedral of the Moors', the church is noted for its lofty stone Perpendicular spire attached to the N.E. corner of the nave. The chancel was rebuilt by Prichard and Seddon in 1861. The 18th-century S. porch is Classical, with a grand pilastered doorway. The inner door is Gothic, as is the huge barn-like nave, which retains its box pews and three-decker pulpit.

NEVERN † St Brynach ★
2ml3km E. of Newport, Pembrokeshire
OS *SN083400* **GPS** *52.02548N, 4.79514W*

This pilgrim church stands on an attractive ancient site, now snug in a hamlet by the River Nyfer, with a view of the Prescellys from the churchyard. A 15th-century cruciform building, it was very well restored by R. J. Withers in 1863. The W. tower is low and battlemented. Inside is a 5th-century Ogham stone and a 10th-century stone carved with a cross. Outside, the great Celtic high cross dates from c. 1000, and there are some fine slate tombs.

NICHOLASTON † St Nicholas ★
Gower Peninsula, above E. end of Oxwich Bay
OS *SS512884* **GPS** *51.57508N, 4.14796W*

A true late Victorian period piece by G. E. Halliday in 1892–4, the church has great charm. No expense has been spared, and it shows. The elaborately carved reredos with polychromatic arcading was by William Clarke, who also carved the apostles' heads over the S. door. Burlison & Grylls did some pleasant glass. On the pulpit are statues of Keble, Liddon and Pusey, and there is a copper baptismal font.

OLD RADNOR † St Stephen ★★
3ml4km E. of New Radnor, Powys
OS *SO249590* **GPS** *52.22487N, 3.0996W*

The tower and beacon turret of this outstanding medieval church are a sturdy landmark for miles westward. It is a perfect Victorian restoration of a fine Perpendicular church. The E. end was entirely rebuilt by F. Preedy of Worcester, and a vast window with Hardman glass was inserted in 1882; there is good late 15th-century glass in the vestry. The carved organ case, c. 1500, is the oldest in Britain. The intricately carved screen, once painted, is now highly polished, and the Tudor roofs are wonderful. The sturdy medieval choir-stalls and medieval tiles have been supplemented by Godwin. The font is a huge lump of dolerite, and there is an interesting Easter Sepulchre in the N. chapel, an 18th-century painting of Moses and Aaron, and some interesting tombs and hatchments. Views of the church from the surrounding countryside are perfectly complemented by the views from the churchyard.

△ **OLD RADNOR: ST STEPHEN** – *the beacon turret pokes up above the tower*

OXWICH † St Illtud ★
Gower Peninsula
OS *SS504861* **GPS** *51.55406N, 4.15908W*

It is well worth visiting this little church, standing in woodland at the very edge of the cliff on the right arm of the bay. The big tower looms out of a green gloom of sycamore, and the church is entered through the W. door under it. The diminutive chancel has a lovely 14th-century tomb and a ceiling painted at the expense of Dame Lilian Baylis of the Old Vic fame; the 1926 chancel screen is by Gerald Cogswell. The two 13th- and 14th-century slabs in the porch bear the names of former rectors. On the N. wall is a recessed tomb with ogee arch, which contains effigies of a knight and his lady, made from sand bound with plaster.

△ **PARTRISHOW: ST ISSUI** – *the 12th-century church stands on a steep bank overlooking the beautiful Vale of Grwyney in Powys*

PARTRISHOW
† St Issui ★★
Also spelt Patricio;
5m/8km N. of Abergavenny, Powys
OS *SO278224* **GPS** *51.89579N, 3.04952W*

Up a remote valley, on a bluff overlooking the Vale of Grwyney, stands a 12th-century two-cell church of remarkable appeal. Approached through Caroe's excellent stone lych gate, the church, with its famous rood screen of c. 1500, was well restored by him in 1908. The two stone altars in front of the screen are a remarkable survival. On the W. wall is painted a memento mori, a comic skeleton with a spade. The monuments include several by the Brutes, distinguished by elegant lettering and charmingly unsophisticated decoration. The huge font is pre-Conquest.

PEMBREY † St Illtud
Adjoins Burry Port to W., Carmarthenshire
OS *SN428012* **GPS** *51.68765N, 4.27472W*

This is a late 13th-century church enlarged with a 14th-century tower that was a landmark for navigators in the treacherous waters of the Burry Estuary. The nave is 16th-century, as is the timber barrel-vaulted roof. There are many unusual maritime memorials and monuments: a niece of the Empress Josephine Buonaparte and many others lost at sea – mariners and passengers alike.

PENALLY † St Nicholas
1m/2km S.W. of Tenby, Pembrokeshire
OS *SS117991* **GPS** *51.65978N, 4.72291W*

The village is reputedly the birth- and burial-place of St Teilo (c. 500–560), first bishop of Llandaff. The well-proportioned cruciform church was rebuilt in the 13th century, and has a barrel-vaulted roof and later W. tower. There are two notable Celtic high crosses in the S. transept: one of 850–900 and the other of 900–950.

PENARTH † St Augustine ★★
3m/4km S. of Cardiff
OS *ST188720* **GPS** *51.44153N, 3.16927W*

Sited on a headland, with a magnificent view over Cardiff Bay, the tiny old church

△ **PARTRISHOW: ST ISSUI** – *the intricately carved rood screen dates from about 1500; it was carefully restored in 1908 by W. D. Caroe*

was replaced in 1865–6 with one of William Butterfield's finest buildings at a cost of £10,000. The tough exterior is in grey Radyr stone, the tall saddleback tower in striking contrast with the humble one it replaced. The interior is an extraordinary exercise in Geometrical polychromy, pink Radyr stone, red sandstone and yellowish Bath stone. Characteristic fittings include a splendid reredos.

PENMON PRIORY † St Seiriol ★★

3m/4km N.E. of Beaumaris, Isle of Anglesey
OS *SH630807* **GPS** *53.30574N, 4.05698W*

The church stands near the top of Anglesey, overlooking the approaches to the Menai Straits. The prior's house, dortoir (dormitory) and ruined refectory survive. The low tower with its pyramidal roof and the present nave and transepts are 12th-century, dark and deeply impressive. Note the bold carving in the crossing arches and the much-weathered dragon in the tympanum of the S. door. Arcading survives in the S. transept. The font was once a cross base, and there are Celtic crosses of c. 1000. The priory was given to the Austin Priors in 1414. The 19th-century chancel, rebuilt by Weightman and Hadfield, seems light and papery by contrast.

PENNANT MELANGELL

† St Melangell ★★

2m/3km W. of Llangynog, Powys
OS *SJ024265* **GPS** *52.82763N, 3.4498W*

Set in a circular churchyard in a remote valley in the Berwyn Hills, the church is of outstanding interest. Its origins go back to the 8th century; the simple church itself has its roots in the 12th century, but has been much rebuilt. The square tower, with a pyramidal roof surmounted by a wooden belfry, was rebuilt in 1877. The porch is dated 1737. The Perpendicular rood screen remains – part of its loft is carved with scenes illustrating the legend of St Melangell. The saint's 12th-century stone shrine was reconstructed in 1958 from fragments embedded in the church walls. The tomb chest and gabled superstructure stand on arches, supported on six columns; the capitals, arches and gables

△ **PENNANT MELANGELL: ST MELANGELL** – *the fabric of the building has been much restored since the 12th century, the tower and belfry being entirely rebuilt in 1877*

are ornamented with rich Romanesque carving. The tomb chest itself was probably covered in precious metals and jewels, and the whole stands about 10 feet high. It has been moved to stand E. of the altar.

PENNARD † St Mary

Gower Peninsula, 4m/6km W. of Mumbles Head
OS *SS565887* **GPS** *51.57922N, 4.07164W*

A puzzling medieval church that replaced – so it was claimed – an earlier church inundated by the sands of Pennard Burrows. The 16th-century date has now been amended to the 13th century. The whole church is white-washed outside, and has a plain but pleasing interior with a curious inverted hull-like chancel roof.

PRESTEIGNE † St Andrew ★★

5m/8km S. of Knighton, Powys
OS *SO315645* **GPS** *52.27498N, 3.00433W*

A fine church of great interest in wonderful border countryside, it incorporates Saxon and Norman work and is mainly late 14th-century, the chancel rebuilt in the mid-15th century. J. L. Pearson restored the church in 1889–91. There is a small, possibly Roman, relief of St Andrew high over the W. window, and in the S. aisle windows is some unusual tracery. On the N. wall inside is an early 16th-century Flemish tapestry of outstanding interest: it depicts Christ's entrance into Jerusalem.

RHULEN † St David

Powys
OS *SO137498* **GPS** *52.14012N, 3.26139W*

A rustic little whitewashed church, it has a ship-lapped wooden belfry and dates from the late 13th to early 14th century, with an octagonal font of c. 1400. It has a delightful setting on the edge of a valley above two streams.

RHYL † St Thomas

Denbighshire
OS *SJ010815* **GPS** *53.32128N, 3.4876W*

By Sir George Gilbert Scott, 1861–9, this is a good sandstone Victorian Gothic Revival town church in Early English style. Its spire stands high above the flat estuary. It was built to accommodate the influx of holidaymakers brought about by the opening of the Chester–Holyhead railway. The interior is lofty and dignified.

RUG † Rug Chapel ★★

Denbighshire
OS *SJ064438* **GPS** *52.98423N, 3.39425W*
CADW

One of Denbighshire's little treasures – a mid-17th-century chapel built for William Salesbury, Royalist Governor of Denbigh Castle. The chapel is outwardly plain, but inside no surface has escaped the attention of the wood-carvers. Roof beams, panels and pew ends are decorated with beasts, angels, foliage and flowers, all highly and authentically coloured.

RUTHIN † St Peter

Denbighshire
OS *SJ123583* **GPS** *53.11545N, 3.31071W*

A fine collegiate church restored by R. K. Penson, 1856, who added the distinctive spire. The magnificent Tudor carved roofs and bosses were reputedly given by Henry VII. The fine wrought-iron churchyard gates, 1727, are by Robert and John Davies of Bersham.

ST BRIDE'S MAJOR † St Bridget ★

3m/4km S. of Bridgend, Vale of Glamorgan
OS *SS894750* **GPS** *51.46326N, 3.59342W*

Rebuilt in the 14th century and over-restored in 1885, the church is best known for the remarkable medieval Butler family tomb, which incorporates a square-headed Tudor window. It is to John Butler, d. 1540, and his wife Jane Bassett, and at the base are their four children. Behind the altar stands a very interesting carved burial slab to Sir John le Botiler, his feet resting on a wyvern. There is a second carved slab in the chancel with canopy; and also of note a wall monument to John Wyndham, d. 1697, and his wife Jane Strode, still with some original colour.

ST BRIDE'S SUPER-ELY † St Bride

5m/8km W. of Cardiff
OS *ST096776* **GPS** *51.49031N, 3.30234W*

In a rural setting W. of Cardiff, the church has a saddleback tower, Norman doorway and recut chancel arch. Inside is a lovely 17th-century Italian statue of the Madonna.

ST DONATS † St Donat

2m/3km W. of Llantwit Major, Vale of Glamorgan
OS *SS933680* **GPS** *51.40167N, 3.53451W*

The church stands at the foot of the sloping rise to St Donat's Castle, now Atlantic College. It is a modest Norman and later building. In the Lady Chapel there are memorials and splendid tombs to the Stradling family. The lectern is of interest – an ambo, medieval Breton in origin. Outside is a late 15th-century calvary on the S. side of churchyard.

ST FAGAN'S † St Mary

4m/6km W. of Cardiff
OS *ST121772* **GPS** *51.48715N, 3.26712W*

An attractive church set near the castle, it was well restored by G. E. Street in 1859–60. Inside is a fine 14th-century sedilia. Fittings by Street include pulpit, font cover, seating and tower screen.

ST ISHMAEL (nr Kidwelly) † St Ishmael ★

3m/4km W. of Kidwelly, Carmarthenshire
OS *SN362084* **GPS** *51.7503N, 4.37416W*

This is a fine site overlooking estuaries. The church has a tough and primitive exterior, mostly late 13th-century with an added N. aisle, and an offset low saddleback tower. The interior was thoroughly Victorianized by R. K. Penson, 1860.

ST ISHMAEL'S (nr Milford Haven) † St Ishmael

5m/8km W. of Milford Haven, Pembrokeshire
OS *SM830067* **GPS** *51.71729N, 5.14271W*

Hidden among the trees in Monk Haven Valley with a path descending to the sands, this is a secret little 13th-century church with Victorianized interior and a pretty carved memorial of 1631.

SKENFRITH † St Bridget ★

6m/10km N.W. of Monmouth
OS *SO456203* **GPS** *51.87902N, 2.79157W*

A little bit of Herefordshire can be seen infiltrating the border in this beautiful and remote corner of Monmouthshire. The massively buttressed, square W. tower has a splendid stepped two-stage timber belfry of Herefordshire type. The nave, tower and chancel are all 13th-century. In the N. aisle is the elaborate 1557 tomb of John Morgan, last Governor of the 'Three Castles' (Skenfrith, White and Grosmont), and a lovely Jacobean pew of the Morgan family. The most remarkable possession is a magnificent 16th-century cope.

STACKPOLE ELIDOR
† St James and St Elidyr

3m/4km S. of Pembroke, Pembrokeshire
OS *SR987973* **GPS** *51.63844N, 4.91013W*

The church has a delightful site in a little valley close to a stream. Surprisingly, it is approached through an Art Nouveau lych gate of 1898. This, and much else of this cherished church, commemorates the family living at Stackpole Court, now demolished. It was kindly restored in 1851 by Sir George Gilbert Scott, who rebuilt the nave and retained the original vaulted transepts and Norman tower. There are some exceptional monuments and very good family hatchments.

TENBY † St Mary ★★

9m/15km E. of Pembroke, Pembrokeshire
OS *SN134004* **GPS** *51.67174N, 4.69958W*

This is a splendid and almost complete Perpendicular rebuilding of the 13th-century church. The tall 13th-century tower, topped by an octagonal spire, almost as tall again, is at an angle between the chancel and nave. The big S. porch is c. 1500, as is the ogee-arched W. door. The barrel-roofed nave is separated by arcades of five deeply moulded arches from the mid-15th-century N. aisle and the later 15th-century S. aisle with open roof and W. window; the glass is by Kempe. The 1634 pulpit was recently restored. The E. end is a complete surprise, but its drama is undermined by the absence of a chancel screen. The chancel was lengthened in about 1470, and a flight of steps constructed across it up to the sanctuary; the walls were also raised and the wagon roof put on. There are some fine monuments.

TOWYN † St Mary

2m/3km N.E. of Abergele, Conwy
OS *SH973794* **GPS** *53.30184N, 3.5418W*

A very satisfying grouping of church, vicarage and school by Street, 1872–3. The church has a well-proportioned buttressed crossing tower with a steep saddleback roof. The tiling on the roof is distinctive and there are excellent original fittings inside.

TREDUNNOCK † St Andrew

4m/6km S. of Usk, Monmouthshire
OS *ST379948* **GPS** *51.64913N, 2.89782W*

With tiny Norman windows in the chancel, an old roof and a carved stone font of 1662, this is a modest but charming church. Above the font is a 2nd-century Roman funerary inscription found in the churchyard. The sensitive restoration of 1910 is commemorated in an inscription by Eric Gill.

TRELYSTAN † All Saints

3m/4km S.E. of Welshpool, Powys
OS *SJ263039* **GPS** *52.62821N, 3.08948W*

A sweet little building, thickly surrounded by yews, the church is delightfully set on the edge of woods and reached over fields by a track. It was re-cased with brick-infilled timber framing in 1856, but retains its fine Perpendicular roof. The highly melodramatic E. window is perhaps by David Evans. A tiny Gothic barrel organ of 1827 is still in playing order.

TYWYN † St Cadfan ★

10m/16km W. of Machynlleth, Gwynedd
OS *SH588009* **GPS** *52.58801N, 4.08533W*

On the site of a clas, the church's Norman origins can be seen in the nave arcades and clerestory windows. The central crossing tower collapsed in the late 17th century, and was rebuilt at the W. end in the 18th century. A 19th-century restoration rebuilt the tower in its original central position. Of special interest inside is the Cadfan Stone in the N.W. corner – the inscriptions are said to be the earliest of their type in Welsh. In the chancel are medieval effigies of a knight and a priest.

USK † St Mary ★★
Monmouthshire
OS *SO378008* **GPS** *51.70257N, 2.90016W*

The original church, built for a priory of Benedictine nuns c. 1135, was cruciform, with an apsidal chancel and central tower. The N. aisle was added for the use of the parish in the 13th century and rebuilt in the 15th. The chancel and transepts eventually disappeared, so that the sanctuary is now beneath the tower. The nave was lengthened westward by T. H. Wyatt in 1844. The two fine late Gothic porches were added in the 15th century. A restored medieval screen runs across nave and aisle, and attached to it is a brass plate bearing the oldest Welsh epitaph extant. The 1862 organ, built by Gray and Davidson for Llandaff Cathedral, is a stunning object and deserves a better position; the case was designed by Seddon. On the W. wall is a curious 17th-century epitaph, and outside some interesting tombs in the churchyard.

WORTHENBURY † St Deiniol ★
6m/10km S.E. of Wrexham
OS *SJ418462* **GPS** *53.01022N, 2.86758W*

A splendid Georgian church in warm red brick by Richard Trubshaw, 1736–9, with a grand W. tower and apsidal chancel. The perfectly preserved interior has two box pews with the Puleston family crest, complete with cast-iron fireplaces. Nearly all the fittings are original, giving a concise picture of the social pecking order in the church.

WREXHAM † St Giles ★★
Temple Row, Wrexham
OS *SJ335501* **GPS** *53.04419N, 2.99256W*

This splendid church stands withdrawn behind fine iron gates of c. 1720 by Davies, in an atmospheric churchyard with narrow passages leading off it. The noble, early 16th-century tower combines strength and dignity of outline with great richness of detail; the rest of the church is its equal in splendour if not in refinement. Flying angel bosses ornament the good Tudor nave ceiling, and over the chancel arch are the remnants of a medieval Last Judgment painting. The apsidal chancel was refitted in 1914 by Sir T. G. Jackson. There is a large, overbearing monument in the N. aisle by Roubiliac. A famous benefactor was Elihu Yale, d. 1721, founder of Yale University, who is buried in the churchyard. In the 1920s a reproduction of Wrexham tower was built on the campus.

YNYSCYNHAEARN † St Cynhaerarn ★
2m/3km E. of Criccieth, Gwynedd
OS *SH525387* **GPS** *52.92623N, 4.1945W*

On the edge of marshland outside Criccieth is this little church of the 12th and 16th centuries. It is remarkable for its late Georgian interior of 1830 with almost intact fittings, including three-decker pulpit, box pews, and benches painted with family and house names. Mariners, rope-makers and mercantile pilots are buried here, alongside Jack Ystumllyn, the 'little black slave', and harpist David Owen, 'David of the White Rock', d. 1741, composer of the *Rising of the Lark*.

SCOTLAND

Scotland is a country of contrast and drama, with an indented coastline of some 6,000 miles and some of the most uninhabited and rugged terrain in the British Isles. Geographically the country is divided into three main areas: Highlands, Midlands and Lowlands. And around the entire Scottish coastline are some 700 islands – 94 populated – distributed principally between the Hebrides, Orkney and Shetland, with clusters in the Firth of Clyde, Solway Firth and Firth of Forth.

The Highlands – whose southern boundary is determined by its namesake fault-line (running approximately from Arran to just south of Aberdeen) – is a region of fjord-like sea lochs, glaciated valleys, high moorland to the north-west, inland lochs and rugged mountains. This region also includes the Western Isles, or Outer Hebrides, for the most part peaty, treeless and agricultural. An adjunct to the Highlands on the east is the coastal plain that straddles Moray and Aberdeenshire. With its upland intrusions, notably the Ochil and Sidlaw hills, this is good farming land: the regional capital is Aberdeen, home to the North Sea oil industry.

The Midlands, bordered by fault-lines north and south, has rich lowland farming, forestry and, to the south, the industrial area of Glasgow and Clydeside and the administrative capital Edinburgh. The Lowlands lies south of Glasgow and Edinburgh. With its gentle upland profile, the terrain is less dramatic than the rugged mountains and high moorlands of the Highlands. Dotted with historic towns – Hawick, Kelso, Selkirk – the Lowlands landscape is redolent of border raids and historical lawlessness.

Scotland's history is turbulent: the Vikings, the English under Edward I, Edward II, Edward III, Edward Seymour, Lord Protector, and Cromwell all left their mark. The Reformation was to play a pivotal part in determining Scotland's political and religious future: from 1599 John Knox became the de-facto leader of the Reformation, imbuing Scottish Protestantism with a strong Calvinistic form. And from 1637, religious division became a major source of conflict, internally and externally.

Charles I's imposition of the English prayer book was a catalyst for violent opposition, resulting in the first National Covenant of 1638 – a commitment to the preservation of Presbyterianism as the sole Scottish religion. For several years during the English Civil War, the Covenanters constituted Scotland's ruling group, sending an army south to fight for the Parliamentarian cause. Thereafter Scottish Catholics – mostly Royalist and from the Highlands, and led by James Graham, 1st Marquess of Montrose, took up arms against the Covenanters, sparking a bitter civil war, the legacy of which would be deep-seated religious, political and cultural divisions.

Cromwell's successful annexation of Scotland effectively put an end to the influence of the Presbyterian Kirk party,

◁ **LOCHAWE: ST CONAN** – *this work of the early 20th century is a medley of architectural forms, a quixotic and eclectic interplay of Celtic, Romanesque and Gothic*

but bitter divisions continued, despite the establishment of a Presbyterian Church of Scotland in the time of William and Mary. The internal strife within Presbyterianism culminated in the Disruption of 1843, when a third of the Church of Scotland broke away to form the Free Church. Scottish Catholicism, outlawed from the Reformation onwards, gradually emerged from the highways and byways after the passing of the Catholic Relief Acts of 1778 and 1829, and Catholic presence in Scotland was boosted by Irish Catholic immigrants fleeing from the Great Famine. This transition can be seen at the secret Catholic church at Tynet, a church disguised as a barn at a time when, although legal, Catholic practices were still regarded with deep suspicion. From a slightly later date, the Catholic church at Preshome proclaimed more publicly – albeit modestly – its right to exist.

Today the Protestant church in Scotland is made up of the established Church of Scotland, the United Free Church (represented in this chapter by the delightful Chalmers Memorial Church at Port Seton), the United Presbyterian Church and the Scottish Episcopal Church.

Many church buildings did not escape lightly, and fabrics bear witness to these turbulent times. After the Reformation it was not uncommon for medieval churches to be divided up to accommodate simultaneous preaching, as at St Giles in Edinburgh. In other large burgh churches, for example at Haddington, Dundee and Aberdeen, where the burgh church was contiguous with the urban parish, the subdivisions were more to do with large rises in population. The more isolated churches tended to escape the consequences of the Reformation. Stobo Kirk has survived remarkably intact, as has Orkney's splendid St Magnus, Kirkwall. Rather more surprisingly, considering its proximity to Edinburgh, so has the splendid Norman church of St Cuthbert, Dalmeny. Neither Paisley Abbey nor St Mary's Haddington fared so well, but were outstandingly restored.

Of the Norman churches featured, St Athernase at Leuchars has fine stone carving, and the nave at Dunfermline

0
20 miles
0
20 km
Orkney Islands
Kirkwall
Lambholm
Cape Wrath
Dunnet
John O'Groats
Durness
Thurso
Wick
Eoropaidh
Isle of Lewis
A857
Outer Hebrides
Stornoway
A859
The Minch
A894
A838
A897
A9
Lairg
A839
A835
Golspie
Dornoch
Ullapool
A836
Harris
Rodel
North Uist
The Little Minch
A832
Cromarty
Forres
Elgin
Tynet
Cullen
Preshome
Strathpeffer
Fortrose
Dyke
Pluscarden
Benbecula
Portree
A896
INVERNESS
MORAY
Huntly
Isle of Skye
HIGHLAND
A97
A96
A90
outh Uist
A87
A887
Aviemore
A939
Barra
ABERDEEN
Mallaig
A82
A93
Braemar
A830
A86
Inner Hebrides
Arbuthnott
Fort William
A93
ANGUS
A9
A861
Cortachy
Brechin
Tobermory
A828
A82
Kirriemuir
Aberfeldy
A926
Tiree
Dunkeld
A92
Craignure
PERTH & KINROSS
Fowlis
DUNDEE
OBAN
Iona
Isle of Mull
Dalmally
Fowlis Wester
PERTH
Leuchars
A816
A82
Dunning
St Andrews
Inveraray
STIRLING
ARGYLL & BUTE
A886
Clachan of Glendaruel
See enlarged area
Jura
A83
GLASGOW
EDINBURGH
Paisley Abbey
Cranshaws
Islay
Millport
Kilbirnie
A'Chleit
Hallyne
PEEBLES
Arran
M77
Biggar
Stobo
Shiskine
Symington
A71
Lamington
Bowden
Kelso
EAST AYRSHIRE
SCOTTISH BORDERS
Campbeltown
A701
A76
Durisdeer
MOFFAT
SOUTH AYRSHIRE
DUMFRIES & GALLOWAY
A74(M)
A7
A714
DUMFRIES
Newton Stewart
A7
Stranraer
A75
CARLISLE
M6
Cruggleton

△ **STOBO KIRK** – *though harled to form a rather austere exterior, at its core the church is a welcome pre-Reformation survivor of the early 12th century*

Abbey is superb: Birnie Kirk has some nice Norman surprises inside. Coming forward in time, the medieval is well represented by St Machar's Cathedral in Old Aberdeen, the lovely St Mungo's Cathedral in Glasgow, more starkly at Rodel's St Clement on the Isle of Harris, and monastically at Pluscarden Abbey. And nowhere in the country can one see better the definitive form of post-Reformation church ordering than at Cromarty, nor a better example of a simple preaching space than at Torosay.

The Victorians took a hand in much good Gothic Revival and restoration: there are exceptionally fine examples of William Butterfield's work, notably at Millport on the Isle of Cumbrae, Ninian Comper at Kirriemuir and Aberdeen, Sir Robert Lorimer, notably at Paisley Abbey, St Giles in Edinburgh and St Mary's Whitekirk, and Sir Robert Anderson's charming church at Kelso. Sir George Gilbert Scott did much to put right English vandalism at St Mary's, Dundee, and, slightly later, very good work by Peter MacGregor Chalmers at Paisley and St Andrews, Holy Trinity. Not everything Victorian was good – the horrid destruction of the Norman nave of St Athernase being a particular low point. The 20th century is represented by one church in particular, the extraordinary and moving Italian Chapel, created by prisoners of war at Lambholm, Orkney.

Good Victorian glass by Morris and Co, Burne-Jones, Strachan and others can be seen in abundance: Kelvinside Hillhead in Glasgow, Haddington, Dundee St Mary's, Brechin Cathedral. There are exceptional examples of 20th-century glass too: Sadie McClellan, Br. Gilbert and Dom Ninian Stone at Pluscarden Abbey, Crear McCartney at Linlithgow, Biggar and Stirling, and, notable at St Mungo's Cathedral in Glasgow, a Millennium Window by John Clark.

Like Wales, Scotland is being treated as one entire chapter in this book. The churches have been selected to give as broad as possible a picture of the best of Scottish church architecture.

ABERDEEN
† Cathedral of St Machar (parochial) ★★
The Chanonry, Old Aberdeen
OS *NJ939087* **GPS** *57.1699N, 2.1022W*

Delightfully set in the old town and, despite the absence of the central tower, transepts and choir, St Machar's is an impressive building of the 14th–16th centuries. The W. front is notable, with stocky twin towers topped by octagonal spires flanking the nave. The inside is severely scraped, but nevertheless has considerable appeal, the E. and W. arcades having massive round piers supporting simple Gothic arches. The flat roof, designed by J. Winter, was completed in the early 16th century and is ornamented with heraldic devices to kings, nobility, a pope and other clerics. The glass by Strachan is excellent.

ABERDEEN † Chapel of the Convent of St Margaret of Scotland
Between Spital and Froghall
OS *NJ940074* **GPS** *57.1575N, 2.0999W*

A pleasing Scoto-Catholic church of 1869, it contains many examples of Sir Ninian Comper's work (his father was the priest here) including St Nicholas's Chapel, 1892, and its excellent glass.

ABERDEEN † Greyfriars John Knox ★
Queen Street
OS *NJ942064* **GPS** *57.1487N, 2.0960W*

A rebuilding on a monumental scale of the 16th-century Franciscan church to designs by A. Marshall Mackenzie, 1903, the church forms the S.W. corner of Marischal College. The tower is an explosion of Gothic Revival, its pinnacles and a heavily crocketed slender spire piercing the city skyline – very busy but satisfying. Light and airy inside, the E. window comes from the old church; Kempe made the glass for this and several other windows.

ABERDEEN † King's College Chapel ★
College Bounds, Old Aberdeen
OS *NJ939081* **GPS** *57.1642N, 2.1016W*

A chapel of 1500, it is integral to King's campus quadrangle and unmissable with its distinctive crown spire. Inside are excellent stalls and a screen, possibly by John Fendour, who did the ceiling at St Machar's. The crown steeple is a curious mixture of Gothic and Rennaisance, and the window tracery is free flowing Curvilinear – perhaps Flemish in inspiration.

ABERDEEN † Kirk of St Nicholas
Between Schoolhill and Back Wynd
OS *NJ940063* **GPS** *57.1476N, 2.0993W*

Little remains of the medieval church founded by Bishop Elphinstone in the 15th century: the interior reflects many post-Reformation changes – in this case the nave (the West Kirk) and choir (the East Kirk) being walled off from each other so two preachers could preach simultaneously. The nave was rebuilt to plans by James Gibb, 1755, and the choir was replaced, 1837, and later rebuilt after a fire in 1875; the medieval tower was also replaced at the same time. The medieval N. transept contains a chapel to the oil industry, with very good contemporary glass by Shona McInnes, and contemporary woodwork by Tim Stead.

ABERDOUR † St Fillian
7m/12km E. of Dunfermline, Fife
OS *NT193854* **GPS** *56.0552N, 3.2970W*

The church stands on the N. shore of the Firth of Forth, adjacent to Aberdour Castle. The N. wall of the nave and chancel are Norman. The rest has been restored well, the S. arcade having 16th-century round piers. The birdcage belfry is late 16th-century. Inside is a memorial to Robert Blair, 1666, chaplain to Charles I.

ABERFELDY
† St Mary / Grandtully Chapel ★
2m/3km N.E. of Aberfeldy, near Grandtully Castle, Perth & Kinross
OS *NN886506* **GPS** *56.6343N, 3.8162W*
Historic Scotland

A church of the 16th century, it is remotely set on a rise, with grand views. Its long, low whitewashed exterior gives the appearance of a croft, but inside is an unexpected treasure, a fine painted barrel-vaulted wooden ceiling of the 1630s. Stewart Arms, heraldic panels, biblical scenes and Evangelists are all vividly painted in tempera. The church is cared for by Historic Scotland.

A'CHLEIT
† Killean/Kilchenzie Parish Church
10m/16km N. of Campbeltown, Argyll & Bute
OS *NR681418* **GPS** *55.6144N, 5.6837W*

A mainly Georgian building of 1787–91, this remote church is outstandingly set on a promontory of volcanic rock that juts out into the sea, with views W. to the Isle of Islay. As with many Scottish churches, the outside is harled; the belfry is a Victorian addition.

ALLOA † St Mungo
5m/8km E. of Stirling, Clackmannanshire
OS *NS883926* **GPS** *56.1135N, 3.7971W*

A Gothic Revival church by J. G. Graham, 1817–19, in a once prosperous port town, St Mungo's is considered to be the high point of the Revival movement in Scotland. Laid to a T-plan, its exterior is castellated: the tower has ornamental finials and diagonal traceried flying buttresses that support a crocketed spire. The outside is very pleasing – unlike the interior, which has been unsympathetically altered.

ARBUTHNOTT † St Ternan ★
20m/30km S. of Aberdeen, Aberdeenshire
OS *NO801746* **GPS** *56.8628N, 2.3271W*

This is a small rural pre-Reformation parish church of great charm. The chancel is 13th-century, the nave slightly later. The bell tower, modelled on the Irish round tower, dates from c. 1500. Inside, in the former Lady Chapel are effigies and memorials to the Arbuthnott family. The illuminated *Arbuthnott Missal*, dating from the late 15th century, was written by James Sibbald, an incumbent of the church, and is believed to be the only surviving one of its kind in Scotland. A major restoration took place in the late 19th century, following a fire.

BARRA † Cille Bharra (Kilbarr Church) ★
N. tip of Barra Island, Outer Hebrides
OS *NF705073* **GPS** *57.0395N, 7.4343W*

Not to be missed: the setting is stupendous. Here are remains of an 11th-century church, and an intact c. 15th-century N. chapel in which stands a replica of the 9th-century Kilbar Stone and some late medieval grave-slabs. Compton MacKenzie, author of *Whisky Galore*, is buried in the churchyard, from which there are sweeping views of white sand beaches and nearby Eriskay and S. Uist.

BIGGAR † Biggar Kirk
12m/19km W. of Peebles, South Lanarkshire
OS *NT040378* **GPS** *55.6251N, 3.5254W*

Collegiate – the last of its kind before the Reformation – and cruciform in plan, Biggar Kirk was rebuilt in 1546. The interior is impressive, though savagely scraped in the 1930s with wooden wagon ceilings. The stained glass of note is by William Wilson and Crear McCartney. The W. wall has diagonal buttressing, and the squat central tower has a turreted staircase.

BOWDEN † Bowden Kirk ★★
2m/3km S. of Melrose, Scottish Borders
OS *NT554301* **GPS** *55.5631N, 2.7081W*

The church is remotely situated. Outwardly an architectural curiosity, the long narrow nave leads to a raised chancel that looks as if it wanted to be a tower, but couldn't quite pluck up the courage. The N. wall, the archway of the organ loft and some vaulting are all that remain of the 1400 church. The elevated chancel was built in 1909, over the burial vault of the Roxburghes. Inside, and of great interest, is the 1611 laird's loft. This was originaly constructed at the E. end, straddling the N. transept arch, but has since been moved closer to the chancel arch. In the graveyard is a good collection of stones, bearing carved symbols of mortality common in Scottish burial places in the 18th century – skulls, crossed bones and hourglasses.

BRAEMAR † St Margaret of Scotland
50m/80km W. of Aberdeen, Aberdeenshire
OS *NO152913* **GPS** *57.0057N, 3.3973W*

Forlorn and boarded up, this excellent but unassuming and largely unaltered example of Comper's work deserves better. Built 1899–1907, it replaced a Victorian wooden church, and its main purpose was to cater for the large number of English visitors to the area. Gothic Revival in Early English style, the locally sourced granite gives a pleasing polychromatic effect. The traceried windows are particularly of note.

◁ **ABERDEEN: CATHEDRAL OF ST MACHAR** – *with its simple, sturdy arcading, three-light east window and flat roof, the nave of the church has a satisfying and harmonious geometry*

BRECHIN † Brechin Cathedral and Round Tower ★

20m/30km N.E. of Dundee, Angus
OS *NO596600* **GPS** *56.7307N, 2.6615W*

The Round Tower at Brechin Cathedral dates from the 11th century, one of only two in Scotland, and shows a strong Celtic Irish influence. The doorway is formed of slabs rather than quoins, and is richly ornamented with a beaded motif and carved crucifix above. The conical cap was replaced in the 14th century by an octagonal cap-room. It was incorporated into the cathedral building of c. 1250 and later. A substantial and ill-informed rebuilding of the cathedral, 1806, swept away both transepts, and constructed aisles that obscured the clerestory windows. This was much remedied by reconstruction in 1900–02 by John Honeyman, who restored the cathedral to its pre-1806 plan. Inside is much good glass by Morris & Co, D. Strachan, W. Wilson and others. Of note too are a Viking Hogback stone, Pictish cross slab and 12th-century font.

CLACHAN OF GLENDARUEL
† St Modan / Kilmodan Kirk

15m/24km S. of Inverary, Argyll & Bute
OS *NR995841* **GPS** *56.0086N, 5.2174W*

A post-Reformation church of 1783 in grand scenery near Loch Riddan, it incorporates stone from an earlier church of 1610. It is simple classical in style, with a pedimented S. front surmounted by an open-framed belfry – very similar to the church at A'Chleit. The interior layout is largely unchanged – a central octagonal pulpit, three-panelled lairds' galleries, and long communion tables at the front of the pews. Outside are several carved late medieval grave slabs of the West Highland school of stone carving.

CORTACHY † Cortachy Parish Church

17m/27km N. of Dundee, Angus
OS *NO395597* **GPS** *56.7252N, 2.9893W*

An estate church of 1828, it stands in a lovely setting close to Cortachy Castle. Externally the building is Gothic Revival in red ashlar, the Perpendicular windows of which are more elaborate than would be expected in a church of such modest proportions. The nave is embattled with finials, and the W. gable has open carved stonework. Inside are memorials to the 9th and 12th earls of Airlie. The apsidal E. end is actually the Airlie family burial vault.

CRAIGNURE † Torosay Church

Isle of Mull, Argyll & Bute
OS *NM721367* **GPS** *56.4678N, 5.7002W*

This is a 1783 church of complete simplicity, small, harled and whitewashed outside, with external stairs leading to the galleries. The interior is a 'preaching box' – a term that does not do justice to the Presbyterian tradition of simple worship. The W. and E. galleries and all the lower seating are arranged in respect of the S. pulpit. There is a complete absence of distracting decoration: dignified and simple.

CRANSHAWS
† Cranshaws Parish Church ★

25m/40km E. of Edinburgh, Scottish Borders
OS *NT692618* **GPS** *55.8487N, 2.4932W*

In rolling Border uplands, this is a rural church by George Fortune of 1899. Replacing an older Georgian building, it is a delightful piece of neo-Romanesque, with fine detailing to the gabled porch, windows and apsidal E. end with carved corbels; the W. gable has a pleasing circular window and birdcage belfry. The main roof timbers have stencilled decoration, and a miniature laird's loft is set near the apse: much good detailing inside.

CRICHTON
† Crichton Collegiate Church ★

8m/13km S.E. of Edinburgh, Midlothian
OS *NT380616* **GPS** *55.8438N, 2.9903W*

A small lane leads to the remains of this former and impressive church, which stands on a steep hillside overlooking a river valley. Only the central tower, transepts and choir survive of the 1449 church. In 1825 it was re-ordered in a very odd way. An imposing pulpit was erected on the S. wall, and galleries and pews installed in transepts and choir, accommodating some 600 people. The galleries have been removed, though the focal point of the church is still westward. The plain stone vaulted roofs are very pleasing. It is owned and maintained by a Trust, which recently restored the 19th-century stained glass.

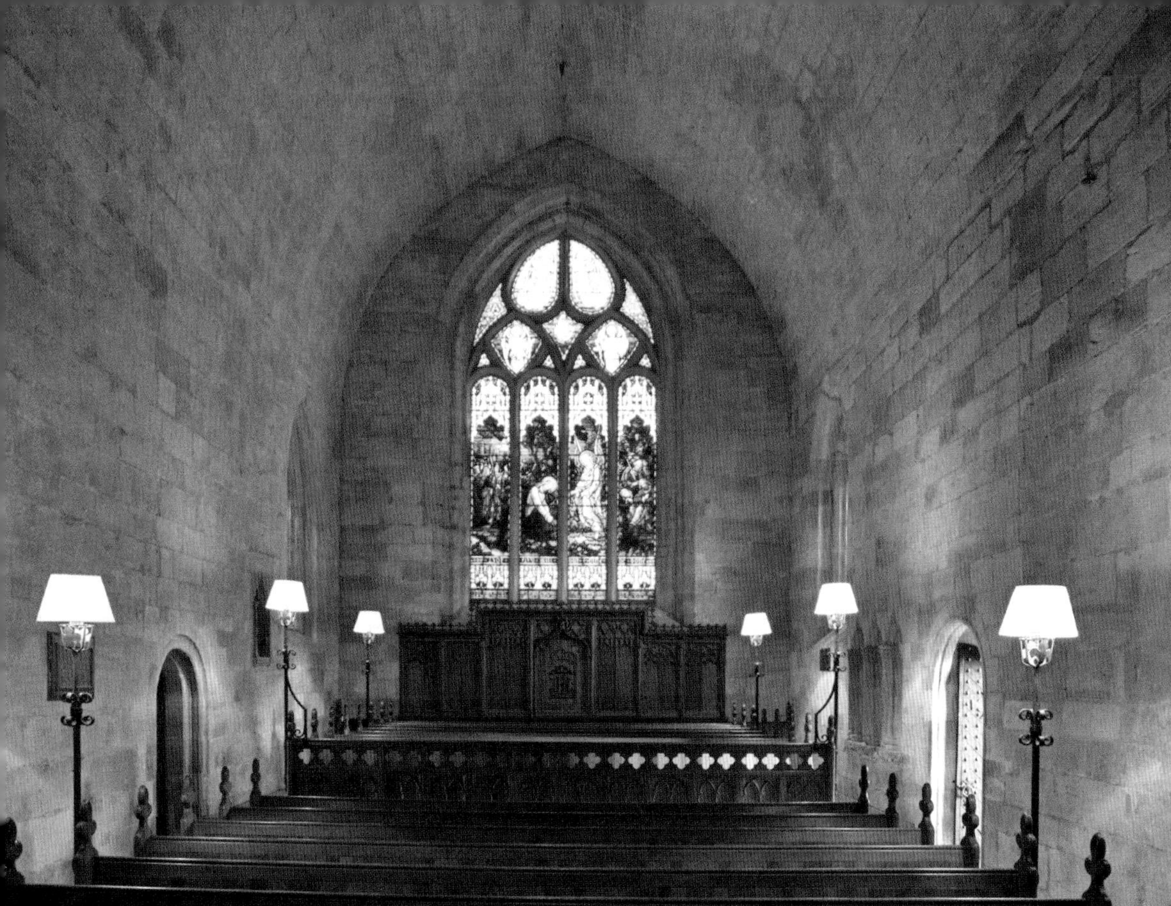

△ **CRICHTON COLLEGIATE CHURCH** – *unusually, the pews in the choir face westward, broadly in the direction of the pulpit, which in the 19th century was placed high on the south wall*

CROMARTY

† East Parish Church ★★

15m/24km N.E. of Inverness, Highland

OS *NH790672* **GPS** *57.6790N, 4.0291W*

This T-plan church is one of the most complete examples of post-Reformation church layout in Scotland. The harled whitewashed exterior, with mostly domestic-scale windows, is thought to have been built over a medieval rectangular church. The inside gives a striking impression of the move from sacramental worship to preaching the Word. A grand Victorian panelled octagonal pulpit with tester stands over a reader's desk, on the S. wall. The N. aisle, E. and W. arms of the church are galleried with box pews and open pews – one painted, and several numbered in accordance with the rental of pews. Of other interest inside: a 15th-century carved grave-slab, a funeral hatchment, and wooden coat and hat pegs.

CRUGGLETON † Cruggleton Church

12m/19km S. of Newton Stewart, Dumfries & Galloway

OS *NX477428* **GPS** *54.7571N, 4.3668W*

The church is in a stone-walled enclosure set in a field, not far from the village of Whithorn. It is two-celled, of Norman origin and rebuilt in 1890. The door in the plain round-arched S. doorway has good iron stud and strapwork. The interior is dimly lit by a few narrow windows, with a rough flagstone floor and good plain Norman chancel arch with clustered piers. It is atmospherically rustic, even if rather gloomy.

CULLEN

† St Mary the Virgin (Cullen Old Kirk) ★

40m/60km E. of Inverness, Moray

OS *NJ507663* **GPS** *57.6844N, 2.8279W*

An interesting conglomeration of styles in an outwardly ordinary 18th- to 19th-century church. Dating from the 13th century, the choir and nave now form E. and W. aisles.

△ **CULROSS ABBEY** – *at the top of a slope above the village of Culross, the church occupies a prominent position and is formed from the surviving parts of a Cistercian abbey*

The S. aisle and chancel are 16th century, the N. aisle 18th century. The prominent 1602 laird's loft is in the E. aisle. There is a Sacrament House c. 1550, with fine carved panelling, and ornate tombs to the Ogilvies, one with a recumbent knight. In the S. aisle – formerly St Anne's Chapel – are various mural monuments of interest, and a wall niche with recumbent figure.

CULROSS

† Culross Abbey Parish Church ★★

6m/10km W. of Dunfermline, Fife
OS *NS988862* **GPS** *56.0583N, 3.6253W*
Historic Scotland

This extensive site comprises the monastic ruins, maintained by Historic Scotland, and above, the former Cistercian abbey church, set over a delightful village. Dating from the 13th century, the bulk of the church is formed of the old chancel and choir of the abbey church, and W. tower of c. 1500, and is distinguished by broad transepts. Above the W. door are two green men. In the N. transept is the Bruce Vault, 1642, with a monumental memorial to Sir George Bruce and his wife Margaret Primrose, eight alabaster kneeling figures of their adult children at the base, and a large memorial to Sir Robert Preston and his wife Elizabeth, c. 1832. In an archway linking the nave and N. transept are two mutilated recumbent figures. This is a church full of interest.

DALMALLY † Glenorchy Parish Church / Church of Dysart

17m/24km E. of Oban, Argyll & Bute
OS *NN167275* **GPS** *56.4042N, 4.9711W*

A church of 1811 by James Elliott for the Earl of Breadalbane, this is early Gothic Revival, octagonal in plan, with an adjoining tower whose finials match those on the church buttresses. The cream harling on the outside, with finials and details picked out in black, gives the external appearance an air of 'Strawberry Hill Gothick'. The octagonal roof is supported by an ingenious spider's web of roof beams. Outside are interesting grave-slabs.

DALMENY † St Cuthbert ★★
7m/12km W. of Edinburgh
OS *NT144774* **GPS** *55.9827N, 3.3725W*

Close by the Forth Bridge on the banks of the Firth of Forth stands this fine Norman church, in which everything except the tower of c. 1937 and the Rosebury Aisle, 1617, is remarkably unchanged. The choir and apse arches are notable, with fine zigzag carving on their several orders, and similarly decorated rib vaulting, with carved corbels. Outside are many carved corbels, and the S. doorway is particularly good, with ornate decoration and carving on the three principal orders, and above a blind arcade of interlaced arches under carved corbels – reminiscent of stone carving at St Athernase in Leuchars, and perhaps by the same masons.

DIRLETON † St Andrew ★
20m/35km N.E. of Edinburgh, East Lothian
OS *NT512842* **GPS** *56.0484N, 2.7840W*

Built in the early 17th century, this capricious building, sheltered by trees and built of red sandstone, looks as if it were assembled from a kit. The nave and chancel are long and low, and, midway along the S. wall, the Archerfield Aisle – Scottish Rennaissance in style – juts out unexpectedly, like a misplaced transept. At the W. end stands the tower, the final stage of which was added in 1825, crowned with overhanging parapets supporting four pinnacles at each corner – reminiscent of Ludwig II's Bavarian confections. The overall effect is charming.

DORNOCH † Dornoch Cathedral
30m/50km N. of Inverness, Highland
OS *NH797896* **GPS** *57.8804N, 4.0299W*

A bulky, solid building of the 13th century, Dornoch Cathedral has seen many changes. A clan feud in 1570 led to the destruction by fire of the nave. Partially re-roofed in 1616, it was only fully and controversially repaired in the 1830s by the Countess of Sutherland, whose estate architect, chosen in preference to the architect William Burn, demolished the largely intact medieval nave and aisles and replaced them with a single narrow nave. Of note are the Carnegie stained-glass windows, and other 19th- to 20th-century glass.

DUDDINGSTON
† Duddingston Parish Church ★
By Duddingston Loch and Arthur's Seat, Edinburgh
OS *NT283726* **GPS** *55.9411N, 3.1490W*

This interesting church dates from the 12th century with additions, principally the N. Prestonfield Aisle, 1631. It is situated on the S.E. slopes of Arthur's Seat, with very fine views all around, on the edge of a small loch. Of note is the Norman doorway, with chevrons, and chancel arch; also note the stained-glass memorial window to the wife of Alan Pinkerton, founder of Pinkerton's Detective Agency. At the entrance to the site is a gatehouse, used as a watch post against body-snatchers – a 19th-century problem attested to here by the use of heavy lockfast tombs. The outside of the church is ornamented with emphatic pinnacles on the nave.

DUMFRIES
† Crichton Memorial Church ★
1m/2km S. of Dumfries
OS *NX982740* **GPS** *55.0509N, 3.5942W*

This church was built 1890–97 by Sydney Mitchell for the use of staff and patients at the nearby hospital. A building on the grand scale, it is a good example of Gothic Revival, in rich red sandstone. The W. front, with lancet windows and crocketed finials, suggests a French Gothic influence.

DUNBLANE † St Blane's Cathedral ★★
5m/8km N. of Stirling
OS *NN781013* **GPS** *56.1894N, 3.9650W*

In 1853 John Ruskin wrote of the cathedral, "I know not anything so perfect in its simplicity and so beautiful, as far as it reaches, in all the Gothic with which I am acquainted." The only trace of the original 12th-century church is the base of the tower, incorporated into the S. aisle. Much of the church is 13th-century, the upper stages of the tower 13th- to late 15th-century. The partially destroyed nave was restored in the late 1900s by Sir Robert Rowan Anderson. Inside are 15th-century misericords and fine fittings by Anderson and Sir Robert Lorimer, stained glass by Strachan, and a Jesse window by Clayton and Bell. The W. front is particularly impressive.

DUNDEE † St Andrew ★
St Andrew's Place
OS *NO404306* **GPS** *56.4646N, 2.9680W*

The only example of a 'Trades' church in Scotland, funded by the City Trade Corporations and completed in 1744. A touch of Wren seems to have found its way into Samuel Bell's design, which features Venetian windows complete with swags: oddly flamboyant for a Presbyterian church at the time. The stained glass is interesting, much of which depicts the various city Trades Corporations. The nearby octagonal chapel was used by the Glasites, a sect led by the deposed Rev. John Glas that denounced any form of State involvement with religious matters.

DUNDEE † St Mary ★
Nethergate
OS *NO401301* **GPS** *56.4596N, 2.9722W*

This city church has a chequered history. It has nothing to thank the English for: sacked in 1303, its replacement was again partially destroyed by them in the 16th and 17th centuries. Subsequent rebuilding and extending of the church, 1789, saw four congregations under one roof, until fire destroyed all but the tower and nave. Sir George Gilbert Scott restored the church in 1870. The inside is galleried, with a fine E. window by Morris and Burne-Jones. The result is a pleasing and dignified Gothic Revival building.

DUNFERMLINE
† Dunfermline Abbey ★★
12m/19km N.W. of Edinburgh, Fife
OS *NT089873* **GPS** *56.0699N, 3.4639W*
Historic Scotland

Two churches in one is the distinctive character of this unusual building. The W. part is the magnificent Norman nave of the original abbey church (now braced by bulky external flying buttresses), a soaring space whose arcades are supported by massive Norman piers, some of which have deeply incised chevrons. This part is in the care of Historic Scotland. The only jarring note here is a feeble and ill-proportioned Georgian tower and spire. The E. end by contrast is parochial, an 1817–21 rebuilding of the derelict choir and sanctuary of the old abbey church, during which remains believed to be those of Robert the Bruce were discovered – now interred in the 'new' church. Adjacent are substantial remnants of the former monastery and Royal Palace, birthplace of Charles I.

DUNKELD
† Dunkeld Cathedral Parish Church
12m/19km N. of Perth, Perth & Kinross
OS *NO023425* **GPS** *56.5651N, 3.5899W*

Like Dunfermline Abbey, this is a church in two halves, situated picturesquely on the banks of the River Tay. The W. end comprises a roofless former nave of the 14th century, whose fine Early English arcades, aisles, clerestory and elaborate window tracery give a good impression of the original form. The W. tower is 15th-century Gothic. The restored choir and chancel – W. Dunn and R. Watson, 1908 – are good Gothic Revival, and at the E. end is a pleasing Perpendicular window. This restoration reversed a clumsy earlier attempt initiated by the 4th Duke of Atholl. Inside are interesting carved stones and effigies. Of note are the Apostle Stone, the tomb of Alexander Stewart, a headless effigy of a bishop and Pictish stone carving.

DUNNET † St Mary
8m/13km E. of Thurso, Highland
OS *ND219711* **GPS** *58.6215N, 3.3449W*

At the most northerly point of mainland Scotland is a modest medieval limewashed church, traces of whose 12th-century origins can be discerned in its mostly 16th-century structure. A simple, long, low building, its distinctive feature is a low, saddlebacked tower at the W. end. Timothy Pont, whose maps of Scotland are the earliest of their kind based on original surveys, was minister here from 1601–14.

DUNNING † St Serf ★
6m/10km S.W. of Perth
OS *NO019144* **GPS** *56.3126N, 3.5873W*

In a small quiet town in the valley of Strathearn, with the Ochil Hills to the S., St Serf's is late 11th- to early 12th-century. Its square saddlebacked tower, with simple arched window openings, is unmistakable.

Traces of a Saxon doorway can be seen in the N. wall, and evidence of a typical Saxon-style high-pitched nave can be seen in the gable outline on the E. side of the tower. Inside the style is Early English, but all re-ordered with galleries, box pews and pulpit on the S. wall. The old chancel contains a rare treasure: an intricately carved sandstone Pictish cross, thought to have stood overlooking Forteviot, an ancient Pictish royal settlement.

DURISDEER † Durisdeer Parish Church

20ml/30km N. of Dumfries
OS *NS893037* **GPS** *55.3156N, 3.7443W*

The exterior of this extensive 1720s church is deceptive. The W. end was a two-storey session house for the Duke of Queensbury, whose ancestor the 1st Duke built the sumptuous Queensbury Aisle or mausoleum against the previous church building. Inside are galleries, box pews and pulpit, and, visible through a window behind the pulpit, the mausoleum, which is entered through an exterior doorway. There are marble floors, a carved canopy supported on marble columns, and on the back wall a large marble memorial to the 2nd Duke and his wife Mary.

DYKE † Dyke Parish Church

20ml/30km E. of Inverness, Moray
OS *NH990584* **GPS** *57.6043N, 3.6915W*

Near Brodie Castle is this church of 1781, with a birdcage belfry. Inside all is to the original plan, with three-decker pulpit (the tester is now hidden above a new ceiling), panelled gallery and pews grouped around the pulpit. The present church hall, accessed through a narrow corridor from the E. end, was originally an 18th-century mausoleum.

EAST SALTOUN
† St Michael (Saltoun Parish Church)

15ml/24km E. of Edinburgh, East Lothian
OS *NT474678* **GPS** *55.9011N, 2.8420W*

A T-plan Gothic Revival church by John Fletcher Campbell, 1805 (possibly to plans by Robert Burn), the church is a cheerful battlemented and finialled sandstone building, with S. tower set in the middle of the S. wall. Of interest is the Fletcher family vault. An 1885 reordering of the church removed the galleries.

EDINBURGH † Canongate Kirk ★

Canongate
OS *NT264738* **GPS** *55.9517N, 3.1795W*

A Dutch-gabled front marks out this simple, dignified church adjacent to Holyrood Palace. Built by James I, using someone else's money, as the chapel of the Order of the Thistle, it was formerly the nave of Holyrood Abbey. Significant alterations took place in the 20th century, notably the removal of the galleries from the transepts, and the opening up of the apse. The interior is lit by large clear-glazed windows: very pleasing, light, and highly coloured.

EDINBURGH
† North Leith Parish Church

Madeira Street, by Prince Regent Street
OS *NT262765* **GPS** *55.9758N, 3.1831W*

This Georgian church of 1816 by William Burn forms a distinctive and elegant end to Prince Regent Street. In Greek Revival style, with pedimented Ionic portico and three-stage tower, it is a much better effort than Burn's restoration of St Giles. Inside, fluted Ionic columns support elegantly curved galleries. The pulpit is simple classical, with tester and gilded eagle finial, and everything is painted and gilded.

EDINBURGH † St Cuthbert ★★

King's Stables Road
OS *NT248735* **GPS** *55.9495N, 3.2055W*

A church by James Wier, 1773–5, St Cuthbert was rebuilt in 1892–5 by Hippolyte Blanc, retaining the original Georgian tower and steeple. The resulting building, situated below Edinburgh Castle, is a striking blend of neo- Byzantine and Renaissance Revival, with which the earlier W. tower sits rather uncomfortably. The E. end is formed of a grand domed apse, flanked by Renaissance towers. The interior has ornate touches: mosaics to the chancel and apse ceilings, a run of alabaster carving based on Leonardo da Vinci's Last Supper in the apse, rich detail in the altar, pulpit and font. Ballantyne and Gardner did the coloured glass, with the exception of the David and Goliath window by Tiffany of New York.

△ **FORRES: ST LAURENCE** – *a spacious and highly impressive piece of neo-Gothic, using stone quarried locally, near to Elgin*

EDINBURGH † St Giles Cathedral ★

Between High Street and Parliament Square
OS *NT257735* **GPS** *55.9496N, 3.1909W*

St Giles is an imposing building of 12th-century origin in the city's Royal Mile, much rebuilt in the 14th, 15th and 16th centuries. Its crowned spire, a statement of Stewart ambition, is one of the landmarks of the city. The original plan was cruciform, but ad hoc additions of aisle and chapels have created a very complex structure. Post-Reformation uses of the church included four church congregations, a fire station, police offices, a store for the guillotine and a prison. William Burn's clumsy 1829 restoration encased the whole building in textureless ashlar, and only in the late 19th century was a more informed attempt made to create a more coherent building. Sir Robert Lorimer's 1911 Gothic Revival Thistle Chapel is of particular interest, as is the Preston Aisle which houses a copy of the National Covenant. In the Chepman Aisle is a recessed monument to James Graham, Marquis of Montrose.

ELGIN † Birnie Kirk

At Paddockhaugh, 2m/3km S. of Elgin, Moray
OS *NJ206587* **GPS** *57.6114N, 3.3299W*

A short distance from Elgin close to the River Lossie, this is a simple Norman church of great appeal, originally the cathedral of the bishops of Moray. Outwardly Georgian and rather plain, inside there are good Norman features: the chancel arch is plain but well proportioned, and there are deeply splayed round arched windows. An ancient bell is kept in the church, as is an 18th-century calf-skin-bound Bible, and in the churchyard is a carved Pictish stone.

ELGIN † St Giles ★

30m/50km E. of Inverness, Moray
OS *NJ215628* **GPS** *57.6487N, 3.3155W*

An unmissable feature of Elgin's city centre, the church stands in the centre of a broad former medieval market place, a high point in an area of good Georgian town houses now with the usual dreary 1980s high street shop frontages. This Greek Revival church by Archibald Simpson, 1825–8, has two distinct fronts, the W. being well proportioned Doric, while the E. is pilastered. Over the E. front is a single-stage tower bearing a columnar drum modelled on the Choragic Monument of Lysicrates, an icon of Greek Revival architecture. Inside, a panelled gallery runs round three sides, and the E. wall has imposing pilasters, but the interest here is the quality of the exterior.

EOROPAIDH † St Moluag
N.W. tip of the Isle of Lewis, Outer Hebrides
OS *NB519651* **GPS** *58.5037N, 6.2601W*

A lonely, isolated stone church in croft land on the N.W. of the island, it is of uncertain date, but probably 12th century. For centuries it lay roofless and ruined, until its c. 1912 restoration by J. S. Richardson. This is a building whose appeal lies in its uninterrupted simplicity and beautiful island setting.

FORRES † St Laurence ★★
22m/35km E. of Inverness, Moray
OS *NJ035588* **GPS** *57.6096N, 3.6151W*

Built between 1904 and 1906, this is a large, striking church of spacious nave and N. aisle by John Robertson; an outstanding example of neo-Gothic, with touches of the Byzantine to be seen in the marble pillars of the octagonal Caen stone pulpit and the baptistry with its marble font. The ceiling is impressive – a broad single span in pitch pine, arch braced with open tracery in the woodwork above. The S. arcade is formed of cylindrical piers that also support the gallery over the S. aisle. A wide chancel arch frames the E. end, and there is good glass by Strachan. The exterior has strong vertical emphasis, soaring pinnacles and finials – all very well proportioned.

FORTROSE † St Andrew
7m/12km N.E. of Inverness, Highland
OS *NH727563* **GPS** *57.5796N, 4.1293W*

In a delightful cliff-top setting and close to the remains of Fortrose Cathedral, the church was built in 1828, a single-cell structure with bold pinnacles set with jaunty finials, and windows with Decorated timber tracery. The apse was added in 1907. Described by some as externally 'dumpy', the interior is remarkably well-proportioned, generously lit by the nave and chancel windows. The chancel arch is broad, and in the chancel is a carved reredos of the Last Supper. At the W. end is a traceried stone screen leading to the baptistry.

FOWLIS † Fowlis Easter Parish Church ★
Kirk Road, Fowlis; 5m/8km W. of central Dundee
OS *NO322334* **GPS** *56.4883N, 3.1024W*

Originally dedicated to St Marnock, this is a simple 15th-century medieval church, with substantial pre-Reformation wood-panel paintings. Of note is the original rood screen, now sited in the nave, on which are depicted the Crucifixion, the Trinity, the Virgin, John the Baptist and St Catherine. For a short while in the 16th century the church was collegiate. A curiosity is the 'jougs' – iron collars used to restrain wrongdoers, still hanging from oak doors.

FOWLIS WESTER † St Bean
10m/16km W. of Perth, Perth and Kinross
OS *NN928240* **GPS** *56.3968N, 3.7382W*

A much altered 13th-century church; Georgian tinkering effectively lost the original plan and detail. J. Jeffrey Waddell 'restored' the church in 1927 to a speculative medieval plan. Not unpleasing inside, with an arched-braced wagon roof and good plain stonework, but the main interest is the Pictish cross slabs which are housed inside the church.

GLASGOW
† Kelvinside Hillhead Parish Church ★★
Observatory Road
OS *NS566673* **GPS** *55.8775N, 4.2933W*

By Douglas and Sellars, 1875–6, and based on Sainte Chapelle, Paris, in smart Glasgow suburbs. The church is rectangular with an apsidal E. end: both nave and apse are lit by tall Decorated windows with distinctive gables standing proud of the parapet. A good wheel window is set above a gracious W. entrance with lofty gable. Inside is a wonderful space uninterrupted by freestanding columns. The stained glass is very good – the best is by Morris and Co. and Burne-Jones – and there is a good marble font with carved cover, and a carved Austrian oak pulpit.

△ **HADDINGTON: ST MARY** – *while the church dates from the 14th century, its magnificent interior owes a debt to the late 20th century, when the choir was magnificently restored*

GLASGOW † St Andrew's R.C. Cathedral

Between Clyde Street and Fox Street
OS *NS590647* **GPS** *55.8557N, 4.2528W*

Built on the banks of the River Clyde to serve the needs of Irish immigrants in Glasgow, this church by James Gillespie Graham, 1816, occupies a narrow site with modest semi-octagonal towers flanking the W. window. It reflects the caution used in constructing Catholic churches before the Catholic Relief Act of 1829. The 1871 and 1892 alterations were by E. W. and P. P. Pugin. Painted and gilded chevrons decorate the chancel arch, and in the sanctuary are a marble altar and reredos. The pulpit is of polychromatic marble, and the Lady Chapel and Chapel of Our Lord have fine Caen stone altars.

GLASGOW † St Mungo's Cathedral ★★

Between Wishart Street and Castle Street
OS *NS602655* **GPS** *55.8629N, 4.2345W*

The cathedral is mostly from the 12th and 13th centuries, with a large 15th-century tower and spire. Its history is one of the usual post-Reformation subdivisions and 19th-century restorations, but there is much of great interest here, and though the interior was savagely scraped, it remains a fine example of Scottish medieval church architecture, one of a few to have survived the Reformation relatively intact. The finely vaulted crypt or lower church was constructed in the mid-13th century to house the tomb of St Kentigern: this lies beneath the choir (the whole church being built on a sloping site). Of note too are the richly carved pulpitum, c. 1400, and the Blackadder Aisle, c. 1500, with well-carved ceiling bosses. The narrow high nave, with triforium and clerestorey, is an impressive space, and there are many fine monuments throughout the church. Stained glass dates from the 14th century on, but particularly impressive is the Millennium Window by John Clark, a masterpiece of technical ingenuity and creativity in oceanic blues.

HADDINGTON † St Mary ★★

15m/24km E. of Edinburgh, East Lothian
OS *NT518736* **GPS** *55.9533N, 2.7720W*

One of Britain's most significant 20th-century restorations took place here – Lindsay & Partners' 1970s reconstruction and restoration of the choir, destroyed by the English in 1548. Seamlessly re-uniting nave and choir, it is difficult to tell the join. The church was collegiate, and dates mostly from the 14th century, although traces of 13th-century style can be seen in the triple-arched tower windows and the fine round arched W. double doorway, over which is set a good free-flowing Curvilinear window. Curvilinear is the dominant tracery here, with some very good glass by Burne-Jones and Sax Shaw. The Lauderdale Aisle has a magnificent memorial to Lord Thirlstane, d. 1595. The warm welcome afforded to visitors is thoroughly in keeping with the ecumenical character of the church.

HALLYNE † Lyne Church

4m/7km W. of Peebles, Scottish Borders
OS *NT191405* **GPS** *55.6515N, 3.2859W*

This is a small church of 1640 in an attractive rural setting, restored in the late 19th and 20th centuries. The church retains canopied pews, a pulpit from 1644 and the medieval font. The E. window has simple Y-tracery.

HUNTLY † St Margaret R.C.

30m/50km N.W. of Aberdeen, Aberdeenshire
OS *NJ528401* **GPS** *57.4493N, 2.7876W*

A very curious and interesting church building, mixing a classical pilastered portico with an ornate Spanish Baroque tower, and constructed to an octagonal plan by William Robertson in 1834. The interior is lit by a series of lunette windows and set under an impressive domed ceiling decorated with Spanish religious paintings contemporary to the time.

INVERARY
† Glenary/Inverary Parish Church

50m/80km N.W. of Glasgow
OS *NN095084* **GPS** *56.2302N, 5.0734W*

Another curious background: it is a plain Georgian town church by Robert Mylne, 1802, divided by an internal wall with the two halves respectively housing a Gaelic- and English-speaking congregation, and was provided for by the 5th Duke of Argyll. The Gaelic half – Glenary Parish – is now used as a church hall, and in the English half – Inverary Parish – is a good pulpit copied from one in the baptistry in Pisa.

INVERNESS
† Cathedral Church of St Andrew **

Bishops Road
OS *NH664448* **GPS** *57.4745N, 4.2291W*

An outwardly unexciting Victorian Gothic Revival building with French influence by Alexander Ross, with the exception of the main doorway, whose gable has fine pierced Geometric/Curvilinear tracery. Inside is sumptuous, especially for a town with such strong Presbyterian traditions. The narthex is separated from the nave by a good traceried stone screen; the piers of the nave arcades are of polished red granite. Dividing the nave from the choir chancel is a fine oak screen by Sir Robert Lorimer, 1923. The choir stalls are of Austrian oak, and the roof is decorated with stencilled motifs. In the apse, the altar front is of serpentine marble, with alabaster panels: the reredos is of Caen stone. Stained glass is by Hardman & Co.

INVERNESS † Old High Kirk

Between Church Street and river
OS *NH664455* **GPS** *57.4801N, 4.2288W*

Prettily situated amongst a scattering of churches along the banks of the River Ness as it runs through Inverness, the Old High Kirk is the city's oldest, although only the lower section of the tower dates back to the 14th century. The main body of the church is 18th-century with 19th-century additions. Inside are galleries and box pews, and many items associated with the Queen's Own Cameron Highlanders Regiment. In front of the pulpit is displayed a first edition of the King James Bible. The chancel is floored with marble from Iona, and there is glass by Strachan. Worth seeing outside is the 1660 Robertson burial enclosure.

INVERNESS † St Stephen

Corner of Southside Road and Old Edinburgh Road
OS *NH670447* **GPS** *57.4731N, 4.2188W*

An unassuming but pleasant Arts and Crafts Gothic church by W. L. Carruthers, 1897, the building consists of nave, N. transept and apse. There is good stained glass by Ballentine & Son; the pulpit is carved from local oak.

CROMARTY: EAST PARISH CHURCH – *a modest building that reflects the post-Reformation change in worship in Scotland and the new T-plan layout of its churches* ▷

△ **KIRKWALL: CATHEDRAL OF ST MAGNUS**
– a mix of Norman and early Gothic

IONA † Iona Abbey ★★

E. side of Iona island, Argyll & Bute; 40m/65km W. of Oban
OS *NM286245* **GPS** *56.3350N, 6.3914W*

This is one of Scotland's most sacred sites. The present abbey building dates from c. 1200, and lay in ruins from the Reformation until 1899, when the Duke of Argyll transferred ownership to a cathedral trust. Repairs began in 1902, but the bulk of the restoration of conventual buildings took place between 1938, when the Iona community was first established, and 1965. The abbey building is cruciform, with a 12th-century N. transept, early 13th-century nave, 15th-century S. transept and rebuilt crossing tower. There are effigies of Abbots Mackinnon and Mackenzie and a marble effigy of George Douglas Campbell, 8th Duke of Argyll, and his wife Ina McNeill. The inside is generally plain, almost severe, but despite the many tourists, retains a moving devotional atmosphere.

IONA † St Oran's Chapel

E. side of Iona island, Argyll & Bute; 40m/65km W. of Oban
OS *NM285244* **GPS** *56.3344N, 6.3929W*

A small chapel of the 9th/10th century, it was restored in the 19th century and stands amidst the burial places of kings and clan chiefs such as Kenneth MacAlpin, of the 9th century, and successive Scottish kings to the mid-1000s. One simple incised Celtic cross in the area dates from the 9th century. Of note is the early Norman doorway, with chunky dogtooth carving, and, inside, a well-carved 15th-century wall recess. John Smith, a celebrated Scottish leader of the Labour Party is buried here; his epitaph reads "An Honest Man's The Noblest Work of God".

KELSO † St Andrew ★

By Kelso Abbey ruins, Scottish Borders
OS *NT727337* **GPS** *55.5966N, 2.4336W*

A very good small Victorian church of 1869 by Sir Robert Rowan Anderson, and much underrated, it is tucked away on a bluff overlooking the River Tweed. The nave and chancel are well-proportioned, and there is a distinctive slender tower and spire. The chancel ceiling is subtly stencilled, there is a good carved stone font with marble columns and inset panels showing Christ the Good Shepherd and the Apostles, and a carved reredos. The nave roof is scissor-braced, and has round clerestory windows. The E. window glass is by Anderson, and there is other glass by Strachan.

KILBIRNIE † Old Parish Church

18m/29km S.W. of Glasgow, North Ayrshire
OS *NS314536* **GPS** *55.7468N, 4.6865W*

An interesting but perplexing building externally and internally, the church dates from the 15th century, with post-Reformation aisles for two branches of the Crawford family and an early 20th-century transept and entrance. The outside is a jumble of stepped and Dutch gables, and inside is some exceptional woodwork: the c. 1705 canopied Crawford Loft with family Arms is particularly fine, as is the more modest Ladyland Loft.

△ **LAMBHOLM: ITALIAN CHAPEL** – *a vibrant church made from extremely modest means by prisoners during the Second World War*

KIRKWALL

† Cathedral of St Magnus ★★

Corner of Broad Street and Palace Road, Orkney
OS *HY449108* **GPS** *58.9814N, 2.9588W*

Founded in the 12th century, the cathedral is a striking building of polychromatic sandstone, the resting place of St Magnus, a Norse earl of Orkney. The architectural mix is exciting – doughty Romanesque with Early English Gothic. Note the Y-tracery on the W. window, and the fine gabled Gothic W. doorway to which nature has added her own decorative erosive touches. The inside is full of grand stonework on a monumental scale, an exciting space crammed with ornamented blind arcades, an imposing Romanesque triforium with deep cut clerestory above, and solid round piers. There are interesting memorials within, notably the tomb of John Rae, Arctic explorer.

KIRRIEMUIR † St Mary ★

15m/24km N. of Dundee
OS *NO383543* **GPS** *56.6770N, 3.0081W*

A well-detailed Gothic Revival church of 1903–5. Curvilinear Gothic with an Arts and Crafts overlay, it is a good example of Comper's work in Scotland. Externally the details are very fine: a step-gabled S. porch, finialed buttresses and corbelling under the tower parapet. Nothing fussy – an essay in coherent design. Comper's furnishing is consistent with the exterior. His stained glass includes a memorial to his father. Pictish carved stones were found here at the time of the demolition of the earlier church.

LAMBHOLM † Italian Chapel ★★

7m/12km S. of Kirkwall, Orkney
OS *HY488006* **GPS** *58.8899N, 2.8895W*

An extraordinary and moving Baroque statement in tin, plasterboard and concrete: the chapel was built by Italian prisoners of war, led by Domenico Chiocchetti. Inside is a masterpiece of improvisation and make-do: tin for the lanterns, plasterboard for the panelling, moulded concrete for the altar and altar rails – and everywhere trompe l'oeil painting. The screen is wrought iron, made by

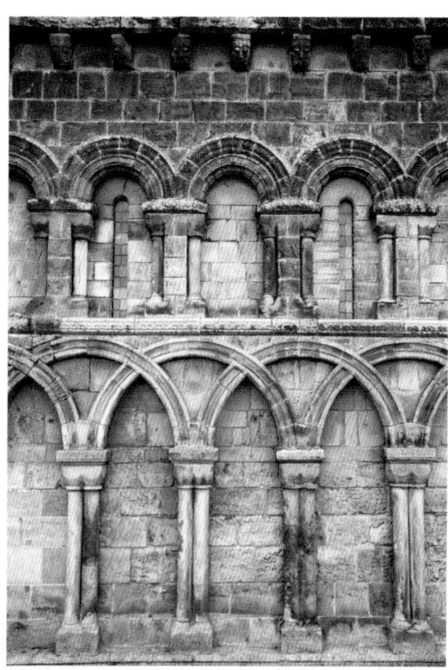

△ **LEUCHARS: ST ATHERNASE** – *interlaced blind arcading of the 12th century*

Palumbo from reinforcing rods for concrete, and the cement façade is by Bruttapasta. No-one can fail to be touched by the hallowed atmosphere of this place – a symbol of reconciliation and peace.

LAMINGTON † St Ninian

20m/32km W. of Peebles, South Lanarkshire
OS *NS978309* **GPS** *55.5615N, 3.6217W*

This rather plain rectangular church of 1721 holds a detail of surprising interest; a 12th-century doorway incorporated into the S. wall. The doorway is missing its columns now, but some bold lozenge carving remains on an inner order, and the archway has rustic relief chevrons, some dogtooth and pellets. It's tempting to speculate on what else of the earlier church might be concealed elsewhere in the 'new' church.

LARGO † Largo Kirk

10m/16km N.E. of Kirkcaldy, Fife
OS *NO423034* **GPS** *56.2204N, 2.9309W*

A cruciform church of 1817, it incorporates a 15th-century tower and chancel. The interior is light and welcoming, with a spacious W. gallery, a gallery in the S. transept, hammer-beam supports to the transepts and a good Georgian pulpit with tester. Of particular note are the many monuments: principally to Admiral Wood, who used to be rowed between the church and his residence on a specially constructed canal; to James Wilson, one of six men who signed both the Declaration of Independence and the Constitution of the USA; and to Alexander Selkirk, the eponymous hero of Daniel Defoe's Robinson Crusoe. Church records show that Selkirk was rebuked in front of the congregation for his "scandalous carriage". A locally made model of Admiral Wood's ship the 'Yellow Caravel' is in the S. transept. And in an enclosure in the churchyard is a carved Pictish stone.

LEUCHARS † St Athernase ★★

5m/8km S. of Dundee, Fife
OS *NO455213* **GPS** *56.3817N, 2.8835W*

Unmistakable on a rise in the town centre, St Athernase has two distinct sections: the nave, and the chancel and apse. This latter part dates from the late 12th century, and its excellent carved stonework may be by the same masons who worked on St Cuthbert's at Dalmeny. Although plain inside, the outside has ornate blind arcading, rising in two tiers, surmounted by a very good corbel table. The lower blind arcades on the chancel are interlaced. The octagonal tower is later, mid-18th century with a cruet-like belfry. The mid-19th century saw the original nave being demolished, its replacement a clumsy neo-Romanesque affair by John Milne. Overlook this, and gaze through the well-carved chancel arch to the apse: this is the Norman spirit of St Athernase.

LINLITHGOW † St Michael ★★

15m/24km W. of Edinburgh, West Lothian
OS *NT002772* **GPS** *55.9781N, 3.6003W*

St Michael's was built over a period of a hundred years, from the mid-15th to mid-16th century, and is prettily situated next to the palace. The church is Gothic, the interior luminous with light from three glorious Perpendicular windows in the apse, and a fine array of clerestory, triforium and

△ **LOCHAWE: ST CONAN** – *the work of siblings Walter and Helen Cambell, St Conan's has a particularly fine apse at the east end of the chancel, Romanesque in influence more than in style*

transeptual windows. The nave arcades are formed of well-proportioned clustered piers, and the nave and apse are undivided, with a rib-vaulted roof. The 1992 stained glass in St Katherine's aisle, set into wonderful flamboyant free-flowing tracery, is outstanding – a Pentecostal theme by Crear McCartney, and one eventually gets used to the strange aluminium business on the tower, which replaced the original crown spire.

LINLITHGOW † St Michael R.C.

15m/24km W. of Edinburgh, West Lothian
OS *NT005773* **GPS** *55.9788N, 3.5948W*

A simple and elegant small church of 1894, St Michael's was built to a design by Peter Paul Pugin, to cater for an increasing Irish immigrant population. The church, close to Linlithlow Loch, has the characteristic Pugin free-flowing Curvilinear Gothic tracery, and is a nice example of simple Gothic Revival on a restricted budget.

LINLITHGOW † St Peter

15m/24km W. of Edinburgh, West Lothian
OS *NT000770* **GPS** *55.9761N, 3.6039W*

Tucked between two houses and set back from the high street, this delightful miniature Byzantine basilica by J. Walker Todd, 1928, was built as a memorial to Bishop Walpole of Edinbugh and his wife Mildred – an unexpected gem with a semi-circular apse and central cupola.

LOCHAWE † St Conan ★★

10m/16km N. of Inverary, Argyll & Bute
OS *NN115267* **GPS** *56.3953N, 5.0541W*

An ebullient and wonderfully eccentric church, 1907–34, by Walter Cambell and his sister Helen, combining the Romanesque, Celtic and Gothic with abandon. The result is a surprisingly good church, whose jumbled S. exterior is covered with carved ornamentation, animals, ribbed buttresses, Arts and Crafts finials and the like; the N.W. cloister garth is a delightfully free Arts and Crafts interpretation of Romanesque. Inside the predominant theme is rough-cut Romanesque and early pointed. The chancel is very fine, with an E. arcade leading to an ambulatorium – all lit by tall clear-glazed windows. The S. aisle is dramatic with splashes of light and dark mysterious chapels; the Bruce Chapel contains an unnervingly lifelike and oversized effigy of Robert the Bruce, one of whose bones is interred here. Outside, the best viewpoints both of the church and the glorious surrounding countryside are from the S. terraces that lead down to the lochside.

MILLPORT † Cathedral of the Isles ★★

Isle of Cumbrae, Argyll & Bute
OS *NS165552* **GPS** *55.7557N, 4.9245W*

A world away from the nearby coastal conurbations of the Firth of Clyde is William Butterfield's 1851 church for George Boyle, 6th Earl of Glasgow. The church was built as a group with a theological college, nowadays used as a retreat centre. The tall slender spire, 123 feet high, gives the impression of a large building, but the church is in fact small, the nave being some 20 by 40 feet. Gilded iron gates lead open to the chancel, separated from the nave by an airy traceried arch with rood cross, supported by polished granite columns. Butterfield's skilful use of coloured floor and wall tiles is excellent without being too busy, and is well balanced by a simple altar. Altogether a fine church, with excellent music too.

MOFFAT † St Andrew

Church Gate, Moffat, Dumfries & Galloway
OS *NT084051* **GPS** *55.3316N, 3.4448W*

A big church of red sandstone, 1887, by J. Starforth, in a former spa town, St Andrew's is distinguished by a grand tower with external staircase. The imposing entrance is flanked by turreted buttresses, and the nave is lit by two tiers of windows – altogether a church built to impress, but inside much simpler. Extensive W., S. and E. galleries are supported on cast iron columns in an open space whose focus is on the ornate W. pulpit.

MONTROSE
† Old and St Andrew's Parish Church

30m/50km N.E. of Dundee, Angus
OS *NO715577* **GPS** *56.7105N, 2.4660W*

Situated on the high street of this former busy sea-port, the spire of the church by James Gillespie Graham, 1834, is an arresting sight: Gothic in spirit, it is based on the tower of St James at Louth in Lincolnshire, the base supported by open-tracery ribs from the prominent finials – everything crocketed and well-detailed. The body of the church is by John Gibson, 1791–3.

PAISLEY † Paisley Abbey ★★

Abbey Close, 4m/7km W. of Glasgow
OS *NS485639* **GPS** *55.8450N, 4.4203W*

A remarkable and welcoming church of noble proportions, mercifully set slightly apart from a brutal 1960s city centre redevelopment. The present abbey is a testament to informed restoration and reconstruction. From the mid-16th century until the mid-1800s the abbey was neglected, sacked for building materials and suffered from general decay. Restoration was undertaken over 60 years by a number of distinguished architects: Sir Rowan Anderson the transepts, crossing and lower tower sections; P. MacGregor Chalmers, Sir Robert Lorimer and Alfred Lochhead the tower choir and E. end. The result is inspiring – the original high nave with elaborate triforium and clerestory and traces of earlier Norman work merges seamlessly with the crossing and choir's breathtaking fan-vaulting, and great Curvilinear E. window. It is surely the most convincing recreation of medieval architecture in the country.

◁ **PAISLEY ABBEY** – *restoration work, which has gone on throughout the 20th century, has returned to this church its remarkable transepts and chancel*

PEEBLES † Old Parish Church

High Street

OS *NT250403* **GPS** *55.6513N, 3.1932W*

The late 19th-century church dominates the west end of this pleasant town's high street, with a crown spire tower and broad step-gabled W. front. The interior is large; the nave with broad S., W. and N. galleries all under a sweeping arch-braced wooden ceiling, and a wide chancel arch. Flanking the entrance is contemporary glass by Crear McCartney.

PERTH † Cathedral of St Ninian ★

Atholl Street

OS *NO114239* **GPS** *56.3992N, 3.4359W*

Another church building by William Butterfield, 1850–90, the proportions of St Ninian's suffer from the absence of the originally planned but incompleted W. tower. J. L. Pearson demolished this, replacing it with a gabled W. front and flanking octagonal pinnacles. Despite a somewhat jumbled exterior, the church is worth visiting for its fine interior details: glass by Butterfield, an impressively proportioned sanctuary with high altar of Cornish granite and baldacchino above, ornately carved canon's stall and rood loft by Comper, Pearson's pulpit – all contribute to a fine and well-detailed interior.

PERTH † St John

St John's Place

OS *NO119235* **GPS** *56.3959N, 3.4281W*

This broad cruciform church dates from c. 1440. Victorian street 'improvements' led to the loss of the medieval S. porch, sacristy and part of the N. transept, but much of the original fabric remains, notably the roof and clustered piers of the choir, the nave with octagonal piers to the arcades, and the lower part of the N.W. Halkerston Tower. The demolished upper part of the tower was restored by Sir Robert Lorimer. Of note is the central tower, with a ribbed broach spire.

PLUSCARDEN † Pluscarden Abbey ★★

35m/55km E. of Inverness, Moray

OS *NJ142575* **GPS** *57.6001N, 3.4359W*

Although the monastic enclosure limits what the visitor may see, this is one of Scotland's unmissable churches. Set in a peaceful, remote wooded valley S.W. of Elgin is an ancient priory founded by the Valliscaulians in the 13th century. After the Reformation, the priory was granted to the Setons, and monastic occupation ceased at the end of the 16th century. In 1948 Lord Colum Crichton-Stuart gave the priory and estates to the monks of Prinknash. Although much had been lost, the medieval transepts, crossing, tower and choir survive, and the nave foundations can be traced in the grass to the W. Traces of 15th-century decoration can be seen in the transept aisles, both of which have remains of good stone carving and ornamentation. The choir and sanctuary contain traces of architectural styles – late Romanesque and Early English, and obvious changes in window openings – that suggest building by trial and error, which was common at the time. There is outstanding stained glass here: Sadie McClellan designed the N. transept window glass, pioneering the use of 'dalles de verre', a modern technique of concrete or epoxy resin and slabs of coloured glass. Two monks in the community, Br. Gilbert and Dom Ninian Stone, are noted for their stained glass, and Br. Gilbert's leaded glass and dalle de vere glass is to be found in many of the abbey windows: good work too by Crear McCartney, in leaded glass.

PORT SETON
† Chalmers Memorial Church

10m/16km E. of Edinburgh

OS *NT403756* **GPS** *55.9705N, 2.9576W*

An Arts and Crafts church by Sydney Mitchell, 1904, this is a Free Church (formed after the 1843 Disruption of the Church of Scotland). A hexagonal slate-hung spire ascends from the saddleback tower, and the main body of the church has typical Arts and Crafts dormer windows. Inside, the nave roof is stencilled in blues and creams. Altogether a charming, simple building.

PRESHOME † St Gregory R.C. ★★

40m/65km E. of Inverness

OS *NJ409614* **GPS** *57.6391N, 2.9899W*

In gentle countryside S. of the Moray Firth stands an externally modest church built five years after the Catholic Relief Bill, by Fr. John Reid, 1788. This close to the Act,

the building does not externally overstate its ecclesiastical function, but inside is a different matter entirely. The semi-octagonal chancel is vividly coloured with stencilled decoration. The high altar front is carved multi-coloured marble, and behind is a canopied painted and gilded reredos of St Gregory. The stencilling extends round the chancel arch into the nave, where the marble columned communion rails echo the high altar. P. P. Pugin attended to some of the internal details of this captivating church – Rome in the Braes of Enzie.

RODEL † St Clement ☆

S. tip of Harris, Outer Hebrides
OS *NG047831* **GPS** *57.7409N, 6.9633W*
Historic Scotland

St Clements is one of the Western Isles' most impressive medieval buildings, remotely set by the coast, a bulky cruciform 16th-century church with a 'Gaelic' feel to its design. Inside is a recessed wall to Alexander MacLoud, founder of the church: finely carved, it includes depictions of a 16th-century sailing ship, hunting scenes and biblical scenes. In the N. transept are carved medieval grave slabs, and in the nave is a heavily weathered stone wheel cross. Outside on the tower are carvings of a Sheela-na-Gig and corresponding male figure.

ROSLIN † Rosslyn Chapel / Collegiate Chapel of St Matthew ☆

8m/13km S. of Edinburgh, Midlothian
OS *NT274630* **GPS** *55.8554N, 3.1599W*

A medieval chapel of 1446 in the ownership of the St Clair family since its founding. It is a work that never reached its intended original plan, but the chapel is still a substantial fabric, full of remarkable detailed stone carving that fell into disuse at the time of Cromwell. David Bryce started restoration work in 1862, since which time conservation and restoration have been ongoing. It is a difficult building to read, suffering from wild speculation about its Masonic connections, and latterly the nonsensical Da Vinci Code, but the 15th-century carvings are extraordinary. Masonic imagery, the inverted angel and Apprentice Pillar, farming scenes, knights, the Nativity, green men and patterned motifs erupt dizzyingly from every surface. The chapel is in use by an Episcopalian congregation.

ST ANDREWS † Holy Trinity ☆☆

15m/24km S.E. of Dundee, Fife
OS *NO509166* **GPS** *56.3398N, 2.7955W*

With only the tower and a few piers remaining from the the 15th century, and a 16th-century spire, St Andrew's was restored by Peter MacGregor Chalmers, one of Scotland's most eminent church restorers and an expert on Scottish medieval church architecture – an expertise that led, as in Paisley Abbey, to a restoration that is difficult to distinguish from the original. The nave and chancel are one open space, with arcades of round piers (some original), and the E. window is good Curvilinear. The wooden wagon roof extends the length of the church, and in the S. aisle is a marble wall memorial to Archbishop Sharp, murdered by Covenanters in 1679.

ST MONANS
† St Monans Parish Church ☆

Village also spelt St Monance; 20m/32km S. of Dundee, Fife
OS *NO522014* **GPS** *56.2031N, 2.7713W*

In a magnificent setting overlooking the harbour on the Fife coastline is a broad-shouldered church of the 12th/13th century. Three restorations, 1826, 1899 and 1955, have more or less restored the pre-Reformation look of the church with its stubby spire, although the lack of a nave – maybe never constructed – gives the church a slightly lopsided appearance. Inside, the seafaring tradition of the area is seen in the 19th-century ship models suspended from the transept vaults. The old choir is finely vaulted, but the 20th-century reordering is odd and overcrowded – pulpit against the N. wall and everywhere crammed with pews.

SHISKINE † St Molio ☆

Isle of Arran, North Ayrshire
OS *NR909294* **GPS** *55.5137N, 5.3118W*

Peacefully set inland on the Isle of Arran, St Molio's was built in 1889 by Sir John James Burnet, a contemporary of Charles Rennie Mackintosh, in Romanesque revival style with distinctive Arts and Crafts features prominent in the catslide roofs and porch, whose ruddy paintwork echoes the reddish sandstone of the church. Very pleasant inside, with arch braced wooden roofs and timber arcading, and the N. end a medieval graveslab set into a buttress.

STIRLING † Church of the Holy Rood ★
St John Street
OS *NS792937* **GPS** *56.1208N, 3.9445W*

A grand Scottish burgh church of the mid-1400s to the 16th century, it suffers undeservedly from its proximity to the castle. Unusual and prized features are the original oak-beam roof, choir and semi-octagonal apsidal E. end. The nave has traces of 12th-century origins in round arcade piers, but the predominant theme here is excellent Scottish Gothic. The Reformation inadvertently prevented the loss of the fine oak roof (only revealed in 1936 behind a plaster ceiling) with the scrapping of plans to build a central tower, associated crossing and transepts. There is good modern glass by Crear McCartney, 1993.

STOBO † Stobo Kirk ★
4m/7km S.W. of Peebles, Scottish Borders
OS *NT182376* **GPS** *55.6256N, 3.2995W*

One of Scotland's oldest Border churches, in a beautiful setting, Stobo Kirk dates from c. 1120, and survived the Reformation unscathed. Rising in height from the chancel to the saddlebacked, part-Norman W. tower, its good Norman S. doorway has been protected by a 16th-century porch, and there are Norman windows in the chancel. The N. chapel is later, contemporary with the porch – a curious round stone-vaulted space in which stand 14th- and 15th-century slabs. The outside, though severely harled, has a simple appeal, and near the S. porch entrance is a 1723 gravestone to John Noble, musketeer.

STRATHPEFFER † St Anne
10m/16km N.W. of Inverness, Highland
OS *NH483580* **GPS** *57.5868N, 4.5387W*

In a fashionable Victorian resort, St Anne's (John Robertson, 1892) was built as a memorial to Anne, Duchess of Sutherland. A notable feature is the round bell tower with its tiled conical cap: it contains a carillon of eight tubular bells struck by wooden hammers. The interior is all late Victorian – dark stained pine pews, pitch pine moulded beams, cedar in the choir and chancel. The 1916 altar is marble and alabaster; the reredos and pulpit are Caen stone and alabaster.

SYMINGTON † Symington Parish Church
20m/32km S.W. of Glasgow, South Ayrshire
OS *NS384314* **GPS** *55.5494N, 4.5628W*

A church whose Norman origins were not obvious until a 1919 restoration by MacGregor Chalmers. It had been much altered in the 18th century with additions of a N. extension, galleries and pews. Chalmers removed most of the galleries and the plaster ceiling that concealed an oak-beam roof. There are three small 12th-century windows with dogtooth carving in the chancel, and a deeply splayed 12th-century priest's door.

TYNET † St Ninian
40m/65km E. of Inverness, Moray
OS *NJ379613* **GPS** *57.6369N, 3.0420W*

A clandestine Catholic church of 1755, St Ninian's looks intentionally like no more than a long, low barn. Originally thatched, it acquired glazed windows and a tiled roof in 1779 and is the oldest post-Reformation Catholic church in Scotland.

WHITEKIRK † St Mary ★
25m/40km N.E. of Edinburgh, East Lothian
OS *NT597817* **GPS** *56.0249, -2.6493*

A prominent sandstone church of great appeal, St Mary's is a rural village church of 12th century origins, with a 15th-century rib-vaulted choir, tower crossing and a stone barrel-vaulted chancel. The church retains a Norman feel, although the chancel and choir arches are the only obvious internal signs of 12th-century work; the windows are Y-traceried. Sir Robert Lorimer restored the church after a fire of 1914. The three-stage tower, with dividing string-courses and corbelled parapet, once housed a columbarium.

THE ISLE OF MAN

The Isle of Man is rich in variety of natural scenery. It is a mixture of Ulster and Cornwall to look at; there are mountains and moors down its middle, whence streams splash to the sea through wooded glens. High fuchsias and veronicas grow by stone cottages, sub-tropical trees and shrubs flourish in those parts that are sheltered from the prevailing south-west gales. The building stone of most of the island is slate of various colours, and there is a certain amount of soft red sandstone in Peel and good grey limestone at Castletown. The northern point of the island has a rich, swampy district called the Curragh, which tails off into a flat sandy tract. Elsewhere the coast is mostly high cliffs.

The Celtic Church was founded in the Isle of Man in about the 5th or 6th century, and influenced by missionaries from Ireland. Their churchyard crosses survive and all seventeen old parish churches of the island, despite many rebuildings, have retained the plain, rectangular plan of Celtic times. In the 8th and 9th centuries the island was invaded by Scandinavian pagans; soon converted, their cross-slabs display both pagan legends and Christian themes. The crosses at Kirk Maughold, the Thor Cross at Kirk Bride, and the Odin Cross at Kirk Andreas are particularly interesting. Under the Norwegians the western islands of Scotland (Sodor) and the island of Man became a single diocese c. 1135, and Man remained Norwegian until 1266. Its Church was controlled directly by Rome until the Reformation. Only two considerable medieval buildings remain. They are St German's Cathedral on an island off the west coast of the fishing port of Peel, and Rushden Abbey. But both are ruins. The Manx Gothic was more like Irish Gothic than English.

The Reformation proceeded slowly in Man, and its Church remained 'high' church until the beginning of the 19th century. Church architecture, as opposed to antiquities, begins with Georgian times. The famous and saintly bishop, Thomas Wilson, who occupied the see from 1698 until his death in 1755, and his successor Bishop Hildesley, were responsible for the restoration and refitting of all old churches. In Bishop Wilson's time there was a Manx Baroque style which may be seen in the west front of Ballaugh Old Church. The Gothic Revival came early to the island, and may have received its impetus first from the castellated building by George Steuart, built as a house for the Duke of Atholl, the island's owner and governor at the end of the 18th century, and now known as the Castle Mona Hotel, Douglas. People who fell into debt used to flee to the Isle of Man at this period and build themselves

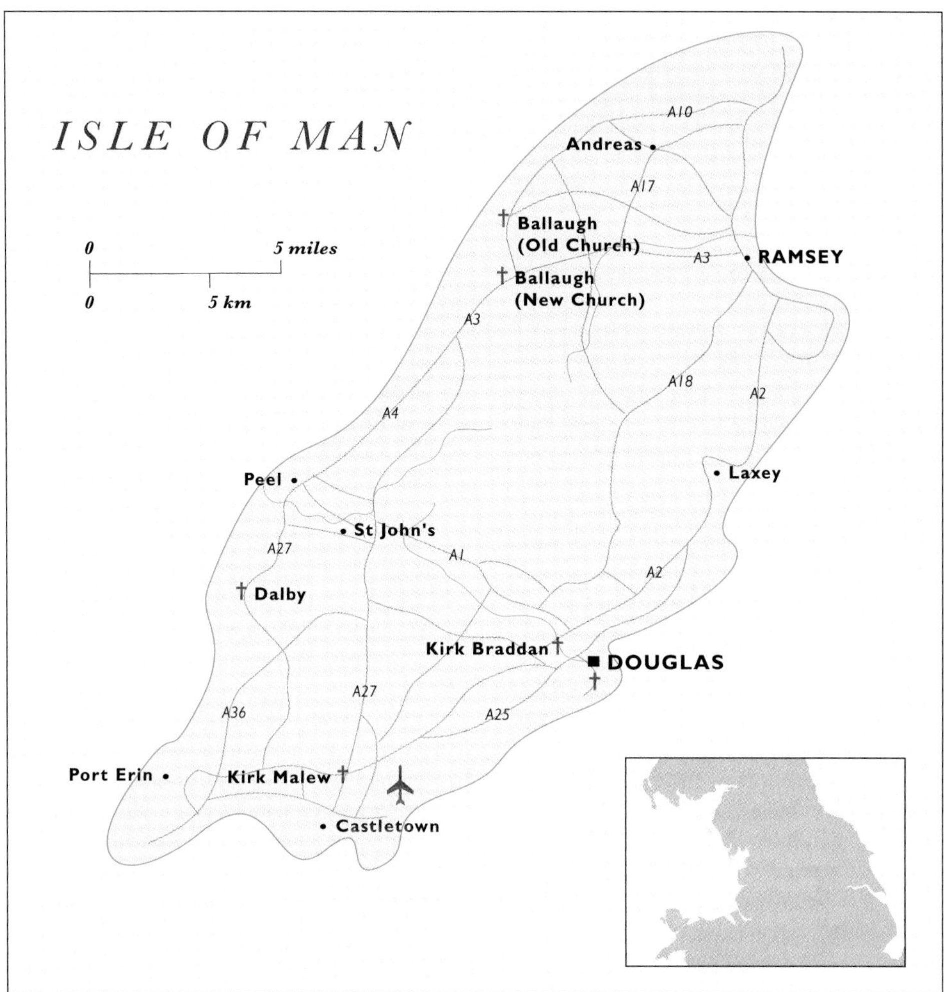

castellated mansions. A Manx Gothic Revival style established itself, and the work of John Welch in the 1820s and 30s is really distinguished.

After the debtors, the visitors: in the 19th century Douglas became the chief town, and churches in North-of-England Victorian style, typical of Castletown, the old capital, began to appear all over the island. Those which seem most distinguished are listed.

Man is 227 square miles, slightly bigger than Rutland, and has 17 ancient parishes. Its Bishop has a say in the government of the island and a seat in the Tynwald Court. Its churches are many and small. Though none of the earlier ones may have much architectural distinction, they have a storm-resisting, prayer-soaked holiness about them. Most old churches were heavily restored, and only two retain their Georgian fittings.

BALLAUGH † St Mary, New Church ★

7ml11km W. of Ramsey

OS *SC345939* **GPS** *54.313787N, 4.545673W*

By John Welch, 1832. The exterior is an impressive attempt in local stone to produce Boston Stump reduced in scale. (See St Botolph, Lincolnshire.)

BALLAUGH † St Mary, Old Church

7ml11km W. of Ramsey

(the old church is about 1ml2km N. of Ballaugh)

OS *SC340957* **GPS** *54.329932N, 4.553447W*

An old church to which Bishop Wilson added a W. gable and bellcote in 1717, in simple and strange Baroque style. Subsequent restoration removed the galleries and chancel extension. Inside there is an 11th-century Runic Cross, which reads *'Ouliabr Loitulfsunr raisti krs thana aftir Ulb sun Sin'* (Olaf Liotulfson erected this cross to the memory of his son Ulf). There is also a sandstone font built into a windowsill, with a Manx inscription – *'Ta un Chiarn, un Credjue, un Vashtey, un Jee as Ayr jeh ooilley'* (There is one Lord, one Faith, one Baptism, one God and Father of all).

DALBY † St James

4ml6km S. of Peel

OS *SC220783* **GPS** *54.170597N, 4.728646W*

A beautiful setting in a remote hamlet on the W. Coast; the church dates from 1840, by John Welch. The W. end and porch are ornamented with many pinnacles. Otherwise the church has a domestic look.

DOUGLAS † St George ★

Upper Church Street

OS *SC379755* **GPS** *54.149389N, 4.4836W*

Built 1761–80 by a local builder who was sent to Whitehaven to copy the church of St James. The interior was much restored in 1910, when the upper galleries were removed and the church extended.

DOUGLAS † St Ninian ★

Glencrutchery Road

OS *SC380772* **GPS** *54.164964N, 4.482900W*

This is a sensitive local stone rendering of late Gothic by W. D. Caroe, 1914, freely treated with a spacious and impressive interior. Henry Bloom Noble, who provided the funds to build the church, stipulated that it be 'served by clergyman of Evangelical and Protestant principles'. A new community hall is within the main building.

KIRK BRADDAN
† St Braddan, Old Church ★

1ml2km N.W. of Douglas

OS *SC364768* **GPS** *54.160865N, 4.507165W*

The mother church of Douglas is in a beautiful wooded valley by the River Dhoo. The churchyard is full of Georgian headstones, dominated by an obelisk to Lord Henry Murray, designed by Steuart. The tower dates from 1773, and the interior has high pews, galleries, clear glass and monuments on the walls – very complete Georgian. Several Celtic and Norse crosses found elsewhere in the parish are now housed here. The church is still occasionally used for services, and is run by the friends of Old Kirk Braddan.

KIRK MALEW † St Lupus or St Moluag

1ml2km S.W. of Ballasalla

OS *SC268694* **GPS** *54.091694N, 4.649229W*

This is what all the old Manx churches were like before Victorian restoration: outside, a whitewashed rectangle in fields; inside, box pews and Georgian fittings, and an 18th-century N. transept.

THE CHANNEL ISLANDS

The islands, much nearer to France than they are to England, are the last remaining part of the Duchy of Normandy to owe allegiance to the English Crown. The islands were converted by the same Celtic missionaries who established churches in Cornwall and Brittany, and the ancient parish churches are a curious mixture of styles which link them both with the West Country and with Northern France.

Until 1569, the islands were under the jurisdiction of the Bishop of Coutances in Normandy, but in that year were transferred to the diocese of Winchester. The religious links of the islands, however, were with the Calvinist Protestants of France, many of whom sought exile there. Though nominally Anglican from the mid-17th century, there were major variations from the normal standards of Anglican worship. The surplice was not worn by the clergy, the use of fonts was abandoned, and the churches had no permanent communion tables. On the quarterly Sacrament Sundays, as in the Scottish and Dutch Calvinist churches, a long table was placed in front of the pulpit around which the communicants sat, and these tables still survive in three Jersey churches. It was not until well into the 19th century that churches in the Channel Islands began to adopt forms of worship familiar to congregations in England.

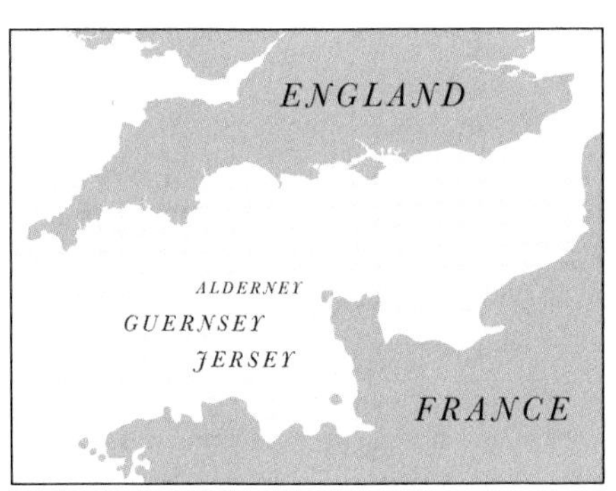

The islands are organized into two bailiwicks: Guernsey (including the outlying islands of Alderney, Herm and Sark); and Jersey. They are very different in character. Jersey, though it still has a few rural enclaves and substantial farmhouses, has been heavily developed over the past century as a popular resort for holidaymakers and as a haven for tax exiles. The capital, St Helier, is a rather drab seaside town, though its tree-lined Royal Square, in which the principal government buildings are located, is reminiscent of squares in small French provincial towns. Guernsey, though largely built up and so dedicated to the growing of tomatoes that from the air the main island looks like one vast greenhouse, is much less cosmopolitan. The capital, St Peter Port, in which the narrow and winding streets rise almost vertically from the harbour, is a delightful town of distinguished late 18th- and early 19th-century buildings. Alderney is even quieter, and Sark, still ruled by its Seigneur, remains wholly feudal. Each bailiwick has its own courts and parliament and forms a deanery within the diocese of Winchester, over which the Dean has a large measure of quasi-episcopal authority.

The churches of the Channel Islands are humble buildings, much enlarged during the medieval period and rather too heavily (and unimaginatively) restored in the 19th century. Jersey was divided into 12 pre-Reformation parishes, and Guernsey, excluding the outlying islands, into 10. These still remain the units of local adminstration in the islands, both civil and ecclesiastical, as they were in England and Wales before 1894. A notable feature of the islands' churches is the crudeness of their construction, especially the roofs, which generally consist of plain and steeply pitched stone vaults. When the population expanded in the 18th and 19th centuries, a number of new churches were built, but none of any great distinction. Local or minor English architects were mostly used, and even when this was not the case, as with St Simon's in St Helier and St Stephen's in St Peter Port, both designed by G. F. Bodley, the buildings were left incomplete or substantially modified through lack of funds. Neither building ranks as among that architect's best work. The only distinguished Victorian churches are Scott's replacement St Anne's in Alderney and Pugin's English Roman Catholic Church in St Peter Port.

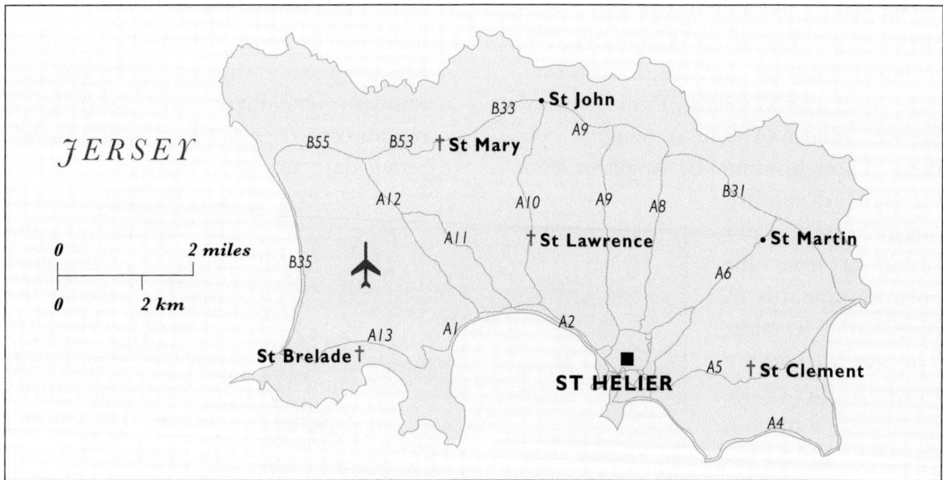

Bailiwick of Jersey

ST BRELADE † St Brendan/Branmalader

St Brelade's Bay **GPS** *49.1841N, 2.2029W*

A 12th-century cruciform church with low central saddleback tower and a large W. porch, to which aisles were added later on the N. sides of both nave and chancel; the transept roof-line was retained, giving a strange effect to the exterior. The interior walls and stone vaults have been savagely scraped. To the S. of the chancel in the churchyard is the 'Fisherman's Chapel', a small oratory of uncertain date containing a series of medieval frescoes covering the walls and vaulted roof.

ST CLEMENT † St Clement

La Grande Route de Saint-Clément
GPS *49.1738N, 2.0567W*

Restoration in 1880 revealed a remarkable series of wall-paintings, including St Michael and the Dragon on the N. wall of the nave, a hunting scene in the S. transept, and two female saints, Barbara and Margaret, in the N. transept. There is a handsome 15th-century font and a long 17th-century communion table. The nave is 12th-century, the chancel and transepts 15th-century.

ST LAWRENCE † St Lawrence

La Route de l'Église **GPS** *49.2146N, 2.1415W*

The church dates substantially from the 14th and 15th centuries, with further additions on the eve of the Reformation. The impressive Hamptonne Chapel, added in 1524, has a vaulted roof with bosses. There is a long 17th-century communion table.

ST MARY † St Mary the Virgin
La Route de Sainte-Marie
GPS *49.235N, 2.1737W*

The N. nave and both chancels are medieval; the S. nave dates from the restoration of 1838–42. The tower has an 18th-century spire and spirelets, like Vale in Guernsey. There are several decent 17th- and 18th-century wall tables and a long 17th-century communion table.

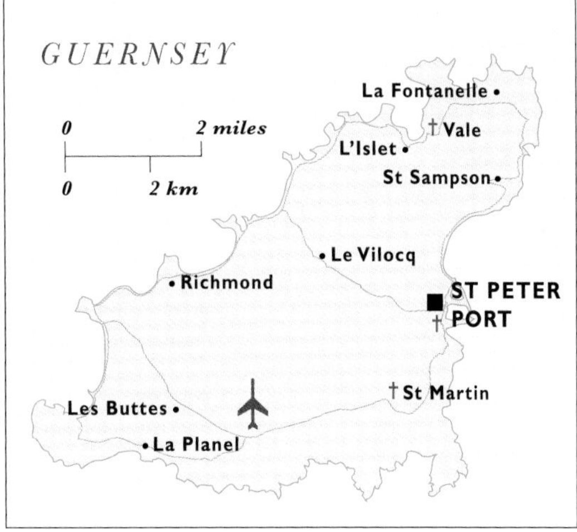

Bailiwick of Guernsey

ST MARTIN † St Martin
La Bellieuse **GPS** *49.4382N, 2.5544W*

A large double nave and chancel church with tower and spire between the S. nave and S. chancel; the 15th-century S. porch has an elaborately carved outer doorway, and there is also a 15th-century octagonal font. The pulpit is dated 1657, and the contemporary reading desk has been cut down to serve as a lectern. This is one of several Guernsey churches retaining its 17th-century poor-box.

ST PETER PORT † Holy Trinity
Trinity Square **GPS** *49.4522N, 2.5405W*

This is a simple Classical church of 1789 with a double row of windows on the N. and S. sides and with a gabled W. front in the Dutch style. The interior has a plain plastered ceiling, galleries and a shallow E. apse. Until very recently it retained, alone in the Channel Islands, a complete set of box pews set chapel-fashion with no central aisle.

ST PETER PORT † St Peter
Church Hill **GPS** *49.4546N, 2.5363W*

The most distinguished and substantial of the ancient parish churches in the Channel Islands, the church is now rather strangely shaped, having been extended on a confined site in the town centre. St Martin's has a central tower and spire, a very short nave and chancel, both with N. and S. aisles, a short N. transept and a long S. transept of three bays with an E. aisle of the same length. Though much of the structure is 13th–15th century, the interior was well restored in 1886 and given a series of plaster vaults. There is a wide range of 17th–19th century wall tablets to most of the leading families in Guernsey.

VALE † St Michael ★
L'Abbaye **GPS** *49.493N, 2.539W*

A large double nave and chancel church; S.W. tower has 18th-century spire and spirelets. The church dates from the 12th to the 14th centuries and is the best-preserved medieval fabric in the Channel Islands. The arcaded S. chancel has an elaborate ribbed vault and the 16th-century porch is also vaulted. There are unusual hood moulds over the windows in the N. nave and both W. doorways.

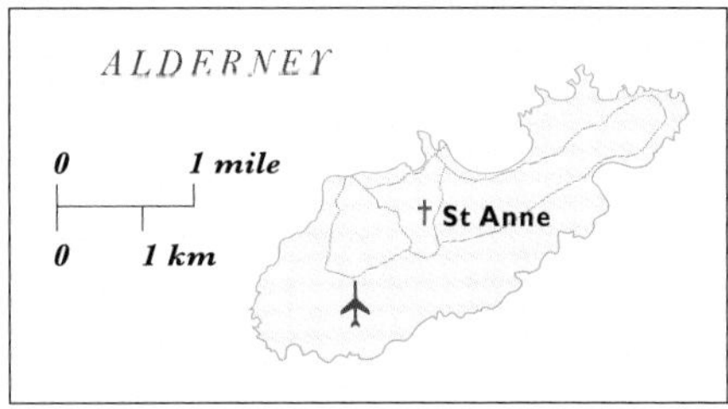

ALDERNEY † St Anne
Between Le Pre and Victoria Street, St Anne
GPS *49.7154N, 2.20466W*

The church was rebuilt in 1847–50 to designs by George Gilbert Scott. Cruciform church in Early English style, it has a squat central tower, pyramidal spire and apsidal chancel. In composition it is sympathetic to the architectural traditions of the Channel Islands and the furnishings are of high quality.

ambulatory
semicircular or polygonal aisle enclosing an apse

Anglo-Saxon
period from c. 500–1066

apse
vaulted semicircular or polygonal end of a chancel or a chapel

arcade
range of arches supported on piers or columns, free-standing; or, blind arcade, the same attached to a wall

arch
curved spanning of an opening, as opposed to a straight, horizontal lintel; these are the key types for church architecture:

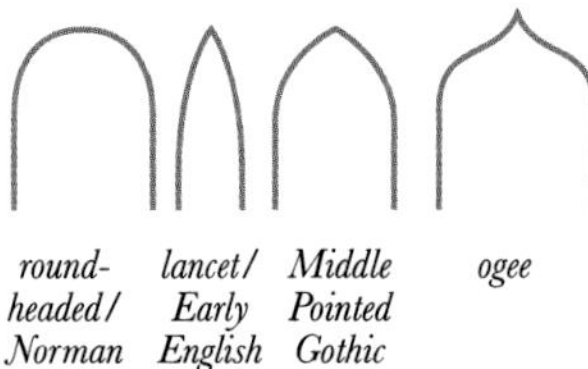

round-headed/ Norman *lancet/ Early English* *Middle Pointed Gothic* *ogee*

arch-brace
see roof

architrave
lowest of the three main parts of the entablature of an order

ashlar
masonry of large blocks wrought to even faces and square edges

aumbrey
recess or cupboard to hold sacred vessels for Mass and Communion

baldacchino
canopy supported on columns

ballflower
globular flower of three petals enclosing a small ball. A decoration used in the first quarter of the 14th century.

baluster
small pillar or column of fanciful outline

balustrade
series of balusters supporting a handrail or coping

basilica
in medieval architecture an aisled church with a clerestory

batter
wall with an inclined face

battlement
parapet with a series of indentations or embrasures with raised portions or merlons between (also called crenellation)

bays
internal compartments of a building; each divided from the other not by solid walls but by division only marked in the side walls (columns, pilasters, etc) or the ceiling (beams, etc). Also external divisions of a building by fenestration.

bedesman
carved praying figure, often situtated at the foot of an effigy on a tomb

bell-cote
turret usually on the W. end of a church to carry the bells

billet
Norman ornamental motif made up of short raised rectangles placed at regular intervals

block capital
Romanesque capital cut from a cube by having the lower angles rounded off to the circular shaft below (also called cushion capital)

boss
knob or projection usually placed to cover the intersection of ribs in a vault or anlges between wooden roof timbers

box pew
pew with a high wooden enclosure

brace
see roof

broach
see spire

buttress
mass of brickwork or masonry projecting from or built against a wall to give additional strength
flying buttress: arch or half arch transmitting the thrust of a vault or roof from the upper part of a wall to an outer support or buttress

cable moulding
moulding imitating a twisted cord

camber
slight rise or upward curve of an otherwise horizontal structure

campanile
isolated bell tower, separate or partially so from the main body of the church

canopy
ornamental covering above an altar, pulpit, niche, etc

canopy of honour
highly decorated portion of the nave roof above the rood

capital
head or top part of a column

cartouche
tablet with an ornate frame, usually enclosing an inscription

caryatid
column in the form of a human figure

ceilure
panelled and adorned part of a wagon-roof above the rood or altar

chalice
small cup used in the Communion service or at Mass

chamfer
surface made by cutting across the square angle of a stone block, piece of wood, etc, at an angle of 45 degrees to the two other surfaces

chancel
part of the E. end of a church in which the altar is placed, usually applied to the main body of the church E. of the crossing; it may include a choir and sanctuary

chancel arch
arch at the W. end of the chancel

chapel
a separate space within a church, with its own dedication and altar

chantry chapel
chapel attached to or inside a church endowed for the saying of Masses for the soul of the founder or some other individual

chapel of ease
a church that lies within a parish but is not the main parish church

chevron
sculptured moulding forming a zigzag

choir
that part of the church where divine service is sung; often placed at the W. end of the chancel

ciborium
a cup-shaped vessel or shrine with an arched cover

clas
Welsh: a mother church with monastic buildings

Classical
here used as the term for Greek and Roman architecture and any subsequent styles copying it

clerestory
upper storey of the nave walls of a church, pierced by windows

clunch
locally found or quarried lumps of rock, chalk or clay, used with mortar to form walls

coade stone
artificial (cast) stone made in the late 18th century and the early 19th century by Coade and Seely in London

cob
walling material made of mixed clay and straw

coffering
decorating a ceiling with sunk square or polygonal ornamental panels

collar-beam
see roof

colonnade
range of columns

Commissioners' church
the Church Building Commission operated from 1818 to 1856 and established many churches with government funds

coping
capping or covering to a wall

corbel
stone support projecting from an internal or external wall, often carved

corbel table
series of corbels, occurring just below the roof eaves externally or internally, often seen in Norman buildings

Corinthian
see Orders

cornice
in classical architecture the top section of the entablature. Also for a projecting decorative feature along the top of a wall, arch, etc.

cove, coving
concave under-surface in the nature of a hollow moulding but on a larger scale

crest, cresting
ornamental finish along the top of a screen, etc

crocket, crocketing
decorative features placed on the sloping sides of spires, pinnacles, gables, etc in Gothic architecture, carved in various leaf shapes and placed at regular intervals

crossing
space at the intersection of nave, chancel, and transepts

crown-post
see roof

crypt
underground room usually below the E. end of a church

cupola
small polygonal or circular domed turret crowning a roof

cushion capital
see block capital

cusp
in tracery, the small pointed member between two lobes of a trefoil, quatrefoil, etc

decalogue
list of the Ten Commandments

Decorated
historical division of English Gothic architecture covering the mid-13th to mid-14th century

diaper work
surface decoration composed of square or lozenge shapes

Doric
see orders

dormer (window)
window placed vertically in the sloping plane of a roof

dripstone
see hood-mould

drum
circular or polygonal vertical wall of a dome or cupola

Early English
historical division of English Gothic architecture roughly covering the mid-12th to mid-13th century

Easter Sepulchre
recess with tomb-chest usually in the wall of a chancel, the tomb-chest to receive an effigy of Christ for Easter celebrations

eaves
underpart of a sloping roof overhanging a wall

embattled
a building with battlements

embrasures
indented portions of a battlement; contrast with merlons

encaustic tiles
earthenware glazed and decorated tiles used for paving

engaged columns
columns attached to, or partly sunk into, a wall

entablature
in classical architecture the whole of the horizontal members above a column (that is architrave, frieze, and cornice)

entasis
very slight convex deviation from a straight line; used on Greek columns and sometimes on spires to prevent an optical illusion of concavity

epitaph
hanging wall monument

escutcheon
shield for armorial bearings

faience
decorated glazed earthenware

fan vault
see vault

festoon
carved garland of flowers and fruit suspended at both ends

fillet
narrow flat band running down a shaft or along a roll moulding

finial
in Gothic architecture the top of a pinnacle, gable, or bench-end carved into a leaf or leaf-like form

flamboyant
properly the last phase of French Gothic architecture where the window tracery takes on wavy undulating lines

flèche
slender wooden spire on the centre of a roof (also called spirelet)

flushwork
decorative scheme using alternately flint and contrasting incised stonework to form a pattern or letters

fluting
vertical channelling in the shaft of a column

flying buttress
see buttress

foliated
carved with leaf shapes

fresco
wall-painting on wet plaster

frieze
a wide band of continuous painting or relief sculpture

frontal
covering of the front of an altar

gable
triangular upper section of a wall at end of a pitched roof; *see also* roof

gallery
in church architecture, the upper storey above an aisle, sometimes opened in arches to the nave

gargoyle
water spout projecting from the parapet of a wall or tower; carved into a human or animal shape

Geometrical
see tracery

Gothic
architectural style characterised by pointed arches, ribbed vaulting, flying buttresses, spacious arcades and clerestory windows, which flourished from the 12th to 16th centuries

Gothic Revival/Neo-Gothic
mid-18th- to late 19th-century movement to revive medieval Gothic architecture, in contrast to the prevailing Classical styles

Gothic Survival
the inclusion of certain Gothic details on some buildings in the 17th century, deemed as 'survival' rather than part of the definitive Gothic Revival movement

'Gothick'
idiosyncratic style of the mid-18th century, exemplified by Horace Walpole's villa at Strawberry Hill in Twickenham

Green Man
motif of a face sprouting with foliage

groin
sharp edge at the meeting of two cells of a cross-vault

groined vault
see vault

grotesque
carved ornamental stone human or animal feature on the exterior of a church

hagioscope
see squint

hammer-beam
see roof

hatchment
board with armorial bearings

helm roof
see roof

Herefordshire School
a group of masons who worked on a number of churches in the Herefordshire area in the 12th century; their most celebrated work is at Kilpeck

hipped roof
see roof

hood-mould
projecting moulding above an arch or a lintel to throw off water (also called dripstone or label)

hogback stone
Anglo-Scandinavian style of grave marker, dating from the time of Danish settlement in the 9th–10th centuries, found in Scotland and Northern England

impost
brackets in walls, usually formed of mouldings, on which the ends of an arch rest

ionic
see orders

Jacobean
early 17th-century style, associated with the reign of King James I, which adopted Renaissance motifs in architecture and furnishings

jamb
straight side of an archway, doorway, or window

keystone
middle stone in an arch

king-post
see roof

lancet window
slender pointed-arched window; *see also* arch

Laudian
relating to the early 17th-century period of reform and High Church standards within the Church of England promulgated by Archbishop William Laud

lean-to roof
roof with one slope only, built against a higher wall

lierne
see vault

lintel
horizontal beam or stone bridging an opening

lych gate
wooden or stone gate structure with a roof and open sides placed at the entrance to a churchyard to provide space for the reception of a coffin – lych is the Saxon word for corpse

mandorla
upright almond-shaped frame to surround an image of Christ enthroned; a device used mostly but not exclusively in medieval art; synomymous with vesica

merlons
raised portions of a battlement, also known as crenellations; contrast with embrasures

miserere
see misericord

misericord
bracket placed on the underside of a hinged choir stall seat which, when turned up, provided the occupant of the seat with a support during long periods of standing (also called miserere)

mullion
vertical post or upright dividing a window into two or more 'lights'

nave
the central, principal space of the church; contrast with chancel and transepts

narthex
a chamber, porch or separated area usually at the W. end of a church

newel
central post in a circular or winding staircase; also the principal post when a flight of stairs meets a landing

Neo-Gothic
see Gothic Revival

Norman
period from 1066 to the mid-12th century, its architecture characterised by round columns and round-headed arches

Norman Revival
style based on Norman architecture adopted in the 18th and 19th centuries; an offshoot of the Gothic Revival

order
in Classical architecture: column with base, shaft, capital and entablature according to one of the following styles: Greek Doric, Roman Doric, Tuscan Doric, Ionic, Corinthian, Composite.

Oxford Movement
mid-19th-century movement associated with Oxford University, which developed into Anglo Catholicism. Also known as the Tractarian Movement.

Palladian
architecture following the ideas and principles of Andrea Palladio, 1518–80; effectively, a rigid revisiting of Classicism

parapet
low wall surmounting a tower or roof

parclose (screen)
screen enclosing and separating from the main body of the church a private chapel that usually honours a particular person or family

parvise
room over a church porch. Often used as a school-house or store room.

pele tower
fortified watch tower – many were built in the N. of England in the 15th century

Perpendicular
historical division of English Gothic architecture roughly covering the period from 1350 to 1530; characterised by a stress on verticality and linearity

pier
strong, solid support, frequently square in section or of composite section (compound pier)

Pietà
sculptural representation of the Virgin Mary cradling the dead body of Jesus

pilaster
shallow pier attached to a wall

pinnacle
ornamental form crowning a spire, tower, buttress, etc, usually of steep pyramidal, conical or similar shape

piscina
basin for washing the Communion or Mass vessels, provided with a drain. Generally set in or against the wall to the S. of an altar.

plate tracery
see tracery

plinth
projecting base of a wall or column, generally chamfered or moulded at the top

poppyhead
ornament of leaf and flower type used to decorate the tops of bench-ends

portico
centre-piece of a house or a church with classical detached or attached columns and a pediment

porticus
Anglo-Saxon side chapel

principal
see roof

priory
monastic house whose head is a prior or prioress, not an abbot or abbess

pulpitum
stone rood screen in a major church

purlin
see roof

quarry
in stained-glass work, a small diamond-shaped piece of glass

queen-posts
see roof

quoins
dressed stones at the angles of a building, set for decorative effect; St Benet's, Paul's Wharf in London is a good example

rafter
see roof

reredos
decorative structure, such as a painting, sculpture or relief carving, displayed behind an altar

respond
a half-pier sunk into a wall to support an arch, much as an ordinary pier would; often found at the end of an arcade or at either side of a chancel arch

retable
the frame enclosing a painting, sculpture or carved relief standing behind and attached to an altar

Reticulated tracery
see tracery

rib vault
see vault

Rococo
last phase of the Baroque style, current in most Continental countries between c. 1720 and c. 1760

Romanesque
style of architecture current in the 11th and 12th centuries (in England more usually called Norman)

rood
large cross or crucifix hung over a rood screen at the chancel entrance

rood loft
singing gallery on top of the rood screen, often supported by a coving

rood screen
see screen

rood stairs
stairs to give access to the rood loft

roof
roof shapes:
gable, or pitched: simple roof form, with two sloping faces and triangular gable walls at each end
hipped: roof with sloped instead of vertical ends (ie four sloping sides)
saddleback: tower roof shaped like an ordinary gabled timber roof
helm: steeply pitched tower roof with four equal sloping faces that rise from gables on each of the four walls of the tower; the sloping faces are set at 45 degree angles to the tower walls
wagon: roof in which, through closely set rafters with arched braces, the appearance of the inside of a canvas over a wagon is achieved; they can be panelled or plastered (ceiled) or left uncovered – Cornwall and Devon have many examples
roof construction:
king-post: upright timber connecting a tie-beam with the apex of the roof
queen-posts: two upright timbers placed symmetrically on a tie-beam or collar-beam.
crown-post: upright timber connecting a tie-beam to a collar-beam; braces usually rise from the crown-post to the collar-beam too.

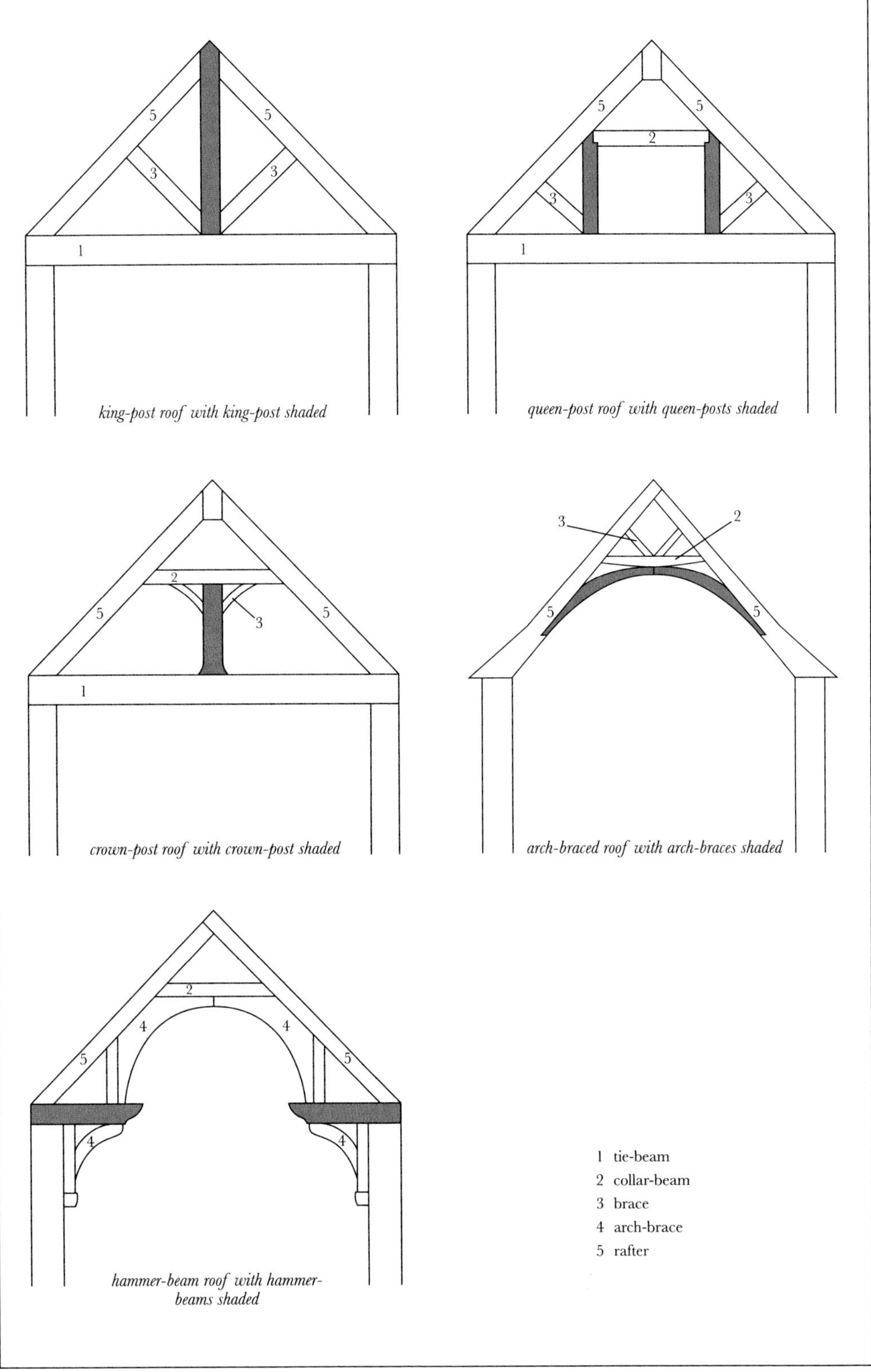
5
5
3
3
1
king-post roof with king-post shaded
5
5
2
3
3
1
queen-post roof with queen-posts shaded
2
5
3
5
1
crown-post roof with crown-post shaded
3
2
5
5
arch-braced roof with arch-braces shaded
2
4
4
5
5
4
4
hammer-beam roof with hammer-beams shaded
1 tie-beam
2 collar-beam
3 brace
4 arch-brace
5 rafter

arch-braced: a pair of curved braces forming an arch that are used as supports for a collar-beam
hammer-beam: horizontal brackets projecting at right angles from the tops of opposite walls to carry arched braces or struts and arched braces to support a collar-beam
The principal types of church roof construction are illustrated on the previous page

rose window
circular window with tracery suggesting the form of a rose

rubble
building stones, not square or hewn, nor laid in regular courses

rustication
Ashlar-work of blocks with the margins only wrought and the faces rough or specially rock-faced: or ashlar-work of smooth-faced blocks with the joints greatly emphasized (smooth rustication). If only the horizontal joints are emphasized it is called banded rustication.

saddleback
see roof

sanctuary
area around the main altar of a church (*see* presbytery)

scagliola
material composed of cement and colouring matter to imitate marble

scraped
reference to the propensity for church restorers in the Victorian age to scrape away the plaster surface on especially the interior walls to reveal the stonework, which was often then pointed with cement; the scraping itself frequently damaged the stone whilst also destroying the plaster and any painting contained thereon

screen
parclose screen: screen separating a chapel from the rest of a church
rood screen: screen at the W. end of a chancel; above it on the rood-beam was the rood

sedilia
seats for the priests (usually three) on the S. side of the chancel

seven-sacrament font
seven-sided font, with symbols of baptism and the other sacraments

Sheela-na-Gig
carving in a grotesque, caricaturelike form of a naked female prominently displaying exaggerated vulva

shingles
wooden tiles used as roofing or as a covering to walls and spires

sill
lower horizontal part of the frame of a window

sounding board
horizontal board or canopy over a pulpit. Also called tester.

spandrel
roughly triangular surface between one side of an arch, the horizontal drawn from its apex, and the vertical drawn from its springer; also the surface between two arches

spire
tall pyramidal or conical pointed erection often built on top of a tower, turret, etc
broach Spire: spire which is generally octagonal in plan rising from the top or parapet of a square tower; a small inclined piece of masonry covers the vacant triangular space at each of the four angles of the square and is carried up to a point along the diagonal sides of the octagon
needle Spire: thin spire rising from the centre of a tower roof, well inside the parapet

spirelet
see flèche

splay
chamfer, usually of the jamb of a window

springing
level at which an arch rises from its supports

squarson
term for a clergyman who was also squire of a parish

squinch
arch or system of concentric arches thrown across the angle between two walls to support a superstructure – for example a dome

squint
hole cut in a wall or through a pier to allow a view of the main altar from places whence it could not otherwise be seen (also called hagioscope)

stall
carved seat, one in a row, made of wood or stone

steeple
the tower or spire of a church

stiff-leaf
Early English type of foliage ornament of many-lobed shapes

stoup
vessel for the reception of holy water, usually placed near a door

string course
projecting horizontal band or moulding set in the surface of a wall

strut
see roof

stucco
plasterwork

swag
festoon formed by a carved piece of cloth suspended from both ends

tabernacle
richly ornamented niche or free-standing canopy. Usually contains the Holy Sacrament.

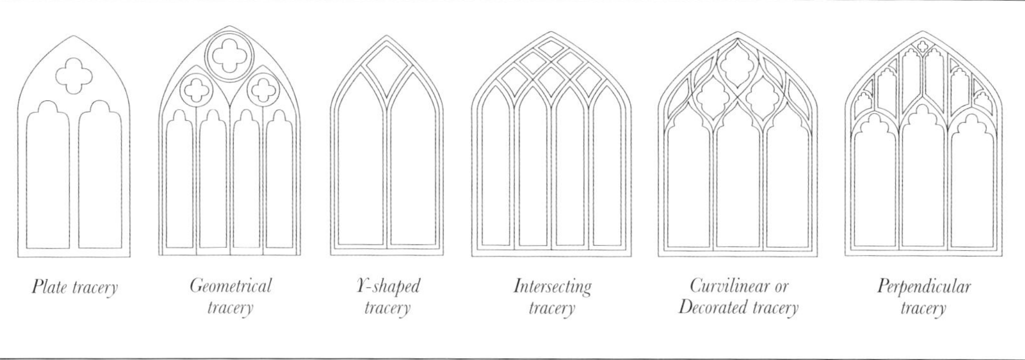
Plate tracery — Geometrical tracery — Y-shaped tracery — Intersecting tracery — Curvilinear or Decorated tracery — Perpendicular tracery

terracotta
burnt clay, unglazed

tester
see sounding board

three-decker pulpit
pulpit with clerk's stall and reading desk placed below each other

tie-beam
see roof

timber-framing
method of construction where walls are built of timber frame-work with the spaces filled in by plaster or brickwork. Sometimes the timber is covered over with plaster or boarding laid horizontally.

tomb-chest
chest-shaped stone coffin, the most usual medieval form of funeral monument

tracery
interesting ribwork in the upper part of a window, or used decoratively in blank arches, on vaults, etc.
Plate tracery: early form of tracery where decoratively shaped openings are cut through the solid stone infilling in the head of a window
Bar tracery: intersecting ribwork made up of slender shafts, continuing the lines of the mullions of windows up to a decorative mesh in the head of the window
Geometrical tracery: consists chiefly of circles or foiled circles
Y-tracery: tracery in which the mullion of a window branches out into two curved bars, thus forming a Y shape
Intersecting tracery: tracery in which each mullion of a window branches out into two curved bars in such a way that every one of them runs concentrically with the others against the arch of the whole window; the result is that every light of the window is a lancet and every two, three, four, etc, lights together form a pointed arch
Reticulated tracery: tracery consisting entirely of circles drawn at the top and bottom into ogee shapes so that a net-like appearance results.
Curvilinear, or Decorated tracery: characterised by the use of continuous flowing lines of tracery
Perpendicular tracery: characterised by repeated perpendicular mullions rising to a curved arch, the mullions crossed at intervals by horizontal transoms producing repeated vertical recangles
The most common forms of tracery are illustrated in the diagram above

Tractarian
see Oxford Movement

transept
the transverse section of a cruciform church, normally at the tower crossing and separating the nave from the chancel

Transitional
architectural period of transition from Norman to Early English, c. 1175–1200, stylistically a mix of Norman and Gothic

transom
horizontal bar across the opening of a window

transverse arch
arch separating one bay of a vault from the next

triforium
arcaded wall passage or blank arcading facing the nave at the height of the aisle roof and below the clerestory windows

trophy
sculptured group of arms or armour, used as a memorial of victory

turret
very small tower, round or polygonal in plan

tympanum
space between the lintel of a doorway and the arch above it

undercroft
vaulted room, sometimes underground, below a church or chapel

vault
basically an arched roof, though the forms in which it has developed are manyfold; the main types mentioned in this book are barrel, fan, lierne, rib and tierceron:

barrel (or tunnel) vault: vault of semicircular section; Devon and Cornwall have lots of examples, such as at St John the Baptist in Ashton
cross-vault: vault of two tunnel vaults of identical shape intersecting each other at right angles
fan vault: vault where all ribs springing from one springer are of the same length, the same distance from the next, and the same curvature; a good example is St Mary's at Sherbone in Dorset
lierne vault: an elaboration of a rib vault with the addition of tertiary ribs – that is, ribs which do not spring either from one of the main springers or the central boss; a good example is St Helen's in Norwich
rib vault: vault with diagonal ribs projecting along the groins
tierceron vault: another variation of a rib vault with the addition only of secondary ribs – that is, ribs which issue from one of the main springers or the central boss and lead to a place on a ridge-rib; St Helen's in Norwich also has tiercerons. *See also* transverse arch

venetian window
window with three openings, the central one arched and wider than those on the outside

vesica
see mandorla

voussoir
wedge-shaped stone used in arch construction; the central voussoir is the key stone

wagon roof
see roof

wainscot
timber lining to walls

wall plate
a longitudinal timber on top of a wall on which sit the roof's rafters

weather-boarding
overlapping horizontal boards, covering a timber-framed wall

weepers
small figures placed in niches along the sides of some medieval tombs (also called mourners)

wheel window
circular window whose mullions radiate from a central point like spokes on a wheel

The publishers would like to thank all the many church wardens and rectors who helped provide access and information for this edition.

PHOTOGRAPHY CREDITS

Michael Ellis
Bedfordshire, Berkshire, Buckinghamshire, Cambridgeshire, Cheshire, Cornwall, Derbyshire (except p180), Devon, Dorset, Essex (except p243), Hampshire & Isle of Wight, Hertfordshire, Kent (except p334, 342–3), Lancashire, Leicestershire, London, Norfolk, Northamptonshire (except p486), Nottinghamshire, Oxfordshire, Rutland, Somerset and Bristol, Staffordshire, Suffolk (except p611, 632), Surrey, Sussex (East and West; except p662, 675), Warwickshire & West Midlands (except p680), Wiltshire (except p696), Worcestershire; also photographs on pages 12, 15, 18, 21, 22, 32 , 35, 42, 45, 46, 48, 50, 55, 60, 65, 69, 72

Richard Surman
Cumbria, Durham, Gloucestershire, Herefordshire, Lincolnshire, Northumberland and Tyne & Wear, Shropshire, Yorkshire (E. Riding, North, South and West), Wales, Scotland; also photographs on pages 8, 77, 180, 243, 334, 342–3, 486, 611, 632, 662, 675, 680, 696

CARTOGRAPHY AND DIAGRAMS
All maps by Rosalyn Ellis at Thameside Media
Glossary diagrams by Thameside Media
Church diagrams in Sir John Betjeman's Introduction are from the original edition, with reference to *The Ground Plan of the English Parish Church*, by A. Hamilton Thompson (1911)

DESIGN AND EDITORIAL
Thameside Media
www.thamesidemedia.com